THE LAW OF NON-INTE...
ARMED CONFL...

LIBRARY – ORDINARY LOAN
This book should be returned or renewed by the date below. Failure to return books promptly will result in fines and affect your borrowing rights.

T 020 7919 7150
lending@gold.ac.uk

Goldsmiths
UNIVERSITY OF LONDON

GOLDSMITHS

8703823129

The Law of Non-International Armed Conflict

SANDESH SIVAKUMARAN

UNIVERSITY PRESS

Great Clarendon Street, Oxford, OX2 6DP,
United Kingdom

Oxford University Press is a department of the University of Oxford.
It furthers the University's objective of excellence in research, scholarship,
and education by publishing worldwide. Oxford is a registered trade mark of
Oxford University press in the UK and in certain other countries

© Sandesh Sivakumaran 2012

The moral rights of the author have been asserted

First Edition published in 2012
First published in paperback 2014
Impression: 1

All rights reserved. No part of this publication may be reproduced, stored in
a retrieval system, or transmitted, in any form or by any means,without the
prior permission in writing of Oxford University Press, or as expressly permitted
by law, by licence or under terms agreed with the appropriate reprographics
rights organization. Enquiries concerning reproduction outside the scope of the
above should be sent to the Rights Department, Oxford University Press, at the
address above

You must not circulate this work in any other form
and you must impose this same condition on any acquirer

Crown copyright material is reproduced under Class Licence
Number C01P0000148 with the permission of OPSI
and the Queen's Printer for Scotland

Published in the United States of America by Oxford University Press
198 Madison Avenue, New York, NY 10016, United States of America

British Library Cataloguing in Publication Data
Data available

Library of Congress Cataloging in Publication Data
Data available

ISBN 978–0–19–923979–5 (hbk.)
ISBN 978–0–19–872228–1 (pbk.)

Printed in Great Britain by
Lightning Source UK Ltd.

Links to third party websites are provided by Oxford in good faith and
for information only. Oxford disclaims any responsibility for the materials
contained in any third party website referenced in this work.

341.68 SIV

7/14

To my parents

Preface

One of the most pleasurable aspects of the writing process has been the drafting of this preface. It comes at a time when the text has been largely completed and it allows me to thank the very many people who have helped me throughout the writing process. As this book is my only sole-authored work, it also affords me an opportunity to thank—in writing and in public—those who have helped me in my career.

My first thanks must go to Professor Susan Marks, who not only taught me international law and international human rights law many a year ago but introduced this topic to me. Since my time as a student, I have had the pleasure of working closely with Sir Daniel Bethlehem, Judge Dame Rosalyn Higgins, Ian Martin, Judge Mohammed Shahabuddeen, and Judge Peter Tomka. Each of them proved influential in the development of my thinking and I remain grateful for the assistance and support they provided during the formative stages of my career.

Numerous colleagues at the School of Law, University of Nottingham, as well as the School itself, have proven supportive of this project. Professor Robert Cryer, in particular, then at Nottingham, was supportive of the project even prior to my realization that it was a book project. His advice throughout the writing process has proven invaluable.

Avner Gidron, Emanuela-Chiara Gillard, Simon Meisenberg, Niki Moss, and persons who should remain anonymous, assisted in the location of state and non-state armed group commitments and practice. Dr Olivier Bangerter and the staff of Geneva Call generously shared with me their own collections of non-confidential commitments of armed groups and Jonathan Somer drew my attention to various practices of armed groups. Given that one of the key features of this work is the consideration of the practice of armed groups, I am grateful to each of them for their contribution.

A small research grant from the British Academy allowed me to explore the public archives of the International Committee of the Red Cross. I am grateful to the British Academy for the funding of this aspect of the work, and to Fabrizio Bensi, the ICRC archivist, for his assistance.

In the course of writing the book, I spoke to members and former members of parties to conflicts, representatives of international organizations, and staff of non-governmental organizations, all on issues relating to the law of non-international armed conflict. Many of these conversations were off the record and meetings at which some of the issues were discussed took place under the Chatham House rule. Accordingly, details of my conversations with these individuals are limited; however, they very much inform the work. I am grateful to them all for the opportunity to discuss my thoughts.

Some of the ideas that are to be found in the book have previously been set out in various articles and book chapters. Various presentations on issues surrounding the law of non-international armed conflict and on armed groups have also proven beneficial to the development of the work. Thanks go to my various interlocutors in this regard, too many to name individually.

Likewise, I am grateful to Marko Divac Öberg, Almut Gadow de Mayor, Leila Jelali, Subramaniam Lingeswaran, and Shankari Sivakumaran, all of whom assisted me with the translation of foreign language materials. Dr Giovanna Frisso and Adamantia Rachovitsa took on the unenviable task of checking the footnotes. I am grateful to them, too, for their conscientious work in this regard.

Pascal Bongard, Anthea Roberts, and Jonathan Somer read parts of the book and offered me valuable suggestions. The late Judge Antonio Cassese, Professor Robert Cryer, Professor Dino Kritsiotis, Dr Marko Milanovic, and Dr Jelena Pejic took on the onerous task of reading the entire manuscript. Their close reading of the text and detailed suggestions proved extremely helpful and the work is the better for their comments. I am immensely grateful to each of them for taking the time and trouble to read the voluminous manuscript. Nino pushed me to take my ideas as far as they could go, indeed further than I thought possible. His advice, generosity, and friendship are sorely missed, as is his inestimable contribution to the development of this area of the law.

The award of the 2009–10 Antonio Cassese Prize, by the Board of Editors of the *Journal of International Criminal Justice*, funded the completion of the work. I am grateful to the Board for the honour and hope that the book lives up to their expectation.

The final stages of the book were completed in Melbourne and Geneva. Dr Alison Duxbury and Professor Gerry Simpson arranged my visit at Melbourne Law School and the Asia-Pacific Centre for Military Law, while Dr Thomas Schultz did likewise in Geneva. I had very enjoyable stays in both places and am grateful for their hospitality and assistance.

Thanks are also due to Merel Alstein, Anthony Hinton, John Louth, Caroline Quinnell, Rebecca Smith, and Fiona Stables at Oxford University Press. OUP was kind enough to contract the book at a very early stage and then allow me to write undisturbed and without time pressure. The book took longer than expected to write and turned out to be considerably lengthier than anticipated. I am grateful to John and his colleagues for allowing me as much time and space as I needed to set out my ideas. I could not have had more accommodating editors.

Finally, it is to my parents that I owe the greatest thanks. This book is dedicated to them.

Contents–Summary

Table of Cases	xix
Table of Instruments	xxvi
List of Abbreviations	xxxiv
List of Acronyms of Armed Groups	xxxvi
Introduction	1

PART I: REGULATING NON-INTERNATIONAL ARMED CONFLICTS

1. Ad-hoc Regulation	9
2. Systematic Regulation through International Humanitarian Law	30
3. Regulation through a Body of International Law	54
4. The Sources of the Law of Non-International Armed Conflict	101

PART II: THE SUBSTANTIVE LAW OF NON-INTERNATIONAL ARMED CONFLICT

5. Identifying a Non-International Armed Conflict: Armed Conflicts and Internal Tensions and Disturbances	155
6. Identifying a Non-International Armed Conflict: International and Non-International Armed Conflicts	212
7. Scope of Application	236
8. Protection of Civilians and Persons *Hors de Combat*	255
9. Conduct of Hostilities	336
10. Implementation and Non-Judicial Enforcement	430
11. Judicial Enforcement	475

PART III: MOVING FORWARD

12. Developments Needed in the Law	513
Conclusion	568
Select Bibliography	571
Index	619

Contents–Detailed

Table of Cases	xix
Table of Instruments	xxvi
List of Abbreviations	xxxiv
List of Acronyms of Armed Groups	xxxvi

Introduction   1
   Nature of the law   2
   Armed groups   3
   Practice   4
   Goals   5
   A note to the reader   5

PART I: REGULATING NON-INTERNATIONAL ARMED CONFLICTS

1. Ad-hoc Regulation   9
   1. Introduction   9
   2. Recognition of belligerency   9
      2.1 The concept of recognition   9
      2.2 Consequences of recognition   14
      2.3 Instances of recognition   17
   3. Instructions and agreements   20
      3.1 Instructions   21
      3.2 Agreements   25
      3.3 Advantages and drawbacks   28
   4. Conclusion   29

2. Systematic Regulation through International Humanitarian Law   30
   1. Introduction   30
   2. The International Committee of the Red Cross and International Conferences of the Red Cross   30
   3. The Diplomatic Conference of 1949   40
   4. The period 1949–74   42
   5. The Diplomatic Conference of 1974–7   49
   6. Post-1977 initiatives   52
   7. Conclusion   53

3. Regulation through a Body of International Law   54
   1. Introduction   54
   2. Drawing on the law of international armed conflict   55
      2.1 Customary international humanitarian law   55
      2.2 Conventional international humanitarian law   61
      2.3 Methodological difficulties with regulation by drawing on the law of international armed conflict   65
         2.3.1 Scope and content   66
         2.3.2 Levels of protection   68
         2.3.3 International and non-international armed conflicts   69

Contents–Detailed

	3. International criminal law	77
	3.1 The war crimes–international humanitarian law nexus	77
	3.2 Methodological concerns with the use of war crimes law	78
	3.2.1 The norms	79
	3.2.2 The enforcement function	82
	4. International human rights law	83
	4.1 Applicability of international human rights law	83
	4.2 Application of international human rights law	87
	4.2.1 Normative content	87
	4.2.2 Interpretation	88
	4.2.3 Direct regulation	93
	5. Conclusion	99
4.	**The Sources of the Law of Non-International Armed Conflict**	**101**
	1. Introduction	101
	2. The traditional sources	101
	2.1 Treaties	101
	2.2 Custom	102
	2.2.1 Methodology	102
	2.2.2 Customary rules	105
	3. The less traditional 'sources'	107
	3.1 Nature of the commitments	108
	3.1.1 Propaganda?	108
	3.1.2 Normative status	109
	3.1.3 An interpretational tool	110
	3.1.4 Commitments and compliance	112
	3.2 The commitments	113
	3.2.1 Unilateral declarations	113
	Declarations of states	113
	Parallel declarations	114
	Declarations of national liberation movements	118
	Declarations of non-state armed groups	118
	Purported accession	118
	Declarations to the ICRC	119
	General declarations	120
	Declarations on particular rules	122
	Declarations on human rights law	123
	3.2.2 Agreements	124
	Agreements on international humanitarian law	125
	Agreements on international humanitarian law and human rights law	129
	Agreements on human rights law	131
	Other agreements	132
	3.2.3 Instructions, codes of conduct, and internal regulations	133
	3.2.4 Legislation	139
	3.2.5 Other important materials	141
	Responses to reports of fact-finding missions	141
	Press releases and other ad hoc statements	141
	Expressions of motivations for taking up arms	142
	3.3 Non-exhaustive list of commitments	143
	4. Conclusion	152

PART II: THE SUBSTANTIVE LAW OF NON-INTERNATIONAL ARMED CONFLICT

5. **Identifying a Non-International Armed Conflict: Armed Conflicts and Internal Tensions and Disturbances** — 155
   1. Introduction — 155
   2. The non-definition approach — 156
      - 2.1 The Diplomatic Conference of 1949 — 156
      - 2.2 Advantages and disadvantages of the lack of definition — 162
   3. The definition approach — 164
      - 3.1 Intensity of violence — 167
      - 3.2 Organization of the armed group — 170
         - 3.2.1 Indicia of organization — 170
         - 3.2.2 Organization in practice — 172
         - 3.2.3 Responsible command — 174
         - 3.2.4 Rationale for organization — 176
      - 3.3 Governmental authorities — 180
      - 3.4 Non-requisites — 180
   4. Prerequisites for particular rules to apply — 182
      - 4.1 Protocol II, Additional to the Geneva Conventions of 1949 — 182
         - 4.1.1 State armed forces — 184
         - 4.1.2 Organized armed groups and responsible command — 184
         - 4.1.3 Territorial control — 185
         - 4.1.4 Sustained and concerted military operations — 188
         - 4.1.5 Implementation of the Protocol — 188
         - 4.1.6 Concluding thoughts — 190
      - 4.2 Rome Statute of the International Criminal Court — 192
      - 4.3 Recognition of belligerency — 195
   5. Characterization of the violence — 196
      - 5.1 The decision-maker — 196
      - 5.2 Recognition of an armed conflict — 200
      - 5.3 Characterization of the armed group — 204
      - 5.4 Legal status and legitimacy — 205
   6. Conclusion — 210

6. **Identifying a Non-International Armed Conflict: International and Non-International Armed Conflicts** — 212
   1. Introduction — 212
   2. Wars of national liberation — 212
      - 2.1 Historical regulation — 212
      - 2.2 Defining wars of national liberation — 216
   3. Outside state intervention — 222
      - 3.1 Intervention through troops — 222
      - 3.2 State control over an armed group — 225
   4. Transnational armed conflicts — 228
   5. Conclusion — 234

7. **Scope of Application** — 236
   1. Introduction — 236
   2. Personal scope of application — 236

2.1 Non-state armed groups and conventional international humanitarian law	236
2.2 Equality of obligation, reciprocity, and asymmetry	242
2.3 Intra-party protection	246
3. Geographical scope of application	250
4. Temporal scope of application	252

8. Protection of Civilians and Persons *Hors de Combat* — 255

1. Introduction	255
2. Humane treatment	255
2.1 The principle	255
2.2 Non-discrimination	258
2.3 Specific prohibitions deriving from the principle of humane treatment	259
2.3.1 Violence to life and person	259
Murder	260
Torture	261
Cruel and inhuman treatment	262
2.3.2 Outrages upon personal dignity	263
2.3.3 Sexual violence	264
2.3.4 Slavery and the slave trade	268
2.3.5 Taking of hostages	268
2.3.6 Collective punishments	271
3. Persons benefitting from particular protections	273
3.1 Wounded, sick, and shipwrecked	273
3.2 Medical and religious personnel	277
3.3 Dead persons	280
3.4 Missing persons	284
3.5 Displaced persons	285
3.5.1 Prohibition on forced displacement	285
Exceptions to the prohibition on forcible transfer	287
Modalities of displacement	288
3.5.2 Treatment of internally displaced persons	289
3.5.3 Return of internally displaced persons	291
3.6 Interned and detained persons	292
3.6.1 Obligations to be respected as a minimum	293
3.6.2 Obligations dependent on capacity	295
3.6.3 Specificities of non-international armed conflict	296
3.6.4 Release of prisoners	300
3.6.5 Legal basis for security detention/internment	301
3.7 Persons subject to the criminal process	305
3.7.1 A regularly constituted court	305
3.7.2 Due process guarantees	306
Identifying the obligations	306
Content of the obligations	308
3.7.3 Capital punishment	310
3.8 Journalists	311
3.9 Women	313
3.10 Children	315
3.10.1 General	315
3.10.2 Child soldiers	316

	The obligations	317
	The relevant age	320
	Human rights law	323
3.11	Peacekeeping missions	324
	3.11.1 International humanitarian law protections	324
	3.11.2 The Convention on the Safety of United Nations and Associated Personnel	327
	3.11.3 Application of international humanitarian law to UN forces	328
3.12	Humanitarian assistance missions	328
4. Humanitarian assistance		329
5. Conclusion		334

9. Conduct of Hostilities — 336

1. Introduction — 336
2. Targeting — 337
    2.1 Underlying principles — 337
    2.2 Attacks against the civilian population — 338
        2.2.1 Attacks on civilians — 338
        2.2.2 Attacks on civilian objects — 342
            Protections afforded to civilian objects — 342
        2.2.3 Defining civilian objects — 344
    2.3 Indiscriminate attacks — 347
    2.4 Disproportionate attacks — 349
    2.5 Precautions — 351
        2.5.1 Precautions in planning and carrying out attacks — 351
        2.5.2 Precautions against the effects of attacks — 356
    2.6 Beneficiaries of protection — 357
        2.6.1 Context — 357
        2.6.2 Categories of persons — 359
            Members of state armed forces and military wing of armed group — 359
            Civilians taking a direct part in hostilities — 362
        2.6.3 The notion of direct participation in hostilities — 363
            Interpretive Guidance — 363
            Types of acts — 364
        2.6.4 Loss of protection — 365
            State armed forces and military wing of armed group — 365
            Civilians taking a direct part in hostilities — 367
            Views of armed groups — 368
            A more humanitarian approach? — 370
        2.6.5 Conclusion — 372
    2.7 Investigations relating to losses of life — 372
    2.8 Objects benefiting from particular protections — 373
        2.8.1 Medical units and transports — 373
        2.8.2 Cultural property — 375
            Definition of cultural property — 376
            Application to non-international armed conflict — 376
            The protections — 377
                Hague Convention on Cultural Property — 377
                Additional Protocol II — 379

Second Protocol to the Hague Convention on Cultural Property	379
Customary international law	381
2.8.3 Dams, dykes, and nuclear electrical generating stations	381
2.8.4 Protected zones	383
3. Means of combat	386
3.1 Introduction	386
3.2 The general rules	387
3.2.1 Unnecessary suffering or superfluous injury	387
3.2.2 Discrimination	390
3.3 Specifically prohibited weapons	392
3.3.1 Poison and poisoned weapons	392
3.3.2 Biological and bacteriological weapons	393
3.3.3 Gas and chemical weapons	394
3.3.4 Incendiary weapons	397
3.3.5 Laser weapons designed to cause permanent blindness	399
3.3.6 Explosive bullets	400
3.3.7 Expanding bullets	401
3.3.8 Booby-traps and anti-personnel mines	404
Booby-traps	404
Anti-personnel mines	404
The Amended Mines Protocol	405
The Ottawa Convention	407
3.3.9 Cluster munitions	409
3.3.10 Non-detectable fragments	410
3.3.11 Explosive remnants of war	411
4. Methods of combat	412
4.1 Denial of quarter	412
4.2 Flags of truce and surrender	415
4.3 Improper use of emblems and uniforms	416
4.3.1 Neutral or protected emblems and uniforms	416
4.3.2 Enemy emblems and uniforms	417
4.4 Perfidy	418
4.5 Human shields	420
4.5.1 Involuntary human shields	420
4.5.2 Voluntary human shields	422
4.6 Starvation of civilians	423
4.6.1 Starvation	423
4.6.2 Objects indispensable to the survival of the civilian population	424
4.7 Pillage	426
4.8 Wanton destruction	428
5. Conclusion	428
10. Implementation and Non-Judicial Enforcement	**430**
1. Introduction	430
2. Internal mechanisms	431
2.1 Dissemination	431
2.1.1 Importance of dissemination	431
2.1.2 States, non-state armed groups, and civilians	432
2.1.3 Modalities of dissemination	433

2.2 Instruction	434
2.3 Legal advice	437
2.4 Manuals, codes of conduct, and internal regulations	438
2.4.1 State measures	438
2.4.2 Non-state armed group measures	438
2.5 Unilateral declarations and bilateral agreements	442
2.6 Sanctions	445
3. Responses to the other side: belligerent reprisals	448
3.1 Prohibited belligerent reprisals	449
3.2 Restrictions on the use of belligerent reprisals	453
3.3 Continued use of belligerent reprisals	455
4. Third parties	457
4.1 Protecting Powers	457
4.2 Fact-finding	459
4.2.1 The International Humanitarian Fact-Finding Commission	459
4.2.2 Other fact-finding initiatives	462
4.3 United Nations entities	465
4.3.1 The Security Council	465
4.3.2 The General Assembly	466
4.3.3 Human rights mechanisms	467
4.4 The International Committee of the Red Cross	467
4.4.1 The institution	467
4.4.2 Activities	468
4.4.3 Modalities	471
4.5 Human rights non-governmental organizations	472
5. Conclusion	473
11. Judicial Enforcement	**475**
1. Introduction	475
2. War crimes	475
3. International criminal courts and tribunals	478
3.1 The International Criminal Tribunal for the former Yugoslavia	478
3.2 The International Criminal Tribunal for Rwanda	479
3.3 The International Criminal Court	481
3.3.1 Jurisdiction	483
3.3.2 Impact	484
3.4 The Special Court for Sierra Leone	487
4. Domestic criminal courts	488
4.1 1860s to mid-1990s	489
4.1.1 Prosecutions	489
4.1.2 National legislation	490
4.2 Mid-1990s to present	494
4.2.1 Conventional law	494
4.2.2 Domestic legislation	494
4.2.3 Trials in national courts	496
4.2.4 Trials in courts of states not involved in the conflict	498
5. Human rights courts	500
5.1 Enforcement of international humanitarian law	501
5.2 Enforcement of human rights law	503

        6. Non-enforcement: amnesties   505
        7. Conclusion   509

                        PART III: MOVING FORWARD

12. **Developments Needed in the Law**   513
        1. Introduction   513
        2. Substantive norms   513
            2.1 Combatant immunity and prisoners of war   513
                2.1.1 Combatant immunity   514
                2.1.2 Prisoners of war   521
            2.2 The natural environment   526
            2.3 Territory under the control of the non-state armed group 529
        3. Enforcement and implementation of the law   532
            3.1 Office of the Special Representative of the Secretary
                General for Children and Armed Conflict and the Security
                Council Working Group on Children and Armed Conflict   533
            3.2 Geneva Call   538
                3.2.1 The Deed of Commitment   539
                3.2.2 Monitoring   539
                3.2.3 Beyond anti-personnel mines   541
            3.3 Engaging compliance   542
                3.3.1 Influencing others   542
                3.3.2 Legitimacy concerns   546
            3.4 Courts of non-state armed groups   549
                3.4.1 Examples   550
                3.4.2 Potential importance   555
                3.4.3 Legitimacy and recognition   557
                3.4.4 Towards greater engagement   562
        4. Methodology: armed groups and the creation of the law   562
        5. A concrete proposal   564

Conclusion   568

Bibliography   571
Index   619

Table of Cases

EUROPEAN COURT OF HUMAN RIGHTS

Abuyeva and others v Russia, Application No 27065/05, Judgment, 2 December 2010 94
Al-Jedda v the United Kingdom, Application No 27021/08, Judgment, 7 July 2011 90
Al-Skeini and others v the United Kingdom, Application No 55721/07, Judgment,
   7 July 2011 372
Ergi v Turkey, Application No 23818/94, Judgment, 28 July 1998...504
Isayeva v Russia, Application No 57950/00, Judgment, 24 February
   2005.. 92, 93, 372, 373, 504
Isayeva, Yusopova and Bazayeva v Russia, Application Nos 57947/00, 57948/00 and
   57949/00, Judgment, 24 February 2005 93
Kaya v Turkey [1998] ECHR 10 ....92, 373
Kerimova and others v Russia, Application No 17170/04 and others, Judgment,
   3 May 2011 372
Korbely v Hungary, Application No 9174/02, Judgment, 19 September 2008 ....93, 413
Loizidou v Turkey (1993) 23 EHRR 513...219, 560
McCann and others v United Kingdom, Application No 18984/91, Judgment,
   27 September 1995 85
Van Anraat v the Netherlands, Application No 65389/09, Decision as to Admissibility,
   6 July 2010 394
Varnava and others v Turkey, Application No 16064/90 and others, Judgment,
   18 September 2009 ....92, 94

INTER-AMERICAN COURT OF HUMAN RIGHTS

Bámaca-Velásquez v Guatemala, Merits, Ser C No 70, 25 November 2000 ....502, 503
Ituango Massacres v Colombia, Preliminary Objections, Merits, Reparations and Costs,
   Judgment, 1 July 2006 502
Las Palmeras v Colombia, Preliminary Objections, Ser C No 67, 4 February 2000 502
Mapiripán Massacre v Colombia, Merits, Reparations and Costs, Judgment, 15 September
   2005..502
Myrna Mack Chang v Guatemala, Merits, Ser C No 101, 25 November 2003 92
Serrano-Cruz Sisters v El Salvador, Preliminary Objections, Judgment, 23 November 2004..........502

INTERNATIONAL COURT OF JUSTICE

*Application of the Convention on the Prevention and Punishment of the Crime of Genocide
   (Bosnia and Herzegovina v Serbia and Montenegro), Judgment* [2007]
   ICJ Rep 43..110, 225, 227
*Armed Activities on the Territory of the Congo (Democratic Republic of the Congo v Uganda),
   Judgment* [2005] ICJ Rep 168 84
*Corfu Channel (United Kingdom of Great Britain and Northern Ireland v Albania),
   Judgment* [1949] ICJ Rep 4 55
Frontier Dispute (Burkina Faso v Mali), Judgment [1986] ICJ Rep 554 110
LaGrand (Germany v United States of America), Judgment [2001] ICJ Rep 466 242
*Legal Consequences for States of the Continued Presence of South Africa in Namibia
   (South West Africa) notwithstanding Security Council Resolution 276 (1970),
   Advisory Opinion* [1971] ICJ Rep 16 ....530, 560
*Legal Consequences of the Construction of a Wall in the Occupied Palestinian Territory,
   Advisory Opinion* [2004] ICJ Rep 136 ....84, 91, 109

Legality of the Threat or Use of Nuclear Weapons, Advisory Opinion [1996] ICJ
Rep 226 .... 84, 91, 337, 348, 388, 390, 391, 527
*Military and Paramilitary Activities in and against Nicaragua (Nicaragua v United
States of America), Judgment* [1986] ICJ Rep 14 .... 55, 57, 103, 105,
110, 223, 225–6, 227, 228, 236, 255
Nuclear Tests (Australia v France), Judgment [1974] ICJ Rep 253 ....110, 114
Western Sahara, Advisory Opinion [1975] ICJ Rep 12...218

INTERNATIONAL CRIMINAL COURT

Prosecutor v Abu Garda, ICC-02/05-02/09, Decision on the Confirmation of Charges,
8 February 2010 (*Abu Garda* Decision on the Confirmation
of Charges).. 324, 325, 329, 344
Prosecutor v Al-Bashir, ICC-02/05-01/09, Decision on the Prosecution's Application
for a Warrant of Arrest against Omar Hassan Ahmad Al Bashir, 4 March 2009
(*Al-Bashir* Decision on Arrest Warrant) 177, 180, 181, 188, 195
Prosecutor v Bemba Gombo, ICC-01/05-01/08, Decision pursuant to Article 61(7)(a)
and (b) of the Rome Statute on the Charges of the Prosecutor against Jean-Pierre
Bemba Gombo, 15 June 2009 (*Bemba Gombo* Rule 61 Decision).......................175, 176, 177,
195, 447, 554, 557, 559
Prosecutor v Katanga and Chui, ICC-01/04-01/07, Decision on the Confirmation
of Charges, 30 September 2008 (*Katanga* Decision on the Confirmation
of Charges) 171, 175, 181, 188, 249, 339
Prosecutor v Kony, Otti, Odhiambo, Ongwen, ICC-02/04-01/05, Decision on the
Admissibility of the Case under Article 19(1) of the Statute, 10 March 2009......................486
Prosecutor v Lubanga, ICC-01/04-01/06, Decision on the Confirmation of Charges,
29 January 2007 (*Lubanga* Decision on the Confirmation of Charges)................165, 166, 168,
170, 177, 195, 226, 317, 318, 319
Prosecutor v Lubanga, ICC-01/04-01/06, Judgment, 14 March 2012 (*Lubanga*
Trial Judgment)...175, 318

INTERNATIONAL CRIMINAL TRIBUNAL FOR
THE FORMER YUGOSLAVIA

Prosecutor v Ademi and Norac, IT-04-78-PT, Decision for Referral to the Authorities
of the Republic of Croatia pursuant to Rule 11*bis*, 14 September 2005 497
Prosecutor v Aleksovski, IT-95-14/1-T, Judgment, 25 June 1999 (*Aleksovski* Trial
Judgment) 258, 263, 264, 293, 477
Prosecutor v Blagojević and Jokić, IT-02-60-T, Judgment, 17 January 2005 (*Blagojević* Trial
Judgment) 367
Prosecutor v Blaškić, IT-95-14-T, Judgment, 3 March 2000
(*Blaškić* Trial Judgment)... 224, 226, 227, 228, 262, 269, 420
Prosecutor v Blaškić, IT-95-14-A, Judgment, 29 July 2004 269
Prosecutor v Boškoski and Tarčulovski, IT-04-82-PT, Decision on Johan Tarčulovski's
Motion Challenging Jurisdiction, 1 June 2005...197
Prosecutor v Boškoski and Tarčulovski, IT-04-82-T, Judgment, 10 July 2008 (*Boškoski* Trial
Judgment) 162, 168, 170, 171, 174, 177, 179, 185, 188, 189, 442
Prosecutor v Boškoski and Tarčulovski, IT-04-82-A, Judgment, 19 May 2010 (*Boškoski*
Appeal Judgment) 168, 170, 171
Prosecutor v Brđanin and Talić, IT-99-36-AR73.9, Decision on Interlocutory Appeal,
11 December 2002 313
Prosecutor v Brđanin, IT-99-36-T, Judgment, 1 September 2004 (*Brđanin* Trial
Judgment)..261, 262
Prosecutor v Delalić, Mucić, Delić and Landžo, IT-96-21-T Judgment, 16 November 1998
(*Delalić* Trial Judgment).....................................81, 89, 168, 176, 177, 249, 20, 261, 262, 477

Prosecutor v Delalić, Mucić, Delić and Landžo, IT-96-21-A, Judgment,
20 February 2001 (*Delalić* Appeal Judgment) 57, 175, 176
Prosecutor v Đorđević, IT-05-87/1-T, Judgment, 23 February 2011
(*Đorđević* Trial Judgment) 170, 171, 287, 554
Prosecutor v Furundžija, IT-95-17/1-T, Judgment, 10 December 1998
(*Furundžija* Trial Judgment) 262, 263, 265
Prosecutor v Furundžija, IT-95-17/1-A, Judgment, 21 July 2000 262
Prosecutor v Galić, IT-98-29-T, Judgment and Opinion, 5 December 2003
(*Galić* Trial Judgment) 57, 58, 339, 348, 351, 361, 366
Prosecutor v Galić, IT-98-29-A, Judgment, 30 November 2006
(*Galić* Appeal Judgment) 61, 341, 348, 438
Prosecutor v Gotovina, Čermak and Markač, IT-06-90-T, Judgment, 15 April 2011 253
Prosecutor v Halilović, IT-01-48-T, Judgment, 16 November 2005
(*Halilović* Trial Judgment) 57, 361, 367
Prosecutor v Haradinaj, Balaj and Brahimaj, IT-04-84-T, Judgment, 3 April 2008
(*Haradinaj* Trial Judgment) 165, 167, 168, 170, 171, 177, 178, 309
Prosecutor v Haradinaj, Balaj and Brahimaj, IT-04-84-A, Judgment, 19 July 2010
(*Haradinaj* Appeal Judgment) 485
Prosecutor v Hadžihasanović, Alagić and Kubura, IT-01-47-PT, Decision on Joint
Challenge to Jurisdiction, 12 November 2002 180
Prosecutor v Hadžihasanović, Alagić and Kubura, IT-01-47-AR72, Decision on
Interlocutory Appeal Challenging Jurisdiction in Relation to Command
Responsibility, 16 July 2003 .... 175, 557
Prosecutor v Hadžihasanović and Kubura, IT-01-47-T, Decision on Motions for
Acquittal pursuant to Rules 98*bis* of the Rules of Procedure and Evidence,
27 September 2004 58
Prosecutor v Hadžihasanović and Kubura, IT-01-47-AR73.3, Decision on Joint Defence
Interlocutory Appeal of Trial Chamber Decision on Rule 98*bis* Motions for Acquittal,
11 March 2005 (*Hadžihasanović* Interlocutory Appeal on 98*bis* Decision) 58, 60, 61,
82, 342, 375, 426, 427, 428
Prosecutor v Hadžihasanović and Kubura, IT-01-47-T, Judgment, 15 March 2006
(*Hadžihasanović* Trial Judgment) 58, 79, 349
Prosecutor v Halilović, IT-01-48-T, Judgment, 16 November 2005
(*Halilović* Trial Judgment) 57, 361, 367
Prosecutor v Karadžić, IT-95-5/18-PT, Decision on Six Preliminary Motions Challenging
Jurisdiction, 28 April 2009 269
Prosecutor v Kordić and Čerkez, IT-95-14/2-T, Judgment, 26 February 2001
(*Kordić* Trial Judgment) 224, 227, 228, 262, 269, 420, 557
Prosecutor v Kordić and Čerkez, IT-95-14/2-A, Judgment, 17 December 2004
(*Kordić* Appeal Judgment) 167, 227, 228, 339, 376, 426, 478
Prosecutor v Kovačević, IT-01-42/2-I, Decision on Referral of Case pursuant to
Rule 11bis, 17 November 2006 497
Prosecutor v Krnojelac, IT-97-25-T, Judgment, 15 March 2002
(*Krnojelac* Trial Judgment) 89, 261, 262, 263, 268
Prosecutor v Krnojelac, IT-97-25-A, Judgment, 17 September 2003 286
Prosecutor v Krstić, IT-98-33-T, Judgment, 2 August 2001 260
Prosecutor v Kunarac, Kovač and Vuković, IT-96-23-T and IT-96-23/1-T, Judgment,
22 February 2001 (*Kunarac* Trial Judgment) 88, 89, 95, 262, 263,
264, 265, 266, 268
Prosecutor v Kunarac, Kovač and Vuković, IT-96-23 and IT-96-23/1-A, Judgment,
12 June 2002 (*Kunarac* Appeal Judgment) 261, 262, 263, 264, 265, 266, 268
Prosecutor v Kupreškić, Kupreškić, Kupreškić, Josipović, Papić and Šantić, IT-95-16-T,
Judgment, 14 January 2000 (*Kupreškić* Trial Judgment) 55, 77, 104, 244, 337,
349, 452, 453, 455, 456, 475
Prosecutor v Kvočka, Radić, Žigić, and Prcać, IT-98-30/1-T, Judgment,
2 November 2001 (*Kvočka* Trial Judgment) 260, 262, 264

Prosecutor v Limaj, IT-03-66-T, Judgment, 30 November 2005 (*Limaj* Trial
 Judgment) 66, 167, 168, 170, 171, 172, 174, 178,
  179, 182, 262, 293, 309
Prosecutor v Martić, IT-95-11-R61, Decision, 8 March 1996 (*Martić* Rule
 61 Decision).. 58, 341, 450, 452
Prosecutor v Martić, IT-95-11-T, Judgment, 12 June 2007 (*Martić* Trial
 Judgment) 391, 392, 449, 453, 454, 455, 532
Prosecutor v Martić, IT-95-11-A, Judgment, 8 October 2008 (*Martić* Appeal
 Judgment) 391, 452
Prosecutor v Milosević, IT-02-54-T, Decision on Motion for Judgment of Acquittal,
 16 June 2004 (*Milosević* Decision on Motion for Acquittal)......................... 168, 170, 171, 180
Prosecutor v Mrkšić, Radić and Šljivančanin, IT-95-13/1-T, Judgment,
 27 September 2007,..299
Prosecutor v Mrkšić, Radić and Šljivančanin, IT-95-13/1-A, Judgment, 5 May 2009,
 Appeal 519
Prosecutor v Naletilić and Martinović, IT-98-34-T, Judgment, 31 March 2003
 (*Naletilić* Trial Judgment).. 225, 227, 228, 262
Prosecutor v Orić, IT-03-68-T, Judgment, 30 June 2006..174
Prosecutor v Rajić and Andrić, IT-95-12-R61, Review of the Indictment pursuant
 to Rule 61 of the Rules of Procedure and Evidence, 13 September 1996 225
Prosecutor v Simić, IT-95-9-PT, Decision on the Prosecution Motion under
 Rule 73 for a Ruling Concerning the Testimony of a Witness, 27 July 1999 472
Prosecutor v Simić, Tadić and Zarić, IT-95-9-T, Judgment, 17 October 2003
 (*Simić* Trial Judgment)...80, 286
Prosecutor v Stakić, IT-97-24-T, Judgment, 31 July 2003 (*Stakić* Trial Judgment) 286
Prosecutor v Stakić, IT-97-24-A, Judgment, 22 March 2006 (*Stakić* Appeal
 Judgment) 80, 286, 288, 289
Prosecutor v Stanković, IT-96-23/2-PT, Decision on Referral of Case under Rule 11bis,
 17 May 2005 497
Prosecutor v Strugar, IT-01-42-T, Judgment, 31 January 2005
 (*Strugar* Trial Judgment) 58, 60, 66, 342, 367, 375, 428

Prosecutor v Strugar, IT-01-42-A, Judgment, 17 July 2008 364

Prosecutor v Tadić, IT-94-1-AR72, Decision on the Defence Motion for Interlocutory
 Appeal on Jurisdiction, 2 October 1995 (*Tadić* Decision on Interlocutory
 Appeal on Jurisdiction)......................... 55, 57, 60, 73, 77, 78, 82, 102, 104, 105, 107, 110,
  111, 155, 164, 165, 166, 167, 180, 193, 194, 195, 210, 223,
  232, 250, 252, 256, 255, 257, 259, 339, 342, 348, 351, 352,
  355, 375, 378, 383, 387, 394, 395, 419, 420, 443, 445,
  452, 459, 477, 478, 479, 490, 569
Prosecutor v Tadić, IT-94-1-T, Opinion and Judgment, 7 May 1997
 (*Tadić* Trial Judgment)... 165, 167, 168, 226, 364
Prosecutor v Tadić, IT-94-1-A, Judgment, 15 July 1999
 (*Tadić* Appeal Judgment) 222, 226, 227, 228, 249
Prosecutor v Vasiljević, IT-98-32-T, Judgment, 29 November 2002..260

INTERNATIONAL CRIMINAL TRIBUNAL FOR RWANDA

Gacumbitsi v the Prosecutor (*Gacumbitsi* Appeal Judgment), ICTR-2001-64-A, Judgment,
 7 July 2006 265
Prosecutor v Akayesu, ICTR-96-4-T, Judgment, 2 September 1998 (*Akayesu* Trial
 Judgment) 109, 165, 170, 175, 177, 179, 180, 186,
  187, 188, 199, 250, 257, 265, 362, 481
Prosecutor v Bagaragaza, ICTR-2005-86-R11bis, Decision on the Prosecution
 Motion for Referral to the Kingdom of Norway, 19 May 2006 498
Prosecutor v Bagosora, Kabiligi, Ntabakuze and Nsengiyuma, ICTR-98-41-T,
 Judgment and Sentence, 18 December 2008 (*Bagosora* Trial Judgment) 326, 361

Prosecutor v Gatete, ICTR-2000-61-R11*bis*, Decision on Prosecutor's Request
for Referral to the Republic of Rwanda, 17 November 2008...498
Prosecutor v Kayishema and Ruzindana, ICTR-95-1-T, 21 May 1999
(*Kayishema* Trial Judgment) 252, 366
Prosecutor v Munyeshyaka, ICTR-2005-87-I, Decision on Prosecutor's Request
for Referral of Wenceslas Munyeshyaka's Indictment to France..498
Prosecutor v Musema, ICTR-96-13-T, Judgment and Sentence,
27 January 2000 (*Musema* Trial Judgment).. 174, 180, 186, 232
Prosecutor v Rutaganda, ICTR-96-3, Judgment and Sentence, 6 December 1999
(*Rutaganda* Trial Judgment) 363, 366
Prosecutor v Semanza, ICTR-97-20-T, Judgment and Sentence, 15 May 2003
(*Semanza* Trial Judgment)...363
Prosecutor v Uwinkindi, ICTR-2001-75-R11*bis*, Decision on Prosecutor's Request
for Referral to the Republic of Rwanda, 28 June 2011 498

PERMANENT COURT OF INTERNATIONAL JUSTICE

Jurisdiction of the Courts of Danzig [1928] PCIJ Series B, No 15 242

POST WORLD WAR II CASES

Trial of Lieutenant General Kurt Maelzer, XI Law Reports of Trials of War Criminals 53..............263
*Trial of the Major War Criminals before the International Military Tribunals, Nuremberg,
14 November 1945-1 October 1946* 476, 477
Trial of Wilhelm List and others (*The Hostages Trial*), VIII Law Reports of
Trials of War Criminals..269

SPECIAL COURT FOR SIERRA LEONE

Prosecutor v Brima, Kamara and Kanu, SCSL-04-16-T, Judgment, 20 June 2007
(*AFRC* Trial Judgment).. 165, 272, 317, 318, 319, 320, 341, 426
Prosecutor v Fofana and Kondewa, SCSL-04-14-T, Judgment, 2 August 2007
(*CDF* Trial Judgment).. 165, 175, 180, 272, 317, 318, 319,
320, 362, 413, 426
Prosecutor v Fofana and Kondewa, SCSL-04-14-A, Judgment, 28 May 2008
(*CDF* Appeal Judgment) 272, 319, 320
Prosecutor v Kallon and Kamara, SCSL-2004-15-AR72(E), SCSL-2004-160AR72(E),
Decision on Challenge to Jurisdiction: Lomé Amnesty Accord,
13 March 2004 ....109, 239, 509
Prosecutor v Kondewa, SCSL-2004-14-AR72(E), Decision on Lack of Jurisdiction/Abuse
of Process: Amnesty provided by the Lomé Accord 508, 509
Prosecutor v Norman, SCSL-2004-14-AR72(E), Decision on Preliminary Motion Based
on Lack of Jurisdiction (Child Recruitment), 31 May 2004 ....239, 319, 487
Prosecutor v Sesay, Kallon and Gbao, SCSL-04-15-T, Judgment, 2 March 2009
(*RUF* Trial Judgment)...66, 134, 166, 179, 186, 187, 246, 247,
256, 257, 264, 266, 267, 269, 272, 299, 309, 317, 318,
319, 320, 324, 325, 326, 328, 329, 358,
368, 427, 428, 439, 442, 529
Prosecutor v Sesay, Kallon and Gbao, SCSL-04-15-A, Judgment, 26 October 2009
(*RUF* Appeal Judgment)..269, 270, 326

SPECIAL TRIBUNAL FOR LEBANON

CH/AC/2010/02, Decision on Appeal of Pre-Trial Judge's Order regarding Jurisdiction
and Standing, 10 November 2010 104

NATIONAL COURTS

Belgium

Ministère Public and Others v B and C, Belgian Military Court, Judgment of
20 November 1997 498
Public Prosecutor v GW, Conseil de Guerre (Brussels), Judgment of 18 May 1966 490

Canada

R v Brocklebank, Judgment of 2 April 1996 498

Chile

Osvaldo Romo Meno, Appeal Court of Santiago, No. 13.597-94, 26 September 1994 496

Colombia

Decision C-225/95, Constitutional Court, 18 May 1995 (*Constitutional Conformity of Protocol II*) 26, 106, 109, 201, 209, 336, 393, 394, 402, 404, 419, 507, 514
Decision T-025, Constitutional Court, 22 January 2004 288
Decision C-291/07, Constitutional Court, 25 April 2007 ....105, 378

Croatia

Prosecutor v Rajko Radulovic and others, K-15/95, Judgment of 26 May 1997 497

Denmark

Refik Sarić, Judgmnet of 22 November 1994 ....499, 500

France

In re Javor, Cour de Cassation, 26 March 1996 500
Munyeshyaka, Cour de Cassation, 6 January 1998 500

Iraq

Al Anfal, Iraqi High Tribunal, Case no 1/CSecond/2006, 24 June 2007 497

Israel

Public Committee Against Torture in Israel v Government of Israel, HCJ 769/02,
11 December 2005 .... 61, 93, 336, 351, 360, 362, 363, 364, 365, 367, 370, 422

Japan

Ryuichi Shimoda et al v The State (1963) 32 ILR 626 389

Kosovo

Prosecutor v Gashi, Mustafa, Mustafa and Mehmeti, Decision of 16 July 2003 ......302, 303

Netherlands

Prosecutor v Knesević, Arnhem District Court, Military Chamber, Decision
No 05/07805-95, 21 February 1996 ....493, 499
Prosecutor v Knesević, Hoge Raad der Nederlanded, Strafkamer, No 3717,
11 November 1997 493
Prosecutor v X and Y, Hague District Court, 14 October 2005 ....493, 499

Peru

Peru v Guzmán Reinoso and others, National Criminal Chamber, No 650-03,
    13 October 2006 189

Russia

Presidential Decrees and Federal Government's Resolution on the Situation in Chechnya,
    Judgment of 31 July 1995 .... 201, 202

South Africa

*The Azanian Peoples Organization (AZAPO) and others v The President of the Republic of
    South Africa and others*, CCT 17/96, 25 July 1996 .... 201, 507

Switzerland

G (Grabez), Military Tribunal, Division 1, Lausanne, 18 April 1997 .... 493, 499
Niyonteze, Military Tribunal, Division 2, Lausanne, 30 April 1999 .... 232, 493, 499
Niyonteze, Military Appeal Tribunal 1A, Geneva, 26 May 2000 493
Niyonteze, Cassation Military Tribunal, 27 April 2001 493

United Kingdom

HH and others v Secretary of State for the Home Department [2008] UKAIT 22 166

United States

Ambrose Light (1885) 25 Fed Rep 408 17
Baldy v Hunter (1969) 171 US 388 560
Hamdan v Rumsfeld (2006) 126 S Ct 2749 .... 61, 202, 232, 307, 309
Holder, Attorney General, et al v Humanitarian Law Project, et al (2010) 130
    S Ct 2705 .... 533, 547, 548
Horn v Lockhart (1873) 84 US 570 531
Prize Cases (1862) 67 US 635 520
Texas v White (1868) 74 US 700 .... 530, 560
Thorington v Smith (1868) 8 Wall 1 531
The Three Friends (1897) 166 US 1 .... 13, 16
Trial of Henry Wirz, HR Ex Doc No 23, 40th Cong, 2nd Sess (1867) 239, 489, 508
United States of America v Omar Ahmed Khadr, Stipulation of Fact, 13 October 2010 518

Table of Instruments

Additional Protocol I, *see* Protocol I Additional to the Geneva Conventions of 12 August 1949 and Relating to the Protection of Victims of International Armed Conflicts 1977

Additional Protocol II, *see* Protocol II Additional to the Geneva Conventions of 12 August 1949 and Relating to the Protection of Victims of Non-International Armed Conflicts 1977

African Charter on Human and Peoples' Rights 1981
- Article 27 83
- Article 60 503
- Article 61 503

African Charter on the Rights and Welfare of the Child 1990.......................................320

African Union Convention for the Protection and Assistance of Internally Displaced Persons in Africa 2009 (Kampala Convention)................................ 101, 208, 290, 291, 547, 568

Amended Mines Protocol 1996, *see* Convention on Prohibitions or Restrictions on the Use of Certain Conventional Weapons Which May be Deemed to be Excessively Injurious or to Have Indiscriminate Effects 1980, Amended Protocol II

American Convention on Human Rights 1969 502
- Article 4 501
- Article 8 306
- Article 31 502

Biological Weapons Convention 1972, *see* Convention on the Prohibition of the Development, Production and Stockpiling of Bacteriological (Biological) and Toxin Weapons and on their Destruction 1972

Blinding Laser Weapons Protocol 1995, *see* Convention on Prohibitions or Restrictions on the Use of Certain Conventional Weapons Which May be Deemed to be Excessively Injurious or to Have Indiscriminate Effects 1980, Protocol IV

Charter of the United Nations 1945 (UN Charter) 45, 217, 218, 324, 325, 326, 327, 328, 329

Chemical Weapons Convention 1993, *see* Convention on the Prohibition of the Development, Production, Stockpiling and Use of Chemical Weapons and on their Destruction 1993

Convention against Torture and Other Cruel, Inhuman or Degrading Treatment or Punishment 1984 89
- Article 1 ....261, 262

Convention on Cluster Munitions 2008 .... 62, 83, 101, 240, 360, 409, 410, 494

Convention on the Privileges and Immunities of the UN 1946...................................327

Convention on Prohibitions or Restrictions on the Use of Certain Conventional Weapons Which May be Deemed to be Excessively Injurious or to Have Indiscriminate Effects 1980 (Conventional Weapons Convention/CCW)...............62, 63, 135, 399, 400, 406, 411, 429, 495
- Amended Article 1 .... 62, 101, 208, 236, 399, 400, 411, 412
- Amended Protocol II on Prohibitions or Restrictions on the Use of Mines, Booby-Traps, and Other Devices 1996 (Amended Mines Protocol) 404, 405
  - Article 1 .... 62, 208, 236, 405, 407
  - Article 2 ....344, 404
  - Article 3 .... 338, 342, 347, 348, 349, 351, 354, 387, 390, 404, 449, 452, 494
  - Article 7 404
- Protocol I on Non-Detectable Fragments 1980 (Non-Detectable Fragments Protocol) 63, 410
- Protocol II on Prohibitions or Restrictions on the Use of Mines, Booby-Traps and Other Devices 1980 (Mines Protocol) 62, 63, 125, 127, 406, 429

Table of Instruments

Protocol III on Prohibitions or Restrictions on the Use of Incendiary Weapons 1980
(Incendiary Weapons Protocol) 63, 338, 342, 344, 353, 397
Protocol IV on Blinding Laser Weapons 1995 (Blinding Laser Weapons Protocol) 63, 399, 400
Protocol V on Explosive Remnants of War 2003 .... 57, 411, 412

Convention on the Prohibition of the Development, Production and Stockpiling
of Bacteriological (Biological) and Toxin Weapons and on their Destruction 1972
(Biological Weapons Convention/BWC) 101, 393

Convention on the Prohibition of the Development, Production, Stockpiling and
Use of Chemical Weapons and on their Destruction 1993 (Chemical Weapons
Convention/CWC) 101, 395, 494
   Article 1 .... 61, 62, 395, 396

Convention on the Prohibition of Military or Any Other Hostile Use of
Environmental Modification Techniques 1976 (ENMOD Convention) 526–7
Convention on the Rights of the Child 1989 .... 101, 132, 150, 322, 467, 568
   Article 38 .... 79, 87, 317
   Article 41 317
Optional Protocol to the Convention on the Rights of the Child on the involvement
of children in armed conflict 2000 .... 101, 124, 323, 324, 467, 568
   Article 1 .... 88, 317, 320
   Article 2 .... 88, 320
   Article 3 .... 88, 320
   Article 4 .... 87, 88, 208, 237, 320

Convention on the Rights of Persons with Disabilities 2006 87
Convention on the Safety of UN and Associated Personnel 1994
(UN Safety Convention) 325, 327, 498

Conventional Weapons Convention 1980, *see* Convention on Prohibitions or Restrictions on the Use of Certain Conventional Weapons Which May be Deemed to be Excessively Injurious or to Have Indiscriminate Effects 1980

Cultural Property Convention, *see* Hague Convention for the Protection of Cultural Property in the Event of Armed Conflict 1954

ENMOD Convention 1976, *see* Convention on the Prohibition of Military or Any Other Hostile Use of Environmental Modification Techniques 1976

European Convention for the Protection of Human Rights and Fundamental Freedoms
1950 (ECHR)
   Article 2 .... 94, 370
   Article 5 90
   Article 6 306
   Article 15 83

Geneva Convention for the Amelioration of the Condition of the Wounded in
Armies in the Field 1864 .... 24, 30, 31, 33, 85, 140, 149, 202, 248, 273, 431, 444, 468, 539
   Article 6 247
   Additional Articles relating to the Condition of the Wounded in War 1868 33
Geneva Convention for the Amelioration of the Condition of the Wounded and Sick
in Armies in the Field 1906 .... 33, 114, 115, 202
   Article 1 247
Geneva Convention for the Amelioration of the Condition of the Wounded and Sick in
Armies in the Field 1929 .... 35, 36, 37, 38, 40, 59, 112, 116, 119, 149,
.... 196, 200, 247, 459, 523
Geneva Conventions 1949 (generally) 33, 47, 49, 86, 111, 114, 116, 117,
.... 118, 119, 120, 121, 122, 123, 126, 132, 133, 135, 144, 145,
.... 146, 147, 148, 149, 150, 151, 179, 202, 203, 207, 213, 219, 241,
.... 242, 270, 300, 328, 434, 438, 439, 441, 443, 444,
.... 488, 490, 491, 503, 523, 524, 562, 568

Geneva Convention (I) for the Amelioration of the Condition of the Wounded and
Sick in Armed Forces in the Field 1949 (Geneva Convention I/GC I/First Geneva
Convention) 74, 125, 126, 273
    Common Article 1 .... 240, 241
    Common Article 2 .... 47, 63, 119, 212
    Common Article 3 .... 1, 5, 30, 41, 42, 43, 44, 47, 48, 49, 51, 53,
                                      54, 55, 56, 57, 59, 61, 62, 63, 66, 67, 74, 157, 78, 87, 91,
                               101, 105, 109, 111, 116, 119, 121, 124, 126, 128, 142, 144,
                               145, 146, 147, 148, 151, 155, 156–64, 164–9, 174, 177,
                               181, 182, 184, 185, 189, 191, 192, 198, 203, 204, 207, 209,
                               213, 229, 230, 231, 232, 236, 239, 244, 248, 249, 250, 252,
                               255, 257, 258, 259, 260, 263, 267, 28, 271, 273, 275, 276,
                               277, 292, 305, 306, 307, 308, 313, 334, 336, 338, 392, 394,
                               406, 411, 428, 431, 444, 450–1, 458, 460, 469, 470, 473, 475,
                               476, 477, 479, 481, 482, 487, 491, 493, 498, 499, 501, 502, 503,
                               508, 519, 521, 524, 568
    Article 8 457
    Article 9 457
    Article 10 457
    Article 11 457
    Article 12 .... 247, 248
    Article 13 247
    Article 17 .... 74, 281, 282
    Article 23 385
    Article 46 449
    Article 47 .... 431, 432
    Article 49 .... 475, 477
    Article 52 459
    Article 60 213
Geneva Convention (II) for the Amelioration of the Condition of Wounded,
Sick and Shipwrecked Members of Armed Forces at Sea 1949 (Geneva
Convention II/GC II) 74, 125, 126, 273
    Common Article 1 ....*see* Geneva Convention (I)
    Common Article 2 ....*see* Geneva Convention (I)
    Common Article 3 ....*see* Geneva Convention (I)
    Article 8 457
    Article 9 457
    Article 10 457
    Article 11 457
    Article 47 449
    Article 48 .... 431, 432
    Article 50 .... 475, 477
    Article 53 459
    Article 59 213
Geneva Convention (IV) Relative to the Protection of Civilian Persons in Time of War 1949
(Geneva Convention IV/GC IV) 125, 126, 127, 213, 302, 491, 499
    Common Article 1 ....*see* Geneva Convention (I)
    Common Article 2 ....*see* Geneva Convention (I)
    Common Article 3 ....*see* Geneva Convention (I)
    Article 4 249
    Article 9 457
    Article 10 457
    Article 11 457
    Article 12 457
    Article 14 385
    Article 15 385
    Article 33 449

Table of Instruments xxix

Article 42 .... 90, 302
Article 43 302
Article 49 .... 68, 285, 287
Article 55 213
Articles 71–76 517
Article 78 302
Article 132 302
Article 144 ....431, 432
Article 146 ....475, 477
Article 149 459

Geneva Convention Relative to the Treatment of
Prisoners of War 1929 .... 35, 36, 37, 38, 40, 112, 116, 119, 149,
.... 196, 200, 263, 444, 457, 469, 523

Geneva Convention (III) Relative to the Treatment of Prisoners of War 1949
(Geneva Convention III/GC III) 125, 127, 142, 147, 213, 298,
.... 299, 300, 499, 524, 525

    Common Article 1 ....*see* Geneva Convention (I)
    Common Article 2 ....*see* Geneva Convention (I)
    Common Article 3 ....*see* Geneva Convention (I)
    Article 4 .... 214, 249, 311, 312, 519, 521, 524
    Article 8 457
    Article 9 457
    Article 10 457
    Article 11 457
    Article 13 ....449, 519
    Article 21 90
    Article 41 477
    Articles 58–68 521
    Articles 82–108 517
    Article 111 525
    Article 121 93
    Article 127 ....431, 432
    Article 129 ....475, 477
    Article 132 459
    Article 139 213

Geneva Gas Protocol 1925, *see* Protocol for the Prohibition of the Use of
Asphyxiating, Poisonous or Other Gases, and of Bacteriological Methods of Warfare 1925

Guiding Principles on Internal Displacement 1998 .... 101, 151, 289, 502, 565, 568
    Principle 6(2) 80
    Principle 6(3) 288
    Principle 7(1) 288
    Principle 12 290
    Principle 15(d) 290
    Principle 16 284
    Principle 20 290
    Principle 25(2) 332
    Principle 28 291
    Principle 29 291
    Principle 30 291

Hague Convention for the Protection of Cultural Property in the Event
of Armed Conflict 1954 (Cultural Property Convention/CPC) 101, 328, 375, 377, 429, 568
    Article 1 376
    Article 4 .... 377, 427, 449, 452
    Article 11 378
    Article 19 .... 42, 43, 54, 56, 63, 64, 208, 236, 376, 379, 433, 443

Article 21 457
Article 25 431
Second Protocol to the Hague Convention for the Protection of Cultural Property in the Event of
Armed Conflict 1999 (Second Protocol) 101, 375, 494, 568
    Article 1 .... 237, 344
    Article 3 .... 62, 377
    Article 4 380
    Article 6 .... 342, 354, 380
    Article 7 .... 349, 351, 353, 354, 380
    Article 8 356
    Article 10 379
    Article 11 .... 237, 379
    Article 13 .... 379, 380
    Article 16 498
    Article 22 .... 62, 208, 237, 377
Hague Convention (IV) Respecting the Laws and Customs of War on Land 1907
(Hague Convention IV/Fourth Hague Convention) 244, 479
Hague Declaration (IV-3) Concerning Expanding Bullets 1899 .... 401, 402
Hague Regulations Concerning the Laws and Customs of War on Land 1907 .... 34, 58
    Article 22 387
    Article 25 58
    Article 26 354
    Article 27 381
    Article 43 530
    Article 50 271
    Article 52 529
    Article 53 529
    Article 55 529
ICTR Statute, *see* Statute of the International Criminal Tribunal for the Prosecution of Persons Responsible for Genocide and Other Serious Violations of International Humanitarian Law Committed in the Territory of Rwanda and Rwandan citizens responsible for genocide and other such violations committed in the territory of neighbouring States, between 1 January 1994 and 31 December 1994 (1994)

ICTY Statute, *see* Statute of the International Tribunal for the Prosecution of Persons Responsible for Serious Violations of International Humanitarian Law Committed in the Territory of the Former Yugoslavia since 1991 (1993)

ILO Convention concerning the Prohibition and Immediate Action for the Elimination of the Worst Forms of Child Labour (C182) 1999 320

Incendiary Weapons Protocol, *see* Convention on Prohibitions or Restrictions on the Use of Certain Conventional Weapons Which May be Deemed to be Excessively Injurious or to Have Indiscriminate Effects 1980

International Convention against the Taking of Hostages 1979
    Article 1 269
    Article 12 269
International Convention for the Protection of All Persons from Enforced
Disappearance 2006 506
    Article 18 87
    Article 24(2) 87, 282
International Covenant on Civil and Political Rights 1966 .... 85, 87
    Preamble 86
    Article 4 .... 83, 84, 307–8
    Article 6 91
    Article 9 302

Table of Instruments

Article 14 .... 91, 310
Article 15 91

Second Optional Protocol to the International Covenant on Civil and Political
Rights on the Abolition of the Death Penalty 1989 311
International Covenant on Economic, Social and Cultural Rights 1966 .... 85, 86

Mines Protocol 1980, *see* Convention on Prohibitions or Restrictions on the Use of Certain Conventional Weapons Which May be Deemed to be Excessively Injurious or to Have Indiscriminate Effects 1980, Protocol II

Non-Detectable Fragments Protocol, *see* Convention on Prohibitions or Restrictions on the Use of Certain Conventional Weapons Which May be Deemed to be Excessively Injurious or to Have Indiscriminate Effects 1980, Protocol I

Optional Protocol to the Convention on the Rights of the Child on the involvement of children in armed conflict 2000, *see* Convention on the Rights of the Child 1989

Ottawa Convention on the Prohibition of the Use, Stockpiling, Production and
Transfer of Anti-Personnel Mines and on their Destruction 1997 .... 101, 240, 243,
.... 244, 390, 392, 407–8, 429, 494, 495, 539, 541, 542, 543, 545

Article 1 .... 62, 238, 407

Protocol I Additional to the Geneva Conventions of 12 August 1949 and Relating
to the Protection of Victims of International Armed Conflicts 1977
(Additional Protocol I/AP I) 51, 53, 58, 59, 64, 70, 117, 118, 120, 121,
.... 125, 126, 127, 132, 135, 147, 148, 150, 151, 179, 202, 209, 233,
.... 299, 328, 438, 439, 491, 503

Article 1(4) 214–22
Article 5 457
Article 8 .... 274, 278, 373
Article 10 248
Article 13 374
Article 20 449
Article 32 .... 282, 284
Article 35 526
Article 37 .... 418, 419
Article 43 368
Article 44 519
Article 48 337
Article 50 .... 58, 359, 423
Article 51 .... 58, 347, 349, 362, 421, 422, 449
Article 52 .... 58, 344
Article 53 449
Article 54 .... 423, 425, 426, 449
Article 55 .... 449, 526
Article 56 .... 69, 382, 383, 449
Article 57 .... 79, 504
Article 60 .... 383, 384
Article 72 83
Article 75 .... 302, 307
Article 76 310
Article 77 .... 68, 79, 316
Article 79 311
Article 82 437
Article 90 459–62
Article 96(3) 113, 220–2

Protocol II Additional to the Geneva Conventions of 12 August 1949 and Relating to
the Protection of Victims of Non-International Armed Conflicts 1977
(Additional Protocol II/AP II) 1, 5, 36, 51, 52, 53, 54, 56, 58, 59, 61,

.... 63, 64, 66, 67, 70, 74, 78, 79, 94, 97, 98, 101, 105, 111, 117, 118,
.... 120, 121, 132, 135, 142, 145, 146, 148, 150, 151, 152, 155, 182,
.... 198, 202, 207, 208, 209, 230, 232, 236, 239, 242, 328, 329, 334, 336,
.... 337, 428, 434, 438, 439, 450, 451, 452, 460, 469, 475, 476, 479,
.... 482, 487, 490, 491, 498, 499, 503, 563, 568

   Preamble 83, 86
   Article 1 .... 51, 66, 67, 97, 162, 164, 182–92, 196, 197, 210, 217, 229, 231, 232, 244, 250
   Article 2 .... 248, 251, 258, 259
   Part II 255
   Article 4 .... 51, 87, 187, 257, 258, 259, 260, 313, 452, 481, 521,
   Article 4(1) 412,
   Article 4(2) 263, 264, 268, 271, 314, 341, 427, 526,
   Article 4(3) 68, 74, 75, 79, 315, 542
   Article 5(1) 51, 74, 252, 293–5, 298, 301
   Article 5(2) 74, 75, 293, 295–6, 298, 301, 314
   Article 5(3) 296
   Article 6 .... 51, 91, 249, 252, 301, 305–10, 314, 316, 506–8, 520, 521, 552, 553, 561
   Article 7 .... 51, 74, 75, 248, 274–5
   Article 8 .... 51, 74, 75, 276, 280
   Article 9 .... 51, 74, 278, 279
   Article 10 .... 51, 74, 278, 279, 280
   Article 11 .... 51, 74, 373, 374
   Article 12 .... 51, 74, 374, 375, 700
   Article 13 .... 51, 57, 74, 337, 338, 341, 351, 362, 366, 367, 420
   Article 14 .... 51, 332, 423, 425, 526
   Article 15 .... 51, 69, 381–3
   Article 16 .... 51, 375, 376, 377, 379, 526
   Article 17 .... 51, 68, 75, 80, 252, 285, 286, 287, 288
   Article 18 .... 51, 252, 329–34
   Article 19 432

Protocol III Additional to the Geneva Conventions of 12 August 1949 and Relating
to the Adoption of an Additional Distinctive Emblem 2005 (Additional
Protocol III/APIII) 374, 416–7

Protocol for the Prohibition of the Use of Asphyxiating, Poisonous or
Other Gases, and of Bacteriological Methods of Warfare 1925 (Geneva
Gas Protocol 1925) 393, 394, 395, 396

Protocol to the Convention on Duties and Rights of States in the Event of
Civil Strife 1957 20

Rome Statute 1998, *see* Statute of the International Criminal Court 1998

Second Hague Protocol 1999, *see* Hague Convention for the Protection of Cultural Property in the
Event of Armed Conflict 1954, Second Protocol

St Petersburg Declaration Renouncing the Use, in Time of War, of Explosive
Projectiles Under 400 Grammes Weight 1868 .... 85, 244, 387, 388, 400–1

Statute of the International Criminal Court 1998
(Rome Statute/ICC Statute) 60, 63, 64, 71, 101, 106, 429, 488, 494
   Article 1 78
   Article 8 .... 62, 63, 164, 483, 495
   Article 8(2)(b)(iv) 79, 350
   Article 8(2)(b)(x) 249
   Article 8(2)(b)(xi) 249
   Article 8(2)(b)(xiii) 249
   Article 8(2)(b)(xvii) 63, 64
   Article 8(2)(b)(xviii) 63, 64
   Article 8(2)(b)(xix) 63, 64

Article 8(2)(b)(xx) 390, 391
Article 8(2)(b)(xxiii) 421
Article 8(2)(c) 67, 192, 193, 257, 258, 482
Article 8(2)(c)(i) 259, 260
Article 8(2)(c)(ii) 263
Article 8(2)(c)(iii) 268
Article 8(2)(d) 195
Article 8(2)(e) 67, 106, 192–5, 482
Article 8(2)(e)(i) 339
Article 8(2)(e)(ii) 279, 342, 374
Article 8(2)(e)(iii) 324, 328, 329, 342
Article 8(2)(e)(iv) 105, 305, 342, 373, 375
Article 8(2)(e)(vi) 265
Article 8(2)(e)(vii) 79, 316, 317
Article 8(2)(e)(viii) 80, 285, 287
Article 8(2)(e)(ix) 71, 249, 418, 419, 420
Article 8(2)(e)(x) 412
Article 8(2)(e)(xi) 249, 260
Article 8(2)(e)(xii) 71, 249, 428
Article 8(2)(e)(xiv) 396
Article 8(2)(e)(xv) 403
Article 8(2)(f) 192, 195
Article 9(3) 288
Article 10 81
Article 13 483
Article 14 483
Article 15 483
Article 17 486
Article 26 323

Statute of the International Tribunal for the Prosecution of Persons Responsible for Serious Violations of International Humanitarian Law Committed in the Territory of the Former Yugoslavia since 1991 (1993) (ICTY Statute)
  Article 2 479
  Article 3 ....57, 428, 479
  Article 4 479
  Article 5 479

Statute of the International Criminal Tribunal for the Prosecution of Persons Responsible for Genocide and Other Serious Violations of International Humanitarian Law Committed in the Territory of Rwanda and Rwandan citizens responsible for genocide and other such violations committed in the territory of neighbouring States, between 1 January 1994 and 31 December 1994 (1994) (ICTR Statute)
  Article 4 ....56, 257, 268, 271, 427, 480, 481

Statute of the Special Court for Sierra Leone 2002 (SCSL Statute)
  Article 3 ....257, 268, 271, 427, 487
  Article 4 ....79, 316, 487

UN Charter, *see* Charter of the United Nations 1945

UN Convention on the Law of the Sea 1982 (UNCLOS) 528

UN Convention on Privileges and Immunities, *see* Convention on the Privileges and Immunities of the United Nations 1946

UN Safety Convention, *see* Convention on the Safety of UN and Associated Personnel 1994

Universal Declaration of Human Rights 1948 ....45, 85, 86, 87, 329

Vienna Convention on the Law of Treaties 1969
  Article 34 240
  Article 35 240
  Article 36 240

List of Abbreviations

Additional Protocol I	Protocol Additional to the Geneva Conventions of 12 August 1949, and Relating to the Protection of Victims of International Armed Conflicts (Protocol I), of 8 June 1977
Additional Protocol II	Protocol Additional to the Geneva Conventions of 12 August 1949, and Relating to the Protection of Victims of Non-International Armed Conflicts (Protocol II), of 8 June 1977
AJIL	*American Journal of International Law*
ASIL Proceedings	*Proceedings of the Annual Meeting of the American Society of International Law*
BYIL	*British Yearbook of International Law*
CARHRIHL	Comprehensive Agreement on Respect for Human Rights and International Humanitarian Law
CICR	Comité International de la Croix-Rouge
Common Article 3	Article 3 common to the four Geneva Conventions of 1949
DRC	Democratic Republic of the Congo
EJIL	*European Journal of International Law*
FYROM	Former Yugoslav Republic of Macedonia
GA	General Assembly
GYIL	*German Yearbook of International Law*
HRLR	*Human Rights Law Review*
HRQ	*Human Rights Quarterly*
ICC	International Criminal Court
ICCPR	International Covenant on Civil and Political Rights
ICESCR	International Covenant on Economic, Social and Cultural Rights
ICJ	International Court of Justice
ICLQ	*International and Comparative Law Quarterly*
ICRC	International Committee of the Red Cross
ICTR	International Criminal Tribunal for Rwanda
ICTY	International Criminal Tribunal for the former Yugoslavia
IJRL	*International Journal of Refugee Law*
ILM	*International Legal Materials*
IRRC	*International Review of the Red Cross*
ISAF	International Security Assistance Force
IYHR	*Israel Yearbook on Human Rights*
JCSL	*Journal of Conflict and Security Law*
JICJ	*Journal of International Criminal Justice*
LJIL	*Leiden Journal of International Law*
MONUSCO	United Nations Organization Stabilization Mission
NATO	North Atlantic Treaty Organization
NGO	non-governmental organization
NQHR	*Netherlands Quarterly of Human Rights*
NYIL	*Netherlands Yearbook of International Law*
OECD	Organization for Economic Co-operation and Development
OLS	Operation Lifeline Sudan
ONUSAL	United Nations Observer Mission in El Salvador
OP-CRC	Optional Protocol to the Convention on the Rights of the Child on the Involvement of Children in Armed Conflict
RBDI	*Revue Belge de Droit International*

RdC	*Recueil des Cours de l'Académie de Droit International*
RICR	*Revue Internationale de la Croix-Rouge*
RSQ	*Refugee Survey Quarterly*
SC	Security Council
SCSL	Special Court for Sierra Leone
SRSG-CAAC	Special Representative of the Secretary-General for Children and Armed Conflict
UN	United Nations
UNAMA	United Nations Assistance Mission in Afghanistan
UNAMID	United Nations–African Union Mission in Darfur
UNAMSIL	United Nations Mission in Sierra Leone
UNEF II	United Nations Emergency Force
UNESCO	United Nations Educational, Scientific and Cultural Organization
UNHCR	United Nations High Commissioner for Refugees
UNMIK	United Nations Interim Administration in Kosovo
UNOSOM II	United Nations Operation in Somalia
UNTAET	United Nations Transitional Administration in East Timor
YIHL	*Yearbook of International Humanitarian Law*
VCLT	Vienna Convention on the Law of Treaties

List of Acronyms of Armed Groups

AFRC	Armed Forces Revolutionary Council
ALN	Armée de Libération Nationale
ANC	African National Congress
ANC-ZAPU	African National Council—Zimbabwe African People's Union
APRD	Armée Populaire pour la Restauration de la République et la Démocratie
ASNLF	Aceh Sumatra National Liberation Front
AUC	Autodefensas Unidas de Colombia
BIAF	Bangsamoro Islamic Armed Force
CDF	Civil Defence Force
CNA	Chin National Army
CNDD-FDD	National Council for the Defence of Democracy-Forces for the Defence of Democracy
CNDP	National Congress for the Defence of the People
CNF	Chin National Front
CPLA	Chinese People's Liberation Army
CPN-M	Communist Party of Nepal-Maoist
EAM	National Liberation Front
ELAS	Greek People's National Liberation Army
ELN	Ejército de Liberación Nacional
ESF	Eastern Sudan Front
EZLN	Ejército Zapatista de Liberación Nacional
FARC	Fuerzas Armadas Revolucionarias de Colombia
FDLR	Forces Démocratiques de Libération du Rwanda
FLEC	Front for the Liberation of the Enclave of Cabinda
FLN	Front de Libération Nationale
FMLN	Frente Farabundo Martí para la Liberación Nacional
FNLA	Frente Nacional de Libertação de Angola
FRELIMO	Frente de Libertação de Moçambique
GAM	Free Aceh Movement
GPRA	Provisional Government of the Algerian Republic
HPG	Hêzên Parastina Gel
IRA	Irish Republican Army
JEM	Justice and Equality Movement
KDP	Kurdistan Democratic Party
KLA	Kosovo Liberation Army
KNA	Karen National Army
KNLA	Karen National Liberation Army
KNPP	Karenni National Progressive Party
KNU	Karen National Union
LRA/M	Lord's Resistance Army / Movement
LTTE	Liberation Tigers of Tamil Eelam
LURD	Liberians United for Reconciliation and Democracy
MILF	Moro Islamic Liberation Front
MLC	Mouvement pour la Libération du Congo
MNJ	Mouvement des Nigériens pour la Justice
MNLF	Moro National Liberation Front
MODEL	Movement for Democracy in Liberia
MPLA	Movimento Popular de Libertação de Angola

MRTA	Movimiento Revolucionario Tupac Amaru
NDFP	National Democratic Front of the Philippines
NLA	National Liberation Army
NLF	National Liberation Front
NPA	New People's Army
NPFL	National Patriotic Front of Liberia
NRA	National Resistance Army
NRM	National Resistance Movement
NTC	National Transitional Council
ONLF	Ogaden National Liberation Front
PDKI	Democratic Party of Iranian Kurdistan
PKK	Kurdistan Workers' Party
PLO	Palestine Liberation Organization
PSLF	Palaung State Liberation Front
PUK	Patriotic Union of Kurdistan
RCD	Rally for Congolese Democracy
RENAMO	Resistência Nacional Moçambicana
RPF	Rwandan Patriotic Front
RUF	Revolutionary United Front
SLA	Sudan Liberation Army
SLM	Sudan Liberation Movement
SLM/A	Sudan Liberation Movement/Army
SLM-Unity	Sudan Liberation Movement-Unity
SPLA	Sudan People's Liberation Army
SPLM	Sudan People's Liberation Movement
SPLM/A	Sudan People's Liberation Movement/Army
SWAPO	South West Africa People's Organization
UNITA	União Nacional para a Independência Total de Angola
URNG	Unidad Revolucionaria Nacional Guatemalteca

Introduction

The vast majority of armed conflicts that are fought today are not of an international character.[1] This fact is well-appreciated but the literature on the law of armed conflict continues to focus disproportionately on international armed conflicts. The leading texts in the area devote a single chapter to non-international armed conflicts, which is usually tucked away at the end of the volume.[2] Things are slowly starting to change, and in recent years, a few works have been published on particular aspects of the law applicable in non-international armed conflict.[3] A variety of older works exist also on specific aspects of the law;[4] however, these have been largely overtaken by events. There is only one recent work that covers much of the breadth of the law of non-international armed conflict.[5]

Historically, the relative neglect for analyses of the law applicable in non-international armed conflict could have been considered an allegory to the state of the law on point. For many years, a detailed body of international humanitarian law regulated international armed conflicts as compared with a minimum of humanitarian rules that regulated non-international armed conflicts. Not infrequently, it continues to be suggested that non-international armed conflicts are governed by only a minimum of norms, with Article 3 common to the four Geneva Conventions of 1949 and Protocol II Additional to the 1949 Geneva Conventions of 1977 being deemed to constitute the majority of rules and the law on the conduct of hostilities being considered minimal.[6] However, the international humanitarian law that regulates non-international armed conflicts has developed considerably since 1977 and it has been suggested that, today, in many salient areas, it is almost as developed as that which

---

[1] Throughout the work, the term 'non-international armed conflict' is used rather than 'internal armed conflict' in order to capture armed conflicts that are not fought wholly within the boundaries of a state. The disadvantage of this terminology is that it suggests, incorrectly, that there is a single category of armed conflict and if it is not international in character, by default it is non-international. See S Sivakumaran, 'Re-envisaging the International Law of Internal Armed Conflict: A Rejoinder to Gabriella Blum' (2011) 22 *EJIL* 273.

[2] See eg the important works by APV Rogers, *Law on the Battlefield* (Manchester University Press, 2004); LC Green, *The Contemporary Law of Armed Conflict* (Manchester University Press, 2008); D Fleck (ed), *The Handbook of International Humanitarian Law* (Oxford University Press, 2008).

[3] See, in particular, L Zegveld, *The Accountability of Armed Opposition Groups in International Law* (Cambridge University Press, 2002); L Perna, *The Formation of the Treaty Law of Non-International Armed Conflicts* (Martinus Nijhoff, 2006); E La Haye, *War Crimes in Internal Armed Conflicts* (Cambridge University Press, 2008); A Cullen, *The Concept of Non-International Armed Conflict in International Humanitarian Law* (Cambridge University Press, 2010); E Crawford, *The Treatment of Combatants and Insurgents under the Law of Armed Conflict* (Oxford University Press, 2010).

[4] See, in particular, RA Falk (ed), *The International Law of Civil War* (Johns Hopkins Press, 1971); JN Moore, *Law and Civil War in the Modern World* (Johns Hopkins University Press, 1974); JE Bond, *The Rules of Riot* (Princeton University Press, 1974); K Suter, *The International Law of Guerrilla Warfare* (St Martins Press, 1984).

[5] L Moir, *The Law of Internal Armed Conflict* (Cambridge University Press, 2002).

[6] See eg Outcome of the Expert Consultation on the Issue of Protecting the Human Rights of Civilians in Armed Conflict: Report of the Office of the United Nations High Commissioner for Human Rights, A/HRC/11/31, 4 June 2009, para 24.

regulates international armed conflicts.[7] In light of these varying characterizations, this work considers, and analyses, the law that governs non-international armed conflicts.

Nature of the law

In order to understand the law of non-international armed conflict, the manner in which it has developed needs to be considered. The regulation of non-international armed conflict has taken various forms: from ad hoc regulation to systematic regulation; from regulation principally by conventional law, to regulation equally, or predominantly, by customary law; from the driving force of the International Committee of the Red Cross, to the important contributions of international courts and tribunals. A common feature of each of these approaches has been that the law of international armed conflict is treated as the standard to which the law of non-international armed conflict should aim. Yet, it is not at all clear that the law of international armed conflict *should* be the standard to which the law of non-international armed conflict aspires. After all, international armed conflicts and their non-international counterparts are of different sorts. There may be particularities of non-international armed conflicts that warrant different solutions to those presented by the law of international armed conflict. Equally, the solutions offered by the law of international armed conflict may be entirely inappropriate, or not the most appropriate, for application to non-international armed conflicts.

A second interesting feature of the law that regulates non-international armed conflicts relates to its nature. Whereas, historically, the applicable law was one of international humanitarian law alone, today, other bodies of international law, in particular international human rights law and international criminal law, play an important role. For this reason, at various points throughout the work, reference is made to 'the law of non-international armed conflict' rather than simply to international humanitarian law. However, international humanitarian law continues to constitute the bulk of the law of non-international armed conflict and, as already indicated, for many years, it constituted the only law that regulated non-international armed conflicts. As such, in the part of the book on historical regulation, as well as in other relevant places, reference will be made to international humanitarian law, the international humanitarian law of non-international armed conflict, or an associated term. More recently, international human rights law has been proposed as an appropriate body of law by which to regulate non-international armed conflicts. Accordingly, in the relevant section, reference will be made to the proposed human rights law of non-international armed conflict. However, to reiterate, today, international criminal law and international human rights law have become linked inextricably with international humanitarian law in the regulation of non-international armed conflict. Together, these three branches have led to the creation of an inclusive body of law: 'the law of non-international armed conflict'.

The methodology by which the law has been created is crucial for understanding the substance of the law of non-international armed conflict. The manner in which the rules have been created has had an important effect, both positive and negative, on the substantive rules themselves. Many rules exist by reason of their having been

---

[7] See, in particular, J-M Henckaerts and L Doswald-Beck, *Customary International Humanitarian Law: Volumes I and II* (Cambridge University Press, 2005).

modelled on the rules of international armed conflict; others are more developed, having been influenced by international human rights law or international criminal law. Yet, a number of rules have been transplanted from the law of international armed conflict to the law of non-international armed conflict without sufficient tailoring to meet the specificities of the situation; still others have been drawn from international human rights law without sufficient appreciation of the differing context. Accordingly, the manner in which the law of non-international armed conflict has developed and its impact on the substantive rules are an important part of the work.

Armed groups

One of the distinguishing features between international and non-international armed conflicts is the actors that take part in them. Non-international armed conflicts are fought between armed forces of states ('states') and the military wings of non-state armed groups ('non-state armed groups' or 'armed groups') or between armed groups. Thus, at least one half of the actors that take part in non-international armed conflicts are non-state actors. This fact is also well-appreciated, but its consequences have not been acted upon. In particular, the law and the legal literature focus predominantly on states parties to non-international armed conflicts. Relatively little is known about the structure and workings of armed groups, at least from a legal perspective, yet the structure and workings of armed groups impact on the operation of the law; the ability of armed groups to comply with the law is not always taken into account in fashioning the rules; and the views of armed groups on the law are even less well known. More general manifestations of this focus include failing to engage with non-state armed groups on humanitarian norms, overlooking the practice of armed groups, and viewing them solely as a problem rather than also as part of the solution.

This oversight, partly deliberate and partly accidental, can be readily explained. The law of non-international armed conflict is part of public international law and public international law remains rather statist in character. Compounding this state-centric focus is the fact that non-international armed conflicts involve non-state actors that are *challenging* states. Thus, states often view their opponents as illegitimate and characterize them as criminals, traitors, and terrorists. However, as non-international armed conflicts, by definition, include non-state actors, and the law of non-international armed conflict operates on the principle of equality of obligation of the belligerents, that law should have certain characteristics that are different to those of general public international law. Furthermore, although a tension will exist between engaging armed groups and legitimizing or affording them a certain status, this tension has to be factored into the law. It cannot serve to justify ignoring or overlooking armed groups.

For these reasons, this work incorporates the perspectives of armed groups on the law.[8] In particular, it includes commitments armed groups have made on respect for the law, as well their views on, and critiques of, the law. It is self-evident that the views, commitments, and motivations of states should be considered in a work on the law of international armed conflict; the same should be true of states and non-state armed groups alike in a work on the law of non-international armed conflict. Accordingly, to consider the views of armed groups is not to sentimentalize them, to be naïve as to their

---

[8] All translations are unofficial by the author unless indicated otherwise.

motives, or to fail to see them as violators of the law. One of the most influential of all military strategists, Sun Tzu, highlighted the necessity of understanding the enemy and its capabilities, tactics, and cultures of war, in order to understand how the enemy fights.[9] Similar considerations arise as to the compliance of states and non-state armed groups with the law. Only by understanding what the parties think of the rules, why they comply with them, and why they do not, can the law be better tailored to meet the specificities of non-international armed conflicts.

Practice

In light of the above, it is evident that the practice of non-international armed conflicts has to be considered. It has been suggested that:

> The laws of war are strange not only in their subject matter, which to many people seems a contradiction in terms, but also in their methodology. There is little tradition of disciplined and reasoned assessment of how the laws of war have operated in practice... In short, the study of the law needs to be integrated with the study of history: if not it is inadequate.[10]

Even if this work does not fully live up to the injunction, it is hoped that it goes some way towards meeting the point. Practice has been selected to illustrate the operation of rules as well as their violation. Violations of the law tend to be publicized and good practice overlooked. Publication of violations alone can give the impression that the law is consistently violated and never respected. To some extent, this is true of international law more generally. However, with the law of armed conflict, a focus on violations could lead parties to believe that the law is meaningless, bringing with it devastating consequences. Accordingly, instances of respect, or purported respect, for the law have been included.

The examples that have been selected should not be taken as a reflection of the general behaviour of the state or armed group. To note that, on one occasion, a particular non-state armed group respected a particular rule cannot be taken to mean that that group always respected that rule, let alone the law more generally. Similarly, to draw on a particular state's violation of a rule is not to characterize that state as a persistent violator of that rule or of the law. Examples have been selected from different armed conflicts and relating to different parties in order to avoid giving this impression. Reliance has been placed primarily on the statements of the parties to the conflict themselves, with media reports and reports of non-governmental organizations being kept to a minimum. However, as the statements emanate from one side, they must be treated with caution, as must allegations made by one party against another. Nonetheless, accusations are useful as they provide an indication of the accusing party's view of the facts and, more importantly, of the law. It is possible, though, that the situation took place in a manner different from that presented. There may also be debate as to the precise character of a particular conflict, even whether the situation amounted to an armed conflict at all. Such debates are inherent in light of the approach taken by the law to the characterization of violence.

---

[9] S Tzu, *The Art of War* (Oxford University Press, 1963).
[10] A Roberts, 'Land Warfare: From Hague to Nuremberg', in M Howard, GJ Andreopoulos, and MR Shulman (eds), *The Laws of War: Constraints on Warfare in the Western World* (Yale University Press, 1994) 116, 117.

Goals

In sum, the book has two principal goals. First, it seeks to ascertain the content of the law of non-international armed conflict, when it applies, and how it is enforced, while subjecting it all to critical analysis. In order to understand the substantive content, the methodology by which the law is created and the changes to the methodology over time also have to be considered. As will be seen, the methodology by which the law has been created has had a fundamental impact on the substance of the law itself. The practical operation of the law is illustrated through examples of respect for, and violation of, the rules by parties to conflicts. Second, the book seeks to incorporate the views of both parties to conflicts—states as well as armed groups—on the law. As non-international armed conflicts involve armed groups, their views on the law are just as important as those of states. Their views are gleaned primarily through a consideration of their ad hoc commitments and other statements.

Throughout the course of the book, various assumptions and conventional wisdom are tested. Among the more prevalent assumptions that have emerged over time are that the first line of defence against the application of the law is denial of the existence of an armed conflict;[11] that the application of common Article 3 has been uncommon;[12] that Protocol II Additional to the Geneva Conventions of 1949 has never been applied,[13] or that its application has been rare;[14] that bilateral agreements on matters of international humanitarian law are seldom concluded in non-international armed conflicts;[15] and that non-state armed groups will not commit to respect the law because the law was created by the states against which they are in conflict.[16] Each of these propositions is intuitively appealing, but they are nevertheless assumptions and will be tested in the course of the work.

A note to the reader

The book is structured in three parts. Part I explores the approaches taken by international law to the regulation of non-international armed conflicts. It considers the ad hoc approaches of regulation through recognition of belligerency and regulation through instructions, unilateral declarations, and bilateral agreements. It also considers the systematic regulation of non-international armed conflict through international humanitarian law. It then analyses the transformation in the regulation of non-international armed conflicts which took place in the mid-1990s, drawing on the role of international human rights law and international criminal law, and on the modelling on the

---

[11] RR Baxter, 'Some Existing Problems of Humanitarian Law' (1975) 14 *Military Law and Law of War Review* 297, 298; T Meron, *Human Rights in Internal Strife: Their International Protection* (Grotius Publications, 1987) 43 (on common Article 3).

[12] Moir, *Internal Armed Conflict*, above note 5, 120.

[13] C Tomuschat, *Human Rights: Between Idealism and Realism* (Oxford University Press, 2008) 306; A Paulus and M Vashakmadze, 'Asymmetrical Warfare and the Notion of Armed Conflict—A Tentative Conceptualization' (2009) 91 *IRRC* 95, 103.

[14] D Turns, 'The Law of Armed Conflict (International Humanitarian Law)', in MD Evans (ed), *International Law* (Oxford University Press, 2010) 814, 823; Cullen, *The Concept of Non-International Armed Conflict*, above note 3, 110.

[15] Moir, *Internal Armed Conflict*, above note 5, 64.

[16] A Cassese, 'The Status of Rebels under the 1977 Geneva Protocol on Non-International Armed Conflicts' (1981) 30 *ICLQ* 416, 429–30; La Haye, *War Crimes*, above note 3, 120.

law of international armed conflict. Finally, it discusses the sources of the law of non-international armed conflict focusing in particular on non-traditional 'sources'.

Part II is devoted to the substantive law of non-international armed conflict. It identifies when a non-international armed conflict can be said to exist, contrasting older approaches of not defining an armed conflict with more recent approaches of defining an armed conflict. It distinguishes between internal tensions and non-international armed conflicts, and between non-international armed conflicts and international armed conflicts. It also considers the recently posited notion of a transnational armed conflict. Part II then turns to the scope of application of the law, exploring its temporal, geographical, and personal extent. The rules relating to the treatment of civilians and persons *hors de combat* are then considered, followed by the rules on the conduct of hostilities. The implementation and enforcement of the law of non-international armed conflict concludes the Part on the substantive law.

Part III considers the ways in which the law of non-international armed conflict needs to move forward. It sets out proposals for filling gaps in the substantive law, offers possibilities for improving the implementation and enforcement of the law, and posits an alternative to the traditional means by which the law is created.

Each of the three parts can be read on their own or in conjunction with any other part. Part I concerns histories and methodologies and thus may be of interest to the general international lawyer. It should also appeal to the international humanitarian lawyer as the methodology by which the law has been created has had important effects on the substantive content of the rules. Part II is designed to provide a critical analysis of the black-letter law and will be of interest to those dealing with situations of non-international armed conflict in an academic or professional capacity. Part III may, again, be of more general appeal both to the international lawyer and the international humanitarian lawyer, particularly for those with an interest in developing the law.

PART I

REGULATING NON-INTERNATIONAL ARMED CONFLICTS

1
Ad-hoc Regulation

1. Introduction

The laws and customs of war, including those that govern what are today described as non-international armed conflicts, are of ancient origin. They have been described as being 'as old an institution as war itself'.[1] The modern period of regulation of armed conflict dates back to the nineteenth century and it is from that period onwards that is the focus of this Part. However, the nineteenth, and much of the twentieth, centuries were characterized by a general reluctance on the part of states to regulate non-international armed conflicts through international law. Two ideas, in particular, informed this reluctance. First, the war-making power was considered a sovereign prerogative and, accordingly, only states could declare and fight wars. To upgrade violence that involved non-state armed groups to the category of war, even civil war, was deemed to be upgrading the legal status of rebels. Second, situations of internal violence were considered to be within the *domaine réservé* of states and therefore a matter for the affected state alone. As such, the legal regulation of non-international armed conflict that existed was ad hoc in character and took two principal forms—recognition of belligerency and regulation through bilateral agreement or unilateral declaration. These two forms of regulation are the subject of this chapter. The systematic regulation of non-international armed conflict through international humanitarian law is considered in Chapter 2.

2. Recognition of belligerency

2.1 The concept of recognition

Historically, in general terms, intra-state violence was categorized into three types: rebellion, insurgency, and belligerency. The principal distinction between the three related to the intensity of the violence. A rebellion involved violence that was of limited duration and which could be rapidly suppressed by the police without the need to resort to military units.[2] A rebellion was a matter for the parent state, and the rebels remained subject to domestic law, including prosecution for its violation.[3] Other states were prohibited from providing assistance to the rebels, such assistance potentially amounting to an intervention and thus violating the duty of non-interference in the

---

[1] I Harding, 'The Origins and Effectiveness of the Geneva Conventions for the Protection of War Victims' (1973) 13 *IRRC* 283, 285.
[2] RA Falk, 'Janus Tormented: The International Law of Internal War', in JN Rosenau (ed), *International Aspects of Civil Strife* (Princeton University Press, 1964) 185, 197; L Kotzsch, *The Concept of War in Contemporary History and International Law* (Droz, 1956) 230.
[3] E Castrén, *Civil War* (Suomalainen Tiedeakatemia, 1966) 21 and 97; HA Wilson, *International Law and the Use of Force* (Clarendon Press, 1988) 23; L Moir, *The Law of Internal Armed Conflict* (Cambridge University Press, 2002) 4.

domestic affairs of a state.[4] These other states remained free to assist the incumbent government.[5]

An insurgency involved serious violence coupled with the inability of the government to suppress the violence.[6] Thus, an insurgency, in contrast to a rebellion, featured extended violence, usually in terms of duration, geographical scope, and numbers, and in which the outcome was in doubt.[7] Beyond these broad indicia there was little that allowed for objective characterization of a situation as one of insurgency. Situations that gave rise to recognition of insurgency were fluid and there was abundant room for discretion on the part of the recognizing state. Recognition of a situation as insurgency allowed the recognizing state to acknowledge the violence while leaving open its response to the violence and its relations with the insurgents. Recognition of insurgency created 'a factual relation in the meaning that legal rights and duties as between insurgents and outside States exist[ed] only in so far as they [we]re expressly conceded and agreed upon for reasons of convenience, of humanity, or of economic interest'.[8] Recognition of insurgency did not give rise to a *specific* set of rights and obligations.[9] Thus, to search for a definition of insurgency, or for objective criteria against which a state of insurgency would be judged, is to misconstrue its nature. Flexibility was paramount.

Situations of belligerency were rather different. Recognition of belligerency on the part of the parent state led to the violence being regulated by the law of war, while recognition on the part of other states led to application of the law of neutrality.[10] According to the classic statement on point, belligerency required 'the existence of a *de facto* political organization of the insurgents, sufficient in character, population and resources, to constitute it, if left to itself, a State among the nations, reasonably capable of discharging the duties of a State; the actual employment of military forces on each side, acting in accordance with the rules and customs of war'.[11] This statement was adopted almost wholesale by US President Grant in 1870 in the context of internal violence in Cuba.[12]

The same sorts of considerations are to be found in an 1867 opinion of the British Law Officers, considerations that were understood as reflecting 'statements of general principle'.[13] These considerations, in deciding whether or not to recognize belligerency, included:

whether the insurrection has or has not assumed the dimensions of war, and whether the legitimate interests of the neutral State do, or do not, require that she should claim from both

---

[4] Kotzsch, *Concept of War*, above note 2, 231; Wilson, *Use of Force*, above note 3, 23.
[5] Falk, Janus Tormented, above note 2, 198; Wilson, *Use of Force*, above note 3, 23–4; HW Briggs, *The Law of Nations* (Crofts, 1938) 992.
[6] Castrén, *Civil War*, above note 3, 211.
[7] Ibid, 24 and 28.
[8] H Lauterpacht, *Recognition in International Law* (Cambridge University Press, 1947) 277. See also A Cullen, *The Concept of Non-International Armed Conflict in International Humanitarian Law* (Cambridge University Press, 2010) 11–12.
[9] CC Hyde, *International Law Chiefly as Interpreted and Applied by the United States* (Little, Brown, and Co, 1922) 82; T Chen, *The International Law of Recognition* (Stevens and Sons, 1951) 399–400; Lauterpacht, *Recognition*, above note 8, 270 and 276–7; E Castrén, 'Recognition of Insurgency' (1965) 5 *Indian Journal of International Law* 443, 446; Falk, Janus Tormented, above note 2, 199.
[10] On the consequences of recognition of belligerency, see below, 14–16.
[11] H Wheaton, *Elements of International Law* (RH Dana ed) (London, 1866) 35 fn 15.
[12] See Special Message of President Grant, 13 June 1870, reproduced in JB Moore, *A Digest of International Law, Volume 1* (Government Printing Office, 1906) 194–5.
[13] HA Smith, *Great Britain and the Law of Nations, Volume I: States* (PS King and Son, 1932) 262.

parties the performance towards her of the obligations incident to the status of a belligerent...
the length of time during which the contest has existed; the number, order, and discipline of the
rebel forces; their subordination to a *de facto* existing Government, capable of maintaining
international relations with foreign States; the acts of the Government against which the rebels
are in arms, both with respect to the rebels themselves and to foreign States.[14]

On the basis of the various statements and opinions issued during the latter part of the
nineteenth century, a number of criteria can be discerned as being required before
belligerency would be recognized. There must have existed: (1) a civil war 'accompanied by a state of general hostilities'; (2) 'occupation and a measure of orderly administration of a substantial part of national territory by the insurgents'; (3) observance of
the laws and customs of war by the purported belligerent group 'acting under a
responsible authority'; and, rather more controversially, (4) 'the practical necessity for
third States to define their attitude to the civil war'.[15]

The precise degree to which each of the criteria had to be satisfied was the subject of
much debate. As to the requirement of 'a state of general hostilities', for example, there
was some suggestion that the disturbances be of such proportions as to have 'developed
into a civil war'.[16] US President Grant, referring to the violence in Cuba in 1875, thus
noted that the hostilities must 'take the contest out of the category of a mere rebellious
insurrection, or occasional skirmishes, and place it on the terrible footing of war'.[17]
Others, however, placed the emphasis elsewhere, requiring 'an armed conflict of a
general (as distinguished from purely local) character'.[18] On this basis, the violence in
Brazil in 1894 was not recognized as belligerency, as the insurgents consisted solely of
units of the navy.[19] Emphasis was also placed on different aspects of the hostilities, for
example its duration,[20] the military power at issue,[21] and the means by which the
destruction was brought about.[22] These differing emphases foreshadowed more recent
views expressed on the notion of a non-international armed conflict.[23] Best reflecting
the position is the communication from the British Foreign Secretary to the British
Ambassador in Constantinople, written in the context of the 1825 Greek rebellion
against Turkey, who noted that 'a certain degree of force and consistency acquired by
any mass of population engaged in war entitled that population to be treated as a
belligerent'.[24] This generality of statement is also reminiscent of present-day debates on
the definition of a non-international armed conflict.[25]

---

[14] Opinion of the Law Officers (JB Karslake, CJ Selwyn, and R Phillimore), 14 August 1867, reproduced in A McNair, *International Law Opinions, Selected and Annotated, Volume One: Peace* (Cambridge University Press, 1956) 143, 144.

[15] L Oppenheim, *International Law, A Treatise: Volume II* (H Lauterpacht ed) (Longman, 1952) 249–50. See also Lauterpacht, *Recognition*, above note 8, 176.

[16] Castrén, *Civil War*, above note 3, 177. See also H Kelsen, *Principles of International Law* (Rinehart and Co, 1952) 291.

[17] Seventh Annual Message of President Grant, 7 December 1875, reproduced in Moore, *Digest*, above note 12, 197.

[18] Lord McNair and AD Watts, *The Legal Effects of War* (Cambridge University Press, 1966) 32.

[19] Lauterpacht, *Recognition*, above note 8, 176 fn 2.

[20] Kotzsch, *Concept of War*, above note 2, 221–2.

[21] G Schwarzenberger, *International Law as Applied by International Courts and Tribunals, Volume II: The Law of Armed Conflict* (Stevens and Sons, 1968) 708.

[22] Kelsen, *Principles of International Law*, above note 16, 291.

[23] See Chapter 5.

[24] Quoted in WE Hall, *A Treatise on International Law* (A Pearce Higgins ed) (Clarendon Press, 1924) 38 fn 1.

[25] See below, 164–80.

A similar divergence of opinion existed on the second requirement, namely occupation and orderly administration. On one view, it was the organization of the armed group that was crucial, and provided the armed group was organized, it need not have been in the nature of a government or have the characteristics of a state.[26] However, this was very much the minority position. The preponderant view required that the armed group have a government or quasi-government in place,[27] even that the belligerents must have 'acquired all characteristics of a state'.[28] Thus, Great Britain did not recognize as belligerency the violence in Brazil in the 1890s due to its view that the rebels had not set up a *de facto* government.[29] Similarly, the United States did not recognize the same situation as belligerency in part due to its view that the rebels' 'provisional government was not intact and was not improving either in organization or in effectiveness'.[30] Along similar lines, France did not recognize Polish insurgents as belligerents during the violence of 1864, the French President explaining to the Senate:

> The Poles in arms have no government, not even a *de facto* government, for one cannot accord this title to an assembly of a few men whose names are a mystery and whose location is unknown. Neither is it possible to regard as an army those bands and parties who fight, sometimes in one place and sometimes in another, always courageously but without common direction, under a variety of chiefs who do not recognize a single superior . . .[31]

As to the observance of the law of war on the part of the putative belligerents, which constituted the third requirement, again, differences of opinion existed as to where the emphasis lay. Some argued that the hostilities should be conducted in accordance with the rules of warfare, pointing out that '[h]e who wants to benefit from international law must show that he respects it'.[32] Others focused on the *capacity* of the insurgents to act in accordance with the rules of warfare, arguing that it is not possible to demand any such guarantees in advance.[33] Similar sorts of debates exist today as to whether the armed group needs to have the capacity to implement the law or whether the law actually needs to be implemented in order for certain rules to enter into force.[34]

The fourth requirement, the practical necessity of states not involved in the violence to define their attitude to the violence, was even more controversial in that its very

---

[26] Castrén, *Civil War*, above note 3, 178, 181–2; McNair and Watts, *Legal Effects of War*, above note 18, 32.

[27] Kelsen, *Principles of International Law*, above note 16, 291; Schwarzenberger, above note 21, 708; JE Bond, *The Rules of Riot* (Princeton University Press, 1974) 34; D Schindler, 'State of War, Belligerency, Armed Conflict', in A Cassese (ed), *The New Humanitarian Law of Armed Conflict* (Editoriale Scientifica, 1979) 3; Cullen, *The Concept of Non-International Armed Conflict*, above note 8, 19.

[28] M Greenspan, *The Modern Law of Land Warfare* (University of California Press, 1959) 18. See also JH Beale Jr, 'The Recognition of Cuban Belligerency' (1895–6) 9 *Harvard Law Review* 406, 407; Chen, *Recognition*, above note 9, 364.

[29] Opinion of the Law Officers (Russell and Rigby), 13 October 1893, excerpted in A McNair, *International Law Opinions, Selected and Annotated, Volume Two: Peace* (Cambridge University Press, 1956) 393.

[30] Cable of Secretary of State Gresham to Minister to Brazil Thompson to inform Admiral da Gama who had requested recognition as belligerents, 5 February 1894, reproduced in Moore, *Digest*, above note 12, 205.

[31] Statement of President Stourm to the French Senate, quoted in C Zorgbibe, 'Sources of the Recognition of Belligerent Status' (1977) 17 *IRRC* 111, 121.

[32] Schwarzenberger, *International Law*, above note 21, 708. See also Zorgbibe, Belligerent Status, above note 31, 123 (allowing for 'isolated minor infractions'); Schindler, State of War, above note 27, 3.

[33] Castrén, *Civil War*, above note 3, 179. See also at 138. See further Kotzsch, *Concept of War*, above note 2, 221–2.

[34] See below, 188–9.

existence as a prerequisite to recognition was disputed. For some, the requirement served to distinguish genuine instances of recognition, in situations that called for it, from those that were intended to aid the putative belligerent.[35] On this view, belligerency could only be recognized when the link between the violence and the recognizing state was such that it was 'necessary' for the recognizing state to determine its treatment of the parties to the violence.[36] Thus, the violence must have impinged upon the rights or interests of the recognizing state,[37] as recognition was 'a reasonable measure of self-protection'.[38] In practice, the rights and interests in question were considered to be impinged only when the violence had a maritime element and interfered with maritime commerce, when the violence occurred in border regions, or when citizens were in need of protection.[39] However, not everyone took the view that this was actually a requirement.[40] An article on point in the draft Institut de Droit International resolution was rejected,[41] and states occasionally granted recognition without any real interest in the violence. For example, Peru reportedly recognized Cuban insurgents in 1869 'simply because of its openly proclaimed intention to cause trouble for Spain'.[42] To be sure, states frequently refrained from recognizing the situation as one of belligerency due to a lack of interest in the matter. For example, the British Law Officers noted that Great Britain had 'not thought fit to recognize belligerency [in Madagascar in 1895], because there was no occasion for it in the interests of Great Britain'.[43] Along similar lines, US President Grant refused to recognize Cuban insurgents as belligerents in 1875 in part because it was not necessary to do so, necessity being defined as 'when the interests and rights of another Government or of its people are so far affected by a pending civil conflict as to require a definition of its relations to the parties thereto'.[44] An interest in the violence, or in the state in which the violence took place, thus provided a useful indication as to whether or not recognition would be granted.[45] However, it does not follow from this that an interest was a prerequisite to granting recognition.

Three, arguably four, criteria were thus required to exist before belligerency could be recognized. However, the requirements were susceptible to differing interpretation, sometimes vastly so. Indeed, the terms were so open to interpretation that it has been

---

[35] Lauterpacht, *Oppenheim*, above note 15, 249–50.
[36] TJ Lawrence, *The Principles of International Law* (MacMillan, 1895) 304.
[37] *The Three Friends* (1897) 166 US 1, 63; Hall, *Treatise*, above note 24, 39. See also Kotzsch, *Concept of War*, above note 2, 223; Greenspan, *Law of Land Warfare*, above note 28, 19; Falk, Janus Tormented, above note 2, 208.
[38] Hall, *Treatise*, above note 24, 39.
[39] TA Walker, *Science of International Law* (CJ Clay and Sons, 1893) 116; Lawrence, *Principles*, above note 36, 304; Wheaton, *Elements of International Law*, above note 11, 35 fn 15; Hyde, *International Law*, above note 9, 81; Hall, *Treatise*, above note 24, 39, 40; Moir, *Internal Armed Conflict*, above note 3, 9.
[40] It is missing from lists of the requirements for the recognition of belligerency. See eg Kelsen, *Principles*, above note 16, 291; McNair and Watts, *The Legal Effects of War*, above note 18, 32; Schindler, State of War, above note 27, 3. See also Zorgbibe, Belligerent Status, above note 31, 124, who considers this 'requirement' to have 'little basis'.
[41] Institut de Droit International, 'Droits et devoirs des Puissances étrangères, au cas de mouvement insurrectionnel, envers les gouvernements établis et reconnus qui sont aux prises avec l'insurrection' (Neuchâtel, 1900) Article 8. See Zorgbibe, Belligerent Status, above note 31, 124.
[42] Zorgbibe, ibid.
[43] Opinion of the Law Officers (RT Reid and F Lockwood), 26 April 1895, reproduced in McNair, *International Law Opinions*, above note 29, 371.
[44] Seventh Annual Message of President Grant, 7 December 1875, reproduced in Moore, *Digest*, above note 12, 196.
[45] Smith, *Great Britain and the Law of Nations*, above note 13, 261–2.

suggested that, in practice, recognition of belligerency took place more on the basis of diplomatic expediency than for reasons of law.[46] It is certainly true that self-interest motivated recognition rather than a desire to mitigate the humanitarian suffering of individuals caught up in the conflict.[47] This is perhaps unsurprising given that states took the view that matters of belligerency and neutrality were, to use the language of an 1867 opinion of the British Law Officers, 'of great delicacy and grave importance'.[48] However, this meant that the definition, insofar as there was one, remained subject to political expediency.

2.2 Consequences of recognition

Upon recognition of insurgency, subject to the intention of the recognizing state, the insurgents tended to be granted rights in respect of the territory which they controlled vis-à-vis the recognizing state. Outside that territory, however, few, if any, rights were accorded to them.[49] For example, insurgents could demand payment for the use of ports which they controlled,[50] and they could prevent supplies from crossing territory under their control in order to stop them reaching the state.[51] However, insurgents were not authorized to stop and search foreign vessels on the high seas.[52] States that recognized insurgency neither prosecuted nor executed insurgents upon capture,[53] nor did they treat insurgents as pirates provided the insurgents carried out their actions against vessels of the parent state.[54] However, the British Law Officers considered the treatment of insurgents to be 'a very delicate question',[55] and the matter tended to be left to the discretion of the state concerned.[56] What is particularly important for the purposes of this chapter is that recognition of insurgency did not automatically give rise to the application of the law of war.[57] A situation was not recognized as insurgency in order to bring about the application of a body of law to regulate the violence; rather, it was recognized in order to regulate the relationship between the insurgents and the recognizing state. Even such regulation was ad hoc in nature and the precise contours of the relationship between the insurgents and the recognizing state could not be

---

[46] E Luard, 'Civil Conflicts in Modern International Relations', in E Luard (ed), *The International Regulation of Civil Wars* (Thames and Hudson, 1972) 7, 20; Wilson, *Use of Force*, above note 3, 26. See also Hall, *Treatise*, above note 24, 37–9; DA Elder, 'The Historical Background of Common Article 3 of the Geneva Convention of 1949' (1979) 11 *Case Western Reserve Journal of International Law* 37, 39–40. But cf Lauterpacht, *Recognition*, above note 8, 186.

[47] Subject to rare exceptions. See below, 15.

[48] Opinion of the Law Officers (JB Karslake, CJ Selwyn, and R Phillimore), 14 August 1867, reproduced in McNair, *International Law Opinions*, above note 14, 143, 144.

[49] Greenspan, *Law of Land Warfare*, above note 28, 620; Castrén, *Civil War*, above note 3, 211–12.

[50] SC Neff, *War and the Law of Nations* (Cambridge University Press, 2005) 269.

[51] Greenspan, *Law of Land Warfare*, above note 28, 620; Wilson, *Use of Force*, above note 3, 24–5.

[52] Greenspan, *Law of Land Warfare*, above note 28, 620; Wilson, *Use of Force*, above note 3, 24–5.

[53] Chen, *Recognition*, above note 9, 333–5; Greenspan, *Law of Land Warfare*, above note 28, 602–1; Castrén, *Civil War*, above note 3, 171; Neff, *War and the Law of Nations*, above note 50, 269.

[54] See the opinions of the British Law Officers, reproduced in Lauterpacht, *Recognition*, above note 8, 310–28. See also Chen, *Recognition*, above note 9, 333–5; Castrén, Recognition, above note 9, 453; McNair and Watts, *Legal Effects of War*, above note 18, 31.

[55] Opinion of the Law Officers (C Robinson, S Shepherd, and R Gifford), 7 October 1817, reproduced in McNair, *International Law Opinions*, above note 29, 333–4.

[56] See the statement of the US Secretary of State, speaking of vessels of the Haitian insurgents in 1869, reproduced in Moore, *A Digest of International Law, Volume II* (Government Printing Office, 1906) 1085.

[57] Castrén, *Civil War*, above note 3, 207–23; Cullen, *The Concept of Non-International Armed Conflict*, above note 8, 12–13.

determined in advance. Much depended on the view of the recognizing state. In sum, it was the need to clarify the legal relationship and not a desire for humanitarian protection that brought about recognition of insurgency.

Things were similar, but also different, insofar as recognition of belligerency was concerned. Through recognition of belligerency, the situation was recognized as a civil war; however, the effects of recognition differed depending on the identity of the recognizing entity. If a state other than the parent state recognized the situation as belligerency, it was required to act as a neutral and could not offer assistance to either party.[58] It could, however, trade with both the belligerents and the state. Thus, in 1861, the British Law Officers approved of the 'opening of postal relations with the Confederate American States' following British recognition of belligerency.[59] Recognizing states were also exempt from paying customs duties to the state if the duties had already been paid to the belligerents.[60] The advantages gained by recognition of belligerency thus had to be weighed against the drawbacks, for example the souring of diplomatic relations with the parent state, and the obligation to act as a neutral. As with recognition of insurgency, it was self-interest that motivated recognition.[61]

Only on rare occasions did humanitarian concerns feature in the decision to recognize belligerency, these occasions being the exception rather than the rule. During the Greek war of independence in the 1820s, the British Foreign Secretary explained that Britain's acknowledgment of the Greeks as belligerents was done 'not out of any partiality to the Greeks, but because we think it for the Interest of humanity to compel *all* belligerents to observe the usages by which the spirit of civilization has mitigated the practice of War' and that the alternative 'could have no other effect than to convert the contest which has been brought ... into one of a regular and civilized character, into one of indiscriminate rapine and massacre'.[62] A century later, during the Spanish civil war (1936-9), for some time, the Spanish Government's objection to the insurgents being recognized as belligerents related to their employment of 'methods of warfare contrary to principles of humanity'.[63]

The consequences of recognizing belligerency were not binding on states that had not granted recognition.[64] Accordingly, recognition of belligerency on the part of states other than the parent state left the parent state free to treat members of the armed group as traitors.[65] However, widespread recognition on the part of states served to induce the parent state to grant recognition.[66] Likewise, if the parent state recognized belligerency, other states were not bound by the law of neutrality, although the parent state was bound by the law of neutrality in relation to these other states.[67]

---

[58] Moir, *Internal Armed Conflict*, above note 3, 7; Schwarzenberger, *International Law*, above note 21, 691.

[59] Opinion of the Law Officers (WM Atherton, R Palmer, and R Phillimore), 25 June 1861, noted in McNair, *International Law Opinions*, above note 14, 146.

[60] Opinion of the Law Officers (R Phillimore), 11 May 1865, reproduced in McNair, *International Law Opinions*, above note 29, 398.

[61] Walker, *Science*, above note 39, 115; Moir, *Internal Armed Conflict*, above note 3, 8–11.

[62] Dispatch of Canning to Wellesley, 31 December 1824 (emphasis removed), reproduced in Smith, *Great Britain and the Law of Nations*, above note 13, 294, 296.

[63] Lauterpacht, *Recognition*, above note 8, 251 fn 2.

[64] Ibid, 246; Greenspan, *Law of Land Warfare*, above note 28, 19.

[65] Lauterpacht, *Oppenheim*, above note 15, 251; G Abi-Saab, 'Non-International Armed Conflicts', in UNESCO (ed), *International Dimensions of Humanitarian Law* (UNESCO, 1988) 217, 218.

[66] Greenspan, *Law of Land Warfare*, above note 28, 19; Castrén, *Civil War*, above note 3, 144; Zorgbibe, Belligerent Status, above note 31, 112–13.

[67] Schwarzenberger, *International Law*, above note 21, 703; McNair and Watts, *Legal Effects of War*, above note 18, 33.

If the parent state recognized the situation as belligerency, the law of war regulated the civil war.[68] Accordingly, members of the armed group were treated as combatants with all its implications, for example combatant immunity and benefitting from prisoner of war status if captured.[69] This reflected the view expressed by Vattel a century earlier:

[W]henever a large body of citizens believe themselves justified in resisting the sovereign, and are sufficiently strong to take to arms, war should be carried on between them and the sovereign in the same manner as between two different Nations, and the belligerents should have recourse to the same means for preventing the excesses of war and for re-establishing peace as are used in other wars.[70]

However, actual instances of recognition of belligerency on the part of the parent state were infrequent. Such recognition was considered 'a sign of... weakness' and likely to enhance the 'prestige' of the armed group.[71] The transformation in the rights and obligations of the various parties also militated against recognition by the parent state.[72] For example, upon recognition of belligerency, the belligerents were able to institute blockades, stop and search vessels, confiscate contraband, convene prize courts, and obtain credit.[73] Only when the parent state would benefit from recognizing belligerency did recognition prove forthcoming. This was done, for example, in order to protect the interests of the state in the territory under the control of the armed group and to protect the state's maritime activities,[74] or to prevent a claim being brought against the parent state by other states in respect of acts of the belligerents.[75] Again, then, it was self-interest that motivated recognition of belligerency by the parent state and not a desire to accord humanitarian protection to those caught up in the violence.

Despite the self-interest inherent in recognition, it was through recognition of belligerency that non-international armed conflicts—civil wars as they were then called—were regulated by international law. This ad hoc approach to regulation and total dependence on states greatly influenced the first systematic regulation of non-international armed conflicts through conventional law, a matter that will be considered in Chapter 2.

---

[68] Falk, *Janus Tormented*, above note 2, 205; Castrén, *Civil War*, above note 3, 152; HM Blix, 'Contemporary Aspects of Recognition' (1970-II) 130 *RdC* 587, 618.
[69] Opinion of the Law Officers (RT Reid and F Lockwood), 26 April 1895, reproduced in McNair, *International Law Opinions*, above note 29, 371. See also Lawrence, *Principles*, above note 36, 303; Kelsen, *Principles*, above note 16, 292; Castrén, *Civil War*, above note 3, 156; RR Baxter, 'Ius in Bello Interno: The Present and Future Law', in JN Moore (ed), *Law and Civil War in the Modern World* (Johns Hopkins University Press, 1974) 518, 519.
[70] E de Vattel, *The Law of Nations or the Principles of Natural Law, Volume 3* (CG Fenwick trans) (Carnegie Institution, 1916) 339.
[71] Chen, *Recognition*, above note 9, 371. See also Zorgbibe, Belligerent Status, above note 31, 112.
[72] Chen, *Recognition*, above note 9, 371.
[73] *The Three Friends* (1897) 166 US 1, 63; Wheaton, *Elements*, above note 11, 37 fn 15; Chen, *Recognition*, above note 9, 371; Falk, *Janus Tormented*, above note 2, 205.
[74] Wheaton, *Elements*, above note 11, 37 fn 15; Abi-Saab, Non-International Armed Conflicts, above note 65, 218.
[75] Correspondence between Secretary of State Seward and Minister to England Adams, 12 June 1861, quoted in Moore, *Digest*, above note 12, 185; Wheaton, *Elements*, above note 11, 37 fn 15; Hall, *Treatise*, above note 24, 37; Kelsen, *Principles*, above note 16, 292; Moir, *Internal Armed Conflict*, above note 3, 10–11. But see the opinions of the Law Officers, reproduced in A McNair, *International Law Opinions*, above note 29, 244–72 for the exclusion of liability on far broader grounds. See also, in this regard, the view of Lauterpacht, *Recognition*, above note 8, 247–50.

2.3 Instances of recognition

Actual instances of recognition of insurgency and belligerency were relatively few in number. The principal cases of recognition included, on the part of Great Britain, recognition of belligerency during the Spanish-American war (1814–25), the violence in Greece (1821–5), the US civil war (1861–5), the Bonny River (1870), and in the Transvaal (1899);[76] and recognition of insurgency in Madagascar (1895).[77] On the part of the United States, instances of recognition of insurgency included those of Cuba (1868–78, 1895–7),[78] Colombia (1885–6),[79] Haiti (1888–9),[80] and Brazil (1893–4).[81] As the list illustrates, it was primarily the United States that recognized insurgency and it did so in respect of violence taking place on the American continent. However, it is difficult to draw any definitive conclusions from the practice given the lack of clarity surrounding the concept of recognition,[82] the late introduction of the concept of recognition of insurgency, and the assimilation of recognition of belligerency to that of recognition of independence. What is apparent is that the concepts of recognition of insurgency and belligerency rose and fell during the nineteenth century, with belligerency not being recognized, most notably, during the Spanish civil war (1936–9).

Several armed conflicts that were fought during the twentieth century *could* have given rise to recognition of belligerency since recognition took different forms. States may explicitly proclaim that they recognize the situation as a civil war, or that they recognize the armed group as belligerents, as Bolivia did in relation to a Chilean armed group in 1891 and Peru did in relation to a Cuban armed group in 1869.[83] Along these lines, the 'Declaration of War' of 12 August 1967 of the Nigerian Federal Government in respect of the Biafran secessionist authorities could have amounted to recognition of belligerency. However, it was not intended in that manner by the parent state and it was not interpreted in that manner by outside states.

States other than the parent state may also recognize belligerency through acting as neutrals.[84] Thus, the British declaration of neutrality of 13 May 1861, which was issued during the US civil war, amounted to recognition of belligerency. That Proclamation provided that:

whereas hostilities have unhappily commenced between the Government of the United States of America and certain States styling themselves the Confederate States of America;

---

[76] Smith, *Great Britain and the Law of Nations*, above note 13, 302–12; Moore, *Digest*, above note 12, 205; Opinion of the Queen's Advocate [Travers Twiss] to Earl Granville, 29 September 1870, reproduced in Lauterpacht, *Recognition*, above note 8, 205.

[77] Moore, *Digest*, above note 12, 205.

[78] See ibid, 193–200, 242.

[79] In the case of the *Ambrose Light* 25 Fed Rep 408, 443, the court considered that the Secretary of State had impliedly recognized the situation as one of belligerency. This was disputed by the Secretary of State. See ibid, 200.

[80] Ibid, 201.

[81] Ibid, 201–5.

[82] From the British perspective, the opinions of the Law Officers provide a useful sense of what was known about recognition of belligerency and insurgency. A perusal of the opinions over the years indicates that, at first, things were rather arbitrary but, over time, the practice became rather consistent. See generally, McNair, *International Law Opinions*, above note 29, 325–71.

[83] Lauterpacht, *Recognition*, above note 8, 177 fn 1.

[84] HA Smith, 'Some Problems of the Spanish Civil War' (1937) 18 *BYIL* 17, 21–2.

And whereas we, being at Peace with the Government of the United States, have declared our Royal determination to maintain a strict and impartial neutrality in the contest between the said contesting Parties...⁸⁵

Formal proclamations of neutrality are not required; what is crucial is that the state intends to act as a neutral and indicates its intention to act in that manner. Accordingly, recognition of belligerency may come about as a response to an act of one of the parties involved in the violence, for example through acquiescence to a blockade. Thus, in an 1867 opinion, the British Law Officers took the view that 'a blockade implies the existence of war, and of two belligerents at least' and that if a government 'declared a formal blockade, it would have no reason to complain if foreign States simply recognized the rebels as belligerents'.⁸⁶ Accordingly, Great Britain recognized belligerency following the Spanish blockade of ports in San Domingo in 1864, of Venezuelan ports in 1871, and of Haitian ports in 1876.⁸⁷

Similarly, insofar as the parent state is concerned, the imposition of a blockade, or the acceptance of a blockade by the armed group, would constitute recognition given that the proclamation of a blockade is 'an assertion of belligerent status'.⁸⁸ Thus, in 1862, the US Supreme Court held that '[t]he proclamation of blockade is itself official and conclusive evidence... that a state of war existed'.⁸⁹ Along similar lines, two years later, the British Law Officers took the view that, through the Spanish Government's notification of blockade during the insurrection of St Domingo, 'they virtually asserted, by that very act, the existence of such a state of war'.⁹⁰ On this basis, the institution of a blockade by the Federal Government of Nigeria of Biafran-controlled ports could have been viewed by outside states as recognition of belligerency on the part of the Federal Government. The same could be said of Israel's naval blockade of Gaza.⁹¹ Likewise, the blockade instituted by the Spanish Government in 1936 of insurgent-controlled ports could have been considered by outside states as the Spanish Government recognizing a situation of belligerency.⁹² Indeed, during the Spanish civil war, the insurgents requested recognition as belligerents:

---

⁸⁵ Lauterpacht, *Recognition*, above note 8, 177 fn 3.
⁸⁶ Opinion of the Law Officers (JB Karslake, CJ Selwyn, and R Phillimore), 14 August 1867, reproduced in McNair, *International Law Opinions*, above note 14, 143, 144. See also, on the Carlist revolution in Spain (1874), PC Jessup, 'The Spanish Rebellion and International Law' (1936–7) 15 *Foreign Affairs* 260, 273.
⁸⁷ This was the consistent advice of the law officers. See the Opinions of the Law Officers (R Palmer, RP Collier, and R Phillimore), 22 August 1864 and 22 November 1864, reproduced in McNair, *International Law Opinions*, above note 14, 140–3; Opinion of the Queen's Advocate [Travers Twiss], 28 June 1871, reproduced in Lauterpacht, *Recognition*, above note 8, 202–3; Opinion of the Law Officers of the Crown [John Holker, Hardinge S Giffard] and Dr Deane to the Earl of Derby, 6 May 1876, reproduced in ibid, 209–10.
⁸⁸ Chen, *Recognition*, above note 9, 384. See also McNair, *International Law Opinions*, above note 14, 138; Castrén, *Civil War*, above note 3, 147; Kotzsch, *Concept of War*, above note 2, 234; McNair and Watts, *Legal Effects of War*, above note 18, 31–2.
⁸⁹ *Prize Cases* (1862) 67 US 635.
⁹⁰ Opinion of the Law Officers (Palmer, Collier, Phillimore), 22 August 1864, in Smith, *Great Britain and the Law of Nations*, above note 13, 313, 314.
⁹¹ On which, see The Public Commission to Examine the Maritime Incident of 31 May 2010, The Turkel Commission, Report: Part One.
⁹² The question of recognition of belligerency in the context of the Spanish Civil War has given rise to much comment. See eg PC Jessup, 'The Spanish Rebellion and International Law' (1936–7) 15 *Foreign Affairs* 260; JW Garner, 'Questions of International Law in the Spanish Civil War' (1937) 31 *AJIL* 66; NJ Padelford, 'International Law and the Spanish Civil War' (1937) 31 *AJIL* 226; VA O'Rourke, 'Recognition of Belligerency and the Spanish War' (1937) 31 *AJIL* 398; HA Smith, 'Some

The National Government... deem the grant of belligerent rights to be a right. There exist to a full extent in National Spain the conditions necessary to request that it may be recognized:

(a) The possession of, and full sway over, a portion of the national Spanish territory which greatly exceeds that held by the enemy.
(b) A legal and regular Government which *de facto* exercises over the said portion of territory the rights inherent in sovereignty.
(c) A regular land and air army, perfectly organized and subject to a strict military discipline, which affords a guarantee of order... respecting and causing to be respected with the utmost scrupulousness the laws and customs of warfare...[93]

Other acts of the parent state that gave rise to recognition of belligerency included the seizure of vessels that breached a blockade or which carried contraband,[94] and the application of certain types of neutrality legislation.[95] On the basis of these precedents, the French visitation of ships of outside states and seizure of cargo during the Algerian war of independence (1954–62) could have been interpreted as recognition of belligerency on the part of France.[96] Indeed, in 1960, the Provisional Government of the Algerian Republic argued that 'the French Government, despite its official thesis that the Algerian conflict is a "domestic matter", has taken upon itself the prerogatives of belligerence'.[97] However, outside states did not interpret France's actions in this manner.

Thus, in the conflicts in Biafra, Spain, Gaza, and Algeria, acts undertaken by the parent state could have been interpreted as recognition of belligerency. Indeed, it is likely that, were those acts carried out in the nineteenth century, they would have been interpreted in such a manner. Although there has been some suggestion that belligerency was, in fact, recognized in some of these conflicts,[98] and while it certainly could have been, it was not. Today, the various acts have been divorced from recognition of belligerency and it would seem that belligerency would have to be recognized explicitly in order for its consequences to take effect. As the report of the Turkel Commission notes, recognition of the applicability of the law on naval blockades to non-international armed conflicts 'should not be interpreted in any way to suggest that the historic doctrine of "belligerency" is applicable or appropriate'.[99]

That being said, reports of the death of recognition of belligerency and insurgency have long been exaggerated. It is true that, at least since 1949, and more likely since 1899, there have not been any cases of recognition of belligerency or insurgency and the 1949 Geneva Conventions had a role to play in this decline, with a new legal regime

---

Problems of the Spanish Civil War' (1937) 18 *BYIL* 17; JW Garner, 'Recognition of Belligerency' (1938) 32 *AJIL* 106.

[93] Note of 2 August 1938, published in *The Times* (UK), 22 August 1938, reproduced in Lauterpacht, *Recognition*, above note 8, 251 fn 2.

[94] Hall, *Treatise*, above note 24, 43; Castrén, *Civil War*, above note 3, 147–8.

[95] Chen, *Recognition*, above note 9, 387–90.

[96] M Bedjaoui, *Law and the Algerian Revolution* (International Association of Democratic Lawyers, 1961) 143 and 151–9.

[97] *White Paper on the Application of the Geneva Conventions of 1949 to the French-Algerian Conflict* (Algerian Office, May 1960) 18.

[98] Zorgbibe, Belligerent Status, above note 31, 112; I Detter, *The Law of War* (Cambridge University Press, 2000) 40; EL Nwogugu, 'The Nigerian Civil War: A Case Study in the Law of War' (1974) 14 *Indian Journal of International Law* 13; Bedjaoui, *Law and the Algerian Revolution*, above note 96, 143 and 151–9; F Bugnion, '*Jus ad Bellum, Jus in Bello* and Non-International Armed Conflicts' (2003) 6 *YIHL* 167, 181.

[99] Turkel Commission, Report, above note 91, para 42 fn 147.

regulating non-international armed conflicts. However, it does not follow that regulation through recognition of belligerency has been 'abandoned'.[100] More accurate is the description of the Government of Colombia in 1999, that '[t]he institution of belligerence... is in practise obviously in disuse'.[101] Nothing prevents a state from explicitly recognizing a situation as one of belligerency or insurgency in the future.[102] Common Article 3 certainly does not preclude such recognition.[103] As Switzerland observed at the 1949 Diplomatic Conference, '[t]he question of belligerency is completely outside [the] scope of the provisions and of the solutions proposed in the four Conventions'.[104] This was made abundantly clear through a resolution adopted at the Diplomatic Conference, which provides that '[t]he Conference considers that the conditions under which a Party to a conflict can be recognized as a belligerent by Powers not taking part in this conflict, are governed by the general rules of international law on the subject and are in no way modified by the Geneva Conventions'.[105] Similarly, the 1957 Protocol to the Havana Convention on Duties and Rights of States in the Event of Civil Strife also refers to recognition of belligerency, providing for the application of certain rules in situations in which belligerency has not been recognized.[106] Recognition also continues to be canvassed from time to time.[107] Likewise, although belligerency has not been recognized, various other concepts have crept into the practice, such as recognition of the 'legitimate interlocutor... representing the... people' and 'legitimate representative of the... people', both statements made by outside states in the course of the 2011 conflict in Libya.[108]

3. Instructions and agreements

During the nineteenth and early twentieth centuries, internal violence was not regulated solely through recognition of belligerency. It was also regulated through ad hoc agreements which were concluded between the warring parties and through instructions or declarations which were issued to the state armed forces or the non-state armed group. This form of regulation was not at all infrequent—albeit many examples remain hidden—and it continues to be used today.

---

[100] This is the view of Detter, *Law of War*, above note 98, 43.
[101] Ministry of Foreign Affairs of Colombia, 'Recognition of State of War Respecting the FARC (Fuerzas Armadas Revolucionarias de Colombia)', 16 June 1999, reprinted in (1999) 2 *YIHL* 440, 441.
[102] See RW Gomulkiewicz, 'International Law Governing Aid to Opposition Groups in Civil War: Resurrecting the Standards of Belligerency' (1988) 63 *Washington Law Review* 43; YM Lootsteen, 'The Concept of Belligerency in International Law' (2000) 166 *Military Law Review* 109, 127; Bugnion, *Jus ad Bellum*, above note 98, 192.
[103] Castrén, *Civil War*, above note 3, 85–6; McNair and Watts, *Legal Effects of War*, above note 18, 33.
[104] *Final Record of the Diplomatic Conference of 1949* (Federal Political Department, Berne), Vol II-B, 336 (Switzerland).
[105] Ibid, Vol I, 362.
[106] See also below, 195–6, 209.
[107] Ibid.
[108] See eg Written Statement of the [UK]Foreign Secretary to Parliament, 13 May 2011; Statement of [German] Foreign Minister, Guido Westerwelle, 13 June 2011, quoted in 'Germany Recognises Libyan Rebels as Sole Government', BBC News, 13 June 2011. Various states later recognized the NTC as the 'legitimate governing authority in Libya'. See Fourth Meeting of the Libya Contact Group, Chair's Statement, 15 July 2011.

3.1 Instructions

During the Swiss civil war of 1847, which was fought between the Federal Government of Switzerland and the Sonderbund, the Commander of the Federal Army, General Dufour (who would go on to chair the Committee of Five, the predecessor of the International Committee of the Red Cross (ICRC)), issued several instructions to his forces on the conduct of hostilities and treatment of persons caught up in the fighting. In his 'Recommandations sur la conduite à tenir envers les habitants et les troupes', he instructed:

> Encourage troops urgently to behave with restraint and not to engage in abuse that would only irritate a population that one should instead try to bring back gently, in order to have fewer enemies to fight and to come to a quicker solution. In particular, with the hostages that could be needed to be taken, be more attentive, and treat them well at the headquarters; so that nothing fails to meet their needs.
>
> Prevent at all costs the violation of churches and religious institutions in order to remove, if possible, the denominational character that one tries to give to this war. Go as far as not quartering troops in these establishments and placing safeguards there.
>
> Also place safeguards to ensure respect for the properties of judges and public officials.
>
> If a troop is in retreat, treat its wounded in the same way as our own and have for them all the respect due to their misfortune.
>
> Disarm the prisoners, but without causing them any harm or insult. Treat them, on the contrary, as well as possible to disabuse them. Let them go home if they solemnly swear to lay down their uniforms and not to take up arms again.
>
> If violence is exercised, let it not be from our side, so that we cannot be blamed for any such thing. Let all the blame weigh on the opposing party. No reprisals of that kind: they can only aggravate our cause.
>
> After a battle, hold the fury of the soldier; spare the vanquished. Nothing gives more honour to the victorious troops, and, in a civil war, nothing is more conducive to the submission of the opposing party. Nothing, on the contrary, infuriates and entrenches it more in its resistance than the opposite conduct. It is necessary, however strong one is, to dread the despair of his enemy.[109]

---

[109] Reproduced in O Reverdin, *La Guerre du Sonderbund vue par le Général Dufour, Juin 1847–Avril 1848* (Éditions du Journal de Genève, 1987) 43–5. The original reads:

> Engager les troupes, de la manière la plus instante, à se conduire avec modération et à ne pas se livrer à de mauvais traitements qui ne feraient qu'irriter une population qu'il faut plutôt tâcher de ramener par la douceur, pour avoir moins d'ennemis à combattre et arrive à une plus prompte solution. En particulier, avec les otages que l'on pourrait être dans la nécessité de prendre, redouble d'égards, et les faire bien traiter au quartier général; que rien ne manque à leurs besoins.
>
> Empêcher à tout prix la violation des églises et des établissements religieux, pour faire disparaître, si possible, le caractère confessionnel que l'on s'efforce de donner à cette guerre. Pousser l'attention jusqu'à ne point loger de troupes dans ces établissements et y poser des sauvegardes.
>
> Mettre aussi des sauvegardes pour faire respecter les propriétés des magistrats et fonctionnaires publics.
>
> Si une troupe est repoussée, faire soigner ses blessés comme les nôtres memes, et avoir pour eux tous les égards dus au malheur.
>
> Désarmer les prisonniers, mais ne leur faire aucun mal, ni leur addresser aucune injure. Les traiter, au contraire, aussi bien que possible pour les désabuser. Les laisser rentrer chez eux s'ils s'engagent sur l'honneur à poser leurs uniformes et à ne pas reprendre les armes.
>
> S'il s'exerce des violences, que ce ne soit pas de notre côté, et qu'on n'ait rien de pareil à nous reprocher. S'il doit y en avoir, que tout l'odieux en pèse sur le parti opposé. Point de représailles de ce genre; elles ne peuvent que gâter notre cause.
>
> Après un combat, retenir la fureur du soldat; épargner les vaincus. Rien ne fait plus d'honneur à une troupe victorieuse, et, dans une guerre civile, rien ne dispose d'avantage le

In his Proclamation to the Army, which was issued the following day, General Dufour enjoined:

> Soldiers, you must leave this struggle not only victorious, but also beyond reproach. People must say about you: they fought valiantly when they had to, but they appeared humane and generous throughout.
>
> I place in your keeping the children, the women, the aged, and the ministers of religion. He who raises a hand against an inoffensive person dishonours himself and tarnishes his flag. Prisoners, and the wounded above all, are entitled to your respect and compassion, the more so because you have often been with them in the same camps.[110]

Both these instructions were informed by his declaration that 'he would never forget that he was fighting against his countrymen'.[111]

General Dufour's instructions were by no means an isolated instance of instructions being issued on the conduct of hostilities and the treatment of individuals. In the same year in which General Dufour made his pronouncements, 1847, US General Winfield Scott issued General Orders No 20, which constituted 'a supplemental code' to the 'rules and articles of war'. General Orders No 20 envisaged punishment of:

> Assassination; murder; malicious stabbing or maiming; rape; malicious assault and battery; robbery; theft; the wanton desecration of churches, cemeteries or other religious edifices and fixtures, and the destruction, except by order of a superior officer, of public or private property...[112]

During the US civil war (1861–5), various other General Orders were issued, which regulated the conduct of Union (Government) troops. General Orders No 8 and No 13, issued in 1861 by General Halleck as Commanding General of the Department of the Missouri, provided that captured members of the Confederate forces were to be treated as prisoners of war and set out the precise treatment to be afforded to them.[113] General McDowell ordered that the taking of private property was forbidden, as was indiscriminate firing on enemy outposts.[114] However, other orders authorized actions that would have been considered violations of the laws of war. For example, General Milroy issued an order that threatened to shoot guerrillas that had engaged in robbery and to destroy their homes.[115] Major General Butler ordered that a woman who insulted or showed contempt for Union forces was to be treated as 'a woman of the town plying her avocation'.[116]

> parti opposé à la soumission. Rien, au contraire, ne l'exaspère, et ne le pousse aux derniers termes de la résistance, comme une conduite oppose. Il faut, quelque fort qu'on soit, redouter le désespoir de son ennemi.

[110] Proclamation to the Army, 5 November 1847, reproduced in ibid, 42–3. The original reads:

> Soldats, il faut sortir de cette lutte non seulement victorieux, mais encore sans reproches. Il faut qu'on puisse dire de vous: ils ont vaillamment combattu quand il l'a fallu, mais ils se sont montrés partout humains et généreux.

[111] See F Siordet, 'The Geneva Conventions and Civil War' (1950) III *RICR Supplement* 132, 135.

[112] General Orders No 20, 19 February 1847, excerpted in RR Baxter, 'The First Modern Codification of the Law of War: Francis Lieber and General Orders No 100' (1963) 3 *IRRC* 171, 187.

[113] General Orders No 8, 26 November 1861; General Orders No 13, 4 December 1861.

[114] GB Davis, 'Doctor Francis Lieber's Instructions for the Government of Armies in the Field' (1907) 1 *AJIL* 13, 14. For other examples, see MH Hoffman, 'The Customary Law of Non-International Armed Conflict' (1990) 30 *IRRC* 322, 323–5.

[115] US War Department, *The War of the Rebellion: A Compilation of the Official Records of the Union and Confederate Armies, Series 3, Volume 2* (Government Printing Office, 1886) 943–4.

[116] General Orders No 28, 15 May 1862, reproduced in ibid, *Series 1, Volume 15*, 426.

It was during the US civil war that one of the most famous humanitarian instruments was issued—the Lieber Code. General Orders No 100, or Instructions for the Government of Armies of the United States in the Field, to give it its full title, was prepared by Francis Lieber and promulgated by President Lincoln in 1863, during the civil war.[117] The Lieber Code consisted of some 157 articles and regulated the conduct of the Union forces on such issues as the treatment of persons and objects, the conduct of hostilities, and the conclusion of hostilities. The Code was criticized at first by the Confederates:

Order No. 100 is a confused, unasserted, and undiscriminating compilation from the opinion of the publicists of the last two centuries, some of which are obsolete, others repudiated; and a military commander under this code may pursue a line of conduct in accordance with principles of justice, faith, and honor, or he may justify conduct correspondent with the warfare of the barbarous hordes...[118]

Particular rules were also criticized, for example the lawfulness of the starvation of belligerents, armed and unarmed. The definition of military necessity was the subject of particular criticism and the Union forces were considered to have:

adopted a barbarous system of warfare on the pretext of a military necessity. It is in this code of military necessity that the acts of atrocity and violence which have been committed by the officers of the United States and have shocked the moral sense of civilized nations are to find an apology and defense.[119]

However, certain rules that were set out in the Code were accepted:

These principles condemn the murder of non-combatants; the pillage of the farms and houses of persons who are not engaged in the war; the destruction of implements of husbandry, growing crops, mills, houses, fruit trees... the expulsion of old men, women, and children, with limited supplies of money and clothing from their homes; the violation of cartels relative to the exchange of prisoners; the detention of prisoners for weeks and months, and even years, after their exchanges...[120]

The Confederates also utilized the Code themselves.[121] The Code would also go on to be used by the armed forces of the United States in the insurrection in the Philippines (1899–1901).[122] The Lieber Code was thus immensely important and was adopted during a civil war, albeit one in which belligerency had been recognized, and later used in another.

It was not just the Swiss civil war and the United States civil war that witnessed the issuance of instructions. During the third Carlist war in the 1870s, orders were issued by the Northern Army on the treatment of the wounded and sick. An order of 1873 read:

---

[117] Instructions for the Government of Armies of the United States in the Field, 24 April 1863 (Lieber Code).
[118] Letter of James A Seddon, Confederate Secretary of War, to Hon Robert Ould, Agent of Exchange, 24 June 1863, reprinted in RS Hartigan, *Lieber's Code and the Law of War* (Precedent, 1983) 120.
[119] Ibid, 123.
[120] Ibid, 122.
[121] F Freidel, 'Francis Lieber and the Codification of the International Law of War', in R Durand and J Meurant (eds), *Préludes et Pionniers: Les Précurseurs de la Croix-Rouge* (Société Henry Dunant, 1991) 43.
[122] Ibid.

I order today by telegram, to all leaders who are under my command, that any Carlist invalid be considered sacred and that any wounded person taken prisoner on the battlefield be pardoned.[123]

A second order, issued some weeks after the first, clarified:

To ensure that all leaders are clear where they stand in relation to the wounded, His Excellency, the Commander in Chief decided:
Only the wounded who have specifically requested a pardon shall be deemed pardoned, but this must not prevent all those who have not requested a pardon to be assisted with all the respect demanded by their condition and by humanitarian sentiment. The recommendation of His Excellency is addressed not only to the leaders and local authorities, but also the philanthropic organisation of the Red Cross so that all the enemy wounded are to be treated with zeal.[124]

Instructions of this character did not emanate from the state side alone. Just days prior to the promulgation of the Lieber Code, during the Polish insurrection of 1863–4, the armed group that was involved in the violence issued instructions for doctors in the field. These instructions included provisions on the wounded and sick, including *inter alia* that '[t]he enemy's wounded must be treated with the same care as our own'.[125] Half a century later, during the Russian revolution and civil war (1917–21), orders were given which also had a humanitarian component. The President of the Military Revolutionary Council of the Republic and of the People's Commissariat for War and the Navy ordered that '[i]n no case shall prisoners who have surrendered or who have been captured be shot'.[126] A later order repeated the injunction and also provided that 'any infringement of the present order shall be reported without delay, so that the military revolutionary court may immediately proceed to the scene of the offence'.[127]

Thus, numerous examples exist of instructions being given to the armed forces or the armed group that have elements of what today would be described as the law of armed conflict. Furthermore, some of these examples pre-date the Lieber Code. However, it was the Lieber Code, together with the 1864 Geneva Convention for the Amelioration of the Condition of the Wounded in Armies in the Field,[128] that generated the modern period of regulation of armed conflict.

---

[123] Order of Le général en chef, Pavia, Armée du Nord, 26 February 1873, reproduced in 'La Guerre Civile' (1873–4) 5 *Bulletin International des Sociétés de Secours aux Militaires Blessés* 34, 39. The original reads: 'J'ordonne aujourd'hui par télégramme, à tous les chefs de colonne qui sont sous mon commandement, qu'on considère comme sacrée la personne de tout malade carliste et qu'on gracie tout blessé fait prisonnier sur le champ de bataille.'

[124] Ordre general pour l'armée, Le colonel chef d'état-major, 17 March 1873, reproduced in ibid. The original reads:

Afin que tous les chefs de colonne sachent clairement à quoi s'en tenir par rapport aux blesses, S. Exc. le général en chef decide:
Ne sera considéré comme gracié que le blessé qui aura expressément demandé sa grace, mais cela ne doit point empêcher que tous ceux qui ne l'auront pas demandée soient assistés avec tous les égards que réclament leur état et le sentiment humanitaire. Cette recommendation de Son Excellence s'addresse non-seulement aux chefs de colonne et aux autorités locales, mais aussi à la philanthropique association de la Croix rouge, afin que tous les blesses de l'ennemi soient soignés avec zèle.

[125] Instructions for Doctors in the Field, 14 April 1863, quoted in R Bierzanek, 'Humanitarian Law in Armed Conflicts: The Doctrine and Practice of Polish Insurgents in the 19th Century' (1977) 17 *IRRC* 128, 131.

[126] Order of the Day No 92, 1 May 1919, reproduced in M Veuthey, 'Military Instructions on the Treatment of Prisoners in Guerrilla Warfare' (1972) 12 *IRRC* 125, 133.

[127] Order of the Day No 126, 18 July 1919, reproduced in ibid.

[128] On which, see Chapter 2.

3.2 Agreements

In addition to issuing instructions, agreements were sometimes concluded between the warring parties. For example, as early as the US war of independence (1776), the Commander in Chief of the British forces, Sir James Robertson, wrote to General Washington of the US forces:

Sir, having received a commission from the King who appointed me Commander in Chief of his forces in this country, one of the first steps that I am taking is to convince you of my desire to conduct war according to the rules of humanity, and the examples that the most civilised nations provide to us. I make this declaration of my resolution in the hope of finding a similar disposition on your side. To achieve this goal, let us agree to prevent or punish any violations of the rules of war, each within the sphere of our command.[129]

General Washington responded favourably to the letter,[130] and the exchange amounts to an agreement to conduct the conflict according to the law of war.

Two agreements of a more traditional sort were concluded in 1820 during the Colombian war of independence. The first, an armistice treaty, provided that the parties would enter into a treaty which would regulate the war 'in conformity with the rights of Man, and the most generous, wise, and humane practices observed by civilised Nations'.[131] That treaty, on the regularization of the war, which was concluded a few days later between Simón Bolívar and Pedro Briceño Méndez, provided in part:

Article 2. Every member or agent of an armed force captured on the battlefield, even before the battle is decided, shall be kept as a prisoner of war, and shall be treated and respected according to his rank until he is exchanged...

Article 4. Members and agents of an armed force who are apprehended wounded or sick, in or outside hospitals, shall not be prisoners of war and shall be free to return to the flags to which they belong after recovering...

Article 11. The inhabitants of villages which are alternately occupied by the forces of both Governments shall be highly respected and shall enjoy extensive and absolute freedom and security, whatever their opinions, positions, services or conduct with respect to the belligerent parties may be or may have been.

Article 12. The bodies of those who gloriously end their journeys on the battlefields, or in any combat, clash, encounter between the armed forces of the two governments shall receive the last honours of burial, or be cremated when their numbers or time pressures do not permit the former. The victorious army or force shall be obliged to perform this sacred duty of which it can only be relieved by very serious and extraordinary circumstances, immediately notifying the authorities of the territory where the bodies are in order that they do so. Bodies which are claimed

---

[129] J Siotis, *Le Droit de la Guerre et les Conflits Armés d'un Caractère Non-International* (Librairie Générale de Droit et de Jurisprudence, 1958) 60, quoting GF De Martens, *Causes Célèbres du Droit des Gens, Volume III* (Leipzig, 1827) 313. The original reads:

Monsieur, ayant reçu une commission du Roi qui me nomme Commandant en Chef de ses forces dans ce pays, un des premiers soins que je prends, c'est de vous convaincre de mon désir de faire la guerre conformément aux règles tracées par l'humanité, et aux exemples que nous recommandent les Nations les plus civilisées. Je vous fais cette déclaration de ma résolution dans l'espoir de trouver une disposition analogue de votre côté. Pour atteindre ce but, convenons de prévenir ou de punir toutes les violations des règles de la guerre, chacun dans la sphère de notre commandement.

[130] Ibid.
[131] Tratado de Armisticio y Suspensión de Armas, 25 November 1820 (1820–1) 71 *Consolidated Treaty Series* 281.

from either side, by the government or by private individuals cannot be refused, and any communications necessary for their transport shall be granted.[132]

Simón Bolívar also issued instructions to his forces to respect the law of war. In particular, he noted that 'even when our enemies break those rules, we must respect them, so that the glory of Colombia is not stained with blood'.[133]

During the Colombian civil war of 1860–1, agreements were reached between the warring parties, which included provisions on *inter alia* the exchange of the wounded and sick, the treatment of prisoners of war, and amnesty to members of the armed group. The Pacto de Chinchiná provided that it was agreed:

1. That the war between the army of Cauca and the [army] which I command shall be fought in accordance with the principles of the Ius Gentium.
2. That no more blood shall be spilt than that shed at the time of combat, not permitting senior officers and non-commissioned officers to carry out acts of atrocity or killing on individuals who have surrendered.
3. That no blood shall be shed in pursuit either, except where fugitives put up armed resistance.
4. That prisoners of war if they are of chief officer or officer rank shall be given a passport to travel to any place they wish provided they give their word of honour not to take up arms again against Antioquia or other states under the general government, and if they are of non-commissioned rank shall be set free immediately to return to their homes.
5. The wounded who are left in the field and captured in pursuit shall receive medical care and attention as if they belonged to the army of Antioquia, and the treatment called-for by humanity and civilisation and the good relations that have existed between Antioquia and Cauca.[134]

---

[132] The original reads:

Article 2. Todo militar o dependiente de un ejército tomado en el campo de batalla, aun antes de decidirse ésta, se conservará y guardará como prisionero de guerra, y será tratado y respetado conforme a su grado hasta lograr su canje....

Article 4. Los militares o dependientes de un ejército que se aprehendan heridos o enfermos en los hospitales, o fuera de ellos, no serán prisioneros de guerra y tendrán libertad para restituirse a las banderas a que pertenezcan, luego que se hayan restablecido...

Article 11. Los habitantes de los pueblos que alternativamente se ocuparen por las armas de ambos gobiernos serán altamente respetados, y gozarán de una absoluta libertad y seguridad, sean cuales fueren o hayan sido sus opiniones, destinos, servicios y conducta con respecto a las partes beligerantes.

Article 12. Los cadáveres de los que gloriosamente terminen su carrera en los campos de batalla, o en cualquier combate, choque o encuentro entre las armas de los dos gobiernos, recibirán los últimos honores de la sepultura, o se quemarán cuando por su número, o por la premura del tiempo, no pueda hacerse lo primero. El ejército o cuerpo vencedor será el obligado a cumplir con este sagrado deber, del cual, sólo por una circunstancia muy grave y singular podrá descargarse, avisándolo inmediatamente a las autoridades del territorio en que se hallan para que lo hagan. Los cadáveres que de una y otra parte se reclamen por el gobierno o por los particulares no podrán negarse, y se concederá la comunicación necesaria para transportarlos.

Tratado de Regularización de la Guerra, 26 November 1820, Articles 2, 4, 11, 12. French version published in (1820–1) 71 *Consolidated Treaty Series* 291.

[133] Proclamation of 25 April 1821, quoted in *Constitutional Conformity of Protocol II*, C-225/95, para 9, reproduced and translated in M Sassòli, AA Bouvier, and A Quintin, *How Does Law Protect in War? Volume III* (ICRC, 2011) 2240.

[134] El Pacto de Chinchiná, 27 August 1860, quoted in A Valencia Villa, *La Humanización de la Guerra: Derecho Internacional Humanitario y Conflicto Armado en Colombia* (Ediciones Uniandes, 1991) 98. The original text reads:

However, the agreement was concluded between generals who were involved in the fighting and was not accepted by the President. A later agreement contained provisions on amnesty:

Art. 3. The Governor of the State of Cauca shall grant a complete amnesty to all those involved in the political uprisings against the Government of the State that have taken place, and guarantees the safety of citizens who have been hostile toward him.

Art. 4. The general Government shall grant an amnesty to all those involved in the uprisings of Cauca against national law.[135]

The importance of regulating non-international armed conflicts was thus recognized over a century prior to the 1949 Geneva Conventions and well before the adoption of the Lieber Code in 1863. It was also recognized that the special nature of civil wars called for their particular regulation. Thus, an article was proposed for inclusion in the 1820 Tratado de Regularización de la Guerra, which provided that '[i]t is in civil war that the application of the law of nations should have its greatest scope and that humanity claims most imperatively the application of its precepts'.[136] Along similar lines, in 1847, General Dufour was minded to recall the fact that he was fighting against his fellow compatriots: 'when the fighting is ended, we shall all be thankful not to have lost sight of the fact that the struggle was between fellow Confederates and that we listened to the voice of compassion.'[137] That civil wars are of a particular nature has also been recognized in instruments adopted more recently. For example, the 1967 instructions issued to the state armed forces during the attempted secession of Biafra from Nigeria noted that '[y]ou must . . . remember that you are not fighting a war with a foreign enemy. Nor are you fighting a religious war or Jihad. You are only subduing the

1. En que la guerra entre el ejército del Cauca y el que yo comando se hará conforme a los principios del derecho de gentes;
2. Que no se derramará más sangre que la que haya en el momento del combate sin permitir a los jefes oficiales y clases de tropa, ejecuten actos de atrocidad y muertes en individuos rendidos;
3. Que en la persecución tampoco se derramará sangre, excepto el caso de que los fugitivos resistan con las armas;
4. Que a los prisioneros de guerra, si pertenecen a la clase de jefes y oficiales se les dará su pasaporte para donde los exijan siempre que ofrezcan bajo palabra de honor no volver a tomar las armas contra Antioquia o los otros estados sometidos al gobierno general, y si pertenecen a la clase de tropa se les pondrá en libertad inmediatamente para que regresen a sus casas;
5. Los heridos que queden en el campo y se tomen en la persecución serán curados y atendidos como si perteneciesen al ejército de Antioquia, y tratados como lo exigen la humanidad y la civilización y las buenas relaciones que han existido entre Antioquia y el Cauca.

[135] La Esponsión de Manizales, 29 August 1860, reproduced in Valencia Villa, ibid, 104. The original text reads:

Art. 3. El señor Gobernador del Estado del Cauca, otorgará una amnistía completa, a todos los comprometidos con los movimientos políticos ocurridos contra el Gobierno del Estado, i garantiza la seguridad de los ciudadanos que le han sido hostiles.

Art. 4. El Gobierno jeneral otorgará una amnistía a favor de todos los comprometidos en los movimientos del Cauca contra las leyes nacionales.

[136] H Valencia Villa, 'The Law of Armed Conflict and its Application in Colombia' (1990) 30 *IRRC* 5, 6.

[137] Instructions of General Dufour, 4 November 1847, reproduced in 'An Example of Humanity' (1976) 16 *IRRC* 94, 95.

rebellion of Lt.-Col. Odumegwu-Ojukwu and his clique. You must not do anything that will endanger the future unity of the country'.[138]

3.3 Advantages and drawbacks

Regulation through instruction or bilateral agreement suffered from several drawbacks. Only those conflicts in which the instructions were issued or agreements concluded were regulated, resulting in the lack of systematic regulation of non-international armed conflicts. Should the parties have decided not to conclude an agreement or to issue instructions, regulation was not forthcoming unless belligerency was recognized. Regulation through instruction or agreement was also partial. This was recognized by one of the founders of the ICRC, Henry Dunant, in his observation in 1862 that '[i]t is the more important to reach an agreement and concert measures in advance, because when hostilities once begin, the belligerents are already ill-disposed to each other, and thenceforth regard all questions from the one limited standpoint of their own subjects'.[139] Furthermore, instructions and orders were not always humanitarian in their nature. Orders such as that of Major General Butler had a severe negative effect on those who were caught up in the hostilities.

Despite these drawbacks, regulation through instruction or agreement also had its advantages. Contrary to the view of Henry Dunant, agreements that were concluded during an armed conflict could be more realistic than those that were concluded during peacetime, as there is a danger that 'in times of peace...the minds of men in dealing with military affairs turn rather to the ideal than the practical'.[140] Instructions that are drawn up during an armed conflict also allow for the norms to be brought into force to be tailored to the specificities of the situation at hand. Thus the Lieber Code has been described as 'emphas[izing] those norms important to the Union'.[141] The norms are also likely to be formulated in language that can be readily understood by those involved in the fighting rather than being of an unintelligible legal sort.[142]

Regardless of the merits and the disadvantages of regulation through instruction and agreement, writing in 1914, Jules Basdevant considered the conclusion of ad hoc agreements to be 'hardly likely'.[143] Some decades later, experts who were consulted by UN Secretary-General U Thant 'doubted whether...optional agreements could in fact be concluded, especially at a time when the conflict has already erupted'.[144] This continues to be the view today, with such agreements being considered 'rare', 'either because the states are concerned about indirectly granting armed groups legitimacy, or because the parties do not want to commit themselves to more than the minimum for fear of their own members being prosecuted, or because the intention of one of both

---

[138] Operational Code of Conduct for the Nigerian Army, issued July 1967, reproduced in AHM Kirk-Greene, *Crisis and Conflict in Nigeria, A Documentary Sourcebook 1966–1969* (Oxford University Press, 1971) 455, 456.

[139] H Dunant, *A Memory of Solferino* (reprinted and translated, ICRC, 1986) 126.

[140] GB Davis, 'Doctor Francis Lieber's Instructions for the Government of Armies in the Field' (1907) 1 *AJIL* 13, 25, citing Colonel Birkhimer, *Military Government and Martial Law*.

[141] T Meron, 'Francis Lieber's Code and Principles of Humanity' (1998) 36 *Columbia Journal of Transnational Law* 269, 281.

[142] See further below, 439–40.

[143] J Basdevant, 'A Little-Known Convention on the Law of War' (1974) 14 *IRRC* 344, 354.

[144] Respect for Human Rights in Armed Conflicts: Report of the Secretary-General, A/8052, 18 September 1970, para 163.

parties to respect international humanitarian law is not sincere'.[145] Yet, as Chapter 4 demonstrates,[146] ad hoc agreements continue to be concluded and instructions issued at a reasonably healthy rate. Thus, it was the view of the United Kingdom at the 1949 Diplomatic Conference which turned out to be somewhat correct, noting (albeit a little too optimistically) that 'if civil war developed to considerable proportions, there would be an inclination on both sides to introduce, by special agreements, as many as possible of the provisions of the Convention'.[147]

4. Conclusion

During the period in question, non-international armed conflicts were regulated in two principal ways, namely through recognition of belligerency and through instruction or agreement. Recognition of belligerency suffered from a number of difficulties. Although it required the existence of certain factors, precisely what those factors were and to what degree they had to be satisfied was a matter of dispute. Recognition was also a self-serving exercise, whether by the parent state or by other states, and the entry into force of the law of war was very much a secondary consideration. In addition to these difficulties, the parent state and every other state had to decide for itself whether, in its view, belligerency should be recognized. This decentralized approach meant that the very same situation was treated by some states as a civil war and by others as insurgency or rebellion. Regulation through instruction or agreement was similarly decentralized, resting entirely on the discretion of the parties to the conflict. Although issued or concluded in many a non-international armed conflict, in just as many others, they were not forthcoming. Nonetheless, regulation through instruction and agreement is important and it is unfortunate that this form of regulation has been largely ignored.

In light of the drawbacks of ad hoc regulation, and the serious effects of non-international armed conflicts, there was a deliberate attempt to regulate non-international armed conflicts systematically through international humanitarian law.

---

[145] A-M La Rosa and C Wuerzner, 'Armed Groups, Sanctions and the Implementation of International Humanitarian Law' (2008) 90 *IRRC* 327, 332–3. See also D Fleck, 'Ruses of War and Prohibition of Perfidy' (1974) 13 *Military Law and the Law of War Review* 269, 297; C Smith, 'Special Agreements to Apply the Geneva Conventions in Internal Armed Conflicts: The Lessons of Darfur' (2007) 2 *Irish Yearbook of International Law* 91, 94.

[146] See below, 124–33.

[147] *Final Record*, above note 104, Vol II-B, 98.

2
Systematic Regulation through International Humanitarian Law

1. Introduction

At around the same time as the Lieber Code was being drafted, in 1863,[1] another formative event was taking place, an event that would prove equally as important in the regulation of armed conflict. The Battle of Solferino was fought between the French and Austrian armies in 1859. Having witnessed the aftermath of the battle, which saw thousands of wounded soldiers being left to die on the battlefield without any attempt to provide them with medical treatment, Henry Dunant published his influential *Un Souvenir de Solferino* recounting his experiences and proposing the creation of relief societies that would provide care to the wounded in wartime.[2] Dunant's text was well-received and led to the formation of the 'Committee of Five' (which comprised General Guillaume-Henri Dufour, Gustave Moynier, Louis Appia, Théodore Maunoir, and Henry Dunant), later to become the International Committee of the Red Cross, to consider the proposals.[3] This, in turn, led to the convening of an international conference in 1863, which adopted the proposal to create national relief societies. The following year, in 1864, a diplomatic conference was convened by the Swiss Federal Council, which adopted the Geneva Convention for the Amelioration of the Condition of the Wounded in Armies in the Field.[4] In time, this would lead to the Diplomatic Conference of 1949 and the adoption of common Article 3 of the Geneva Conventions.[5] Several other instruments would also follow. It is this systematic regulation of non-international armed conflict through international humanitarian law that is the focus of this chapter.

2. The International Committee of the Red Cross and International Conferences of the Red Cross

The International Committee of the Red Cross (ICRC or Committee) was initially reluctant to accept that it or the 1864 Geneva Convention had a role to play in times of civil war. The minutes of the second meeting of the ICRC noted that:

[t]he Committee agreed, first and foremost, that, in its opinion, no action should be contemplated during civil wars, and that the [national] Committees should concern themselves only with European wars. After a few years' experience, the welfare scheme, once universally adopted

---

[1] On which, see above, 23.
[2] H Dunant, *Un Souvenir de Solferino* (Genève, 1862); H Dunant, *A Memory of Solferino* (reprinted and translated, ICRC, 1986).
[3] The Committee of Five would later be known as the International Committee for the Relief of Wounded Combatants and still later as the International Committee of the Red Cross.
[4] For a detailed history, see P Boissier, *History of the International Committee of the Red Cross: From Solferino to Tsushima* (Henri Dunant Institute, 1985).
[5] On which, see chapter 3.

and established, could of course be extended in various ways, but for the moment we should confine ourselves to the question of large-scale conflicts between European Powers.[6]

This decision was not made simply for reasons of practicality or to allow the Committee to gain experience. As Gustave Moynier wrote elsewhere in 1870, '[n]eedless to say, we are not talking about civil wars; international laws are not applicable to them'.[7] Likewise, the Committee wrote in 1875 that the 1864 Geneva Convention does not bind states parties in respect of their own subjects.[8] However, by 1876, Moynier and the Committee had changed their minds, taking the view that nothing in the text of the 1864 Convention suggested that it was limited to wars being fought between the contracting parties. Rather, the obligations were framed in neutral terms. They also opined that the Convention was not in the nature of 'a commercial treaty or a postal convention', but was more of 'a code of ethics' or 'recognition of certain laws of a higher order'.[9] Moynier reasoned further that, as the Convention did not work on the basis of reciprocity, the contracting parties remained under an obligation to respect the Convention even if they faced rebels.[10]

Even prior to this change of position, it had been agreed that *national* Red Cross societies had a role to play in time of civil war.[11] During the Carlist war of 1872–6, certain members of the Spanish Red Cross had expressed the view that, as the Red Cross 'draws its origin from an international document, recognized by a diplomatic convention, its aim should be confined to relieving the suffering resulting from large-scale international conflicts'. However, they also noted that '[i]t is very hard to accept that our compatriots, however misguided, can be treated more harshly than foreigners; it is cruel to tell us that we should calmly watch the blood flowing from their wounds without helping them by using the means prepared for the benefit of enemy soldiers ... Blood, once spilt, effaces the colours that the wounded wore during the fight'.[12] Accordingly, national Red Cross societies did offer their services to parties to civil wars as well as in other situations of internal violence, for example in Cuba (1897), during the Boer War (1899–1902), in Venezuela (1903), Nicaragua (1909), Honduras (1911), and China (1912).[13]

---

[6] Meeting of 17 February 1863, minutes reprinted and translated in (1963) 3 *IRRC* 63, 67.
[7] G Moynier, *Étude sur la Convention de Genève* (Paris, 1870) 304 ('Nous ne parlons pas, cela va sans dire, des guerres civiles; les lois internationales ne leur sont pas applicables').
[8] 'L'Insurrection dans la Herzégovine' (1875–October) 6 *Bulletin International des Sociétés de Secours aux Militaires Blessés* 175, 175 ('cette Convention ne le lie pas envers ses propres sujets').
[9] G Ador and G Moynier, for the International Committee of the Red Cross, 'Les Destinées de la Convention de Genève pendant la Guerre de Serbie' (1876–October) 7 *Bulletin International des Sociétés de Secours aux Militaires Blessés* 165, 168 ('un code de morale'); G Moynier, *La Croix-Rouge: Son Passé et Son Avenir* (Paris, Sandoz and Thuillier, 1882) 219 ('une reconnaissance de certaines lois d'ordre supérieur').
[10] Moynier, ibid, 218–19.
[11] See Boissier, *History*, above note 4, 298–300.
[12] 'La Charité dans la Guerre Civile' (1870–July) 1 *Bulletin International des Sociétés de Secours aux Militaires Blessés* 175, 175–6 ('puisque l'association tire son origine d'un acte international, reconnu par une convention diplomatique, son objet doit être circonscrit au soulagement des malheurs provenant des grands conflits internationaux'; 'il est bien dur d'admettre que nos compatriotes, même complètement égarés, puissent être traités plus rigoureusement que les étrangers; il est cruel de nous dire, que nous devons voir avec calme le sang couler de leurs blessures, sans nous empresser de faire usage pour les secourir de ressources préparées en faveur de soldats ennemis ... le sang, une fois versé, efface les couleurs que le blessé portait pendant le combat'). The English translation is taken from Boissier, *History*, above note 4, 298.
[13] Statement of the United States, *Compte-Rendu de la Neuvième Conférence International de la Croix-Rouge Tenue à Washington du 7 au 17 mai 1912*, ICRC Archives CR 22/32, 26–7.

A more formalized approach to Red Cross involvement in civil wars was suggested to the Ninth International Conference of the Red Cross in 1912. Two reports were submitted to the delegates to the Conference, on the role of the Red Cross in civil war. A report by the American Red Cross, entitled 'The Role of the Red Cross in Case of Civil War or of Insurrection', contained a draft international convention on the subject. A second report, on 'Measures to be taken by the Red Cross in a Country in a State of Insurrection, to enable this Institution to Fulfil its Functions towards the two Belligerent parties without violating its neutrality' by the Cuban Red Cross, also considered the role of national Red Cross societies.[14] These proposals were not favourably received. Reflecting the prevailing sentiment of the time,[15] the Russian delegate stated rather forcefully:

As a delegate of the Imperial Government, I believe and declare that the Imperial Government cannot be a contracting party in any manner or form or even a negotiating party to any agreement or declaration on this subject and I believe this subject, given its grave political nature, cannot even be a matter for discussion in an exclusively humanitarian and peaceful conference.

I further believe that the Red Cross societies could have no duty to perform towards insurgent gangs or revolutionaries which can only be considered as criminals by the laws of my country... any offer of services, whether direct or indirect, from Red Cross societies to insurgents or revolutionaries could only be viewed as a breach of friendly relations, as an unfriendly act, likely to encourage and foment sedition and rebellion in a country.[16]

Delegates debated the proposals contained in the reports, although the proposals themselves were not put to a vote. The delegate of the American Red Cross stressed that the offering of services on the part of national Red Cross societies of neutral states could not be taken as constituting recognition of belligerency and was only a humanitarian gesture.[17] The delegate stated: '[t]he only topic under consideration here is providing human beings who are suffering in a civil war with the same aid you would give to the wounded and sick of foreign and hostile armies in recognised international war.'[18] He also noted that none of the states that were involved in violence objected to the American Red Cross' furnishing of assistance; indeed, on the contrary, they were appreciative of the assistance rendered.[19] Responding to the objection of the delegate

---

[14] 'Le Rôle de la Croix-Rouge en Cas de Guerre Civile ou d'Insurrection', *Compte-Rendu*, ibid, 4–13; 'Mesures à Prendre par la Croix-Rouge dans un Pays en État d'Insurrection permettant à cette Institution d'Accomplir ses Fonctions entre les deux Belligérants sans Manquer à la Neutralité', ibid, 14–15.
[15] F Siordet, 'The Geneva Conventions and Civil War' (1950) III *RICR Supplement* 132, 138.
[16] Statement of Russia, *Compte-Rendu de la Neuvième Conférence*, above note 13, 2–3. The original reads:

En qualité de délégué du Gouvernement Impérial je considère et déclare que le Gouvernement Impérial ne saurait dans aucun cas ni sous aucune forme être partie contractante ou même seulement partie discusante à aucun accord ou voeu à ce sujet et j'estime que ce sujet, vu son caractère de gravité politique ne saurait même devenir matière à discussion au sein d'une Conférence exclusivement humanitaire et pacifique.

Je considère en outre que les sociétés de la Croix-Rouge ne sauraient avoir de devoir à remplir auprès des bandes insurgées ou de révolutionnaires lesquelles ne peuvent être considérées par les lois de mon pays que comme des criminels... tout offre de service, direct ou indirect des sociétés de la Croix-Rouge à des insurgés ou révolutionnaires ne pourrait être envisagé que comme une violation des relations amicales, que comme un "unfriendly act" tendant à encourager et à fomenter dans un pays la sédition et la rébellion.

[17] Statement of the United States, ibid, 21.
[18] Ibid. The original reads: 'Il ne s'agit ici que du problème de porter aux êtres humains qui souffrent dans une guerre civile, les mêmes secours que vous accorderiez aux blessés et aux malades des armées étrangères et hostiles dans la guerre internationale reconnue.'
[19] Ibid, 26–7.

of Russia concerning the criminal nature of the opposing party involved in a civil war, the delegate of the United States noted:

> In times of international conflict, we now compete in our efforts to improve the condition of enemies that fate has thrown in our power... Will we say that our adversaries in civil conflicts, that those who are close to us, our fathers, our sons, our brothers, should be treated, will be treated with less respect, less benevolence, less affection than our outside enemies?[20]

Ultimately, the matter was left undecided.

The subject arose once again, in 1921, at the Tenth International Conference of the Red Cross, which took place following the Russian revolution and civil war (1917–21) and after the conclusion of the Hungarian revolution (1919), in both of which the ICRC had played a role.[21] In 1918, following the Russian revolution and during the civil war, the Council of People's Commissars issued a decree informing the ICRC and all states parties to the Geneva Convention 'that this Convention in its first version [1864] as well as in subsequent versions [1868, 1906], and all the other Conventions and international agreements relating to the Red Cross to which Russia was an adherent until October 1917, are recognized and will be maintained by the Russian Soviet Government and that the Red Cross Society retains all rights and prerogatives based on the said conventions and agreements'.[22] This followed an earlier decree which purported to abolish the Russian Red Cross.[23] In certain respects, the 1864 Convention contained greater protection than that afforded by the 1949 Geneva Conventions, with persons and objects involved in the treatment of the wounded and sick being treated as neutrals.[24] The Bureau established to liquidate the Russian Red Cross confirmed to the ICRC Delegate in Petrograd that:

> [a]ll the prerogatives of the Red Cross are preserved. Given the current needs in relation to the return of prisoners of war and care for the disabled, the work of the Red Cross continues to be practised in its entirety. All that once belonged to it is rendered until the end of the war.[25]

During the 1919 Hungarian revolution, the ICRC delegate noted the problem of the lack of 'possibility of invoking an article of the Geneva Convention, however obscure and inadequate' in times of civil war.[26] Furthermore, a former delegate of the Hungarian Red Cross queried how a foreigner could 'be justified in becoming involved in political activity which the traditional principles of law see as a purely internal affair?

---

[20] Ibid, 28–9. The original reads: 'En temps de conflit international nous rivalisons maintenant dans nos efforts d'améliorer la condition des ennemis que le sort a jetés en notre pouvoir... Nous faudra-t-il dire que nos adversaires de luttes civiles, que ceux qui nous sont proches, nos pères, nos fils, nos frères devraient être traités, seront traités avec moins d'égards, moins de bienveillance, moins d'affection que nos ennemis du dehors?'

[21] On which, see CICR, *Rapport Général du Comité International de la Croix-Rouge sur son activité de 1912 à 1920* (CICR, 1921) 185–208; A Durand, *From Sarajevo to Hiroshima: History of the International Committee of the Red Cross* (Henry Dunant Institute, 1984) 99–110 and 126–38.

[22] Decree of 2 June 1918, ICRC Archives Mis 1/5 (Frick). English translation taken from Durand, *History of the International Committee of the Red Cross*, above note 21, 100–2.

[23] Decree of 6 January 1918, ICRC Archives Mis 1/5 (Frick).

[24] Articles 1 and 2.

[25] Letter from the Bureau of Liquidation to the ICRC Delegate in Petrograd, undated, ICRC Archives Mis 1/5 (Frick). The original reads: 'Toutes les prérogatives de la Croix-Rouge russe, comme partie de la Société internationale de la Croix-Rouge, sont conservées. Etant donné les nécessités actuelles en rapport avec le retour des prisonniers de guerre et les soins à donner aux invalides, l'activité de la Croix-Rouge continue à s'exercer dans sa totalité. Tout ce qui lui appartenait autrefois lui est rendu jusqu'au moment de la liquidation définitive de la guerre.' See also L'Ordonnance du Soviet des Commissaires du Peuple, 7 August 1918, ibid.

[26] Quoted in Durand, *History of the International Committee of the Red Cross*, above note 21, 127.

The problem was to get the People's Commissars to recognize this point and extend the principles of the Geneva Convention, hitherto applicable only to war between nations, to apply to the class struggle'.[27] The People's Commissar did issue a decree on the role of the ICRC, which included the provision that '[e]verything must be done to enable the International Red Cross to perform its humanitarian duties without let or hindrance in the territory of the Hungarian Soviet Republic, for only thus will it be able to afford assistance to the wounded, sick and prisoners of war'.[28]

In its report to the Tenth Conference, the ICRC reflected on its experience in Russia and Hungary, opining that Red Cross institutions have a role to play in civil war and reflecting that, civil wars, if continued, gradually become regular wars.[29] The Tenth Conference also had before it reports of various national Red Cross societies on the role that they had played during civil wars.[30] The Tenth Conference did not pursue the idea of a convention applicable in time of civil war, but did adopt Resolution XIV, entitled 'Civil War'. The Resolution affirmed the 'right and duty' of the Red Cross 'of affording relief in case of civil war and social and revolutionary disturbances'. The Resolution also recognized that 'all victims of civil war or of such disturbances are, without any exception whatsoever, entitled to relief, in conformity with the general principles of the Red Cross'.[31] The Resolution went on to note that, 'the state of civil war cannot justify violation of International Law' and that 'political detainees in time of civil war should be considered and treated in accordance with the principles which inspired those who drew up the 1907 Hague Convention'.[32] This latter point would turn out to foreshadow similar arguments made in respect of captured fighters in times of non-international armed conflict.[33]

The principles contained in the Resolution were put into action almost immediately, in the civil war in the plebiscite of Upper Silesia (1921), in the violence in Ireland (1922), and during the Spanish civil war (1936–9), among other situations.[34] Indeed, the resolution was used so frequently during the inter-war period as a basis upon which to intervene, that it has been described as 'an unofficial convention in a non-international war'[35] and as 'one of the most important texts in the history of the Red Cross'.[36]

However, the Resolution also limited the possibility of direct involvement on the part of the ICRC. The Resolution provided that, '[i]n every country in which civil war breaks out, it is the National Red Cross Society of the country which, in the first place, is responsible for dealing, in the most complete manner, with the relief needs of the victims'. It was only in limited 'exceptional cases' that the ICRC could intervene directly with the parties to the conflict. These exceptional cases were of two sorts, namely (1) 'by reason of the inability or unwillingness of [the national Red Cross] Society to request foreign aid or accept an offer of relief received through the

---

[27] Ibid, 127.
[28] Decree of 10 April 1919, reproduced in (1919–May) 1 *RICR* 604.
[29] CICR, *Rapport Général 1912 à 1920*, above note 21, 208 ('[l]a guerre civile devant, si elle se prolongeait, devenir peu à peu une guerre régulière').
[30] See in particular, the reports of the national Red Cross societies of Finland, Italy, Portugal, Russia, and Turkey.
[31] Xth International Red Cross Conference, Geneva, 1921, Resolution XIV, 'Civil War'.
[32] Ibid.
[33] See below, 521–6.
[34] On which, see Durand, *History of the International Committee of the Red Cross*, above note 26, 200–2, 225–30, 317–69.
[35] Ibid.
[36] F Bugnion, *The International Committee of the Red Cross and the Protection of War Victims* (ICRC, 2003) 262.

intermediary of the International Committee of the Red Cross [and] the unrelieved suffering caused by civil war imperatively demands alleviation' and (2) '[s]hould all forms of Government and National Red Cross be dissolved in a country engaged in civil war'.[37]

On this basis, upon requests from third parties for the ICRC to involve itself in the civil wars in Ireland (1922) and Bulgaria (1923), the ICRC responded that, following the Resolution adopted at the Tenth Conference, it could only intervene in certain special conditions.[38] It was only following the inability of the British Red Cross Society to act in relation to the situation in Ireland in 1922—the President of the British Red Cross Society responded to a letter from the ICRC that 'in view of the very delicate political situation that exists in Ireland, my Society feels that it cannot at the moment take any action in the matter'[39]—that the ICRC involved itself. Indeed, in the ICRC letter that prompted this statement, the ICRC noted that, if intervention on the part of the British Red Cross did not appear possible, it would consider whether there was a need for direct intervention on the part of the ICRC in accordance with the Resolution.[40] The limited possibility for ICRC action was mitigated by the fact that, in many an instance, national Red Cross societies had become integrated with the state establishment to such an extent that the view of the state was also invariably the view of the national society.[41] Thus, in these situations, the national Red Cross society proved unwilling to act.

Some years after the adoption of the two Geneva Conventions in 1929, the ICRC engaged in a study on the difficulties and deficiencies of the Geneva Conventions. It invited national Red Cross societies to send experts to a meeting designed for the revision and possible extension of the Conventions. One of the issues to be considered was the extension of the scope of application of the 1929 Conventions to include civil wars. The ICRC decided that, although 'desirable', the Conventions could not be amended to include civil war: '[i]n such cases we are not in the presence of two States parties to the Convention, and each entitled to claim its protection, but in actual fact to two factions of the same country.' However, the invited experts took the view that the 'humanitarian principles' of the Convention 'must be respected under all circumstances, even when it is not juridically applicable'.[42]

Civil wars were again considered at an International Conference of the Red Cross, this time at the Sixteenth Conference, in 1938, at which time the Spanish civil war was still raging. The ICRC submitted a report to the Conference on its work in the conflicts in Upper Silesia, Ireland, and Spain. The report contained a draft resolution on the protection of civilians, the wounded and sick, and prisoners, as well as intervention in a civil war on the part of national Red Cross societies and the ICRC.[43] The draft

---

[37] Resolution XIV, 'Civil War', above note 31.
[38] See eg Letter of 21 December 1923 of the Vice-President of the ICRC, ICRC Archives, CR 22/12 (concerning Bulgaria); Letter of 28 June 1921, ICRC Archives, CR 22 (84)/2 (concerning Ireland).
[39] Letter from the President of the British Red Cross to the ICRC, 13 December 1922, ICRC Archives, CR 22 (84)/73.
[40] Letter from the ICRC to the President of the British Red Cross, 4 December 1922, ICRC Archives, CR 22(84)/66.
[41] This is apparent from a perusal of the ICRC archives. See also, reaching a similar conclusion, G Best, *Humanity in Warfare* (Methuen, 1983) 141.
[42] Report on the Interpretation, Revision and Extension of the Geneva Convention of July 27, 1929 (June 1938) 7–8.
[43] Report of the ICRC to the XVIth International Red Cross Conference, London, June 1938, 'Le Role et l'action de la Croix-Rouge en Temps de Guerre Civile', reproduced in (1938–February) 20 *RICR* 97.

resolution contained a clause, an equivalent of which would become a standard provision in later instruments: '[s]uch action, whatever the form it may take, shall in no case be considered as the recognition of a state of war or of belligerence, nor as help furnished to one or other of the hostile parties.'[44]

The Legal Commission of the International Conference paid close attention to the ICRC report and to problems arising in civil wars. It opined that 'in civil war the great humanitarian principles which are the soul of the Red Cross should be increasingly applied, not only to the wounded, sick and prisoners of war, but also to non-combatants, and to children in particular',[45] and noted that '[t]he value of laying down definite rules both for the application of the principles of Geneva and for the intervention of the Red Cross in civil war did not escape the Commission'. However, it took the view that, given that the Spanish civil war was then ongoing, 'the moment would hardly be propitious for laying down stable principles'. The report of the ICRC was also considered to raise 'delicate juridical problems' which required further study and, importantly, study on the part of governments.[46] Accordingly, the Legal Commission requested 'the International Committee, in the light of its practical experience, to pursue the study of all problems relating to the work of the Red Cross in civil war or revolution'.[47] Ultimately, the plenary Conference adopted a Resolution, entitled 'Role and Activity of the Red Cross in time of Civil War'. The norms contained in that Resolution have an interesting parallel with the norms that would later be included in Protocol II Additional to the 1949 Geneva Conventions, of 1977.[48] The Resolution provided that the Conference:

requests the International Committee and the national Red Cross Societies to endeavour to obtain:

(a) the application of the humanitarian principles which were formulated in the Geneva Convention of 1929 and the Xth Hague Convention of 1907, especially as regards the treatment of the wounded, the sick, and prisoners of war, and the safety of medical personnel and medical stores;
(b) humane treatment for all political prisoners, their exchange and, so far as possible, their release;
(c) respect of the life and liberty of non-combatants;
(d) facilities for the transmission of news of a personal nature and for the re-union of families;
(e) effective measures for the protection of children.

The Conference requests the International Committee, making use of its practical experience, to continue the general study of the problems raised by civil war as regards the Red Cross, and to submit the results of its study to the next International Red Cross Conference.[49]

The ICRC did study the matter and consulted with national Red Cross societies and governmental experts, convening meetings of both. The Commission for the Study of the Conventions, which was tasked with the project, proposed to the Preliminary Conference of National Red Cross Societies in 1946 that, in respect of the 1929 Geneva Convention on the Wounded and Sick in Armies in the Field, 'in case of Civil

---

[44] Ibid.
[45] Sixteenth International Red Cross Conference, London, 1938: Report, 83.
[46] Ibid, 82–3.
[47] Ibid, 83.
[48] On Additional Protocol II, see below, 182–92.
[49] XVIth International Red Cross Conference, London, 1938, Resolution XIV, 'Role and Activity of the Red Cross in time of Civil War'.

War within the frontiers of a State the adversaries should be invited to declare their readiness to apply the principles of the Convention, subject to reciprocity being observed'.[50] For its part, the Preliminary Conference went further than the proposal, recommending that an article be included at the start of a revised Geneva Convention, which provided *inter alia* that, '[i]n the case of armed conflict within the borders of a State, the Convention shall also be applied by each of the adverse Parties, unless one of them announces expressly its intention to the contrary'.[51] The Preliminary Conference thus suggested the application of a revised Convention in its entirety rather than solely its underlying principles. It also presumed applicability rather than inviting the parties to declare their acceptance. The Preliminary Conference based its proposal on the hope that 'no State or insurgent body would venture to proclaim, in the face of world opinion, its intention of disregarding the laws of humanity'.[52]

As regards the 1929 Geneva Convention Relative to the Treatment of Prisoners of War, the Preliminary Conference agreed to add to its revised scope of application that 'these provisions must be applied ... in principle, in case of civil war'.[53] It also suggested that the revised Geneva Conventions should include a provision on the activities of national Red Cross societies along the lines that, '[i]n case of the occupation of a country, or in case of civil war, the Red Cross shall be authorized to extend its care to all wounded, without distinction of the party to which they may belong'.[54] In this regard, the President of the ICRC expressed the view that 'future Red Cross activities must rest on a firmer basis than agreements concluded for each particular case'.[55] A systematic, rather than ad hoc, approach to the regulation of non-international armed conflict was thus recognized as necessary.

At the 1947 Conference of Government Experts, the proposals of the Preliminary Conference of National Red Cross Societies were considered. As to a revised Convention on the Wounded and Sick in Armies in the Field, the Conference of Government Experts agreed insertion of the language: '[i]n case of civil war, in any part of the home or colonial territory of a Contracting Party, the principles of the Convention shall be equally applied by the said Party, subject to the adverse Party also conforming thereto.'[56] Much the same was agreed in respect of a revised Prisoners of War Convention and a new convention on the protection of civilian enemy aliens in time of war.[57] Unlike the Preliminary Conference, then, the Government Experts took the view that it was the principles of the Conventions rather than the Conventions themselves that would be applicable in civil wars, and even then, application of the principles was subject to conformity on the part of the armed group. In the view of one delegate, 'it should be clearly understood that the humanitarian obligations stipulated by the present Article should entail no juridical consequences in respect of the legal status of any body claiming governmental authority, but not recognized by another Government as enjoying such authority'.[58] That view continues today and can be

---

[50] ICRC, Report on the Work of the Preliminary Conference of National Red Cross Societies for the Study of the Conventions and of Various Problems Relative to the Red Cross (Geneva, July 26–August 3, 1946) (ICRC, 1947) 15 (emphasis removed).
[51] Ibid, 15.
[52] Ibid, 15.
[53] Ibid, 70.
[54] Ibid, 105.
[55] Ibid, 107.
[56] ICRC, Report on the Work of the Conference of Government Experts for the Study of the Conventions for the Protection of War Victims (Geneva, April 14–26, 1947) (ICRC, 1947) 8.
[57] Ibid, 8, 103, and 272.
[58] Ibid, 9.

found in most conventional instruments applicable in non-international armed conflict, although doubts still surround such sentiments at the political level.[59]

On the basis of the conclusions reached at the Conference of Government Experts, the ICRC drew up texts and submitted them to the Commission for the Study of the Conventions, which made certain revisions to the texts before approving them. The ICRC then submitted the approved texts to national Red Cross societies and to states signatories to the 1929 Geneva Conventions, with a view to discussing the texts at the Seventeenth International Conference of the Red Cross, in 1948, in Stockholm.[60] The relevant provisions of the draft Conventions read:

> In all cases of armed conflict which are not of an international character, especially cases of civil war, colonial conflicts, or wars of religion, which may occur in the territory of one or more of the High Contracting Parties, the implementing of the principles of the present Convention shall be obligatory for each of the adversaries. The application of the Convention in these circumstances shall in nowise depend on the legal status of the parties to the conflict and shall have no effect on that status.[61]

In its accompanying report, the ICRC noted that the provision was based on the proposal of the Conference of Government Experts but that application was no longer contingent on the adverse party conforming thereto. It was felt that '[t]he condition of reciprocity might... render this... valueless, as one Party could always allege that its adversary disregarded some specific clause of the Convention'.[62] Delegates' concern about the legal status of the parties was also reflected in the text.

An error in the English translation of the provision contributed to confusion as to whether the principles of the Conventions were to be applied, or, rather, whether the provisions themselves were applicable. The French text of the provision, which was distributed to national Red Cross societies and states signatories, referred to 'les dispositions de la présente Convention',[63] but the term 'les dispositions' was translated as 'principles' rather than 'provisions'. This was an error of translation rather than anything more substantive.[64]

Thus, it was the 'provisions approach' that was followed. However, this led to criticism by one delegate at the Stockholm Conference, who felt that it was 'utterly impossible for any Government whatsoever to agree to [the Convention] being adopted as a whole in each armed conflict which might arise' and noted 'the impossibility of applying this article in all armed conflicts'.[65] The delegate's attempt to substitute 'the humanitarian principles of the present Convention' for the 'provisions of the present Convention' failed, as did an attempt to reintroduce the condition of reciprocity.[66]

---

[59] See below, 546–9.
[60] ICRC, *Draft Revised or New Conventions for the Protection of War Victims* (ICRC, 1948) 2.
[61] Article 2. See ibid, 5, 34–5, 52, 153–4, 222.
[62] Ibid, 6.
[63] CICR, *Projets de Conventions Revisées ou Nouvelles Protégeant les Victimes de la Guerre* (CICR, Mai 1948) 6.
[64] See *XVIIe Conférence Internationale de la Croix-Rouge (Stockholm, Août 1948), Commission Juridique, Sténogramme des Séances* (Janvier 1949) 46 ('Il y a une erreur de traduction'). Cf DA Elder, 'The Historical Background of Common Article 3 of the Geneva Convention of 1949' (1979) 11 *Case Western Reserve Journal of International Law* 37, 43, who considers the change a substantive one. Elder's view has been followed in the literature.
[65] Seventeenth International Red Cross Conference: Stockholm, 1948, Report, 72 and 71 (Greece).
[66] *Commission Juridique, Sténogramme des Séances*, above note 64, 38–47 and 55.

The reference to 'especially cases of civil war, colonial conflicts, or wars of religion' was deleted from the text, 'because too rigid a definition might allow belligerents to escape their obligations, by claiming that the conflict in which they were involved was not provided for',[67] and because those were simply types of wars that fell within existing legal categories.[68] The former point continues to have resonance today in respect of the particular legal regime that applies to wars of national liberation.[69]

Accordingly, the relevant provision of the draft Convention on the Wounded and Sick of Armed Forces in the Field, and the draft Convention on the Wounded, Sick and Shipwrecked Members of Armed Forces on Sea, as adopted by the Stockholm Conference in 1948, read:

In all cases of armed conflict not of an international character which may occur in the territory of one or more of the High Contracting Parties, each of the adversaries shall be bound to implement the provisions of the present Convention. The Convention shall be applicable in these circumstances, whatever the legal status of the Parties to the conflict and without prejudice thereto.[70]

The relevant provision of the draft Convention on the Treatment of Prisoners of War and the draft Convention for the Protection of Civilian Persons in Time of War, as adopted by the Stockholm Conference in 1948, differed. Those draft Conventions provided that:

[i]n all cases of armed conflict not of an international character which may occur in the territory of one or more of the High Contracting Parties, each of *the Parties to the conflict* shall be bound to implement the provisions of the present Convention, *subject to the adverse party likewise acting in obedience thereto.* The Convention shall be applicable in these circumstances, whatever the legal status of the Parties to the conflict and without prejudice thereto.[71]

In addition to the change that was made to the Conventions on the Wounded and Sick, the element of reciprocity was reintroduced to the Prisoners of War and Civilians Conventions.[72] The drafts of the four Conventions were circulated to states in anticipation of the Diplomatic Conference that was envisaged to be held in 1949.[73] However, in proposals that were circulated to states also in advance of the Diplomatic Conference, the ICRC suggested deletion of the reciprocity clause, reiterating its view that any such clause may render application of the Convention 'completely stultified' as '[o]ne of the parties to the conflict could always assert, as would be all too easy in a war of this nature, that the adversary was not observing such and such a provision of the Convention'.[74]

---

[67] ICRC, *The Geneva Conventions of August 12, 1949: Analysis for the Use of National Red Cross Societies, Volume II* (ICRC, 1950) 6.
[68] *Commission Juridique, Sténogramme des Séances*, above note 64, 40–5.
[69] On which, see below, 212–22.
[70] ICRC, *Revised and New Draft Conventions for the Protection of War Victims* (ICRC, 1948) 10 and 32 respectively.
[71] Ibid, 51–2 and 114 (emphasis in original, reflecting the amendments made by the Stockholm Conference).
[72] *Commission Juridique, Sténogramme des Séances*, above note 64, 36–57. See in particular the statements of Greece.
[73] *Remarks and Proposals submitted by the International Commission of the Red Cross: Document for the Consideration of Governments invited by the Swiss Federal Council to attend the Diplomatic Conference at Geneva (April 21, 1949)* (Geneva, 1949) 5.
[74] Ibid, 38.

3. The Diplomatic Conference of 1949

A Diplomatic Conference was convened, as envisaged, in 1949, under the auspices of the Swiss Federal Council, in order to consider revisions to the 1929 Geneva Conventions and the Xth Hague Convention of 1907, and to conclude a new Convention on the protection of civilians in time of war.[75] The Stockholm drafts, as amended, were put before the Diplomatic Conference. According to one delegate, '[n]o other issue has given rise to such a long discussion and to such a detailed and exhaustive study as the question of the extension of the Convention to war victims of conflicts not of an international character'.[76] Similar statements have been made at every subsequent diplomatic conference that considered the issue.

At the Diplomatic Conference, a number of states took the view that civil wars (or armed conflicts not of an international character, as they would soon be called) should not be regulated through international law. For example, the United Kingdom 'did not believe it possible to oblige a State to apply the Conventions to situations which were not war, declared or not, as this idea is defined by international law ... their application to civil war would strike at the root of national sovereignty and endanger national security, quite apart from the practical difficulty' in applying them.[77] The Burmese delegate expressed particularly strong views on the matter, stating that '[t]he proposed Convention should not give legal status to insurgents who sought by undemocratic methods, to overthrow a legally constituted government by force of arms' and that 'the Eastern countries he represented in the Special Committee [which was tasked with reaching agreement on the situations in which the Conventions would apply] could not agree to an extension of the Conventions to civil war, and if such a provision were included, they would not be able to sign the Conventions'.[78] The Burmese delegate thus proposed deletion of the article on non-international armed conflicts, stating that its inclusion was 'a very serious danger to sovereignty and civilian rights' and '[t]o give international recognition to insurgency would certainly be as grave an error as recognition of aggression'.[79] In his view, inclusion of the article would 'only be an incentive to armed conflicts with all their terrible effects'.[80]

Other delegates took the view that non-international armed conflicts should be regulated by international law. Hungary, for example, stated that 'the essential aim of the Conference was to extend the field of action of the Convention as much as possible for the protection of the victims of conflicts',[81] while Mexico opined that 'the rights of the State should not be placed above all humanitarian considerations' and that '[o]ften civil war was more cruel than international war'.[82] The USSR was equally as forceful as Burma, but, in a turnaround from the position it expressed at the Ninth International Conference of the Red Cross in 1912,[83] to the opposite effect. The USSR stated that civil wars 'were often accompanied by violations of international law and were characterized by cruelty of all kinds. The suffering of the population in the instance of civil and colonial wars was as distressing as that which led Henry Dunant to realize the need for regulating the laws of warfare'.[84]

---

[75] Letter of the Federal Political Department of Switzerland to states parties to the Geneva Conventions of 1929 and the Xth Hague Convention of 1907, 11 May 1948, reproduced in *Final Record of the Diplomatic Conference of Geneva of 1949* (Federal Political Department, Berne) Vol I, 147.
[76] Ibid, Vol II-B, 325 (USSR).   [77] Ibid, 10.   [78] Ibid, 15 and 102.
[79] Ibid, 327.   [80] Ibid, 329.   [81] Ibid, 11.
[82] Ibid, 11.   [83] See above, 32.
[84] *Final Record*, above note 75, Vol II-B, 14. See also the interjection at 325–7.

The vast majority of states were in favour of extending regulation to non-international armed conflict, with a vote on point being passed by 10 votes in favour, one against, and one abstention.[85] The Report of the Special Committee provided that the Committee 'almost unanimously agreed that the four Conventions should contain a clause extending at least part of their benefits to non-international war', that '[c]ivil wars sometimes leave the most painful wounds in the organism of nations and their healing is most difficult', and that 'it was in the well-conceived interest of the Parties to the conflict, and above them of the country which they desired to serve, to reduce the excesses and horrors of such conflicts to the greatest possible extent'.[86] However, there was considerable disagreement as to precisely which such conflicts should be regulated as well as how they should be regulated. A number of states preferred to regulate non-international armed conflicts through the continued use of recognition of belligerency or a variant thereof, while others proposed extending regulation to conflicts that did not reach the level of belligerency. A way through the impasse was only reached by leaving the notion of non-international armed conflict undefined and approaching the matter through the lens of the rules that would be applicable. However, it is evident from the discussion of states that the level of violence at issue was akin to the notion of an insurgency.[87] The provision of the Geneva Conventions that regulates non-international armed conflicts, common Article 3 as ultimately adopted, provides:

In the case of armed conflict not of an international character occurring in the territory of one of the High Contracting Parties, each Party to the conflict shall be bound to apply, as a minimum, the following provisions:

(1) Persons taking no active part in the hostilities, including members of armed forces who have laid down their arms and those placed 'hors de combat' by sickness, wounds, detention, or any other cause, shall in all circumstances be treated humanely, without any adverse distinction founded on race, colour, religion or faith, sex, birth or wealth, or any other similar criteria.

To this end, the following acts are and shall remain prohibited at any time and in any place whatsoever with respect to the above-mentioned persons:

(a) violence to life and person, in particular murder of all kinds, mutilation, cruel treatment and torture;
(b) taking of hostages;
(c) outrages upon personal dignity, in particular humiliating and degrading treatment;
(d) the passing of sentences and the carrying out of executions without previous judgment pronounced by a regularly constituted court, affording all the judicial guarantees which are recognized as indispensable by civilized peoples.

(2) The wounded and sick shall be collected and cared for.

An impartial humanitarian body, such as the International Committee of the Red Cross, may offer its services to the Parties to the conflict.

The Parties to the conflict should further endeavour to bring into force, by means of special agreements, all or part of the other provisions of the present Convention.

The application of the preceding provisions shall not affect the legal status of the Parties to the conflict.

The rules that were considered applicable in non-international armed conflicts were thus few in number and in type and were taken from an intended preamble to the Civilians Convention, a preamble that reflected the underlying principles of the

---

[85] Ibid, 45. [86] Ibid, 124. [87] This is considered in detail in Chapter 5.

Convention.[88] Indeed, during the Conference, the USSR criticized common Article 3 as constituting a 'convention in miniature', opining that:

[i]t would hardly seem possible to summarize in twenty-five lines the four hundred Articles of the four Conventions... Such a procedure would inevitably entail the renunciation of many provisions drawn up by the Conference for the protection of war victims.[89]

Nonetheless, it was the 'principles' rather than the 'provisions' approach that was ultimately adopted. The approach would prove important, for a recurring question has been to what extent detailed rules and proscriptions can be read into the more general statements of law.[90]

4. The period 1949–74

In the period that followed the 1949 Diplomatic Conference, the minimal regulation of non-international armed conflict was recognized as problematic.[91] Accordingly, further attempts were made to provide protections to those caught up in non-international armed conflicts. The ICRC convened conferences of experts, in 1953, on the question of assistance to political detainees; in 1955, on the application of humanitarian principles in internal disturbances; and in 1962, on aid to victims in internal conflicts or disturbances.[92] From the latter, an influential definition of a non-international armed conflict emerged along with indicia that should be considered when deciding whether or not such a conflict exists.[93] In 1956, the ICRC also drew up 'Draft Rules for the Limitation of the Dangers Incurred by the Civilian Population in Time of War', which were intended to apply to international and non-international armed conflicts alike.[94] The Draft Rules contained provisions on protection for the civilian population in the context of targeting, and were adopted by the Nineteenth International Conference of the Red Cross in 1957.[95] However, states failed to act upon them and they gained little traction.

At around the same time, a convention was being drafted under the auspices of UNESCO on the protection of cultural property, which became the 1954 Hague Convention for the Protection of Cultural Property in the Event of Armed Conflict. Article 19 of that Convention provides:

---

[88] See the view of the Chairman: *Final Record*, above note 75, Vol II-A, 696.

[89] Ibid, Vol II-B, 98 (USSR). See also at 326. Today, the phrase 'a convention in miniature' is used in a positive sense to describe common Article 3. See eg JS Pictet (ed), *The Geneva Conventions of 12 August 1949, Commentary: IV Geneva Convention Relative to the Protection of Civilian Persons in Time of War* (ICRC, 1958) 34; Elder, Common Article 3, above note 64, 38; G Abi-Saab, 'Non-International Armed Conflicts', in UNESCO (ed), *International Dimensions of Humanitarian Law* (UNESCO, 1988) 217, 221; L Moir, *The Law of Internal Armed Conflict* (Cambridge University Press, 2002) 31.

[90] See eg on the law relating to precautions, below, 351–7.

[91] See eg B Jakovljević and J Patrnogić, 'The Urgent Need to Apply the Rules of Humanitarian Law to So-Called Internal Armed Conflicts' (1961) 1 *IRRC* 250.

[92] 'Commission of Experts for the Examination of the Question of Assistance to Political Detainees' (1953) 6 *RICR Supplement* 124; 'Report of the Commission of Experts for the Study of the Question of the Application of Humanitarian Principles in the Event of Internal Disturbances', in ICRC, Annual Report 1955 (ICRC, 1956) 75; 'Humanitarian Aid to the Victims of Internal Conflicts: Meeting of a Commission of Experts in Geneva' (1963) 3 *IRRC* 79.

[93] Ibid, 82. See generally below, 164–80.

[94] Article 2(b). On the Draft Rules, see K Suter, *An International Law of Guerrilla Warfare* (St Martin's Press, 1984) 91–6.

[95] See *Final Record Concerning the Draft Rules for the Limitation of the Dangers Incurred by the Civilian Population in Time of War* (ICRC, April 1958).

1. In the event of an armed conflict not of an international character occurring within the territory of one of the High Contracting Parties, each party to the conflict shall be bound to apply, as, a minimum, the provisions of the present Convention which relate to respect for cultural property.
2. The parties to the conflict shall endeavour to bring into force, by means of special agreements, all or part of the other provisions of the present Convention.
3. The United Nations Educational, Scientific and Cultural Organization may offer its services to the parties to the conflict.
4. The application of the preceding provisions shall not affect the legal status of the parties to the conflict.

The article was modelled on common Article 3,[96] as is clear from the language of the text.

A few years later, in 1965, a resolution was adopted by the Twentieth International Conference of the Red Cross, which 'urge[d] the ICRC to continue its work with the aim of strengthening the humanitarian assistance of the Red Cross to victims of non-international conflicts'.[97] Another resolution contained certain principles that were applicable to 'all Governments and other authorities responsible for action in armed conflicts [which] should conform at least to the following principles':

that the right of the parties to a conflict to adopt means of injuring the enemy is not unlimited;
that it is prohibited to launch attacks against the civilian population as such;
that distinction must be made at all times between persons taking part in the hostilities and members of the civilian population to the effect that the latter be spared as much as possible;
that the general principles of the Law of War apply to nuclear and similar weapons.[98]

The Resolution was initially drawn up with international armed conflicts in mind, that being the mandate of the Commission charged with considering the matter. However, it was made clear that it was without prejudice to the rules applicable in non-international armed conflict. An attempt expressly to limit the scope of the Resolution to international armed conflicts failed and the Resolution has since been interpreted as applying also to non-international armed conflicts.[99]

With the adumbration of the 1956 Draft Rules and the 1965 Resolution, there was a considered attempt to regulate the conduct of hostilities in non-international armed conflicts, common Article 3 lacking any rules on point. This was also reflected in the more general study of the ICRC on the laws and customs applicable in armed conflicts, which was being conducted during the same period. That study noted:

[W]hile international wars involving the application of [the Geneva] Conventions have been few since 1945, non-international wars have been frequent and deadly. In these the only rules applicable are the few basic rules contained in [common] Article 3...; these moreover mainly concern the treatment of persons in enemy hands, not the conduct of hostilities. However valuable this Article 3, which was a veritable victory in 1949, succeeding internal conflicts have demonstrated that it was inadequate to ensure the human person all the necessary protection.[100]

---

[96] *Actes de la Conférence Convoquée par l'Organisation des Nations Unies pour l'Éducation, la Science et la Culture tenue à la Haye du 21 Avril au 14 Mai* (La Haye, 1961) Documents de Travail, 323.
[97] Twentieth International Red Cross Conference, Vienna, 1965, Resolution XXXI, 'Protection of Victims of Non-International Conflicts'.
[98] Ibid, Resolution XXVIII, 'Protection of Civilian Populations against the Dangers of Indiscriminate Warfare', reproduced in (1967) 7 *IRRC* 305, 305.
[99] Twentieth International Conference of the Red Cross, Report, Vienna, 2–9 October 1965, 84–7.
[100] Reaffirmation and Development of the Law and Customs Applicable in Armed Conflicts: Report submitted by the International Committee of the Red Cross (May 1969) 8. See also at 97–8.

The ICRC proposed developing common Article 3, to include 'respect of the red cross sign, hospitals, medical personnel or members of National Red Cross Societies; the treatment of regular combatants; relief for military or civilian detainees; blockade; [and] supervision'. The experts consulted 'recognized that most of [the proposals] were not aimed at the formulation of entirely new rules but at defining norms implicitly contained in Article 3, and more especially the fundamental principle of humane treatment'.[101] Thus, the general statements of common Article 3 were considered to contain within them rules of greater detail.

A specific report of the ICRC on the protection of victims of non-international armed conflicts was submitted to the Twenty-first International Conference of the Red Cross in 1969.[102] At that Conference, a number of important resolutions were adopted. Resolution XVII, on the 'Protection of Victims of Non-International Armed Conflicts', noted that the number of non-international armed conflicts were increasing and that common Article 3 'ha[d] already rendered great service in protecting the victims of these conflicts' but 'experience has brought out certain points on the basis of which this Article could be made more specific or supplemented'. Accordingly, the Conference 'ask[ed] the ICRC to devote special attention to this problem within the framework of the more general studies it has started to develop [on] humanitarian law, in particular with the co-operation of Government experts'.[103] A Resolution was also adopted on the specific issue of the 'Status of Combatants in Non-International Armed Conflicts', again calling for the ICRC to consider the issue.[104] Another Resolution encouraged the ICRC's work on the more general issue of the applicable laws and customs of war.[105]

The year 1969 also saw the Institut de Droit International adopt a Resolution on 'The Distinction Between Military Objectives and Non-Military Objects in General and Particularly the Problems Associated with Weapons of Mass Destruction'. Once again, the subject of the Resolution was the conduct of hostilities rather than the protection of persons *hors de combat*. The rules were considered to apply to 'any *de jure* or *de facto* government, or by any other authority responsible for the conduct of hostilities',[106] thus indicating its applicability to non-international armed conflicts.

At around the same time, the UN also became interested in the subject of human rights in armed conflicts. The International Conference on Human Rights, held in 1968 in Tehran, adopted a Resolution, which opined 'that the Red Cross Geneva Conventions of 1949 are not sufficiently broad in scope to cover all armed conflicts'. Accordingly, the Resolution requested 'the General Assembly to invite the Secretary-General to study' steps that could be taken to apply better international humanitarian law 'in all armed conflicts' and to consider the need for additional instruments or revision of existing instruments.[107] The General Assembly, in turn, adopted Resolution

---

[101] Ibid, 104.
[102] 'Protection of Victims of Non-International Conflicts' (1969) 9 *IRRC* 343.
[103] XXIst International Red Cross Conference, Istanbul, 1969, Resolution XVII, 'Protection of Victims of Non-International Armed Conflicts'.
[104] Ibid, Resolution XVIII, 'Status of Combatants in Non-International Armed Conflicts'.
[105] Ibid, Resolution XIII, 'Reaffirmation and Development of the Laws and Customs Applicable in Armed Conflicts'.
[106] Preamble.
[107] International Conference on Human Rights, Resolution XXIII, 12 May 1968. For an analysis of the build up to the Resolution, see Suter, *Guerrilla Warfare*, above note 94, Chapter 2.

2444 (XXIII) which recognized 'the necessity of applying basic humanitarian principles in all armed conflicts'. The Resolution was modelled on the 1965 Resolution of the Twentieth International Conference of the Red Cross and affirmed:

(a) That the right of the parties to a conflict to adopt means of injuring the enemy is not unlimited;
(b) That it is prohibited to launch attacks against the civilian populations as such;
(c) That distinction must be made at all times between persons taking part in the hostilities and members of the civilian population to the effect that the latter be spared as much as possible;[108]

The Resolution also invited the Secretary-General to consider steps that could be taken to secure greater respect for international humanitarian law 'in all armed conflicts' and to consider whether there was a need for additional humanitarian law again 'in all armed conflicts'.[109]

Two years later, the General Assembly adopted Resolution 2675 (XXV), which recognized 'the need for measures to ensure the better protection of human rights in armed conflicts of all types' and which affirmed 'the following basic principles for the protection of civilian populations in armed conflicts':[110]

1. Fundamental human rights, as accepted in international law and laid down in international instruments, continue to apply fully in situations of armed conflict.
2. In the conduct of military operations during armed conflicts, a distinction must be made at all times between persons actively taking part in the hostilities and civilian populations.
3. In the conduct of military operations, every effort should be made to spare civilian populations from the ravages of war, and all necessary precautions should be taken to avoid injury, loss or damage to civilian populations.
4. Civilian populations as such should not be the object of military operations.
5. Dwellings and other installations that are used only by civilian populations should not be the object of military operations.
6. Places or areas designated for the sole protection of civilians, such as hospital zones or similar refuges, should not be the object of military operations.
7. Civilian populations, or individual members thereof, should not be the object of reprisals, forcible transfers or other assaults on their integrity.
8. The provision of international relief to civilian populations is in conformity with the humanitarian principles of the Charter of the United Nations, the Universal Declaration of Human Rights and other international instruments in the field of human rights. The Declaration of Principles for International Humanitarian Relief to the Civilian Population in Disaster Situations, as laid down in resolution XXVI adopted by the twenty-first International Conference of the Red Cross, shall apply in situations of armed conflict, and all parties to a conflict should make every effort to facilitate this application.[111]

---

[108] GA Res 2444 (XXIII) (1968). [109] Ibid.
[110] GA Res 2675 (XXV) (1970). [111] Ibid.

The years 1969 and 1970 also saw two important reports from UN Secretary-General U Thant.[112] The 1969 report summarized the state of the international humanitarian law that governed armed conflicts and presented observations on the better implementation of that law, while the 1970 report proposed developments of that law.[113] With respect to non-international armed conflicts, the 1969 report largely drew on the work of the ICRC. It noted that there was a 'need to extend the scope of certain parts of existing humanitarian law to cover internal armed conflicts' and suggested the elaboration of a new instrument.[114] The 1970 report, described as 'one of the most important contributions to the debate on the updating of the law of armed conflicts',[115] proposed further defining the concept of non-international armed conflict, noted the need for an international agency to be mandated to determine the existence of a non-international armed conflict, expressed the importance of defining the concept of 'persons taking no active part in the hostilities' (something that would take a further 40 years), and argued that additional provisions were needed to regulate non-international armed conflicts.[116]

The Secretary-General also published the comments of governments on the 1969 and 1970 reports, comments which were largely supportive of the reports. The comments of three states are particularly relevant as they foreshadowed what would turn out to be ongoing debates. The Dominican Republic queried whether '[i]t might...be appropriate to consider the possibility of drawing up *a single instrument* containing a suitable updated version of the provisions of the various Conventions signed between 1899 and the present'.[117] Norway 'question[ed] the desirability of maintaining a rigid distinction between international conflicts and armed conflicts not of an international character'.[118] Likewise, Sweden considered whether that distinction should be abolished.[119] Comments along these lines would continue to be expressed in the lead-up to the 1974–7 Diplomatic Conference.

Returning to the activities of the ICRC, government experts were consulted in 1970 on the subject of the protection of victims of non-international armed conflicts.[120] The reports of the consultations were intended to feed into the work of the Secretary-General on human rights in armed conflicts,[121] and the Secretary-General's report duly drew heavily on the work of the ICRC. A Conference of Red Cross Experts and a Conference of Government Experts were convened in 1971, and the topic was again

---

[112] Respect for Human Rights in Armed Conflicts: Report of the Secretary-General, A/7720, 20 November 1969; Respect for Human Rights in Armed Conflicts: Report of the Secretary-General, A/8052, 18 September 1970.

[113] Suter, *Guerrilla Warfare*, above note 94, 57.

[114] *Respect for Human Rights in Armed Conflicts*, A/7720, above note 112, paras 134 and 177. See also the comment of Norway, 82.

[115] Suter, *Guerrilla Warfare*, above note 94, 63.

[116] *Respect for Human Rights in Armed Conflicts*, A/8052, above note 112, paras 127–65.

[117] Respect for Human Rights in Armed Conflicts: Report of the Secretary-General, A/8318 and Add.3, at 29.

[118] Ibid, Add.3, 6.

[119] Ibid, 54.

[120] Preliminary Report on the Consultations of Experts Concerning Non-International Conflict and Guerrilla Warfare (Geneva, July 1970); Report on the Consultation of Experts concerning Non-International Conflict and Guerrilla Warfare (1970). The views are summarized in Conference of Government Experts on the Reaffirmation and Development of International Humanitarian Law Applicable in Armed Conflicts (Geneva, 24 May–12 June 1971): Submitted by the International Committee of the Red Cross (1971) Part V: Protection of Victims of Non-International Armed Conflicts.

[121] Ibid, 8 fn 4.

considered.¹²² In preparation for the Conferences, the ICRC drew up a report on the protection of victims of non-international armed conflicts,¹²³ in which it proposed to clarify the definition of a non-international armed conflict and to 'reaffirm and develop Article 3 by a series of appropriate rules... concretized in the form of an additional Protocol to Article 3'.¹²⁴ It also drew up a report on the rules that were applicable in guerrilla warfare and proposed 'the drafting of standard minimum rules which would be applicable in all conflicts not corresponding entirely to the conventional definition envisaged in Articles 2 and 3 of the Geneva Conventions and which—and herein lies the original aspect of such rules—would in no way influence the designation of the conflict or the legal status of the parties'.¹²⁵

At the 1971 Conference of Government Experts itself, while the distinction drawn in common Articles 2 and 3 of the Geneva Conventions between international and non-international armed conflicts was questioned by some delegates, others preferred maintaining the division.¹²⁶ Similar debates were had in the various commissions of the Conference. The Commission on the protection of the wounded and sick initially opted for a single instrument applicable in both types of armed conflict. However, it later opted for separate instruments for international and non-international armed conflicts in light of the Geneva Conventions treating the two situations differently.¹²⁷ It was decided that the proposed instrument on the protection of the wounded and sick in non-international armed conflicts had to include a greater number of provisions than its counterpart on international armed conflicts given that common Article 3 was far less detailed that the relevant Geneva Conventions. On the other hand, it was recognized that the proposed instrument 'could contain only basic principles without entering too much into technical details'.¹²⁸ In many respects, however, the rule that was drafted for application in international armed conflicts was simply incorporated for application in non-international armed conflicts without more. Again, this would foreshadow the approach taken at the 1974–7 Diplomatic Conference.¹²⁹ The Commission that was considering rules on the protection of victims of non-international armed conflicts recognized that there was a need to develop and supplement the provisions contained in common Article 3.¹³⁰ It considered the merits of drawing up a definition of non-international armed conflict, the issue of objective determination of the existence of such a conflict, and the content of a protocol applicable in non-international armed conflict. There was much discussion on all of the issues, and a variety of views were expressed; however, little was reached by way of conclusion.

---

¹²² ICRC, Conference of Red Cross Experts on the Reaffirmation and Development of International Humanitarian Law Applicable in Armed Conflicts (The Hague, 1–6 March 1971) Report on the Work of the Conference (April 1971).
¹²³ Protection of Victims of Non-International Armed Conflicts, above note 120.
¹²⁴ Ibid, 11 (emphasis removed).
¹²⁵ Ibid, Part VI: Rules Applicable in Guerrilla Warfare, 50 (emphasis removed).
¹²⁶ Conference of Government Experts on the Reaffirmation and Development of International Humanitarian Law Applicable in Armed Conflicts (Geneva, 24 May–12 June 1971): Report on the Work of the Conference (ICRC, August 1971) 20 paras 21–2, 35 paras 111–12, 36 paras 133–4. On the Conference, see F Kalshoven, 'The Conference of Government Experts on the Reaffirmation and Development of International Humanitarian Law Applicable in Armed Conflicts, 24 May–12 June, 1971' (1972) 3 *NYIL* 18.
¹²⁷ Report on the Work of the 1971 Conference, above note 126, 23–4 para 41.
¹²⁸ Ibid, 27 para 71. For the text of the Protocol, see 30 (Annex II).
¹²⁹ See below, 49–52.
¹³⁰ Report on the Work of the 1971 Conference, above note 126, 34 para 99.

Accordingly, a second session of the Conference of Government Experts took place in 1972, before which was placed a draft Additional Protocol to common Article 3 drawn up by the ICRC.[131] The draft Protocol 'contained identical, or at least very similar, provisions on certain subjects' as the draft Additional Protocol on international armed conflict, and the question of adopting a single protocol or two protocols was again debated with the majority of experts opting for two protocols.[132] The Conference considered in detail the scope of application of the intended Protocol and its substantive content. With considerable foresight, it was recognized that 'the final decisions to be taken depended on two basic hypotheses. Either the definition chosen could allow for a wide field of application, in which case the rules for protection would no doubt be more limited, or the definition could be narrowed, in which case greater latitude might be allowed in applying the protection'.[133] The ICRC draft also treated certain 'special cases' differently. In situations in which the non-state armed group had a government which exercised 'effective power' over a quantum of territory, the law of international armed conflict was considered applicable.[134] The law of international armed conflict was also deemed applicable in cases of intervention on the part of an outside state on behalf of the armed group in respect of fighting between the parent state and the outside state.[135] However, neither 'special case' met with the approval of the Conference.

On the basis of the discussions that took place at the various conferences, the ICRC drew up draft Additional Protocols in 1973 and produced a commentary thereto.[136] These provided a basis for discussion at the Twenty-second International Conference of the Red Cross in 1973. Debates similar to those that took place at the Conference of Government Experts were had, namely whether a single instrument should govern international and non-international armed conflicts alike, and on the relationship between the scope of application of the Protocol and the provisions that may be adopted and relating to the choice between a limited scope with a 'full set of rules' and a broader scope with basic provisions.[137] A diplomatic conference was then convened by the Swiss Federal Council in 1974, which would run until 1977.

The period between 1949 and 1974 thus saw numerous proposals to regulate better non-international armed conflicts. Three themes emerge from the various proposals. First, there was a concerted effort to move away from only regulating the treatment of

---

[131] ICRC, Conference of Government Experts on the Reaffirmation and Development of International Humanitarian Law Applicable in Armed Conflicts, Geneva, 3 May–3 June 1972 (Second Session): I Basic Texts, Documentary Material Submitted by the International Committee of the Red Cross (Geneva, January 1972); Conference of Government Experts on the Reaffirmation and Development of International Humanitarian Law Applicable in Armed Conflicts (Second Session, 3 May–3 June 1972): Report on the Work of the Conference, Volume I (Geneva, July 1972). On the Conference, see F Kalshoven, 'The Conference of Government Experts on the Reaffirmation and Development of International Humanitarian Law Applicable in Armed Conflicts (Second Session), 3 May–2 June, 1972' (1972) 3 *NYIL* 18.

[132] Report on the Work of the 1972 Conference, above note 131, 61–3 and 27.

[133] 'Reaffirmation and Development of International Humanitarian Law Applicable in Armed Conflicts: Conference of Government Experts [Second Session]' (1973) 13 *IRRC* 61, 67. See also Kalshoven, 1972 Conference of Government Experts, above note 131, 56. See below, 156–62.

[134] ICRC, Conference of Government Experts on the Reaffirmation and Development of International Humanitarian Law Applicable in Armed Conflicts, Geneva, 3 May–3 June 1972 (second session): II Commentary, Part Two (January 1972) 84–6.

[135] Ibid, 87–9. On which subject, see below, 222–8.

[136] Draft Additional Protocols (June 1973); ICRC, *Draft Additional Protocols to the Geneva Conventions of August 12, 1949: Commentary* (October 1973).

[137] Report on the Study by the XXIInd International Conference of the Red Cross of the Draft Additional Protocols to the Geneva Conventions of August 12, 1949 (January 1974) 23.

persons *hors de combat* and to include the regulation of the conduct of hostilities. Second, there were suggestions to move away from the international/non-international distinction, set out in the Geneva Conventions, and to have certain rules apply to all armed conflicts in equal measure. At the very least, this meant drawing on the more established rules of international armed conflicts to regulate non-international armed conflicts. Third, there was recognition that the general statements of common Article 3 implicitly contained within them detailed rules. All three themes re-emerged at the 1974–7 Diplomatic Conference.

5. The Diplomatic Conference of 1974–7

The Draft Additional Protocol II that was put before the Diplomatic Conference in 1974 was 'drawn from the [Geneva] Conventions and from Draft Protocol I, but adapted to the specific conditions of non-international armed conflicts, and hence in most cases simplified'.[138] Although a simplified text, Draft Additional Protocol II contained a substantial body of norms that were applicable in non-international armed conflicts and was similar to Draft Additional Protocol I. As with the Government Experts, opinions of delegates to the Diplomatic Conference on the norms to be contained in a Protocol on non-international armed conflicts varied considerably.

At one end of the spectrum, certain delegations favoured the inclusion of a single additional protocol that would encompass international and non-international armed conflicts alike.[139] These delegates considered anything else to be 'selective humanitarianism'.[140] However, not all delegations agreed, with some arguing that the distinction was valid based on the differences between the two types of conflicts.[141] Delegates of this view indicated that the two Protocols should be kept entirely separate.[142] Others expressed some sympathy with the single protocol approach, but considered the idea to be 'far ahead of its time' and that 'realism dictated otherwise'.[143] For its part, the ICRC stated that it had respected 'the distinction, well established in public international law, between those armed conflicts, in conformity with the wish expressed by the vast majority of experts consulted' and '[i]n order to take into account the fundamentally different political aspects which existed between international and non-international armed conflicts'.[144] Intermediate views were also expressed, according to which the rules relating to non-international armed conflicts should 'closely resemble' those applicable in international conflicts,[145] that 'whenever possible the two protocols should be on identical lines',[146] and that it was 'important to avoid differences in the treatment of victims depending on the nature of the conflict'.[147]

---

[138] *Commentary on the Draft Additional Protocols*, above note 136, 2.
[139] *Official Records of the Diplomatic Conference on the Reaffirmation and Development of International Humanitarian Law Applicable in Armed Conflicts, Geneva (1974–1977)* (Federal Political Department, Berne, 1978) Vol 5, 91 para 3 (Norway); 149 para 40 (Australia); 193 para 54 (Syria); Vol 8, 218 para 17 (New Zealand); Vol 5, 186 para 15 (Finland).
[140] Ibid, Vol 8, 217 para 12 (Norway).
[141] Ibid, Vol 5, 130 para 19 (Portugal); Vol 8, 221 para 33 (Romania); Vol 11, 248 para 18 (Indonesia).
[142] Ibid, 108 para 40 (Monaco).
[143] Ibid, Vol 8, 232 para 17 (Nigeria).
[144] Ibid, 202 para 4.
[145] Ibid, Vol 5, 142 para 7 (Sweden). See also Vol 5, 202 para 47 (International Commission of Jurists).
[146] Ibid, 186 para 15 (Finland). See also Vol 11, 249 para 21 (Norway).
[147] Ibid, Vol 5, 92 para 8 (Egypt); Vol 5, 142 para 6 (Sweden).

At the other end of the spectrum, some delegations took the view that, as it had been decided that wars of national liberation would fall within the scope of Additional Protocol I, a protocol on non-international armed conflict no longer served a purpose.[148] Many other delegations emphasized state sovereignty and considered that '[t]he automatic application to internal conflicts of regulations applicable in international conflicts might have negative results and entail violation of international law and national sovereignty'.[149] Characteristic of this position was the statement of India, which:

> raised strong objections to the very idea of a second protocol on the ground that once the national liberation movements had been included in paragraph 2 of Part I of draft Protocol I, giving them the status of international conflicts, then Protocol II would not be necessary, since any other conflict taking place within the territory of a sovereign State would be an internal conflict, and any international instrument designed to regulate non-international conflicts might in actual application impede the settlement of the conflict and lead to external interference.[150]

In light of these differing views and given the concern that ultimately no protocol would be adopted, a substantial protocol that had been adopted at the committee stage and which was modelled on Additional Protocol I was watered down in order to ensure its adoption. Pakistan played an important role in ensuring that a compromise text—a 'simplified draft'[151]—would be passed. The delegate's explanation of the compromise text is worth quoting in large part. In his words:

> During contacts with many ... delegations of both developed and under-privileged countries ... it had realized that there was considerable dissatisfaction with the length of the text as well as with the fact that it ventured into domains which they considered sacrosanct and inappropriate for inclusion in an international instrument. A cross-section of opinion firmly held the view that the text entered into unnecessary details, rendering it not only cumbersome but difficult to understand and to apply in the peculiar circumstances of a non-international conflict.
>
> Perceiving, therefore, that such views might endanger its adoption or ratification, and after consultation with other delegations, the delegation of Pakistan had prepared a version of Protocol II ... which, while simplified, adhered to the original language ... It was based on the following theses: its provisions must be acceptable to all and, therefore, of obvious practical benefit; the provisions must be within the perceived capacity of those involved to apply them and, therefore, precise and simple; they should not appear to affect the sovereignty of any State Party or the responsibility of its Government to maintain law and order and defend national unity, nor be able to be invoked to justify any outside intervention; nothing in the Protocol should suggest that dissidents must be treated legally other than as rebels; and lastly, there should be no automatic repetition of the more comprehensive provisions, such as those on civil defence, found in Protocol I. To include such provisions would risk changing the material field of application to such an extent that States would either fail to ratify Protocol II or tend to argue for its non-application in situations falling within its scope, thereby leaving the victims of those conflicts without adequate protection.[152]

The provisions versus principles debate again reared its head.

---

[148] Ibid, 345–6 paras 50–4, 379–81 paras 4–8; Vol 8, 224 para 48 (all India); Vol 5, 351 para 76 (Philippines). See also Vol 5, 381 para 9 (Iraq). On wars of national liberation, see below, 212–22.
[149] Ibid, 103 para 15 (Romania).
[150] Ibid, 345 para 50. See also Vol 5, 351 para 76 (Philippines); Vol 8, 224 para 48 (India).
[151] Ibid, Vol 7, 311 para 159.
[152] Ibid, Vol 7, 61 paras 10–11. See also DP Forsythe, 'Legal Management of Internal War: The 1977 Protocol on Non-International Armed Conflicts' (1978) 72 *AJIL* 272, 277–82.

The draft protocol was thus 'simplified', with a number of provisions being reduced or deleted. For some, this was a significant reduction; for others, little was lost.[153] There is an element of truth in both positions. There was a significant reduction in the number of provisions. The Protocol, as adopted, contained 28 articles, compared to 102 articles in Additional Protocol I and 47 articles in the draft Protocol that was originally before the Conference. However, comparing the number of articles in the Protocols can be misleading. Relatively few concepts were omitted in their entirety: those that were being limited to prohibitions on certain belligerent reprisals, on the unnecessary suffering principle, and on perfidy; and provisions on civil defence forces, the creation of an information bureau, and an impartial body offering its services to the parties to the conflict. The other deletions related, rather, to the fleshing out of the various concepts, with the core of the concepts remaining intact. For example, a lengthy article on the safeguard of an enemy *hors de combat* was deleted, but a provision on quarter remained. A substantial article on penal prosecutions was reduced and the provision that prohibited the carrying out of capital punishment before the end of hostilities was deleted. Similarly, provisions on the wounded and sick were reduced but the core protections remained.[154] Thus, if the text, as adopted, is compared with the text that was put before the Diplomatic Conference, it is evident that the vast majority of the core of the protections remained intact; the provisions themselves, however, were adopted in attenuated form.

The Protocol, as adopted, provides for norms on humane treatment, similar to, but more developed than, those contained in common Article 3:[155] protections for the wounded and sick, again in more detail than those contained in common Article 3, and including protections for those that take care of the wounded and sick;[156] protections for persons whose liberty has been restricted;[157] protections for persons subject to the criminal process, again in greater detail than those contained in common Article 3;[158] a prohibition on the forced movement of civilians;[159] norms on relief societies and relief action;[160] and certain concise rules on the conduct of hostilities.[161] However, the Protocol would only apply to non-international armed conflicts 'which take place in the territory of a High Contracting Party between its armed forces and dissident armed forces or other organized armed groups which, under responsible command, exercise such control over a part of its territory as to enable them to carry out sustained and concerted military operations and to implement this Protocol'.[162]

Between this threshold of application, the reductions made to the substantive provisions, and the general feelings surrounding the regulation of non-international

---

[153] See, for the former view, Forsythe, ibid, 283; 'Application of Humanitarian Law in Noninternational Armed Conflicts: Remarks by René Kosirnik' (1991) 85 *ASIL Procs* 96, 97; M Bothe, KJ Partsch, and WA Solf, *New Rules for Victims of Armed Conflicts* (Martinus Nijhoff, 1982) 608. Cf, for the latter view, A Eide, 'The New Humanitarian Law in Non-International Armed Conflict', in A Cassese (ed), *The New Humanitarian Law of Armed Conflict* (Editoriale Scientifica, 1979) 277; 'Determining Customary International Law Relative to the Conduct of Hostilities in Non-International Armed Conflicts: Remarks of WJ Fenrick' (1987) 2 *American University Journal of International Law and Policy* 471, 474; Moir, *Internal Armed Conflict*, above note 89, 94.

[154] For contemporaneous accounts of the drafting of Additional Protocol II, see Forsythe, Legal Management, above note 152; F Kalshoven, 'Reaffirmation and Development of International Humanitarian Law Applicable in Armed Conflicts: The Diplomatic Conference, Geneva, 1974–1977, Part I: Combatants and Civilians' (1977) 8 *NYIL* 107; Eide, The New Humanitarian Law, above note 153 277.

[155] Article 4.   [156] Articles 7–12.   [157] Article 5.   [158] Article 6.
[159] Article 17.   [160] Article 18.   [161] Articles 13–16.
[162] Article 1(1), on which, see below, 182–92.

armed conflicts, Additional Protocol II has borne the brunt of severe criticism. However, much of the criticism is unfair given that the threshold need not be interpreted in the manner that it has,[163] and given that the Protocol was a significant advance on that which existed prior to its conclusion. Nonetheless, it remains the case that the Protocol that was adopted in 1977 is a weaker version of the draft that was before the Diplomatic Conference in 1974 and of the draft that was adopted during the Committee stage of the Conference. Several important areas also remained without regulation.

6. Post-1977 initiatives

In light of the difficulties surrounding the regulation of non-international armed conflicts as expressed at the Diplomatic Conference, and because of the general views that surrounded Additional Protocol II, few attempts were made to regulate non-international armed conflicts in the period following the Diplomatic Conference. Diplomatic conferences, and even private initiatives, proved infrequent.

The most important initiative that emerged during this period was the 1990 Declaration on the Rules of International Humanitarian Law governing the Conduct of Hostilities in Non-International Armed Conflicts of the Institute of International Humanitarian Law. Given that Additional Protocol II contained only a few concise provisions on the conduct of hostilities, the Declaration contained a useful list of principles and rules which had either crystallized or were in the process of emerging.[164] The Declaration contained the principles of distinction and unnecessary suffering. It provided for prohibitions on attacks against the civilian population and against civilian objects, the requirement of precautions, and the prohibition of perfidy. The Declaration also included prohibitions and restrictions on the use of certain weapons, namely chemical weapons, expanding bullets, poison, mines and booby-traps, and incendiary weapons. Although a private initiative, the Declaration would prove important. It has been taken by courts and tribunals to reflect the state of the law, and it has served as a means by which the conduct of parties to non-international armed conflicts would be judged.[165]

A second private initiative was that of the 'Fundamental Standards of Humanity' or 'Minimum Humanitarian Standards'. This initiative was designed to address a gap that was considered to exist when states derogated from human rights treaties but when international humanitarian law was yet to apply.[166] Through the initiative, a group of experts adopted a Declaration on Minimum Humanitarian Standards in 1990.[167] The Declaration was transmitted to the UN for adoption by states but has since stalled.

Despite being private initiatives, the two Declarations are important. It should be recalled that the law of armed conflict has a history of rules later being accepted which first emerged 'from the pens of scholarly advocates'.[168]

---

[163] See ibid. [164] Preamble. [165] See below, 105–6.
[166] See T Meron, 'On the Inadequate Reach of Humanitarian and Human Rights Law and the Need for a New Instrument' (1983) 77 *AJIL* 589.
[167] See A Eide, A Rosas, and T Meron, 'Combating Lawlessness in Gray Zone Conflicts through Minimum Humanitarian Standards' (1995) 89 *AJIL* 215.
[168] JE Bond, 'Application of the Law of War to Internal Conflicts' (1973) 3 *Georgia Journal of International and Comparative Law* 345, 345.

7. Conclusion

In light of the limits of ad hoc regulation, the need to regulate non-international armed conflicts systematically through international humanitarian law was recognized. A neat, linear transition from ad hoc regulation to systematic regulation did not take place given that ad hoc commitments continued to be issued, indeed were actively sought, during attempts to systematize regulation. As with much of the 'Geneva' aspects of international humanitarian law, initial proposals to regulate systematically non-international armed conflicts emanated from the ICRC. Several attempts had to be made with various objections being raised by different states and entities at different points in time. After considerable effort by the ICRC, and following considerable practice on the part of the ICRC and of national Red Cross societies, the 1949 Diplomatic Conference adopted common Article 3, an article that broke new ground.

Despite the success, common Article 3 was soon recognized as being limited. In light of the failings of common Article 3, shortly after it was adopted, attempts were made to increase the content of the international humanitarian law that would govern non-international armed conflicts. Conferences of Government Experts were convened on point in the 1950s and 1960s. The UN International Conference on Human Rights in Tehran in 1968 proved influential, leading as it did to two General Assembly resolutions on the basic humanitarian principles applicable in *all* conflicts. Further conferences of Government Experts in the 1970s led to the convening of a Diplomatic Conference in 1974 that would run until 1977 and which adopted the Protocols Additional to the 1949 Geneva Conventions.

Two themes ran consistently through the conferences of Government Experts and the Diplomatic Conferences. First was the issue of whether *principles* of the law of international armed conflict would apply to non-international armed conflicts, or, rather, whether the *provisions* of the law of international armed conflict would apply. There was considerable debate on point in the lead-up to the 1949 Diplomatic Conference with one or other approach being adopted at various meetings. At the Diplomatic Conference itself, the principles approach was adopted, but only after the Conference failed to reach agreement on the situations in which the provisions would be applicable. Importantly, the principles were not of an entirely loose and vague general sort, but took the form of certain concrete propositions. The principles versus provisions debate would take on a different form in the years following the Diplomatic Conference, the issue being the extent to which detailed rules could be read into the more general principles contained in common Article 3 and Additional Protocol II.

The second theme that ran through this period was whether, and if so to what extent, non-international armed conflicts should be regulated in the same manner as international armed conflicts. The issue was raised primarily in the period leading up to the 1974–7 Diplomatic Conference and at that Conference, in the context of whether a single protocol should apply to both types of armed conflict. Views were split; however, the majority position was that two separate protocols should be concluded in order to regulate the two types of conflict. Nonetheless, the two protocols approach was ameliorated significantly given that the protocol regulating non-international armed conflict was based on, and drew from, the protocol regulating international armed conflict. This too had important consequences, which would come to the fore in the period commencing in the mid-1990s, which forms the subject of the next chapter.

3
Regulation through a Body of International Law

1. Introduction

As discussed in the previous chapter, in the post-1949 period, there was a concerted effort to move away from regulation of non-international armed conflict on an ad hoc basis. Regulation through ad hoc commitments continued—as with the 1967 Operational Code of Conduct issued by the Federal Government of Nigeria during the attempted secession of Biafra; and through the 1960 accession to the Geneva Conventions on the part of the Provisional Government of the Algerian Republic during the Algerian war of independence—but they continued to suffer from the limits of ad hoc-ism and partiality.[1] The systematic regulation of non-international armed conflict involved attempts at assimilating the law of non-international armed conflict to the law of international armed conflict. However, these attempts by and large did not succeed. In the period between 1949 and the mid-1990s, only a minimum of conventional international humanitarian law rules governed non-international armed conflicts, namely common Article 3 of the 1949 Geneva Conventions, Article 19 of the 1954 Hague Convention on Cultural Property, and Protocol II Additional to the Geneva Conventions of 1977. Each instrument was an advance on that which existed previously, but each also provided for only a minimum of protection for those caught up in non-international armed conflicts. Common Article 3 did not contain any rules on the conduct of hostilities. Article 19 of the Hague Convention on Cultural Property is necessarily limited in subject matter, being contained in a treaty devoted to the protection of cultural property. Additional Protocol II, still the only international humanitarian law treaty devoted solely to non-international armed conflict, represents a pared-back version of earlier drafts. The customary international humanitarian law that governed non-international armed conflict was even less clear.

All this changed dramatically in the mid-1990s. Whereas previously, rules were initiated by non-state bodies and concluded in diplomatic conferences, in the 1990s, judicial bodies entered the arena. These were primarily international judicial bodies, but certain national courts also played an important role. Concerns relating to state sovereignty thus featured far less strongly and were secondary to a desire to increase humanitarian protection. The relevant judicial bodies transformed the law of non-international armed conflict primarily through drawing on the law of international armed conflict, either analogizing the law of non-international armed conflict to it, or extending its scope of application to cover non-international armed conflicts. These developments were later confirmed in large part, in diplomatic conferences. Suggestions to this effect posited in the previous decades[2] were finally implemented.

[1] See Chapter 4.   [2] See Chapter 2.

Given that the relevant judicial bodies were international *criminal* tribunals, shaping of the law of non-international armed conflict took place largely through international criminal law.

International human rights law had also developed considerably by the mid-1990s, as compared with 1949 or 1977. Accordingly, regard was also had to international human rights law when developing the law of non-international armed conflict. Indeed, through the influence of international criminal law and international human rights law, the law that governs non-international armed conflict today can be described as a body of international law rather than solely a body of international humanitarian law, although international humanitarian law continues to constitute its bulk.

2. Drawing on the law of international armed conflict

2.1 Customary international humanitarian law

It is the identification of the customary international humanitarian law rules that govern non-international armed conflict, in particular, that has developed since the mid-1990s. Up until that point in time, the view that there were more than simply a handful of customary rules applicable in non-international armed conflict was never seriously entertained and identifying even those rules proved problematic. It was generally agreed by the mid-1980s that there existed at least some customary rules of non-international armed conflict. However, identification of those rules proved more elusive. The International Court of Justice (ICJ) in *Nicaragua* took the view that the rules contained in common Article 3 reflected 'elementary considerations of humanity' applicable in international and non-international armed conflicts alike.[3] This led to expressions of surprise on the part of many, but more due to the lack of citation of state practice and *opinio juris* on the part of the Court than to its actual conclusion.[4] Beyond common Article 3, the position was even less clear. General Assembly Resolutions 2444 (XXIII) and 2675 (XXV), with their various protections for the civilian population, were considered to reflect the state of customary international law applicable to all armed conflicts.[5] However, the customary status of a prohibition on belligerent reprisals, as contained in GA Res 2675 (XXV), was disputed some 30 years later,[6] suggesting that not every principle contained in the resolutions reflected

---

[3] *Military and Paramilitary Activities In and Against Nicaragua (Nicaragua v United States of America)* [1986] ICJ Rep 14, para 218. The Court had spoken in 1949 of 'elementary considerations of humanity, even more exacting in peace than in war'; however, the precise content of those considerations were not then identified. See *Corfu Channel (United Kingdom v Albania)* [1949] ICJ Rep 4, 22.

[4] See eg the Dissenting Opinion of Judge Jennings in *Nicaragua*, above note 3, 537–8; T Meron, *Human Rights and Humanitarian Norms as Customary Law* (Clarendon Press, 1989) 36; PH Kooijmans, 'In the Shadowland between Civil War and Civil Strife: Some Reflections on the Standard-Setting Process', in AJM Delissen and GJ Tanja (eds), *Humanitarian Law of Armed Conflict, Challenges Ahead: Essays in Honour of Frits Kalshoven* (Martinus Nijhoff, 1991) 225, 229.

[5] On GA Res 2444 (XXIII) (1968), see eg the United States, excerpted in (1973) 67 *AJIL* 122; *Prosecutor v Tadić*, IT-94-1-AR72, Decision on the Defence Motion for Interlocutory Appeal on Jurisdiction, 2 October 1995, paras 110–12. On GA Res 2675 (XXV) (1970), see eg Denmark, Third Committee, General Assembly, 25th Session, 1785th Meeting, 11 November 1970, (1970) UNGA Official Records (Third Committee) 281; *Tadić* Decision on Interlocutory Appeal on Jurisdiction, paras 110–12. The United Kingdom considers GA Res 2675 (XXV) to be 'evidence of state practice': UK Ministry of Defence, *The Manual of the Law of Armed Conflict* (Oxford University Press, 2004) 391.

[6] Cf *Prosecutor v Kupreškić et al*, IT-95-16-T, Judgment, 14 January 2000, paras 527–36, with UK *Manual of the Law of Armed Conflict*, above note 5, 421 fn 62. See below, 452.

customary international law. Leading commentators expressed their views on the customary status of particular Additional Protocol II provisions, but the relevant provisions were few and far between and the views were not always consistent with one another.[7] There had been some suggestion that the basic rules of international humanitarian law were of customary status in respect of large-scale non-international armed conflicts.[8] However, as late as 1994, the Commission of Experts appointed to investigate violations of international humanitarian law committed in the former Yugoslavia wrote that '[i]t is unlikely that there is any body of customary international law applicable to internal armed conflict which does not find its root in' common Article 3, Additional Protocol II, and Article 19 of the Hague Convention on Cultural Property.[9] Thus, precisely which rules beyond common Article 3 had customary status was unclear and did not benefit from uniform agreement.

Since the mid-1990s, the customary international humanitarian law rules that have been identified as applicable in non-international armed conflicts have grown dramatically. Although there remains some debate as to precisely which rules have customary status, that there is a sizeable body of custom is no longer questioned. This is due, primarily, to two important contributions, namely the jurisprudence of the International Criminal Tribunal for the former Yugoslavia (ICTY) and the 2005 Customary International Humanitarian Law study concluded under the auspices of the International Committee of the Red Cross (ICRC).[10] Other lists of customary international humanitarian law rules also exist and should not be overlooked.[11] The creation of the International Criminal Tribunal for Rwanda (ICTR) in 1994, with its explicit criminalization of violations of common Article 3 and of Article 4 of Additional Protocol II, also proved important.[12]

In ascertaining the customary international humanitarian law applicable in non-international armed conflicts, the general approach, whether explicit or implicit, has been to analogize to the law of international armed conflict, while also referring to the

---

[7] Cf Meron, *Human Rights and Humanitarian Norms*, above note 4, 72 fn 199; A Cassese, 'The Geneva Protocols of 1977 on the Humanitarian Law of Armed Conflict and Customary International Law' (1984) 3 *UCLA Pacific Basin Law Journal* 55, 112–13; C Greenwood, 'Customary Law Status of the 1977 Geneva Protocols', in AJM Delissen and GJ Tanja (eds), *Humanitarian Law of Armed Conflict Challenges Ahead: Essays in Honour of Frits Kalshoven* (Martinus Nijhoff, 1991) 93, 113. See also, setting out the position of the United States, 'The United States Position on the Relation of Customary International Law to the 1977 Protocols Additional to the 1949 Geneva Conventions: Remarks of Michael J Matheson' (1987) 2 *American University Journal of International Law and Policy* 419.

[8] See A Cassese, 'The Spanish Civil War and the Development of Customary Law concerning Internal Armed Conflict', in A Cassese (ed), *Current Problems in International Law: Essays on UN Law and the Law of Armed Conflict* (Giuffré, 1975) 287–8. See also T Hoffman, 'The Gentle Humanizer of Humanitarian Law—Antonio Cassese and the Creation of the Customary Law of Non-International Armed Conflict', in C Stahn and L van den Herik (eds), *Future Perspectives on International Criminal Justice* (TMC Asser Press, 2010) 58, 58–63.

[9] Final Report of the Commission of Experts established pursuant to Security Council Resolution 780 (1992), S/1994/674, 27 May 1994, para 52.

[10] J-M Henckaerts and L Doswald-Beck, *Customary International Humanitarian Law: Volumes I and II* (Cambridge University Press, 2005). The study, conducted pursuant to a mandate from the 1995 International Conference of the Red Cross and Red Crescent, took nearly 10 years to conclude and involved some 150 experts. See Meeting of the Intergovernmental Group of Experts for the Protection of War Victims, Geneva (23–27 January 1995), Recommendation II, reproduced in (1995) 77 *IRRC* 33, 34; J-M Henckaerts, 'Customary International Humanitarian Law: A Response to US Comments' (2007) 89 *IRRC* 473, 474.

[11] See eg Report of the International Commission of Inquiry on Darfur to the Secretary-General, S/2005/60, 1 February 2005, para 166.

[12] Statute of the ICTR, Article 4, annexed to SC Res 955 (1994). See Report of the Secretary-General pursuant to Paragraph 5 of Security Council Resolution 955 (1994), S/1995/134, 13 February 1995, paras 11–12.

traditional elements of state practice and *opinio juris* to support the conclusion reached. The ground-breaking *Tadić* Decision on Interlocutory Appeal on Jurisdiction is illustrative of this approach. As the ICTY Appeals Chamber questioned:

> Why protect civilians from belligerent violence, or ban rape, torture or the wanton destruction of hospitals, churches, museums or private property, as well as proscribe weapons causing unnecessary suffering when two sovereign States are engaged in war, and yet refrain from enacting the same bans or providing the same protection when armed violence has erupted 'only' within the territory of a sovereign State?[13]

Or, as was put so eloquently later on in the Decision:

> elementary considerations of humanity and common sense make it preposterous that the use by States of weapons prohibited in armed conflicts between themselves be allowed when States try to put down rebellion by their own nationals on their own territory. *What is inhumane and consequently proscribed, in international wars, cannot but be inhumane and inadmissible in civil strife.*[14]

Decades earlier, at the Diplomatic Conference of 1949, the USSR advocated a similar approach: '[i]nhuman treatment of human beings and any other acts which would be condemned in the case of international war between States should likewise be condemned in the instance of civil war.'[15] However, it was not to be. Likewise, the attempt to regulate all types of armed conflicts through a single Protocol failed in the 1970s but largely succeeded in the 1990s through identification of rules of customary international law. This modelling on the law of international armed conflict has been the consistent approach of the ICTY. In *Delalić et al*, the Appeals Chamber argued that, 'to maintain a distinction between the two legal regimes and their criminal consequences in respect of similarly egregious acts because of the difference in nature of the conflicts would ignore the very purpose of the Geneva Conventions, which is to protect the dignity of the human person'.[16] The *Halilović* Trial Chamber went further, stating that, '[w]hen an accused is charged with violation of Article 3 of the Statute, based on a violation of Common Article 3, it is immaterial whether the armed conflict was international or non-international in nature ... there is no need for the Trial Chamber to define the nature of the conflict in the present case'.[17] The reason for the Trial Chamber's position was that common Article 3, as a reflection of customary international law, applies in all armed conflicts.[18]

Pursuant to this approach, the ICTY has read into the customary equivalents of sparse Additional Protocol II provisions, all the detail of the customary rules of international armed conflict. For example, Article 13(2) of Additional Protocol II reads, in a rather concise fashion: '[t]he civilian population as such, as well as individual civilians, shall not be the object of attack.' The customary equivalent of the provision has been interpreted by the ICTY to include a prohibition on indiscriminate attacks;[19]

---

[13] *Tadić* Decision on Interlocutory Appeal on Jurisdiction, para 97.
[14] Ibid, para 119 (emphasis added). Not everyone agreed with this position. For contemporaneous reactions, see eg C Greenwood, 'International Humanitarian Law and the *Tadić* Case' (1996) 7 *EJIL* 265, 278; GR Watson, 'The Humanitarian Law of the Yugoslavia War Crimes Tribunal: Jurisdiction in *Prosecutor v Tadić*' (1995–6) 36 *Virginia Journal of International Law* 687, 713–15; C Warbrick and P Rowe, 'The International Criminal Tribunal for Yugoslavia: The Decision of the Appeals Chamber on the Interlocutory Appeal on Jurisdiction in the *Tadić* Case' (1996) 45 *ICLQ* 691, 701.
[15] *Final Record of the Diplomatic Conference of Geneva of 1949* (Federal Political Department, Berne), Vol II-B, 98.
[16] *Prosecutor v Delalić et al*, IT-96-21-A, Judgment, 20 February 2001, para 172.
[17] *Prosecutor v Halilović*, IT-01-48-T, Judgment, 16 November 2005, para 25.
[18] See *Nicaragua*, above note 3, para 218.
[19] *Prosecutor v Galić*, IT-98-29-T, Judgment and Opinion, 5 December 2003, para 57.

a prohibition on disproportionate attacks,[20] which itself has been interpreted as giving rise to a requirement that certain precautions be taken;[21] and a prohibition on attacks against civilian objects,[22] which, in turn, has given rise to a prohibition on the 'wanton destruction of cities, towns or villages, or devastation not justified by military necessity'.[23] These more detailed rules stem from the law of international armed conflict, in particular from Additional Protocol I and the Hague Regulations.[24] The ICTY has thus taken the view that the succinct provisions of Additional Protocol II contain within them more detailed rules, at least at the level of customary international humanitarian law. This position supports the view of Additional Protocol II, noted above, as containing the core concepts and rules, lacking only in detail.[25] Detailed provisions were thus read into the more general rules of the relevant instrument. In this sense, at least at the level of judicial interpretation, the principles versus provisions debate is of lesser importance.[26]

The general position of the ICTY was that there exists a common body of law applicable to both sorts of armed conflict and which is derived from the international humanitarian law that governs international armed conflict. This reflects the position taken by the ICTY Office of the Prosecutor (OTP), which has been to argue that 'the essential substance of the detailed [Additional Protocol I] provisions concerning unlawful attacks applicable to international conflicts is also contained in the single relevant sentence in APII [Additional Protocol II] which is applicable to internal conflicts. This is a conscious effort on the part of the OTP, successful to date, to argue that the law concerning unlawful attacks against civilians is, in substance, the same in both international and internal conflicts'.[27] In fact, the approach has not been limited to the rules on targeting but has been adapted to the law of non-international armed conflict more generally. Thus, in *Martić*, a Trial Chamber held that '[t]here exists, at present, a corpus of customary international law applicable to all armed conflicts irrespective of their characterisation as international or non-international armed conflicts'.[28]

A similar approach was adopted, albeit implicitly, by the Customary International Humanitarian Law study. Although the study did not set out any particular novel approach to the determination of the content of customary international humanitarian law,[29] the manner in which that determination took place suggests that it, too, derived the rules from the law of international armed conflict. The study compiles all the relevant practice (treaties, military manuals, national legislation, case-law, and the like)

---

[20] *Prosecutor v Hadžihasanović and Kubura*, IT-01-47-T, Judgment, 15 March 2006, para 45.
[21] *Galić*, Trial Judgment, above note 19, para 58.
[22] *Prosecutor v Hadžihasanović and Kubura*, IT-01-47-T, Decision on Motions for Acquittal Pursuant to Rule 98*bis* of the Rules of Procedure and Evidence, 27 September 2004, para 98; *Prosecutor v Strugar*, IT-01-42-T, Judgment, 31 January 2005, para 225.
[23] *Prosecutor v Hadžihasanović and Kubura*, IT-01-47-AR73.3, Decision on Joint Defence Interlocutory Appeal of Trial Chamber Decision on Rule 98*bis* Motions for Acquittal, 11 March 2005, paras 29–30; *Strugar*, Trial Judgment, para 228.
[24] Additional Protocol I, Articles 50–2; Hague Regulations, Article 25.
[25] See above, 51.
[26] On the debate, see Chapter 2.
[27] WJ Fenrick, 'The Prosecution of Unlawful Attack Cases before the ICTY' (2004) 7 *YIHL* 153, 166.
[28] *Prosecutor v Martić*, IT-95-11-R61, Decision, 8 March 1996, para 11. See S Boelaert-Suominen, 'The Yugoslavia Tribunal and the Common Core of Humanitarian Law Applicable to all Armed Conflicts' (2000) 13 *LJIL* 619.
[29] For a statement as to its approach, see *Customary International Humanitarian Law, Volume I: Rules*, above note 10, xxxi.

on a particular issue without separating out that relating to an international armed conflict from that relating to a non-international armed conflict.[30] The rules identified from this practice are divided into those pertaining to international and non-international armed conflicts, but by and large, single rules cover both conflicts and it is only in rare cases that the rule diverges as between the two.[31] Given that, historically, international armed conflicts benefited from far greater legal regulation than non-international armed conflicts, the law of international armed conflict has been extended to regulate non-international armed conflict rather than a separate body of law independently emerging. Thus, in their introduction to the study, the authors note that 'the gaps in the regulation of the conduct of hostilities in Additional Protocol II have largely been filled through State practice, which has led to the creation of rules parallel to those in Additional Protocol I, but applicable as customary law to non-international armed conflicts'.[32] Although the study was set out in this manner because state practice was judged as not making the distinction, certain value judgements did have to be made, such as the weight to be given to state military manuals that did not delineate their scope of application. Many of these manuals were drawn up at a time in which there was little by way of international humanitarian law applicable in non-international armed conflict. Accordingly, materials that were drawn up for use in one context, namely international armed conflicts, were utilized to regulate a different context, namely non-international armed conflicts. Implicit in the study is, then, an approach of looking to situations of international armed conflict for guidance.

It is not just the ICTY and the Customary International Humanitarian Law study that have adopted the approach of looking to the international humanitarian law of international armed conflict. The Inter-American Commission on Human Rights has expressly stated that '[m]any of the rules in Protocol I, which applies only to international armed conflicts, are particularly useful referents for interpreting the substantive content of similar, but less detailed, provisions in Protocol II and common Article 3'.[33] The Human Rights Division of the United Nations Observer Mission in El Salvador (ONUSAL) also applied various provisions of Additional Protocol I by analogy to the non-international armed conflict in El Salvador and judged the conduct of the parties against them.[34] This was done prior to the creation of the ICTY and before the idea of a study on Customary International Humanitarian Law was conceived. Indeed, during the civil war in Paraguay in 1948, the ICRC and national Red Cross societies used provisions of the 1929 Geneva Convention for the relief of the wounded and sick by analogy, a use which caused 'legitimate pride'.[35] More generally, as the following chapter indicates, prior to the conclusion of common Article 3, the approach was necessarily one of analogy to the law of international armed conflict in extracting

---

[30] See ibid, *Volume II: Practice*.
[31] Ibid, *Volume I: Rules*.
[32] Ibid, xxix.
[33] Inter-American Commission on Human Rights, Third Report on the Human Rights Situation in Colombia, OEA/Ser.L/V/II.102, Doc.9 rev.1, 26 February 1999, Chapter IV, para 44. See also L Zegveld, *The Accountability of Armed Opposition Groups in International Law* (Cambridge University Press, 2002) 79–81.
[34] See eg Second Report of the United Nations Observer Mission in El Salvador, A/46/658-S/23222, 15 November 1991, para 69 fn 18; Third Report of the United Nations Observer Mission in El Salvador, A/46/876-S/23580, 19 February 1992, para 131; Zegveld, *Armed Opposition Groups*, above note 33, 78–9.
[35] The analogy in question was the use of neutral relief aircraft contained in Article 18 of the 1929 Convention. See Letter of ICRC Delegate Dunand to the Vice-President of the ICRC, 15 June 1947, ICRC Archives CR 22(43)/34.

commitments from the warring parties, given that international humanitarian law simply did not regulate non-international armed conflicts on a systematic basis. However, it is largely through the jurisprudence of the ICTY and the Customary International Humanitarian Law study that the customary international humanitarian law applicable to non-international armed conflict has been identified and developed.

The ICTY has identified a substantial body of customary international humanitarian law that is applicable equally to all armed conflicts. In the area of the conduct of hostilities, various chambers have held that such rules as the prohibition on attacks against civilians,[36] and attacks against civilian objects,[37] the wanton destruction of property,[38] the protection of cultural property,[39] the prohibitions on the destruction of religious objects,[40] plunder, and pillage,[41] and the prohibition on the use of chemical weapons[42] are all of customary status and applicable to international and non-international armed conflicts alike. Although, at first, the Tribunal was criticized for going too far,[43] such criticisms have since faded.[44] States themselves have drawn up a list of war crimes applicable in non-international armed conflicts, by implication affirming a list of customary international humanitarian law rules applicable therein. The approach of *Tadić*, by which the law of non-international armed conflict would look to the law of international armed conflict, 'was put to the vote of the community of States'[45] and passed.

Although there has been some hesitation surrounding particular war crimes and criticism that certain violations really should have found their place on the list of war crimes in the Rome Statute,[46] the debates tend to turn on the criminalization of the rule rather than its applicability to non-international armed conflict. Similar criticisms of the ICTY jurisprudence are often directed at the so-called 'fourth *Tadić* condition', namely that violation of the particular rule 'must entail, under customary or conventional law, the individual criminal responsibility of the person breaching the rule', rather than any of the first three '*Tadić* conditions', namely the violation of a rule of international humanitarian law, the customary or conventional nature of that rule, and the severity of the violation.[47] Accordingly, it is generally recognized that there exists a

---

[36] See eg *Tadić* Decision on Interlocutory Appeal on Jurisdiction, above note 5, paras 100–18; *Strugar*, Trial Judgment, above note 23, paras 220–2.

[37] See eg *Strugar*, ibid, paras 223–6; *Hadžihasanović*, Decision on Interlocutory Appeal of Rule 98*bis* Decision, above note 23, paras 26–30.

[38] See eg *Strugar*, ibid, paras 227–8; *Hadžihasanović*, ibid, paras 26–30.

[39] See eg Strugar, ibid, paras 229–30; *Hadžihasanović*, ibid, paras 44–8.

[40] See eg *Hadžihasanović*, ibid, paras 47–8.

[41] See eg ibid, paras 37–8.

[42] *Tadić* Decision on Interlocutory Appeal on Jurisdiction, above note 5, paras 120–4.

[43] See eg Greenwood, *Tadić*, above note 14, 278; Watson, *Tadić*, above note 14, 713–15; Warbrick and Rowe, *Tadić*, above note 14, 701.

[44] But see A Zahar, 'Civilizing Civil War: Writing Morality as Law at the ICTY', in B Swart, A Zahar, and G Sluiter (eds), *The Legacy of the International Criminal Tribunal for the former Yugoslavia* (Oxford University Press, 2011) 469.

[45] C Kress, 'War Crimes Committed in Non-International Armed Conflict and the Emerging System of International Criminal Justice' (2000) 30 *IYHR* 104, 107. See also AM Danner, 'When Courts Make Law: How the International Criminal Tribunals Recast the Laws of War' (2006) 59 *Vanderbilt Law Review* 1.

[46] See eg R Cryer, *Prosecuting International Crimes* (Cambridge University Press, 2005) 283; A Cassese, 'The Statute of the International Criminal Court: Some Preliminary Reflections' (1999) 10 *EJIL* 144, 152–3; Kress, War Crimes, above note 45, 134–6.

[47] The 'four *Tadić* conditions' are set out in *Tadić* Decision on Interlocutory Appeal on Jurisdiction, above note 5, para 94. For criticism of the fourth *Tadić* condition, see eg G Mettraux, *International Crimes and the ad hoc Tribunals* (Oxford University Press, 2005) 51–2; Greenwood, *Tadić*, above note 14, 279–80. For criticism of the application of the fourth *Tadić* condition to

sizeable body of customary international humanitarian law applicable to non-international armed conflict.

Such a conclusion is supported by the Customary International Humanitarian Law study. One of the purposes of the study was 'to determine whether customary international law regulates non-international armed conflict in more detail than does treaty law and if so, to what extent'.[48] The study found that of 161 rules of customary international humanitarian law, the vast majority of them are or may be applicable in non-international armed conflict.[49] Although there has been some criticism over particular rules and aspects of the methodology,[50] the general tenor of the study has not been criticized, nor has its conclusion that a large number of international humanitarian law rules are applicable to situations of non-international armed conflict.[51] Accordingly, it is of undoubted importance, as demonstrated by its citation in judgments of leading courts and tribunals almost immediately after publication.[52] The existence of a substantial body of customary international humanitarian law governing non-international armed conflict and extending beyond the norms contained in common Article 3 and Additional Protocol II is, most importantly, recognized by states and non-state armed groups.[53]

2.2 Conventional international humanitarian law

A transformation has also taken place at the level of conventional law. Conventional international humanitarian law instruments concluded since the mid-1990s regulate non-international armed conflicts almost as a matter of course. This is not to say that international armed conflicts and their non-international counterparts are always treated alike; on occasion, their regulation varies. However, the more recent international humanitarian law treaties do apply systematically to both sorts of armed conflict.

Some conventions treat international and non-international armed conflicts exactly alike. The 1993 Chemical Weapons Convention, for example, regulates the two types of armed conflict in precisely the same manner. Article 1 of that Convention provides that '[e]ach State Party to this Convention undertakes never under any circumstances' to act in a particular manner. The phrase 'never under any circumstances' covers all types of armed

---

particular rules, see eg *Prosecutor v Galić*, IT-98-29-A, Judgment, 30 November 2006, Separate and Partially Dissenting Opinion of Judge Schomburg, paras 4–22.

[48] J-M Henckaerts, 'Study on Customary International Humanitarian Law: A Contribution to the Understanding and Respect for the Rule of Law in Armed Conflict' (2005) 87 *IRRC* 175, 178.

[49] *Customary International Humanitarian Law, Volume I: Rules*, above note 10.

[50] See eg the criticism of the United States relating to the application to internal armed conflict of Rules 31, 45 and 78 of the Customary International Humanitarian Law Study: JB Bellinger III and WJ Haynes II, 'A US Government Response to the International Committee of the Red Cross Study *Customary International Humanitarian Law*' (2007) 89 *IRRC* 443. See also eg GH Aldrich, 'Customary International Humanitarian Law—An Interpretation on Behalf of the International Committee of the Red Cross' (2005) LXXVI *BYIL* 503; Y Dinstein, 'The ICRC Customary International Humanitarian Law Study' (2006) 36 *IYHR* 1; the symposium in (2006) 11 *JCSL* 163–291; E Wilmshurst and S Breau (eds), *Perspectives on the ICRC Study on Customary International Humanitarian Law* (Cambridge University Press, 2007).

[51] See eg Aldrich, Customary International Humanitarian Law, above note 50, 523; Dinstein, Customary International Humanitarian Law, above note 50, 1; E Newalsing, 'Book Review': Jean-Marie Henckaerts and L Doswald-Beck (eds), *Customary International Humanitarian Law*' (2008) 21 *LJIL* 255, 277.

[52] See eg *Hadžihasanović* Decision on Interlocutory Appeal of Rule 98*bis* Decision, above note 23; *Hamdan v Rumsfeld* (2006) 126 S Ct 2749, 2797; *Public Committee Against Torture in Israel v Government of Israel* HCJ 769/02.

[53] See generally Chapter 4.

conflict and was considered to render unnecessary a scope of application clause.[54] This is also true of the 1997 Ottawa Convention on Anti-Personnel Mines, and the 2008 Cluster Munitions Convention, both of which use similar language.[55] Also regulating non-international and international armed conflicts alike are the 1999 Second Protocol to the Hague Convention on Cultural Property,[56] and the 2003 Protocol on Explosive Remnants of War (Protocol V to the Convention on Certain Conventional Weapons).[57] Other conventions treat the two sorts of armed conflicts in different ways but still regulate both. For example, the 1998 Rome Statute of the International Criminal Court (Rome Statute) contains two lists of war crimes, those applicable in international armed conflict and those applicable in non-international armed conflict, with the former list being more extensive than the latter.[58] Either way, treaties drafted today regulate non-international armed conflict almost as a matter of course.

Furthermore, certain treaties that were adopted prior to the mid-1990s have since been amended to bring non-international armed conflicts within their scope of application or to extend their regulation. The 1980 Convention on Certain Conventional Weapons is the prime example of this approach. During the first Review Conference for the Convention in 1996, Protocol II to the Convention, the Mines Protocol, was amended to include non-international armed conflicts within its scope. The original limitation to international armed conflicts was recognized as a shortcoming, given that the majority of casualties of anti-personnel mines were to be found in states involved in non-international armed conflicts. As Spain put it, speaking on behalf of the European Union, 'it was precisely in such conflicts, the most common kind at present, that the indiscriminate use of anti-personnel mines occurred most frequently and had the most devastating effects on innocent civilians'.[59] Accordingly, the scope of application of the Protocol was amended to be the same as that of common Article 3.[60]

Some years later, in 2001, the framework Convention itself was amended, precisely so as to apply in non-international armed conflicts. Again, the scope of application of common Article 3 was used,[61] and the amendment benefitted from broad support.[62]

---

[54] A Gioia, 'The Chemical Weapons Convention and its Application in Time of Armed Conflict', in M Bothe, N Ronzitti, and A Rosas (eds), *The New Chemical Weapons Convention—Implementation and Prospects* (Kluwer Law International, 1998) 397, 381–3; WH Boothby, *Weapons and the Law of Armed Conflict* (Oxford University Press, 2009) 321.

[55] On the Ottawa Convention, see Article 1; S Maslen, *Commentaries on Arms Control Treaties: Volume I* (Oxford University Press, 2005) 74–7; Boothby, *Weapons*, above note 54, 322. On the Cluster Munitions Convention, see Article 1; K Hulme, 'The 2008 Cluster Munitions Convention: Stepping Outside the CCW Framework (Again)' (2009) 58 *ICLQ* 219, 221–2.

[56] Articles 3 and 22(1). See R O'Keefe, *The Protection of Cultural Property in Armed Conflict* (Cambridge University Press, 2006) 246.

[57] Article 1(3).

[58] Article 8.

[59] CCW/CONF.I/SR.2 (1996) 4 para 16, in 'Review Conference of the States Parties to the Convention on the Prohibitions or Restrictions on the Use of Certain Conventional Weapons which may be Deemed to be Excessively Injurious or to have Indiscriminate Effects, Final Document, Part II', CCW/CONF.I/16 (Part II). See MJ Matheson, 'The Revision of the Mines Protocol' (1997) 91 *AJIL* 158, 159; JH McCall Jr, 'Infernal Machines and Hidden Death: International Law and Limits on the Indiscriminate Use of Land Mine Warfare' (1994–5) 24 *Georgia Journal of International and Comparative Law* 229, 264.

[60] Article 1(2).

[61] Article 1. See generally D Kaye and SA Solomon, 'The Second Review Conference of the 1980 Convention on Certain Conventional Weapons' (2002) 96 *AJIL* 922, 928–31.

[62] See generally 'Second Review Conference of the States Parties to the Convention on Prohibitions or Restrictions on the Use of Certain Conventional Weapons which May be Deemed to be Excessively Injurious or to have Indiscriminate Effects', CCW/CONF.II/2.

Accordingly, Protocols I–IV to the framework Convention are applicable to non-international armed conflicts for states that ratify the amendment to the framework Convention.[63] Indeed, even prior to the amendment, certain states had taken the view that the Convention should apply to non-international armed conflicts. When the President of the United States transmitted the original Convention to the Senate for its advice and consent as to ratification, in 1994, the President proposed that ratification should be accompanied by a declaration that the United States would apply the Convention 'to all armed conflicts referred to in Articles 2 and 3 common to the Geneva Conventions of 12 August 1949'.[64] In turn, the Senate, in giving its advice and consent, stated as a priority for strengthening the Protocol '[a]n expansion of the scope . . . to include internal armed conflicts'.[65] Upon ratification of the Convention, other states, too, indicated that they would apply the Convention to armed conflicts referred to in common Article 3.[66] The general trend, then, insofar as international humanitarian law treaties are concerned, is to make them applicable to non-international armed conflicts as well as international armed conflicts.

This extension is based on the modelling approach described above, for when drafting an international humanitarian law treaty, it is the international armed conflict that treaty negotiators have in mind. This is necessarily the case with 'older' treaties, in that they were intended to apply solely to international armed conflicts, with their extension to non-international armed conflicts coming about at a later date through amendment. However, even in respect of treaties which are intended to govern both international and non-international armed conflicts, the template used is that of the international armed conflict.

That the international armed conflict is viewed as the archetypal armed conflict is evident from two instruments—the Rome Statute and the 1954 Hague Convention on Cultural Property. Article 8 of the Rome Statute contains two lists of war crimes: those applicable in international armed conflict and those applicable in non-international armed conflict. The list of war crimes in non-international armed conflict that do not relate to violations of common Article 3 is largely drawn from the list of war crimes applicable in international armed conflicts,[67] and not from Additional Protocol II. This is also true of the amendments to the Rome Statute made at the 2010 Review Conference of the Statute of the International Criminal Court. In proposing to add the use of certain weapons to the list of war crimes applicable in non-international armed conflict, Belgium provided as its justification the fact that '[t]he use of the weapons listed in this draft amendment is already incriminated by [Article 8(2)(b)

---

[63] The amendment entered into force on 18 May 2004. For the view that Protocol IV is applicable to non-international armed conflict even outside ratification of the amendment, see L Doswald-Beck, 'New Protocol on Blinding Laser Weapons' (1996) 36 *IRRC* 272.

[64] Reproduced in (1994) 88 *AJIL* 748, 751.

[65] Resolution of Ratification, para 3(c)(3), 141 Congressional Record S4568, S4569 (24 March 1995), cited in Matheson, Mines Protocol, above note 59, 160.

[66] See the reservation of France and the Declaration made on accession of Israel, in D Schindler and J Toman, *The Laws of Armed Conflict* (Nijhoff, 2004) 217 and 218 respectively.

[67] M Bothe, 'War Crimes', in A Cassese, P Gaeta, and JRWD Jones (eds), *The Rome Statute of the International Criminal Court: A Commentary* (Oxford University Press, 2002) 379, 417–18; A Zimmermann, 'Preliminary Remarks on para 2(c)–(f) and para 3: War crimes committed in an armed conflict not of an international character', in O Triffterer (ed), *Commentary on the Rome Statute of the International Criminal Court: Observers' Notes, Article by Article* (Beck, 2008) 475, 476–7; H von Hebel and D Robinson, 'Crimes within the Jurisdiction of the Court', in RS Lee (ed), *The International Criminal Court: The Making of the Rome Statute, Issues, Negotiations, Results* (Kluwer Law International, 1999) 79, 119.

(xvii)–(xix)] of the Statute in case of an international armed conflict'.[68] The preamble to the resolution amending the Statute reflects this point, repeating on numerous occasions that the crimes intended for inclusion are already criminalized in the Rome Statute in international armed conflicts.[69] Thus, the model was, and remains, that of the law of international armed conflict.

The same approach is evident, for less fortunate reasons, in the Hague Convention on Cultural Property. That Convention contains a number of rules relating to the protection of cultural property in situations of armed conflict. Article 19 provides that, '[i]n the event of an armed conflict not of an international character occurring within the territory of one of the High Contracting Parties, each party to the conflict shall be bound to apply, as a minimum, the provisions of the present Convention which relate to respect for cultural property'. The provision is not a model of clarity; quite what is meant by the provisions that relate to 'respect for cultural property' is unclear.[70] This suggests that even treaties that are intended to be applicable to all armed conflicts are actually designed for international armed conflicts, with their application to non-international armed conflicts tagged on at the end. The fact that application to non-international armed conflict is contained in an article separate from the scope of application clause and at the end of the treaty also supports such a conclusion.

The model of the international armed conflict holds true for the sole treaty that applies to non-international armed conflict alone. Additional Protocol II, modelled as it was on Additional Protocol I, took as its starting point the law of international armed conflict. Indeed, the question was not so much *whether* to assimilate Additional Protocol II to Additional Protocol I, but *how far* the assimilation should go.[71] This approach led to something of a debate at the Diplomatic Conference. Some delegates took the view that the two Protocols should 'closely resemble'[72] one another, or mirror one another to the largest extent possible.[73] Others took the view that such an approach would be inappropriate.[74] One delegate recognized that 'several of the complexities of draft Protocol II were attributable to their having been discussed by experts too familiar with similar provisions in draft Protocol I'.[75] These positions should not always be taken at face value given that some delegations wanted little or no regulation of non-international armed conflict, while others favoured a single protocol applicable to all armed conflicts. However, ultimately, the approach adopted was one of drawing on Additional Protocol I.[76]

---

[68] Res ICC-ASP/8/Res.6, Annex III: Belgium: Proposal of Amendment, 26 November 2009. The proposal was supported by Austria, Argentina, Bolivia, Bulgaria, Burundi, Cambodia, Cyprus, Germany, Ireland, Latvia, Lithuania, Luxembourg, Mauritius, Mexico, Romania, Samoa, Slovenia, and Switzerland.

[69] Res RC/Res.5, 10 June 2010. On the amendment process, see A Alamuddin and P Webb, 'Expanding Jurisdiction over War Crimes under Article 8 of the ICC Statute' (2010) 8 *JICJ* 1219.

[70] On the various positions, see below, 376–7.

[71] F Kalshoven, 'The Conference of Government Experts on the Reaffirmation and Development of International Humanitarian Law Applicable in Armed Conflicts (Second Session), 3 May–2 June, 1972' (1972) 3 *NYIL* 18, 55.

[72] *Official Records of the Diplomatic Conference on the Reaffirmation and Development of International Humanitarian Law Applicable in Armed Conflicts, Geneva (1974–1977)* (Federal Political Department, 1978) Vol 5, 142 para 7 (Sweden). See also Vol 11, 209 para 42 (Australia); Vol 11, 208 para 39 (FRG).

[73] Ibid, Vol 11, 249 para 21 (Norway). See also Vol 5, 186 para 15 (Finland).

[74] Ibid, Vol 14, 67 para 72 (United States); Vol 8, 221 para 33 (Romania); Vol 11, 248 para 18 (Indonesia).

[75] Ibid, Vol 5, 184 para 6 (Canada).

[76] See the table in M Bothe, KJ Partsch, and WA Solf, *New Rules for Victims of Armed Conflicts* (Martinus Nijhoff, 1982) 641. See above, 49–52.

What these examples demonstrate is that, when drafting an international humanitarian law treaty, the negotiators have in mind international armed conflicts as the archetypal situation. The rules are then extended to apply to non-international armed conflicts, or non-international armed conflicts are added on to the scope of application clause of the treaty. This is despite the fact that non-international armed conflicts are more numerous than their international counterparts.

Ultimately, then, it is from the law of international armed conflict that the law of non-international armed conflict has emerged. That the general approach in the development of the international humanitarian law of non-international armed conflict has been to model on the international humanitarian law of international armed conflict is unsurprising. It reflects similar statements made in the 1960s and 1970s by private bodies and progressive states.[77] It spilled over into the mainstream in later decades, primarily through the work of judicial bodies that were not constrained by concerns of state sovereignty. To extend a law to cover an analogous situation is also markedly easier than to create a new law, and in many ways there was no feasible alternative to regulation by analogy. At another level, the traditional view has been that it is the law of international armed conflict that represents the high watermark of regulation and the standard towards which to aim. As the introduction to the Customary International Humanitarian Law study notes, it is simply a matter of '[c]ommon sense' that the relevant rules 'should be equally applicable in international and non-international armed conflicts'.[78] This is demonstrated in the ever-increasing tendency to call for a uniform body of international humanitarian law and the removal of the international/non-international distinction.[79] Thus, an alternative to the modelling approach was not sought.

2.3 Methodological difficulties with regulation by drawing on the law of international armed conflict

Despite being the predominant approach, regulating non-international armed conflict by looking to the law of international armed conflict suffers from a number of difficulties. These difficulties exist in three particular areas, namely the close relationship between the situations in which particular norms apply and the content of those norms, the differing levels of protection afforded by the law of international armed conflict and the law of non-international armed conflict on the same subject matter, and the differences between international and non-international armed conflicts themselves.

---

[77] See Chapter 2.
[78] *Customary International Humanitarian Law, Volume I: Rules*, above note 10, xxix. See also W Abresch, 'A Human Rights Law of Internal Armed Conflict: The European Court of Human Rights in Chechnya' (2005) 16 *EJIL* 741, 742.
[79] See, to varying degrees: J Stewart, 'Toward a Single Definition of Armed Conflict in International Humanitarian law: A Critique of Internationalized Armed Conflict' (2003) 85 *IRRC* 313; L Moir, 'Towards the Unification of International Humanitarian Law?', in R Burchill, ND White, and J Morris (eds), *International Conflict and Security Law: Essays in Memory of Hilaire McCoubrey* (Cambridge University Press, 2005) 108; A Duxbury, 'Drawing Lines in the Sand—Characterising Conflicts for the Purposes of Teaching International Humanitarian Law' (2007) 8 *Melbourne Journal of International Law* 259, 266–8; E Crawford, 'Unequal before the Law: The Case for the Elimination of the Distinction between International and Non-International Armed Conflicts' (2007) 20 *LJIL* 441.

2.3.1 Scope and content

There is an 'intimate nexus'[80] between the situations in which the international humanitarian law of non-international armed conflict applies and its normative content. Thus, the report of the 1972 Conference of Government Experts reads: '[t]he interdependence of the [draft] Protocol [II]'s field of application and its content was repeatedly stressed',[81] and the same was true of interventions of certain delegates at the 1974–7 Diplomatic Conference.[82] For example, the ICRC stated that the material field of application of the Protocol was its 'cornerstone ... for on its scope the whole contents of the instrument would depend'.[83] Similarly, as Canada put it, '[t]he key to the height of threshold we suggest lies in the expression "to implement this Protocol", for the threshold of the Protocol will now clearly depend upon the contents of the Protocol'.[84] Indeed, during the Diplomatic Conference, many delegates were unwilling to express their position on the applicability and content of particular rules without first knowing the threshold for application of the Protocol.[85] The scope–content nexus is also clear from the text of Additional Protocol II itself, with Article 1, entitled 'Material field of application', expressly linking application of the Protocol to the ability of the armed group to implement it.[86]

The scope–content nexus of the law of non-international armed conflict deserves some consideration given the tendency in recent years, by some highly influential bodies, to lower the threshold for the applicability of the norms while simultaneously increasing the normative content. In considering whether certain rules of international humanitarian law are applicable to a non-international armed conflict, the ICTY has taken the view that it need only determine whether there existed an armed conflict at the time in question. It has dispensed with the further issue of whether the Additional Protocol II threshold criteria are satisfied. Thus, customary rules of Additional Protocol II have been applied to all non-international armed conflicts and not simply those meeting the higher threshold of the Protocol.[87] Occasionally, the ICTY seems to go so far as to indicate that the Additional Protocol II threshold is not required even for application of Additional Protocol II *qua* treaty,[88] but such a position would be incorrect. Not all courts have opted for this approach, however, with the Special Court for Sierra Leone distinguishing between violations of common Article 3 and Additional Protocol II and requiring that the additional threshold criteria be proven in respect of violations of the latter.[89] Nonetheless, the general trend of 'reading out' the strict Additional Protocol II threshold is continued in the Rome Statute, an important

---

[80] The phrase is that of GIAD Draper, 'Humanitarian Law and Internal Armed Conflicts' (1983) 13 *Georgia Journal of International and Comparative Law* 253, 270.
[81] 'Reaffirmation and Development of International Humanitarian Law Applicable in Armed Conflicts: Conference of Government Experts [Second Session]' (1973) 13 *IRRC* 61, 64.
[82] See eg *Official Records*, above note 72, Vol 11, 248 para 17 (Indonesia); Vol 11, 249 para 19 (Denmark).
[83] Ibid, Vol 8, 203 para 11.
[84] Ibid, Vol 7, 77. See also Vol 8, 204 para 15 (ICRC); Vol 9, 234 para 52 (ICRC).
[85] See eg ibid, Vol 11, 248 para 17 (Indonesia); Vol 11, 249 para 19 (Denmark); Vol 8, 210 para 42 (France). See also Conference of Government Experts [Second Session], above note 81, 64.
[86] See below, 185–7.
[87] See eg *Strugar* Trial Judgment, above note 22, 220–2, 227–33. On the Additional Protocol II threshold, see below, 182–92.
[88] See *Prosecutor v Limaj, Bala and Musliu*, IT-03-66-T, Judgment, 30 November 2005, paras 88–90.
[89] See eg *Prosecutor v Sesay, Kallon and Gbao*, SCSL-04-15-T, Judgment, 2 March 2009, paras 96–7 and 978–81.

point given its ratification by states. The list of war crimes in non-international armed conflict is split into violations of common Article 3 (Article 8(2)(c) of the Rome Statute) and other serious violations of the law of non-international armed conflict (Article 8(2)(e)). There is some confusion as to whether the latter provision is subject to a higher threshold than the former, given that it applies in a 'protracted armed conflict'.[90] However, the better view is that it is not; and even if it is, the threshold is certainly not that of Additional Protocol II.[91] This trend of omitting the Additional Protocol II threshold is taken further in the Customary International Humanitarian Law study which does not introduce any threshold for the application of the various rules identified because it was determined that states did not make that distinction in practice.[92]

The scope–content nexus was originally considered important so as to make the rules amenable to states. Thus, speaking to Additional Protocol II, the United Kingdom noted at the 1974–7 Diplomatic Conference that:

> [t]he underlying difficulty was that of striking the right balance between scope and content. If the level of application was set so high that only the 'classical' civil war was covered, Protocol II would be useless; if it was set so low that it covered police action against sporadic criminal or terrorist acts, it was unlikely to be accepted by states. The obligations imposed on States and dissidents should not be so vague as to be nugatory, or so high as to set an impossible standard.[93]

As will be discussed, purported sovereignty concerns are to be treated with some caution.[94] However, the scope–content nexus is important for a different reason. Increasing the normative content while simultaneously reducing or removing any threshold brings with it a danger of overloading. At some stage, a tipping point will be reached whereby the normative content overwhelms the capacity of the parties to the conflict, in particular the non-state armed group. To increase the obligations to such an extent that the armed group is unable to meet them does not serve a useful purpose. The danger is that the armed group cannot comply with the rules which may, in turn, lead to non-compliance on the part of the state and violations spiralling out of control. The issue of the capabilities of non-state armed groups is discussed in further detail below.[95]

Alternatively, increasing the normative content may have the effect of raising the threshold at which a non-international armed conflict exists. As will be seen in Chapter 5, a non-international armed conflict is defined by reference to a certain intensity of violence and a certain measure of organization of the armed group.[96] The latter is judged, in part, on the ability of the armed group to implement the law and to enforce breaches of it.[97] Accordingly, to increase the content of the law is to require a greater degree of organization on the part of the armed group, raising the threshold at which a conflict will exist. Just as scope affects content, content affects scope. Indeed, at the 1972 Conference of Government Experts, it was said that 'in order to solve the

---

[90] Rome Statute, Article 8(2)(f).
[91] See, for further detail, below, 192–5.
[92] This has been criticized. See M Bothe, 'Customary International Humanitarian Law: Some Reflections on the ICRC Study' (2005) 8 *YIHL* 143, 175.
[93] *Official Records*, above note 82, Vol 8, 236 para 37. See also T Meron, *Human Rights in Internal Strife: Their International Protection* (Grotius, 1987) 152.
[94] See below, 70–1.
[95] See below, 72–6.
[96] See below, 164–80.
[97] Additional Protocol II, Article 1(1); *Limaj* Trial Judgment, above note 88, paras 113–17. See below, 170–1 and 176–80.

problem of the definition [of non-international armed conflict]... the essential thing was to define the rights and duties of the combatants involved...; once this was done, it would be possible to find a definition adequately circumscribing the situations to be envisaged'.[98] If the increased content of the law does raise the threshold for a non-international armed conflict to exist that may prove problematic. Although that is not *necessarily* a bad thing—the law of non-international armed conflict should only enter into force when the parties to the conflict are able to comply with it;[99] below that level, international human rights law would be the applicable law—it is not always appreciated that this will be the consequence.

The scope–content nexus is an important one. Its balance has been recalibrated in recent years and this has potential downsides. However, the recalibration is not inherently negative. Much depends on when the law enters into force, the capabilities of the parties, and the substantive norms themselves.

2.3.2 Levels of protection

A further concern with the regulation of non-international armed conflict by looking to the law of international armed conflict is that, in certain, albeit very few, areas, the international humanitarian law of non-international armed conflict has the potential to offer greater protection than the international humanitarian law of international armed conflict. By transposing the latter into the former, these greater protections have been reduced. Three examples serve to illustrate the point. Insofar as child soldiers are concerned, Additional Protocol II provides that, 'children who have not attained the age of fifteen years shall neither be recruited in the armed forces or groups nor allowed to take part in hostilities'.[100] This stands in contrast with Additional Protocol I, which provides that, '[t]he Parties to the conflict shall take all feasible measures in order that children who have not attained the age of fifteen years do not take a direct part in hostilities and, in particular, they shall refrain from recruiting them into their armed forces'.[101] This latter provision is weaker in two respects than its non-international counterpart. It requires only that 'all feasible measures' be taken and it prohibits only 'direct' participation in hostilities. As will be discussed below, other instruments relating to child soldiers draw on the standard of the law of international armed conflict and not non-international armed conflict, thus weakening the relevant protections.[102]

A second example of the law of non-international armed conflict offering greater protection relates to the prohibition on deportation. In international humanitarian law applicable in international armed conflict, the prohibition on deportation applies only from occupied territory.[103] In international humanitarian law applicable in non-international armed conflict, the prohibition on deportation applies in respect of territory generally, provided the threshold of Additional Protocol II is met.[104] Familiarity with the law of international armed conflict has led to suggestions that a

---

[98] Conference of Government Experts on the Reaffirmation and Development of International Humanitarian Law Applicable in Armed Conflicts (Second Session, 3 May–3 June 1972): Report on the Work of the Conference, Volume I (July 1972) 64 para 2.25.
[99] See below, 72–3.
[100] Additional Protocol II, Article 4(3)(c).
[101] Additional Protocol I, Article 77(2).
[102] See below, 79 and 317.
[103] Fourth Geneva Convention, Article 49.
[104] Additional Protocol II, Article 17(2).

prohibition on deportation in non-international armed conflict simply does not exist in light of occupation not being an accepted notion.[105]

The two examples considered immediately above exist at the level of conventional international humanitarian law. The same approach can also be seen at the level of customary international humanitarian law in relation to a different norm, namely the protection of works and installations containing dangerous forces. In non-international armed conflict, Additional Protocol II prohibits the targeting of certain listed objects containing dangerous forces if it would lead to the release of dangerous forces that would cause severe losses among the civilian population. This is the case even if the objects in question are military objectives.[106] The equivalent rule in Additional Protocol I is rather different. That rule also provides for a prohibition on the targeting of certain listed objects, but goes on to note that the protection shall cease if the object 'is used for other than its normal function and in regular, significant and direct support of military operations and if such attack is the only feasible way to terminate such support'.[107] Conventional international humanitarian law thus affords greater protection to the objects in situations of non-international armed conflict than it does in international armed conflict. Yet, the Customary International Humanitarian Law study provides that it is the content of the conventional rule of *international* armed conflict that applies at the level of custom to both international and non-international armed conflicts. This is despite the fact that the prohibition in Additional Protocol II is absolute and does not contain a provision on the cessation of protection. Furthermore, the military manuals of a number of states also contain an absolute prohibition on the targeting of the listed objects in non-international armed conflicts, while accepting that protection may cease in international armed conflicts.[108] Likewise, reservations made by states in respect of the Additional Protocol I provision have not been made in respect of the Additional Protocol II provision.[109] In the context of this norm, drawing on the law of international armed conflict to regulate non-international armed conflicts, while failing to appreciate the differences between the two sets of rules, has weakened the protection of the relevant rule.[110] The position of the Customary study is to be treated with caution.

2.3.3 International and non-international armed conflicts

There is much to be said for modelling the law of non-international armed conflict on the law of international armed conflict. Many norms can be applied in both sorts of conflicts without any difficulty and, at least insofar as those rules are concerned, there is no reason for a differentiation between the two sorts of conflicts. Much of the law of targeting or relating to the humane treatment of persons *hors de combat* falls into this category. As the USSR delegate queried in 1949:

I should be very glad if the supporters of [the alternative position] would explain why, in the case of conflicts of a non-international character, it would be impossible to apply the provisions of the Wounded and Sick Convention or those of the Civilians Convention, which stipulate, for

---

[105] See below, 286.
[106] Additional Protocol II, Article 15.
[107] Additional Protocol I, Article 56(2).
[108] Article 15. See the military manuals of Argentina, Canada, and Netherlands, quoted in *Customary International Humanitarian Law, Volume II: Practice*, above note 10, 814–40.
[109] See the reservations of France and the United Kingdom, in Schindler and Toman, above note 66, 801 and 817.
[110] See further, below, 381–3.

instance, that civilian hospitals may in no circumstances be attacked, and that women and children shall at all times enjoy particular respect and protection, that, in order to bring relief to the civilian population, the unrestricted transport and distribution of various shipments, such as medicines and medical equipment, shall be guaranteed.[111]

However, the application of other norms to non-international armed conflict may be more difficult. As Romania put it at the 1974–7 Diplomatic Conference, '[t]here was a fundamental difference between international and non-international armed conflicts, and it would be a mistake automatically to transpose the provisions of draft Protocol I to draft Protocol II'.[112] Such difficulty arises with respect to three particular classes of norms.

One set of norms may be considered inapplicable in non-international armed conflict by the state concerned for reasons of sovereignty. The prohibition on perfidy and the prohibition on wanton destruction may be considered to fall into this category. A lengthy debate took place during the 1974–7 Diplomatic Conference as to the applicability of the prohibition on perfidy to non-international armed conflict. It was said, for example, that if the Protocol set out that 'killing by resort to perfidy was prohibited, it might be deduced *a contrario* that killing without resort to such methods was allowable',[113] and that any clause on point would appear 'to indicate that there were two ways of rebelling against a legitimate Government: a legal way of killing, injuring or capturing soldiers belonging to the government forces, and an illegal way'.[114] Similarly, it has been said of wanton destruction, that is to say, the prohibition on the destruction or seizure of property of an adversary unless demanded by imperative military necessity, that, 'no state would accept that "imperative military necessity" is a principle that the forces fighting to overthrow the state's government may in any way benefit from'.[115] Indeed, it has been suggested that to make any rule that contains an element of military necessity or proportionality applicable to non-international armed conflicts would be objectionable to states as the rule would 'weaken the hand of [the] government's forces'.[116] For related reasons, some states have been uncomfortable with the use of the word 'reprisal' in the context of belligerent reprisals and preferred alternative formulations, such as 'measures of retaliation comparable to reprisals',[117] 'actions similar to those of reprisal',[118] or 'acts of extreme retaliation'.[119] The concern was that, from a political point of view, the word 'reprisal' 'gave the Parties to a conflict a status under international law which they had no right to claim'.[120] However, sovereignty concerns can be overstated. They are put forward by some states but not by others; they are raised in respect of certain rules but not others, and oftentimes they indicate a more general concern surrounding the regulation of non-international armed conflict rather than principled objection to the particular rule at hand. The strength of such concerns has also been ameliorated significantly in recent years, primarily by acceptance of the list of war crimes in non-international armed conflict over which the International Criminal Court (ICC) has jurisdiction, such list being approved by states. The list includes the very crimes of

---

[111] *Final Record*, above note 15, Vol II-B, 326.
[112] *Official Records*, above note 72, Vol 8, 221 para 33.
[113] Ibid, Vol 15, 215 para 35 (FRG) (emphasis removed).
[114] Ibid, 217 para 49 (Canada).
[115] Zahar, Civil War, above note 44, 467, 500.
[116] Ibid, 502.
[117] *Official Records*, above note 72, Vol 8, 325 para 11 (FRG); Vol 14, 177 para 41 (United Kingdom). See also Vol 11, 561 paras 73–6 (Canada, on behalf of the Working Group).
[118] Ibid, Vol 11, 336 para 53 (Canada).
[119] Ibid, 336 para 53 (Canada).
[120] Ibid, Vol 8, 325 para 11 (FRG).

'[k]illing or wounding treacherously a combatant adversary' and wanton destruction.[121] It should also be recalled that the law of non-international armed conflict does not provide the parties to the conflict with a right to undertake certain actions. Rather, it prohibits certain actions and regulates other conduct should the parties choose to engage in particular endeavours.

One sovereignty concern that has had, and continues to have, a very real impact on the substantive law of non-international armed conflict relates to the lack of combatant privilege. Pursuant to this idea, combatants have the authority to participate in hostilities. Accordingly, they cannot be prosecuted for taking part in hostilities and committing lawful acts of war. Importantly, however, the notion of combatant, and therefore also the combatant privilege, is limited to international armed conflicts. States are unwilling to afford the combatant privilege to members of non-state armed groups that fight against them. Instead, they leave open the possibility of prosecuting such members for treason, sedition, or some other offence under domestic law. For this reason, the law of non-international armed conflict cannot be exactly equivalent to the law of international armed conflict. The lack of combatant immunity in non-international armed conflict is recognized as a hurdle for advocating compliance with the law on the part of non-state armed groups. If members of armed groups are to be prosecuted regardless of their compliance with international humanitarian law, there is little incentive for them to comply with it. This is a matter that will be re-visited in Chapter 12 as it is an area in which further work is needed.

A second set of norms may be considered inapplicable to non-international armed conflict due to the fine line that exists between situations of internal tensions and disturbances and non-international armed conflicts. The use of certain weapons may be lawful in the former situation making the prohibition on their use in the latter more difficult. Falling into this category are expanding bullets. Thus, it has been said that these weapons are widely used in situations of internal tensions and disturbances so as to minimize injury to persons located nearby,[122] and to stop the target instantaneously.[123] Given the fine line between such situations and situations of non-international armed conflict, it has been suggested that they should not be prohibited in the latter. However, the concern is overstated, for once the situation has been identified as a non-international armed conflict, the prohibition enters into force. Furthermore, the matter is rendered less important today following the 2010 amendment of the Rome Statute to include a prohibition on the use of expanding bullets in non-international armed conflicts.[124] Although there may be valid uses for expanding bullets during non-international armed conflicts—to control a riot in a detention camp or in a hostage-rescue operation being the two classic examples[125]—the same is also true of international armed conflicts. Thus, the nature of the armed conflict as international or non-international is not the determining factor. Rather, it is whether there should be exceptions to the prohibition on the use of expanding bullets in certain situations. Accordingly, the idea that there is a category of norms that is not applicable to non-international armed conflict for reasons along these lines is not particularly sound.

---

[121] Article 8(2)(e)(ix) and (xii).
[122] Steering Committee for Human Rights, *Study on Human Rights Protection during Situations of Armed Conflict, Internal Disturbances and Tensions*, DH-DEV(2002)1, 18 March 2001 (Document prepared by F Hampson) para 32.
[123] International Institute of Humanitarian Law, *The Manual on the Law of Non-International Armed Conflict With Commentary* (Sanremo, 2006) 35.
[124] However, difficulties still arise. See further below, 401–3.
[125] On which see ibid.

A third set of norms that are potentially problematic are those that depend on the capacity of the actors taking part in non-international armed conflicts. The limited capabilities of the actor in question may mean that it is unable to comply with the substance of a particular norm. Care needs to be taken when drawing on the law of international armed conflict given that non-international armed conflicts, by definition, involve at least one non-state armed group. At the 1974–7 Diplomatic Conference, at which Additional Protocol II was negotiated, a concern was adduced on the part of a number of states relating to whether non-state armed groups had the capacity to comply with the rules being drafted.[126] Denmark, for example, cautioned against 'extend[ing] the scope of the rules applicable in certain armed conflicts beyond what the parties to the conflict were able to observe' as this 'would have the effect of weakening confidence in international law as a useful means of promoting respect for human rights in armed conflicts'.[127] Concern has also been expressed as to whether non-state armed groups would be able to apply the Geneva Conventions as a whole.[128]

Although it has been suggested that the 'legal relevance' of capability issues should not be stressed,[129] concerns relating to capacity need to be taken seriously, not least because they emanate from some armed groups themselves. For example, in 2010, the Moro Islamic Liberation Front (MILF) of the Philippines indicated that it had 'a lot of difficulties' in enforcing its law on child soldiers, given that an 'essential requirement is resources' and that '[o]ther concrete measures have had to be postponed due to a lack of the required resources'.[130] For its part, the Polisario Front of Western Sahara stated, also in 2010, that it does not have the financial resources to institute projects for the benefit of children.[131] Another armed group indicated in 2011 that the training and education of its fighters may be an issue. During times of minimal fighting, it is able to train and educate fighters, including on such issues as how to engage with the civilian population; however, during times of intense fighting, training is limited to combat and does not extend to other issues, which may lead in turn to a greater number of transgressions and violations.[132] These are not new concerns. For example, in 1965, when the National Liberation Front (FLN) of Viet Nam informed the ICRC that it did not consider itself bound by the Geneva Conventions, it stated that the Conventions 'contain articles which neither strictly correspond to our action, nor to the organisation of the armed forces of the FLN, which is why the FLN cannot mechanically apply the Convention[s]'.[133] The latter point alludes to the lack of possibility of compliance.

---

[126] *Official Records*, above note 72, Vol 7, 61 para 11 (Pakistan); Vol 8, 309 para 55 (India); Vol 8, 337 para 71 (Canada); Vol 8, 339–40 para 82 (Iran); Vol 8, 340 para 87 (India); Vol 8, 345 para 18 (Italy).
[127] Ibid, Vol 5, 124 para 39.
[128] B Jakovlević and J Patrnogić, 'The Urgent Need to Apply the Rule of Humanitarian Law to so-called Internal Armed Conflicts' (1961) 1 *IRRC* 250, 256–7. See also, in the context of national liberation movements, RR Baxter, 'The Geneva Conventions of 1949 and Wars of National Liberation', in MC Bassiouni (ed), *International Terrorism and Political Crimes* (Thomas, 1975) 121, 125.
[129] Zegveld, *Armed Opposition Groups*, above note 33, 34.
[130] Geneva Call (ed), *In Their Words: Perspectives of Armed Non-State Actors on the Protection of Children from the Effects of Armed Conflict* (Geneva Call, 2010) 26.
[131] Ibid, 29.
[132] Information provided to author.
[133] Letter from Chef de la Représentation Permanente du FLN du Sud-Vietnam en URSS to Representative of the ICRC, 16 October 1965, ICRC Archives B AG 202 223-005 (Russian original and French translation). The original reads: '[c]es Conventions contiennent des articles qui ne correspondent absolument pas à notre action, ni à l'organisation des forces armées du FNL, et c'est pourquoi le FNL ne peut pas appliquer mécaniquement cette Convention.'

Furthermore, in 2001, the Sudan People's Liberation Movement/Army (SPLM/A) made a similar capacity point in the context of humanitarian norms more generally:

> The SPLM/A is fully conscious of the fact that although it is a non-state actor, the world has come to expect from it humanitarian standards, approaching if not on a par with those expected of sovereign governments. This constitutes a daunting challenge and a tremendous burden for our Movement, and unless the international community comes to our aid with increased levels of humanitarian assistance, especially in the field of health, education and human resources development, we will not be able to continue to live up to those high expectations.[134]

Issues of capacity are thus important. However, it is also important not to overstate the point. The danger of overloading is not true of all non-state armed groups; some have significant capabilities and have indicated that capacity is simply not a problem. A representative of one armed group indicated in 2011 that the group complies with international humanitarian law unless compliance proves 'impossible', but there have not been any instances of impossibility to date.[135] At the Diplomatic Conference of 1974–7, the Frente de Libertação de Moçambique (FRELIMO) of Mozambique stated that 'despite disparities in the resources of the parties involved, nothing prevents the national liberation movements from respecting the principles of humanitarian law' and that '[t]he essential requirement...was not the technical apparatus or the material means, but the will to apply the principles of humanitarian law'.[136]

What all this demonstrates is that armed groups have varying degrees of capability. They are not monolithic entities. As with states, the term 'armed group' captures a wide array of actors, from those in control of a sizeable tract of territory and which act as *de facto* states, to those that barely meet the international humanitarian law requirement of organization. Some engage solely in guerrilla tactics; others, albeit far fewer, have air and sea capabilities, as was the case with the Liberation Tigers of Tamil Eelam (LTTE) of Sri Lanka. Many armed groups are divided into military wings, intelligence wings, and political wings, the latter often based abroad; and some armed groups have human rights, relief, and social divisions.[137] These differing capacities of non-state armed groups have consequences for the normative content of particular rules.

Many of the concerns surrounding the capabilities of non-state armed groups would be less problematic if the content of the more demanding norms were 'translated' to meet the particularities of a non-international armed conflict. Instead of focusing exclusively on the passage from the 1995 *Tadić* Decision on Interlocutory Appeal on Jurisdiction to the effect that, what is prohibited in international armed conflict cannot but be prohibited in internal armed conflict,[138] equal attention should be paid to a later passage which makes clear that 'this extension has not taken place in the form of a full and mechanical transplant of those rules to internal conflicts; rather, the general essence of those rules, and not the detailed regulation they may contain, has become applicable to internal conflicts'.[139] This could be effected in a number of different ways.

---

[134] Statement of the Sudan People's Liberation Movement/Army on the Occasion of the Signing and Depositing to Geneva Call Deed of Commitment to Ban Landmines, 4 October 2001.

[135] Information provided to author.

[136] *Official Records*, above note 72, Vol 8, 32 para 46 and 36 para 18.

[137] For example, the LTTE's political wing was based in London; the Front de Libération Nationale (FLN) of Algeria had an office in New York; the Frente Farabundo Martí para la Liberación Nacional (FMLN) of El Salvador had a Secretariat for the Promotion and Protection of Human Rights; the Sudan People's Liberation Movement (SPLM) had a relief wing.

[138] *Tadić* Decision on Interlocutory Appeal on Jurisdiction, above note 5, para 119.

[139] Ibid, para 126.

One option is to identify the core of a norm which would remain intact and applicable in non-international armed conflict. Outside that core, there would be room for interpretation so as to make the obligation achievable for armed groups. The idea that a norm contains a core alongside associated obligations already finds expression in certain conventional rules. For example, Article 5(1) of Additional Protocol II contains the core of the protections afforded to detained persons, providing that 'the following provisions shall be respected as a minimum'.[140] Beyond these minimum core rules, other obligations arise, but they are dependent on the capacity of the detaining entity: '[t]hose who are responsible for the internment or detention of the persons referred to in paragraph 1 shall also, *within the limits of their capabilities*, respect the following provisions.'[141] This follows on from the idea expressed at the 1949 Diplomatic Conference that the problem is not so much a lack of ability to comply with entire norms; rather it is the inability of armed groups to comply with norms to the same degree as that of states.[142]

A second, related, option is to have a general norm and more specific norms linked with that general norm. There is usually little problem at the level of generality: '[t]he civilian population as such, as well as individual civilians, shall not be the object of attack', for example, or 'children shall be provided with the care and aid they require'.[143] It is at the level of detail that difficulties can arise. This can be illustrated through a norm that is included in common Article 3, Additional Protocol II, and the international humanitarian law applicable in international armed conflict, namely protection of the wounded and sick. Common Article 3 provides, without more, '[t]he wounded and sick shall be collected and cared for'.[144] Additional Protocol II puts some flesh on these bare bones, containing as it does an entire part on the wounded, sick, and shipwrecked.[145] It refers to respect and protection for the wounded and sick, their humane treatment, and medical care;[146] searching for and collection of the wounded and sick;[147] and specific protection for medical and religious personnel and medical units and transports.[148] The international humanitarian law of international armed conflict contains two entire conventions on the wounded and sick. Those Conventions, in addition to providing for the general protections that find reflection in common Article 3 and Additional Protocol II, contain such requirements as medical examination prior to the burial or cremation of the dead and the creation of a Graves Registration Service.[149] It is these minutiae that go beyond the capabilities of many a non-state armed group. Thus, the ICRC had suggested in 1969 that, '[g]uerrillas and their opponents should conform to the same rules' but '[t]he more restricted facilities of the former should ... be taken into account and general principles established which both Parties could apply'.[150]

A third option is to use clauses such as those already found in some conventional norms. A number of Additional Protocol II provisions explicitly take into account the capacity of the actor, through reference to 'all appropriate steps', 'within the limits of their capabilities', 'to the fullest extent practicable', 'all possible measures', and the

---

[140] Additional Protocol II, Article 5(1).   [141] Ibid, Article 5(2) (emphasis added).
[142] *Final Record*, above note 15, Vol II-B, 326 (USSR).
[143] Additional Protocol II, Articles 13(2) and 4(3).   [144] Common Article 3(2).
[145] Part III.   [146] Article 7.   [147] Article 8.   [148] Articles 9–12.
[149] First Geneva Convention, Article 17.
[150] Reaffirmation and Development of the Laws and Customs Applicable in Armed Conflicts: Report submitted by the International Committee of the Red Cross (May 1969) 118.

like.¹⁵¹ Generally speaking, there has not been any objection to these provisions,¹⁵² nor should there be provided they are interpreted in a sensible manner. Indeed, at the 1974–7 Diplomatic Conference, the 'apparent tendency to tone down the imperative obligation... by using such phrases as "within the limits of their capabilities"' was criticized, not because of the move from absolute to relative obligations, but because 'it was a recognized general principle that no one was compelled to do the impossible'.¹⁵³

That 'recognized general principle' constitutes a fourth option. A provision would be formulated in its usual terms, but there would be general recognition that respect for it would be dependent on the capability of the actor. Along these lines, the 1947 Conference of Government Experts suggested that 'derogations should be implicitly allowed whenever belligerents plead, in all good faith, inability to meet their obligations'.¹⁵⁴ Along associated lines, UN Secretary-General U Thant suggested that:

[a]ppropriate provisions might be envisaged to the effect that the laws and customs of war should be fully applied save in exceptional and compelling circumstances due to lack of facilities... such circumstances might have to be notified to the parties the conflict concerned, which may involve the International Committee of the Red Cross. However, it should be made clear that [other] humanitarian rules or principles... may never be disregarded.¹⁵⁵

To allow derogations to be made, be they implicit or notified, goes too far in the opposite direction. They would be incompatible with the protective function of international humanitarian law and the notion of equality of obligation of belligerents. However, the suggestions do usefully illustrate the point being made. It has also been recognized that certain states themselves may have difficulty in applying certain rules to the fullest possible extent. Thus, the Eritrea-Ethiopia Claims Commission has held, in the context of an international armed conflict, that when assessing what was meant by 'required' medical care, it was aware that both states had 'very limited resources'.¹⁵⁶

What each of these options has in common is that there has to be a certain 'shaping' of the norm. This shaping could take different forms in the context of different rules. For example, insofar as trials are concerned, according to common Article 3, the courts in question have to be 'regularly constituted'.¹⁵⁷ If this is interpreted as requiring legal enactment, the interpretation should not be limited to *state* law, for that would render the courts of non-state armed groups inherently unlawful. Rather, it should be enough that courts of armed groups are established pursuant to a 'law' issued by the armed group. Similarly, due process guarantees should be interpreted in a way that both respects the minimum core—the essence of a fair trial—but is achievable by the armed group. As the Frente Farabundo Martí para la Liberación Nacional (FMLN) argued in 1988 during the conflict in El Salvador: 'the type of tribunal and law required by

---

¹⁵¹ Additional Protocol II, Article 4(3)(b) ('all appropriate steps shall be taken'); Article 5(2) ('within the limits of their capabilities'); Article 7(2) ('to the fullest extent practicable'); Article 8 ('all possible measures'); Article 17 ('all possible measures').
¹⁵² On the contrary. See eg *Official Records*, above note 72, Vol 8, 337 para 71 (Canada); Vol 8, 339–40 para 82 (Iran).
¹⁵³ Ibid, 345 para 18 (Italy).
¹⁵⁴ *Remarks and Proposals submitted by the International Commission of the Red Cross: Document for the Consideration of Governments invited by the Swiss Federal Council to attend the Diplomatic Conference at Geneva (April 21, 1949)* (1949) 37–8.
¹⁵⁵ Respect for Human Rights in Armed Conflicts: Report of the Secretary-General, A/8052, 18 September 1970, para 181.
¹⁵⁶ Eritrea-Ethiopia Claims Commission, *Partial Award: Prisoners of War-Eritrea's Claim 17* (2003) 42 *ILM* 1083, 1104 para 117.
¹⁵⁷ Common Article 3(1)(d).

Protocol II have to be adapted to the conditions and capacity of the contending party; the particular mechanisms necessary for defense must be adjusted to the real possibilities of the zone where the trial is held.'[158] Such courts and legislation would still be assessed against the standards of international law. However, they cannot be deemed *inherently* incompatible with the law of armed conflict, for example requiring state courts or standards that can never be satisfied. As has been noted more generally, '[t]o require that a group respect a rule that the State makes it impossible to comply with makes a nonsense of the law'.[159]

Similarly, in the context of internment, this has to take place pursuant to a legal basis, the basis in question usually being domestic legislation. Internment also has to be reviewed by a court or administrative body. Both the legislation and the review mechanism will likely be state legislation and a state court or administrative body insofar as the state party is concerned. For the non-state armed group, it may take the form of state or non-state armed group legislation and a non-state armed group court or administrative body.[160] The notions of legislation and of courts have to be interpreted as including the bodies and materials of states and non-state armed groups alike. Any other interpretation renders the relevant law unworkable in practice. Again, this is not to suggest that all non-state armed group legislation or bodies will meet international standards. When judged against the standards of the law of armed conflict, some may be found wanting. However, the law cannot be drafted and interpreted in such a way as to make compliance on the part of the non-state armed group impossible. That does not serve a useful purpose. A balance needs to be found by which the requisite standards are maintained while also making them achievable for the parties to the conflict.

None of this is to suggest that if the law was tailored in the manner suggested there would be a sudden transformation in rates of compliance. Other factors also play crucial roles insofar as compliance is concerned.[161] However, the law needs to play its part in encouraging compliance. It should be reiterated that difficulties of capacity only apply in respect of certain norms; others, particularly prohibition-type norms, can be applied irrespective of capacity. It should also be recalled that armed groups have varying capacities. An armed group in effective control over a sizeable portion of state territory and that has established some sort of administration may well be able to comply with all relevant norms.[162] Furthermore, problems of capacity are not limited to non-state armed groups; they may also be true of certain states.

It is understandable why the international humanitarian law of international armed conflict formed the reference point for the regulation of non-international armed conflict. It would be more difficult to conjure up new rules than to apply existing rules to a different situation; it may even have proven impossible given the reticence of states. However, it is not immediately apparent that the international humanitarian law of

---

[158] FMLN, *The Legitimacy of Our Methods of Struggle* (Inkworks Press, 1988) 20. See generally below, 549–62.

[159] F Hampson, 'Fundamental Guarantees', in E Wilmshurst and SC Breau (eds), *Perspectives on the ICRC Study on Customary International Humanitarian law* (Cambridge University Press, 2007) 282, 287 fn 20.

[160] See below, 303–4.

[161] See generally O Bangerter, 'Reasons Why Armed Groups Choose to Respect International Humanitarian Law or Not' (2011) 93 *IRRC* 353.

[162] *Final Record*, above note 15, Vol II-B, 13 (Canada); ICRC, Conference of Government Experts on the Reaffirmation and Development of International Humanitarian Law Applicable in Armed Conflicts, Geneva, 3 May–3 June 1972 (second session): II Commentary, Part Two (January 1972) 84–6.

international armed conflict *should* be the law on which the international humanitarian law of non-international armed conflict is modelled. It is one thing to seek to reach the level of protection that that body of law affords; it is another altogether to model the rules upon it. In particular, the analogy approach has meant that where an appropriate analogy cannot be drawn, such as with the law of belligerent occupation or combatant immunity, the matter has been left largely unregulated.[163]

3. International criminal law

The second means by which the international humanitarian law of non-international armed conflict has developed has been through the development of international criminal law relating to war crimes. International criminal law is a useful means by which international humanitarian law may be enforced.[164] International criminal law has been utilized to enforce international humanitarian law and to sanction those who commit serious violations of it. Indeed, on one view, international criminal law is the most important means of enforcement of international humanitarian law.[165] Using international criminal law to enforce international humanitarian law could also have an impact on other means of enforcement. For example, an ICTY Trial Chamber held that in light of the existence of international criminal law, resort to belligerent reprisals could no longer be justified.[166] However, the use of international criminal law in this context has not been limited to the realm of enforcement. There is a far closer, and more complex, relationship between international humanitarian law and international criminal law than simply operation at the level of enforcement.

3.1 The war crimes–international humanitarian law nexus

War crimes law comprises the secondary rules to the primary rules of international humanitarian law.[167] Usually, there is relatively little interaction between the primary and the secondary rules, with the rules relating to state responsibility, for example, tending not to affect the content of the primary rules. However, insofar as international criminal law and international humanitarian law are concerned, there is an extremely close relationship between the two. After all, a war crime is essentially a serious violation of international humanitarian law, which entails the individual criminal responsibility of the violator.[168] Accordingly, the international criminal tribunals have had to interpret international humanitarian law provisions in order to pronounce on the guilt or innocence of individuals accused of war crimes. Thus, it has been through the lens of war crimes that certain rules of international humanitarian law were first shown to be applicable to non-international armed conflicts. This is true, for example, of the many rules in the area of the conduct of hostilities to which conventional

---

[163] See S Sivakumaran, 'Re-envisioning the International Law of Internal Armed Conflict' (2011) 22 *EJIL* 219. See further Chapter 12.
[164] See Chapter 11.
[165] A Cassese, 'On the Current Trends towards Criminal Prosecution and Punishment of Breaches of International Humanitarian Law' (1998) 9 *EJIL* 2, 17.
[166] *Kupreškić* Trial Judgment, above note 6, para 530. See further below, 448.
[167] Bothe, War Crimes, above note 67, 381.
[168] See *Tadić* Decision on Interlocutory Appeal on Jurisdiction, above note 5, para 94. See generally G Abi-Saab, 'The Concept of "War Crimes"', in S Yee and W Tieya (eds), *International Law and the Post-Cold War World: Essays in Honour of Li Haopei* (Routledge, 2001) 99, 112. See below, 475–8.

international humanitarian law of non-international armed conflict remains limited.[169] It has also been through the lens of war crimes that existing rules of international humanitarian law applicable to non-international armed conflicts have been fleshed out.[170] Historically, war crimes used to refer to the regulation of violations of international humanitarian law rather than their definition; by contrast, today, they are as much about definition as they are regulation.[171] These interpretations have provided useful guidance in understanding the relevant rule of international humanitarian law.

Even one of the most fundamental issues, the very definition of a non-international armed conflict, has been aided immeasurably by international criminal law. As will be seen in Chapter 5, for many years, a neat, authoritative definition of a non-international armed conflict proved elusive, with neither common Article 3 nor Additional Protocol II defining the term. The influential ICRC Commentaries on the 1949 Geneva Conventions had the potential to mislead as their 'convenient criteria' for the identification of a non-international armed conflict were no more than a collation of the proposals made during the 1949 Diplomatic Conference, all of which were rejected.[172] Furthermore, the criteria were suggested at a time during the Diplomatic Conference when the full body of international humanitarian law was considered applicable and not the far fewer rules of common Article 3 alone. Although various definitions had been put forward by commentators and other bodies, none proved sufficiently authoritative. It was only in 1995 with the *Tadić* Decision on Interlocutory Appeal on Jurisdiction that an authoritative definition was finally encapsulated. Subsequent ICTY jurisprudence has set out indicia that may be utilized in determining whether or not an armed conflict exists.[173]

Indeed, one of the major achievements of the international criminal tribunals has been the development of international *humanitarian* law. Just as international human rights law rejuvenated international humanitarian law in the late 1960s and early 1970s, international criminal law reinvigorated international humanitarian law in the mid-1990s and 2000s. Without the jurisprudence of the international criminal tribunals, the law of non-international armed conflict would not be what it is today. Accordingly, it is not an overstatement to suggest that the law of non-international armed conflict cannot be understood without detailed consideration of the jurisprudence of the international criminal tribunals. This will become apparent from the discussion on the substantive norms in Part II.

3.2 Methodological concerns with the use of war crimes law

All that being said, just as there are important differences between international armed conflicts and non-international armed conflicts, so too are there important differences between international humanitarian law and international criminal law. International criminal law relates to 'the most serious crimes of international concern',[174] and war

---

[169] See Chapter 9. [170] See eg above, 57–8.
[171] M Sassòli, 'Humanitarian Law and International Criminal law', in A Cassese et al (eds), *The Oxford Companion to International Criminal Justice* (Oxford University Press, 2009) 111, 111–12.
[172] A former ICRC Director for International Law and Cooperation has also taken the view that the ICRC Commentaries on this point (as well as certain other points) 'must be viewed with serious reservations'. F Bugnion, *The International Committee of the Red Cross and the Protection of War Victims* (ICRC, 2003) 344.
[173] See below, 164.
[174] Rome Statute, Article 1.

crimes give rise to individual criminal responsibility. Thus, the war crime is sometimes drawn up, or interpreted, in a narrower manner than its international humanitarian law equivalent.[175] This is unsurprising; in certain instances, it may even be necessary. However, it does mean that care needs to be taken before transposing from international criminal law to international humanitarian law.

3.2.1 The norms

In many areas, the law on war crimes acts as a *renvoi* to international humanitarian law.[176] In these instances, there should be little by way of difficulty of application of international criminal law to international humanitarian law. However, the international criminal law standard is not always coterminous with the international humanitarian law standard, as illustrated through the following examples. As noted above,[177] the relevant provision of Additional Protocol II on child soldiers provides that, 'children who have not attained the age of fifteen years shall neither be recruited in the armed forces or groups nor allowed to take part in hostilities'.[178] This stands in contrast with the equivalent war crime as well as the equivalent provisions in the international humanitarian law of international armed conflict and in international human rights law, all of which are narrower.[179] The war crime relates to '[c]onscripting or enlisting children under the age of fifteen years into armed forces or groups or using them to participate actively in hostilities'.[180] Whereas Additional Protocol II prohibits children from taking *any* part in hostilities, only an aspect of that prohibition has been criminalized, namely the *active* participation of children in hostilities. Given that the approach to the list of war crimes in non-international armed conflict in the Rome Statute was to draw not from Additional Protocol II, but the list of war crimes in international armed conflict,[181] the criminal prohibition adopts the weaker standard of the law of international armed conflict.

The war crime of the disproportionate attack is also drafted in a narrower manner than the international humanitarian law prohibition. Article 57 of Additional Protocol I prohibits attacks 'which may be expected to cause incidental loss of civilian life, injury to civilians, damage to civilian objects, or a combination thereof, which would be excessive in relation to the concrete and direct military advantage anticipated'.[182] This is considered applicable to non-international armed conflict through customary international law.[183] The Rome Statute lists as a war crime in international armed conflict such attacks which are 'clearly excessive in relation to the concrete and direct overall military advantage anticipated'.[184] The insertion of the words 'clearly' and 'overall' creates a higher threshold for the war crime as compared with the international

---

[175] On other differences, and their impact on international *criminal* law, see D Robinson, 'The Identity Crisis of International Criminal Law' (2008) 21 *LJIL* 925, 946–55.
[176] R Cryer, 'The Interplay of Human Rights and Humanitarian Law: The Approach of the ICTY' (2010) 14 *JCSL* 511, 516.
[177] See above, 68.
[178] Additional Protocol II, Article 4(3)(c).
[179] Additional Protocol I, Article 77(2); Convention on the Rights of the Child, Article 38(2).
[180] Rome Statute, Article 8(2)(e)(vii). See also Statute of the Special Court for Sierra Leone, Article 4(c).
[181] See above, 63.
[182] Additional Protocol I, Article 57(2)(a)(iii).
[183] See eg *Hadžihasanović* Trial Judgment, above note 20, para 45; *Customary International Humanitarian Law*, Rule 14.
[184] Rome Statute, Article 8(2)(b)(iv).

humanitarian law norm.[185] Accordingly, future case-law of the ICC on point should not be taken as a reflection of the international humanitarian law standard. Indeed, it may be that that provision is not even reflective of customary international criminal law on point; rather it goes to the delimitation of the crime for the purposes of the ICC alone. It may be that this higher standard is appropriate for the ICC, which 'does not merely deal with outlawing certain military conduct, but with the criminalization of individual behaviour'.[186] On this view, the inclusion of the word 'clearly' is needed and at any rate 'does not entail a significant new hurdle, since prosecution would in any event be viable only in cases where the proportionality requirement was clearly breached'.[187] To the extent that that position is correct, it should be catered for within prosecutorial discretion rather than as an element of the offence. A prosecutor may have prosecuted only those instances in which it was clear; now, the prosecutor may seek to prosecute only those instances in which it is abundantly clear. Incorporation of such language shifts the standard utilized. For the purposes of this section, the more pressing concern is that the 'clearly excessive' and 'overall' standards will be translated from international criminal law back to international humanitarian law to form the requisite standard of the law of non-international armed conflict, altering the balance between military necessity and humanity found in that rule at present.[188]

A third example relates to forced displacement. The forced displacement of the civilian population, or individual members thereof, is prohibited in international humanitarian law.[189] The prohibition covers both deportation, that is to say, 'the forced displacement of persons by expulsion or other forms of coercion from the area in which they are lawfully present, across a *de jure* state border or, in certain circumstances, a *de facto* border, without grounds permitted under international law',[190] as well as forcible transfer, namely 'a forced removal or displacement of people from one area to another which may take place within the same national borders'.[191] The prohibition on forcible transfer is subject to two exceptions: 'security of the civilians involved' and 'imperative military reasons'.[192] The two exceptions do not apply to the prohibition on deportation, which is absolute.[193] The prohibition on forced displacement, as criminalized in the Rome Statute, is different. The prohibition on deportation is not separated out from the prohibition on forcible transfer and the two exceptions of the security of the civilians involved and imperative military reasons apply to both.[194] This difference should not be translated across to the international humanitarian law arena.

Accordingly, international humanitarian law rules and their associated war crimes are closely related. However, the interpretation of the latter cannot always be taken to

---

[185] von Hebel and Robinson, Crimes, above note 67, 79, 111; R Arnold, 'War Crimes—para. 2(b)(iv)', in O Triffterer (ed), *Commentary on the Rome Statute of the International Criminal Court: Observers' Notes, Article by Article* (Beck, 2008) 338, 339.
[186] D Pfirter, 'Article 8(2)(b)(iv)', in RS Lee (ed), *The International Criminal Court: Elements of Crimes and Rules of Procedure and Evidence* (Transnational, 2001) 148.
[187] R Cryer et al, *An Introduction to International Criminal Law and Procedure* (Cambridge University Press, 2010) 300. See also Arnold, War Crimes, above note 185, 341.
[188] See also the concern expressed by the ICRC at the Rome Conference: A/CONF.183/INF/10, 13 July 1998.
[189] Additional Protocol II, Article 17.
[190] *Prosecutor v Stakić*, IT-97-24-A, Judgment, 22 March 2006, para 278.
[191] *Prosecutor v Simić, Tadić and Zarić*, IT-95-9-T, Judgment, 17 October 2003, para 122.
[192] Additional Protocol II, Article 17; Guiding Principles on Internal Displacement, Principle 6(2).
[193] Additional Protocol II, Article 17.
[194] Article 8(2)(e)(viii).

inform the former. If appropriate care is not taken, interpretations of the war crime could end up narrowing the protections afforded by international humanitarian law. There is some suggestion that this concern may be overstated, or at least that the risk has not yet materialized.[195] That may be true; however, it is too early for any definite conclusions to be reached. Certainly insofar as the law relating to child soldiers is concerned, there does seem to be a generalized assumption that the prohibition is on *active* participation in hostilities rather than *any* participation in hostilities. The broader danger remains that, if states and non-state armed groups realize that they can move beyond the international humanitarian law prohibition to a certain degree without risking prosecution, they will seek to do so, even if such a move constitutes a violation of international humanitarian law.

At another level, even if the international humanitarian law prohibition and the international criminal law proscription are framed in an identical manner, the two may still not be coterminous with one another. A war crime amounts to a *serious* violation of international humanitarian law. A violation of the international humanitarian law rule may thus be committed without it reaching the gravity of a war crime. This is illustrated in the *Delalić* Trial Judgment, with the Trial Chamber considering an allegation of plunder in respect of money and other valuables taken from detainees:

the evidence before the Trial Chamber fails to demonstrate that any property taken from the detainees in the Čelebići prison-camp was of sufficient monetary value for its unlawful appropriation to involve grave consequences for the victims. Accordingly, it is the Trial Chamber's opinion that the offences, as alleged, cannot be considered to constitute such serious violations of international humanitarian law that they fall within the subject matter jurisdiction of the International Tribunal pursuant to Article 1 of the Statute.[196]

The use of international criminal law, which provides the secondary rules, to interpret the primary rules of international humanitarian law also represents a departure from the usual order of things. It may give the impression that 'all behaviour in armed conflict is either a war crime or lawful'.[197] It is also an instance of working backwards, looking at the primary rules through a very particular lens.[198] Resort to international criminal law in this manner may also have the unintended effect of freezing international humanitarian law. Developments in international humanitarian law may take place only when the ICC has an opportunity to pronounce on the matter, and, given the importance of the *nullum crimen sine lege* principle, opportunity for development may be limited.[199] This too would be a potential unintended impact of international criminal law. The concern should be ameliorated by the provision in the Rome Statute which provides that nothing in the Statute 'shall be interpreted as limiting or prejudicing in any way existing or developing rules of international law for purposes other than this Statute'.[200] It remains to be seen whether the provision will indeed satisfy these concerns.

---

[195] Sassòli, Humanitarian Law, above note 171, 117. See also Cryer, Interplay, above note 176, 516–17.
[196] *Prosecutor v Delalić, Mucić, Delić, and Landžo*, IT-96-21-T, Judgment, 16 November 1998, para 1154.
[197] M Sassòli, 'The Implementation of International Humanitarian Law: Current and Inherent Challenges' (2007) 10 *YIHL* 45, 54.
[198] See D Turns, 'At the "Vanishing Point" of International Humanitarian Law: Methods and Means of Warfare in Non-International Armed Conflicts' (2002) 45 *GYIL* 115.
[199] Sassòli, Humanitarian Law, above note 171, 117.
[200] Article 10.

3.2.2 The enforcement function

Dangers also arise with the enforcement function of international criminal law. If criminal prosecutions are brought for violation of ad hoc agreements that are concluded between the parties to the conflict,[201] this may lead to fewer such agreements being concluded. The possibility of criminal prosecution on the basis of ad hoc agreements arose in the *Tadić* Decision on Interlocutory Appeal on Jurisdiction, in which the Appeals Chamber took the view that 'a rule of conventional international law' that was binding on the parties to the conflict at the time of the alleged offence and not in conflict with peremptory norms of international law could form the basis of a criminal prosecution.[202] In practice, however, prosecutions have not taken place in respect of violations of agreements themselves. Rather, agreements have been used in different ways, for example, as a means by which to bring into force certain other treaty provisions which would then form the basis of the prosecution, for their normative content, as evidence of the fact that violations of international humanitarian law attracted criminal sanction, and as evidence of the characterization of the armed conflict.[203] From the perspective of international humanitarian law, the conclusion of ad hoc agreements is to be encouraged, given that, for example, they may bring into play rules over and above those that are otherwise applicable. Accordingly, it may prove a disservice to prosecute their violation unless a clause on criminal responsibility is included to that effect in the agreement. In the specific case of the 22 May 1992 Agreement to which the *Tadić* Decision on Interlocutory Appeal was referring, prosecution of its violation was appropriate given that the Agreement provided: '[e]ach party undertakes, when it is informed, in particular by the ICRC, of any allegation of violations of international humanitarian law, to open an enquiry promptly and pursue it conscientiously, and to take the necessary steps to put an end to the alleged violations or prevent their recurrence *and to punish those responsible* in accordance with the law in force.'[204] However, without a reference of this sort, care should be taken before instituting prosecutions for fear of limiting the conclusion of such agreements in the future.

Ultimately, criminal enforcement of international humanitarian law is immensely useful. However, it is not a cure for all the world's ills: '[t]he success or failure of international humanitarian law must be measured in terms of lives saved and injuries not suffered. It is not measured by the number of prosecutions or the number of convictions.'[205] A final concern, then, is that enforcement through criminal law, whether international or national, will eclipse other forms of enforcement.[206] This would be problematic given the limited reach of criminal mechanisms; after all, international criminal enforcement 'hinges on, and depends upon, the goodwill of states'.[207] In some respects, the enforcement function of international criminal law may

---

[201] On which, see above, 25–8 and below, 124–33, 442–5.
[202] *Tadić* Decision on Interlocutory Appeal on Jurisdiction, above note 5, paras 94 and 143. See generally paras 94–137.
[203] See *Hadžihasanović* Decision on Interlocutory Appeal of Rule 98*bis* Decision, above note 23, para 28 fn 51; *Tadić* Decision on Interlocutory Appeal on Jurisdiction, above note 5, paras 73 and 136. See generally L Vierucci, '"Special Agreements" between Conflicting Parties in the Case-law of the ICTY', in B Swart, A Zahar, and G Sluiter (eds), *The Legacy of the International Criminal Tribunal for the former Yugoslavia* (Oxford University Press, 2011) 401.
[204] Article 5(2) (emphasis added).
[205] WJ Fenrick, 'The Law Applicable to Targeting and Proportionality After Operation Allied Force: A View from the Outside' (2000) 3 *YIHL* 53, 79–80.
[206] Sassòli, Humanitarian Law, above note 171, 117–19.
[207] Cassese, Current Trends, above note 165, 4 (emphasis removed).

prove beneficial. If criminal law proved so successful that it could eclipse resort to belligerent reprisals, that would be cause for celebration. However, criminal enforcement should not eclipse other forms of enforcement, such as by third states, the UN, or NGOs. Equally, it should not prevent the creation of new mechanisms of enforcement. These concerns are very real ones. Parties to the conflict may deprive outside entities from engaging with particular individuals or accessing particular areas for fear that they may be called to testify in later war crimes trials.[208] Negotiating an ad hoc agreement with a fighter could lead to that fighter being considered aware of the existence of a particular international humanitarian law norm leading to the prosecution of the fighter,[209] leading to a decrease in the conclusion of such agreements. To rely exclusively on criminal sanction would be unfortunate, as ultimately '[p]rosecution and punishment of those who violate the law cannot be a substitute for preventing violations. Attention needs to shift from repression of those who violate the law to the area of prevention'.[210]

4. International human rights law

The third means by which the law of non-international armed conflict has emerged has been through resort to international human rights law. A brief history is in order in this respect.

4.1 Applicability of international human rights law

Today, it is widely accepted that international human rights law applies in situations of armed conflict. This is the view expressed in the principal international humanitarian law instruments. For example, the Preamble to Additional Protocol II recalls that 'international instruments relating to human rights offer a basic protection to the human person'.[211] The Cluster Munitions Convention is even more explicit, referring to the Convention on the Rights of Persons with Disabilities in its preamble, and to human rights law in its provision on victim assistance.[212] The principal international human rights law treaties are equally clear. For example, the International Covenant on Civil and Political Rights provides that a state party to the Covenant may derogate from certain of its obligations '[i]n time of public emergency which threatens the life of the nation', a phrase that implicitly includes armed conflict.[213] The consequence of this derogation clause is that non-derogable provisions continue to bind the state in times of armed conflict. Certain other human rights treaties, the African Charter on Human and Peoples' Rights for one, do not contain derogation clauses. In respect of these treaties, no derogation is permitted and the whole host of human rights obligations

---

[208] Sassòli, Humanitarian Law, above note 171, 117–18.
[209] A Clapham, 'The Rights and Responsibilities of Armed Non-State Actors: The Legal Landscape and Issues Surrounding Engagement', Ownership of Norms Project—Toward a Better Protection of Civilians in Armed Conflicts, February 2010, 36.
[210] H Spieker, 'Twenty-five Years after the Adoption of Additional Protocol II: Breakthrough or Failure of Humanitarian Legal Protection' (2001) 4 *YIHL* 129, 165.
[211] Additional Protocol II, Preamble. See also Additional Protocol I, Article 72.
[212] Article 5.
[213] International Covenant on Civil and Political Rights, Article 4. The European Convention of Human Rights, Article 15 and the African Charter on Human and Peoples Rights, Article 27 specifically mention 'war'.

remains applicable in time of armed conflict.[214] As the ICJ put it: 'the protection offered by human rights conventions does not cease in case of armed conflict, save through the effect of provisions for derogation of the kind to be found in Article 4 of the International Covenant on Civil and Political Rights.'[215]

The view that international human rights law continues to apply in time of armed conflict is also accepted by the vast majority of states, a wide range of international courts and tribunals, and other international law bodies.[216] This is the predominant, but not unanimous, view.[217] The applicability of international human rights law to situations of non-international armed conflict is also well accepted. Indeed, some go so far as to suggest that its application to non-international armed conflict is even more pertinent than to international armed conflict,[218] and its application has been accepted by those otherwise sceptical of the applicability of international human rights law to armed conflicts.[219]

In previous years, international humanitarian law and international human rights law were kept separate and there was little by way of interaction between the two.[220] After all, international humanitarian law and international human rights law are different bodies of law, and to describe international humanitarian law as the human rights law of armed conflict is apt to mislead.[221] Thus, the applicability of international human rights law to situations of armed conflict was not always assured. Although the

---

[214] African Commission on Human and Peoples' Rights, *Commission Nationale des Droits de l'Homme et des Libertés v Chad*, No 74/92, 9th Annual Activity Report 1995–6, para 21; African Commission on Human and People's Rights, *Communications 279/03—Sudan Human Rights Organization and The Sudan, 296/05—Centre of Housing Rights and Evictions/The Sudan*, 45th Ordinary Session, 13–27 May 2009, para 167.

[215] *Legal Consequences of the Construction of a Wall in the Occupied Palestinian Territory*, Advisory Opinion [2004] ICJ Rep 136, para 106. See also *Case Concerning Armed Activities on the Territory of the Congo (Democratic Republic of the Congo v Uganda)* [2005] ICJ Rep 168, para 216; *Legality of the Threat or Use of Nuclear Weapons*, Advisory Opinion [1996] ICJ Rep 226, para 25 (on the ICCPR).

[216] See eg *Nuclear Weapons*, above note 215, 226, para 25; *Wall*, above note 215, 136, para 106; *Armed Activities on the Territory of the Congo*, above note 215, para 216; *Commission Nationale des Droits de l'Homme et des Libertés v Chad*, above note 214, para 21; Fragmentation of International Law: Difficulties arising from the Diversification and Expansion of International Law, Report of the Study Group of the International Law Commission, A/CN.4/L.682, 13 April 2006, para 104; Human Rights Committee, General Comment No 31, 'Nature of the General Legal Obligation Imposed on States Parties to the Covenant', CCPR/C/21/Rev.1/Add.13, 2004, para 11. See also the various views expressed in the written and oral pleadings in the *Nuclear Weapons* and *Wall* advisory opinions.

[217] For the opposing view, see Response of the United States to Request for Precautionary Measures—Detainees in Guantanamo Bay, Cuba, 15 April 2002 (2002) 41 *ILM* 1015; MJ Dennis, 'Application of Human Rights Treaties Extraterritorially in Times of Armed Conflict and Military Occupation' (2005) 99 *AJIL* 119; B Bowring, 'Fragmentation, *Lex Specialis* and the Tensions in the Jurisprudence of the European Court of Human Rights' (2009) 14 *JCSL* 485.

[218] Abresch, Human Rights Law of Internal Armed Conflict, above note 78, 746–50; H Krieger, 'A Conflict of Norms: The Relationship between Humanitarian law and Human Rights Law in the ICRC Customary Law Study' (2006) 11 *JCSL* 265, 273–5; C Droege, 'Elective Affinities? Human Rights and Humanitarian Law' (2008) 90 *IRRC* 501, 527; K Watkin, 'Controlling the Use of Force: A Role for Human Rights Norms in Contemporary Armed Conflict' (2004) 98 *AJIL* 1, 25–7.

[219] GIAD Draper, 'Humanitarian Law and Human Rights', in MA Meyer and H McCoubrey (eds), *Reflections on Law and Armed Conflicts: The Selected Works on the Laws of War by the late Professor Colonel GIAD Draper OBE* (Kluwer Law International, 1998) 145, 147 and 148–9.

[220] See eg AH Robertson, 'Humanitarian Law and Human Rights', in C Swinarski (ed), *Studies and Essays on International Humanitarian Law and Red Cross Principles in Honour of Jean Pictet* (ICRC, 1984) 793; R Kolb, 'The Relationship between International Humanitarian Law and Human Rights Law: A Brief History of the 1948 Universal Declaration of Human Rights and the 1949 Geneva Convention' (1998) 38 *IRRC* 409.

[221] See Y Dinstein, 'International Humanitarian Law as *Lex Specialis*', in G Ravasi and GL Beruto (eds), *International Humanitarian Law and Other Legal Regimes: Interplay in Situations of Violence* (Nagard, 2005) 103, 103.

two bodies of law share some of the same purposes, they have differing origins and remain distinct. These positions are well rehearsed and can be set out in brief.[222]

First, international human rights law flourished in the immediate aftermath of the Second World War, with the adoption of the Universal Declaration of Human Rights. It has since been followed by the two International Covenants as well as numerous other treaties, declarations, and the like. International humanitarian law's first flourish took place in the 1860s with the conclusion of the Lieber Code (1863), the 1864 Geneva Convention, and the St Petersburg Declaration on Explosive Projectiles (1868).[223] Second, international human rights law largely developed within the UN system while international humanitarian law developed outside that system, primarily through its guardian, the ICRC. The ICRC was wary of associating itself with the—politicized—UN. For its part, the UN, having outlawed the threat or use of force in its Charter, was concerned about considering the law that applies during war lest it be thought that such outlawry was doomed from the outset. Such was the concern that the International Law Commission, tasked by the UN with codifying and progressively developing international law, felt unable to place the revision of the law of armed conflict on its work agenda despite the urgent need for its revision as evidenced by the Second World War.[224] Indeed, on one view, the very term 'international humanitarian law' has its origins in the reluctance to use the term 'law of war' after the conclusion of the UN Charter.[225]

Third, and most important, whereas international humanitarian law applies as between two or more competing factions engaged in an armed conflict (between states and armed groups or between armed groups), international human rights law regulates the relationship between the state and the individual. International humanitarian law operates on the basis of equality of obligation as between the parties to the conflict;[226] the fundamental premise of international human rights law is the unequal relationship between the governor and the governed. Human rights law also presupposes the capacity of an actor to carry out a range of governmental functions, functions which international humanitarian law does not regulate and many non-state parties would be unable to implement.

Fourth, the two bodies of law differ in their approach to the substance of certain norms because of the different realities that each was primarily crafted to regulate. International human rights law prides itself on the right not to be arbitrarily deprived of life, viewing it as the supreme right on which all others are built.[227] International humanitarian law accepts the killing of combatants and fighters and tolerates the killing of civilians in certain limited circumstances. International humanitarian law balances

---

[222] See eg L Doswald-Beck and S Vité, 'International Humanitarian Law and Human Rights Law' (1993) 33 *IRRC* 94; H-P Gasser, 'International Humanitarian Law and Human Rights Law in Non-international Armed Conflict: Joint Venture or Mutual Exclusion?' (2002) 45 *GYIL* 149.

[223] See D Schindler, 'Human Rights and Humanitarian Law' (1981–2) 31 *American University Law Review* 935, 935–6.

[224] See *1949 Yearbook of the International Law Commission* (UN, 1956) 281, para 18.

[225] T Meron, 'Convergence of International Humanitarian Law and Human Rights Law', in D Warner (ed), *Human Rights and Humanitarian Law* (Martinus Nijhoff, 1997) 97, 98.

[226] See below, 242–4.

[227] Human Rights Committee, *De Guerrero v Colombia*, Communication No R.11/45, 31 March 1982, UN Doc A/37/40, 137, para 13.1; European Court of Human Rights, *McCann and Others v UK*, Application No 18984/91, Judgment, 27 September 1995, para 147; African Commission on Human and People's Rights, *Communications 279/03—Sudan Human Rights Organization and The Sudan, 296/05—Centre of Housing Rights and Evictions/The Sudan*, 45th Ordinary Session 2009, para 146.

military necessity with the dictates of humanity in situations of armed conflict; international human rights law consists of obligations, principally injunctions, which are binding on states.[228]

Given these differences, there was little interaction between the two bodies of law in the period immediately after 1945. Some of the most influential instruments of both bodies were adopted at around the same time, the Universal Declaration of Human Rights was adopted in 1948 and the four Geneva Conventions in 1949. Yet few persons participated in the drafting of both sets of instruments and the impact of the one on the other was minimal.[229] It took until 1968 and the International Conference on Human Rights in Tehran for the two bodies of law to come into close contact with one another.[230] The Conference led to a 'renaissance'[231] of international humanitarian law, which had become stagnant, and provided the 'impetus' for the diplomatic conference that led to the Additional Protocols.[232] The Tehran Conference and subsequent resolutions also 'underscored the close relations between human rights law and international humanitarian law; and they gave formal expression to the concern of the United Nations (UN) for international humanitarian law and its obligation to work for respect for international humanitarian law by parties to an armed conflict'.[233] Ever since the Tehran Conference, there has been greater interaction between international human rights and humanitarian law.[234]

With the benefit of hindsight, the mutual influence of the two sets of rules and the close association between the bodies working with them may be considered unsurprising given that they share similar goals, namely respect for, and dignity of, the human person.[235] The idea of human dignity is at the very heart of international human rights law, human rights being derived from the 'inherent dignity of the human person'.[236] In international humanitarian law, the impact of human dignity can be seen in such concrete prohibitions as 'outrages upon personal dignity', and is infused more broadly throughout that body of law, with the entire body of the law able to be 'traced back to the obligation to respect human dignity'.[237] The Martens clause, for example, a residual clause contained in most humanitarian law instruments, provides that 'in cases not covered by the law in force, the human person remains under the protection of the principles of humanity and the dictates of the public conscience'.[238]

---

[228] Doswald-Beck and Vité, Humanitarian Law and Human Rights Law, above note 222, 95–105.
[229] Gasser, Humanitarian Law and Human Rights Law, above note 222, 152–3; Kolb, Humanitarian Law and Human Rights Law, above note 220.
[230] See above, 44–6.
[231] T Meron, 'The Humanization of Humanitarian Law' (2000) 94 *AJIL* 239, 247.
[232] D Schindler, Human Rights and Humanitarian Law, above note 223, 938. See also Gasser, Humanitarian Law and Human Rights Law, above note 222, 154.
[233] Gasser, ibid, 154.
[234] Doswald-Beck and Vité, Humanitarian Law and Human Rights Law, above note 222, 105; C Droege, 'The Interplay between International Humanitarian Law and International Human Rights Law in Situations of Armed Conflict' (2007) 40 *Israel Law Review* 310, 315–17.
[235] See Robertson, Humanitarian Law and Human Rights, above note 220, 795; Meron, Convergence, above note 225, 100.
[236] ICCPR, Preamble; ICESCR, Preamble.
[237] Gasser, Humanitarian Law and Human Rights Law, above note 222, 155.
[238] See eg Additional Protocol II, Preamble.

4.2 Application of international human rights law

Far more difficult than the applicability of international human rights law to situations of non-international armed conflict is its actual application therein.[239] To introduce human rights into the equation may be to upset the delicate balance between humanity and military necessity that is at play in international humanitarian law. The precise relationship between international human rights law and international humanitarian law is thus still unsettled. International human rights law has been used in situations of non-international armed conflict in a number of different ways, three of which are considered below.

4.2.1 Normative content

International human rights law has been drawn upon to shape the normative content of the international humanitarian law applicable in non-international armed conflict.[240] During the Diplomatic Conference of 1974–7, the Federal Republic of Germany said that '[d]raft Protocol II was designed to establish, in all cases, a minimum standard of humanitarian protection in order to safeguard, in time of armed conflict, fundamental human rights on a level in accordance with the international covenants on human rights'.[241] Italy also opined that '[d]raft Protocol II was closely linked to all the international rules relating to human rights and could contribute to the application of certain ideas which had received increasing support since the adoption' of the Universal Declaration.[242] Thus, the fundamental guarantees clause of Additional Protocol II, which prohibits murder, torture, and the like, and the article on due process guarantees, develop common Article 3 and are inspired by international human rights law.[243]

It is not just international human rights law that has influenced international humanitarian law; the reverse is also true. The non-derogable provisions of the International Covenant on Civil and Political rights 'closely resemble[] the fundamental guarantees codified by humanitarian law treaties',[244] suggesting the influence of the latter on the former. The Convention on the Rights of Persons with Disabilities contains express reference to respect for international humanitarian law,[245] while the Convention for the Protection of All Persons from Enforced Disappearance also contains multiple references to international humanitarian law, and certain of its provisions were influenced by international humanitarian law.[246] More concretely, the Convention on the Rights of the Child requires states parties to 'respect and to ensure respect for rules of international humanitarian law applicable to them in armed conflicts which are relevant to the child'.[247] The Optional Protocol thereto on the Involvement of Children in Armed Conflict, unusually for a human rights instrument, refers to non-state armed groups,

---

[239] See generally N Lubell, 'Challenges in Applying Human Rights Law to Armed Conflict' (2005) 87 *IRRC* 737.
[240] See generally Meron, Humanization, above note 231.
[241] *Official Records*, above note 72, Vol 5, 132, para 26.
[242] Ibid, Vol 8, 223, para 46.
[243] Y Sandoz, C Swinarski, and B Zimmermann (eds), *Commentary on the Additional Protocols of 8 June 1977 to the Geneva Conventions of 12 August 1949* (ICRC, 1987) 1369 and 1397.
[244] Gasser, Humanitarian Law and Human Rights Law, above note 222, 157. Cf common Article 3 with Article 4 of the ICCPR.
[245] Article 11.
[246] Articles 18 and 24(2). See Droege, Interplay, above note 234, 343.
[247] Convention on the Rights of the Child, Article 38(1).

namely that they 'should not, under any circumstances, recruit or use in hostilities persons under the age of 18 years'.[248]

One potential downside of referring to humanitarian law ideas in human rights instruments is that the humanitarian law norm may be inserted into a different context, such context impeding the utility of the norm.[249] This is exemplified by the aforementioned Optional Protocol to the Convention on the Rights of the Child. Insofar as states are concerned, the Optional Protocol contains a prohibition on using children under the age of 18 years to take a *direct part* in hostilities and *compulsorily* recruiting them into their armed forces.[250] Children under the age of 18 years can enter into 'schools operated by or under the control of the armed forces'.[251] This should be compared with the prohibition in respect of non-state armed groups which relates to *all* forms of recruitment and use of children under the age of 18 years.[252] This departs from the principle of equality of obligation of the parties to the conflict, so important for international humanitarian law, by which all parties to the armed conflict are treated alike in terms of their substantive obligations.[253] Departure from this principle along the lines of the Optional Protocol may prove objectionable to non-state armed groups as it purports to create more onerous standards on them as compared with the states against which they are in conflict. Thus, the National Democratic Front of the Philippines (NDFP), in a 2008 letter to UN Secretary-General Ban Ki-Moon, expressed concern that standards are being imposed upon it 'that are not even made absolutely applicable to States'.[254] Another armed group has questioned why the state against which it is fighting is allowed to recruit children under the age of 18 into its military academy.[255]

4.2.2 Interpretation

International human rights law has also been used as an interpretational tool, to interpret provisions of international humanitarian law. International human rights law concepts have been used to define similar concepts in international humanitarian law, as was the case with the definition of torture.[256] The use of torture is prohibited in international humanitarian law, in respect of both states and non-state armed groups. However, a definition of torture is not to be found in international humanitarian law instruments. Torture is defined in international human rights law, in the

---

[248] Optional Protocol to the Convention on the Rights of the Child on the Involvement of Children in Armed Conflict, Article 4(1).
[249] On other difficulties with the international human rights law/international humanitarian law relationship, see Krieger, Conflict of Norms, above note 218; NK Modirzadeh, 'The Dark Sides of Convergence: A Pro-Civilian Critique of the Extraterritorial Application of Human Rights Law in Armed Conflict', in RA Pedrozo (ed), *The War in Iraq: A Legal Analysis* (Volume 86 *International Law Studies*, Naval War College, Newport, 2010) 349.
[250] Articles 1 and 2.
[251] Article 3.
[252] Article 4.
[253] See below, 242–4.
[254] NDFP, Letter to UN Secretary-General Ban Ki-Moon, 24 November 2008.
[255] E Decrey Warner, J Somer, and P Bongard, 'Armed Non-State Actors and Humanitarian Norms: Lessons from the Geneva Call Experience', in B Perrin (ed), *Modern Warfare: Armed Groups, Private Militaries, Humanitarian Organizations, and the Law* (University of British Columbia Press, 2012) 73, 81.
[256] *Prosecutor v Kunarac, Kovac and Vukovic*, IT-96-23-T and IT-96-23/1-T, Judgment, 22 February 2001, paras 465–97.

Convention against Torture, and certain ICTY Trial Chambers have held that the Convention against Torture definition could be used to define torture for the purposes of international humanitarian law.[257]

Resort to international human rights law in this regard can pose certain difficulties. When norms of international human rights law complement those of international humanitarian law, use of the human rights norm is likely rather useful. There may be a lack of precedent in international humanitarian law, or a convergence between the two bodies in terms of 'goals, values and terminology'.[258] However, even at the level of complementary norms, application directly from the one to the other may not be appropriate. Some tailoring of the norm may be needed, for it may be appropriate in one context but inappropriate in another.[259] As the ICTY recognized, 'notions developed in the field of human rights can be transposed in international humanitarian law only if they take into consideration the specificities of the latter body of law',[260] for the two bodies diverge in terms of the identity and role of the actors as well as sanctions for their violation.[261] Thus, in the specific case of the definition of torture, other ICTY Trial Chambers noted that 'the definition of an offence is largely a function of the environment in which it develops' and held that the Convention against Torture definition could only be 'an interpretational aid'.[262]

In the majority of situations, a particular norm will exist both in international human rights law as well as in international humanitarian law. In such instances, the precise relationship between the two norms will have to be ascertained. This is usually done on the basis of the *lex specialis* rule. However, as this term has been understood in different ways,[263] it is of greater utility to focus on the operation of the rule rather than on questions of terminology. Two principles serve as a guide to its operation.[264] The first principle applies in the event of a conflict of norms. In this situation, the specific rule modifies the general rule to the extent of the inconsistency between them. The general rule does not fall away; it remains in the background and is applicable to the extent that it does not conflict with the specific rule. The second principle applies when the norms are consistent with one another but one norm is of greater specificity than the other or is more tailored to the particular circumstances at hand. In this situation, the more specific rule is but an application of the general rule. Although it may be useful to distinguish between these two principles, a firm distinction is difficult to draw and somewhat artificial. It may also be difficult to ascertain the identity of the

---

[257] See eg *Delalić et al* Trial Judgment, above note 196, para 459.
[258] *Kunarac* Trial Judgment, above note 256, para 467.
[259] See Lubell, Challenges, above note 239, 745–6.
[260] *Kunarac* Trial Judgment, above note 256, para 471. See also *Prosecutor v Krnojelac*, IT-97-25-T, Judgment, 15 March 2002, para 181.
[261] *Kunarac* Trial Judgment, above note 256, para 470.
[262] *Kunarac*, ibid, paras 469–70, 482. See generally, S Sivakumaran, 'Torture in International Human Rights and International Humanitarian Law: The Actor and the Ad Hoc Tribunals' (2005) 18 *LJIL* 541.
[263] See A Lindroos, 'Addressing Norm Conflicts in a Fragmented Legal System: The Doctrine of Lex Specialis' (2005) 74 *Nordic Journal of International Law* 27; N Prud'homme, '*Lex Specialis*: Oversimplifying a More Complex and Multifaceted Relationship?' (2007) 40 *Israel Law Review* 356; C McCarthy, 'Legal Conclusion or Interpretive Process? *Lex Specialis* and the Applicability of International Human Rights Standards', in R Arnold and N Quénivet (eds), *International Humanitarian Law and Human Rights Law* (Martinus Nijhoff, 2008) 101; M Milanović, 'A Norm Conflict Perspective on the Relationship between International Humanitarian Law and Human Rights Law' (2009) 14 *JCSL* 459, 473–6.
[264] See generally, *Fragmentation of International Law*, above note 216, paras 56–8.

special rule as compared with the general rule. Nonetheless, it is useful to consider the operation of the two principles.

The first principle relates to the modification of the general rule by the specific rule to the extent of any inconsistency between them. A useful example of the operation of this principle relates to the law on internment. International humanitarian law allows for internment in certain situations.[265] A regional body of human rights law on the other hand, the European Convention on Human Rights, provides for the right to liberty and security of the person and provides for a certain number of limited exceptions to the right, of which internment is not one.[266] Thus, there is a conflict of norms, at least for Council of Europe states, between the rules of international humanitarian law that allow for internment and those of European human rights law that do not. Which of the two constitutes the general rule and which the specific rule thus needs to be identified.

As the rules of international humanitarian law on point were tailored for the specific situation—the Fourth Geneva Convention providing that '[t]he internment or placing in assigned residence of protected persons may be ordered only if the security of the Detaining Power makes it absolutely necessary'[267]—the international humanitarian law rules on point constitute the *leges speciales*. It is those rules that are better tailored to meet the specificities of armed conflicts, with the security concerns that arise in such times and which do not exist to the same extent in times of peace. Likewise, Article 21 of the Third Geneva Convention provides for the internment of prisoners of war, an instance with respect to which human rights law does not specifically legislate. Those provisions accordingly constitute the *leges speciales* in relation to the more general rules of human rights law on liberty and security of the person.[268] This is not to suggest that human rights law on point disappears. Rather, it continues to apply save for the inconsistency. Thus, the right to liberty and security of the person continues to apply in times of armed conflict subject to the exceptions provided for in international humanitarian law.

However, in the *Al-Jedda* case, the European Court of Human Rights took a different view. It held that, as international humanitarian law does not contain an obligation to intern, providing only for a power to do so, and the European Convention provides for an obligation to respect the liberty and security of the person, a conflict of norms does not arise.[269] States may satisfy their obligations under both international humanitarian law and human rights law by not interning persons. While sound as a matter of formal legal argumentation, the approach effectively reads out any power on the part of states to intern persons through international humanitarian law, a far-reaching and controversial proposition.[270] Indeed, the Court itself seemed to acknowledge this when it noted that, in its view, internment pursuant to the Fourth Geneva Convention was 'a measure of last resort', seemingly leaving open the possibility of internment.[271]

The second principle relates to the application of the more specific rule as a detailed or tailored version of the general rule. In this situation, a conflict does not exist between

---

[265] See below, 301–5.   [266] ECHR, Article 5(1).   [267] Article 42.
[268] Cf Milanović, Norm Conflict, above note 263, 474–6.
[269] *Al-Jedda v the United Kingdom*, Application No 27021/08, Judgment, 7 July 2011, para 107. The issue was framed as a law of belligerent occupation issue. However, it has equal resonance for the law of non-international armed conflict.
[270] See J Pejic, 'The European Court of Human Rights' *Al-Jedda* Judgment: The Oversight of International Humanitarian Law' (2011) 93 *IRRC* 837.
[271] *Al-Jedda*, above note 269, para 107.

the two rules. Rather, one provision is the more detailed version of the other or the more appropriate in the circumstances. Sometimes, international humanitarian law will offer greater protection, for example in the area of the prohibition of medical experimentation. More pertinent for this chapter, which considers the way in which the law of non-international armed conflict has developed, in part by drawing upon international human rights law, are the instances in which international human rights law offers greater protection than international humanitarian law. An instance in this regard is the prohibition on sentence and execution prior to a fair trial. The International Covenant on Civil and Political Rights provides for a lengthy list of fair trial guarantees.[272] For its part, common Article 3 requires the provision of 'judicial guarantees which are recognized as indispensable by civilized peoples'. A list of the required guarantees is not provided. Additional Protocol II contains such a list but that list is not self-contained, referring as it does to 'all necessary rights and means of defence'.[273] In order to interpret that clause, it becomes necessary to turn to the relevant rules of international human rights law, which form the more specific rules on point. In this situation, a conflict does not exist between the relevant rules of international human rights law and the associated rules of international humanitarian law. One contains a detailed body of regulation; the other, somewhat vague standards. In order to give content to the general rule, resort needs to be had to its more specific counterpart. Precisely how this relationship plays out in the situation of trials is considered in Chapter 8.[274]

The principle operates at its clearest when there is a phrase in the relevant provision to which the principle can attach. An example in this regard is the right to life. Article 6 of the International Covenant on Civil and Political Rights protects against the arbitrary deprivation of life. This begs the question of when a deprivation of life will be considered arbitrary. Does the use of nuclear weapons in armed conflict, for example, constitute an arbitrary deprivation of life? The ICJ has considered this issue:

In principle, the right not arbitrarily to be deprived of one's life applies also in hostilities. The test of what is an arbitrary deprivation of life, however, then falls to be determined by the applicable *lex specialis*, namely the law applicable in armed conflict which is designed to regulate the conduct of hostilities. Thus, whether a particular loss of life, through the use of a certain weapon in warfare, is to be considered an arbitrary deprivation of life contrary to Article 6 of the Covenant, can only be decided by reference to the law applicable in armed conflict and not deduced from the terms of the Covenant itself.[275]

In this instance, the relevant rules of international humanitarian law constituted the *leges speciales* and so trumped, to the extent of the inconsistency, the equivalent rule found in international human rights law. The ICJ is not suggesting that the body of international humanitarian law as such always constitutes the *lex specialis*.[276] The ICJ was considering one particular right—the right to life—and one particular aspect of that right—its compatibility with the use of nuclear weapons. It does not follow that the entire body of international human rights law is the *lex generalis* and the full corpus of international humanitarian law the *lex specialis*. Generalizations cannot be made at

---

[272] ICCPR, Articles 14–15.   [273] Additional Protocol II, Article 6(2)(a).
[274] Below, 306–10.   [275] *Nuclear Weapons*, above note 215, 226, para 25.
[276] It is true that the Court stated in *Wall*, above note 215, para 106: 'In order to answer the question put to it, the Court will have to take into consideration both these branches of international law, namely human rights law and, as *lex specialis*, international humanitarian law.' However, the words 'In order to answer the question put to it' suggest the context-specific nature of the statement.

the level of the overarching body; it comes down to an analysis of the individual rule.[277] The competing rules have to be identified and the specificity between them ascertained in relation to the particular situation at hand. Should the relevant rule of international human rights law—or, for that matter, any other body of law, such as international environmental law—contain the more specific rule, it would modify the general rule of international humanitarian law to the extent of the inconsistency between them. However, a word of caution is in order in the use of international human rights law or another body of international law in this manner. Absence of a norm in international humanitarian law cannot automatically be filled by a norm present in another body of international law such as international human rights law, as silence cannot always be equated with a gap in protection. Sometimes, the silence may be deliberate.[278] Equally, the presumption that the norm that grants greater protection is the more specific norm and can thus be applied by way of the *lex specialis* rule, while attractive, is not always entirely accurate.[279] The precise level of protection to be found in international humanitarian law may have been intended for various reasons.

This second principle is of particular utility when there is a 'gap' in international humanitarian law. The existence of a gap also illustrates the care that needs to be taken in filling it. The obligation to investigate certain losses of life is illustrative both of such a gap and the requisite care. Although a duty to investigate losses of life at the hands of state forces does not appear in the text of the principal human rights treaties, it has been read into certain of its provisions. The regional human rights courts, for example, have held that the obligation to protect the right to life coupled with a state's duty to secure convention rights implies that 'there should be some form of effective official investigation when individuals have been killed as a result of the use of force'.[280] The investigation is required to be prompt, thorough, and effective and should be undertaken by an independent and impartial body.[281] An investigation seeks to avoid the creation of a climate of impunity, which so often provides the setting for further violations. It also 'allows authorities to learn from any mistake and avoid violations in the future'.[282] The obligation to investigate does not cease just because the loss of life occurred during a military operation: 'neither the prevalence of violent armed clashes nor the high incidence of fatalities can displace the obligation'.[283] Although the European Court of Human Rights has led the way in this regard, other regional bodies have made similar pronouncements and the work of regional institutions has had an important influence on international human rights law. By contrast, the general obligation to investigate all losses of life does not form part of the corpus of

---

[277] G Gaggioli and R Kolb, 'A Right to Life in Armed Conflicts? The Contribution of the European Court of Human Rights' (2007) 37 *Israel Yearbook on Human Rights* 115, 119–20; Krieger, Conflict of Norms, above note 218, 271; Milanović, Norm Conflict, above note 263, 462–5.

[278] LM Olson, 'Practical Challenges of Implementing the Complementarity between International Humanitarian and Human Rights Law—Demonstrated by the Procedural Regulation of Internment in Non-International Armed Conflict' (2007–9) 40 *Case Western Reserve Journal of International Law* 437, 454.

[279] See Milanović, Norm Conflict, above note 263.

[280] *Isayeva v Russia*, Application No 57950/00, Judgment, 24 February 2005, para 209. See also *Myrna Mack Chang v Guatemala*, Ser C No 101, 25 November 2003, para 157; *Commission Nationale des Droits de l'Homme et des Libertés v Chad*, No 74/92, 9th Annual Activity Report 1995–6, para 22.

[281] See eg General Comment No 31, above note 216, para 15; *Isayeva*, above note 280, paras 209–14; *Varnava and others v Turkey*, Application No 16064/90 and others, Judgment, 18 September 2009, para 191.

[282] L Doswald-Beck, 'The Right to Life in Armed Conflict: Does International Humanitarian Law Provide All the Answers?' (2006) 88 *IRRC* 881, 887.

[283] *Kaya v Turkey* [1998] ECHR para 91.

international humanitarian law. In certain specified situations—such as in the case of deaths of prisoners of war,[284] or in relation to war crimes[285]—there is a duty to investigate, but no general duty to investigate all losses of life exists. There are certainly cogent reasons as to why international humanitarian law should contain such a requirement, and of late, there is some authority for the existence of such a general duty in certain situations.[286] Indeed, it has been suggested that 'a bona fide interpretation of IHL must come to the same conclusion—that is, any suspected violation of IHL needs to be properly investigated for the reasons stated by the [human rights] treaty bodies'.[287] However, there are also cogent practical reasons why international humanitarian law cannot contain a duty to investigate all losses of life, given the reality of armed conflicts. It would seem, then, that international humanitarian law is moving in this direction but that it is not there just yet. Until such time, international human rights law fills the gap to the extent appropriate.[288]

4.2.3 Direct regulation

More controversially, human rights law has been used directly to regulate non-international armed conflict rather than to inform regulation through international humanitarian law. This 'human rights law of non-international armed conflict' is primarily a construct of scholars and has flourished in the literature in recent years.[289] Proponents of the idea point to the judgments of the European Court of Human Rights in *Isayeva* and *Isayeva, Yusupova and Bazayeva* for support.[290] Whether the European Court considered the situation in the two *Isayeva* cases to be a non-international armed conflict or, rather, a state of internal tensions and disturbances is unclear. It is equally unclear whether the Court was implicitly applying international humanitarian law or, rather, applying human rights law, given the lack of explicit pronouncement on point and the contradictory indications within the judgment. For example, while the European Court used the language of international humanitarian law, speaking of 'legitimate targets', 'disproportionality in the weapons used', and 'illegal armed insurgency',[291] it also referred to 'law-enforcement' and being 'outside wartime'.[292] Furthermore, on occasion, the European Court of Human Rights has considered, and applied, issues of international humanitarian law, namely the notion of direct participation in hostilities and the law of surrender in the context of alleged violations of the European Convention.[293] Nevertheless, the predominant view is that

---

[284] Third Geneva Convention, Article 121.
[285] See MN Schmitt, 'Investigating Violations of International Law in Armed Conflict' (2011) 2 *Harvard National Security Journal* 31, 35–48.
[286] *Public Committee Against Torture in Israel*, above note 52, para 40. See also Report of the Special Rapporteur on Extrajudicial, Summary or Arbitrary Executions, E/CN.4/2006/53, 8 March 2006, para 34.
[287] Doswald-Beck, Right to Life, above note 282, 889.
[288] See Droege, Interplay, above note 234, 352. But cf Schmitt, Investigating Violations, above note 285, 51–6.
[289] See, in particular, Abresch, Human Rights Law of Internal Armed Conflict, above note 78; FF Martin, 'Using International Human Rights Law for Establishing a Unified Use of Force Rule in the Law of Armed Conflict' (2001) 64 *Saskatchewan Law Review* 347.
[290] *Isayeva, Yusupova and Bazayeva v Russia*, Application Nos 57947/00, 57948/00 and 57949/00, Judgment, 24 February 2005; *Isayeva*, above note 280.
[291] *Isayeva, Yusupova and Bazayeva*, above note 290, paras 175 and 197; *Isayeva*, above note 280, para 180 respectively.
[292] *Isayeva*, ibid, para 191.
[293] See *Korbely v Hungary*, Application No 9174/02, Judgment, 19 September 2008, paras 86–94.

the European Court was directly applying human rights law in these cases to regulate a non-international armed conflict,[294] a suggestion which is strengthened by a Separate Opinion in a related case.[295] Furthermore, in a later case, the Grand Chamber of the European Court stated that Article 2 of the European Convention 'must be interpreted in so far as possible in light of the general principles of international law, including the rules of international humanitarian law which play an indispensable and universally-accepted role in mitigating the savagery and inhumanity of armed conflict'.[296] On this view, it is human rights law that directly regulates the situation, albeit as interpreted by international humanitarian law.

The 'human rights law of non-international armed conflict' approach can be usefully broken down into two schools of thought. The 'unification' school takes the view that there should be a unified body of law applicable in situations of peace and non-international armed conflict, regardless of the intensity of that conflict.[297] The 'threshold' school seeks to split up the law of non-international armed conflict depending on the intensity of the violence. A non-international armed conflict of a low intensity would be regulated by international human rights law; a high-intensity non-international armed conflict would be governed by international humanitarian law; the separating threshold would be that of Additional Protocol II.[298] Both schools are premised on common ideas, namely that there is little by way of international humanitarian law that regulates non-international armed conflict,[299] that international humanitarian law suffers from a lack of specificity,[300] that states rarely accept that an armed conflict is taking place thus denying the very applicability of international humanitarian law,[301] and that the relationships inherent in a non-international armed conflict can be considered akin to those present in human rights law.[302]

The use of international human rights law in this manner is of a different order to the other uses considered above. Rather than utilizing human rights law to influence or interpret international humanitarian law, human rights law is being posited as a means of directly regulating non-international armed conflict. This would be a fundamental shift in the regulation of non-international armed conflict.[303]

---

[294] See Abresch, Human Rights Law of Internal Armed Conflict, above note 78; Krieger, Conflict of Norms, above note 218, 275; Gaggioli and Kolb, Right to Life, above note 277, 124–7; C Tomuschat, 'Human Rights and International Humanitarian Law' (2010) 21 *EJIL* 15, 19–20.

[295] *Abuyeva and Others v Russia*, Application No 27065/05, Judgment, 2 December 2010, Concurring Opinion of Judge Malinverni, joined by Judges Rozakis and Spielmann.

[296] *Varnava and Others v Turkey*, Application Nos 16064/90 and others, Judgment, 18 September 2009, para 185.

[297] Abresch, Human Rights Law of Internal Armed Conflict, above note 78; Martin, Using International Human Rights Law, above note 289.

[298] See, to varying degrees, Gaggioli and Kolb, Right to Life, above note 277, 158–62; D Kretzmer, 'Rethinking the Application of IHL in Non-International Armed Conflicts' (2009) 42 *Israel Law Review* 8, 42. See also C Kreß, 'Some Reflections on the International Legal Framework Governing Transnational Armed Conflict' (2010) 15 *JCSL* 245, 262.

[299] Abresch, Human Rights Law of Internal Armed Conflict, above note 78, 746–50; Lubell, Challenges, above note 239, 746. See also Outcome of the Expert Consultation on the Issue of Protecting the Human Rights of Civilians in Armed Conflict: Report of the Office of the United Nations High Commissioner for Human Rights, A/HRC/11/31, 4 June 2009, para 24.

[300] Abresch, Human Rights Law of Internal Armed Conflict, above note 78, 746–7; Krieger, Conflict of Norms, above note 218, 274.

[301] Abresch, Human Rights Law of Internal Armed Conflict, above note 78, 756; Krieger, Conflict of Norms, above note 218, 275.

[302] Krieger, ibid, 275.

[303] The use of human rights monitoring mechanisms to enforce the law of non-international armed conflict is considered in Chapter 10.

There is, however, a fundamental difference between international human rights law and international humanitarian law that makes the direct regulation of non-international armed conflict by international human rights law rather difficult. The difference is the principle of equality of obligation of belligerents. That principle is fundamental to international humanitarian law,[304] including the international humanitarian law of non-international armed conflict.[305] The principle holds that all parties to an armed conflict have the same rights and obligations as a matter of law, irrespective of the 'justness' of the cause; the idea being that if one side is not bound by particular rules, the side that is bound will not comply with them. Given that, traditionally, international human rights law governs the relationship between the state and the individual, with the individual considered the beneficiary of the right and the state the guarantor of the obligation, international human rights law does not contain an idea corresponding to that of equality of belligerents. As the *Kunarac* Trial Chamber observed, 'international humanitarian law purports to apply equally to and expressly bind all parties to the armed conflict whereas, in contrast, human rights law generally applies to only one party, namely the state involved, and its agents'.[306] Difficulties arise, then, in the regulation of non-international armed conflict directly through international human rights law. If international human rights law is not binding on the non-state armed group, then regulation through human rights law would be inappropriate as it would be binding on only one of the parties to the conflict, with the other side being left unregulated by human rights law; in a conflict between armed groups, neither side would be regulated through human rights law.

The traditional view of human rights law was that it was binding on the state alone and not the non-state armed group. In recent years, there has been suggestion that, in certain situations, non-state armed groups may have human rights obligations.[307] A number of theoretical bases have been put forward to explain how and why non-state armed groups may be bound by international human rights law: (1) equality of obligation—if one party is bound by an obligation, so too must the other side be bound;[308] (2) as intrinsic principles, whether expressed as a 'demand of the international community',[309] as 'one of the great principles of international law' observable in 'borderline situations outside the normal configurations of inter-State relationships',[310] or as an 'integral part of [the] international order for the maintenance and reestablishment

---

[304] H Lauterpacht, 'The Limits of the Operation of the Law of War' (1953) 30 *BYIL* 206; C Greenwood, 'The Relationship between *Jus ad Bellum* and *Jus in Bello*' (1983) 9 *Review of International Studies* 221. See below, 242–4.

[305] See ICRC, *Commentary on the Additional Protocols*, above note 243, 1345; F Bugnion, '*Jus ad Bellum*, *Jus in Bello* and Non-International Armed Conflicts' (2003) 6 *YIHL* 167; M Sassòli, '*Ius ad Bellum* and *Ius in Bello*: The Separation between the Legality of the Use of Force and Humanitarian Rules to be Respected in Warfare—Crucial or Outdated?', in MN Schmitt and J Pejić (eds), *International Law and Armed Conflict: Exploring the Faultlines, Essays in Honour of Yoram Dinstein* (Martinus Nijhoff, 2007) 241, 254–7.

[306] *Kunarac* Trial Judgment, above note 256, para 470.

[307] See, in particular, A Clapham, *Human Rights Obligations of Non-State Actors* (Oxford University Press, 2006) Chapter 7.

[308] C Tomuschat, 'The Applicability of Human Rights Law to Insurgent Movements', in H Fischer et al (eds), *Krisensicherung und Humanitarer Schutz—Crisis Management and Humanitarian Protection: Festschrift für Dieter Fleck* (Berliner Wissenschaftsverlag, Berlin, 2004) 573, 576.

[309] See eg Report of the Special Rapporteur on extrajudicial, summary or arbitrary executions, Mission to Sri Lanka, E/CN.4/2006/53/Add.5, 27 March 2006, para 25; Report of four Special Rapporteurs, Mission to Lebanon and Israel, A/HRC/2/7, 2 October 2006, para 19.

[310] Tomuschat, Applicability, above note 308, 586–7.

of peace and security';³¹¹ (3) obligations as the correlative of rights³¹²—if non-state armed groups benefit from human rights, they must also be subject to obligations; and (4) through effective control over territory.³¹³ This latter explanation has attracted the most support and represents, by some margin, the predominant view to date.³¹⁴ It is sometimes expressed as an *expectation* of the international community,³¹⁵ while at other times as a *binding legal obligation* on the part of the non-state armed group.³¹⁶ To these theoretical bases may be added, rather more simply, holding non-state armed groups to their commitments. Non-state armed groups issue unilateral declarations, draw up charters, conclude bilateral agreements, and the like, on human rights matters. There is a fair amount of practice on point, from states and non-state armed groups themselves,³¹⁷ and these can be considered binding on the non-state armed group, an issue that is discussed in Chapter 4.³¹⁸

By and large, the view that non-state armed groups have human rights obligations has been expressed by UN bodies and truth commissions. This should come as no surprise for it is often at this level that novel concepts are first introduced before later being accepted by states. In addition, states themselves have sometimes taken the position that non-state armed groups are bound by human rights obligations. For example, Guatemala argued before the Guatemalan Commission for Historical Clarification that 'it was unacceptable to appraise the conduct of their security forces by

---

³¹¹ Institut de Droit International, The Application of International Humanitarian Law and Fundamental Human Rights, in Armed Conflicts in which Non-State Entities are Parties (Session of Berlin, 1999) Article III.

³¹² D Fleck, 'Humanitarian Protection Against Non-State Actors', in JA Fowein et al (eds), *Verhandeln für den Frieden—Negotiating for Peace: Liber Amicorum Tono Eitel* (Springer, Berlin, 2003) 69, 79.

³¹³ Report of the Special Rapporteur on extrajudicial, summary or arbitrary executions, E/CN.4/2005/7, 22 December 2004, para 76.

³¹⁴ The approach taken by the Special Rapporteur on extrajudicial, summary or arbitrary executions, ibid, has been adopted in later reports of the Special Procedures mechanisms of the Human Rights Council. See eg Human Rights in Palestine and Other Occupied Arab Territories, Report of the United Nations Fact-Finding Mission on the Gaza Conflict, A/HRC/12/48, 25 September 2009, paras 305 and 1370; Report of four special procedures mechanisms, Mission to Lebanon and Israel, A/HRC/2/7, para 19; Report of the Special Rapporteur on extrajudicial, summary or arbitrary executions, Mission to Sri Lanka, E/CN.4/2006/53/Add.5, 27 March 2006, paras 26–7; Human Rights Situation in Palestine and Other Occupied Arab Territories, A/HRC/10/22, 29 May 2009, para 22; Report of the Secretary-General's Panel of Experts on Accountability in Sri Lanka, 31 March 2011, para 181. The territorial control approach also benefits from academic support. See eg NS Rodley, 'Can Armed Opposition Groups Violate Human Rights?', in KE Mahoney and P Mahoney, *Human Rights in the Twenty-first Century* (Martinus Nijhoff, 1993) 297, 298, 300, 313; Zegveld, *Armed Opposition Groups*, above note 33, 149; C Ryngaert, 'Human Rights Obligations of Armed Groups' [2008] *RBDI* 355, 361, 375, and 380–2.

³¹⁵ Report of the Special Rapporteur on extrajudicial, summary or arbitrary executions, E/CN.4/2005/7, 22 December 2004, para 76; Report of four special procedures mechanisms, Mission to Lebanon and Israel, A/HRC/2/7, para 19; Report of the Special Rapporteur on extrajudicial, summary or arbitrary executions, Mission to Sri Lanka, E/CN.4/2006/53/Add.5, 27 March 2006, paras 26–7.

³¹⁶ Report on the Gaza Conflict, above note 314, paras 305 and 1370; Human Rights Situation in Palestine and Other Occupied Arab Territories, above note 314, para 22; Report of the International Commission of Inquiry to investigate all alleged violations of international human rights law in the Libyan Arab Jamahiriya, A/HRC/17/44, 1 June 2011, para 72.

³¹⁷ For the practice, see Chapter 4. See also Fleck, Humanitarian Protection, above note 312, 69; Clapham, *Human Rights Obligations of Non-State Actors*, above note 307, 281–9; A Clapham, 'Human Rights Obligations of Non-State Actors in Conflict Situations' (2006) 88 *IRRC* 491.

³¹⁸ See also A Roberts and S Sivakumaran, 'Lawmaking by Non-State Actors: Engaging Armed Groups in the Creation of International Humanitarian Law' (2012) 37 *Yale Journal of International Law* 107.

stricter standards than the conduct of the guerrilla forces'.[319] Similarly, the Armed Forces of the Philippines are reported to have 'regularly lodge[d] complaints about human rights violations by the rebel forces with the independent Human Rights Commission'.[320] More prevalent are bilateral agreements between a state and an opposing non-state armed group in which the agreement reconfirms that both parties have human rights obligations. Given that states are one of the parties to these agreements, they may be considered to be assenting to the idea of human rights obligations on the part of certain non-state armed groups. The practice on point is considered in Chapter 4.[321] At this stage, it suffices to note that, on the basis of this practice, a number of states—at the very least El Salvador, Guatemala, Liberia, Nepal, Papua New Guinea, the Philippines, Sierra Leone, and Sudan—can be considered to have taken the view that certain non-state armed groups do indeed have obligations under international human rights law, at least when the conflict has been taking place for a certain duration and reached a certain intensity.

The lack of equality of obligation in international human rights law is not, then, an insurmountable obstacle to regulation through international human rights law. There is a fair amount of practice to suggest that, at least in certain limited situations, armed groups have obligations pursuant to international human rights law. More problematic is the fact that the method by which international human rights law binds non-state armed groups may not fit with the situations in which human rights law purports to regulate non-international armed conflict. As indicated above, the most accepted means by which human rights law is considered binding on non-state armed groups is through territorial control. When armed groups are in effective control over a certain quantum of territory, human rights obligations are considered to attach to them. Below this threshold, armed groups may not be under an obligation to comply with human rights obligations. Yet, human rights law purports to regulate non-international armed conflict in precisely the reverse situation, either below the level of an Additional Protocol II armed conflict, when the non-state armed group does not exercise territorial control, or in all situations.[322] Without consideration of the differences between international human rights law and international humanitarian law, application of the former may defeat the purpose for which it is intended to be used, or make it less useful than would be the case were it tailored to fit the particularities of the situation.

In relation to the suggestion that international humanitarian law would apply in an Additional Protocol II conflict and international human rights law in a conflict below the level of Additional Protocol II,[323] as will be seen in Chapter 5, the difference between the two sorts of conflict is not at all large. In particular, vast amounts of territory need not be controlled by the armed group in order to trigger Additional Protocol II. Rather, what is required is that the armed group exercise such territorial control as to enable it to carry out sustained and concerted military operations and to implement the Protocol.[324] Furthermore, in situations in which the armed group exercises control over large swathes of a state's territory, international human rights law may be better placed to regulate the situation in addition to international humanitarian law. In order for armed groups to control territory at that level, the conflict has

---

[319] Tomuschat, Applicability, above note 308, 576.
[320] Koojmans, Shadowland, above note 4, 245 fn 43.
[321] See especially below, 129–32.   [322] See above, 94.
[323] Gaggioli and Kolb, Right to Life, above note 277, 158–62; Kreß, Transnational Armed Conflict, above note 298, 262; Kretzmer, Non-International Armed Conflicts, above note 298, 42.
[324] See below, 185–7.

usually reached a stage at which, while fighting continues, a certain 'peace' exists in parts of the territory. The situation in a large part of the territory under the control of the armed group will thus be normalized to a certain degree. In that situation, international humanitarian law will continue to regulate the relations between the parties to the armed conflict, whereas international human rights law will, at least on a *de facto* basis, govern the way in which the non-state armed group treats persons under its control. The LTTE control of the north and east of Sri Lanka in the late 1990s and early 2000s, the Fuerzas Armadas Revolucionarias de Colombia (FARC) control of a sizeable part of Colombia following the 1998 cession of territory by the Government, and the SPLM control over south Sudan in the 2000s, are but three examples of this relatively 'normalized' situation. Fighting continued in all three states; however, there was also a largely normalized, albeit abnormal, situation in tracts of the territory under the LTTE, FARC, and SPLM control. In sum, the Additional Protocol II standard is not the appropriate one by which to divide human rights law from international humanitarian law as the applicable law.

Furthermore, it is not immediately apparent why international human rights law *should* directly regulate non-international armed conflict. Direct regulation of non-international armed conflict through international human rights law is premised on the idea that there is a lack of content and specificity on the part of international humanitarian law.[325] This explains why international human rights law is suggested to regulate non-international armed conflicts but not international armed conflicts.[326] However, this premise is open to challenge. As will be seen in Part II, there is a substantial body of law that regulates non-international armed conflicts. Although the applicability of some of the rules may be open to question, the vast majority of them have been accepted by states. The need for regulation through international human rights law is often suggested for the law of targeting in particular.[327] Yet, this is an area in which international humanitarian law offers detailed rules. The situation is often described as if it was 1977 and Additional Protocol II had just been concluded with its minimal rules on the means and methods of warfare.[328] Yet, there is customary international humanitarian law on point, and even if the Customary International Humanitarian Law study may be faulted, it cannot be criticized for holding that the principal rules on targeting apply to non-international armed conflict. This is a position that has been recognized by courts and tribunals, influential bodies, and, most importantly, states and non-state armed groups, in many cases years before the study was concluded.[329] Furthermore, it would be difficult, if not impossible, to fight an armed conflict exclusively under an international human rights law paradigm. This is not to suggest

---

[325] See above, 94.
[326] Abresch, Human Rights Law of Internal Armed Conflict, above note 78, 746; Droege, Elective Affinities, above note 218, 527; C Tomuschat, 'Human Rights and International Humanitarian Law' (2010) 21 *EJIL* 15, 20.
[327] See eg Abresch, Human Rights Law of Internal Armed Conflict, above note 78; M Sassòli and LM Olson, 'The Relationship between International Humanitarian and Human Rights Law Where it Matters: Admissible Killing and Internment of Fighters in Non-International Armed Conflicts' (2008) 90 *IRRC* 599.
[328] See eg the description in Abresch, Human Rights Law of Internal Armed Conflict, above note 78, 746–50; Lubell, Challenges, above note 239, 746; A Paulus and M Vashakmadze, 'Asymmetrical War and the Notion of Armed Conflict—A Tentative Conceptualization' (2009) 91 *IRRC* 95, 112; 'Outcome of the Expert Consultation on the Issue of Protecting the Human Rights of Civilians in Armed Conflict: Report of the Office of the United Nations High Commissioner for Human Rights', A/HRC/11/31, 4 June 2009, para 24.
[329] See Chapter 4.

that international human rights law has nothing to offer. As this section has shown, it may be helpful in a number of different ways. However, there should not be a rush to judgement that international human rights law holds the answer to all the problems.

5. Conclusion

The period since the mid-1990s has witnessed a wholesale transformation in the regulation of non-international armed conflict. Prior to the mid-1990s, there existed relatively little by way of applicable conventional and customary international law. Today there exists a substantial body of international law—conventional and customary alike—that governs non-international armed conflicts. This body has developed along three principal lines. First, the international humanitarian law of non-international armed conflict has been modelled on, and assimilated to, the international humanitarian law of international armed conflict. The international humanitarian law of international armed conflict is considered the high watermark of legal regulation, the pinnacle to which the international humanitarian law of non-international armed conflict should aspire. Second, the law of non-international armed conflict has been elaborated through international criminal law, which has filled in some of its substantive content. Third, it has drawn on international human rights law. The impact of these three approaches is that, today, international criminal law and international human rights law have become inextricably linked with international humanitarian law in the regulation of non-international armed conflict. Together, these three approaches have led to the creation of a 'law of non-international armed conflict'.

The law developed along these three lines primarily because of the resistance of states to the direct regulation of non-international armed conflict through international humanitarian law. Thus, it was only through these creative means that the law could be developed. States have been far less reluctant to regulate the conduct of international armed conflict; thus, historically, that branch of law has been more advanced than its non-international counterpart. In light of the criticism of the international/non-international armed conflict distinction and the advantages of a uniform body of international humanitarian law, modelling on the law of international armed conflict made considerable sense. Likewise, in the period between 1949 and the mid-1990s, the development of international human rights law gained far greater traction than did the international humanitarian law of non-international armed conflict. Given the similarities between international human rights law and the 'Geneva' aspects of international humanitarian law, and the existence of working enforcement mechanisms, international human rights law proved attractive in the regulation of non-international armed conflict. The huge growth of international criminal law since the mid-1990s, coupled with the close relationship between international criminal law and international humanitarian law, meant that that body, too, proved useful in regulating non-international armed conflict.

However, each of these approaches suffers from certain limitations and gives rise to certain difficulties. This is due, primarily, to the existing focus on the similarities between international armed conflicts and non-international armed conflicts, and between international humanitarian law on the one side and international criminal law and international human rights law on the other. Insufficient attention has been paid to the differences between each of them. The primary difference between an international and a non-international armed conflict is the actors that take part in them. The difference is obvious, yet the implications of this difference have not been followed through. The differing actors involved in the two types of armed conflict suggest that, at the very least, certain legal norms cannot be transposed directly from the international armed conflict to the non-international armed conflict without some modification. Translation and not transplantation is in order.

The differences between international humanitarian law on the one hand and international criminal law and international human rights law on the other also pose certain difficulties. International criminal law gives rise to individual criminal responsibility and, accordingly, certain provisions of war crimes law are interpreted in a narrower fashion than their international humanitarian law counterparts. If care is not taken, this narrower reading of a war crime will replace the broader interpretation of the international humanitarian law rule. Complexities also arise in the use of international human rights law. International human rights law was originally designed to govern the state–individual relationship, with the state the bearer of the obligation and the individual the possessor of the right. If international human rights law is to be applied directly in situations of non-international armed conflict, this vertical relationship will require re-thinking.

These differences do not suggest that the existing approaches of regulation by analogy and resort to other bodies of international law have been misplaced, nor do they call for a wholesale transformation of the applicable law. They do, however, require a certain care to be taken before moving from the one to the other. They also require analysis in order to identify whether there are gaps in need of regulation. Resort would also be had to other areas of the law which may inform the situation. More generally, understanding of the workings of non-state armed groups would be developed and greater regard would be had to the practice of non-international armed conflicts in order to establish whether or not a particular rule 'worked'. All this is considered, as appropriate, in Part II on the substantive law of non-international armed conflict and in Part III on moving forward.

4
The Sources of the Law of Non-International Armed Conflict

1. Introduction

The law of non-international armed conflict is part of public international law. Accordingly, the sources of the law of non-international armed conflict are the same as those of general public international law. They comprise treaties, custom, and general principles, and as a subsidiary means for determining the law, judicial decisions and the writings of publicists.[1] In addition to these well-accepted sources and subsidiary means of law-determination, a whole host of other materials also influences the behaviour of parties to non-international armed conflicts. These materials are equally as important as the well-accepted sources of general international law. This chapter considers the traditional sources and subsidiary means of law-determination. As they are less well-known, the chapter pays particular attention to the other materials of states and non-state armed groups that influence their behaviour, namely their ad hoc commitments. Ad hoc commitments of states and armed groups include agreements concluded between the warring parties, unilateral declarations, and instructions or regulations that are internal to a party. The role, normative status, and potential utility of these ad hoc commitments will be explored.

2. The traditional sources

2.1 Treaties

At the conventional level, the international humanitarian law of non-international armed conflict includes common Article 3, Additional Protocol II, the Hague Convention on Cultural Property, and its Second Protocol. It also includes various weapons treaties, notably the Chemical Weapons Convention, the Biological Weapons Convention, the Convention on Certain Conventional Weapons (as amended) and the various Protocols thereto, the Ottawa Convention on Anti-Personnel Mines, and the Cluster Munitions Convention. Instruments belonging to other areas of international law also have a role to play in non-international armed conflict, principally the Convention on the Rights of the Child and the Optional Protocol thereto on children and armed conflict, the Guiding Principles on Internal Displacement, and the Rome Statute of the International Criminal Court. At the regional level, additional instruments regulate non-international armed conflict, including the African Union Convention on Internal Displacement and the Cairo Declaration on Human Rights in

---

[1] Statute of the International Court of Justice, Article 38. See R Cryer, 'Of Custom, Treaties, Scholars and the Gavel: The Influence of the International Criminal Tribunals on the ICRC Customary Law Study' (2006) 11 *JCSL* 239.

Islam.² The idea that there are but a few treaty norms applicable to non-international armed conflicts is thus entirely mistaken.

2.2 Custom

An even more substantial body of law applicable in non-international armed conflict exists at the customary level.

2.2.1 Methodology

The methodology by which the customary law of non-international armed conflict is created is largely the same as that in which custom in general international law is created.³ It is largely the same as, rather than identical to, the determination of general customary international law given that, in highly normative areas such as the law of armed conflict, greater regard is had for *opinio juris* and for what ought to be the law than is otherwise the case.⁴ The focus tends also to be on verbal rather than physical acts. This is evident from the *Tadić* Decision on Interlocutory Appeal on Jurisdiction, which observed that, 'on account of the inherent nature of this subject-matter, reliance must primarily be placed on such elements as official pronouncements of States, military manuals and judicial decisions', as well as from the Customary International Humanitarian Law study, which also focused on military manuals and the like, albeit indicating that the approach it was taking was a 'classic one'.⁵

Situations of armed conflict are also atypical in that reactions of states that are not involved in the conflict to violations of the law tend to be more forthcoming than in other situations. These reactions are important as they demonstrate the views of the outside state on the law. For example, following the conclusion of the armed conflict in Sri Lanka in 2009, the United States assessed the conduct of the parties to that conflict. In so doing, it set out its own view of the customary international law status of certain rules relating to the conduct of hostilities. It observed:

> The customary laws of war also require all parties to a conflict to comply with the principles of distinction and proportionality in the conduct of hostilities. The principle of distinction holds that civilians and civilian objects (such as hospitals and schools) are generally immune from direct attack, though civilians lose this immunity if they take direct part in hostilities. The principle of proportionality prohibits attacks that may cause incidental loss of life, injury or damage to civilians that would be excessive in relation to the concrete and direct military advantage anticipated. The civilian population must not be used to shield military objectives or operations from attack, and parties must take all practicable precautions, taking into account military and humanitarian considerations, to minimize incidental death, injury and damage to civilians.⁶

---

² African Union Convention for the Protection and Assistance of Internally Displaced Persons in Africa (not yet in force); Cairo Declaration on Human Rights in Islam, Article 3.

³ See the methodology used in J-M Henckaerts and L Doswald-Beck, *Customary International Humanitarian Law, Volume I: Rules* (Cambridge University Press, 2005) xxxi–xlv.

⁴ See AE Roberts, 'Traditional and Modern Approaches to Customary International Law: A Reconciliation' (2001) 95 *AJIL* 757; *Customary International Humanitarian Law, Volume I: Rules*, above note 3, xlii.

⁵ *Prosecutor v Tadić*, IT-94-1-AR72, Decision on the Defence Motion for Interlocutory Appeal on Jurisdiction, 2 October 1995, para. 99; *Customary International Humanitarian Law, Volume I: Rules*, above note 3, xxxii.

⁶ US Department of State, Report to Congress on Incidents During the Recent Conflict in Sri Lanka (2009) 7.

Likewise, one party to the conflict may allege that the other side has violated the law of non-international armed conflict by committing certain actions. These allegations demonstrate the belief of the accusing party as to the existence of the particular rules. For example, during the final stages of the conflict in Sri Lanka in 2009, a Sri Lankan Government Minister stated before the UN Human Rights Council:

> Hostage taking in a conflict situation is, as you know, a clear violation of international humanitarian law... It is our fervent appeal, through you Mr President, to the members and observers of this Council and to the world at large, to bring any influence you might have to bear on the LTTE [Liberation Tigers of Tamil Eelam], to apply whatever pressure you can to permit these civilians—these innocent hostages—to move to safety.[7]

Parties also tend to make statements on their own conduct during the conflict more frequently than they do in other areas. For example, in relation to the fight against Al-Qaeda, which branches of the US Government have considered to be a non-international armed conflict,[8] the Legal Advisor of the Department of State indicated that:

> this Administration has carefully reviewed the rules governing targeting operations to ensure that these operations are conducted consistently with law of war principles, including:
>
> - First, the principle of *distinction*, which requires that attacks be limited to military objectives and that civilians or civilian objects shall not be the object of the attack; and
> - Second, the principle of *proportionality*, which prohibits attacks that may be expected to cause incidental loss of civilian life, injury to civilians, damage to civilian objects, or a combination thereof, that would be excessive in relation to the concrete and direct military advantage anticipated.
>
> In U.S. operations against al-Qaeda and its associated forces—including lethal operations conducted with the use of unmanned aerial vehicles—great care is taken to adhere to these principles in both planning and execution, to ensure that only legitimate objectives are targeted and that collateral damage is kept to a minimum.[9]

Given that many of the relevant rules are not to be found in conventional instruments applicable in non-international armed conflict, statements such as these are important for demonstrating the views of parties to conflicts on the substance of customary international law.

Just as important are the denials of parties that they undertook particular acts that violate a customary rule. Alternatively, a party may justify the acts through the existence of an exception to the customary rule. In both situations, the denial serves to confirm the existence of the rule rather than to put its customary status into question.[10] Thus, when the parties to the Spanish civil war denied that they had attacked the civilian population, claiming instead that they had attacked military objectives,[11] this served to

---

[7] Statement to the UN Human Rights Council by Minister Mahinda Samarasinghe, 2 March 2009.
[8] See below, 232.
[9] HH Koh, 'The Obama Administration and International Law', Speech at the Annual Meeting of the American Society of International Law, 25 March 2010. See also HH Koh, 'The Lawfulness of the US Operation against Osama bin Laden', Opinio Juris Blog, 19 May 2011.
[10] *Military and Paramilitary Activities In and Against Nicaragua (Nicaragua v United States of America)* [1986] ICJ Rep 14, para 186.
[11] See the various statements quoted in A Cassese, 'The Spanish Civil War and the Development of Customary Law Concerning Internal Armed Conflicts', in A Cassese (ed), *The Human Dimension of International Law: Selected Papers* (Oxford University Press, 2008) 128, 139–40.

support the claim that there was a rule of customary international law that prohibited the targeting of civilians.

Determining the existence of customary international law is notoriously difficult. In practice, the existence of a customary rule tends to be posited by a court, tribunal, or other influential body, and later accepted or rejected by states. For example, the holding by the International Criminal Tribunal for the former Yugoslavia (ICTY) in *Tadić* that the customary law of non-international armed conflict was a good deal more developed than had generally been thought and violation of that law gave rise to individual criminal responsibility was largely accepted by states at the Rome Conference.[12] By contrast, the view of the ICTY in *Kupreškić* that the use of belligerent reprisals against civilians was prohibited in customary international law was not accepted by certain states.[13] Thus, it has been remarked that '[t]he combination of a string of decisions... coupled with the implicit acceptance or acquiescence of all the international subjects concerned, clearly indicates the existence of the practice and *opinio juris* necessary for holding that a customary rule of international law has evolved'.[14] This is a good description of what happens in practice, even if it differs from the orthodox accounts of how customary international law is created.

It also explains why the Customary International Humanitarian Law study concluded under the auspices of the International Committee of the Red Cross (ICRC) and the jurisprudence of the ICTY are so important. Both the study and the jurisprudence indicate that very many norms of customary international humanitarian law regulate non-international armed conflict.[15] This has met with some scepticism on the part of certain states and commentators,[16] with the possibility of a backlash reducing the progress that has been made in the area. However, the Customary International Humanitarian Law study has been cited with approval by a number of courts and the jurisprudence of the ICTY has been followed in other arenas. Indeed, it may well be that, in practice, albeit not in law, the findings of the study will reverse the presumption as to the existence of a customary norm. Traditionally, the burden of proof lies on the entity that argues that a customary rule exists. The fact that the study identifies the existence of a particular customary norm may serve to satisfy this burden, albeit only for practical purposes. It will then be incumbent on the party that argues that no such customary norm exists to prove its case.[17]

To the extent that it can be demonstrated that certain norms suggested by the study or the jurisprudence of the ICTY do not in fact have customary status, it does not follow that only a few norms of customary international humanitarian law govern non-international armed conflicts. Very many norms have been determined to be of customary status irrespective of the Customary International Humanitarian Law study and the jurisprudence of the ICTY.

---

[12] C Kress, 'War Crimes Committed in Non-International Armed Conflict and the Emerging System of International Criminal Justice' (2000) 30 *IYHR* 104, 107.

[13] See UK Ministry of Defence, *The Manual of the Law of Armed Conflict* (Oxford University Press, 2004) 43 fn 62.

[14] Special Tribunal for Lebanon, CH/AC/2010/02, Decision on Appeal of Pre-Trial Judge's Order regarding Jurisdiction and Standing, 10 November 2010, para 47.

[15] *Customary International Humanitarian Law*, above note 3.

[16] See eg JB Bellinger III and WJ Haynes II, 'A US Government Response to the International Committee of the Red Cross Study *Customary International Humanitarian Law*' (2007) 89 *IRRC* 443.

[17] See eg the approach taken in the Report of the Secretary-General's Panel of Experts on Accountability in Sri Lanka, 31 March 2011, para 183.

2.2.2 Customary rules

The norms contained in common Article 3 have been accepted as having passed into customary international law at least since the International Court of Justice (ICJ)'s 1986 judgment in *Nicaragua*.[18] Criticisms of its finding in this regard did not relate to the conclusion so much as its lack of citation of state practice and *opinio juris*,[19] and its holding has since been reiterated on numerous occasions. At least the 'core' of Additional Protocol II has similarly been accepted as having passed into customary international law.[20] So too certain rules for the protection of cultural property.[21] Thus, the obligations of humane treatment, care for the wounded and sick, and respect for cultural property, as well as the prohibitions of murder, torture, and cruel treatment, rape, humiliating and degrading treatment, the taking of hostages, summary execution, collective punishments, acts of terrorism, slavery, and pillage are all of customary status.

The customary international humanitarian law of non-international armed conflict is by no means limited to norms relating to humane treatment. A number of rules regulating the conduct of hostilities are likewise accepted as having customary status. The principles contained in General Assembly Resolution 2444 (XXIII) were considered to reflect customary international law by influential states at the time of the Resolution's adoption.[22] Various international and regional bodies have held likewise.[23] Thus, the rule that the right of the parties to adopt means of injury is not unlimited, the prohibition of attacks against civilians, and the principle of distinction are all of customary status. The same has been suggested of General Assembly Resolution 2675 (XXV), which elaborates on Resolution 2444.[24] Thus, the principle of distinction, the prohibition on attacks against civilians and civilian objects, the requirement to take precautions, the prohibition on forcible transfer of civilians, and the provision of humanitarian relief, all have the status of norms of customary international law.[25]

The 1990 Declaration of the International Institute of Humanitarian Law on the Rules of International Humanitarian Law governing the Conduct of Hostilities in

---

[18] *Nicaragua*, above note 10, 114 para 218.

[19] See above, 55.

[20] Report of the Secretary-General on the Establishment of a Special Court for Sierra Leone, S/2000/915, 4 October 2000, para 14; 'The United States Position on the Relation of Customary International Law to the 1977 Protocols Additional to the 1949 Geneva Conventions: Remarks of Michael J Matheson' (1987) 2 *American University Journal of International Law and Policy* 419.

[21] Rome Statute, Article 8(2)(e)(iv); Constitutional Court of Colombia, Decision C-291/07, para 6.1, reproduced and translated in M Sassòli, AA Bouvier, and A Quintin, *How Does Law Protect in War? Volume III* (ICRC, 2011) 2255.

[22] United States, in Third Committee, General Assembly, 23rd Session, 1634th Meeting, 10 December 1968 (1968) UNGA Official Records (Third Committee) 2. See also the letter from the US Department of Defence, excerpted in (1973) 67 *AJIL* 122.

[23] Inter-American Commission on Human Rights, Third Report on the Human Rights Situation in Colombia, OEA/Ser.L/V/II.102, Doc.9 rev.1, 26 February 1999, Chapter IV, para 39; *Colombia v Jose Alexis Fuentes Guerrero et al*, Case 11.519, Report No 61/99, OEA/Ser.L/V/II.95, Doc.7 rev.446, 13 April 1999, paras 37–8; *Ignacio Ellacuria et al v El Salvador*, Case 10.488, Report No 136/99, 22 December 1999, paras 158–9. See also *Tadić* Decision on Interlocutory Appeal on Jurisdiction, above note 5, paras 111–12.

[24] Denmark, in Third Committee, General Assembly, 25th Session, 1785th Meeting, 11 November 1970, (1970) UNGA Official Records (Third Committee) 281; *Fuentes Guerrero*, above note 23, paras 37–8; *Ignacio Ellacuria et al v El Salvador*, above note 23, paras 158–9. See also *Tadić* Decision on Interlocutory Appeal on Jurisdiction, above note 5, paras 111–12.

[25] There is more dispute surrounding the customary status of a prohibition on belligerent reprisals against the civilian population. See below, 452.

Non-International Armed Conflicts has also been considered to reflect customary international law, and has been described as 'the most authoritative expression of international legal opinion in this field'.[26] As this was the holding of the Colombian Constitutional Court, it amounts to the practice of at least one state. Furthermore, during the conflict in El Salvador, in 1991, the United Nations Observer Mission in El Salvador (ONUSAL) judged the conduct of the Government of El Salvador and the Frente Farabundo Martí para la Liberación Nacional (FMLN) against the norms contained in the Declaration.[27] Thus, although the Preamble to the Declaration provides that the 'principles and norms' contained therein are 'crystallized or . . . emergent rules of international law', the rules that were emergent when the Declaration was being drafted must have been considered to have crystallized by the time they were utilized by the relevant bodies. On this basis, the prohibitions and restrictions on the use of certain weapons also have customary status, as do certain rules relating to targeting.

The list of war crimes contained in the Rome Statute also reflects customary international law, albeit in some instances framed in a narrower manner than the relevant rules of international humanitarian law.[28] The drafters of the Rome Statute intended that the Statute would contain only customary international law crimes.[29] Thus the war crimes contained therein necessarily have customary status. In this regard, a distinction has to be drawn between evidencing the customary nature of particular rules from their inclusion in a treaty and the prior decision of states to include only customary norms in a treaty. The Rome Statute is an example of the latter situation and is thus free from difficulties relating to the Baxter paradox.[30] In order that the war crime is of customary status, the underlying prohibition must also have been of customary status. Accordingly, any norms that did not have customary status before the Rome Conference can be considered to have crystallized during the Conference.[31] Thus, the prohibitions on attacks against the civilian population, attacks on objects and personnel bearing the protected emblem, attacks on humanitarian assistance or peacekeeping personnel and objects, and attacks on religious, educational, and certain other objects, are all of customary status. So too are the prohibitions on pillage; sexual violence; mutilation; conscripting, enlisting, or using children to participate actively in hostilities; ordering displacement; killing or wounding treacherously; declaring that no quarter shall be given; and wanton destruction.[32] Following the amendment to the Rome Statute, the prohibitions on the use of poison and poisoned weapons, expanding bullets, and certain gases can also be added to this list.[33]

These conclusions are supported by the list of rules found to reflect customary international humanitarian law applicable in non-international armed conflict in other

---

[26] *Constitutional Conformity of Protocol II*, C-225/95, para 23, reproduced and translated in M Sassòli and AA Bouvier, *How Does Law Protect in War? Volume II* (ICRC, 2006) 2240.

[27] Third Report of the United Nations Observer Mission in El Salvador, A/46/876-S/23580, 19 February 1992, para 131.

[28] See above, 78–81.

[29] H von Hebel and D Robinson. 'Crimes within the Jurisdiction of the Court', in RS Lee (ed), *The International Criminal Court: The Making of the Rome Statute, Issues, Negotiations, Results* (Kluwer, 1999) 79, 104.

[30] On which, see RR Baxter, 'Multilateral Treaties as Evidence of Customary International Law' (1965–6) 41 *BYIL* 275.

[31] See, on the child soldiers provision, R Cryer, *Prosecuting International Crimes* (Cambridge University Press, 2005) 283.

[32] Rome Statute, Article 8(2)(e).

[33] Amendment to the Rome Statute, RC/Res.5.

important documents.³⁴ Thus, even leaving aside the important contributions of the ICTY and the Customary International Humanitarian Law study, there exists a substantial body of customary international humanitarian law that is applicable to non-international armed conflict, and which has been recognized by states. This body includes rules on humane treatment and the protection of civilians and persons *hors de combat*, as well as prohibitions on the use of certain means and methods of warfare.

The customary status of particular rules is considered on a rule-by-rule basis in Chapters 8 and 9.

3. The less traditional 'sources'

States and non-state armed groups frequently recognize the applicability of international humanitarian law, international human rights law, or other rules of international law to the conflict in which they are involved. Recognition takes place in a number of ways, principally through the issuance of an ad hoc commitment. Although there is not always a clear division between the various forms of commitment, they can usefully be grouped along the following lines. Ad hoc commitments can be sub-divided into unilateral declarations; bilateral agreements between the parties or between one of the parties and a UN entity or non-governmental organization, or trilateral agreements between the parties and an outside entity; codes of conduct, instructions, or regulations that are internal to the group; and legislation. These ad hoc commitments do not feature in the traditional list of the sources of international law. However, in light of their normative character and potential importance, they are considered here under the rubric of 'less traditional "sources"'.

The existence of these less traditional 'sources', especially those of non-state armed groups, tends to be overlooked. This is not a conscious decision on the part of the international community. Rather, they are forgotten because, oftentimes, they do not have a counterpart in international armed conflict. The modelling approach considered in Chapter 3 affects not only the substantive rules but also the methodology by which those rules are determined. As the model is that of the international armed conflict, only materials associated with international armed conflicts are considered; materials associated with non-state armed groups go unnoticed. There are, of course, exceptions. The 22 May 1992 Agreement concluded between the warring factions in the conflict in Bosnia has been utilized to varying degrees as the basis for criminal prosecution by the ICTY.³⁵ The 1995 *Tadić* Decision on Interlocutory Appeal on Jurisdiction also considered the commitments of non-state armed groups. However, these are the exceptions that prove the rule. The materials of non-state armed groups have not, by and large, been taken into account in the development of the law of non-international armed conflict. The developments that have taken place, at both the conventional and customary levels, have been largely statist in character and there has been little participation by non-state armed groups in the development of the law. As a consequence, at least one half of the actors involved in non-international armed conflicts did not

---

³⁴ See eg Report of the International Commission of Inquiry on Darfur to the Secretary-General, S/2005/60, 1 February 2005, para 166.
³⁵ Agreement of 22 May 1992, reproduced in M Sassòli, AA Bouvier, and A Qunitin, *How Does Law Protect in War? Volume II* (ICRC, 2011) 1717. For the varying use by the ICTY, see L Vierucci, '"Special Agreements" between Conflicting Parties in the Case-law of the ICTY', in B Swart, A Zahar, and G Sluiter (eds), *The Legacy of the International Criminal Tribunal for the former Yugoslavia* (Oxford University Press, 2011) 401.

participate in the formation of the relevant rules. This is particularly unfortunate given that overlooking these materials has led to the emergence of certain assumptions,[36] and certain understandings of the law have been skewed. Re-working the methodology by which the law is created is discussed further in Chapter 12.

3.1 Nature of the commitments

3.1.1 Propaganda?

Two points immediately arise in respect of ad hoc commitments, particularly those of armed groups. First, are they merely propaganda or do they deserve to be taken seriously? Second, if they are to be taken seriously, what is their normative status? As to the first point, it is difficult, if not impossible, to declare in advance whether or not a commitment is issued for propaganda purposes or because the party intends to follow it, nor are the two possibilities mutually exclusive. Much will depend on whether or not the commitment is actually followed in practice. Regardless, the same uncertainty arises in respect of states; and it applies with respect to ratification of treaties as much as it does issuance of ad hoc commitments. Furthermore, a number of distinct situations can be identified: the commitment is followed; it is followed to an extent; it is not followed; and it is unclear whether or not the commitment is followed. It is submitted that, in the first two situations, the commitment needs to be taken seriously. In the last situation, the commitment should be taken seriously, subject to further investigation. This comports with the idea of good faith. Only when the commitment is not followed should the presumption be that it was issued for propaganda purposes. Even in this situation, as in the three others, the commitment can still be used in different ways. It can be used by outside observers to engage with the party that issued the commitment. For example, the United Nations Assistance Mission in Afghanistan (UNAMA) has engaged with the Taliban of Afghanistan, in part, using the Taliban's statements on the protection of civilians and its Code of Conduct.[37] It can also be used by local populations to complain to the issuing party. For example, the frontline manual of the National Transitional Council of Libya, which was issued in 2011 during the conflict, set out a procedure for persons seeking to complain about breaches of the rules on detention also contained in the manual.[38] It may even constitute part of an ongoing dialogue on the law. For example, the 2011 Eid message of the Taliban on the taking of precautions is considered by some to be part of an ongoing, albeit indirect, dialogue between the Taliban and UNAMA.[39] There is little question that certain commitments are issued by parties without any intention to comply with them; however, this cannot be used to tarnish all commitments by all parties. Ad hoc commitments should not be automatically dismissed out of hand because they are ad hoc in character or because they emanate from armed groups. In many cases, they deserve to be taken seriously.

---

[36] See above, 5.
[37] See eg UNAMA, Afghanistan: Midyear Report 2011 Protection of Civilians in Armed Conflict (July 2011) 11–13.
[38] National Transitional Council Manual, 19 May 2011. See I Scobbie, 'Operationalising the Law of Armed Conflict for Dissident Forces in Libya', EJIL:Talk! Blog, 31 August 2011.
[39] K Clark, 'Two Eid Messages from the Warring Leaders', Afghanistan Analysts Network, 6 November 2011.

3.1.2 Normative status

The normative status of ad hoc commitments, in particular those of armed groups, is unsettled.[40] The legal status of bilateral agreements is uncertain. In some instances, international courts have considered them binding on the parties and akin to treaties. For example, the ICTY has relied upon the 22 May 1992 agreement in different ways, primarily as a means by which to bring into force certain other treaty provisions which could then form the basis of prosecution.[41] Similarly, the International Commission of Inquiry on Darfur noted that the Sudan Liberation Movement/Army (SLM/A) and the Justice and Equality Movement (JEM) 'possess under customary international law the power to enter into binding international agreements (*jus contrahendi*), and have entered into various internationally binding agreements with the Government' on issues pertaining to international humanitarian law.[42] For its part, the Security Council has demanded that armed groups comply with obligations contained in bilateral agreements concluded between those groups and the state.[43] However, other courts have taken the view that only states can create international obligations and that, therefore, agreements involving armed groups do not amount to treaties and are not binding under international law. Along these lines, the Colombian Constitutional Court held that common Article 3 agreements 'are not, strictly speaking, treaties, as they are not established between entities subject to public international law but between the parties to an internal conflict, which are subject to international humanitarian law'.[44] Similarly, the Special Court for Sierra Leone held that the Lomé Agreement between the Government of Sierra Leone and the Revolutionary United Front (RUF) was not a treaty because it was signed by the government and an armed group.[45]

As with bilateral agreements, the legal status of unilateral declarations of armed groups is unsettled. On occasion, international courts have referred favourably to undertakings by armed groups.[46] For example, in the *Akayesu* Trial Judgment, the International Criminal Tribunal for Rwanda (ICTR) noted that the Rwandese Patriotic Front had 'stated to the International Committee of the Red Cross that it was bound by the rules of international humanitarian law'.[47] UN entities also have treated unilateral declarations of armed groups as binding upon the groups and have called upon the international community to monitor and enforce them.[48] However, considerable

---

[40] See generally A Roberts and S Sivakumaran, 'Lawmaking by Non-State Actors: Engaging Armed Groups in the Creation of International Humanitarian Law' (2012) 37 *Yale Journal of International Law* 107. On the normative status of peace agreements, see C Bell, 'Peace Agreements: Their Nature and Legal Status' (2006) 100 *AJIL* 373; C Bell, *On the Law of Peace* (Oxford University Press, 2008).

[41] See above, 107.

[42] Darfur Commission Report, above note 34, para 174.

[43] See eg SC Res 1127 (1997) on UNITA and the Lusaka Protocol.

[44] *Constitutional Conformity of Protocol II*, above note 26, 2240, para 17.

[45] *Prosecutor v Kallon and Kamara*, SCSL-2004-15-AR72(E) and SCSL-2004-16-AR72(E), Decision on Challenge to Jurisdiction: Lomé Accord Amnesty, 13 March 2004, paras 45–50. For criticism, see A Cassese, 'The Special Court and International Law: The Decision Concerning the Lomé Agreement Amnesty' (2004) 2 *JICJ* 1130, 1134–5; Bell, Peace Agreements, above note 40, 387.

[46] See eg on the PLO declaration, *Legal Consequences of the Construction of a Wall in the Occupied Palestinian Territory*, Advisory Opinion, [2004] ICJ Rep 136, 173, para 91.

[47] *Prosecutor v Akayesu*, ICTR-96-4-T, Judgment, 2 September 1998, para 627.

[48] See eg Additional Report of the Special Representative of the Secretary-General for Children and Armed Conflict, E/CN.4/2000/71, 9 February 2000, para 20; Report of the Special Rapporteur on Extrajudicial, Summary or Arbitrary Executions, Mission to Sri Lanka, E/CN.4/2006/53/Add.5, 27 March 2006, para 30.

uncertainty surrounds the normative status of unilateral declarations of states.[49] Accordingly, it is to be expected that even more uncertainty exists in relation to unilateral declarations of non-state armed groups.

The legal status of the various materials listed, other than bilateral agreements and unilateral declarations, is also unsettled. In the *Tadić* Decision on Interlocutory Appeal on Jurisdiction, the ICTY Appeals Chamber took into account the commitments of armed groups in holding that customary international humanitarian law rules regulated non-international armed conflicts.[50] However, since *Tadić*, the ICTY has not resorted to the practice of armed groups aside from the 22 May 1992 Agreement. The Customary International Humanitarian Law study concluded under the auspices of the ICRC collected and listed practice of armed groups,[51] but under the heading of 'other practice', and did not use this practice in the determination of the existence of customary rules. This was explained by the lack of clarity surrounding the legal significance of the practice of armed groups.[52] Elsewhere, however, one of the authors of the study has advocated the inclusion of the practice of non-state armed groups in the determination of customary rules.[53]

The normative status of the various commitments is thus unsettled. However, as will be discussed below, there is good reason to treat ad hoc commitments of armed groups as well as those of states as binding under international law. A more general role for armed groups in the development of international law is discussed further in Chapter 12.

3.1.3 An interpretational tool

Leaving aside the normative status of the commitments of non-state armed groups, their existence must be acknowledged and used to inform interpretations of the law. They are useful for providing a sense of what has proven acceptable and in which areas there is contestation.[54] It would become apparent, for example, that a prohibition on the use of anti-personnel mines is acceptable to a great many armed groups, with 41 armed non-state actors signing Geneva Call's Deed of Commitment and numerous others prohibiting the use of mines through internal regulations and the like.[55] It would also become clear that particular disagreement surrounds the individuals who may be lawfully targeted.[56] Having regard to the practice and materials of armed groups and states would provide a far better sense of the state of the law and the likelihood for

---

[49] Cf *Nuclear Tests (Australia v France)* [1974] ICJ Rep 253, paras 43–6; *Case Concerning the Frontier Dispute (Burkina Faso/Republic of Mali)* [1986] ICJ Rep 554, paras 39–40; *Nicaragua*, above note 10, para 261; *Application of the Convention on the Prevention and Punishment of the Crime of Genocide (Bosnia and Herzegovina v Serbia and Montenegro)* [2007] ICJ Rep 43, paras 377–8.

[50] *Tadić* Decision on Interlocutory Appeal on Jurisdiction, above note 5, paras 102, 103, and 107.

[51] See, for a selection of this practice, *Customary International Humanitarian Law, Volume II: Practice*, above note 3, 64, 77, 115, 126, 356, 412, 778, 870, 2882, and 3610.

[52] Ibid, *Volume I*, xxxvi.

[53] J-M Henckaerts, 'Binding Armed Opposition Groups through Humanitarian Treaty Law and Customary Law' (2003) 27 *Collegium* 123, 128.

[54] See S Sivakumaran, 'Lessons for the Law of Armed Conflict from Commitments of Armed Groups: Identification of Legitimate Targets and Prisoners of War' (2011) 93 *IRRC* 463.

[55] Geneva Call is a Geneva-based organization dedicated to engaging 'armed non-state actors' in respecting and adhering to humanitarian norms, See the practice available at <http://www.genevacall.org/resources/nsas-statements/nsas-statements-2.htm>. For more on Geneva Call, see below, 538–42.

[56] See below, 368–70.

compliance with particular norms. It would also challenge traditional conceptions in a number of areas.

First, ad hoc commitments on the part of states that are actually involved in non-international armed conflicts to apply international humanitarian law are far more numerous than is imagined. The traditional assumption that states do not recognize the existence of non-international armed conflicts on their territory, or that they will not agree to apply international humanitarian law, is thus mistaken.[57] The same is true of the assumption that non-state armed groups do not commit to respect the law.[58]

Second, these commitments date back a century. They are not a construct of the post-*Tadić* period, or even the post-1949 Geneva Conventions period. Thus, the *Tadić* 'revolution' is supported by numerous other instances of state application of international humanitarian law in non-international armed conflicts.

Third and most importantly, the commitments do not relate to common Article 3 and Additional Protocol II alone. Prior to 1949 and 1977, commitments necessarily had to be made to the law of international armed conflict, and states and non-state armed groups proved willing to so commit. In the period after 1949 and 1977, states remained willing to commit to apply the Geneva Conventions as a whole or international humanitarian law as a whole, or the principles thereof, despite being under no obligation to do so. States and non-state armed groups thus not infrequently commit to applying more than is actually required of them by the law in force at the relevant point in time. This has included commitments to apply the law relating to the means and methods of warfare. Again, this has an impact on the normative content of the law of non-international armed conflict, even if not as a matter of customary international law. The commitments provide an indication of what states and non-state armed groups are willing to accept in conflicts in which they are involved.

Fourth, at a certain point in time during the conflict, states may consider the non-state armed group bound by human rights law. Usually, this comes at a time in which the armed group exercises control over territory and the conflict has been ongoing for a certain duration. Armed groups themselves tend to commit to abide by international human rights law at an earlier point in time, sometimes in the very early stages of a conflict. This is important in light of the uncertainty that surrounds whether, and if so, when, armed groups are bound by human rights obligations.[59]

Finally, it should be noted that states may, and do, change their mind. For example, the Russian Government spoke out against Red Cross involvement in civil wars in 1912; by 1949, the USSR was in favour of detailed regulation of non-international armed conflict; more recently, Russia seems to have reverted to its earlier position.[60] The Government of Colombia has accepted and denied the existence of an armed conflict at various points in time.[61] The United States has accepted certain rules of international humanitarian law as norms of customary international law but has also retreated from that position. For example, in 1986, the Deputy Legal Advisor at the Department of State set out the position of the United States on the Additional Protocols,[62] and this was relied upon in a 2005 US

---

[57] See generally below, 200–4.   [58] See below, 241–2.
[59] See above, 95–97.   [60] See above, 32, 42, and below, 546.
[61] See eg below, 202 and 205.
[62] 'The United States Position on the Relation of Customary International Law to the 1977 Protocols Additional to the 1949 Geneva Conventions: Remarks of Michael J Matheson' (1987) 2 *American University Journal of International Law and Policy* 419.

military manual.⁶³ However, an errata sheet was later published, indicating that '[t]his information was taken from an article written by Michael Matheson in 1986. It takes an overly broad view of the US position and as a result may cause some confusion as to US policy'.⁶⁴ Yet, in 1912, it was the US delegation that was the leading advocate of Red Cross involvement in times of non-international armed conflict.⁶⁵ By 2011, the United States would seem to have reverted to a slightly broader position.⁶⁶ Despite the change in position of states at various points in time, regard may still be had for the acceptance of the norm on the part of the relevant state, particularly if that norm became a norm of a customary international law in the interim. Later rejection of the customary norm will not have an effect on the status of that rule even in respect of the now-objecting state.

Ad hoc commitments are thus of an uncertain normative status. Nonetheless, they remain useful in providing a sense of which rules are readily accepted and which are less well-accepted and for informing the interpretation of particular rules. Accordingly, in Part II, ad hoc commitments are used to illustrate acceptance or violation of a particular rule, but not to determine whether or not the rule is one of customary international law. Furthermore, as indicated above, the weight to be given to a particular commitment will depend on the extent to which it is followed.⁶⁷

3.1.4 Commitments and compliance

Committing to respect international humanitarian law, international human rights law, or particular rules thereof should not be confused with compliance with the law. In a number of the armed conflicts in which commitments were made, violations were rife. During the Spanish civil war, for example, the Junta declared it would observe and respect the Geneva Conventions on the wounded and sick, and on prisoners of war. However, that commitment has been considered 'more an attempt to obtain some form of international status than a serious intention to abide by any legal commitments'.⁶⁸ During the armed conflicts in the former Yugoslavia, ICRC delegates would prove to have reservations about the utility of concluding bilateral agreements between the warring parties due to 'the treachery encountered in the field in spite of all the firm promises made on both sides'.⁶⁹ Indeed, one ICRC delegate described the position as '[t]hey bombard each other, they sign, they bombard each other again and sign again, and so on'.⁷⁰ As indicated above, certain commitments may be issued for purely political reasons or for propaganda purposes with the armed group having no intention whatsoever to follow them. However, the same is true of states and, ultimately, an individual commitment by an individual state or armed group will have to be assessed on its own terms. However, in general, while issuing a commitment does not equal

---

⁶³ International and Operational Law Department, *Operational Law Handbook* (2005).
⁶⁴ Quoted in C Garraway, 'The Use and Abuse of Military Manuals' (2004) 7 *YIHL* 425, 437.
⁶⁵ See above, 32–3.
⁶⁶ See the statements of the State Department Legal Advisor, above note 9. See also US Report on Sri Lanka, above note 6, 51.
⁶⁷ See above, 108.
⁶⁸ F Bugnion, *The International Committee of the Red Cross and the Protection of War Victims* (ICRC, 2003) 270. See also J Siotis, *Le Droit de la Guerre et les Conflits Armés d'un Caractère Non-International* (Librairie Général de Droit et de Jurisprudence, 1958) 156.
⁶⁹ Quoted in M Mercier, *Crimes without Punishment: Humanitarian Action in Former Yugoslavia* (Pluto Press, 1995) 35.
⁷⁰ Ibid, 37.

compliance, it can be a first step towards compliance, and issuing commitments and concluding agreements has led to an increased compliance in certain instances.[71]

In order to illustrate the various points set out above, in light of the oft-expressed view that they are not often concluded,[72] and given that many of them are difficult to locate, the section that follows contains excerpts from a variety of ad hoc commitments of states and non-state armed groups.

3.2 The commitments

3.2.1 Unilateral declarations

States and non-state armed groups frequently issue unilateral declarations to indicate their agreement to abide by international humanitarian law obligations. For example, several states and armed groups have provided commitments to UN entities on the disarmament, demobilization, and reintegration of child soldiers pursuant to Security Council instruction and which contain commitments to international humanitarian law norms.[73] Geneva Call has created a Deed of Commitment that can be signed by 'armed non-state actors'.[74] At the time of writing, the Deed on Anti-Personnel Mines, which *inter alia* prohibits the use of anti-personnel mines and requires co-operation in, and undertaking of, mine action, had attracted some 41 signatures. Geneva Call has also drawn up a second deed, on children and armed non-state actors, and at the time of writing was in the process of adopting a third, on sexual and gender-based violence. Unilateral declarations of adherence to Additional Protocol I, purportedly pursuant to Article 96(3) of that Protocol, have also been issued.[75] Unilateral declarations are issued even more frequently on an ad hoc basis.

Declarations of states

From time to time, states issue unilateral declarations on matters of international humanitarian law during non-international armed conflicts. For example, in 1964, during the post-independence armed conflicts that were raging in the Democratic Republic of the Congo (DRC), the Prime Minister of the DRC declared that:

[f]or humanitarian reasons, and with a view to reassuring, in so far as necessary, the civilian population which might fear that it is in danger, the Congolese Government wishes to state that the Congolese Air Force will limit its action to military objectives.

In this matter, the Congolese Government desires not only to protect human lives but also to respect the Geneva Convention. It also expects the rebels and makes an urgent appeal to them to that effect to act in the same manner.

As a practical measure, the Congolese Government suggests that International Red Cross observers come to check on the extent to which the Geneva Convention is being respected, particularly in the matter of the treatment of prisoners and the ban against taking hostages.

Independently of the pacification campaign it has launched and which will be vigorously continued since its repeated appeals for conciliation have not been heeded, the Congolese Government is also determined to prevent false reports from being used to threaten the innocent

---

[71] See Chapter 12. [72] See above, 5.
[73] See the list of action plans concluded by states and state-sponsored militias in Children and Armed Conflict: Report of the Secretary General, A/63/785-S/2009/158, 26 March 2009, para 148.
[74] See Chapter 12.
[75] For example, the NDFP Declaration of Undertaking to Apply the Geneva Conventions of 1949 and Protocol I of 1977, addressed to the Swiss Federal Council, 5 July 1996; NDFP Declaration of Undertaking to Apply the Geneva Conventions of 1949 and Protocol I of 1977, addressed to the ICRC, 5 July 1996.

civilian population with reprisals. It hopes that this unequivocal communiqué will ensure respect for international conventions.[76]

Numerous other ad hoc commitments have been provided to the ICRC. For example, following the revolution in Guatemala in 1954, the government that came to power gave an assurance to the ICRC delegate that he would be able to visit persons interned and detained as a result of the conflict.[77] The visits were conducted pursuant to the 1949 Geneva Conventions.[78] Prior to taking power, the Government, as the then armed group, had sent a telegram to the ICRC which read:

Invoking humanitarian principles and international treaties we shall be grateful for aid in personnel equipment medicine plasma etc immediate attention for wounded on both sides in revolution against arbenz government . . . provisional government places at disposal of worthy institution the airports at chiquimula and esquipulas in republic of guatemala.[79]

At around the same time, the incumbent government had also called for ICRC intervention.[80] During the conflict in Afghanistan during the Cold War (1979–89), the President 'assured the ICRC that he would respect the principles of the Geneva Conventions under all circumstances and that all armed forces on Afghan territory would comply with their obligations under the Conventions'.[81]

In certain situations, unilateral declarations of states are considered binding upon them. Whether or not they are viewed in this manner depends on the intention of the author of the declaration and how the declaration is understood by other actors.[82] Although, in general, binding unilateral declarations are restrictively conceived,[83] in situations of non-international armed conflict, when a state issues a declaration on humanitarian norms indicating that it will or will not act in a particular manner, such declarations should be viewed as binding.

Parallel declarations

Unilateral commitments are sometimes issued by the opposing parties along identical, or largely similar, lines. These parallel commitments tend to be issued when the parties are unwilling or unable to conclude a bilateral agreement on the subject. There is a long history of parallel unilateral declarations being issued. For example, during the conflict in the plebiscite of Upper Silesia in 1921, both parties agreed to an ICRC proposal to respect persons wearing an armband bearing the insignia of the ICRC and stamped by the relevant military authority.[84] The proposal was based on the 1906 Geneva

---

[76] Public Statement of the Prime Minister, Dr Moise Tshombe, 21 October 1964, ICRC Archives B AG 202 229-006, reproduced at (1965) 59 *AJIL* 616 (emphases omitted). See also Letter from the Prime Minister, Dr Moise Tshombe to the President of the ICRC, 22 October 1964, ibid.

[77] Letter from ICRC Delegate Jequier to the ICRC in Geneva, 15 July 1954, ICRC Archives B AG 200 086.

[78] Letter from ICRC Delegate Jequier to SE Monsieur George Adán Serrano, Ministre de l'Intérieur et de la Justice, 23 July 1954, ICRC Archives, ibid.

[79] Telegram from Carlos Salazar, Secretario de relaciones exteriores and Luis Valladares y Aycinena, Secretaro de gobernacion to ICRC, 26 June 1954, ICRC Archives, ibid. The English translation is taken from a similar telegram sent to the American Red Cross, in ibid. The latter omits reference to 'international treaties'.

[80] Letter from the Consul Général Représentant Permanent de Guatemala auprès de l'Office Européen des Nations Unies to M. Gallopin, Directeur du CICR, 25 June 1954, ICRC Archives, ibid.

[81] ICRC, Annual Report 1980 (ICRC, 1981) 44.

[82] *Nuclear Tests* [1974] ICJ Rep 253, paras 43–6.

[83] Ibid, para 44.

[84] For the proposal, see Letter from Lucien Cramer to Général [Hoefer] and Letter from Lucien Cramer to M Korfanty, 20 June 1921, reproduced in (1921) 3 *RICR* 691, Annexes 14 and 14*bis*. For

Convention.⁸⁵ Both parties also expressed their willingness to assist the ICRC in its work. M Korfanty, of the Polish side, stated:

I the undersigned hereby declare myself prepared to allow the delegates of the International Committee of the Red Cross to visit without restriction all prison camps and to work according to the principles of the Red Cross.

They will also be allowed to help children, women and the elderly by giving them the aid and supplies necessary for their existence, under the responsibility of the International Committee.⁸⁶

General Hoefer, of the German side, also issued a commitment:

On behalf of all the commands of the Selbstschutz of Upper Silesia, which are under my command, I am willing to facilitate in any way the implementation of the work of the members of the International Committee of the Red Cross...

I will immediately give to all my subordinate commands the order to give the fullest assistance to all the people who will be incontestably recognised as representatives of the International Committee of the Red Cross.⁸⁷

Some 15 years later, at the outset of the Spanish civil war, in 1936, the Spanish Government issued a statement which provided that:

[t]he Spanish Government, having received and heard Mr. Marcel Junod representing the International Red Cross, agrees to receive two delegations of the International Committee, delegations one of which will operate in Madrid and Barcelona, and the other in Burgos and Seville. Their mission will be to protect and create respect for the sign of the Red Cross by both parties and facilitate the humanitarian work of this institution.

The government looks favorably upon the creation of an information section for prisoners of war and civilians under the responsibility of the said delegations, and accepts the possibility of an exchange of some non-combatants amongst them, especially women and children.⁸⁸

---

the commitments, see Letter from Korfanty to the ICRC in Oppeln, 27 June 1921, and the oral commitment of General Hoefer reported in the Telegram of the ICRC Delegate in Oppeln to the ICRC in Geneva, 30 June 1921, ICRC Archives CR 22-5/111/85, and/128ter, reproduced respectively in (1921) 3 *RICR* 691, Annexes 16, 17 and 17*bis*.

⁸⁵ Letter from President of the ICRC to ICRC Delegate in Upper Silesia, 24 June 1921, ICRC Archives CR 22-8/48; (1921) 3 *RICR* 691, Annex 15.

⁸⁶ Letter from M Korfanty, 2 June 1921, reproduced in (1921) 3 *RICR* 691, Annex I. The original reads:

Je soussigné me déclare prêt à autoriser les délégués du Comité international de la Croix-Rouge à visiter sans restriction tous les camps de prisonniers et à y travailler suivant les principes de la Croix-Rouge.

Ils seront autorisés, également, à secourir les enfants, les femmes et les vieillards en leur distribuant sous la responsabilité du Comité international, les secours et approvisionnements qui sont nécessaires à leur existence.

⁸⁷ Letter from General Hoefer, Chef du Selbstschutz de la Haute-Silésie, 1 June 1921, reproduced in (1921) 3 *RICR* 691, Annex II. The original reads:

Au nom de tous les commandements du Selbstschutz de la Haute-Silésie, qui se trouvent sous mes ordres, je me déclare prêt à faciliter par tous les moyens la mise en oeuvre de l'activité des membres du Comité international de la Croix-Rouge...

Je donnerai immédiatement à tous les commandements qui me sont soumis l'ordre de prêter leur assistance la plus large à toutes les personnes qui seront incontestablement reconnues comme représentants du Comité international de la Croix-Rouge.

⁸⁸ Accord de José Giral, Le Président du Conseil des Ministres, 3 September 1936, reproduced in (1936) 18 *RICR* 749, Annex II. The original reads:

Le Gouvernement espagnol, après avoir reçu et entendu M. Marcel Junod, en représentation de la Croix-Rouge internationale, accepte l'envoi d'une double délégation du Comité international, délégations qui exerceront leur activité à Madrid et à Barcelone d'une part et à

For its part, the Burgos National Defence Junta issued a statement which provided *inter alia* that:

[i]t stands ready to observe and respect, as it always has and as it still will at every moment, the Geneva Convention regarding the wounded, the sick and the prisoners of war.

Before considering the question of hostages and their exchange, it would like to state that it did not have recourse to this process that has not been applied to the military or civilian population, or to women and children, but on the other hand it had to deplore the loss of the most prominent and the most distinguished personalities of national and global life who were shot or murdered. However, inspired by the loftiest sentiments of humanity, it agrees that women, children and young people not liable to military service who express the desire can leave the area placed under its dependence to go abroad or the area of the government of Madrid, provided that the same permission is granted in the other camp for women, children and young people who in the same circumstances wish to go abroad or to the area of the government of Burgos.[89]

The content of other parallel commitments has been largely identical. For example, during the conflict in the Dominican Republic in 1965, both sides gave the ICRC delegate in the Dominican Republic an oral commitment to respect the Geneva Conventions.[90] Likewise, during the conflict in Lebanon in 1958, both parties committed to the ICRC to apply and respect common Article 3.[91] Along similar lines, during the conflict in the Yemen in the 1960s, both the Royalist side and the Republican side made a commitment to the ICRC delegates. Following a visit from the ICRC delegates, Mohamed El-Badr, freshly deposed and fighting against the Government that had taken power, wrote to the President of the ICRC indicating that:

[w]e take this opportunity to assure you that we greatly appreciate ... the humanitarian efforts of the International Red Cross organization and we also assure you that the principles of this organisation are the object of our esteem and respect. Accordingly, we have ordered our armed forces to respect these principles and everything related to them, leaving aside political issues.[92]

Burgos et Séville d'autre part. Leur mission sera celle de protéger et de faire respecter le signe de la croix-rouge par les deux parties et de faciliter le travail humanitaire de cette institution.

Le Gouvernement voit avec sympathie la création d'une section d'informations à la charge desdites délégations auprès des prisonniers de guerre ou civils et il admet la possibilité d'un échange de quelques-uns d'entre eux non combatants, spécialement de femmes et d'enfants.

[89] Miguel Cabanellas, Junte de Défense Nationale d'Espagne, 15 September 1936, reproduced in (1936) 18 *RICR* 749, Annex IV. The original reads:

Elle se déclare prête à observer et à respecter, comme elle l'a toujours fait et comme elle le fait encore à chaque instant, la Convention de Genève concernant les blessés de guerre, les malades et les prisonniers.

Avant de considérer la question des otages et de leur échange, elle tient à déclarer qu'elle n'a pas eu recours à ce procédé qui n'a été appliqué ni à la population militaire ou civile, ni aux femmes et aux enfants, mais par contre qu'elle a eu à déplorer la perte des personnalités les plus en vue et les plus distinguées de la vie nationale et mondiale, qui ont été fusillées ou assassinées. Cependant, s'inspirant des sentiments les plus élevés d'humanité, elle accepte que les femmes, les enfants et les jeunes gens non astreints au service militaire qui en exprimeraient le désir puissent abandonner la zone placée sous sa dépendance pour gagner l'étranger ou la zone du gouvernement de Madrid, pour autant que la même autorisation soit accordée dans l'autre camp aux femmes, enfants et jeunes gens qui, dans les mêmes circonstances, désireraient gagner l'étranger ou la zone du Gouvernement de Burgos.

[90] Telegram from ICRC Delegate Jequier to the ICRC in Geneva, 19 May 1965, ICRC Archives B AG 251 170. See also ICRC, Annual Report 1965 (ICRC, 1966) 37.

[91] Note of ICRC Delegate de Traz to ICRC, 16 June 1958; Note, 20 June 1958, ICRC Archives B AG 200 115-001. See also CICR, 'L'Action de Secours du CICR au Liban et l'Art 3 des Conventions de Genève de 1949'.

[92] Letter from El-Badr to the President of the ICRC, 2 January 1963. Arabic original and French translation in ICRC Archives B AG 200 226. The original reads:

The principles in question apparently related to 'the essential humanitarian principles of the Geneva Conventions, concerning the treatment of the wounded and prisoners'.[93] The commitment was also broadcast by the Imam over the radio.[94] Following a separate meeting with different ICRC delegates, the new Government headed by Al-Moushir Abdullah El-Sallal indicated that:

[o]n behalf of the government of the Yemen Arab Republic, we declare: to respect the humanitarian principles enshrined in the Geneva Convention of 1949 regarding the Red Cross and the Red Crescent and we promise to respect their applications.[95]

More recently, in 1991, during the conflict in Croatia, the various parties stated that they:

undertake to respect and ensure respect of International Humanitarian Law and remind all Fighting Units of their obligation to apply the following fundamental principles:

— wounded and ill persons must be helped and protected in all circumstances,
— all arrested persons, and notably combatants who have surrendered, must be treated with humanity,
— all detaining authorities must ensure the protection of the prisoners,
— the civilian population and civilian property must not be attacked,
— the Red Cross emblem must be respected. It may be used only to designate sanitary troops or buildings as well as persons and vehicles belonging to this service,
— all Red Cross personnel and medical personnel assisting civilian populations and persons hors de combat must be granted the necessary freedom of movement to achieve their tasks,
— unconditional support for the action of the ICRC in favour of the victims

support unreservedly the humanitarian action of the Red Cross and in particular of the International Committee of the Red Cross (ICRC).[96]

During the conflict in Bosnia (1992–5), the parties likewise signed unilateral commitments that mirrored one another and which provided that:

all parties to the conflict are bound to comply with their obligations under International Humanitarian Law and in particular the Geneva Conventions of 1949 and the Additional Protocols thereto, and that persons who commit or order the commission of grave breaches are individually responsible.[97]

Nous profitons de cette occasion pour vous assurer que nous estimons grandement et depuis fort longtemps les efforts humanitaires déployés par l'organisation de la Croix-Rouge international et nous vous assurons également que les principes de cette organisation sont l'objet de toute notre estime et respect. En conséquence, nous avons donné l'ordre à nos armées de respecter ces principes et tout ce qui s'y attache, en laissant de côté les questions politiques.

[93] Letter from the President of the ICRC to the Ambassador of the Yemen in Jeddah, 28 January 1963, ICRC Archives B AG 200 226, referring to the Letter from El-Badr.
[94] Archive Note, 2 April 1963, ICRC Archives B AG 200 226.
[95] Written Statement from Président de la République arabe yéménite, Al-Mousir Abdullah El-Sallal, 28 January 1963. Arabic original and French translation in ICRC Archives B AG 200 226. The original reads:

Au nom du Gouvernement de la République arabe yéménite, nous déclarons: estimer les principes humanitaires, inscrits dans la Convention de Genève de 1949 concernant la Croix-Rouge et le Croissant-Rouge et nous promettons de respecter ses applications.

[96] The Hague Statement on Respect of Humanitarian Principles, 5 November 1991, reproduced in J-F Berger, *The Humanitarian Diplomacy of the ICRC and the Conflict in Croatia (1991–1992)* (ICRC, 1995) Annex 4.
[97] The London International Conference: Programme of Action on Humanitarian Issues Agreed between the Co-Chairmen to the Conference and the Parties to the Conflict, 27 August 1992, para 3(i).

If, as indicated above, unilateral declarations issued by states on international humanitarian law during a non-international armed conflict are treated as binding,[98] so too must unilateral declarations of non-state armed groups be considered binding. The alternative is that the state would be bound but not the armed group; yet the state may well have issued its declaration on the condition that the non-state armed group would also do so. This may be done for reasons of equality of obligation and not wishing to place constraints on itself to which the opposing party would not also be subject. This is particularly important where the parties are agreeing to be bound by obligations to which they are not already bound, for example to the law of *international* armed conflict.

Declarations of national liberation movements

In the late 1970s and early 1980s, various national liberation movements committed to abiding by international humanitarian law. In 1981, the South West Africa People's Organization (SWAPO) declared that 'it intends to respect and be guided by the rules of the four Geneva Conventions of 12 August 1949 for the protection of the victims of armed conflicts and the 1977 additional Protocol relating to the protection of victims of international armed conflicts (Protocol I)'.[99] One year earlier, and along similar lines, the União Nacional para a Independência Total de Angola (UNITA) committed 'to the Geneva Conventions and ... to the fundamental rules of international law applicable in armed conflicts'.[100] The African National Council—Zimbabwe African People's Union (ANC-ZAPU) also undertook to apply the Geneva Conventions and Additional Protocol I,[101] while the Polisario Front of Western Sahara committed to respect the Geneva Conventions.[102] In 1989, the Palestine Liberation Organization (PLO) submitted a declaration to the depositary, which provided that 'the Executive Committee of the Palestine Liberation Organization, entrusted with the functions of the Government of the State of Palestine by decision of the Palestine National Council, decided, on 4 May 1989, to adhere to the Four Geneva Conventions of 12 August 1949 and the two Protocols additional thereto'. This purported accession was not accepted by the depositary. However, it noted that the PLO's 'unilateral declaration of application of the four Geneva Conventions and of the additional Protocol I made on 7 June 1982 ... remains valid'.[103]

Declarations of non-state armed groups

The vast majority of unilateral declarations that are issued in times of non-international armed conflict emanate from non-state armed groups. This is unsurprising given that states have the opportunity to demonstrate their consent to be bound by particular rules through ratification of treaties. Non-state armed groups cannot ratify treaties and thus, their acceptance of particular rules necessarily takes place in an ad hoc manner.

Purported accession

The strongest form of a unilateral declaration of an armed group is an attempt to accede to the Geneva Conventions or a related conventional instrument. On one occasion, a

---

[98] See above, 114.
[99] South West Africa People's Organisation, Declaration to the International Committee of the Red Cross, 15 July 1981.
[100] Declaration by UNITA, 25 July 1980 [to ICRC], (1980) 20 *IRRC* 320.
[101] ICRC, Annual Report 1977 (ICRC, 1978) 16.
[102] ICRC, Annual Report 1975 (ICRC, 1976) 8.
[103] Note of Information [of the Depositary], 13 September 1989.

purported accession has succeeded, with the 1960 attempt of the Provisional Government of the Algerian Republic to the Geneva Conventions to accede being accepted by a number of states.[104] However, that was an exceptional instance and attempted accessions by non-state entities will usually be rejected. Prior to its accession, the Provisional Government and the Front de Libération Nationale (FLN) made a number of commitments to respect common Article 3 and the Geneva Conventions as a whole. For example, on 16 February 1956, a representative of the FLN in Paris assured the ICRC delegate that 'leaders of the [FLN] are doing whatever is in their power to respect and ensure respect for the fundamental rules of humanity'.[105] One week later, the FLN wrote to the ICRC indicating:

> With reference to Article 2, paragraph 3 of the Geneva Convention, we are prepared to implement the provisions of this Convention to all French prisoners of war taken by the National Liberation Army, subject to reciprocity on the part of the government of the French Republic.[106]

The Provisional Government also set out a White Paper on the application of the Geneva Conventions to the armed conflict.[107]

Declarations to the ICRC

Of greater frequency than attempted accessions are commitments that are made to the ICRC. Numerous examples exist of non-state armed groups issuing unilateral declarations that accept international humanitarian law generally or the Geneva Conventions in particular. For example, during the Greek civil war, in 1945, the National Liberation Front (EAM) and Greek People's National Liberation Army (ELAS) committed to apply the 1929 Geneva Conventions.[108] During the conflict in Hungary in 1956, President Szigethy of the Gyor Committee gave a commitment to the ICRC delegate to apply the Geneva Conventions during the civil war. He also promised to issue an order to his troops in this regard.[109] However, the National Liberation Committee of Sopron refused to issue a similar commitment.[110] Decades later, the Hungarian Supreme Court would affirm the applicability of common Article 3 to the events of

---

[104] Instruments of Accession of the Algerian Republic to the Geneva Conventions of August 12, 1949 (registered at Berne, 20 June 1960). This is reproduced in M Bedjaoui, *Law and the Algerian Revolution* (International Association of Democratic Lawyers, 1961) 199.
[105] Note de Dossier, 16 February 1956, ICRC Archives 225 008-002. The original reads: 'les dirigeants du front de libération nationale font de qui est en leur pouvoir respecter ou faire respecter les règles essentielles d'humanité.'
[106] Lettre de la Délégation Algérienne, représentant le Front de Libération Nationale et l'Armée de Libération Nationale à Monsieur David de Traz, Représentant Spécial du Comité International de la Croix-Rouge, 23 February 1956, ICRC Archives B AG 202 008-001. The original reads:

> Nous référant à l'article 2, troisième paragraphe de la Convention de Genève, nous sommes prêts à appliquer les dispositions de ladite Convention à tous les prisonniers de guerre français pris par l'Armée de Libération Nationale, sous réserve de réciprocité de la part du Gouvernement de la République Française.

[107] *White Paper on the Application of the Geneva Conventions of 1949 to the French-Algerian Conflict* (Algerian Office, New York, 1960).
[108] Telegram of ICRC delegate to ICRC, 29 January 1945, ICRC Archives G44/53c-236.
[109] Rapport de M Beckh sur sa Mission a Vienne, a Budapest et en Hongrie Occidentale, 15 November 1956, ICRC Archives B AG 251 094-004.
[110] Proces Verbal de Telephone de M Beckh et M Borsinger, 2 November 1956, ICRC Archives, ibid.

1956.[111] In 1958, Fidel Castro, then Commander in Chief of an armed group fighting against the forces of Cuban President Batista, wrote to the ICRC indicating:

> Let me be clear that... all Laws of War are respected here and injured enemies treated with the greatest degree of humanity possible in the current battle conditions...[112]

Castro reiterated his intention to apply the Geneva Conventions to captured fighters upon his victory.[113] Immediately prior to the attempted secession of Biafra from Nigeria (1967–70), the Biafran authorities assured the ICRC that it 'proposed to apply the Geneva Conventions in the event of a conflict'.[114] More recently, in 1994, the Rwandese Patriotic Front (RPF) committed to the ICRC to respect international humanitarian law.[115] The FMLN of El Salvador did likewise in 1985.[116]

Commitments to the ICRC are usually made orally to visiting delegates or in writing to ICRC Headquarters in Geneva. As such, it is unlikely that these commitments are made for propaganda purposes. This is not to suggest that they will inevitably be followed, given that they may be made for reputational reasons or as a result of political pressure. However, their sometimes private and confidential nature suggests that they are not issued in order to influence the international community, as demonstrated by the fact that many of the commitments are not well known and some of them are buried in the ICRC archives.

General declarations

Commitments are not always addressed to the ICRC. They are sometimes addressed to UN bodies or to the Depositary of the Geneva Conventions. For example, in 1988, the LTTE of Sri Lanka committed to abide by the Geneva Conventions and Additional Protocols in a letter to the members of the forty-fourth session of the UN Commission on Human Rights. In the letter, the LTTE stated:

> On this date we have transmitted our notice of acceptance of the Geneva Conventions I–IV of 1949 and the Protocols I and II to the Geneva Conventions to United Nations Headquarters and to the International Committee of the Red Cross.[117]

Just a few years later, in 1991, the National Democratic Front of the Philippines (NDFP):

---

[111] See (2000) 3 *YIHL* 518–9.

[112] Letter from Fidel Castro, 24 July 1958, ICRC Archives B AG 200 060. The original reads:

> Debo hacer constar que,... aquí se respetan todas las leyes de la Guerra y se trata a los heridos enemigos con el máximo de humanidad posible en las condiciones actuales de la lucha...

[113] Oral Commitment of Fidel Castro to the ICRC Delegate in Cuba, 10 January 1959, in Rapport No 3 de P Jequier à CICR, 14 January 1959, ICRC Archives B AG 200 060.

[114] ICRC, Annual Report 1967 (ICRC, 1968) 36.

[115] Report of the Special Rapporteur on extrajudicial, summary, or arbitrary executions, Mission to Rwanda, E/CN.4/1994/7/Add.1, 11 August 1993, para 26.

[116] ICRC, Annual Report 1985 (ICRC, 1986) 36.

[117] Letter from Vellupillai Prabhakaran, Leader, Liberation Tigers of Tamil Eelam, to Members and Observers, United Nations Commission on Human Rights, Forty-fourth session, 24 February 1988. See also Press Release, International Secretariat, Liberation Tigers of Tamil Eelam, 18 February 1992; Letter from Velummylum Manoharan, Representative, LTTE International Secretariat, to Honourable Judges of the US Court of Appeal District of Colombia Circuit, undated, published in *Sunday Times* (Sri Lanka), 16 November 1997.

formally declare[d] its adherence to international humanitarian law, especially Article 3 common to the Geneva Conventions as well as Protocol II additional to said conventions, in the conduct of the armed conflict in the Philippines.[118]

In 1996, it also committed to the Geneva Conventions and Additional Protocol I.[119] The commitments were made to the Swiss Government as depositary of the Geneva Conventions and Additional Protocols, as well as to the ICRC. They were also publicized relatively widely.

For its part, in 1995, the Kurdistan Workers' Party (PKK) of Turkey made a commitment to the UN, in which it stated that:

[i]n its conflict with the Turkish state forces, the PKK undertakes to respect the Geneva Conventions of 1949 and the First Protocol of 1977 regarding the conduct of hostilities and the protection of the victims of war and to treat those obligations as having the force of law within its own forces and the areas within its control.[120]

Commitments may also be made to the public at large. For example, in 1995, and again in 2004, the Ejército de Liberación Nacional (ELN) of Colombia declared its respect for international humanitarian law, indicating that its conduct 'is inspired by the clear understanding that the rules of International Humanitarian Law are absolutely and universally applicable and binding'.[121] The Coordinadora Nacional Guerrillera, Simón Bolívar, issued a resolution in 1987 providing that:

[t]he struggle for the right to life. As guerrilla organisations we commit ourselves to respecting the Ius Gentium, the Geneva agreements and to making the military confrontation which today takes place in the country humane, and we ask the government and its army to equally respect the rules of international humanitarian law.

We reject the practices of torture, disappearances and undertake to offer treatment to captured enemies and to respect the civilian population and its property in military conflict.

We reject assassinations and threats against members of the UP, other political and social movements and important democratic figures who are directly responsible for State security agencies and the State's paramilitary machine, and believe that in order to stop this slaughter a mass public response must be fostered and perpetrators must be punished.[122]

---

[118] NDFP Declaration of Adherence to International Humanitarian Law, 15 August 1991, reproduced in NDFP, *Declaration of Undertaking to Apply the Geneva Conventions of 1949 and Protocol I of 1977* (NDFP Human Rights Monitoring Committee Booklet No 6) 98.
[119] NDFP Declaration of Undertaking to Apply the Geneva Conventions of 1949 and Protocol I of 1977, 5 July 1996, in ibid, 9.
[120] PKK Statement to the United Nations, 24 January 1995.
[121] Comando Central, Ejército de Liberación Nacional, Foro Internacional: Minas antipersonales y Acuerdos Humanitarios, 4 June 2004. See also the radio address on the Declaration on International Humanitarian Law, 15 July 1995.
[122] Resolución Política de la Cumbre Constitutiva de la Coordinadora Nacional Guerrillera Simón Bolívar, October 1987, reproduced in Oficina del Alto Comisionado para la Paz et al (eds), *Derecho Internacional Humanitario Aplicado: Casos de Colombia, El Salvador, Guatemala, Yugoslavia y Ruanda* (CICR, 1998) 273. The original reads:

La lucha por el derecho a la vida. Como organizaciones guerrilleras nos comprometemos a respetar el Derecho de Gentes, los acuerdos de Ginebra y a humanizer la confrontación bélica que hoy se da en el país y exigimos que el goberino y su ejército también respeten las normas del derecho internacional humanitaro.

Rechazamos las prácticas de las torturas, las desapariciones, y nos comprometemos a dar un trato a los enemigos capturados y a respetar la población civil y sus bienes en la contienda militar.

Rechazamos los asesinatos y las amenazas contra los miembros de la UP, los demás movimientos políticos y sociales y las personalidades democráticas, cuyos responsables directos son los organismos de seguridad del Estado y sus aparatos paramilitares, y

In the conflicts in the former Yugoslavia in the late 1990s and early 2000s, the National Liberation Army (NLA) of the Former Yugoslav Republic of Macedonia stated that '[t]he General Staff and the entire UÇK respect and will always respect the Geneva Convention during their operations'.[123] The Kosovo Liberation Army (KLA) indicated that it 'has stated before and repeats that we have respected and continue to respect all international conventions of war and peace',[124] and that it 'recognizes and respects the international acts of the United Nations and the Conventions on war'.[125] In 1994, the Ejército Zapatista de Liberación Nacional (EZLN) of Mexico declared 'now and forever that we are subject to that which is stipulated by the Laws of War of the Geneva Conventions'.[126] A decade later, in 2004, the Communist Party of Nepal-Maoist (CPN-M) stated that '[o]ur Party has been committed to the fundamental norms of human right[s] and Geneva Convention [sic] since the historic initiation of the People's War'.[127] The Movimiento Revolucionario Tupac Amaru (MRTA) likewise indicated in 1996 that it 'has respected and will respect the Geneva Convention on internal conflicts'.[128]

Declarations of this sort have to be treated with a degree of caution. Some may be made for political and propaganda purposes. For example, the commitment of the LTTE was not followed on the ground. However, others may be made for genuine reasons. For example, the MRTA indicated that it issued its commitment in order to distinguish itself from the Sendero Luminoso, which was also involved in the conflict in Peru at the relevant time and which committed numerous atrocities.[129] Thus, as discussed above, each declaration needs to be treated on its own terms.

Declarations on particular rules
As an alternative, or in addition, to commitments to international humanitarian law generally, commitments are also made in respect of particular rules. For example, in 2008, JEM and the Sudan Liberation Movement-Unity (SLM-Unity), both of Darfur, committed to particular norms of international humanitarian law. They stated:

We will do our utmost to guarantee the protection of civilian populations in accordance with the principles of human rights and international humanitarian law. In collaboration with

    consideramos que para frenar esta matazón es necesario impulsar la más amplia movilización de las masa y castigar a los culpables.

[123] Ali Ahmeti, Political Representative, UÇK General Staff, Untitled Document, 8 May 2001, Exhibit P00507.E in ICTY *Boškoski* trial. See also Ali Ahmeti, National Liberation Army Commander, Ideas for Conducting the Operation, Exhibit P00487 in ICTY *Boškoski* trial.
[124] Political Statement No 11 of the Kosova Liberation Army, 5 October 1998, reproduced as 'UCK Confirms Respect for International Conventions', *Pristina Koha Ditore*, 6 October 1998, Exhibit P48 in ICTY *Limaj* trial (ICTY translation). See also, Memorandum of the General Staff of the Kosovo Liberation Army Sent to the Relevant Institutions of the International Community, undated, reproduced in UCK Sends 'Memorandum' to International Community, *Pristina Bujku*, 17 October 1998, ibid (ICTY translation).
[125] Political Statement of the KLA, 27 April 1998, Exhibit P328, Annex 12, in ICTY *Haradinaj* trial.
[126] Declaration of War of the Zapatista National Liberation Army (EZLN), Communiqué of 2 January 1994, reproduced and translated in B Clarke and C Ross (eds), *Voice of Fire: Communiqués and Interviews from the Zapatista National Liberation Army* (Freedom Voices, 2000) 31, 32. See also EZLN General Command, Declaración de la Selva Lacandona, 1993.
[127] Appeal of the Communist Party of Nepal (Maoist), 16 March 2004.
[128] Communique No 4, December 1996. See also Letter from the National Directorate of the MRTA to Cardinal Juan Lanázari Ricketts, 26 March 1989.
[129] See MRTA, *Con las Masas y las Armas, Conquistando el Porvenir: Notas sobre la Historia del MRTA* (MRTA, 1990).

UNICEF, we will adopt measures ensuring protection of children in Darfur. We also affirm the principles of freedom of movement.

We reaffirm our commitment to refrain from targeting or forcibly displacing civilian populations, destroying civilian infrastructure, recruiting children for military operations, and to hold to account perpetrators of acts of rape and other forms of gender based violence. We recognize that placing military assets and personnel in close proximity to civilian areas increases the risk that civilians will be caught up in hostilities or even targeted. We will therefore continue our policy of maintaining a proper physical separation between our armed forces and the civilian population. We also continue to commit to curtailing the militarization of IDP/refugee camps.

We reaffirm our commitment to clearly instructing our personnel on the ground regarding their obligations under human rights and international humanitarian law.[130]

A year later, in 2009, the Houthi of Yemen stated:

[W]e would like to confirm again that... in this imposed war we commit to the humanitarian international laws with regard to protecting civilians and dealing with the hostages and the neutral associations and entities like the international and aid organizations and media.[131]

Commitments of this sort are partial in nature given that they are made in respect of specific rules alone. However, the advantage of such commitments is that they are focused on particular issues arising during the conflict in question. Furthermore, commitments to international humanitarian law generally have the downside that the group in question may not fully appreciate all the obligations to which it has committed. The group may also not have the ability to comply with the various obligations that it is now required to follow. Thus, although more holistic commitments are perhaps of greater appeal to the international community, commitments to abide by particular rules may have a greater influence in practice.[132]

Declarations on human rights law

Unilateral declarations of non-state armed groups may also contain commitments to respect human rights law. For example, the Ogaden National Liberation Front (ONLF) of Ethiopia stated that it 'confirms that we shall adhere to all relevant international agreements on human rights including the Universal Declaration on Human Rights'.[133] As part of its 2004 commitment on international humanitarian law, the CPN-M of Nepal also indicated that '[o]ur Party has been expressing its commitment not only on the Geneva Convention in relation to the war but also on the international declarations in relation to the human rights. And at the present concrete condition, we want to clarify that if there is a concrete proposal for us through the international human right convention, our approach will be positive on that'.[134] For its part, during the conflict in Sierra Leone, the RUF indicated that '[w]e affirm and uphold the principle of a responsible press freedom, in particular, and of Human Rights and fundamental freedoms for all without distinction as to race, sex, language,

---

[130] Statement by the Opposition Movements [JEM and SLM-Unity], undated (published on 11 July 2008).
[131] Letter from Abdulmalik al Houthi to Dr Mohammed Al-Mikhlafi [Head of the Yemeni Observatory for Human Rights], undated (published on 4 September 2009). See also Letter from Abd al-Malik Badr al-Din Al-houthi to Human Rights Watch, 29/Jumada II/1430.
[132] See also M Sassòli, 'The Implementation of International Humanitarian Law: Current and Inherent Challenges' (2007) 10 *YIHL* 45, 64.
[133] Political Programme of the Ogaden National Liberation Front (ONLF), undated.
[134] Appeal of the Communist Party of Nepal (Maoist), 16 March 2004.

or religion, in general'.¹³⁵ As indicated above, the JEM and SLM-Unity of Sudan also provided that '[w]e will do our utmost to guarantee the protection of civilian populations in accordance with the principles of human rights and international humanitarian law'.¹³⁶

Action plans concluded between armed groups and UN entities on the disarmament, demobilization, and reintegration of child soldiers are also important for the commitments they contain to abide by human rights law. For example, the 2009 Action Plan between the Moro Islamic Liberation Front (MILF) and the UN in the Philippines contains a clause:

Stressing acceptance and commitment of the Moro Islamic Liberation Front (MILF), to the obligations under International Humanitarian Law, International Human Rights Law, specifically the Optional Protocol to the Convention on the Rights of the Child (CRC) on the involvement of children in armed conflict, and relevant UN Security Council Resolutions... to promote and protect the rights of the child and other relevant policies and agreements.¹³⁷

Commitments to abide by human rights law are important given the uncertainty as to whether or not, and if so, to what degree, armed groups have human rights obligations.¹³⁸ If a group commits to be bound by international human rights law, that commitment may vest human rights obligations in the group in the same way as a commitment to abide by international humanitarian law is treated as binding on the group.¹³⁹ However, the drawbacks of uncertainty of knowledge and capacity also arise.

In sum, unilateral declarations of both states and non-state armed groups may prove important. Although some declarations may be issued for propaganda purposes and with no intention of being followed, others may not be issued for such purposes, rather being issued with every intention of being followed. Sweeping generalizations cannot be made; each commitment will have to be assessed on its own terms. Many such declarations should also be considered binding as a matter of law.

3.2.2 Agreements

Unilateral declarations are by no means the only form of ad hoc commitment that is issued in times of non-international armed conflict. Agreements are not infrequently concluded between states, non-state armed groups, and international organizations on issues of international humanitarian law. This should not come as a surprise given the existence of similar agreements dating back to at least 1820.¹⁴⁰ Common Article 3 also exhorts parties to conflicts to conclude agreements through which humanitarian law

---

¹³⁵ 'Lasting Peace in Sierra Leone: The Revolutionary United Front Sierra Leone (RUF/SL) Perspective and Vision', undated.
¹³⁶ Statement by the Opposition Movements, above note 130.
¹³⁷ Action Plan between the Moro Islamic Liberation Front (MILF) and the United Nations in the Philippines regarding the Issue of Recruitment and Use of Child Soldiers in the Armed Conflict in Mindanao, 1 August 2009. See also Action Plan between the Sudan People's Liberation Army and the United Nations regarding Children Associated with the SPLA in Southern Sudan, 20 November 2009.
¹³⁸ See above, 95–7.
¹³⁹ See above, 118.
¹⁴⁰ Tratado de Regularización de la Guerra, 26 November 1820, reproduced in (1820–1) 71 *Consolidated Treaty Series* 291.

norms other than those contained in the Article are brought into force. This notion of a special agreement is thus a broad one and encompasses any agreement which brings into force additional humanitarian law norms. It includes agreements specifically designated as special agreements as well as more general agreements on human rights and humanitarian law. Peace agreements between states and armed groups also increasingly contain humanitarian law commitments.[141]

Agreements on international humanitarian law

The most well-known ad hoc international humanitarian law agreements are those concluded between the parties to the armed conflicts in Bosnia (1992–5) and Croatia (1991–5). The Memorandum of Understanding of 27 November 1991 relating to the conflict in Croatia provided that:

(1) Wounded and sick

All wounded and sick on land shall be treated in accordance with the provisions of the First Geneva Convention of 12 August 1949.

(2) Wounded, sick and shipwrecked at sea

All wounded, sick and shipwrecked at sea shall be treated in accordance with the provisions of the Second Geneva Convention of 12 August 1949.

(3) Captured combatants

Captured combatants shall enjoy the treatment provided for by the Third Geneva Convention of 12 August 1949.

(4) Civilians in the power of the adverse party

Civilians who are in the power of the adverse party and who are deprived of their liberty for reasons related to the armed conflict shall benefit from the rules relating to the treatment of internees laid down in the Fourth Geneva Convention of 12 August 1949 (Articles 79 to 149).

All civilians shall be treated in accordance with Articles 72 to 79 of Additional Protocol I.

(5) Protection of the civilian population against certain consequences of hostilities

The civilian population is protected by Articles 13 to 26 of the Fourth Geneva Convention of 12 August 1949.

(6) Conduct of hostilities

Hostilities shall be conducted in accordance with Article 35 to 42 and Articles 48 to 58 of Additional Protocol I, and the Protocol on Prohibition or Restrictions on the Use of Mines, Booby Traps and Other Devices annexed to the 1980 Weapons Convention.

(7) Establishment of protected zones

The parties agree that for the establishment of protected zones, the annexed standard draft agreement shall be used as a basis for negotiations.

(8) Tracing of missing persons

The parties agree to set up a Joint Commission to trace missing persons; the Joint Commission will be made up of representatives of the parties concerned, all Red Cross organizations concerned and in particular the Yugoslav Red Cross, the Croatian Red Cross and the Serbian Red Cross with ICRC participation.

(9) Assistance to the civilian population

The parties shall allow the free passage of all consignments of medicines and medical supplies, essential foodstuffs and clothing which are destined exclusively for the other

---

[141] See generally C Bell, *Peace Agreements and Human Rights* (Oxford University Press, 2000).

party's civilian population, it being understood that both parties are entitled to verify that the consignments are not diverted from their destination.

They shall consent to and cooperate with operations to provide the civilian population with exclusively humanitarian, impartial and nondiscriminatory assistance. All facilities will be given in particular to the ICRC.

(10) Red Cross emblem

The parties undertake to comply with the rules relating to the use of the Red Cross emblem. In particular, they shall ensure that these rules are observed by all persons under their authority. The parties shall repress any misuse of the emblem and any attack on persons or property under its protection.[142]

The Agreement of 22 May 1992 relating to the conflict in Bosnia contained similar provisions. It provided that '[t]he parties commit themselves to respect and to ensure respect for the Article 3 of the four Geneva Conventions of 12 August 1949'. It also noted specifically the common Article 3 clause pursuant to which 'the Parties agree to bring into force the following provisions':

2.1. Wounded, sick and shipwrecked
The treatment provided to the wounded, sick and shipwrecked shall be in accordance with the provisions of the First and Second Geneva Conventions of 12 August 1949, in particular:

— All the wounded, sick and shipwrecked, whether or not they have taken part in the armed conflict, shall be respected and protected.
— In all circumstances, they shall be treated humanely and shall receive, to the fullest extent practicable and with the least possible delay, the medical care and attention required by their condition. There shall be no distinction among them founded on any grounds other than medical ones.

2.2. Protection of *hospitals and other medical units*
Hospitals and other medical units, including medical transportation may in no circumstances be attacked, they shall at all times be respected and protected. They may not be used to shield combatants, military objectives or operations from attacks.

The protection shall not cease unless they are used to commit military acts. However, the protection may only cease after due warning and a reasonable time limit to cease military activities.

2.3. Civilian population
The civilians and the civilian population are protected by Articles 13 to 34 of the Fourth Geneva Convention of 12 August 1949. The civilian population and individual civilians shall enjoy general protection against the dangers arising from military operations. They shall not be the object of attack. Acts or threats of violence the primary purpose of which is to spread terror among the civilian population are prohibited.

All civilians shall be treated in accordance with Articles 72 to 79 of Additional Protocol I. Civilians who are in the power of an adverse party and who are deprived of their liberty for reasons related to the armed conflict shall benefit from the rules relating to the treatment of internees laid down in the Fourth Geneva Convention of 12 August 1949.

In the treatment of the civilian population there shall be no adverse distinction founded on race, religion or faith, or any other similar criteria.

---

[142] Memorandum of Understanding, 27 November 1991, reproduced in M Sassòli, AA Bouvier, and A Quintin, *How Does Law Protect in War? Volume III* (ICRC, Geneva, 2011) 1713.

The displacement of the civilian population shall not be ordered unless the security of the civilians involved or imperative military reasons so demand. Should such displacements have to be carried out, all possible measures shall be taken in order that the civilian population may be received under satisfactory conditions of shelter, hygiene, health, safety and nutrition.

The International Committee of the Red Cross (ICRC) shall have free access to civilians in all places, particularly in places of internment or detention, in order to fulfil its humanitarian mandate according to the Fourth Geneva Convention of 12 August 1949.

2.4. Captured combatants
Captured combatants shall enjoy the treatment provided for by the Third Geneva Convention. The International Committee of the Red Cross (ICRC) shall have free access to all captured combatants in order to fulfil its humanitarian mandate according to the Third Geneva Convention of 12 August 1949.

2.5. Conduct of hostilities
Hostilities shall be conducted in the respect of the laws of armed conflict, particularly in accordance with Articles 35 to 42 and Articles 48 to 58 of Additional Protocol I, and the Protocol on the prohibition or Restriction on the Use of Mines, Booby Traps and other Devices annexed to the 1980 Weapons Convention. In order to promote the protection of the civilian population, combatants are obliged to distinguish themselves from the civilian population.

2.6. Assistance to the civilian population
The Parties shall allow the free passage of all consignments of medicines and medical supplies, essential foodstuffs and clothing which are destined exclusively to the civilian population.

They shall consent to and cooperate with operations to provide the civilian population with exclusively humanitarian, impartial and non-discriminatory assistance. All facilities will be given in particular to the ICRC.

3. Red Cross Emblem
The Red Cross emblem shall be respected. The Parties undertake to use the emblem only to identify medical units and personnel and to comply with the other rules of international humanitarian law relating to the use of the Red Cross emblem and shall repress any misuse of the emblem or attacks on persons or property under its protection.[143]

Another agreement was concluded the following day, relating to the exchange of lists of prisoners with a view to their release and the evacuation of certain persons.[144] A third agreement was concluded some weeks later and related to the activities of the ICRC in delivering humanitarian assistance to vulnerable groups, providing medical assistance, and accessing prisoners. It also contained the parties' agreement to provide security guarantees to the ICRC in order to enable it to carry out its work.[145]

Numerous other ad hoc agreements exist, including those concluded between the Government of Colombia and the Fuerzas Armadas Revolucionarias de Colombia (FARC) in 2001,[146] the Government of the Philippines and the MILF in 2002,[147] the Government of Uganda and the Lord's Resistance Army/Movement (LRA/M) in 2006,[148] the Government of Liberia and the National Patriotic Front of Liberia

---

[143] Reproduced in M Sassòli, AA Bouvier, and A Quintin, *How Does Law Protect in War? Volume III* (ICRC, 2011) 1717. On which, see B Jakovljević, 'The Agreement of May 22, 1992, on the Implementation of International Humanitarian Law in the Armed Conflict in Bosnia-Herzegovina' [1992] *Jugoslovenska Revija Za Medunarodno Pravo* 212.

[144] Agreement of 23 May 1992.

[145] Agreement of 6 June 1992.

[146] Government-FARC Humanitarian Exchange Accord, 2 June 2001.

[147] Implementing Guidelines on the Humanitarian, Rehabilitation and Development Aspects of the GRP-MILF Tripoli Agreement on Peace of 2001, 7 May 2002.

[148] Cessation of Hostilities Agreement, Addendum I, 1 November 2006; Agreement on a Permanent Ceasefire, 23 February 2008.

(NPFL) in 1993,[149] the Government of Sudan and the Eastern Sudan Front in 2006,[150] and the Government of Sudan, JEM, and SLM in 2004.[151] Thus, far from infrequently, states that are actually involved in non-international armed conflicts accept the applicability of a wide range of humanitarian law norms to the conflict in question. Two agreements, in particular, stand out. The 2002 Agreement on the Protection of Civilians and Civilian Facilities, concluded between the Government of Sudan and the Sudan People's Liberation Movement (SPLM), provides that:

[t]he Government of the Republic of Sudan (GOS) and the Sudan People's Liberation Movement (SPLM) (hereafter referred to as the 'Parties') reconfirm their obligations under international law, including common Article 3 of the 1949 Geneva Conventions, to take constant care to protect the civilian population, civilians and civilian objects against the dangers arising from military operations. In this context, the Parties specifically commit themselves:

a) to refrain from targeting or intentionally attacking non-combatant civilians;
b) to refrain from targeting or intentionally attacking civilian objects or facilities, such as schools, hospitals, religious premises, health and food distribution centers, or relief operations, or objects or facilities indispensable to the survival of the civilian population and of a civilian nature;
c) to refrain from endangering the safety of civilians by intentionally using them as 'human shields' or by using civilian facilities such as hospitals or schools to shield otherwise lawful military targets; and
d) to take all precautions feasible to avoid incidental loss of civilian life, injury to civilians, and danger to civilian objects.

Military operations include, but are not limited to, air attacks, artillery attacks, ground attacks, ambushes and intentional military activity or other uses of force that could result in the killing or injury of persons or damage or destruction of property.[152]

Along largely similar lines, the 2009 Agreement on the Civilian Protection Component of the International Monitoring Team, between the Government of the Philippines and the MILF provides that:

[t]he Parties reconfirm their obligations under humanitarian law and human rights law to take constant care to protect the civilian population and civilian properties against the dangers arising in armed conflict situations. In this context, the Parties commit themselves to:

a) Refrain from intentionally targeting or attacking non-combatants, prevent suffering of the civilian population and avoid acts that would cause collateral damage to civilians;
b) Refrain from targeting or intentionally attacking civilian properties or facilities such as schools, hospitals, religious premises, health and food distribution centers, or relief operations, or objects or facilities indispensable to the survival of the civilian population and of a civilian nature;

---

[149] Cotonou Accord between Interim Government of National Unity (IGNU) of Liberia, National Patriotic Front of Liberia (NPFL) and the United Movement of Liberia for Democracy (ULIMO), 25 July 1993.
[150] Agreement to Create a Conducive Atmosphere for Peace, 19 June 2006.
[151] Agreement on Humanitarian Ceasefire on the Conflict in Darfur, 8 April 2004; Protocol between the Government of Sudan (GoS), the Sudan Liberation Movement/Army (SLM/A) and the Justice and Equality Movement (JEM) on the Improvement of the Humanitarian Situation in Darfur, 9 November 2004; Protocol between the Government of Sudan (GoS), the Sudan Liberation Movement/Army (SLM/A) and the Justice and Equality Movement (JEM) on the Enhancement of the Security Situation in Darfur in Accordance with the N'Djamena Agreement, 9 November 2004.
[152] Agreement between the Government of the Republic of Sudan and the Sudan People's Liberation Movement to Protect Non-Combatant Civilians and Civilian Facilities from Military Attack, 10 March 2002.

c) Take all necessary actions to facilitate the provision of relief supplies to affected communities;
d) Take all precautions feasible to avoid incidental loss of civilian life, injury to civilians, and danger to civilian objects;
e) Ensure that all protective and relief actions shall be undertaken in a purely nondiscriminatory basis covering all affected communities.[153]

The similarities between the two agreements are evident.

Agreements on international humanitarian law and human rights law

In addition to agreements on international humanitarian law, other agreements contain a mix of international humanitarian law and human rights law norms. For example, the 1998 Comprehensive Agreement on Respect for Human Rights and International Humanitarian Law (CARHRIHL) between the Government of the Philippines and the NDFP contains a lengthy list of human rights and humanitarian law guarantees. Insofar as international humanitarian law is concerned, the Agreement provides that the following acts are prohibited:

Article 3

1. violence to life and person, particularly killing or causing injury, being subjected to physical or mental torture, mutilation, corporal punishment, cruel or degrading treatment and all acts of violence and reprisals, including hostage-taking, and acts against the physical well-being, dignity, political convictions and other human rights;
2. holding anyone responsible for an act that she/he has not committed and punishing anyone without complying with all the requisites of due process;
3. ...
4. desecration of the remains of those who have died in the course of the armed conflict or while under detention, and breach of duty to tender immediately such remains to their families or to give them decent burial;
5. ...
6. ...
7. practices that cause or allow the forcible evacuations or forcible reconcentration of civilians, unless the security of the civilians involved or imperative military reasons so demand; the emergence and increase of internally displaced families and communities, and the destruction of the lives and property of the civilian population;

Article 4

1. Persons hors de combat and those who do not take a direct part in hostilities are entitled to respect for their lives, dignity, human rights, political convictions and their moral and physical integrity and shall be protected in all circumstances and treated humanely without any adverse distinction founded on race, color, faith, sex, birth, social standing or any other similar criteria.
2. The wounded and the sick shall be collected and cared for by the party to the armed conflict which has them in its custody or responsibility.

---

[153] Agreement on the Civilian Protection Component of the International Monitoring Team, 27 October 2009.

3. Neutral persons or entities and medical personnel, including persons of humanitarian and/or medical organizations like the International Committee of the Red Cross (ICRC), shall be protected and respected. The establishments, facilities, transport and equipments of these persons, entities and organizations; objects bearing the emblem of the red cross and the flag of peaceful intention; and historic monuments, cultural objects and places of worship shall likewise be protected.
4. Civilian population and civilians shall be treated as such and shall be distinguished from combatants and, together with their property, shall not be the object of attack. They shall likewise be protected against indiscriminate aerial bombardment, strafing, artillery fire, mortar fire, arson, bulldozing and other similar forms of destroying lives and property, from the use of explosives as well as the stockpiling near or in their midst, and the use of chemical and biological weapons.
5. Civilians shall have the right to demand appropriate disciplinary actions against abuses arising from the failure of the Parties to the armed conflict to observe the principles and standards of international humanitarian law.
6. All persons deprived of their liberty for reasons related to the armed conflict shall be treated humanely, provided with adequate food and drinking water, and be afforded safeguards as regards to health and hygiene, and be confined in a secure place. Sufficient information shall be made available concerning persons who have been deprived of their liberty. On humanitarian or other reasonable grounds, such persons deprived of liberty shall be considered for safe release.
7. The ICRC and other humanitarian and/or medical entities shall be granted facilitation and assistance to enable them to care for the sick and the wounded and to undertake their humanitarian missions and activities.
8. Personnel and facilities of schools, the medical profession, religious institutions and places of worship, voluntary evacuation centers, programs and projects of relief and development shall not be the target of any attack. The persons of said entities shall be guaranteed their safety.
9. Every possible measure shall be taken, without delay, to search for and collect the wounded, sick and missing persons and to protect them from any harm and ill treatment, to ensure their adequate care and to search for the dead, prevent despoliation and mutilation and to dispose of them with respect.

...

Article 9

Internally displaced families and communities shall have the right to return to their places of abode and livelihood, to demand all possible assistance necessary to restore them to their normal lives and to be indemnified for damages suffered due to injuries and loss of lives.

Article 10

The Parties shall provide special attention to women and children to ensure their physical and moral integrity. Children shall not be allowed to take part in hostilities.

Article 11

Medical, religious and other humanitarian organizations and their personnel shall not carry out other tasks inimical to any of the Parties. Neither shall they be compelled to carry out tasks which are not compatible with their humanitarian tasks. Under no circumstances shall any person be punished for having carried out medical activities compatible with the principles of medical ethics, regardless of whoever is benefitting from such medical activities.

Article 12

Civilian population shall have the right to be protected against the risks and dangers posed by the presence of military camps in urban centers and other protected areas.[154]

The 1990 Agreement on Human Rights between the Government of El Salvador and the FMLN, although containing human rights law norms alone, provides in its Preamble that:

for the purposes of the present political agreement, 'human rights' shall mean those rights recognized by the Salvadorian legal system, including treaties to which El Salvador is a party, and by the declarations and principles on human rights *and humanitarian law* adopted by the United Nations and the Organization of American States.[155]

Likewise, the 1994 Comprehensive Agreement on Human Rights between the Government of Guatemala and the Unidad Revolucionaria Nacional Guatemalteca (URNG), although principally a human rights agreement, contains the provision that:

[u]ntil such time as the firm and lasting peace agreement is signed, both Parties recognize the need to put a stop to suffering of the civilian population and to respect the human rights of those wounded, captured and those who have remained out of combat.[156]

For its part, the 2002 Implementing Guidelines on the Humanitarian, Rehabilitation and Development Aspects of the GRP-MILF [Government of Philippines-Moro Islamic Liberation Front] Tripoli Agreement on Peace of 2001 contains a general commitment to international humanitarian law and international human rights law as well as commitments to specific norms.[157]

Agreements on human rights law

Other agreements are of a broader sort but include commitments to respect human rights. These agreements are more numerous than the previous category and include agreements between the Government of Liberia, Liberians United for Reconciliation and Democracy (LURD), and Movement for Democracy in Liberia (MODEL) in 2003;[158] the Government of Nepal and the CPN-M in 2005;[159] the Government of Papua New Guinea and the relevant parties in 1997 and 1998;[160] and the Government of the Philippines and the MILF in 2009.[161] The language used in these agreements is of particular interest. The parties 'reiterate', 'reconfirm', and 'reaffirm' their obligations, all of which suggest that the relevant human rights obligations are not being created by the agreement but existed even prior to the conclusion of the agreement.

---

[154] 16 March 1998.
[155] Agreement on Human Rights, 26 July 1990, A/44/971-S/21541, Annex, 16 August 1990 (emphasis added).
[156] Agreement of 29 March 1994, Article IX(1).
[157] 7 May 2002, Article 4.
[158] Peace Agreement between the Government of Liberia (GOL), The Liberians United for Reconciliation and Democracy (LURD), The Movement for Democracy in Liberia (MODEL) and the Political Parties, 18 August 2003, Article XII.
[159] 12-Point Understanding reached between the Seven Political Parties and Nepal Communisty Party (Maoists), 22 November 2005, Point 8.
[160] Burnham Truce, 10 October 1997; Lincoln Agreement on Peace, Security and Development on Bougainville, 23 January 1998, Article 1.
[161] GRP/MILF, Agreement on the Civilian Protection Component of the International Monitoring Team, 27 October 2009.

Still other agreements do not contain concrete commitments on the part of the relevant parties but recall human rights in their preambular provisions or condemn violations of human rights.[162] Nonetheless, some of these preambular references are considered by the parties to represent concrete commitments. For example, the Preamble to the 1996 Abidjan Peace Agreement between the Government of Sierra Leone and the RUF provided that the parties are '[c]ommitted to promoting... full respect for human rights and humanitarian laws'.[163] The RUF later indicated that, in its view, this meant that both the Government and the RUF 'had committed themselves to the promotion of popular participation in government and full respect for human rights and humanitarian laws'.[164]

Commitments bringing into force international humanitarian law or international human rights law are also to be found in ceasefire or peace agreements. Such agreements include those concluded between the Government of Nepal and the CPN-M in 2006,[165] the Government of Burundi and the Palipehutu-FNL also in 2006,[166] the Government of Liberia and LURD in 2003,[167] the Government of Uganda and the National Resistance Movement (NRM) in 1985,[168] the Government of Sri Lanka and the LTTE in 2002,[169] the Government of Sudan and the Eastern Sudan Front in 2006;[170] and the Government of Sudan, the SLM, and the JEM also in 2006.[171]

Other agreements

Agreements are also concluded between non-state armed groups and UN entities, or between non-state armed groups and non-governmental organizations that contain the group's commitment to international humanitarian law or international human rights law. For example, in the Agreement on Ground Rules relating to Operation Lifeline Sudan, the SPLM, the SPLM-Unity, and the South Sudan Independence Movement each:

express[ed] our support for the following international humanitarian conventions and their principles, namely: (i) Convention on the Rights of the Child 1989; (ii) Geneva Conventions of 1949 and the 1977 Protocols additional to the Geneva Conventions.[172]

In some cases, tripartite agreements are entered into by states, armed groups, and UN entities, such as the 2002 Memorandum of Understanding between the Government

---

[162] Abidjan Peace Agreement, 30 November 1996; Protocol between the Government of Sudan (GoS), the Sudan Liberation Movement/Army (SLM/A) and the Justice and Equality Movement (JEM) on the Improvement of the Humanitarian Situation in Darfur, 9 November 2004.
[163] Abidjan Peace Agreement, 30 November 1996.
[164] 'Lasting Peace in Sierra Leone: The Revolutionary United Front Sierra Leone (RUF/SL) Perspective and Vision', undated.
[165] Ceasefire Code of Conduct, 25 May 2006, Preamble and Article 7.
[166] Comprehensive Ceasefire Agreement, 7 September 2006, Article II.
[167] Agreement on Ceasefire and Cessation of Hostilities between the Government of the Republic of Liberia and Liberians United for Reconciliation and Democracy and the Movement for Democracy in Liberia, 17 June 2003, Points 5 and 9; Comprehensive Peace Agreement between the Government of Liberia, the Liberians United for Reconciliation and Democracy, the Movement for Democracy in Liberia, and the Political Parties, 18 August 2003, Article XV.
[168] Nairobi Peace Agreement, 17 December 1985, Article 1(i).
[169] Ceasefire Agreement, 2002, Articles 1.2, 2.1, 2.2.
[170] Eastern Sudan Peace Agreement, 14 October 2006, Article 6.
[171] Darfur Peace Agreement, 5 May 2006, Articles 1(7) and 3.
[172] SPLM-United/Operation Lifeline Sudan, Agreement on Ground Rules, May 1996; SPLM/Operation Lifeline Sudan, Agreement on Ground Rules, 3 July 1995; South Sudan Independence Movement Operation/Lifeline Sudan, Agreement on Ground Rules, 5 August 1995.

of Sudan, the SPLM, and the United Nations regarding UN Mine Action Support to Sudan.[173]

Agreements between armed groups may also prove instructive. For example, in the Acte d'Engagement concluded between various armed groups fighting in the DRC, a commitment is made to 'strict observation of the rules of international humanitarian law and human rights law'.[174]

Bilateral agreements concluded between the warring parties are particularly important given the equality of obligation that arises through the agreement. As with unilateral declarations, agreements can be broad and all-encompassing or concluded to address specific problems arising out of the conflict. They may also be used to bring into force rules that would otherwise be inapplicable to the conflict. The mere existence of an agreement will not suffice, as is evident from the numerous atrocities committed during the conflicts in the former Yugoslavia despite the existence of the Memorandum of Understanding of 27 November 1991 and the 22 May 1992 Agreement. However, at other times, the existence of an agreement will prove important. For example, the NDFP frequently refers to the CARHRIHL in the context of its activities.[175] Ultimately, as with unilateral declarations, the importance of an agreement or lack thereof has to be judged on an individual basis.

3.2.3 Instructions, codes of conduct, and internal regulations

In addition to unilateral declarations and bilateral or trilateral agreements, during times of non-international armed conflict, states may issue ad hoc instructions or regulations to its armed forces on matters of international humanitarian law. For example, in 1967, during the attempted secession of Biafra, the Federal Government of Nigeria issued an Operational Code of Conduct, which provided in relevant part:

I direct all officers and men to observe strictly the following rules during operations (These instructions must be read in conjunction with the Geneva Convention):

   a. Under no circumstances should pregnant women be illtreated or killed.
   b. Children must not be molested or killed. They will be protected and cared for.
   c. Youths and school children may not be attacked unless they are engaged in open hostility against Federal Government Forces. They should be given all protection and care.
   d. Hospitals, hospital staff and patients should not be tampered with or molested.
   e. Soldiers who surrender will not be killed. They are to be disarmed and treated as prisoners of war. They are entitled in all circumstances to humane treatment and respect for their person and their honour.
   f. No property, building, etc, will be destroyed maliciously.
   g. Churches and Mosques must not be desecrated.
   h. No looting of any kind. (A good soldier will never loot).
   i. Women will be protected against any attack on their person, honour and in particular against rape or any form of indecent assault.
   j. Male civilians who are hostile to the Federal Forces are to be dealt with firmly but fairly. They must be humanely treated.
   k. All military and civilians wounded will be given necessary medical attention and care. They must be respected and protected in all circumstances.

---

[173] Memorandum of Understanding, 19 September 2002.
[174] Article III ('Observation stricte des règles du droit international humanitaire et des droits de l'Homme').
[175] See eg the statement of a New People's Army spokesperson, 'NPA did not violate CARHRIHL in using Landmine in Cagayan Ambush', 28 January 2011.

l. Foreign nationals on legitimate business will not be molested, but mercenaries will not be spared: they are the worst of enemies.[176]

The Federal Government had previously assured the ICRC that it 'proposed to apply the Geneva Conventions in the event of a conflict'.[177]

Non-state armed groups also issue instructions, codes of conduct, and regulations to their members. These materials regulate the behaviour of members of the group in their relations with other members and with persons external to the group. They do not relate solely to issues of international humanitarian law; indeed, some codes and regulations do not relate to the law of armed conflict at all.[178] Others do so implicitly, containing rules that have an equivalent in the law of armed conflict.

Perhaps the classic codes of conduct are those of the Chinese People's Liberation Army (CPLA), with its 'Three Main Rules of Discipline' and 'Eight Points of Attention', reissued in 1947.[179] The Three Main Rules of Discipline provided:

(1) Obey orders in all your actions
(2) Do not take a single needle or piece of thread from the masses
(3) Turn in everything captured.

The Eight Points for Attention provided:

(1) Speak politely
(2) Pay fairly for what you buy
(3) Return everything you borrow
(4) Pay for anything you damage
(5) Do not hit or swear at people
(6) Do not damage crops
(7) Do not take liberties with women
(8) Do not ill-treat captives.

These codes have since been adopted by a variety of groups, including the RUF of Sierra Leone;[180] the New People's Army (NPA), the armed wing of the NDFP;[181] and the National Resistance Army (NRA) of Uganda.[182]

A variety of other groups have or had codes of conduct or internal regulations with a humanitarian component. For example, the 'Ten Commandments' of 1954 of the (Algerian) Armée de Libération Nationale, which fought for independence from France, included the rule: 'to comply with the principles of Islam and international law in the destruction of enemy forces.'[183] The Sendero Luminoso had a code of

---

[176] Operational Code of Conduct for the Nigerian Army, reprinted in AHM Kirk-Greene, *Crisis and Conflict in Nigeria* (Oxford University Press, 1971) 455, 456.
[177] ICRC, Annual Report 1967 (ICRC, 1968) 36.
[178] See eg Kosovo Liberation Army, *Interim Regulations on the Organization of Internal Affairs in the Army*, Prishtina, 1998.
[179] Three Main Rules of Discipline (1927; reissued 1947); Six Points for Attention (1928; reissued in 1947 as the Eight Points for Attention). See also the Four Policies for the Lenient Treatment of Captives (1928).
[180] RUF, Eight Codes of Conduct, reproduced in *Prosecutor v Sesay, Kallon and Gbao*, SCSL-04-15-T, Judgment, 2 March 2009, para 705. See below, 442.
[181] Basic Rules of the New People's Army, 29 March 1969, NDFP, *Declaration of Undertaking to Apply the Geneva Conventions of 1949 and Protocol I of 1977* (NDFP Human Rights Monitoring Committee Booklet No 6) 85.
[182] National Resistance Army Code of Conduct, reprinted in OO Amaza, *Museveni's Long March from Guerrilla to Statesman* (Fountain, 1998) 246.
[183] Les Dix Commandements (1954) 1 *El Moudjahadid*. The original reads: '[s]e conformer aux principes de l'Islam et aux lois internationales dans la destruction des forces ennemies.'

conduct which included the instructions: 'Do not steal', 'Return what you borrow', 'Do not mistreat prisoners', and 'respect the property of farmers.'[184] The Military Code of Conduct of the Mouvement pour la Libération du Congo (MLC) of the Central African Republic reportedly provided for 'the protection of civilians and respect for human rights and international humanitarian law in all circumstances'.[185] The KLA indicated in 1998 that:

[f]rom the start, we had our own internal rules for our operation. These clearly lay down that the UCK recognizes the Geneva Convention and the conventions governing the conduct of war, even though it has not been offered the chance of signing them, as it would have done.[186]

For its part, JEM of Darfur's Army Penal Code provides that 'international Human Rights and Geneva Conventions and its Protocols have supremacy over JEM laws'.[187] The SPLM committed internally to respecting the Convention on Certain Conventional Weapons,[188] while its 1984 Penal and Disciplinary Rules provided that '[t]he SPLA as an organised and disciplined Army, shall observe and be bound by internationally recognized humanitarian standards for the conduct of warfare'.[189] The Chin National Front (CNF) of Burma has a lengthy code of conduct, which is based on the Geneva Conventions.[190]

In 1996, the ELN of Colombia set out certain rules to be followed by its fighters:

1. In times of war, [the ELN] will work to reduce to the maximum unnecessary human sacrifice and suffering by the enemy; this is because combatants will limit their actions to complete only the mission they have been entrusted with; and at all times, they will respect the combatant's ethical code, specifically the rules of behavior of the International Committee of the Red Cross.
2. [The ELN] will give humanitarian treatment to enemies who have surrendered or been wounded in combat and will respect their dignity and provide them with the aid necessary for their condition.
3. Within our ranks, we will not permit or tolerate abuses against the population; they are our reason for being and our relationship with them should be above reproach.
4. Our revolutionary ethic obligates us to be rigorous in avoiding military actions that can harm civilians and our people. This is the essence of our ethics and behavior.
5. It is important to underscore that during armed conflict there are unforseen circumstances and critical situations that can overcome the best intentions. But we, the ELN, are willing to discuss attitudes that, after appropriate analysis, may be punishable if

---

[184] Reproduced in JM Weinstein, *Inside Rebellion* (Cambridge University Press, 2007) 152.
[185] Referred to in *Prosecutor v Bemba Gombo*, ICC-01/05-01/08, Conclusions de la Defense en Reponse a l'Acte d'Accusation Amende du 30 Mars 2009, para 239 fn 161.
[186] Krasniqi Explains UCK's Origins, Structure, Pristina *Koha Ditore*, 12 July 1998, Exhibit P48 in ICTY *Limaj* trial (ICTY translation).
[187] Report of the Panel of Experts established pursuant to Resolution 1591 (2005) concerning the Sudan Issues 29 October 2009: A Response from JEM, 18 November 2009.
[188] Formation of New Sudan Authority on Landmines, 9 May 2004, referring to Doc.CM/1884 (LX11) Annex II.
[189] SPLM/A, Penal and Disciplinary Rules, 4 July 1984, Section 30(2), quoted in *Customary International Humanitarian Law, Volume II: Practice*, above note 3, 2632 fn 367.
[190] Chin National Front, Code, undated (attributed to 1998).

they merit such action, in accordance with our rules of conduct and internal regulations.[191]

The 1995 Código de Guerra of the ELN contains norms of greater specificity:

Respect for the civilian population

— During combat civilians shall not be taken as human shields, that is to say no hostages shall be taken.
— Where the enemy carries civilians as hostages in its movements, efforts shall be made not to harm these in our attacks on enemy forces.
— Military operations shall be carried out selectively on enemy targets, avoiding indiscriminate range of its impact.
— Damage related to civilian property and facilities is to be avoided and reparations offered where possible.
— The civilian population shall be informed of mined areas.
— No actions shall be carried out for the sole purpose of intimidating the population.
— The civilian population shall not be forcibly displaced from combat zones.
— Nobody under the age of 15 shall be incorporated into the permanent military forces; they may join other revolutionary ranks not involved in active hostilities.
— Those who participate in paramilitary groups and their property shall no longer be considered civilians or civilian property.
— The organisation makes political arrests in order to raise awareness of its political proposals ensuring that detainees are treated with respect and informing their next of kin of their situation.

Limits to the methods and means of warfare

— When carrying out acts of sabotage, no facilities which are of greater use to the community than to the enemy shall be hit.
— In acts of sabotage every effort shall be made to minimise damage to the environment.
— No religious facilities, cultural heritage or infrastructure containing dangerous forces such as water dams or nuclear material shall be attacked.
— No toxic gases shall be used nor water poisoned.
— In combat zones vehicles and facilities marked with the Red Cross symbol shall be respected. The use of this symbol by our troops to mislead the enemy is prohibited.
— The force's commanding officers shall prevent plundering and pillage. Once enemy positions have surrendered they shall arrange recovery of any goods that the force may require.

Treating prisoners with dignity

— Killing or injuring an adversary who has surrendered or is out of action is prohibited.
— Prisoners of war shall be treated humanely and receive medical care. Their possessions shall be seized temporarily.
— The number and names of the captured shall be published.
— The handover of prisoners to the Red Cross shall be sought after a short period of captivity.
— Mercenaries and spies shall not benefit from the entitlements guaranteed to prisoners of war.[192]

---

[191] Comando Central del ELN, Manuel Pérez Martínez, Nicolás Rodríguez Bautista, Antonio García, 'Nuestra Ética En La Doctrina Militar' (1996), reproduced and translated in Human Rights Watch, *War Without Quarter: Colombia and International Humanitarian Law* (1998) Chapter V.
[192] 15 July 1995. The Spanish original reads:
Respeto a la Población Civil
— Durante el combate no se tomará a civiles como escudo de protección.

The Sources of the Law of Non-International Armed Conflict   137

For its part, the FARC has explicitly noted that, while it does not use 'technical terms of International Humanitarian Law … some of its documents establish rules which seek to protect the civilian population from the conflict, establishing criteria which mirror the basic principles of Humanitarian Law, such as the distinction between combatant and non-combatant and the immunity of the civilian population'.[193] One such document is its 'Normas de comportamiento con las masas', which provides:

1. Our everyday behaviour and the plans we pursue must be derived from the interests of the people.
2. We must respect the ideas and political, philosophical and religious attitudes of the population and particularly the culture and autonomy of indigenous communities and other ethnic minorities.
3. We must not prevent the exercise of the [right to] vote, nor force people to vote.
4. In planning and implementing politico-military work and in our everyday movements the security of working people, of their homes and their property must be taken into consideration.

— Cuando el enemigo lleve civiles como rehenes en sus desplazamientos, se procurrá no hacerles daño con nuestros ataques a la fuerza enemiga.
— Las operaciones militares se desarrollarán en forma selectiva sobre objetivos enemigos, evitando el alcance indiscriminado de sus efectos.
— Se buscará evitar daños conexos a los bienes e instalaciones civiles y se procura hacer las reparaciones posibles.
— Se informará a la población civil de las áreas minadas.
— No se realizarán acciones con el único fin de atemorizar a la población.
— No se forzará el desplazamiento de población civil de las zonas de combate.
— No se incorporarán menores de 15 años a la fuerza militar permanente. Se podrán integrar a otras actividades revolucionarias diferentes a la participación en hostilidades.
— Las personas participantes en los grupos paramilitares y sus bienes dejarán de ser considerados como población y bienes civiles.
— La Organización hace detenciònes políticas con el fin de hacer conocer sus planteamientos, garantizando a los detenidos un trato respetuoso e informando a sus familiares de la situación en que se hallan.

Limitacion a los Medios y Metodos de Guerra

— Al desarrollar acciones de sabataje no se afectarán instalaciones que le sirvan más a la comunidad que al enemigo.
— Los sabotajes se realizarán evitando al máximo el daño sobre el medio ambiente.
— No se atacarán instalaciones religiosas, bienes culturales ni obras de infraestructura que contengan fuerzas peligrosas, como aguas represadas o material nuclear.
— No se usarán gases venenosos ni se envenenarán las aguas.
— En zonas de combate se respetarán los vehículos y las instalaciones que contengan el símbolo de la Cruz Roja. Está prohibido a nuestras fuerzas utilizar este símbolo para engañar al enemigo.
— Los comandantes de la fuerza evitarán el saqueo y el pillaje; una vez rendida la posición enemiga, organizarán la recuperación de los bienes que requiera la fuerza.

Trato Digno a los Prisioneros

— Está prohibido matar o herir a un adversario que se rinda o que está fuera de combate.
— Los prisioneros de guerra tendrán un trato humanitario, asistencia sanitaria y se les requisarán sus pertenencias temporalmente.
— Se informará públicamente sobre el número y nombre de los capturados, se buscará entregar los prisioneros a la Cruz Roja y que sea un cautiverio breve.
— Ni a los mercenarios, ni a los espías se les darán las garantías propias de los prisioneros de guerra; se les brindará trato humanitario.

[193] A La Poblacion Civil, in FARC-EP Comisión Internacional, *Beligerencia: Suplemento*, 10.

5. We must respect the various steps which our supporters take to keep secret their relationship with us.
6. Internal discipline and work with the masses must prioritise care for innocent and/or friendly people in order that our wrongdoing or omissions do not play into the hands of terrorism and the official army and its paramilitaries' hatred.
7. Wherever and whenever the masses are attacked by the official army or by paramilitaries, with bombardments or destruction of their property, we must proactively denounce and fight these terrorist activities, so that the people feel supported by us.
8. Any kind of abuse or killing proven to have been committed against the population will be considered a criminal offence.
9. We must not impose things on the masses. We must ensure that they regard our arms as theirs.
10. Complaints from the community about agressions by combatants or other persons must be investigated exhaustively, relying on the judgment of the community.
11. Chiefs and combatants must study and follow the Rules of International Humanitarian Law where appropriate for the conditions of our revolutionary war.
12. Should it be necessary to detain any member or supporter of a sister organisation for an alleged or proven breach, the case and where possible the individual must be handed over to that organisation.
13. In any event our most basic principle is respect for the right to life.
14. Chiefs and combatants should remember that executions may only be carried out for very serious offences by the enemies of the people and only with express authorisation for each individual case from the appropriate higher levels of command of each organisation. In all cases the evidence has to be reviewed and decisions have to be taken collectively. Senior officers must make a record detailing the evidence.
15. Alcoholism, drug addiction, theft and dishonesty are counter-revolutionary vices which damage public confidence in us.
16. We must avoid abusing people's confidence and generosity, and not demand goods for personal use.[194]

---

[194] Normas de comportamiento con las masas (released in 1998). The Spanish original provides:
1. Nuestro comportamiento diarios y los planes que nos rigen deben partir de los intereses del pueblo.
2. Debemos respetar las ideas y actitudes políticas, filosóficas y religiosas de la población y particularmente la cultura y la autonomía de las comunidades indígenas y de otras minorías étnicas.
3. No debemos impedir el ejercicio del voto, ni obligar al pueblo a votar.
4. En los planes de trabajo político-militar, en su desarrollo y en los desplazamientos diarios, se deben tener en cuenta la seguridad de las gentes trabajadoras, de sus hogares y sus bienes.
5. Debemos respetar las diferentes medidas que tomen los colaboradores para mantener el secreto de su relación con nosotros.
6. La disciplina interna y el trabajo de masas deben privilegiar el cuidado con la gente inocente y/o amiga, para que por nuestra mala acción u omisión, no quede a merced del terrorismo y del odio del ejército oficial y sus paramilitares.
7. En todo lugar y momento en que las masas sean agredidas por el ejército oficial y los paramilitares, con bombardeos y destrucción de sus bienes, debemos ser activos en la denuncia y el combate a estas actividades terroristas, para que el pueblo se sienta respaldado por nosotros.
8. Se considera un delito el asesinato y toda clase de atropellos que se comprueben, cometidos contra la población.
9. De nuestra parte no debe haber imposiciones a las masas. Debemos procurar que vean nuestras armas como suyas.

The internal regulations of the MRTA also contained humanitarian norms, including: '[e]very combatant must duly hand over to his command any enemy taken prisoner without subjecting them to mistreatment or allowing them to be abused by other guerrilla fighters' and '[c]ombatants are not to establish unauthorized contact with the population. Much less must they use, steal or damage their property, nor attack the population's traditions, customs, morals or way of life.'[195] Another set of examples are the various Codes of Conduct of the Taliban of Afghanistan, the most recent version of which was issued in 2010, and which contained norms that also violate international humanitarian law.[196]

Internal codes and regulations are particularly important as they are intended primarily for internal consumption. Although they may become publicly available, the primary audience is the members of the group themselves. Some groups also publicize certain regulations to local communities in order to encourage reporting of breaches, thus strengthening the superior's control over lower-ranking individuals.[197] Given that codes and regulations are intended to be internal to the group, they may well amount to group policy rather than law. Despite this, they remain important given that even policy can bolster or be contrary to international law. Accordingly, internal measures can illustrate the extent to which certain norms are accepted by the group in question. Insofar as codes and regulations of states are concerned, they have also been used as examples of state practice to determine the existence of customary rules.

3.2.4 Legislation

During times of non-international armed conflict, states may issue domestic legislation on matters of international humanitarian law. For example, in 1918, following the Russian revolution and during the civil war, the Council of People's Commissars issued

10. Los reclamos de la comunidad sobre agresiones de combatientes u otras personas, deben ser investigados exhaustivamente contando con el criterio de la comunidad.
11. Los mandos y combatientes deben estudiar y practicar las Normas del Derecho Internacional Humanitario acordes a las condiciones de nuestra guerra revolucionaria.
12. En caso de que sea necesario retener a cualquier persona por presunta o comprobada falta, siendo este militante o simpatizante de una organización hermana, se debe entregar a esta última el caso y en lo posible la persona.
13. En cualquier caso nuestro principio fundamental es el respeto por el derecho a la vida.
14. Los mandos y combatientes deben tener en cuenta que los ajusticiamientos sólo se pueden hacer por delitos muy graves de los enemigos del pueblo y con autorización expresa para cada caso, por parte de las instancias superiores de dirección de cada organización. En todos los casos hay que confrontar pruebas y las decisiones deben ser asumidas colectivamente, los jefes deben dejar actas con constancias de las pruebas.
15. El alcoholismo, la drogadicción, el robo, la deshonestidad, son vicios contrarrevolucionarios que lesionan la confianza de nuestro pueblo.
16. Debemos evitar los abusos de la confianza y la generosidad de la gente; no exigiendo bienes para beneficio personal.

[195] Movimiento Revolucionario Tupac Amaru, Reglamento, Articles 62 and 70. See also Article 74. Article 62 reads: 'Todo combatiente debe entregar oportunamente a su mando, al enemigo hecho prisionero sin hacerlo victim de maltratos, ni propiciar sean injuriados por lose demás guerrilleros.' Article 70 provides: 'Los combatientes no peuden establecer contacto con la población sin autorización. Menos aún pueden hacer uso, robar o dañar los bienes de ésta, ni atentar contra las tradiciones, costumbres, moral y forma de vida de la población.'
[196] Taliban Code of Conduct (2006, 2009, 2010).
[197] O Bangerter, 'Do As You Are Told': On Codes of Conduct of Insurgents and Other Measures to Enforce Behaviour (Small Arms Survey, Geneva, forthcoming 2012).

a decree on the applicability of the 1864 Geneva Convention.[198] During the Hungarian revolution of 1919, the People's Commissar issued a decree, which provided that '[e]verything must be done to enable the International Red Cross to perform its humanitarian duties without let or hindrance in the territory of the Hungarian Soviet Republic, for only thus will it be able to afford assistance to the wounded, sick and prisoners of war'.[199] A second decree proclaimed the 'absolute equality of treatment of the wounded of all nationalities and... the duty of doctors sent to the theatre of war, to treat enemy soldiers as nationals',[200] while a third decree provided that:

[a]nyone, but especially the military and political authorities, must grant to the Society of the Hungarian Red Cross, to all its institutions, bodies, and staff, treatment in accordance with its neutrality, ensure its effective protection due to its neutrality and support its work.[201]

Together, the various decrees reflected elements of the 1864 Geneva Convention and the Recommendations adopted at the 1863 Conference.

Just as states enact legislation, so too do non-state armed groups. The state in which the conflict is taking place will likely challenge the characterization of the materials as 'legislation' and will contest its binding nature. Nonetheless, for the armed group and for individuals living in territory under armed group control, the legislation will prove important. Legislation is enacted particularly by armed groups that exercise control over territory or which constitute *de facto* states.[202] Such groups tend to have detailed penal codes that apply to the territory under their control.[203] Other groups enact constitutions or issue other sorts of legislation.[204] As with codes of conduct, much of this material fails to refer to the law of armed conflict by name, but they relate to concepts that are the subject of that law. Other legislation does refer to matters of the law of armed conflict by name or concerns human rights issues or the protection of displaced persons.[205] Legislation differs from codes of conduct and internal regulations in that it is enacted in order to regulate the conduct of persons residing in the area in question, rather than governing the behaviour of members of the armed group alone.

As with internal codes and regulations, legislation of states and armed groups amounts to practice of the state and the group. Thus, it, too, demonstrates the extent to which particular humanitarian norms are accepted.

---

[198] Ordonnance of 2 June 1918, ICRC Archives Mis 1/5 (Frick).
[199] Ordonnance du Commissariat du people pour les Affaires Étrangères No 2086 concernant la Situation juridique de la Croix Rouge International de Genève dans la République des Conseils de Hongrie, 10 April 1919, ICRC Archives Mis.4 5/67, reproduced in (1919) 1 *RICR* 604. English translation taken from A Durand, *From Sarajevo to Hiroshima: History of the International Committee of the Red Cross* (Henry Dunant Institute, 1984) 128–9.
[200] Degree of 26 April 1919, cited in CICR, *Rapport Général du Comité International de la Croix-Rouge sur son activité de 1912 à 1920* (Genève, 1921) 195. The original reads: 'l'égalité absolue de traitement des blessés de toute nationalité et reconnaît l'obligation pour les médecins envoyés sur le théâtre de la guerre, de soigner les soldats ennemis comme les nationaux.'
[201] Decree No 62 du Commissariat du Peuple pour le Bien Public et les Affaires Sanitaires, 9 July 1919, ICRC Archives Mis.4 5/134. The original reads:

Quiconque, mais surtout les autorités militaries et politiques, doit accorder à la Société de la Croix Rouge Hongroise, à toutes ses institutions, ses organes, ainsi, qu'à son personnel un traitement confrome à son caractère de neutralité, lui assurer une protection efficace, due à sa neutralité et appuyer son activité.

[202] See E Guevara, *Guerrilla Warfare* (Penguin, 1969) 82 and 95.
[203] See eg Communist Party of Nepal–Maoist, Public Legal Code 2060 (2003/2004).
[204] See eg Liberation Tigers of Tamil Eelam, Tamil Eelam Child Protection Act (Act No 3 of 2006).
[205] See eg Ejército Zapatista de Liberación Nacional, Revolutionary Women's Law.

3.2.5 Other important materials

Three further categories of materials are important, even though they do not always consist of commitments in the legal sense of the term. These materials give an indication of the views of armed groups on the law and may set out the group's position on a particular point. Accordingly, they may prove useful.

Responses to reports of fact-finding missions

States and non-state armed groups sometimes respond to reports of UN special rapporteurs or reports of human rights organizations, challenging particular facts or interpretations of the law.[206] Given that states are encouraged to engage in such dialogue,[207] non-state armed groups should also be encouraged to enter into a conversation with the relevant body, particularly where the response does not take the form of an outright and unreasoned denial.

Press releases and other ad hoc statements

Non-state armed groups have also entered the information age, maintaining websites and even twitter accounts. Websites of armed groups often contain press releases and other statements setting out the group's position on various international humanitarian law issues. Statements may also be issued through other organizations.[208] Some statements are of considerable detail and rather lengthy.[209]

Some statements describe the practice of the relevant party and come very close to, if not actually constituting, a formal commitment. For example, during the violence in Ireland in 1922, the Irish Republican Government stated that the Irish Republican Army (IRA) 'grants to the enemy, as the army of the Britannic Kingdom, the benefit of the customs and laws of war'.[210] During the civil war in Greece (1946–9), the Provisional Democratic Government sent a lengthy letter to the ICRC indicating the humanitarian measures it had taken. It is worth quoting from the letter in part:

During this war, the duty of each belligerent side is to respect certain principles of humanity...

We will quote some examples which show the dedication of the Democratic Army to the institutions of justice and humanity. The soldiers of the traitorous army of Athens, taken prisoner by the Democratic Army, are released. Thus far thousands of combatants have been released and

---

[206] For example: Letter from Insurgent Comandante Marcos [of the EZLN] to 'Asma Jahangir, Special Correspondent [sic] of the UN for Extrajudicial, Summary or Arbitrary Executions', 19 July 1999, reproduced in B Clarke and C Ross (eds), *Voice of Fire: Communiqués and Interviews from the Zapatista National Liberation Army* (Freedom Voices, 2000) 116; KNU Press Statement on Report of UNSG, 27 April 2009; Report of the Panel of Experts established pursuant to Resolution 1591 (2005) concerning the Sudan Issued 2 October 2009: A Response from JEM, 16 November 2009; NDFP Letter to UN Secretary-General Ban Ki Moon, 24 November 2008.

[207] P Alston, J Morgan-Foster, and W Abresch, 'The Competence of the UN Human Rights Council and its Special Procedures in relation to Armed Conflicts: Extrajudicial Executions in the "War on Terror"' (2008) 19 *EJIL* 183, 185–90.

[208] For example: Statement of the Opposition Movements, above note 130.

[209] For example, FMLN, *The Legitimacy of Our Methods of Struggle* (Inkworks Press, 1988) (a 24-page booklet); the *White Paper on the Application of the Geneva Conventions of 1949 to the French-Algerian Conflict* (Algerian Office, New York, 1960) (an 85-page booklet).

[210] Mémoire du Gouvernement de la République Irlandaise au Comité International de la Croix-Rouge, 13 March 1923, 5, ICRC Archives CR 22 (84)/1. The original reads: 'accorde à l'ennemi, comme Armée du Roi Britannique, le bénéfice des usages et lois de guerre.'

even officers of the monarcho-fascist military units. Their wounded find in our care such treatment and aid that we sometimes cannot give to our wounded because of lack of resources...[211]

More recently, in 2011, during the violence in Libya, the Interim Transitional National Council declared that it 'would like to reiterate that its policies strictly adhere to the "Geneva Convention relative to the treatment of Prisoners of War"',[212] which may perhaps be taken to reflect an actual commitment to abide by the Third Geneva Convention.[213] Along similar lines, in 1988, the FMLN of El Salvador stated that it 'endeavors to assure that its methods of struggle comply with the stipulations of Article 3 Common of [sic] the Geneva Conventions and Additional Protocol II'.[214] This too may perhaps be taken to reflect an actual commitment to abide by common Article 3 and Additional Protocol II.

Similar considerations arise in respect of statements on human rights law. For example, a 1999 communiqué of the General Staff of the KLA provided that, '[i]t is a duty and an obligation for all the KLA effective to respect the human rights and the international conventions that regulate them even in peace time'.[215] The SPLM stated that '[t]he Movement stands in support and respect of international Conventions on human rights and similar international protocols on human rights' and '[t]he Movement shall adhere to and respect internationally accepted norms and standards of human rights and shall protect and respect the rights and civil liberties of all persons resident in the New Sudan without prejudice based on race, tribe, religion or gender'.[216] A 2000 declaration of the Revolutionary Workers' Party of the Philippines/Revolutionary Proletarian Army-Alex Boncayao Brigade (RPM-P/RPA-ABB) read, '[w]e believe that while we are fighting to achieve full human development and social progress, we must respect the lives of the people and of nature—uphold and promote human rights, and protect the environment'.[217]

Expressions of motivations for taking up arms

Upon the outbreak of violence, the putative armed group frequently sets out the reasons why it has taken up arms. These explanations may also prove useful as giving an insight into the group, assuming that such statements are not issued for purely

---

[211] Letter from the President of the Provisional Democratic Government, Markos, to the ICRC, 23 December 1947, ICRC Archives G 44/53c-237. The original reads:

> Au cours de cette guerre, le devoir de chaque côté belligérant est de respecter certains principes d'humanité...
>
> Nous citerons quelques exemples qui montrent le dévouement de l'Armée démocratique aux institutions de la justice et de l'humanité. Les soldats de l'armée-traitre d'Athènes, faits prisonniers par l'Armée démocratique sont libérés. C'est ainsi que jusqu'à présent des milliers de combattants ont été libérés et même des officiers des unités militaires monarchofascistes. Leurs blessés trouvent chez nous de tels soins et une telle aide que nous ne pouvons parfois donner à nos blessés, faute du manque de moyens...

[212] The Treatment of Detainees and Prisoners, 25 March 2011.
[213] See also the statements of the Council: A Vision of a Democratic Libya (undated); untitled statement, 22 March 2011.
[214] FMLN, *The Legitimacy of Our Methods of Struggle*, above note 209, 7.
[215] Communique of the KLA General Staff, reproduced as 'Text of Ceku Communique Urging Serbs to Remain', 18 August 1999, Exhibit P48 in ICTY *Limaj* trial (ICTY translation).
[216] Fifteen Point Programme of the SPLM, Point 13.
[217] Declaration of the RPM-P/RPA-ABB against the use and production of landmines, 21 March 2000.

political reasons.[218] Not infrequently, among the reasons that are given are that human rights violations are taking place in the state in question as is ongoing discrimination, as was the case with a 1990 statement of Charles Taylor's NPFL.[219] Accordingly, following on from these explanations, it is not at all unusual for armed groups to state that the future state will respect human rights and international law. For example, during the 2011 violence in Libya, the National Transitional Council (NTC) issued a statement in which it provided that:

[t]he interim national council will be guided by the following in our continuing march to freedom, through espousing the principles of political democracy. We recognise without reservation our obligation to:

...

8. Build a democratic Libya whose international and regional relationships will be based upon:

a. ...

b. A state which will uphold the values of international justice, citizenship, the respect of international humanitarian law and human rights declarations, as well as condemning authoritarian and despotic regimes. The interests and rights of foreign nationals and companies will be protected. Immigration, residency and citizenship will be managed by government institutions, respecting the principles and rights of political asylum and public liberties.[220]

The NTC also requested from an expatriate group of Libyan lawyers advice on the applicable law of armed conflict as it did not want to 'act like Qadhafi and his forces'.[221]

More recently, the 1999 Statute of the MLC provided that '[t]he MLC is a political-military movement aimed at the overthrow of the dictatorial regime in order to establish a democratic state based on free and fair elections in accordance with human rights and individual freedoms'.[222]

These expressions of motivations constitute important 'hooks' on which to engage the armed group. For example, if an armed group commits violations of the law, it could usefully be reminded of the reason why it is fighting, namely to stand up against violations in the first place. Furthermore, a declaration on point on the part of the NTC of Libya was used by the UN International Commission of Inquiry to support its conclusion that in certain situations the Council was bound by international human rights law.[223]

3.3 Non-exhaustive list of commitments

Table 4.1 illustrates the very many armed conflicts in which the applicability of the law of non-international armed conflict has been recognized, either by the state, the non-state armed group, or both parties to the conflict.[224]

---

[218] On which see above, 108.
[219] First Policy Statement of Mr Charles Ghankay Taylor, Leader of the National Patriotic Front of Liberia, 1 January 1990.
[220] See eg National Transitional Council, *A vision of a democratic Libya*, 29 March 2011.
[221] Quoted in Scobbie, above note 38.
[222] Statuts du Mouvement de Libération du Congo, 30 Juin 1999, Article 3. The original reads: 'Le MLC est un mouvement politico-militaire qui vise le renversement du régime dictatorial en vue d'instaurer un Etat Démocratique sur base des élections libres et transparentes dans le respect des droits de l'homme et des libertés individuelles.'
[223] Report of the International Commission of Inquiry to investigate all alleged violations of international human rights law in the Libyan Arab Jamahiriya, A/HRC/17/44, 1 June 2011, para 72.
[224] All dates are approximate and are included only to convey a sense of the time period in question. They are taken from various sources, principally reports of the ICRC and the Uppsala Armed Conflict Dataset.

Table 4.1 List of commitments

Conflict	Party	Form of commitment	Substance of commitment
Afghanistan (1979–89)	USSR-backed Government	Parallel commitments	Agreement on the transfer and Internment in a neutral country of Soviet soldiers detained by Afghan opposition movements
		Commitment to ICRC	Geneva Conventions
	Mujahadeen	Parallel commitments	Agreement on the transfer and internment in a neutral country of Soviet soldiers detained by Afghan opposition movements
Afghanistan (post-2001)	Government		
	Taliban	Code of conduct	Equivalent to certain norms. Also contrary to certain norms
Algerian war of independence, 1954-62 (France)	France	Communiqué	Common Article 3
	FLN/Provisional Government	Unilateral declaration	Geneva Conventions
		Accession to Geneva Conventions	Geneva Conventions
		Code of conduct	Equivalent to certain norms
Angola (war of independence, 1961–75)	Government		
	UNITA	Unilateral declaration	Geneva Conventions; fundamental rules of international law applicable in armed conflicts
Bosnia (1992–5)	Various parties	Ad hoc agreements	Geneva Conventions and listed rules; prisoner exchange; humanitarian assistance
		Parallel unilateral declarations	International humanitarian law
Burundi (1993–2005)	Government	Ceasefire agreement	Specific norms
	FNL	Ceasefire agreement	Specific norms
China (1946–9)	Government		
	CPLA	Internal regulations	Equivalent to certain norms
Colombia (war of independence, 1820)	Briceño Méndez forces	Bilateral agreement	Specific norms
	Bolivar forces	Proclamation to troops	Law of war

Colombia (1860–1)	Confederación Granadina	Bilateral agreements	Specific norms
	Forces of Cipriano de Mosquera	Bilateral agreements	Specific norms
Colombia (1964–ongoing)	Government	Court judgment	Additional Protocol II
		Government recognition	Common Article 3; Additional Protocol II
		Bilateral agreement with FARC	Humanitarian exchange
	ELN	Unilateral declaration	International humanitarian law
		Internal regulations	Specific norms
	FARC	Internal regulations	Specific norms
		Bilateral agreement with Government	Humanitarian exchange
	Coordinadora Guerrillera Simón Bolívar	Unilateral declaration	International humanitarian law
Croatia (1991–5)	Various parties	Memorandum of Understanding	Geneva Conventions and listed rules
		Unilateral declarations	International humanitarian law
		Instructions to troops	International humanitarian law
		Bilateral agreements	Protected zones; prisoner exchanges
Cuba (1958–9)	Government	Commitment to ICRC	Laws of war
	Rebels (led by Castro)	Request to ICRC	Collection of wounded
		Declaration by Castro to Government forces	Surrender; humane treatment; protection
Dominican Republic (1965)	Junta	Parallel oral commitments to ICRC	Geneva Conventions
	Forces of General Imbert	Truce	Collection of wounded and dead
DRC (Katanga, 1960–2)	Government	Letter to Depositary	Confirmation of party status to Geneva Conventions
	Katangan authorities		
DRC (1964)	Government	Letter to ICRC	Geneva Conventions
	Armed group	Public statement	Geneva Conventions
DRC (2000s)	Government		
	MLC	Internal regulations	International humanitarian law; International human rights law

Continued

Table 4.1 Continued

Conflict	Party	Form of commitment	Substance of commitment
	Various groups	Ad hoc agreement	International humanitarian law; International human rights law
El Salvador (1980–91)	Government	Bilateral agreement	Human rights and international humanitarian law
	FMLN	Unilateral declaration	Common Article 3; Additional Protocol II
		Unilateral declaration	Specific norms
		Bilateral agreement	Human rights and international humanitarian law
Ethiopia (1994–ongoing)	Government		
	ONLF	Statement	International agreements on human rights
Former Yugoslav Republic of Macedonia (2001)	Government	Unilateral declaration	Geneva Convention
	NLA	Internal regulations	Geneva Convention
Greece (1946–9)	Government		
	ELM/ELAS	Oral assurance to ICRC	Geneva Conventions
Guatemala (1954)	Government	Request to ICRC	ICRC intervention
	Armed group	Commitment to ICRC	Request for assistance
Guatemala (1982–95)	Government	Bilateral agreement	International human rights law
	URNG	Bilateral agreement	International human rights law
Hungary (1919)	People's Commissar	Decrees	ICRC to carry out its mandate; neutrality of Hungarian Red Cross; respect for wounded
Hungary (1956)	Government	Agreement with ICRC and Hungarian Red Cross	Distribution of relief; recognition of traditional ICRC activities
	Gyor Committee	Oral commitment to ICRC	Geneva Conventions
Indonesia (1975–2006)	Government	Memorandum of Understanding	Human rights
	GAM	Memorandum of Understanding	Human rights

Ireland (1922–3)	Government	Statement to ICRC	Apply laws of war to enemy forces
	IRA		
Lebanon (1958)	Government	Commitment to ICRC	Respect for common Article 3
	Armed group	Commitment to ICRC	Respect for common Article 3
Liberia (2002–3)	Government	Ceasefire agreement	Human rights
	LURD	Peace agreement	International humanitarian law
Liberia (1989–96)	Government	Peace agreement	Specific norms
	NPFL	Peace agreement	Specific norms
Libya (2011)	Government	Unilateral declarations	Geneva Convention relative to Treatment of Prisoners of War; prohibition on anti-personnel mines
	Interim Transitional National Council		
Mexico (1994)	Government	Unilateral declaration	Laws of war
	EZLN	Internal regulations	Women's rights
Myanmar/Burma (2000s)	Government	Unilateral declarations	Child soldiers
	KNPP/KNA		Anti-personnel mines
	KNU/KNLA	Unilateral declarations	Child soldiers
			Anti-personnel mines
	CNF	Code of conduct	Specific norms
Namibia (1966–88)	Government of South Africa	Unilateral declaration	Geneva Conventions and Additional Protocol I
	SWAPO	Ceasefire agreement	Specific norms
		Action plan with UN	Child soldiers
Nepal (1996–2006)	Government	Ceasefire agreement	Specific norms
	CPN-M	Unilateral declaration	Human rights; Geneva Conventions
		Action plan with UN	Child soldiers

Continued

Table 4.1 Continued

Conflict	Party	Form of commitment	Substance of commitment
Nicaragua (1979–90)	Government	Commitment to ICRC	Observe and apply international humanitarian law
	Contras		
Nigeria (1967–70)	Government	Instructions for armed forces	Geneva Conventions and listed norms
		Commitment to ICRC	Geneva Conventions
	Biafra	Commitment to ICRC	Geneva Conventions
Peru (1980–99)	Government	Internal regulations	Equivalent to certain norms
	Sendero Luminoso		
Peru (1984–96)	Government	Unilateral declarations	Geneva Convention on internal conflicts
	MRTA		
Philippines (1969–96)	Government	Unilateral declaration	
	MNLF		
Philippines (1973–ongoing)	Government	Acceptance of applicability	Additional Protocol II
		Bilateral agreement	International humanitarian law and international human rights law
	NDFP	Unilateral declaration	International humanitarian law 'especially Article 3 common to the Geneva Conventions as well as Protocol II additional to said conventions'
		Unilateral declaration	Geneva Conventions and Additional Protocol I
		Bilateral agreement	International humanitarian law and international human rights law
		Internal regulations	Equivalent to certain norms
Philippines (1976–ongoing)	Government	Bilateral agreements	International humanitarian law and international human rights law; listed norms
	MILF	Bilateral agreements	International humanitarian law and international human rights law; listed norms
		Action plan with UN	Child soldiers

Poland (1863–4)	Government	Instructions	Treatment of wounded and sick
	Armed group		
Russian revolution and civil war (1917–20)	Council of People's Commissars	Commitment to ICRC Decree Orders	Geneva Convention Geneva Convention Treatment of prisoners
Russia (first Chechen conflict, 1994–6)	Government Chechen groups	Court judgment	Additional Protocol II
Rwanda (1990–4)	Government RPF	Commitment to ICRC	International humanitarian law
Rwanda/DRC (1994–ongoing)	Government FDLR		
Serbia (Kosovo 1998–9)	Serbia KLA	Unilateral declaration Internal regulations	International humanitarian law International humanitarian law and international human rights law
Sierra Leone (1991–2002)	Government RUF	Peace agreement Peace agreement Statement Statement Code of conduct	International humanitarian law International humanitarian law International humanitarian law (through peace agreement) International human rights law Equivalent to certain norms
Somalia (1979)	Government ABBO Liberation Front	Commitment to ICRC	Humanitarian principles of Geneva Conventions
Spain (1936–9)	Government Franco forces	Unilateral declaration Unilateral declaration	Respect for the emblem, creation of prisoner information bureau Application of 1929 Geneva Conventions
Sri Lanka (1983–2009)	Government	Ceasefire agreement	Specific norms

Continued

Table 4.1 Continued

Conflict	Party	Form of commitment	Substance of commitment
Sri Lanka (1983–2009)	LTTE	Ceasefire agreement	Specific norms
		Unilateral declarations	Geneva Conventions and Additional Protocols
		Child Protection Act	Child soldiers
Sudan (1983–2005)	Government	Bilateral agreement	Specific norms
	SPLM/A	Bilateral agreement	Specific norms
		Trilateral agreement (Government, SPLM, UN)	Mine action
		Ground Rules (Operation Lifeline Sudan)	Convention on the Rights of the Child; Geneva Conventions; Additional Protocols
		Internal regulations	International humanitarian law; Convention on Certain Conventional Weapons; human rights
		Action plan with UN	Child soldiers
Sudan (2005–6)	Government	Bilateral agreement	Specific norms
	ESF	Bilateral agreement	Specific norms
Sudan (2003–ongoing)	Government	Bilateral agreements	Specific norms
	JEM	Bilateral agreements	Specific norms
		Memorandum of Understanding with UNICEF	Child soldiers
		Unilateral declaration	Specific norms
		Army Penal Code	Human rights; Geneva Conventions
	SLM/A	Various bilateral agreements	Specific norms
		Unilateral declaration	Specific norms
Switzerland (1847)	Government Sonderbund	Instructions to troops	Specific norms
Tajikistan (1992–7)	Government	Instructions to troops	International humanitarian law

Turkey (1984–ongoing)	Government	Unilateral declaration	Geneva Conventions; Additional Protocol I
	PKK		
Uganda (1981–6)	Government	Peace agreement	Common Article 3
	NRM	Peace agreement	Common Article 3
		Internal regulations	Equivalent to certain norms
Uganda (1988–ongoing)	Government	Cessation of hostilities agreement	Specific norms
	LRA		
United States (1776)	Great Britain	Exchange of letters	Laws of war
	United States	Exchange of letters	Laws of war
United States civil war (1861–5)	Union forces	Internal regulation (Lieber Code)	Specific norms
	Confederates		
Upper Silesia (1921)	Polish armed groups (in territory of Upper Silesia)	Commitment to ICRC	ICRC to carry out its work; respect persons wearing Red Cross armband
	German armed groups (in territory of Upper Silesia)	Commitment to ICRC	ICRC to carry out its work; respect persons wearing Red Cross armband
Yemen (1962–7)	Government	Commitment to ICRC	Geneva Conventions
	Royalists	Commitment to ICRC	Humanitarian principles of Geneva Conventions concerning the treatment of wounded and prisoners
Yemen (2004–ongoing)	Government		International humanitarian law
	Houthi	Letter to Human Rights Watch	Guiding Principles on Internal Displacement
Western Sahara (1975–89)	Polisario	Unilateral declaration	Geneva Conventions

4. Conclusion

There is a substantial body of international humanitarian law, conventional and customary in nature, that regulates non-international armed conflicts. These rules have largely been accepted by states and non-state armed groups alike. Although dispute continues to exist at the level of particular rules, the fact that there exists a substantial body of law is no longer disputed. Importantly, this body includes norms relating, to humane treatment, the protection of civilians and persons *hors de combat*, targeting, and the prohibition on the use of certain means and methods of combat.

The applicability of international rules to non-international armed conflicts is supported by the practice of states and non-state armed groups that are actually involved in non-international armed conflicts. For example, states involved in non-international armed conflicts have issued instructions to their forces to abide by particular rules. They have concluded bilateral agreements with the non-state armed group against which they are fighting and in which both parties recommit to abide by international humanitarian law or particular norms contained therein. Likewise, non-state armed groups have committed to comply with international humanitarian law, particular listed norms, and international human rights law.

These ad hoc commitments are often hidden and overlooked. Thus, it is often thought that non-state armed groups do not and will not commit to abide by the law of non-international armed conflict, that special agreements envisaged in common Article 3 are not concluded, and that states do not accept the increased normative content of the law of non-international armed conflict. Accordingly, the picture is presented as if it were 1977 and Additional Protocol II had just been concluded with its relatively limited substantive content. As this chapter has demonstrated, the situation is altogether different.

Ad hoc commitments on the part of parties to the conflict are crucial as they provide an indication of which norms are accepted, and which are more disputed. They ought to be studied more carefully than they are at present and taken into account in the creation of the law. Ultimately, it is only by considering the views of all parties to a non-international armed conflict that the body of law applicable therein can become truly fit for purpose.

In Part II, the substantive law of non-international armed conflict will be considered. The customary status of particular rules will be noted primarily along the lines set out above, and as a secondary basis, by reference to the Customary International Humanitarian Law study and the jurisprudence of the ICTY. The commitments and practice of armed groups will be used to illustrate compliance with or violation of, and to demonstrate acceptance of or departure from, particular rules. They will not be used to argue that a particular norm has customary international law status.

PART II

THE SUBSTANTIVE LAW OF NON-INTERNATIONAL ARMED CONFLICT

5
Identifying a Non-International Armed Conflict: Armed Conflicts and Internal Tensions and Disturbances

1. Introduction

The definition of an armed conflict not of an international character, or at least the ability to identify when such a conflict exists, is crucial for the application of the law of non-international armed conflict. Since 1949, a functional approach has been taken to the applicability of the law. It applies irrespective of terminology, recognition by the parties, or consent. A factual situation, that of a non-international armed conflict, brings the law of non-international armed conflict into play. For such a foundational issue, determining whether or not a non-international armed conflict exists has proven surprisingly difficult. Indeed, it has been remarked that '[o]ne of the most assured things that might be said about the words "armed conflict not of an international character" is that no one can say with assurance precisely what meaning they were intended to convey'.[1]

For decades, an authoritative definition of a non-international armed conflict proved elusive. A lack of definition provided parties to conflicts maximum flexibility to characterize the situation as they saw fit. However, the advantage of flexibility was simultaneously a disadvantage, allowing for the situation to be characterized according to the political interests of the actors concerned, sometimes in complete variance with the facts on the ground. It was only in 1995 that a neat definition was encapsulated, with the Appeals Chamber of the International Criminal Tribunal for the former Yugoslavia (ICTY) in the *Tadić* Decision on Interlocutory Appeal on Jurisdiction holding that 'an armed conflict exists whenever there is a resort to armed force between States or protracted armed violence between governmental authorities and organized armed groups or between such groups within a State'.[2] This definition has since been adopted by a variety of influential actors and is widely recognized as authoritative. It defines the notion of an armed conflict for the purposes of Article 3 common to the four Geneva Conventions of 1949 as well as the notion of a non-international armed conflict in customary international law. In order for particular rules of international humanitarian law to apply, however, such as those found in Protocol II Additional to the 1949 Geneva Conventions of 1977, a conflict will have to exhibit certain additional attributes, over and above those needed to be satisfied for the showing of a non-international armed conflict.

---

[1] T Farer, 'Humanitarian Law and Armed Conflicts: Toward the Definition of "International Armed Conflict"' (1971) 71 *Columbia Law Review* 37, 43 (emphasis omitted).
[2] *Prosecutor v Tadić*, IT-94-1-AR72, Decision on the Defence Motion for Interlocutory Appeal on Jurisdiction, 2 October 1995, para 70.

Despite the *Tadić* definition, uncertainty continues to surround the identification of a non-international armed conflict. Debate continues to exist as to whether or not a particular situation amounts to a non-international armed conflict, albeit the debate is now framed around the facts that aid identification of an armed conflict rather than the definition of an armed conflict itself.

Equally as important as the definition of a non-international armed conflict, perhaps even more important, is the identity of the actor that characterizes the situation. The parties to the violence have a vested interest in its characterization. The state may seek to downplay the violence while the non-state armed group may tend towards its exaggeration. The state may also view the armed group as criminals or terrorists and any violence to which it resorts as mere disturbances or criminal acts. Accordingly, the parties are frequently unable to provide an impartial assessment of the situation. Characterization of the violence by a neutral observer has the benefit of impartiality. However, it may have minimal impact on the parties to the conflict. Quite who decides whether or not the situation amounts to an armed conflict is thus crucial.

This chapter considers these various issues, principally the definition and identification of a non-international armed conflict and the identity of the actors that qualify the situation. Associated issues, such as the legal status and legitimacy of the armed group, are also explored.

2. The non-definition approach

2.1 The Diplomatic Conference of 1949

In light of the decentralized, subjective, and ad hoc approach to recognition of belligerency,[3] a deliberate attempt was made to move away from regulation through recognition during what may be described as the period of systematicity.[4] In the period leading up to the Diplomatic Conference of 1949 and during the Conference, attempts were made to define a non-international armed conflict.[5] However, differences of opinion between the delegates meant that a definition did not prove forthcoming.

The original text relating to non-international armed conflict that was put before the Diplomatic Conference and which would become common Article 3 of the Geneva Conventions provided that:

[i]n all cases of armed conflict not of an international character which may occur in the territory of one or more of the High Contracting Parties, each of the adversaries shall be bound to implement the provisions of the present Convention [, subject to the adverse party likewise acting in obedience thereto[6]]. The Convention shall be applicable in these circumstances, whatever the legal status of the Parties to the conflict and without prejudice thereto.[7]

---

[3] See above, 9–20.
[4] See Chapter 2.
[5] For accounts of the drafting of common Article 3, see DA Elder, 'The Historical Background of Common Article 3 of the Geneva Conventions of 1949' (1979) 11 *Case Western Journal of International Law* 37; L Moir, *The Law of Internal Armed Conflict* (Cambridge University Press, 2002) 30–88; L Perna, *The Formation of the Treaty Law of Non-International Armed Conflicts* (Martinus Nijhoff, 2006) 49–60; A Cullen, *The Concept of Non-International Armed Conflict in International Humanitarian Law* (Cambridge University Press, 2010) 25–61.
[6] The text in square brackets was included in the Draft Prisoners of War Convention and the Draft Civilians Convention alone. See *Final Record of the Diplomatic Conference of Geneva of 1949* (Federal Political Department, Berne) Vol I, 73 and 113.
[7] Ibid, Vol I, 47 and 61.

Delegates expressed differing views on this text. Some took the view that the (Geneva) Conventions should apply to all cases of armed conflict not of an international character; others took precisely the opposite position, namely that the Conventions should not apply to any such conflicts.⁸ Of particular interest for the purposes of this chapter are the differing views that were expressed on the definition of a non-international armed conflict.

One approach that was put to the Committee tasked with considering articles common to all four Geneva Conventions (the Joint Committee), and a Sub-Committee thereof known as the Special Committee, was to focus on certain attributes of the non-state party (the armed group). France, for example, suggested the application of the relevant Convention 'if the adverse Party possesses an organized military force, an authority responsible for its acts acting within a defined territory and having the means of observing and enforcing the Convention'.⁹ This met with the approval of other states, some of which made suggestions along similar lines. Italy approved of the French proposal and suggested that 'in cases which were not provided for under the French proposal, the Parties to the conflict should be bound to respect the humanitarian principles embodied in the Preamble of the draft Civilians Convention'.¹⁰ This would have had the effect that those armed groups that had the capacity to observe the Geneva Conventions were under an obligation to do so while those that did not were under an obligation to respect the principles of the Conventions. Spain also supported the French proposal, but preferred the language: 'the Conventions should only be applied in cases where the legal government was obliged to have recourse to the regular military forces against insurgents organized as military and in possession of a part of the national territory.'¹¹ Spain thus considered the armed group as one important element of the situation, another being recourse to the military on the part of the state.

Other states preferred the elements required to be satisfied before belligerency could be recognized. For example, the United States proposed that regulation be subject to the following requirements:

— that the insurgents must have an organization purporting to have the characteristics of a State;
— that the insurgent civil authority must exercise *de facto* authority over persons within a determinate territory;
— that the armed forces must act under the direction of the organized civil authority and be prepared to observe the ordinary laws of war;
— that the insurgent civil authority must agree to be bound by the provisions of the Convention.¹²

This was interpreted by Canada as referring to situations 'of effective control of a substantial portion of the national territory by the rebels, who had set up something resembling a civil administration'.¹³ Despite the differences between the Italian, Spanish, and US proposals, all sought to identify objective elements, the presence of which would suggest the existence of a non-international armed conflict.

By contrast, other delegates preferred to continue to utilize the doctrine of recognition of belligerency. For example, Australia proposed that the Conventions would be applicable provided:

---

⁸ See ibid, Vol II-B, 121 (Report of the Special Committee of the Joint Committee).
⁹ Ibid, Vol III, 27.   ¹⁰ Ibid, Vol II-B, 121.
¹¹ Ibid.   ¹² Ibid. See also at 12.   ¹³ Ibid, 13.

(1) that the *de jure* Government has recognized the insurgents as belligerents; or

(2) that the *de jure* Government has claimed for itself the rights of a belligerent; or

(3) that the *de jure* Government has accorded the insurgents recognition as belligerents for the purposes only of the present Convention;[14]

Australia proposed a fourth option that did not relate to recognition of belligerency, namely '(4) that the dispute has been admitted to the Agenda of the Security Council or the General Assembly of the United Nations as being a threat to international peace, a breach of the peace, or an act of aggression'.[15] However, this was criticized as subjecting the decision of the government of the state in which the violence had broken out to the United Nations.[16] As noted in the introduction to this chapter, the identity of the actor that decides whether or not a non-international armed conflict exists, and as a result, on the applicability of the law of non-international armed conflict, is an important one. It is an issue that will be returned to below.[17] Contrary to the proposal of Australia, continued use of the doctrine of recognition of belligerency was also criticized, with Norway expressing the hope 'that the Conference would agree that purely humanitarian rules should be applied in armed conflicts independently of any recognition of belligerency'.[18]

On the basis of the various interjections, members of the Special Committee largely agreed that the Conventions should cover non-international armed conflicts and that the concept of a non-international armed conflict needed greater clarification. A vote along these lines was passed with 10 in favour, one against, and one abstention.[19] Beyond these generalities, however, consensus was limited and a Working Party was set up to forge the way ahead. A first proposal of the Working Party merged elements of the French, Australian, and US proposals. The proposal read, in salient part:

(1) In the case of armed conflict not of an international character occurring in the territory of one of the High Contracting Parties, each Party to the conflict shall be bound to implement the provisions of the present Convention, provided:

   a) that the *de jure* government has recognized the status of belligerency of the adverse party, without restrictions, or for the sole purposes of the application of the present Convention, or

   b) that the adverse party presents the characteristics of a State, in particular, that it possesses an organized military force, that it is under the direction of an organized civil authority which exercises *de facto* governmental functions over the population of a determinate portion of the national territory, and that it has the means of enforcing the Convention, and of complying with the laws and customs of war; application of the Convention in these circumstances shall in no wise depend upon the legal status of the parties to the conflict.

(2) This obligation presupposes, furthermore, in all circumstances, that the adverse party declares itself bound by the present Convention, and, as is the *de jure* government, by the laws and customs of war (and that it complies with above conditions in fact).[20]

---

[14] Ibid, 121, and Vol III, 27.   [15] Ibid, Vol II-B, 121.
[16] Ibid, 42 (United States).   [17] See 196–204.
[18] *Final Record*, above note 6, Vol II-B, 11.
[19] Ibid, 121.   [20] Ibid, 124.

A second proposal of the Working Party took into account suggestions made by other members of the Special Committee. This second proposal differed as between the Civilians Convention and the three other Conventions. As to the former, the text read:

In the case of armed conflict not of an international character occurring in the territory of one of the High Contracting Parties, the Parties to the conflict should endeavour to bring into force, by means of special agreements, all or part of the provisions of the present Convention, and in all circumstances shall act in accordance with the underlying humanitarian principles of the present Convention.[21]

As to the three other Conventions, the approach of the first proposal was followed with some amendments. In particular, the requirement that the adverse party 'presents the characteristics of a State' was deleted as it was considered to give rise to 'the impression that the rebels already constitute a subject in international law'.[22] Similarly, the requirement that the adverse parties declare themselves bound by the Convention was rephrased as it presupposed 'a legal personality which they could not possess'.[23] Insofar as these three Conventions were concerned, the approach remained to provide criteria by which the existence of a non-international armed conflict would be judged, and, in the alternative, to resort to recognition of belligerency.

However, the criteria against which the existence of a conflict was to be judged were criticized as being so onerous as to be satisfied only rarely, with the International Committee of the Red Cross (ICRC) going so far as to suggest that the text 'could never have been applied in any recent case of civil war'.[24] The criteria were also criticized as lacking an objective basis for determining whether or not they had been fulfilled, with the consequence that the matter would essentially be left to the discretion of the *de jure* government.[25]

In light of these criticisms, a suggestion was made for the Working Party to alter its approach. Instead of delineating the situations in which the Conventions would apply, the various provisions of the Conventions that would be applicable should be identified.[26] Hence, the report of the Joint Committee describes the choice as being between 'restrict[ing] the cases of conflicts not of an international character, to which the Conventions should apply' and 'restrict[ing] the ... provisions to be applied in the case of a conflict which was not of an international character'.[27]

A second Working Party was created to consider the issue and opted for the latter approach, having failed to reach agreement on the former. The second Working Party adopted the language of 'armed conflict not of an international character' without any further elaboration, and drew up a list of minimum rules that would be applicable in such conflicts, the rules being taken from a proposed preamble to the Civilians Convention. The rules were largely the same as those which were finally adopted. The proposal read:

Paragraph 1.—In the case of armed conflict not of an international character occurring in the territory of one of the High Contracting Parties, each Party to the conflict shall be bound to apply, as a minimum, the following provisions:

(1) Persons taking no active part in the hostilities, and those placed hors de combat by sickness, wounds, captivity or any other cause, shall be treated humanely in all circumstances and without discrimination.

---

[21] Ibid, 125.   [22] Ibid, 47 (Italy).   [23] Ibid.   [24] Ibid, 48.
[25] Ibid, 123 (Report of the Special Committee to the Joint Committee).
[26] Ibid, 49 (Monaco).   [27] Ibid, 76.

To this end, the following acts are and shall remain prohibited with respect to the above-mentioned persons:

a) violence to life and person, in particular murder of all kinds, mutilation, cruel treatment and torture;
b) taking of hostages;
c) outrages upon personal dignity, in particular, humiliating and degrading treatment;
d) the passing of sentences and the carrying out of executions without previous judgment pronounced by a regularly constituted court, affording all the judicial guarantees which are recognized as indispensable by civilized peoples.

(2) The wounded and sick shall be collected and cared for.
(3) No adverse discrimination shall be practised on the basis of differences of race, colour, religion or faith, sex, birth or wealth.

Paragraph 2.—An impartial humanitarian body, such as the International Committee of the Red Cross, may offer its services to the Parties to the conflict.

Paragraph 3.—The Parties to the conflict should further endeavour to bring into force, by means of special agreements, all or part of the other provisions of the present Convention.

Paragraph 4.—The application of the preceding provisions shall not affect the legal status of the parties to the conflict.[28]

The principal criticism of this proposal, and more generally the approach adopted by the second Working Party, was that it failed to take into account those situations that 'resembled international wars sufficiently close to justify, in the general interest, the application to them of the provisions' of the Geneva Conventions.[29]

Nevertheless, after some modification in the Special Committee, a vote was taken on the text of the second Working Party as modified. It was rejected by five votes in favour and five votes against, with the delegate presiding over the meeting abstaining; the rules of the Diplomatic Conference being unclear as to whether, in such cases, the tie could be broken by the vote of the presiding delegate. The presiding delegate did indicate, however, that had he not been presiding over the meeting, he would have voted in favour of the text.[30] A vote was then taken on the second proposal of the first Working Party. This, too, was rejected, this time by seven votes to four.[31] In light of this outcome, the Special Committee put before its parent body, the Joint Committee, the second proposal of the first Working Party, the proposal of the second Working Party, as modified, and a proposal of the USSR that had also been rejected.[32] In the Joint Committee, the modified proposal of the second Working Party was adopted by 21 votes in favour, 6 votes against, and 14 abstentions.[33] At plenary, after much discussion, the proposal was adopted by 34 votes to 12, with one abstention,[34] and became the famous 'common Article 3'.

Having reviewed the drafting history of common Article 3, it is easy to understand why leading commentators have opined that '[n]o one has been completely sure as to what factual situations the article applies' and [i]t is difficult to know where the border line should properly be drawn'.[35] The phrase 'armed conflict not of an international

---

[28] Ibid, 125–6. [29] Ibid, 124 (Report of the Special Committee to the Joint Committee).
[30] Ibid, 127. [31] Ibid, 123–4.
[32] For the text of the proposal of the USSR, see ibid, 127. This was rejected, with one vote in favour and nine against. See ibid, 100.
[33] Ibid, 37. [34] Ibid, 339.
[35] DP Forsythe, 'Legal Management of Internal War: The 1977 Protocol on Non-International Armed Conflicts' (1978) 72 *AJIL* 272, 273; GIAD Draper, 'The Geneva Conventions of 1949' (1965-I) 114 *RdC* 63, 82.

character' was introduced into the legal lexicon without explanation. Indeed, the drafting history suggests that this was deliberate and the scope of application of common Article 3 left open on purpose, as every attempt to elaborate or to provide guidance led to disagreement and lack of consensus. It was only through creative ambiguity that agreement could be reached.

It does not follow from the lack of definition that the notion of an armed conflict not of an international character and the scope of application of common Article 3 is entirely uncertain. Even if a precise definition did not prove forthcoming, a range of situations to which common Article 3 is applicable can be discerned.

It has been suggested in the literature that common Article 3 operates in situations that are at the level of a 'civil war',[36] or in conditions akin to belligerency.[37] However, each of the two suggestions has the potential to mislead. Although the terminology of civil war was used by the Joint Committee to describe the threshold at which common Article 3 applies,[38] it was used as a means of distinguishing the requisite degree of violence from riots and disturbances. It was not used as a term of art or to describe a situation equivalent to the recognition of belligerency. Thus, the same report of the Joint Committee goes on to query 'at what point should the suppression of the rising be regarded as a civil war? What criterion should be adopted?'[39] Accordingly, common Article 3 was not intended to apply only at the level of a civil war in the legal sense of the term.

Likewise, the threshold of common Article 3 is not the same as that at which belligerency could be recognized. The possibility of recognizing a situation as belligerency continued even after the conclusion of the Diplomatic Conference. This was made clear through a resolution passed by the Diplomatic Conference, which provided that '[t]he Conference considers that the conditions under which a Party to a conflict can be recognized as a belligerent by Powers not taking part in this conflict, are governed by the general rules of international law on the subject and are in no way modified by the Geneva Conventions'.[40] Furthermore, the text, '[t]he application of the preceding provisions shall not affect the legal status of the Parties to the conflict', was introduced into common Article 3 precisely so as to prevent the claim that the operation of common Article 3 amounted to recognition of belligerency.[41] Proposals to regulate non-international armed conflict through recognition of belligerency, along the lines of the Australian proposal, also failed.[42] All this, coupled with the approach of reducing the applicable provisions in order to broaden the scope of application of the Article,[43] demonstrates that common Article 3 was not intended to apply only in situations in which belligerency could be recognized.[44]

---

[36] JAC Gutteridge, 'The Geneva Conventions of 1949' (1949) 26 *BYIL* 294, 300; Cullen, *Concept of Non-International Armed Conflict*, above note 5, 26–7, 49, and 54.
[37] Cullen, ibid, 49; JE Bond, *The Rules of Riot* (Princeton University Press, 1974) 53.
[38] *Final Record*, above note 6, Vol II-B, 129 (Report drawn up by the Joint Committee and presented to the Plenary Assembly).
[39] Ibid. Cf Cullen, *Concept of Non-International Armed Conflict*, above note 5, 49–51.
[40] Resolution 10, in *Final Record*, above note 6, Vol I, 362.
[41] Gutteridge, Geneva Conventions, above note 36, 301; F Siordet, 'The Geneva Conventions and Civil War' (1950) 3 *IRRC Supplement* 201, 212; E Castrén, *Civil War* (Suomalainen Tiedeakatemia, 1966) 88. See also below, 207.
[42] See above, 157.
[43] See above, 159–60.
[44] Cf the view of Cullen, *Concept of Non-International Armed Conflict*, above note 5, 49–51.

Rather, common Article 3 operates at a lower level and includes situations of insurgency.⁴⁵ As the Inter-American Commission on Human Rights observed in *Tablada*, '[i]t is important to understand that application of Common Article 3 does not require the existence of large-scale and generalized hostilities or a situation comparable to a civil war in which dissident armed groups exercise control over parts of national territory'.⁴⁶

At the other end of the spectrum, it is equally evident that common Article 3 was not designed to operate at the level of internal tensions and disturbances. Although this is nowhere to be found in the text of common Article 3 itself, states indicated that an armed conflict did not include 'a mere riot or disturbances caused by bandits',⁴⁷ situations of 'disorder, anarchy or brigandage',⁴⁸ an 'uprising',⁴⁹ or 'mere strife'.⁵⁰ Indeed, a clause in a later instrument, Additional Protocol II, which provides that it 'shall not apply to situations of internal disturbances and tensions',⁵¹ is considered to be designed more for common Article 3 than the Additional Protocol.⁵² Accordingly, it is difficult to agree with the exhortation in the ICRC Commentaries, subsequently adopted by various courts and tribunals,⁵³ that common Article 3 should be applied 'as wide[ly] as possible' including in situations of banditry.⁵⁴ It is equally difficult to agree with the 'convenient criteria' set out in the ICRC Commentaries for the identification of a non-international armed conflict, despite the fact that they too are repeated in the jurisprudence of international courts and tribunals,⁵⁵ for the reasons set out above.⁵⁶ Nonetheless, they do play a useful, evidentiary role in that, while their absence does not suggest that a non-international armed conflict does not exist, their presence suggests the existence of an armed conflict.

2.2 Advantages and disadvantages of the lack of definition

The lack of definition of an armed conflict not of an international character, and the associated lack of clarity surrounding precisely when the law of non-international armed conflict applies, has been the subject of considerable criticism. It has been suggested that the absence of a definition has allowed states to deny the existence of

---

⁴⁵ See *The Law of War on Land being Part III of the Manual of Military Law* (HMSO, 1958) 6; L Kotzsch, *The Concept of War in Contemporary History and International Law* (Droz, 1956) 238 fn 73.
⁴⁶ *Juan Carlos Abella v Argentina*, Case 11.137, 18 November 1997, OEA/Ser.L/V/II.98, Doc.6 rev, 13 April 1998, para 152 (emphasis omitted).
⁴⁷ *Final Record*, above note 6, Vol II-B, 129 (Report of the Joint Committee to the Plenary Assembly).
⁴⁸ Ibid, 10 (France).
⁴⁹ Ibid, 11 (Norway).
⁵⁰ Ibid, 121 (various unnamed delegations).
⁵¹ Additional Protocol II, Article 1(2).
⁵² G Abi-Saab, 'Non-International Armed Conflicts', in UNESCO (ed), *International Dimensions of Humanitarian Law* (UNESCO, 1988) 217, 229. See also *Official Records of the Diplomatic Conference on the Reaffirmation and Development of International Humanitarian Law Applicable in Armed Conflicts, Geneva (1974–1977)* (Federal Political Department, 1978) Vol 7, 239 (GDR).
⁵³ *Prosecutor v Milošević*, IT-02-54-T, Decision on Motion for Judgment of Acquittal, 16 June 2004, para 19; *Abella*, above note 46, para 152.
⁵⁴ JS Pictet (ed), *The Geneva Conventions of 12 August 1949, Commentary: IV Geneva Convention Relative to the Protection of Civilian Persons in Time of War* (ICRC, 1958) 36. See also Moir, *Internal Armed Conflict*, above note 5, 35–6; C Kreß, 'Some Reflections on the International Legal Framework Governing Transnational Armed Conflicts' (2010) 15 *JCSL* 245, 261.
⁵⁵ See eg *Prosecutor v Boškoski and Tarčulovski*, IT-04-82-T, Judgment, 10 July 2008, para 176.
⁵⁶ See also below, 180–1.

an armed conflict,[57] and has prevented the application of common Article 3.[58] There is certainly truth in these propositions, although it is equally true that the lack of definition has allowed for a broad interpretation of the notion of a non-international armed conflict.[59]

Indeed, there are advantages in not defining a non-international armed conflict. The difficulties that are inherent in drawing up a definition are avoided, for example the dangers of over- and under-inclusivity, potentially leading to borderline cases falling outside the scope of the definition.[60] As one of the experts at the 1972 Conference of Government Experts noted, 'all definitions contained ambiguities; the more they were defined and reaffirmed the more difficult it would become to have the [law] applied and the easier it would become to avoid applying it'.[61] A definition, in this context at least, would also serve to shift the debate rather than resolve it in its entirety. In deciding whether or not a situation amounts to an armed conflict, the discussion would move from the definition of an armed conflict to whether the elements of that definition have been satisfied. A government that denies the existence of an armed conflict will not accept its existence were a definition to exist; rather, it will deny the existence of the requisite elements of the definition.

The question is, then, whether the advantages of the absence of a definition outweigh the disadvantages. To the extent that there remains debate following the existence of a definition, the debate becomes circumscribed by the definition; it is forced to take place within the framework of the definition. Thus, a definition of a non-international armed conflict leaves less room for the parties to argue that such a conflict does or does not exist; it 'diminish[es] the arbitrary evaluation left to each government',[62] and at a certain point, plausible deniability is lost. A definition is particularly important when seeking to challenge the characterization of one of the parties to the violence. It is more difficult to challenge a determination that a situation does not amount to a non-international armed conflict when there is no agreement as to its definition. For example, the lack of definition allowed Portugal to declare at the time of signing the Geneva Conventions:

As there is no actual definition of what is meant by a conflict not of an international character, and as, in case this term is intended to refer solely to civil war, it is not clearly laid down at what moment an armed rebellion within a country should be considered as having become a civil war, Portugal reserves the right not to apply the provisions of Article 3, in so far as they may be contrary to the provisions of Portuguese law, in all territories subject to her sovereignty in any part of the world.[63]

---

[57] Conference of Government Experts on the Reaffirmation and Development of International Humanitarian Law Applicable in Armed Conflicts (Geneva, 24 May–12 June 1971): Submitted by the International Committee of the Red Cross (1971) Part V: Protection of Victims of Non-International Armed Conflicts, 43.

[58] Minimum Humanitarian Standards: Analytical Report of the Secretary-General submitted pursuant to Commission on Human Rights Resolution 1997/21, E/CN.4/1998/87, 5 January 1988, para 74; Moir, *Internal Armed Conflict*, above note 5, 34; Cullen, *Concept of Non-International Armed Conflict*, above note 5, 57.

[59] Draper, Geneva Conventions, above note 35, 87; Moir, *Internal Armed Conflict*, above note 54, 32.

[60] D Ciobanu, 'The Concept and the Determination of the Existence of Armed Conflicts Not of an International Character' (1975) 58 *Rivista di Diritto Internazionale* 43, 48.

[61] 'Reaffirmation and Development of International Humanitarian Law Applicable in Armed Conflicts: Conference of Government Experts [Second Session]' (1973) 13 *IRRC* 61, 65.

[62] Protection of Victims of Non-International Armed Conflicts, above note 57, 41.

[63] *Final Record*, above note 6, Vol I, 351. Portugal did not enter this reservation at the time of ratification.

The absence of a definition thus proved unfortunate.

3. The definition approach

The inability to define precisely and authoritatively what was meant by an armed conflict not of an international character lasted up until 1995. Various definitions had been posited in the interim, and certain core elements were common to the various definitions, but each failed to gain sufficient traction to make it sufficiently authoritative. Treaties concluded in the period between 1949 and 1995 simply adopted the 'armed conflict not of an international character' formula of common Article 3 without more.[64] For its part, Additional Protocol II, concluded in 1977, referred to the notion of a non-international armed conflict, which it left undefined, but also required certain criteria additional to that concept in order for the Protocol to apply.[65] In this way, Additional Protocol II is of the same mould as other treaties concluded during the period, aside from the additional criteria that are required to exist in order for the instrument to apply.

The requirement of Additional Protocol II that additional criteria be satisfied also introduced the idea of different types of non-international armed conflict for the purposes of international humanitarian law: the 'ordinary' non-international armed conflict (ie a common Article 3 conflict, which is described in the section that follows as a 'non-international armed conflict *simpliciter*'),[66] and the Additional Protocol II-type armed conflict. Things would become even more complex with the adoption of the Rome Statute of the International Criminal Court (Rome Statute) in 1998 and the possible existence of a third type of non-international armed conflict. These issues are considered further in Section 4 below. For now, the notion of a non-international armed conflict *simpliciter* will be considered.

In 1995, a precise definition of a non-international armed conflict was set out by the ICTY Appeals Chamber in the *Tadić* Decision on Interlocutory Appeal on Jurisdiction. In that Decision, the Appeals Chamber observed that 'an armed conflict exists whenever there is a resort to armed force between States or protracted armed violence between governmental authorities and organized armed groups or between such groups within a State'.[67] The core elements that featured in the various definitions that had been posited previously were thus encapsulated in a neat and concise definition. An armed conflict not of an international character is, then, 'protracted armed violence between governmental authorities and organized armed groups or between such groups'. Whether the conflict has to be fought 'within a state' is considered below.[68]

---

[64] Hague Convention for the Protection of Cultural Property in the Event of Armed Conflict, Article 19.

[65] Article 1. The Additional Protocol II threshold is considered more fully below, 182 et seq.

[66] The terminology of non-international armed conflict *simpliciter* is used in order to distinguish the 'ordinary' non-international armed conflict from the non-international armed conflict that is required to satisfy certain additional elements in order for particular rules to apply. A non-international armed conflict *simpliciter* is the same as a common Article 3 conflict. However, it is not described in that way, given that it would suggest that it applies only to common Article 3 and not to other bodies of international law. In subsequent chapters, when a distinction does not need to be drawn between different types of non-international armed conflict, the simpler language of 'non-international armed conflict' will be used.

[67] *Tadić* Decision on Interlocutory Appeal on Jurisdiction, above note 2, para 70.

[68] Chapter 6, 228–32.

The *Tadić* definition thus singles out two particular characteristics of the situation in order for it to be considered a non-international armed conflict *simpliciter*—the violence and the actors taking part in the violence.[69] When the *Tadić* Trial Chamber came to apply the definition of the Appeals Chamber to the facts of the case, it noted that '[t]he test applied by the Appeals Chamber... focuses on two aspects of a conflict: the intensity of the conflict and the organization of the parties' and that it was these two aspects that differentiated a non-international armed conflict from internal tensions and disturbances.[70] The dual concepts of intensity of violence and organization of the armed group have since been a constant refrain in the jurisprudence of the ad hoc international criminal tribunals.[71]

These two concepts have a long and distinguished history. According to Vattel: '[w]hen a party is formed within the State which cease to obey the sovereign and is strong enough to make a stand against him, or when a Republic is divided into two opposite factions, and both sides take up arms, there exists a civil war.'[72] Likewise, a former British Foreign Secretary, George Canning, once described belligerency as 'a certain degree of force and consistency acquired by a mass of population engaged in war'.[73] An influential report of a 1962 Conference of Government Experts convened by the ICRC also provided that the existence of a non-international armed conflict cannot be denied if:

the *hostile action*, directed against a legal government, is *of a collective character and consists of a minimum amount of organization*. In this respect and without these circumstances being necessarily cumulative, one should take into account such factors as the length of the conflict, the number and framework of the rebel groups, their installation or action on a part of the territory, the degree of the insecurity, the existence of victims, the methods employed by the legal government to re-establish order, etc.[74]

Likewise, in 1972, the ICRC suggested to the Conference of Government Experts the language: 'hostilities of a collective nature are in action between organized armed forces under the command of a responsible authority.'[75] Along similar lines, the ICRC

---

[69] See also International Law Association Committee on the Use of Force, Final Report on the Meaning of Armed Conflict in International Law (2010).

[70] *Prosecutor v Tadić*, IT-94-1-T, Opinion and Judgment, 7 May 1997, para 562.

[71] See eg *Prosecutor v Haradinaj, Balaj and Brahimaj*, IT-04-84-T, Judgment, 3 April 2008, para 38; *Prosecutor v Jean-Paul Akayesu*, Case No ICTR-96-4-T, Judgment, 2 September 1998, para 620; *Prosecutor v Brima, Kamara and Kanu*, SCSL-04-16-T, Judgment, 20 June 2007, para 244; *Prosecutor v Fofana and Kondewa*, SCSL-04-14-T, Judgment, 2 August 2007, para 124. See also *Prosecutor v Thomas Lubanga Dyilo*, ICC-01/04-01/06, Decision on the Confirmation of Charges, 29 January 2007, para 233.

[72] E de Vattel, *The Law of Nations or the Principles of Natural Law, Volume 3* (CG Fenwick trans) (Carnegie Institution, 1916) 338 (emphasis removed).

[73] Statement by the British Foreign Secretary to its Ambassador in Constantinople in the context of the 1825 Greek rebellion, quoted in WE Hall, *A Treatise on International Law* (A Pearce Higgins ed) (Clarendon Press, 1924) 38 fn 1.

[74] ICRC, 'Humanitarian Aid to the Victims of Internal Conflicts: Meeting of a Commission of Experts in Geneva' (1963) 3 *IRRC* 79, 82–3 (emphases added). This formulation was adopted in Reaffirmation and Development of the Laws and Customs Applicable in Armed Conflicts: Report submitted by the International Committee of the Red Cross (May 1969) 99–100; Respect for Human Rights in Armed Conflicts: Report of the Secretary-General, A/8052, 18 September 1970, para 134; Protection of Victims of Non-International Armed Conflicts, above note 57, 45–8; Conference of Government Experts on the Reaffirmation and Development of International Humanitarian Law Applicable in Armed Conflicts (Geneva, 24 May–12 June 1971): Report on the Work of the Conference (ICRC, August 1971) 39, para 170.

[75] ICRC, Conference of Government Experts on the Reaffirmation and Development of International Humanitarian Law Applicable in Armed Conflicts, Geneva, 3 May–3 June 1972 (second

Commentary on Additional Protocol II notes that 'the expression "armed conflict"... introduces a material criterion: the existence of open hostilities between armed forces which are organized to a greater or lesser degree'.[76] Expressed in different ways, then, the requirements of intensity and organization are central features of definitions of non-international armed conflict and are of longstanding origin.[77] Thus, even though the precise *Tadić* formulation was set out in 1995, its component elements are steeped in history. What the ICTY managed to do was to encapsulate in a brief sentence the core elements of a definition that had been recognized decades and centuries earlier.

What is particularly important about the *Tadić* definition, over and above those of previous definitions, is the authority of the entity from which it emanated and the traction it has since gathered. The definition caught on, and in the years since it was adumbrated, it has been widely recited. The precise formulation set out in the *Tadić* Decision has been adopted by other international criminal courts such as the Special Court for Sierra Leone (SCSL) and the International Criminal Court (ICC).[78] Importantly, it has also been utilized outside of international criminal law circles, such as by international commissions of inquiry and fact-finding missions,[79] special procedures mechanisms of the Human Rights Council,[80] the International Law Commission,[81] national courts,[82] national legislation,[83] state military manuals,[84] and the ICRC.[85] It has been used to define a non-international armed conflict for the purposes of *inter alia* asylum law and the law of treaties.[86] Thus, the definition is as pertinent for international humanitarian law, international human rights law, international refugee law, and general public international law, as it is for international criminal law.

---

session): II Commentary, Part Two, Documentary Material Submitted by the International Committee of the Red Cross (Geneva, January 1972) 4.

[76] Y Sandoz, C Swinarski, and B Zimmermann (eds), *Commentary on the Additional Protocols of 8 June 1977 to the Geneva Conventions of 12 August 1949* (ICRC, 1987) 1319. See also Pictet (ed), *Commentary on the Fourth Geneva Convention*, above note 54, 36.

[77] See also the various definitions of commentators. For example, D Ciobanu, 'The Concept and the Determination of the Existence of Armed Conflicts Not of an International Character' (1975) 58 *Rivista di Diritto Internazionale* 43, 56; S Junod, 'Additional Protocol II: History and Scope' (1983–4) 33 *American University Law Review* 29, 30; C Greenwood, 'Scope of Application of Humanitarian Law', in D Fleck (ed), *The Handbook of Humanitarian Law in Armed Conflicts* (Oxford University Press, 1995) 39, 47–9.

[78] See eg *Prosecutor v Sesay, Kallon and Gbao*, SCSL-04-15-T, Judgment, 2 March 2009, para 95; *Lubanga* Decision on the Confirmation of Charges, above note 71, para 233.

[79] See eg Report of the Secretary-General's Panel of Experts on Accountability in Sri Lanka, 31 March 2011, para 181; Report of the International Commission of Inquiry to Investigate All Alleged Violations of International Human Rights Law in the Libyan Arab Jamahiriya, A/HRC/17/44, 1 June 2011, para 63.

[80] See eg Report on the Situation of Human Rights in Somalia, E/CN.4/1997/88, 3 March 1997, paras 53–4; Final Report of the Special Rapporteur on Terrorism and Human Rights, E/CN.4/Sub.2/2004/40, 25 June 2004, fn 23. See also Children and Armed Conflict: Report of the Secretary-General, A/62/609-S/2007/757, 21 December 2007, para 5 fn 2.

[81] First Report on the Effects of Armed Conflicts on Treaties, A/CN.4/627, 22 March 2010, para 30 (Draft Article 2(b)).

[82] See eg *HH and Others v Secretary of State for the Home Department* [2008] UKAIT 22.

[83] See eg [Philippines] Act on Crimes against International Humanitarian Law, Genocide, and other Crimes against Humanity, section 3(c).

[84] UK Ministry of Defence, *The Manual of the Law of Armed Conflict* (Oxford University Press, 2004) 29.

[85] 'How is the Term "Armed Conflict" Defined in International Humanitarian Law?: International Committee of the Red Cross (ICRC) Opinion Paper', March 2008, 4.

[86] *HH and Others v Secretary of State for the Home Department* [2008] UKAIT 22; First Report on the Effects of Armed Conflicts on Treaties, A/CN.4/627, 22 March 2010, para 30 (Draft Article 2(b)).

In considering whether the requisite levels of intensity and organization have been met, the ad hoc international criminal tribunals have been careful to note that the matter can only be assessed on a case-by-case basis.[87] Nonetheless, indicia that demonstrate their existence can be identified in the abstract and these indicia are considered below. A word of caution is in order in this regard. Both the ICTY and the International Criminal Tribunal for Rwanda (ICTR) were dealing with large-scale non-international armed conflicts and, as such, many of the same indicia may not be present in smaller and shorter conflicts.

3.1 Intensity of violence

The requirement that the violence be of a certain level of intensity can be interpreted in a myriad of different ways. It could relate to the number of incidents of violence or the consequent number of deaths, injuries, or damage to property. Alternatively, it could be judged against the number of persons involved in the fighting and the military hardware used. Equally, it could involve consideration of the geographic spread of the violence or its duration. It could be assessed against a combination of the above or relate to something entirely different.

The approach taken by the *Tadić* Appeals Chamber may suggest that the principal determining factor is one of duration, given that the Appeals Chamber referred to the idea of '*protracted* armed violence', rather than violence of a particular intensity, and referred to the fact that fighting 'began in 1991, continued through the summer of 1992... and persists to this day'.[88] In some senses, this is reminiscent of recognition of insurgency, which essentially concerned violence that continued for an extended period of time.[89] On the basis of duration alone, a short period of fighting, for example some 30 hours in the case of *La Tablada*, would not amount to a non-international armed conflict.[90]

However, duration alone was not, and cannot be, determinative. A criterion of duration has been questioned as, by definition, it can be established only after a certain quantum of time.[91] Furthermore, the Appeals Chamber added the words 'large-scale' to the requirement of protraction to convey a sense of magnitude: '[t]here has been protracted, large-scale violence between the armed forces of different States and between governmental forces and organized insurgent groups.'[92] Thus, although the choice of the term 'protraction' to describe the violence has been interpreted as suggesting that a threshold of violence is not required,[93] the Appeals Chamber couples protraction with scale precisely in order to require violence of a certain magnitude. This is also the way in which the *Tadić* Trial Chamber understood the requirement, considering the protracted nature of the violence to be an element of the overall question of the intensity of the violence.[94] Subsequent case-law likewise confirms

---

[87] See eg *Prosecutor v Limaj, Bala and Musliu*, IT-03-66-T, Judgment, 30 November 2005, para 90.
[88] *Tadić* Decision on Interlocutory Appeal, above note 2, para 70 (emphasis added).
[89] See above, 10.
[90] Cf *Abella*, above note 46.
[91] ICRC, *Draft Additional Protocols to the Geneva Conventions of August 12, 1949: Commentary* (October 1973) 133.
[92] *Tadić* Decision on Interlocutory Appeal, above note 2, para 70. See also *Prosecutor v Kordić and Čerkez*, IT-95-14/2-A, Judgment, 17 December 2004, para 341.
[93] APV Rogers, *Law on the Battlefield* (Manchester University Press, 2004) 218–19; APV Rogers, 'Unequal Combat and the Law of War' (2004) 7 *YIHL* 3, 8; Moir, *Internal Armed Conflict*, above note 5, 43.
[94] *Tadić* Trial Judgment, above note 70, para 562. See also *Haradinaj* Trial Judgment, above note 71, para 40. For an early view along similar lines, see Castrén, *Civil War*, above note 41, 28.

that a whole host of factors are relevant for the assessment of intensity. Intensity is, then, a much broader notion of which duration forms but part.

Nonetheless, the role that duration plays should not be understated. Indeed, a criticism of the older definitions that focused on the elements of intensity and organization alone was that the element of duration had been insufficiently emphasized.[95] With the focus returning to the criteria of intensity and organization, the *Boškoski* Trial Chamber has recalled that, 'care is needed not to lose sight of the requirement for protracted armed violence in the case of an internal armed conflict, when assessing the intensity of the conflict'.[96] This reminder is important, not least because, as duration is an aspect of the intensity of violence, violence of a relatively brief duration may still amount to a non-international armed conflict provided that other indicia suggesting intensity are present to a significant degree.[97] Likewise, violence of a moderate intensity may amount to an armed conflict if it takes place over an extended duration.

Various indicia exist, which can assist in deciding whether or not the violence has reached the requisite level of intensity. These are simply indicia; thus the fact that one or even many of them do not exist does not mean that a non-international armed conflict is not taking place. This is crucial to bear in mind, not least because the indicia are taken from instances of high-intensity non-international armed conflicts and may not be features of low-level conflicts. These indicia include the number of incidents and the level, length, and duration of the violence,[98] the geographical spread of the violence,[99] the deaths, injuries, and damage caused by the violence,[100] the mobilization of individuals and the distribution of weapons to them,[101] the weapons used by the parties,[102] the conclusion of ceasefire and peace agreements,[103] the involvement of third parties, whether the United Nations Security Council or other outside entities,[104] the prosecution of offences applicable only in armed conflicts,[105] and the granting of amnesties.[106] Derogations from human rights treaties and declarations of states of

---

[95] Conference of Government Experts on the Reaffirmation and Development of International Humanitarian Law Applicable in Armed Conflicts (Geneva, 24 May–12 June 1971): Report on the Work of the Conference (ICRC, August 1971) 39, para 164.
[96] *Boškoski* Trial Judgment, above note 55, para 175, seemingly endorsed by the Appeals Chamber in *Prosecutor v Boškoski and Tarčulovski*, IT-04-82-A, Judgment, 19 May 2010, para 21.
[97] ILA Report on Armed Conflict, above note 69, 30.
[98] *Tadić* Trial Judgment, above note 70, paras 565–6; *Prosecutor v Delalić, Mucić, Delić and Landžo*, IT-96-21-T, Judgment, 16 November 1998, para 189; Prosecutor v *Milošević*, IT-02-54-T, Decision on Motion for Judgment of Acquittal, 16 June 2004, para 28; *Limaj* Trial Judgment, above note 87, paras 135–67; *Haradinaj* Trial Judgment, above note 71, para 49; *Boškoski* Trial Judgment, above note 55, paras 216–34, 243; *Boškoski* Appeal Judgment, above note 96, para 22; *Lubanga* Decision on the Confirmation of Charges, above note 71, para 235.
[99] *Milošević* Decision on Motion for Acquittal, above note 98, para 29; *Boškoski* Trial Judgment, above note 55, paras 216–34, 243; *Boškoski* Appeal Judgment, above note 96, para 22.
[100] *Tadić* Trial Judgment, above note 70, paras 565–6; *Limaj* Trial Judgment, above note 87, paras 135–167; *Lubanga* Decision on the Confirmation of Charges, above note 71, para 235.
[101] *Delalić* Trial Judgment, above note 98, para 188; *Milošević* Decision on Motion for Acquittal, above note 98, para 30; *Limaj* Trial Judgment, above note 87, paras 135–67.
[102] *Milošević* Decision on Motion for Acquittal, para 31; *Limaj* Trial Judgment, paras 135–67; *Haradinaj* Trial Judgment, para 49; *Boškoski* Trial Judgment, paras 213–22; *Boškoski* Appeal Judgment, para 22.
[103] *Boškoski* Trial Judgment, paras 232–4 and 243; *Boškoski* Appeal Judgment, para 22.
[104] *Tadić* Trial Judgment, para 567; *Delalić* Trial Judgment, para 190; *Haradinaj* Trial Judgment, para 49; *Boškoski* Trial Judgment, paras 220–4, 232–4, 243; *Boškoski* Appeal Judgment, para 22; *Lubanga* Decision on the confirmation of charges, para 235.
[105] *Boškoski* Trial Judgment, paras 243 and 247; *Boškoski* Appeal Judgment, para 22.
[106] *Boškoski* Trial Judgment, paras 243 and 247; *Boškoski* Appeal Judgment, para 22.

emergency may also constitute indicia of an armed conflict depending on the reasons provided for them.

Of particular significance is the use of armed forces on the part of the state rather than the use of its police force.[107] This reflects the position of the Netherlands at the 1974–7 Diplomatic Conference, which opined that 'draft Protocol II would not be applicable in situations of conflict that were being dealt with by police forces using normal police methods and equipment, but that it would become applicable as soon as the authorities were forced to seek substantial assistance from military units or to hand full responsibility for dealing with the conflict over to the armed forces'.[108] However, care needs to be taken in this regard, for the police may continue to be used in non-international armed conflicts, while the armed forces may support the police in times of internal tensions or other emergencies. Accordingly, while a useful indicia, use of the armed forces cannot be determinative.

In the *Tablada* case, the Inter-American Commission held:

> What differentiates the events at the La Tablada base from [internal disturbances] are the concerted nature of the hostile acts undertaken by the attackers, the direct involvement of governmental armed forces, and the nature and level of the violence attending the events in question. More particularly, the attackers involved carefully planned, coordinated and executed an armed attack, i.e., a military operation, against a quintessential military objective—a military base. The officer in charge of the La Tablada base sought, as was his duty, to repulse the attackers, and President Alfonsín, exercising his constitutional authority as Commander-in-Chief of the armed forces, ordered that military action be taken to recapture the base and subdue the attackers.
>
> The Commission concludes therefore that, despite its brief duration [agreed by the parties to be approximately 30 hours], the violent clash between the attackers and members of the Argentine armed forces triggered application of the provisions of Common Article 3, as well as other rules relevant to the conduct of internal hostilities.[109]

Although the final conclusion of the Commission seems misplaced in light of the extremely brief duration of the events in question, the test adopted by the Commission and the indicia considered in the assessment of the situation are sound. Thus, although the conclusion of the *Tablada* case may appear to suggest that the approach taken differs from that taken by the ICTY, this is not in fact the case. What differs is not the elements of organization and intensity, nor is it the indicia used to establish those elements, but the conclusion reached.[110]

Numerous indicia thus exist which assist in the determination of whether or not the intensity of the violence surpasses the threshold required for a non-international armed conflict. Essentially, the existence or non-existence of the various indicia need to be weighed against one another and a decision taken as to whether or not the requisite threshold of intensity has been met. Much turns on the specificities of a particular situation and, aside

---

[107] *Boškoski and Tarčulovski* Trial Judgment, paras 243, 245–6; *Boškoski and Tarčulovski* Appeal Judgment, para 22. See also ICRC, 'Armed Conflicts Linked to the Disintegration of State Structures, Preparatory Document Drafted by the International Committee of the Red Cross for the First Periodical Meeting on International Humanitarian Law', 19–23 January 1998; 'How is the Term "Armed Conflict" Defined in International Humanitarian Law?: International Committee of the Red Cross (ICRC) Opinion Paper', March 2008, 3.
[108] *Official Records*, above note 52, Vol 8, 222, para 39 (Netherlands).
[109] *Abella*, above note 46, paras 154–6.
[110] Cf C Kress, 'The 1999 Crisis in East Timor and the Threshold of the Law on War Crimes' (2002) 13 *Criminal Law Forum* 409, 417, juxtaposing the *Tadić* and *Tabalda* tests.

from identifying the various indicia, it is difficult to make any determinations in the abstract.

3.2 Organization of the armed group

The second constitutive element of a non-international armed conflict is that of organization, more specifically the organization of the armed group. The state's armed forces are presumed to meet the requisite level of organization. However, on occasion, such as in cases of state disintegration, the degree of organization of the state's armed forces may also have to be assessed in order to clarify whether the requisite level is met.

The precise degree of organization required of the armed group is rather opaque. For example, the *Akayesu* Trial Chamber referred to armed forces 'organized to a greater or lesser extent', while the *Limaj* Trial Chamber noted that 'some degree of organization by the parties will suffice'.[111] Commentators similarly refer to 'a modicum of organization', a 'minimum' level of organization, and a level of organization that 'must not be exaggerated'.[112] Thus, the threshold is not all that high.

3.2.1 Indicia of organization

As with the criterion of intensity, certain indicia can be identified that assist in determining whether or not the requisite level of organization has been met. Again, as with the element of intensity, these are simply indicia. The lack of existence of one or even many of them does not mean that a non-international armed conflict is not taking place. This is important not least because the indicia are taken from instances of high-intensity non-international armed conflicts and may not be a feature of low-level conflicts. The *Boškoski* Trial Chamber usefully groups these indicia into those that: indicate a command structure; suggest that the group can carry out organized military operations; indicate logistical ability; relate to the implementation of obligations of international humanitarian law; and demonstrate the ability to speak with a unified voice.[113] More specifically, within the group, the indicia include the existence of an official command structure,[114] headquarters,[115] uniforms,[116] discrete roles and responsibilities of differing entities,[117] the modes of communication used,[118]

---

[111] *Akayesu* Trial Judgment, above note 71, para 620; *Limaj* Trial Judgment, above note 87, para 89. See also *Final Record*, above note 6, Vol II-B, 335 (delegate of Switzerland).
[112] Draper, Geneva Conventions, above note 35, 90; D Schindler, 'The Different Types of Armed Conflicts According to the Geneva Conventions and Protocols' (1979-II) 163 *RdC* 117, 147; Kress, East Timor, above note 110, 416.
[113] *Boškoski* Trial Judgment, above note 55, paras 199–203. See also *Prosecutor v Đorđević*, IT-05-87/1-T, Judgment, 23 February 2011, paras 1537–78.
[114] *Milošević* Decision on Motion for Acquittal, above note 98, para 23; *Limaj* Trial Judgment, paras 97, 110; *Haradinaj* Trial Judgment, paras 60 and 65–8; *Boškoski* Trial Judgment, para 271; *Boškoski* Appeal Judgment, para 23; *Đorđević* Trial Judgment, paras 1541–3.
[115] *Milošević* Decision on Motion for Acquittal, para 23; *Haradinaj* Trial Judgment, paras 60 and 65–8.
[116] *Limaj* Trial Judgment, para 123; *Boškoski* Trial Judgment, para 285; *Đorđević* Trial Judgment, paras 1562–3.
[117] *Limaj* Trial Judgment, paras 100–1.
[118] Ibid, para 103; *Boškoski* Trial Judgment, para 269; *Đorđević* Trial Judgment, paras 1569–70.

and whether military training is afforded to members of the group.[119] External relations, such as undertaking negotiations with third parties,[120] and requiring permits to cross checkpoints,[121] also constitute evidence of organization. The ability to operate within designated zones,[122] control territory,[123] procure, transport, and distribute arms,[124] recruit new members,[125] and co-ordinate actions,[126] all provide evidence of organization. The existence of internal regulations[127] and disciplinary procedures[128] are also important.

The armed group itself may set out the ways in which it is organized. For example, the National Liberation Army (NLA) which fought in the Former Yugoslav Republic of Macedonia in 2001 indicated:

Bearing in mind the need to inform national and international public opinion that the National Liberation Army/UÇK/has met conditions for its legalisation, we hereby:
DECLARE

1. The National Liberation Army functions as a disciplined military organisation, as evinced by the Internal Rules of the UÇK, as well the rules on the work and authority of the staffs, commands, units, officers and men;
2. The National Liberation Army has its own uniforms, ranks and insignia, which are worn in accordance with the Rules on the Wearing of Uniforms;
3. The method of organisation of the UÇK, as well as living and working conditions within the UÇK in line with current regulations, ensure that the UÇK conducts its operations in accordance with the stipulations of international law, fully respected by all members, and especially the General Staff;
4. The General Staff and the entire UÇK respect and will always respect the Geneva Convention during their operations.[129]

Statements along these lines may prove important as evidencing the view of the armed group in question. However, they will have to be assessed against the facts on the ground and, in the case of inconsistency between the two, it will be the facts on the ground that prove determinative.

---

[119] *Haradinaj* Trial Judgment, paras 60, 86; *Boškoski* Trial Judgment, para 284; *Boškoski* Appeal Judgment, para 23; *Đorđević* Trial Judgment, paras 1560–1.
[120] *Limaj* Trial Judgment, paras 125–9; *Haradinaj* Trial Judgment, para 60; *Boškoski* Trial Judgment, para 289; *Boškoski* Appeal Judgment, para 23; *Đorđević* Trial Judgment, para 1576.
[121] *Limaj* Trial Judgment, para 145; *Haradinaj* Trial Judgment, paras 71–2.
[122] *Milošević* Decision on Motion for Acquittal, para 23; *Limaj* Trial Judgment, para 95.
[123] *Haradinaj* Trial Judgment, paras 60, 70–5; *Đorđević* Trial Judgment, para 1557; *Lubanga* Decision on the Confirmation of Charges, para 236.
[124] *Milošević* Decision on Motion for Acquittal, para 23; *Haradinaj* Trial Judgment, paras 60, 76–82; *Boškoski* Trial Judgment, paras 281 and 286; *Boškoski* Appeal Judgment, para 23; *Đorđević* Trial Judgment, paras 1566–8.
[125] *Limaj* Trial Judgment, para 118; *Haradinaj* Trial Judgment, para 60.
[126] *Limaj* Trial Judgment, para 108; *Haradinaj* Trial Judgment, para 60.
[127] *Limaj* Trial Judgment, para 110; *Đorđević* Trial Judgment, paras 1571–2.
[128] *Limaj* Trial Judgment, paras 113–17; *Haradinaj* Trial Judgment, para 60; *Boškoski* Trial Judgment, paras 274–5; *Boškoski* Appeal Judgment, para 23; *Đorđević* Trial Judgment, paras 1573–5; *Prosecutor v Katanga and Chui*, ICC-01/04-01/07, Decision on the Confirmation of Charges, 30 September 2008, para 239.
[129] Ali Ahmeti, Political Representative, UÇK General Staff, Untitled Document, 8 May 2001, Exhibit P00507.E in ICTY *Boškoski* trial.It should be noted that the acronym UÇK was used by both the Kosovo Liberation Army and the National Liberation Army (Macedonia). According to the ICTY, 'National Liberation Army in Albanian is *Ushtria Çlirimtare Kombëtare* (acronym UÇK), while Kosovo Liberation Army in Albanian is *Ushtria Çlirimtare e Kosovës* (acronym UÇK)': *Boškoski* Trial Judgment, para 273 fn 1185.

3.2.2 Organization in practice

The context in which the armed group operates must be borne in mind when assessing its degree of organization. For example, armed groups will usually be underground organizations that operate in conditions of secrecy and that are faced with military operations by the state.[130] For these reasons, the structure of the group and the identity of all its members may not be known. Accordingly, the indicia set out above and, by implication, the degree of organization will differ as between an armed group that operates underground and state armed forces that are operating out in the open.

At the outset of the violence, armed groups not infrequently fail to meet the requisite degree of organization. Unless the 'group' is made up of dissident forces, namely a segment of the state armed forces that are rebelling against the state, it will usually start out as a loose association of individuals. For example, the Chief of Staff of the NLA of the Former Yugoslav Republic of Macedonia noted in 2001 that, '[i]n the early stages of the war, the NLA was a number of small groups operating without co-ordination. When I became Chief of Staff, I began to organise the brigades. The NLA consisted of six brigades which were constantly developing'.[131] Similarly, the 'armed group' that was involved in the conflict in Libya in 2011 initially comprised 'ordinary' individuals who were supporting the opposition to President Gaddafi,[132] and, at the outset of the violence, there was little by way of structure or organization. It is only with time that the co-ordination, cohesion, and structure of the 'group' develop. Indeed, as early as 1937, Mao Tse-Tung wrote that:

> all guerrilla bands that spring from the masses of the people suffer from lack of organization at the time of their formation... As the war progresses... leaders will gradually overcome the lack of discipline, which at first prevails; they will establish discipline in their forces, strengthening them and increasing their combat efficiency.[133]

To the extent that any categorization can be made, armed groups tend to be organized along two lines. The first is the pyramidal structure, with clearly defined chains of command. For example, the New People's Army (NPA), the armed wing of the National Democratic Front of the Philippines (NDFP), which, at the time of writing, was fighting against the Government of the Philippines, consists of regular mobile forces, guerrilla units, militia and self-defence units, and armed city partisans.[134] Regular mobile forces are constructed along the following lines: a squad of five to 10 fighters in addition to the squad leader; a platoon, consisting of two to three squads in addition to the platoon leader; a company, made up of two to three platoons plus the company commander; a battalion, comprising two to three companies in addition to the battalion commander; a regiment, consisting of two to three battalions and the regiment commander; a division, comprising two to three regiments in addition to the division commander; a corps, namely two to three divisions with the corps commander; and the army,

---

[130] *Limaj* Trial Judgment, para 171.
[131] Witness Statement of Gzim Ostreni, Chief of NLA General Staff, para 20, Exhibit P00497.E in ICTY *Boškoski* trial.
[132] Report of the International Commission of Inquiry to investigate all alleged violations of international human rights law in the Libyan Arab Jamahiriya, A/HRC/17/44, 1 June 2011, para 56.
[133] M Tse-Tung, *On Guerrilla Warfare* (SB Griffith trans) (Anchor Press, 1978) 42.
[134] 'Basic Rules of the New People's Army', Principle VIII, Point 1, reproduced in NDFP, *Declaration of Undertaking to Apply the Geneva Conventions of 1949 and Protocol I of 1977* (NDFP Human Rights Monitoring Committee Booklet No 6) 85, 93.

namely two to three corps and the army commanders.[135] The Political Bureau and Central Committee direct 'all formations of the armed units'.[136] The National Operations Command implements national policies and military plans, while the Regional, Provincial, and District Operations Command do so in respect of regional, provincial, and district policies and military plans respectively.[137] Similarly, the Armée de Libération Nationale (ALN) of Algeria, which fought for independence from France between 1954 and 1962, was highly structured with a strict chain of command, designated zones of operation, uniforms and insignia, and military regulations.[138] It was structured along the lines of battalions, companies, sections, and units.[139] The same was true of the Sudan People's Liberation Army (SPLA) which fought against the Government of Sudan between 1983 and 2005.[140]

Groups organized along these lines should be contrasted with the second set of groups, which are broadly speaking decentralized and benefit from less clearly delineated roles and responsibilities. In his classic work on guerrilla warfare, Mao noted:

In orthodox warfare...a certain degree of initiative is accorded subordinates, but in principle, command is centralized.... In the case of guerrilla warfare, this is not only undesirable but impossible. Only adjacent guerrilla units can coordinate their activities to any degree...there are no strictures on the extent of guerrilla activity nor is it primarily characterized by the quality of cooperation of many units.[141]

Groups of this nature tend to be structured horizontally with power distributed among the various units. For example, it has been suggested that '[k]nowledgeable experts consider that the Taliban's armed forces were not comparable to an organized army, since they had no strategic military plans, or decision-making power and they resorted to guerrilla tactics'.[142] The forces of the Taliban of Afghanistan, which has fought against the Government of Afghanistan and the International Security Assistance Force (ISAF) in the post-2001 period, are also considered to have 'no organized, uniformed military, no strategic military plans, and no formal command and control structure characteristic of a regular military'.[143] This decentralization does not mean that the groups do not meet the international humanitarian law requirement of organization. Even decentralized armed groups may be organized, for an armed group will find it difficult to function—carry out hostilities, enforce orders, mete out internal discipline, and the like—without some semblance of a structure.[144] The misunderstanding arises

---

[135] Ibid, Principle VIII, Point 2.
[136] Ibid, Principle VII, Point 1.
[137] Ibid, Principle VII, Points 1–4.
[138] See M Bedjaoui, *Law and the Algerian Revolution* (International Association of Democratic Lawyers, 1961) 46–55.
[139] First Congress of the Algerian Front of National Liberation, 20 August 1956, in *White Paper on the Application of the Geneva Conventions of 1949 to the French-Algerian Conflict* (Algerian Office, New York, 1960) Appendix III.
[140] A Vinci, *Armed Groups and the Balance of Power* (Routledge, 2009) 18.
[141] Tse-Tung, *On Guerrilla Warfare*, above note 133, 48.
[142] J Toman, 'The Status of Al Qaeda/Taliban Detainees under the Geneva Conventions' (2003) 32 *IYHR* 271, 284.
[143] WH Parks, 'Combatants', in MN Schmitt (ed), *The War in Afghanistan: A Legal Analysis* (Volume 85, International Law Studies, Naval War College, 2009) 247, 258.
[144] O Bangerter, 'Disseminating and Implementing International Humanitarian Law within Organized Armed Groups: Measures Armed Groups can Take to Improve Respect for International Humanitarian Law', in International Institute of Humanitarian Law (ed), *Non-State Actors and International Humanitarian Law* (FrancoAngeli, 2010) 187, 188–9; JK Kleffner, 'The Collective Accountability of Organized Armed Groups for System Crimes', in H van der Wilt and

from comparing the organization of the armed group to that of the state's armed forces. Thus, the Taliban is viewed as 'not comparable to an organized army', and as not having a 'formal command and control structure characteristic of a regular military'. However, this comparison with the state armed forces is misleading as it skews the notion of organization.

Indeed, many of the difficulties that emerge in this area of the law arise as a result of the structure and organization of the armed group being compared to that of the state's armed forces. Such an approach posits the structure of the state armed forces as the archetype to be followed by the armed group. If judged in this way, the armed group will invariably suffer from a lack of organization. The quintessential form of organization—highly structured lines of command present in state armed forces—is thus converted into the only form of organization, with the result that anything else translates into a lack of organization. Yet, this is precisely the comparison that tends to be made by outside observers. For example, during the 1974–7 Diplomatic Conference, the ICRC indicated that there should be 'no difference in the degree of organization' between state armed forces and non-state armed groups.[145]

The point is recognized from time to time. For example, the ICRC Commentary on Additional Protocol II notes the requirement of 'some degree of organization' and goes on to express the view that 'this does not necessarily mean that there is a hierarchical system of military organization similar to that of regular armed forces'.[146] It is also noted, on occasion, in the jurisprudence.[147] It needs to be borne in mind at all times.

3.2.3 Responsible command

Inherent in the idea of organization is the notion of responsible command. Although the requirement is not always spelt out in the relevant texts, it is implicit in the very notion of the organization of the armed group. An early ICRC draft of Additional Protocol II, which was intended to have the same scope of application as common Article 3 and not the higher threshold which was subsequently adopted, made explicit reference to the idea of 'organized armed forces under the command of a responsible authority'.[148] Similarly, the ICRC commentary on the draft provided that the armed group 'must be organized, *thus implying* that [it is] subject to a sufficiently firm discipline that will ensure respect, in the conduct of the hostilities, of the provisions laid down in the Protocol'.[149] Along similar lines, the *Hadžihasanović* Appeals Chamber considered that 'military organization implies responsible command'; indeed, that 'there cannot be an organized military force save on the basis of responsible

---

A Nollkaemper (eds), *System Criminality in International Law* (Cambridge University Press, 2009) 238, 243.

[145] *Official Records*, above note 52, Vol 8, 204, para 15.
[146] ICRC *Commentary on the Additional Protocols*, above note 76, 1352.
[147] *Limaj* Trial Judgment, above note 87, para 89; *Prosecutor v Orić*, IT-03-68-T, Judgment, 30 June 2006, para 254; *Boškoski* Trial Judgment, above note 55, para 197; *Prosecutor v Musema*, ICTR-96-13-T, Judgment and Sentence, 27 January 2000, para 257.
[148] Conference of Government Experts on the Reaffirmation and Development of International Humanitarian Law Applicable in Armed Conflicts (Second Session, 3 May–3 June 1972): Report on the Work of the Conference, Volume II (July 1972) 16. See also Volume I, para 2.9.
[149] ICRC, *Draft Additional Protocols to the Geneva Conventions of August 12, 1949: Commentary* (October 1973) 132 (emphasis added). See also ICRC, Conference of Government Experts, above note 148, Commentary, Part Two, Documentary Material Submitted by the International Committee of the Red Cross (January 1972) 6.

command'.¹⁵⁰ The reverse proposition has also been expressed. Thus, when the *Akayesu* Trial Chamber came to consider the meaning of responsible command, it noted that '[t]he armed forces opposing the government must be under responsible command, which entails a degree of organization within the armed group or dissident armed forces',¹⁵¹ and an ICC Pre-Trial Chamber found that specified armed groups 'had a certain degree of organisation, insofar as such groups acted under a responsible command and had an operative internal disciplinary system'.¹⁵² On either approach, ideas of organization and responsible command are inextricably linked: '[o]nly when such a structure exists can the leaders train the members of the group, give clear orders and instructions, be informed of the actions of subordinates and react promptly to them.'¹⁵³ Thus, the notion of responsible command is inherent in a non-state party fighting in a non-international armed conflict, being derived as it is from the requirement of organization.¹⁵⁴

It may be thought that horizontal or decentralized armed groups, while organized, do not have a responsible command. Thus, it has been suggested that '[t]he requirement of the existence of an individual commander may not be easy to meet in some guerrilla movements which operate under a collegial authority'.¹⁵⁵ However, that is to misconstrue the idea of responsible command. Just as the organization of the armed group may take different forms, so too may responsible command. Responsible command is not the same as command responsibility, albeit the two are linked.¹⁵⁶ Responsible command does not, in and of itself, imply a hierarchical pyramidal structure with one individual at the top. It simply requires that there be some sort of relationship of effective control by which one individual has the power to control the acts of another, in particular the power to prevent or punish particular acts of that other individual.¹⁵⁷ This is usually described as a superior–subordinate relationship; however, care needs to be taken if utilizing this terminology as it, too, posits the notion of a clearly defined hierarchy when in fact it is being used to describe a relationship of effective control. Rather clearer, the Rome Statute refers to the idea of a 'person effectively acting as a military commander' and notions of 'effective authority and control'.¹⁵⁸ However, an ICC Pre-Trial Chamber has interpreted this as referring to

---

¹⁵⁰ *Prosecutor v Hadžihasanović, Alagić, and Kubura*, IT-01-47-AR72, Decision on Interlocutory Appeal Challenging Jurisdiction in Relation to Command Responsibility, 16 July 2003, paras 17 and 16.

¹⁵¹ *Akayesu* Trial Judgment, above note 71, para 626. See also *Fofana and Kondewa* Trial Judgment, above note 71, para 127.

¹⁵² *Katanga* Decision on the Confirmation of Charges, above note 128, para 239. See also *Prosecutor v Bemba Gombo*, ICC-01/05-01/08, Decision Pursuant to Article 61(7)(a) and (b) of the Rome Statute on the Charges of the Prosecutor Against Jean-Pierre Bemba Gombo, 15 June 2009, para 234.

¹⁵³ A-M La Rosa and C Wuerzner, 'Armed Groups, Sanctions and the Implementation of International Humanitarian Law' (2008) 90 *IRRC* 327, 329. See also Kleffner, Armed Groups, above note 144, 243.

¹⁵⁴ See also Report of the International Commission of Inquiry to investigate all alleged violations of international human rights law in the Libyan Arab Jamahiriya, A/HRC/17/44, 1 June 2011, para 64. Cf *Prosecutor v Lubanga*, ICC-01/04/-01/06, Trial Judgment, 14 March 2012, 536; Cullen, *Concept of Non-International Armed Conflict*, above note 5, 149 and 155, both taking the view that responsible command is a construct of Additional Protocol II.

¹⁵⁵ Respect for Human Rights in Armed Conflicts: Report of the Secretary-General, A/8052, 18 September 1970, para 176.

¹⁵⁶ *Hadžihasanović* Decision on Command Responsibility, above note 150, para 22.

¹⁵⁷ See eg *Prosecutor v Delalić, Mucic, Delic and Landžo*, IT-96-21-A, Judgment, 20 February 2001, para 378.

¹⁵⁸ Article 28.

groups 'that follow a structure of military hierarchy or a chain of command'.[159] Yet there is no reason for such an interpretation. The Rome Statute does not require it, and it excludes groups which, while utilizing relationships of effective control, do not follow a strict chain of command.[160] While such groups may be in the minority, the typical situation should not be converted into a condition precedent.

It is well-accepted that a *de jure* superior position does not necessarily give rise to effective control.[161] The reverse proposition is also accepted, namely that effective control does not necessarily require a *de jure* superior position. Although it is true that '"effective control" is generally a manifestation of a superior–subordinate relationship between the suspect and the forces or subordinates in a *de jure* or *de facto* hierarchical relationship (chain of command)',[162] and that '[t]he ability to exercise effective control . . . will almost invariably not be satisfied unless such a relationship of subordination exists',[163] the almost invariable situation does indeed exist. The ICTY Appeals Chamber acknowledged as much when it considered the example 'of two persons of equal status or rank . . . in fact exercis[ing] "effective control"'.[164] However, it went on to note that the doctrine of command responsibility was not intended to apply to persons of equal status.[165] Regardless of the correctness of that position, persons of equal rank controlling one another could well satisfy the notion of responsible command. Accordingly, even horizontally structured armed groups can satisfy the element of responsible command.

What is important is that there are individuals who are 'capable of ensuring generally the execution of . . . orders, including, as far as possible, respect of the laws and customs of war',[166] regardless of whether they are also in a superior–subordinate relationship.

3.2.4 Rationale for organization

Just as important as the indicia of organization are the reasons why organization is a prerequisite for the existence of a party to a non-international armed conflict. An armed group may be organized for one purpose, such as conducting large-scale violence, but not for another, such as being able to comply with the law. The reason why a certain level of organization is a prerequisite will thus affect the weight to be afforded to the various indicia noted above. For example, if organization is required in order to demonstrate that the group has the ability to carry out intense hostilities, factors such as the ability to procure, distribute, and use weaponry should be the crucial indicia. However, if organization is required in order that the group be able to enforce international humanitarian law, factors such as the existence of disciplinary procedures and internal regulations should take priority.

---

[159] *Bemba Gombo* Decision on Confirmation of Charges, above note 152, para 410.
[160] See generally M Osiel, 'The Banality of Good: Aligning Incentives Against Mass Atrocity' (2005) 105 *Columbia Law Review* 1751.
[161] See eg *Delalić* Trial Judgment, above note 98, para 354.
[162] *Bemba Gombo* Decision on Confirmation of Charges, above note 152, para 414.
[163] *Delalić* Appeal Judgment, above note 157, para 303.
[164] Ibid, para 303.
[165] Ibid.
[166] Respect for Human Rights in Armed Conflicts: Report of the Secretary-General, A/8052, 18 September 1970, para 176. See also Conference of Government Experts on the Reaffirmation and Development of International Humanitarian Law Applicable in Armed Conflicts (Geneva, 24 May–12 June 1971): Submitted by the International Committee of the Red Cross (Geneva, 1971) Part VI: Rules Applicable in Guerrilla Warfare, 13.

The requirement of organization exists for three principal reasons. First, the requisite intensity of violence may depend on the armed group being organized to a certain degree,[167] as may its duration.[168] ICC pre-trial chambers have thus opined that the reference to organized armed groups 'focuses on the need for the[m] ... to have the ability to plan and carry out military operations for a prolonged period of time'.[169] Second, organization suggests that the violence is of a collective character,[170] rather than being carried out by random individuals. Thus, the *Delalić* Trial Chamber noted that it is 'in order to distinguish from cases of civil unrest or terrorist activities [that] the emphasis is on the protracted extent of the armed violence and the extent of organisation of the parties involved'.[171] Third, the armed group is required to be organized in order that it can comply with the law of armed conflict. Thus, the International Law Association Committee on the Use of Force has noted that the 'underlying theme' within the requirement of organization 'is that there must be a sufficient level of organisation through a command structure in order for the basic requirements of Common Article 3 to the 1949 Geneva Conventions to be implemented'.[172]

Of the three reasons, it is suggested that it is the latter two that should be considered the more important. If the armed group is required to be organized in order to evidence its ability to conduct violence at a certain level of intensity, then the issue is really one of intensity alone. Organization for the purposes of the collective character of the violence is important as it distinguishes violence on the part of isolated individuals from violence on the part of a group. An armed conflict is fought between two or more 'parties' and it is, in part, this notion of parties to the conflict that distinguishes an armed conflict from internal tensions and disturbances. The notion of parties to the conflict also brings with it responsibility on both sides. In practical terms, in order for the law of non-international armed conflict to be respected, the parties must be able—rather than simply willing—to comply with it. Indeed, it was recognized by the 1971 Conference of Government Experts, albeit in the context of guerrilla warfare, that, '[t]he condition of respecting the laws and customs of war is absolutely fundamental and should be given a top position in an interpretative Protocol'.[173] Yet, many of the indicia of organization identified above go to the intensity of the violence rather than compliance with the law. This suggests that, at least insofar as the international criminal tribunals are concerned, organization for the purposes of intensity of the violence is rather more important than organization for the purposes of compliance with the law. Indeed, it has been suggested that the '*Tadić* formulation has no requirement that armed groups ... be capable of

---

[167] *Akayesu* Trial Judgment, above note 71, para 626; *Haradinaj* Trial Judgment, above note 71, para 60.
[168] International Law Association Report Armed Conflict, above note 69, 30.
[169] *Lubanga* Decision on the Confirmation of Charges, para 234; *Bemba Gombo* Decision on the Confirmation of Charges para 233; *Prosecutor v Al-Bashir*, ICC-02/05-01/09, Decision on the Prosecution's Application for a Warrant of Arrest against Omar Hassan Ahmad Al Bashir, 4 March 2009, para 60.
[170] 'How is the Term "Armed Conflict" Defined in International Humanitarian Law?: International Committee of the Red Cross (ICRC) Opinion Paper', March 2008, 3; Moir, *Law of Internal Armed Conflict*, above note 5, 36.
[171] *Delalić* Trial Judgment, above note 98, para 184. Terrorist acts may also factor into the intensity of the violence. See *Boškoski* Trial Judgment, above note 55, paras 184–90.
[172] International Law Association Report Armed Conflict, above note 69, 29.
[173] Conference of Government Experts on the Reaffirmation and Development of International Humanitarian Law Applicable in Armed Conflicts (Geneva, 24 May–12 June 1971): Submitted by the International Committee of the Red Cross (Geneva, 1971) Part VI: Rules Applicable in Guerrilla Warfare, 16 (emphasis removed).

meeting IHL obligations'.[174] Although this overstates the point, organization of the armed group for the purposes of implementation and enforcement of the law should play a more central role.

Organization for the purposes of the implementation and enforcement of the law does not require that there be perfect compliance with it. It is the *ability* to enforce the law that is crucial rather than willingness to enforce it or actual enforcement. While actual implementation of the law remains the best evidence of ability to implement it, neither isolated violations, systematic violations, nor group policies to violate the law necessitate the conclusion that the group lacked the ability to enforce it. Thus, although it has been suggested that, '[i]f members of an armed group consistently violate the law of war and are not punished, that is strong evidence that the group does not qualify as "armed forces", since it fails to meet the criterion of an internal disciplinary system',[175] that conclusion should not be reached too readily. For example, the Resistência Nacional Moçambicana (RENAMO) looted civilian property and engaged in various killings, which led to its being characterized by the Government of Mozambique as armed bandits and by commentators as a 'disorganised movement of thieves'.[176] However, RENAMO 'was a highly centralised operation, with each of its many units connected by radio to the central command'.[177]

When the ability of the armed group to implement and enforce the law has been considered, it has been downgraded in importance. During the drafting of common Article 3, for example, there was some discussion of the armed group being in a position to implement the Conventions;[178] however, it came to nothing. The 1972 ICRC draft of Additional Protocol II included a provision which provided that, '[a]rmed forces shall be organized and subject to an appropriate internal disciplinary system. Such disciplinary system shall enforce respect of the present rules and of the other rules applicable in armed conflicts'.[179] This met with some doubt on the part of government experts 'because it would raise serious difficulties for the party opposed to the legal government'.[180] Explaining the point at the 1974–7 Diplomatic Conference, the ICRC stated that 'insurgent armed forces had to have an organic structure, in other words, they must be endowed with a system of competence and responsibility and subjected to a system of internal discipline as implied by article 36—measures for execution—which stipulated that each Party to the conflict should take measures to ensure observance of the Protocol by its military and civilian agents and persons subject to its authority'.[181] However, the position was not adopted. Decades later, the *Haradinaj* Trial Chamber found that the Kosovo Liberation Army (KLA) was organized for the purposes of a non-international armed conflict, while also finding that, in the early part of the conflict, discipline of KLA soldiers did 'not appear to have been a significant concern for the KLA', that the KLA 'had no courts, judges, or prisons', and that the KLA had 'no system for disciplining KLA soldiers'.[182] Similarly, before the *Limaj* Trial

---

[174] International Law Association Report Armed Conflict, above note 69, 15.
[175] Rogers, Unequal Combat, above note 93, 16.
[176] See JM Weinstein, *Inside Rebellion: The Politics of Insurgent Violence* (Cambridge University Press, 2007) 230.
[177] Ibid.
[178] *Final Record*, above note 6, Vol II-B, 43.
[179] Article 39, reproduced in Conference of Government Experts on the Reaffirmation and Development of International Humanitarian Law Applicable in Armed Conflicts (Second Session, 3 May–3 June 1972): Report on the Work of the Conference, Volume II (Geneva, July 1972) 6.
[180] Ibid, 110 para 2.439.
[181] *Official Records*, above note 52, Vol 8, 204, para 15. See also Vol 9, 234, para 52.
[182] *Haradinaj* Trial Judgment, above note 71, para 69.

Chamber, the defence argued that 'the law does not require the impossible and that, in order to be bound by international humanitarian law, a party to a conflict must be able to implement international humanitarian law and, at the bare minimum, must possess: a basic understanding of the principles laid down in Common Article 3, a capacity to disseminate rules, and a method of sanctioning breaches'.[183] However, the Trial Chamber indicated that it 'does not share this view' and that 'some degree' of organization would suffice,[184] again suggesting that ability to impose discipline was a factor of lesser importance.

Yet, most non-state armed groups possess some sort of internal disciplinary system, usually to sanction non-compliance with orders and to enforce violations of their internal regulations and codes of conduct.[185] For example, the *RUF* Trial Judgment indicates that 'the RUF's disciplinary system was critical to maintaining its operation as a cohesive military organisation, particularly as the force grew with the addition of captured civilians trained as fighters'.[186] Furthermore, the existence of an internal disciplinary system is crucial insofar as actual enforcement, rather than simply applicability, of the law of armed conflict is concerned. Some groups have recognized this, with the NDFP stating in 1996 that '[t]he NDFP and the forces it herein represents accept the principle of command responsibility for the system of discipline to ensure respect for the rules of international humanitarian law and punish those who break them'.[187] Along similar lines, in 1995, the Kurdistan Workers' Party (PKK) indicated that '[i]t has adopted a system of discipline to ensure respect for these rules [the Geneva Conventions and Additional Protocol I] and the punishment of those who break them. It accepts the principle of command responsibility'.[188] While the internal disciplinary system of an armed group need not be greatly developed,[189] at least a semblance is required as part of its organization. Organization for the purposes of the enforcement of the law is equally as important as, indeed even more important than, organization for the purposes of the intensity of the violence.

The lack of importance attributed to an internal disciplinary system at present should not be taken to extremes. There is some jurisprudence and commentary that stresses the importance of organization for the purposes of compliance with the law of armed conflict.[190] The notion of responsible command within the element of organization has also re-focused things. Thus, the *Hadžihasanović* Trial Chamber noted that '[t]he existence of a responsible command implies some degree of organization... [i]t means an organization capable, on the one hand, of planning and carrying out

---

[183] *Limaj* Trial Judgment, above note 87, para 88.
[184] Ibid, para 89.
[185] See below, 445–8 and 549–55.
[186] *RUF* Trial Judgment, above note 78, para 706.
[187] NDFP Declaration of Undertaking to Apply the Geneva Conventions of 1949 and Protocol I of 1977, 5 July 1996, reproduced in NDFP, *Declaration of Undertaking to Apply the Geneva Conventions of 1949 and Protocol I of 1977* (NDFP Human Rights Monitoring Committee Booklet No 6) 13.
[188] PKK Statement to the United Nations, 24 January 1995.
[189] Kress, East Timor, above note 110, 417.
[190] See *Akayesu* Trial Judgment, above note 71, para 626; *Boškoski* Trial Judgment, above note 55, para 196; Draper, Geneva Conventions, above note 35, 90; Moir, *Internal Armed Conflict*, above note 5, 36; E La Haye, *War Crimes in Internal Armed Conflicts* (Cambridge University Press, 2008) 8; L Zegveld, *The Accountability of Armed Opposition Groups in International Law* (Cambridge University Press, 2002) 135 and 140.

sustained and concerted military operations, and on the other, of imposing discipline in the name of a *de facto* authority'.[191] Nonetheless, it is deserving of greater weight.

3.3 Governmental authorities

A third aspect of the *Tadić* definition is also important, namely the notion of 'governmental authorities'. Governmental authorities are usually the armed forces of the state, the reference to armed forces including '*all* the armed forces—including those which under some national systems might not be called regular forces'. However, armed forces do not include 'other governmental agencies the members of which may be armed', for example, 'the police, customs and other similar organizations',[192] as long as, it should be noted, they are not formally incorporated into the armed forces or do not in fact fight alongside the armed forces.

Thus, when non-international armed conflicts are described as being fought between a state and a non-state armed group, the reference to the state is a short-form for the armed forces of the state or the governmental authorities of the state. It would also include state-sponsored militias. Similarly, in respect of armed groups with multiple wings and/or divisions, reference to the armed group is usually to the military wing of the armed group.

3.4 Non-requisites

Just as important as the prerequisite elements of intensity and organization are the elements that are not required for a non-international armed conflict *simpliciter* to exist. Certain of the elements may, however, be required in order for particular rules of international humanitarian law to apply.[193]

A number of influential bodies have suggested that territorial control on the part of the armed group is a prerequisite for a non-international armed conflict *simpliciter*.[194] However, it is submitted that such territorial control is not at all determinative.[195] The source of this confusion may be the ICRC Commentaries on common Article 3, which is sometimes cited as authority for the proposition that territorial control is required.[196] However, the ICRC Commentaries contain a compilation of proposals made at the 1949 Diplomatic Conference, of which the requirement of territorial control was one,

---

[191] *Prosecutor v Hadžihasanović, Alagić and Kubura*, IT-01-47-PT, Decision on Joint Challenge to Jurisdiction, 12 November 2002, para 87, quoting ICRC, *Commentary on the Additional Protocols*, para 4463 (emphasis omitted).

[192] *Official Records*, above note 52, Vol 10, 40, para 91. See also 94. See also *Akayesu* Trial Judgment, above note 71, para 625; *Musema* Trial Judgment, para 256; *Fofana and Kondewa* Trial Judgment, above note 71, para 127.

[193] See below, 182 et seq.

[194] *Akayesu* Trial Judgment, above note 71, para 619; *Al-Bashir* Decision on Arrest Warrant, above note 169, paras 59–65; Report of the International Commission of Inquiry on Darfur to the Secretary-General, S/2005/60, 1 February 2005, paras 75 and 157; Report of the International Commission of Inquiry to investigate all alleged violations of international human rights law in the Libyan Arab Jamahiriya, A/HRC/17/44, 1 June 2011, para 64; J Pictet (ed), *The Geneva Conventions of 12 August 1949, Commentary: I Geneva Convention for the Amelioration of the Condition of the Wounded and Sick in Armed Forces in the Field* (ICRC, 1952) 49–50.

[195] See *Milosević* Decision on Motion for Acquittal, above note 53, para 36. See also Schindler, Armed Conflicts, above note 112, 146; Moir, *Internal Armed Conflict*, above note 5, 38; K Dörmann, *Elements of War Crimes under the Rome Statute of the International Criminal Court: Sources and Commentary* (Cambridge University Press, 2003) 386–7; La Haye, *War Crimes*, above note 190, 13; R Cryer, 'The Definitions of International Crimes in the *Al Bashir* Arrest Warrant Decision' (2009) 7 *JICJ* 283, 285–6.

[196] See eg *Akayesu* Trial Judgment, above note 71, paras 619–20.

and none of which garnered enough support to be adopted.[197] Furthermore, the suggestions were made at a point during the Diplomatic Conference when the entire body of international humanitarian law was proposed to apply and not only the minimum rules contained in common Article 3. Accordingly, to utilize one of the suggestions made at that time—that of territorial control—is to take it out of context. Although territorial control on the part of the armed group is certainly useful as *evidence* of the intensity of the violence and the organization of the armed group, lack of territorial control demonstrates neither lack of intensity of violence nor lack of organization of the armed group.

Particular rules of international humanitarian law, namely Additional Protocol II, may require that the armed group exercise territorial control;[198] however, territorial control is not required for the existence of a non-international armed conflict below that threshold. Thus, when ICC pre-trial chambers note that specified armed groups 'had the capacity to plan and carry out sustained and concerted military operations, insofar as they held control of parts of the territory of the Ituri District',[199] and that 'control over the territory by the relevant organised armed groups has been a key factor in determining whether they had the ability to carry out military operations for a prolonged period of time',[200] it is submitted that they should be understood as meaning that territorial control was *evidence* of the ability of the armed group in these regards and not that territorial control is a required *condition* for such. A means of proof must not be turned into a condition precedent.

A second purported requirement is that governmental forces must be a party to the violence in order for the violence to be characterized as a non-international armed conflict.[201] Again, Additional Protocol II requires that governmental forces be a party to the violence,[202] but nothing in the text of common Article 3 or in its drafting history suggests that that Article was intended to be limited to such conflicts. Accordingly, it is generally accepted that a non-international armed conflict may also be fought between two or more organized armed groups.[203] Indeed, even at a time in which the doctrine of recognition of belligerency was utilized, it was accepted that a civil war could be fought between armed groups or their equivalents. On this basis, Great Britain recognized as belligerents rival chiefs in the Bonny River in 1870.[204] The situation of Lebanon in the 1980s and Somalia in the 1990s are more recent examples of non-international armed

---

[197] A former ICRC Director for International Law and Cooperation has also taken the view that the ICRC Commentaries on this point (as well as certain other points) 'must be viewed with serious reservations'. F Bugnion, *The International Committee of the Red Cross and the Protection of War Victims* (ICRC, Geneva, 2003) 344.

[198] On Additional Protocol II, see below, 182 et seq.

[199] *Katanga and Chui* Decision on the Confirmation of Charges, above note 128, para 239.

[200] *Al-Bashir* Decision on Arrest Warrant, above note 169, para 60.

[201] ICRC, 'Armed Conflicts Linked to the Disintegration of State Structures, Preparatory Document Drafted by the ICRC for the First Periodical Meeting on International Humanitarian Law' (Geneva, 19–23 January 1998); Cullen, *Concept of Non-International Armed Conflict*, above note 5, 146 (speaking of civil wars).

[202] Article 1, on which see below, 184.

[203] This is the view of the United Kingdom: UK Ministry of Defence, *The Manual of the Law of Armed Conflict* (Oxford University Press, 2004) 31. See also Draper, Geneva Conventions, above note 35, 86; C Greenwood, 'Scope of Application of Humanitarian Law', in D Fleck (ed), *The Handbook of Humanitarian Law in Armed Conflicts* (Oxford University Press, Oxford, 1995) 39, 48; Moir, *Internal Armed Conflict*, above note 5, 39–40; Rogers, *Law on the Battlefield*, above note 93, 221.

[204] Opinion of the Queen's Advocate [Travers Twiss] to Earl Granville, 29 September 1870, reproduced in H Lauterpacht, *Recognition in International Law* (Cambridge University Press, 1947) 205. See also the view of Lauterpacht, ibid, 175.

conflicts that did not involve government forces. The involvement of governmental forces is not, then, integral to the concept of a non-international armed conflict, although it is an important aspect of an Additional Protocol II conflict.[205]

A third requirement that is sometimes cited is that an armed group should fight with a particular motive in mind, usually a political motive. In this context, it should be noted that the motives of the armed group, as indeed the motives of the state, are irrelevant to the decision as to whether or not a non-international armed conflict exists.[206] Armed groups may, and do, fight for different reasons. Some seek to create a new state, others to overthrow the government, still others for greater autonomy. Some fight to claim a share of natural resources; others wish to engage in ethnic cleansing, to pillage, or to terrorize. The reasons that motivate the fighting are irrelevant insofar as the existence of a non-international armed conflict is concerned.

4. Prerequisites for particular rules to apply

A non-international armed conflict *simpliciter* is judged by reference to two elements: the intensity of the violence and the organization of the non-state armed group. Once a non-international armed conflict *simpliciter* exists, a body of international law comes into force that regulates the conflict.[207] However, as alluded to in the previous section, in order for particular rules of conventional international humanitarian law to come into force, certain additional conditions need to be satisfied. The additional criteria are the subject of this part.

4.1 Protocol II, Additional to the Geneva Conventions of 1949

Two decades after the adoption of the 1949 Geneva Conventions, it became apparent that non-international armed conflicts were in need of further regulation.[208] The ICRC commenced work on the subject and a Diplomatic Conference on the Reaffirmation and Development of International Humanitarian Law was convened in 1974. The text of the Protocol that was put before the Diplomatic Conference and drafted by the ICRC provided that it would apply 'to all armed conflicts not covered by Article 2 common to the Geneva Conventions of 12 August 1949, taking place between armed forces or other organized armed groups under responsible command'.[209] The Protocol was intended to have the same scope of application as common Article 3. The only requirement explicitly set out in the text, namely that the armed groups be organized and under responsible command, spelt out what was implicit in the notion of an armed conflict not of an international character.[210]

However, a number of states took the view that the scope of application of the Protocol would benefit from further elaboration. Some states pushed for a definition of the term 'non-international armed conflicts'.[211] Others suggested adding 'elements such as duration, degree of intensity of the conflict, and area of occupation by the

---

[205] On which, see below, 184.
[206] *Limaj* Trial Judgment, above note 87, para 171.
[207] For the content of that body, see Chapters 8 and 9. For its scope of application, see Chapter 7.
[208] The issue is considered in greater detail in Chapter 2, 42 et seq.
[209] Draft Protocol Additional to Geneva Conventions of August 12, 1949, and relating to the Protection of Victims of Non-International Armed Conflicts, Article 1(1), in *Official Records*, above note 52, Vol I, Part Three, 33.
[210] See above, 174–5.
[211] *Official Records*, above note 52, Vol 8, 209, para 40 (France). See also 212, para 57 (Viet-Nam).

adverse party',[212] or referencing 'identifiable combatants occupying some territory and carrying on an armed conflict with an obvious degree of intensity'.[213] Among the more detailed proposals, Pakistan proposed an amendment to the scope of application clause which required that:

(a) Organized armed forces engage in hostile acts against the authorities in power and the authorities in power employ their own armed forces in response.

(b) The hostilities are of some intensity and continue for a reasonable period of time.

(c) The armed forces opposing the authorities in power occupy a part of the territory of the High Contracting Party.

(d) The armed forces opposing the authorities in power are represented by a responsible authority and declare their intention of observing the humanitarian rules laid down in Article 3, common to the Geneva Conventions, and in the present Protocol.[214]

Along similar lines, the Brazilian amendment required:

(a) Organized armed forces or other organized armed groups under a responsible and identifiable authority, and clearly distinguished from the civilian population, perform acts hostile to the established authorities to which the latter respond by using their armed forces; and

(b) Forces hostile to the Government exert continuous and effective control over a non-negligible part of the territory.[215]

Others favoured the ICRC draft but pressed for clarity on the terms used therein, namely 'responsible command' and 'armed forces or other organized armed groups under responsible command'.[216] Along these lines, the Spanish amendment suggested including the phrase, after the words 'responsible command', 'effectively exercised in such a way as to guarantee its readiness and ability to observe and enforce observance of the rules of humanitarian law in force'.[217] Still others considered the ICRC definition eminently satisfactory and opposed the introduction of any new criteria.[218] Norway thus proposed that the Protocol should apply in the situations referred to in common Article 3 without more.[219]

The Committee mandated to consider the Protocol applicable in non-international armed conflicts referred the scope of application clause to a working group, which in turn established a sub-working group 'to carry out informal consultations among delegations with a view to agreeing a text'.[220] The sub-working group carried out the desired consultations—which unfortunately are not documented in the published records—and the text it prepared was approved by the working group and then by the Committee.[221] The text of Article 1, as adopted, read:[222]

---

[212] Ibid, Vol 5, 104, para 17 (Indonesia). See also Vol 4, 7 (Indonesia).
[213] Ibid, Vol 5, 149, para 42 (Australia).
[214] Ibid, Vol 4, 6.
[215] Ibid, 8.
[216] Ibid, Vol 8, 209, para 37 (Spain); 231, para 11 (Argentina).
[217] Ibid, Vol 4, 7.
[218] Ibid, Vol 8, 208, para 33 (Belgium); 216, para 10 (Austria); 219, para 26 (Switzerland); 223, para 45 (Italy); Vol 4, 8. See also at 10 (Philippines).
[219] Ibid, Vol 4, 9.
[220] Ibid, Vol 10, 39, para 89.
[221] Ibid, 39, paras 90 and 91; Vol 8, 287, para 11.
[222] Ibid, Vol 10, 40, para 92.

1. The present Protocol, which develops and supplements Article 3 common to the Geneva Conventions of 12 August 1949 without modifying its existing conditions of application, shall apply to all armed conflicts which are not covered by article 1 of Protocol I and which take place in the territory of a High Contracting Party between its armed forces and dissident armed forces or other organized groups which, under responsible command, exercise such control over a part of its territory as to enable them to carry out sustained and concerted military operations and to implement the present Protocol.

2. The present Protocol shall not apply to situations of internal disturbances and tensions, such as riots, isolated and sporadic acts of violence and other acts of a similar nature, as not being armed conflicts.

This was ultimately adopted by 58 votes in favour, 5 votes against, and 29 abstentions.[223]

The scope of application clause of Additional Protocol II is a much misunderstood provision. Bearing in mind the counsel of the chairman of the working group that 'it would be extremely inadvisable to seek to interpret' the provision as it 'represented a very fragile consensus reached only after lengthy consideration',[224] this section will do precisely that. In particular, it will consider the extent to which Additional Protocol II contains requirements additional to those required for a non-international armed conflict *simpliciter* to exist in order for the Protocol to be applicable.

4.1.1 State armed forces

One very real prerequisite of Additional Protocol II is that governmental forces must be a party to the conflict. Additional Protocol II requires that the conflict be between the armed forces of a High Contracting Party and 'dissident armed forces or other organized armed groups'.[225] Thus, the Protocol applies to a conflict that is fought between the armed forces of a state and that part of the armed forces that rises up against it, as well as to a conflict between the armed forces and a non-state armed group. An armed conflict between armed groups is not covered by the Protocol. Indeed, Austria found it 'hard to see how Protocol II could be applied without Government forces being involved'.[226] However, it is the Austrian position that is difficult to understand. If the Protocol can be applied by an armed group that is fighting against the state, there would seem to be no reason why it cannot be applied by an armed group that is fighting against another armed group. The inapplicability of the Protocol to such conflicts is a major failing of the Protocol.

4.1.2 Organized armed groups and responsible command

As discussed above,[227] both the requirement of organization and the associated idea of 'responsible command' are fundamental to the very notion of a non-international armed conflict. Thus, during the 1974–7 Diplomatic Conference, Norway opined that 'there could not be an armed conflict in the sense of [common Article 3] except in cases where hostilities broke out between armed forces or other organized groups under responsible command'.[228] Nonetheless, there is a difference in the *degree* of

---

[223] Ibid, Vol 7, 70, para 65. [224] Ibid, 66, para 38. [225] Article 1.
[226] *Official Records*, above note 52, Vol 8, 216, para 9.
[227] See above, 170–80. [228] *Official Records*, above note 52, Vol 8, 217, para 13.

organization required of an armed group for the purposes of the existence of a non-international armed conflict *simpliciter* and for a non-international armed conflict to which Additional Protocol II applies. Additional Protocol II requires a higher degree of organization on the part of the armed group as compared with a common Article 3 conflict, the difference in organization being 'logical in view of the more detailed rules of international humanitarian law that apply in Additional Protocol II conflicts... By contrast, Common Article 3 reflects basic humanitarian protections, and a party to an armed conflict only needs a minimal degree of organisation to ensure their application'.[229] There is thus a close nexus between the organization of the armed group and the content of the applicable law. As the substantive law of non-international armed conflict increases, presenting more numerous and greater obligations on armed groups, the degree of organization required of them also increases.[230]

4.1.3 Territorial control

A second additional requirement for the applicability of the Protocol relates to territorial control on the part of the armed group. The orthodox view holds that the non-state armed group must exercise control over a sizeable part of territory in order for Additional Protocol II to apply.[231] In terms of the amount of territory required to be in the hands of the armed group, views at the Diplomatic Conference ranged from 'non-negligible' through to 'fairly-large', 'substantial', and 'considerable'.[232] Some states, such as Indonesia, took the view that the opposition forces should 'exercise continuous and effective control over a substantial or non-negligible part of its territory for such a prolonged period as to enable them to carry out sustained and concerted military operations of a high intensity and to implement this Protocol'.[233] By contrast, others considered that a requirement of territorial control was 'useless' as it 'opened the door to conflicting interpretations which would make it impossible to implement' the Protocol.[234] For Egypt, the requirement of territorial control:

was too restrictive in view of the nature of modern, and particular guerrilla, warfare. In armed conflict situations characterized by high mobility, territorial control continuously changed hands, sometimes alternating between day and night, to the point of becoming meaningless. Other forms of intense armed conflict, such as urban guerrilla armed conflict would not fulfil the requirement of territorial control. Such a requirement would then exclude from the ambit of Protocol II many, if not most, of the contemporary types of internal armed conflict and would confine it to the relatively rare cases of characterized civil war; it would thus severely limit its real significance and usefulness.[235]

So how much territory is required to be under the control of the armed group? To phrase the question in this manner, and to focus on the quantitative dimension of territorial control, is to misconstrue the nature of the requirement. As the wording of the provision makes clear, there is no requirement of territorial control in and of itself; rather, what is required is that the armed group 'exercise such control over a part of its

---

[229] *Boškoski* Trial Judgment, above note 55, para 197.
[230] See above, 66–8.
[231] See eg International Law Association Report on Armed Conflict, above note 69, 12.
[232] *Official Records*, above note 52, Vol 8, 213, para 60 (Vietnam); Vol 7, 71, para 71 (Indonesia); Vol 4, 8 (Brazil); Vol 7, 84 (Cameroon).
[233] Ibid, Vol 7, 71, para 71 (Indonesia).
[234] Ibid, 67, para 47 (Syria). See also 82 (Kenya).
[235] Ibid, Vol 8, 235, para 32.

territory as to enable [it] to carry out sustained and concerted military operations and to implement the... Protocol'.²³⁶ The key phrase is 'exercise *such control* over a part of its territory *as to* enable' the group. Thus Vietnam considered that territorial control 'was proof of the seriousness and high degree of intensity of the hostilities', while Canada observed that '[t]he key to the height of threshold... lies in the expression "to implement this Protocol"'.²³⁷ Territorial control is, then, an enabling element, one that demonstrates the ability of the armed group. It is a qualitative issue rather than a quantitative one.²³⁸ The *Akayesu* Trial Judgment reflects the position best in noting that the armed group 'must be able to dominate a *sufficient* part of the territory *so as to* maintain sustained and concerted military operations and to apply Additional Protocol II'.²³⁹ Although 'sufficient' is a less clear descriptor than 'substantial', for sufficiency is not an objective standard, it is precisely this inherently variable quality of the term that best fits the rationale behind the requirement and reflects the language of the Protocol. It serves to refocus attention away from the territorial control and towards the military operations and the ability of the armed group to apply the Protocol. It is the intensity of the violence and the ability to comply with the substantive law that is determinative, and not the quantum of territory controlled.

Insofar as implementation of the Protocol is concerned, only two Protocol rules require some form of territorial control—those relating to the detention and internment of persons and the requirement of due process guarantees in the convening of courts. Other rules, such as the fundamental guarantees and the prohibition on attacks against the civilian population, are not dependent on the armed group exercising territorial control. Yet both rules are also rather nuanced. In certain cases, the armed group will not take any prisoners, releasing them instead after confiscating their weapons and providing them with a lecture.²⁴⁰ In other cases, detainees will be transferred across a border to a friendly state in which the armed group is located.²⁴¹ With respect to due process guarantees, the law of non-international armed conflict does not require courts to be convened; only that persons are not to be sentenced prior to a fair trial. Mobile courts may also be used. Furthermore, if an armed group decides not to detain or intern persons and not to sentence individuals, they will be able to implement the Protocol without exercising any territorial control. In this situation, despite the absence of territorial control on the part of the armed group, it is submitted that the Protocol requirement would be met. It follows from the requirement that the armed group 'exercise such control over a part of its territory *as to* enable [it] to carry out sustained and concerted military operations and to implement the... Protocol' that if the armed group can do so without the enabling element, the requirement is still satisfied. The defining aspect of the Protocol is the intensity of the violence and the implementation of the Protocol and not the territorial control.²⁴²

---

²³⁶ Additional Protocol II, Article 1.
²³⁷ *Official Records*, above note 52, Vol 8, 213, para 60; Vol 7, 77.
²³⁸ See S Junod, 'Additional Protocol II: History and Scope' (1983–4) 33 *American University Law Review* 29, 37; M Bothe, KJ Partsch, and WA Solf, *New Rules for Victims of Armed Conflicts* (Martinus Nijhoff, 1982) 627. See also, hinting at this approach, C Kress, 'War Crimes Committed in Non-International Armed Conflict and the Emerging System of International Criminal Justice' (2000) 30 *Israel Yearbook on Human Rights* 103, 120; Kress, East Timor, above note 110, 417–18. The point is recognized in, but criticized by, Moir, *Internal Armed Conflict*, above note 5, 108.
²³⁹ *Akayesu* Trial Judgment, above note 71, para 626 (emphasis added).
²⁴⁰ See below, 297 and 300–1.
²⁴¹ See below, 297.
²⁴² In a number of cases, ICTR and SCSL Trial Chambers have de-linked territorial control from the ability to implement the Protocol. See eg *Akayesu* Trial Judgment, above note 71, para 623; *Musema* Trial Judgment, above note 147, para 254; *RUF* Trial Judgment, above note 78, para 97.

Should armed groups choose to detain prisoners or convene courts, as they often do, the amount of territory needed to be under the control of the armed group in order to enable them to do so will be minimal. Thus, the *RUF* Trial Chamber held that 'the RUF had the capacity to implement the provisions of Additional Protocol II on the territory that they seized and controlled'.[243] Large swathes of the country need not be controlled by the armed group in order for it to be able to house prisoners or to convene courts. In this respect, the Protocol requirement will be satisfied with even minimal territorial control. Likewise, the actual territory that is under the control of the armed group need not be fixed but could vary, with one village being controlled one day and a neighbouring village the next. Thus, when the International Commission of Inquiry on Darfur noted that, in 2005, the Sudan Liberation Movement/Army (SLM/A) exercised control over 'certain rural areas' but 'given its operation as a mobile guerrilla group, these areas of control are not fixed',[244] such control may very well suffice for the purposes of the Protocol. Provided the armed forces of the state are prevented from controlling the relevant area, as with the declaration of 'no go areas' which have their intended effect and which allow the group to carry out hostilities and implement the Protocol, the Additional Protocol II requirement would also be satisfied.[245] As the ICRC Commentary on Additional Protocol II indicates, 'the extent of territory' the non-state armed group 'can claim to control will be that which escapes the control of the government armed forces',[246] a statement that was followed by the *Akayesu* Trial Chamber.[247] Complete and effective control over territory is thus not required of the armed group.[248] Accordingly, it is by no means the case that, as '[g]uerrilla troops ... mostly lack any air forces ... more often than not guerrilla troops cannot pretend to be in control of a given area in the sense required by Article 1' of the Protocol.[249]

The essential point is that it is the ability to carry out sustained and concerted military operations and to implement the Protocol that is the crucial feature of the Protocol and not the quantum of territory controlled by the armed group. The territorial control is an enabling element for the operations and the implementation of the Protocol. Thus, it is linked to the substance of the rules themselves. This is evident from Switzerland's assessment in 1987 as to the applicability of the Protocol to the armed conflict in El Salvador. Switzerland indicated that the Protocol was applicable 'because the guerrilla movement exercises a level of control over certain parts of the territory which enable it to take care of the sick and wounded, treat prisoners humanely and also comply with the other provisions contained in Article 4 of the Protocol'.[250]

---

[243] *RUF* Trial Judgment, ibid, para 978.
[244] Darfur Commission Report, above note 194, para 132.
[245] Cf LC Green, 'Low-Intensity Conflict and the Law' (1996–7) 3 *ILSA Journal of International and Comparative Law* 493, 506, who takes the view that 'no go areas' are insufficient.
[246] ICRC, *Commentary on the Additional Protocols*, above note 76, 1353. See also, in the context of national liberation movements, G Abi-Saab, 'Wars of National Liberation and the Laws of War' (1972) 3 *Annales d'Etudes Internationales* 93, 97.
[247] *Akayesu* Trial Judgment, above note 71, para 626.
[248] Cf H McCoubrey, *International Humanitarian Law* (Dartmouth, 1990) 172, who takes the view that 'quasi-governmental control of territory' is required.
[249] C Tomuschat, *Human Rights: Between Idealism and Realism* (Oxford University Press, 2008) 305–6.
[250] 'Law of Armed Conflicts: Conditions Governing the Application of Protocol II Additional to the 1949 Geneva Conventions (case of El Salvador)' (1987) 43 *Annuaire Suisse de Droit International* 185, reproduced and translated in M Sassòli, AA Bouvier, and A Qunitin, *How Does Law Protect in War? Volume II* (ICRC, 2011) 1330.

4.1.4 Sustained and concerted military operations

Given that territorial control is required, in part, in order that the armed group be enabled to carry out 'sustained and concerted military operations', it is important to understand what that phrase means. On one view, sustained and concerted military operations require a higher level of intensity of violence than that required for an armed conflict *simpliciter*. Thus, the requirement has been described as '[p]erhaps the most significant' of the Protocol criteria.[251] Indeed, according to the *Boškoski* Trial Chamber, 'the degree of organization required to engage in "protracted violence" is lower than the degree of organization required to carry out "sustained and concerted military operations"'.[252] There is also some suggestion that the operations must be 'continuous and planned'.[253]

Whether the notion of sustained and concerted military operations does indeed presuppose a higher level of violence than protracted armed violence depends in large part on the meaning attributed to the latter concept.[254] Sustained is an element of duration and means ongoing rather than non-stop; and this notion is covered by the idea of protraction. Thus, it is not entirely clear that the Additional Protocol II notion does require a greater level of violence than that required for a non-international armed conflict *simpliciter*. This view is supported implicitly by a number of ICC pre-trial chamber decisions, which have utilized the language of Additional Protocol II, referring to notions of sustained and concerted military operations,[255] even though the Additional Protocol II standard need not be met for the purposes of the ICC.[256] This suggests that the level of violence required for a non-international armed conflict *simpliciter* is the same as that required by Additional Protocol II, namely sustained and concerted military operations or protracted armed violence.

A final uncertainty surrounding sustained and concerted military operations relates to whether the armed group has to be in a position to carry out sustained and concerted military operations or whether it actually has to carry out the relevant operations. The phrase 'to enable' could be interpreted in either manner: either the territorial control assists the group with its actual carrying out of operations, or it imbues it with the ability to do so.

4.1.5 Implementation of the Protocol

The same question arises in relation to the implementation of the Protocol. The language 'as to enable [the armed group] to implement this Protocol' could be

---

[251] Cullen, *Concept of Non-International Armed Conflict*, above note 5, 103.

[252] *Boškoski* Trial Judgment, above note 55, para 197. See also A Zimmermann, 'Preliminary Remarks on para 2(c)–(f) and para 3: War Crimes Committed in an Armed Conflict not of an International Character', in O Triffterer (ed), *Commentary on the Rome Statute of the International Criminal Court: Observers' Notes, Article by Article* (Beck, 2008) 475, 501; Cullen, *Concept of Non-International Armed Conflict*, above note 5, 128 and 142.

[253] *Akayesu* Trial Judgment, above note 71, para 626. See also *Niyonteze*, Military Court of Cassation, Decision of 26 May 2000, reproduced in M Sassòli, AA Bouvier, and A Quintin, *How Does Law Protect in War? Volume III* (ICRC, 2011) 2233, 2208. Cf M Bothe, 'Article 3 and Protocol II: Case Studies of Nigeria and El Salvador' (1981–2) 31 *American University Law Review* 899, 906.

[254] On which, see above, 167–70.

[255] *Katanga* Decision on the Confirmation of Charges, above note 128, para 239; *Al-Bashir* Decision on Arrest Warrant, para 59.

[256] See below, 192–3.

interpreted as requiring the ability of the group to implement the Protocol or it could require its actual implementation. The equivalent issue was considered during the 1949 Diplomatic Conference, with the United States querying the position whereby the armed group 'possessed the means for enforcing the Convention but was not disposed to do so', to which France proposed the requirement of 'an authority responsible for its acts acting within a defined territory, and declaring their readiness to observe and to enforce the Convention'.[257] However, these proposals came to nothing and the UK Military Manual considers the matter 'unclear'.[258]

Despite this purported lack of clarity, it is submitted that it must be the ability to implement the Protocol that is decisive. It would be circular, to say the least, were the Protocol to be applicable only in situations in which the armed group actually implements it. One domestic court has taken this position, holding that systematic violations of international humanitarian law suggested a lack of responsible command for the purposes of Additional Protocol II,[259] and by implication an inability to implement the Protocol. However, great care needs to be taken before reaching such a conclusion, as it may simply be that the Protocol is being violated rather than not being in force.[260] Any other approach too readily excuses the parties for their wrongful conduct.

Ability to implement the Protocol rather than its actual implementation also best reflects the drafting history of the provision. During the 1972 Conference of Government Experts, which led to the drafting of Additional Protocol II, various proposals were made, including that 'the Parties to the conflict have the material means of observing and ensuring the observance of the obligations of common Article 3 and of this Protocol',[261] and that the responsible command has 'effective authority ensuring its desire and ability to ensure observance of the rules of Humanitarian Law in force'.[262] Likewise, in early drafts of common Article 3, it was stated that, '[t]he condition of reciprocity might . . . render [application] . . . valueless, as one Party could always allege that its adversary disregarded some specific clause of the Convention'.[263]

Subsequent practice is along similar lines. For example, Switzerland took the view that the question is one of ability to implement the Protocol; 'whether or not they [the Frente Farabundo Martí para la Liberación Nacional (FMLN) of El Salvador] do so effectively is of little importance'.[264] Ability to implement the Protocol rather than its actual implementation is also evident from the *Boškoski* Trial Judgment, which speaks of the armed group possessing 'the organisational *ability* to comply with the obligations of international humanitarian law'.[265]

---

[257] *Final Record*, above note 6, Vol II-B, 43.
[258] UK Ministry of Defence, *The Manual of the Law of Armed Conflict* (Oxford University Press, 2004) 32 fn 22.
[259] *Peru v Guzmán Reinoso and Others*, No 650-03, Peru, Judgment of the National Criminal Chamber, 13 October 2006 [ILDC 670 (PE 2006) para 470].
[260] See *Boškoski* Trial Judgment, para 205.
[261] Proposal CE/COM II/14, in ICRC, Conference of Government Experts on the Reaffirmation and Development of International Humanitarian Law Applicable in Armed Conflicts, Second Session, 3 May–3 June 1972: Report on the Work of the Conference: Volume II (Geneva, July 1972) 35–6.
[262] Proposal CE/COM II/18, in ibid, 36.
[263] ICRC, Draft Revised or New Conventions for the Protection of War Victims (ICRC, 1948) 6. See also Remarks and Proposals submitted by the International Commission of the Red Cross: Document for the Consideration of Governments invited by the Swiss Federal Council to attend the Diplomatic Conference at Geneva (April 21, 1949) (1949) 38.
[264] 'Law of Armed Conflicts: Conditions Governing the Application of Protocol II Additional to the 1949 Geneva Conventions (case of El Salvador)', above note 250.
[265] *Boškoski* Trial Judgment, para 205.

4.1.6 Concluding thoughts

The scope of application clause of Additional Protocol II gave rise to negative reaction at the Diplomatic Conference. Some states considered that the conditions set out were 'so numerous and so stringent' as to make the Protocol govern 'only a very limited number of internal conflicts',[266] and others took the view that the scope of application clause rendered the Protocol 'worthless'.[267] Indeed, the report of the US delegation to the Diplomatic Conference provided that, '[g]iven all of these qualifications, it will be a dull and unimaginative government that will be unable to find an excuse not to apply the Protocol to its own international [*sic*: non-international] armed conflict'.[268] Other states, however, took the view that the clause served the purpose of limiting regulation of conflicts that were of a 'significant intensity',[269] while others yet expressed the position that the 'qualifications are a reflection of the factual and practical circumstances that would in fact have to exist if a Party to the conflict could be expected to implement the provisions of the Protocol'.[270] So many different opinions were expressed on the threshold that it has been suggested that 'it is impossible to trace any common understanding'.[271]

It is thus unfortunate that the scope of application clause has been interpreted in the manner that it has, higher than some at the Diplomatic Conference intended it to be, and contrary to the wording of the provision itself. While the scope of application clause of the Protocol certainly has its disadvantages, such as the requirement that a state's armed forces be a party to the conflict, it is the subsequent and unnecessary interpretation of the clause that has limited its scope of application. This interpretation of Additional Protocol II has had a negative impact on the practice of states. For example, for many years Colombia refused to ratify Additional Protocol II for fear that to do so would be to recognize the armed groups as belligerents and grant them status.[272] This followed the commonly held view that the Additional Protocol II threshold presupposed the existence of the conditions required for the recognition of belligerency.[273] Yet that is not the case and while it is certainly true that some states at the Diplomatic Conference took this view,[274] many others did not.[275]

In light of the numerous eminent views to the contrary, it is worth reiterating the salient point that has been submitted: what is required is not that the armed group

---

[266] *Official Records*, above note 52, Vol 7, 100 (Italy). See also Vol 7, 84 (Cameroon).
[267] Ibid, Vol 7, 199, para 30 (Syria).
[268] 'Report of the US Delegation to the 1974–77 Diplomatic Conference to the Secretary of State' (1978) 72 *AJIL* 405, 407.
[269] *Official Records*, above note 52, Vol 7, 304, para 121 (United Kingdom).
[270] Ibid, 77 (Canada).
[271] Cullen, *Concept of Non-International Armed Conflict*, above note 5, 101.
[272] H Valencia Villa, 'The Law of Armed Conflict and its Application in Colombia' (1990) 30 *IRRC* 5, 10; D García-Peña Jaramillo, 'Humanitarian Protection in Non-International Conflicts: A Case Study of Colombia' (2000) 30 *IYHR* 179, 182–3.
[273] See eg T Meron, 'On the Inadequate Reach of Humanitarian and Human Rights Law and the Need for a New Instrument' (1983) 77 *AJIL* 589, 599; LC Green, *The Contemporary Law of Armed Conflict* (Manchester University Press, 2000) 66–7; GH Aldrich, 'The Laws of War on Land' (2000) 94 *AJIL* 42, 60; R Provost, *International Human Rights and Humanitarian Law* (Cambridge University Press, 2002) 264; La Haye, *War Crimes*, above note 190, 44. Rare exceptions are J Pictet, *Development and Principles of International Humanitarian Law* (Martinus Nijhoff, 1985) 48; Abi-Saab, Non-International Armed Conflicts, above note 52, 228; A Carrillo-Suárez, '*Hors de Logique*: Contemporary Issues in International Humanitarian Law as Applied to Internal Armed Conflict' (1999) 15 *American University International Law Review* 1, 67–90.
[274] See eg *Official Records*, above note 52, Vol 7, 300, para 104 (Switzerland).
[275] See eg ibid, 79 (Ecuador).

exercise territorial control in and of itself but that it exercises such territorial control as to enable it to carry out hostilities and implement the Protocol. The requirement is a qualitative one rather than a quantitative one. Furthermore, Additional Protocol II is in no way tantamount to recognition of belligerency. As was seen in Chapter 1, one of the conditions that have to be satisfied before belligerency could be recognized is the existence of a government or quasi-government on the part of the armed group. At the very least, there had to be a civil administration in place.[276] Additional Protocol II does not require any of this; it only requires a responsible command on the part of the armed group. This, in turn, would mean that conflicts such as those between the Federal Republic of Yugoslavia and the KLA between 1998 and 1999, or between Sudan and the Justice and Equality Movement (JEM) and the SLM/A in Darfur during the late 2000s, would satisfy the Additional Protocol II requirements.

Accordingly, if read properly, aside from the requirement of governmental forces, the Protocol does not contain any criteria that are not inherent in a non-international armed conflict *simpliciter*; heightened the criteria may be, but they are not *qualitatively* different. Indeed, the then Legal Advisor of the US State Department stated: 'I believe that the United States should make clear when it ratifies Protocol II that it will apply the Protocol to all conflicts covered by common article 3 of the 1949 Geneva Conventions, and only such conflicts, which will include all non-international armed conflicts as traditionally defined, but of course not internal disturbances, riots or sporadic acts of violence.'[277] One of the 'Recommended Understandings and Reservations' in the President's transmittal of the Protocol to the Senate, read: '[t]he United States declares that it will apply this Protocol only to those conflicts covered by Article 3 common to the Geneva Conventions of 12 August 1949 and to all such conflicts, and encourages all other States to do likewise.'[278] Although the United States did not become party to Additional Protocol II, its position on point is an important one, for it suggests that the Protocol can be implemented in a non-international armed conflict *simpliciter*.

The Protocol also contains one very real advantage. For the first time, it explicitly includes the requirement that the armed group be able to comply with the relevant rules of international humanitarian law. It also makes clear the inextricable link between the scope of application of the rules and their substantive content.[279] Thus, contrary to many a view,[280] the threshold of Additional Protocol II is a positive one and should be welcomed.

---

[276] See above, 12.
[277] 'The Position of the United States on Current Law of War Agreements: Remarks of Judge Abraham D Sofaer, Legal Adviser, United States Department of State, January 22, 1987' (1987) 2 *American University Journal of International Law and Policy* 460, 462. See also 'The United States Position on the Relation of Customary International Law to the 1977 Protocols Additional to the 1949 Geneva Conventions: Remarks of Michael J Matheson' (1987) 2 *American University Journal of International Law and Policy* 419, 430.
[278] *Message from the President of the United States Transmitting the Protocol II Additional to the Geneva Conventions of August 12, 1949, and Relating to the Protection of Victims of Noninternational Armed Conflicts, Concluded at Geneva on June 10, 1977* (US Government Printing Office, 1987) 7.
[279] See above, 185–7. Cf Moir, *Internal Armed Conflict*, above note 5, 108, who considers this to be a difficulty with the Protocol.
[280] See eg Meron, Inadequate Reach, above note 273, 599; Moir, *Internal Armed Conflict*, above note 5, 108; Provost, *International Human Rights and Humanitarian Law*, above note 273, 264; La Haye, *War Crimes*, above note 190, 46; Cullen, *Concept of Non-International Armed Conflict*, above note 5, 105–6.

The scope of application of Additional Protocol II is of lesser importance today, given the fact that the majority of norms contained in the Protocol are of customary status and are considered to be of customary status even in conflicts below the Protocol threshold. Thus, both the ICTY and the Customary International Humanitarian Law study take the view that the customary norms of Additional Protocol II apply to all non-international armed conflicts and that numerous other norms also apply to all non-international armed conflicts.[281] However, that position is not altogether clear,[282] and the 'correct' Additional Protocol II threshold remains important for the applicability of the conventional instrument as well as to assist in ratification of the instrument.

4.2 Rome Statute of the International Criminal Court

The second conventional instrument that may require that certain criteria be satisfied over and above the requirements for a non-international armed conflict *simpliciter* is the Rome Statute of the International Criminal Court (Rome Statute or Statute). The Rome Statute uses a combination of the definition and non-definition approaches discussed above. Article 8(2)(c) of the Statute, which essentially reproduces the rules contained in common Article 3, applies to armed conflicts not of an international character.[283] Article 8(2)(e) of the Statute, which contains certain other rules that are applicable in non-international armed conflicts, applies to 'armed conflicts that take place in the territory of a State when there is protracted armed conflict between governmental authorities and organized armed groups or between such groups'.[284] The reference to non-international armed conflict in Article 8(2)(c) of the Statute must be understood and interpreted along the lines set out above.[285] Accordingly, it refers implicitly to the elements of organization and intensity with all that those elements entail.[286] More difficult is whether the reference to 'protracted armed conflict' in Article 8(2)(f) of the Statute was intended to introduce an additional qualifying element of duration or whether it was simply poor drafting.[287]

In order to address this question, it is necessary to consider how the phrase found its way into the Statute at all. Early drafts of the Statute contained all war crimes applicable in non-international armed conflicts in a single provision.[288] Violations of common Article 3 were not separated out from violations of other rules of non-international armed conflict and consequently there was no distinction between their respective spheres of application. However, not all delegations at the Rome Diplomatic Conference viewed this in a positive light, with some states preferring a higher threshold for violations of the rules that were not contained in common Article 3, a threshold along the lines of that set out in Additional Protocol II.[289] Accordingly, the Conference Bureau proposed raising the threshold for those rules to that of Additional Protocol

---

[281] See above, 66–7. [282] Ibid. [283] Rome Statute, Article 8(2)(d).
[284] Ibid, Article 8(2)(f). [285] See above, 164–82. [286] Ibid.
[287] See for a more detailed consideration of this issue, S Sivakumaran, 'Identifying an Armed Conflict Not of an International Character', in C Stahn and G Sluiter (eds), *The Emerging Practice of the International Criminal Court* (Martinus Nijhoff, 2009) 363; A Cullen, 'The Definition of Non-International Armed Conflict in the Rome Statute of the International Criminal Court' (2008) 12 *JCSL* 419.
[288] This was the position as late as the Bureau discussion paper of 6 July 1998, the statute being adopted some 11 days later. See A/CONF.183/C.1/L.53.
[289] A/CONF.183/C.1/SR.26, para 115 (Egypt); A/CONF.183/C.1/SR.28, para 64 (Sudan); A/CONF.183/C.1/SR.27, para 21 (Bahrain).

II.²⁹⁰ This, in turn, led to criticism by a number of states, which took the view that too high a threshold had been set,²⁹¹ a threshold that would exclude conflicts fought between armed groups and conflicts in which the armed group did not exercise territorial control.²⁹² Other states, however, welcomed the new threshold.²⁹³ Sierra Leone expressed reservations about the newly posited threshold and proposed that the relevant provision apply to 'armed conflicts that take place in a territory of a State when there is protracted armed conflict between governmental authorities and organized armed groups or between such groups'.²⁹⁴ This proposal received the support of a number of states,²⁹⁵ and ultimately found its way into the Statute.

Aside from the discrepancy between the phrase 'protracted armed violence' and the phrase 'protracted armed conflict', the proposal of Sierra Leone, as subsequently used in the Statute of the International Criminal Court, is the very same definition of a non-international armed conflict as set out in the *Tadić* Decision on Interlocutory Appeal. Were it not for this discrepancy, it could be said without controversy that the *Tadić* definition, Article 8(2)(c), and Article 8(2)(e) all have the same material scope of application.

The discrepancy makes such a conclusion slightly more difficult. On one view, the language creates a new threshold, distinguishing the 'mere' armed conflict from the 'protracted' armed conflict.²⁹⁶ On this view, the change was a deliberate one, precisely so as to distinguish the material scope of application of Article 8(2)(c) from Article 8(2)(e). Thus, Bosnia and Herzegovina expressed its concern over the raising of the threshold, but opined that 'if a different threshold had to be established, the wording proposed by the delegation of Sierra Leone would be acceptable'.²⁹⁷

However, a number of points tend toward the conclusion that the Diplomatic Conference did not intend to create a new threshold. There is no question that the Sierra Leonan proposal is taken from the *Tadić* definition, and the deliberate substitution of the phrase 'protracted armed violence', as used in *Tadić*, with 'protracted armed conflict', as used in the Statute, makes little sense. To define an 'armed conflict' by reference to a 'protracted armed conflict' is singularly unhelpful, for if an armed conflict is defined, in part, as protracted armed violence, then a protracted armed conflict is simply protracted, protracted armed violence.²⁹⁸ The additional 'protracted' adds little or no value. The manner in which the text came about should also be recalled. The

---

²⁹⁰ A/CONF.183/C.1/L.59, 7. See also the remarks of the Coordinator, introducing that document: A/CONF.183/C.1/SR.33, para 7.
²⁹¹ A/CONF.183/C.1/SR.33, para 18 (Switzerland); para 24 (United States); para 68 (Germany); A/CONF.183/C.1/SR.35, para 37 (Finland); para 67 (Canada); para 68 (Denmark); para 76 (Estonia).
²⁹² A/CONF.183/C.1/SR.33, para 14 (Austria on behalf of the Member States of the European Union); A/CONF.183/C.1/SR.34, para 60 (South Africa on behalf of the Member States of the Southern African Development Community); para 107 (Australia); A/CONF.183/C.1/SR.35, para 49 (Tanzania); A/CONF.183/C.1/SR.36, para 2 (Norway); para 52 (ICRC); A/CONF.183/INF/11, 2 (ICRC).
²⁹³ A/CONF.183/C.1/SR.33, para 40 (China); A/CONF.183/C.1/SR.35, para 73 (Portugal).
²⁹⁴ A/CONF.183/C.1/SR.35, para 8. See also the written proposal at: A/CONF.183/C.1/L.62.
²⁹⁵ A/CONF.183/C.1/SR.35, para 23 (Uganda); para 80 (Solomon Islands); A/CONF.183/C.1/SR.36, para 30 (Slovenia); para 42 (Bosnia and Herzegovina).
²⁹⁶ L Condorelli, 'War Crimes and Internal Conflicts in the Statute of the International Criminal Court', in M Politi and G Nesi (eds), *The Rome Statute of the International Criminal Court* (Ashgate, 2001) 107, 112–13; M Sassòli and AA Bouvier, *How Does Law Protect in War? Volume I* (ICRC, 2006) 110; Provost, *International Human Rights and Humanitarian Law*, above note 273, 268–9.
²⁹⁷ A/CONF.183/C.1/SR.36, para 42.
²⁹⁸ K Dörmann, *Elements of War Crimes under the Rome Statute of the International Criminal Court: Sources and Commentary* (Cambridge University Press, 2003) 441.

proposal of Sierra Leone was a response to the Bureau draft, which reproduced the higher threshold of Additional Protocol II and which was, in turn, a reaction to the views of a few states. It was not in and of itself an attempt to create a new threshold.[299] This is evident from the speech during which the proposal was introduced:

> *Mr. Dabor* (Sierra Leone) said that his delegation urged that sections C and D should be included in the new article 5 *quater*,[[300]] but it had reservations, for example, regarding the *chapeau* to section D, which referred to organized armed groups that exercised 'control over a part of [a State party's] territory'. That wording was very restrictive: in his own country, for example, the rebel forces did not occupy a territory. Thus, as presently drafted, section D would exclude the type of internal conflict presently taking place in Sierra Leone. His delegation therefore proposed that the second sentence of the *chapeau* be replaced by the text: 'It applies to armed conflicts that take place in a territory of a State when there is protracted armed conflict between governmental authorities and organized armed groups or between such groups'.[301]

The French text of the speech more clearly points to this conclusion, for it is *identical* to the corresponding portion of the *Tadić* definition. The speech reads in relevant part:

> Elle s'applique aux conflits armés qui ont lieu sur le territoire d'un État dès lors qu'il existe *un conflit armé prolongé entre les autorités gouvernementales et des groupes armés organisés ou entre de tels groupes*.[302]

The relevant part of the *Tadić* Decision on Interlocutory Appeal reads:

> ... nous estimons qu'un conflit armé existe chaque fois qu'il y a recours à la force armée entre Etats ou *un conflit armé prolongé entre les autorités gouvernementales et des groupes armés organisés ou entre de tels groupes* au sein d'un Etat.[303]

Thus, if the French text of the speech were followed, the intention would quite clearly seem to have been to have the *Tadić* definition adopted.[304] It may come down to a simple issue of translation: 'conflit armé' was translated as 'armed conflict' rather than 'armed violence'.

The intention of other states present at the Diplomatic Conference should also be borne in mind. In light of the number of non-international armed conflicts that take place, a large number of states considered it essential to include in the Statute provisions on war crimes in non-international armed conflicts.[305] To impose a threshold, such as that contained in the Bureau proposal, that would have the effect of preventing a good number of these conflicts from falling within Article 8(2)(e) of the Statute would have been contrary to the intention of these states. Thus, several states welcomed the proposal of Sierra Leone for this very reason. Uganda, for example, supported the proposal, noting that '[w]hether or not the perpetrators controlled territory was

---

[299] Kress, War Crimes, above note 238, 117–18.

[300] Article 5 *quater*, Section C would become Article 8(2)(c) of the Statute while Article 5 *quarter*, Section D is equivalent to Article 8(2)(e) of the Statute.

[301] A/CONF.183/C.1/SR.35, para 8.

[302] Ibid (emphasis added). The written proposal was worded differently but to similar effect: 'Elle s'applique aux conflits armés qui opposent de manière prolongée sur le territoire d'un Etat les autorités gouvernementales à des groupes armés organisés ou ces groupes entre eux' (A/CONF.183/C.1/L.62).

[303] *Tadić* Decision on Interlocutory Appeal on Judgment, above note 2, para 70 (emphasis added).

[304] See Kress, East Timor, above note 110, 419; Kress, War Crimes, above note 238, 118. However, it should be noted that it was the English version of the *Tadić* Decision that was authoritative. See the Separate Declaration of Judge Deschênes on the Defence Motion for Interlocutory Appeal on Jurisdiction, above note 2.

[305] See e.g. A/CONF.183/C.1/SR.25, para 10 (South Africa on behalf of Member States of the Southern African Development Community). See further below, 481–2.

immaterial'.³⁰⁶ The Solomon Islands stated that the Bureau proposal 'did not take account of the sort of contemporary conflict that the Court was designed to address. If the *chapeau* was retained, it should be amended to cover armed conflict between armed groups, as suggested by the representative of Sierra Leone'.³⁰⁷

Despite these various indications, pre-trial chambers of the ICC have taken a different view. In the view of the *Lubanga* Pre-Trial Chamber, Article 8(2)(f) with its reference to 'protracted armed conflict between . . . organized armed groups' 'focuses on the need for the armed groups in question to have the ability to plan and carry out military operations for a prolonged period of time'.³⁰⁸ This sentence is important for it mirrors the Pre-Trial Chamber's understanding of the *Tadić* definition but goes on to add the words 'for a prolonged period of time'. At first sight, the additional language suggests that a new threshold has indeed been created for the application of Article 8(2)(f), with duration playing a greater role than before. Closer inspection, however, may suggest that there is no greater focus on duration than there was in the *Tadić* Decision on Interlocutory Appeal. The original, French, text of *Lubanga* refers to 'prolongée', the same word used in the French text of *Tadić*,³⁰⁹ the English original of which was 'protracted'. So 'protracted' was translated as 'prolongée', which was translated back as 'prolonged'. Thus, for these purposes, the words 'protracted' and 'prolonged' were considered interchangeable and as has already been seen, the *Tadić* definition contains an element of protraction, albeit as part of the broader notion of intensity. That being said, the notion of prolongation is starting to take on a life of its own,³¹⁰ and one pre-trial chamber considers it to be an additional element.³¹¹ It has even been suggested by a pre-trial chamber that the (potentially) more restrictive standard of Article 8(2)(f) could be used to interpret the threshold of application of Article 8(2)(d).³¹² To the extent that this would raise the threshold of Article 8(2)(d), it would be incorrect. Article 8(2)(d) refers simply to 'armed conflicts not of an international character', a term interpreted in the *Tadić* Decision on Interlocutory Appeal and discussed above. That Article does not contain a requirement that the conflict, as opposed to the violence, be protracted.

4.3 Recognition of belligerency

Although recognition of belligerency has fallen into disuse,³¹³ the possibility continues to be canvassed on occasion. The possibility of recognizing a situation as belligerency was explicitly kept open by the 1949 Diplomatic Conference.³¹⁴ The non-state armed group may appeal for recognition as a belligerent. For example, in December 1960, the Provisional Government of the Algerian Republic appealed to 'the Atlantic powers' to recognize its status as a belligerent.³¹⁵ Likewise, during the Spanish civil war (1936–9), General Franco appealed to states not involved in the violence for recognition as a

---

[306] A/CONF.183/C.1/SR.35. para 23.
[307] A/CONF.183/C.1/SR.35, para 80.
[308] *Lubanga* Decision on Confirmation of Charges, para 234. See also *Al-Bashir* Decision on Arrest Warrant, para 60; *Bemba Gombo* Decision on Confirmation of Charges, para 233.
[309] *Tadić* Decision on Interlocutory Appeal, para 70.
[310] See *Al-Bashir* Decision on Arrest Warrant, paras 60–70.
[311] *Bemba Gombo* Decision on Confirmation of Charges, para 235.
[312] Ibid, para 235.
[313] See above, 17–20.
[314] Resolution 10, in *Final Record*, above note 6, Vol I, 362.
[315] See Bedjaoui, *Algerian Revolution*, above note 138, 179.

belligerent.³¹⁶ States, too, may speculate on the possibility of recognizing a situation as belligerency. For example, in 2008, President Chavez of Venezuela proposed that Colombia recognize the Fuerzas Armadas Revolucionarias de Colombia (FARC) as belligerents, a proposal that was supported by the Venezuelan National Assembly.³¹⁷ A former President of Colombia himself reportedly proposed granting the status of 'restricted belligerence' to the FARC, the status being considered akin to the recognition of belligerency but without the consequences for states not involved in the violence.³¹⁸ Thus, a situation may still be recognized as belligerency, albeit the reasons for doing so are altogether less clear.³¹⁹

5. Characterization of the violence

5.1 The decision-maker

Just as important as the definition of a non-international armed conflict is the identity of the actor that decides whether or not the situation amounts to a non-international armed conflict. In the specific context of Additional Protocol II, the identity of the entity that would decide whether or not the Protocol threshold had been surpassed featured prominently in the discussions of states at the 1974–7 Diplomatic Conference. Some states took the view that it was the High Contracting Party on whose territory the conflict was taking place that would take the decision.³²⁰ Thus, Colombia proposed inclusion of the language: '[t]he determination of the conditions ... shall be a matter for the State in which the conflict occurs',³²¹ while Romania opined that '[t]he automatic application to internal conflicts of regulations applicable in international conflicts might have negative results and entail violation of international law and national sovereignty'.³²² Brazil, in a more neutral but less practical fashion, took the view that both the state concerned and the head of the non-state armed group should make the decision.³²³ Other states argued that an objective determination of the situation was in order and that 'there was no room for any subjective assessment'.³²⁴ These differing views were maintained up until the end of the Diplomatic Conference. For example, Chile voted against the scope of application clause of the Protocol as 'its application was determined by criteria whose definition by States other than the State in whose territory the armed conflict was taking place would constitute interference in

---

³¹⁶ See NJ Padelford, *International Law and Diplomacy in the Spanish Civil Strife* (Macmillan, 1939) 597–8; A Cassese, 'The Spanish Civil War and the Development of Customary Law concerning Internal Armed Conflicts', in A Cassese (ed), *Current Problems of International Law* (Giuffrè, 1975) 287, 288–9.
³¹⁷ K Janicke, 'Venezuela Legislature Supports Belligerent Status for Colombian Rebels', Venezuelan Analysis, 19 January 2008. See also 'Answer of H.E. the Minister of Foreign Affairs Guillermo Fernando to the questions as posed in the proposal of summons no. 142, Recognition of state of war respecting the FARC', reproduced in (1999) 2 *YIHL* 440, 441.
³¹⁸ D García-Peña Jaramillo, 'Humanitarian Protection in Non-International Conflicts: A Case Study of Colombia' (2000) 30 *IYHR* 179, 193.
³¹⁹ For the prerequisites and consequences, see above, 11–16.
³²⁰ *Official Records*, above note 52, Vol 10, 94 and Vol 8, 286, para 7 (Brazil); Vol 8, 286, para 9 and Vol 8, 288, para 16 (Romania); Vol 7, 70, para 67 (Saudi Arabia); Vol 7, 84 (Tanzania); Vol 8, 230, para 7 (Yugoslavia); Vol 7, 232 (Chile).
³²¹ Ibid, Vol 7, 66, para 39.
³²² Ibid, Vol 5, 103, para 15.
³²³ See ibid, Vol 4, 12.
³²⁴ Ibid, Vol 8, 290, para 26 (Italy). See also Vol 8, 290, para 21 (Switzerland); Vol 8, 291, para 28 (Belgium); Vol 8, 292, para 32 (United States). See also Vol 8, 203, para 12 (ICRC).

the internal affairs of that State and consequently an infringement of its sovereignty'.[325] Argentina voted likewise but for precisely the opposite reason, arguing that the Protocol 'has been seriously compromised by the fact that it includes no safeguard clause providing for a mechanism or reasonably objective parameters for determining in each case whether the conditions for the application of the Protocol have been met'.[326]

The discussions surrounding the application of Additional Protocol II are symptomatic of a more general issue, namely who decides whether or not the violence amounts to an armed conflict. It has long been recognized that no authoritative impartial arbiter exists and that, as a result, every relevant actor determines the issue for itself. It has also been recognized that, ideally, the violence ought to be characterized by a neutral decision-maker with no vested interest in the situation.[327] The government that is involved in the violence may have a tendency to downplay the situation in order to demonstrate to the world, and its own people, that it remains in charge. Thus, it may characterize the situation as troubles or unrest, and the armed group as criminals or terrorists. For example, during the first part of the Algerian war of independence in the 1950s, France described the Armée de Libération Nationale (ALN), the armed wing of the Front de Libération Nationale (FLN), as 'criminals and brigands' and the situation as a 'police operation'.[328] The armed group, on the other hand, may exaggerate the scale of the violence in order to establish itself on the scene, to indicate that it should be taken seriously and be treated as a negotiating partner, and to seek to demonstrate that the government has lost control. The situation may be characterized very differently years later, at which time members of the armed group may argue that the situation was not an armed conflict in order to avoid liability for war crimes,[329] and the state may accept the existence of an armed conflict.[330] However, during the violence itself, which constitutes the crucial point in time, the parties have vested interests. They tend to be partial and unwilling or unable to judge the situation in an objective manner. Accordingly, the situation ought to be characterized by a neutral decision-maker.

Several difficulties arise with such a proposition. The government may consider any such decision-maker, or decision, as interference in the internal affairs of the state. For this reason, any outside entity may be hesitant to characterize the situation. Furthermore, any determination by an outside entity may not hold great weight to the parties involved in the violence. Accordingly, the characterization of the violence may have little practical effect.

The identity of the neutral decision-maker also raises difficult issues. In the past, various third parties judged the existence of a non-international armed conflict. However, none can be relied upon to make such a determination on a systematic basis. States that are not involved in the violence have sometimes taken on this role. For example, in 1987, Switzerland expressed its view that the violence in El Salvador involving the FMLN not only amounted to a non-international armed conflict, but surpassed the Additional Protocol II threshold.[331] Similarly, in 1994, Germany indicated that the violence in Turkey involving the PKK amounted to an armed conflict

---

[325] Ibid, Vol 7, 72, para 75.
[326] Ibid, Vol 7, 75.
[327] See eg 'Protection of Victims of Non-International Conflicts' (1969) 9 *IRRC* 343, 345.
[328] Bedjaoui, *Algerian Revolution*, above note 138, 142. For further examples, see below, 200–1 and 204–5.
[329] See eg the arguments made in the *Boškoski and Tarčulovski* case: Decision on Johan Tarčulovski's Motion Challenging Jurisdiction, IT-04-82-PT, 1 June 2005, para 6.
[330] See eg the admission of Guatemala as to its liability for war crimes: (2000) 3 *YIHL* 516.
[331] 'Law of Armed Conflicts: Conditions Governing the Application of Protocol II Additional to the 1949 Geneva Covnentions (case of El Salvador)', above note 250.

for the purposes of common Article 3.[332] However, states that are not involved in the violence cannot be presumed to be neutral third parties, for many will have an interest in the outcome of the conflict, whether for political, ideological, or other reasons. Other states may be hesitant to express any view on point for fear of jeopardizing diplomatic relations.

International or regional organizations could, and do, make determinations as to the characterization of the situation. The General Assembly may adopt a resolution indicating that, in its view, the situation amounts to an armed conflict.[333] Alternatively, the existence of an armed conflict will be recognized implicitly through condemnations of violations of international humanitarian law in a particular state.[334] However, international and regional organizations also have to maintain goodwill with their member states and some determinations have been revoked following criticism by the states in question. For example, in one report, UN Secretary-General Kofi Annan classified the violence in one state as a 'conflict' and described certain groups as insurgency groups. Two corrigenda followed in which references to 'Chechen insurgency groups' were amended to read 'Chechen illegal armed groups', and a statement was included to the effect that 'the situation' in Chechnya 'is not an armed conflict within the meaning of the Geneva Conventions and the Additional Protocols thereto'.[335] A reference to a 'conflict' in Northern Ireland was amended along similar lines.[336] Some decades earlier, in 1955, France noted of the UN's concern over the situation in Algeria that Algeria is 'an integral part of French territory' and that 'in a matter which is essentially within its domestic jurisdiction my Government refuses to accept any intervention of the United Nations which would be in defiance of the provisions of the Charter. It will consider as null and void any recommendation which the General Assembly might make on the matter'.[337] Accordingly, as with states not involved in the conflict, it cannot be assumed that international and regional organizations will be willing to characterize each and every situation of violence.

The ICRC, the pre-eminent body working in this area,[338] could make the determination, and proposals have been made to mandate the ICRC with this function.[339] However, in the past, the ICRC has chosen not to take on this role as a matter of course in order to avoid politicizing its work.[340] This position has been

---

[332] See 'Reply by the Federal Government to the written question submitted by Bundestag member Vera Wollenberger and the parliamentary party of the Alliance 90/Greens', reproduced and translated in M Sassòli, AA Bouvier, and A Quintin, *How Does Law Protect in War? Volume III* (ICRC, 2011) 2288.

[333] See eg GA Res 37/185 (1982) and GA Res 40/140 (1985), on El Salvador and Guatemala respectively.

[334] See eg the Statement of the Commission on Human Rights, Situation of Human Rights in the Republic of Chechnya of the Russian Federation, E/CN.4/1996/177, 24 April 1996, 362–3.

[335] Children and Armed Conflict: Report of the Secretary-General, A/58/546-S/2003/1053, 10 November 2003, para 61 and Annex II; Children and Armed Conflict: Report of the Secretary-General, A/58/546/Corr.2-S/2003/1053/Corr.2, 19 April 2004.

[336] Children and Armed Conflict: Report of the Secretary-General, A/58/546-S/2003/1053, 30 October 2003, para 58; Children and Armed Conflict: Report of the Secretary-General, A/58/546/Corr.1-S/2003/1053/Corr.1, 20 February 2004.

[337] General Assembly, 10th Session, 530th Meeting, 30 September 1955, (1955) 10 UNGA Official Records 193 and 196. See also Security Council, 11th Year, 729th Meeting, 26 June 1956, (1956) UNSC Official Records 5 and 16–18.

[338] On which see below, 467 et seq.

[339] See Respect for Human Rights in Armed Conflicts: Report of the Secretary-General, A/8052, 18 September 1970, para 160(b).

[340] Conference of Government Experts on the Reaffirmation and Development of International Humanitarian Law Applicable in Armed Conflicts (Geneva, 24 May–12 June 1971): Submitted by the

criticized,³⁴¹ but it is in conformity with the ICRC's desire towards neutrality and perceptions of neutrality. To recognize publicly a situation as a non-international armed conflict, or alternatively as internal tensions and disturbances, may be considered by the government or the non-state armed group as favouring the other side. For example, when the ICRC attempted to involve itself in the situation in Northern Ireland in 1922, it met with a frosty response from the Minister of Foreign Affairs of the Irish Free State: 'Refuse [to] discuss measures considered necessary by my Government to repress rebellion in Ireland. They are internal in character... Your attempt to intervene [is a] hostile act excusable only by ignorance of facts or false information from [an] anti-Irish source.'³⁴² This may lead to the party impeding the work of the ICRC. The ICRC does characterize the situation for internal purposes, however, and may, from time to time, do so publicly as with the 2011 violence in Libya;³⁴³ but it does not do so on a systematic basis.³⁴⁴

International courts and tribunals could adjudge the situation. For example, the International Criminal Tribunal for Rwanda (ICTR) has stressed that 'the ascertainment of the intensity of a non-international conflict does not depend on the subjective judgment of the parties to the conflict'.³⁴⁵ Determinations necessarily have to be made if war crimes are alleged. However, relatively few situations arise before international criminal courts and tribunals, and those that do may arise many years after the violence first commences. The International Court of Justice (ICJ) could have a role to play in this regard. Indeed, at the 1949 Diplomatic Conference, a Resolution was adopted, recommending that 'in the case of a dispute relating to the interpretation *or application* of the present Conventions which cannot be settled by other means, the High Contracting Parties concerned endeavour to agree between themselves to refer such dispute to the International Court of Justice'.³⁴⁶ However, this has not been followed through in practice and jurisdictional constraints of the ICJ may make it rare. The Resolution does, however, indicate the importance of a neutral decision-maker in deciding on the application of international humanitarian law and, as a consequence, the existence of an armed conflict. This issue needs to be given serious consideration, perhaps with a group of eminent jurists taking on the role, or a new organization being established in order to do so.³⁴⁷

International Committee of the Red Cross (1971) Part V: Protection of Victims of Non-International Armed Conflicts, 42.

³⁴¹ Conference of Government Experts on the Reaffirmation and Development of International Humanitarian Law Applicable in Armed Conflicts (Geneva, 24 May–12 June 1971): Report on the Work of the Conference (ICRC, August 1971) 43, paras 214–16.

³⁴² Telegram from the Minister of Foreign Affairs, Desmond Fitzgerald, to President of the International Committee of the Red Cross, Gustave Ador, 23 January 1923, ICRC Archives CR 22 (84)/89. English translation taken from A Durand, *History of the International Committee of the Red Cross: From Sarajevo to Hiroshima* (Henry Dunant Institute, Geneva, 1984) 227.

³⁴³ See eg ICRC, 'Libya: Urgent to Apply the Rules of War', 10 March 2011.

³⁴⁴ See SR Ratner, 'Law Promotion Beyond Law Talk: The Red Cross, Persuasion and the Laws of War' (2011) 22 *EJIL* 459, 474–7.

³⁴⁵ *Akayesu* Trial Judgment, para 603. See also Inter-American Commission on Human Rights, Report on Terrorism and Human Rights, OEA/Ser.L/V/II.116 Doc.5 rev.1 corr, 22 October 2002, para 59.

³⁴⁶ Resolution 1, in *Final Record*, above note 6, Vol I, 361 (emphasis added).

³⁴⁷ See also the various proposals in Respect for Human Rights in Armed Conflicts: Report of the Secretary-General, A/8052, 18 September 1970, paras 145 and 161; Conference of Government Experts on the Reaffirmation and Development of International Humanitarian Law Applicable in Armed Conflicts (Geneva, 24 May–12 June 1971): Submitted by the International Committee of the Red Cross (1971) Part V: Protection of Victims of Non-International Armed Conflicts, 40.

5.2 Recognition of an armed conflict

As indicated above, each of the parties to the violence will have a vested interest in its characterization. Accordingly, it is often suggested that governments invariably deny the existence of an armed conflict on their territory: 'the first line of defense against international humanitarian law is to deny that it applies at all.'[348] This observation was first made in respect of international humanitarian law generally and not specifically the law of non-international armed conflict. However, it has since been reiterated with non-international armed conflicts in mind.[349] Indeed, in the context of the law of non-international armed conflict, the UK Military Manual notes that 'states have been, and always will be, reluctant to admit that a state of armed conflict exists'.[350] As early as 1922 it was recognized that:

> one can rarely find a government that wants to recognise officially a civil war in its country before being overthrown or placed in an unfavourable situation. As a general rule, a government, dealing with internal unrest, shall always assert that it is just a simple riot.[351]

Those holding this view can point to numerous examples to support their position. For example, in 1947, during the conflict in Greece, in response to an appeal from the ICRC, the Minister of Foreign Affairs responded:

> The application of the Conventions in question [of 1929] and the intervention of the ICRC assumes the existence of an international war, or at least a civil war. However, these conditions do not occur now in Greece where, quite simply, a number of people rose against the laws of the state, [and] formed gangs that engage in common crimes in the midst of subversive activities...[352]

The United Kingdom did not recognize the existence of an armed conflict in Kenya, Malaya, or Cyprus in the 1950s, or in Northern Ireland in the context of the post-1969 violence against the Provisional Irish Republican Army.[353] Indeed, upon a request of

---

[348] RR Baxter, 'Some Existing Problems of Humanitarian Law' (1975) 14 *Military Law and the Law of War Review* 297, 298.

[349] See Draper, Geneva Conventions, above note 35, 88; T Meron, *Human Rights in Internal Strife: Their International Protection* (Grotius Publications, 1987) 43; C Greenwood, 'International Humanitarian Law (Laws of War)', in C Greenwood, *Essays on War in International Law* (Cameron May, 2006) para 5.13.

[350] UK Ministry of Defence, *The Manual of the Law of Armed Conflict* (Oxford University Press, 2004) 384.

[351] Rapport M Lodygeusky for the ICRC, 5 May 1922, ICRC Archives CR 22/1. The original reads:

> on trouvera difficilement un gouvernement qui veuille reconnaître officiellement le fait de la guerre civile dans son pays, avant d'être renversé ou placé dans une situation défavorable. Comme règle générale, un gouvernement, ayant affaire à des troubles intérieurs, affirmera toujours qu'il ne s'agit que d'une simple émeute.

[352] Letter from Minister of Foreign Affairs and Vice-President of the Council of Ministers to ICRC Delegate in Greece, 8 March 1947, ICRC Archives G44/53c-236. The original reads:

> l'application des conventions en question [of 1929] et l'intervention du CICR supposent l'existence d'une guerre internationale, ou du moins d'une guerre civile. Cependant, ces conditions ne se présentent pas actuellement en Grèce où, tout simplement, un nombre de personnes, s'étant soulevé contre les lois de L'Etat, ont formé des bandes qui se livrent à des délits de droit commun au milieu d'une activité subversive...

See also the Letter of 3 May 1947, ibid.

[353] GIAD Draper, *The Red Cross Conventions* (Stevens and Sons, 1958) 15 fn 47; M Veuthey, 'Les Conflits Armés de Caractère Non-International et le Droit Humanitaire', in A Cassese (ed), *Current Problems of International Law: Essays on UN Law and on the Laws of Armed Conflict* (Giuffrè, 1975) 179, 246.

the ICRC to visit internment and detention camps in Kenya in 1955, the ICRC was informed that there were insufficient grounds for its involvement and that 'the problems in Kenya are of a rather special kind'.[354] Equally, Portugal did not recognize the existence of an armed conflict in Mozambique or Angola in the 1960s and 1970s in the period leading up to their independence.[355] More recently, mention can be made of the position of Turkey, which argued in 2005 that the violence between it and the PKK was a matter of law-enforcement against a terrorist organization.[356] Similarly, in the early 2000s, Russia denied the existence of an armed conflict in Chechnya.[357] For its part, in 1999, Colombia stated that '[t]he Government has not and will not recognise the state of war with any subversive groupings, which operate within the country'.[358] Numerous examples along similar lines may also be cited.

However, the picture is altogether more nuanced than these examples alone suggest. Although there is frequently denial as to the existence of an armed conflict, denial is not always undertaken in bad faith, as there may be legitimate disagreement as to the characterization of the situation. For example, although controversial, the position of the United Kingdom that the situation in Northern Ireland amounted to 'troubles' and not a non-international armed conflict had the support of distinguished commentators.[359] Similarly, characterization of the violence at La Tablada in 1989 as a non-international armed conflict by the Inter-American Commission on Human Rights[360] has been criticized by commentators.[361] On this basis, Argentina would have had legitimate grounds to deny the existence of an armed conflict. Accordingly, not every denial of the existence of a non-international armed conflict can be assumed to be erroneous or in bad faith, although denials for such reasons certainly do exist.

Furthermore, oftentimes, the state concerned will recognize the existence of a non-international armed conflict. If the matter is raised before a domestic court, for example, a judicial organ may make a pronouncement on the existence of a conflict and the applicability of international humanitarian law thereto. This was true, for example, of the South African Constitutional Court relating to the violence between the Government and the African National Congress (ANC), the Russian Constitutional Court on the violence in Chechnya in 1994–6, the Colombian Constitutional Court on the violence in Colombia, and, in a not uncontroversial pronouncement, the US Supreme Court on the 'war on terror'.[362]

---

[354] See Letter from ICRC to Colonel GIAD Draper, 6 December 1956; Letter from the Vice-President of the ICRC to the Vice-Chairman of the Executive Committee of the British Red Cross Society, 12 August 1955; Letter of the Vice Chairman of the British Red Cross Society to the Vice-President of the ICRC, 9 August 1955; all in ICRC Archives, B AG 2001 08.

[355] Bond, *Rules of Riot*, above note 37, 59–60.

[356] Letter from Ambassador Türkekul Kurttekn in response to the characterization of the PKK, Landmine Monitor Report, 15 December 2005.

[357] See Children and Armed Conflict: Report of the Secretary-General, A/58/546-S/2003/1053, 10 November 2003, para 61 and Annex II; Children and Armed Conflict: Report of the Secretary-General, A/58/546/Corr.2-S/2003/1053/Corr.2, 19 April 2004.

[358] 'Answer of H.E. the Minister of Foreign Affairs Guillermo Fernando to the questions as posed in the proposal of summons no. 142, Recognition of state of war respecting the FARC', reproduced in (1999) 2 *YIHL* 440. The Government did, however, recognize the applicability of international humanitarian law. See at 441.

[359] See eg Rogers, *Law on the Battlefield*, above note 93, 216.

[360] *Abella*, above note 46.

[361] Zegveld, *Armed Opposition Groups*, above note 190, 138.

[362] *The Azanian Peoples Organization (AZAPO) and Others v The President of the Republic of South Africa and Others*, CCT 17/96, 25 July 1996; Constitutional Conformity of Protocol II, C-225/95, reproduced and translated in M Sassòli, AA Bouvier, and A Quintin, *How Does Law Protect in War? Volume III* (ICRC, Geneva, 2011) 2240; Presidential Decrees and Federal Government's Resolution

State recognition of the existence of an armed conflict is by no means limited to judicial organs; political organs have also accepted its existence. For example, in 1998, the Government of Colombia recognized the existence of a non-international armed conflict and the applicability of international humanitarian law thereto,[363] and did so again in 2011.[364] According to the International Commission of Inquiry on Darfur, which published its report in 2005, '[a]ll the parties to the conflict—the Government of the Sudan, SLA and JEM—have recognized that this is an internal armed conflict'.[365] Similarly, representatives of the Philippine armed forces told the Special Rapporteur on torture in 1991 that 'conditions "short of war" indeed prevailed in certain areas and that, therefore, the Protocol [Additional Protocol II] could be applicable'.[366] Likewise, an order issued to troops in Tajikistan in 1996 provided that, '[t]aking into consideration the actual conduct of hostilities of a non-international character by the Republic of Tajikistan against illegal armed units', government troops are to 'be strictly guided by the standards and principles of IHL contained in Geneva Conventions of 1949, and both Additional Protocols'.[367] Furthermore, following the declaration of secession on the part of Biafran authorities, in 1967, the Federal Government of Nigeria declared 'war'.[368]

More frequent than direct statements is implicit acceptance of the existence of an armed conflict through recognition of the applicability of international humanitarian law. This takes place in particular through unilateral declarations, or commitments to the ICRC, and has a long history. For example, in 1918, following the Russian revolution and during the civil war, the Council of People's Commissars (the Government) issued a decree recognizing the applicability of the 1864 and 1906 Geneva Conventions.[369] During the Hungarian revolution of 1919, the People's Commissar issued a number of decrees which, together, reflected elements of the 1864 Geneva Convention and the Recommendations adopted at the 1863 Conference.[370] During the conflict in the plebiscite of Upper Silesia in 1921, both parties made commitments to the ICRC, allowing it to visit prisoners without restriction, to distribute relief, and to

---

on the Situation in Chechnya, Judgment of 31 July 1995, reproduced and translated in ibid, 2468; *Hamdan v Rumsfeld* (2006) 126 S Ct 2749.

[363] See 'Third Report on the Human Rights Situation in Colombia', OEA/Ser.L/V/II.102, Doc 9 Rev.1, 26 February 1999, Chapter IV, paras 20–1. See also 'Answer of H.E. the Minister of Foreign Affairs Guillermo Fernando to the questions as posed in the proposal of summons no. 142, Recognition of state of war respecting the FARC', reproduced in (1999) 2 *YIHL* 440, 441.

[364] 'Colombia's Victims Law: Feeling Their Pain', *The Economist*, 4 June 2011, 58.

[365] Darfur Commission Report, above note 194, para 76.

[366] Report of the Special Rapporteur on torture and other cruel, inhuman or degrading treatment or punishment, E/CN.4/1991/17, 10 January 1991, para 266.

[367] Order of the Commander and Head of the Department of the Interior Troops of the Ministry of Internal Affairs of the Republic of Tajikistan No 26, 23 April 1996, quoted in La Haye, *War Crimes*, above note 190, 60.

[368] Declaration of War, 12 August 1967.

[369] Ordonnance of 2 June 1918, ICRC Archives Mis 1/5 (Frick). See Durand, *History of the International Committee of the Red Cross*, above note 342, 100–2. See also Letter from the Bureau of Liquidation to the ICRC Delegate in Petrograd, undated, ICRC Archives Mis 1/5 (Frick). See also L'Ordonnance du Soviet des Commissaires du Peuple, 7 August 1918, ibid.

[370] Ordonnance du Commissariat du peuple pour les Affaires Étrangères No 2086 concernant la Situation Juridique de la Croix Rouge International de Genève dans la République des Conseils de Hongrie, 10 April 1919, ICRC Archives Mis.4 5/67, reproduced in (1919) 1 *RICR* 604; Decree of 26 April 1919, cited in CICR, *Rapport Général 1912–1920* (Genève, 1921) 195; Decree No 62 du Commissariat du Peuple pour le Bien Public et les Affaires Sanitaires, 9 July 1919, ICRC Archives Mis.4 5/134. For the text, see above, 140.

assist it in its work.³⁷¹ At the outset of the Spanish civil war, in 1936, the Spanish Government issued a statement which recognized the applicability of particular norms and the work of the ICRC.³⁷²

During the revolution in Guatemala in 1954, the Minister of Foreign Affairs requested ICRC intervention.³⁷³ During the Hungarian uprising of 1956, the ICRC and the Hungarian Red Cross concluded an agreement, which was ratified by the Government of Hungary, pursuant to which the ICRC would distribute humanitarian relief and which recognized the ICRC's activities under the Geneva Conventions.³⁷⁴ Similarly, during the conflict in Lebanon in 1958, the Government agreed to respect common Article 3.³⁷⁵ During the post-independence conflicts taking place in the Democratic Republic of the Congo (DRC), in 1961, at the request of the ICRC delegate in the DRC, the Government issued a letter confirming its participation in the Geneva Conventions.³⁷⁶ A few years later in 1964, in relation to an associated conflict, the Government issued a public statement and wrote to the ICRC 'in order to make clear the desire of the [Government] to abide by the Geneva Conventions and to show our respect for generous humanitarian measures which would avoid needless suffering by civilians'.³⁷⁷ During the armed conflicts in the Yemen in the 1960s and in the Dominican Republic in 1965, all concerned parties, both the deposed governments and the new governments, committed to the ICRC to apply the Geneva Conventions or the principles contained therein.³⁷⁸

During the attempted secession of Biafra from Nigeria (1967–70), the Government issued an Operational Code of Conduct to all officers and members of the armed forces, noting that it was 'honour bound to observe the rules of the Geneva Convention', and which set out particular provisions on the conduct of hostilities and the treatment of civilians and persons *hors de combat*.³⁷⁹ The Government had previously assured the ICRC that it 'proposed to apply the Geneva Conventions in the event of a conflict'.³⁸⁰ During the Algerian War of Independence, in February 1955, the French Prime Minister Mendès-France accepted the ICRC's proposal to visit detention camps.³⁸¹

---

³⁷¹ Letter from Korfanty to ICRC Delegates; Letter from Hoefer to ICRC Delegates, 1 June 1921, ICRC Archives CR 22-5/26 and/76, reproduced in (1921) 3 *RICR* 691, Annexes 1 and 2.

³⁷² Accord de José Giral, Le Président du Conseil des Ministres, 3 September 1936, reproduced in (1936) 18 *RICR* 749, Annex II.

³⁷³ Letter from the Consul Général Représentant Permanent de Guatemala auprès de l'Office Européen des Nations Unies to M. Gallopin, Directeur du CICR, 25 June 1954, ICRC Archives B AG 200 086.

³⁷⁴ 16 November 1956. English translation in (1956) IX *RICR Supplement* 214, 215.

³⁷⁵ Note of ICRC Delegate de Traz to ICRC, 16 June 1958; Note, 20 June 1958; ICRC Archives B AG 200 115-001.

³⁷⁶ Letter from Minister of Foreign Affairs, Republic of Congo, to Political Department, Berne, 20 February 1961, ICRC Archives B AG 202 229-00.

³⁷⁷ Letter from Prime Minister Dr Moise Tshombe of the Democratic Republic of the Congo to the President of the International Committee of the Red Cross, 22 October 1964, ICRC Archives B AG 202 229-006, reproduced in (1965) 59 *AJIL* 615.

³⁷⁸ Letter from El-Badr to the President of the ICRC, 2 January 1963; Written Statement of Président de la République Arabe Yéménite Al-Moushir Abdullah El-Sallal, 28 January 1963 (both Yemen, ICRC Archives, B AG 200 226); Oral commitment of General Imbert and Junta Government, noted in Telegram from ICRC Delegate Jequier to the ICRC in Geneva, 19 May 1965, ICRC Archives B AG 251 170.

³⁷⁹ Operational Code of Conduct for the Nigerian Army, reproduced in AHM Kirk-Greene, *Crisis and Conflict in Nigeria: A Documentary Sourcebook 1966–1969, Volume I* (Oxford University Press, 1971) 455, 456.

³⁸⁰ ICRC, Annual Report 1967 (ICRC, 1968) 36.

³⁸¹ Letter from P Mendès-France to Monsieur WH Michel, Comité International de la Croix-Rouge, 2 Feburary 1955, ICRC Archives B AG 225 008-002.

This was confirmed the following year by Prime Minister Guy Mollet, who issued a communiqué stating:

> In conformity with Article 3 of the Geneva Conventions regarding armed conflicts not of an international character, which arise in the territory of one of the contracting parties, the International Committee of the Red Cross has offered its services to the French Government. The French Government authorized it to send a mission to Algeria... [382]

Furthermore, when the violence has been ongoing for an extended period, the Government may indicate its acceptance of the law of armed conflict through conclusion of a bilateral agreement with the non-state armed group on point. There are numerous examples of such agreements, which were discussed in Chapter 4.[383]

Thus, while intuitively appealing, it is not the case that states systematically deny the existence of an armed conflict on their territory. Denial certainly takes place; the aforementioned examples are testament to that. However, states also accept that they are involved in an armed conflict, not infrequently characterizing it as a non-international armed conflict, whether directly or indirectly. This acceptance may take place only after the violence has raged for an extended period, but that is a vastly different proposition from the one that suggests that denial is the norm. Governments may also allege the existence of an armed conflict when the weight of opinion suggests otherwise. The most-high profile such instance is the US-led 'war on terror', but this is not a new tendency, with other governments having adopted similar views in the past.[384]

5.3 Characterization of the armed group

An issue that is associated with the characterization of the violence is the characterization of the non-state armed group. States have a tendency to label non-state armed groups against which they are in conflict as bandits and criminals in an attempt to delegitimize them. In this, there is nothing new. During the Nineteenth International Conference of the Red Cross in 1912, at which proposals were being considered on the role of the Red Cross in time of civil war, the Russian delegate opined that 'Red Cross Societies have no duty whatever to fulfil toward rebel or revolutionary troops, which the laws of my country can only consider as criminal'.[385] Similarly, during the Hungarian Revolution of 1919, the People's Commissar for Foreign Affairs, Béla Kun, described the armed group as 'bandits'.[386] Characterization of the armed group as a terrorist group is the modern day equivalent of the bandit. For example, Turkey maintains that the PKK is not a non-state armed group but a terrorist organization and that '[t]he use of terms such as "rebels" or "armed non-state actors"' to describe them gives 'a wrong

---

[382] Communiqué de presse [of Prime Minister Guy Mollet, 23 June 1956], ICRC Archives B AG 202 008-001. A slightly different text also appears in Bedjaoui, *Algerian Revolution*, above note 138, 213

[383] See above, 124–33.

[384] See J Moreillon, 'The International Committee of the Red Cross and the Protection of Political Detainees' (1975) 15 *IRRC* 171, 177; M Bothe, 'Article 3 and Protocol II: Case Studies of Nigeria and El Salvador' (1981–2) 31 *American University Law Review* 899, 900.

[385] Declaration of M le General Yermolow, *Compte-Rendu de la Neuvieme Conférence Internationale de la Croix-Rouge Tenue à Washington du 7 au 17 mai 1912*, ICRC Archives CR 22/32, 45. The French original reads: 'les sociétés de la Croix-Rouge ne sauraient avoir de devoir à remplir auprès des bandes insurgées ou de révolutionnaires lesquelles ne peuvent être considérées par les lois de mon pays que comme des criminels.'

[386] Statement of Béla Kun, 27 June 1919, quoted and translated in Durand, *History of the International Committee of the Red Cross*, above note 342, 132–3.

indication about the real nature of a terrorist organization'.[387] Similarly, in 2005, President Uribe of Colombia stated that 'in Colombia there is a very serious social problem that we must solve, but the actions of the violent groups cannot be framed nor defined as actions within an internal armed conflict. It is a terrorist threat'.[388] Likewise, during the violence in Libya in 2011, President Gaddafi characterized the armed group as terrorists and as Al-Qaeda.[389] The difference between characterizing members of the armed group as bandits in earlier times, and as terrorists today, is the associated regime that comes with the characterization of individuals as terrorists. In addition to the de-legitimization of the group, the terrorist label may carry with it travel bans and sanctions, not only by the state that is involved in the violence but by other states and organizations.[390] A perusal of the terrorist lists maintained by the United Nations, the European Union, and the United States reveals that, of the groups that are listed as terrorists, many are also non-state armed groups that are fighting in non-international armed conflicts. This is true, for example, of the NPA, the PKK, the FARC and National Liberation Army (ELN) of Colombia, and, prior to its defeat, the Liberation Tigers of Tamil Eelam (LTTE) of Sri Lanka.[391]

Unsurprisingly, groups that have been listed as terrorists have reacted strongly against such a characterization. The LTTE, for example, responded to the decision of the United States to list it as a terrorist group as 'unfair, unfounded and irresponsible' and warned that it would encourage the Government of Sri Lanka to 'pursue its policy of war and military repression against the Tamils and thereby escalate the present conflict'.[392] Along related lines, the NDFP has taken the view that '[b]y using the "terrorist" label to blackmail the NDFP, the US and GRP [Government of the Philippines] are preventing the resumption of formal talks and are scuttling the peace negotiations'.[393]

5.4 Legal status and legitimacy

States are invariably concerned with not affording non-state armed groups any legitimacy or legal status, including legitimacy or status that may attach through the application of international humanitarian law.[394] Thus, at the 1949 Diplomatic Conference, '[t]he French Delegation considered that signatory Governments who were confronted with an insurgent movement would be in a dilemma: either they would never apply the clauses of the Conventions, or they would implicitly recognize

---

[387] Letter from Ambassador Türkekul Kurttekn in response to the characterization of the PKK, Landmine Monitor Report, 15 December 2005.
[388] Intervention of President Uribe, Forum on 'Internal Conflict or Terrorist Threat?', Chía, Colombia, 26 April 2005, quoted in D Roa-Castro, 'Mine Action in the Midst of Internal Conflict: The Colombian Case' in Geneva Call, *Mine Action in the Midst of Internal Conflict* (2005) 15, 17. See also 'Colombia's victims law: Feeling their pain', *The Economist*, 4 June 2011, 58.
[389] See eg I Black, 'Libya Rebels Rejects Al-Qaida Spin', *The Guardian* (UK), 1 March 2011.
[390] See eg Council Common Position 2009/67/CFSP, OJL23, 26 January 2009, 37.
[391] Council Common Position 2009/67/CFSP, 26 January 2009.
[392] Political Committee of the LTTE, Special Press Release, 10 October 1997.
[393] JM Sison, 'Introduction', in NDFP, *Declaration of Undertaking to Apply the Geneva Conventions of 1949 and Protocol I of 1977* (NDFP Human Rights Monitoring Committee Booklet No 6) 4–5.
[394] Meron, *Internal Strife*, above note 349, 38; PH Kooijmans, 'In the Shadowland between Civil War and Civil Strife: Some Reflections on the Standard-Setting Process', in AJM Delissen and GJ Tanja (eds), *Humanitarian Law of Armed Conflict, Challenges Ahead: Essays in Honour of Frits Kalshoven* (Martinus Nijhoff, 1991) 225, 228.

that the adverse party had a character which was tantamount to that of a State'.[395] Although significantly overstating the point, the mindset it portrays is telling.

Concerns surrounding the affording of legal status through the application of international humanitarian law stem from the fact that, historically, non-international armed conflicts were regulated by international humanitarian law upon recognition of a situation as belligerency by the parent state.[396] Thus, states did not want to suggest that the reverse proposition was also true, namely that application of international humanitarian law to the violence in question was tantamount to recognition of belligerency. Accordingly, concern was expressed that a provision such as common Article 3, 'might reinforce the position of a group of insurgents, in having it considered as a belligerent'.[397] For example, at the 1949 Diplomatic Conference, the United Kingdom spoke out against application of the Geneva Conventions to internal violence, in part because this 'would appear to give the status of belligerents to insurgents'.[398] Another cause for concern was that some sort of legal status may be the central goal of the non-state armed group, that 'status is the prize for which fighting is waged'.[399]

States did have some basis to be concerned given the suggestion that, if a government orders its forces to apply international humanitarian law, this suffices to afford recognition of belligerency to the non-state armed group.[400] However, there was also authority to the contrary, with the Lieber Code providing that:

[w]hen humanity induces the adoption of the rules of regular war toward rebels, whether the adoption is partial or entire, it does in no way whatever imply a partial or complete acknowledgement of their government, if they have set up one, or of them, as an independent and sovereign power. Neutrals have no right to make the adoption of the rules of war by the assailed government toward rebels the ground of their own acknowledgment of the revolted people as an independent power.[401]

Francis Lieber had noted previously, in 1861, that the exchange of prisoners between state forces and the non-state armed group, and the acceptance of a flag of truce, did not constitute recognition of the belligerent character of the armed group,[402] points that have since been stressed.[403]

---

[395] *Final Record*, above note 6, Vol II-B, 78. See also *Official Records*, above note 52, Vol 7, 219, paras 124 and 126 (Zaire).

[396] See above, 9–20.

[397] ICRC, *The Geneva Conventions of August 12, 1949: Analysis for the Use of National Red Cross Societies, Volume II* (ICRC, 1950) 6.

[398] *Final Record*, above note 6, Vol II-B, 10.

[399] E van Cleef Greenberg, 'Law and the Conduct of the Algerian Revolution' (1970) 11 *Harvard International Law Journal* 37, 70.

[400] NJ Padelford, 'International Law and the Spanish Civil War' (1937) 31 *AJIL* 226, 229. See also Bedjaoui, *Algerian Revolution*, above note 138, 173–5 (on the Hague law rather than the Geneva law); La Haye, *War Crimes*, above note 190, 36 (on granting rebels the status of prisoners of war).

[401] Article 152. See also Article 153.

[402] Letter from Francis Lieber to Attorney General Bates, published as 'The Disposal of Prisoners: Would the Exchange of Prisoners Amount to a Partial Acknowledgment of the Insurgents as Belligerents, According to International Law?', *New York Times*, 19 August 1861, 3, quoted in RR Baxter, 'The First Modern Codification of the Law of War: Francis Lieber and General Orders No 100' (1963) 3 *IRRC* 171, 177.

[403] Institut de Droit International, 'Droits et devoirs des Puissances étrangères, au cas de mouvement insurrectionnel, envers les gouvernements établis et reconnus qui sont aux prises avec l'insurrection' (Neuchâtel, 1900) Article 4(2); Conference of Government Experts on the Reaffirmation and Development of International Humanitarian Law Applicable in Armed Conflicts (Geneva, 24 May–12 June 1971): Submitted by the International Committee of the Red Cross (Geneva, 1971) Part V: Protection of Victims of Non-International Armed Conflicts, 65; *Official Records*, above note 52, Vol 8, 227, para 68 (ICRC).

Given these concerns and the divergence in views on point, at the 1947 Conference of Government Experts, one expert noted that, 'it should be clearly understood that the humanitarian obligations stipulated by' what was to become common Article 3 'should entail no juridical consequences in respect of the legal status of any body claiming governmental authority, but not recognized by another Government as enjoying such authority'.[404] This view proved influential and is reflected in the final sentence of common Article 3: '[t]he application of the preceding provisions shall not affect the legal status of the Parties to the conflict.' As the ICRC has noted, as a consequence of this clause, 'the insurgents are prevented from taking advantage of the fact that they respect the principles of the Convention, to secure recognition as a belligerent Power'.[405]

However, even the final sentence of common Article 3 could not assuage the concerns of all states. Burma, which was strongly against any form of international regulation of non-international armed conflict, took the view that the language of the final sentence was 'an attempt to safeguard the legal status of the *de jure* government'. However, the sentence was 'only a bait... Whether or not you safeguard the legal status of the *de jure* government, the mere inclusion of this Article in an international Convention will automatically give the insurgents a status as high as the legal status which is denied to them. It can easily be imagined that this paragraph is going to be an encouragement and an incentive to the insurgents'.[406] This view should be contrasted with that of the USSR, which was at the opposite end of the spectrum from Burma, and which took the view that the clause was 'redundant... since the legal status of [the] Parties would in no way be affected'.[407] For its part, Norway praised the 'sound innovation' of the clause, stating that '[i]f the application of the Convention entailed no consequence as regards the legal status of opposing parties, that meant that the Convention must be applied even where the opposing parties were not recognized as belligerents'.[408]

In the process leading up to the drafting of Additional Protocol II, the 1971 Conference of Government Experts took the view that the caveat on legal status should appear in the instrument under consideration and the report of the Conference provides that '[t]his principle is considered as an essential guarantee by the State, and it must remain inviolate if the desired results are to be achieved'.[409] Accordingly, the draft put before the 1974–7 Diplomatic Conference by the ICRC included an article relating to the legal status of the parties to the conflict, which was based on the equivalent language of common Article 3.[410] This read:

The legal status of the parties to the conflict or that of the territories on which they exercise authority shall not be affected by the application of the provisions of the present Protocol, or by all or part of the provisions of the Geneva Conventions of August 12, 1949, and of the Additional

---

[404] ICRC, Report on the Work of the Conference of Government Experts for the Study of the Conventions for the Protection of War Victims (Geneva, April 14–26, 1947) (1947) 9.

[405] ICRC, *The Geneva Conventions of August 12, 1949: Analysis for the Use of National Red Cross Societies, Volume II* (ICRC, 1950) 8.

[406] *Final Record*, above note 6, Vol II-B, 330 (Burma).

[407] Ibid, 98 (USSR).

[408] Ibid, 11 (Norway).

[409] ICRC, Conference of Government Experts on the Reaffirmation and Development of International Humanitarian Law Applicable in Armed Conflicts, Geneva, 24 May–12 June 1971 (1971) Vol 5, 52.

[410] *Official Records*, above note 52, Vol 8, 227, para 67 (ICRC). See also ICRC, *Draft Additional Protocols to the Geneva Conventions of August 12, 1949: Commentary* (1973) 134.

Protocol relating to the protection of victims of international armed conflicts brought into force in accordance with Article 38 or by the conclusion of any agreement provided for in the Geneva Conventions and their Additional Protocols.

This provision was intended to shore up the conclusion that application of the instrument 'would not therefore constitute a recognition, even implicitly, of belligerency, and would have no effect whatsoever on the legal qualification of the relations between the parties to the conflict'.[411] Shortly before Additional Protocol II was adopted, however, it became clear that there was considerable resistance to the Protocol, which may have affected the chances of its adoption and later ratification. As such, various changes were made to the Protocol so as to maximize its chances of passing.[412] One of the principles governing the amendments was that 'nothing in the Protocol should suggest that dissidents must be treated legally other than as rebels'.[413] Accordingly, all references to 'parties to the conflict' were removed, including, somewhat ironically, the provision quoted above.[414] Despite the deletion, some states continued to take the view that Additional Protocol II could give legal or political legitimacy to armed groups.[415] However, it is generally accepted that the principle underlying the provision remains intact.[416]

In the years since Additional Protocol II was concluded, numerous instruments which regulate non-international armed conflicts have been adopted, which include a provision indicating that the legal status of the parties to the conflict is not affected by application of the instrument. This is true primarily of international humanitarian law instruments in the area.[417] However, the presence of such a provision is by no means limited to international humanitarian law instruments alone. Instruments in the areas of human rights and internal displacement, which are applicable to non-international armed conflicts, also contain such a provision,[418] as do ad hoc bilateral agreements concluded between states and opposing non-state armed groups.[419] Even instruments designed for application to non-state armed groups alone contain such a clause,[420] their inclusion designed 'so as not to alarm states'.[421] This is important given that the

---

[411] Ibid, 134. [412] See above, 50–1.
[413] *Official Records*, above note 52, Vol 7, 61, para 11 (Pakistan).
[414] See ICRC, *Commentary on the Additional Protocols*, above note 76, 1339.
[415] 'The United States Position on the Relation of Customary International Law to the 1977 Protocols Additional to the 1949 Geneva Conventions: Remarks of Michael J Matheson' (1987) 2 *American University Journal of International Law and Policy* 419, 429, referring to the views of some 'Third World governments'.
[416] See eg Bothe, Partsch, and Solf, *New Rules for Victims of Armed Conflicts,* above note 238, 632.
[417] Second Hague Protocol for the Protection of of Cultural Property in the Event of Armed Conflict (1999), Article 22(6); Convention on Certain Conventional Weapons (1980), Amended Article 1(6); Amended Protocol II on Prohibitions or Restrictions on the Use of Mines, Booby-Traps and Other Devices (1996), Article 1(6). See also Hague Convention for the Protection of Cultural Property in the Event of Armed Conflict (1954), Article 19(4).
[418] Optional Protocol to the Convention on the Rights of the Child on the Involvement of Children in Armed Conflicts (2000), Article 4(3); African Union Convention for the Protection and Assistance of Internally Displaced Persons in Africa (2009), Article 7.
[419] See eg Government-FARC Humanitarian Exchange Accord, 2 June 2001; Agreement of 22 May 1992 [Bosnia], reproduced in M Sassòli, AA Bouvier, and A Qunitin, *How Does Law Protect in War? Volume II* (ICRC, 2011) 1717.
[420] Deed of Commitment under Geneva Call for Adherence to a Total Ban on Anti-Personnel Mines and for Cooperation in Mine Action, Article 6. See also Declaration of the Second Meeting of Signatories to Geneva Call's 'Deed of Commitment for Adherence to a Total Ban on Anti-Personnel Mines and for Cooperation in Mine Action', 19 June 2009. On Geneva Call, see below, 538–42.
[421] Mine Ban Education Workshop in Southern Sudan: Report of Proceedings and Recommendations (Geneva Call, Geneva, 2003) 33.

occasional armed group does envisage a link between compliance with norms and recognition of belligerency, with the NDFP considering its 1996 Declaration of Adherence to Additional Protocol I to be 'significant because it has raised to a new and higher level the efforts of the revolutionary government and movement represented by the NDFP to gain international diplomatic recognition for their status of belligerency'.[422]

As noted above, the clause was initially drafted in order to avoid the application of international humanitarian law being considered to constitute recognition of belligerency.[423] It was not drafted with general notions of legal status or legitimacy in mind. However, the meaning of the clause has changed over time, it now being used to assuage more general concerns surrounding notions of legal status and legitimacy. Thus, the Colombian Constitutional Court has noted that '[i]t is...wrong to assume, as some...have done, that by implementing Protocol II the State of Colombia would be conferring legitimacy upon irregular armed groups, since application of the humanitarian rules has no effect on the legal status of the parties'.[424] Likewise, in 2011, President Santos of Colombia indicated that recognition of the existence of an armed conflict did not amount to recognizing the FARC as belligerents.[425] Some years earlier, in 2003, a commander of the SPLM/A 'encouraged [the NGO] Geneva Call to make clear to armed groups that signature [of its] Deed of Commitment does not change in any way their legal status or lend legitimacy to their struggles'.[426]

Whereas, ordinarily, rights and obligations follow from legal status, the caveat in question seeks to divorce the relationship between the two. It seeks to bind the non-state armed group by certain rules without granting the group any special status by way of those rules. However, to some extent, a certain status is afforded to the non-state armed group through the application of international humanitarian law. This increased status follows inevitably from the move from internal tensions and disturbances to armed conflict. However, it arises from the facts rather than from the application of the law. The increased status also has to be weighed against the obligations to which the armed group becomes subject. In this sense, there is a 'serious contradiction dictated by opposing political motivations. Article 3 has two souls: one is humanitarian and open to insurgents; the other favours respect for State sovereignty and is thus opposed to the rebels'.[427]

In general, the principle that the legal status of the parties to the conflict is not affected by the application of the relevant international law is crucial for states and accepted by many non-state armed groups. Provided such a clause is present, the concerns of many states seem satisfied. Whereas states have now accepted that the application of the law of non-international armed conflict to the non-state armed group does not legitimize the group or afford it legal status, the same is not true of engagement with non-state armed groups, even on matters of the law of armed conflict. In the area of engagement, concerns of legal status and legitimacy continue to arise.[428]

---

[422] JM Sison, 'Introduction', in NDFP, *Declaration of Undertaking to Apply the Geneva Conventions of 1949 and Protocol I of 1977* (NDFP Human Rights Monitoring Committee Booklet No 6) 3.
[423] See above, 207.
[424] *Constitutional Conformity of Protocol II*, C-225/95, above note 362, 2240.
[425] 'Colombia's victims law: Feeling their pain', *The Economist*, 4 June 2011.
[426] Mine Ban Education Workshop in Southern Sudan: Report of Proceedings and Recommendations (Geneva Call, Geneva, 2003) 33.
[427] A Cassese, 'Civil War and International Law', reprinted in A Cassese, *The Human Dimension of International Law: Selected Papers* (Oxford University Press, 2008) 110, 119 (emphasis omitted).
[428] See below, 546–9.

6. Conclusion

For many years, a concise and authoritative definition of a non-international armed conflict did not exist. Attempts were made to define the term at diplomatic conferences but consensus could not be reached. Definitions were posited at meetings of experts and by commentators; however, they failed to gain sufficient traction to make any one of them authoritative. Nonetheless, a range of situations that fell within the term could be identified and the core elements of a definition of non-international armed conflict had been identified and accepted. It was only in 1995 with the *Tadić* Decision on Interlocutory Appeal on Jurisdiction that the term was defined in an authoritative manner and widely followed. The *Tadić* Decision defines a non-international armed conflict by reference to two elements: intensity of violence and organization of the armed group. Subsequent ICTY jurisprudence has elucidated these two elements and provided indicia against which the elements can be assessed. An international criminal tribunal thus proved critical in the elucidation of the notion of a non-international armed conflict, basing itself on elements that were generally accepted as constituting key features of the violence.

Despite organization of the armed group comprising one of the two elements of a non-international armed conflict, insufficient attention has been paid to armed groups, their structure, and workings. Little attention has been paid to why it is that organization of the armed group is an element of the definition of a non-international armed conflict. Even less has been paid to the relationship between organization and enforcement of the law. Furthermore, the notion of responsible command is traditionally interpreted by reference to a hierarchical pyramidal structure which does not always map onto the structure of armed groups. The structure of armed groups is also often compared with that of the armed forces of the state, skewing the notion of organization. The important nexus between the scope of application of the law and its substantive content also remains under-explored. In sum, the element of organization and the workings of armed groups are only just starting to be understood.

A further complexity arises in ascertaining whether or not particular conventional rules are applicable to the non-international armed conflict in question. Additional Protocol II requires that the non-international armed conflict be of a particular sort before it applies. The principal addition is that the armed group exercises 'such control over a part of its territory as to enable [it] to carry out sustained and concerted military operations and to implement the present Protocol'. This phrase has been interpreted in a very particular manner, one which goes against the text of the instrument itself. The scope of application of the Rome Statute has also given rise to debate. The Rome Statute provides that certain rules will apply in 'protracted armed conflicts' but the meaning of the phrase has proven open to debate.

Accordingly, while significant advancements have been made on the notion of a non-international armed conflict, for such a foundational issue, considerable uncertainties remain.

Ascertaining whether or not a non-international armed conflict exists continues to be the subject of dispute, primarily due to the lack of a neutral party both able and willing to take on the role of characterizing the violence. This has led to a number of states denying the existence of a non-international armed conflict. However, examples of denial need to be compared against examples of acceptance of involvement in an armed conflict. Only in this way will a more complete picture of the situation become apparent.

The identification of a non-international armed conflict operates at another level, namely the distinction between a non-international armed conflict and an international armed conflict. The issue arises because what may seem to be a non-international armed conflict may turn out to be an international armed conflict. This is the subject of the next chapter.

6

Identifying a Non-International Armed Conflict: International and Non-International Armed Conflicts

1. Introduction

Non-international armed conflicts frequently contain some sort of international element. The non-state armed group may be based at the border regions, straddling an international boundary, and crossing into another state. The armed forces of the state may raid neighbouring territory if part of the non-state armed group is located abroad. Fighting may take place between a non-state armed group that is based in one state and state armed forces that are based in another, despite the states not being adjacent to one another. Outside states[1] may support the forces of the state involved in the violence or the fighters of a non-state armed group, whether through financial or logistical means. Outside states may intervene militarily in the conflict to prop up one side or another. What is seemingly a non-international armed conflict may, then, turn out to be an international one, or, at least, governed by the law of international armed conflict.

An armed conflict that appears to be a non-international one may in fact be subject to the law of international armed conflict in three principal situations. First, the parent state may recognize the situation as amounting to belligerency. Recognition of belligerency was considered in Chapter 1 and will not feature further here. Second, the armed conflict may be a war of national liberation as that phrase is understood in international law, namely involving a national liberation movement that is fighting against a racist regime, colonial domination, or alien occupation. Third, an outside state may intervene in the conflict. Not all forms of intervention on the part of an outside state will transform a non-international armed conflict into an international one. Two forms that may have this effect are the involvement of troops of an outside state in the hostilities on the side of the armed group, and control over the non-state armed group on the part of an outside state. This chapter considers these second and third transformative possibilities. The possible category of 'transnational armed conflict', referring to armed conflicts that are fought between a state and a non-state armed group across an international border, is also considered.

2. Wars of national liberation

2.1 Historical regulation

The 1949 Geneva Conventions treated wars of national liberation as non-international armed conflicts. Article 2, common to the four Geneva Conventions, provides that: '[a]lthough one of the Powers in conflict may not be a party to the present Convention,

---

[1] This is sometimes described as the involvement of a 'third' state. However, as there is no 'second' state, the language of 'outside' state is used.

the Powers who are parties thereto shall remain bound but it in their mutual relations. They shall furthermore be bound by the Convention in relation to the said Power, if the latter accepts and applies the provisions thereof.' It had been suggested that the reference to 'Powers' in that Article included national liberation movements.[2] The same argument was made in respect of common Article 60/59/139/155 of the Geneva Conventions, which provide that '[f]rom the date of its coming into force, [the relevant Convention] shall be open to any Power in whose name the present Convention has not been signed, to accede to this Convention'.[3] However, the interpretation of the articles along these lines has not been generally accepted, the term 'Power' being considered to refer to states alone.[4] This is supported by early drafts of the Conventions, which treated civil wars, colonial conflicts, and wars of religion together, all as examples of non-international armed conflicts.[5] It was also the view of states at the 1949 Diplomatic Conference.[6] Thus, wars of national liberation were considered non-international armed conflicts and subject to common Article 3 alone.

This minimal regulation of wars of national liberation was increasingly questioned in the 1960s and 1970s, with new states, created from a wave of decolonization, pushing for an alteration in the manner in which wars of national liberation were regulated. In the UN General Assembly, numerous resolutions were adopted which called on states to apply the Third Geneva Convention on Prisoners of War to particular armed conflicts that were considered wars of national liberation or to apply the Third and Fourth Geneva Conventions in them.[7] Statements of principle were also adopted; for example, General Assembly Resolution 3103 (XXVIII) provided that 'armed conflicts involving the struggle of peoples against colonial and alien domination and racist regimes are to be regarded as international armed conflicts in the sense of the 1949 Geneva Conventions'.[8] The resolutions are not a model of consistency, with some calling solely for the application of the Third Geneva Convention, others for the application of the principles of the Geneva Conventions, and still others for captured fighters to be treated as prisoners of war.[9] Nevertheless, the general thrust of the resolutions was clear: wars of national liberation could no longer be treated as akin to other non-international armed conflicts.

---

[2] G Abi-Saab, 'Wars of National Liberation and the Laws of War' (1972) 3 *Annales d'Etudes Internationales* 93, 103–4; D Schindler, 'The Different Types of Armed Conflicts According to the Geneva Conventions and Protocols' (1979-II) 163 *RdC* 117, 135–6; N Higgins, *Regulating the Use of Force in Wars of National Liberation: The Need for a New Regime* (Martinus Nijhoff, 2010) 93–7.

[3] Ibid.

[4] See the interpretation in JS Pictet (ed), *The Geneva Conventions of 12 August 1949: Commentary, III Geneva Convention Relative to the Treatment of Prisoners of War* (ICRC, 1960) 24–7; RR Baxter, 'The Geneva Conventions of 1949 and Wars of National Liberation', in MC Bassiouni (ed), *International Terrorism and Political Crimes* (Thomas, 1975) 120, 123; A Cassese, 'Wars of National Liberation and Humanitarian Law', in C Swinarski (ed), *Studies and Essays on International Humanitarian Law and Red Cross Principles in Honour of Jean Pictet* (ICRC, 1984) 313, 316; A Rosas, *The Legal Status of Prisoners of War* (Suomalainen Tiedeakatemia, 1976) 263.

[5] See eg Revision of the Geneva Convention of July 27, 1929, for the Relief of the Wounded and Sick in Armies in the Field, Article 2, in ICRC, *Draft Revised or New Conventions for the Protection of War Victims* (May 1948) 6.

[6] See eg *Final Record of the Diplomatic Conference of Geneva of 1949* (Federal Political Department, Berne) Vol II-B, 325–7 (USSR) and 332–3 (Mexico).

[7] See eg GA Res 2446 (XXIII) (1968), GA Res 2621 (XXV) (1970), GA Res 2678 (XXV) (1970), GA Res 2871 (XXVI) (1971).

[8] GA Res 3103 (XXVIII) (1973).

[9] Rosas, *Prisoners of War*, above note 4, 265.

The debates that were taking place at the General Assembly translated across to the humanitarian law arena. At the Twenty-first International Conference of the Red Cross in 1969, a resolution was passed which provided that 'combatants and resistance movements who participated in non-international armed conflicts and who conform to the provisions of Article 4 of the Third Geneva Convention on 12 August 1949 should when captured be protected against any inhumanity and brutality and receive treatment similar to that which that Convention lays down for prisoners of war'.[10] By the time of the 1971 Conference of Government Experts, 'most of the experts... who spoke on this subject considered that wars of liberation were international armed conflicts'.[11] At the Diplomatic Conference of 1974–7, quite how wars of national liberation were to be regulated gave rise to a heated controversy, taking up almost the entire 1974 session.[12]

The draft Protocol on international armed conflicts that was put before the Diplomatic Conference provided that:

[t]he present Protocol, which supplements the Geneva Conventions of August 12, 1949, for the Protection of War Victims, shall apply in the situations referred to in Article 2 common to these Conventions.[13]

Common Article 2, in turn, reads in relevant part: 'the present Convention shall apply to all cases of declared war or of any other armed conflict which may arise between two or more of the High Contracting Parties, even if the state of war is not recognized by one of them.' The initial Protocol thus treated wars of national liberation as non-international armed conflicts. However, this was unacceptable to a number of states. Accordingly, a group of socialist and African states proposed the inclusion of a paragraph which provided that:

[t]he international armed conflicts referred to in Article 2 common to the Conventions include also conflicts where peoples fight against colonial and alien domination and against racist regimes.[14]

An alternative amendment, put forward by a group of 15 states of varying persuasions, proposed the additional language:

The situations referred to in the preceding paragraph include armed struggles waged by peoples in the exercise of their right of self-determination as enshrined in the Charter of the United Nations

---

[10] Resolution XVIII, in XXIst International Conference of the Red Cross: Report, Istanbul 1969, 100.
[11] ICRC, Conference of Government Experts on the Reaffirmation and Development of International Humanitarian Law Applicable in Armed Conflicts: Report on the Work of the Conference (August 1971) 54, para 321.
[12] See, on the first session, F Kalshoven, 'The First Session of the Diplomatic Conference on Reaffirmation and Development of International Humanitarian Law Applicable in Armed Conflicts, Geneva, 20 February–29 March 1974' (1974) 5 *NYIL* 3; DP Forsythe, 'The 1974 Diplomatic Conference on Humanitarian Law: Some Observations' (1975) 69 *AJIL* 77; G Abi-Saab, 'Wars of National Liberation and the Development of Humanitarian Law', in RJ Akkerman, PJ van Krieken, and CO Pannenborg (eds), *Declarations on Principles* (AW Sijthoff, 1977) 143, 153–60; G Abi-Saab, 'Wars of National Liberation in the Geneva Conventions and Protocols' (1979-IV) 165 *RdC* 353, 374–84.
[13] Article 1, in *Official Records of the Diplomatic Conference on the Reaffirmation and Development of International Humanitarian Law Applicable in Armed Conflicts, Geneva (1974–1977)* (Federal Political Department, 1978) Vol I, 3.
[14] Ibid, Vol 3, 5.

and defined by the Declaration on Principles of International Law concerning Friendly Relations and Cooperation among States in accordance with the Charter of the United Nations.[15]

As described by one of the participants to the Diplomatic Conference, the difference between the two amendments was

> mainly one of approach: whereas under the first version certain named situations would be included among the international armed conflicts, the second provided an abstract definition which, in the eyes of its authors, would of course lead to exactly the same situations being deemed international armed conflicts as the proponents of the more specific formula had in mind but which, on the other hand, could be used to cover other situations as well.[16]

Advocates of the two amendments argued that the international law on point had changed subsequent to the 1949 Diplomatic Conference, primarily through the General Assembly resolutions considered above, and that international law now treated wars of national liberation as subject to the law of international armed conflict.[17] It was argued that '[p]articipants were... not being asked to accept anything new; it was merely proposed that they should affirm explicitly in the field of humanitarian law what they had already accepted as binding law within the United Nations and within general international law'.[18] It was also contended that the Diplomatic Conference was tasked with bringing the Geneva Conventions up to date, which included regulating wars of national liberation in an appropriate manner.[19]

However, some of the participants at the Diplomatic Conference viewed the amendments in an unfavourable light. Certain states took the view that armed groups fighting in wars of national liberation (national liberation movements) lacked the capacity to comply with all the requirements of the Geneva Conventions.[20] Others maintained that wars of national liberation were non-international conflicts and 'to include them in Protocol I would disrupt the whole system of the Geneva Conventions'.[21] Still others suggested that international humanitarian law 'should never vary according to the motives of those engaged in a particular armed struggle' and thus wars of national liberation could not be regulated in a special manner.[22] Others yet considered it 'doubtful whether the effect of the United Nations General Assembly

---

[15] Ibid. This amendment followed a similar proposal made at the second session of the Conference of Government Experts. See Proposal CE/COM IV/74, in ICRC, Conference of Government Experts on the Reaffirmation and Development of International Humanitarian Law Applicable in Armed Conflicts, Second Session, 3 May–3 June 1972, Report on the Work of the Conference: Volume 2 (July 1972) 114.

[16] Kalshoven, Diplomatic Conference, above note 12, 29.

[17] *Official Records*, above note 13, Vol 8, 8, para 8 (Egypt); 10, paras 24–6 (Norway); 17, para 1 (USSR).

[18] Ibid, 8, para 10 (Egypt). See also 9, para 17 (Yugoslavia).

[19] Ibid, 8, paras 9, 11 (Egypt); 13, para 42 (United Republic of Tanzania); 45, para 12 (Senegal); 9, para 19 (Yugoslavia).

[20] Ibid, 11, para 32 and 31, para 42 (Belgium); 25, para 4 (USA); 29, para 25 (United Kingdom). But cf 21, para 27 (Poland); 32, para 46 and 36, para 18 (FRELIMO); 35, para 14 (Ukranian Soviet Socialist Republic); 38, para 34 (PLO); 39, para 41 (Guinea-Bissau). See also Abi-Saab, Development, above note 12, 159–60.

[21] *Official Records*, above note 13, Vol 8, 22, para 37 (Italy). See also 13, para 44 (United Kingdom). But cf 21, para 29 (Venezuela); 27, para 17 (China); 28, para 23 (Syrian Arab Republic); 31, para 41 (Brazil).

[22] Ibid, 13, para 45 (United Kingdom). See also 14, para 49 (France); 19, para 13 (Switerland); 19, para 16 (Canada); 37, para 22 (Denmark). But cf 15, para 53 (Romania); 21, para 26 (Poland).

resolutions had been to transform that positive law'.²³ Objections were also made to the concepts of 'self-determination' and 'peoples', considering them vague.²⁴

On the basis of these objections, a counter-proposal was made by Western states, which read:

1. The High Contracting Parties undertake to respect and to ensure respect for the present Protocol in all circumstances.
2. The present Protocol shall apply in the situations referred to in Article 2 common to the Geneva Conventions of 12 August 1949, for the Protection of War Victims.
3. In cases not included in this present Protocol or in other instruments of conventional law, civilians and combatants remain under the protection and the authority of the principles of international law, as they result from established custom, from the principles of humanity and the dictates of public conscience.²⁵

After some negotiation, a compromise was reached between the supporters of the first two amendments, which resulted in their merger. The compromise provided that the Protocol on international armed conflicts would regulate:

armed conflicts where peoples fight against colonial and alien domination and against racist régimes in the exercise of their right of self-determination, as enshrined in the Charter of the United Nations and defined by the Declaration of Principles of International Law concerning Friendly Relations and Cooperation among States in accordance with the Charter of the United Nations.²⁶

After further debate, this compromise text was combined with the proposed amendment of the Western states. Following another amendment—the language of 'colonial and alien domination' was replaced by 'colonial domination and alien occupation'²⁷—a vote was taken in committee and was adopted by 70 votes in favour, 21 against, and 13 abstentions.²⁸ At the plenary, the article was adopted with 80 votes in favour, 1 against, and 11 abstentions. Accordingly, pursuant to Article 1(4) of Additional Protocol I, certain armed conflicts that are fought between a state and an armed group (national liberation movement) are regulated by the law of international armed conflict. It has been suggested that Article 1(4) has passed into the corpus of customary norms;²⁹ however, given the controversy surrounding such conflicts, this is overly optimistic.³⁰

2.2 Defining wars of national liberation

Article 1(4), as adopted, provides:

The situations referred to in the preceding paragraph [which are subject to the law of international armed conflict] include armed conflicts in which peoples are fighting against colonial

---

²³ Ibid, 28, para 21 (Monaco). See the discussion in A Cullen, *The Concept of Non-International Armed Conflict in International Humanitarian Law* (Cambridge University Press, 2010) Chapter 3.
²⁴ *Official Records*, above note 13, Vol 8, 13–14, para 46 (United Kingdom); 14, para 51 (United States of America); 26, para 10 (Ireland); 31, para 42 (Brazil). But cf 15, para 53 (Romania).
²⁵ Ibid, Vol 3, 6.
²⁶ Ibid, 7.
²⁷ See ibid, Vol 8, 99, para 16 (Argentina).
²⁸ Ibid, 102, para 42.
²⁹ Abi-Saab, *RdC*, above note 12, 371–2; A Cassese, 'The Geneva Protocols of 1977 on the Humanitarian Law of Armed Conflict and Customary International Law' (1984) 3 *UCLA Pacific Basin Law Journal* 55, 68–71.
³⁰ See also C Greenwood, 'Scope of Application of Humanitarian Law', in D Fleck (ed), *The Handbook of Humanitarian Law in Armed Conflicts* (Oxford University Press, 1995) 39, 49.

domination and alien occupation and against racist régimes in the exercise of their right of self-determination, as enshrined in the Charter of the United Nations and the Declaration on Principles of International Law concerning Friendly Relations and Co-operation among States in accordance with the Charter of the United Nations.[31]

In order for an armed conflict to constitute a war of national liberation for the purposes of the law of international armed conflict, a number of prerequisites must be satisfied. Just as important, the armed conflict need not satisfy certain other elements.

First and foremost, there must be an armed conflict. The level of violence needed to exist before the situation can be considered a war of national liberation has been disputed. Some states suggested that the conflict had to reach 'a certain level of intensity',[32] or that the requisite level of intensity was the same as that required for the application of Additional Protocol II.[33] However, no such requirement found its way into the text and accordingly, no set level of intensity is required for the application of Article 1(4).[34] This puts the situation closer to an international armed conflict, for which only a minimum level of violence is required,[35] as compared to a non-international armed conflict, for which the violence should indeed reach a certain level of intensity.[36] In practice, as with non-international armed conflicts, the state will be unlikely to recognize the situation as an armed conflict until the violence reaches a certain level of duration. That said, unlike non-international armed conflicts, states will likely never consider themselves to be fighting a war of national liberation.[37]

The second requirement is that one of the parties to the violence must be a 'peoples'. Third, the 'peoples' must be fighting 'in the exercise of their right of self-determination'. Fourth, and crucially, the fighting must be against 'colonial domination', 'alien occupation', and 'racist regimes'. The precise meaning of these terms is rather elusive. In general terms, colonial domination refers to traditional ideas of colonialism.[38] The concept of racist regimes is broader than apartheid practised in South Africa but is narrower than any racial discrimination.[39] The idea of alien occupation corresponds to that of 'colonies of settlement'; it is not coterminous with belligerent occupation.[40] The choice of terminology was influenced by, and directed at, particular situations then in existence. References to 'colonial domination' and 'racist regimes' were aimed at 'South Africa, Namibia (South West Africa), Rhodesia, and the Portuguese colonies', while the

---

[31] Additional Protocol I, Article 1(4).
[32] *Official Records*, above note 13, Vol 8, 109, para 26 (United States). See also Rosas, *Prisoners of War*, above note 4, 272–3.
[33] Declaration of the UK on signature of the Additional Protocols, in D Schindler and J Toman, *The Laws of Armed Conflict* (Martinus Nijhoff, 2004) 814–15. On the Additional Protocol II threshold, see above, 182 et seq.
[34] Y Sandoz, C Swinarski, and B Zimmermann (eds), *Commentary on the Additional Protocols of 8 June 1977 to the Geneva Conventions of 12 August 1949* (ICRC, 1987) 55; Abi-Saab, *RdC*, above note 12, 413–14; Wilson, *International Law and the Use of Force by National Liberation Movements* (Clarendon Press, 1988) 166.
[35] Pictet, *Commentary on the Third Geneva Convention*, above note 4, 23.
[36] See above, 167–70.
[37] See below, 220.
[38] Abi-Saab, *RdC*, above note 12, 394.
[39] See M Bothe, KJ Partsch, and WA Solf, *New Rules for Victims of Armed Conflicts* (Martinus Nijhoff, 1982) 50; Wilson, *National Liberation Movements*, above note 34, 167.
[40] Abi-Saab, Development, above note 12, 163 fn 39; Abi-Saab, *RdC*, above note 12, 394–6; Bothe, Partsch, and Solf, above note 39, 51–2; Schindler, Armed Conflicts, above note 2, 137–8; Rosas, *Prisoners of War*, above note 4, 272–3.

reference to 'alien occupation' was directed at Israel.[41] Accordingly, Article 1(4) has been described as 'dated', the argument being that once the situations to which the provision was directed are resolved, and many have been, the provision ceases to be of use.[42] This is true to a certain extent. However, other situations exist that arguably fall within the scope of the Protocol, one such candidate being Western Sahara.[43] Indeed, the Aceh Sumatra National Liberation Front (ASNLF) argued that it was fighting a war of 'self-determination [on behalf of] the people of Aceh Sumatra' against the Government of Indonesia in respect of the 'decolonization of the Dutch East Indies alias "Indonesia" which has not been decolonized legally and properly in accordance with the purpose and meaning of the Charter of the United Nations, with the principles and procedures of International Law, and with the UN Resolution on the Granting of Independence to Colonial Countries and Peoples'.[44] Should that argument have proven correct, the Aceh situation may have fallen within the scope of Article 1(4). Furthermore, it is far from inconceivable that a racist regime will come into existence in the future.

Of greater importance is whether the scope of application of the Protocol is in fact limited to conflicts against 'colonial domination', 'alien occupation', and 'racist regimes', or whether an armed conflict that is fought for the purposes of exercising the right to self-determination more broadly is enough to trigger the application of the provision. The issue is important given that many non-state armed groups argue that they are fighting for self-determination, that they are national liberation movements, and that their fights fall within the scope of the Protocol. These groups tend not to make the further argument that they are fighting against colonial domination, alien occupation, and racist regimes. For example the Ogaden National Liberation Front (ONLF) of Ethiopia was mandated, by its declaration of formation, *inter alia* '[t]o reclaim our inherent right to national self-determination' and has stated that the 'Ogaden issue is not a border dispute between two neighbors, Ethiopia and Somalia, as held by the former, but rather a conflict between a colonized people and their colonizer'.[45] Similarly, the Oromo Liberation Front, also of Ethiopia, has indicated that '[t]he protracted armed resistance under the leadership of the Front is an act of self-defense exercised by the Oromo people against successive Ethiopian governments... who forcibly deny their right to self-determination'.[46] Likewise, in 1997, the Liberation Tigers of Tamil Eelam (LTTE) argued that it was 'a national liberation movement, which is presently involved in armed conflict with the government of Sri Lanka in order to realize the right of the Tamils of Sri Lanka for self-determination on the island of Sri Lanka'.[47] Along similar lines, in 1994, the Sudan People's Liberation Movement (SPLM) stated that it was 'committed to fight and achieve the right and exercise of

---

[41] RR Baxter, 'Humanitarian Law or Humanitarian Politics? The 1974 Diplomatic Conference on Humanitarian Law' (1975) 16 *Harvard International Law Journal* 1, 12. See also Schindler, Armed Conflicts, above note 2, 137–8; Wilson, *National Liberation Movements*, above note 34, 168.

[42] Baxter, Wars of National Liberation, above note 4, 132; Cassese, Wars of National Liberation, above note 4, 319; Rosas, *Prisoners of War*, above note 4, 274.

[43] This would seem to be the effect of the International Court of Justice's Advisory Opinion in *Western Sahara* [1975] ICJ Rep 12.

[44] ASNLF, 'The Aims of the ASNLF', previously available at the ASNLF website.

[45] 'Political Programme of the Ogaden National Liberation Front (ONLF)', Part I and Part 2, Article 4B.

[46] Oromo Liberation Front, 'Major Policies'.

[47] Letter from Velummylum Manoharan, Representative, LTTE International Secretariat, to Honourable Judges of the US Court of Appeal District of Colombia Circuit (undated), published in *Sunday Times* (Sri Lanka), 16 November 1997.

self-determination for the oppressed people of the New Sudan'.⁴⁸ For its part, the National Democratic Front of the Philippines (NDFP) argues that the violence it is engaged in 'involves the struggle for self-determination and the people's war for national liberation and comes within the purview of Article I, paragraph 4 of Protocol I'.⁴⁹ The Fuerzas Armadas Revolucionarias de Colombia (FARC) has made similar arguments.⁵⁰ However, these groups tend not to fight against entities that may be considered colonial powers, alien occupiers, or racist regimes in the sense envisaged by the Protocol. Accordingly, whether the Protocol applies to these conflicts will depend on whether it governs wars for self-determination more broadly. The issue is also important given the right to internal self-determination. It is well-established that, in certain situations, if the right to internal self-determination is denied, a claim to external self-determination may arise.⁵¹ This may result in a conflict being fought along these lines. It is not unlikely that such situations will exist in the future.

In order to answer that question, Article 1 of Additional Protocol I needs to be considered. That Article reads in relevant part:

3. This Protocol, which supplements the Geneva Conventions of 12 August 1949 for the protection of war victims, shall apply in the situations referred to in Article 2 common to those Conventions.
4. The situations referred to in the preceding paragraph *include* armed conflicts in which peoples are fighting against colonial domination . . . ⁵²

During the Diplomatic Conference, Australia opined that 'if paragraphs [3 and 4 of Article 1] were taken together and if the word "include" . . . was taken literally, the list could be interpreted as not being exhaustive'.⁵³ The paragraphs could be read as providing that, in addition to inter-state armed conflicts (paragraph 3), conflicts against colonial domination, alien occupation, and racist regimes are to be covered by the law of international armed conflict (paragraph 4). Alternatively, as in the view of Australia, the paragraphs could be read along the lines that the law of international armed conflict will cover inter-state armed conflicts (paragraph 3), as well as other conflicts, including those against colonial domination, alien occupation, and racist regimes (paragraph 4). The latter view certainly accords with 'the spirit of the Protocol and the Conventions'.⁵⁴ However, it goes against the drafting history of the Article and has not been taken up in practice.⁵⁵ Thus, regardless of the merit of particular conflicts, Article 1(4)

---

⁴⁸ SPLM, *A Major Watershed: SPLM/SPLA First National Convention, Resolutions, Appointments and Protocol* (SPLM, New Sudan, March/April 1994). See also SPLM Political Secretariat, 'Vision and Programme of the Sudan People's Liberation Movement (SPLM)', March 1998, Section 3: Objectives of the SPLM.
⁴⁹ NDFP Declaration of Undertaking to Apply the Geneva Conventions of 1949 and Protocol I of 1977, 5 July 1996, reproduced in NDFP, *Declaration of Undertaking to Apply the Geneva Conventions of 1949 and Protocol I of 1977* (NDFP Human Rights Monitoring Committee Booklet No 6) 10.
⁵⁰ FARC-EP Comisión Internacional, *Beligerancia: Suplemento*, 3.
⁵¹ See eg *Loizidou v Turkey* (1993) 23 EHRR 513, Concurring Opinion of Judge Wildhaber, Joined by Judge Ryssdal.
⁵² Emphasis added.
⁵³ *Official Records*, above note 13, Vol 5, 228, para 14 (Australia).
⁵⁴ Abi-Saab, *RdC*, above note 12, 398. See also Cassese, Wars of National Liberation, above note 4, 317–18.
⁵⁵ Bothe, Partsch, and Solf, above note 39, 50 fn 19a; ICRC, *Commentary on the Additional Protocols*, above note 34, 54–5; Wilson, *National Liberation Movements*, above note 34, 168; R Provost, *International Human Rights and Humanitarian Law* (Cambridge University Press, 2002) 256.

is limited to conflicts that are fought against colonial domination, alien occupation, and racist regimes.

Lest this be considered unfortunate, it should be recalled that not a single state has acknowledged, nor will they acknowledge, being involved in a war of national liberation as that would be tantamount to accepting that they are colonial powers, alien occupiers, or racist regimes. Even if the provision were extended to cover self-determination more broadly, no state will acknowledge that it is fighting to suppress that right. Of course, that does not make the position correct and the problems of self-characterization of violence have already been discussed.[56]

Even if the terms of Article 1(4) are met, a further condition must be satisfied. One of the principal concerns expressed by Western states during the Diplomatic Conference was that the application of international humanitarian law to wars of national liberation would result in the rules being imposed on states but not on national liberation movements.[57] Accordingly, a provision was added to Additional Protocol I by which the national liberation movement is required to undertake to apply the Geneva Conventions and the Additional Protocol. Rather unusually, the provision was drafted during informal consultations among delegates and without reference to a working group.[58] Furthermore, a vote was taken on the provision in Committee without discussion of its substance, a decision that proved controversial.[59] Despite the controversy, the provision was adopted at the Committee stage by 50 votes in favour, 0 against, and 14 abstentions.[60] In plenary, the provision was adopted by 93 votes in favour, 1 against, and 2 abstentions.[61] The provision—Article 96(3)—provides that '[t]he authority representing a people engaged against a High Contracting Party in an armed conflict of the type referred to in Article 1, paragraph 4, may undertake to apply the Conventions and this Protocol in relation to that conflict by means of a unilateral declaration addressed to the depositary'.

An Article 96(3) declaration contains two key elements. First, the author of the declaration must be an authority representing a people. Although the text refers to '*the* authority', a declaration should not be limited to a single authority provided there is more than one authority representing or purporting to represent a people. In the case of multiple national liberation movements, each with their own domestic constituencies, each may make an Article 96(3) declaration, whether jointly or severally.[62] However, were the national liberation movements to fight one another, as was the case with the Movimento Popular de Libertação de Angola (MPLA), the Frente Nacional de Libertação de Angola (FNLA), and the União Nacional para a Independência Total de Angola (UNITA), following the independence of Angola, this would take the conflict outside the scope of Article 96(3), given its reference to an engagement 'against a High Contracting Party'. Such a conflict would be a non-international armed conflict between the various movements. The second element is that the declaration must be addressed to the depositary, namely the Swiss Federal Council. Thus, at a formal level,

---

[56] Above, 197.
[57] Abi-Saab, Development, above note 12, 162.
[58] *Official Records*, above note 13, Vol 9, 364, para 61. See Bothe, Partsch, and Solf, above note 39, 555.
[59] See eg *Official Records*, above note 13, Vol 9, 365–7, paras 67, 72, 73, 74, 78, 79, 81.
[60] Ibid, 365, para 71.
[61] Ibid, Vol 6, 353, para 75.
[62] See ICRC, *Commentary on the Additional Protocols*, above note 34, 1088–9; R Ranjeva, 'Peoples and National Liberation Movements', in M Bedjaoui, *International Law: Achievements and Prospects* (Martinus Nijhoff, Dordrecht, 1991) 101, 108.

at least, declarations addressed to the ICRC, a UN entity, or another body would not satisfy the Article 96(3) requirement. However, if the only thing impeding the validity of the declaration is the entity to which it is addressed, it would be overly formalistic to require the declaration to be resubmitted to the depositary.[63] Although, as a strict matter of law, the declaration has to be addressed to the depositary, what should be the crucial feature is the public nature of the declaration and that the parent state has knowledge of its existence.

It has been suggested that no declarations pursuant to Article 96(3) have been made.[64] However, this is not the case, and attempts have indeed been made by some groups to issue Article 96(3) declarations. For example, the NDFP sought to deposit a unilateral declaration and there are reports that certain Chechen armed groups have done likewise.[65] However, none of the declarations have been successful to date.[66] Some do not take effect because the states against which the groups are in conflict are not parties to Additional Protocol I; hence there is no High Contracting Party involved in the conflict. Thus, the 1996 NDFP declaration of acceptance could not be effectual due to the fact that the Philippines was not a party to Additional Protocol I. The fact that Article 1(4) does not reflect customary international law also militates against the successful issuance of these declarations. Other declarations are issued in relation to states that are not considered to be colonial dominators, alien occupiers, or racist regimes. Regardless, it is unfortunate that Article 96(3) declarations remain hidden.

Once the conditions of Article 1(4) and Article 96(3) are met, the Geneva Conventions and Additional Protocol I enter into force in respect of the national liberation movement. The national liberation movement then has the same rights and obligations as the state against which it is in conflict.[67]

Certain conditions are *not* required for the application of Article 1(4) or for an Article 96(3) declaration to take effect. The national liberation movement need not control territory,[68] as it obtains its authority from the people it represents and not from the territory it controls.[69] Similarly, national liberation movements do not need to be recognized by a regional intergovernmental organization in order for Article 1(4) to apply or for the purposes of an Article 96(3) declaration.[70] A proposal was made to this effect during the Diplomatic Conference;[71] however, it was not adopted. Recognition would serve to limit application given that certain regions do not benefit from a regional inter-governmental organization, and national liberation movements that fight against a member state of a regional inter-governmental organization may not be recognized by the organization, as was the case with the Polisario Front of

---

[63] Abi-Saab, *RdC*, above note 12, fn 113.
[64] See eg V Bílková, 'Treat Them as They Deserve?! Three Approaches to Armed Opposition Groups under Current International Law' (2010) 4 *Human Rights and International Legal Discourse* 111, 120.
[65] NDFP Declaration of Undertaking to Apply the Geneva Conventions of 1949 and Protocol I of 1977, 5 July 1996. On Chechnya, see N Quénivet, 'The Moscow Hostage Crisis in the Light of the Armed Conflict in Chechnya' (2001) 4 *YIHL* 348, 353.
[66] Higgins, *Regulating the Use of Force*, above note 2, 119, referring to a 2007 communication of the Deputy Head of the Treaty Section of the Federal Department of Foreign Affairs of Switzerland.
[67] Article 96(3).
[68] Wilson, *National Liberation Movements*, above note 34, 166. Cf Y Dinstein, 'Commentary' (1981–2) 31 *American University Law Review* 849, 850–1.
[69] Abi-Saab, *RdC*, above note 12, 410–12; Provost, *International Human Rights and Humanitarian Law*, above note 55, 256–60.
[70] ICRC *Commentary on the Additional Protocols*, above note 34, 53 and 1088–9.
[71] *Official Records*, above note 13, Vol 3, 8 (Turkey).

Western Sahara.[72] Thus, although some states require recognition by a regional intergovernmental organization,[73] it is not a requirement as a matter of law, although in practice, recognition would be of help.

The approach taken to national liberation movements and non-state armed groups are thus fundamentally different. Non-state armed groups are required to possess a certain degree of organization in order for the law of non-international armed conflict to apply. They must also carry out a certain level of violence. National liberation movements are treated rather differently. They are judged on the basis of their representing a people. Furthermore, the possibility of national liberation movements committing themselves to respect international humanitarian law is built into the architecture of the conventional instruments. Article 96(3) of Additional Protocol I explicitly envisages the submission of a declaration to the depositary. Non-state armed groups may also publish declarations committing to apply international humanitarian law, but such declarations remain outside the traditional architecture of international humanitarian law. Nonetheless, the practical effect of the law governing wars of national liberation is extremely limited.

3. Outside state intervention

The involvement of an outside state in non-international armed conflicts is not at all unusual. During the Cold War, some form of outside state involvement was almost a feature of seemingly non-international armed conflicts. This has continued despite the conclusion of the Cold War. The involvement of outside states takes a number of different forms. It includes the provision of finance, arms, and equipment; the training and instruction of combat personnel; assistance with logistics or tactics; and the actual provision of troops. It is not the case that each of these forms of involvement suffices to transform a non-international armed conflict into an international one or to subject the conflict to the law of international armed conflict. The situations in which they do so are the subject of the section that follows.

3.1 Intervention through troops

The intervention of an outside state with its troops[74] is by no means an infrequent occurrence. To take two recent examples, NATO was involved in the post-2001 armed conflict in Afghanistan, in part, at the request of the Government of Afghanistan; NATO was also involved in the 2011 armed conflict in Libya, which started out between the Government of Libya and the Transitional National Council.

An armed conflict that appears, at first sight, to be a non-international armed conflict may nevertheless be subject to the law of international armed conflict when an outside state 'intervenes in that conflict through its troops'.[75] The party on whose side the outside state intervenes will be determinative in identifying the applicable law.

There are two principal approaches to the impact of intervention through troops on the characterization of a conflict. The first approach holds that the conflict has to be

---

[72] Schindler, Armed Conflicts, above note 2, 142–3; Abi-Saab, *RdC*, above note 12, 408–9.
[73] *Official Records*, above note 13, Vol 6, 55, para 121 (Turkey); 62–3 (Indonesia); Vol 9, 366, para 76 (Mauritania); 375, para 29 (Oman). See also Declaration of Belgium on ratification of the Additional Protocols, in Schindler and Toman, above note 33, 796.
[74] As will be discussed below, this is not limited to ground troops.
[75] *Prosecutor v Tadić*, IT-94-1-A, Judgment, 15 July 1999, para 84.

divided into its component parts. The theory of pairings is utilized, such that intervention by an outside state on the side of the government forces does not transform the conflict into an international one because the fighting remains between a state and a non-state armed group.[76] By contrast, when an outside state intervenes on the side of the armed group, the fighting that takes place between the government forces and the outside state is subject to the law of international armed conflict, while the fighting that ensues between the government forces and the non-state armed group remains subject to the law of non-international armed conflict. Thus, in respect of NATO's 1999 intervention in Kosovo, Germany took the view that the conflict between NATO and the Federal Republic of Yugoslavia was an international armed conflict, while the conflict between the Federal Republic of Yugoslavia and the Kosovo Liberation Army (KLA) was a non-international armed conflict.[77] This had also been the approach taken by the International Court of Justice (ICJ) in its 1986 judgment in *Nicaragua*, with the conflict between the Government of Nicaragua and the contras being considered a non-international armed conflict and the conflict between the United States and Nicaragua an international armed conflict.[78] Such a possibility was also left open by the International Criminal Tribunal for the former Yugoslavia (ICTY) in *Tadić*.[79] This 'pairings' approach makes considerable sense, for it best reflects the actual relationships between the various warring parties and, in theory at least, the various parties are distinct from one another. It also makes practical sense, given that the parent government may be unlikely to afford combatant immunity to captured fighters of the armed group, which would be the consequence were the entire conflict to be considered an international one.

The second approach holds that intervention on the part of troops of an outside state renders the entire armed conflict international in character, irrespective of the side on which the outside state intervenes. This approach had been posited from time to time at conferences of government experts in the late 1960s and early 1970s.[80] However, it had been rejected for fear that it would serve to encourage armed groups to resort to outside assistance.[81] The position re-emerged in the 1990s in the jurisprudence of the

---

[76] Conference of Government Experts on the Reaffirmation and Development of International Humanitarian Law Applicable in Armed Conflicts (Geneva, 24 May–12 June 1971): Submitted by the International Committee of the Red Cross (1971) Part V: Protection of Victims of Non-International Armed Conflicts, 19; D Bindschedler-Robert, 'A Reconsideration of the Law of Armed Conflicts', in *The Law of Armed Conflicts* (Carnegie Endowment for International Peace, 1971) 52–3; Schindler, Armed Conflicts, above note 2, 150; L Moir, *The Law of Internal Armed Conflict* (Cambridge University Press, 2002) 51.

[77] See (1999) 2 *YIHL* 325, 364.

[78] *Military and Paramilitary Activities in and against Nicaragua* [1986] ICJ Rep 14, para 219.

[79] *Prosecutor v Tadić*, IT-94-1-AR72, Decision on the Defence Motion for Interlocutory Appeal on Jurisdiction, 2 October 1995, para 72.

[80] 'Protection of Victims of Non-International Conflicts' (1969) 9 *IRRC* 343, 346; ICRC, Reaffirmation and Development of the Laws and Customs Applicable in Armed Conflicts (May 1969) 101; Conference of Government Experts on the Reaffirmation and Development of International Humanitarian Law Applicable in Armed Conflicts (Geneva, 24 May–12 June 1971): Submitted by the International Committee of the Red Cross (1971) Part V: Protection of Victims of Non-International Armed Conflicts, 19; Respect for Human Rights in Armed Conflicts: Report of the Secretary-General, A/8052, 18 September 1970, para 146. See also T Farer, 'Humanitarian Law and Armed Conflicts: Toward the Definition of "International Armed Conflict"' (1971) 71 *Columbia Law Review* 37, 69; H-P Gasser, 'Internationalized Non-International Armed Conflicts: Case Studies of Afghanistan, Kampuchea, and Lebanon' (1983–4) 33 *American University Law Review* 145, 147.

[81] ICRC, Conference of Government Experts on the Reaffirmation and Development of International Humanitarian Law Applicable in Armed Conflicts (Geneva, 24 May–12 June 1971): Report on the Work of the Conference (August 1971) paras 290 and 301. See also ICRC, Conference of

ICTY. Certain ICTY trial chambers have even suggested that involvement of foreign troops in one fight could have the effect of internationalizing another, separate fight.[82] Thus, in *Kordić and Čerkez*, the Trial Chamber found that the Croatian Army, by fighting Serb forces in Bosnia, internationalized the conflict between Bosnian Croats and Bosnian Muslims as it 'freed up' Bosnian Croats who would otherwise have had to fight Serb forces as well.[83] This extends things considerably.[84] This second approach is easier to apply on the ground than the pairings approach, as it may not always be possible to distinguish between the various parties. However, in practice, states may be unwilling to afford combatant immunity to captured fighters of the armed group. It is understandable why the ICTY took the view that it did, given the facts of the conflicts in the former Yugoslavia. Nonetheless, as Judge Shahabuddeen has observed, 'it is difficult to see why an on-going internal armed conflict should suddenly and necessarily lose that character altogether because of foreign intervention'.[85] Furthermore, there are limits to extrapolating from one situation, in this case the conflicts in the former Yugoslavia, to another, or to generalize from a particular situation.

It is submitted that neither the 'pairings' approach nor the 'complete internationalization' approach can be applied satisfactorily to each and every situation. The facts of one particular intervention may point to the pairings approach whereas those of another may point to the complete internationalization approach. For example, if an outside state intervenes on the side of the government, the conflict remains a non-international one, as the relationship on both fronts is one of a state fighting a non-state armed group. If an outside state intervenes on the side of the non-state armed group against the government, much will turn on the relationship between the intervening state and the non-state armed group. If there is little interaction between them, in essence, two distinct armed conflicts are being fought, one between the non-state armed group and the government and the other between the government and the intervening state. In such a situation, it would be sensible to adopt the pairings approach. If, on the other hand, there is a close relationship between the armed group and the intervening state, with the actions of the two being closely related and coordinated, it would be sensible to adopt the complete internationalization approach, even if the close relation and coordination does not amount to the state exercising overall control over the armed group.[86] The crucial question is whether a single armed conflict is being fought, albeit with multiple actors participating in it, or whether parallel armed conflicts are taking place, albeit with some associations between them. In the end, the facts will prove decisive. The situation in Libya during the 2011 violence is

---

Government Experts on the Reaffirmation and Development of International Humanitarian Law Applicable in Armed Conflicts, Second Session (3 May–3 June 1972), Report on the Work of the Conference, Volume I (July 1972) 97–100.

[82] *Prosecutor v Blaskić*, IT-95-14-T, Judgment, 3 March 2000, para 94; *Prosecutor v Kordić and Čerkez*, IT-95-14/2-T, Judgment, 26 February 2001, paras 108–9. See also GH Aldrich, 'The Laws of War on Land' (2000) 94 *AJIL* 42, 63; C Byron, 'Armed Conflicts: International or Non-International?' (2001) 6 *JCSL* 63, 82.

[83] *Kordić and Čerkez* Trial Judgment, paras 108–9.

[84] See J Stewart, 'Towards a Single Definition of Armed Conflict in International Humanitarian Law: A Critique of Internationalized Armed Conflict' (2003) 85 *IRRC* 313, 328–33.

[85] *Blaskić* Trial Judgment, Declaration of Judge Shahabuddeen. See also C Greenwood, 'International Humanitarian Law and the *Tadić* Case' (1996) 7 *EJIL* 265, 269–72.

[86] On which, see below, 225–8. See, on NATO's 1999 intervention in Kosovo, C Greenwood, 'The Applicability of International Humanitarian Law and the Law of Neutrality to the Kosovo Campaign', in AE Wall (ed), *Legal and Ethical Lessons of NATO's Kosovo Campaign* (Volume 78 International Law Studies, Naval War College, 2002) 35, 44–6.

a case in point. Pursuant to Security Council Resolution 1973 (2011), NATO intervened in the hostilities in Libya in order to protect civilians. It did so on the side of the forces of the National Transitional Council (NTC) against the forces of the Government of President Gaddafi. The question that arises is whether the involvement of NATO internationalized the entire conflict or whether an international armed conflict existed between NATO and the Government of Libya alongside a non-international armed conflict that existed between the Government of Libya and the NTC. The answer depends on the relationship between NATO and the NTC, on which the facts are murky.

From the jurisprudence of the ICTY, the nature and level of the outside state troop participation necessary in order to modify the character of the conflict can be identified. The ICTY has considered the presence of soldiers and units on the territory in question, even if not in every area, to be determinative.[87] In *Rajić*, the Trial Chamber held that the 'significant and continuous military action' of the intervening troops was sufficient to internationalize the armed conflict.[88] The Trial Chamber referred to the 5,000–7,000 troops of the Croatian army that were located on Bosnian territory to support the Bosnian Croats and which were involved in the conflict against Bosnian government forces.[89] Intervention through troops is not limited to ground forces but would include support through air forces, for example in the form of a bombing campaign.[90] Thus, the NATO air campaign in Libya during the 2011 conflict could have served to internationalize that conflict, although as indicated above, this depends on the relationship between NATO and the NTC and associated forces. It has also been suggested that it is necessary to consider such factors as the 'dimensions, scope and duration of a foreign military intervention, the foreign state's direct participation in the hostilities, the nature of the states and political entities involved in the conflict [and] their recognition by other states'.[91] It is, then, essentially a fact-based issue for determination.

3.2 State control over an armed group

Intervention with troops is not the only way through which outside state intervention in a non-international armed conflict transforms it into an international armed conflict. If an outside state controls the armed group, that control may serve to transform the conflict into an international one. Quite what level of control is required to transform the situation has proven controversial.

In *Nicaragua*, the ICJ had to consider whether the United States' support for the contra rebels of Nicaragua meant that the acts of the contras could be attributed to the United States for the purposes of state responsibility. The Court set out two tests to determine the issue.[92] The Court noted that, first, it had to determine 'whether or not the relationship of the contras to the US Government was so much one of dependence

---

[87] *Prosecutor v Naletilić and Martinović*, IT-98-34-T, Judgment, 31 March 2003, paras 191, 194.
[88] *Prosecutor v Rajić and Andrić*, IT-95-12-R61, Review of the Indictment pursuant to Rule 61 of the Rules of Procedure and Evidence, 13 September 1996, para 13.
[89] Ibid.
[90] R Cryer, 'The Fine Art of Friendship: *Jus in Bello* in Afghanistan' (2002) 7 *JCSL* 37, 44–5.
[91] T Meron, 'Classification of Armed Conflict in the former Yugoslavia: *Nicaragua*'s Fallout' (1998) 92 *AJIL* 236, 241.
[92] See *Case Concerning the Application of the Convention on the Prevention and Punishment of the Crime of (Bosnia Herzegovina v Serbia and Montenegro)* [2007] ICJ Rep 43, paras 384–407; M Milanović, 'State Responsibility for Genocide' (2006) 17 *EJIL* 553, 576.

on the one side and control on the other that it would be right to equate the contras, for legal purposes, with an organ of the US Government, or as acting on behalf of that Government'.[93] Answering the question in the negative, the Court then went on to consider a second test, namely whether the United States 'had effective control of the military or paramilitary operations in the course of which the alleged violations were committed'.[94] Although the tests were set out in order to determine state responsibility, they have been considered relevant for the internationalization of an armed conflict.[95] According to the Appeals Chamber in *Tadić*, a common issue connects state responsibility with the internationalization of an armed conflict, namely:

> the question . . . of establishing the criteria for the legal imputability to a State of acts performed by individuals not having the status of State officials. In the one case these acts, if they prove to be attributable to a State, will give rise to the international responsibility of that State; in the other case, they will ensure that the armed conflict must be classified as international.[96]

This commonality has been questioned;[97] however, irrespective of its correctness, what is better accepted is the test set out by the *Tadić* Appeals Chamber on the internationalization of an armed conflict. The Appeals Chamber held that, in order for a non-international armed conflict to be rendered international through the control exercised by an outside state over an armed group, the state should exercise:

> overall control over the group, not only by equipping and financing the group, but also by coordinating or helping in the general planning of its military activity . . . However, it is not necessary that, in addition, the State should also issue, either to the head or to members of the group, instructions for the commission of specific acts contrary to international law.[98]

The Appeals Chamber continued:

> Under international law it is by no means necessary that the controlling authorities should plan all the operations of the units dependent on them, choose their targets, or give specific instructions concerning the conduct of military operations and any alleged violations of international humanitarian law. The control required by international law may be deemed to exist when a State (or, in the context of an armed conflict, the Party to the conflict) *has a role in organizing, coordinating or planning the military actions* of the military group, in addition to financing, training and equipping or providing operational support to that group.[99]

The holding of the Appeals Chamber has been followed in the subsequent jurisprudence of the ICTY,[100] by the International Criminal Court (ICC),[101] and in the

---

[93] *Nicaragura*, above note 78, 62, para 109.
[94] Ibid, 65, para 115.
[95] *Tadić* Trial Judgment, paras 585–607; *Tadić* Appeal Judgment, paras 103–4. See also A Cassese, 'The *Nicaragua* and *Tadić* Tests Revisited in Light of the ICJ Judgment on Genocide in Bosnia' (2007) 18 *EJIL* 649; M Spinedi, 'On the Non-Attribution of the Bosnian Serbs' Conduct to Serbia' (2007) 5 *JICJ* 829.
[96] *Tadić* Appeal Judgment, para 104.
[97] Ibid, Separate Opinion of Judge Shahabuddeen, paras 17–18. See also Meron, Classification, above note 91, 236–40; C Greenwood, 'The Development of International Humanitarian Law by the International Criminal Tribunal for the Former Yugoslavia' (1998) 2 *Max Planck Yearbook of United Nations Law* 97, 119–21; Milanović, State Responsibility, above note 92, 576 and 585.
[98] *Tadić* Appeal Judgment, para 131.
[99] Ibid, para 137. The *Tadić* Appeals Chamber also set out tests for the exercise of control, not over an armed group, but over private individuals or groups that are not organized military, as well as for the assimilation of individuals to state organs.
[100] See eg *Blaskić* Trial Judgment, paras 96–123.
[101] *Prosecutor v Lubanga Dyilo*, ICC-01/04-01/06, Decision on the Confirmation of Charges, 29 January 2007, paras 210–11.

reports of commissions of inquiry.[102] In the *Bosnia Genocide* case, the ICJ noted that '[i]nsofar as the "overall control" test is employed to determine whether or not an armed conflict is international ... it may well be that the test is applicable and suitable', although the Court reserved its position on the point as the matter was not at issue before it.[103]

It is submitted that, ultimately, the disagreement as to whether the relevant test is one of 'effective control' or, rather, whether it is one of 'overall control' disguises what is in fact the real question. As Judge Shahabuddeen indicated in *Blaskić*, the real question relates to 'the degree of control which is effective in any set of circumstances to enable the impugned state to use force against the other state through the intermediary of the foreign military entity concerned'.[104] It is this notion of a proxy that transforms what seems to be a conflict that is fought between a state and an armed group into a conflict that is actually being fought between states. The involvement of an outside state in a non-international armed conflict, even without the presence of the troops of that state on the ground, may thus amount to an international armed conflict because, in reality, the fight is between two states albeit through the use of a proxy. Viewed in this manner, the 'dependence and control' test of the Court seems too strict, while the 'organization and coordination' test of the Tribunal seems not strict enough.

Ultimately, the relationship between an outside state and an armed group could take a number of forms and the conflict could still amount to one that is fought between two states. The armed group could be an agent of the outside state, the agency relationship being such that the principal carries out the violence albeit through its agent. The armed group could be identified with the armed forces of the outside state to such a degree that it proves impossible to distinguish between the two. This may arise due to a seamless relationship between the two, for example through the sharing of key positions, or the ease of transfer of individuals from one entity to the other. The armed group could be so dependent on the outside state for financing, direction, and strategy that its actions amount to those of the state. Ultimately, then, whether framed in terms of effective control, overall control, or something entirely different, it comes down to the question identified by Judge Shahabuddeen, namely whether the degree of control is such that the one state is, in essence, using force against another state. Accordingly, it is not an 'overall' or 'effective' control test that would resolve the issue but the facts on the ground and the indicia at play.

What has to be determined is whether the armed group is acting as a proxy for the state, or rather whether the two are but extremely close allies. In this regard, the indicia that have been used by the Court and the Tribunal are pertinent. The indicia that aid determination of the issue include the creation of the armed group by the outside state;[105] the transfer of officials from the armed forces of the outside state to the armed group;[106] the appointment by the outside state of individuals at high-level positions within the armed group,[107] or the sharing of forces;[108] financing,[109] or the payment of

---

[102] Report of the International Commission of Inquiry on Darfur to the Secretary-General, S/2005/60, 1 February 2005, para 123; Independent International Fact-Finding Mission on the Conflict in Georgia, Report: Volume II, September 2009, 301–4.
[103] *Bosnia Genocide*, above note 92, para 404.
[104] *Blaskić* Trial Judgment, Declaration of Judge Shahabuddeen (emphasis removed).
[105] *Nicaragua*, above note 78, 54–5, para 94.
[106] *Tadić* Appeal Judgment, para 150; *Kordić* Trial Judgment, paras 124–32. See also *Kordić* Appeal Judgment, paras 362–9.
[107] *Nicaragua*, 63 (political leaders); *Naletilić* Trial Judgment, para 201.
[108] *Blaskić* Trial Judgment, para 114.
[109] *Naletilić* Trial Judgment, para 199.

wages of members of the armed group by the outside state;[110] the shared military objectives and strategies of the outside state and the armed group;[111] the identical structure and ranks of the outside state and the armed group;[112] and the direction, supervision, or command of the armed group by the outside state,[113] the coordination of decisions,[114] or the dependence of the armed group on the state.[115] The *Tadić* Appeals Chamber also indicated that '[w]here the controlling State in question is an adjacent State with territorial ambitions on the State where the conflict is taking place, and the controlling State is attempting to achieve its territorial enlargement through the armed forces which it controls, it may be easier to establish the threshold'.[116] These indicia are eminently useful. However, a certain care needs to be taken when considering them. When a state disintegrates and new states are formed on the relevant territory, 'the armed forces of the former central State necessarily have many links with the former central authorities which are now foreign authorities. As such links are inherent in the situation, they are not necessarily an indication of control'.[117] This will be particularly true of such things as identical structure and ranks as between the state and the armed group.

4. Transnational armed conflicts

It has been suggested in recent years that, in addition to international armed conflicts and non-international armed conflicts, a third type of armed conflict exists, one that is extra-state or transnational in character.[118] These conflicts, which are fought between a state and a non-state armed group and which straddle an international border, are considered to be of a sufficiently different character from both non-international armed conflicts and international armed conflicts as to warrant their different regulation. In 2002, the Government of the United States took the view that such conflicts were neither international armed conflicts, as they did not involve two or more High Contracting Parties, nor were they non-international armed conflicts, as they were not purely internal in character.[119] Contrary to that determination, it is submitted that

---

[110] *Tadić* Appeal Judgment, para 150; *Kordić* Trial Judgment, para 127; *Kordić* Appeal Judgment, para 366; *Naletilić* Trial Judgment, para 199.
[111] *Tadić* Appeal Judgment, para 151; *Blaskić* Trial Judgment, para 108; *Naletilić* Trial Judgment, paras 200–1.
[112] *Tadić* Appeal Judgment, para 151.
[113] *Tadić* Appeal Judgment, para 151; *Naletilić* Trial Judgment, paras 197–202.
[114] *Naletilić* Trial Judgment, para 200.
[115] *Nicaragua*, 62, para 109.
[116] *Tadić* Appeal Judgment, para 140. See also *Kordić* Trial Judgment, paras 124–5, 133–7, and 142. See also *Kordić* Appeal Judgment, paras 366–7, 370.
[117] M Sassòli, 'The Legal Qualification of the Conflicts in the Former Yugoslavia: Double Standards or New Horizons for International Humanitarian Law?', in S Yee and W Tieya (eds), *International Law in the Post-Cold War World: Essays in Memory of Li Haopei* (Routledge, 2001) 307, 327.
[118] See, in particular, RS Schöndorf, 'Extra-State Armed Conflicts: Is there a Need for a New Legal Regime?' (2004) 37 *New York University Journal of International Law and Politics* 1; G Corn and E Talbot, 'Transnational Armed Conflict: A Principled Approach to the Regulation of Counter-Terror Combat Operations' (2009) 42 *Israel Law Review* 46. See also C Kreß, 'Some Reflections on the International Legal Framework Governing Transnational Armed Conflicts' (2010) 15 *JCSL* 245.
[119] US Department of Justice Office of Legal Counsel, Memorandum for Alberto R Gonzales Counsel to the President, and William J Haynes II General Counsel of the Department of Defense, Re: Application of Treaties and Laws to al Qaeda and Taliban Detainees, 22 January 2002, reprinted in KJ Greenberg and JL Dratel (eds), *The Torture Papers* (Cambridge University Press, 2005) 81; Memorandum for the Vice President and Others, 7 February 2002, reprinted in ibid, 134.

the better view is that, from a legal standpoint, such conflicts are but a subset of the category of non-international armed conflict, even if, from a descriptive perspective, they can be characterized as transnational armed conflicts.

The law of non-international armed conflict does not require that the violence be of a purely internal character, that is to say confined within the borders of a single state. The language of certain instruments may, at first sight, point towards this conclusion; however such language has the potential to mislead, the emphasis laying elsewhere. Common Article 3 refers to cases 'of armed conflict not of an international character occurring in the territory of one of the High Contracting Parties', while Additional Protocol II references armed conflicts 'which take place in the territory of a High Contracting Party'.[120] The references to territory in these instruments were included in order to distinguish between armed conflicts that take place on the territory of states parties to the Conventions and Protocol and armed conflicts that take place on the territory of non-states parties.[121] The Conventions and Protocol are applicable to the former but not to the latter. The emphasis thus lies on the phrase 'High Contracting Parties' rather than on 'one of' or 'a'.

Such a conclusion is reached through a consideration of the drafting history of the provisions. The 1946 Preliminary Conference of National Red Cross Societies proposed the application of the Conventions '[i]n the case of armed conflict within the borders of a State',[122] and the accompanying report likewise referred to civil wars 'within the frontiers of a State'.[123] The rules were thus considered to apply to conflicts that were wholly internal in character. However, that scope of application was rejected. The report on the 1947 Conference of Government Experts, for example, provided that '[t]he treaty stipulations in question are binding upon the contracting party, on the sole condition that they be applied by the adverse party, *wherever the civil war may take place*'.[124] Furthermore, the 1948 draft Convention provided that the non-international armed conflict 'may occur in the territory of *one or more* of the High Contracting Parties'.[125] This was considered and approved by the International Conference of the Red Cross in Stockholm,[126] and it was these drafts that were put before the Diplomatic Conference of 1949. The fact that the language emphasized above was included in the drafts suggests that it was a direct response to the earlier drafts that required the violence to be wholly internal. It also suggests that, contrary to certain views, the fact that a civil

---

[120] Common Article 3; Additional Protocol II, Article 1.
[121] M Sassòli, 'Transnational Armed Groups and International Humanitarian Law', Harvard University Program on Humanitarian Policy and Conflict Research, Occasional Paper Series, Winter 2006, No 6, 9; N Melzer, *Targeted Killing in International Law* (Oxford University Press, 2008) 258. But cf Moir, *Internal Armed Conflict*, above note 76, 31; A Paulus and M Vashakmadze, 'Asymmetrical War and the Notion of Armed Conflict—A Tentative Conceptualization' (2009) 91 *IRRC* 95, 110; R Geiß, 'Armed Violence in Fragile States: Low-Intensity Conflicts, Spillover Conflicts, and Sporadic Law Enforcement Operations by Third Parties' (2009) 91 *IRRC* 127, 137–8; L Arimatsu, 'Territory, Boundaries and the Law of Armed Conflict' (2009) 12 *YIHL* 157, 186.
[122] ICRC, Report on the Work of the Preliminary Conference of National Red Cross Societies for the study of the Conventions and of various Problems relative to the Red Cross (Geneva, July 26–August 3, 1946) (1947) 15.
[123] Ibid.
[124] ICRC, Report on the Work of the Conference of Government Experts for the Study of the Conventions for the Protection of War Victims (Geneva, April 14–26, 1947) (1947) 9 (emphasis added).
[125] ICRC, *Draft Revised or New Conventions for the Protection of War Victims* (1948) 5 (emphasis added).
[126] See ICRC, *Revised and New Draft Conventions for the Protection of War Victims* (1948) 10, 32, 51–2, 114.

war may cross an international border was expressly considered at the relevant time and it was not simply presumed that civil wars would be confined to the territory of a single state. Indeed, civil wars that took place immediately prior to the Diplomatic Conference had a cross-border element; for example, Portuguese ports were used by the rebels during the Spanish civil war (1936–9).[127] The wording that would emerge from the Diplomatic Conference varied from that put before it. However, nothing in the records suggest that the change resulted from the view that the violence should be confined within the boundaries of a single state.[128] The delimitation that was sought was between states parties and non-states parties and the modified wording resulted from the usual workings of diplomatic conferences. Importantly, the treaty rules do not refer to armed conflicts fought within a *single* High Contracting Party or within the territory of one High Contracting Party *alone*, both of which would suggest territorial limits.

Today, with the universal ratification of common Article 3 through state ratification of at least one of the Geneva Conventions, the reference to High Contracting Parties has lost much of its importance; all states are parties to common Article 3. Thus, the ICRC has noted that 'any armed conflict between governmental armed forces and armed groups or between such groups cannot but take place on the territory of one of the Parties to the Convention'.[129] The point retains some importance insofar as Additional Protocol II is concerned, although this is mitigated by the customary status of many of the Additional Protocol II norms.[130]

The conclusion that the violence need not be confined within the borders of a single state can be reached through a different line of reasoning. A non-international armed conflict that spills outside territorial boundaries, and a conflict that is fought on territorial waters but which extends to the high seas, would both remain covered by common Article 3, even that part of the fighting that takes place outside state territory. Likewise, conflicts with a more clearly defined cross-border element are covered by the conventional rules, provided they involve a High Contracting Party. It is not at all unusual for members of a non-state armed group to be based in the border regions of a neighbouring state. For example, in the 2000s, members of the FARC were based at the Colombia/Ecuador border in Ecuadorian territory, and Colombian forces entered Ecuadorian territory to fight FARC fighters who were based there. Similarly, the Lord's Resistance Army (LRA) had a base in South Sudan and would cross the border into Uganda to carry out hostilities. Decades earlier, during the Algerian war of independence, the Armée de Libération Nationale (ALN) had bases in Tunisia, from which attacks were launched against French troops in Algeria.[131] Despite their very real cross-border elements, the non-international character of the Colombia/FARC armed conflict or the Uganda/LRA armed conflict is not seriously challenged.[132]

---

[127] AVW Thomas and AJ Thomas Jr, 'International Legal Aspects of the Civil War in Spain, 1936–39', in RA Falk (ed), *The International Law of Civil War* (Johns Hopkins Press, 1971) 111, 114.

[128] See also, reaching the same conclusion, Melzer, *Targeted Killing*, above note 121, 257; J Pejić, 'The Protective Scope of Common Article 3: More than Meets the Eye' (2011) 93 *IRRC* 189, 199–200.

[129] 'How is the Term "Armed Conflict" Defined in International Humanitarian Law?: International Committee of the Red Cross (ICRC) Opinion Paper', March 2008, 3. See also Melzer, *Targeted Killing*, above note 121, 259; N Lubell, *Extraterritorial Use of Force against Non-State Actors* (Oxford University Press, 2010) 101–4.

[130] See generally Chapters 8 and 9.

[131] A Fraleigh, 'The Algerian Revolution as a Case Study in International Law', in RA Falk (ed), *The International Law of Civil War* (Johns Hopkins University Press, 1971) 179, 206.

[132] See, for additional examples, Schöndorf, Extra-State Armed Conflicts, above note 118, 9; Melzer, *Targeted Killing*, above note 121, 260.

The line of reasoning set out above in respect of common Article 3 may, it is submitted, apply equally to Additional Protocol II. That Protocol provides that it 'shall apply to all armed conflicts which...take place in the territory of a High Contracting Party between its armed forces and dissident armed forces or other organized armed groups' subject to the existence of certain conditions. This formulation has been taken to mean that the Protocol is inapplicable to 'transnational' armed conflicts, as such conflicts do not '"take place" in the territory of *a* High Contracting Party between *its* armed forces and dissident armed forces or other organized armed groups'.[133] However, it is submitted that, provided some part of the hostilities takes place on the territory of a High Contracting Party, the conflict may be governed by Additional Protocol II. Thus, if a non-state armed group that is based in state A, commits hostilities that amount to an armed conflict on the territory of the High Contracting Party B, the Protocol requirements are satisfied. The conflict takes place in the territory of a High Contracting Party and is fought between its armed forces and an armed group. The question then becomes whether the Protocol is applicable to those parts of the hostilities that take place in state A. It would be curious to hold that those hostilities are not governed by the Protocol with the applicable law being modified at the border. Furthermore, the provision can be read as stating that, provided the conflict takes place in the territory of a High Contracting Party (state B) between that Party's armed forces and an armed group, the Protocol governs all hostilities relating to the conflict, including those outside the territory of the Party. The focus is thus placed on the words 'armed conflicts' rather than 'in the territory' and 'its armed forces'. Once the conditions of the provision are met, the Protocol is applicable to all aspects of the conflict, regardless of whether or not the hostilities cross a geographical border.

What does constitute a potential hurdle to the applicability of Additional Protocol II to transnational armed conflicts is whether the conflict is fought between High Contracting Party X against non-state armed group Y in the territory of state Y. In this situation, a conflict is not taking place in the territory of a High Contracting Party between *its* armed forces and an armed group. However, it is curious for the Protocol not to apply to such a conflict when it would be applicable were the conflict to move to the territory of state X. The location of the fighting should not prove determinative.

A further difficulty is the requirement that the armed group 'exercise such control over a part of [the High Contracting Party's] territory as to enable them to carry out sustained and concerted military operations and to implement this Protocol'. In many a transnational conflict, the armed group will be unlikely to exercise such territorial control. However, this will not always be the case, with the FARC, for example, controlling territory within Colombia while being based in part in Venezuela. Furthermore, it should be recalled that the territorial control is to be exercised 'as to enable' the group to carry out the requisite level of hostilities and implement the Protocol. As discussed above,[134] this can be satisfied with a minimum of territorial control. Thus, it is submitted, Additional Protocol II may be applicable to certain transnational armed conflicts.

Certain leading definitions of a non-international armed conflict have limited the concept to violence that is contained within the boundaries of a state. The *Tadić* definition, for example, provides that 'an armed conflict exists whenever there is a resort to armed force between States or protracted armed violence between governmental

---

[133] Pejić, Common Article 3, above note 128, 201. See also Lubell, *Extraterritorial Use of Force*, above note 129, 100.
[134] See above, 185–7.

authorities and organized armed groups or between such groups within a State'.[135] Similarly, the ICTR has held that a non-international armed conflict is one in which the 'government of a single state [is] in conflict with one or more armed factions within its territory'.[136] However, this is likely due to the fact that, to date, the 'classic' non-international armed conflict has been of the internal variety. Conflicts with a certain overspill have been far from infrequent, but these too have been conceived as internal. Indeed, the ICTR made its pronouncement while the Statute of the Tribunal gives it jurisdiction to try violations of international humanitarian law committed within Rwanda as well as outside Rwanda and in the territory of 'neighbouring states',[137] thus recognizing the 'transnational' aspect of the conflict. The Tribunal also had jurisdiction over certain violations of Additional Protocol II with the same geographical spread. This supports the position set out above, with overspill simply being considered a normal part of an 'internal' conflict and in respect of common Article 3 as well as Additional Protocol II. In sum, it is evident that non-international armed conflicts include both those conflicts that are purely internal in character and those that straddle an international boundary. What separates the non-international armed conflict from the international armed conflict is not its geographical location but the parties to the two sorts of conflicts.[138]

The issue was taken to its extreme with the 'war on terror'. Initially, in early 2002, the US Government under the Bush administration indicated that the 'war against terrorism' was an armed conflict but that it fell into a gap between an international armed conflict and a non-international armed conflict.[139] However, in 2006, the US Supreme Court held that the conflict against Al-Qaeda was a non-international one, noting that non-international armed conflicts are those that do not involve 'a clash between nations'.[140] This correctly focuses the issue on the parties to the violence. However, the precise means by which the Supreme Court reached this conclusion is more open to question. The relevant test considered above must be satisfied, namely the violence must reach a certain level and the armed group must be organized to a certain degree. It is insufficient to hold that an armed conflict exists and because the conflict is not an international one it must be a non-international one. That is not how non-international armed conflicts are identified.[141] Since 2006, various branches of the US Government have indicated that the fight against Al-Qaeda is a non-international armed conflict,[142] although at other times, other branches do not specify the nature of the conflict.[143]

---

[135] *Tadić* Decision on Interlocutory Appeal on Jurisdiction, above note 79, para 70.
[136] *Musema* Trial Judgment, para 247. See also *Niyonteze*, Military Court of Cassation, Decision of 26 May 2000, reproduced in M Sassòli, AA Bouvier, and A Quintin, *How Does Law Protect in War? Volume III* (ICRC, 2011) 2208.
[137] ICTR Statute, Article 1. See Sassòli, Transnational Armed Groups, above note 121, 9.
[138] L Zegveld, *The Accountability of Armed Opposition Groups in International Law* (Cambridge University Press, 2002) 136.
[139] See Memorandum for Alberto Gonzales, above note 119, 81; Memorandum for the Vice President, ibid, 134.
[140] *Hamdan v Rumsfeld* (2006) 126 S Ct 2749, 2757.
[141] See D Kritsiotis, 'The Tremors of Tadić' (2010) 43 *Israel Law Review* 262; S Sivakumaran, 'Re-envisaging the International Law of Internal Armed Conflict: A Rejoinder to Gabriella Blum' (2011) 22 *EJIL* 273.
[142] See eg 'National report submitted in accordance with paragraph 15 (a) of the annex to Human Rights Council resolution 5/1: United States', A/HRC/WG.6/9/USA/1, 23 August 2010, para 84.
[143] See eg HH Koh, 'The Obama Administration and International Law', Speech at the Annual Meeting of the American Society of International Law, 25 March 2010; JO Brennan, 'Strengthening

Dispute has also arisen as to whether there is one armed conflict—a global conflict without defined territorial limits—between the United States and Al-Qaeda;[144] multiple armed conflicts between the United States and Al-Qaeda, for example in Afghanistan, in the Arabian Peninsula, and the like; an armed conflict between the United States and Al-Qaeda in one country but not another; or no armed conflicts aside from those in Afghanistan and Iraq, rather law-enforcement operations against Al-Qaeda.[145] The issue is important as terrorist attacks in and of themselves do not amount to an armed conflict. Thus, on ratification of Additional Protocol I, the United Kingdom introduced a reservation providing that 'the term "armed conflict" of itself and in its context denotes a situation of a kind which is not constituted by the commission of ordinary crimes including acts of terrorism whether concerted or in isolation'.[146]

As indicated above, a non-international armed conflict can have overspill and the overspill remains part of the core conflict. Thus, a conflict between the Governments of Afghanistan, the United States, and others, on the one side, and the Taliban and Al-Qaeda in Afghanistan, on the other, that spills over into Pakistan, remains a non-international armed conflict, including that part which is fought in Pakistan. There is but one conflict that is fought in two places.

Things have the potential to differ where there is not an overspill conflict but where an armed group, such as Al-Qaeda, is based in two or more states. In such a situation, what needs to be established is whether Al-Qaeda in its various locations—Afghanistan, the Arabian Peninsula, and the like—constitutes different groups or whether they are parts of the same group.[147] If it is the same group, then it is submitted that a single conflict exists, albeit the actor is located in different states, as there is a nexus between the violence in the different places. On this basis, a single non-international armed conflict would be fought between the United States and Al-Qaeda, in Afghanistan and in the Arabian Peninsula, with overspill, for example in Pakistan. As it is a single group, its acts in its different locations could be aggregated to determine the intensity of the violence. To take a less controversial example, there is a single non-international armed conflict taking place between the Government of Colombia and the FARC despite the FARC being located in Colombia, and, at various points in time, in the border regions of its neighbour to the north, Venezuela, and to the south, Ecuador. If, on the other hand, Al-Qaeda is not one group but constitutes different groups and affiliates,[148] operating on different territories albeit under the same name, then different situations exist and each would have to satisfy the requisite levels of intensity and organization to amount to non-international armed conflicts. As the groups are different, their acts could not be aggregated to determine the intensity of the violence in question. On this basis, a non-international armed conflict would be fought between the United States and Al-Qaeda in Afghanistan, for example, with overspill in Pakistan, but law-enforcement operations

---

Our Security by Adhering to Our Values and Laws', Speech at Harvard Law School, 16 September 2011.

[144] Authorization for Use of Military Force, 18 September 2001. See also Koh, ibid; Brennan, ibid.

[145] 'International Humanitarian Law and the Challenges of Contemporary Armed Conflicts, Document Prepared by the International Committee of the Red Cross for the 30th International Conference of the Red Cross and Red Crescent, Geneva, Switzerland, 26–30 November 2007' (2007) 89 *IRRC* 719, 724–6.

[146] Reservation of 28 January 1998.

[147] For one view, see Report of the Special Rapporteur on Extrajudicial, Summary or Arbitrary Executions: Study on Targeted Killings, A/HRC/14/24/Add.6, 28 May 2010, para 55.

[148] The language of 'al-Qaida and its affiliates and adherents', which is sometimes used by the United States, would point in this direction. See eg the United States' *National Strategy for Counterterrorism* (June 2011). See further, Lubell, *Extraterritorial Use of Force*, above note 129, 118–20.

would be taking place in the Arabian Peninsula, again to take an example, as the level of violence in the former passes the requisite threshold but in the latter does not.

Three key points thus emerge. First, the facts will prove determinative and many of the controversies are, in fact, factual ones despite being framed as legal ones. If the facts surrounding the identity and structure of Al-Qaeda could be ascertained,[149] many of the legal points fall into place. Second and importantly, the key feature is the nature and identity of the group(s) and not the territory on which they are based. Third, a conflict must have a territorial base whether a single territory, a core territory plus overspill onto different territory, or multiple territories; a global non-international armed conflict does not exist, at least as a matter of law.

Accordingly, the US 'armed conflict with Al-Qaeda', to the extent that it amounts to an armed conflict at all—and that is an important caveat—is of a non-international character. It, too, is an armed conflict that is fought between a state and a non-state armed group which crosses international borders. What differentiates that conflict from the cross-border conflicts such as those involving the LRA and the FARC is that the warring parties are not located in adjacent states and this makes things somewhat unusual. The cross-border element is, then, of a different *degree* of geographical proximity to the typical cross-border non-international armed conflict but it is not of a different *type* as to necessitate it being treated in an altogether different manner.

5. Conclusion

An armed conflict that appears, at first sight, to be a non-international one may amount to an international armed conflict, or at least be subject to the law that governs international armed conflicts, in three distinct ways. First, the parent state may recognize the situation as belligerency. Such a possibility remains today and is canvassed from time to time. However, recognition of belligerency has not taken place since the turn of the last century.

A second way in which the conflict will be regulated by the law of international armed conflict is if it amounts to a war of national liberation. These conflicts are defined narrowly by international humanitarian law, constituting only those conflicts that are fought against colonial domination, alien occupation, and racist regimes. Conflicts falling outside those three categories, including those otherwise fought in pursuance of the right to self-determination, remain subject to the law of non-international armed conflict. Thus, although many an armed group contends that it is fighting for the right to self-determination, this does not, of itself, mean that the conflict is an international one. Furthermore, given that states do not accept that they are a colonial dominator, alien occupier, or racist regime, the impact of the legal regime that governs wars of national liberation is limited.

The most common way in which a non-international armed conflict will be transformed into an international one is through intervention on the part of an outside state. This takes two forms: intervention through the troops of an outside state and outside state control over a non-state armed group. In respect of both forms of intervention, the facts will prove decisive.

---

[149] On which, see eg the debate between Bruce Hoffman and Marc Sageman in 'The Myth of Grassroots Terrorism' (2008) 87 *Foreign Affairs* 133 and 'The Reality of Grass-Roots Terrorism' (2008) 87 *Foreign Affairs* 163.

In recent years, a third type of armed conflict has been posited, one that is described as a transnational armed conflict or an extra-state conflict. Proponents of this category of conflict take the view that they are neither international armed conflicts, as they are fought between a state and a non-state armed group, nor are they non-international armed conflicts, as they cross a state boundary. However, such conflicts are no more than a subset of non-international armed conflicts. Traditional 'internal' armed conflicts have not infrequently had some sort of cross-border component, with the armed group being based on the territory of an adjacent state, or their being some sort of 'overspill'. Although certain recent non-international armed conflicts have involved states and armed groups that are not situated in adjacent territory, the difference is one of degree rather than type.

Having explored the notion of a non-international armed conflict, the remainder of this Part considers the substantive law that governs such conflicts, as well as the scope of application of that law.

7
Scope of Application

1. Introduction

Before considering the substantive rules of the law of non-international armed conflict, it is crucial to ascertain the situations in which the rules apply. This turns, in large part, on the situation being identified as a non-international armed conflict, an issue that was considered in the previous two chapters. In addition to the existence of a non-international armed conflict, other important issues have to be considered, namely the personal, geographic, and temporal scope of application of the rules. In other words, it needs to be established to whom the law applies, both the persons that benefit from it and the persons who are bound by it, the geographical reach of the law, as well as its temporal limits. These issues are the subject of this chapter.

2. Personal scope of application

It is a fundamental rule of international law that treaties are binding on parties to them.[1] Thus, conventional international humanitarian law is binding on states that are parties to them. It is also widely accepted that customary international humanitarian law is binding on states and non-state armed groups alike.[2] A more difficult question has proven to be how conventional international humanitarian law binds non-state armed groups when they are not parties to the relevant instruments.

2.1 Non-state armed groups and conventional international humanitarian law

Certain instruments are clearly intended to bind non-state armed groups. Common Article 3, the Hague Convention on Cultural Property, the amended Convention on Certain Conventional Weapons, and Amended Protocol II to that Convention all provide that 'each party to the conflict shall be bound to apply' certain rules.[3] The phrase '[e]ach party' refers to states parties to the conflict as well as non-state parties to the conflict. Additional Protocol II does not contain any such reference, a provision to this effect being deleted at the 1974–7 Diplomatic Conference. However, the provision was deleted because states were concerned with affording non-state armed groups recognition and status and not because the Protocol was intended to bind states alone.[4] Accordingly, Additional Protocol II was also intended to bind states and armed groups alike.

---

[1] Vienna Convention on the Law of Treaties, Article 26.
[2] See eg *Military and Paramilitary Activities in and against Nicaragua* [1986] ICJ Rep 14, 113–14.
[3] Common Article 3; Hague Convention on Cultural Property, Article 19; Convention on Certain Conventional Weapons, Amended Article 1(3); Amended Protocol II to the Convention on Certain Conventional Weapons, Article 1(3).
[4] See Y Sandoz, C Swinarski, and B Zimmermann (eds), *Commentary on the Additional Protocols of 8 June 1977 to the Geneva Conventions of 12 August 1949* (ICRC, 1987) 1345; G Abi-Saab,

Other instruments may originally have been intended to bind states alone, but this was due to an oversight, subsequently corrected, rather than as a result of any policy. The Second Protocol to the Hague Convention on Cultural Property, which governs international and non-international armed conflicts alike, uses the term 'Party', but defines it as 'a State Party to this Protocol'.[5] Thus, the phrase 'Parties to the Conflict' in the Protocol refers to states that are both parties to the Protocol and parties to the conflict,[6] rather than to states and non-state armed groups. At the final plenary meeting of the drafting of the Protocol, the Chairman of the Drafting Committee stated that '[t]he Drafting Committee considered that the term "parties to a conflict" could also apply to non-State parties to a conflict by virtue of Article 22 which provides that the Second Protocol applies to non-international armed conflicts and that this Protocol is to be interpreted in that sense'.[7] This is a useful clarification. However, it may be that only certain usages of the phrase 'parties to the conflict' include armed groups. For example, Article 11(9) of the Protocol provides for communication with the International Committee of the Blue Shield by Parties to the conflict, and it is not clear whether this would include non-state armed groups.[8] It is unlikely that this was the intention, as provisions relating to interaction with states or international organizations are usually limited to states.[9] Furthermore, during the Diplomatic Conference that adopted the 1954 Hague Convention on Cultural Property, the United Kingdom opined that '[i]n the event of civil war, the party which opposes the legitimate government is not recognised and therefore cannot be bound by the Convention. If an organisation such as UNESCO entered into contact with insurgent troops, that would confer a certain legality to the movement'.[10]

Still other instruments were not intended to bind non-state armed groups directly but to bind states in respect of non-state armed groups. The Optional Protocol to the Convention on the Rights of the Child on the Involvement of Children in Armed Conflict is one such instrument and provides that '[a]rmed groups that are distinct from the armed forces of a State should not, under any circumstances, recruit or use in hostilities persons under the age of 18 years'.[11] The provision does not purport to create obligations for armed groups. Rather, the drafters intended the provision to bind states alone and to create obligations for states in respect of armed groups.[12] The

'Non-International Armed Conflicts', in UNESCO (ed), *International Dimensions of Humanitarian Law* (UNESCO, 1988) 217, 231; L Moir, *The Law of Internal Armed Conflict* (Cambridge University Press, 2002) 96.

[5] Article 1(a).

[6] UNESCO, Diplomatic Conference on the Second Protocol to the Hague Convention for the Protection of Cultural Property in the Event of Armed Conflict: Summary Report (1999) para 36.

[7] Ibid, para 36. See also J-M Henckaerts, 'New Rules for the Protection of Cultural Property in Armed Conflict' (1999) 81 *IRRC* 593, 618–19.

[8] Henckaerts, ibid, 619 fn 65.

[9] See eg Protocol on Explosive Remnants of War, Protocol V to the Convention on Certain Conventional Weapons, which applies to non-international armed conflict (Article 1(3)) and limits its provisions on co-operation and assistance to 'High Contracting Parties' (Articles 6–11).

[10] *Actes de la Conférence Convoquée par l'Organisation des Nations Unies pour l'Éducation, la Science et la Culture tenue à la Haye du 21 Avril au 14 Mai* (La Haye, 1961) Procès-Verbaux de la Conférence, para 649. The original reads: '[e]n cas de guerre civile, la Partie qui s'oppose au Gouvernement légitime ne serait pas reconnue et ne pourrait donc être liée par la Convention. Si un organisme tel que l'Unesco entrait en rapport avec une troupe insurgée, cette démarche conférerait une certain légalité à ce mouvement.'

[11] Article 4(1).

[12] R Brett, 'Non-Governmental Human Rights Organizations and International Humanitarian Law' (1998) 38 *IRRC* 531, 534.

International Committee of the Red Cross (ICRC) had argued that the better approach was to use the language of 'all parties to the conflict', considering this to bind armed groups and states alike by the Protocol;[13] however, that suggestion was not followed.

The situation regarding certain other instruments is less clear. The Ottawa Convention on Anti-Personnel Mines, which is applicable in situations of non-international armed conflict, provides that '[e]ach State Party' undertakes never to do certain things,[14] and nowhere is there reference to non-state armed groups or 'parties to the conflict'. The efforts of the International Campaign to Ban Landmines and of Colombia to include non-state armed groups within the framework of the Convention proved unsuccessful.[15] The same is true of the Convention on Cluster Munitions.[16] That Convention does contain reference to armed groups, but only in its Preamble: '*[r]esolved* also that armed groups distinct from the armed forces of a State shall not, under any circumstances, be permitted to engage in any activity prohibited to a State Party to this Convention.' This is a considerable step forward being the first time that an international humanitarian law treaty contains express reference to 'armed groups'. However, this makes it all the more surprising that the obligations arising from the Convention are limited to states parties.

The lack of explicit application to non-state armed groups has proven problematic for certain states that are involved in non-international armed conflicts. For example, Sri Lanka expressed the view that it would only ratify the Ottawa Convention when the Liberation Tigers of Tamil Eelam (LTTE) made a similar commitment; and Sudan ratified the Ottawa Convention only after the Sudan People's Liberation Movement/Army (SPLM/A) signed a commitment, which in large part reflected the Ottawa Convention.[17] These examples also demonstrate the importance of the notion of equality of obligation, an issue that is considered below.[18] States parties to the Ottawa Convention in general have recognized the need for engagement with non-state armed groups on the prohibition of anti-personnel mines.[19]

The question that follows is how these conventional instruments purport to bind non-state armed groups when the groups are not parties to the instruments.[20] At one stage, it was thought that the instruments bind states parties but not armed groups against which those states are in conflict.[21] The orthodox view was that a non-state armed group is bound by international humanitarian law only when it 'choose[s] to

---

[13] D Helle, 'Optional Protocol on the Involvement of Children in Armed Conflict to the Convention on the Rights of the Child' (2000) 82 *IRRC* 797, 807.

[14] Article 1.

[15] See S Maslen, *Commentaries on Arms Control Treaties: Volume I* (Oxford University Press, 2005) 67 and 77–8.

[16] See G Nystuen and SC Maslen, *The Convention on Cluster Munitions: A Commentary* (Oxford University Press, 2010) 64–5; B Docherty, 'Breaking New Ground: The Convention on Cluster Munitions and the Evolution of International Humanitarian Law' (2009) 31 *HRQ* 934, 961–2.

[17] E Decrey Warner, J Somer, and P Bongard, 'Armed Non-State Actors and Humanitarian Norms: Lessons from the Geneva Call Experience', in B Perrin (ed), *Modern Warfare: Armed Groups, Private Militaries, Humanitarian Organizations, and the Law* (University of British Columbia Press, 2012) 73, 79.

[18] See below, 242 et seq.

[19] Declaration of the Third Meeting of the States Parties (Managua Declaration) 2001, para 12.

[20] For a more detailed consideration of the issue, see S Sivakumaran, 'Binding Armed Opposition Groups' (2006) 55 *ICLQ* 369, from which the following paragraphs are derived.

[21] See eg *Final Record of the Diplomatic Conference of Geneva of 1949* (Federal Political Department, Berne) Vol II-B, 79 (United States, France), 94 (United Kingdom, Australia); *Official Records of the Diplomatic Conference on the Reaffirmation and Development of International Humanitarian Law Applicable in Armed Conflicts, Geneva (1974–1977)* (Federal Political Department, 1978) Vol 7, 79 (Colombia). See also *Actes de la Conférence*, above note 10, para 150 (India).

announce its adherence',[22] and that '[i]nsofar as [common] Article 3 purports to bind the insurgent party to the conflict to apply its provisions, its legal efficacy may be doubted'.[23] Today, it is firmly accepted that international humanitarian law binds states and armed groups alike.[24] Several explanations have been put forward to explain quite how this takes place. The difficulties that arise are illustrated by the suggestion that purporting to bind non-state armed groups by treaty instruments is 'legal heresy but... necessary heresy'.[25]

Some of the explanations that have been put forward are of limited use in that they bind non-state armed groups only by certain norms. For example, it is well-accepted that non-state armed groups are bound by customary international humanitarian law.[26] However, that explanation is necessarily limited to norms that have customary status. The limitations of this explanation are less extensive today, but it would not explain how non-state armed groups were bound by various rules before they gained customary status, for example the rules of Additional Protocol II prior to the mid-1990s. Equally, it is unable to explain how armed groups are bound by rules that are not of customary status, or how it is that members of armed groups may be prosecuted on the basis of conventional law.

Other explanations are limited in that they bind only certain types of non-state armed groups. For example, international humanitarian law is considered to be binding on armed groups that claim to represent the state. Such a claim may be explicit: 'if the responsible authority at [its] head exercises effective sovereignty, it is bound by the very fact that it claims to represent the country, or part of the country.'[27] This was the view taken by a Judge Advocate General in the *Wirz* trial at the end of the US civil war: 'the moment they [the Confederates] asked a place among nations they were bound to recognize and obey those laws international which are and of necessity must be applicable alike to all.'[28] The argument may also be implicit, manifested through territorial control.[29] Both variations are problematic in that they purport to bind an entity on the basis of that entity's claim to represent the state. Even more problematically, the explanation does not bind non-state armed groups that do not control territory, or do not exercise effective sovereignty, and do not purport to represent the state. As discussed in Chapter 5, non-state armed groups need not do any of these

---

[22] G von Glahn, 'The Protection of Human Rights in Time of Armed Conflicts' (1971) 1 *IYHR* 208, 217. See also RR Baxter, 'Forces for Compliance with the Law of War' (1964) 58 *ASIL Proceedings* 82, 87.
[23] RT Yingling and RW Ginnane, 'The Geneva Conventions of 1949' (1952) 46 *AJIL* 393, 396. See also ICRC, *The Geneva Conventions of August 12, 1949: Analysis for the Use of National Red Cross Societies, Volume II* (ICRC, 1950) 6.
[24] See eg *Prosecutor v Norman*, SCSL-2004-14-AR72(E), Decision on Preliminary Motion Based on Lack of Jurisdiction (Child Recruitment), Decision of 31 May 2004, para 22; *Juan Carlos Abella v Argentina*, Case 11.137, 18 November 1997, OEA/Ser.L/V/II.98, Doc 6 rev, 13 April 1998, para 174.
[25] F Siordet, 'The Geneva Conventions and Civil War' (1950) III *RICR Supplement* 166, 168.
[26] *Prosecutor v Kallon and Kamara*, SCSL-2004-15-AR72(E) and SCSL-2004-16-AR72(E), Decision on Challenge to Jurisdiction, Lomé Accord Amnesty, 13 March 2004, para 47; Report of the International Commission of Inquiry on Darfur to the Secretary-General, S/2005/60, 1 February 2005, para 172.
[27] JS Pictet (ed), *The Geneva Conventions of 12 August 1949: Commentary, III Geneva Convention Relative to the Treatment of Prisoners of War* (ICRC, Geneva, 1960) 37.
[28] *Trial of Henry Wirz*, HR Ex Doc No 23, 40th Cong, 2nd Sess (1867) 764.
[29] L Zegveld, *The Accountability of Armed Opposition Groups in International Law* (Cambridge University Press, 2002) 15.

things in order to be involved in a non-international armed conflict and for international humanitarian law to be binding on them.[30]

For some time, the answer was thought to lie in the binding nature of treaties on third parties. It was suggested that resort could be had to the Vienna Convention on the Law of Treaties (VCLT) and its rules on the binding nature of treaties on third parties.[31] Article 34 of the VCLT provides that '[a] treaty does not create either obligations or rights for a third State without its consent'. However, this is subject to Articles 35 and 36, Article 35 providing that a third party may be subject to treaty obligations if the parties to the treaty 'intend the provision to be the means of establishing the obligation' and the third party itself 'expressly accepts that obligation in writing'. Article 36 provides that a third party may benefit from rights that are contained in a treaty provided that the parties to the treaty 'intend the provision to accord that right' to the third party and the third party 'assent[s] thereto'. Unlike the case of obligations, the assent of the third parties can be presumed.

The difficulty with the explanation, aside from the rules of the VCLT being extended to non-state actors, is that it does not explain how non-state armed groups that do not accept the rights and obligations of international humanitarian law would be bound by the rules. The binding nature of the rules is dependent entirely on the will of the parties. Non-state armed groups that do not consider themselves bound—the very groups that are most in need of being bound—would not be bound. On this basis the National Liberation Front (FLN) of Viet Nam, the Fuerzas Armadas Revolucionarias de Colombia (FARC), and the Frente Farabundo Martí para la Liberación Nacional (FMLN) of El Salvador would not have been bound.[32] A further limitation of this explanation is that the parties to the treaty must 'intend the provision to be the means of establishing the obligation'. As noted above, the drafters and states parties of certain treaties—the Ottawa Convention and the Cluster Munitions Convention in particular—seemingly did not intend non-state armed groups to be bound by the relevant Conventions. Accordingly, while usefully binding some non-state armed groups, or obligating compliance with certain international humanitarian law rules, these explanations are of limited value.

This is not to suggest that non-state armed groups are not bound by conventional international humanitarian law. Rather, the explanation lies elsewhere. When a state ratifies a treaty, it does so not only on behalf of the state but also on behalf of all individuals within its jurisdiction.[33] Thus, the law of armed conflict binds not only states but individuals.[34] Indeed, it has been noted that 'the entire law of war is based on the assumption that its commands are binding not only upon States but also upon their nationals, whether members of their armed forces or not'.[35] This notion of state ratification relates to ratification of the treaty at the *international* level and not, more narrowly, at the level of domestic implementation. For this reason, the ICRC suggested for inclusion in Article 1 of the Geneva Conventions, the language, '[t]he High

---

[30] See above, 180–2.
[31] A Cassese, 'The Status of Rebels under the 1977 Geneva Protocol on Non-International Armed Conflicts' (1981) 30 *ICLQ* 416; Moir, *Internal Armed Conflict*, above note 4, 52–3 and 96–9.
[32] See the objections of the FLN, FARC, and FMLN, below, 562–3.
[33] Abi-Saab, Non-International Armed Conflicts, above note 4, 231; ICRC, *Commentary on the Additional Protocols*, above note 4, 1345; C Lysaght, 'The Scope of Protocol II and its Relation to Common Article 3 of the Geneva Conventions of 1949 and other Human Rights Instruments' (1983) 33 *American University Law Review* 9, 12; Zegveld, *Accountability*, above note 29, 15–17.
[34] *The Law of War on Land being Part III of the Manual of Military Law* (HMSO, 1958) 1.
[35] L Oppenheim, *International Law: Volume I* (H Lauterpacht (ed)) (Longmans, 1955) 341.

Contracting Parties undertake, *in the name of their peoples*, to respect and to ensure respect for the present Convention in all circumstances'.[36] The ICRC took the view that this would stress that the 'undertakings are subscribed to by Governments in the name of their peoples' and that this would 'facilitate the implementing of the... Convention, especially in case of civil war'.[37] The fact that certain individuals group together and challenge the authority of the state does not impact upon the binding nature of the rules upon them. This explanation, that the armed group is bound by state ratification of conventional instruments, found favour among some delegates both at the Diplomatic Conference of 1949[38] and at the Diplomatic Conference of 1974–7.[39] It was also on this basis that the ICRC considered the FLN of Viet Nam bound by the Geneva Conventions.[40]

Two principal criticisms have been levelled at this explanation. First, in many legal systems a state does not bind its citizens simply by ratifying a treaty; rather, the treaty only becomes binding upon incorporation into domestic law. If incorporation does not take place, the non-state armed group would not be bound by the treaty. Thus, it is said that what is at stake is not whether armed groups are subjects of domestic law but their regulation by international law.[41] Second, it is suggested that it is problematic to bind the armed group by the state's ratification of an international humanitarian law instrument given that armed groups are unlikely to comply with laws that are formulated by the very governments against which they are fighting.[42]

These two criticisms are misplaced. As to the first, international humanitarian law instruments are binding on the non-state armed group not through domestic law but *directly* through international law. Thus, it is irrelevant for these purposes whether or not the international instrument has been incorporated into domestic law.[43] It is

---

[36] ICRC, *Draft Revised or New Conventions for the Protection of War Victims* (Geneva, May 1948) 4 (emphasis added).
[37] Ibid, 5.
[38] *Final Record*, above note 21, Vol II-B, 94 (Greece).
[39] *Official Records*, above note 21, Vol 8, 239, para 55 (ICRC); Vol 9, 234, para 54 (ICRC); Vol 9, 238, para 9 (Mongolia); Vol 14, 314, paras 22 and 24 (USSR).
[40] Letter from the Vice-President of the ICRC to Président, Front National de Libération du Sud-Vietnam, 14 June 1965, ICRC Archives B AG 202 223-005 ('[q]uant au Front national de libération, il se trouve également lié par les engagements souscrits au nom du Vietnam'). See also Appeal to the National Front of Liberation of South Viet Nam, reproduced in 'Respect for the Rules of Humanity in Viet Nam' (1965) 5 *IRRC* 417, 417.
[41] M Bothe, KJ Partsch, and WA Solf, *New Rules for Victims of Armed Conflicts: Commentary on the Two 1977 Protocols Additional to the Geneva Conventions of 1949* (Martinus Nijhoff, 1982) 700; Cassese, Status of Rebels, above note 31, 429; T Fleiner-Gerster and MA Meyer, 'New Developments in Humanitarian Law: A Challenge to the Concept of Sovereignty' (1985) 34 *ICLQ* 267, 272 and 277; T Meron, *Human Rights in Internal Strife: Their International Protection* (Grotius, 1987) 39; J Klabbers, '(I Can't Get No) Recognition: Subjects Doctrine and the Emergence of Non-State Actors', in J Petman and J Klabbers (eds), *Nordic Cosmopolitanism: Essays in International Law for Martti Koskenniemi* (Martinus Nijhoff, 2003) 351, 358; A Bellal, G Giacca, and S Casey-Maslen, 'International Law and Armed Non-State Actors in Afghanistan' (2011) 93 *ICRC* 47, 55–6.
[42] Cassese, Status of Rebels, above note 31, 429–30; Moir, *Internal Armed Conflict*, above note 4, 53–5; R Baxter, 'Ius in Bello Interno', in JN Moore (ed), *Law and Civil War in the Modern World* (Johns Hopkins University Press, Baltimore, 1974) 518, 527–8; Zegveld, *Accountability*, above note 29, 16; J-M Henckaerts, 'Binding Armed Opposition Groups Through Humanitarian Treaty Law and Customary Law' (2003) 27 *Collegium* 123, 126–7; Klabbers, Recognition, above note 41, 359 and 362; Y Dinstein, 'The Interaction between Customary International Law and Treaties' (2006) 322 *RdC* 243, 343–4; E La Haye, *War Crimes in Internal Armed Conflicts* (Cambridge University Press, 2008) 120.
[43] Describing this notion as 'legislative jurisdiction' in Sivakumaran, Binding Armed Opposition Groups, above note 20, seems to have caused confusion and is omitted here.

well-accepted that certain treaties create rights and obligations directly upon individuals, irrespective of whether or not they have been incorporated in domestic law. This much is evident from the *Jurisdiction of the Courts of Danzig* advisory opinion of the Permanent Court of International Justice and more recently the *LaGrand* Judgment of the International Court of Justice (ICJ).[44] It has also been affirmed in relation to substantive international criminal law, with the International Law Commission noting of the Nuremberg Principles, 'international law may impose duties on individuals directly without any interposition of internal law'.[45] Although this refers to the international criminalization of the rules and not their binding nature as such, in order to be able to prosecute individuals for the breach of certain rules, they must necessarily have been binding upon them in the first place. Thus, the above statements also stand for the proposition that conventional international humanitarian law binds individuals regardless of whether or not the relevant instrument has been incorporated into domestic law. Conventional international humanitarian law binds individuals directly without the need for incorporation into domestic law.

As to the second criticism, the underlying concern is that non-state armed groups will not consider themselves bound by rules of international humanitarian law as these rules have been formulated by the governments against which they are now in conflict. This is intuitively appealing; however, practice suggests that the concern is overstated. There are certainly instances of non-state armed groups arguing that they are not bound by particular rules because they did not have a role in their formation. This was true of the FLN with respect to the Geneva Conventions, the FARC on Additional Protocol II, and the FMLN on specific norms.[46] However, the objection on the part of each of these groups lay in their lack of input into the rule and not the role played by the opposing side in its formation. Furthermore, these instances are offset by the significantly more numerous instances in which non-state armed groups have expressly stated that they consider themselves bound by, or will follow, international humanitarian law.[47] Even if the non-state armed group may declare certain state legislation null and void, it tends not to do so of the rules relating to the law of armed conflict. Accordingly, it is quite clear that non-state armed groups are bound by international humanitarian law instruments despite not being parties to them.

2.2 Equality of obligation, reciprocity, and asymmetry

The international humanitarian law of non-international armed conflict binds 'each party to the conflict', namely the state and the non-state armed group or, if the conflict is fought between armed groups, the armed groups. Equality of obligation, or as it is more commonly described, equality of belligerents, is a principle that is fundamental to international humanitarian law,[48] including the international humanitarian law of

---

[44] *Jurisdiction of the Courts of Danzig* [1928] PCIJ Series B, No 15, 18–26; *LaGrand* [2001] ICJ Rep 466, para 77.
[45] Report of the International Law Commission covering its second session, 5 June–29 July 1950, A/1316 (1950), Formulation of the Nürnberg Principles, para 99. See also 1954 Draft Code of Offences against the Peace and Security of Mankind, Article 1; Draft Code of Crimes against the Peace and Security of Mankind, Article 2, and Commentary of the ILC thereto, in *Yearbook of the International Law Commission*, 1996, Volume II, Part Two, A/CN.4/Ser.A/1996/Add.1 (Part 2), 19.
[46] Above, 240.
[47] See generally Chapter 4.
[48] See H Lauterpacht, 'The Limits of the Operation of the Law of War' (1953) 30 *BYIL* 206; C Greenwood, 'The Relationship between *Jus ad Bellum* and *Jus in Bello*' (1983) 9 *Review of International Studies* 221.

non-international armed conflict.⁴⁹ The principle holds that all parties to an armed conflict have the same rights and obligations as a matter of law, irrespective of the 'justness' of their cause; the idea being that if one side is not bound by particular rules, the side that is bound will not comply with them. The principle also aims to ensure that both sides treat civilians and civilian objects in the same manner. It has been suggested that the principle is unworkable in non-international armed conflicts as members of the armed group remain subject to domestic criminal law and may be prosecuted for taking part in the hostilities.⁵⁰ However, this is true only of domestic law, through which the member of the armed group may be prosecuted. Insofar as international humanitarian law is concerned, the principle of equality of obligation remains intact.⁵¹ Challenges to application of the principle in non-international armed conflict are ameliorated further with prosecution not taking place for mere participation in hostilities, or amnesty being granted to members of the armed group, in some large-scale non-international armed conflicts.⁵² That being said, the lack of formal combatant immunity in the law of non-international armed conflict is a considerable obstacle to encouraging respect for the law.

Equality of obligation has been urged by parties to conflicts also in respect of human rights law components of the law of non-international armed conflict. For example, Guatemala argued before the Guatemalan Commission for Historical Clarification that 'it was unacceptable to appraise the conduct of their security forces by stricter standards than the conduct of the guerrilla forces',⁵³ the reference to stricter standards being to human rights law. Arguments of equality of obligation are made in particular by non-state armed groups, through their criticism of unequal obligations. For example, in 2008 and again in 2011, the National Democratic Front of the Philippines (NDFP) criticized the unequal obligations of states and non-state armed groups in the law relating to child soldiers.⁵⁴ For much the same reason, a commander of the Sudan People's Liberation Army (SPLA) 'raised some concern' to Geneva Call 'about the "inequity"' of the differential obligations as between the Geneva Call Deed of Commitment on Anti-Personnel Mines 'for armed groups' and the Ottawa Convention for

---

⁴⁹ See ICRC, *Commentary on the Additional Protocols*, above note 4, 1345; F Bugnion, '*Jus ad Bellum, Jus in Bello* and Non-International Armed Conflicts' (2003) 6 *YIHL* 167; M Sassòli, '*Ius ad Bellum* and *Ius in Bello*: The Separation between the Legality of the Use of Force and Humanitarian Rules to be Respected in Warfare—Crucial or Outdated?', in M Schmitt and J Pejić (eds), *International Law and Armed Conflict: Exploring the Faultlines, Essays in Honour of Yoram Dinstein* (Martinus Nijhoff, 2007) 241, 254–7.

⁵⁰ L Doswald-Beck, 'The Right to Life in Armed Conflict: Does International Humanitarian Law Provide all the Answers?' (2006) 864 *IRRC* 881, 903; J Kleffner, 'From "Belligerents" to "Fighters" and Civilians Directly Participating in Hostilities—On the Principle of Distinction in Non-International Armed Conflicts One Hundred Years After the Second Hague Peace Conference' (2007) LIV *NILR* 315, 322–3. For a more nuanced view, see J Somer, 'Jungle Justice: Passing Sentence on the Equality of Belligerents in Non-International Armed Conflict' (2007) 89 *IRRC* 655, 659–64.

⁵¹ Sassòli, *Ius ad Bellum*, above note 49, 241.

⁵² See below, 514–20.

⁵³ C Tomuschat, 'The Applicability of Human Rights Law to Insurgent Movements', in H Fischer et al (eds), *Krisensicherung und Humanitarer Schutz—Crisis Management and Humanitarian Protection: Festschrift für Dieter Fleck* (Berliner Wissenschaftsverlag, 2004) 573, 576.

⁵⁴ Letter to UN Secretary-General Ban Ki-Moon on Children in Armed Conflict from LG Jalandoni, Member of the NDFP National Executive Committee and Chairperson of the NDFP Negotiating Panel, 24 November 2008; Letter to Ms Coomaraswamy [Special Representative of the Secretary-General for Children and Armed Conflict] from the Chairperson of the NDFP Human Rights Monitoring Committee, 7 April 2011.

states, the two instruments defining the prohibited mines in different ways.[55] There is far less difficulty in respect of the latter example, given that the non-state armed group is choosing to become a party to the relevant commitment. The armed group is thus consenting to be bound by a more onerous obligation than the obligation to which the state is subject. The element of choice reduces the disparity of obligation. This also explains why a number of armed groups have signed Geneva Call's Deed despite the states against which they are fighting not being a party to the Ottawa Convention. Where, however, the disparity of obligation arises from the creation of rules on the part of states and there is no element of consent on the part of the armed group, such as with the child soldiers example, the disparity may be perceived as problematic. Equality of obligation in international humanitarian law is also important for states. Thus, as discussed earlier, some states have refused to ratify certain instruments without the non-state armed group making an equivalent commitment.[56]

It is crucial to distinguish ideas of equality of obligation from related ideas of reciprocity and asymmetry. Reciprocity is itself a multi-faceted notion. In its strongest form, *de jure* reciprocity was used in the law of armed conflict to ensure that a particular rule applied to a conflict only if all parties to the conflict were also parties to the relevant rule. Such was the case with the St Petersburg Declaration on Explosive Projectiles of 1868 and the Fourth Hague Convention of 1907.[57] *De jure* reciprocity is not used in this sense today and has never been used in this manner in instruments that regulate non-international armed conflict.[58] It has been suggested that Additional Protocol II implicitly adopted this approach in requiring the adverse party actually to implement the Protocol, in order for it to enter into force.[59] However, as discussed in Chapter 5, the Protocol cannot be interpreted in that manner, and requires the armed group simply to exercise such territorial control as to *enable* it to implement the Protocol.[60]

A less strong, but still restrictive, form of reciprocity provides that the relevant rule of international humanitarian law is applicable only if the other party agrees to apply the rule. Language along these lines was suggested for common Article 3—'[i]n case of civil war, in any part of the home or colonial territory of a Contracting Party, the principles of the Convention shall be equally applied by the said Party, subject to the adverse Party also conforming thereto'[61]—but was rejected as rendering the principles valueless for ease of objection.[62] Thus, *de jure* reciprocity is not an aspect of the law of

---

[55] SM Santos Jr, 'A Critical Reflection on the Geneva Call Instrument and Approach in Engaging Armed Groups on Humanitarian Norms: A Southern Perspective', Paper for the Armed Groups Conference, Vancouver, 13–15 Novermber 2003, 12.

[56] Above, 238.

[57] Declaration Renouncing the Use, in Time of War, of Explosive Projectiles Under 400 Grammes Weight (1868); Hague Convention (IV) respecting the Laws and Customs of War on Land (1907), Article 2.

[58] See the discussion in *Prosecutor v Kupreškić*, IT-95-16-T, Judgment, 14 January 2000, paras 515–19, on the nature of international humanitarian law generally.

[59] F Kalshoven, *Constraints on the Waging of War* (ICRC, 1987) 139; PH Kooijmans, 'In the Shadowland of Civil War and Civil Strife: Some Reflections on the Standard-Setting Process', in AJM Delissen and GJ Tanja (eds), *Humanitarian Law of Armed Conflict, Challenges Ahead: Essays in Honour of Frits Kalshoven* (Nijhoff, Dordrecht, 1991) 225, 233.

[60] See above 185–7.

[61] ICRC, Report on the Work of the Conference of Government Experts for the Study of the Conventions for the Protection of War Victims (Geneva, April 14–26, 1947) (1947) 8. See also XVIIe Conférence Internationale de la Croix-Rouge (Stockholm, août 1948) Commission Juridique, Sténogramme des Séances (Janvier 1949) 36–57.

[62] ICRC, Draft Revised or New Conventions for the Protection of War Victims (ICRC, 1948) 6. See also Commission Juridique, above note 61, 36–57.

non-international armed conflict. However, when parties make unilateral commitments, these are sometimes framed as being dependent on a reciprocal commitment being made by the other side.[63]

The only form of reciprocity that underlies international humanitarian law today, and that remains important, is *de facto* reciprocity. *De facto* reciprocity relates to one of the parties to the conflict respecting the law in the hope that it will induce the other party similarly to respect the law. This is particularly true in relation to international humanitarian law rules that govern the conduct of hostilities, aimed at protecting the civilian population and civilian objects, and of rules on the treatment of detainees, with the treatment of prisoners of one side affecting the treatment of those of the other.[64] For example, during the US war of independence of 1776, George Washington was reported to have 'warned the British commanding general that American policy towards British prisoners of war would parallel British treatment of American prisoners'.[65] Along these lines, UN Secretary-General Ban Ki-Moon has suggested that '[t]he incentives for armed groups to comply with the law should be emphasized, including increased likelihood of reciprocal respect for the law by opposing parties'.[66] Reciprocity in this sense is more 'of a sociological order' than a principle of international law,[67] but it is important nonetheless.[68]

Reciprocity and equality of obligation also differ from ideas of asymmetry and factual inequality. Parties to a non-international armed conflict usually have vastly differing capabilities. The phrase 'equality of belligerents' is, then, something of a misnomer; it is not the parties which are equal but their obligations. In a typical non-international armed conflict, the armed forces of the state will have superior capabilities over the non-state armed group. The state armed forces will usually have an air force whereas the non-state armed group will rely on land capabilities. There are, of course, exceptions; the LTTE, for example, had an air wing and a sea wing; the Bosnian Serb forces also had significant capabilities. However, by and large, the state will have superior capabilities to the non-state armed group. Thus, a fighter of the rebel forces during the 2011 violence in Libya is reported as stating: '[t]here is no comparison between our weapons and theirs [the government's]. They're trained, they're organized. They got their training in Russia and I don't know where. We're not an army, we're the people and even if we had weapons, we wouldn't even know how to use them.'[69] This asymmetry or factual inequality does not render nugatory the idea of *de facto* reciprocity. For example, it has been noted that 'attacks on civilians by air force or commando units have a decided influence on the treatment awaiting captured pilots and guerrilla fighters, such treatment in turn sometimes resulting in fiercer attacks

---

[63] See eg Lettre de la délégation algérienne au Caire à David de Traz, 23 février 1956, quoted in F Perret, 'L'action du Comité International de la Croix-Rouge pendant la Guerre d'Algérie (1954–1962)' (2004) 86 *IRRC* 917, 926. See further below, 523.

[64] See O Bangerter, 'Reasons Why Armed Groups Choose to Respect International Humanitarian Law or Not' (2011) 93 *IRRC* 353, 366–7.

[65] BM Carnahan, 'Reason, Retaliation, and Rhetoric: Jefferson and the Quest for Humanity in War' (1993) 139 *Military Law Review* 83, 91.

[66] Report of the Secretary-General on the Protection of Civilians in Armed Conflict, S/2009/277, 29 May 2009, para 41.

[67] Reaffirmation and Development of the Laws and Customs Applicable in Armed Conflicts: Report submitted by the International Committee of the Red Cross (May 1969) 83.

[68] See generally, R Provost, *International Human Rights and Humanitarian Law* (Cambridge University Press, 2002) Part II.

[69] Muhammad al-Houni, a 25-year-old fighter, quoted in A Shadid, 'Qaddafi Forces Bear Down on Strategic Town as Rebels Flee', *International Herald Tribune*, 10 March 2011.

against civilians'.⁷⁰ Furthermore, as the report of the 1971 Conference of Government Experts puts it: 'reciprocity did not mean that respect for the rules would have the same complexion on one side as on the other; it was necessary to take into account the possibilities on either side. What was important was that there should be the greatest possible measure of reciprocity, and that it should be applied in all good faith.'⁷¹ Thus the idea of *de facto* reciprocity is not incompatible with an asymmetrical conflict.

Ideas of equality of obligation, *de facto* reciprocity, and asymmetry are interlinked. Non-international armed conflicts, almost by their nature, are asymmetrical. This state of affairs is, or at least should be, taken into account in the formation of the rules. Asymmetry may make respect for particular norms on the part of the armed group more difficult or more onerous. However, difficulties resulting from lack of capacity can be ameliorated in different ways.⁷² It may even be that the parties agree between themselves that one side will not carry out certain actions or will be afforded certain treatment on condition that the other does not carry out different actions.⁷³ Here too there is equality of obligation, albeit not of the traditional sort and not in respect of the same obligation.

As the obligations arising in non-international armed conflict are not dependent on *de jure* reciprocity, they continue even in situations in which there is no *de facto* reciprocity. Violation of the rules on the part of one side does not excuse compliance on the part of the other side. *Tu quoque* is not a defence. Thus, although the role of reciprocity in the law of non-international armed conflict is sometimes questioned,⁷⁴ it is only *de jure* reciprocity that does not exist. Both *de facto* reciprocity and equality of obligation are principles that are important for the application of the law.

2.3 Intra-party protection

In addition to the norms by which parties to the conflict are bound, it is necessary to consider to whom they are obligated. In particular, a question arises as to whether or not the law of non-international armed conflict regulates the conduct between a party to the conflict and its *own* forces. The issue is raised because violence sometimes takes place within a non-state armed group. For example, members of an armed group who wish to disassociate themselves with the group may be killed if they attempt to leave.⁷⁵ Others may be killed if they are suspected of conniving with the opposing side.⁷⁶ Members of non-state armed groups, in particular female members, may also be raped or sexually abused by other members of the group.⁷⁷

---

⁷⁰ M Veuthey, 'Guerrilla Warfare and Humanitarian Law' (1976) 16 *IRRC* 277, 283–4.
⁷¹ ICRC, Conference of Government Experts on the Reaffirmation and Development of International Humanitarian Law Applicable in Armed Conflicts, Geneva, 24 May–12 June 1971, Report on the Work of the Conference (August 1971) 55–6, para 343.
⁷² See above, 73–6.
⁷³ See G Blum, 'Re-envisaging the International Law of Internal Armed Conflict: A Reply to Sandesh Sivakumaran' (2011) 22 *EJIL* 265, 270.
⁷⁴ See eg Outcome of the Expert Consultation on the Issue of Protecting the Human Rights of Civilians in Armed Conflict: Report of the Office of the United Nations High Commissioner for Human Rights, A/HRC/11/31, 4 June 2009, para 24; Blum, Reply, above note 73, 269–71.
⁷⁵ Guatemala: Memory of Silence, A/53/928, Annex, 27 April 1999, para 133.
⁷⁶ *Prosecutor v Sesay, Kallon and Gbao*, SCSL-04-15-T, Judgment, 2 March 2009, para 1399; Guatemala: Memory of Silence, above note 75, para 133.
⁷⁷ D Mazurana, *Women in Armed Opposition Groups Speak on War, Protection and Obligations under International Humanitarian and Human Rights Law* (Geneva Call, 2008) 44.

It is generally assumed that international humanitarian law operates only as between parties to a conflict. In non-international armed conflicts, this relates to the relationship between states and non-state armed groups, or between opposing armed groups. International humanitarian law has not traditionally been viewed as governing relations within the group. The commonly held view is that references to the obligation to protect presupposed that a party would take care of its own forces and that the aim of international humanitarian law in this regard was to ensure that the party would also take care of the other side. On this basis, the *RUF* Trial Chamber held that the law 'was never intended to criminalize acts of violence committed by one member of an armed group against another' and that 'a different approach would constitute an inappropriate re-conceptualisation of a fundamental principle of international humanitarian law'.[78]

However, it is submitted that things are not quite as self-evident as the traditional position suggests. It is instructive to consider the relevant provisions in their historical context. The first Geneva Convention, the 1864 Convention for the Amelioration of the Condition of the Wounded in Armies in the Field, provided that '[w]ounded or sick combatants, *to whatever nation they may belong*, shall be collected and cared for'.[79] Along similar lines, the 1906 Geneva Convention provided that '[o]fficers, soldiers, and other persons officially attached to armies, who are sick or wounded, shall be respected and cared for, *without distinction of nationality, by the belligerent in whose power they are*',[80] and the 1929 Geneva Convention used similar language.[81] Given that these three Conventions applied at a time in which the classic inter-state war was fought between two opposing sides of different nationalities, the protection afforded to members of armed forces from acts of their fellow comrades becomes apparent. Thus, Gustave Moynier, in his Commentary on the 1864 Convention, noted in this context that it was intended that persons should not be distinguished on the grounds of their nationality.[82] As put in the ICRC Commentary on the First Geneva Convention of 1949, the principle to be derived from these three provisions is that, 'when faced with suffering no distinction should be drawn between brothers-in-arms, enemy and allies'.[83]

This idea is carried through to the 1949 Geneva Conventions relating to the condition of the wounded and the sick. Article 12 of the First Geneva Convention, for example, provides in relevant part that '[m]embers of the armed forces and other persons mentioned in the following Article, who are wounded or sick, shall be respected and protected in all circumstances'. Article 13 goes on to list six categories of individuals, four of which do not require a specific relationship on the part of the protected, and which include '[m]embers of the armed forces of a Party to the conflict'. The same is true of Articles 12 and 13 of the Second Geneva Convention. Any doubt that 'in all circumstances' means 'in all circumstances' rather than 'in all circumstances save for intra-party relations' is resolved by the ICRC Commentary to the First Geneva Convention:

---

[78] *RUF* Trial Judgment, above note 76, para 1453. See also P Rowe, 'The Obligation of a State under International Law to Protect Members of its Own Armed Forces during Armed Conflict or Occupation' (2006) 9 *YIHL* 3, 23.
[79] Article 6 (emphasis added).
[80] Article 1 (emphasis added).
[81] Convention for the Amelioration of the Condition of the Wounded and Sick in Armies in the Field, 1929, Article 1.
[82] G Moynier, *Étude sur la Convention de Genève* (Paris, 1870) 201.
[83] J Pictet (ed), *The Geneva Conventions of 12 August 1949, Commentary: I Geneva Convention for the Amelioration of the Condition of the Wounded and Sick in Armed Forces in the Field* (ICRC, Geneva, 1952) 55.

The obligation embodied in this paragraph (paragraph 1 [of Article 12]) is general in character. It is applicable 'in all circumstances'. *The wounded are to be respected just as much when they are with their own army* or in no man's land as when they have fallen into the hands of the enemy.[84]

Although it is not always made clear that the provisions were intended to address the issue of intra-party protection, what is clear is that states were not assumed to look after their own forces leaving only their treatment of the other side in need of regulation. After all, the 1864 Geneva Convention was a direct response to the Battle of Solferino, at which wounded soldiers of both sides were left to die.[85]

For its part, common Article 3 provides that '[t]he wounded and sick shall be collected and cared for', without any limitations. Additional Protocol II provides for its application to 'all persons affected by an armed conflict',[86] and its substantive provisions include that '[a]ll the wounded, sick and shipwrecked, whether or not they have taken part in the armed conflict, shall be respected and protected' and '[t]here shall be no distinction among them founded on any grounds other than medical ones'.[87] The equivalent provision of Additional Protocol I, Article 10, provides that '[a]ll the wounded, sick and shipwrecked, *to whichever Party they belong*, shall be respected and protected',[88] again suggesting intra-party protection. Thus, it is submitted that the provisions relating to the wounded and sick apply within the party to the conflict as well as outside the party.

It is submitted further that intra-group protections are not limited to the wounded and sick alone.[89] Common Article 3 provides for humane treatment to persons taking no active part in the hostilities and prohibits certain conduct. It does not contain any limitation to one side or another.[90] On the contrary, it provides for humane treatment 'in all circumstances'. As the ICRC Commentary puts it, '[t]he wording adopted could not be more definite...No possible loophole is left; there can be no excuse, no attenuating circumstances'.[91] As long as the individual concerned is not taking an active part in hostilities, they should be protected by the provisions of common Article 3. The interpretation of the phrase active (or direct) participation in hostilities, used in this context, differs from that used in the context of the conduct of hostilities.[92]

Certain other provisions apply more clearly to intra-party relations. For example, the prohibition on the use of child soldiers in hostilities is designed to protect children who are associated with a party to the conflict from certain forms of treatment by that party.[93] Thus, the International Criminal Court (ICC) has noted that the associated war crime 'can be committed by a perpetrator against individuals in his own party to

---

[84] Ibid, 135.
[85] See H Dunant, *A Memory of Solferino* (reprinted and translated, ICRC, 1986).
[86] Article 2(1).
[87] Article 7.
[88] Article 10 (emphasis added).
[89] See E David, *Principes de Droit des Conflits Armés* (Bruylant, 2002) 229, para 1.205.
[90] Ibid. Cf P Rowe, 'The Obligation of a State under International Law to Protect Members of its Own Armed Forces during Armed Conflict or Occupation' (2006) 9 *YIHL* 3, 17.
[91] Pictet, *Commentary on the Third Geneva Convention*, above note 27, 39.
[92] See ICRC, *Interpretive Guidance on the Notion of Direct Participation in Hostilities under International Humanitarian Law* (ICRC, May 2009) 11. On the notion in the conduct of hostilities, see below, 363 et seq.
[93] M Cottier, 'Article 8(2)(b)(xxvi)', in O Triffterer (ed), *Commentary on the Rome Statute of the International Criminal Court* (Beck, München, 2008) 466; Rowe, Obligation to Protect, above note 90, 17–18.

the conflict'.⁹⁴ The requirement relating to trial by a regularly constituted court offering fair trial guarantees⁹⁵ similarly applies to anyone being tried by one of the parties to the conflict, whether a member of the party that is convening the trial, a member of the opposing forces, or a civilian. Sexual violence is prohibited, whether against civilians, members of the armed forces, or the armed group. These examples evidence the transformation that international humanitarian law has undergone, moving away from 'a series of reciprocal promises between parties to a conflict' towards 'the duty of any party toward victims of conflict'.⁹⁶ This is confirmed by the manner in which many of the rules of customary international humanitarian law have been framed by the Customary International Humanitarian Law study; certain actions are simply prohibited. Accordingly, it is submitted that certain provisions regulate the intra-party relationship.

This is not to suggest that international humanitarian law in its entirety protects members of parties to the conflict from intra-party violence. Many provisions of international humanitarian law do require a particular relationship between the relevant individuals. Prisoners of war, for the purposes of the Third Geneva Convention, are defined as persons falling within the specified list and 'who have fallen into the power of the enemy'.⁹⁷ Many of the provisions of the Fourth Geneva Convention are limited to protected persons, namely those 'in the hands of a Party to the conflict or Occupying Power of which they are not nationals'.⁹⁸ However, even these provisions have undergone something of a modification in recent years, protected persons being defined on the basis of allegiance rather than nationality, the focus not being on 'formal bonds and purely legal relations' but on 'the substance of relations'.⁹⁹ This has relevance to the situation at hand given that members of the armed group or armed forces may not actually have allegiance to the group or force but may be made up, for example, of conscripts or abductees.

The same is true of international criminal law provisions, many of which require a specific victim-perpetrator relationship. The Rome Statute, for example, limits certain offences to when they are carried out against 'persons who are in the power of an adverse party', 'individuals belonging to the hostile nation or army', or 'the enemy'.¹⁰⁰ In non-international armed conflicts, the Rome Statute criminalizes '[k]illing or wounding treacherously a combatant *adversary*', '[d]estroying or seizing the property of an *adversary*', and '[s]ubjecting persons who are in the power of *another party* to the conflict to physical mutilation'.¹⁰¹ However, other provisions do not specify any such relationship. Those crimes may posit a particular victim, for example 'persons taking no active part in the hostilities', but they do not specify a particular victim–perpetrator relationship. The juxtaposition of the two sets of provisions strengthens the case for the aforementioned interpretation of common Article 3 and other related norms.

---

⁹⁴ *Prosecutor v Katanga and Chui*, ICC-01/04-01/07, Decision on the Confirmation of Charges, 30 September 2008, para 248.
⁹⁵ Additional Protocol II, Article 6.
⁹⁶ R Cryer et al, *An Introduction to International Criminal Law and Procedure* (Cambridge University Press, 2010) 288 and fn 133.
⁹⁷ See Third Geneva Convention, Article 4.
⁹⁸ Fourth Geneva Convention, Article 4.
⁹⁹ *Prosecutor v Tadic*, IT-94-1-A, Judgment, 15 July 1999, para 168. See also *Prosecutor v Delalić et al*, IT-96-21-T, Judgment, 16 November 1998, para 265.
¹⁰⁰ Rome Statute, Article 8(2)(b)(x), (xi), and (xiii) respectively.
¹⁰¹ Ibid, Article 8(2)(e)(ix), (xii), and (xi) respectively (emphases added).

3. Geographical scope of application

A second issue that arises in terms of the scope of application of the law of non-international armed conflict relates to the geographical boundaries within which the law applies. Common Article 3 provides, '[i]n the case of armed conflict not of an international character occurring in the territory of one of the High Contracting Parties, each Party to the conflict shall be bound to apply, as a minimum, the following provisions'. Reference to the territory of a High Contracting Party is also made in the scope of application clause of Additional Protocol II.[102] These references could be taken as suggesting that the relevant provisions apply in the entire territory of the state involved in the armed conflict. The ad hoc international criminal tribunals have been of this view, with the ICTY Appeals Chamber in the *Tadić* Decision on Interlocutory Appeal holding that 'international humanitarian law continues to apply in ... the whole territory under the control of a party, whether or not actual combat takes place there'.[103] Other influential actors have since adopted this position.[104]

However, it seems unlikely that the international humanitarian law of armed conflict should always apply in the entire territory of the state in which the conflict takes place. A non-international armed conflict that is confined to a small part of a large state should not render international humanitarian law applicable throughout that state. That approach makes little sense if the conflict is self-contained. Along similar lines, the 1972 Conference of Government Experts took the view that it was 'inconceivable that, in the case of a disturbance in one specific part of a territory (in a town, for instance) the whole territory of the State should be subjected to the application of the Protocol'.[105] If reference is made to international human rights law, in which derogations may be made from human rights treaties in situations of public emergency which threaten the life of the nation, and which include non-international armed conflicts, the derogation may be required to be geographically circumscribed. For example, the Human Rights Committee has required that the derogation measures are 'limited to the extent strictly required by the exigencies of the situation' and that this includes its geographical coverage.[106] To be sure, in certain non-international armed conflicts, it may be entirely appropriate for international humanitarian law to apply throughout the country, certainly if the violence rages throughout the territory. However, this will not always be the case, with some conflicts seeing fighting limited to territorially circumscribed regions. For example, the armed conflict between the Moro Islamic Liberation Front (MILF) and the Government of the Philippines is limited to Mindanao. At the other

---

[102] Article 1.

[103] *Prosecutor v Tadić*, IT-94-1-AR72, Decision on the Defence Motion for Interlocutory Appeal on Jurisdiction, 2 October 1995, para 70. See also *Prosecutor v Jean-Paul Akayesu*, Case No ICTR-96-4-T, Judgment, 2 September 1998, para 635. See further C Greenwood, 'Scope of Application of Humanitarian Law', in D Fleck (ed), *The Handbook of Humanitarian Law in Armed Conflicts* (Oxford University Press, 1995) 39, 51.

[104] See eg Report on the Situation of Human Rights in Somalia, E/CN.4/1997/88, 3 March 1997, para 55; Inter-American Commission on Human Rights, Report on Terrorism and Human Rights, OEA/Ser.L/V/II.116 Doc 5 rev 1 corr, 22 October 2002, para 60.

[105] Conference of Government Experts on the Reaffirmation and Development of International Humanitarian Law Applicable in Armed Conflicts (Second Session, 3 May–3 June 1972): Report on the Work of the Conference, Volume I (July 1972) 68, para 2.59.

[106] Human Rights Committee, *General Comment No 29: States of Emergency (Article 4)*, CCPR/C/21/Rev.1/Add.11, 31 August 2001, para 4. See also the Siracusa Principles on the Limitation and Derogation of Provisions in the International Covenant on Civil and Political Rights, E/CN.4/1984/4, para 51.

end of the spectrum, the application of the law of armed conflict cannot be limited to the classical battlefield. In some non-international armed conflicts, a traditional battlefield does not exist, and even if one does exist, fighting or detention may take place away from the battlefield. Applying international humanitarian law to the entire territory of the state in which the conflict takes place may thus be overly broad.

It may also be overly narrow. The law of non-international armed conflict extends to fighters who are located in the border regions of another state despite not being present in the territory in which the conflict is taking place. The applicable law does not suddenly cease when it reaches a territorial frontier, nor is it transformed into the law of international armed conflict when it crosses the border.[107] Similarly, the higher echelons of a non-state armed group, who are not infrequently based outside the state in which the conflict takes place, would be subject to the international humanitarian law of non-international armed conflict by reason of their involvement in the armed conflict. Thus, if it can be established that the United States is involved in an armed conflict against Al-Qaeda,[108] the targeting of Osama bin Laden would be judged by reference to international humanitarian law. The fact that the targeting took place while bin Laden was in Pakistan is of little significance insofar as the *application* of the law is concerned.[109] However, it is submitted that, as a matter of *lex ferenda*, the *specificities* of the law should be tailored to take into account the fact that the individuals in question are far removed from the geographic site of the conflict. For example, insofar as the rules on targeting are concerned, the individuals in question should be subject only to force that is 'absolutely necessary', even if they are fighters.[110] Ultimately, though, their location does not immunize them from the operation of the law and all this suggests the need to move away from geographic-based ideas of applicability of the law.

The geographic focus essentially constitutes the drawing of arbitrary boundaries. A better approach would be to require a certain nexus between the conduct at issue and the applicable law. The language of Additional Protocol II itself provides such a nexus: the 'Protocol shall be applied ... to all persons *affected* by an armed conflict'.[111] The ICRC Commentary makes clear that 'the applicability of the Protocol follows from a criteria [*sic*] related to persons, and not to places',[112] and takes into account the criticism made at the 1972 Conference of Government Experts relating to violence in a small part of a state's territory. The ICRC Commentary to its 1973 draft Protocol provides further explanation of the approach taken:

> The Protocol shall apply to all persons affected in one way or another by the armed conflict, either because they would be exposed to the dangers resulting from the armed conflict, whether or not they participated in the hostilities, or because they are taking part in the hostilities and therefore must abide by certain rules of behaviour with regard to adverse armed forces and to the civilian population ... What is important is that persons affected by the armed conflict should be entitled to the protection of the Protocol, wherever they might be. Thus, a person arrested in some place far from the combat zone for an act committed in connection with the armed conflict ought to be protected ...[113]

---

[107] See above, 230.
[108] On which, see above, 232–4.
[109] It does, however, make a difference to the *jus ad bellum*.
[110] See below, 370–2.
[111] Article 2(1) (emphasis added).
[112] ICRC, *Commentary on the Additional Protocols*, above note 4, 1360.
[113] ICRC, *Draft Additional Protocols to the Geneva Conventions of August 12, 1949: Commentary* (October 1973) 134.

There is already some evidence of this in the law. For example, the international humanitarian law provisions on 'persons whose liberty has been restricted' apply only to those deprived of their liberty 'for reasons related to the armed conflict'.[114] The provisions on penal prosecution likewise apply to criminal offences 'related to the armed conflict'.[115] The same is true of the displacement of the civilian population, which 'shall not be ordered for reasons related to the conflict'.[116] Insofar as national relief societies are concerned, they may offer their services 'in relation to the victims of the armed conflict'.[117] For its part, the *Kayishema* Trial Judgment notes:

> Violations of these international instruments [common Article 3 and Protocol II] could be committed outside the theatre of combat. For example, the captured members of the RPF [Rwandan Patriotic Front] may be brought to any location within the territory of Rwanda and could be under the control or in the hands of persons who are not members of the armed forces. Therefore, every crime should be considered on a case-by-case basis taking into account the material evidence presented by the Prosecution.[118]

While utilizing a location-based approach, the Trial Chamber also recognizes the importance of considering the personal nexus. Thus, a focus on persons, objects, and the like that are affected by the armed conflict and the conduct at issue rather than any geographic location would prove a more appropriate solution to the question of the geographic scope of application of the law.[119]

The disadvantage of such an approach is the lack of bright-line rules or guidance as to its outer limits. Applicability outside the core fighting areas will have to be determined on a case-by-case basis, which may lead to a greater degree of difficulty in its application on the ground. Nonetheless, it is submitted that the advantages resulting from a nexus-based approach to the application of the law outweigh the difficulties faced in implementation. Location will continue to be an important factor, however, and it may affect the substance of a rule.[120]

4. Temporal scope of application

A third issue that arises relates to the temporal scope of application of the law of non-international armed conflict. That law modifies the applicable law of peace upon the outbreak of a non-international armed conflict.[121] The time at which it ceases is a rather more difficult issue. The conventional rules again fail to provide any guidance on point.

The ICRC Commentary on Additional Protocol II provides that the law is no longer applicable 'after the end of hostilities'.[122] It is not quite clear whether this is a reference to the cessation of active hostilities, usually through the conclusion of a ceasefire agreement, or the general close of hostilities, usually through a peace agreement. To the 1972 Conference of Government Experts, the ICRC suggested that the draft

---

[114] Additional Protocol II, Article 5.
[115] Ibid, Article 6.
[116] Ibid, Article 17.
[117] Ibid, Article 18(1).
[118] *Prosecutor v Kayishema and Ruzindana*, ICTR-95-1-T, Judgment, 21 May 1999, para 176.
[119] See also L Arimatsu, 'Territory, Boundaries and the Law of Armed Conflict' (2009) 12 *YIHL* 157, 189.
[120] See further below, 370–1.
[121] *Tadić* Decision on Interlocutory Appeal on Jurisdiction, above note 103, para 70.
[122] ICRC, *Commentary on the Additional Protocols*, above note 4, 1360.

Additional Protocol 'shall cease to be applied at the end of hostilities, that is when a general cease-fire is declared'; however, a similar proposal made for the application of international humanitarian law to 'cease to apply upon the general cessation of military operations' at the 1974–7 Diplomatic Conference was not adopted.[123] Given that many ceasefire agreements specifically provide for the continued application of international humanitarian law,[124] in practice, the law of non-international armed conflict continues to operate beyond the cessation of active hostilities. The operation of certain aspects of international humanitarian law beyond the cessation of hostilities also supports this conclusion.[125] An alternative approach, then, would be for the operation of international humanitarian law to cease upon the general close of hostilities, at which time peaceful relations would resume between the parties. This is usually done through a peace agreement. Thus, the *Tadić* Appeals Chamber took the view that the law 'extends beyond the cessation of hostilities until...a peaceful settlement is achieved'.[126]

Ultimately, the applicability of the law of non-international armed conflict turns on whether or not a non-international armed conflict continues to exist at the relevant time. If it does, the law of non-international armed conflict continues to operate; if it does not, the law ceases. That explains why the law of non-international armed conflict continues to exist even following the conclusion of a ceasefire agreement, as violence of the requisite intensity may continue to exist. This was the case, for example, in the conflict in Sri Lanka in which a ceasefire agreement was concluded in 2002,[127] and following which fighting continued. Thus, in situations in which the conflict ceases to exist following the conclusion of a ceasefire agreement and absent the conclusion of a peace agreement, the law of non-international armed conflict will cease to apply. Likewise, when the fighting declines up until the point that it dissipates entirely, the law of non-international armed conflict will cease to apply.[128] The exact moment in time at which the law of non-international armed conflict would cease to operate in such a situation would have to be judged on a case-by-case basis as against the facts on the ground. Just as the law of non-international armed conflict commences upon the existence of certain facts (an armed conflict) so too should it cease to apply upon the non-existence of certain facts (the lack of an armed conflict). Usually, this will be attested to through the conclusion of a peace agreement; however, the lack of a peace agreement cannot be considered determinative.

Application of the international humanitarian law of non-international armed conflict would also cease upon a complete military victory by one of the parties. Non-international armed conflicts rarely end in complete victories and defeats;

---

[123] ICRC, Conference of Government Experts on the Reaffirmation and Development of International Humanitarian Law Applicable in Armed Conflicts, Geneva, 3 May–3 June 1972 (second session): II Commentary, Part Two, Documentary Material Submitted by the International Committee of the Red Cross (January 1972) 8; *Official Records*, above note 21, Vol 4, 12.

[124] See above, 132.

[125] *Tadić* Decision on Interlocutory Appeal on Jurisdiction, above note 103, para 67; D Jinks, 'The Temporal Scope of Application of International Humanitarian Law in Contemporary Conflicts', Background Paper prepared for the Informal High-Level Expert Meeting on the Reaffirmation and Development of International Humanitarian Law, Cambridge, 27–29 January 2003.

[126] *Tadić* Decision on Interlocutory Appeal on Jurisdiction, above note 103, para 70.

[127] Agreement on a Ceasefire between the Government of the Democratic Socialist Republic of Sri Lanka and the Liberation Tigers of Tamil Eelam, 22 February 2002.

[128] Cf *Prosecutor v Gotovina, Čermak and Markač*, IT-06-90-T, Judgment, 15 April 2011, para 1694.

however, on occasion, these do occur. Thus, upon the Government of Sri Lanka's defeat of the LTTE in 2009, the application of international humanitarian law ceased. However, the military victory must be complete; remnants of fighting following victory should not continue to take place, otherwise the law of non-international armed conflict would continue to apply.

8

Protection of Civilians and Persons *Hors de Combat*

1. Introduction

This chapter is the first of two that explore the substantive rules that are applicable in non-international armed conflict. It focuses on the rules relating to the protection of civilians and persons *hors de combat*. Application of these rules to non-international armed conflict has a long and distinguished history. Rules of this sort were included in the instructions of General Dufour issued during the Swiss civil war in 1847 and are to be found in the Tratado de Regularización of 1820 concluded during the Colombian war of independence.[1] It is also rules of this sort that were included in the first systematic regulation of non-international armed conflict, namely common Article 3 of the 1949 Geneva Conventions.

Today, there are very many rules that relate to the treatment of persons and these may be loosely divided into three categories: the principle of humane treatment and specific rules deriving from that principle; rules that relate to the protection of particular categories of persons, for example the wounded and sick, the missing and the dead, and the detained; and rules on humanitarian assistance. Each of these categories is considered in turn. The rules relating to the conduct of hostilities, which also contains protections for civilians, is considered in the following chapter.

2. Humane treatment

2.1 The principle

The principle of humane treatment is the basic principle that informs international humanitarian law relating to the treatment of persons in the power of the adversary, whether civilians or persons *hors de combat*. Common Article 3 provides that persons who do not take an active part in hostilities 'shall in all circumstances be treated humanely'.[2] Additional Protocol II contains an entire part on 'humane treatment', setting out fundamental guarantees in respect of such persons.[3] The principle of humane treatment is also a norm of customary international law.[4]

The principle of humane treatment is generally accepted by parties to conflicts and is a frequent component of instructions issued to the armed forces and codes of conduct internal to the armed group. For example, during the Swiss civil war of 1847, General

---

[1] See above, 21–2 and 25–6.
[2] Common Article 3(1).
[3] Additional Protocol II, Part II.
[4] See eg *Military and Paramilitary Activities In and Against Nicaragua (Nicaragua v United States of America)* [1986] ICJ Rep 14, 114, paras 218–20; *Prosecutor v Tadić*, IT-94-1-AR72, Decision on the Defence Motion for Interlocutory Appeal on Jurisdiction, 2 October 1995, para 98; Customary International Humanitarian Law, Rule 87.

Dufour instructed: '[d]isarm the prisoners of war, but do them no harm and do not insult them. On the contrary, treat them as well as possible so as to set them right. Allow them to return home if they promise, on their honor, to put aside their uniforms and not to take up arms again.'[5] During the armed conflict in Niger (2007–9), members of the Mouvement des Nigériens pour la Justice (MNJ) 'were required to swear an oath on the Qur'an that included not harming civilians or damaging their possessions'.[6] The Eight Points for Attention of the Chinese People's Liberation Army (CPLA) issued in 1947 provided '[d]on't ill-treat captives',[7] an injunction also contained in the codes of conduct of the Revolutionary United Front (RUF) of Sierra Leone,[8] and the National Democratic Front of the Philippines (NDFP).[9] Along similar lines, the Code of Conduct of the National Resistance Army (NRA) of Uganda provided: '[n]ever abuse, insult, shout at, or beat any member of the public',[10] and President Museveni of Uganda, previously head of the NRA, has recounted the necessity of 'not mistreat[ing] civilians'.[11] For its part, according to Jean-Pierre Bemba Gombo, 'the MLC [Mouvement pour la Libération du Congo] know that the golden rule enshrined in the Code of Conduct in our army is the protection of civilians and respect for human rights and international humanitarian law in all circumstances'.[12]

The obligation to treat persons humanely also appears in ad hoc, ceasefire, and peace agreements. For example, the 1998 Comprehensive Agreement on Respect for Human Rights and International Humanitarian Law between the Government of the Philippines and the NDFP provided that: '[p]ersons *hors de combat* and those who do not take a direct part in hostilities are entitled to respect for their lives, dignity, human rights, political convictions and their moral and physical integrity and shall be protected in all circumstances and treated humanely without any adverse distinction founded on race, color, faith, sex, birth, social standing or any other similar criteria.'[13] The 2002 Ceasefire Agreement between the Government of Sri Lanka and the Liberation Tigers of Tamil Eelam (LTTE) provided: '[t]he Parties shall in accordance with international law abstain from hostile acts against the civilian population, including such acts as torture, intimidation, abduction, extortion and harassment.'[14] In the Acte d'Engagement, various armed groups in the Democratic Republic of the Congo (DRC) committed to '[s]top acts of violence, abuse, discrimination and exclusion in all forms, against civilian populations, especially women and children, the elderly and

---

[5] Recommandations sur la conduite à tenir envers les habitants et les troupes, reproduced in O Reverdin, *La Guerre du Sonderbund vue par le Général Dufour, Juin 1847–Avril 1848* (Éditions du Journal de Genève, 1987) 43.

[6] O Bangerter, 'Talking to Armed Groups' (2011) 37 *Forced Migration Review* 7, 8.

[7] Eight Points for Attention, in M Tse-Tung, *Selected Works of Mao Tse-Tung, Volume IV* (Foreign Languages Press, 1969) 155.

[8] Reproduced in *Prosecutor v Sesay, Kallon and Gbao*, SCSL-04-15-T, Judgment, 2 March 2009, para 705.

[9] Basic Rules of the New People's Army, Principle IV, reproduced in NDFP, *Declaration of Undertaking to Apply the Geneva Conventions of 1949 and Protocol I of 1977* (NDFP Human Rights Monitoring Committee Booklet No 6) 85, 90.

[10] The National Resistance Army Code of Conduct, reprinted in OO Amaza, *Museveni's Long March from Guerrilla to Statesman* (Kampala, 1998) 246.

[11] YK Museveni, 'The Strategy of Protracted People's War: Uganda' [November–December 2008] *Military Review* 4, 9.

[12] *Prosecutor v Bemba Gombo*, ICC-01/05-01/08, Conclusions de la Défense en Réponse à l'Acte d'Accusation Amendé du 30 Mars 2009, para 239 fn 161.

[13] Part IV, Article 4(1).

[14] Article 2(1).

disabled persons'.[15] Pursuant to a 2006 agreement between the Government of Sudan and the Eastern Sudan Front (ESF), the parties agreed to '[r]efrain from all acts of violence against civilians, as well as threats directed at them and their forceful displacement', and the Peace Agreement concluded between the same parties contained an obligation to refrain from exposing 'civilians to any form of violence, harassment, intimidation, and forced displacement'.[16] A 2004 agreement between the Government of Sudan and the Justice and Equality Movement (JEM) likewise provided that, '[d]uring the cease-fire, each party shall: . . . Refrain from any act of violence or any other abuse on civilian populations'.[17]

Some of these commitments cannot be taken at face value given that they were not followed in practice. For example, the RUF did far worse to civilians than harass and intimidate them.[18] Both the Government of Sri Lanka and the LTTE committed hostile acts against the civilian population.[19] Other commitments, however, were followed, such as the instructions of General Dufour. Thus, each commitment has to be judged on its own terms.

Certain concrete obligations have been derived from the principle of humane treatment and are contained in the text of the instruments themselves, namely prohibitions on violence to life and person, the taking of hostages, outrages upon personal dignity, sentence or execution without fair trial, collective punishments, acts of terrorism, slavery, and pillage.[20] Threats to undertake each of the foregoing are equally prohibited.[21] Given that the obligations are to be found in common Article 3 and Article 4 of Additional Protocol II, they are all of customary international law status.[22] They are considered in detail below.

Detailed exposition of the principle of humane treatment had been considered 'pointless' for want of being self-evident and 'dangerous' for fear of imposing unintended limitations.[23] However, a contrary view held that lack of exposition could lead to an over-abundance of freedom being afforded to the parties to the conflict.[24] Accordingly, a happy medium needed to be found which provided guidance to the parties to the conflict while not unduly constraining the breadth of the principle. Today, a different concern surrounds exposition of the principle. There is a tendency to focus on the concrete manifestations of the principle to the exclusion of the principle itself. While the concrete manifestations are crucial, also crucial is the continued

---

[15] Acte d'Engagement, Article III ('[a]rrêt des actes de violence, d'exaction, de discrimination et d'exclusion, sous toutes formes, à l'égard des populations civiles, particulièrement les femmes et les enfants, les personnes âgées et les personnes avec handicapes').

[16] 19 June 2006; Article 25, para 91.

[17] Agreement on Humanitarian Ceasefire on the Conflict in Darfur, 8 April 2004, Article 2.

[18] See *RUF* Trial Judgment, above note 8; Witness to Truth: Report of the Sierra Leone Truth and Reconciliation Commission (2004).

[19] See eg, relating to the final stages of the conflict, Report of the Secretary-General's Panel of Experts on Accountability in Sri Lanka, 31 March 2011.

[20] Common Article 3; Additional Protocol II, Article 4(1).

[21] Additional Protocol II, Article 4(1).

[22] *Nicaragua*, above note 4, 114, paras 218–19 (common Article 3); Rome Statute, Article 8(2)(c) (common Article 3); ICTR Statute, Article 4; SCSL Statute, Article 3; *Tadić* Decision on Interlocutory Appeal on Jurisdiction, above note 4, para 98; Report of the Secretary-General on the Establishment of a Special Court for Sierra Leone, S/2000/915, 4 October 2000, para 14; *Prosecutor v Akayesu*, ICTR-96-4-T, Judgment, 2 September 1998, para 610; Customary International Humanitarian Law, Rules 88–105.

[23] J Pictet (ed), *The Geneva Conventions of 12 August 1949, Commentary: I Geneva Convention for the Amelioration of the Condition of the Wounded and Sick in Armed Forces in the Field* (ICRC, 1952) 53.

[24] DA Elder, 'The Historical Background of Common Article 3 of The Geneva Convention of 1949' (1979) 11 *Case Western Reserve Journal of International Law* 37, 61.

operation of the broader principle. This becomes apparent if certain words are omitted from common Article 3: '[p]ersons taking no active part in the hostilities... shall in all circumstances be treated humanely... *To this end* the following acts are and shall remain prohibited...'[25] The words emphasized indicate that the primary obligation is one of humane treatment and the prohibitions that are derived from it are merely manifestations of the obligation. This, in turn, means that more can be read into the principle than the listed prohibitions alone. Thus, although international criminal law limits itself to criminalizing the particular manifestations of the principle,[26] the international humanitarian law obligation is far broader.[27] Accordingly, although such things as the prohibition on enforced disappearances and the prohibition on forced labour are not to be found in the treaty lists of the manifestations of humane treatment, they are nonetheless aspects of the required treatment.[28]

The principle of humane treatment is limited to '[p]ersons taking no active part in the hostilities, including members of armed forces who have laid down their arms and those placed *hors de combat* by sickness, wounds, detention, or any other cause'.[29] This raises the issue of whether the reference to 'members of armed forces who have laid down their arms' relates to individual members or to the armed forces as a group. As the text uses the word 'who'—referring to the individual—rather than 'which' or 'that'—referring to the armed forces, it must be a reference to individual members.[30] A proposal by the United Kingdom to the 1949 Diplomatic Conference to replace the word 'who' with the word 'which', 'to indicate that the armed forces as a whole must lay down their arms', was rejected.[31] Further, it is highly unlikely, albeit not impossible, that the armed forces as a whole, rather than individuals or groups of individuals within the armed forces, will be placed *hors de combat* through sickness, wounds, or detention.

2.2 Non-discrimination

The principle of humane treatment operates 'without any adverse distinction founded on race, colour, religion or faith, sex, birth or wealth, or any other similar criteria'.[32] To the list of prohibited distinctions contained in common Article 3, Additional Protocol II adds the grounds of language, political or other opinion, and national or social origin.[33] The general requirement of non-discrimination in the context of humane treatment has customary status, even if each and every adverse distinction listed has not attained such a status.[34]

---

[25] Common Article 3 (emphasis added).
[26] For example, Rome Statute, Article 8(2)(c).
[27] See *Prosecutor v Aleksovski*, IT-95-14/1-T, Judgment, 25 June 1999, para 49; L Moir, 'Violations of Common Article 3 of the Geneva Conventions', in J Doria, H-P Gasser, and MC Bassiouni (eds), *The Legal Regime of the International Criminal Court: Essays in Honour of Professor Igor Blishchenko* (Martinus Nijhoff, 2009) 619, 620.
[28] See also the broader list in International Institute of Humanitarian Law (IIHL), *The Manual on the Law of Non-International Armed Conflict With Commentary* (Sanremo, 2006) 14.
[29] Common Article 3; Rome Statute, Article 8(2)(c). See also Additional Protocol II, Article 4(1).
[30] Pictet, *Commentary on the First Geneva Convention*, above note 23, 53.
[31] *Final Record of the Diplomatic Conference of Geneva of 1949* (Federal Political Department, Berne) Vol II-B, 100.
[32] Common Article 3.
[33] Additional Protocol II, Articles 2(1) and 4(1).
[34] See IIHL Manual, above note 28, 15. Cf Customary International Humanitarian Law, Rule 88, listing all mentioned grounds.

Notable by way of its omission from common Article 3 is distinction on the basis of 'nationality'. The International Committee of the Red Cross (ICRC) suggested its inclusion at the 1949 Diplomatic Conference.[35] However, states cast doubt on its inclusion, pointing to differences afforded to nationals and non-nationals enshrined in national legislation,[36] and due to the desire to treat non-nationals differently from nationals in times of armed conflict.[37] According to the ICRC Commentary on common Article 3, distinction on the basis of nationality in non-international armed conflicts is 'of less importance' than other grounds of distinction; nationality may fall under the category of 'other similar criteria'; and, at any rate, non-nationals still benefit from the guarantees of humane treatment.[38] By the time of the 1974–7 Diplomatic Conference, a nationality-related concept was accepted for inclusion, albeit in the form of national origin rather than nationality itself.[39] Despite its inclusion, it does not prohibit a party from taking 'special security measures in the case of persons of foreign nationality'.[40] The severity of an offence may also vary depending on whether or not it was committed by a national or a non-national.[41]

Discrimination based on nationality has nevertheless been a feature of some non-international armed conflicts. For example, during the armed conflict arising from the Soviet intervention in Afghanistan in 1979, the treatment of prisoners varied according to their religion and nationality. African prisoners as well as Muslim prisoners 'were integrated into the resistance or freed but kept under surveillance'; however, 'foreign non-Muslim prisoners were summarily executed'.[42] Different treatment was also afforded to 'Afghan conscripts, members of the Afghan Communist Party, important persons, or members of the foreign armed forces'.[43] Thus, the prohibition on discrimination on particular grounds, particularly insofar as detained persons are concern, is an important one.

2.3 Specific prohibitions deriving from the principle of humane treatment

2.3.1 *Violence to life and person*

Violence to life and person against persons in the power of the adversary is prohibited in conventional and customary international humanitarian law.[44] Accordingly, acts such as murder, mutilation, cruel treatment, torture, medical or scientific experimentation,

---

[35] *Final Record*, above note 31, Vol II-B, 94 (ICRC).
[36] Ibid (United States).
[37] Ibid (France).
[38] Pictet, *Commentary on the First Geneva Convention*, above note 23, 55–6. See also F Siordet, 'The Geneva Conventions and Civil War' (1950) 3 *IRRC Supplement* 201, 214.
[39] Articles 2(1) and 4(1).
[40] *Official Records of the Diplomatic Conference on the Reaffirmation and Development of International Humanitarian Law Applicable in Armed Conflicts, Geneva (1974–1977)* (Federal Political Department, 1978) Vol 8, 210, para 45 (ICRC).
[41] Ibid.
[42] Report on the Situation of Human Rights in Afghanistan, E/CN.4/1985/21, 19 February 1985, para 103. The characterization of the conflict is, though, open to question.
[43] Ibid, para 164. See also, in the context of the armed conflicts fought by Imperial Germany: IV Hull, 'Prisoners in Colonial Warfare: The Imperial German Example', in S Scheipers (ed), *Prisoners in War* (Oxford University Press, 2010) 157, 166–8.
[44] Common Article 3; Additional Protocol II, Article 4; Rome Statute, Article 8(2)(c)(i); *Nicaragua*, above note 4, 114, paras 218–19; Report of the Secretary-General on the establishment of a Special Court for Sierra Leone, S/2000/915, 4 October 2000, para 14.

and corporal punishment are prohibited.[45] As with the manifestations of the principle of humane treatment, these are simply illustrations of the prohibited violence. The general prohibition is one of violence to life and person and the underlying principle in this area is that of bodily integrity. As General Assembly Resolution 2675 (XXV) puts it: '[c]ivilian populations, or individual members thereof, should not be the object of... assaults on their integrity.'[46] This includes both the physical and mental health of the individual in question.[47] Care was taken not to go into too much detail on the basis that 'the more specific and complete a list tries to be, the more restrictive it becomes'.[48] Accordingly, although the language of 'violence to life and person' may be insufficiently precise for international criminal law purposes—thus the *Vasiljević* Trial Chamber acquitted the defendant of that charge[49]—its open-ended nature is important for the law of armed conflict.

Certain acts are singled out in the international humanitarian law instruments for especial mention.

Murder

Murder is a crime that 'is clearly understood and well defined in the domestic law of every State'.[50] Murder has been defined as the 'death of the victim resulting from an act or omission of the accused committed with the intention to kill or cause serious bodily harm which he/she should reasonably have known might lead to death'.[51] The prohibition on murder is largely the same as that on wilful killing.[52]

A prohibition on murder or killing is to be found in numerous codes of conduct, instructions, and bilateral agreements. For example, the manifesto of the CPLA provided that members of the army were not to 'kill or humiliate any of Chiang Kai-shek's army officers and men who lay down their arms'.[53] Similarly, the Code of Conduct of the NRA included the injunction: '[n]ever kill any member of the public or any captured prisoners, as the guns should only be reserved for armed enemies or opponents.'[54] President Museveni of Uganda, previously Head of the NRA, has recounted the importance of the prohibition on killing civilians:

> don't kill civilians! Civilians should not be killed if they are not armed—even if they are for the government—you scare them away, [tell them] 'Don't come back here. If we find you here again, you'll see.' The fellow will just run away. You don't have to kill. And that, by the way, is also part of building the prestige of the revolutionary movement. Because the word goes around, 'These people are not killers! They could have killed me. They captured me. I was in their control but they told me to go away'.[55]

---

[45] Common Article 3; Rome Statute, Article 8(2)(c)(i) and 8(2)(e)(xi); Additional Protocol II, Article 4(2).
[46] GA Res 2675 (XXV) (1970).
[47] Additional Protocol II, Article 4(2)(a).
[48] Pictet, *Commentary on the First Geneva Convention*, above note 23, 54.
[49] See *Prosecutor v Vasiljević*, IT-98-32-T, Judgment, 29 November 2002, paras 193–204.
[50] A Zimmermann, 'War Crimes—Article 8 para. 2(c)(i)', in O Triffterer (ed), *Commentary on the Rome Statute of the International Criminal Court: Observers' Notes, Article by article* (Nomos Verlagsgesellschaft, 1999) 273.
[51] *Prosecutor v Krstić*, IT-98-33-T, Judgment, 2 August 2001, para 485. The definition was cited with approval by the *Kvočka* Appeals Chamber: *Prosecutor v Kvočka*, IT-98-30/1-T, Judgment, 2 November 2001, para 259.
[52] *Prosecutor v Delalić et al*, IT-96-21-T, Judgment, 16 November 1998, para 422.
[53] Manifesto of the Chinese People's Liberation Army, in M Tse-Tung, *Selected Works of Mao Tse-Tung, Volume IV* (Foreign Languages Press, 1969) 147, 151.
[54] National Resistance Army Code of Conduct, above note 10.
[55] Museveni, Strategy, above note 11, 8.

The Code of the Chin National Front (CNF) also provides for an obligation not to kill or hurt civilians or detainees.[56] The Operational Code of Conduct issued in 1967 to the armed forces of the Federal Republic of Nigeria during the attempted secession of Biafra provided that '[u]nder no circumstances should pregnant women be illtreated or killed', that '[c]hildren must not be molested or killed', and that '[s]oldiers who surrender will not be killed'.[57] The Code was found by an independent observer mission to have been followed by Federal troops.[58] Numerous ad hoc and ceasefire agreements also contained a prohibition on murder, killing, or summary executions.[59] Nonetheless, as is all too well known, the killing of persons in the power of the adversary is commonplace. Indeed, despite the commitments set out above, writing elsewhere, Mao Tse-Tung advocated the killing of prisoners: '[i]t is best to require the prisoners first to hand over their weapons, and then to disperse them, or to execute them.'[60] The frequency of violations makes examples too numerous to mention.

Torture

For the purposes of international humanitarian law and international criminal law in situations of non-international armed conflict, torture is defined as the intentional infliction of severe pain or suffering for a particular listed purpose.[61] The definition is based on the Convention against Torture but is not identical to it. In particular, the individual committing the act need not be a 'public official or other person acting in an official capacity'.[62] This is crucial given that, otherwise, members of armed groups may not fall within the definition,[63] and it illustrates the importance of not transposing from one body of the law automatically to another without having regard to the specificities of each of those bodies.[64]

Torture is distinguishable from other forms of mistreatment on the basis of the purpose for which it is carried out, as well as the severity of the pain or suffering that results.[65] The prohibited purposes include obtaining information or a confession; punishing, intimidating, or coercing either the victim or a third person; and

---

[56] Chin National Front, Code, undated (attributed to 1998).

[57] Operational Code of Conduct for the Nigerian Army, para 4(b), July 1967, issued by Major-General Yakubu Gowon, Head of the Federal Military Government, Commander-in-Chief of the Armed Forces Of the Federal Republic of Nigeria, reproduced in AHM Kirk-Greene, *Crisis and Conflict in Nigeria: A Documentary Sourcebook 1966–1969: Volume I* (Oxford University Press, 1971) 455, 456.

[58] Report of the Observer Team to Nigeria, 24 September to 23 November 1968, Presented to Parliament by the Secretary of State for Foreign and Commonwealth Affairs by Command of Her Majesty (HMSO, January 1969) 12.

[59] See eg Comprehensive Agreement on Human Rights and International Humanitarian Law between the Government of the Philippines and the National Democratic Front, Part IV, Article 3(1); Comprehensive Ceasefire Agreement between the Government of the Republic of Burundi and the Palipehutu-FNL, 7 September 2006, Article 1.1.5.

[60] M Tse-Tung, *Basic Tactics* (Pall Mall Press, 1967) 98.

[61] See *Prosecutor v Kunarac et al*, IT-96-23-A and IT-96-23/1-A, Judgment, 12 June 2002, para 142. See also ICC Elements of Crimes, Article 8(2)(c)(i).

[62] *Kunarac* Appeal Judgment, above note 61, para 148. Cf Convention against Torture, Article 1.

[63] See S Sivakumaran, 'Torture in International Human Rights and International Humanitarian Law: The Actor and the Ad Hoc Tribunals' (2005) 18 *LJIL* 541.

[64] See above, 65–77.

[65] *Prosecutor v Krnojelac*, IT-97-25-T, Judgment, 15 March 2002, paras 180–1; *Delalić* Trial Judgment, above note 52, para 470; *Prosecutor v Brđanin*, IT-99-36-T, Judgment, 1 September 2004, paras 483, 486.

discrimination on any ground.⁶⁶ It remains unclear whether other prohibited purposes are included, in particular that of humiliation,⁶⁷ or whether, rather, that is separately prohibited. The prohibited purpose need not be the sole or even principal purpose for inflicting the pain or suffering. That the pain or suffering was inflicted for any prohibited purpose renders its infliction also for other purposes irrelevant.⁶⁸

The pain or suffering must be severe,⁶⁹ although the level of severity can only be assessed on a case-by-case basis. What can be stated in the abstract is that neither permanent injury nor visible injury is required,⁷⁰ and the pain or suffering may be physical or mental.⁷¹ In assessing the severity of the suffering, regard must be had to an objective determination of the mistreatment, as well as such subjective criteria as the actual effect of the act or omission on the victim;⁷² the victim's age, sex, and health;⁷³ the victim's 'specific social, cultural and religious background';⁷⁴ and 'the nature and context of the infliction of pain, the premeditation and institutionalisation of the ill-treatment, the physical condition of the victim, the manner and method used, and the position of inferiority of the victim'.⁷⁵

Cruel and inhuman treatment

The term 'cruel treatment' is largely synonymous with that of 'inhuman treatment'.⁷⁶ The ICTY has defined cruel treatment as 'an intentional act or omission... which causes serious mental or physical suffering or injury or constitutes a serious attack on human dignity'.⁷⁷ It need not be carried out for a listed purpose as is the case with the definition of torture. For its part, the Elements of Crimes of the International Criminal Court (ICC) refers to the infliction of 'severe physical or mental pain or suffering upon one or more persons'.⁷⁸ The assessment of seriousness is a relative one: '[a]ll the factual circumstances must be taken into account, including the nature of the act or omission, the context in which it occurs, its duration and/or repetition, the physical, mental and

---

⁶⁶ *Prosecutor v Kunarac et al*, IT-96-23-T and IT-96-23/1-T, Judgment, 22 February 2001, para 485. See also *Krnojelac* Trial Judgment, above note 65, para 185; *Prosecutor v Limaj*, IT-03-66-T, Judgment, 30 November 2005, para 239; ICC Elements of Crimes, Article 8(2)(c)(i)-4.

⁶⁷ For inclusion of humiliation, see *Prosecutor v Kvočka et al*, IT-98-30/1-T, Judgment, 2 November 2001, para 141; *Prosecutor v Furundžija*, IT-95-17/1-T, Judgment, 10 December 1998, para 162; *Prosecutor v Furundžija*, IT-95-17/1-A, Judgment, 21 July 2000, para 111. But cf *Krnojelac* Trial Judgment, above note 65, para 186; ICC Elements of Crimes, Article 8(2)(c)(i)-4, from which humiliation is absent.

⁶⁸ *Delalić* Trial Judgment, above note 52, para 470; *Kvočka* Trial Judgment, above note 67, para 153; *Kunarac* Appeal Judgment, above note 61, para 155; *Brđanin* Trial Judgment, above note 65, para 487.

⁶⁹ Convention against Torture, Article 1; ICC Elements of Crimes, Article 8(2)(c)(i)-4.

⁷⁰ *Brđanin* Trial Judgment, above note 65, para 484.

⁷¹ *Kunarac* Appeal Judgment, above note 61, para 142.

⁷² *Kvočka* Trial Judgment, above note 67, para 143. See also *Brđanin* Trial Judgment, above note 65, para 484; *Limaj* Trial Judgment, above note 66, para 237.

⁷³ *Kvočka* Trial Judgment, above note 67, para 143. See also *Brđanin* Trial Judgment, above note 65, para 484; *Limaj* Trial Judgment, above note 66, para 237.

⁷⁴ *Limaj* Trial Judgment, above note 66, para 237. See also *Delalić* Trial Judgment, above note 52, para 495.

⁷⁵ *Krnojelac* Trial Judgment, above note 65, para 182. See also *Limaj* Trial Judgment, above note 66, para 237.

⁷⁶ *Delalić* Trial Judgment, above note 52, para 552; *Prosecutor v Blaškić*, Judgment, IT-95-14-T (3 March 2000) para 186; *Prosecutor v Kordić and Čerkez*, IT-95-14/2-T, Judgment, 26 February 2001, para 265.

⁷⁷ *Delalić* Trial Judgment, above note 52, para 552. See also *Kordić* Trial Judgment, above note 76, para 265; *Prosecutor v Naletilić and Martinović*, IT-98-34-T, Judgment, 31 March 2003, para 246.

⁷⁸ ICC Elements of Crimes, Article 8(2)(c)(i)-3.

moral effects of the act on the victim and the personal circumstances of the victim, including age, sex and health.'[79] Importantly, there is no significant temporal element; the suffering need not be 'lasting' as long as it is both 'real and serious'.[80]

2.3.2 Outrages upon personal dignity

Outrages upon personal dignity are prohibited in conventional and customary international law.[81] According to the ICTY, outrages upon personal dignity are essentially a subset of the broader prohibition on inhuman treatment.[82] The *Furundžija* Trial Chamber thus noted that the prohibition is 'intended to shield human beings from outrages upon their personal dignity, whether such outrages are carried out by unlawfully attacking the body or by humiliating and debasing the honour, the self-respect or the mental well-being of a person'.[83] Despite the suggestion of the ICTY, the prohibition on inhuman treatment and the prohibition on outrages upon personal dignity are of different sorts. Whereas inhuman treatment revolves around ideas of integrity of the body and mind, outrages upon personal dignity relate to ideas of dignity. Indeed, it was originally linked to notions of protection from 'public curiosity'.[84] This is confirmed by the ICC Elements of Crimes, which does not define inhuman treatment by reference to an attack on human dignity, as does the ICTY.[85] Thus, while the notions of outrages upon personal dignity and inhuman treatment are related, they are conceptually different.

As with violence to life and person, the listed treaty proscriptions are but examples of outrages upon personal dignity. The prohibition would include such things as 'publicly parading captured personnel in a manner subjecting them to ridicule and insult',[86] and forcing individuals to eat food prohibited by their religion.[87] Certain examples of outrages upon personal dignity that are listed in conventional instruments fit better under other headings. Thus, the prohibitions on rape and enforced prostitution, considered outrages upon personal dignity,[88] are better considered as sexual offences in their own right in order to capture the particular harm resulting from the acts.

Outrages upon person dignity are closely linked with, and sometimes described as, humiliating and degrading treatment. Thus common Article 3 prohibits 'outrages upon personal dignity, in particular, humiliating and degrading treatment'. These forms of treatment have been defined as acts or omissions that cause humiliation, degradation, or attacks on human dignity.[89] The acts or omissions need not result in actual harm;

---

[79] *Krnojelac* Trial Judgment, above note 65, para 131.
[80] Ibid.
[81] Common Article 3; Rome Statute, Article 8(2)(c)(ii); Additional Protocol II, Article 4(2)(e); *Nicaragua*, above note 4, 114, para 218; Report of the Secretary-General on the establishment of a Special Court for Sierra Leone, S/2000/915, 4 October 2000, para 14.
[82] *Prosecutor v Aleksovski*, IT-95-14/1-A, Judgment, 24 March 2000, para 26; *Kunarac* Trial Judgment, above note 66, para 502.
[83] *Furundžija* Trial Judgment, above note 67, para 183.
[84] On which, see 1929 Geneva Convention relative to the Treatment of Prisoners of War, Article 2; *Trial of Lieutenant General Kurt Maelzer*, XI Law Reports of Trials of War Criminals 53.
[85] ICC Elements of Crimes, Article 8(2)(c)(i)-3. See above, 262.
[86] IIHL Manual, above note 28, 16.
[87] K Dörmann, *Elements of War Crimes under the Rome Statute of the International Criminal Court: Sources and Commentary* (Cambridge University Press, 2003) 315.
[88] Additional Protocol II, Article 4(2)(e).
[89] *Kunarac* Trial Judgment, above note 66, para 514. This met with the approval of the Appeals Chamber: *Kunarac* Appeal Judgment, above note 61, para 163. See also ICC Elements of Crimes, Article 8(2)(c)(ii)-1.

instead, it is enough that they cause suffering.[90] This is judged both objectively and subjectively. Objectively, the act should cause humiliation, degradation, or an attack on human dignity,[91] and will depend on such factors as the 'form, severity and duration of the violence [and] the intensity and duration of the physical or mental suffering'.[92] Subjectively, the individual's 'temperament or sensitivity' should be taken into account,[93] as should the 'cultural background' of the victim.[94] There is no 'minimum temporal requirement'; the humiliation must be more then 'fleeting' but need not be 'lasting'.[95]

For the purposes of the criminalization of the prohibition, that is to say the war crime of committing outrages upon personal dignity, the humiliation is required to be serious.[96] However, this is likely a distinction between the international criminal law prohibition and its international humanitarian law counterpart.[97] This is not to say that each and every act that results in humiliation or degradation will automatically amount to a violation of international humanitarian law; a threshold of suffering will still have to be utilized. However, that threshold will differ as between what constitutes a violation of international humanitarian law and what amounts to a war crime.

It has been suggested that the category of outrages upon personal dignity is 'an anachronism of chivalry' and 'out of place in a listing of proscribed inhumane activities'.[98] However, the prohibition does play an important role given that acts that debase personal dignity continue to occur in times of non-international armed conflict. In order to prevent such acts taking place, certain armed groups have issued instructions that seek to prohibit such acts. For example, the Manifesto of the CPLA contained an instruction not to 'humiliate any of Chiang Kai-Shek's army officers and men who lay down their arms'.[99] The CPLA's Eight Points of Attention provided '[d]ont hit or swear at people',[100] and the Eight Codes of Conduct of the RUF similarly provided '[d]o not hate or swear at people'.[101] Likewise, the Comprehensive Agreement on Human Rights and International Humanitarian Law between the Government of the Philippines and the NDFP prohibited acts against the dignity of persons, and against the moral integrity of persons.[102]

2.3.3 Sexual violence

Rape, enforced prostitution, indecent assault, and threats thereof are all prohibited in Additional Protocol II.[103] Their proscription also reflects norms of customary

---

[90] *Aleksovski* Trial Judgment, above note 27, para 56.
[91] *Kunarac* Trial Judgment, above note 66, para 507.
[92] *Aleksovski* Trial Judgment, above note 27, para 57.
[93] *Kvočka* Trial Judgment, above note 67, para 167.
[94] ICC Elements of Crimes, Article 8(2)(c)(ii)-1, fn.
[95] *Kunarac* Trial Judgment, above note 66, para 501. But cf *Aleksovski* Trial Judgment, above note 27, para 56.
[96] *Kunarac* Trial Judgment, above note 66, para 503.
[97] On which see above, 78–81.
[98] Elder, above note 24, 63.
[99] Manifesto of the Chinese People's Liberation Army, above note 53.
[100] On the Reissue of the Three Main Rules of Discipline and the Eight Points for Attention, Instruction of the General Headquarters of the Chinese People's Liberation Army, 10 October 1947, above note 7.
[101] Reproduced in *RUF* Trial Judgment, above note 8, para 705. As the Eight Codes of the RUF was based on those of the CPLA, it is unclear whether the injunction was intended also to read 'hit'.
[102] Part IV, Articles 3(1) and 4(1).
[103] Additional Protocol II, Article 4(2)(e) and (h).

international humanitarian law.[104] Although contained under the rubric of outrages upon personal dignity, as indicated above, the prohibition is a sub-category in its own right under the broader rubric of humane treatment. This is now accepted, with the Rome Statute listing rape, sexual slavery, enforced prostitution, forced pregnancy, enforced sterilization, and other forms of sexual violence as war crimes in their own right, rather than as a subset of the prohibition on outrages upon personal dignity.[105]

Rape has been defined in a number of different ways in the jurisprudence of the ICTY and International Criminal Tribunal for Rwanda (ICTR). The *Akayesu* Trial Chamber held that rape could be defined as 'a physical invasion of a sexual nature, committed on a person under circumstances which are coercive'. Reference to coercive circumstances included physical force, '[t]hreats, intimidation, extortion and other forms of duress which prey on fear or desperation'.[106] This conceptual approach to the definition was upheld in a number of cases, but was not followed by the ICTY in *Furundžija*, which opted for a more mechanical approach. The *Furundžija* Trial Chamber defined rape as 'the sexual penetration, however slight (a) of the vagina or anus of the victim by the penis of the perpetrator or any other object used by the perpetrator; or (b) of the mouth of the victim by the penis of the perpetrator' where the penetration occurs through 'coercion or force or threat of force against the victim or a third person'.[107] A third approach, in *Kunarac*, was to define the element of coercion by reference to lack of consent: where 'such sexual penetration occurs without the consent of the victim. Consent for this purpose must be consent given voluntarily, as a result of the victim's free will, assessed in the context of the surrounding circumstances'.[108] The surrounding circumstances in war crimes cases were considered to be 'almost universally coercive. That is to say, true consent will not be possible'.[109] A middle position was adopted by the ICTR Appeals Chamber in *Gacumbitsi*, pursuant to which lack of consent is an element of the offence, but this may be proved 'by proving the existence of coercive circumstances under which meaningful consent is not possible'.[110] Accordingly, a variety of approaches have been set out to define rape and to define consent. For its part, the ICC Elements of Crimes requires:

1. The perpetrator invaded the body of a person by conduct resulting in penetration, however slight, of any part of the body of the victim or of the perpetrator with a sexual organ, or of the anal or genital opening of the victim with any object or any other part of the body.
2. The invasion was committed by force, or by threat of force or coercion, such as that caused by fear of violence, duress, detention, psychological oppression or abuse of power,

---

[104] Rome Statute, Article 8(2)(e)(vi); Customary International Humanitarian Law, Rule 93; Report of the Secretary-General on the establishment of a Special Court for Sierra Leone, S/2000/915, 4 October 2000, para 14.
[105] Rome Statute, Article 8(2)(e)(vi).
[106] *Akayesu* Trial Judgment, above note 22, paras 598 and 688.
[107] *Furundžija* Trial Judgment, above note 67, para 185.
[108] *Kunarac* Trial Judgment, above note 66, para 460; *Kunarac* Appeal Judgment, above note 61, para 127.
[109] Ibid, para 130.
[110] *Gacumbitsi v the Prosecutor*, ICTR-2001-64-A, Judgment, 7 July 2006, para 155. See generally W Schomburg and I Peterson, 'Genuine Consent to Sexual Violence under International Criminal Law' (2007) 101 *AJIL* 121.

against such person or another person, or by taking advantage of a coercive environment, or the invasion was committed against a person incapable of giving genuine consent.[111]

Sexual slavery is comprised of two elements: the element of enslavement and the element of the sexual nature of the enslavement. As to the first, the ICC Elements of Crimes provides that '[t]he perpetrator exercised any or all of the powers attaching to the right of ownership over one or more persons, such as by purchasing, selling, lending or bartering such a person or persons, or by imposing on them a similar deprivation of liberty'.[112] This follows the jurisprudence of the ICTY which held that enslavement consisted of 'the exercise of any or all of the powers attaching to the right of ownership over a person'.[113] Factors that go to the determination of enslavement include 'control of someone's movement, control of physical environment, psychological control, measures taken to prevent or deter escape, force, threat of force or coercion, duration, assertion of exclusivity, subjection to cruel treatment and abuse, control of sexuality and forced labour'.[114] The specific crime of sexual slavery as distinct from that of enslavement emanates from the second element, namely that '[t]he perpetrator caused such person or persons to engage in one or more acts of a sexual nature'.[115] As the Special Court for Sierra Leone (SCSL) has noted, the specific crime of sexual slavery is 'designed to draw attention to serious crimes that have been historically overlooked and to recognise the particular nature of sexual violence that has been used, often with impunity, as a tactic of war to humiliate, dominate and instil fear in victims, their families and communities during armed conflict'.[116]

Enforced prostitution has been defined as:

1. The perpetrator caused one or more persons to engage in one or more acts of a sexual nature by force, or by threat of force or coercion, such as that caused by fear of violence, duress, detention, psychological oppression or abuse of power, against such person or persons or another person, or by taking advantage of a coercive environment or such person's or persons' incapacity to give genuine consent.

2. The perpetrator or another person obtained or expected to obtain pecuniary or other advantage in exchange for or in connection with the acts of a sexual nature.[117]

Forced pregnancy is defined in the Elements of Crimes as '[t]he perpetrator confined one or more women forcibly made pregnant, with the intent of affecting the ethnic composition of any population or carrying out other grave violations of international law'.[118] The latter clause of the crime is important as it does not limit the crime to ethnic conflicts or crimes against ethnic groups during a conflict.

---

[111] ICC Elements of Crimes, Article 8(2)(e)(vi)-1 (fn omitted).
[112] Article 8(2)(e)(vi)-2.
[113] *Kunarac* Trial Judgment, above note 66, para 540; *Kunarac* Appeal Judgment, above note 61, paras 116–18. See V Oosterveld, 'Sexual Slavery and the International Criminal Court Advancing International Law' (2003–4) 25 *Michigan Journal of International Law* 605.
[114] *Kunarac* Appeal Judgment, above note 61, para 119, approving the holding of the Trial Chamber. See also *RUF* Trial Judgment, above note 8, para 160.
[115] Article 8(2)(e)(vi)-2.
[116] *RUF* Trial Judgment, above note 8, para 156.
[117] ICC Elements of Crimes, Article 8(2)(e)(vi)-3.
[118] Ibid, Article 8(2)(e)(vi)-4.

The crux of the crime of enforced sterilization is that '[t]he perpetrator deprived one or more persons of biological reproductive capacity'.[119] This may take various forms, including mutilation of the genitals, castration, or beatings resulting in failure of reproductive capacity, as well as failure of reproductive capacity being the consequence of other acts, such as repeated rape.

The abovementioned crimes are not the only crimes of sexual violence that are prohibited in times of non-international armed conflict. The war crime of 'any other form of sexual violence' covers acts of sexual violence 'of a gravity comparable to that of a serious violation of [common] article 3'.[120] This residual category would include such acts as sexual mutilation not falling within enforced sterilization, forced nudity, and enforced masturbation, all of which are common in situations of non-international armed conflict. Furthermore, it is important to recall that international criminal law is not the same as international humanitarian law,[121] the principle of legality requiring it to be of great specificity. Thus, it is not only the war crimes that are set out immediately above, in their specific confines that are prohibited in times of non-international armed conflict, but sexual violence more generally.

All the offences apart from forced pregnancy are gender neutral.[122] The ICC Elements of Crimes expressly notes that the word 'invasion' in the definition of rape 'is intended to be broad enough to be gender neutral'.[123] This is important given the numerous instances of sexual violence committed against men and boys in armed conflicts.

Codes of conduct of armed groups not infrequently contain mention of the prohibition on rape and other forms of sexual violence. Although the language of rape and sexual violence may not be used, the codes instead using language understood by fighters, it is clear that it is that which is prohibited. Thus, the Eight Points for Attention of the CPLA instructed members not to 'take liberties with women'.[124] The Eight Points for Attention adopted by the NDFP and the Eight Codes of Conduct adopted by the RUF provided likewise;[125] however, in actuality, there were numerous instances of rape and sexual violence on the part of the RUF.[126] Similarly, the Code of Conduct of the NRA of Uganda provided: '[n]ever develop illegitimate relationship[s] with any woman because there are no women as such waiting for passing soldiers yet many women are wives, or daughters of somebody somewhere. Any illegitimate relationship is bound to harm our good relations with the public.'[127] President Museveni of Uganda, previously Head of the NRA, has recounted the importance of the injunction of 'not tak[ing] liberties with women'.[128] The Code of the CNF prohibits rape, sexual abuse, and sexual harassment.[129] The Code of Conduct issued by the Nigerian Government in 1967 during the attempted secession of Biafra required that '[w]omen will be protected against any attack on their person, honour and in particular against rape or any form of indecent assault',[130] a code that was found to have been followed by an independent observer mission.[131] Ceasefire agreements also

---

[119] Ibid, Article 8(2)(e)(vi)-5.   [120] Ibid, Article 8(2)(e)(vi)-6.   [121] See above, 78–81.
[122] See S Sivakumaran, 'Sexual Violence against Men in Armed Conflict' (2007) 18 *EJIL* 253.
[123] ICC Elements of Crimes, Article 8(2)(e)(vi)-1, fn. See also *RUF* Trial Judgment, above note 8, para 146.
[124] Eight Points for Attention, above note 7.
[125] 'Basic Rules of the New People's Army', above note 9, Principle IV. The Eight Codes of Conduct of the RUF is reproduced in *RUF* Trial Judgment, above note 8, para 705.
[126] See eg *RUF* Trial Judgment, ibid, paras 1283–308, 1575–82.
[127] National Resistance Army Code of Conduct, above note 10.
[128] Museveni, Strategy, above note 11, 9.
[129] Chin National Front, Code, above note 56.
[130] Operational Code of Conduct for the Nigerian Army, above note 56, para 4(i).
[131] Report of the Observer Team to Nigeria, above note 58, 12.

contain a prohibition on sexual violence.[132] For their part, JEM and the Sudan Liberation Army (SLA) have 'reaffirm[ed] our commitment...to hold to account perpetrators of acts of rape and other forms of gender based violence'.[133] This reaffirmation bolsters an earlier finding of the UN International Commission of Inquiry that there were 'few cases reported of rebels committing rape and sexual violence' and that 'during its own investigations of incidents involving rebels, the Commission did not find any cases of rape committed by the rebels'.[134]

2.3.4 Slavery and the slave trade

Slavery and the slave trade in all their forms are prohibited both in conventional and customary international law.[135] Threats to enslave are equally prohibited.[136] Slavery has been defined as 'the exercise of any or all of the powers attaching to the right of ownership over a person'.[137] Factors that indicate slavery include 'control of someone's movement, control of physical environment, psychological control, measures taken to prevent or deter escape, force, threat of force or coercion, duration, assertion of exclusivity, subjection to cruel treatment and abuse, control of sexuality and forced labour'.[138] The phrase 'slavery and the slave trade in all their forms' was taken from the Slavery Convention and includes 'certain institutions and practices comparable to slavery, such as servitude for the payments of debts, serfdom, the purchase of wives and the exploitation of child labour'.[139] Today, 'contemporary forms of slavery', such as sale into marriage, would fall within the scope of the prohibition. The 'trafficking in persons, particularly women and children, for sexual or any other unlawful purposes' would be another pertinent example.[140]

2.3.5 Taking of hostages

The taking of hostages is prohibited in conventional and customary international humanitarian law,[141] as are threats thereof.[142] The inclusion of this prohibition in common Article 3 was considered innovative in 1949, prohibiting as it did practices

---

[132] See eg Comprehensive Ceasefire Agreement between the Government of the Republic of Burundi and the Palipehutu-FNL, 7 September 2006, Article 1.1.5.

[133] 'Statement by the Opposition Movements [JEM and SLM-Unity]', undated (published on 11 July 2008).

[134] Report of the International Commission of Inquiry on Darfur to the United Nations Secretary-General, paras 335 and 355.

[135] Additional Protocol II, Article 4(2)(f); *Krnojelac* Trial Judgment, above note 65, para 353; Customary International Humanitarian Law, Rule 94; Report of the Secretary-General on the establishment of a Special Court for Sierra Leone, S/2000/915, 4 October 2000, para 14.

[136] Additional Protocol II, Article 4(2)(h).

[137] *Kunarac* Trial Judgment, above note 66, para 539; *Kunarac* Appeal Judgment, above note 61, para 117. A slight variation to the wording was introduced at para 118.

[138] *Kunarac* Trial Judgment, above note 66, para 543; *Kunarac* Appeal Judgment, above note 61, para 119.

[139] Y Sandoz, C Swinarski, and B Zimmermann (eds), *Commentary on the Additional Protocols of 8 June 1977 to the Geneva Conventions of 12 August 1949* (ICRC, 1987) 1376.

[140] IIHL *Manual*, above note 28, 17.

[141] Common Article 3; Additional Protocol II, Article 4(2)(c); Rome Statute, Article 8(2)(c)(iii); ICTR Statute, Article 4(c); SCSL Statute, Article 3(c); Customary International Humanitarian Law, Rule 96; *Nicaragua*, above note 4, 114, para 218; Report of the Secretary-General on the establishment of a Special Court for Sierra Leone, S/2000/915, 4 October 2000, para 14.

[142] Additional Protocol II, Article 4(2)(h).

that were then in common use,[143] as evident by the Trial Judgment in *Wilhelm List and Others*, which observed that hostages could be taken and executed as a 'last resort'.[144] The 1979 Convention against the Taking of Hostages provides a useful definition of the act:

> Any person who seizes or detains and threatens to kill, to injure or to continue to detain another person (hereinafter referred to as the 'hostage') in order to compel a third party, namely, a State, an international intergovernmental organization, a natural or juridical person, or a group of persons, to do or abstain from doing any act as an explicit or implicit condition for the release of the hostage commits the offence of taking of hostages ('hostage-taking') within the meaning of this Convention.[145]

Even though the Convention was not drafted with an armed conflict in mind—indeed, it expressly provides for its inapplicability to certain such situations[146]—the definition contained therein has been considered appropriate for application in time of armed conflict.[147] Accordingly, the crux of the prohibition is the seizure, detention, or holding hostage of one or more persons, coupled with a threat to kill or continue to detain them, with the intention of compelling a third party to act in particular way.[148] The threat must be 'to kill, to injure or continue to detain' the detained individuals but it may be explicit or implicit.[149] The precise means by which the individual enters the custody of the hostage-taker is immaterial; it may be through lawful means such as detention or internment or through unlawful means such as abduction.[150] As the *RUF* Appeals Chamber put it, 'the precise means by which the individual falls into the hands of the perpetrator is not the defining characteristic of the offence; it is, rather, a secondary feature'.[151] Hostage-taking is not a one-off event but a continuing act; the name of the offence being misleading in this regard. Accordingly, the intention to compel need not be present at the time of the original detention; it may form at a later point in time.[152] Thus, an initially lawful detention could later turn into an unlawful taking of hostages if, at one moment in time, there is seizure, detention, or holding of an individual; a threat to kill or to continue to detain; both with the intention of compelling a third party to act in a particular manner.[153]

The prohibition against the taking of hostages is an important one. A well-known example of hostage-taking during a non-international armed conflict was the RUF taking hostage peacekeepers of the United Nations Mission in Sierra Leone

---

[143] Pictet, *Commentary on the First Geneva Convention*, above note 23, 54.
[144] *The Hostages Trial, Trial of Wilhelm List and Others*, VIII Law Reports of Trials of War Criminals 34, 61 (in the context of occupied territories). On which, see KJ Heller, *The Nuremberg Military Tribunals and the Origins of International Criminal Law* (Oxford University Press, 2011) 214–17.
[145] International Convention against the Taking of Hostages, Article 1(1).
[146] Ibid, Article 12.
[147] *Prosecutor v Sesay, Kallon and Gbao*, SCSL-04-15-A, Judgment, 26 October 2009, para 579.
[148] ICC Elements of Crimes, Article 8(2)(c)(iii); *RUF* Trial Judgment, above note 8, para 240.
[149] *RUF* Trial Judgment, ibid, para 242; *Prosecutor v Blaškić*, IT-95-14-A, Judgment, 29 July 2004, para 639.
[150] *RUF* Appeal Judgment, above note 147, para 598. But cf *Blaškić* Trial Judgment, above note 76, para 187; *Kordić* Trial Judgment, above note 76, paras 319–20; *Prosecutor v Karadžić*, IT-95-5/18-PT, Decision on Six Preliminary Motions Challenging Jurisdiction, 28 April 2009, para 65. See generally, S Sivakumaran, 'War Crimes before the Special Court for Sierra Leone' (2010) 8 *JICJ* 1009, 1031–3.
[151] *RUF* Appeal Judgment, above note 147, para 598.
[152] Ibid, para 597. See also JL Lambert, *Terrorism and Hostages in International Law: A Commentary on the Hostages Convention 1979* (Grotius, 1990) 83.
[153] Sivakumaran, War Crimes, above note 150, 1031–3.

(UNAMSIL) in order to exert pressure for the release of its leader Foday Sankoh.[154] The prohibition is also well-accepted. For example, in 1964, during the post-independence conflicts in the DRC, the Government invited the ICRC to ascertain its compliance with the Geneva Conventions, in particular 'in the matter of the treatment of prisoners and the ban against taking hostages'.[155] The prohibition is also well recognized by armed groups. For example, the Ejército Zapatista de Liberación Nacional (EZLN) of Mexico stated in a 1994 speech, '[d]on't fear for your belongings or your lives. We respect you and your freedom. In case of problems we aren't going to take hostages, nor will we take anyone by force to protect us. In such case as we may have to leave or to fight we guarantee that we won't take civilians with us, nor hostages'.[156] To related effect, in 2002, the Moro Islamic Liberation Front (MILF) of the Philippines condemned 'all Kidnap-for-Ransom Activities' and instructed its armed wing 'to arrest, and take drastic action against the perpetrators of this heinous crime, until these criminal activities are neutralized and stopped in MILF areas'.[157] The CNF of Burma has also prohibited the use of hostages.[158] The prohibition is also contained in a variety of ad hoc and ceasefire agreements.[159]

The Fuerzas Armadas Revolucionarias de Colombia (FARC) and the Ejército de Liberación Nacional (ELN), also of Colombia, both notorious for their taking of hostages, have denied doing so, characterizing their holding of individuals as permissible to recover taxes. For example, the ELN has stated that it is 'permissible to recover war taxes, and to detain persons who refuse to pay them as a form of pressure in order to obtain payment. These detentions cannot be considered "hostage-taking", because we never use these persons as shields during hostilities'.[160] The FARC has made similar arguments, taxing certain individuals and providing that '[t]hose who do not comply with this demand will be retained. Their release will depend on the payment of the sum that will be determined', although the FARC has also claimed the right to take hostages.[161] These two examples demonstrate the importance of committing not simply to the terminology of the norm, but to its substance.

Other groups have considered that they have a right to take hostages, with the authorities of Katanga in 1964 initially 'threaten[ing] to execute foreign residents who would henceforth be considered as "hostages", in the event of towns being bombed by the Leopoldville forces'. The Katangan authorities later indicated that 'all foreigners

---

[154] *RUF* Appeal Judgment, above note 147, paras 550–601.
[155] Public Statement of the Prime Minister of the Democratic Republic of the Congo, 21 October 1964, reproduced in (1965) 59 *AJIL* 614, 616.
[156] 'Speech by an Indigenous Guerrilla', later published in *La Jornada*, 19 January 1994, reproduced and translated in B Clarke and C Ross (eds), *Voice of Fire: Communiqués and Interviews from the Zapatista National Liberation Army* (Freedom Voices, 2000) 39.
[157] 'Resolution to reiterate MILF policy of strongly and continuously condemning all kidnap for ransom activities in Mindanao and everywhere, and to take drastic action against the perpetrators of this heinous crime in all MILF areas', 6 February 2002, available at the website of Geneva Call <http://www.genevacall.org/>.
[158] Chin National Front, Code, above note 56.
[159] Agreement on Ceasefire and Cessation of Hostilities between the Government of the Republic of Liberia and Liberians United for Reconciliation and Democracy and the Movement for Democracy in Liberia, 17 June 2003, Point 9; Government of Sierra Leone/RUF, Agreement of 10 November 2000, Article 9; Comprehensive Agreement on Human Rights and International Humanitarian Law between the Government of the Philippines and the National Democratic Front, Part IV, Article 3(1).
[160] N Rodríguez Bautista, 'Qué es humanizar el conflict colombiano?, 1 May 1996', quoted in P Gassmann, 'Colombia: Persuading Belligerents to Comply with International Norms', in S Chesterman (ed), *Civilians in War* (Lynne Rienner Publishers, 2001) 67, 73.
[161] FARC, 'Communiqué of 26 April 2000', quoted in ibid, fn 14.

would in future be considered as "prisoners of war"'.¹⁶² For its part, the Houthi armed group in Yemen has accepted that it engages in the taking of hostages but has stated that it 'ensure[s] it that all hostages are being treated and dealt [with] in a proper manner maintaining their dignity, mental and physical safety' and that 'our treatment to the hostages are [*sic*] based on our religious principles and does not contradict at all neither the Humanitarian international law and conventions with regard to the hostages... and as we clarified above we treat them so much better than what is provided in the laws and conventions'.¹⁶³

2.3.6 Collective punishments

Parties to non-international armed conflicts not infrequently resort to collective punishments. For example, the inhabitants of a village may be expelled for supporting the state or the non-state armed group. During the Algerian war of independence, 'if an attack took place, the nearest village was considered collectively responsible'.¹⁶⁴ Along similar lines, the 1951 Emergency Regulations enacted by the United Kingdom in Malaya provided that:

[i]n any case where a competent authority has a reason to believe that within any area any person has been murdered or dangerously or fatally wounded by unlawful attack, or terrorism or any property has been destroyed or damaged unlawfully or by terrorism, he may order that a fine be levied collectively from the assessable inhabitants of such area, or any part thereof... unless such inhabitants can show that:

(a) they had not an opportunity of preventing the offense or arresting the offender; or
(b) they have used all reasonable means to bring the offender to justice.¹⁶⁵

It has been suggested that common Article 3 prohibits collective punishments through the principle of humane treatment, the prohibition on the taking of hostages, and the requirement of judicial guarantees.¹⁶⁶ However, each of these principles and prohibitions can be respected while still undertaking a collective punishment. Thus, they cannot serve to prohibit the institution of collective punishments. Collective punishments are, however, prohibited through other instruments, as are threats thereof.¹⁶⁷ Although the prohibition is not to be found in the Rome Statute,¹⁶⁸ it has long been considered a rule of customary international humanitarian law.¹⁶⁹ This was the view, for example, of Cameroon at the 1974–7 Diplomatic Conference.¹⁷⁰

---

¹⁶² (1965) 59 *AJIL* 614, 618.
¹⁶³ Letter from Abdulmalik al Houthi to Dr Mohammed Al-Mikhlafi (Head of the Yemeni Observatory for Human Rights), undated (published on 4 September 2009).
¹⁶⁴ R Branche, 'The French in Algeria: Can There be Prisoners of War in a "Domestic" Operation?', in S Scheipers (ed), *Prisoners in War* (Oxford University Press, 2010) 173, 177.
¹⁶⁵ Emergency Regulations, section 17DA(2)(ii). The UK used similar regulations in Kenya and Cyprus; however, it did not consider these situations to amount to non-international armed conflicts.
¹⁶⁶ ICRC, 'Humanitarian Aid to the Victims of Internal Conflicts: Meeting of a Commission of Experts in Geneva' (1963) 3 *IRRC* 79, 85.
¹⁶⁷ Additional Protocol II, Article 4(2)(b) and (h).
¹⁶⁸ On which, see S Darcy, 'Prosecuting the War Crime of Collective Punishment: Is it Time to Amend the Rome Statute?' (2010) 8 *JICJ* 29, 46.
¹⁶⁹ Hague Regulations, Article 50; ICTR Statute, Article 4(b); SCSL Statute, Article 3(b); Customary International Humanitarian Law, Rule 103; Report of the Secretary-General on the establishment of a Special Court for Sierra Leone, S/2000/915, 4 October 2000, para 14.
¹⁷⁰ *Official Records*, above note 40, Vol 9, 455.

The prohibition rests on the premise of individual responsibility, the idea being that 'responsibility is personal in nature and that no one may be punished for an act he or she has not personally committed'.[171] The fact that the relevant individual was a member of a particular collective should not, by itself, lead to punishment. The prohibition is a broad one, covering all forms of punishment including 'fine[s], confinement or a loss of property or rights' and is not limited to punishments handed out by courts of law.[172] Indeed, the Additional Protocol II prohibition was re-located from its original position in the provision on penal prosecutions to the provision on fundamental guarantees so as not to limit the application of the principle to the penal context.[173] The concern also explains the change in terminology from 'collective penalties' to 'collective punishments'.[174]

The Appeals Chamber of the SCSL has described collective punishments as 'the indiscriminate punishment imposed collectively on persons for omissions or acts for which some or none of them may or may not have been responsible'.[175] This followed differing definitions on the part of trial chambers of the Special Court.[176] The existence of multiple definitions may be explained by the uncertainty surrounding the exact focus of the prohibition and the inability to identify precisely what it is that the prohibition seeks to prevent. There are two principal aspects to the prohibition, namely the nature of the punishment, whether collective rather than individual, and targeted or indiscriminate; and the identity of the victim, whether they did or did not commit the act in question, whether they were perceived as committing the act in question, or whether there was a failure to identify the responsible individual. The various definitions have differed on whether to stress the nature of the punishment—and if so, whether to focus on its indiscriminate,[177] or collective,[178] character—or whether to focus on the identity of the victim—and if so, whether to concentrate on the lack of identification on the part of the perpetrator,[179] or precisely what the victim has,[180] or is perceived to have,[181] done. It is submitted that collective punishments are best characterized as punishments that are imposed on a group of persons for actions of particular individuals. Thus, the focus of the offence should be on the punishment rather than on the individual victim, although the identity of the victim certainly has a role to play; and on the collective, rather than indiscriminate, nature of the punishment.[182]

---

[171] *Prosecutor v Brima, Kamara, and Kanu*, IT-04-16-T, Judgment, 20 June 2007, para 678 (*AFRC* Trial Judgment). See also *Prosecutor v Fofana and Kondewa*, SCSL-04-14-T, Judgment, 2 August 2007, para 178 fn 222 (CDF Trial Judgment).

[172] *CDF* Trial Judgment, ibid, paras 181 and 222.

[173] *Official Records*, above note 40, Vol 10, 130.

[174] Ibid, Vol 7, 87–8.

[175] *Prosecutor v Fofana and Kondewa*, SCSL-04-14-A, Judgment, 28 May 2008, para 224 (*CDF* Appeal Judgment).

[176] *AFRC* Trial Judgment, above note 171, para 676; *CDF* Trial Judgment, above note 171, para 180; *CDF* Appeal Judgment, above note 175, Partially Dissenting Opinion of Justice Winter, para 46.

[177] *AFRC* Trial Judgment, para 676; *CDF* Appeal Judgment, para 224; *CDF* Appeal Judgment, Partially Dissenting Opinion of Justice Winter, para 46.

[178] *AFRC* Trial Judgment, para 676; *CDF* Trial Judgment, para 180; *CDF* Appeal Judgment, para 224.

[179] *AFRC* Trial Judgment, para 680.

[180] Ibid, para 676 (have not); *CDF* Trial Judgment, para 180 (have not); *CDF* Appeal Judgment, para 224 (some or none of them may or may not have; responsibility rather than commission).

[181] *CDF* Appeal Judgment, Partially Dissenting Opinion of Justice Winter, para 46; *RUF* Trial Judgment, para 127.

[182] See, for further detail, Sivakumaran, War Crimes, above note 150, 1020–4.

3. Persons benefitting from particular protections

In addition to the principle of humane treatment and the obligations that derive from that principle, additional protections are afforded to particular categories of individuals. These include the wounded, sick, and shipwrecked; medical and religious personnel; the dead and the missing; the displaced; the interned and detained; persons subject to the criminal process; journalists; women; children; peacekeepers; and humanitarian assistance personnel. Each of these categories of persons is considered in turn.

3.1 Wounded, sick, and shipwrecked

The treatment of the wounded and sick has been at the heart of international humanitarian law since its modern inception. It was, after all, the sight of wounded soldiers left on the battlefield at Solferino that led Henry Dunant to appeal for the creation of relief societies that would provide care to the wounded in wartime.[183]

Common Article 3 provides that '[t]he wounded and sick shall be collected and cared for'. As this obligation arises in respect of persons who do not take an active part in hostilities, it includes the civilian wounded and sick as well as wounded and sick fighters. The obligation is of customary status.[184] The common Article 3 obligation has the advantage of brevity while reflecting the 'salient principles' of the Geneva Convention on the Wounded and the Sick.[185] However, the succinct wording may also be criticized as 'not enough to guarantee the protection of the wounded and sick and to safeguard the position of those who minister to them'.[186] Yet, a statement along similar lines contained in the 1864 Geneva Convention attracted the criticism: '[a]sking us to sign a promise to respect and protect the wounded is almost like inviting an honest man to undertake in writing not to put his hand into his neighbour's pocket' and proposals for revisions to the Convention suggested deletion of the provision 'as superfluous if not offensive'.[187] With the benefit of hindsight, it is clear that even self-evident propositions need codification. Accordingly, Additional Protocol II developed the common Article 3 obligation. It seeks to 'make explicit what was implicit in the very simple general statement... by formulating a number of derivative rules specifying the protection to be given to medical personnel, units and installations, the standard of care, and so forth'.[188] Today, these are recognized to have passed into customary international law.[189]

---

[183] H Dunant, *A Memory of Solferino* (reprinted and translated, ICRC, 1986) 115.

[184] *Nicaragua*, above note 4, 114, para 218; Customary International Humanitarian Law, Rule 10.

[185] GIAD Draper, 'Humanitarian Law and Internal Armed Conflicts' (1983) 13 *Georgia Journal of International and Comparative Law* 253, 270. See also WA Solf, 'Development of the Protection of the Wounded, Sick and Shipwrecked under the Protocols Additional to the 1949 Geneva Conventions', in C Swinarski (ed), *Studies and Essays on International Humanitarian Law and Red Cross Principles in Honour of Jean Pictet* (ICRC, 1984) 237, 239.

[186] RR Baxter, 'Ius in Bello Interno', in JN Moore (ed), *Law and Civil War in the Modern World* (Johns Hopkins University Press, 1974) 518, 529. See also Conference of Government Experts on the Reaffirmation and Development of International Humanitarian Law Applicable in Armed Conflicts (Geneva, 24 May–12 June 1971): Submitted by the International Committee of the Red Cross (1971) Part V: Protection of Victims of Non-International Armed Conflicts, 53.

[187] Arnold, *Study on the Geneva Convention*, cited in P Boissier, *History of the International Committee of the Red Cross: From Solferino to Tsushima* (Henry Dunant Institute, 1985) 202–3.

[188] *Official Records*, above note 40, Vol 11, 209, para 43 (United States).

[189] See below, 275.

The meaning of 'wounded, sick and shipwrecked' is the same in the law of non-international armed conflict as it is in the law of international armed conflict.[190] Additional Protocol I defines the 'wounded' and 'sick' in broad terms to mean 'persons, whether military or civilian, who, because of trauma, disease or other physical or mental disorder or disability, are in need of medical assistance or care and who refrain from any act of hostility'.[191] However, the terms are narrower than their everyday meanings given that they are limited to persons who refrain from acts of hostility: '[a] person who has broken his leg is not wounded in the sense of the Protocol if he continues to shoot.'[192] Thus, although the terminology used is that of the wounded and sick, it is more accurate to refer to persons 'rendered helpless by wounds and sickness'.[193]

Four principles guide the treatment to be afforded to the wounded, sick, and shipwrecked: 'respect, protection, humane treatment and medical care'.[194] According to Article 7(1) of Additional Protocol II, '[a]ll the wounded, sick and shipwrecked, whether or not they have taken part in the armed conflict, shall be respected and protected'.[195] To respect, in this context, means 'to spare, not to attack'; to protect is 'to come to someone's defence, to lend help and support'.[196] The latter implies 'taking measures to remove the wounded, sick and shipwrecked, if possible, from the scene of combat and shelter them, and to ensure that they are effectively respected'.[197] As noted above, provided they refrain from acts of hostility, military wounded fall within the definition of the wounded. Thus, to kill wounded fighters who are placed *hors de combat* as a result of their wounds is to violate the relevant law.[198] Hospitals that house military wounded are similarly protected from attack.

Article 7(2) of Additional Protocol II provides: '[i]n all circumstances they shall be treated humanely and shall receive, to the fullest possible extent practicable and with the least possible delay, the medical care and attention required by their condition.'[199] This means that the wounded and sick should be afforded medical care and, at the very least, should not be left wilfully without medical care.[200] In dealing with the wounded and sick, the only permitted distinction is that of medical need.[201] These obligations can be derived from the principle of protection and the requirement of humane

---

[190] See eg the Statement of Understanding of Canada made at the time of ratification, and the Declaration of the US on signature of the Additional Protocols, in D Schindler and J Toman, *The Laws of Armed Conflict* (Nijhoff, 2004) 798 and 818; UK Ministry of Defence, *The Manual of the Law of Armed Conflict* (Oxford University Press, 2004) 406; ICRC, *Commentary on the Additional Protocols*, above note 139, 1405 and 1408–9.

[191] Additional Protocol I, Article 8.

[192] ICRC, *Commentary on the Additional Protocols*, above note 139, 118. However, the terms are also broader as they are considered to include persons who, in the ordinary sense of the terms, are neither wounded nor sick, namely 'maternity cases, new-born babies and other persons who may be in need of immediate medical assistance or care, such as the infirm or expectant mothers, and who refrain from any act of hostility'. Additional Protocol I, Article 8.

[193] As was suggested in 1911, by JW Spaight, *War Rights on Land* (1911) 421.

[194] ICRC, *Commentary on the Additional Protocols*, above note 139, 1408. See also Pictet, *Commentary on the First Geneva Convention*, above note 23, 135.

[195] Additional Protocol II, Article 7(1).

[196] ICRC, *Commentary on the Additional Protocols*, above note 139, 1408. See also Pictet, *Commentary on the First Geneva Convention*, above note 23, 134–5.

[197] ICRC, *Commentary on the Additional Protocols*, above note 139, 1408. See also Pictet, *Commentary on the First Geneva Convention*, above note 23, 134–5.

[198] For just such an instance, see *Avilan et al v Colombia*, Case 11.142, Report No 26/97, 30 September 1997, OEA/Ser.L/V/II.98, doc.6 rev, 13 April 1998, paras 131–42.

[199] Additional Protocol II, Article 7(2).

[200] UK Manual, above note 190, 122.

[201] Additional Protocol II, Article 7(2).

treatment and may be deemed an authoritative interpretation of that which is required by common Article 3. For reasons that are self-evident, the obligation is one of means rather than result. The nature and extent of the care is dependent upon the practicalities of the situation, as is clear from the phrase 'to the fullest possible extent practicable'. That phrase was included 'as a matter of realism, in order to take into account the means and personnel available'.[202] Practicability includes both the capabilities of the parties and the situation at hand. Each of these obligations is a norm of customary international law.[203]

Operation of the principles of respect, protection, humane treatment, and medical care are illustrated by a 1958 telegram to the ICRC from Fidel Castro, then leader of an armed group fighting against the Cuban Government headed by General Batista:

> After the latest battle in the Sierra Maestra, a great many wounded Batista soldiers remain in our hands. It has always been the rebels' custom to care for enemy soldiers wounded in the fighting in our improvised hospitals, thereby saving the lives of many of them. This time, however, we cannot put our humanitarian principles fully into practice because there are too many casualties. For lack of beds, seriously wounded soldiers are lying on the ground, without even a blanket, and we are unable to provide them with the food which their condition requires. Medicines are in short supply... We have publicly proposed that a commission of the Cuban Red Cross should come to fetch the wounded and have stated that we are ready to hand them over so that they can receive the treatment they need...[204]

There exists other practice on point. For example, the 1994 Declaration of War of the EZLN of Mexico provided: '[r]espect the lives of prisoners and turn in the wounded to the International Red Cross for medical attention.'[205] Similarly, during the attempted secession of Biafra, an Operational Code of Conduct was issued to the Nigerian Federal Army in 1967, which provided *inter alia* that '[h]ospitals, hospital staff and patients should not be tampered with or molested' and that '[a]ll military and civilians wounded will be given necessary medical attention and care. They must be respected and protected in all circumstances'.[206] An independent observer mission found that the Code was being followed by Federal troops.[207] Along similar lines, in 1988, the Frente Farabundo Martí para la Liberación Nacional (FMLN) of El Salvador indicated that it gave 'wounded government troops the same medical care that the FMLN combatants receive'.[208] The CNF Code provides for a similar obligation, namely that its members 'and its medics... must render help to wounded or sick civilians or enemies and treat them equally as they treat their fellow CNF soldiers'.[209] Che Guevara also indicated that '[t]he wounded should be cared for

---

[202] ICRC, *Commentary on the Additional Protocols*, above note 139, 1410.
[203] See the view of Customary International Humanitarian Law, Rule 110. Cf JP Benoit, 'Mistreatment of the Wounded, Sick and Shipwrecked by the ICRC Study on Customary International Humanitarian Law' (2008) 11 *YIHL* 175, 210–12.
[204] Telegram from Fidel Castro, Commander-in-Chief of the Rebel Army, 3 July 1958, ICRC Archives B AG 200 060. The English translation is taken from F Perret, 'Activities of the International Committee of the Red Cross in Cuba 1958–1962' (1998) 38 *IRRC* 655, 656–7. The appeal was reiterated in a Telegram from Castro, 6 July 1958, ICRC Archives B AG 200 060.
[205] 'Declaration of War of the Zapatista National Liberation Army (EZLN)', Communiqué of 2 January 1994, reproduced and translated in B Clarke and C Ross (eds), *Voice of Fire: Communiqués and Interviews from the Zapatista National Liberation Army* (Freedom Voices, 2000) 31, 32. See also EZLN General Command, Declaración de la Selva Lacandona, 1993.
[206] Operational Code of Conduct for the Nigerian Army, above note 57, para 4(e).
[207] Report of the Observer Team to Nigeria, above note 58, 12.
[208] FMLN, *The Legitimacy of Our Methods of Struggle* (Inkworks Press, 1988) 7.
[209] Chin National Front, Code, above note 56.

with all possible resources at the time of the action'.²¹⁰ The 1991 Hague Statement on Respect of Humanitarian Principles, signed during the conflict in the former Yugoslavia, likewise provided that the 'wounded and ill persons must be helped and protected in all circumstances'.²¹¹ The 22 May 1992 Agreement concluded between the parties to the conflict in Bosnia also provided for the respect and protection of, and medical care and attention for, the wounded and sick,²¹² although this too was violated quite significantly. The NRA of Uganda's Code of Conduct also provided: '[o]ffer medical treatment to the members of the public who may be in the territory of your unit.'²¹³ The ELN of Colombia issued rules in 1996 which provided, *inter alia*, that the ELN 'will give humanitarian treatment to enemies who have surrendered or been wounded in combat and will respect their dignity and provide them with the aid necessary for their condition'.²¹⁴

An associated obligation is contained in Article 8 of Additional Protocol II: '[w]henever circumstances permit, and particularly after an engagement, all possible measures shall be taken, without delay, to search for and collect the wounded, sick and shipwrecked, to protect them against pillage and ill-treatment, [and] to ensure their adequate care.'²¹⁵ The obligations of protection and ensuring adequate care are reflections of the four guiding principles considered above and are of customary status.²¹⁶ They are also linked to the requirement of humane treatment to be afforded to all persons *hors de combat*.²¹⁷ The only requirement additional to that contained in common Article 3 is thus the obligation to search for the wounded, sick, and shipwrecked. The obligation is couched in language that reflects the temporal and practical constraints of the situation. This includes the capacities of the parties to the conflict ('all possible measures') and the specificities of the situation at hand ('whenever circumstances permit'). The Protocol is thus cognizant of the capabilities of the parties to the conflict.²¹⁸ This obligation, too, is of customary status,²¹⁹ and has been followed in bilateral agreements²²⁰ and internal instructions.²²¹

To this obligation, the Customary International Humanitarian Law study adds the obligation to take all possible measures to evacuate the wounded, sick, and shipwrecked when circumstances permit.²²² Although the customary status of the norm has been

---

²¹⁰ E Guevara, *Guerrilla Warfare* (Penguin, 1969) 29.
²¹¹ 5 November 1991, reproduced in J-F Berger, *The Humanitarian Diplomacy of the ICRC and the Conflict in Croatia 1991–2* (ICRC, 1995) 59.
²¹² Agreement of 22 May 1992, Article 2.2, reproduced in M Sassòli, AA Bouvier, and A Qunitin, *How Does Law Protect in War? Volume II* (ICRC, 2011) 1717.
²¹³ National Resistance Army Code of Conduct, above note 10.
²¹⁴ Comando Central del ELN, Manuel Pérez Martínez, Nicolás Rodríguez Bautista, Antonio García, 'Nuestra Ética En La Doctrina Militar' (1996), reproduced and translated in Human Rights Watch, *War Without Quarter: Colombia and International Humanitarian Law* (1998) Chapter V.
²¹⁵ Additional Protocol II, Article 8.
²¹⁶ See the view of Customary International Humanitarian Law, Rules 109 and 111. Cf Benoit, above note 203, 214–15.
²¹⁷ On which see above, 255–72.
²¹⁸ On which see above, 72–6 .
²¹⁹ Customary International Humanitarian Law, Rule 109.
²²⁰ Comprehensive Agreement on Respect for Human Rights and International Humanitarian Law between the Government of the Philippines and the National Democratic Front, Part IV, Article 4(2) and (9).
²²¹ National Transitional Council, Rules on the Treatment of Detainees, 19 May 2011. See I Scobbie, 'Operationalising the Law of Armed Conflict for Dissident Forces in Libya', EJIL: Talk! Blog, 31 August 2011.
²²² Customary International Humanitarian Law, Rule 109.

questioned,[223] the obligation to evacuate the wounded and sick follows on from the obligations to search for and collect the wounded and sick. This is particularly true in cases in which the requisite care cannot be afforded by the relevant party to the conflict. In practice, truces are not infrequently concluded to allow for the collection and evacuation of the wounded and the dead. For example, during the violence in the Dominican Republic in 1965, the ICRC delegate reached agreement with the heads of the Government Junta and the Constitutional Junta over a 24-hour truce to allow for evacuation of the wounded and collection of the dead.[224] The ICRC reported that some 2,000 dead bodies and 5,000 wounded persons were evacuated.[225] On a related point, Kwame Nkrumah indicated that '[t]he wounded should, if possible, be carried to a safe place for treatment'.[226] For its part, a military commander of the Communist Party of Nepal-Maoist (CPN-M) set out instructions to be followed during a raid in 2005. One such instruction was that '[t]he injured and sick must be passed to the safe places outside, they should not be kept... for a long time'.[227] The customary obligation in respect of evacuation of the wounded has also been recognized by certain states. In this regard, in 2009, during the armed conflict in Sri Lanka, upon the ICRC reporting that it was unable to evacuate the wounded and sick, the UK Secretary of State for International Development stated that, '[o]ver the last four months alone, the ICRC has evacuated by ship over 14,000 sick and wounded people. Denying this life-saving evacuation and medical treatment is a fundamental violation of International Humanitarian Law'.[228] Thus, the obligation has been interpreted as containing both a negative component, namely a duty not to obstruct evacuation, as well as a positive one, namely a duty to evacuate. Parties to conflicts have also concluded ad hoc bilateral agreements on the exchange of the wounded and sick,[229] and the evacuation of the wounded and sick.[230] As this additional customary obligation, too, is subject to the prevailing circumstances and the various constraints, it should not prove unduly onerous.

3.2 Medical and religious personnel

The protection of medical personnel derives from the obligations arising in respect of the wounded and sick.[231] In order that the wounded and sick be afforded medical care, it follows that those affording the care should themselves be protected. Thus, it has been suggested that the obligation to protect medical personnel is implicit in common Article 3.[232] This goes too far; however, resolution of the issue is less necessary today

---

[223] Benoit, above note 203, 199–203.
[224] See 'External Activities: Santo Domingo' (1965) 5 *IRRC* 303. See also 'How a Humanitarian Truce was Brought About in Santo Domingo' (1965) 5 *IRRC* 362–4.
[225] Procès-verbaux du Comité, Séances Plénières, 3 June 1965, ICRC Archives, B AG 251 170.
[226] K Nkrumah, *Handbook of Revolutionary Warfare* (Panaf Books, 1968) 119.
[227] Pasang, *Red Strides of History* (Agnipariksha Janaprakashan Griha, 2008) 206.
[228] Statement of Secretary of State for International Development, Douglas Alexander, 15 May 2009.
[229] See eg Government-FARC Humanitarian Exchange Accord, 2 June 2001.
[230] Croatia/Yugoslav People's Army, Agreement on Humanitarian Convoy to Evacuate Wounded and Sick from Vukovar Hospital, 18 November 1991; Agreement between the Catalan Parliament and the ICRC, 8 December 1936. See also the commitment made in The London International Conference: Programme of Action on Humanitarian Issues Agreed between the Co-Chairmen to the Conference and the Parties to the Conflict, 27 August 1992.
[231] ICRC, *Commentary on the Additional Protocols*, above note 139, 124.
[232] Ibid, 1418.

given that the protections have been made explicit in Additional Protocol II,[233] and reflect customary international law.[234]

Medical personnel are defined in Additional Protocol I, in general terms, as those 'persons assigned, by a Party to the conflict, exclusively to the medical purposes . . . or to the administration of medical units or to the operation or administration of medical transports',[235] this aspect of the definition being applicable equally to non-international armed conflict.[236] Two elements inform the definition, namely those of exclusivity and assignment. The element of exclusivity means that 'protected medical personnel cannot spend any time on different activities as long as they are assigned to medical tasks'.[237] To engage in activities not of a medical nature may take the individuals concerned outside the definition. The element of assignment requires that a party to the conflict recognize the individuals concerned as medical personnel or authorize them to act in such a manner and implies that the party exercises a certain level of control over them.[238] Legislation itself is not strictly required, any 'expression of attachment by the responsible leadership' serving to suffice.[239] Thus, not every doctor, nurse, or other person engaged in medical activities falls within the international humanitarian law definition of medical personnel,[240] though they would benefit from the protections afforded to civilians generally. Religious personnel are also defined in Additional Protocol I,[241] and similar issues arise.

Medical and religious personnel benefit from various protections. These continue for the duration of their mission.[242] Additional Protocol II provides that '[m]edical and religious personnel shall be respected and protected and shall be granted all available help for the performance of their duties'.[243] The latter clause is evidently context-dependent. Furthermore, '[t]hey shall not be compelled to carry out tasks which are not compatible with their humanitarian mission.' The obligations of respect and protect were used in this context in order to formulate 'in concrete terms the consequences one wishes to draw' from the more abstract obligations of neutrality or inviolability.[244] The meaning to be attributed to the requirements of respect and protect have been discussed in the context of the wounded and sick,[245] and are applicable equally here. At the very least, medical and religious personnel are not to be made the object of attack. The Rome Statute also offers protections, listing as a war crime, 'intentionally directing attacks against . . . personnel using the distinctive emblems of the Geneva Conventions

---

[233] Additional Protocol II, Articles 9 and 10.
[234] See the view of Council of the International Institute of Humanitarian Law, Declaration on the Rules of International Humanitarian Law Governing the Conduct of Hostilities in Non-International Armed Conflicts (San Remo, 7 April 1990) A5; Customary International Humanitarian Law, Rule 25.
[235] Additional Protocol I, Article 8(c).
[236] See eg Declaration of the US on signature of the Additional Protocols, in Schindler and Toman, above note 190, 818; M Bothe, KJ Partsch, and WA Solf, *New Rules for Victims of Armed Conflicts* (Martinus Nijhoff, 1982) 655–6.
[237] ICRC, *Commentary on the Additional Protocols*, above note 139, 125.
[238] F Kalshoven, 'International Humanitarian Law and Violation of Medical Neutrality', in F Kalshoven, *Reflections on the Law of War: Collected Essays* (Nijhoff, 2007) 1011–12.
[239] S Lunze, 'Serving God and Caesar: Religious Personnel and their Protection in Armed Conflict' (2004) 86 *IRRC* 69, 79.
[240] ICRC, *Commentary on the Additional Protocols*, above note 139, 126.
[241] Additional Protocol I, Article 8(d).
[242] ICRC, *Commentary on the Additional Protocols*, above note 139, 1421.
[243] Article 9(1). See also Customary International Humanitarian Law, Rule 25 (respected and protected).
[244] F Kalshoven, 'International Humanitarian Law and Violation of Medical Neutrality', in F Kalshoven (ed), *Reflections on the Law of War: Collected Essays* (Nijhoff, 2007) 1002.
[245] Above, 274.

in conformity with international law'.²⁴⁶ This prohibition is sometimes violated, such violations being condemned, thus supporting the status of the prohibition. For example, the El Salvadorian armed forces killing of a nurse working in an FMLN hospital was described by the El Salvador Truth Commission as 'a violation of international humanitarian law'.²⁴⁷ Commitments have also been made on point. For example, an unnamed armed group 'told the ICRC that it had issued orders to its forces not to direct attacks against religious and medical personnel and objects'.²⁴⁸ Norms on point also feature in bilateral agreements.²⁴⁹ Mirroring the provision on medical assistance to the wounded and sick, Additional Protocol II provides that, '[i]n the performance of their duties medical personnel may not be required to give priority to any person except on medical grounds'.²⁵⁰

As noted above, the terms 'medical and religious personnel' are defined in a particular manner. However, certain protections are afforded to *any* person involved in medical activities even if they do not satisfy the international humanitarian law definition of medical personnel. Additional Protocol II provides that '[u]nder no circumstances shall any person be punished for having carried out medical activities compatible with medical ethics, regardless of the person benefitting therefrom'.²⁵¹ The only qualification is that the medical activity be compatible with medical ethics.²⁵² Additional Protocol II also provides that '[p]ersons engaged in medical activities shall neither be compelled to perform acts or to carry out work contrary to, nor be compelled to refrain from acts required by, the rules of medical ethics or other rules designed for the benefit of the wounded and sick, or this Protocol'.²⁵³ Such acts would include the administration of behavioural modification drugs, the carrying out of medical experiments on persons, and the like.²⁵⁴ These rules have been suggested to be of customary status,²⁵⁵ and are to be found in ad hoc agreements.²⁵⁶

Protections are also afforded to persons involved in medical activities in respect of their professional obligations relating to information they may come to possess concerning the wounded and sick in their care. International humanitarian law seeks to strike a balance between maintaining doctor-patient confidentiality and state sovereignty;²⁵⁷ however, whether it has managed to do so is open to question. Subject to national law on point, professional obligations are to be respected and failure to divulge

---

²⁴⁶ Article 8(2)(e)(ii).
²⁴⁷ Report of the UN Commission on the Truth for El Salvador, S/25500, Annex, 1 April 1993, 87 and 89.
²⁴⁸ JM Henckaerts and L Doswald-Beck, *Customary International Humanitarian Law, Volume II: Practice* (Cambridge University Press, 2005) 507.
²⁴⁹ Comprehensive Agreement on Respect for Human Rights and International Humanitarian Law between the Government of the Philippines and the National Democratic Front, Part IV, Article 4(3) and (8).
²⁵⁰ Additional Protocol II, Article 9(2).
²⁵¹ Ibid, Article 10(1).
²⁵² On the question of medical ethics in time of armed conflict, see the Regulations in Time of Armed Conflict of the World Medical Association and the Rules Governing the Care of Sick and Wounded, Particularly in Time of Conflict, both adopted by the 10th World Medical Assembly, Havana, October 1956; JK Kleffner, 'Protection of the Wounded, Sick, and Shipwrecked', in D Fleck (ed), *The Handbook of International Humanitarian Law* (Oxford University Press, 2008) 348.
²⁵³ Additional Protocol II, Article 10(2).
²⁵⁴ ICRC, *Commentary on the Additional Protocols*, above note 139, 1427.
²⁵⁵ Customary International Humanitarian Law, Rule 26.
²⁵⁶ Comprehensive Agreement on Respect for Human Rights and International Humanitarian Law between the Government of the Philippines and the National Democratic Front, Part IV, Article 11.
²⁵⁷ ICRC, *Commentary on the Additional Protocols*, above note 139, 1425.

information learned may not result in a penalty.[258] However, subjecting the rule to national law has the potential to vitiate entirely the protection, and some states have accordingly described the deference to national law as to be 'deeply regretted' and 'dangerous'.[259] A specific example on point is that of the United States, which is by no means unique in this regard, which considered a reservation to the provision to be appropriate in order 'to preserve the ability of the U.S. Armed Forces to control the actions of their medical personnel, who might otherwise feel entitled to invoke these provisions to disregard, under the guise of "medical ethics", the priorities and restrictions established by higher authority'.[260]

3.3 Dead persons

Additional Protocol II provides that, '[w]henever circumstances permit, and particularly after an engagement, all possible measures shall be taken, without delay... to search for the dead, prevent their being despoiled, and decently dispose of them'.[261] These obligations were described at the Diplomatic Conference of 1974–7 as 'even more important in non-international conflicts than in international conflicts'.[262] They are of customary status.[263]

There are thus three related obligations. First, there is an obligation to search for the dead. The customary equivalent of the rule extends beyond searching for the dead and includes the collection and evacuation of the dead.[264] Although these latter two obligations are not contained in the treaty provision, they follow on from the obligation to search for the dead. Part of the reason behind the obligation to search for the dead is precisely so as to collect and evacuate them. It is also similar to the obligation to search for the wounded, sick, and shipwrecked.[265] In practice, search, collection, and evacuation of the dead and of the wounded are all treated together, with truces not infrequently being concluded to allow for the collection and evacuation of the wounded and dead. For example, during the violence in the Dominican Republic in 1965, the ICRC delegate reached agreement with the heads of the Government Junta and the Constitutional Junta over a 24-hour truce to allow for evacuation of the wounded and collection of the dead.[266] Collection of the dead may also be provided for in ceasefire agreements, as was the case in the 1992 agreement between the Government of Rwanda and the Rwandan Patriotic Front (RPF),[267] and ad hoc agreements, as between

---

[258] Additional Protocol II, Article 10(3) and (4).
[259] *Official Records*, above note 40, Vol 11, 513, para 2 (Norway). See also UK *Manual*, above note 190, 406 fn 108.
[260] Letter of Submittal [of Additional Protocol II] from the Secretary of State to the President, Detailed Analysis of Article 10, in *Message from the President of the United States Transmitting the Protocol II Additional to the Geneva Conventions of August 12, 1949, and Relating to the Protection of Victims of Noninternational Armed Conflicts, Concluded at Geneva on June 10, 1977* (US Government Printing Office, 1987) 5.
[261] Additional Protocol II, Article 8.
[262] *Official Records*, above note 40, Vol 11, 268, para 73 (Canada).
[263] Customary International Humanitarian Law, Rules 112, 113, and 115.
[264] Customary International Humanitarian Law, Rule 112.
[265] On which see above, 276.
[266] See 'External Activities: Santo Domingo' (1965) 5 *IRRC* 303. See also 'How a Humanitarian Truce was Brought About in Santo Domingo' (1965) 5 *IRRC* 362–4. See above, 277.
[267] The N'Sele Ceasefire Agreement between the Government of the Rwandese Republic and the Rwandese Patriotic Front, as amended at Gbadolite, 16 September 1991, and at Arusha, 12 July 1992, Article 2(5).

the Government of Philippines and the NDFP.[268] Should one party to the conflict find bodies of fighters of the other side, these are not infrequently handed over, such as happened on several occasions during the conflict in Sri Lanka between the Government and the LTTE.[269] One armed group, the National Liberation Army (NLA) of the Former Yugoslav Republic of Macedonia, also indicated that it issued instructions to its forces 'to not take advantage of the situation when the opponent was removing its killed soldiers from the terrain'.[270]

Second, there is an obligation to prevent the dead from being despoiled, which is a well established rule of customary international law.[271] The rule against despoliation protects the dead from pillage and the theft of personal items, as well as from mutilation or mistreatment. Accordingly, dragging the bodies of the dead through the streets, as was done in Somalia,[272] and mutilating dead bodies, whether for taking body parts as 'souvenirs' in Afghanistan,[273] or as proof of death to collect a reward in Colombia,[274] would all constitute violations of the obligation not to despoil. Despoliation of the dead may also amount to the war crime of outrages upon personal dignity, with the ICC Elements of Crimes explicitly noting that the crime can be committed against dead persons.[275]

Third, there is an obligation to dispose of the dead in a decent manner, by which may be implied burial in accordance with the 'rites of the faith of the deceased'.[276] Thus, following the United States' targeting of Osama bin Laden in 2011, in what branches of the US Government considers to be a non-international armed conflict, bin Laden was buried 'in strict conformance with Islamic precepts and practices'.[277] The obligation of decent disposal of the dead is a longstanding one. For example, the Tratado de Regularización de la Guerra, concluded during the Colombian war of independence of 1820, provided:

The bodies of those who gloriously end their journeys on the battlefields, or in any combat, clash, encounter between the armed forces of the two governments shall receive the last honours of burial or be cremated when their numbers or time pressures do not permit the former. The victorious army or force shall be obliged to perform this sacred duty of which it can only be relieved by very serious and extraordinary circumstances, immediately notifying the authorities of the territory where the bodies are in order that they do so. Bodies which are claimed from either side, by the government or private individuals cannot be refused and any communications necessary for their transport shall be granted.[278]

---

[268] Comprehensive Agreement on Respect for Human Rights and International Humanitarian Law between the Government of the Philippines and the National Democratic Front, Part IV, Article 4(9).
[269] See eg 'Tamil Tigers' Bodies Handed Over', *BBC News*, 24 July 2008.
[270] Witness Statement of Gzim Ostreni, Chief of NLA General Staff, para 51, Exhibit P00497.E in ICTY *Boškoski* trial.
[271] See UK Manual, above note 190, 134 fn 72; Customary International Humanitarian Law, Rule 113.
[272] See HW Elliott, 'Dead and Wounded', in R Gutman, D Reiff, and A Dworkin (eds), *Crimes of War* (WW Norton and Co, 2007) 152, 154.
[273] See L Mogelson, 'A Beast in the Heart of Every Fighting Man', *New York Times Magazine*, 27 April 2011, detailing allegations made against members of the so-called 'kill team' in Afghanistan.
[274] See J McDermott, 'FARC Rallies its Battered Troops', *BBC News*, 2 March 2009.
[275] ICC Elements of Crimes, Article 8(2)(c)(ii), fn 57.
[276] H McCoubrey, *International Humanitarian Law* (Dartmouth, 1990) 178. See First Geneva Convention, Article 17.
[277] Counter-terrorism advisor John O Brennan, quoted in N Schmidle, 'Getting Bin Laden', *The New Yorker*, 8 August 2011.
[278] Tratado de Regularización de la Guerra, 26 November 1820, Article 12. French translation published in (1820–1) 71 *Consolidated Treaty Series* 291. The original reads:

Along similar lines, the 1994 Declaration on Measures for A Political Settlement of the Georgian/Abkhaz Conflict provided for obligations in relation to 'reburial of the dead'.[279] The Customary International Humanitarian Law study, without any real explanation or supporting practice, extends the obligation to include respect for and proper maintenance of the graves of the dead.[280] Respect for graves can be considered akin to the prohibition on despoliation of the dead, albeit a broader obligation, and would prohibit the digging up of graves in order to hide casualties and the flattening of grave sites. The latter, while pertinent, is more difficult to explain.

Each of the three obligations is limited by the circumstances in which the deaths arose and the immediate aftermath of the deaths. For example, the sheer numbers involved may mean that the dead have to be buried in mass graves, albeit as a last resort;[281] or the lack of an appropriate religious leader in the area in question may prevent the administration of the rites of the faith of the deceased. The reference to the 'circumstances' must also be understood as including the capacity of the parties to the conflict, both in terms of the search for, and the burial of, the dead. It would also include the intensity of the fighting at the relevant time. Thus, in many situations, a simple burial in a mound of earth or under stones would have to suffice to meet the obligations of the parties. Mass graves used to dump and hide bodies following the commission of an atrocity clearly would not suffice. Furthermore, no circumstance would allow for the actual despoliation of the dead on the part of one of the parties to the conflict. In this sense, the negative obligation not to interfere with the body exists irrespective of circumstance or capacity. The obligations arise '[w]henever circumstances permit, and particularly after an engagement' and 'without delay'. However, it may prove militarily impossible to do so until days after the conclusion of an engagement, depending on the situation at hand.[282]

Three further obligations are considered to arise in the context of the dead. First, parties are to record information about the missing and the dead.[283] This obligation is linked to the right to truth in the context of enforced disappearances,[284] and the general principle that guides the equivalent provisions of Additional Protocol I, namely that the parties 'shall be prompted mainly by the right of families to know the fate of their relatives'.[285] The right to truth is a norm that is gaining greater currency in the international human rights law field and its impact on the law of non-international

> Los cadáveres de los que gloriosamente terminen su carrera en los campos de batalla, o en cualquier combate, choque o encuentro entre las armas de los dos gobiernos, recibirán los últimos honores de la sepultura, o se quemarán cuando por su número, o por la premura del tiempo, no pueda hacerse lo primero. El ejército o cuerpo vencedor será el obligado a cumplir con este sagrado deber, del cual, sólo por una circunstancia muy grave y singular podrá descargarse, avisándolo inmediatamente a las autoridades del territorio en que se hallan para que lo hagan. Los cadáveres que de una y otra parte se reclamen por el gobierno o por los particulares no podrán negarse, y se concederá la comunicación necesaria para transportarlos.

[279] 4 April 1994, Article 9. See also Comprehensive Agreement on Respect for Human Rights and International Humanitarian Law between the Government of the Philippines and the National Democratic Front, Part IV, Article 4(9).

[280] Customary International Humanitarian Law, Rule 115. See *Customary International Humanitarian Law, Volume I: Rules*, above note 248, 415–16.

[281] See, in this regard, First Geneva Convention, Article 17.

[282] See Spaight, above note 193, 430.

[283] Customary International Humanitarian Law, Rule 116; GA Res 3220 (XXIX) (1974) ('provide', rather than 'record', information).

[284] International Convention for the Protection of All Persons from Enforced Disappearance, Article 24(2).

[285] Additional Protocol I, Article 32.

armed conflict is likely to increase. Second, parties are to mark graves.[286] This is linked to, and would clearly assist in, the obligation to search for the dead and the missing. It is also linked to the third obligation, namely that parties must endeavour to facilitate the return of the remains of the dead upon the request of the party to the conflict to which they belong or upon the request of the next of kin.[287]

Each of these three further obligations is considered to arise through customary international law. The General Assembly has also called upon parties to armed conflicts, regardless of the character of the conflict, to abide by them. However, the normative status of all three obligations is open to question, with the Customary International Humanitarian Law study noting of the third obligation that 'it is not clear whether this arises from a sense of legal obligation'.[288] Despite the uncertainty, there is much to be said for each of them. As indicated, each obligation is associated with other norms. Some commitments on point have also been made by parties to conflicts.[289] As early as 1820, for example, the Tratado de Regularización de la Guerra provided that '[b]odies which are claimed from either side, by the government or private individuals cannot be refused and any communications necessary for their transport shall be granted'.[290] There is also growing acceptance of the applicability of the various obligations to non-international armed conflicts.[291] For example, during the 2011 violence in Libya, the National Transitional Council (NTC) issued 'Rules on the treatment of detainees' to its forces. One aspect of the rules provided for an '[a]ttempt to identify the dead'. The Rules continued: 'If this is not possible, then record (and if possible, photograph) the personal possessions with which the body is buried. This is to help with subsequent attempts to identify the person. Records of the dead and the location of their burial should be sent to the ICRC.'[292] Over and above that which is required by the law, the CNF of Burma requires that '[i]f a prisoner of war dies while under the control of the Chin National Front, the Chin National Front officer in charge should investigate the reason for the death and should sign and declare it. The officer-in-charge should write the name, age, burial place and reason for the death and should report to [superior] officer'.[293]

These three obligations are also subject to the capabilities of the parties to the conflict.[294] Whereas the state may be able to record information about the dead in a central depositary and search relevant databases, this may not be true of the armed group. Nonetheless, the armed group will be able to record information in a different form. The obligations of recording information and marking graves are required 'with a view to the identification of the dead'.[295] This is to take place prior to burial using such

---

[286] Customary International Humanitarian Law, Rule 116; GA Res 3220 (XXIX) (1974) (locate and mark).
[287] Customary International Humanitarian Law, Rule 114; GA Res 3220 (XXIX) (1974) (limited to families of the dead).
[288] *Customary International Humanitarian Law, Volume I: Rules*, above note 248, 414.
[289] Comprehensive Agreement on Respect for Human Rights and International Humanitarian Law between the Government of the Philippines and the National Democratic Front, Part IV, Article 3(4).
[290] Tratado de Regularización de la Guerra, 26 November 1820, Article 12. French translation published in (1820–1) 71 *Consolidated Treaty Series* 291. The original reads: 'Los cadáveres que de una y otra parte se reclamen por el gobierno o por los particulares no podrán negarse, y se concederá la comunicación necesaria para transportarlos.'
[291] See IIHL *Manual*, above note 28, 54–5.
[292] National Transitional Council, Rules on the Treatment of Detainees, 19 May 2011. See Scobbie, above note 221.
[293] Chin National Front, Code, above note 56, Article 10 (unofficial translation).
[294] Customary International Humanitarian Law, Rule 116.
[295] Ibid.

means as 'collecting one half of the double identity disk, autopsies, the recording of autopsies, the establishment of death certificates, the recording of the disposal of the dead, burial in individual graves, prohibition of collective graves without prior identification, and the proper marking of graves. Practice also suggests that exhumation combined with the application of forensic methods, including DNA testing, may be an appropriate method of identifying the dead after burial'.[296] Clearly, many of these means will be beyond the capacities of the armed group. However, armed groups may be able to carry out acts akin to the NTC or CNF, which would assist in the later identification of the deceased.

3.4 Missing persons

General Assembly Resolution 3220 (XXIX), which applies to armed conflicts of all types, calls on parties to the conflict to provide information about missing persons. Additional Protocol I, which is applicable in international armed conflicts, also provides for 'the right of families to know the fate of their relatives',[297] a desire which is no less true in times of non-international armed conflict. A right to information is also emerging in international human rights law and is contained in the Guiding Principles on Internal Displacement.[298] Ad hoc commitments have also been made in this regard. For example, in a 2002 Agreement between the Government of the Philippines (GRP) and the MILF, the parties commit '[i]n conformity with international humanitarian law' to 'provide information, through the tracing mechanism of the ICRC, to families of all persons who are unaccounted for. The GRP and MILF will cooperate fully in determining the identity, whereabouts, and fate of those missing persons'.[299] It has also been suggested that parties to the conflict shall, whenever circumstances permit, search for persons who have been reported missing.[300] This is akin to the obligation to search for the dead. Indeed, the two are linked, given that at the relevant time it will not be known whether the relevant individual is missing or dead. Again, there is practice on point from non-international armed conflicts.[301]

No obligations along the lines set out above are contained in any of the conventional instruments that regulate non-international armed conflict. However, a customary norm has been posited according to which '[e]ach party to the conflict must take all feasible measures to account for persons reported missing as a result of armed conflict and must provide their family members with any information it has on their fate'.[302] Reference to 'account for' would necessitate a search being undertaken. Thus, the

---

[296] *Customary International Humanitarian Law, Volume I: Rules*, above note 248, 419–20.
[297] Article 32.
[298] Guiding Principles, Principle 16.
[299] Implementing Guidelines on the Humanitarian, Rehabilitation and Development Aspects of the GRP-MILF Tripoli Agreement on Peace of 2001, 7 May 2002, Article IV(4). See also Government of Nepal/CPN-M, Ceasefire Code of Conduct, 25 May 2006, Article 17; Ratko Mladić, Order to Commands [transmission of ceasefire agreement], 23 December 1994, Exhibit 5D01043.E in ICTY *Popović* trial; Memorandum of Understanding, 27 November 1991, Article 8 [Croatia], reproduced in M Sassòli, AA Bouvier, and A Quintin, *How Does Law Protect in War? Volume III* (International Committee of the Red Cross, Geneva, 2011) 1761.
[300] Comprehensive Agreement on Respect for Human Rights and International Humanitarian Law between the Government of the Philippines and the National Democratic Front, Part IV, Article 4(9); IIHL *Manual*, above note 28, 54. See also Guiding Principles on Internal Displacement, Principle 16.
[301] See eg Declaration on Measures for a Political Settlement of the Georgian/Abkhaz Conflict Signed on 4 April 1994, Article 9.
[302] Customary International Humanitarian Law, Rule 117.

purported customary rule contains both the obligation to provide information and the obligation to search for missing persons. It, too, is subject to the capabilities of the parties to the conflict. In light of the close relationship between this rule and other customary rules, and the link between norms in various bodies of law, if it is not already a rule of customary international law, it is on its way to becoming one.

3.5 Displaced persons
3.5.1 Prohibition on forced displacement

Displacement of the civilian population is a particular problem during non-international armed conflicts. It is an inherent part of ethnic cleansing. It may also be used by one party as a means by which to deprive the other party of its support in particular localities. The prevalence of forced displacement may explain why the relevant provision in the Rome Statute is the only one that deviates from the approach of incorporating offences from the equivalent article on international armed conflict, instead drawing on Additional Protocol II.[303] That said, the Additional Protocol II provision was based on the equivalent provision in the Fourth Geneva Convention.[304] As such, the international humanitarian law of international armed conflict once again influenced the international humanitarian law of non-international armed conflict.[305] Furthermore, although the provision in the Rome Statute drew from Additional Protocol II, as will be discussed below, it was modified to become akin to the rule applicable in international armed conflict.

The forced displacement of the civilian population, or individual members thereof, is prohibited in customary international law.[306] Common Article 3 does not contain an explicit prohibition on point, but certain displacements, depending on their nature and the way in which they are carried out, have the potential to violate the prohibitions on violence to life and person and outrages upon personal dignity.[307] Additional Protocol II and the Rome Statute do contain provisions on point, but they are limited to a prohibition on the *ordering* of forced displacement.[308] Ordering in this context is to be construed broadly, interpreted in the sense of a deliberate action on the part of the relevant party, in order to distinguish it from voluntary movement on the part of the civilian population. This is consistent with the original proposal put forth at the 1972 Conference of Government Experts which related to the displacement being 'ordered or compelled'.[309] It is also consistent with the jurisprudence of the ICTY on deportation, which has focused on the forced, coercive, or involuntary character of the

---

[303] D Robinson and H von Hebel, 'War Crimes in Internal Armed Conflicts: Article 8 of the ICC Statute' (1999) 2 *YIHL* 193, 203.
[304] ICRC, *Commentary on the Additional Protocols*, above note 139, 1472.
[305] On which see generally above, 55 et seq.
[306] Rome Statute, Article 8(2)(e)(viii); GA Res 2675 (XXV) (1970); Customary International Humanitarian Law, Rule 129B; Darfur Commission Report, above note 134, para 166.
[307] AM de Zayas, 'International Law and Mass Population Transfers' (1975) 16 *Harvard International Law Journal* 207, 220–1.
[308] Additional Protocol II, Article 17; Rome Statute, Article 8(2)(e)(viii). See J Willms, 'Without Order, Anything Goes? The Prohibition of Forced Displacement in Non-International Armed Conflict' (2009) 91 *IRRC* 547.
[309] ICRC, Conference of Government Experts on the Reaffirmation and Development of International Humanitarian Law Applicable in Armed Conflicts: Report on the Work of the Conference, Volume I (1972) para 2.503 and Volume II, 50. See also Fourth Geneva Convention, Article 49, on which the provision is based; GA Res 2675 (XXV) (1970).

displacement.³¹⁰ Just as the prohibition on ordering that there shall be no survivors has been interpreted as also prohibiting declaring that there shall be no survivors and conducting hostilities on that basis,³¹¹ so too should the prohibition on ordering the displacement of the civilian population be interpreted in such a manner. Thus, it is not limited to the person at the top of the chain of command who issues the initial order, but includes the low-level official who implements the instruction, forcing the individuals out of their homes, or individuals who commit other acts with the intention of forcing the civilian population to leave. The practice is along these lines. For example, a former officer in the Forces Démocratiques de Libération du Rwanda (FDLR) recounted in 2009 that he 'personally saw a telegram in which President [of the FDLR] Murwanashyaka told commanders that they should attack villages to force civilians to flee'.³¹² Along similar lines, the RUF of Sierra Leone sent 'letters announcing their imminent arrival in particular towns or villages' so as to generate panic among inhabitants.³¹³ At any rate, there is no room for the argument that, in non-international armed conflicts, governments have 'the right to transfer part of the civilian population from one region to another if they considered it necessary', as was the view espoused by at least one state during the 1974–7 Diplomatic Conference.³¹⁴

The prohibition on forced displacement is intended to safeguard 'the right and aspiration of individuals to live in their communities and homes without outside interference'.³¹⁵ It covers both deportation—'the forced displacement of persons by expulsion or other forms of coercion from the area in which they are lawfully present, across a *de jure* state border or, in certain circumstances, a *de facto* border, without grounds permitted under international law'³¹⁶—as well as forcible transfer—'a forced removal or displacement of people from one area to another which may take place within the same national borders'.³¹⁷ The prohibition against deportation is important, as it is sometimes thought, incorrectly, that deportation is irrelevant in the context of non-international armed conflict.³¹⁸ That view confuses the crossing of a border for the purposes of the characterization of the conflict with the crossing of a border by the civilian population as a result of the conflict. Practice has also shown that cross-border transfers may take place in non-international armed conflicts. Although Additional Protocol II does not use the term 'deportation', the prohibition on compelling civilians 'to leave their own territory for reasons connected with the conflict' is precisely that.³¹⁹

Despite the prohibition, forced displacement is commonplace. It takes place for various reasons, including for the purposes of ethnic cleansing. For example, during the conflicts in the former Yugoslavia, the forced displacements were part of the ethnic cleansing that was carried out; indeed, the displacement was considered 'the essence' of the ethnic cleansing.³²⁰ It also takes place in order to increase support for the armed

---

[310] See eg *Prosecutor v Stakić*, IT-97-24-A, Judgment, 22 March 2006, para 279.
[311] See below, 412.
[312] Quoted in 'FDLR Inc: Congo's Multinational Rebels', *BBC News*, 18 November 2009.
[313] D Keen, *Conflict and Collusion in Sierra Leone* (International Peace Academy, 2005) 42.
[314] *Official Records*, above note 40, Vol 14, 225, para 50 (Canada).
[315] *Prosecutor v Krnojelac*, IT-97-25-A, Judgment, 17 September 2003, para 218.
[316] *Stakić* Appeal Judgment, above note 310, para 278.
[317] *Prosecutor v Simić, Tadić, and Zarić*, IT-95-9-T, Judgment, 17 October 2003, para 122.
[318] This was the view, for example, of the second Working Party: *Final Record*, above note 31, Vol II-B, 83.
[319] Article 17(2).
[320] Interim Report of the Commission of Experts Established Pursuant to Security Council Resolution 780 (1992), S/25274, 26 January 1993, para 55; *Prosecutor v Stakić*, IT-97-24-T, Judgment, 31 July 2003, para 664.

group or armed forces. For example, the LTTE expropriated land from certain civilians in territory under its control in order to increase the proportion of persons in its territory who were sympathetic to its cause.[321] Persons may also be forcibly displaced as retaliatory measures against the opposing party to the conflict, as was true in Colombia.[322]

Exceptions to the prohibition on forcible transfer

The prohibition on forcible transfer is subject to two exceptions: 'security of the civilians involved' and 'imperative military reasons'.[323] Concern has been expressed that these exceptions may be abused by parties to a conflict.[324] The danger does exist; however, at least in the latter case, the word 'imperative' creates a very high threshold to be overcome before displacement may be ordered and rules out displacement for political reasons or displacement resulting from one side's 'own unlawful activity'.[325] The two exceptions do not apply to the prohibition on deportation, which is framed in absolute terms: '[c]ivilians shall not be compelled to leave their own territory for reasons connected with the conflict.'[326]

The exceptions in international criminal law are slightly different. First, the prohibition on deportation is not separated out from the prohibition on forcible transfer.[327] Accordingly, deportation, too, is subject to the two exceptions of security of the civilians involved and imperative military reasons. Insofar as the international criminal law proscription is concerned, then, greater freedom is afforded to the displacing entity than in international humanitarian law. This is consistent with the idea that international criminal law may provide for more exacting standards in certain situations before criminalization will result.[328] It is also a consequence of the influence of the law of international armed conflict, with the Fourth Geneva Convention allowing evacuations involving the displacement of persons 'outside the bounds of the occupied territory' in certain limited situations.[329] However, it is important that the international humanitarian law prohibition is not 'read down' to the weaker level of the international criminal law equivalent. Yet, this may be what ends up happening in practice if it is realized that no, or limited, sanctions follow from violating the international humanitarian law prohibition but keeping within the international criminal law standard. The wording of the Customary International Humanitarian Law study rule is unfortunately misleading in this regard,[330] as it too suggests that the exceptions apply to all forms of displacement, even in situations of non-international armed conflict. This is mitigated somewhat by the commentary to the relevant rule, which notes that 'evacuations may never involve displacement outside the national territory';[331] but the rule itself should

---

[321] US Department of State, Annual Report on International Religious Freedom 2001, 540.
[322] Former FARC member, in *Armed Non-State Actors and the Protection of Internally Displaced People* (Geneva Call and IDMC, June 2011) 14.
[323] Additional Protocol II, Article 17(1); Guiding Principles on Internal Displacement, Principle 6(2); Customary International Humanitarian Law, Rule 129B.
[324] *Official Records*, above note 40, Vol 14, 229, para 4 (Norway).
[325] See, respectively, ICRC, *Commentary on the Additional Protocols*, above note 139, 1473; *Stakić* Appeal Judgment, above note 310, para 287.
[326] Additional Protocol II, Article 17(2).
[327] Rome Statute, Article 8(2)(e)(viii); *Prosecutor v Đorđević*, IT-05-87/1-T, Judgment, 23 February 2011, para 1613 fn 6017. See above, 80.
[328] Above, 78–81.
[329] Fourth Geneva Convention, Article 49.
[330] Customary International Humanitarian Law, Rule 129B.
[331] *Customary International Humanitarian Law, Volume I: Rules*, above note 248, 461.

be formulated along these lines. A second difference is that, at least insofar as the ICC Elements of Crimes are concerned, the exception is one of 'military necessity', with the qualifier 'imperative' being omitted.[332] Again, this should not be translated across to the international humanitarian law arena. It should not even be applied by the ICC for it is contrary to the wording of the Rome Statute provision itself, and Article 9(3) of the Statute requires the Elements to be consistent with the Statute. In case of inconsistency, the Statute will trump the Elements.

If displacement is lawful, whether for reasons of security of the civilians involved or for imperative military reasons, the displacement should not last for any longer than is required. This is a derivative of the exceptions themselves. Once the prevailing reasons of security or military necessity cease to exist, the situation should be returned to its pre-existing state.[333]

Modalities of displacement

Certain rules also exist on the modalities of the displacement. The Guiding Principles on Internal Displacement provide that: '[p]rior to any decision requiring the displacement of persons, the authorities concerned shall ensure that all feasible alternatives are explored in order to avoid displacement altogether. Where no alternatives exist, all measures shall be taken to minimize displacement and its adverse effects.'[334] Although the Guiding Principles constitute soft law, they have proven important and influential and are followed by a number of states and courts.[335] Not only does this particular Principle provide useful guidance on the modalities of displacement, but, taken as it is from international human rights law, a World Bank operational directive, and certain OECD guidelines,[336] it reveals that when looking to interpret certain provisions of international humanitarian law, resort should be had not only to international human rights law, but to all relevant material.[337] Of course, the differences between the situations in which the materials would apply need to be considered. Thus, when the Annotations to the Guiding Principles refer to '[c]omprehensive and holistic impact assessments',[338] this cannot be taken too far. What may be possible in time of peace, when planning for a construction project, for example, will not always be possible in time of armed conflict. Similarly, what may be possible for a state, with its department for the environment, for planning, and the like, may not be possible for the non-state armed group.

A further rule on the modalities of displacement, in both conventional and customary international law, is that if displacement does take place, 'all possible measures shall be taken in order that the civilian population may be received under satisfactory conditions of shelter, hygiene, health, safety and nutrition'.[339]

Finally, it should be noted that not every instance of displacement will violate international humanitarian law. For example, the fact that individuals are fearful of a particular situation and thus depart from the relevant area does not automatically mean

---

[332] ICC Elements of Crimes, Article 8(2)(e)(viii)-2.
[333] *Stakić* Appeal Judgment, above note 310, para 284; Customary International Humanitarian Law, Rule 132; Guiding Principles, Principle 6(3).
[334] Principle 7(1).
[335] See eg Colombian Constitutional Court, Decision T-025, 22 January 2004.
[336] W Kälin, *Guiding Principles on Internal Displacement: Annotations* (ASIL, 2008) 38–9.
[337] See further Chapter 12.
[338] Kälin, above note 336, 39.
[339] Additional Protocol II, Article 17(1). Customary International Humanitarian Law, Rule 131 adds 'members of the same family are not [to be] separated'.

that a violation has occurred. The prohibition is one of *forcible* displacement; it does not prohibit the voluntary movement of individuals. However, a careful assessment needs to take place as to whether or not the movement is truly voluntary. As the ICTY Appeals Chamber has noted, '[f]actors other than force itself may render an act involuntary, such as taking advantage of coercive circumstances'.[340] Consent will also play an important role: 'consent must be real in the sense that it is given voluntarily and as a result of the individual's free will, assessed in the light of the surrounding circumstances.'[341] Mere presence or participation of a humanitarian agency in the displacement does not render an involuntary movement voluntary.[342] As in many other areas of the law, much will turn on the facts.

3.5.2 Treatment of internally displaced persons

An influential definition of internally displaced persons can be found in the Guiding Principles on Internal Displacement:

Persons or groups of persons who have been forced or obliged to flee or to leave their homes or places of habitual residence, in particular as a result of or in order to avoid the effects of armed conflict, situations of generalized violence, violations of human rights or natural or human-made disasters, and who have not crossed an internationally recognized state border.[343]

For the purposes of this book, the focus is on that subset of internally displaced persons who are created or affected by non-international armed conflict.

Internally displaced persons are civilians (unless they are 'fighters'[344]) and benefit from the protections afforded to civilians, whether through international humanitarian law or other bodies of international law.[345] Thus, norms on humane treatment, protections from attack, and the like all attach to internally displaced persons in the same way as they do civilians who are not displaced. Commitments of the parties to the conflict to respect international humanitarian law thus also benefit internally displaced persons.

In addition to the protections that are afforded by international humanitarian law and other bodies of international law, internally displaced persons benefit from the Guiding Principles. These are, as the name suggests, principles or soft law and not binding obligations. That said, many of the Principles are based on hard law and are binding, albeit through the treaty and customary law provisions on which they are based rather than through the Guiding Principles. The particular utility of the Guiding Principles comes into play where gaps exist in the protections afforded by the various bodies of hard law, whether due to a lack of norms, a lack of specificity of norms, or problems with the scope of application of the norms.[346]

---

[340] *Stakić* Appeal Judgment, above note 310, para 279.
[341] Ibid.
[342] Ibid, para 286.
[343] Guiding Principles, para 2.
[344] The term is that of the IIHL *Manual*, above note 28, 4 and 5. It is used here to describe members of the state armed forces and members of the military wing of the non-state armed group. Unlike the Manual, it does not include civilians who take a direct part in hostilities.
[345] J-P Lavoyer, 'Comments on the Guiding Principles on Internal Displacement' (1998) 38 *IRRC* 467; 'Internally Displaced Persons: The Mandate and Role of the International Committee of the Red Cross' (2000) 82 *IRRC* 491.
[346] On the gaps, see Report of the Representative of the Secretary-General for Internally Displaced Persons, 'Compilation and Analysis of Legal Norms', E/CN.4/1996/52/Add.2, 5 December 1995, paras 410–15.

For example, pursuant to the Guiding Principles, internally displaced persons have a right not to be 'interned in or confined to a camp' unless 'exceptional circumstances' render it 'absolutely necessary'.[347] They also benefit from '[t]he right to be protected against forcible return to or resettlement in any place where their life, safety, liberty or health would be at risk'.[348] This is innovative in particular in its application to non-state armed groups. Personal identification documents are also to be provided by the state or the non-state armed group.[349] It may be concluded from this that both the parent state and other states should recognize documents issued by non-state armed groups for these purposes.

The Guiding Principles have had practical effect. They have been supported by inter-governmental organizations,[350] formed the basis of states' domestic legislation,[351] and are used by influential bodies to assess the conduct of states. For example, the Inter-American Commission on Human Rights has described the Guiding Principles as 'provid[ing] authoritative guidance to the Commission on how the law should be interpreted and applied during all phases of displacement'.[352] Thus, at least in certain instances, the Guiding Principles have been transformed into binding law or treated as binding law. However, not all states fully support the Guiding Principles.[353] Insofar as non-state armed groups and *de facto* entities are concerned, they too have been rather supportive. For example, the *de facto* President of Abkhazia suggested translating the Guiding Principles into local languages,[354] and trainings have been conducted on the Guiding Principles to armed groups.[355] Occasional reference is made to the Guiding Principles in bilateral agreements between the state and the non-state armed group;[356] and armed groups, on occasion, signal their intent to comply with the Principles in unilateral declarations.[357] However, such instances are far fewer than instances of commitments to international humanitarian law.[358] Thus, protections afforded to internally displaced persons through international humanitarian law more generally should not be overlooked, and, in many situations, it may be more appropriate to interpret international humanitarian law in light of the Guiding Principles rather than to use the Guiding Principles as the basis from which to work.

The 2009 African Union Convention for the Protection and Assistance of Internally Displaced Persons in Africa is also useful in this regard for its consideration of the obligations of states parties, armed groups, and other relevant non-state actors. States

---

[347] Principle 12.   [348] Principle 15(d).   [349] Principle 20.

[350] See eg GA Res 62/153 (2007) para 10.

[351] See R Cohen, 'The Guiding Principles on Internal Displacement: An Innovation in International Standard Setting' (2004) 10 *Global Governance* 459, 467–71; S Carr, 'From Theory to Practice: National and Regional Application of the Guiding Principles' (2009) 21 *IJRL* 34.

[352] Inter-American Commission on Human Rights, Third Report on the Human Rights Situation in Colombia, OEA/Ser.L/V/II.102, Doc.9 rev.1, 26 February 1999, Chapter VI, para 10.

[353] See S Bagshaw, 'Internally Displaced Persons at the Fifty-Fourth Session of the United Nations Commission on Human Rights, 16 March–24 April 1998' (1998) 10 *IJRL* 548; Cohen, Guiding Principles, above note 351, 472–5; C Phuong, *The International Protection of Internally Displaced Persons* (Cambridge University Press, 2004) 71–2.

[354] Report of the Representative of the Secretary General on internally displaced persons, E/CN.4/2003/86, 21 January 2003, para 28.

[355] G Zeender, 'Engaging Armed Non-State Actors on Internally Displaced Persons Protection' (2005) 24 *RSQ* 96, 105–6; Cohen, Guiding Principles, above note 351, 471.

[356] Protocol on the Establishment of Humanitarian Assistance in Darfur, Annexed to the Agreement on Humanitarian Ceasefire, 8 April 2004; Darfur Peace Agreement, 5 May 2006, Article 21, para 177.

[357] Letter from Abd al-Malik Badr al-Din Al-houthi [Houthi (Yemen)] to Human Rights Watch, 29/Jumada II/1430.

[358] On which see above, 124–33.

parties have obligations relating to protection from internal displacement,[359] and to protection and assistance towards internally displaced persons.[360] The Convention also provides that '[m]embers of armed groups shall be prohibited from' carrying out certain acts, including arbitrary displacement, impeding assistance to the internally displaced, restricting their freedom of movement, recruiting child soldiers and forcibly recruiting any persons, and denying internally displaced persons the right to live in satisfactory conditions.[361] A debate arose as to whether directly referencing armed groups in a treaty would be tantamount to providing them with a certain legal status.[362] Hence, the Convention contains a provision that the relevant obligations 'shall not, in any way whatsoever, be construed as affording legal status or legitimizing or recognizing armed groups'.[363] As discussed in Chapter 5,[364] providing such a provision is present, states are less wary of purporting to regulate the conduct of non-state armed groups in pertinent international instruments.

3.5.3 Return of internally displaced persons

Internally displaced persons have a right to return to the place from which they were displaced. Although an explicit right to return in conventional international humanitarian law is found only in relation to occupied territory,[365] a right to return can be 'inferred *a fortiori* following unlawful displacement'.[366] If the initial displacement was unlawful, by necessity there must be a right to return to the place from which displacement took place; otherwise, the illegality would be concretized permanently. If the displacement was lawful, being rendered for particular security or imperative military reasons, once those reasons cease to exist, again return becomes appropriate. However, nowhere is this explicitly stated, and conventional international humanitarian law instruments are recognized as containing gaps in this regard.[367] That said, the Customary International Humanitarian Law study posits a customary rule relating to the right of displaced persons to return.[368] The Guiding Principles also contain obligations on the right to return,[369] and there is considerable practice to support the notion. For example, the LTTE of Sri Lanka made a commitment in 1998 that 'the movement of displaced populations who wanted to return to areas now under government control would not be impeded'.[370] This commitment was not followed in the final stages of the conflict.[371] In the Acte d'Engagement, between various armed groups

---

[359] Article 4. At the time of writing, the Convention had not entered into force.
[360] Articles 5 and 9.
[361] Article 7(5).
[362] AB Birganie, 'An African Initiative for the Protection of the Rights of Internally Displaced People' (2010) 10 *HRLR* 179, 189.
[363] Article 7(1).
[364] Above, 209.
[365] Fourth Geneva Convention, Article 49.
[366] E-C Gillard, 'The Role of International Humanitarian Law in the Protection of Internally Displaced Persons' (2005) 24 *RSQ* 37, 42.
[367] See J Kallenberger, 'Sixty Years of the Geneva Conventions: Learning from the Past to Better Face the Future', Address at the Ceremony to Celebrate the 60th Anniversary of the Geneva Conventions, 12 August 2009.
[368] Customary International Humanitarian Law, Rule 132.
[369] Principles 28–30. See Kälin, above note 336, 127–43.
[370] Protection of children affected by armed conflict: Note by the Secretary-General, A/53/482, 12 October 1998, para 64.
[371] See Report of the Secretary-General's Panel of Experts on Accountability in Sri Lanka, 31 March 2011, para 98.

in the Democratic Republic of the Congo, a commitment was made to '[t]he establishment of a commission to oversee the return of internally displaced persons and their resettlement in their home environments in collaboration with the UN and other humanitarian organisations'.[372] The parties to the conflict in the former Yugoslavia also made a commitment, in 1992, that 'refugees and displaced persons should be allowed to return voluntarily and safely to their places of origin'.[373] Numerous ad hoc agreements also reference the right to return on the part of internally displaced persons and contain provisions on providing the necessary security and environmental conditions to allow them to return. This tends to be almost a standard component of ceasefire and peace agreements.[374]

3.6 Interned and detained persons

Affording protection to persons who are deprived of their liberty in non-international armed conflicts, principally those who are detained or interned, is of considerable importance given that ideologies and emotions may be aroused,[375] and that detainees are by definition in a particular situation of vulnerability vis-à-vis their captors. For example, detained persons may be abused not only by their guards but also by civilians living close to the detention facilities. Accordingly, common Article 3, and more particularly, Additional Protocol II, contain detailed rules on the protections to be afforded to persons who are deprived of their liberty. The norms are also of customary international law status and additional customary norms relate to the treatment of detainees.[376]

---

[372] Acte d'Engagement, Article III ('La mise en place d'une commission chargée de superviser le retour des déplacés internes et leur réinstallation dans leurs milieux d'origine avec la collaboration des Nations-Unies et des autres organisations à caractère humanitaire').

[373] The London International Conference: Programme of Action on Humanitarian Issues Agreed between the Co-Chairmen to the Conference and the Parties to the Conflict, 27 August 1992.

[374] See eg Protocol on Refugees [Tajikistan/United Tajik Opposition], 21 January 1997; Accord de Paix entre le Gouvernement de la Republique Centrafricaine et le mouvements politico-militaires ci-après désignés: Front Democratique du Peuple Centrafricain (FDPC), Union des Forces Democratiques pour le Rassemblement, Article 3(3); Agreement on Ceasefire and Cessation of Hostilities between the Government of the Republic of Liberia and Liberians United for Reconciliation and Democracy and the Movement for Democracy in Liberia, 17 June 2003, Point 5; Peace Agreement between the Government of Liberia (GOL), The Liberians United for Reconciliation and Democracy (LURD), The Movement for Democracy in Liberia (MODEL) and the Political Parties Accra, Ghana, 18 August 2003, Article XIV(4). See also Programme of Action on Humanitarian Issues agreed between the Co-Chairmen to the Conference and the Parties to the Conflict, 27 August 1992; 12-Point Understanding reached between the Seven Political Parties and Nepal Communist Party (Maoists), 22 November 2005, Point 5; Implementing Guidelines on the Humanitarian, Rehabilitation and Development Aspects of the GRP-MILF Tripoli Agreement on Peace of 2001, 7 May 2002, Article VI(1); [Government of Sudan/Eastern Sudan Front] Agreement to Create a Conducive Atmosphere for Peace, 19 June 2006; [Government of Sudan/Eastern Sudan Front] Eastern Sudan Peace Agreement, 14 October 2006, Article 25, para 93; Agreement between the Government of Sudan, the Sudan Liberation Movement, and the Justice and Equality of Movement', 25 April 2004, Article 4(g); Protocol between the Government of Sudan (GoS), the Sudan Liberation Movement/Army (SLM/A) and the Justice and Equality Movement (JEM) on the Improvement of the Humanitarian Situation in Darfur, 9 November 2004, Article 2; [Georgia/Russia/Abkhazia/UNHCR] Quadripartite Agreement on Voluntary Return of Refugees and Displaced Persons signed on 4 April 1994, S/1994/397; Comprehensive Agreement on Respect for Human Rights and International Humanitarian Law between the Government of the Philippines and the National Democratic Front, Part IV, Article 9.

[375] LC Green, *The Contemporary Law of Armed Conflict* (Manchester University Press, 2000) 327.

[376] Customary International Humanitarian Law, Rules 118–28.

Certain Additional Protocol II norms on the treatment of detained persons are required to be respected 'as a minimum'. Others are to be respected 'within the limits of the[] capabilities' of the detaining entity.[377] As a result, the location of a particular provision within Additional Protocol II proved important and contentious. However, the schema set out in the Protocol is somewhat misleading, as although certain provisions are listed as to be respected as a minimum, their actual content will vary depending on the situation at hand. Similarly, certain provisions that are listed as being dependent on the capacity of the detaining entity do not turn on notions of capacity at all. The obligations to be respected as a minimum will be considered first before turning to the obligations that are dependent on the capacity of the detaining entity. As a preliminary point, it should be noted that the provisions cover all persons who have been interned or detained, whether civilian or fighter, as long as the deprivation of liberty results from the armed conflict; 'ordinary' prisoners do not fall within the protections of the Article.[378]

3.6.1 Obligations to be respected as a minimum

The obligation of humane treatment arises in respect of all persons who are *hors de combat*,[379] which thus includes interned and detained persons. This means that the prohibitions on such acts as violence to life, outrages upon personal dignity, collective punishments, and the like are all equally relevant in this context.[380]

Persons whose liberty has been restricted shall, 'to the same extent as the local civilian population, be provided with food and drinking water and be afforded safeguards as regards health and hygiene and protection against the rigours of the climate and the dangers of the armed conflict'.[381] The obligation is to be respected as a minimum, but the actual content of the obligation will vary depending on the local conditions. The variable nature of the content results from the view that it would be 'unreasonable to demand a higher standard of treatment for detainees than that enjoyed by local civilians'.[382] This does not mean that, if local civilians have insufficient food and water, so too will detained persons, as, in such circumstances, the detaining party may be under an obligation to facilitate humanitarian assistance.[383] Poor conditions of detention, particularly through inadequate food and water or lack of medical treatment, may also amount to a violation of the prohibition on inhuman treatment.[384] Nonetheless, the standards of the civilian population then prevailing will be a factor in assessing the treatment to be afforded to detained persons.[385]

In practice, the relevant comparator tends to be that of the fighters in question rather than the local civilian population. British treatment of captured fighters during the Boer war of 1899–1902 was along these lines.[386] Similarly, French fighters who were detained by the Armée de Libération Nationale (ALN) during the Algerian war of

---

[377] Article 5(1) and (2) respectively.
[378] See *Official Records*, above note 40, Vol 8, 336, para 65 (ICRC); ICRC, *Commentary on the Additional Protocols*, above note 139, 1386; Bothe, Partsch, and Solf, above note 236, 645.
[379] See above, 255.
[380] On which see above, 259–72.
[381] Additional Protocol II, Article 5(1)(b).
[382] L Moir, *The Law of Internal Armed Conflict* (Cambridge University Press, 2002) 113.
[383] On which see below, 329–34.
[384] See eg *Limaj* Trial Judgment, above note 66, paras 288–9.
[385] *Aleksovski* Trial Judgment, above note 27, paras 173 and 182.
[386] Spaight, above note 193, 275.

independence (1954–62) indicated that they were subject to the same conditions as the ALN: '[w]e ate as they did. We slept where they slept and we followed them when they moved.'[387] More recently, in 1988, the FMLN indicated that it gave 'wounded government troops the same medical care that the FMLN combatants receive'.[388] Other armed groups have also indicated that they treat captured fighters on the same basis as their own fighters. This comports with the standard set out in the 1874 Brussels Declaration, which provided that, in the absence of a bilateral agreement between the parties to the conflict on the treatment of prisoners of war, 'prisoners of war shall be treated as regards food and clothing, on the same footing as the troops of the Government which capture them'.[389] However, it has been suggested that the comparator should be the local civilian population given that guerrilla fighters may live under harsher conditions.[390] While this may be true, it is unlikely to be followed in practice.

The equivalent customary rules have been framed in an absolute manner—'[p]ersons deprived of their liberty must be provided with adequate food, water, clothing, shelter and medical attention'; '[p]ersons deprived of their liberty must be held in premises which are removed from the combat zone and which safeguard their health and hygiene'[391]—as are certain commitments by the parties.[392] Nonetheless, as the rules are based on the treaty obligation, and in light of the difficulties resulting from any absolute obligations in this regard, in practice, the local conditions prevailing at the relevant time will have to be considered. This is recognized by the commentary to the customary rule, which provides that, in respect of food, water, clothing, shelter, and medical attention, the content of the obligation will vary depending on the local conditions,[393] although, in respect of premises 'removed from the combat zone and which safeguard...health and hygiene', there is no such recognition.[394]

Other provisions that are to be respected as a minimum include allowing detainees 'to receive individual or collective relief';[395] 'to practise their religion and, if requested and appropriate, to receive spiritual assistance from persons, such as chaplains, performing religious functions';[396] and 'if made to work, [to] have the benefit of working conditions and safeguards similar to those enjoyed by the local civilian population'.[397] The actual content of the latter obligation is thus dependent on the local conditions, while the receipt of spiritual assistance is limited to 'appropriate' situations. Thus, as before, although Additional Protocol II requires each of these provisions to be respected 'at a minimum', their actual content will prove variable.

In addition to the conventional obligations, the Customary International Humanitarian Law study posits the existence of a customary norm by which '[t]he personal

---

[387] Interview with French soldiers, *France Soir*, 21 October 1958, quoted in *White Paper on the Application of the Geneva Conventions of 1949 to the French-Algerian Conflict* (Algerian Office, 1960) 16. See also 17.
[388] FMLN, above note 208, 7.
[389] Project for an International Declaration concerning the Laws and Customs of War, Brussels, 1874, Article 27. See also Spaight, above note 193, 285.
[390] Bothe, Partsch, and Solf, above note 236, 647.
[391] Customary International Humanitarian Law, Rules 118 and 121.
[392] Comprehensive Agreement on Respect for Human Rights and International Humanitarian Law between the Government of the Philippines and the National Democratic Front, Part IV, Article 4(6).
[393] *Customary International Humanitarian Law, Volume I: Rules*, above note 248, 430.
[394] Ibid, 435–7.
[395] Additional Protocol II, Article 5(1)(c).
[396] Ibid, Article 5(1)(d); Customary International Humanitarian Law, Rule 127 (respect for personal convictions and religious practices).
[397] Additional Protocol II, Article 5(1)(e).

details of persons deprived of their liberty must be recorded'.[398] Although the customary status of such a norm may be queried, bilateral agreements concluded between the parties sometimes contain a provision on point.[399] Furthermore, there is other practice on point, with the NTC of Libya in 2011 requiring a 'capture card' be completed following the detention of an individual and a copy of the card to be sent to the ICRC.[400] Drafters of the NTC guidance indicated that they included such a requirement due to the customary status of the requirement to record the personal details of detained persons.[401] The obligation would also facilitate search for the missing and would assist the prohibition on enforced disappearances.[402] Accordingly, the existence of such a norm would be welcome.

3.6.2 Obligations dependent on capacity

During the drafting of Additional Protocol II, it was recognized that certain provisions could not be respected at all times but depended on the means available to the parties to the conflict.[403] The fact that these obligations are dependent on capacity should not, however, be taken as a means by which 'to deny arbitrarily to the victims the enjoyment of the rights mentioned'.[404] The provisions that follow are to be respected 'within the limits of [the] capabilities'[405] of the detaining entity. The first such provision is that, '[e]xcept when men and women of a family are accommodated together, women shall be held in quarters separated from those of men and shall be under the immediate supervision of women'.[406] This serves to protect women from sexual violence and guard against outrages upon personal dignity.[407] However, the views of the detainees themselves should be considered in this regard, for if there is solely one male or one female among a group of detainees, that individual may not wish to be detained in isolation. Detainees are also to be 'allowed to send and receive letters and cards, the number of which may be limited by competent authority if it deems necessary'.[408] The ability to send and receive messages allows detainees contact with the outside world. It is also invaluable for the families of detainees to receive word that the detainees are alive and to maintain contact with them. Visits by family members would also prove beneficial in this regard. In addition, detainees 'shall have the benefit of medical examinations';[409] and upon their release, 'necessary measures to ensure their safety shall be taken'.[410] Both obligations are required to safeguard the life and health of the individuals concerned.

---

[398] Customary International Humanitarian Law, Rule 123.
[399] Comprehensive Agreement on Respect for Human Rights and International Humanitarian Law between the Government of the Philippines and the National Democratic Front, Part IV, Article 4(6).
[400] National Transitional Council, Rules on the Treatment of Detainees, 19 May 2011. See Scobbie, above note 221.
[401] Ibid.
[402] *Customary International Humanitarian Law, Volume I: Rules*, above note 248, 439–42.
[403] JE Bond, 'Application of the Law of War to Internal Conflicts' (1973) 3 *Georgia Journal of International and Comparative Law* 345, 376–7.
[404] Bothe, Partsch, and Solf, above note 236, 647.
[405] Article 5(2).
[406] Article 5(2)(a). See also Customary International Humanitarian Law, Rule 118.
[407] See further below, 314.
[408] Article 5(2)(b). See also Customary International Humanitarian Law, Rule 125.
[409] Article 5(2)(d).
[410] Article 5(4).

Two other obligations exist that are deserving of particular comment. First, 'places of internment and detention shall not be located close to the combat zone. [The interned and detained] shall be evacuated when the places where they are interned or detained become particularly exposed to danger arising out of the armed conflict, if their evacuation can be carried out under adequate conditions of safety'.[411] It has been suggested that it 'may well be unduly onerous to satisfy this requirement' given the fluid nature of non-international armed conflicts.[412] This will be true, particularly in instances of mobile warfare in the context of which there does not tend to be a combat zone as such. However, the difficulties inherent in meeting the obligation are taken into consideration in the obligation itself, with it being subject to the capabilities of the detaining entity. As such, the obligation is already tailored to meet the fluidity of the situation.

Second, the 'physical or mental health and integrity' of interned and detained persons 'shall not be endangered by any unjustified act or omission'. Accordingly, 'it is prohibited to subject' interned and detained persons 'to any medical procedure which is not indicated by the state of health of the person concerned, and which is not consistent with the generally accepted medical standards applied to free persons under similar medical circumstances'.[413] It is generally considered surprising, and unfortunate, that this obligation is subject to the capabilities of the detaining power.[414] However, this is not as important as would seem at first sight, for much of the obligation is not at all dependent on the capabilities of the detaining entity. Those aspects of the obligation would have to be respected as a minimum. It is also important to recall that the general principle of humane treatment remains applicable and includes a prohibition on medical experimentation.[415]

3.6.3 Specificities of non-international armed conflict

The rules surrounding treatment and conditions of detention are not infrequently raised as going above and beyond the capabilities of the parties.[416] In general, the obligations in respect of detained and interned persons are not at all unduly onerous, as a number of guarantees are explicitly made subject to the capabilities of the detaining power. Hence, it is difficult to agree with the view that the mobile nature of most non-international armed conflicts makes it inherently difficult or impossible for detained persons to be treated in accordance with international humanitarian law. Control over a small tract of territory, or the odd town or village throughout the country, may very well suffice to allow the armed group to afford the requisite guarantees.

However, in certain situations, a party to a non-international armed conflict, usually the armed group, may have to desist from taking prisoners if it cannot provide the requisite guarantees. In this regard, some armed groups have expressly stated to the

---

[411] Article 5(2)(c).
[412] LC Green, *The Contemporary Law of Armed Conflict* (Manchester University Press, 2000) 328.
[413] Additional Protocol II, Article 5(2)(e). See also Customary International Humanitarian Law, Rule 92.
[414] See eg WA Solf, 'Development of the protection of the wounded, sick and shipwrecked under the Protocols Additional to the 1949 Geneva Conventions', in C Swinarski (ed), *Studies and Essays on International Humanitarian Law and Red Cross Principles in Honour of Jean Pictet* (International Committee of the Red Cross, Geneva, 1984) 237, 242–3; Moir, *Internal Armed Conflict*, above note 382, 112.
[415] Additional Protocol II, Article 5(3).
[416] See eg JE Bond, *The Rules of Riot* (Princeton University Press, 1974) 117–18.

ICRC that they execute captured members of the state armed forces due to the inability to detain them.[417] The release of prisoners by other armed groups, as in the instances discussed below, may also have been influenced by the difficulties experienced in detaining them. Writing in 1968, Kwame Nkrumah, for example, indicated that '[t]he question of prisoners, particularly during the initial stages of revolutionary warfare poses a number of problems. A small unit of guerrillas, sometimes without even a base camp, cannot spare time, energy or supplies in looking after them. It is sometimes necessary to abandon them after seizing their weapons and supplies. In general, they should be treated as humanely as possible'.[418] According to Nkrumah, humane treatment of prisoners also serves a military purpose: '[i]f the enemy retains the hope that he can save his life by surrendering, his will to fight will be considerably reduced. On the other hand, if the enemy is unaware of the moderate and humane treatment given by guerrillas to prisoners, he will fight with greater fury, in the belief that there is no escape.'[419]

Insofar as the conditions of detention are concerned, it is important to bear in mind that the conditions usually provided by state forces are not necessarily the model to be followed by non-state armed groups. State-of-the-art detention facilities are not required. Rather, detention may take the form of quite basic facilities or improvised facilities provided—and this is an important proviso—that the guarantees surrounding the conditions of detention are met. Even fixed detention centres are not strictly required, a point that should not go unnoticed given the practice. For example, during the Algerian war of independence (1954–62), 'because the FLN [Front de Libération Nationale] bases were mobile and FLN control over territory often insecure, permanent camps were not created. Some prisoners were detained in Morocco or Tunisia or shuttled in small groups from place to place within Algeria'.[420] Similarly, as one journalist who was briefly detained by the Taliban of Afghanistan in 2010 recounted: '[t]he word prison usually implies a thick-walled building with gates, padlocks and guards. But in the Taliban concept of a jail, the gate doesn't exist. The jailer was the gate, the prison cell, the executioner and sometimes, if you were lucky, your friend ... Wherever he was, the cell went with him. It could be a cave or a room in a farmer's house.'[421] Fixed detention facilities are the preferred option, but none of the forms of detention just mentioned are inherently unlawful. What is required is that the requisite guarantees be met, and it will be far more difficult to meet the guarantees of humane treatment, to safeguard health and hygiene, to afford protection from the climate, and the like, in instances of mobile detention.

There is considerable practice in support of the humane treatment of detainees. Codes of conduct of armed groups, in particular, contain rules on point. The CPLA, in its 1947 Eight Points for Attention, provided: '[d]on't ill-treat captives.'[422] It also set out Five Policies for Lenient Treatment of Captives, which included the injunctions

---

[417] See the examples in *Customary International Humanitarian Law, Volume II: Practice*, above note 248, 976–7.
[418] Nkrumah, above note 226, 113. See also E Guevara, *Guerrilla Warfare* (Penguin, 1969) 49.
[419] Ibid, 113–14.
[420] E van Cleef Greenberg, 'Law and the Conduct of the Algerian Revolution' (1970) 11 *Harvard International Law Journal* 37, 60 (internal citations omitted). See also *White Paper on the Application of the Geneva Conventions of 1949 to the French-Algerian Conflict* (Algerian Office, 1960) 16. R Maison, 'The French in Algeria: Can there be Prisoners of War in a "Domestic" Operation?', in S Scheipers (ed), *Prisoners in War* (Oxford University Press, Oxford, 2010) 173, 183.
[421] G Abdul-Ahad, 'Five Days Inside a Taliban Jail', *The Guardian* (UK), 25 November 2010.
[422] Eight Points for Attention, above note 7.

'[d]o not kill or injure captives', '[d]o not hit, swear at, maltreat or insult captives', and '[d]o not confiscate the private property of captives'.[423] The NRA of Uganda's Code of Conduct provided: '[n]ever kill any member of the public or any captured prisoners, as the guns should only be reserved for armed enemies or opponents.'[424] The 1982 Code of Conduct for members of the Sendero Luminoso of Peru included the injunction '[d]o not mistreat prisoners'.[425] The RUF of Sierra Leone stated that '[w]e have learnt the value of treating captives and prisoners of war with utmost civility',[426] and its Eight Codes of Conduct provided '[d]o not ill-treat captives'.[427] The EZLN of Mexico issued an order in 1994 to its forces to '[r]espect the lives of prisoners and turn in the wounded to the International Red Cross for medical attention'.[428] The FMLN of El Salvador reported in 1988 that it treated detained persons 'in accord with that stipulated by Article 5 of [Additional] Protocol II'.[429] During the post-independence violence in the DRC, in 1964, the Government invited the ICRC to ascertain its compliance with the Geneva Conventions, in particular 'in the matter of the treatment of prisoners'.[430] More recently, in 1991, during the conflict in Croatia, the parties committed that 'all arrested persons, and notably combatants who have surrendered, must be treated with humanity' and that 'all detaining authorities must ensure the protection of the prisoners'.[431] The Code of the CNF of Burma contains very many norms on the treatment of detained persons, including obligations to protect them; to provide special protection for female prisoners; to provide adequate food, water, and medical treatment; to return confiscated property prior to release; and to equality of treatment.[432] During the 2011 violence in Libya, the National Transitional Council issued 'Rules on the treatment of detainees', which provided *inter alia* for humane treatment, medical treatment, detention centres, and the recording of the details of detainees.[433] It also issued a statement, which is worth reproducing in large part:

The TNC would like to reiterate that its policies strictly adhere to the 'Geneva Convention relative to the treatment of Prisoners of War'...The council conveys its regret for some individual incidents that had occurred during the first few days of the revolution and guarantees that this would not be repeated. Clear codes of conduct have been issued from the National Interim council and include:

1. Any Libyan caught whether they be military personnel or citizens recruited to cause sabotage and spread chaos, should not be titled as 'Prisoner' but as a Libyan brother (or sister) who has been deceived.

---

[423] See H Xiaodong, 'The Chinese Humanitarian Heritage and the Dissemination of and Education in International Humanitarian Law in the Chinese People's Liberation Army' (2001) 83 *IRRC* 141, 144–5.
[424] National Resistance Army Code of Conduct, above note 10.
[425] Code of 1982. Reproduced in J Weinstein, *Inside Rebellion: The Politics of Insurgent Violence* (Cambridge University Press, 2007) 152.
[426] RUF, 'Footpaths to Democracy: Toward a New Sierra Leone', 1995.
[427] Reproduced in *RUF* Trial Judgment, above note 8, para 705.
[428] 'Declaration of War of the Zapatista National Liberation Army (EZLN)', Communique of 2 January 1994, reproduced and translated in B Clarke and C Ross (eds), *Voice of Fire: Communiqués and Interviews from the Zapatista National Liberation Army* (Freedom Voices, 2000) 31, 32.
[429] FMLN, above note 208, 9.
[430] Public Statement, above note 155.
[431] The Hague Statement on Respect of Humanitarian Principles, 5 November 1991, reproduced in Berger, above note 211, 59.
[432] Chin National Front, Code, above note 56, Articles 1–15 (unofficial translation).
[433] National Transitional Council, Rules on the Treatment of Detainees, 19 May 2011. See Scobbie, above note 221.

2. All prisoners and detainees will be provided with food, water and necessary medical assistance and will be treated humanely, without the use of aggression in any form. The TNC will vow to punish those who violate this code and will allow local and international human rights organizations to freely visit and talk to the detainees and prisoners at any time.
3. Detainees and prisoners will be allowed to contact their relatives and arrangements will be made to allow them to return home without any restrictions or conditions... [434]

Another armed group indicated in 2011 that it releases all foreign detainees, ill persons, and persons over the age of 55.[435]

Despite all these statements and injunctions, the practice of some of these very groups is entirely inconsistent with their statements and codes. For example, the RUF treated detainees extremely poorly.[436] Detainees were treated extremely poorly also in the conflict in Croatia.[437] Writing elsewhere, Mao Tse-Tung advocated the killing of prisoners: '[i]t is best to require the prisoners first to hand over their weapons, and then to disperse them, or to execute them.'[438] Also problematic is the 2009 Code of Conduct of the Taliban of Afghanistan, which provided that '[i]f the captive is a Director (in a governmental office) a Commander, a District Administrator or a higher ranking official than them, or a foreign Muslim, the Imam and his deputy will decide whether the captive will be punished, executed or released in the framework of prisoners exchange'; and that '[i]f an infidel warrior has been captured, his fate (execution, release in prisoner exchange, release following negotiations, or release upon payment in case the Muslims need money) will be decided by the Imam and his deputy'.[439] However, in respect of other groups, practice contrary to their codes does not necessarily mean that the group was not genuinely seeking to address the conduct. Codes of conduct and internal regulations can be aimed at changing existing practices and issued to address standing concerns. Indeed, it makes little sense to issue a code of conduct on matters that are not raised by the conflict in question. Thus, violation of a provision of the code does not necessarily mean that the group was not genuinely seeking to address contrary practice. Each commitment needs to be assessed on its own terms and against the practice of the group.

Furthermore, in many instances, the provisions of a code are indeed followed. The New People's Army (NPA), the military wing of the NDFP, stated in 2004: '[w]e must treat captives leniently in accordance with the Geneva Convention and Protocol I and demonstrate that we treat well those who surrender or are rendered incapable of fighting in the course of combat.'[440] On this basis, according to the NDFP, in 2010, four members of the Philippine National Police Special Action Force, who were wounded in an attack by the NPA, 'were treated as prisoners of war (POWs) and were given first aid by the NPA. In accordance with the NDFP policy on the treatment

---

[434] Interim Transitional National Council, 'The Treatment of Detainees and Prisoners', 25 March 2011.
[435] Information provided to author.
[436] See eg *RUF* Trial Judgment, above note 8, paras 1109–1115.
[437] See eg *Prosecutor v Mrkšić, Radić, and Šljivančanin*, IT-95-13/1-T, Judgment, 27 September 2007.
[438] M Tse-Tung, *Basic Tactics* (Pall Mall Press, 1967) 98.
[439] Code of Conduct for the Mujahideen, Articles 8 and 9, 9 May 2009, reproduced and translated in M Sassòli, AA Bouvier, and A Quintin, *How Does Law Protect in War? Volume III* (ICRC, Geneva, 2011) 2325.
[440] 'Fight for National Liberation, Democracy and Peace through Protracted People's War', 29 March 2004, reproduced in (2004) 7 *YIHL* 552. See also its statement in (2005) 8 *YIHL* 484.

of POWs, the NPA decided to release them immediately so that they could be brought to the nearest hospitals in Antipolo City'.⁴⁴¹ This also comports with the 1998 Comprehensive Agreement on Respect for Human Rights and International Humanitarian Law concluded between the NDFP and the Government of the Philippines which provides for the humane treatment of detainees and notes that '[o]n humanitarian or other reasonable grounds, such persons deprived of liberty shall be considered for safe release'.⁴⁴²

Nonetheless, the treatment of prisoners is an area in which violations of the law are commonplace. Allegations of mistreatment by one party against the other also abound. For example, the JEM of Darfur alleged mistreatment of detainees and inhuman conditions of detention on the part of the Government of Sudan. In 2009, it noted that 'Khartoum is signatory to the Four Conventions of Geneva one of whom [*sic*] concerns us as Prisoners of war', alleged that '[i]n accordance with those Conventions, Khartoum is in direct breach of international laws', and appealed to the UN Special Rapporteur on human rights in Sudan 'to ensure that those who are currently under detention are treated humanely and in line with international conventions'.⁴⁴³ Similarly, during the violence in Libya in 2011, the Interim Transitional National Council alleged that the conditions in which detainees were held by the Government of Libya 'are in clear gross violation of international humanitarian laws'.⁴⁴⁴

3.6.4 Release of prisoners

There is a variety of practice on the release of prisoners. During the Boer war of 1899–1902, Boer commanders released captured fighters having found it impossible to detain them.⁴⁴⁵ Decades later, Che Guevara indicated that prisoners should be freed. This, too, was done for military reasons:

> What can never be done is to keep prisoners, unless a secure base of operations, invulnerable to the enemy, has been established. Otherwise, the prisoner will become a dangerous menace to the security of the inhabitants of the region or to the guerrilla band itself because of the information that he can give upon rejoining the enemy army. If he has not been a notorious criminal, he should be set free after receiving a lecture.⁴⁴⁶

Fidel Castro, then head of an armed group fighting against the forces of President Batista of Cuba, stated: '[w]e return prisoners without even intimidating them. We do not exchange them, you understand; not one of ours has ever been returned in the field. But we just disarm our enemies when we capture them and send them back through the Cuban Red Cross.' Along similar lines, Raul Castro addressed captured Batistianos:

> We hope that you will stay with us and fight against the master who so ill-used you. If you decide to refuse this invitation—and I am not going to repeat it—you will be delivered to the Cuban Red Cross tomorrow. Once you are under Batista's orders again, we hope that you will not take up arms against us. But, if you do, remember this: 'We took you this time. We can take you

---

⁴⁴¹ NDFP Human Rights Monitoring Committee, 'NDFP denies use of anti-personnel mines, emphasizes adherence to international humanitarian law', 24 April 2010.
⁴⁴² Comprehensive Agreement on Respect for Human Rights and International Humanitarian Law between the Government of the Philippines and the National Democratic Front, Part IV, Article 4(6).
⁴⁴³ 'A Letter from JEM Prisoners of War in Khartoum to the UN Human Rights Rapporteur to Sudan', 3 June 2009.
⁴⁴⁴ Urgent Press Release, 6 April 2011.
⁴⁴⁵ Spaight, above note 193, 89.
⁴⁴⁶ E Guevara, *Guerrilla Warfare* (Penguin, 1969) 49.

again. And when we do, we will not frighten or torture or kill you, any more than we are doing to you at this moment. If you are captured a second time or even a third by us, we will again return you exactly as we are doing now.'[447]

The CNF of Burma also provides for the release of prisoners in its Code, an exception being made for persons accused of war crimes. It provides:

As per the nature of [the] revolution that the Chin National Front is waging, prisoners of war should not be detained for [a] long period of time. After interrogating, educating about Democracy and persuading them to support the Chin National movement, the prisoners of war should be immediately released. This should be practiced as the Chin National Front's standard for detaining prisoners of war.[448]

Prisoners have also been released pursuant to agreements, on an ad hoc basis, and through exchanges of prisoners.[449] Two points emerge from the practice. First, it is not at all the case that armed groups inevitably kill prisoners who they are unable to detain; in a not insignificant number of cases, they are released. Second, a military advantage may also be served by releasing such prisoners, as it evidences the humanity of the group.

3.6.5 Legal basis for security detention/internment

The law relating to conditions of detention is reasonably clear, if not always followed in practice. Rather less clear is the legal basis for security (administrative) detention or internment. Internment or security detention are those forms of detention that are imposed by the executive rather than the judiciary and which are preventive in nature, usually for reasons of security rather than on the basis of a criminal charge.[450] International humanitarian law does not provide an explicit legal basis for internment in situations of non-international armed conflict, although it does reference the practice suggesting that the requisite legal basis is implicitly contained therein.[451] Thus, in 1988, the FMLN adopted the view of Americas Watch that 'Protocol II, Article 5, implies that the parties have the authority to intern or detain persons for reasons related to the armed conflict'.[452] It is also recognized that the power to detain 'flows from the practice of armed conflict and the logic of IHL that parties to a conflict may capture persons deemed to pose a serious security threat and that such persons may be interned as long as they continue to pose a threat'.[453] The power to detain is also a corollary of the power to target individuals during armed conflict.[454] However, as all this is only implicit in international humanitarian law, the modalities of internment lie elsewhere. For its part, international human rights law contains a prohibition on

---

[447] Quoted in D Chapelle, 'How Castro Won', in TN Greene (ed), *The Guerrilla—And How to Fight Him* (Praeger, 1967) 218, 223. See also below, 414–5.
[448] Chin National Front, Code, above note 56, Article 14 (unofficial translation). Article 15 contains the exception in the case of war crimes.
[449] See eg Agreement on the Release and Transfer of Prisoners, 1 October 1992 [Bosnia]; JEM, 'Sudan, Darfur rebels agree prisoner swap', 17 February 2009; JEM, 'JEM announces release of 60 Sudanese soldiers during Doha talks', 29 May 2009.
[450] See ICRC, *Commentary on the Additional Protocols*, above note 139, 875.
[451] Additional Protocol II, Articles 5 and 6.
[452] FMLN, above note 208, 8, quoting Americas Watch, *The Civilian Toll 1986–7* (1987) 148.
[453] 'Expert Meeting on Procedural Safeguards for Security Detention in Non-International Armed Conflict' (2009) 91 *IRRC* 859, 863.
[454] C Kreß, 'Some Reflections on the International Legal Framework Governing Transnational Armed Conflicts' (2010) 15 *JCSL* 245, 263–4.

arbitrary deprivation of liberty.[455] What is considered arbitrary will be determined by the context.

The law of *international* armed conflict contains explicit provisions on internment, both in the territory of a party to the conflict and in occupied territory. That body of law provides that persons may be interned if 'absolutely necessary' in the former case, or for 'imperative reasons of security' in the latter.[456] It also provides that internees must be released as soon as the reasons that gave rise to the internment no longer exist, and that a review process is required to take place.[457] It has been suggested that this framework could also be applied in situations of non-international armed conflict.[458] Indeed, it has been so utilized, on occasion, in practice. A 1991 Memorandum of Understanding concluded between the parties to the conflict in Croatia provided that: '[c]ivilians who are in the power of the adverse party and who are deprived of their liberty for reasons related to the armed conflict shall benefit from the rules relating to the treatment of internees laid down in the Fourth Geneva Convention of 12 August 1949 (Articles 79 to 149).'[459] A weaker standard was used by the District Court of Pristina, with its holding that 'a genuine suspicion that the person concerned is a threat to the security of the detaining authority or those whom it represents in the conflict' would suffice.[460] For its part, in 1999, the Inter-American Commission on Human Rights stated in the context of internment by Colombian armed groups that 'international humanitarian law also prohibits the detention or internment of civilians except where necessary for imperative reasons of security'.[461] The standard of 'imperative reasons of security' is considered to constitute 'a workable balance between the need to protect personal liberty and the detaining authority's need to protect against activity seriously prejudicial to its security'.[462] However, it is left to the interning power to interpret the notion of 'imperative reasons of security'.[463]

Should resort be had to the law of international armed conflict as a basis from which to proceed, it would be important to appreciate the differences between the situations in which that body of law applies and non-international armed conflict. For example, what constitutes 'absolute necessity' in the territory of a party to the conflict and 'imperative' reasons of security in an occupied territory may be different. As the ICRC Commentary to the Fourth Geneva Convention notes, '[i]n occupied territories the internment of protected persons should be even more exceptional than it is inside the territory of the Parties to the conflict'.[464] That said, it should be recalled that internment is itself one of the 'severest measures of control' and that its 'exceptional character

---

[455] See eg ICCPR, Article 9(1).
[456] Fourth Geneva Convention, Articles 42 and 78.
[457] Ibid, Articles 132 and 43, 78 and Additional Protocol I, Article 75 (3).
[458] Expert Meeting, above note 453, 864; Kreß, above note 454, 263–4. Cf JB Bellinger III and VM Padmanabhan, 'Detention Operations in Contemporary Conflicts: Four Challenges for the Geneva Conventions and other Existing Law' (2011) 105 *AJIL* 201, 214.
[459] 27 November 1991, Article 4, reproduced in M Sassòli, AA Bouvier, and A Quintin, *How Does Law Protect in War? Volume III* (ICRC, 2011) 1713.
[460] *Prosecutor v Gashi, Mustafa, Mustafa, and Mehmeti*, Decision of 16 July 2003 (2003) 6 *YIHL* 594, 598.
[461] Inter-American Commission on Human Rights, Third Report on the Human Rights Situation in Colombia, OEA/Ser.L/V/II.102, Doc.9 rev.1, 26 February 1999, Chapter IV, para 122.
[462] J Pejić, 'The Protective Scope of Common Article 3: More than Meets the Eye' (2011) 93 *IRRC* 189, 209.
[463] JS Pictet (ed), *The Geneva Conventions of 12 August 1949, Commentary: IV Geneva Convention Relative to the Protection of Civilian Persons in Time of War* (ICRC, 1958) 257.
[464] Ibid, 367.

must be preserved'.⁴⁶⁵ Perhaps for this reason, in the case of spies, the NDFP indicated in 1989 that 'preventive arrest is prohibited. Arrest based on mere suspicion without firm evidence is prohibited even if the stated aim is to ensure the security of the Party and the revolution'.⁴⁶⁶

Although it has been queried 'how a non-State actor can exercise the inherent right to intern',⁴⁶⁷ it is submitted that it is not so much about a right to intern as it is about the need to regulate the existing practice of parties to non-international armed conflicts. Insofar as the modalities of internment, in particular the procedural protections that accompany internment, are concerned, state legislation would govern detention by state armed forces, while legislation of the non-state armed group may suffice for the purposes of non-state armed group detention. Indeed, a number of armed groups have enacted rules on offences, arrest, and trial,⁴⁶⁸ and these could and should be developed to include the modalities for internment. Alternatively, a non-state armed group may utilize the relevant state law on point to regulate its internment. For example, in 2011, the National Transitional Council of Libya used the Libyan Criminal Code and not its own law, albeit in the context of detention of fighters and not internment.⁴⁶⁹ On a more general note, references to the state in the law of non-international armed conflict will usually have to be interpreted along the lines of party to the conflict, thus including the non-state armed group. For example, when state legislation is mentioned, this would have to be read to include the legislation of non-state armed groups.

Insofar as the procedural protections to be afforded to interned persons are concerned, the detaining power, whether the state or the non-state armed group, is required to review the internment through an independent and impartial mechanism. Review is considered 'the most important procedural safeguard against arbitrary detention'.⁴⁷⁰ Indeed, the lack of a framework by which internees could have their detention independently reviewed led to the District Court of Pristina finding unlawful detention on the part of members of the KLA.⁴⁷¹ Such review may be undertaken by a judicial or administrative body; its precise character is less important than its independent and impartial nature. What is crucial is that it should have the power to order the release of the interned individual. It is also important that a political organ of the party to the conflict not be able to overrule it. Along the lines indicated above, it is submitted that the review mechanism should not be limited to state courts or administrative bodies, but should include those of the non-state armed group. For example, in 1972, the NDFP adopted a 'Guide for Enacting the People's Democratic Government' which included a chapter on people's courts and a chapter on the rights and duties of citizens.

---

⁴⁶⁵ Ibid, 257 and 368.
⁴⁶⁶ NDFP, 'Rules in the Investigation and Prosecution of Suspected Enemy Spies', in NDFP, *Declaration of Undertaking to Apply the Geneva Conventions of 1949 and Protocol I of 1977* (NDFP Human Rights Monitoring Committee Booklet No 6) 158. It should be noted that it is not entirely clear whether the preventive arrest in question relates to the criminal process or to internment.
⁴⁶⁷ Expert Meeting, above note 453, 870, which goes on to note the power of non-state armed groups to intern.
⁴⁶⁸ See eg the SPLA Act, 2003; Laws of the New Sudan, The Penal Code, 1994; CPN-M, Public Legal Code, 2060 (2003/2004); LTTE Penal Code; NDFP, Rules in the Investigation and Prosecution of Suspected Enemy Spies, above note 466.
⁴⁶⁹ Procedure on Detaining or Capturing People, Frontline Manual, 19 May 2011. See Scobbie, above note 221.
⁴⁷⁰ Expert Meeting, above note 453, 877.
⁴⁷¹ *Gashi*, above note 460.

Detailed procedures are also in place for the convening of trials.[472] This procedural framework could be extended to monitor cases of internment. Likewise, in 2003, the CPN-M drew up a legal code which included various offences and a brief criminal procedure.[473] This too could be adapted to monitor cases of internment. An administrative rather than a judicial process could also be adopted by the non-state armed group, which may be well within the capabilities of most groups.[474]

Concerns of legitimacy and legality may arise over courts or other mechanisms of non-state armed groups, as indeed they may with respect to non-state armed group 'legislation'. These concerns are considered in Chapter 12.[475] However, in this context, it should be borne in mind that 'any rules or guidelines regarding internment must be formulated in a way that would allow them to be implemented in a realistic way in the different types of [non-international armed conflicts], by both States and non-State actors'.[476]

Aside from regular review of the internment, it will be incumbent on the detaining power to afford other procedural guarantees. The ICRC has set out 15 norms that, in its view, should apply to interned persons. These include that internment is an exceptional measure and is not an alternative to criminal proceedings, that it be ordered on an individual and not a collective basis, and that it cease as soon as the reasons for its ordering cease.[477] Each of these norms follows from the very nature of internment. Other applicable norms include that reasons for the internment are to be provided to the interned, that the interned individual has a right to challenge the internment and a right to periodic review of the internment, and that review take place by an impartial and independent body.[478] The latter two norms are accepted guarantees in the context of internment; the former is required in order that the internment be open to challenge on the part of the interned.

There is some practice, of interest, in this regard, with the 1998 Comprehensive Agreement on Respect for Human Rights and International Humanitarian Law between the Government of the Philippines and the NDFP prohibiting:

denial of the right of relatives and duly authorized representatives of a person deprived of liberty for reasons related to the armed conflict to inquire whether a person is in custody or under detention, the reasons for the detention, under what circumstances the person in custody is being detained, and to request directly or through mutually acceptable intermediaries for his/her orderly and expeditious release.[479]

However, practice of this sort is in the minority and internment remains an area in which both the law and the practice need to be developed.

---

[472] Guide for Enacting the People's Democratic Government, reproduced in NDFP, *Declaration of Undertaking to Apply the Geneva Conventions of 1949 and Protocol I of 1977* (NDFP Human Rights Monitoring Committee Booklet No 6) 78.

[473] CPN-M, Public Legal Code, 2060 (2003/2004).

[474] M Sassòli and LM Olson, 'The Relationship between International Humanitarian and Human Rights Law where it Matters: Admissible Killing and Internment of Fighters in Non-International Armed Conflicts' (2008) 90 *IRRC* 599, 623. See also J Pejić, 'Procedural Principles and Safeguards for Internment/Administrative Detention in Armed Conflict and Other Situations of Violence' (2005) 87 *IRRC* 375, 387, recommending the establishment of an 'independent and impartial' body.

[475] Below, 557–62.

[476] Expert Meeting, above note 453, 862. See also Pejić, Protective Scope, above note 463, 207.

[477] Pejić, Procedural Principles, above note 474, which was adopted as the ICRC position. See 'International Humanitarian Law and the Challenges of Contemporary Armed Conflicts' (2007) 89 *IRRC* 719, 730.

[478] Ibid.

[479] Part IV, Article 3(6).

As indicated above, it follows from the very nature of internment that, once the conditions giving rise to the internment cease, the individuals should be released. Such release is a frequent component of ceasefire and peace agreements.[480] It may also be considered a norm of customary international law.[481]

3.7 Persons subject to the criminal process

International humanitarian law prohibits any sentencing or execution before a fair trial is conducted by a regularly constituted court for persons accused of crimes related to the armed conflict. The obligation is both a conventional and customary one.[482] Practice on point is mixed. The obligation is frequently violated with summary execution being commonplace in times of non-international armed conflict. Parties may also expressly declare a policy of summary execution or judgment. For example, in 1994, the EZLN of Mexico provided in an order to its forces: '[i]nitiate summary judgments against soldiers of the Mexican Federal Army and the political police who have received courses and who have been trained, assisted or paid by foreigners whether within or outside our nation; against those accused of betraying our Homeland and against all those who repress and mistreat the civilian population and rob or assault the good of the people.'[483] On the other hand, the NDFP indicated as early as 1969 that 'all accused shall be given a just trial',[484] and the bilateral agreement between the NDFP and the Government of the Philippines requires the affording of 'all the requisites of due process'.[485] Likewise Che Guevara indicated that '[e]xcept in special situations, there ought to be no execution of justice without giving the criminal an opportunity to clear himself'.[486]

Two critical issues arise. First, the meaning of trial by a 'regularly constituted court'; and, second, the due process guarantees that are required. The creation of a court and convening of a trial are sometimes considered beyond the capacity of non-state armed groups. As will be seen, this is by no means the case, provided the requisite guarantees are interpreted in an appropriate manner.

3.7.1 A regularly constituted court

Common Article 3(1)(d) provides for judgment by a 'regularly constituted court'. Insofar as states are concerned, this should not be overly problematic, although controversies do arise. For armed groups, however, this may prove rather more difficult as their courts are necessarily ad hoc in nature. Thus, reference to regular constitution was omitted from Additional Protocol II, given the view that 'it was unlikely that a

---

[480] See below, 519–20.
[481] Customary International Humanitarian Law, Rule 128C.
[482] Common Article 3; Additional Protocol II, Article 6; Rome Statute, Article 8(2)(c)(iv); Customary International Humanitarian Law, Rule 100.
[483] 'Declaration of War of the Zapatista National Liberation Army (EZLN)', communiqué of 2 January 1994, reproduced and translated in B Clarke and C Ross (eds), *Voice of Fire: Communiqués and Interviews from the Zapatista National Liberation Army* (Freedom Voices, 2000) 31, 32.
[484] Basic Rules of the New People's Army, above note 9.
[485] Comprehensive Agreement on Respect for Human Rights and International Humanitarian Law between the Government of the Philippines and the National Democratic Front, Part IV, Article 3(2).
[486] E Guevara, *Guerrilla Warfare* (Penguin, 1969) 29.

court could be "regularly constituted" under national law by an insurgent party'.[487] Much turns, then, on the meaning of a regularly constituted court.

Various views exist in this regard.[488] The Customary International Humanitarian Law study defines a regularly constituted court as one which 'has been established and organised in accordance with the laws and procedures already in force in a country'.[489] This would exclude the courts of armed groups established pursuant to their own 'law' as well as state courts concluded on an ad hoc basis. However, other interpretations have been offered. The ICC Elements of Crimes defines 'regularly constituted' by reference to 'the essential guarantees of independence and impartiality'.[490] Approaching the issue from an altogether different perspective, it has been suggested that whether a court of an armed group is regularly constituted should not be 'construed too literally', '[g]uerrillas, after all, are not apt to carry black robes and white wigs in their back packs'; rather, the test should be one of appropriateness, 'whether the appropriate authorities, acting under appropriate powers, created the court according to appropriate standards'.[491] It is submitted that the regularly constituted requirement should be interpreted as meaning 'established by law', to use the phrasing of human rights instruments,[492] but reference to law in this context should not be limited to state law. This would allow the courts of non-state armed groups to satisfy the necessary criterion.[493] As Nigeria noted at the 1974–7 Diplomatic Conference, if an armed group is sufficiently organized as to be a party to a conflict and observe the rules of humanitarian law, it may be sufficiently organized as to enact laws and a legal basis for its courts.[494] This has been borne out in practice with very many non-state armed groups convening courts pursuant to their own law.[495]

3.7.2 Due process guarantees

Identifying the obligations

Identifying the due process guarantees required of courts in times of armed conflict can be a tricky endeavour. Common Article 3 requires 'judicial guarantees which are recognized as indispensable by civilized peoples'; however, no list of such guarantees is to be found in the Article itself. Although several states at the 1949 Diplomatic

---

[487] ICRC, *Commentary on the Additional Protocols*, above note 139, 1398.

[488] See generally J Somer, 'Jungle Justice: Passing Sentence on the Equality of Belligerents in Non-International Armed Conflict' (2007) 89 *IRRC* 655, 671–6; S Sivakumaran, 'Courts of Armed Opposition Groups: Fair Trials or Summary Justice?' (2009) 7 *JICJ* 489, 498–500.

[489] *Customary International Humanitarian Law, Volume I: Rules*, above note 248, 355. This was cited with approval in *Hamdan v Rumsfeld* (2006) 126 S Ct 2749, 2797.

[490] ICC Elements of Crimes, Article 8(2)(c)(iv). See also *Hamdan*, above note 489, 2797–8.

[491] JE Bond, 'Application of the Law of War to Internal Conflicts' (1973) 3 *Georgia Journal of International and Comparative Law* 345, 372. See also C Byron, *War Crimes and Crimes against Humanity in the Rome Statute of the International Criminal Court* (Manchester University Press, 2009) 180.

[492] European Convention on Human Rights, Article 6(1); American Convention on Human Rights, Article 8(1).

[493] Cf A-M La Rosa and C Wuerzner, 'Armed groups, sanctions and the implementation of international humanitarian law' (2008) 90 *IRRC* 327, 340; *Prosecutor v Bemba Gombo*, ICC-01/05-01/08-406, Amicus Curiae Observations on Superior Responsibility submitted pursuant to Rule 103 of the Rules of Procedure and Evidence, 20 April 2009, paras 22–3.

[494] *Official Records*, above note 248, Vol 8, 360, para 20.

[495] See below, 550–5.

Conference were in favour of compiling a list of requisite guarantees,[496] such a list did not prove forthcoming.

In ascertaining the guarantees that are considered indispensable by civilized peoples, the starting point is Article 6 of Additional Protocol II. That provision does contain a list of 'essential guarantees of independence and impartiality' which are applicable during non-international armed conflicts. In introducing what was to become Article 6 at the Diplomatic Conference, the ICRC highlighted the link between that provision and common Article 3,[497] and a link between the two is also evident from the ICC Elements of Crimes.[498] Indeed, during the Rome Conference, Colombia observed that Article 6, 'which establishes an indispensable minimum of judicial guarantees during time of war', may be useful in drawing up the elements of the common Article 3(1)(d) offence.[499]

A second approach to identifying the indispensable guarantees is to look to the fair trial rights of the law of international armed conflict, in particular those that are set out in the fundamental guarantees clause of Additional Protocol I, which apply, as a safety net, to any person who does not enjoy more favourable protection through the Geneva Conventions or Additional Protocol I.[500] There is much to be said for this position. After all, common Article 3 started life as a preambular provision to the Civilians Convention, designed to reflect the spirit of that Convention.[501] Thus, when interpreting common Article 3, it is natural to turn to the Conventions and Additional Protocol I.[502] Such an approach reflects suggestions made in 1949 to incorporate into what was to become common Article 3 some of the provisions on fair trial rights in the law of international armed conflict.[503] It also has the benefit of judicial support, with a plurality of the US Supreme Court in *Hamdan* taking the view that common Article 3 should be interpreted in this context by reference to Article 75 of Additional Protocol I.[504] Ultimately, it reflects the interconnected nature of the various due process guarantees that are dispersed throughout international humanitarian law.

A third approach is to draw on the fair trial standards of international human rights law. As discussed in Chapter 3, international human rights law has a role to play in the regulation of non-international armed conflict in general and in the present context in particular.[505] Article 6 of Additional Protocol II was 'largely based on' the International Covenant on Civil and Political Rights (ICCPR).[506] Indeed, during the drafting process, a number of delegates supported what was to become Article 6 for the very reason that it reflected provisions of the ICCPR,[507] with one state going so far as to

---

[496] *Final Record*, above note 31, Vol II-B, 78 and 84 (France); 49 and 84 (Italy); 83 (United States).
[497] *Official Records*, above note 40, Vol 8, 357, para 3 (ICRC).
[498] See K Dörmann, 'Preparatory Commission for the International Criminal Court: the Elements of War Crimes' (2000) 82 *IRRC* 771.
[499] Proposal submitted by Colombia, PCNICC/1999/WGEC/DP.15. For a similar view, see Zimmermann, above note 50, 492.
[500] Article 75(4).
[501] *Final Record*, above note 31, Vol II-A, 696. On common Article 3 see above, 40–2.
[502] JE Bond, 'Internal Conflict and Article Three of the Geneva Conventions' (1971–2) 48 *Denver Law Journal* 263, 282–3.
[503] *Final Record*, above note 31, Vol II-B, 49 and 84 (Italy); 83 and 90 (United States).
[504] *Hamdan*, above note 489, 2797.
[505] See in particular above, 90–1.
[506] ICRC, *Commentary on the Additional Protocols*, above note 139, 1397. See also Bothe, Partsch, and Solf, above note 236, 650.
[507] *Official Records*, above note 40, Vol 8, 347, para 27 (Iran); 350, para 41 and Vol 9, 312, para 39 (Belgium).

submit an amendment to Article 6 in order to harmonize it with the ICCPR.[508] Thus, the ICCPR could be used to discern the requisite standards.

There are, then, three ways through which to identify the due process guarantees afforded by common Article 3. When drawing on any of the three approaches, it is important to bear in mind the particular context in which the instrument applies. Additional Protocol II applies in conflicts in which the armed group exercises such territorial control as to enable it to implement the Protocol; the Geneva Conventions and Additional Protocol I apply to conflicts usually fought between states; and human rights law traditionally regulates the relationship between the state and the individual. As such, the content of none of these instruments can be transported wholesale into a non-international armed conflict *simpliciter*.[509] That would destroy the nexus between the scope of application and the content of the rule,[510] and it may create obligations that exceed the capabilities of the parties. This does not mean that the guarantees themselves are inapplicable or should be interpreted in such a way as to render them meaningless. Rather, they need to be interpreted in a manner which respects their substance while also making compliance with them possible. It should be kept in mind that, '[i]f humanitarian considerations dominate to the exclusion of the capacity of the insurgents... then the proposed rules are divorced from reality'.[511]

Content of the obligations

In determining the content of the due process guarantees, as noted above, the starting point is Article 6 of Additional Protocol II. This provides for the accused to be notified 'without delay' of the allegations against him, the requirement of individual penal responsibility, affording the accused 'all necessary rights and means of defence', the principles of *nullum crime sine lege* and *nulla poena sine lege*, the presumption of innocence, the right to be present at trial, and the prohibition on compulsory testifying or confessing of guilt. Subject to one exception, these guarantees are not affected by the intensity of the conflict or the capabilities of the parties. They are, in some senses, intangible rights. The exception is the 'necessary rights and means of defence', which requires the provision of certain resources and which, accordingly, may prove difficult for certain parties. Ultimately, much turns on the precise meaning of the phrase.

During the drafting of the ICC Elements of Crimes, the inclusion of a list of specific rights and means of defence was proposed and the list was not challenged on the basis of its inapplicability to, or impracticality in, non-international armed conflict. As such, the list stands as a useful guide to understanding the meaning of the phrase 'necessary rights and means of defence'. It is convenient to reproduce the list in relevant part:

- The right to be brought promptly before a judge or other officer authorized by law to exercise judicial power;
- The right to be entitled to take proceedings before a court, in order that that court may decide without delay on the lawfulness of his detention and order his release;
- The right to have adequate time and facilities for the preparation of his defence and to communicate with counsel of his own choosing;
- The right to defend himself/herself in person or through legal assistance;

---

[508] Ibid, Vol 8, 349, para 38 (GDR).
[509] On the notion of a non-international armed conflict *simpliciter*, see above, 164 fn 66.
[510] On which see above, 66–8.
[511] GIAD Draper, 'Humanitarian Law and Internal Armed Conflicts' (1983) 13 *Georgia Journal of International and Comparative Law* 253, 264.

- The right to be tried without undue delay;
- The right to present and examine witnesses;
- The right to an interpreter.[512]

As with the due process guarantees generally, then, many of these rights and means of defence do not depend on the capacities of the parties to the conflict. Others, however, are context- and capacity-dependent, notably the right to present witnesses, the right to legal assistance, the associated right to counsel of one's own choosing, and the right to adequate time and facilities for the preparation of the defence. These could prove beyond the reach of many an armed group in particular. Understanding the particular context in which the case is set, however, should not make these difficulties insurmountable for all groups.

That some due process guarantees may be interpreted in a way that both respects their substance yet modifies them so as to take into account the particular nature of the conflict should not be cause for concern, as there is a history of their differential interpretation based on the exigencies of the situation.[513] At any rate, the very use of the word 'adequate' in the right to adequate time and facilities for the preparation of the defence denotes an inherently variable standard. As the Human Rights Committee has confirmed, '[t]he determination of what constitutes "adequate time and facilities" requires an assessment of the individual circumstances of each case'.[514]

Interpretation of the rules, of course, has its limits. At some point, rights cease to be modified and start to be breached. This means that some armed groups may be unable to meet the requisite standards, particularly if they do not exercise even a modicum of territorial control. That control over territory is linked to the ability to conduct trials is demonstrated in the observation of a SCSL Trial Chamber that 'instances of systematic discipline of fighters for crimes committed against civilians occurred in locations where the RUF had a relatively stable control over that territory'.[515] Some non-state armed groups do not possess any territorial control and it may be harder to envisage their holding fair trials. Along these lines, the FARC reportedly took the view that 'no mobile guerrilla force can satisfy the demands for minimum judicial guarantees as contained in Article 6 of Additional Protocol II'.[516]

However, even in conflicts in which the armed group does not exercise territorial control, it should not be assumed that the standards of a fair trial can never be met. As discussed in Chapter 5, a non-international armed conflict presupposes a certain degree of organization on the part of the armed group and one of the indicia of organization is the existence of 'disciplinary rules and mechanisms within the group'.[517] Although this does not require the existence of judicial processes, the greater the degree of organization, the more likely it will be that the disciplinary process is developed. Furthermore, portable or mobile courts could be utilized,[518] as is the case in the DRC in respect of

---

[512] Proposal submitted by Costa Rica, Hungary and Switzerland on Article 8, paragraph 2(c) of the Rome Statute of the International Criminal Court, PCNICC/1999/WGEC/DP.10.

[513] See *Hamdan*, above note 489, 2797–8.

[514] See eg *Thomas v Jamaica*, Communication No 272/1988, CCPR/C/44/D/272/1988, 8 April 1992, para 11.4; *Little v Jamaica*, Communication No 283/1988, CCPR/C/43/D/283/1988, 19 November 1991, para 8.3.

[515] *RUF* Trial Judgment, above note 8, para 707.

[516] P Gassmann, 'Colombia: Persuading Belligerents to Comply with International Norms', in S Chesterman (ed), *Civilians in War* (Lynne Rienner Publishers, 2001) 67, 81.

[517] *Prosecutor v Haradinaj, Balaj and Brahimaj*, IT-04-84-T, Judgment, 3 April 2008, para 60; *Limaj* Trial Judgment, above note 66, para 171. See above, 170–1 and 177–9.

[518] Somer, above note 488, 688.

gender crimes. As has been noted in a different context, '[n]on-state armed group adherence to the rules will necessarily be contextual given the practical and other circumstances in which they most often operate'.[519]

Two additional issues deserve consideration. Article 6(3) of Additional Protocol II provides that '[a] convicted person shall be advised on conviction of his judicial and other remedies and of the time-limits within which they may be exercised'.[520] Whether there is a right to appeal is uncertain. The ICRC draft of Article 6 included such a right,[521] but this was disputed by states and no such right appears in the text of the Additional Protocol as adopted. Human rights law does contain such a right.[522] However, the fact that international humanitarian law instruments are silent on point does not mean that the international human rights law rule constitutes the *lex specialis* and fills the gap. This is one area in which the absence of the norm may have been deliberate.[523] The second issue relates to the notion of 'law' in the context of non-state armed groups and is considered in Chapter 12.[524]

3.7.3 Capital punishment

Certain limitations exist on the use of capital punishment in time of non-international armed conflict. Persons under the age of 18 at the time they committed the offence may not be sentenced to death; pregnant women and mothers of young children may be sentenced to death but the sentence may not be carried out.[525] At the Diplomatic Conference of 1974–7, it had been argued that the death penalty should not even be 'pronounced' against pregnant women,[526] as this would mean that as soon as the baby was born, the mother could be executed.[527] However, the majority of states were not prepared to go that far. The compromise position, as reflected in the text, is that the death penalty shall not be 'carried out' on pregnant women or mothers of young children. This stands in contrast to Additional Protocol I, which contains a recommendation not even to impose the death sentence on such women.[528] Quite what is meant by mothers of 'young children' is unclear.[529] It has been suggested that the reference is to children under seven years of age,[530] or to 'children still young enough to depend on their mother for care'.[531] However, ultimately, the meaning is left for determination by individual parties.

International humanitarian law does not prohibit a sentence of capital punishment or the death penalty from being carried out against any other person for serious violations of that body of norms. In addition, and as discussed above,[532] persons who 'merely' take part in the conflict, even if they respect international humanitarian law

---

[519] Pejić, Protective Scope, above note 462, 207.
[520] Additional Protocol II, Article 6(3).
[521] Article 10(2), in *Official Records*, above note 40, Vol 1, Part III, 36.
[522] See eg ICCPR, Article 14(5).
[523] See generally above, 92.
[524] Below, 561–2.
[525] Additional Protocol II, Article 6(4).
[526] *Official Records*, above note 40, Vol 8, 351, para 50 (Ukraine).
[527] Ibid, 359–60, para 16 (Sweden). See also 363, para 33 (Iran); 363, para 35 (Mongolia); 364, para 38 (Poland).
[528] Additional Protocol I, Article 76(3).
[529] *Official Records*, above note 40, Vol 9, 312, para 42 (United Kingdom); Vol 9, 319, para 82 (Japan).
[530] UK *Manual*, above note 190, 405 fn 96.
[531] LC Green, *The Contemporary Law of Armed Conflict* (Manchester University Press, 2000) 329.
[532] See above, 71.

while doing so, may be subject to the death penalty for any acts of violence they committed for violation of, and pursuant to, domestic law. The position is not changed by international human rights law, as the Second Optional Protocol to the ICCPR, which aims to prohibit the death penalty, allows states to enter a reservation to the Protocol which 'provides for the application of the death penalty in time of war pursuant to a conviction for a most serious crime of a military nature committed during wartime'.[533]

Following the conclusion of hostilities, amnesties and pardons are frequently granted, allowing persons convicted of taking part in the conflict to go free.[534] Thus, agreeing not to sentence members of the armed group to death may go some way towards mitigating the lack of combatant status in non-international armed conflict, particularly if coupled with a later amnesty or pardon. This is a matter that will be considered further in Chapter 12. Precisely such a proposal was made to the 1974–7 Diplomatic Conference,[535] but was not accepted. Revisiting the issue today would be useful, for '[a]ny capital punishment in time of conflict, in relation with the conflict, cannot fail to bring about an increase in tension, vigorous reaction from the enemy and even reprisals'.[536] To take an example, in 2010, the suggestion that the United Nations–African Union Mission in Darfur (UNAMID) would hand over members and supporters of the Sudan Liberation Movement (SLM) wanted by the Government of Sudan to the Government was highly controversial in light of their possibly being sentenced to death.[537]

3.8 Journalists

The term 'journalist' is used in a 'broad sense',[538] and includes 'any correspondent, reporter, photographer, and their technical film, radio and television assistants who are ordinarily engaged in any of these activities as their principal occupation'.[539] This broad notion of a journalist is applicable as much to non-international armed conflicts as it is to international armed conflicts.[540] There are three categories of journalists in armed conflict: those 'engaged on dangerous professional missions' in areas of armed conflict, war correspondents, and those working for media outlets or information services of the armed forces. The latter are members of the armed forces and hence fighters.[541] Journalists 'engaged on dangerous professional missions' and journalists who are 'war correspondents' are civilians, although the latter are afforded prisoner of war status in international armed conflicts.[542]

---

[533] Second Optional Protocol to the International Covenant on Civil and Political Rights, aiming at the abolition of the death penalty, Article 2(1).
[534] See below, 515–20.
[535] Article 10(3) of the ICRC Draft, in *Official Records*, above note 40, Vol 1, Part III, 36.
[536] M Veuthey, 'The Red Cross and Non-International Conflicts' (1970) 10 *IRRC* 411, 417.
[537] 'UNAMID Chief Inches Closer to Handing Over Six IDP Delegates to Khartoum: Report', *Sudan Tribune*, 28 September 2010. See also SLM, 'Darfur Rebel Leader Praises UNAMID Refusal to Handover Kalma Residents', 5 August 2010.
[538] ICRC, *Commentary on the Additional Protocols*, above note 139, 921.
[539] See Draft International Convention for the Protection of Journalists engaged in Dangerous Missions in Areas of Armed Conflict, Article 2(a).
[540] See H-P Gasser, 'The Protection of Journalists Engaged in Dangerous Professional Missions' (1983) 23 *IRRC* 3, 14.
[541] ICRC, *Commentary on the Additional Protocols*, above note 139, 921; LC Green, *The Contemporary Law of Armed Conflict* (Manchester University Press, 2000) 109 fn 33.
[542] Additional Protocol I, Article 79(1) and (2) (journalists engaged on dangerous professional missions); Third Geneva Convention, Article 4(A)(4) (war correspondents); H-P Gasser, 'Protection of

Journalists who are war correspondents are defined in the Third Geneva Convention as '[p]ersons who accompany the armed forces without actually being members thereof... provided that they have received authorization, from the armed forces which they accompany'.[543] In the case of international armed conflict, war correspondents are formally accredited to the armed forces, with the armed forces providing them with an identity card indicating such status.[544] However, it is the authorization that is important, such things as identity cards simply being proof of the authorization.[545] Thus, with respect to a non-state armed group fighting in a non-international armed conflict, it is submitted that the proof of accreditation may be different, for example being of a less formal nature and absent an identity card.

Journalists engaged on dangerous professional missions—'any professional activity—"being on the spot, doing interviews, taking notes, taking photographs or films, sound recording etc. and transmitting them to his newspaper or agency"—exercised in an area affected by hostilities'[546]—are those journalists who are not accredited as war correspondents. Some may have been operating in the territory in question when the conflict broke out and choose to operate as before; others may choose not to operate as war correspondents for whatever reason. These journalists require an identity card that confirms their status. The responsibility for issuing the card rests with the authorities of the state in which the journalists reside or of which they are nationals.[547] Accordingly, the character of the armed conflict on which the journalist is reporting is immaterial for the purposes of the identity card.

As journalists are afforded the protection afforded to civilians, if they take a direct part in hostilities, they lose their immunity for such time as they take a direct part in hostilities.[548] Their activity *qua* journalists or correspondents—reporting on events, investigating abuses by parties to the conflict, and the like—does not constitute taking a direct part in hostilities.[549] This is true even if such reports benefit the other party to the conflict, for example through provoking an international reaction or motivating the civilian population. Thus, attacks on journalists, for example those looking into the conduct of the state armed forces or the conduct of the armed group, would be violations of international law. This stands in contrast to the actual practice of non-international armed conflicts, in which journalists are frequently targeted precisely for being journalists,[550] whether in Afghanistan, Chechnya, or elsewhere. Equally, civilian status is not lost simply by following the armed forces or the armed group, or by riding in military vehicles. However, such individuals may end up casualties of a lawful attack against the military vehicles or armed forces. This is particularly true of journalists who are embedded with a party to the conflict. For this reason, in 1988, the FMLN issued instructions, advising 'members of the press... at no time, nor for any reason [to] board

---

the Civilian Population', in D Fleck (ed), *The Handbook of International Humanitarian Law* (Oxford University Press, 2008) 237, 257.

[543] Third Geneva Convention, Article 4(A)(4).
[544] Ibid; Gasser, Civilian Population, above note 542, 257.
[545] Gasser, Journalists, above note 540, 5.
[546] ICRC, *Commentary on the Additional Protocols*, above note 139, 921.
[547] Gasser, Civilian Population, above note 542, 258.
[548] On which see below, 362–8.
[549] Gasser, Civilian Population, above note 542, 257.
[550] See also SC Res 1738 (2006).

helicopters or any other aircraft of the Armed Forces' in 'an effort to minimize civilian casualties'.[551]

Despite the different legal regimes applicable to journalists who are war correspondents and journalists who are engaged on dangerous professional missions, the two are often conflated. The ICTY, for example, has defined war correspondents as 'individuals who, for any period of time, report (or investigate for the purposes of reporting) from a conflict zone on issues relating to the conflict'.[552] However, in light of the different requirements for the two classes of journalists, the ICTY definition should be limited to the particular context in which it was set out, namely on the issue of compelling journalists to testify in war crimes trials, and should not be applicable to international humanitarian law more broadly.

Media equipment and buildings have the same status, and are subject to the same rules, as civilian objects.[553] Accordingly, provided they do not constitute a military objective, they may not be attacked. Media equipment or buildings that serve a dual purpose, for example a media studio that broadcasts civilian programmes but which is also used by the armed forces to communicate with one another, may constitute military objectives, provided the relevant test is met.[554] Such objectives would then constitute a legitimate target. On this basis, NATO's targeting of the RTS station in Belgrade in 1999 during the conflict in Kosovo was not considered unlawful by the ICTY Committee established to review the NATO campaign;[555] however, the attack remains a controversial one.[556]

Difficult issues surround the broadcasting of propaganda by a civilian broadcasting service, namely whether such broadcasts transform the media station into a military objective. In many cases, the effects of the propaganda will be limited to boosting the morale of the population and the war effort, neither of which are legitimate targets.[557] On the other hand, if the propaganda is of such a nature as to incite war crimes or other crimes under international law, as was the case with Radio Mille Collines during the Rwandan armed conflict and genocide, the broadcaster may be considered to constitute a legitimate target.[558]

3.9 Women

In general terms, women are afforded the same legal protections as men.[559] For example, common Article 3 and Additional Protocol II provide for application of the rules without adverse distinction on the basis of sex.[560] International humanitarian law

---

[551] FMLN, 'Instructions for the Civilian Population', 15 April 1988, reproduced in FMLN, above note 208, Appendix 1.
[552] *Prosecutor v Brdjanin and Talić*, IT-99-36-AR73.9, Decision on Interlocutory Appeal, 11 December 2002, para 29.
[553] On which see below, 342 et seq.
[554] See ibid.
[555] See eg Final Report to the Prosecutor by the Committee Established to Review the NATO Bombing Campaign Against the Federal Republic of Yugoslavia (2000) 39 *ILM* 1257, 1277, paras 71–9. It should be noted that this part of the Kosovo campaign was an international armed conflict. However, the example is one of the most high profile on point.
[556] See eg GH Aldrich, 'Yugoslavia's Television Studios as Military Objectives' (1999) 1 *International Law Forum* 149.
[557] See below, 346. See also Final Report on NATO, above note 555, 1270, para 47.
[558] Cf I Henderson, *The Contemporary Law of Targeting* (Nijhoff, 2009) 138.
[559] See F Krill, 'The Protection of Women in International Humanitarian Law' (1985) 25 *IRRC* 337.
[560] Common Article 3; Additional Protocol II, Article 4.

also recognizes the particular situation of women during times of armed conflict. For example, women whose liberty has been restricted 'shall be held in quarters separated from those of men' unless they are family members, and they 'shall be under the immediate supervision of women'.[561] However, as discussed above, regard should also be had to the wishes of detainees in this regard.[562] At the very least, there should be 'separate sleeping quarters and separate washing facilities'.[563] This is in 'accordance with the most elementary rules of decency' and, to use the formulation of several decades ago, in order to 'protect' female detainees.[564] The norm is considered to be of customary status.[565]

In addition to the particular rules on female detainees, international humanitarian law affords protection to women in other ways. Women are protected from sexual violence, as too are men and children.[566] Expectant mothers are protected, albeit through the provisions on the wounded and sick.[567] Furthermore, the death sentence is prohibited from being carried out on pregnant women and mothers of young children.[568] However, the focus of international humanitarian law in these three areas—pregnant women, mothers, and sexual violence—has been criticized as protecting women 'in terms of their relationship with others and not as individuals in their own right'.[569] This is starting to change, with attention being paid to other aspects of the impact of armed conflict on women,[570] for example in the relationship between women, peace, and security.[571]

One particularly neglected area has been the role of women in armed groups. Women may comprise a sizeable proportion of non-state armed groups; for example, it has been reported that one third of the members of the FARC are women.[572] A number of female members of armed groups have indicated that they joined the group in order to prevent further victimization, especially sexual violence.[573] It has also been suggested that the presence of women in armed groups may lead to a decline in instances of sexual violence being committed by members of the group.[574] The particular experiences of female members of armed groups are only starting to be explored.

---

[561] Additional Protocol II, Article 5(2)(a).
[562] See above, 295.
[563] ICRC, *Commentary on the Additional Protocols*, above note 139, 1390.
[564] JS Pictet (ed), *The Geneva Conventions of 12 August 1949: Commentary, III Geneva Convention Relative to the Treatment of Prisoners of War* (ICRC, Geneva, 1960) 207 and 465 respectively. The Third Geneva Convention provision is equivalent to the Additional Protocol II provision for these purposes.
[565] Customary International Humanitarian Law, Rule 118.
[566] Additional Protocol II, Article 4(2)(e). On which see above, 264–8.
[567] See above, 274 fn 192.
[568] Additional Protocol II, Article 6(4). See above, 310.
[569] JG Gardam and MJ Jarvis, *Women, Armed Conflict and International Law* (Kluwer, 2001) 94. See also J Gardam and H Charlesworth, 'Protection of Women in Armed Conflict' (2000) 22 *HRQ* 148, 149. See further K Engle, 'Judging Sex in War' (2008) 106 *Michigan Law Review* 941.
[570] See eg C Lindsey, *Women Facing War: ICRC Study on the Impact of Armed Conflict on Women* (ICRC, 2001); J Gardam, 'The Neglected Aspect of Women and Armed Conflict—Progressive Development of the Law' (2005) LII *NILR* 197.
[571] SC Res 1325 (2000); *Women, Peace and Security, Study Submitted by the Secretary-General Pursuant to Security Council Resolution 1325 (2000)* (UN, 2002).
[572] 'Leading Farc Commander Surrenders', *BBC News*, 19 May 2008.
[573] Geneva Call, Women in Armed Opposition Groups in Africa and the Promotion of International Humanitarian Law and Human Rights: Report of a Workshop organized in Addis Ababa by Geneva Call and the Program for the Study of International Organization(s), 23–26 November 2005.
[574] EJ Wood, 'Variation in Sexual Violence during War' (2006) 34 *Politics and Society* 307.

3.10 Children

3.10.1 General

Children are a vulnerable segment of the population, particularly in time of armed conflict. Accordingly, one of the key features of Additional Protocol II is its provisions on children.[575] One of the difficulties of the rules relating to children is the divergent views on the age at which a child becomes an adult. In light of the difference in approach at the national level and in different legal traditions, international humanitarian law does not specify the age at which the protections afforded to children cease to apply, although certain provisions do contain specified age limits. In leaving it to the discretion of the parties to the conflict, one state has described the lack of a fixed age as 'dangerous'.[576] That said, writing in 1958, the ICRC Commentary on the Fourth Geneva Convention notes that 'international usage has now settled on an age limit of fifteen years as defining what is meant by "children" when no further description is given'.[577] By 2010, there was a clear trend towards the raising of the age to 18 years, with a UN campaign being launched on 'Zero under 18'.

The general principle on which the international humanitarian law rules on children are based is that children 'be provided with the care and aid they require'.[578] Reflecting this general principle, in 2010, the MILF of the Philippines reported that the Code of Conduct of its armed wing, the Bangsamoro Islamic Armed Force (BIAF), provides 'for the General Staff... to take feasible measures aimed at ensuring the protection of the rights and welfare of children affected by the armed conflict in Mindanao'.[579] Likewise, the Code of Conduct issued by the Federal Government of Nigeria in 1967 during the attempted secession of Biafra provided that '[c]hildren must not be molested or killed. They will be protected and cared for'.[580]

The general international humanitarian law principle relating to children noted above underlies a series of specific rules. Among them are the following: children 'shall receive an education, including religious and moral education, in keeping with the wishes of their parents, or in the absence of parents, of those responsible for their care';[581] 'all appropriate steps shall be taken to facilitate the reunion of families temporarily separated';[582] 'measures shall be taken, if necessary, and whenever possible with the consent of their parents or persons who by law or custom are primarily responsible for their care, to remove children temporarily from the area in which hostilities are taking place to a safer area within the country and ensure that they are accompanied by persons responsible for their safety and well-being';[583] '[t]he death

---

[575] AJM Delissen, 'Legal Protection of Child-Combatants after the Protocols: Reaffirmation, Development or a Step Backwards?', in AJM Delissen and GJ Tanja (eds), *Humanitarian Law of Armed Conflict, Challenges Ahead: Essays in Honour of Frits Kalshoven* (Nijhoff, 1991) 153, 153; Moir, *Internal Armed Conflict*, above note 382, 111.
[576] *Official Records*, above note 40, Vol 15, 82, para 27 (Australia).
[577] Pictet, *Commentary on the Fourth Geneva Convention*, above note 463, 395.
[578] Additional Protocol II, Article 4(3).
[579] Geneva Call (ed), *In Their Words: Perspectives of Armed Non-State Actors on the Protection of Children from the Effects of Armed Conflict* (Geneva Call, 2010) 25.
[580] Operational Code of Conduct for the Nigerian Army, above note 57, para 4(b).
[581] Additional Protocol II, Article 4(3)(a).
[582] Ibid, Article 4(3)(b).
[583] Ibid, Article 4(3)(e).

penalty shall not be pronounced on persons who were under the age of eighteen years at the time of the offence';[584] and children under the age of 15 years continue to benefit from the special protections afforded to them, even if they take a direct part in hostilities and are captured.[585] These rules are also considered to reflect norms of customary international law.[586]

Reflecting these specific obligations, the Karen National Union (KNU) of Burma indicated in 2010 that its armed wing, the Karen National Liberation Army (KNLA), is responsible for guiding children to a safe place in the event of an attack by the Government.[587] In the context of the obligation that children receive an education, makeshift schools have been established by various groups, for example some 50 schools at primary, middle, and high level have been established by the Armée Populaire pour la Restauration de la République et la Démocratie (APRD) of the Central African Republic.[588] The JEM of Sudan has indicated that it pays for school teachers to educate children,[589] while the KNU has an 'Education Department' which has a policy by which 'every child should receive primary education'.[590] For its part, the Democratic Party of Iranian Kurdistan (PDKI) has reported that it maintains 'education centres' in its military camps in which subjects such as human rights and the rights of prisoners of war are taught.[591]

3.10.2 Child soldiers

Given the nature of modern armed conflict, one of the most important protections for children is that 'children who have not attained the age of fifteen years shall neither be recruited in the armed forces or groups nor allowed to take part in hostilities'.[592] The protections are of customary status,[593] even though there remain disputes as to the meaning of certain key terms. The protection in the international humanitarian law of non-international armed conflict is thus stronger than that applicable in international armed conflict, as the latter refers to the rather weaker obligation to take 'all feasible measures' in this regard and is further limited to a prohibition on children taking a 'direct part' in hostilities.[594] This stronger protection for children in non-international armed conflict was inadvertent, rather than being due to its heightened importance or to make recruitment by armed groups more difficult. Despite the inadvertence, it is incorrect to suggest that 'the law as it is worded, allows for the participation of children

---

[584] Ibid, Article 6(4). See also above, 310.
[585] Ibid, Article 4(3)(d).
[586] Report of the Secretary-General on the Establishment of a Special Court for Sierra Leone, S/2000/915, 4 October 2000, para 14; Customary International Humanitarian Law, Rule 135.
[587] *In Their Words*, above note 579, 23.
[588] Ibid, 13.
[589] Ibid, 18. See also 'Report of the Panel of Experts established pursuant to Resolution 1591 (2005) concerning the Sudan Issued 29 October 2009: A Response from JEM', 18 November 2009.
[590] *In Their Words*, above note 579, 21.
[591] Ibid, 28.
[592] Additional Protocol II, Article 4(3)(c).
[593] Report of the Secretary-General on the Establishment of a Special Court for Sierra Leone, S/2000/915, 4 October 2000, para 14 [partially]; Rome Statute, Article 8(2)(e)(vii) [partially]; Statute of the Special Court for Sierra Leone, Article 4 [partially]; Darfur Commission Report, above note 134, para 166.
[594] Additional Protocol I, Article 77.

under 15 years of age in activities that do not amount to an "active participation" in hostilities'.[595]

Far from embracing the stricter prohibition, later treaties, such as the Rome Statute of the International Criminal Court, the Convention on the Rights of the Child, and the relevant Optional Protocol thereto, have all opted for the weaker prohibition even in respect of non-international armed conflicts, limiting the prohibited conduct to taking an active or direct part in hostilities.[596] This undermining of existing standards was recognized, and criticized, during the drafting of those instruments,[597] but to no avail. However, Article 41 of the Convention on the Rights of the Child provides that '[n]othing in the present Convention shall affect any provisions which are more conducive to the realization of the rights of the child'. Thus, states that are parties to both Additional Protocol II and the Convention on the Rights of the Child remain subject to the stricter standards of the Protocol. Furthermore, the relevant rule in the Customary International Humanitarian Law study provides that '[c]hildren must not be allowed to take part in hostilities'.[598] This suggests that the customary prohibition is on all forms of participation in hostilities. However, as this rule is posited also for international armed conflicts and is thus of a broader nature than the applicable instruments, its breadth may be queried in that context.

The obligations

The importance of a prohibition on all forms of participation in hostilities as opposed to a more limited prohibition on direct or active participation in hostilities is demonstrated by the difficulty in drawing a distinction between acts that constitute direct or active participation in hostilities and those that do not. Acts that fall within the definition of active participation include the use of children: in combat;[599] in armed patrols;[600] to guard military objectives;[601] as spies,[602] scouts,[603] bodyguards to commanders,[604] and human shields;[605] to man military

---

[595] *CDF* Trial Judgment, above note 171, Separate and Partially Dissenting Opinion of Justice Itoe, para 12.
[596] Rome Statute, Article 8(2)(e)(vii); Convention on the Rights of the Child, Article 38; Optional Protocol to the Convention on the Rights of the Child on the Involvement of Children in Armed Conflict, Article 1.
[597] See Report of the Working Group on a draft convention on the rights of the child, E/CN.4/1989/48, 2 March 1989, para 612; Report of the working group on a draft optional protocol to the Convention on the Rights of the Child on involvement of children in armed conflicts, E/CN.4/1995/96, 10 February 1995, para 23; Report of the working group on a draft optional protocol to the Convention on the Rights of the Child on involvement of children in armed conflicts on its second session, E/CN.4/1996/102, 21 March 1996, paras 28, 29, 40, 97; Report of the working group on a draft optional protocol to the Convention on the Rights of the Child on involvement of children in armed conflicts on its third session, E/CN.4/1997/96, 13 March 1997, paras 25, 79.
[598] Customary International Humanitarian Law, Rule 137. See also Darfur Commission Report, above note 134, para 166, but cf fn 98.
[599] *RUF* Trial Judgment, above note 8, paras 1710–16; *CDF* Trial Judgment, above note 171, Separate and Partially Dissenting Opinion of Justice Itoe, para 10.
[600] *RUF* Trial Judgment, paras 1717–18.
[601] Ibid; *CDF* Trial Judgment, Separate and Partially Dissenting Opinion of Justice Itoe, para 10. See also *Prosecutor v Thomas Lubanga Dyilo*, ICC-01/04-01/06, Decision on the Confirmation of Charges, 29 January 2007, paras 261–3.
[602] *RUF* Trial Judgment, para 1729; Report of the Preparatory Committee on the Establishment of an International Criminal Court, Addendum, A/CONF.183/2/Add.1, 14 April 1998, 21 fn 12.
[603] Ibid.
[604] *RUF* Trial Judgment, paras 1731–42; *CDF* Trial Judgment, Separate and Partially Dissenting Opinion of Justice Itoe, para 10. See also *Lubanga* Decision on the confirmation of charges, above note 601, paras 261–3.
[605] *AFRC* Trial Judgment, above note 171, para 737. See also para 1266.

checkpoints;[606] and to engage in sabotage.[607] Activities unrelated to the hostilities do not fall within the term and include the use of children: for domestic labour;[608] to forage food;[609] or to undertake 'domesticated jobs of a purely civilian character like cooking, food finding, laundry or running routine errands'.[610] More difficult is the intermediate status—the grey area—of certain support functions. The statement of the *AFRC* Trial Chamber, quoted with approval by the *Lubanga* Trial Chamber, that '*[a]ny* labour or support that gives effect to, or helps maintain, operations in a conflict constitutes active participation', is problematic by reason of its breadth. Accordingly, its determination, also quoted with approval by the *Lubanga* Trial Chamber, that 'carrying loads for the fighting faction, finding and/or acquiring food, ammunition or equipment, acting as decoys, carrying messages, making trails or finding routes... are some examples of active participation as much as actual fighting and combat'[611] should be treated with caution. It may well be that the acting as a decoy, or the finding of ammunition can, in a particular instance, amount to active participation in hostilities. However, that can only be judged on a case-by-case basis and it would be imprudent to pronounce in advance that all these activities, as a matter of course, amount to active participation in hostilities. Many of these activities would, however, fall within the notion of participation in hostilities and would thus be prohibited under the law of non-international armed conflict. Thus, the UN Observer Mission in El Salvador (ONUSAL) held that the prohibition prevented the FMLN from using minors to gather information, transport ammunition, and engage in acts of sabotage.[612]

The approach taken in the *Lubanga* Trial Judgment, by which active participation in hostilities is judged by reference to 'whether the support provided by the child to the combatants exposed him or her to real danger as a potential target',[613] is equally problematic. It gives little guidance to the pertinent actors in advance, as quite what is meant by 'real danger as a potential target' is unclear. The use of children in this regard is prohibited not just because of their exposure to being an object of attack but due to the danger of violence from their own side, their exposure to violence, the psychological effects of participation in conflict, and the like. More problematically, the approach taken suggests that certain activities at a certain point in time would not amount to active participation in hostilities as the child is not exposed to danger as a potential target, but the same activities at a different point in time may well amount to active participation. By the time it is realized that the child may be in real danger, it may well be too late.

The presence of children in the camps of armed groups or the camps of armed forces does not automatically mean that the law of non-international armed conflict is being violated. What is prohibited is participation in hostilities, not all forms of involvement

---

[606] Ibid, para 737; *CDF* Trial Judgment, Separate and Partially Dissenting Opinion of Justice Itoe, para 10; Report on the ICC, above note 602, 21 fn 12.
[607] Ibid.
[608] *RUF* Trial Judgment, para 1730.
[609] Ibid, para 1743.
[610] *CDF* Trial Judgment, Separate and Partially Dissenting Opinion of Justice Itoe, para 13. See also *Lubanga* Decision on the confirmation of charges, para 262; Report on the ICC, above note 602, 21 fn 12.
[611] *AFRC* Trial Judgment, para 737 (emphasis added); *Prosecutor v Lubanga*, ICC-01/04-01/06, Trial Judgment, 14 March 2012, para 624.
[612] Second Report of the United Nations Observer Mission in El Salvador, A/46/658, 15 November 1991, para 116.
[613] *Lubanga* Trial Judgment, para 628. See also paras 820 and 882.

in the armed conflict in general.⁶¹⁴ Thus, families may legitimately move to camps of the armed forces or the armed group in order to seek protection. Similarly, the fact that some 'combatants live with their families, so the children are with their parents',⁶¹⁵ as is the case with the APRD of the Central African Republic, would not amount to a violation. Likewise, the armed forces or the armed group may legitimately look after orphaned children.⁶¹⁶ However, in that situation, the armed forces and the armed group need to refrain from taking advantage of the presence of children and utilizing them in hostilities. The danger is that this very temptation will arise, particularly if the fighting becomes intense and all available resources need to be utilized. Furthermore, the children themselves may want military training or to be involved in the hostilities, a point that is noted by the APRD.⁶¹⁷

In addition to a prohibition on using children to participate in hostilities, international humanitarian law prohibits the recruitment of children. Recruitment comprises conscription and enlistment.⁶¹⁸ Conscription 'implies some use of force', some 'compulsion, albeit in some cases through force of law'.⁶¹⁹ The key element of conscription is one of compulsion, with the precise nature of the compulsion being a secondary consideration. It includes 'the abduction of persons for specific use within an organization' and 'the forced military training of persons'.⁶²⁰ Although the traditional view of conscription 'refers to government policies requiring citizens to serve in their armed forces', in light of the possibility, indeed reality, of conscription into non-state armed groups, the term cannot be interpreted in such a narrow manner.⁶²¹

The enlistment of a child is equally prohibited. Enlistment 'entails accepting and enrolling individuals when they volunteer to join an armed force or group'.⁶²² For the purposes of enlistment, 'there must be a nexus between the act of the [enlistor] and the child joining the armed force or group'.⁶²³ Enlistment 'cannot narrowly be defined as a formal process'; rather, it is to be regarded 'in the broad sense as including any conduct accepting the child as a part of the militia'.⁶²⁴ The crucial test is whether the act in question 'substantially furthers the process of a child's enrolment and acceptance into an armed force or group'.⁶²⁵ This furtherance 'may be a very short process and may constitute a single act' or it may 'be a process involving several acts', for example, '[r]eligious initiation, military training and the signing of a certificate declaring a child fit for combat'.⁶²⁶ It may be a one-off act or a series of continuing acts. The line between enlistment and conscription is not altogether clear, although, ultimately, 'any

---

⁶¹⁴ On the distinction, see below, 363–5. But cf the Principles and Guidelines on Children Associated with Armed Forces of Armed Groups (The Paris Principles) 2007, Section 2.1.
⁶¹⁵ *In Their Words*, above note 579, 13.
⁶¹⁶ See eg 'Prachanda Interview: Full Transcript', BBC News, 13 February 2006. Prachanda was the head of the CPN-M in Nepal. Cf Darfur Commission Report, above note 147, para 416.
⁶¹⁷ *In Their Words*, above note 579, 13.
⁶¹⁸ *Lubanga* Decision on the Confirmation of Charges, above note 601, para 246. See also *Prosecutor v Fofana and Kondewa*, SCSL-04-14-T, Judgment, 2 August 2007, para 191.
⁶¹⁹ *Prosecutor v Norman*, SCSL-2004-14-AR72(E), Decision on Preliminary Motion Based on Lack of Jurisdiction (Child Recruitment), Dissenting Opinion of Justice Robertson, 31 May 2004, paras 1, 5. See also *Prosecutor v Brima, Kamara and Kanu*, SCSL-04-16-T, Judgment, 20 June 2007, para 734.
⁶²⁰ *RUF* Trial Judgment, para 1695.
⁶²¹ *AFRC* Trial Judgment, para 734.
⁶²² Ibid, para 735. See also *Norman* Child Recruitment Decision, Dissenting Opinion of Justice Robertson, paras 5 and 33; *CDF* Appeal Judgment, para 140; *RUF* Trial Judgment, para 185.
⁶²³ *CDF* Appeal Judgment, para 141.
⁶²⁴ Ibid, para 144.
⁶²⁵ *CDF* Appeal Judgment, Partially Dissenting Opinion of Justice Winter, para 11.
⁶²⁶ Ibid, para 12.

distinction between conscription and enlistment is of little practical significance', as 'a child's consent cannot be a valid defence to the crime'.[627]

The relevant age

Considerable debate surrounds the age at which recruitment and use of children in armed conflict is prohibited. At the 1974–7 Diplomatic Conference, some states expressed the view that 18 years was the optimum age;[628] however, 15 years was set as the default position. Such debates re-emerged at the time of the drafting of the Convention on the Rights of the Child and the Rome Statute.[629] In both instances, proponents in favour of 15 years won out, despite the rest of the Convention on the Rights of the Child using the age of 18, reportedly due to the inadequate support for the higher age in customary international law.[630] The debate as to 15 or 18 years of age continues, with considerable movement towards the latter, with the African Charter on the Rights and Welfare of the Child,[631] ILO Convention 182 on the Elimination of Child Labour,[632] and the Committee on the Rights of the Child,[633] all adopting the age of 18, in the case of the Committee, despite the terms of the Convention provision itself.

In the Optional Protocol to the Convention on the Rights of the Child, the age is raised to 18 with respect to the taking of a direct part in hostilities and the compulsory recruitment by the state into its armed forces, and the recruitment or use in hostilities by armed groups.[634] Insofar as voluntary recruitment by states is concerned, the age is raised to 16.[635] No such reduced age limit applies to voluntary recruitment on the part of non-state armed groups. Upon ratification of the Protocol, some states have indicated that they will limit voluntary recruitment to persons aged 18 and over.[636]

The Paris Principles and Guidelines on Children Associated with Armed Forces or Armed Groups also utilizes the age of 18.[637] States and non-state armed groups who enter into action plans with UN entities on the disarmament, demobilization, and reintegration of child soldiers are required to commit to the Paris Principles.[638] Parties

---

[627] Ibid, para 11 fn 1207. See also *AFRC* Trial Judgment, para 735; *CDF* Trial Judgment, para 192; *RUF* Trial Judgment, para 187.

[628] ICRC, *Commentary on the Additional Protocols*, above note 139, 1379–80.

[629] G van Bueren, 'The International Legal Protection of Children in Armed Conflicts' (1994) 43 *ICLQ* 809, 814; D Momtaz, 'War Crimes in Non-International Armed Conflicts Under the Statute of the International Criminal Court' (1999) 2 *YIHL* 177, 184. See M Happold, *Child Soldiers in International Law* (Manchester University Press, 2005).

[630] D Robinson and H von Hebel, 'War Crimes in Internal Armed Conflicts: Article 8 of the ICC Statute' (1999) 2 *YIHL* 193, 203; IIHL *Manual*, above note 28, 49–50.

[631] African Charter on the Rights and Welfare of the Child, Articles 2 and 22(2).

[632] 1999 ILO Convention (182) on the Prohibition of and Immediate Action for the Elimination of the Worst Forms of Child Labour, Articles 2 and 3.

[633] Committee on the Rights of the Child, Concluding Observations: Bhutan, CRC/C/15/Add.157, 9 July 2001, paras 54 and 55; Concluding Observations: Chad, CRC/C/TCD/CO/2, 12 February 2009, para 71.

[634] OP-CRC, Articles 1, 2, and 4. For the debate, see Report of the Working Group on a Draft Optional Protocol to the Convention on the Rights of the Child on Involvement of Children in Armed Conflicts on its Fourth Session, E/CN.4/1998/102, 23 March 1998.

[635] OP-CRC, Article 3.

[636] See eg The Declaration of the Government of Uganda, 6 May 2002.

[637] Paris Principles and Guidelines on Children Associated with Armed Forces or Armed Groups, Section 2.0.

[638] See eg Action Plan between the Moro Islamic Liberation Front (MILF) and the United Nations in the Philippines regarding the Issue of Recruitment and Use of Child Soldiers in the Armed Conflict in Mindanao, 1 August 2009. See also Action Plan between the Sudan People's Liberation Army and

to non-international armed conflicts are also sometimes judged as against the Paris Principles. For example, when the NPA, the armed wing of the NDFP, argued that that it does not recruit or use children, UN Secretary-General Ban Ki-Moon noted that the NPA 'uses the narrow definition of those engaged directly in hostilities and not the definition of children associated with armed forces and groups set in 2007 by The Paris Principles'.[639] The NDFP, in turn, has criticized the Paris Principles as 'overbroad',[640] and as 'not an international instrument'.[641] Given that action plans are entered into under threat of sanction by the Security Council, the Paris Principles are being treated, in effect, as binding law.

A significant amount of practice exists utilizing the standard of 18 years of age. For example, commitments were made on point by the Governments of Burundi and Sudan in 1999 and 2000 respectively.[642] In 1997, the Government of Colombia introduced legislation which limited the participation of children under the age of 18 years.[643] The Government of Myanmar made a commitment to UNICEF that no child under the age of 18 years would be recruited into the military.[644] Numerous states have also committed to the Paris Principles which, as noted above, utilizes the age of 18 years.

Considerable practice also exists on the part of armed groups. In 2006, Colonel Yod Suk, the head of the Shan State Army of Burma, denied using children under the age of 18, stating that '[t]here are no soldiers under 18' and that '[a]ll our soldiers are aged 18 to 50'.[645] In 2010, the entity of Abkhazia reported that it prohibits compulsory recruitment of children under the age of 18 but allows for voluntary recruitment of children between 15 and 18;[646] however, it has also expressed the desire to accede to the Optional Protocol to the Convention on the Rights of the Child, in which case it 'would raise to 18 years the minimum age of voluntary enrolment of persons in the national forces'.[647] Also in 2010, the Polisario Front of Western Sahara and the PDKI both indicated that they had prohibited the recruitment of children under the age of 18 years.[648] The Rally for Congolese Democracy (RCD) in the Democratic Republic did

---

the United Nations regarding Children Associated with the SPLA in Southern Sudan, 20 November 2009.

[639] Report of the Secretary-General on Children and Armed Conflict in the Philippines, S/2010/36, 21 January 2010, para 14.

[640] Letter to UN Secretary-General Ban Ki-Moon on Children in Armed Conflict from LG Jalandoni, Member of the NDFP National Executive Committee and Chairperson of the NDFP Negotiating Panel, 24 November 2008.

[641] Letter to Ms Coomaraswamy [Special Representative of the Secretary-General for Children and Armed Conflict] from the Chairperson of the NDFP Human Rights Monitoring Committee, 7 April 2011.

[642] Protection of Children Affected by Armed Conflict, Report of the Special Representative of the Secretary-General for Children and Armed Conflict, A/54/430, Annex, 1 October 1999, para 98(a) (Burundi); Additional Report of the Special Representative of the Secretary-General for Children and Armed Conflict, E/CN.4/2000/71, 9 February 2000, para 24 (Sudan).

[643] Law 418 of 1997, cited in D García-Peña Jaramillo, 'Humanitarian Protection in Non-International Conflicts: A Case Study of Colombia' (2000) 30 *IYHR* 179, 186; Protection of Children Affected by Armed Conflict, Report of the Special Representative of the Secretary-General for Children and Armed Conflict, A/54/430, Annex, 1 October 1999, para 98(a).

[644] Letter from Myanmar to Human Rights Watch, 12 September 2007, reproduced as an Appendix to Human Rights Watch, *Sold to be Soldiers: The Recruitment and Use of Child Soldiers in Burma* (2007).

[645] Quoted in E Cropley, 'Myanmar Rebel Chief Denies Using Child Soldiers', *Reuters*, 31 January 2006.

[646] *In Their Words*, above note 579, 11.

[647] Ibid, 12.

[648] Ibid, 28 and 29.

likewise in 2000 albeit 'in principle'.[649] The same was true of the RUF and Civil Defence Force (CDF) of Sierra Leone.[650] The APRD of the Central African Republic has prohibited the direct participation of children under the age of 18 'in combat' or 'in any activity directly linked to combat'; however, they are used 'as lookouts',[651] which would constitute participation in hostilities. JEM of Darfur has reported that it uses the standard of 18 years of age,[652] as has the CNF of Burma. In the case of the CNF, this was done prior to the conclusion of the Convention on the Rights of the Child.[653] For its part, the KNU also of Burma has reported that its previous army law on recruitment utilized the age of 16; however, in 2003, it raised the age to 18 and promulgated and distributed an order to this effect to its various brigades.[654] The raising of the age limit followed UN and NGO reports that the KNU was using child soldiers.[655] The Karenni National Progressive Party (KNPP) also committed to the age of 18.[656] For its part, the LTTE of Sri Lanka committed not to recruit children under the age of 17, which it later raised to 18, and not to use in combat children under the age of 18.[657] However, it has contrary practice on point, given that its Child Protection Act provided that '[t]he enlistment or involvment of children under the age of 16, whether directly or surreptitiously for combat activity should be expressly avoided', that '[y]ouths aged between 16–17 should not be engaged in direct warfare', and that '[a]n exemption to the provision above can be granted if the parents or guardian of the said individual makes an application, with appropriate affidavits, to the attention of the judiciary via the competent District Authority'.[658] In 1995, the Sudan People's Liberation Movement (SPLM) went so far as to commit itself to abide by the Convention on the Rights of the Child.[659] The Code of Conduct of the BIAF, the armed wing of the MILF, limits membership to persons over the age of 18 years.[660] However, the MILF also reports the reluctance of some members of its community to conform to that age, considering an individual to become an adult 'upon reaching the age of puberty' or considering the age of 18 to be 'part of the so-called anti-insurgency campaign'.[661] The NDFP has indicated that it utilizes the age of 18 for the purposes of combat, and has done so since 1988, prior to the entry into force of the Convention on the Rights of the Child

---

[649] Additional Report of the Special Representative of the Secretary-General for Children and Armed Conflict, E/CN.4/2000/71, 9 February 2000, para 51.
[650] Report of the Special Representative of the Secretary-General for Children and Armed Conflict, A/56/453, 9 October 2001, para 69; Protection of Children Affected by Armed Conflict, Report of the Special Representative of the Secretary-General for Children and Armed Conflict, A/54/430, Annex, 1 October 1999, para 132(g) (RUF and CDF).
[651] *In Their Words*, above note 579, 13.
[652] Ibid, 18, 19.
[653] Ibid, 16. See also Chin, 'Deed of Commitment', 10 March 2009.
[654] KNU Press Statement on Report of UNSG, 27 April 2009. See also KNU/KNLA, Deed of Commitment, 4 March 2007.
[655] *In Their Words*, above note 579, 22.
[656] KNPP/KNA, Deed of Commitment, 13 April 2007.
[657] Report of the Special Representative of the Secretary-General for Children and Armed Conflict, A/53/482, 12 October 1998, para 65; Annual Report of the Special Representative of the Secretary-General for Children and Armed Conflict, A/HRC/9/3, 27 June 2008, para 35.
[658] Article 4(22), (23)(a), (23)(b).
[659] UNICEF, *The State of the World's Children 1996* (Oxford University Press, 1997) 36.
[660] *In Their Words*, above note 579, 25. See also Action Plan between the Moro Islamic Liberation Front (MILF) and the United Nations in the Philippines regarding the Issue of Recruitment and Use of Child Soldiers in the Armed Conflict in Mindanao, 1 August 2009.
[661] *In Their Words*, above note 579, 26.

and Optional Protocol thereto, but children between the ages of 15 and 18 can receive training for self-defence purposes.[662]

The fact that some of these groups—such as the LTTE and the RUF—were notorious for recruiting and using children under the age of 18 to participate in hostilities reveals that their commitments cannot be taken at face value. Furthermore, there are armed groups that do not accept a prohibition in respect of children under the age of 18 years or even under the age of 15 years. Some groups consider the use of children as inevitable due to a desire to increase the number of their fighters. For example, a former high-ranking leader of an unnamed armed group stated in this context: 'if you want to make a large fire, you need lots of wood.'[663] Likewise, a former officer in the FDLR has been reported as stating in 2009 that '[w]e have been losing a lot of troops through DDRRR (the UN's demobilisation programme) so we have to go to schools to get more soldiers. We have no choice'.[664] Nonetheless, the commitments of so many states and non-state armed groups demonstrate the tendency towards utilizing the standard of 18 years of age. Although the law in the area is in a state of flux, there is a marked tendency towards adoption of the standard of 18 years of age.

In addition to the general state of flux surrounding the relevant age, there is also something of a mismatch between international humanitarian law and international criminal law. The International Criminal Court does not have jurisdiction over persons who were under the age of 18 years at the time of the offence.[665] Yet, under international humanitarian law, as it currently stands, children over the age of 15 years may be conscripted, enlisted, or used to participate actively in hostilities. Thus, the effect of the Rome Statute exclusion is that persons between the ages of 15 and 17 can take part in hostilities but may not be tried by the International Criminal Court for war crimes resulting from that participation.[666]

Human rights law

The provision on armed groups in the Optional Protocol to the Convention on the Rights of the Child is an important one. International human rights law is traditionally conceived as governing the state–individual relationship. Accordingly, the obligations of human rights law are addressed to states.[667] To include a provision on armed groups in a human rights instrument is thus novel and is indicative of the trend towards a greater role for international human rights law in the regulation of non-international armed conflict.[668] However, the inclusion of the provision in the Optional Protocol was not a foregone conclusion,[669] and the provision itself does not purport to bind

---

[662] NDFP, *NDFP's Defense of the Rights of the Filipino Child* (NDFP Human Rights Monitoring Committee 2005, Booklet Number 7) 9. See also Executive Committee, Central Committee Communist Party of the Philippines, Memorandum on the Minimum Age Requirement for NPA Fighters, 15 October 1999, reproduced in ibid, Appendix, 72.

[663] Quoted in O Bangerter, 'Reasons Why Armed Groups Choose to Respect International Humanitarian Law or Not' (2011) 93 *IRRC* 353, 354.

[664] Quoted in 'FDLR Inc: Congo's Multinational Rebels', *BBC News*, 18 November 2009.

[665] Rome Statute, Article 26.

[666] A Cassese, 'The Statute of the International Criminal Court: Some Preliminary Reflections' (1999) 10 *EJIL* 144, 153.

[667] See above, 95.

[668] See above, 83 et seq.

[669] See Report of the working group on a draft optional protocol to the Convention on the Rights of the Child on involvement of children in armed conflicts on its third session, E/CN.4/1997/96, 13 March 1997, para 35; Report of the working group on a draft optional protocol to the Convention on the Rights of the Child on involvement of children in armed conflicts on its second session, E/CN.4/1996/102, 21 March 1996, paras 31, 32, and Annex ('New Article A'); Report of the working group

armed groups directly. Rather, it serves to impose a moral obligation upon armed groups and vest the legal obligation in states in respect of armed groups.[670]

From the perspective of international humanitarian law, which operates on the basis of equality of obligation as between the parties to the conflict,[671] the lack of equality of obligation in the Optional Protocol as between the rules that govern states and those that govern armed groups is concerning. The lack of equality of obligation arises in that voluntary recruitment into state forces is allowed for children over the age of 16 but not for non-state armed groups. State armed forces can also operate schools but not armed groups. This 'double standard'[672] may be, and indeed has been, questioned by armed groups. For example, one armed group has questioned why the state against which it is fighting is allowed to recruit children under the age of 18 into its military academy.[673] Another has queried the unequal obligations of states and non-state armed groups in the law relating to child soldiers more generally.[674] However, it is also the case that other non-state armed groups have considered themselves bound by the Optional Protocol.[675]

3.11 Peacekeeping missions

3.11.1 International humanitarian law protections

Persons involved in a peacekeeping mission in accordance with the UN Charter are protected from attack as long as they are entitled to the protection afforded to civilians.[676] Protection is also afforded to installations, material, units, and vehicles of the mission to the extent that they are entitled to the protection afforded to civilian objects.[677] The protection is thus a particularization of the protections that are afforded to civilians and civilian objects.[678] The protections reflect rules of customary international law, as is evident from their inclusion in the Rome Statute.[679]

Three aspects of the protections are in need of further consideration. First, on the prohibited attack, actual damage is not required; it is the very attack that is prohibited.[680] An 'attack' in this context is an 'act of violence',[681] in turn defined as 'a forceful

---

on a draft optional protocol to the Convention on the Rights of the Child on involvement of children in armed conflicts on its fourth session, E/CN.4/1998/102, 23 March 1998, Annex II: Chairman's Perception (Article 3).

[670] D Helle, 'Optional Protocol on the Involvement of Children in Armed Conflict to the Convention on the Rights of the Child' (2000) 82 *IRRC* 797, 806.

[671] See above, 242 et seq.

[672] G Machel, *The Impact of War on Children* (Hurst, 2001) 20; Helle, Optional Protocol, above note 670, 808.

[673] E Decrey Warner, J Somer, and P Bongard, 'Armed Non-State Actors and Humanitarian Norms: Lessons from the Geneva Call Experience', in B Perrin (ed), *Modern Warfare: Armed Groups, Private Militaries, Humanitarian Organizations, and the Law* (University of British Columbia Press, 2012) 73, 81.

[674] See above, 88.

[675] For example, the NPA of the Philippines. See Report of the Secretary-General on Children and Armed Conflict in the Philippines, S/2008/272, 24 April 2008, para 21.

[676] Rome Statute, Article 8(2)(e)(iii); Statute of the Special Court for Sierra Leone, Article 8(2)(e)(iii).

[677] Ibid.

[678] *RUF* Trial Judgment, above note 8, paras 215 and 218.

[679] Article 8(2)(e)(iii). See also Customary International Humanitarian Law, Rule 33.

[680] *RUF* Trial Judgment, para 220; *Prosecutor v Abu Garda*, ICC-02/05-02/09, Decision on the Confirmation of Charges, 8 February 2010, para 65.

[681] *RUF* Trial Judgment, para 220.

interference which endangers the person or impinges on the liberty of the peacekeeper'.[682] This would include the unlawful deprivation of liberty of the relevant person.[683] However, threats alone do not suffice given that 'peacekeepers are by definition deployed in areas of actual or recent armed conflict, often in precarious situations before the warring factions have disarmed and while tensions remain high'.[684]

The second aspect of the protection concerns the meaning of a 'peacekeeping mission in accordance with the Charter of the United Nations'. The traditional understanding of this phrase utilizes a distinction between peacekeeping missions and peace-enforcement missions.[685] Although clear in theory—in addition to differences relating to the consent of the parties and the impartiality of the mission, peacekeeping missions may use force in self-defence while peace-enforcement missions may use force beyond self-defence[686]—the difference is rather more nuanced in practice.[687] Peace-enforcement missions are not characterized as such in their authorizing resolutions and it may be difficult to distinguish them from so-called 'robust' peacekeeping missions. The relevant chapter of the UN Charter pursuant to which they are established is not always of help. Nor are the situations in which the mission is authorized to use force determinative, given that, ever since the second United Nations Emergency Force (UNEF II) in 1973, the notion of self-defence has included 'situations in which peacekeepers were being prevented by armed persons from fulfilling their mandate'.[688] If anything, the distinction lies between peacekeeping missions and coalitions of the willing; as the Brahimi report notes, '[w]here enforcement action is required, it has consistently been entrusted to coalitions of willing States, with the authorization of the Security Council, acting under Chapter VII of the Charter'.[689] However, this distinction is also limited given that, in practice, certain missions do engage in enforcement action. The United Nations Organization Stabilization Mission (MONUSCO) in the Democratic Republic of the Congo in 2011 is a case in point. As such, the requirement should be treated as a formalistic one, namely whether the mission was established lawfully by the United Nations in accordance with the principles and purposes of the United Nations, or otherwise in accordance with the Charter of the United Nations.

The third, and crucial, issue relates to when personnel, installations, material, units, or vehicles of peacekeeping missions are entitled to the protection given to civilians or civilian objects under the law of armed conflict. According to the *RUF* Trial Chamber, 'common sense dictates that peacekeepers are considered to be civilians only insofar as they fall within the definition of civilians laid down for non-combatants in customary international law and under Additional Protocol II . . . namely, that they do not take a

---

[682] Ibid, para 1889. See also Convention on the Safety of United Nations and Associated Personnel, Article 9(1)(a).
[683] See the findings in *RUF* Trial Judgment, paras 1891 and 1897.
[684] Ibid, para 1889.
[685] Ibid, paras 221–31; *Abu Garda* Decision on the Confirmation of Charges, 8 February 2010, para 74; M Cottier, 'Article 8(2)(b)(xxvi)', in O Triffterer (ed), *Commentary on the Rome Statute of the International Criminal Court* (Beck, 2008) 330, 333.
[686] Ibid.
[687] See C Greenwood, 'International Humanitarian Law and United Nations Military Operations' (1998) 1 *YIHL* 3, 10–11.
[688] M Goulding, 'The Evolution of United Nations Peacekeeping' (1993) 69 *International Affairs* 451, 455. See also *RUF* Trial Judgment, para 228.
[689] Report of the Panel on United Nations Peace Operations, A/55/305-S/2000/809, 21 August 2000, para 53.

direct part in hostilities'.[690] Thus, individuals who are involved in a peace-enforcement operation and engaged as combatants or fighters would not benefit from the protection, not because they are not involved in a peacekeeping mission in accordance with the UN Charter, but because they are not entitled to the protection afforded to civilians as a result of their activity.

The use of force in self-defence does not transform a civilian into a fighter.[691] However, care needs to be taken, as 'self-defence can progressively lead to a situation where multinational forces become party to a conflict'.[692] A more difficult issue relates to whether or not force may be used in defence of the discharge of the mandate of the peacekeeping mission without taking the peacekeepers outside the scope of their protection. To pose the question in these terms is somewhat misleading, as the answer will depend on a combination of precisely what the forces are being mandated to do and, more importantly, the facts on the ground. The United Nations Operation in Somalia (UNOSOM II), for example, was mandated *inter alia* '[t]o prevent any resumption of violence and, if necessary, take appropriate action against any faction that violates or threatens to violate the cessation of hostilities', '[t]o seize the small arms of any unauthorized armed elements and to assist in the registration and security of such arms'.[693] In such a situation, the peacekeepers are close to, if they are not actually, fighters. Thus, peacekeepers may be using force in defence of their mandate and be taking a direct part in hostilities at one and the same time. The two are not mutually exclusive. Being mandated to take action against spoilers,[694] provide security, and assist in disarmament,[695] may also be close to the hostilities end of the spectrum.

Ultimately, the facts on the ground will be crucial in determining whether or not the peacekeeping mission will benefit from the protections afforded to civilians and civilian objects. For example, there may be, and frequently is, a gap between the mandate of the peacekeeping mission and the actual conduct of the peacekeepers. Alternatively, the relevant individuals may go in as peacekeepers but be transformed into active participants in an armed conflict depending on the nature of the situation on the ground. Accordingly, as the *RUF* Trial Chamber held:

In determining whether the peacekeeping personnel or objects of a peacekeeping mission are entitled to civilian protection, the Chamber must consider the totality of the circumstances existing at the time of the alleged offence, including, *inter alia*, the relevant Security Council resolutions for the operation, the specific operational mandates, the role and practices actually adopted by the peacekeeping mission during the particular conflict, their rules of engagement and operational orders, the nature of the arms and equipment used by the peacekeeping force, the interaction between the peacekeeping force and the parties involved in the conflict, any use of force between the peacekeeping force and the parties in the conflict, the nature and frequency of such force and the conduct of the alleged victim(s) and their fellow personnel.[696]

---

[690] *RUF* Trial Judgment, para 233.
[691] See eg *Prosecutor v Bagosora, Kabiligi, Ntabakuze and Nsengiyuma*, ICTR-98-41-T, Judgment and Sentence, 18 December 2008, paras 2239 and 2175; *RUF* Trial Judgment, para 233; *Abu Garda* Decision on the Confirmation of Charges, 8 February 2010, para 83.
[692] 'Application of International Humanitarian Law and International Human Rights Law to UN-Mandated Forces: Report on the Expert Meeting on Multinational Peace Operations' (2004) 86 *IRRC* 207, 208.
[693] SC Res 814 (1993).
[694] Report of the Panel on United Nations Peace Operations, A/55/305-S/2000/809, 21 August 2000, para 21.
[695] See eg SC Res 1509 (2003) on the United Nations Mission in Liberia.
[696] *RUF* Trial Judgment, para 234. For the application of this test, see paras 1907–37. This was noted with approval by the Appeals Chamber: *RUF* Appeal Judgment, above note 147, para 529.

If members of the peacekeeping mission take a direct part in hostilities, or the objects of the mission constitute military objectives, the protections afforded to civilians and civilian objects will cease and the personnel or objectives may be targeted. The modalities of the loss of protection from attack, including the duration of the loss, are examined below.[697]

On occasion, agreements have been concluded that are intended to protect peacekeeping forces. During the armed conflict in Bosnia, an agreement was concluded in which the parties undertook 'that they shall within 24 hours issue, publicly, orders which explicitly forbid sniping activities against military personnel, civilians and UN personnel in Saravejo region'. In its Preamble, the Agreement referred to 'Geneva Convention (1949) obligations relating to the protection of civilians in time of war' as well as the Convention on Privileges and Immunity of the United Nations.[698]

3.11.2 The Convention on the Safety of United Nations and Associated Personnel

The 1994 Convention on the Safety of United Nations and Associated Personnel contains protections that are simultaneously broader and narrower than the international humanitarian law protections that are afforded to peacekeepers. The protections are broader in that they explicitly include actions that prevent personnel from 'discharging their mandate'.[699] States parties to the Convention are also to 'take all appropriate measures to ensure the safety and security of United Nations and associated personnel'.[700] However, the protections afforded by the Convention are narrower in that the Convention is limited to 'United Nations and associated personnel, their equipment and premises'. The Optional Protocol to the Convention extends coverage of the Convention to UN operations engaged in the delivery of 'humanitarian, political or development assistance in peacebuilding' or 'delivering emergency humanitarian assistance'.[701]

It was intended that there would be a neat delineation between the scope of the Convention and the scope of international humanitarian law. Personnel would either benefit from the protections of the Convention or would be subject to the protections afforded by international humanitarian law. Thus, the Convention does not apply to enforcement action pursuant to Chapter VII of the UN Charter 'in which any of the personnel are engaged as combatants against organized armed forces and to which the law of international armed conflict applies'.[702] However, this provision does not meet its aims. Reference is made to 'the law of international armed conflict' rather than the 'international law of armed conflict', suggesting that when UN forces are taking part in a non-international armed conflict, the Convention will always be applicable. That is rather curious.

---

[697] On the different standards, see below, 357 et seq.
[698] Agreement on Elimination of Sniping Activities in Sarajevo Region, 14 August 1994.
[699] Convention on the Safety of United Nations and Associated Personnel, Article 7(1).
[700] Ibid, Article 7(2).
[701] Optional Protocol to the Convention on the Safety of United Nations and Associated Personnel, Article II(1).
[702] Convention on the Safety of United Nations and Associated Personnel, Article 2.

3.11.3 Application of international humanitarian law to UN forces

Until 1999, the issue of whether international humanitarian law was binding on UN forces as such proved rather controversial. Agreements concluded between the UN and the host state frequently provided that the UN would ensure that the relevant mission:

> shall conduct its operations in [the host State] with full respect for the *principles and spirit* of the general conventions applicable to the conduct of military personnel. These international conventions include the four Geneva Conventions of 12 August 1949 and their Additional Protocols of 8 June 1977 and the UNESCO Convention of 14 May 1954 on the Protection of Cultural Property in the event of armed conflict.[703]

The UN took the view that, as it was not a party to the relevant conventions, it was not bound by the conventions themselves, and that, furthermore, in deploying peacekeeping forces, it could not be considered a party to an armed conflict.[704] However, other influential bodies considered that international humanitarian law was binding on UN forces.[705] The 'principles and spirit' approach lasted until 1999 at which time UN Secretary-General Kofi Annan issued a bulletin entitled 'Observance by United Nations forces of international humanitarian law'.[706] The Bulletin sets out in concrete terms the 'fundamental principles and rules of international humanitarian law applicable to United Nations forces conducting operations under United Nations command and control',[707] and does not utilize the international/non-international armed conflict distinction. Thus, UN forces 'conducting operations under United Nations command and control' are bound by *inter alia*: rules relating to the protection of the civilian population; rules relating to the means and methods of combat; rules relating to the humane treatment of civilians and persons *hors de combat*; rules on the treatment of detainees; and rules on protection for the wounded and sick. However, the effect of the Bulletin is extremely limited given that it applies to operations that are under UN command and control.

3.12 Humanitarian assistance missions

Persons involved in a humanitarian assistance mission in accordance with the UN Charter are protected from attack as long as they are entitled to the protections that are afforded to civilians.[708] Protection is also afforded to installations, material, units, and vehicles of the mission to the extent that they are entitled to the protection that is afforded to civilian objects.[709] The protection is thus a particularization of the protections afforded to civilians and civilian objects.[710] The protections reflect rules of

---

[703] See eg United Nations and Rwanda, Agreement on the Status of the United Nations Assistance Mission for Rwanda, 5 November 1993, Article 7(a) (emphasis added).

[704] D Shraga, 'The United Nations as an Actor Bound by International Humanitarian Law', in L Condorelli, A-M La Rosa, and S Scherrer (eds), *Les Nations Unies et le Droit International Humanitaire* (Pedone, 1996) 317, 322–3.

[705] See eg Institut de Droit International, 'Conditions of Application of Humanitarian Rules of Armed Conflict to Hostilities in which United Forces May be Engaged' (Zagreb, 1971) Article 2; Institut de Droit International, 'Conditions of Application of Rules, other than Humanitarian Rules, of Armed Conflict to Hostilities in which United Forces may be engaged' (Wiesbaden, 1975) Article 2.

[706] ST/SGB/1999/13, 6 August 1999.

[707] Ibid, Preamble.

[708] Rome Statute, Article 8(2)(e)(iii); Statute of the Special Court for Sierra Leone, Article 8(2)(e)(iii).

[709] Ibid.

[710] *RUF* Trial Judgment, above note 8, paras 215 and 218.

customary international law as is evident from their inclusion in the Rome Statute.[711] The Customary International Humanitarian Law study extends the obligation to one of respect for and protection of humanitarian relief personnel and objects used for humanitarian relief operations.[712]

As with peacekeeping missions, actual damage resulting from the attack is not required; it is the very attack that is prohibited.[713] An 'attack' in this context is an 'act of violence',[714] in turn defined as 'a forceful interference which endangers the person or impinges on the liberty'[715] of the humanitarian assistance personnel. This would include the unlawful deprivation of liberty of the relevant person.[716] In respect of objects that are used in humanitarian assistance missions, it would include such things as destruction and looting. Applying the statement of the *RUF* Trial Chamber to humanitarian assistance personnel, 'common sense dictates that [persons involved in a humanitarian assistance mission] are considered to be civilians only insofar as they fall within the definition of civilians laid down for non-combatants in customary international law and under Additional Protocol II... namely, that they do not take a direct part in hostilities'.[717] Delivering humanitarian aid, or providing humanitarian assistance, cannot be considered taking a direct part in hostilities. The notion of a humanitarian assistance mission is considered immediately below.

4. Humanitarian assistance

Humanitarian assistance may be provided by relief bodies that are located within the state in which the armed conflict takes place, or by relief bodies that are located outside the state in question. Additional Protocol II provides that '[r]elief societies located in the territory of the High Contracting Party... may offer their services for the performance of their traditional functions in relation to the victims of the armed conflict. The civilian population may, even on its own initiative, offer to collect and care for the wounded, sick and shipwrecked'.[718] The notion of a relief society is to be 'understood in its traditional broad sense'.[719] It does not refer solely to national Red Cross and Red Crescent societies, but includes any relief organization located in the territory of the state in question.

Humanitarian relief may also be provided from outside the state in which the fighting is taking place. As the ICJ noted in *Nicaragua*, 'the provision of strictly humanitarian aid to persons or forces in another country... cannot be regarded as unlawful intervention, or as in any other way contrary to international law'.[720] The idea of humanitarian assistance being provided from outside the state is longstanding. General Assembly Resolution 2675 (XXV) provides: '[t]he provision of international relief to civilian populations is in conformity with the humanitarian principles of the Charter of the United Nations, the Universal Declaration of Human Rights and other

---

[711] Article 8(2)(e)(iii).
[712] Customary International Humanitarian Law, Rules 31 and 32.
[713] *RUF* Trial Judgment, para 220; *Abu Garda* Decision on the Confirmation of Charges, 8 February 2010, para 65 (in the context of peacekeeping missions).
[714] *RUF* Trial Judgment, para 220.
[715] Ibid, para 1889.
[716] See the findings in ibid, paras 1891 and 1897.
[717] Ibid, para 233.
[718] Additional Protocol II, Article 18(1).
[719] ICRC *Commentary on the Additional Protocols*, above note 139, 1477.
[720] *Nicaragua*, above note 4, para 242.

international instruments in the field of human rights.'[721] Guiding Principles on humanitarian assistance have also been adopted.[722] For its part, Additional Protocol II provides that, '[i]f the civilian population is suffering undue hardship owing to a lack of the supplies essential for its survival, such as foodstuffs and medical supplies, relief actions for the civilian population which are of an exclusively humanitarian and impartial nature and which are conducted without any adverse distinction shall be undertaken subject to the consent of the High Contracting Party concerned'.[723] The customary norm has been framed along different lines, namely that '[t]he parties to the conflict must allow and facilitate rapid and unimpeded passage of humanitarian relief for civilians in need, which is impartial in character and conducted without any adverse distinction, subject to their right of control'.[724]

Five aspects of humanitarian assistance missions need further consideration, namely the notions of undue hardship, essential supplies, humanitarian and impartial, adverse distinction, and consent. The first four are relatively uncontroversial; the last mentioned is rather more contentious. Undue hardship depends on such factors as the standard of living of the population, their needs resulting from the hostilities, and the extent to which the responsible authorities can meet the needs of the population.[725] Supplies essential for the survival of the civilian population should be read broadly. It means, in essence, 'all acts, activities and the human and material resources for the provision of goods and services of an exclusively humanitarian character, indispensable for the survival and the fulfilment of the essential needs of the victims of disasters'.[726] Goods include food, water, medical supplies, shelter, clothing, and bedding; services would encompass such things as medical services, de-mining, and decontamination.[727] Humanitarian, in this context, refers to alleviation of the condition of the human person, while impartial refers to without discrimination.[728] Impartiality is also linked to the idea of adverse distinction, namely impartiality as to individual victims. Thus, no discrimination should be rendered in respect of the victims, for example, as to whom they are supporting or where their allegiances lie. Distinction can be made only on the basis of the vulnerability of the victim.[729]

These principles are reflected in the Agreement on Ground Rules, which was concluded between Operation Lifeline Sudan (OLS) and various Sudanese armed groups in 1995 and 1996:

1. ... The right to receive humanitarian assistance and to offer it is a fundamental humanitarian principle.

---

[721] GA Res 2675 (XXV) (1970).
[722] GA Res 46/182 (1991).
[723] Additional Protocol II, Article 18.
[724] Customary International Humanitarian Law, Rule 55.
[725] ICRC, *Commentary on the Additional Protocols*, above note 139, 1479.
[726] Institut de Droit International, 'Humanitarian Assistance' (Bruges, 2003) Article I.
[727] See ibid. See also Institute of International Humanitarian Law, Guiding Principles on the Right to Humanitarian Assistance, Principle 9.
[728] P Macalister-Smith, 'Rights and Duties of the Agencies Involved in Providing Humanitarian Assistance and their Personnel in Armed Conflict', in F Kalshoven (ed), *Assisting the Victims of Armed Conflict and Other Disasters* (Martinus Nijhoff, 1989) 103. See also ICRC, *Commentary on the Additional Protocols*, above note 139, 818.
[729] Institut de Droit International, 'Humanitarian Assistance' (Bruges, 2003) Article II(3); MA Meyer, 'Development of the Law Governing Relief Operations', in MA Meyer (ed), *Armed Conflict and the New Law: Aspects of the 1977 Geneva Protocols and the 1981 Weapons Convention* (BIICL, 1989) 209, 215.

2. The guiding principle of OLS and SRRA [Sudan Relief and Rehabilitation Association] is that of humanitarian neutrality—an independent status for humanitarian work beyond political or military considerations. In other words:
    i. Humanitarian aid must be given according to considerations of human need alone. Its granting, or its acceptance must not be made dependent on political factors or upon race, religion, ethnicity or nationality. It must not seek to advance any political agenda. Where humanitarian assistance is inadequate to meet the needs of all, priority must be given to the most vulnerable.
    ii. The passage of humanitarian assistance to populations in need should not be denied even if this requires that aid passes through an area controlled by one party in order to reach the needy in another area, provided that such passage is not used for military advantage.
    iii. Relief assistance is provided solely on the basis of need; those providing assistance do not affiliate themselves to any side in the ongoing conflict.
    iv. The only constraints on responding to humanitarian need should be those of resources and practicality.
3. All humanitarian assistance provided is for the use of identified civilian beneficiaries. Priority must at all time[s] be given to women and children and other vulnerable groups such as the elderly, disabled and displaced people.[730]

Much turns on the fifth aspect, i.e. on consent, and that requirement has been interpreted in a number of different ways. The provision of relief action is framed in mandatory terms in Additional Protocol II: 'relief actions...shall be undertaken' and this has been interpreted along the lines that the government is under an obligation to give its consent.[731] However, the Protocol also makes the provision of relief 'subject to the consent of the High Contracting Party concerned', making it clear that it is dependent on the state.[732] The juxtaposition of the two clauses has led to suggestion that consent is required but that it can only be refused for valid reasons, principally that of military necessity.[733] States, too, have interpreted the provision along these lines. For example, the United States has indicated that it 'would expect that the requirement of consent by the party concerned would not be implemented in an arbitrary manner, and that essential relief shipments would only be restricted or denied for the most compelling and legitimate reasons'.[734] During the conflict in Sri Lanka in 2009, the United States reiterated its view that it 'supports the principle that, subject to the requirements

---

[730] SPLM-United/Operation Lifeline Sudan, Agreement on Ground Rules, May 1996; SPLM/Operation Lifeline Sudan, Agreement on Ground Rules, 3 July 1995; South Sudan Independence Movement/Operation Lifeline Sudan, Agreement on Ground Rules, 5 August 1995.

[731] International Institute for Humanitarian Law, Guiding Principles on the Right to Humanitarian Assistance, Principle 10. See also ICRC, *Commentary on the Additional Protocols*, above note 139, 1479; Gasser, Civilian Population, above note 542, 269; D Plattner, 'Assistance to the Civilian Population: The Development and Present State of International Humanitarian Law' (1992) 32 *IRRC* 249, 260. See also ICRC, 'Humanitarian Aid to the Victims of Internal Conflicts: Meeting of a Commission of Experts in Geneva' (1963) 3 *IRRC* 79, 86–7.

[732] UK Manual, above note 190, 409 fn 129. See also, in a different context, Guiding Principles, GA Res 46/182 (1991), Annex, para 3.

[733] See, to differing degrees, M Bothe, 'Relief Actions: The position of the Recipient State', in F Kalshoven (ed), *Assisting the Victims of Armed Conflict and Other Disasters* (Martinus Nijhoff, 1989) 93–5; H McCoubrey, *International Humanitarian Law* (Dartmouth, 1990) 180; Meyer, above note 729, 221. See also Moir, *Internal Armed Conflict*, above note 382, 119.

[734] Letter of Submittal [of APII] from the Secretary of State to the President, Detailed Analysis of Article 18, in *Message from the President of the United States Transmitting the Protocol II Additional to the Geneva Conventions of August 12, 1949, and Relating to the Protection of Victims of Noninternational Armed Conflicts, Concluded at Geneva on June 10, 1977* (US Government Printing Office, 1987) 6.

of imperative military necessity, impartial relief actions necessary for the survival of the civilian population should be permitted and encouraged'.[735] Similarly, a Recommendation of the Council of Europe Committee of Ministers, in the context of internally displaced persons, provides that parties to the conflict may not 'arbitrarily refuse offers from other states or international organisations to provide such aid'.[736] The Institut de Droit International has approached the question from a different angle, noting that states cannot 'arbitrarily and unjustifiably' reject humanitarian assistance and, in particular, they may not refuse to give consent 'if such refusal is likely to endanger the fundamental human rights of the victims or would amount to a violation of the ban on starvation of civilians as a method of warfare'.[737]

The question that follows relates to the identity of the party in respect of which consent is required, the state, the non-state armed group, or both parties. The text of Additional Protocol II limits consent to that of the High Contracting Party, suggesting that it is *only* the consent of the state that is at issue.[738] Such a view is supported by various General Assembly resolutions that have been adopted on the issue of humanitarian assistance.[739] Although this is true as a matter of 'strict law', in practice it is unrealistic.[740] It is a consequence of the insufficient attention paid to the specificities of non-international armed conflicts and the involvement of armed groups therein at the time of the drafting of the Protocol. In practice, the consent of the non-state armed group will be required in respect of territory over which it exercises control.[741] Thus, a report of UN Secretary-General Kofi Annan notes that '[b]ecause non-State armed groups may exercise de facto control over areas of territory where population groups are in urgent need of humanitarian assistance, negotiating humanitarian access with these armed groups has become integral to the work of humanitarian agencies'.[742] Indeed, in 2011, the Al-Shabaab group refused access to parts of Somalia under its control to humanitarian agencies that sought to provide assistance during the famine.[743]

This is not to suggest that only the consent of the non-state armed group is required in respect of the provision of humanitarian assistance to persons in territory under its control. At the very least, consent of the state will be required in respect of relief action to territory under the control of the non-state armed group if the relief action is to pass

---

[735] US Department of State, Report to Congress on Incidents During the Recent Conflict in Sri Lanka (2009) 51.

[736] Committee of Ministers, Council of Europe, Recommendation Rec(2006)6, 5 April 2006, para 4. See also Guiding Principles on Internal Displacement, Principle 25(2).

[737] Institut de Droit International, 'Humanitarian Assistance' (Bruges, 2003) Article VIII(1). See also *Customary International Humanitarian Law, Volume I: Rules*, above note 248, 197; M Torrelli, 'From Humanitarian Assistance to "Intervention on Humanitarian Grounds"' (1992) 32 *IRRC* 228, 234. See Additional Protocol II, Article 14; Customary International Humanitarian Law, Rule 53.

[738] See also ICRC, *Commentary on the Additional Protocols*, above note 139, 1479; Gasser, Civilian Population, above note 542, 269; Plattner, above note 731, 260.

[739] GA Res 46/182 (1991).

[740] See Bothe, Partsch, and Solf, above note 236, 696; Moir, above note 382, 119.

[741] M Sandvik-Nylund, *Caught in Conflicts: Civilian Victims, Humanitarian Assistance and International Law* (Institute for Human Rights, Turku/Abo, 1998) 35–6; Torrelli, above note 737, 234; Meyer, above note 729, 221.

[742] Report of the Secretary-General on Children and Armed Conflict, S/2002/1299, 26 November 2002, para 17. See also Institut de Droit International, 'Humanitarian Assistance' (Bruges, 2003) Article III(1) and (2).

[743] See eg J Gettleman, 'Somalis Waste Away as Insurgents Block Escape from Famine', *New York Times*, 1 August 2011.

over territory under the state's control. Thus, when the ICRC communicated its intention to provide humanitarian relief by air to Biafra in 1968, the Federal Government of Nigeria appealed 'to all countries which have any influence on the ICRC to urge them not to carry through the action, unprecedented in the history of the Red Cross, of over-flying Nigerian territory and the positions of Federal troops without the agreement of the Government. Such internationally illegal action could lead to grave incidents for which the Nigerian Government cannot be held responsible'.[744] The Federal Government required that all 'relief supplies to rebel-held areas... must be cleared by the Armed Forces and Police after thorough inspection'. This was done in order to prevent 'transportation of arms and other war materials' to the Biafran authorities.[745] For the latter reason, state consent may always be required and not only in instances of passage of the humanitarian relief mission over its territory.[746] Certainly, in practice, 'donor States and international organizations... very rarely provide humanitarian assistance in rebel-controlled areas without the prior consent of the State involved and, when they do so, it is generally with the utmost discretion'.[747] Instances of relief without state consent may be rare, but they do occur, as was reportedly the case of the ICRC providing humanitarian assistance from Sudan to Tigray and Eritrea, then part of Ethiopia.[748] In general, in many instances, the consent of both the state and the non-state armed group will be required.

Not infrequently, the parties concerned do give their consent to the delivery of humanitarian assistance and they do so through bilateral agreements or unilateral declarations on humanitarian assistance. This was true, for example, in respect of the parties to the conflicts in Sudan, the Philippines, Mozambique, Somalia, Sierra Leone, Yemen, and the former Yugoslavia.[749] However, there have been other conflicts in which consent has not been provided. For example, for a period of time during the

---

[744] Statement of 2 September 1968, in AHM Kirk-Greene, *Crisis and Conflict in Nigeria: A Documentary Sourcebook 1966–1969: Volume II* (Oxford University Press, 1971) 315–16.

[745] Federal Government of Nigeria Policy Statement on Relief Supplies to Displaced Persons and Other Civilian Victims of the Civil War, 30 June 1969, reproduced in T Hentsch, *Face au Blocus: la Croix-Rouge International dans Le Nigeria en Guerre (1967–1970)* (Graduate Institute, 1973) Annex VII.

[746] A Eide, 'The New Humanitarian Law in Non-International Armed Conflict', in A Cassese (ed), *The New Humanitarian Law of Armed Conflict* (Editoriale Scientifica, 1979) 277, 294; Bothe, above note 733, 94; RA Stoffels, 'Legal Regulation of Humanitarian Assistance in Armed Conflict: Achievements and Gaps' (2004) 86 *IRRC* 515, 534–5. Cf Moir, *Internal Armed Conflict*, above note 382, 119; Bothe, Partsch, and Solf, *New Rules for Victims*, above note 236, 696–7.

[747] Stoffels, above note 746, 535.

[748] DP Forsythe, 'The International Committee of the Red Cross and Humanitarian Assistance—A Policy Analysis' (1996) 36 *IRRC* 512, 517–18.

[749] See eg SPLM-United/Operation Lifeline Sudan, Agreement on Ground Rules, May 1996; SPLM/Operation Lifeline Sudan, Agreement on Ground Rules, 3 July 1995; South Sudan Independence Movement/Operation Lifeline Sudan, Agreement on Ground Rules, 5 August 1995; RENAMO/Government of Mozambique, Guiding Principles of Humanitarian Assistance, 16 July 1992; [Philippines/MILF] Agreement on the Civilian Protection Component of the International Monitoring Team', 27 October 2009, Article 1(c); Comprehensive Agreement on Respect for Human Rights and International Humanitarian Law between the Government of the Philippines and the National Democratic Front, Part IV, Article 4(7); Agreement of 10 November 2000 between the Government of Sierra Leone and the RUF, Article 5; [Government of Sudan/JEM] Agreement on Humanitarian Ceasefire on the Conflict in Darfur (8 April 2004) and Protocol on the Establishment of Humanitarian Assistance in Darfur annexed thereto; Agreement between the TFG and the ARS, 9 June 2008, Articles 3 and 8; Agreement on a Cease-Fire in the Republic of Yemen, 30 June 1994, annexed to S/1994/778; The London International Conference: Programme of Action on Humanitarian Issues Agreed between the Co-Chairmen to the Conference and the Parties to the Conflict, 27 August 1992.

conflict in Sri Lanka, the Government of Sri Lanka objected to the provision of humanitarian assistance on the part of the Government of India.[750] Equally, there may be general consent to a humanitarian assistance mission but dispute as to the modalities of the operation. For example, during the attempted secession of Biafra, consent was given by the Federal Government of Nigeria and the Biafran authorities for the delivery of humanitarian aid to persons in territory under the control of the Biafran authorities. However, there was considerable dispute as to the modalities for such delivery, with the Federal Government requiring delivery through a land corridor and the Biafran authorities requiring night-time delivery by air.[751] Both had political and military reasons for doing so. When the ICRC did deliver humanitarian relief by air, the Federal Government declared that the ICRC was in Nigeria 'for reasons other than humanitarian' and 'has so sided with the rebels that it has now assumed the role of an agent for the secessionists'.[752] Later on, a relief aircraft was shot down.[753] The consequences of failing to obtain the consent of the relevant authorities, including for the modalities of the operation, can thus be severe. When, at a later point in time, the ICRC committed to flying over federal territory only with authorization from the Federal Government, the ICRC was criticized by the Biafran authorities.[754] The situation is invariably a delicate one.

5. Conclusion

As this chapter has demonstrated, there exists a substantial body of law which protects civilians and persons *hors de combat*. The rules relate largely to humane treatment and particular protections that are afforded to specific groups of persons. The core of the rules stem from common Article 3 and Additional Protocol II, and are of customary status. Other rules apply to non-international armed conflict through customary international law which are not derived from common Article 3 or Additional Protocol II. These rules have been identified by the international criminal tribunals and by the Customary International Humanitarian Law study, and developed by reference to international human rights law and by modelling on the international humanitarian law of international armed conflict. Each of these methods has proven important. It has been through international criminal law that the concepts of outrages upon personal dignity, torture, and the like have been defined and the prohibition on sexual violence expounded. Human rights law has given content to the fair trial guarantees. The international humanitarian law of international armed conflict has been posited for the law relating to internment and it is that same body of law that contains key definitions, such as those of the wounded and sick. Ad hoc commitments have been

---

[750] See DP Verma, 'Humanitarian Assistance to the Tamils in Sri Lanka', in F Kalshoven (ed), *Assisting the Victims of Armed Conflict and Other Disasters* (Martinus Nijhoff, 1989) 139; S Alam, 'Indian Intervention in Sri Lanka and International Law' (1991) 38 *Netherlands International Law Review* 346, 354.

[751] See EI Nwogugu, 'The Nigerian Civil War: A Case Study in the Law of War' (1974) 14 *Indian Journal of International Law* 13, 32–40.

[752] 'Partners in Crime', Lagos Radio talk, in AHM Kirk-Greene, *Crisis and Conflict in Nigeria: A Documentary Sourcebook 1966–1969: Volume II* (Oxford University Press, 1971) 82.

[753] See 'Help to War Victims in Nigeria' (1969) 9 *IRRC* 353, 353–4. See generally, Hentsch, *Face au blocus*, above note 745.

[754] See generally, GA Mudge, 'Starvation as a Means of Warfare' (1969–70) 4 *International Lawyer* 228, 255–64.

made by a number of states and armed groups to respect the various norms. The codes of conduct of some armed groups also reflect certain applicable norms.

The concerns identified in Chapter 3 play out in the law relating to civilians and persons *hors de combat*. International criminal law conflates deportation and forcible transfer and applies the exceptions to both prohibitions. This results in the protections afforded by international criminal law being narrower than those afforded by international humanitarian law. Protections afforded to child soldiers are also weaker in international criminal law and in the international humanitarian law of international armed conflict as compared with the international humanitarian law of non-international armed conflict. The international human rights law rules on point have been criticized by armed groups for not applying the principle of equality of obligation fundamental to international humanitarian law.

That insufficient attention has been paid to the specificities of non-international armed conflicts and the involvement of armed groups therein is also evident from a number of rules. Reference to consent on the part of the state alone in respect of humanitarian assistance has proven unworkable and the situation on the ground has necessitated that the consent of armed groups also be obtained. The possibility of courts being convened by armed groups was raised at the various diplomatic conferences but the issue was not seriously considered, leaving uncertainties as to the understanding of the relevant law to be applied and the notion of regularly constituted courts. Similar issues arise in the context of internment. The capacities of the parties to the conflict are largely taken into account in the rules, with a number of them referring to all feasible measures, within the capacities of the parties to the conflict, and the like. Nonetheless, there remains a danger that not all norms will be able to be complied with by all parties, particularly in the areas of detention and trial. This can be ameliorated provided the norms are interpreted in a manner that affords the necessary protection while also making them able to be complied with on the part of both parties to the conflict.

These various issues also play out in the law relating to the conduct of hostilities, which forms the subject of the next chapter. Despite these various difficulties and unfortunate interpretations, the law of non-international armed conflict relating to the protection of civilians and persons *hors de combat* is substantial. The same is true of the law relating to the conduct of hostilities.

9
Conduct of Hostilities

1. Introduction

Whether international law regulates the conduct of hostilities in non-international armed conflict has long been the subject of dispute. A number of distinguished authors sought to read rules relating to the conduct of hostilities from the protections afforded by common Article 3.[1] A similar view was taken by certain courts and influential bodies.[2] This stems, at least in part, from the idea espoused by some that rules relating to the conduct of hostilities form part of the obligation of humane treatment. For example, during the 1949 Diplomatic Conference, the USSR submitted a proposal based on the principle of humane treatment, which considered the principle to include 'such measures as... [the prohibition on] the destruction of property not rendered absolutely necessary by military operations'.[3] However, other equally distinguished authors took a different view, holding that common Article 3 does not contain rules on the conduct of hostilities.[4] This position was adopted by other courts and influential bodies,[5] and it is a position with which this author agrees. Similar disagreements arose in respect of Additional Protocol II, with some taking the view that that instrument regulates the conduct of hostilities,[6] and others expressing the contrary position.[7] This reflected the various views that were expressed at the 1974–7 Diplomatic Conference,

---

[1] See eg A Cassese, 'The Geneva Protocols of 1977 on the Humanitarian Law of Armed Conflict and Customary International Law' (1984) 3 *UCLA Pacific Basin Law Journal* 55, 107; APV Rogers, *Law on the Battlefield* (Manchester University Press, 2004) 221.

[2] Inter-American Commission on Human Rights, Third Report on the Human Rights Situation in Colombia, OEA/Ser.L/V/II.102, Doc.9 rev.1, 26 February 1999, Chapter IV, para 42; *The Public Committee against Torture in Israel v The Government of Israel*, HCJ 769/02, Judgment, para 30.

[3] *Final Record of the Diplomatic Conference of Geneva of 1949* (Federal Political Department, Berne) Vol II-B, 327.

[4] 'Application of Humanitarian Law in Noninternational Armed Conflicts: Remarks by T Meron' (1991) 85 *ASIL Proceedings* 83, 84; 'Determining Customary International Law Relative to the Conduct of Hostilities in Non-International Armed Conflicts: Remarks of HP Gasser' (1987) 2 *American University Journal of International Law and Policy* 471, 478; 'Determining Customary International Law Relative to the Conduct of Hostilities in Non-International Armed Conflicts: Remarks of Fenrick' (1987) 2 *American University Journal of International Law and Policy* 471, 492–3; D Fleck, 'Humanitarian Protection in Non-International Armed Conflicts: The New Research Project of the International Institute of Humanitarian Law' (2000) 30 *IYHR* 1, 2.

[5] *Constitutional Conformity of Protocol II*, C-225/95, reproduced and translated in M Sassòli, AA Bouvier, and A Quintin, *How Does Law Protect in War? Volume III* (ICRC, 2011) 2240; ICRC, *Interpretive Guidance on the Notion of Direct Participation in Hostilities under International Humanitarian Law* (ICRC, May 2009) 28.

[6] G Abi-Saab, 'Non-International Armed Conflicts', in UNESCO (ed), *International Dimensions of Humanitarian Law* (UNESCO, 1988) 217, 231–2; Y Sandoz, C Swinarski, and B Zimmermann (eds), *Commentary on the Additional Protocols of 8 June 1977 to the Geneva Conventions of 12 August 1949* (ICRC, 1987) 1446; JG Gardam, *Non-Combatant Immunity as a Norm of International Humanitarian Law* (Martinus Nijhoff, 1993) 27; L Moir, *The Law of Internal Armed Conflict* (Cambridge University Press, 2002) 116–17.

[7] Fleck, Humanitarian Protection, above note 4, 2; 'Application of Humanitarian Law in Non International Armed Conflicts: Remarks by R Kosirnik' (1991) 85 *ASIL Proceedings* 83, 96.

with some states questioning whether 'combat provisions...were appropriate in a protocol to be applied mainly within the territory of a single State'.[8]

Decades later, it continues to be written by some commentators that few rules, whether of a conventional or customary nature, govern the conduct of hostilities in non-international armed conflict.[9] As seen in Chapter 3, and as this chapter demonstrates, such views no longer hold true. Additional Protocol II contains rules on the conduct of hostilities, and other conventional instruments that regulate the conduct of hostilities have been extended to include non-international armed conflicts within their scope of application. Still other instruments have been adopted to regulate international and non-international armed conflicts alike. A large number of customary rules also exist on point. Indeed, it has been noted that, in respect of many rules that regulate the conduct of hostilities, 'a differentiation between international and non-international armed conflicts is not really relevant'.[10]

This chapter considers the rules on the conduct of hostilities. It commences with a consideration of the law of targeting, before turning to the rules relating to the means and methods of combat.

2. Targeting

2.1 Underlying principles

The general principle that underlies the law of targeting is that of distinction: 'the Parties to the conflict shall at all times distinguish between the civilian population and combatants and between civilian objects and military objectives.'[11] This is well-accepted as one of the cardinal principles of international humanitarian law.[12] Following on from this, '[t]he civilian population and individual civilians shall enjoy general protection against the dangers arising from military operations'.[13] Indeed, the protection of civilians, whether in international or non-international armed conflict, has been described as 'the bedrock of modern humanitarian law'.[14]

This principle of general protection is reaffirmed in a variety of ad hoc commitments. For example, a 2009 agreement between the Government of the Philippines and the Moro Islamic Liberation Front (MILF) provided that '[t]he parties reconfirm their obligations under humanitarian law and human rights law to take constant care to protect the civilian population and civilian properties against the dangers arising in armed conflict situations'.[15] A 1998 agreement between the Government of the Philippines and the National Democratic Front (NDFP) also provided that:

---

[8] *Official Records of the Diplomatic Conference on the Reaffirmation and Development of International Humanitarian Law Applicable in Armed Conflicts, Geneva (1974–1977)* (Federal Political Department, 1978) Vol 5, 184, para 6 (Canada).
[9] See eg D Turns, 'At the "Vanishing Point" of International Humanitarian Law: Methods and Means of Warfare in Non-International Armed Conflicts' (2002) 45 *GYIL* 115, 120; W Abresch, 'A Human Rights Law of Internal Armed Conflict: The European Court of Human Rights in Chechnya' (2005) 16 *EJIL* 741, 747–51.
[10] D Fleck, 'The Law of Non-International Armed Conflicts', in D Fleck (ed), *The Handbook of International Humanitarian Law* (Oxford University Press, 2008) 605, 608.
[11] Additional Protocol I, Article 48; Customary International Humanitarian Law, Rule 1.
[12] *Legality of the Threat or Use of Nuclear Weapons*, Advisory Opinion [1996] ICJ Rep, para 78.
[13] Additional Protocol II, Article 13(1).
[14] *Prosecutor v Kupreškić et al*, IT-95-16-T, Judgment, 14 January 2000, para 521.
[15] Agreement on the Civilian Protection Component of the International Monitoring Team, 27 October 2009, Article 1.

[c]ivilian population and civilians shall be treated as such and shall be distinguished from combatants and, together with their property, shall not be the object of attack. They shall likewise be protected against indiscriminate aerial bombardment, strafing, artillery fire, mortar fire, arson, bulldozing and other similar forms of destroying lives and property, from the use of explosives as well as the stockpiling near or in their midst, and the use of chemical and biological weapons.[16]

Along largely similar lines, a 2002 agreement between the Government of Sudan and the Sudan People's Liberation Movement (SPLM) provided that the parties 'reconfirm their obligations under international law, including common Article 3 of the 1949 Geneva Conventions, to take constant care to protect the civilian population, civilians and civilian objects against the dangers arising from military operations'.[17] Likewise, the Chief of Staff of the National Liberation Army (NLA), which fought in the former Yugoslav Republic of Macedonia, recounted:

I made aware the brigade commanders of their duty to respect civilians and their property. I reminded [them] that the conflict was between uniformed sides, and that civilians are not part of this conflict. These instructions were included into service regulations and were communicated orally and in writing.[18]

The language of these agreements and statements indicate that the parties were simply reconfirming a pre-existing commitment rather than creating a new commitment through the agreement or statement.

From this underlying principle of general protection, certain concrete rules can be discerned. Thus, Additional Protocol II provides that '[t]he civilian population and individual civilians shall enjoy general protection against the dangers arising from military operations. *To give effect to this protection*, the following rules shall be observed in all circumstances'.[19] In particular, the civilian population and individual civilians shall not be made the object of attack. In addition, indiscriminate attacks are prohibited. These rules reflect the two principal dangers faced by the civilian population in the context of military operations.[20] Rules also exist on avoiding or minimizing incidental losses, and on taking precautions. Despite the prohibitions and the protections, civilians may nonetheless be killed in the context of a lawful attack, and the civilian population may still suffer from the hardships of armed conflict. The existence of losses of life, damage to civilian objects, and the suffering of considerable hardship does not in and of itself indicate that the law has been violated.

2.2 Attacks against the civilian population

2.2.1 Attacks on civilians

An express treaty proscription is that '[t]he civilian population as such, as well as individual civilians, shall not be the object of attack'.[21] The provision thus prohibits

---

[16] Comprehensive Agreement on Respect for Human Rights and International Humanitarian Law, Part IV, Article 4(4).
[17] Agreement between the Government of the Republic of Sudan and the Sudan People's Liberation Movement to Protect Non-Combatant Civilians and Civilian Facilities from Military Attack, 10 March 2002, Article 1.
[18] Witness Statement of Gzim Ostreni, Chief of NLA General Staff, para 51, Exhibit P00497.E in ICTY *Boškoski* trial.
[19] Article 13(1) (emphasis added).
[20] ICRC, *Commentary on the Additional Protocols*, above note 6, 1449.
[21] Additional Protocol II, Article 13(2). See also Convention on Certain Conventional Weapons, Amended Protocol II, Article 3(7); Convention on Certain Conventional Weapons, Protocol III, Article 2(1).

the deliberate targeting of civilians. The equivalent war crime has been interpreted in a narrower manner, with the International Criminal Tribunal for the former Yugoslavia (ICTY) taking the view that, at the time of the armed conflicts in the former Yugoslavia, the war crime of unlawful attacks against civilians required that the attack result in death, serious bodily injury, or equivalent harm.[22] However, the international criminal law standard should not be equated with the international humanitarian law prohibition,[23] which prohibits the attacks themselves, and thus operates irrespective of any ensuing harm. The International Criminal Court (ICC) has confirmed that, for the purposes of the Rome Statute, a crime is committed when an attack on civilians is launched, a specific material result not being required.[24] This brings the international criminal law standard in line with that of international humanitarian law.

The prohibition on attacks against civilians and the civilian population is undoubtedly a norm of customary international law.[25] It is constantly reiterated by parties to non-international armed conflicts, states, and non-state armed groups alike, as well as by third parties.[26] For example, in 1938, in the context of the Spanish civil war and the Sino-Japanese war, the League of Nations adopted a resolution confirming that 'the intentional bombing of civilian population is illegal'.[27] Similar pronouncements had been made by UK Prime Minister Chamberlain in the House of Commons,[28] and in communications of the United Kingdom and France to the Franco forces in Spain.[29] Along similar lines, during the attempted secession of Biafra from Nigeria, the 1968 Code of Operations of the Nigerian Air Force provided that 'non-military targets were not to be bombed and that any gathering of the civilian population was to be spared

---

[22] *Prosecutor v Kordić and Čerkez*, IT-94-14/2-A, Judgment, 17 December 2004, paras 55–68.

[23] See generally above, 78–81.

[24] *Prosecutor v Katanga and Chui*, ICC-01/04-01/07, Decision on the Confirmation of Charges, 30 September 2008, para 270.

[25] See eg Rome Statute, Article 8(2)(e)(i); GA Res 2444 (XXIII) (1968); GA Res 2675 (XXV) (1970); *Prosecutor v Galić*, IT-98-29-T, Judgment and Opinion, 5 December 2003, para 19; *Prosecutor v Tadić*, IT-94-1-AR72, Decision on the Defence Motion for Interlocutory Appeal on Jurisdiction, 2 October 1995, para 127; *Juan Carlos Abella v Argentina*, Case 11.137, OEA/Ser.L/V/II.98, doc.6 rev, 13 April 1998, para 177; *Hugo Bustios Saavedra v Peru*, Case 10.548, Report No 38/97, 16 October 1997, OEA/Ser.L/V/II.98, doc.6 rev, 13 April 1998, para 61; Customary International Humanitarian Law, Rule 1; Report of the International Commission of Inquiry on Darfur to the Secretary-General, S/2005/60, 1 February 2005, para 166; Third Report on Colombia, above note 2, Chapter IV, para 82.

[26] See eg Public Statement of the Prime Minister of the Democratic Republic of the Congo, 21 October 1964, reproduced in (1965) 59 *AJIL* 616; Letter from the Prime Minister of the Democratic Republic of the Congo to the President of the International Committee of the Red Cross, 22 October 1964, reproduced in (1965) 59 *AJIL* 615; Agreement of 22 May 1992, Article 2.3[1], reproduced in M Sassòli, AA Bouvier, and A Quintin, *How Does Law Protect in War? Volume III* (ICRC, 2011) 1717; Memorandum of Understanding, 27 November 1991, para 6, reproduced in ibid, 1761; FMLN, *The Legitimacy of Our Methods of Struggle* (Inkworks Press, 1988) 5; Chin National Front, Code, Article 19, undated (attributed to 1998) (unofficial translation); US Department of State, Report to Congress on Incidents During the Recent Conflict in Sri Lanka (2009) 7.

[27] League of Nations, Assembly, Resolution, 30 September 1938, League of Nations, Official Journal, Special Supplement No 186, Records of the XIXth Ordinary Session of the Assembly, Minutes of the IIIrd Committee, 9–36.

[28] UK Prime Minister Chamberlain, 333 House of Commons Debates, col 1177, 23 March 1938, cited in *Tadić* Decision on Interlocutory Appeal on Jurisdiction, above note 25, para 100. See also UK Prime Minister, 337 House of Commons Debates, cols 937–38, 21 June 1938, cited in ibid. See generally A Cassese, 'The Spanish Civil War and the Development of Customary Law concerning Internal Armed Conflict', in A Cassese (ed), *Current Problems in International Law* (1975) 287.

[29] League of Nations, Official Journal, 104th Session of the Council, Fourth Meeting, 18 January 1939, cited in Cassese, ibid, 300.

from bombing'.³⁰ Likewise, recounting his leadership of the National Resistance Army (NRA) of Uganda, President Museveni noted:

> First of all, you must never attack noncombatants. Never, never, never, never! You would never have heard that Museveni attacked noncombatants, or that Mandela blew up people drinking in a bar. Why do you bother with people in a bar? People in a bar are not political, they are just merrymakers. Why do you target them? Targeting people in a bar is bankrupt.³¹

More recently, in 2008, the Justice and Equality Movement (JEM) of Sudan and the Sudan Liberation Army (SLA) issued a statement, 'reaffirm[ing] our commitment to refrain from targeting...civilian populations'.³² The Ogaden National Liberation Front (ONLF) of Ethiopia likewise '[a]ffirm[ed] our opposition to engaging civilians and non-combatants' and indicated that 'as a matter of policy [it] shall not engage non-combatants or civilian targets'.³³ The parties to the conflict in Croatia, in 1991, also indicated that 'the civilian population and civilian property must not be attacked'.³⁴

The norm can also be found in numerous bilateral agreements concluded between the warring parties. For example, a 2009 agreement between the Government of the Philippines and the MILF provided: '[r]efrain from intentionally targeting or attacking non-combatants.' It even extended to 'avoid[ing] acts that would cause collateral damage to civilians'.³⁵ Along similar lines, the Government of Sudan and the SPLM committed themselves in a bilateral agreement in 2002 'to refrain from targeting or intentionally attacking non-combatant civilians'.³⁶ The prohibition is also found in numerous ad hoc and ceasefire agreements.³⁷

As is all too well known, in practice, civilians are attacked, sometimes by the very parties that issued these commitments. However, importantly, the norm also tends to be confirmed following attacks against the civilian population. For example, following an attack on a bus transporting civilians in 2006, the Liberation Tigers of Tamil Eelam (LTTE) of Sri Lanka released a statement indicating that it 'condemns this attack on the civilian bus. Directly targeting civilians...cannot be justified under any

---

³⁰ Nigerian Air Force, Code of Operations, 14 January 1968, quoted in E La Haye, *War Crimes in Internal Armed Conflicts* (Cambridge University Press, 2008) 60 fn 236. See also its use in the Report of the Observer Team to Nigeria, 24 September to 23 November 1968, Cmnd 3878 (HMSO, 1969) 12.

³¹ YK Museveni, 'The Strategy of Protracted People's War: Uganda' [November–December 2008] *Military Review* 4, 7.

³² 'Statement by the Opposition Movements' [JEM and SLM-Unity], undated (published on 11 July 2008).

³³ Political Programme of the Ogaden National Liberation Front (ONLF), Part 2, Article 2E.

³⁴ The Hague Statement on Respect of Humanitarian Principles, 5 November 1991, reproduced in J-F Berger, *The Humanitarian Diplomacy of the ICRC and the Conflict in Croatia 1991–2* (ICRC, 1995) 59. See also Agreement of 22 May 1992, above note 26, Article 2.3.

³⁵ Agreement on the Civilian Protection Component of the International Monitoring Team, 27 October 2009, Article 1.

³⁶ Agreement between the Government of the Republic of Sudan and the Sudan People's Liberation Movement to Protect Non-Combatant Civilians and Civilian Facilities from Military Attack, 10 March 2002, Article 1.

³⁷ See eg Comprehensive Ceasefire Agreement between the Government of the Republic of Burundi and the Palipehutu-FNL, 7 September 2006, Article 1.1.5; Agreement on Ceasefire and Cessation of Hostilities between the Government of the Republic of Liberia and Liberians United for Reconciliation and Democracy and the Movement for Democracy in Liberia, 17 June 2003, Point 9; Cessation of Hostilities Agreement between the Government of the Republic of Uganda and Lord's Resistance Army/Movement, Addendum I, 1 November 2006, Article 2; [Uganda/Lords Resistance Army] Agreement on a Permanent Ceasefire, 23 February 2008, Article 5(2); Comprehensive Agreement on Respect for Human Rights and International Humanitarian Law [CARHRIHL] between the Government of the Philippines and the National Democratic Front, Part IV, Article 4(4).

circumstances'.[38] The LTTE also stated that it 'never targets civilians who take no active part in the conflict'.[39] Along similar lines, following an attack on the Tongolese football team during the Africa Cup of Nations in Angola in 2010, the Front for the Liberation of the Enclave of Cabinda (FLEC) indicated that the 'attack was not aimed at the Tongolese players but at the Angolan forces at the head of the convoy'.[40] Statements along these lines confirm the existence of the legal obligation not to attack civilians.

One type of attack that is singled out for especial reprobation, although in reality is no more than a subset of the general prohibition, is attacks specifically aimed at terrorizing civilians. Thus, '[a]cts or threats of violence the primary purpose of which is to spread terror among the civilian population are prohibited'.[41] The *Galić* Appeals Chamber took the view that the proscription does not contain a new principle but is an elaboration of the general prohibition on attacks against the civilian population.[42] Examples of acts that are covered by the prohibition and which frequently take place in non-international armed conflicts are car bombs installed in areas frequented by civilians, 'their object being to create panic among the population',[43] and the firing of rockets wantonly to spread fear.[44] The prohibition is not limited to acts that are directed at the human person, but covers 'any action whatsoever designed to terrorize the civilian population'.[45] Thus, death or serious injury is not required, and acts such as the destruction of homes are equally prohibited if their purpose is to instil terror.[46] Indeed, the actual infliction of terror is not an element of the offence.[47] However, legitimate attacks that have the incidental effect of spreading terror would not violate the prohibition. At the Diplomatic Conference of 1974–7, it was remarked that, 'in traditional wars attacks could not fail to spread terror among the civilian population: what should be prohibited...was the intention to do so'.[48] Thus, the acts that are prohibited are those the *primary purpose of which* is to spread terror. Accordingly, the statement in the ICRC Commentary, that the prohibition 'is intended to prohibit acts of violence the primary purpose of which is to spread terror among the civilian population *without offering substantial military advantage*',[49] cannot be taken to mean that should such military advantage accrue, the act ceases to be prohibited.

---

[38] Liberation Tigers of Tamil Eelam Peace Secretariat, Press Release, 15 June 2006, quoted in Report of the Special Rapporteur on extrajudicial, summary or arbitrary executions, Follow-up to Country Recommendations, A/HRC/8/3/Add.3, 14 May 2008, para 66.
[39] Letter from Velummylum Manoharan, Representative, LTTE International Secretariat, to Honourable Judges of the US Court of Appeal District of Colombia Circuit, undated, published in *Sunday Times* (Sri Lanka), 16 November 1997.
[40] Statement of Rodrigues Mingas, Secretary-General of the FLEC, in 'Togo footballers were attacked by mistake, Angolan rebels say', *The Guardian* (UK), 11 January 2010.
[41] Additional Protocol II, Article 4(2)(d) and (h) and Article 13(2).
[42] *Prosecutor v Galić*, IT-98-29-A, Judgment, 30 November 2006, para 87.
[43] UK Ministry of Defence, *The Manual of the Law of Armed Conflict* (Oxford University Press, 2004) 67.
[44] *Prosecutor v Martić*, IT-95-11-I, Rule 61 Decision, 8 March 1996, para 31.
[45] Institut de Droit International, 'The Distinction Between Military Objectives and Non-Military Objects in General and Particularly the Problems Associated with Weapons of Mass Destruction' (Edinburgh, 1969) para 6.
[46] *Prosecutor v Brima, Kamara, and Kanu*, SCSL-04-16-T, Judgment, 20 June 2007, para 670.
[47] *Galić* Appeal Judgment, above note 42, paras 72–3.
[48] *Official Records*, above note 8, Vol 14, 65, para 54 (France).
[49] ICRC, *Commentary on the Additional Protocols*, above note 6, 618 (emphasis added).

2.2.2 Attacks on civilian objects

Protections afforded to civilian objects

An associated prohibition is the prohibition on attacks against civilian objects. Although no conventional international humanitarian law provision that is applicable in non-international armed conflict prohibits attacks on civilian objects in general—and the jurisprudence of the ICTY is misleading in this regard, conflating the relevant provisions of Additional Protocols I and II[50]—the prohibition is very much part of the international humanitarian law of non-international armed conflict. The prohibition applies through the principle of distinction,[51] and as a 'necessary corollary to the protection of the civilian population'.[52] It has been included in subject-specific treaties that apply in non-international armed conflicts,[53] and the Rome Statute criminalizes attacks against a subset of civilian objects.[54] Accordingly, its applicability to non-international armed conflict is well-accepted in general,[55] and as a matter of customary international law.[56] Thus, the United States has observed that '[t]he customary laws of war... require all parties to a conflict to comply with the principles of distinction and proportionality in the conduct of hostilities. The principle of distinction holds that civilians *and civilian objects* (such as hospitals and schools) are generally immune from direct attack'.[57]

As with the prohibition on attacks against civilians, the prohibition on attacks against civilian objects is frequently reiterated by parties to non-international armed conflicts as well as by states that are not involved in conflicts.[58] For example, in 1964, during the post-independence violence that plagued the Democratic Republic of the Congo, the Premier stated that 'I am directing my Air Force to limit its action to military objectives'.[59] The Code of Conduct issued by the Federal Government of Nigeria in 1967 during the attempted secession of Biafra provided that '[n]o property, building, etc, will be destroyed maliciously' and that '[c]hurches and Mosques must not be

---

[50] See eg *Prosecutor v Strugar*, IT-01-42-T, Judgment, 31 January 2005, para 220.
[51] *Prosecutor v Hadžihasanović and Kubura*, IT-01-47-AR73.3, Decision on Joint Defence Interlocutory Appeal of Trial Chamber Decision on Rule 98*bis* Motions for Acquittal, 11 March 2005, para 28; US Report on Sri Lanka, above note 26, 7.
[52] *Hadžihasanović*, ibid, para 98. See also *Strugar* Trial Judgment, above note 50, para 225; Council of the International Institute of Humanitarian Law, Declaration on the Rules of International Humanitarian Law Governing the Conduct of Hostilities in Non-International Armed Conflicts (San Remo, 7 April 1990) A6.
[53] Convention on Certain Conventional Weapons, Amended Protocol II, Article 3(7); Convention on Certain Conventional Weapons, Protocol III, Article 2(1); Second Protocol to the Hague Convention on Cultural Property, Article 6(a).
[54] Rome Statute, Article 8(2)(e)(ii)–(iv).
[55] See eg International Institute of Humanitarian Law, *The Manual on the Law of Non-International Armed Conflict With Commentary* (Sanremo, 2006) 18; IDI Resolution on Distinction, above note 45, paras 1, 4. But cf Steering Committee for Human Rights, *Study on Human Rights Protection during Situations of Armed Conflict, Internal Disturbances and Tensions*, DH-DEV(2002)1, 18 March 2001 (Document prepared by F Hampson) para 54 (considering the matter 'unclear').
[56] See eg GA Res 2675 (XXV) (1970), para 5; *Tadić* Decision on Interlocutory Appeal on Jurisdiction, above note 25, para 127; Customary International Humanitarian Law, Rule 7; Darfur Commission Report, above note 25, para 166.
[57] US Report on Sri Lanka, above note 26, 7 (emphasis added).
[58] See eg UK Prime Minister, 337 House of Commons Debates, cols 937–38, 21 June 1938, cited in *Tadić* Decision on Interlocutory Appeal on Jurisdiction, above note 25, para 100; League of Nations, OJ Spec Supp 183, at 135–6 (1938) (30 September 1938, League of Nations Assembly) cited in ibid, para 101; FMLN, above note 26, 5.
[59] Letter from Prime Minister of the Democratic Republic of the Congo, above note 26. See also Public Statement, ibid.

desecrated'.[60] The Code of the Chin National Front (CNF) prohibits the intentional attack of civilian properties.[61] In a 2009 agreement between the Government of the Philippines and the MILF, the parties committed to '[r]efrain from targeting or intentionally attacking civilian properties or facilities such as schools, hospitals, religious premises, health and food distribution centers, or relief operations, or objects or facilities indispensable to the survival of the civilian population and of a civilian nature'.[62] In a 1998 agreement between the Government of the Philippines and the National Democratic Front of the Philippines, the parties likewise provided:

> Personnel and facilities of schools, the medical profession, religious institutions and places of worship, voluntary evacuation centers, programs and projects of relief and development shall not be the target of any attack.[63]

Along similar lines, the Government of Sudan and the SPLM committed themselves in a bilateral agreement in 2002 'to refrain from targeting or intentionally attacking civilian objects or facilities, such as schools, hospitals, religious premises, health and food distribution centres, or relief operations, or objects or facilities indispensable to the survival of the civilian population and of a civilian nature'.[64] The JEM and SLA of Sudan in 2008 likewise 'reaffirm[ed] our commitment to refrain from targeting… civilian populations [and] destroying civilian infrastructure'.[65] In 1991, during the conflict in Croatia, the parties also committed that 'civilian property must not be attacked'.[66]

However, high-level officials have also called specifically for attacks against civilian objects. For example, President Museveni of Uganda, recalling his leadership of the NRA, noted:

> Attack police stations; attack policemen on duty because they are not in great numbers; blow up infrastructure—railways, power lines, waterworks; attack intelligence staff; scare away government administrators—don't kill civilians![67]

Likewise, Kwame Nkrumah's *Handbook of Revolutionary Warfare* provided that '[c]ommunications, above all, railways, airfields and roads are some of the most suitable objectives for guerrilla attack' and that 'it will be necessary at times to destroy some of the country's assests, such as bridges, crops, buildings, airfields and telephone and telegraphic networks'. However, Nkumrah went on to state that '[o]bviously no more destruction will be carried out than is strictly necessary for the success of military operations'.[68]

---

[60] Operational Code of Conduct for the Nigerian Army, para 4(e), July 1967, reproduced in AHM Kirk-Greene, *Crisis and Conflict in Nigeria: A Documentary Sourcebook 1966–1969: Volume I* (Oxford University Press, 1971) 455, 456.
[61] Chin National Front, Code, above note 26, Article 20 (unofficial translation).
[62] Agreement on the Civilian Protection Component of the International Monitoring Team, 27 October 2009, Article 1.
[63] CARHRIHL, above note 37, Part IV, Article 4(8).
[64] Agreement between the Government of the Republic of Sudan and the Sudan People's Liberation Movement to Protect Non-Combatant Civilians and Civilian Facilities from Military Attack, 10 March 2002, Article 1.
[65] Statement by JEM and SLM-Unity, above note 32.
[66] Hague Statement, above note 34.
[67] Museveni, Strategy, above note 31, 8. See also 6–7.
[68] K Nkrumah, *Handbook of Revolutionary Warfare* (Panaf Books, 1968) 109 and 120.

2.2.3 Defining civilian objects

Given that the term 'civilian objects' is not defined in Additional Protocol II, regard may be had to the definition contained in Additional Protocol I. That Protocol provides that civilian objects are objects that are not military objectives.[69] Military objectives, in turn, are defined as 'those objects which by their nature, location, purpose or use make an effective contribution to military action and whose total or partial destruction, capture or neutralization, in the circumstances ruling at the time, offers a definite military advantage'.[70] That definition has been used in conventional instruments that apply in non-international armed conflict.[71] It has also been utilized by states,[72] and is considered to reflect the customary international law definition.[73]

The definition of a military objective requires an assessment of two elements. First, does the object, by its 'nature, location, purpose or use make an effective contribution to military action'? If so, would its 'total or partial destruction, capture or neutralization, in the circumstances ruling at the time, offer[] a definite military advantage'? Each element contains various subparts. The nature of an object relates to objects that are 'owned or usually controlled' by the armed forces or armed group.[74] Both the 'intrinsic character' of the object and its direct use by the armed forces or armed group will be important for assessing whether the element of nature is satisfied.[75] Location refers to the geographical site of the object.[76] It includes territory as well as certain immovable objects. Purpose relates to the 'intended future use' of the object;[77] and use, the 'present function' of the object.[78] Given that purpose is a part of the definition, the actions of a party to the conflict could make almost any object a military objective. It is thus crucial that purpose be 'predicated on intentions known to guide the adversary, and not on those figured out hypothetically in contingency plans based on a "worst case scenario"'.[79] Destruction or the like must also offer 'a definitive military advantage' and 'in the circumstances ruling at the time'. Accordingly, the test should rarely turn solely on the purpose of the object.[80]

Once the nature, location, purpose, or use of an object has been identified, it is necessary to consider whether it makes an effective contribution to military action. This

---

[69] Additional Protocol I, Article 52(1). See also Customary International Humanitarian Law, Rule 9.
[70] Additional Protocol I, Article 52(2); Customary International Humanitarian Law, Rule 8.
[71] Convention on Certain Conventional Weapons, Amended Protocol II, Article 2(6); Convention on Certain Conventional Weapons, Protocol III, Article 1(3); Second Protocol to the Hague Convention on Cultural Property, Article 1(f).
[72] UK *Manual*, above note 43, 391. See also [US] Military Commissions Act 2009, Section 950(p)(a)(1), subject to the exception below, at 345.
[73] *Prosecutor v Abu Garda*, ICC-02/05-02/09, Decision on the Confirmation of Charges, 8 February 2010, paras 85–9; Eritrea Ethiopia Claims Commission, Partial Award, Western Front, Aerial Bombardment and Related Claims, Eritrea's Claims 1, 3, 5, 9–13, 14, 21, 25, and 26, 19 December 2005, para 113. See also IIHL Manual, above note 55, 6.
[74] I Henderson, *The Contemporary Law of Targeting* (Nijhoff, 2009) 55.
[75] See Y Dinstein, *The Conduct of Hostilities under the Law of International Armed Conflict* (Cambridge University Press, 2004) 88; ICRC, *Commentary on the Additional Protocols*, above note 6, 636.
[76] Ibid.
[77] Ibid. See also UK *Manual*, above note 43, 55–6; EECC Partial Award, above note 73, para 120.
[78] ICRC, *Commentary on the Additional Protocols*, above note 6, 636. See, generally, the discussion in Henderson, above note 74, 54–61.
[79] Dinstein, above note 75, 90.
[80] APV Rogers, 'What is a Legitimate Military Target?', in R Burchill, ND White, and J Morris (eds), *International Conflict and Security Law: Essays in Memory of Hilaire Mcoubrey* (Cambridge University Press, 2005) 160, 175.

requires the existence of 'a proximate nexus' between the object and the 'war-fighting'.[81] A broader view adds the notion of 'war-sustaining capability' to that of 'war-fighting'. This is the view taken in particular by the United States.[82] On this view, economic targets 'that indirectly but effectively support and sustain the enemy's war-fighting capability' could lawfully be attacked.[83] This position is based on the destruction of cotton during the US civil war being held justified by the American-British Claims Commission following the conclusion of the conflict, as the sale of cotton produced funds for the purchase of Confederate arms.[84] However, the particular nexus between the production and sale of cotton during the US civil war and the Confederate forces needs to be borne in mind. The specificities of the Confederates–cotton nexus makes it difficult to extrapolate to other situations, as is evident from the following passage:

That cotton in the insurrectionary States was peculiarly and eminently a legitimate subject for such destruction, from its relation to the enemy's government, as the *great staple* from which were derived the *principal means* of that government for the carrying on of the war, which was the *principal basis* of its credit, the *source* of its military and naval supplies, and on which it *relied* to maintain its independent existence and to carry on the war against the United States. That the control of this staple as to production, sale, and exportation, had been, to a large extent, *assumed by that government*. That by the laws, military orders, and practice of the Confederate States and their authorities, the destruction of cotton, whenever likely to fall into the hands of their enemies, was enjoined and practiced...[85]

Thus, the exceptional relationship between the Confederate forces and the production and sale of cotton is clear. As such, the *Cotton Claims* position cannot support the suggestion that any war-sustaining objects can be attacked.

Furthermore, such an extension broadens to an unacceptable degree the notion of a military objective, as it includes objects that are too far removed from the actual fighting. It has thus been expressly excluded from contemporary restatements of the law.[86] It would also be the start of a slippery slope, as most objects, in some indirect manner, support a party's war-fighting capacity. It has been suggested that the matter is 'not relevant' to non-international armed conflicts;[87] however, the practice of such conflicts indicates that this is not the case. Just a short step further would be the approach advocated by the Frente Farabundo Martí para la Liberación Nacional (FMLN), which justified its attacks on the telecommunications and electrical systems in El Salvador in 1988, in part, on the basis that this forced the government to repair

---

[81] Dinstein, above note 75, 87; MN Schmitt, 'Fault Lines in the Law of Attack', in SC Breau and A Jachec-Neale (eds), *Testing the Boundaries of International Humanitarian Law* (BIICL, 2006) 281.

[82] Military Commissions Act 2009, section 950(p)(a)(1); Military Commission Instruction No 2, section 5D, 30 April 2003; AR Thomas and JC Duncan (eds), *Annotated Supplement to the Commander's Handbook on the Law of Naval Operations* (Volume 73 International Law Studies, Naval War College, 1999) 402, para 8.1.1. See also WH Parks, 'Air War and the Law of War' (1990) 32 *Air Force Law Review* 1, 135–45.

[83] US *Commander's Handbook*, above note 82, 403, para 8.1.1. See also LC Green, *The Contemporary Law of Armed Conflict* (Manchester University Press, 2000) 191.

[84] *Cotton Claims*, in *Papers Relating to the Treaty of Washington, Volume VI* (Government Printing Office, 1874) 53. See its use in US *Commander's Handbook*, above note 82, 403 fn 11, and the military manuals of Australia, Belgium, New Zealand, and the United States, quoted in J-M Henckaerts and L Doswald-Beck, *Customary International Humanitarian Law, Volume II: Practice* (Cambridge University Press, 2005) 217–19. See also EECC Partial Award, above note 73, para 121.

[85] *Cotton Claims*, above note 84, 52–3 (emphasis added).

[86] See *San Remo Manual on International Law Applicable to Armed Conflicts at Sea* (Cambridge University Press, 1995) 117. See also Henderson, above note 74, 142–4.

[87] IIHL *Manual*, above note 55, 6 fn 3.

the systems thus reducing the money available for military purchases.[88] Similarly, just a few years later, in 1991, the Fuerzas Armadas Revolucionarias de Colombia (FARC) recommended attacks on 'civilian factories and trucks' in order to 'destroy the source [of the government's] wealth, so that [it would] be unable to maintain this war over a long period'.[89] Even further removed is the idea that the morale of the civilian population constitutes a contribution to military action and may be targeted.[90] It is certainly true that the support of the civilian population is crucial in non-international armed conflicts, especially those that involve guerrilla warfare. Nevertheless, such factors as destroying the morale of the population can never form the basis of an attack,[91] being too far removed from the notion of contribution to military action. Furthermore, what is at issue is the *military* action and not the political objectives or strategic goals of the conflict,[92] albeit the two may be linked.

Having established that the nature, location, purpose, or use of an object makes an effective contribution to military action, it becomes necessary to consider the second element of the test, namely whether the object's 'total or partial destruction, capture or neutralization, in the circumstances ruling at the time, offers a definite military advantage'. Military advantage relates to gaining ground, weakening the military forces of the adversary, and protecting the party's own forces.[93] A 'definite' military advantage is one that is 'concrete and perceptible' rather than 'hypothetical and speculative'.[94] According to the views of certain states, shared by this author, the advantage may be anticipated 'from the attack as a whole and not only from isolated or particular parts of the attack',[95] that is to say, from more than a single specific incident but less than the entire conflict.[96] As the test is to be judged 'in the circumstances ruling at the time', the very same object may be lawfully attacked at one moment in time but not another. As the scope and objectives of the conflict change, so too may the military objectives.[97] This means that any lists of military objectives can be only indicative at best.

If any of the elements are not satisfied, the object in question will not be a military objective. Given that a civilian object is defined as against a military objective, this means that the object in question will be a civilian object and cannot be attacked.

---

[88] FMLN, above note 26, 14–15. See also Final Report on the Situation of Human Rights in El Salvador, E/CN.4/1985/18, 1 February 1985, para 113.

[89] O Mandan las Fuerzas Armadas o el Presidente de la República, Resistencia Internacional, May 1991, 7, quoted in Human Rights Watch, *War Without Quarter: Colombia and International Humanitarian Law* (1998) Chapter V.

[90] For just such a view, see JM Meyer, 'Tearing Down the Façade: A Critical Look at the Current Law on Targeting the Will of the Enemy and Air Force Doctrine' (2001) 51 *Air Force Law Review* 143.

[91] C Greenwood, 'A Critique of the Additional Protocols to the Geneva Conventions of 1949', in H Durham and TLH McCormack (eds), *The Changing Face of Conflict and the Efficacy of International Humanitarian Law* (Martinus Nijhoff, 1999) 12. See also L Doswald-Beck, 'The Value of the 1977 Geneva Protocols for the Protection of Civilians', in MA Meyer (ed), *Armed Conflict and the New Law* (BIICL, 1989) 137, 155.

[92] Henderson, above note 74, 43.

[93] ICRC, *Commentary on the Additional Protocols*, above note 6, 685 (gaining ground; weakening forces); Henderson, above note 74, 62 (protection). See also, in a different context, M Bothe, KJ Partsch, and WA Solf, *New Rules for Victims of Armed Conflicts* (Martinus Nijhoff, 1982) 196.

[94] Bothe, Partsch, and Solf, ibid, 326.

[95] See eg Declaration of the UK on signature of the Additional Protocols, in D Schindler and J Toman, *The Laws of Armed Conflict* (Nijhoff, 2004) 815. See also the Declarations of Belgium, Italy, and Spain, in ibid 796, 807, and 813. See also EECC Partial Award, above note 73, para 113.

[96] Doswald-Beck, Value, above note 91, 157.

[97] Final Report to the Prosecutor by the Committee Established to Review the NATO Bombing Campaign Against the Federal Republic of Yugoslavia, (2000) 39 ILM 1257, 1266, para 37.

In time of armed conflict, objects that are ordinarily of a purely civilian character may be appropriated also to serve a military function; others may have both functions to begin with. In practice, then, objects may be used both by the civilian population as well as by the armed forces or armed group. These 'dual-use' objects include such things as 'communications systems, transportation systems, petrochemical complexes [and certain] manufacturing plants'.[98] An integrated power grid, for example, will provide power both to the civilian population and to the military. Regardless, there is no special category of 'dual-use' objects in international humanitarian law;[99] and the definition of a military objective remains the same. If the relevant object satisfies the test for a military objective, it becomes a military objective, regardless of its importance for civilians. This does not mean that it can therefore automatically be attacked; the rule on disproportionate attacks may prevent an attack. Conversely, reliance on an object by the civilian population does not mean that that object can never be attacked. Thus the view that 'the destruction of water plants, which unavoidably hits the civilian population most severely, can *never* be justifiable'[100] is framed in rather too absolute a manner, albeit rare will be the situation in which such a plant can be lawfully attacked.

2.3 Indiscriminate attacks

In addition to the prohibition on making the civilian population the object of attack, indiscriminate attacks are prohibited. Indiscriminate attacks are those attacks that are not directed against military objectives. These tend to be of two sorts, namely those that take place through the use of indiscriminate means of combat which 'cannot be directed at a specific military objective' and those that take place through the use of indiscriminate methods of combat, again which 'cannot be directed at a specific military objective'.[101] The prohibition on indiscriminate attacks does not suggest that there are 'means or methods of combat whose use would involve an indiscriminate attack in all circumstances', as the rule requires regard to be had to all the circumstances.[102] It is the use of such means and methods rather than the means and methods themselves that tend to violate the prohibition.[103]

Indiscriminate methods of combat may be divided into failing to identify specific military objectives, and treating 'a number of clearly separate and distinct military objectives collocated with civilians or civilian objects as a single entity, such as carpet-bombing an entire urban area containing dispersed legitimate targets'.[104] The latter prohibition is particularly important in non-international armed conflicts,

---

[98] Ibid.
[99] C Greenwood, 'Current Issues in the Law of Armed Conflict: Weapons, Targets and International Criminal Liability' (1997) 1 *Singapore Journal of International and Comparative Law* 441, 461.
[100] C Tomuschat, *Human Rights: Between Idealism and Realism* (Oxford University Press, 2008) 310 (emphasis added).
[101] Additional Protocol I, Article 51(4); Convention on Certain Conventional Weapons, Amended Protocol II, Article 3(8).
[102] *Official Records*, above note 8, Vol 15, 274, para 55 (Report of Committee III). See also C Lysaght, 'The Attitude of Western Countries', in A Cassese (ed), *The New Humanitarian Law of Armed Conflict* (Editoriale Scientifica, 1979) 349, 363–4; F Kalshoven, 'Arms, Armaments and International Law' (1985-II) 191 *RdC* 183, 246–7.
[103] See below, 390–2.
[104] IIHL *Manual*, above note 55, 21. See Convention on Certain Conventional Weapons, Amended Protocol II, Article 3(9); Additional Protocol I, Article 51(5)(a); Customary International Humanitarian Law, Rule 13.

given that the presence of members of an armed group in a particular area can lead to the destruction of the entire area, even in situations in which the members could be targeted in isolation and on an individual basis. The following example, taken from the 2005 report of the International Commission of Inquiry on Darfur, illustrates the point:

> The [Sudanese] Minister of Defence clearly indicated that he considered the presence of even one rebel sufficient for making the whole village a legitimate military target. The Minister stated that once the Government received information that there were rebels within a certain village, 'it is no longer a civilian locality, it becomes a military target'. In his view, 'a village is a small area, not easy to divide into sections, so the whole village becomes a military target'.[105]

As with attacks against civilian objects, the principal treaty provisions applicable in non-international armed conflict do not explicitly prohibit indiscriminate attacks. Nonetheless, the prohibition applies to non-international armed conflict, operating through the principle of distinction,[106] and as a manifestation of the rule that civilians are not to be made the object of attack.[107] It is also to be found in subject-specific treaties that are applicable in non-international armed conflict.[108] The prohibition is recognized as applying to non-international armed conflicts through customary international law.[109] There is also some practice on point. For example, in 1968, during the attempted secession of Biafra from Nigeria, the Government of Nigeria 'issued instructions to the troops to abstain from indiscriminate bombing'.[110] The Comprehensive Agreement on Respect for Human Rights and International Humanitarian Law concluded in 1998 between the Government of the Philippines and the NDFP provided that civilians and the civilian population shall 'be protected against indiscriminate aerial bombardment'.[111] Referring to the conflict in Sudan in 1993, the German Government stated that 'during military operations, instances occur over and again which violate the international law of war [such as]... the indiscriminate bombing of villages'.[112] Thus, views to the effect that indiscriminate methods of hostilities are both inevitable on the part of the armed group and necessary on the part of the government, as expressed by certain states during the 1974–7 Diplomatic Conference,[113] would today be soundly rejected.

---

[105] Darfur Commission Report, above note 25, para 249.
[106] UK *Manual*, above note 43, 392; IIHL Declaration, above note 52, A1; IIHL *Manual*, above note 55, 20.
[107] *Nuclear Weapons*, above note 12, para 78; *Galić* Appeal Judgment, above note 42, para 132; Bothe, Partsch, and Solf, above note 93, 676.
[108] Convention on Certain Conventional Weapons, Amended Protocol II, Article 3(8)(a).
[109] IIHL Declaration, above note 52, A1; *Tadić* Decision on Interlocutory Appeal on Jurisdiction, above note 25, para 127; *Galić* Trial Judgment, above note 25, para 57; Customary International Humanitarian Law, Rule 11; Darfur Commission Report, above note 25, para 166. See also IIHL *Manual*, above note 55, 20.
[110] M Bothe, 'Article 3 and Protocol II: Case Studies of Nigeria and El Salvador' (1981–2) 31 *American University Law Review* 899, 903.
[111] Part IV, Article 4(4).
[112] Germany, Reply by the government to a question in the Lower House of Parliament, Menschenrechtslage im Sudan, *BT-Drucksache* 12/6513, 28 December 1993, quoted in *Customary International Humanitarian Law, Volume II: Practice*, above note 84, 257, para 76.
[113] See A Eide, 'The New Humanitarian Law in Non-International Armed Conflict', in A Cassese (ed), *The New Humanitarian Law of Armed Conflict* (Editoriale Scientifica, 1979) 277, 291, referring to Canada.

2.4 Disproportionate attacks

Even if a target is a military objective and the strike is discriminate, an attack will not always be lawful. An assessment has to be made as to whether the attack 'may be expected to cause incidental loss of civilian life, injury to civilians, damage to civilian objects, or a combination thereof, which would be excessive in relation to the concrete and direct military advantage anticipated'.[114] If the attack would prove excessive, it is prohibited.

Although this rule on proportionality does not find expression in Additional Protocol II or the Rome Statute, it does find expression in other treaties that are applicable in non-international armed conflict.[115] The rule has also been described as one of the 'general principles' applicable in all conflicts,[116] and as forming part of the principle of distinction or at least its application.[117] It also gives effect to the general rules on the protection of the civilian population.[118] Accordingly, despite suggestion to the contrary,[119] its omission from key texts cannot be taken to suggest its inapplicability to non-international armed conflicts. Indeed, there is much support for the application of the rule to non-international armed conflict, and it is considered a norm of customary international law.[120] For example, in respect of the second Chechen conflict, the United Kingdom noted that any military operations 'must be proportionate and in strict adherence to the rule of law'.[121] Commenting on the final stages of the Sri Lankan armed conflict in 2009, the United States observed that '[t]he customary laws of war also require all parties to a conflict to comply with the principles of distinction and proportionality in the conduct of hostilities'.[122] Likewise, the FMLN of El Salvador reported in 1988 that it had 'suspended some actions because of having foreseen that they could cause damage to the population or to property of a civilian nature that would be excessive in relation to the realizable concrete and direct military advantage'.[123]

This rule of proportionality has its critics. It has been criticized for 'comparing two things for which there is no standard of comparison',[124] and for overlooking the

---

[114] Additional Protocol I, Article 51(5)(b).
[115] Convention on Conventional Weapons, Amended Protocol II, Article 3(8)(c). See also Second Protocol to the Hague Convention on Cultural Property, Article 7(c).
[116] ICRC, *Commentary on the Additional Protocols*, above note 6, 1449.
[117] 'Customary Law and Additional Protocol I to the Geneva Conventions for Protection of War Victims: Future Directions in Light of the U.S. Decision Not to Ratify: Remarks by Hans-Peter Gasser' (1987) 81 *ASIL Proceedings* 26, 33.
[118] Doswald-Beck, Value, above note 91, 154; H Blix, 'Means and Methods of Combat', in UNESCO (ed), *International Dimensions of Humanitarian Law* (UNESCO, 1988) 135, 148.
[119] See J Gardam, *Necessity, Proportionality and the Use of Force by States* (Cambridge University Press, 2004) 125; Moir, *Internal Armed Conflict*, above note 6, 117 fn 140; Hampson *Study*, above note 55, para 54 (considering the matter 'unclear').
[120] See eg Customary International Humanitarian Law, Rule 14; HH Koh, 'The Obama Administration and International Law', Speech at the Annual Meeting of the American Society of International Law, 25 March 2010; *Kupreškić* Trial Judgment, above note 14, para 524; *Prosecutor v Hadžihasanović and Kubura*, IT-01-47-T, Judgment, 15 March 2006, para 45. See also Third report on Colombia, above note 2, Chapter IV, para 77; Darfur Commission Report, above note 25, para 166.
[121] (2002) 73 *BYIL* 955.
[122] US Report on Sri Lanka, above note 26, 7.
[123] FMLN, above note 26, 7.
[124] RR Baxter, 'Criteria of the Prohibition of Weapons in International Law', in *Festschrift für U Scheuner* (1973) 46, cited in A Cassese, 'A Tentative Appraisal of the Old and the New Humanitarian Law of Armed Conflict', in A Cassese (ed), *The New Humanitarian Law of Armed Conflict* (Editoriale Scientifica, 1979) 461, 478. See also Rogers, above note 1, 20; WJ Fenrick, 'The Rule of Proportionality and Protocol I in Conventional Warfare' (1982) 98 *Military Law Review* 91, 102.

'concept of bringing a preponderance of power to bear on a military objective'.[125] There is much truth in the matter. However, it has also been recognized that there is 'no serious alternative'.[126] How, then, is the rule to be applied?

First, the concrete and direct military advantage anticipated from the attack has to be assessed. According to a number of states, the advantage in question relates to that anticipated from the attack as a whole and not from isolated parts thereof.[127] Further the idea of 'advantage' is to be given its normal meaning and is not limited to concepts such as 'ground gained' concepts that are not always applicable in non-international armed conflicts.[128] The military advantage is that which is anticipated; that which actually results may serve as a guide as to that which was anticipated, but cannot be anything more than a guide.

Second, it has to be considered whether the attack will result in loss of civilian life, injury to civilians, damage to civilian objects, or a combination thereof. Traditionally limited to the immediate effects of an attack,[129] it is now accepted that longer-term effects have to be taken into account, such as deaths resulting from the impact of the destruction of the civilian infrastructure.[130] Certainly following the 1990–1 Gulf war, it is no longer feasible to argue that effects resulting from destruction of the civilian infrastructure are not reasonably foreseeable. That the extent of this 'indirect harm' may depend on the 'victim party'[131] is irrelevant, for what is at issue is the injury and damage *anticipated* and not that which actually results.

Once the two opposing criteria have been identified, the test is whether or not the expected damage would be 'excessive' in relation to the military advantage anticipated. The rule on proportionality does not render illegal every incidental injury resulting from an otherwise lawful attack. Heavy losses to the civilian population or significant damage to civilian objects do not automatically render an attack unlawful. Everything turns on whether they were excessive. Some gloss has been put on this test, but care needs to be taken not to distort the intended meaning. Excessive has been described as meaning 'severe',[132] or 'extensive'.[133] However, each of these descriptors modifies the balance inherent in the test. A consequence can be severe or extensive without being excessive, as excessive is a comparative concept while extensive is an absolute one.[134] References to 'clearly excessive', to use the language of the Rome Statute,[135] manifest

---

[125] Parks, Air War, above note 82, 170 (emphasis removed).
[126] Dinstein, *The Conduct of Hostilities*, above note 75, 122.
[127] See eg Declaration of the UK on signature of the Additional Protocols, in Schindler and Toman, *The Laws of Armed Conflict* above note 95, 815. See also the Declarations of Belgium, Germany, Italy, Netherlands, New Zealand, and Spain, in ibid 796, 802, 807, 810, 811, and 813.
[128] IIHL *Manual*, above note 55, 24.
[129] Greenwood, Current Issues, above note 99, 461.
[130] FJ Hampson, 'Means and Methods of Warfare in the Conflict in the Gulf', in P Rowe (ed), *The Gulf War 1990–91 in International and English Law* (Routledge, London, 1993) 89, 100; C Greenwood, 'The Law of Weaponry at the Start of the New Millennium' (1998) 71 *International Law Studies* 185, 202. But cf J Gardam, 'Crimes involving Disproportionate Means and Methods of Warfare under the Statute of the International Criminal Court', in J Doria, H-P Gasser, and MC Bassiouni (eds), *The Legal Regime of the International Criminal Court: Essays in Honour of Professor Igor Blishchenko* (Martinus Nijhoff, 2009) 547–8; J Holland, 'Military Objective and Collateral Damage: Their Relationship and Dynamics' (2004) 7 *YIHL* 35, 61–2.
[131] Greenwood, Current Issues, above note 99, 461.
[132] Fenrick, Proportionality, above note 124, 111.
[133] ICRC, *Commentary on the Additional Protocols*, above note 6, 626.
[134] MN Schmitt, 'Precision Attack and International Humanitarian Law' (2005) 87 *IRRC* 445, 457; C Greenwood, 'International Humanitarian Law (Laws of War)', in C Greenwood, *Essays on War in International Law* (Cameron May, 2006) 111 fn 98.
[135] Rome Statute, Article 8(2)(b)(iv).

disproportionality,[136] and 'no proportionality at all'[137] should similarly be avoided for want of raising the requisite threshold. Accordingly, future case-law of the ICC on point should not be taken as a reflection of the international humanitarian law standard. On the other hand, the commitment in the 2009 Agreement on the Civilian Protection Component of the International Monitoring Team between the Government of the Philippines and the MILF to 'avoid acts that would cause collateral damage to civilians' goes beyond existing standards, because it would prohibit any incidental damage, whether or not it be excessive.[138] The concept of excessive is such that any explanation, even that designed to elucidate the test, may have the effect of distorting rather than clarifying the meaning.

2.5 Precautions

2.5.1 Precautions in planning and carrying out attacks

Neither Additional Protocol II nor the Rome Statute contains rules on precautions. The omission does not mean that the requirement to take precautions is inapplicable to non-international armed conflicts, as it applies through the principles of distinction and proportionality.[139] Rules on precautions may also be implied from the rules on the protection of the civilian population,[140] and from the prohibition on attacking civilians.[141] It is a derivative of the rule that 'the civilian population and individual civilians shall enjoy general protection against the dangers arising from military operations'.[142] Furthermore, rules on precautions are to be found in the subject-specific treaties applicable in non-international conflicts,[143] and in customary international law.[144] For example, the United States has indicated that, under customary international law, 'parties must take all practicable precautions, taking into account military and humanitarian considerations, to minimize incidental death, injury and damage to civilians'.[145]

There is also practice on point by states and armed groups that are involved in non-international armed conflicts. In the context of the Spanish civil war (1936–9), the UK Prime Minister stated that 'reasonable care must be taken in attacking... military objectives so that by carelessness a civilian population in the neighbourhood is not bombed',[146] and the League of Nations took the view that '[a]ny attack on legitimate military objectives must be carried out in such a way that civilian populations in the

---

[136] S Oeter, 'Methods and Means of Combat', in D Fleck (ed), *The Handbook of International Humanitarian Law* (Oxford University Press, 2008) 119, 135.

[137] Schmitt, Fault Lines, above note 81, 293.

[138] Agreement on the Civilian Protection Component of the International Monitoring Team, 27 October 2009, Article 1(a).

[139] *Galić* Trial Judgment, above note 25, para 58; UK *Manual*, above note 43, 393.

[140] ICRC, *Commentary on the Additional Protocols*, above note 6, 1449; IIHL Declaration, above note 52, A8; IHL *Manual*, above note 55, 25; Rogers, *Law on the Battlefield*, above note 1, 231; JF Quéguiner, 'Precautions under the Law Governing the Conduct of Hostilities' (2006) 88 *IRRC* 793, 796.

[141] *Public Committee against Torture*, above note 2, para 26.

[142] Additional Protocol II, Article 13(1).

[143] Convention on Certain Conventional Weapons, Amended Protocol II, Article 3(10); Second Protocol to the Hague Convention on Cultural Property, Article 7(b).

[144] GA Res 2444 (XXIII) (1968); GA Res 2675 (XXV) (1970); Customary International Humanitarian Law, Rule 15; Darfur Commission Report, above note 25, para 166; *Abella*, above note 25, para 177.

[145] US Report on Sri Lanka, above note 26, 7.

[146] UK Prime Minister, *Hansard*, Volume 337, House of Commons Debates, cols 937–8, 21 June 1938, cited in *Tadić* Decision on Interlocutory Appeal on Jurisdiction, above note 25, para 100.

neighbourhood are not bombed through negligence'.[147] Along similar lines, in 1988, during the conflict in El Salvador, the FMLN of El Salvador indicated that it took measures '[t]o take effective precautions to spare the civilian population' during its attacks and set out a variety of measures it had taken in respect of the use of mines, which included preparing maps of mined areas and issuing warnings through FMLN radio stations.[148] More recently, the 2009 Code of Conduct of the Taliban of Afghanistan included a statement that '[t]he Provincial and District authorities, Group leaders and all other Mujahideen should take maximum measures to avoid civilian deaths and injuries, as well as the loss of their vehicles and other properties'.[149] In its 2011 Eid message, the Taliban stated that 'the Mujahideen have to take every step to protect the lives and wealth of ordinary people in accordance with their religious responsibility' and that:

[a]s far as it is pertaining to Mujahideen then they should ward off future civilian casualties by vigorously implementing the following stipulations:
... Scholars should be employed every now and then to preach protection of civilian life, wealth and honor to Mujahideen and promote virtue. All those civilian casualties which are caused or are believed to be caused by Mujahideen should be reported to the superiors.
If civilian casualties are caused in IED strikes, martyrdom attacks and other operations but the Mujahideen of the area repudiate these allegations while all testimonials and evidence point otherwise then all the suspects should be forwarded to the legal offices. If it is irrefutably proven that the blood of innocent Muslims is spilled by the negligence of Mujahideen then a penalty should be implemented in accordance with Shariah after extensive investigation and all steps should be taken to seek the pardon and pleasure of the inheritors and affectee.[150]

However, the Taliban continues to use improvised explosive devices (IEDs), which, as the UN mission in Afghanistan noted in response to the Eid message, results in a significant proportion of civilian casualties.[151]

Commitments to take precautions are also found in ad hoc agreements concluded between the warring parties. A 2009 agreement between the Government of the Philippines and the MILF provided that '[t]he parties reconfirm their obligations under humanitarian law and human rights law to take constant care to protect the civilian population and civilian properties against the dangers arising in armed conflict situations' and in particular to '[t]ake all precautions feasible to avoid incidental loss of civilian life, injury to civilians, and danger to civilian objects'.[152] Similarly, in a 2002 bilateral agreement concluded between the Government of Sudan and the SPLM, the parties 'reconfirm[ed] their obligations under international law, including common Article 3 of the 1949 Geneva Conventions, to take constant care to protect the civilian population, civilians and civilian objects against the dangers arising from military

---

[147] League of Nations, OJ Spec Supp 183, at 135–6 (1938), 30 September 1938, League of Nations Assembly, cited in *Tadić*, ibid, para 101.
[148] FMLN, above note 26, 7 and 24.
[149] Code of Conduct for the Mujahideen, 9 May 2009, Article 46, reproduced and translated in M Sassòli, AA Bouvier, and A Quintin, *How Does Law Protect in War? Volume III* (ICRC, 2011) 2325.
[150] Message of Felicitation of the Esteemed Amir-ul-Momineen [Mullah Mohammad Omar] on the Occassion of Eid-ul-Odha, 5 November 2011.
[151] See J Boone, 'Mullah Omar warns Taliban aginst hurting Afghan civilians', *The Guardian* (UK), 4 November 2011.
[152] Agreement on the Civilian Protection Component of the International Monitoring Team, 27 October 2009, Article 1.

operations'. This included 'tak[ing] all precautions feasible to avoid incidental loss of civilian life, injury to civilians, and danger to civilian objects'.[153]

As is evident from many of these commitments, the obligations recounted simply reconfirm pre-existing law. The general rule is that feasible precautions must be taken to avoid or minimize death and injury to the civilian population and damage to civilian objects. The notion of feasibility is defined in the Incendiary Weapons Protocol as 'those precautions which are practicable or practically possible taking into account all circumstances ruling at the time, including humanitarian and military considerations'.[154] This definition can be, and has been, applied outside the confines of the Protocol.[155] The precautionary measures actually undertaken can take various forms. In its strongest form, certain attacks must not take place or must be stopped. This was reflected in a 2010 statement of the Democratic Party of Iranian Kurdistan (PDKI) that, in 'the 10 years during which we defended ourselves militarily, we never once attacked Iranian forces inside cities or populated areas to avoid civilian casualites'.[156] Similarly, in 1964, during the post-independence violence in the Democratic Republic of the Congo, the Premier stated: 'I am directing my Air Force...not to conduct strikes against cities and important localities which would endanger the civilian population.'[157] Likewise, during the 2011 armed conflict in Libya, the armed group called off an attempt to capture Saif al-Islam Qaddafi, 'in part because of the risk it posed to foreign journalists'.[158] However, the complete cessation of attacks against military objectives in which the civilian population may be affected is not necessarily required and some of these reactions may have gone beyond that which the law requires. Feasible is an inherently variable concept and what is feasible will depend on such factors as the quantity and quality of territorial control exercised. Thus, what is feasible for one party may not be feasible for another, with one party possessing advanced technical capabilities and another not;[159] what is feasible in one conflict may not be feasible in another; and what is feasible at one stage of a conflict may not be feasible at another.

Rules of greater specificity have been derived from the general rule that feasible precautions must be taken. First, parties should 'do everything feasible to verify that the objectives to be attacked' are military objectives.[160] Second, parties should do everything feasible to establish whether or not the attack may be disproportionate.[161] Both of these rules are derivatives of other rules, namely the prohibition on attacks against civilians and civilian objects, and the prohibition on disproportionate attacks. As such, they are of customary status.[162] Thus, in the context of the US operations against

---

[153] Agreement between the Government of the Republic of Sudan and the Sudan People's Liberation Movement to Protect Non-Combatant Civilians and Civilian Facilities from Military Attack, 10 March 2002, Article 1.
[154] Convention on Certain Conventional Weapons, Protocol III, Article 1(5).
[155] See eg its adoption in US Report on Sri Lanka, above note 26, 7. See also APV Rogers, 'Zero-Casualty Warfare' (2000) 82 *IRRC* 165, 175; WH Parks, 'The Protocol on Incendiary Weapons' (1990) 30 *IRRC* 535, 547.
[156] Geneva Call (ed), *In Their Words: Perspectives of Armed Non-State Actors on the Protection of Children from the Effects of Armed Conflict* (Geneva Call, 2010) 28.
[157] Letter from Prime Minister of the Democratic Republic of the Congo, above note 26.
[158] Leader of the rebels, in DD Kirkpatrick, 'Rebels Arm Tripoli Guerrillas and Cut Resources to Capital', *New York Times*, 24 June 2011.
[159] ICRC, *Commentary on the Additional Protocols*, above note 6, 682.
[160] See, in the context of cultural property, Second Protocol to the Hague Convention on Cultural Property, Article 7(a). See more generally, Darfur Commission Report, above note 25, para 166.
[161] See, in the context of cultural property, Second Protocol to the Hague Convention on Cultural Property, Article 7(b and c).
[162] Customary International Humanitarian Law, Rules 16 and 18.

Al-Qaeda, which branches of the US Government have considered a non-international armed conflict, the State Department Legal Adviser indicated that 'great care is taken to adhere to these principles [of distinction and proportionality] in both planning and execution, to ensure that only legitimate objectives are targeted and that collateral damage is kept to a minimum'.[163] Likewise, the CNF of Burma's Code provides that the attacking of military objectives 'without proper analyses or identification...is strictly prohibited. Even while attacking care should be taken to only target [the military objective] without killing civilians or damaging civil[ian] propert[y]'.[164]

Third, '[a]n attack must be cancelled or suspended if it becomes apparent that the target is not a fighter or military objective or is subject to special protection, or if the expected injury to civilians and/or the expected damage to civilian objects would be excessive in relation to the concrete and direct military advantage anticipated'.[165] This rule is derived from the two previous rules and also stems from the prohibition on attacks against civilians and civilian objects and the prohibition on disproportionate attacks. Accordingly, it too is of customary status.[166]

Fourth, '[w]hen a reasonable choice between methods or means used in an attack exists for obtaining a similar military advantage, the methods or means expected to minimise the danger to civilians and civilian objects must be selected'.[167] This would include such factors as 'the timing of an attack' and 'the angle of attack'.[168] Here the capacities of the parties to the conflict have to be borne in mind, as not all parties to conflicts will be able to engage in detailed assessments. Fifth, '[w]hen a reasonable choice is available between several military objectives for obtaining a similar military advantage, the objective expected to minimise the danger to civilians and civilian objects must be selected'.[169] These two rules are specific manifestations of the rule on precautions, namely minimizing death and injury to civilians and damage to civilian objects. They are also linked to the rule on proportionality albeit one step removed. Accordingly, they too are of customary status.[170]

Sixth, an 'effective advance warning shall be given whenever circumstances permit'.[171] Reference to circumstances is linked to 'cases of assault, where surprise may be of the essence'.[172] This, too, has been considered a norm of customary international law.[173] The warning should, if circumstances permit, give enough time for the civilian population to take the necessary measures, for example, to evacuate the area. Warnings

---

[163] HH Koh, 'The Obama Administration and International Law', Speech at the Annual Meeting of the American Society of International Law, 25 March 2010.

[164] Chin National Front, Code, above note 26, Article 21 (unofficial translation).

[165] IIHL *Manual*, above note 55, 25. See, in the context of cultural property, Second Protocol to the Hague Convention on Cultural Property, Article 7(d).

[166] See also Customary International Humanitarian Law, Rule 19.

[167] IIHL *Manual*, above note 55, 25. See also Darfur Commission Report, above note 25, para 166.

[168] Quéguiner, 'Precautions', above note 140, 800–1.

[169] IIHL *Manual*, above note 55, 25.

[170] Customary International Humanitarian Law, Rules 17 and 21. See also Darfur Commission Report, above note 25, para 259.

[171] See, in the context of cultural property, Second Protocol to the Hague Convention on Cultural Property, Article 6(d). See also, in the context of 'emplacement of mines, booby-traps and other devices which may affect the civilian population', Convention on Certain Conventional Weapons, Amended Protocol II, Article 3(11).

[172] Rogers, *Law on the Battlefield*, above note 1, 231. See further Hague Regulations, Article 26.

[173] Customary International Humanitarian Law, Rule 20. Darfur Commission Report, above note 25, para 259. The customary study frames the rule in the negative: 'Each party to the conflict must give effective advance warning of attacks which may affect the civilian population, unless circumstances do not permit.'

may take the form of dropping leaflets from aircraft, radio announcements informing of the intention to attack, or communication through local leaders. The requirement of a warning has been a norm applicable in non-international armed conflict since the time of the Lieber Code,[174] and stands in sharp contrast to General Sherman's view, expressed during the US civil war, that he 'was not bound by the laws of war to give notice of the shelling of Atlanta'.[175]

The question that these rules of greater specificity raise is whether they are legitimate derivations of the general rule that feasible precautions must be taken. After all, the ICTY Appeals Chamber in the *Tadić* Interlocutory Appeal noted that it is the essence of rules that have been transplanted into the law of non-international armed conflicts and not the detail of the law of international armed conflict.[176] It also raises the question of the extent to which detailed rules can be read into principles of greater generality.[177] These are longstanding issues, which have been raised throughout the historical regulation of non-international armed conflicts. As to the precise area in issue, it is submitted that the inferences are legitimate ones, for some of them are closely related to other rules, for example the prohibition on disproportionate attack, and many of them would need to be satisfied in order to respect these other rules. Others have been accepted to apply in non-international armed conflict, albeit in respect of particular subjects, for example the protection of cultural property.

To related effect, albeit along very different lines, the FMLN released instructions to civilians in 1988 in order to avoid civilian casualties. These instructions provided that:

1. The civilian population and members of the press should at no time, nor for any reason board helicopters or any other aircraft of the Armed Forces.
2. The civilian population should abstain from boarding military vehicles, both in the countryside as well as in the cities.
3. Civilian vehicles circulating on the highways should maintain a minimum distance of 50 meters from military convoys and vehicles to thus avoid falling into ambushes.
4. The civilian population should abstain from living in housing located in a 50 meter perimeter of the Armed Forces military garrisons.
5. The civilian population should avoid approaching military installations in the interior of the country and in the cities, since they may be attacked at any time.
6. Civilians should not for any reason serve as guides in the rural areas for the patrols of the government Armed Forces.
7. Civilians who live in the zones of conflict should heed the instructions of the FMLN member responsible for the zone during Armed Forces operations.
8. Drivers should avoid transporting military personnel.

---

[174] Instructions for the Government of Armies of the United States in the Field (Lieber Code), 24 April 1863, Article 18.
[175] Letter from WT Sherman, Major-General Commanding, to General JB Hood, Commanding Army of the Tennessee Confederate Army, 14 September 1864, in US War Department, *The War of the Rebellion: A Compilation of the Official Records of the Union and Confederate Armies, Series 1, Volume 39* (Government Printing Office, 1886) 422.
[176] See above, 73.
[177] See above, 36–42.

9. During the transportation stoppages, press vehicles and those of humanitarian organizations should travel with clear and visible signs and drive at slow speeds. They should follow the instructions of the FMLN.[178]

The instructions are of a different sort as they place the onus on the civilian rather than on the FMLN. Despite that shift in emphasis, the vast majority of the instructions seek to avoid putting civilians in a position in which they could be caught up in a *lawful* attack. Viewed in this light, the instructions complement the notion of precautions in attacks.

2.5.2 Precautions against the effects of attacks

In addition to the precautions required of the attacking party, precautions are also required to be taken by the defending party in relation to the effects of attacks: 'Military commanders and the civilian authorities should do everything that they feasibly can do to protect civilians and civilian objects in their area of control from the effects of war.'[179] Again, the obligations turn on the notion of feasibility and are variable in nature.[180] The rules on precautions against the effects of attacks apply to non-international armed conflicts through customary international law,[181] and as 'a matter of common humanity'.[182] They can also be derived from the principle of protection for the civilian population.

One concrete rule that derives from the general rule and does not depend on feasibility is that 'military installations should not be intentionally placed in the midst of a concentration of civilians with a view to using the latter as a shield or for the purpose of making the adverse party abandon an attack'.[183] A broader version of the rule subject to considerations of feasibility is considered 'arguably' to constitute a norm of customary international law.[184] If it is not already a norm of customary international law, there is a trend towards it becoming one. The rule is linked to the requirement that precautions be taken and to the prohibition on using human shields.[185] There is some practice that supports the application of this rule to non-international armed conflict. For example, in 2008, the JEM and SLM of Sudan issued a statement in which they noted that, '[w]e will do our utmost to guarantee the protection of civilian populations in accordance with the principles of human rights and international humanitarian law'.[186] In particular, '[w]e recognize that placing military assets and personnel in close proximity to civilian areas increases the risk that civilians will be caught up in hostilities or even targeted. We will therefore continue our policy of maintaining a proper physical separation between our armed forces and the civilian population'.[187] Rather weaker was

---

[178] Instructions for the Civilian Population, April 15, 1988, reproduced in FMLN, above note 26, Appendix 1.
[179] UK *Manual*, above note 43, 395. See also IIHL *Manual*, above note 55, 55.
[180] On the meaning of feasibility, see above, 353.
[181] Customary International Humanitarian Law, Rule 22. See also *Kupreškić* Trial Judgment, above note 14, para 524.
[182] UK *Manual*, above note 43, 395.
[183] ICRC, *Commentary on the Additional Protocols*, above note 6, 1449–50. See also IIHL *Manual*, above note 55, 44. See, in the context of cultural property, Second Protocol to the Hague Convention on Cultural Property, Article 8.
[184] Customary International Humanitarian Law, Rule 23.
[185] On which see below, 420–2.
[186] Statement by JEM and SLM-Unity, above note 32.
[187] Ibid.

the commitment contained in a 1998 agreement between the Government of the Philippines and the NDFP, which provided that the '[c]ivilian population shall have the right to be protected against the risks and dangers posed by the presence of military camps in urban centers and other populated areas'.[188] Allegations of practice along these lines have also been condemned. The Forces Démocratiques de Libération du Rwanda (FDLR), for example, 'condemn[ed] the tactics used by the coalition of FARDC, RPA and MONUC [the armed forces of the DRC and Rwanda and the UN forces in Congo] consisting in establishing military positions within the civilian population and shelling with heavy weapons surrounding communities from these positions, endangering ipso facto these people'.[189] For its part, the FARC released a statement on point criticizing the Government of Colombia:

> On 9 July, units of the People's Army-FARC carried out an attack on the police station and on a commando of the army special forces stationed in a residential dwelling in the urban area of the Municipality of Toribio...
>
> We regret death and injury caused to civilians, as well as the damage caused through collateral damage. We would like to point out that the Colombian State alone is responsible for the damage because it kept military personnel and infrastructure amid the civilian population...
>
> By situating military units among residential dwellers, supposedly in order to 'protect the civilian population'—while in fact hoping that insurgents refrain from attacking them because of the presence of members of the civilian population—at a time of intensifying warfare that characterises Colombia at present the Government is violating rules of International Humanitarian Law to which the Colombian State is a signatory...[190]

2.6 Beneficiaries of protection

2.6.1 Context

It is in the nature of non-international armed conflict, that ordinary civilians are relied upon for shelter, food, and water, particularly by non-state armed groups. Thus, Mao Tse-Tung wrote with respect to guerilla warfare that the relationship between guerrillas and the people is like that between fish and water.[191] Accordingly, it can be difficult to distinguish between civilians and fighters and between civilian objects and military objectives. Indeed, at the time of the 1974–7 Diplomatic Conference, states questioned whether affording protection to civilian objects was realistic in situations of non-international armed conflict,[192] and suggested that, as both parties 'generally fight[]

---

[188] CARHRIHL, above note 37, Part IV, Article 12.
[189] FDLR Press Release Nr 04/SE/CD/AUGUST2009, 20 August 2009.
[190] Joint Western Command, FARC-EP, undated. The Spanish original reads:

> El pasado 9 de julio, unidades de las FARC-Ejército del Pueblo, realizamos un ataque a la estación de policía y a un comando de las fuerzas especiales del ejército acantonado dentro de una vivienda del área urbana del municipio de Toribio...
>
> Lamentamos la muerte y heridas causadas a civiles, así como otros daños ocasionados por los efectos colaterales del combate. Señalamos como único responsable de los daños al Estado colombiano, por mantener personal e infraestructura militar en medio de la población civil.
>
> Al ubicar las unidades militares en medio de los pobladores, con el supuesto de 'proteger a la población civil' -cuando en realidad buscan es que por la presencia de la población la insurgencia se abstenga de atacarlos- en un contexto de intensificación de la guerra como el que caracteriza a Colombia, el Gobierno está violando normas del Derecho Internacional Humanitario (DIH), del cual es firmante el Estado colombiano...

[191] M Tse-Tung, *On Guerilla Warfare* (SB Griffith translator (Anchor Press, 1978)) 83. See also E Guevara, *Guerrilla Warfare* (Penguin, 1969) 15.
[192] *Official Records*, above note 8, Vol 7, 140 (New Zealand).

on their own national territory, it would perhaps be inappropriate to suggest to them that they could not deal with certain objects as they saw fit'.[193] Leading commentators have likewise opined that 'seek[ing] to preserve the traditional cleavage between civilians and combatants... is hardly realistic in a conflict on the level of a civil war',[194] and that '[t]he demands of military necessity in internal conflicts might conceivably legitimate some terror tactics not authorized in international conflicts'.[195] The notion of civilians taking a direct part in hostilities could also be interpreted in an extremely broad manner. Thus, state armed forces or groups associated with the state sometimes take the view that civilians who feed and house members of the non-state armed group are taking part in hostilities. This is evident from a 1997 statement of the Autodefensas Unidas de Colombia (AUC):

[T]his is a war of movements which, as such, requires a close relationship between the active groups and the civilian population, to the point that it may be said that all of the inhabitants of a region dominated by any of the armed groups, are potentially combatants. They may well be combatants even in their condition as active sympathizers, who do not take part directly in the conflict but who assume the decisive responsibility of transmitting orders and information, supplying means of communication, providing supplies of all types, infiltrating the enemy, gathering funds, carrying out political activities, etc..., and serving, also, as a connection between the active groups and the population. Also falling into this category are passive sympathizers who take on the task of seeing nothing, hearing nothing and, especially, knowing nothing. The conduct of these persons is motivated by fear, by psychological pressure, by tricks, by convenience or by unconfessed and undeclared sympathy. These unconfessed and undeclared sympathies especially affect those civilian sympathizers who dedicate themselves to commercial activities and who provide supplies (medicine, food, shoes, personal hygiene products, underclothing, personal supplies, etc...) and who voluntarily subsidize those costs which could be referred to as 'petty cash' expenses.[196]

Conversely, members of non-state armed groups sometimes take the view that civilians who do not feed and house them are supporting the state forces. In this sense, both parties take the view that 'if you are not for us then you are against us'.

The notion of 'collaborators' is also used, by which if individuals assist the other side or do not assist the armed group or armed forces in question, they are considered to be 'collaborating' with the opposing party. For example, in the ideology of the Revolutionary United Front (RUF), 'civilians were required and expected to bear the costs of the revolution, for instance by providing food and labour. Consequently, those civilians who resisted the RUF were enemies'.[197] The notion of a collaborator may also depend on such things as the ethnicity of the individual if the armed conflict is an ethnic one, the location of the individual if based in territory controlled by one side or another, and linkages to one or other side. For example, at one stage during the armed conflict in Sierra Leone, the Government took the view that 'all those found behind enemy lines would be considered as rebels' and that 'efforts to flee the capital would be interpreted

---

[193] Ibid, Vol 14, 149, para 41 (Canada). See also 152, para 7 (United States).
[194] LC Green, 'The New Law of Armed Conflict' (1977) 15 *Canadian Yearbook of International Law* 3, 36.
[195] JE Bond, 'Internal Conflict and Article Three of the Geneva Conventions' (1971–2) 48 *Denver Law Journal* 263, 273–4.
[196] Autodefensas Unidas de Colombia, 'Naturaleza Politico-Militar del Movimiento, 26 June 1997, quoted in Third Report on Colombia, above note 2, para 50.
[197] *Prosecutor v Sesay, Kallon and Gbao*, SCSL-04-15-T, Judgment, 2 March 2009, para 709.

as treachery'.[198] However, the law of non-international armed conflict does not contain the notion of a 'collaborator'.

In light of this background, it is important to consider the beneficiaries of protection of the law of targeting. The rules on targeting exist largely for the protection of the civilian population and individual civilians. It is thus necessary to consider the meaning of 'civilians' and to ascertain the extent of their protection. This is an extremely controversial area of the law, and in many respects, there is no 'correct' answer. In 2009, the International Committee of the Red Cross (ICRC) set out 'Interpretive Guidance',[199] which forms the basis of the discussion below. However, as the Guidance itself notes, it does not purport to change existing rules, rather to 'reflect the ICRC's institutional position as to how existing IHL should be interpreted'.[200] Accordingly, the Guidance does not represent binding law, and it has itself proven controversial.[201]

There are three principal aspects to the beneficiaries of protection of the law of targeting. First, it is important to distinguish between different classes of persons given that different classes are treated in entirely distinct ways. The classes of persons in question are civilians as distinct from members of the state armed forces or of the military wing of the armed group; within the category of civilians, between civilians who do and do not take a direct part in hostilities; and within the category of members of the military wing, between *de jure* and *de facto* members. Second, the notion of direct participation in hostilities needs to be considered, both in general terms and with respect to specific acts. Third, when, and the extent to which, protection ceases for the various classes of persons identified needs to be explored.

2.6.2 Categories of persons

Members of state armed forces and military wing of armed group

In the law of international armed conflict, in general terms, civilians are those persons who are not members of the armed forces of the state.[202] In the law of non-international armed conflict, there has been considerably more debate on the issue. Thus, the Customary International Humanitarian Law study notes that 'practice is ambiguous as to whether members of armed opposition groups are considered members of armed forces or civilians'.[203] For many years, the position in the law of international armed conflict was also considered to reflect the position in the law of non-international armed conflict, with civilians being considered persons who are not members of the armed forces of the state. Accordingly, members of the armed group were also considered civilians, albeit civilians taking a direct part in hostilities.[204] This was a consequence of the lack of combatant status in the law of non-international armed conflict coupled with states not wanting to create a special status for armed groups. Thus, international humanitarian law instruments did not contain any mention of the term 'armed groups' or combatants. This has changed over time, with the ICRC, in its 2009 Interpretive Guidance on the notion of direct participation in hostilities, taking

---

[198] D Keen, *Conflict and Collusion in Sierra Leone* (International Peace Academy, 2005) 89 and 227.
[199] ICRC Interpretive Guidance, above note 5.
[200] Ibid, 9.
[201] See, in particular, the symposium in (2010) 42 *New York University Journal of International Law and Politics*.
[202] Additional Protocol I, Article 50(1); Customary International Humanitarian Law, Rule 5.
[203] *Customary International Humanitarian Law: Volume I*, above note 84, 17.
[204] See the criticism in IIHL *Manual*, above note 55, 5.

the view that, for the purposes of the conduct of hostilities, civilians are persons who are neither members of state armed forces nor members of organized armed groups.[205] The vocabulary 'armed groups' has also started to feature in instruments,[206] and the term 'fighter' is used to describe, *inter alia*, members of the military wing of the armed group.[207]

The ICRC Interpretive Guidance defines membership of the military wing of the armed group by reference to 'individuals whose continuous function it is to take a direct part in hostilities ("*continuous combat function*")'.[208] It defines 'continuous combat function', in turn, by reference to involvement in 'the preparation, execution, or command of acts or operations amounting to direct participation in hostilities'. It also includes individuals who are 'recruited, trained and equipped' by the group to 'continuously and directly participate in hostilities on its behalf'. The Guidance goes on to note that '[i]ndividuals who continuously accompany or support an organized armed group, but whose function does not involve direct participation in hostilities, are not members of that group for the purposes of IHL'.[209] It is submitted that the ICRC Guidance unreasonably narrows the notion of membership in the military wing of an armed group.

An alternative approach would be to recognize that membership of the military wing of the armed group can take two distinct forms. The two manifestations of membership are *de jure* membership pursuant to the law of the armed group and *de facto* membership through ongoing direct participation in hostilities. Just as membership of the state armed forces is premised on the idea of formal membership according to national law,[210] so too membership in the military wing of an armed group may be evidenced through the law, albeit the law of the non-state armed group. This is the notion of *de jure* membership. For example, the New People's Army (NPA), the armed wing of the NDFP, has rules on membership. The 'Basic Rules of the New People's Army' provide that '[a]nyone who is physically fit, regardless of age, sex, race, nationality or religion . . . may be a member of a fighting unit of the New People's Army'.[211] Former members of the enemy's ranks may join following investigation and re-education.[212] The Sudan People's Liberation Army (SPLA), the armed wing of the SPLM, also had detailed rules on commissioning, enrolment, and enlistment.[213]

De facto membership refers to ongoing direct participation in hostilities by persons who are not *de jure* members of the military wing of the armed group. An ongoing 'chain of hostilities, with short periods of rest between them', suggests the assumption of fighter status,[214] particularly if the periods of rest serve as preparation for the next

---

[205] ICRC *Interpretive Guidance*, above note 5, 36. See also N Melzer, *Targeted Killing in International Law* (Oxford University Press, 2008) 316–17.
[206] Cluster Munitions Convention, Preamble.
[207] IIHL *Manual*, above note 55, 4 and 5.
[208] ICRC *Interpretive Guidance*, above note 5, 27. On the notion of direct part in hostilities, see below, 363 et seq.
[209] *ICRC Interpretive Guidance*, above note 5, 34.
[210] N Melzer, 'Keeping the Balance between Military Necessity and Humanity: A Response to Four Critiques of the ICRC's Interpretive Guidance on the Notion of Direct Participation in Hostilities' (2010) 42 *New York University Journal of International Law and Politics* 831, 843.
[211] 'Basic Rules of the New People's Army', Principle 3, Point 1, reproduced in NDFP, *Declaration of Undertaking to Apply the Geneva Conventions of 1949 and Protocol I of 1977* (NDFP Human Rights Monitoring Committee Booklet No 6) 85, 90.
[212] Ibid, Principle 3, Point 6.
[213] SPLA Act 2003, Chapter II.
[214] *Public Committee against Torture*, above note 2, para 39.

engagement. These persons, it is submitted, should be considered *de facto* members of the military wing of the armed group as they are sufficiently different from civilians who take an entirely ad hoc part in the hostilities.[215] This proposed approach would not contain an imbalance between the state armed forces and the armed group, as the concern is sometimes expressed,[216] as members of the military wing of the armed group, whether *de jure* or *de facto*, are treated in a different manner from other persons who take a direct part in hostilities, as discussed below. Persons taking a direct part in hostilities on an ad hoc basis are treated in the same manner regardless of on whose side they engage in hostilities.

It has been suggested that factors that indicate an ongoing direct participation in hostilities include 'the activity [of the individual], whether or not the victim was carrying weapons, [and the] clothing, age and gender of the victims at the time of the crime'.[217] While these factors may be of some assistance in certain situations, they should be used with care. Weapons may have been a feature of the society during peacetime; they may be possessed for use in self-defence,[218] self-defence not constituting taking a direct part in hostilities;[219] or they may have been used to prevent looting.[220] Accordingly, their existence should not automatically lead to the conclusion that the bearer was taking a direct part in hostilities. The same is true of age and sex, not least in light of the participation of child and female fighters.

The combination of a *de jure* and *de facto* approach to membership and the transformative possibility from civilian to *de facto* member stands in contrast to the ICRC's Interpretive Guidance. It is submitted that it is to be preferred for three reasons. First, the notion of *de jure* membership of the military wing of the armed group is missing in the Interpretive Guidance and membership is premised on function alone. This assumes that there is an absence of formality in membership of armed groups, an assumption that is misplaced.[221] Second, individuals who do not have a continuous combat function within a group, but who perform other (non-combat or non-continuous combat) functions, are not considered members by the Interpretive Guidance. Such persons may have a logistical role or be tasked with certain support functions. Yet these persons would be considered members of the military wing in the general sense of the term. For example, the Basic Rules of the NPA provide that '[t]he broad majority of members of the New People's Army are armed fighters at all times, although some may be assigned to non-combat work but related to the fighting capacity of the army'.[222] Likewise, Mao Tse-Tung included as members of guerrilla companies, barbers and cooks.[223] Were such persons operating on the side of the state, they would be considered members of the state armed forces and would not benefit from

---

[215] On which see below, 365–8. But cf ICRC *Interpretative Guidance*, above note 5, 27–8.
[216] IIHL *Manual*, above note 55, 5; B Boothby, '"And For Such Time As": The Time Dimension to Direct Participation in Hostilities' (2010) 42 *New York University Journal of International Law and Politics* 741, 757.
[217] *Prosecutor v Halilović*, IT-01-48-T, Judgment, 16 November 2005, para 34; *Galić* Trial Judgment, above note 25, para 50.
[218] APV Rogers, 'Unequal Combat and the Law of War' (2004) 7 *YIHL* 3, 20.
[219] *Prosecutor v Bagosora*, ICTR-98-41-T, Judgment and Sentence, 18 December 2008, paras 2238–9.
[220] Darfur Commission Report, above note 25, para 292.
[221] See also K Watkin, 'Opportunity Lost: Organized Armed Groups and the ICRC "Direct Participation in Hostilities" Interpretive Guidance' (2010) 42 *New York University Journal of International Law and Politics* 641, 674–80.
[222] Basic Rules of the New People's Army, above note 211, Principle 3, Point 8.
[223] *On Guerilla Warfare*, above note 191, Appendix, Table 1.

protection.²²⁴ The same should be true of the armed group. This lack of equivalence between the state armed forces and the military wing of the non-state armed group is concerning. Furthermore, when the Interpretive Guidance notes that '[a] continuous combat function may be openly expressed through the carrying of uniforms, distinctive signs, or certain weapons',²²⁵ it is not so much a continuous combat function that is being demonstrated thereby but membership. Third, the idea of the civilian being transformed into a *de facto* member of the military wing of the armed group, as outlined above, is rejected by the Interpretive Guidance as undermining the conceptual integrity of the categories of civilians, armed forces, and armed groups.²²⁶ Yet, the Interpretive Guidance includes the intriguing statements that a continuous combat function may be identified 'where a person has repeatedly directly participated in hostilities in support of an organized armed group in circumstances indicating that such conduct constitutes a continuous function rather than a spontaneous, sporadic, or temporary role assumed for the duration of a particular operation' and that there is a need to distinguish between members of the armed group and civilians who directly participate in hostilities on a 'merely spontaneous, sporadic or unorganized basis'.²²⁷ Furthermore, the primary author of the Guidance, responding to critiques of the Guidance, explains that its 'criterion of "continuous combat function" is an objective and pragmatic one, which does not impose a rigid and inflexible formula, but requires a contextualized interpretation on a case-by-case basis', speaks of *de facto* members of the armed group who assume a continuous combat function, and notes that 'according to the Interpretive Guidance, the assumption of a continuous combat function does not presuppose constant involvement in combat, nor does it exclude the parallel, or even predominant, exercise of non-combat functions'.²²⁸

Civilians taking a direct part in hostilities

In addition to the distinction between civilians and members of the state armed forces and of the military wing of the armed group, a second distinction needs to be drawn, namely between civilians and civilians who take a direct part in hostilities. In the international humanitarian law of non-international armed conflict, as in the international humanitarian law of international armed conflict, civilians enjoy protection from attack 'unless and for such time as they take a direct part in hostilities'. This is a rule of conventional and customary international law.²²⁹ The notion of taking a 'direct part' in hostilities is synonymous with that of taking an 'active' part in hostilities,²³⁰ conventional instruments referring to both terms. Direct participation in hostilities is not itself

---

²²⁴ Watkin, Opportunity Lost, above note 221, 649 and 691; WH Boothby, 'Direct Participation in Hostilities—A Discussion of the ICRC Interpretive Guidance' (2010) 1 *Journal of International Humanitarian Legal Studies* 143, 153–4; WJ Fenrick, 'ICRC Guidance on Direct Participation in Hostilities' (2009) 12 *YIHL* 287, 290–1.
²²⁵ ICRC *Interpretive Guidance*, above note 5, 35.
²²⁶ Ibid, 28.
²²⁷ Ibid, 35. See also Melzer, Response, above note 210, 890.
²²⁸ Ibid, 890 and 848 respectively. It should be noted that the article provides that it 'reflects the views of the author alone and not necessarily those of the ICRC'.
²²⁹ Additional Protocol II, Article 13(3); Additional Protocol I, Article 51(3); UK *Manual*, above note 43, 389; Customary International Humanitarian Law, Rule 6; *Public Committee against Torture*, above note 2, para 30.
²³⁰ *Prosecutor v Akayesu*, ICTR-96-4-T, Judgment, 2 September 1998, para 629; *Prosecutor v Fofana and Kondewa*, SCSL-04-14-T, Judgment, 2 August 2007, para 131 (*CDF* Trial Judgment); *Abella*, above note 25, para 176; IIHL *Manual*, above note 55, 4; ICRC *Interpretive Guidance*, above note 5, 43.

unlawful under international law, nor does it constitute a crime under international law; however, it may be an offence under domestic law. It also leads to a cessation in certain protections that are afforded by international law.

2.6.3 The notion of direct participation in hostilities

Interpretive Guidance

Given that both the continuous combat function in the test of the ICRC, and the *de facto* membership of the military wing of the armed group in the test posited above, turn on the notion of 'direct participation in hostilities', it is necessary to consider the meaning of that term. That meaning has been aided by the ICRC Interpretive Guidance, which identified three constitutive elements in the notion. First, a certain threshold of harm must be likely to result from the relevant act,[231] the idea being more a qualitative than a quantitative one.[232] Actual harm need not result; what is at issue is the harm that was likely to result.[233] The harm in question relates to adversely affecting 'the military operations or military capacity of a party to an armed conflict' or causing death or injury to protected persons or damage to protected objects.[234] Second, there must be a direct causal link between the act and the harm.[235] Phrased differently, the immediate consequence of the act should be 'the harm done to the enemy at the time and the place where the activity takes place'.[236] A useful working test is thus to assess 'the criticality of the act to the direct application of violence against the enemy'.[237] Third, the act must be designed to cause the threshold of harm.[238] This third element is a matter of a belligerent nexus between the act and the harm.[239] It seeks to separate out the act that takes advantage of the background armed conflict from the act that is connected to the armed conflict. It does not relate to the subjective intention of the relevant actor.[240] Pursuant to the Interpretive Guidance, direct participation includes 'preparations for combat and return from combat'.[241]

---

[231] Ibid, 47–50.
[232] MN Schmitt, 'Deconstructing Direct Participation in Hostilities: The Constitutive Elements' (2010) 42 *New York University Journal of International Law and Politics* 697, 716.
[233] ICRC *Interpretive Guidance*, above note 5, 47.
[234] Ibid. See generally, 47–51. For older statements to similar effect, see ICRC *Commentary on the Additional Protocols*, above note 6, 619. See also 516. This has been adopted by the ICTR in *Prosecutor v Rutaganda*, ICTR-96-3, Judgment and Sentence, 6 December 1999, para 100; *Prosecutor v Semanza*, ICTR-97-20-T, Judgment and Sentence, 15 May 2003, para 366; by the Inter-American Commission on Human Rights in its Third Report on Colombia, above note 2, Chapter IV, para 53; and by Israel, in *Public Committee against Torture*, above note 2, para 33.
[235] ICRC *Interpretive Guidance*, 51–5. For an older statement to similar effect, see ICRC, *Commentary on the Additional Protocols*, above note 6, 1453.
[236] Ibid, 516 on Additional Protocol I. See also Schmitt, DPH, above note 232, 712.
[237] MN Schmitt, '"Direct Participation in Hostilities" and 21st Century Armed Conflict', in H Fischer et al (eds), *Crisis Management and Humanitarian Protection: Festschrift für Dieter Fleck* (Berliner Wissenschafts-Verlag, 2004) 505, 509; MN Schmitt, 'Humanitarian Law and Direct Participation in Hostilities by Private Contractors or Civilian Employees' (2005) 5 *Chicago Journal of International Law* 511, 534.
[238] ICRC *Interpretive Guidance*, above note 5, 58.
[239] Ibid.
[240] Ibid, 59.
[241] Ibid, 67–8. See also *Official Records*, above note 8, Vol 15, 330 (Report to Committee on the Work of the Working Group). See also ICRC, *Commentary on the Additional Protocols*, above note 6, 1453; *Public Committee against Torture*, above note 2, para 34.

Types of acts

In addition to the general guidance on direct participation in hostilities considered immediately above, guidance can also be discerned with respect to specific acts. It is well-accepted that support for, or participation in, the war effort does not constitute taking a direct part in hostilities.[242] At the 1972 Conference of Government Experts, the notion of taking a direct part in hostilities was discussed. It was agreed that equating this with '"tak[ing] part in the fighting or in military operations" was too narrow' while the formula '"participat[ing] in the military effort" too broad'.[243] Similarly, it is agreed that 'mere expression of sympathy' for the cause of one of the parties does not constitute taking a direct part in hostilities.[244] In light of the difficulties in defining the concept, and the varying definitions in state practice,[245] historically, the matter has tended to be considered on a case-by-case basis.[246]

Accordingly, guidance can be identified in relation to specific acts from the jurisprudence of international courts and tribunals. Examples of direct participation that are particularly prevalent in non-international armed conflict include: actual combat; bearing or using arms,[247] with the caveat expressed above; attacking the other side's personnel, materiel, or facilities,[248] including with roadside bombs when on patrol;[249] engaging in the sabotage of military installations or communications;[250] certain forms of intelligence gathering;[251] and acting as human shields.[252] Examples that do not fall within direct participation include: 'working in a munitions factory'[253] or a factory supplying food or clothing to the armed forces;[254] selling food or medicine to the parties;[255] 'serving as messengers';[256] and 'failing to act to prevent an incursion by one of the armed parties'.[257] The reason for these latter actions not constituting direct participation in hostilities is that they do not 'involve acts of violence which pose an immediate threat of actual harm to the adverse party'.[258] Thus, journalists who report on the armed conflict, including publicizing violations by one side or the other, do not

---

[242] ICRC, *Commentary on the Additional Protocols*, above note 6, 619; Rogers, *Law on the Battlefield*, above note 1, 8–9; Third Report on Colombia, above note 2, para 56.

[243] 'Reaffirmation and Development of International Humanitarian Law Applicable in Armed Conflicts: Conference of Government Experts [Second Session]' (1973) 13 *IRRC* 61, 68.

[244] *Monsignor Oscar Arnulfo Romero y Galdamez v El Salvador*, Case 11.481, Report No 37/00, 13 April 2000, para 69. See also *Prosecutor v Strugar*, IT-01-42-A, Judgment, 17 July 2008, para 177; Third Report on Colombia, above note 2, para 56.

[245] See *Customary International Humanitarian Law, Volume I: Rules*, above note 84, 23.

[246] *Prosecutor v Tadić*, IT-94-1-T, Opinion and Judgment, 7 May 1997, para 616; *Strugar* Appeal Judgment, above note 244, para 179.

[247] Ibid, para 177.

[248] Ibid; IIHL *Manual*, above note 55, 4; Direct Participation in Hostilities under International Humanitarian Law: Report prepared by the ICRC (2003).

[249] Rogers, Unequal Combat, above note 218, 19.

[250] IIHL *Manual*, above note 55, 4; DPH Report, above note 248; Rogers, Unequal Combat, above note 218, 19.

[251] *Strugar* Appeal Judgment, above note 244, para 177; IIHL *Manual*, above note 55, 4–5; *Public Committee against Torture*, above note 2, para 35; DPH Report, above note 248.

[252] See also above, 317–18 in the context of child soldiers.

[253] IIHL *Manual*, above note 55, 5; DPH Report, above note 248.

[254] Ibid.

[255] *Strugar* Appeal Judgment, above note 244, para 177; *Public Committee against Torture*, above note 2, para 34. See also Third Report on Colombia, above note 2, para 56.

[256] Rogers, *Law on the Battlefield*, above note 1, 226. See also above, 318, in the context of child soldiers.

[257] Third Report on Colombia, above note 2, para 56; *Strugar* Appeal Judgment, above note 244, para 177.

[258] Third Report on Colombia, above note 2, para 56.

thereby take a direct part in hostilities.[259] Likewise, persons who criticize one side or another do not take a direct part in hostilities in so doing.

More difficult are the borderline situations, such as the individual who drives an ammunition truck, over whom there exists much disagreement.[260] There are two competing approaches to the borderline situation. The first is that it is necessary to err on the side of finding direct participation so as to protect the general civilian population.[261] The diametrically opposed approach is that the notion of direct participation should be restrictively conceived so as to preserve the fundamental principles of distinction and civilian immunity and protect the individual target.[262] The difference in approach stems from the tension within the rule as to the identity of the principal beneficiary, namely whether it is the general civilian population or the individual civilian in question. Identifying that focus would resolve the issue of where the presumption lies.

2.6.4 Loss of protection

It is necessary to draw the distinctions considered above, between civilians, civilians taking a direct part in hostilities, and members of the state armed forces or the military wing of the armed group, as the cessation of protection is different in respect of each category. The situations in which each category loses protection, and the duration for which they so lose, are controversial and various views have been expressed.[263]

State armed forces and military wing of armed group

Members of the military wing of the armed group, be they *de jure* or *de facto* members, may be targeted, it is submitted, at any time, regardless of whether or not they are taking a direct part in the hostilities at the time at which they are targeted.[264] This is important for reasons of parity as between the parties to the conflict,[265] given that members of the state armed forces do not benefit from the protections afforded to civilians and may also be targeted at any time. Although this approach groups individuals together as an armed group and arguably provides that group with a certain status,[266] the idea of an armed group is inherent in the very existence of a non-international armed conflict.

This 'membership' approach benefits from support. It was the approach taken at the Committee stage of the 1974–7 Diplomatic Conference before the substantive provisions of the Protocol were reduced: 'a civilian is anyone who is not a member of the

---

[259] See above, 312.
[260] For the diverging views, see DPH Report, above note 248; Rogers, *Law on the Battlefield*, above note 1, 9; Schmitt, 21st Century Conflict, above note 237, 508; *Public Committee against Torture*, above note 2, para 35; ICRC *Interpretive Guidance*, above note 5, 56.
[261] Schmitt, 21st Century Conflict, above note 237, 509.
[262] Rogers, Unequal Combat, above note 218, 11.
[263] For a range of views, see the reports of the various Expert Meetings on the Notion of Direct Participation in Hostilities, organized by the ICRC and the TMC Asser Institute (2003–8).
[264] ICRC *Interpretive Guidance*, above note 5, 71–2. See also WJ Fenrick, 'The Prosecution of Unlawful Attack Cases before the ICTY' (2004) 7 *YIHL* 153, 170.
[265] See also Boothby, Direct Participation, above note 224, 146–7. This has been criticized from a human rights perspective: Report of the Special Rapporteur on Extrajudicial, Summary or Arbitrary Executions, Study on Targeted Killings, A/HRC/14/24/Add.6, 28 May 2010, paras 65–6.
[266] See, for this criticism, Watkin, Opportunity Lost, above note 221, 643–4. See also Boothby, Direct Participation above note 224, 149–50.

armed forces or of an organized armed group.'[267] The ad hoc international criminal tribunals have likewise affirmed that, '[f]or the purpose of the protection of victims of armed conflict, the term "civilian" is defined negatively as anyone who is not a member of the armed forces or of an organised military group belonging to a party to the conflict'.[268] The ICRC Commentary on Additional Protocol II takes a similar view in its observation that '[t]hose who belong to armed forces or armed groups may be attacked at any time',[269] and the ICRC Interpretive Guidance also utilizes the notion of membership of the armed group.[270] It also fits with the language of the relevant treaties. Additional Protocol II provides that civilians enjoy protection 'unless and for such time as they take a direct part in hostilities';[271] as the individuals in question are not civilians, they may be targeted at any time.

This means that the military commander of an armed group may be targeted, even if they are also the head of the political wing of the group. For example, as late as 2009, the leadership of the FDLR was based in Europe with Ignace Murwanashyaka, President of the FDLR, living in Germany, serving also as 'supreme military commander' and controlling operations.[272] This means that the military commander who also serves as the leader of a government would constitute a legitimate military target. Political figures who are members of the armed forces, or who are involved in the command and control of the armed forces, generally speaking, may then also be legitimate targets of attack. This includes heads of state and other high-ranking government officials involved in the military operations such as ministers of defence. These persons stand in contrast to those heads of state who hold only a figurative or ceremonial commanding position and who would not thus constitute a legitimate target.[273] Whereas in international armed conflicts, attacks against heads of state who also serve as commanders-in-chief have been limited 'as a matter of comity',[274] the same is not true of non-international armed conflicts. On this basis, the killing of Sri Lankan President Ranasinghe Premadasa in 1993, which has been attributed to the LTTE, would not have violated the rule relating to legitimate targets given that the President of Sri Lanka is also the Commander-in-Chief of the Sri Lankan armed forces,[275] and is not purely a ceremonial position. Likewise, the killing of the Minister of State for Defence Ranjan Wijeratne, also attributed to the LTTE, would not have violated the rule on legitimate targets given the role of the Defence Minister in the hostilities. However, the killings of other ministers and members of parliament who were not involved in the hostilities, again attributed to the LTTE, would constitute a violation of the law relating to targets. Although such persons may have had some involvement in the armed conflict—voting in favour of emergency legislation, approving expenditure for

---

[267] Draft Article 25, as adopted by the Committee. See *Official Records*, above note 8, Vol 15, 290 and 320. On the reduction of the Protocol, see above, 49–51.
[268] *Galić* Trial Judgment, above note 25, para 47. See also *Prosecutor v Kayishema and Ruzindana*, ICTR-95-1-T, Judgment, 21 May 1999, para 179; *Prosecutor v Rutaganda*, ICTR-96-3-T, Judgment and Sentence, 6 December 1999, para 100.
[269] ICRC, *Commentary on the Additional Protocols*, above note 6, 1453.
[270] ICRC, *Interpretive Guidance*, above note 5, 31–5.
[271] Additional Protocol II, Article 13(3).
[272] 'FDLR Inc: Congo's Multinational Rebels', *BBC News*, 18 November 2009.
[273] Rogers, Legitimate Target, above note 80, 176–7; Henderson, *Contemperary Law*, above note 74, 110.
[274] Department of the Army, Office of the Judge Advocate General of the Army, Memorandum of Law: Executive Order 12333 and Assassination', 2 November 1989 (written by WH Parks, as reissued) fn 12.
[275] Constitution of the Democratic Socialist Republic of Sri Lanka (1978), section 30(1). The *manner* in which the President was killed may have violated the law.

the armed forces, and the like—such actions relate to the armed conflict more broadly and not the hostilities in particular.

On this basis, members of the political wing of an armed group, or of another wing such as a human rights division, or those involved in the provision of education or services, may not be targeted unless they take a direct part in hostilities. They are to be treated like civilians who take a direct part in hostilities, who are considered immediately below. Much will turn on the facts on the ground and the particular structure of the group. Difficulties of identification may also arise, for example it may be difficult to distinguish between members of the military wing or the political or social wing of an armed group if there is a common uniform across all wings. Although states sometimes argue that the armed group as a whole can be targeted given that 'its instruments of political and social control [are] as legitimate a target as its rocket caches',[276] this goes too far. It would also mean that parallel objects and persons in state structures would not benefit from protection.

Civilians taking a direct part in hostilities

Persons who participate in hostilities on an entirely ad hoc basis are treated in a different manner from members of the armed forces or of the military wing of the armed group. A number of approaches have been suggested regarding these persons. One approach is that such persons have lost immunity and may be targeted at any time, even after concluding their part in the hostilities. This has the advantage of preventing the 'farmer by day, guerrilla by night', 'revolving door' approach, but goes against the very wording of Additional Protocol II with its reference to 'for such time as'. Another approach is that such individuals lose immunity until such time as they demonstrate that they are no longer taking a direct part in hostilities.[277] However, this suffers from the evidential difficulty that would be required for such a showing. A third approach follows the letter of the Protocol: the individual loses immunity 'for such time as' they take a direct part in hostilities. However, this suffers from the 'revolving door' problem.[278]

It is submitted that this third approach is the most satisfactory and there is support for it in the jurisprudence. For example, the Israeli Supreme Court has indicated that '[a] civilian who... commits acts of combat does not lose his status as a civilian, but as long as he is taking a direct part in hostilities he does not enjoy—during that time—the protection granted to a civilian... He is a civilian performing the function of a combatant. As long as he performs that function, he is subject to the risks which that function entails and ceases to enjoy the protection granted to a civilian from attack'.[279] The 'revolving door' problem would be ameliorated by the concept of the *de facto* member of the military wing of the armed group, considered above.

---

[276] State official, quoted in C Tomuschat, 'Human Rights and International Humanitarian Law' (2010) 21 *EJIL* 15, 22 fn 26.

[277] Schmitt, 21st Century Conflict, above note 237, 510; Boothby, '"And For Such Time As"', above note 216, 759–61.

[278] K Watkin, 'Controlling the Use of Force: A Role for Human Rights Norms in Contemporary Armed Conflict' (2004) 98 *AJIL* 1, 17; Boothby, '"And For Such Time As"', above note 216, 755. See generally, Melzer, *Targetted Killing*, above note 205, 346–53.

[279] *Public Committee against Torture*, above note 2, para 31. See also *Strugar* Trial Judgment, above note 50, para 282; *Prosecutor v Blagojević and Jokić*, IT-02-60-T, Judgment, 17 January 2005, para 544; *Halilović* Trial Judgment, above note 217, para 34; *Abella*, above note 25, para 189.

In general terms, members of the police force are to be treated as civilians.[280] However, in times of non-international armed conflict, the police force may be attached to the armed forces, or fall under the auspices of the Ministry of Defence, and used in hostilities. This may also be the case in times of peace. For example, pursuant to the Constitution of Colombia, the police force, together with the armed forces, comprises the security forces and both are controlled by the Ministry of Defence.[281] Thus, when the FARC argues that it may target the police,[282] the legality of such a claim has to be taken seriously. Similarly, in the armed conflict in Darfur, the police force fights alongside the state armed forces, and militia have been incorporated into the police force. In light of such circumstances, the Darfur Commission took the view that the civilian status of the police was 'questionable'.[283] As such, although, in theory, members of the police force are civilians and this will be the presumption, in practice, in a particular conflict, it may be difficult to argue that members of the police force benefit from the protections afforded to the civilian population. Again, much will turn on the structure of the force in the domestic system, and on the facts.

Views of armed groups

The identification of certain classes of persons as legitimate targets is an area in which considerable disagreement lies. For example, in 1988, the FMLN of El Salvador took the position that US military advisors were military objectives given that:

> [t]hey are also participating in the strategic direction of the war... With more and more frequency they are participating personally in the operations. It is undeniable that their contribution has directly contributed to the deepening and development of the hostilities. Therefore, according to Article 43 of Additional Protocol I, these advisors must be considered as combatants and are legitimate military targets.[284]

The Kurdistan Workers' Party (PKK) indicated in 1995 that it:

> regards the following groups as part of the Turkish security forces and, therefore, as legitimate targets of attack:
>
> — members of the Turkish armed forces;
> — members of the Turkish contra-guerrilla forces;
> — members of the Turkish Intelligence Service (MIT);
> — members of the Turkish gendarmerie;
> — village guards.

The PKK does not regard civil servants as members of the security forces, unless they come within one of the above categories.[285]

The NDFP took a largely similar position in 1996, indicating that it:

---

[280] *RUF* Trial Judgment, above note 197, para 87.
[281] Constitution of Colombia (1991) Article 216, cited in A Carrillo-Suárez, 'Hors de Logique: Contemporary Issues in International Humanitarian Law as Applied to Internal Armed Conflict' (1999) 15 *American University International Law Review* 1, 12. See also *RUF* Trial Judgment, above note 197, para 87.
[282] D García-Peña Jaramillo, 'Humanitarian Protection in Non-International Conflicts: A Case Study of Colombia' (2000) 30 *IYHR* 179, 194.
[283] Darfur Commission Report, above note 25, para 422.
[284] FMLN, *Legitimacy*, above note 26, 9–10 (footnote omitted). It should be noted that Additional Protocol I was not applicable to the conflict as a matter of law.
[285] PKK Statement to the United Nations, 24 January 1995.

regards as legitimate targets of military attack the units, personnel and facilities belonging to the following:

a. The Armed Forces of the Philippines;
b. The Philippine National Police;
c. The paramilitary forces; and
d. The intelligence personnel of the foregoing.

It also indicated that '[c]ivil servants of the GRP [Government] are not subject to military attack, unless in specific cases they belong to any of the four abovestated categories'.[286]

These statements reflect the position of the law of armed conflict in certain respects, considering as they do members of the armed forces and the paramilitary forces to be 'legitimate targets of military attack'. The clarifications surrounding civil servants are useful in light of the fact that, in some conflicts, any representative of the state is considered to be a legitimate target. The NDFP's limitation of intelligence personnel to the intelligence personnel of the listed categories is to be welcomed as not considering all intelligence personnel to be legitimate objects of attack. For example, intelligence personnel who are tasked with activities entirely unrelated to the conflict could not be considered legitimate targets of attack, although, in practice, differentiation along these lines may prove difficult. However, the NDFP's limitation is eroded almost entirely with its interpretation of 'intelligence personnel' as including 'casual Government informers, such as peasants who answer when asked by [government] soldiers to identify local CPP [Communist Party of the Philippines] members or someone who calls the police when faced with NPA extortion'.[287] This is extremely broad and certainly inconsistent with international standards.

For its part, in 1998, the Kosovo Liberation Army (KLA) took the view that 'all Serbian forces, whether the police, the military, or armed civilians, are our enemy'.[288] The SPLM/A indicated in 1984 that the following individuals and entities are 'declared enemies of the people and therefore target of the SPLA/SPLM':

a) The incumbent administration of Jaafer Mohammed Nimeiri, its appendages and supporting institutions.

b) Any subsequent reactionary administration that may emerge while the revolutionary war is still being waged.

c) Any individual or group of individuals directly or indirectly cooperating with the autocratic regime in Khartoum in order to sustain or consolidate its rule and to undermine the objectives and efforts of the People's Revolution.

d) Any individual or group of individuals who wage counter-revolutionary war against the SPLA/SPLM or who circulate any subversive literature, verbally or in written form against the SPLA/SPLM with the intent to discredit it or turn public opinion against it.

e) Persons acting as agents or spies for the Sudan Government.

---

[286] NDFP Declaration of Undertaking to Apply the Geneva Conventions of 1949 and Protocol I of 1977, 5 July 1996, reproduced in NDFP, *Declaration of Undertaking to Apply the Geneva Conventions of 1949 and Protocol I of 1977* (NDFP Human Rights Monitoring Committee Booklet No 6) 13.
[287] Report of the Special Rapporteur on extrajudicial, summary or arbitrary executions, A/HRC/8/3/Add.2, 16 April 2008, para 31.
[288] 'Krasniqi Explains UCK's Origins, Structure', Pristina *Koha Ditore*, 12 July 1998, Exhibit P00328 in ICTY *Haradinaj* trial (ICTY translation).

f) Armed bandits that operate to rob ordinary citizens, rape their women or commit any other crime against them, their movable or immovable properties or any other property of the People's revolution.

g) Individuals or groups of people who propagate or advocate ideas, ideologies or philosophies or organize societies and organizations inside the country or abroad, that tend to uphold or perpetuate the oppression of the people or their exploitation by the Khartoum regime or by any other system of similar nature.[289]

Just as with the other mentioned armed groups, the SPLM/A considered a much broader section of society to be legitimate targets of attack. In particular, objects of potential attack include 'individuals directly or indirectly cooperating with' the government and persons who advocate ideas that perpetuate the oppression. This, and other aspects of the SPLM/A position, widens matters considerably and, again, falls short of international standards.

Even more broadly, some armed groups define as a military objective *any* representative of the state. This would include ministries and ministers entirely unrelated to the conduct of the armed conflict and again would clearly violate international humanitarian law.

A more humanitarian approach?

In international human rights law, the right not to be arbitrarily deprived of one's life is central. Indeed, it is the supreme right on which all other rights are built. As such, the protections afforded to the right to life are substantial. The European Convention on Human Rights, for example, provides for the right to life and observes that deprivation of life shall not constitute a violation of the Convention 'when it results from the use of force which is no more than absolutely necessary' in certain specified situations.[290] This rule applies to civilians, members of the armed forces, and members of the non-state armed group alike, such that only force that is 'absolutely necessary' may be directed even against fighters in times of armed conflict. The exact consequences of this rule are yet to be seen but the implication is that lethal force may not be used against fighters in situations in which it is feasible to arrest them. This idea is most developed in the European human rights system; however, it is by no means limited to that system.[291] Accordingly, to kill fighters when it would have been feasible to capture them constitutes a violation of human rights law. This is an important divergence from the position under international humanitarian law, which, as has been discussed, differs as between civilians, civilians taking a direct part in hostilities, and members of the armed forces or the military wing of an armed group.

A similar approach has, however, started to influence international humanitarian law. The Israeli Supreme Court has adopted a view similar to human rights law, indeed drawing on human rights norms, albeit in the context of belligerent occupation.[292] The 2009 ICRC Interpretive Guidance reached a largely similar conclusion, albeit through a different line of reasoning, namely the interplay of the international humanitarian law principles of military necessity and humanity. It suggested that, in light of the principle

---

[289] SPLM/A, Penal and Disciplinary Laws, 4 July 1984, section 29(1)(c), quoted in *Customary International Humanitarian Law, Volume II: Practice*, 126–7.
[290] ECHR, Article 2.
[291] See eg *de Guerrero v Colombia*, Communication No 45/1979, View of 31 March 1982, paras 13.2–3.
[292] *Public Committee against Torture*, above note 2, para 40.

by which no more force should be used than is required to achieve a legitimate military purpose, in certain situations, 'it would defy basic notions of humanity to kill an adversary or to refrain from giving him or her an opportunity to surrender where there manifestly is no necessity for the use of lethal force'.[293] The Guidance makes it clear that a party is not required 'to take additional risks for themselves or the civilian population in order to capture an armed adversary alive', and it recognizes that the approach may not be workable in 'classic battlefield situations involving large-scale confrontations'.[294] It also notes that such an approach is particularly relevant 'where a party to the conflict exercises effective territorial control, most notably in... non-international armed conflicts'.[295]

However, the ICRC position has led to considerable criticism.[296] Three additional concerns may be raised in the specific context of non-international armed conflict, some of which are not inconsistent with the Interpretive Guidance but may be read alongside it. First, the intensity of fighting in certain non-international armed conflicts is as severe as that which exists in international armed conflicts and can involve 'classic battlefield situations'. The final stages of the armed conflict in Sri Lanka in 2009 is an example. Thus, when the Guidance notes that the approach is particularly relevant 'where a party to the conflict exercises effective territorial control, most notably in... non-international armed conflicts',[297] the focus should be on the notion of effective territorial control rather than the notable situation posited for when it may apply. The crucial distinction is not whether the conflict is an international or non-international one but whether there are appropriate situations within either type of conflict in which the approach could be utilized. In many non-international armed conflicts, it may not prove feasible to adopt such a position. One situation in which it may prove appropriate are the areas outside those in which the fighting takes place, as the Guidance indicates, such area not being limited to the notion of the battlefield.[298] In particular, this would be the case for individuals who are located abroad (excluding adjacent border regions), for example members of the political wing of a non-state armed group who control hostilities from abroad. With respect to such individuals, it may be appropriate to apply the human rights law approach. This has the merit of reflecting the realities on the ground; however, it is very much a case of *lex ferenda*.[299] A second area of concern relates to the capacities of the parties to the conflict: '[a] government has the alternative of law enforcement and of applying domestic criminal law, and must therefore plan an operation in such a way so as to maximize the possibility of being able

---

[293] ICRC *Interpretive Guidance*, above note 5, 82.
[294] Ibid, 80, 82, and fn 221.
[295] Ibid, 81. See also K Watkin, 'Assessing Proportionality: Moral Complexity and Legal Rules' (2005) 8 *YIHL* 3, 40–1.
[296] WH Parks, 'Part IX of the ICRC "Direct Participation in Hostilities" Study: No Mandate, No Expertise, and Legally Incorrect' (2010) 42 *New York University Journal of International Law and Politics* 769; MN Schmitt, 'The Interpretive Guidance on the Notion of Direct Participation in Hostilities: A Critical Analysis' (2010) 1 *Harvard National Security Journal* 5, 42; Fenrick, Direct Participation in Hostilities, above note 224, 296–8; D Akande, 'Clearing the Fog of War? The ICRC's Interpretive Guidance on Direct Participation in Hostilities' (2010) 59 *ICLQ* 180, 191–2. But see Melzer, Response, above note 210, 892–912.
[297] ICRC *Interpretive Guidance*, above note 5, 81. See also K Watkin, 'Assessing Proportionality: Moral Complexity and Legal Rules' (2005) 8 *YIHL* 3, 40–1.
[298] C Droege, 'Elective Affinities? Human Rights and Humanitarian Law' (2008) 90 *IRRC* 501, 535–7; C Tomuschat, 'Human Rights and International Humanitarian Law' (2010) 21 *EJIL* 15, 22.
[299] N Lubell, 'Challenges in Applying Human Rights Law to Armed Conflict' (2005) 87 *IRRC* 737, 749–50. See also above, 251.

to arrest persons.'[300] The same is not necessarily true of all armed groups. Third, the consequence of all this is that different standards would be applicable within a single armed conflict, depending on such factors as the location of relevant individuals. This may prove workable; however, identifying the situations in which the human rights law approach is the most appropriate remains difficult and would have to be ascertained on a case-by-case basis.

2.6.5 Conclusion

To summarize, civilians benefit from various protections, including not being made the object of attack. Civilians who take a direct part in hostilities on an ad hoc basis fall outside the scope of these protections for such time as they take a direct part in hostilities. When they cease to take such part, their protections resume. Members of the state armed forces and of the military wing of the non-state armed group are treated in an altogether different manner. They do not benefit from the protections afforded to civilians and may be targeted at any time, although this may be queried as a matter of *lex ferenda*. Membership of the military wing of the non-state armed group, it is submitted, takes two principal forms—*de jure* membership pursuant to the law of the armed group and *de facto* membership, the latter referring to an ongoing chain of hostilities.

2.7 Investigations relating to losses of life

One aspect of the international human rights law rules relating to targeting that is potentially important for the law of armed conflict is the requirement of investigations in respect of certain losses of life. If an individual is killed as a result of the use of force, an investigation has to be carried out. The investigation must be independent and impartial,[301] prompt and expeditious,[302] and involve 'a sufficient element of public scrutiny'.[303] The European Court of Human Rights has held that, '[i]n particular, the authorities must take the reasonable steps available to them to secure the evidence concerning the incident, including, *inter alia*, eyewitness testimony, forensic evidence and, where appropriate, an autopsy which provides a complete and accurate record of injury and an objective analysis of clinical findings, including the cause of death'.[304] The European Court has also acknowledged that 'concrete constraints may compel the use of less effective measures of investigation or may cause an investigation to be delayed'.[305]

A requirement to investigate losses of life cannot be imported into the law of non-international armed conflict without appreciating the different context in which the latter body operates. A requirement to investigate losses of life exists in international

---

[300] M Sassòli, 'Taking Armed Groups Seriously: Ways to Improve their Compliance with International Humanitarian Law' (2010) 1 *International Humanitarian Legal Studies* 5, 19.

[301] Human Rights Committee, General Comment 31, 'Nature of the General Legal Obligation Imposed on States Parties to the Covenant', CCPR/C/21/Rev.1/Add.13, 2004, para 15; *Isayeva v Russia*, Application No 57950/00, Judgment, 24 February 2005, paras 209–14.

[302] *Kerimova and Others v Russia*, Application Nos 17170/04, 20792/04, 22448/04, 23360/04, 5681/05 and 5684/05, Judgment, 3 May 2011, para 265.

[303] Ibid, para 266.

[304] Ibid, para 264.

[305] *Al-Skeini and Others v United Kingdom*, Application No 55721/07, Judgment, 7 July 2011, para 164.

human rights law as death at the hands of state forces is considered exceptional and thus warranting investigation. In times of non-international armed conflict, however, deaths are by no means exceptional; indeed, they may be considered a normal part of the conflict.[306] To require investigations in non-international armed conflicts in respect of 'ordinary' losses of life may result in the obligation 'collaps[ing] under its own procedural weight'.[307] The idea that investigations are required into all deaths that result from non-international armed conflicts is to transplant the international human rights law norm into international humanitarian law without regard for the differences between the situations in which the two sets of rules apply.[308] This suggests that the requirements should apply only to *certain* losses in *certain* situations. However, identifying those losses and situations is difficult and a middle position needs to be found. This may relate to, for example, alleged violations of the law in which persons have lost their lives.[309]

The capabilities of non-state armed groups also need to be borne in mind in this regard. International human rights law was designed for states, thus presuming certain capabilities. Accordingly, non-state armed groups may not be in a position to comply with all the obligations surrounding investigations, for example those relating to evidence-collection and the reconstruction of events, ballistic examination, forensic examination, and autopsy.[310] Arguments of capability are not insurmountable as the discussion on the capabilities of armed groups and the translation of norms demonstrates.[311] Albeit considered in the context of international humanitarian law, similar approaches could be utilized for the purposes of international human rights law. Nonetheless, the potential for overloading is present and should be taken on board.

2.8 Objects benefiting from particular protections

2.8.1 Medical units and transports

Medical units and transports are defined in Additional Protocol I,[312] a definition that can be applied in non-international armed conflicts, as is the case with the definition of the wounded and sick themselves.[313] Additional Protocol II provides that '[m]edical units and transports shall be respected and protected at all times and shall not be the object of attack'.[314] The rule is one of customary international law.[315] These protections derive from the protections that are afforded to the wounded and sick, and regard may be had to the interpretations of 'respect' and 'protect' of the wounded and sick in order to understand the similar protections that are afforded to medical units and

---

[306] D Kretzmer, 'Re-Thinking the Application of IHL in Non-International Armed Conflicts' (2009) 42 *Israel Law Review* 8, 36.
[307] K Watkin, 'Assessing Proportionality: Moral Complexity and Legal Rules' (2005) 8 *YIHL* 3, 40.
[308] See generally above, 65 et seq.
[309] Special Rapporteur on Extrajudicial, summary or arbitrary executions, E/CN.4/2006/53, 8 March 2006, paras 33–43. See also Melzer, *Targetted Killing*, above note 205, 432–3.
[310] See eg *Kaya v Turkey*, Judgment, 19 February 1998, para 89; *Gülec v Turkey*, Judgment, 27 July 1998, paras 78–82; *Isayeva*, above note 301, paras 211–4. See also Second Report of the United Nations Observer Mission in El Salvador, A/46/658, 15 November 1991, para 33.
[311] See above, 72–6.
[312] Additional Protocol I, Article 8.
[313] See above, 274.
[314] Additional Protocol II, Article 11(1).
[315] Rome Statute, Article 8(2)(e)(iv); Customary International Humanitarian Law, Rules 28 and 29.

transports.[316] At the very least, medical units and transports are not to be made the objects of attack. The Rome Statute thus lists as a war crime, '[i]ntentionally directing attacks against...medical units and transport...using the distinctive emblems of the Geneva Conventions in conformity with international law'.[317]

Medical units and transports benefit from the particular protections provided that they are assigned exclusively to medical purposes.[318] While they are so assigned, they are to be respected and protected at all times, including when they are not carrying the wounded and sick. Protection as medical units and transports cease when they are used 'to commit hostile acts, outside their humanitarian function'.[319] Hostile acts include housing fighters and storing arms. For example, in 1962, during the attempted secession of Katanga from the Democratic Republic of the Congo, the UN, which was involved in the situation, stated that the Katangan forces 'regularly abused the Red Cross symbol, employing vehicles painted with red crosses to transport gendarmes and to snipe at United Nations personnel'.[320] In the event that a hostile act is committed, a warning should be given before the unit or transport is attacked. A reasonable period of time between the warning and the attack should be afforded, whenever appropriate,[321] allowing the hostile act to cease,[322] or the wounded and sick to be removed, such time varying according to the particular circumstances at hand. Whether the hostile act renders the unit or transport a legitimate target depends on the law of targeting.[323]

Equipping the medical unit or transport with 'light individual weapons for their own defence or for that of the wounded and sick in their charge', guarding the unit 'by a picket or by sentries or by an escort', the presence of weapons and ammunition in the unit taken from the wounded until disposed of, and 'members of the armed forces or other combatants [who] are in the unit for medical reasons', do not amount to acts harmful to the enemy or hostile acts.[324] In many ways, this is akin to the arming of civilians or the presence of fighters in the civilian population which does not automatically deprive the civilian population of their civilian status. The guidance is to be found in the law of international armed conflict, but its applicability to non-international armed conflict has been suggested by states.[325]

For the protections of medical units and transports to be effective, the objects in question must be identifiable. Identification is made possible through the emblem of the red cross, red crescent, or red crystal.[326] However, '[t]he use of the emblem is optional; medical personnel and medical units and transports are protected in any

---

[316] See above, 274.
[317] Rome Statute, Article 8(2)(e)(ii).
[318] Customary International Humanitarian Law, Rule 28; ICRC, *Commentary on the Additional Protocols*, above note 6, 1433.
[319] Additional Protocol II, Article 11(2); Customary International Humanitarian Law, Rules 28 and 29.
[320] *Yearbook of the United Nations 1961* (UN, 1962) 72–3.
[321] Additional Protocol II, Article 11(2).
[322] Agreement of 22 May 1992, above note 26, Article 2.2.
[323] See above, 342–7.
[324] Additional Protocol I, Article 13(2).
[325] UK *Manual*, above note 43, 407 fn 111.
[326] See Additional Protocol II, Article 12 (red cross and red crescent). Additional Protocol II also includes the emblem of the red lion and sun. However, these have not been used since 1980. In 2005, the emblem of the red crystal was adopted. See Protocol Additional to the Geneva Conventions of 12 August 1949, and Relating to the Adoption of an Additional Distinctive Emblem (Protocol III), of 8 December 2005. See generally F Bugnion, *Red Cross, Red Crescent, Red Crystal* (ICRC, 2007).

event'.[327] The emblem serves an identificatory purpose rather than constituting a prerequisite for protection. It is the responsibility of the 'authority concerned' to display the emblem,[328] such term including both the governmental authorities and the authorities of the non-state armed group.[329] In the case of a non-state armed group, its leaders will be responsible for ensuring the display of the emblem.[330]

Protections afforded to medical units are generally respected, or at least allegations of violations are denied. In this regard, the Customary International Humanitarian Law study notes:

578. In 1991, an armed opposition group denied allegations that a hospital had been shelled. It stated that it had been ordered not to shell the compound in which the field hospital was located at any time and reiterated its intention not only to spare the facility, but to facilitate its supply of food and medicine.

579. In 1993, a faction of an armed opposition group insisted that it had issued orders to its troops not to fire in the vicinity of hospitals and not to enter hospitals with weapons.

580. In 1993, the Minister of Health of a separatist entity complained of a flight breaking the sound barrier over a hospital marked with the red cross, which caused damage, and of the shelling of a hospital.

581. In 1994, in a letter to the ICRC, an armed opposition group reminded the ICRC of the necessity of evacuating its medical facility. The letter pointed out that an officer of a UN peacekeeping mission operating in the country had acknowledged that it was not possible to ensure the security of a medical unit situated so close to a military camp. The officer had added that the belligerents' obligations amounted to refraining from deliberate attacks on the unit only. The ICRC should thus choose a site that was not as close to military installations.[331]

More recently, in 2011, the Taliban of Afghanistan used an ambulance to launch an attack. Following condemnation by the ICRC, the Taliban admitted its use and pledged not to do so again.[332] Statements such as these, consisting of denials and the like, support the existence of a rule prohibiting attacks against medical units and transports. Similar commitments on point can also be found in ad hoc agreements concluded between parties to conflicts.[333]

2.8.2 Cultural property

Cultural property is afforded certain protection in the international humanitarian law of non-international armed conflict. The protections emanate from conventional international law,[334] as well as customary international law,[335] although the precise

---

[327] ICRC, *Commentary on the Additional Protocols*, above note 6, 1440. See also UK *Manual*, above note 43, 407 fn 115.
[328] Additional Protocol II, Article 12.
[329] Cf F Kalshoven, 'International Humanitarian Law and Violation of Medical Neutrality', in F Kalshoven (ed), *Reflections on the Law of War: Collected Essays* (Nijhoff, 2007) 1019.
[330] ICRC, *Commentary on the Additional Protocols*, above note 6, 1441.
[331] *Customary International Humanitarian Law, Volume II: Practice*, above note 84, 535 (footnotes omitted; all taken from 'ICRC archive documents').
[332] UNAMA, Afghanistan: Midyear Report 2011 Protection of Civilians in Armed Conflict (July 2011) 14.
[333] See eg CARHRIHL, above note 37, Part IV, Article 4(3).
[334] 1954 Convention on Cultural Property; Second Protocol to the 1954 Convention; Additional Protocol II, Article 16. See also, in part, Rome Statute, Article 8(2)(e)(iv).
[335] Rome Statute, Article 8(2)(e)(iv); *Tadić* Decision on Interlocutory Appeal on Jurisdiction, above note 25, para 98; *Hadžihasanović* Decision on Appeal of Rule 98*bis* Decision, above note 51, para 46; *Strugar* Trial Judgment, above note 50, para 230; Customary International Humanitarian Law, Rules 38–40; Darfur Commission Report, above note 25, para 166.

scope of the customary obligations is unclear. States have taken the view that the protections afforded to cultural property are particularly important in time of non-international armed conflict,[336] given that, in conflicts with an ethnic or religious character in particular, cultural property is attacked in order to destroy the history, culture, and identity of the ethnic or religious group. The target in such conflicts is not so much the property as the people.[337]

Definition of cultural property

The Hague Convention on Cultural Property contains a detailed definition of cultural property for the purposes of the Convention. The crucial element is that the protected property be 'movable or immovable property of great importance to the cultural heritage of every people', 'buildings whose main and effective purpose is to preserve or exhibit the movable cultural property', or 'centres containing a large amount of cultural property'.[338] The reference to 'the cultural heritage of every people' is ambiguous, as it could be read in the broad sense of 'each and every people', or in the narrow sense of 'mankind'; opinions on point are split.[339] The United Kingdom has adopted a middle position, by which the items are required to be 'of international rather than local importance'.[340] Reference in the Preamble to the Convention 'that damage to cultural property belonging to any people whatsoever means damage to the cultural heritage of all mankind, since each people makes its contribution to the culture of the world' suggests the former view is correct. The Convention definition of cultural property suffers from another difficulty: the requirement that the property be of 'great importance' is subjective, and it is difficult, if not impossible, to set out criteria by which to judge importance.[341] Additional Protocol II defines cultural property somewhat differently.[342] However, the two definitions are more or less the same with any differences generally considered to be superficial.[343]

Application to non-international armed conflict

As noted above, there is a conventional basis for the protections afforded to cultural property in non-international armed conflict. However, the precise scope of the protections is unclear in light of the unfortunate wording of the treaty. Article 19 of the Hague Convention on Cultural Property provides that 'each party to the conflict shall be bound to apply, as a minimum, the provisions of the present Convention which relate to respect for cultural property'. The reference to 'respect for cultural

---

[336] See eg Official Records, above note 8, Vol 7, 115, para 59 (Greece). See also 115–16, paras 61–3, 65–6, 70, 73, and 75. The view was not unanimous: see 115, para 60 (India); 115 para 64 (United States).

[337] PJ Boylan, Review of the Convention for the Protection of Cultural Property in the Event of Armed Conflict, UNESCO Doc. CLT-93/WS/12 (1993) A.8.

[338] Hague Convention on Cultural Property, Article 1.

[339] For the former view, see R O'Keefe, *The Protection of Cultural Property in Armed Conflict* (Cambridge University Press, 2006) 103–4; IIHL *Manual*, above note 55, 57; K Chamberlain, *War and Cultural Heritage* (Institute of Art and Law, 2004) 29; Dinstein, above note 75, 157. For the latter view, see Rogers, above note 1, 140; Green, above note 83, 154 fn 214.

[340] UK *Manual*, above note 43, 71 fn 116.

[341] J Toman, *The Protection of Cultural Property in the Event of Armed Conflict* (Dartmouth, 1996) 50.

[342] Additional Protocol II, Article 16.

[343] *Kordić* Appeal Judgment, above note 22 para 91; ICRC, *Commentary on the Additional Protocols*, above note 6, 1469; R O'Keefe, 'Protection of Cultural Property', in D Fleck (ed), *The Handbook of International Humanitarian Law* (Oxford University Press, 2008) 431, 439–41. Cf *Customary International Humanitarian Law, Volume I: Rules*, above note 84, 130.

property' is unclear. On one view, the reference is to Article 4 alone, Article 4 being titled 'respect for cultural property'.³⁴⁴ Another, more expansive, view holds that the protections afforded by certain other articles also relate to 'respect for cultural property' and therefore apply to non-international armed conflict.³⁴⁵ At any rate, the Convention is considered difficult to apply in non-international armed conflict as it was designed for application in international armed conflicts.³⁴⁶ Both points demonstrate the necessity of designing a Convention for application in non-international armed conflict, or in both international and non-international armed conflicts, rather than tagging on non-international armed conflicts to an instrument designed for international armed conflicts.³⁴⁷

Other conventional instruments also afford protection to cultural property in non-international armed conflict. The Second Protocol to the Hague Convention applies to non-international armed conflicts,³⁴⁸ an extension which proved controversial.³⁴⁹ General international humanitarian law treaties also afford protection, as is the case with Additional Protocol II.³⁵⁰ The Rome Statute is broader but also narrower in its protections with its prohibition on '[i]ntentionally directing attacks against buildings dedicated to religion, education, art, science or charitable purposes, [or] historic monuments... provided they are not military objectives'.³⁵¹ The protection is broader given that not all such buildings will amount to cultural property. However, it is narrower in that only attacks against such buildings are prohibited.

The protections

Hague Convention on Cultural Property

The Hague Convention on Cultural Property affords two levels of protection—general protection and special protection. General protection applies to all cultural property while special protection applies to a subset thereof. The Convention also provides for rules on the transport of cultural property, personnel protecting cultural property, the distinctive emblem, and execution of the Convention.

In terms of general protection, four rules can be discerned. First, parties to the conflict are prohibited from using cultural property or its immediate surroundings 'for purposes which are likely to expose it to destruction or damage',³⁵² an exception being made for imperative military necessity.³⁵³ Imperative military necessity cannot be equated with 'military convenience',³⁵⁴ or even ordinary notions of military necessity. Nor is it the same as the use for military purposes by the other side.³⁵⁵ The former are too broad; the latter too narrow. Rather, imperative military necessity means that 'the

---

³⁴⁴ Rogers, above note 1, 140 fn 48; O'Keefe, above note 339, 98.
³⁴⁵ Toman, above note 341, 214–15; Chamberlain, above note 339, 72.
³⁴⁶ J Hladik, 'The Review Process of the 1954 Hague Convention for the Protection of Cultural Property in the Event of Armed Conflict and its Impact on International Humanitarian Law' (1998) 1 *YIHL* 313, 313.
³⁴⁷ See above, 61–5.
³⁴⁸ Articles 3 and 22(1).
³⁴⁹ UNESCO, Diplomatic Conference on the Second Protocol to the Hague Convention for the Protection of Cultural Property in the Event of Armed Conflict: Summary Report (1999) paras 33–5.
³⁵⁰ Article 16.
³⁵¹ Rome Statute, Article 8(2)(e)(iv).
³⁵² Article 4(1). See also UK *Manual*, above note 43, 393; IIHL *Manual*, above note 55, 56–7.
³⁵³ Article 4(2).
³⁵⁴ See UNESCO Doc CLT-97/CONF.208/3, para 5(ii) and 155 EX/51, Annex, para 14, cited in O'Keefe, above note 339, 123.
³⁵⁵ Ibid, 127.

military objective cannot be reached in any other manner'.[356] This means that when the Khmer Rouge based itself in and around the Angkor Wat in Siem Reap, Cambodia, in 1979 and used it to discourage an attack, it violated the relevant rule.[357] Second, parties are prohibited from directing hostilities against cultural property,[358] again subject to imperative military necessity,[359] an exception that has been criticized.[360] Thus, the 1998 LTTE bombing of the Temple of the Tooth, a UNESCO World Heritage Site that is considered to house a tooth of the Buddha, in Kandy, Sri Lanka, violated the law relating to cultural property. Third, parties are prohibited from carrying out belligerent reprisals against cultural property.[361] Fourth, they are also required to prohibit, prevent, and put a stop to theft, pillage, and misappropriation of, and vandalism against, cultural property, and refrain from requisitioning cultural property,[362] obligations which arise both in respect of the parties' own troops and the general population. This is occasionally done, for example, with certain cultural facilities being secured, such as during the conflict in Bosnia in December 1993, and certain cultural objects being moved, such as a statue of 'Our Lady of Madhu', which is considered to have 'healing and protective properties' during the conflict in Sri Lanka in 2008.[363] Each of these rules is considered to be of customary status.[364] As with other aspects of international humanitarian law, the rules on the protection of cultural property do not cover each and every destruction of cultural property in non-international armed conflict. Thus, the destruction of the Buddhas of Bamiyan during the conflict in Afghanistan did not engage the relevant rules given that the destruction did not relate to the conflict.[365]

The rules on special protection are inapplicable to non-international armed conflicts. The primary benefit of the rules on special protection is that immunity may be waived 'in exceptional cases of *unavoidable* military necessity' and 'only by the officer commanding a force the equivalent of a division in size or larger'.[366] This is not a great loss. Whether greater protection is afforded by 'unavoidable' rather than 'imperative' military necessity is unclear, and thus the only real benefit derives from the level at which the decision is made. Accordingly, special protection is generally considered of little use,[367] and offering only 'extraordinarily minor' protections.[368]

---

[356] KJ Partsch, 'Protection of Cultural Property', in D Fleck (ed), *The Handbook of International Humanitarian Law* (Oxford University Press, 1995) 377, 388. See also Rogers, note 1, 144.

[357] It should be noted that the conflict during the period in question was most likely an international one.

[358] Article 4(1). See also UK *Manual*, above note 43, 393; IIHL *Manual*, above note 55, 56–7.

[359] Article 4(2).

[360] PJ Boylan, Review of the Convention for the Protection of Cultural Property in the Event of Armed Conflict, UNESCO Doc. CLT-93/WS/12 (1993) 4.16.

[361] Article 4(4). On belligerent reprisals, see below, 448 et seq.

[362] Article 4(3). See also UK *Manual*, above note 43, 393 (stealing, misappropriation, confiscation, wilful damage); IIHL *Manual*, above note 55, 56–7 (pillage, seizure, vandalism).

[363] On Bosnia, see *Customary International Humanitarian Law: Volume II*, above note 84, 799; on Sri Lanka, see F Harrison, 'Tamil Tigers Appeal over Shrine', *BBC News*, 18 May 2008.

[364] US *Commander's Handbook*, above note 82, 425, para 8.5.1.6 fn 122; *Tadić* Decision on Interlocutory Appeal on Jurisdiction, above note 25, para 98 (via Article 19); Customary International Humanitarian Law, Rules 38A, 39, 40B; Constitutional Court of Colombia, Decision C-291/07, reproduced and translated in M Sassòli, AA Bouvier, and A Quintin, *How Does Law Protect in War? Volume III* (ICRC, 2011) 2255 (protection of cultural property more generally).

[365] See O'Keefe, above note 339, 98–9. Cf F Francioni and F Lenzerini, 'The Destruction of the Buddhas of Bamiyan and International Law' (2003) 14 EJIL 619, 632–3.

[366] Article 11(2) (emphasis added).

[367] Rogers, above note 1, 142.

[368] O'Keefe, above note 339, 140.

Pursuant to Article 19(3) of the Hague Convention, and modelled on the equivalent clause in common Article 3, UNESCO 'may offer its services to the parties to the conflict'. UNESCO has so offered, albeit only on occasion. For example, during the attempted secession of Biafra from Nigeria (1967–70), UNESCO wrote to the Federal Government of Nigeria indicating that, 'should this be considered desirable, Unesco could offer its services to the Parties to the conflict'.[369] The Federal Government replied that 'it was not inclined to accept an offer of services' but provided an assurance to the Director-General that it 'had scrupulously observed the provisions of the Convention'.[370] UNESCO also issued appeals for compliance during the conflict in the former Yugoslavia.[371]

Additional Protocol II
For its part, Additional Protocol II provides that, '[w]ithout prejudice to the provisions of the Hague Convention... it is prohibited to commit any acts of hostility directed against historic monuments, works of art or places of worship which constitute the cultural or spiritual heritage of peoples, and to use them in support of the military effort'.[372] *Any* act of hostility is thus prohibited, irrespective of military necessity. However, the proposition is not as all-encompassing as may seem at first sight. Some states, on ratification of the Protocol, stated that, 'if the objects protected by this Article are unlawfully used for military purposes they will thereby lose their protection from attacks directed against such unlawful military uses',[373] bringing it closer to the standard of the Hague Convention. Furthermore, for states that are parties to the Hague Convention and Additional Protocol II, the 'without prejudice' clause acts as a *renvoi* to the Hague Convention, giving the latter priority in the event of any inconsistency.[374] Thus, for these parties, the imperative military necessity standard is brought into play. The irony is, then, that participation in the Hague Convention actually serves to weaken the protection otherwise afforded to cultural property.[375]

Second Protocol to the Hague Convention on Cultural Property
Enhanced protection is afforded to certain property through the Second Protocol to the Hague Convention, which applies to non-international armed conflict.[376] The granting of enhanced protection is subject to an elaborate procedure, including approval by a special committee.[377] Cultural property under enhanced protection does not benefit from total immunity. Its immunity may be withdrawn or may be lost 'if, and for as long as, the property has, by its use, become a military objective'.[378] In such a situation, the property may be attacked if: (a) 'the attack is the only feasible means of terminating the use of the property' as a military objective; (b) 'all feasible precautions are taken in the choice of means and methods of attack'; and (c) 'unless

---

[369] UNESCO, *Information on the Implementation of the Convention for the Protection of Cultural Property in Case of Armed Conflict, The Hague 1954* (UNESCO, Paris, 1970) 8.
[370] Ibid.
[371] See O'Keefe, above note 339, 182–4.
[372] Additional Protocol II, Article 16.
[373] Reservations and Declarations made on ratification of the United Kingdom, in Schindler and Toman, above note 95, 317 (in the context of Additional Protocol I).
[374] Resolution 20(IV) of the 1974–7 Diplomatic Conference.
[375] O'Keefe, above note 339, 232.
[376] Article 10.
[377] Article 11.
[378] Article 13(1)(b).

circumstances do not permit' for reasons of 'immediate self-defence', (i) 'the attack is ordered at the highest operational level of command', (ii) 'effective advance warning is issued to the opposing forces requiring the termination of the use' of the cultural property as a military objective, and (iii) 'reasonable time is given to the opposing forces to redress the situation'.[379] Thus, the descriptor 'enhanced protection' has the potential to mislead. The protection is only enhanced in the areas of the level of command that can order an attack, the warning to be given, and time for redress. The underlying ideas surrounding protection and loss thereof remain the same as those of the Hague Convention.[380]

The Second Protocol also gives meaning to the 'imperative military necessity' idea of the Hague Convention. Article 6(a) of the Second Protocol provides that:

waiver on the basis of imperative military necessity pursuant to Article 4 paragraph 2 of the Convention may only be invoked to direct an act of hostility against cultural property when and for as long as:

i. that cultural property has, by its function, been made into a military objective; and
ii. there is no feasible alternative available to obtain a similar military advantage to that offered by directing an act of hostility against that objective.

After much debate, and as a compromise, the word 'function' was used as opposed to the more traditional word 'use', function being broader than use but narrower than location.[381] The 'no feasible alternative' requirement has the important effect that 'when there is a choice between several military objectives and one of them is cultural property, the latter shall not be attacked'.[382] The 'decision to invoke imperative military necessity shall only be taken by an officer commanding a force the equivalent of a battalion in size or larger, or a force smaller in size where circumstances do not permit otherwise'.[383] If there is to be an attack, 'an effective advance warning shall be given whenever circumstances permit'.[384]

Pursuant to Article 6(b) of the Second Protocol, a waiver to 'use cultural property for purposes which are likely to expose it to destruction or damage' may only be invoked 'when and for as long as no choice is possible between such use of the cultural property and another feasible method for obtaining a similar military advantage'. The classic example is 'the case of retreating troops who need to take shelter in a cultural property for defence purposes'.[385]

Under Article 7 of the Second Protocol, precautions must be taken, including to 'do everything feasible to verify that the objectives to be attacked are not cultural property protected under Article 4 of the Convention' and to avoid or at least minimize incidental damage to protected cultural property. Article 7 also calls for refraining 'from deciding to launch any attack which may be expected to cause incidental damage to cultural property protected under Article 4 of the Convention which would be excessive in relation to the concrete and direct military advantage anticipated'.

---

[379] Article 13(2).
[380] See J-M Henckaerts, 'New Rules for the Protection of Cultural Property in Armed Conflict' (1999) 81 *IRRC* 593, 610.
[381] For the debates during the drafting, see ibid, 604–6; O'Keefe, above note 339, 252–3.
[382] Henckaerts, New Rules, above note 380, 601 and 602.
[383] Article 6(c).
[384] Article 6(d).
[385] Henckaerts, New Rules, above note 380, 606.

Customary international law

In addition to the customary norms that are based on the conventional norms and which were considered above, the Customary International Humanitarian Law study posits two additional customary norms in the area of cultural property: '[s]pecial care must be taken in military operations to avoid damage to buildings dedicated to religion, art, science, education or charitable purposes and historic monuments unless they are military objectives' and '[a]ll seizure of or destruction or wilful damage done to institutions dedicated to religion, charity, education, the arts and sciences, historic monuments and works of art and science is prohibited'.[386] The scope of these norms is open to question as the protections are broader than those emanating from the Hague Regulations or the Rome Statute and in respect of objects that are broader than the narrow definition of cultural property.[387] Nonetheless, both protections are linked to existing norms, namely the requirement to take precautions and the prohibition on misappropriation and attacks and may be considered specific manifestations of them.

2.8.3 Dams, dykes, and nuclear electrical generating stations

Additional Protocol II provides that: '[w]orks or installations containing dangerous forces, namely dams, dykes and nuclear electrical generating stations, shall not be made the object of attack, even where these objects are military objectives, if such attack may cause the release of dangerous forces and consequent severe losses among the civilian population.'[388]

Special protection is afforded to such works and installations in light of the 'serious consequences that may ensue if they are destroyed'.[389] The rule does not seek to protect the objects themselves from destruction but the civilian population. Two consequences follow. First, if the attack would not cause the release of dangerous forces, or if that release would not cause severe losses among the civilian population, the attack is not prohibited. Second, if the attack would cause the release of dangerous forces and if that release in turn would cause severe losses among the civilian population, the object may not be attacked even if it is a military objective, for example, 'the anti-aircraft gun on the dyke'.[390] However, what is meant by 'severe' losses it is not altogether clear. What is clear is that it is not a balancing test or a proportionality test between the military value of the object and the effect on civilians. As the United States has indicated: 'If severe losses would result, then the attack is forbidden, no matter how important the target.'[391] The list of objects which shall not be made the object of attack is exhaustive, even though attacking other objects may release equally dangerous forces. The particular case of oil rigs and petroleum refineries was raised during the Diplomatic Conference but not taken up.[392] Similarly, chemical and bacteriological installations are not

---

[386] Rules 38A and 40A.
[387] Cf Hague Regulations, Article 27.
[388] Additional Protocol II, Article 15.
[389] ICRC, *Commentary on the Additional Protocols*, above note 6, 1462.
[390] RR Baxter, 'The Duties of Combatants and the Conduct of Hostilities (Law of The Hague)', in UNESCO (ed), *International Dimensions of Humanitarian Law* (UNESCO, 1988) 93, 120.
[391] 'The Position of the United States on Current Law of War Agreements: Remarks of Judge Abraham D Sofaer, Legal Adviser, United States Department of State, January 22, 1987' (1987) 2 *American University Journal of International Law and Policy* 460, 468.
[392] See *Official Records*, above note 8, Vol 15, 352; ICRC, *Commentary on the Additional Protocols*, above note 6, 1462.

protected under this rule.³⁹³ The ordinary rules on the targeting of military objectives would apply to these classes of objects as a matter of law; however, parties to non-international armed would be advised to bear the prohibition in mind even in respect of non-listed but equally dangerous works and installations.

There has been some suggestion that the rule would not be complied with in times of armed conflict. It is thus revealing that at least one non-state armed group has claimed to have followed the proscription. The FMLN of El Salvador indicated in 1988 that, when it occupied 'the two most important hydro-electric plants in the country', it 'concentrated on annihilating the troops stationed there and damaging the machinery', but did not destroy the dams or dykes 'since they are installations expressly protected by Article 56 of Additional Protocol I',³⁹⁴ a similar provision of the law of international armed conflict.

The Customary International Humanitarian Law study suggests that the customary equivalent of the rule is that: '[p]articular care must be taken if works and installations containing dangerous forces, namely dams, dykes and nuclear electrical generating stations, and other installations located at or in their vicinity are attacked, in order to avoid the release of dangerous forces and consequent severe losses among the civilian population.'³⁹⁵ The framing of this rule is rather curious and it weakens the protections afforded by the conventional rule quite considerably. Pursuant to this purported customary rule, attacks against the listed objects may be carried out if they constitute a military objective subject to 'particular care' being taken. The particular care required is essentially that which is to be undertaken through the ordinary rules on precautions.³⁹⁶ As such, the effect of this rule is to downgrade the protections that are afforded to the listed objects in conventional law and to equate them with ordinary military objectives.

There are two reasons which suggest that this framing is inaccurate. First, the equivalent provision in Additional Protocol I contains rules relating to the cessation of protection for the listed objects in certain instances.³⁹⁷ However, these rules are narrower than the purported scope of the customary rule. Second, and more importantly, the broadened rules relating to the cessation of protection have been extended to non-international armed conflict. Yet, Additional Protocol II is entirely silent on the cessation of protection for the listed objects.³⁹⁸ Furthermore, the military manuals of a number of states reflect the divergence in position, referencing the absolute prohibition on attacking the listed objects in non-international armed conflict while accepting the cessation of protection for the listed objects in international armed conflict.³⁹⁹ Likewise, reservations made by states in respect of the Additional Protocol I provision have not been made in respect of the Additional Protocol II provision.⁴⁰⁰ Thus, the rule diverges between international armed conflicts and non-international armed conflicts. Indeed, when the Deputy Legal Advisor of the (United States) State Department was

---

³⁹³ Green, above note 83, 325.
³⁹⁴ FMLN, above note 26, 15–16.
³⁹⁵ Rule 42.
³⁹⁶ On which see above, 351–6.
³⁹⁷ Article 56(2).
³⁹⁸ See Article 15.
³⁹⁹ See the military manuals of Argentina, Canada, Netherlands, quoted in *Customary International Humanitarian Law, Volume II: Practice*, above note 84, 814–40.
⁴⁰⁰ See the reservations of France and the United Kingdom, in Schindler and Toman, above note 95, 800 and 814.

questioned about the divergent position of the United States concerning the rule in the two types of conflicts, the Legal Advisor responded:

[T]he United States military based its objections on a pragmatic, real-world estimation of the difference between the two situations. The military perceives that in international conflicts, many situations may arise where it is important to attack and destroy parts of an electric power grid, such as a nuclear or hydroelectric generating station. In internal conflicts, on the other hand, such a significant real-world need will not exist. Preserving the military option in international conflicts where such facilities are more likely to become an object of military attack, therefore, is very important.[401]

As such, the two types of conflicts may well be treated differently. The position taken by the Customary International Humanitarian Law study is particularly surprising given that, in respect of other rules, when the Additional Protocol I provision contains exceptions but the Additional Protocol II provision does not, the approach of the study was to indicate that '[i]t is doubtful, however, whether this exception also applies to non-international armed conflicts, because ... Additional Protocol II does not provide for it and there is no practice supporting it'.[402] This is thus an area in which the conflation between the law of international armed conflict and the law of non-international armed conflict has weakened the protections afforded by the latter.[403] For all these reasons, the framing of the purported customary rule by the Customary International Humanitarian Law study must be treated with caution and the Additional Protocol II proscription better reflects the state of customary international law on point.[404]

2.8.4 Protected zones

General Assembly Resolution 2675 (XXV) provides that '[p]laces or areas designated for the sole protection of civilians, such as hospital zones or similar refuges, should not be the object of military operations'. This norm is considered to have the status of customary international law.[405] The principle expressed in the Resolution also reflects the prohibition on the targeting of civilians, civilian objects, and persons *hors de combat*.

Conditions usually attach to the creation of hospital zones. For example, in establishing the Jaffna hospital as a hospital zone in 1990, during the conflict in Sri Lanka, the Government and the LTTE agreed that the hospital compound would be marked with red crosses for identification purposes, no armed personnel would be allowed in the compound, no military vehicle would be stationed there, and only hospital, ICRC, and Sri Lankan Red Cross vehicles would be allowed to enter.[406]

Demilitarized zones are different from hospital zones and the like. Demilitarized zones are established subject to the agreement of the parties.[407] Accordingly, a unilat-

---

[401] 'The United States Position on the Relation of Customary International Law to the 1977 Additional Protocols Additional to the 1949 Geneva Conventions: Remarks of Michael J Matheson' (1987) 2 *American University Journal of International Law and Policy* 419, 434.
[402] *Customary International Humanitarian Law, Volume I: Rules*, above note 84, 192.
[403] See generally above, 68–9.
[404] See Darfur Commission Report, above note 25, para 166.
[405] *Tadić* Decision on Interlocutory Appeal on Jurisdiction, above note 25, para 112; Customary International Humanitarian Law, Rule 35. See also IIHL *Manual*, above note 55, 60.
[406] ICRC Press Release of 6 November 1990, reproduced in M Sassòli, AA Bouvier, and A Quintin, *How Does Law Protect in War? Volume III* (ICRC, 2011) 1652.
[407] Additional Protocol I, Article 60(1); IIHL *Manual*, above note 55, 60.

eral declaration of one party alone will not suffice.[408] The agreement creating the zone usually provides that the zone may not contain any fighters or mobile military materiel, that any fixed military installations within the zone are not to be used to carry out hostile acts, that no hostile acts are to be carried out by persons within the zone, and that any activity linked to the military effort must cease.[409] However, the precise conditions may be varied by the parties to the conflict and the agreement. The United Kingdom has expressed the view that '[t]he other rules on protective zones applicable in international armed conflicts may be applied by analogy to internal armed conflicts'.[410] These conditions are evident from the relevant practice. For example, in the Nairobi Peace Agreement of 1985 between the Government of Uganda and the National Resistance Movement (NRM), provision was made for the city of Kampala to be considered a demilitarized and neutral zone:

(1) The city of Kampala shall be demilitarized and neutralised by removing out of Kampala all troops to be determined by the reconnaissance team. The security of Kampala shall be maintained by the police force which shall have been screened and whose arms shall have been verified by the monitoring/observer force. The Monitoring/observer force shall be adequately represented to ensure the neutrality of Kampala.

(2) The demilitarization arrangements for Kampala shall remain in force until the complete demobilisation of the combatant forces has been achieved through recruitment in the new force established under Article 7 or resettlement of the men and women not so recruited.[411]

Likewise, the 1990 'Act establishing the Demilitarized Zone' in the Ceasefire Agreement between the Government of Nicaragua and the YATAMA Atlantic Front of the Nicaraguan Resistance provided that:

[i]n the demilitarized zone, there shall be no artillery, no offensive troops of any kind, and no militia and no paramilitary or security forces.
. . .
The police of the villages situated within the demilitarized zone shall be disarmed.
. . .
Co-ordination groups shall be established to solve the security problems . . . [412]

If one of the conditions is violated and the zone loses its status as a hospital or demilitarized zone, it continues to benefit from other protections, such as those afforded to medical personnel.[413]

The Customary International Humanitarian Law study suggests that the norm that '[d]irecting an attack against a demilitarised zone agreed upon between the parties to the conflict is prohibited' is a norm of customary international law.[414] The added value of such a finding is unclear given that demilitarized zones are created by the parties to

---

[408] Ibid, 60.
[409] Additional Protocol I, Article 60(3); IIHL *Manual*, above note 55, 60–1 (omitting the final condition).
[410] UK *Manual*, above note 43, 396.
[411] 17 December 1985, Article 13.
[412] Definitive ceasefire agreement between the Government of the Republic of Nicaragua and the 'YATAMA' Atlantic Front of the Nicaraguan Resistance under the auspices of His Eminence Miguel Cardinal Obando y Bravo, Annex, Act Establishing the Demilitarized Zone, 18 April 1990, A/44/941-S/21272, 25 April 1990.
[413] Additional Protocol I, Article 60(7); IIHL *Manual*, above note 55, 60–1.
[414] Rule 36.

the conflict on an ad hoc basis and pursuant to a written agreement. Accordingly, the binding nature of the rules is derived from the agreements themselves and is subject to the terms of the agreement. The customary norm seems only to confirm that parties are not to violate agreements creating demilitarized zones that they have concluded.

The precise intentions behind the creation of hospital and demilitarized zones vary. For example, the creation of such a zone may be designed to protect the area itself,[415] or to protect civilians or persons *hors de combat*, or a subset thereof such as the wounded and sick, within those areas.[416] In practice there have been the traditional zones as envisaged by international humanitarian law—hospital zones for the protection of the military wounded and sick; hospital and safety zones for the protection of the civilian wounded and sick, children, the elderly, expectant mothers, and mothers of young children; and demilitarized zones.[417] Demilitarized zones were set up in a college, a hospital, and a hotel in Dhaka during the secession of Bangladesh from Pakistan in 1971.[418] Several safety zones were established in Nicaragua in 1979 in churches, hospitals, embassies, and near the airport.[419] A hospital was designated a hospital zone in Jaffna, Sri Lanka in 1990.[420] Similarly, in Osijek in Croatia in 1991, a hospital was designated a protected zone, as were a first-aid station and hospital in Dubrovnik. Both were accorded such status following the result of agreements reached between the parties to the conflicts under the auspices of the ICRC.[421]

More recently, a different type of protected zone has been envisaged—'safe areas' or 'safe havens'. These are often created by the international community (the UN Security Council, outside states, or humanitarian agencies) with varying degrees of consent on the part of parties to the conflict. Thus, they do not fall within the traditional idea of the hospital zone or demilitarized zone as envisaged by international humanitarian law, nor do they represent a legal category in their own right. Safe havens were created for the benefit of the Kurdish population in Iraq (1991) by states;[422] and Srebrenica, Sarajevo, Tuzla, Zepa, Gorazde, and Bihac were classified as 'safe areas' in Bosnia (1993) by the UN Security Council.[423] The dangers of such zones are well-known.[424] Although sometimes encouraged,[425] care needs to be taken to prevent creating a false sense of security for those within the zone and implicitly suggesting that those outside the zones are less protected.

---

[415] UK *Manual*, above note 43, 92.
[416] Geneva Convention IV, Articles 14, 15. See also Draft Convention for the Protection of Civilian Populations Against New Engines of War, 1938.
[417] See respectively Geneva Convention I, Article 23; Geneva Convention IV, Articles 14, 15.
[418] Y Sandoz, 'The Establishment of Safety Zones for Persons Displaced within their Country of Origin', in N Al-Nauimi and R Meese, *International Legal Issues Arising under the United Nations Decade of International Law* (Martinus Nijhoff, 1995) 899, 909. See also F Bugnion, *The International Committee of the Red Cross and the Protection of War Victims* (ICRC, 2003) 756–9.
[419] Sandoz, above note 418, 899, 913–14.
[420] See ICRC Press Release, 6 November 1990, reproduced in M Sassòli, AA Bouvier, and A Quintin, *How Does Law Protect in War? Volume III* (ICRC, 2011) 1652.
[421] See M Mercier, *Crimes without Punishment: Humanitarian Action in the Former Yugoslavia* (Pluto Press, 1995) 98–100; J-F Berger, *The Humanitarian Diplomacy of the ICRC and the Conflict in Croatia 1991–2* (ICRC, 1995) 38.
[422] See SC Res 688 (1991); Memorandum of Understanding signed on 18 April 1991 [between Iraq and the UN].
[423] SC Res 819 (1993); SC Res 824 (1993).
[424] See generally, Report of the Secretary-General pursuant to General Assembly Resolution 53/35: The Fall of Srebrenica, A/54/549, 15 November 1999.
[425] See eg SC Res 1296 (2000).

Still another type of zone—the 'open relief centre'—has been used. 'Open relief centres' were established by the UNHCR during the armed conflict in Sri Lanka, with the consent of the Government of Sri Lanka, to assist returnees and displaced persons, the possibility of creating a traditional zone having been considered but rejected for want of feasibility.[426] This was later solidified by way of a written agreement between the UNHCR and the Government of Sri Lanka, and with the LTTE reportedly consenting to the operation of the centre.[427] These centres are neither traditional international humanitarian law zones nor safe havens, although as they comprise internally displaced persons, they do benefit from certain protections.

Yet another type of zone that has arisen in practice is the zone or space for peace. In the case of the Philippines, the Ginapaladtaka Declaration relating to a space for peace and children as zones of peace was initiated by the inhabitants of villages and adopted in meetings with the parties to the conflict. Pursuant to the Declaration, certain villages are to be respected as zones of peace and thus not to be used as a location for fighting, but fighters may continue living within the zone. Peace zones were also envisaged by the Cessation of Hostilities Framework Agreement concluded between the Government of the Republic of Indonesia and the Free Aceh Movement.[428] Such instances differ from, but are related to, the international humanitarian law notion of a protected zone.

3. Means of combat

3.1 Introduction

The 'means of combat' are essentially the weapons that are used in combat. They are distinct from the 'methods of combat' which concern the tactics that are used in combat and which are considered in the following section. The law regulates the means of combat in two distinct ways. First, certain rules apply to all weapons; second, the use of specific weapons is restricted or prohibited. Both approaches have their advantages and disadvantages. The advantage of the 'specific prohibition' approach relates to clarity and relative ease in ascertaining compliance. However, these advantages are off-set by the ease through which a prohibition may be evaded, for example by using a weapon of a similar sort that is not quite caught by the terms of the prohibition. Indeed, 'the more specific the prohibition, the greater the possibility of lawful circumvention of the rule'.[429] The weapons that are banned also tend to be those that are 'not decisive in the battlefield... Whenever the banning of important weapons was envisaged, it was strongly opposed and subsequently never effected'.[430] The advantage of the 'general rules' is that all weapons are subjected to certain rules, both weapons that

---

[426] BS Chimni, 'The Incarceration of Victims: Deconstructing Safety Zones', in N Al-Nauimi and R Meese, *International Legal Issues Arising under the United Nations Decade of International Law* (Martinus Nijhoff, 1995) 823.

[427] Memorandum of Understanding among the Government of the Socialist Republic of Sri Lanka and the Office of the United Nations High Commissioner for Refugees relating to the Repatriation of Sri Lankan Refugees and Displaced Persons, 1 February 1993; Chimni, above note 426.

[428] Article 4.

[429] Paper by Sir David Hughes-Morgan to the Lucerne Conference, cited in F Kalshoven, 'Conventional Weaponry: the Law from St Petersburg to Lucerne and Beyond', in MA Meyer (ed), *Armed Conflict and the New Law* (BIICL, 1989) 251, 259.

[430] A Cassese, 'A Tentative Appraisal of the Old and the New Humanitarian Law of Armed Conflict', in A Cassese (ed), *The New Humanitarian Law of Armed Conflict* (Editoriale Scientifica, 1979) 461, 475.

presently exist and those that may be created in the future. Its weakness lies in its concrete application to a particular weapon: 'it is difficult to find a single example of a weapon which has entered into service during the twentieth century and which is generally agreed to fall foul of' the general rules.[431] The two approaches, as well as their relative advantages and disadvantages, are not new. They were expressed as early as 1899 by the Delegates to the Hague Peace Conference. For example, the United States criticized the specific weapon approach, noting that '[i]n the effort to catch a single detail of construction, it has left the door open to everything else which ingenuity may be able to suggest'.[432] By contrast, the Netherlands opined that '[t]here must be a specified limit and not a general limit. Otherwise, no result will be reached'.[433]

Both the 'general rules' approach and the 'specific prohibition' approach are applicable to international and non-international armed conflicts alike, through conventional and customary international law.

3.2 The general rules

The general, and primary, principle that underlies the law relating to the means of combat is that 'the only legitimate object which States should endeavour to accomplish during war is to weaken the military forces of the enemy'.[434] Accordingly, the right of the parties to the conflict 'to adopt means of injuring the enemy' is not unlimited.[435] Although the principle started out as applying to the law of international armed conflict alone, its application to non-international armed conflicts has since been confirmed.[436] From this general principle, two rules have been derived: weapons should not cause unnecessary suffering or superfluous injury,[437] and weapons should not be indiscriminate. Both of these rules apply to all weapons.

3.2.1 Unnecessary suffering or superfluous injury

Using means of combat 'that are of a nature to cause superfluous injury or unnecessary suffering' to fighters is prohibited.[438] The rule is applicable to non-international armed conflict through conventional and customary international law.[439] It was described by the International Court of Justice as one of the 'cardinal principles' of international

---

[431] Greenwood, Weaponry, above note 130, 198. See also T McCormack, 'From Solferino to Sarajevo: A Continuing Role for International Humanitarian Law?' (1997) 21 *Melbourne University Law Review* 621, 629–31.

[432] JB Scott (ed), *The Proceedings of the Hague Conferences: The Conference of 1899* (Oxford University Press, 1920) 81.

[433] Ibid, 82.

[434] Declaration Renouncing the Use, in Time of War, of Explosive Projectiles Under 400 Grammes Weight (St Petersburg Declaration), Preamble.

[435] Hague Regulations Respecting the Laws and Customs of War on Land, annexed to the 1907 Hague Convention (IV) Respecting the Laws and Customs of War on Land, Article 22; *Nuclear Weapons*, above note 12, 257, para 78.

[436] GA Res 2444 (XXIII) (1968); *Tadić* Defence on Interlocutory Appeal on Jurisdiction, above note 25, para 119.

[437] The two terms will be used interchangeably given that both have been used to translate the French expression 'maux superflus'. See H Meyrowitz, 'The Principle of Superfluous Injury or Unnecessary Suffering' (1994) 34 *IRRC* 98, 104–5.

[438] IIHL *Manual*, above note 55, 12. See also UK *Manual*, above note 43, 103.

[439] Convention on Certain Conventional Weapons, Amended Protocol II, Article 3.3; Customary International Humanitarian Law, Rule 70; IIHL Declaration, above note 52, A3. See also IIHL *Manual*, above note 55, 13.

humanitarian law.[440] It is also a longstanding rule, with the Lieber Code providing that '[m]ilitary necessity does not admit of cruelty—that is, the infliction of suffering for the sake of suffering'.[441]

Unnecessary suffering involves 'some sort of equation between, on the one hand, the degree of injury or suffering inflicted (the humanitarian aspect) and, on the other, the degree of necessity underlying the choice of a particular weapon (the military aspect)'.[442] The concept of suffering is generally agreed to include such things as 'mortality rates, the painfulness or severeness [sic] of wounds, or the incidence of permanent damage or disfigurement'.[443] Today, with greater understanding of psychiatric injury, this too should be covered, although psychological harm would not suffice. Whether or not the social and economic impact on society of the suffering of fighters and combatants should be taken into account is contested.[444] Beyond this general guidance, it has proven impossible to define objectively the idea of suffering from a medical perspective.[445] The military side of the equation includes such things as the capacity of a weapon to disable the enemy, to destroy or neutralize enemy materiel, to restrict movement, interdict lines of communication, weaken resources, and enhance the security of friendly forces.[446] It does not include the capacity of a weapon to cause death rather than disablement or its ability to impact on the morale of the enemy.[447] As the Preamble to the St Petersburg Declaration notes:

Considering
...
That the only legitimate object which States should endeavour to accomplish during war is to weaken the military forces of the enemy;
That for this purpose it is sufficient to disable the greatest possible number of men;
That this object would be exceeded by the employment of arms which uselessly aggravate the sufferings of disabled men, or render their death inevitable;[448]

As is evident from the generality of this description, both the humanitarian and the military aspects of the equation are in need of further clarification. However, this has proven difficult, with an ICRC project to define better the concept of unnecessary suffering being abandoned.[449]

Also difficult is the precise equation between the humanitarian and the military aspects. The test is a balancing exercise, requiring the humanitarian aspect to be

---

[440] *Nuclear Weapons*, above note 12, para 78.
[441] Article 16.
[442] ICRC, Conference of Government Experts on the Use of Certain Conventional Weapons (Lucerne, 24.9–18.10.1974): Report (ICRC, 1975) 9, para 24. See generally A Cassese, 'Weapons Causing Unnecessary Suffering: Are They Prohibited?', reprinted in A Cassese, *The Human Dimension of International Law: Selected Papers* (Oxford University Press, 2008) 192
[443] Lucerne Conference Report, above note 442, 8, para 23.
[444] Cf BM Carnahan and M Robertson, 'The Protocol on "Blinding Laser Weapons": A New Direction for International Humanitarian Law' (1996) 90 *AJIL* 484, 490, with C Greenwood, 'Battlefield Laser Weapons in the Context of the Law on Conventional Weapons', in L Doswald-Beck (ed), *Blinding Weapons* (ICRC, 1993) 71, 76.
[445] ICRC, Conference of Government Experts on the Use of Certain Conventional Weapons (Second Session—Lugano, 28.1–26.2.1976): Report (ICRC, 1976) 140.
[446] Lucerne Conference Report, above note 442, 9, para 25.
[447] Greenwood, Weaponry, above note 130, 195–6.
[448] Declaration Renouncing the Use, in Time of War, of Explosive Projectiles Under 400 Grammes Weight, 1868.
[449] RM Coupland (ed), *The SIrUS Project: Towards a Determination of Which Weapons Cause 'Superfluous Injury or Unnecessary Suffering'* (ICRC, 1997).

weighed against the military aspect.[450] Two consequences follow from this balancing test. First, 'the more effective a weapon is from the military point of view, the less likely it is that the injuries which it causes will be characterized as unnecessary'.[451] Second, that the suffering is 'horrendous' is not enough for a weapon to be prohibited.[452] As the Court in *Shimoda* put it, 'the use of a certain weapon, great as its inhuman result may be, need not be prohibited by international law if it has a great military effect'.[453] It has been suggested that the test is an exercise in proportionality, requiring the suffering caused by the weapon to be proportionate to the military advantage anticipated.[454] However, the balance can be upset without it being disproportionate. Once the humanitarian and military aspects of the weapons are identified, and balanced against one another, if the humanitarian aspect outweighs the military aspect, use of the weapon will be prohibited.

The test is at its clearest when the choice is between weapons, as the results of both may be compared against one another. Thus, 'it is unlawful to use a weapon which causes more suffering or injury than another which offers the same or similar military advantages'.[455] The classic example of the weapons comparison is between a weapon and a weapon that has been altered—a lance as opposed to a lance with a barbed head, or a knife as opposed to a knife with a serrated edge.[456] The principle also applies to the design of a particular weapon. For example, it has been suggested that certain, new, smaller bullets cause more serious injuries than their older counterparts, or the design construction of particular anti-personnel mines may have different effects even though their intended purpose is identical.[457] Application of the unnecessary suffering rule may thus prohibit certain redesigns of weapons. The availability of a weapon will also impact upon the rule as persons are unlikely to be carrying an array of weapons with them.[458] This is even truer of members of armed groups, whose access to different types of weaponry may be limited.

Outside the choice between weapons, application of the unnecessary suffering rule to particular weapons is limited. Indeed, it has been said that the principle 'is to a great extent couched in such vague and uncertain terms as to be barren of practical results'.[459] Arguably, though, it has had some results. The prohibition on the use of

---

[450] See H Meyrowitz, 'The Principle of Superfluous Injury or Unnecessary Suffering' (1994) 34 *IRRC* 98, 109–10; Response by H Blix to paper by Sir David Hughes-Morgan at the Lucerne Conference, cited in F Kalshoven, 'Conventional Weaponry: the Law from St Petersburg to Lucerne and Beyond', in MA Meyer (ed), *Armed Conflict and the New Law* (BIICL, London, 1989) 251, 260; Greenwood, Weaponry, above note 130, 201.

[451] Greenwood, Current Issues, above note 99, 446.

[452] *Nuclear Weapons*, above note 12, Dissenting Opinion of Judge Higgins, 585, para 13; Paper by Sir David Hughes-Morgan to the Lucerne Conference, cited in Kalshoven, Weaponry, above note 450, 259; Greenwood, Weaponry, above note 130, 194.

[453] *Ryuichi Shimoda et al v The State* (1963) 32 *ILR* 626, 634.

[454] Paper by Sir David Hughes-Morgan to the Lucerne Conference, cited in Kalshoven, Weaponry, above note 450, 259–60; S Oeter, 'Methods and Means of Combat', in D Fleck (ed), *The Handbook of Humanitarian Law in Armed Conflicts* (Oxford University Press, 1995) 105, 115; *Customary International Humanitarian Law, Volume I: Rules*, above note 84, 240.

[455] Blix, above note 118, 139.

[456] UK *Manual*, above note 43, 105; [US] Department of the Army, *FM 27-10 The Law of Land Warfare* (Department of the Army, 18 July 1956) 18.

[457] L Doswald-Beck, 'Obstacles to Regulating New Weaponry: Battlefield Laser Weapons', in H Fox and MA Meyer (eds), *Armed Conflict and the New Law, Volume II: Effecting Compliance* (BIICL, 1993) 107, 115.

[458] See F Kalshoven, 'The Soldier and his Golf Clubs', in C Swinarski (ed), *Studies and Essays on International Humanitarian Law and Red Cross Principles in Honour of Jean Pictet* (ICRC, 1984) 369.

[459] Cassese, Unnecessary Suffering, above note 442, 211.

'any weapon the primary effect of which is to injure by fragments which in the human body escape detection by X-rays' is considered by some to be based on the idea that such weapons cause suffering beyond any military purpose.[460] The Preambles to the Ottawa Convention on Anti-personnel Mines and the Convention on Certain Conventional Weapons also refer to the rule. Furthermore, Amended Protocol II to the Convention on Certain Conventional Weapons explicitly prohibits the use of 'any mine, booby-trap or other device which is designed or of a nature to cause superfluous injury or unnecessary suffering'.[461] However, others consider the prohibition on these weapons, and these uses, to be based on other reasons.[462] The precise basis for the prohibitions and restrictions often differs from party to party.

A further issue that needs to be considered relates to whether particular weapons are prohibited because they 'inevitably' cause unnecessary suffering or are of a nature to cause unnecessary suffering, on the one hand; or because they 'normally or typically' do so, on the other.[463] The weapon that inevitably causes unnecessary suffering is prohibited outright. However, rare will be such a weapon, not least because the unnecessary suffering test operates by comparison to other factors. The Rome Statute, albeit in a provision relating to international armed conflict, lists as a war crime the employment of 'weapons, projectiles and material and methods of warfare which are of a nature to cause superfluous injury or unnecessary suffering or which are inherently indiscriminate in violation of the international law of armed conflict'.[464] At first sight, this may suggest that weapons do exist that are of a nature to cause superfluous injury. However, such weapons have to be listed in an annex to the Statute and, to date, none has been listed. The weapon that normally or typically causes unnecessary suffering cannot be prohibited outright, for a situation can be envisaged in which its use does not cause unnecessary suffering, albeit an atypical situation.[465] However, the user of such a weapon bears a heavy burden in using it, given that they will be aware that the normal use of the weapon results in unnecessary suffering. Furthermore, weapons that could have been used in this, legal, manner have arguably sometimes been prohibited outright given their typical nature.

3.2.2 Discrimination

A second rule that applies to all weapons is that the use of weapons that are by their nature indiscriminate is prohibited. Indiscriminate weapons are those that are 'incapable of being specifically directed against fighters or military objectives or which ha[ve] effects on civilians and civilian objects that are uncontrollable'.[466] This is a norm of customary international law.[467] Indeed, the International Court of Justice

---

[460] S Haines, 'Weapons, Means and Methods of Warfare', in E Wilmshurst and SC Breau (eds), *Perspectives on the ICRC Study on Customary International Humanitarian law* (Cambridge University Press, 2007) 258, 273.
[461] Article 3(3).
[462] WH Boothby, *Weapons and the Law of Armed Conflict* (Oxford University Press, 2009) 60 and 115.
[463] Lucerne Conference Report, above note 442, 9–10, para 28.
[464] Rome Statute, Article 8(2)(b)(xx).
[465] Cf Boothby, *Weapons*, above note 462, 62.
[466] IIHL *Manual*, above note 55, 29. See also *Nuclear Weapons*, above note 12, para 78; *Nuclear Weapons*, Dissenting Opinion of Judge Higgins, 588–9, para 24.
[467] Customary International Humanitarian Law, Rule 71. See also IDI Resolution on Distinction, above note 45, para 7.

(ICJ) considered that the rule followed directly from the 'cardinal principle' of distinction.[468]

Despite the prohibition on the use of weapons that are inherently or by their nature indiscriminate, as with unnecessary suffering, it should be queried whether any such weapons exist. As certain experts at the Lucerne Conference of Government Experts noted, 'all conventional weapons could be used in circumstances where the risk of hitting civilians was virtually non-existent'.[469] This would include, for example, the use of such weapons 'against large-scale military objectives, remote from civilians'.[470] Thus, even the V1 and V2 missiles used during the Second World War and the Scud missiles used during the 1990–1 Gulf conflict, often cited in this context,[471] are unlikely to be unlawful in *all* situations, albeit their use in the mentioned conflicts was unlawful. Likewise, although the *Martić* Trial Chamber held that 'the M-87 Orkan is an indiscriminate weapon', the context suggests that it was the particular situation in which the weapon was used that rendered it indiscriminate.[472] This would extend to such weapons as nuclear weapons or bacteriological weapons, which have the potential to be used in limited situations that would affect fighters alone. Indeed, several states at the 1974–7 Diplomatic Conference took the view that 'the definition of indiscriminate attacks... was not intended to mean that there were means of combat the use of which would constitute an indiscriminate attack in all circumstances. The [relevant] paragraph [in Additional Protocol I] did not in itself prohibit the use of any specific weapon, but it took account of the fact that the lawful use of any means of combat depended on the circumstances'.[473] Against such a position, the Rome Statute, albeit in a provision relating to international armed conflict, lists as a war crime the employment of 'weapons, projectiles and material and methods of warfare which are of a nature to cause superfluous injury or unnecessary suffering or which are inherently indiscriminate in violation of the international law of armed conflict'.[474] However, such weapons have to be listed in an annex to the Statute and agreement has not been reached on the existence of any such weapons.

In light of this, it has been suggested that it is not only weapons that are inherently or by their nature indiscriminate that are prohibited, but also weapons 'whose normal or typical use would be one which had indiscriminate effects'.[475] As with the principle of unnecessary suffering,[476] if there do exist weapons that are *inherently* indiscriminate, they would be prohibited. However, as noted above, such weapons will be rare indeed. Weapons the normal or typical use of which is indiscriminate cannot be prohibited outright, for a situation can be envisaged in which their use would not be

---

[468] *Nuclear Weapons*, above note 12, para 78.
[469] Lucerne Conference Report, above note 442, 10, para 30.
[470] FJ Hampson, 'Means and methods of warfare in the conflict in the Gulf', in P Rowe (ed), *The Gulf War 1990–91 in International and English Law* (Routledge, 1993) 89, 103.
[471] UK *Manual*, above note 43, 104; GH Aldrich, 'The Laws of War on Land' (2000) 94 *AJIL* 42, 51; Greenwood, Weaponry, above note 130, 200; A Cassese, 'Means of Warfare: The Traditional and the New Law', in A Cassese (ed), *The New Humanitarian Law of Armed Conflict* (Editoriale Scientifica, 1979) 164; A Cassese, 'The Prohibition of Indiscriminate Means of Warfare', in RJ Akkerman, PJ van Krieken, and CO Pannenborg (eds), *Declarations on Principles: A Quest for Universal Peace* (AW Sijthoff, 1977) 171, 172.
[472] *Prosecutor v Martić*, IT-95-11-T, Judgment, 12 June 2007, para 463. See also *Prosecutor v Martić*, IT-95-11-A, Judgment, 8 October 2008, para 252.
[473] *Official Records*, above note 8, Vol 6, 164, para 119. See also 187 (FRG); 179 (Canada); Vol 15, 274, para 55 (Report of Committee III). See further Blix, above note 118, 145.
[474] Rome Statute, Article 8(2)(b)(xx).
[475] Lucerne Conference Report, above note 442, 10–11, para 31.
[476] See above, 390.

indiscriminate, albeit an atypical situation. However, given that the indiscriminate use of a weapon is prohibited, the normal use of these weapons would be prohibited.

That said, on occasion, the use of certain weapons has been prohibited completely in light of their being indiscriminate in their normal use. For example, the use of anti-personnel mines has been prohibited for states parties to the Ottawa Convention, in part, in light of the indiscriminate nature of the normal use.[477] Anti-personnel mines are not inherently indiscriminate for they may be used in areas frequented only by fighters, their location may be recorded, and they may be retrieved upon conclusion of the hostilities. However, in practice, this is not how they are used and accordingly, on the basis of their normal use, their complete use has been prohibited.

In respect of those weapons that are indiscriminate in their normal use but have not been prohibited outright, a great deal of care needs to be taken before they are used, given that the user of the weapon will be on notice as to the indiscriminate nature of the weapon in its normal use. For example, the *Martić* Trial Chamber noted that 'before the decision was made to once again use this weapon [the M-87 Orkan]...the full impact of using such an indiscriminate weapon was known beyond doubt as a result of the extensive media coverage on...the effects of the [earlier] attack'.[478] Since this concerns the use of the weapon, the relevant rules are those on discrimination and proportionality in attack rather than the legality of the weapon itself.

3.3 Specifically prohibited weapons

3.3.1 Poison and poisoned weapons

The prohibition on the use of poison and poisoned weapons is one of the oldest weapons-related rules of armed conflict. The prohibition is based on the 'perception of its treacherous nature and the fact that poisoned weapons inevitably caused death',[479] and on ideas of honour.[480] In this respect, the prohibition on poisoned weapons falls foul of the prohibition on unnecessary suffering. As General Halleck observed: '[w]e may wound an enemy in order to disable him, but when so disabled, we have no right to take his life; we, therefore, cannot introduce poison into that wound so as, subsequently, to cause his death.'[481] The prohibition is accepted as applying to non-international armed conflicts through customary international law.[482]

The prohibition is not limited to the administration of poison *stricto senso* but includes any use of poison or poisoned weapons. Likewise it is not limited to poisonous chemical agents but would include such things as dead bodies used to poison water supplies. In the words of the Lieber Code, '[t]he use of poison in any manner, be it to poison wells, or food, or arms, is wholly excluded from modern warfare. He that uses it

---

[477] Ottawa Convention, Preamble. On which see below, 404–8.
[478] *Martić* Trial Judgment, above note 472, para 463.
[479] ICRC, Report of the International Committee of the Red Cross for the Review Conference of the 1980 United Nations Convention on Prohibitions or Restrictions on the Use of Certain Conventional Weapons which May be Deemed to be Excessively Injurious or to have Indiscriminate Effects (ICRC, February 1994) 123, 130.
[480] The Laws of War on Land (Oxford Manual), 9 September 1880, Article 8(a).
[481] HW Halleck, *International Law: Or Rules Regulating the Intercourse of States in Peace and War* (S Baker ed)) (C Kegan Paul and Co, 1878) 22.
[482] Amendment to the Rome Statute, RC/Res.5; Customary International Humanitarian Law, Rule 72. See also its acceptance in UK *Manual*, above note 43, 397; IIHL Declaration, above note 52, B3. It had been suggested for inclusion in common Article 3: *Final Record*, above note 3, Vol II-B, 90 (United States).

puts himself out of the pale of the law and usages of war'.[483] The prohibition thus covers bullets laced with poison;[484] the poisoning of wells and water supplies; and the punji stick, a spiked stake covered with poison or excrement, as used in the conflict in Vietnam;[485] to name but three examples. The poisoning of abandoned food by the Confederate forces during the US civil war was described by General Halleck as a 'barbarous act—an act condemned by every civilized nation, ancient and modern'.[486]

3.3.2 Biological and bacteriological weapons

Biological and bacteriological warfare, described as 'so particularly odious that it revolts the conscience of humanity more than any other method of warfare',[487] is prohibited in non-international armed conflict. The 1925 Geneva Gas Protocol provides in relevant part that the High Contracting Parties agree to the prohibition on the 'use of bacteriological methods of warfare and agree to be bound as between themselves according to the terms of this declaration'. The reference to 'as between themselves' indicates that the Protocol was applicable only in wars between states parties to the Protocol. However, in 1970 the UN General Assembly passed a Resolution calling upon parties 'to any armed conflict' to observe the Geneva Gas Protocol.[488] An attempt was made to restrict the scope of the Resolution to international armed conflicts, but this was defeated. Responding to the objection, the United Kingdom stated that 'in any armed conflict, whether international or not, certain minimal standards had to be respected'.[489]

Application of the prohibition to non-international armed conflict is evident from the 1972 Bacteriological Weapons Convention. That Convention provides that states parties undertake 'never in any circumstance to develop, produce, stockpile or otherwise acquire or retain' certain listed agents.[490] Reference to 'in any circumstance' is understood as including non-international armed conflict. Although the Convention does not explicitly prohibit the use of biological or bacteriological weapons, the phrase 'never in any circumstances' has long been recognized as covering use, not least because use is dependent on development and production, both of which are explicitly proscribed. For example, China, in acceding to the Convention, criticized it for failing to prohibit the use of biological weapons 'in explicit terms',[491] suggesting that such use was prohibited albeit only implicitly. At the Fourth Review Conference in 1996, states parties to the Convention confirmed that the Convention prohibits the use of bacteriological weapons.[492] The prohibition on the use of biological and bacteriological weapons is also a norm of customary international law.[493]

---

[483] Instructions for the Government of Armies of the United States in the Field (Lieber Code), 24 April 1863, Article 70. Cf JW Spaight, *War Rights on Land* (1911) 84–5.
[484] W Winthrop, *Military Law and Precedents* (Government Printing Office, 1920) 785.
[485] See JE Bond, *The Rules of Riot* (Princeton University Press, 1974) 142.
[486] General Order No 40, Department of the Mo, 1862, quoted in Winthrop, Arms, above note 484, 785.
[487] Conf.D.120, para 11, quoted in Kalshoven, Arms, above note 102, 221.
[488] GA Res 2677 (XXIV) (1970). See also GA Res 2852 (XXVI) (1971).
[489] A/C.3/SR.1799, 26 November 1970, quoted in *Customary International Humanitarian Law: Volume II*, above note 84, 1538.
[490] Convention on the Prohibition of the Development, Production and Stockpiling of Bacteriological (Biological) and Toxin Weapons and on Their Destruction, Article 1.
[491] Declarations and Reservations to the Biological and Toxin Weapons Convention, Statement of China, paragraph 1.
[492] See Fourth Review Conference of the Parties to the Convention on the Prohibition of the Development, Production and Stockpiling of Bacteriological (Biological) and Toxin Weapons and on their Destruction, Final Document, Part II, Final Declaration.
[493] *Constitutional Conformity of Protocol II*, above note 5, para 23; IIHL Declaration, above note 52, B1; Customary International Humanitarian Law, Rule 73.

3.3.3 Gas and chemical weapons

One of the problems associated with the use of gas and chemical weapons is that, 'once it has been released it is no longer under the control of those employing it'.[494] Thus, a prohibition on 'the use of projectiles the sole object of which is the diffusion of asphyxiating or deleterious gases' in the 1899 Hague Declaration concerning asphyxiating gases, was considered necessary as asphyxiating gases were considered 'barbarous' and endangering civilians.[495]

For similar reasons, the use of certain gases and chemical weapons is prohibited in non-international armed conflict. The 1925 Geneva Gas Protocol prohibits 'the use in war of asphyxiating, poisonous or other gases, and of all analogous liquids, materials or devices'. However, the treaty prohibition applies 'as between' the High Contracting Parties themselves, thus failing to cover situations of non-international armed conflict. The prohibition on the use of gas was suggested for inclusion in common Article 3, but the suggestion was not taken up.[496] Nonetheless, at least since 1988, if not earlier, the prohibition on the use of asphyxiating, poisonous, and other gases, and chemical weapons in non-international armed conflict has been recognized as a norm of customary international law.[497] The use of poison gas during the Yemeni civil war in the 1960s had been condemned by various states. For example, US officials described its use against civilians as 'entirely contrary to the laws of nations' and stated that it was 'clearly contrary to international law'.[498] Similarly, the use of chemical weapons in Angola and Mozambique by the Portuguese military was condemned, in general,[499] and as a violation of common Article 3.[500] If such reactions did not lead to the crystallization of a rule of customary international law prohibiting the use of chemical weapons in non-international armed conflict, reactions to the use of certain gases and chemical weapons by the Iraqi Government against the Kurdish population of Halabja in 1988 did crystallize the prohibition.

In respect of Halabja, the US State Department condemned the deployment of chemical weapons against the Kurds. It noted that '[q]uestions have been raised as to whether the prohibition in the 1925 Geneva Protocol against [chemical weapon] use "in war" applies to [chemical weapon] use in internal conflicts. However, it is clear that such use against the civilian population would be contrary to the customary international law that is applicable to internal armed conflicts, as well as other international agreements'.[501] The then 12 Member States of the European Community issued a

---

[494] Conf.D.120, para 3, quoted in Kalshoven, *Arms*, above note 102, 221 fn 44.
[495] *Proceedings*, above note 432, 366 (Russia), 366 (Denmark), and 283 (Netherlands).
[496] *Final Record*, above note 3, Vol II-B, 90 (United States).
[497] *Tadić* Decision on Interlocutory Appeal on Jurisdiction, above note 25, paras 120–4; *Van Anraat v The Netherlands*, Application No 65389/09, Decision as to Admissibility, 6 July 2010, para 94; Customary International Humanitarian Law, Rule 74; *Constitutional Conformity of Protocol II*, above note 5, para 23; IIHL Declaration, above note 52, B1.
[498] Quoted in AVW Thomas and AJ Thomas, *Legal Limits on the Use of Chemical and Biological Weapons* (Southern Methodist University Press, 1970) 152. See also JN Moore, 'Ratification of the Geneva Protocol on Gas and Bacteriological Warfare: A Legal and Political Analysis' (1972) 58 *Virginia Law Review* 419, 449.
[499] E/CN.4/SR.1232, 262 (Chile) and E/CN.4/SR.1233, 269–70 (Zaire), 272–3 (Tanania), 273–4 (Philippines), 274–5 (Senegal), cited in A Cassese, 'The Prohibition of Indiscriminate Means of Warfare', in RJ Akkerman, PJ van Krieken, and CO Pannenborg (eds), *Declarations on Principles: A Quest for Universal Peace* (AW Sijthoff, 1977) 171, 187 fn 73.
[500] E/CN.4/SR.1233, 271 (Italy) and A/C.1/PV.1953, 37 (Jamaica), cited in ibid, 187 fn 73.
[501] US, Department of State, Press Guidance, 9 September 1988, quoted in *Tadić* Decision on Interlocutory Appeal on Jurisdiction, above note 25, para 122.

declaration providing that '[t]he Twelve are greatly concerned at reports of the alleged use of chemical weapons against the Kurds... They confirm their previous positions, condemning any use of these weapons. They call for respect of international humanitarian law, including the Geneva Protocol of 1925, and Resolutions 612 and 620 of the United Nations Security Council'.[502] For its part, the UK Foreign Office stated that the use of chemical weapons in Halabja amounted to 'a serious and grave violation of the 1925 Geneva Protocol and international humanitarian law'.[503] Likewise, a German parliament resolution 'resolutely rejected the view that the use of poison gas was allowed on one's own territory and in clashes akin to civil wars, assertedly because it was not expressly prohibited by the Geneva Protocol of 1925'.[504] Along similar lines, Sweden stated before the General Assembly:

[t]he large-scale use of chemical weapons against the city of Halabja was a flagrant violation of the 1925 Geneva [Gas] Protocol and of customary international law prohibiting the use of chemical weapons. Such attacks must be universally condemned.[505]

Pursuant to the 1993 Chemical Weapons Convention, states parties undertake 'never under any circumstances', *inter alia*, to develop, produce, acquire, stockpile, retain, transfer, or use chemical weapons.[506] The reference to 'never under any circumstances' also includes non-international armed conflicts.[507] Chemical weapons are defined in the 1993 Convention as, *inter alia*, '[t]oxic chemicals and their precursors, except where intended for purposes not prohibited under this Convention, as long as the types and quantities are consistent with such purposes'.[508] One of the purposes not prohibited is '[l]aw enforcement including domestic riot control purposes',[509] although the use of riot control agents 'as a method of warfare' is prohibited.[510] A question thus arises as to whether riot control agents can be used for law-enforcement purposes *during* a non-international armed conflict, for example to control a riot in a detention camp. Given the phrasing of the relevant provisions, the answer would seem to be in the affirmative.[511] The juxtaposition is between law-enforcement and methods of warfare, not between internal tensions and armed conflicts.[512] Along similar lines, the Customary International Humanitarian Law study considers the relevant customary rule to be that '[t]he use of riot-control agents as a method of warfare is prohibited'.[513] Such a

---

[502] (1988) 4 *European Political Cooperation Documentation Bulletin* 92, quoted in ibid, para 120. For reiteration of this statement see: A/C.1/43/PV.4; A/C.1/43/PV.31; A/C.3/43/SR.49; (1988) 4 *European Political Cooperation Documentation Bulletin* 187, quoted in ibid.
[503] (1988) 59 *BYIL* 579.
[504] (1990) 50 *Zeitschrift Für Ausländisches Öffentliches Recht Und Völkerrecht* 382–3, quoted and translated in *Tadić* Decision on Interlocutory Appeal on Jurisdiction, above note 25, para 121.
[505] A/S-15/PV.2, 1 June 1988, para 89, quoted in *Customary International Humanitarian Law, Volume II: Practice*, above note 84, 1713.
[506] Article I.
[507] W Krutzsch and R Trapp, *A Commentary on the Chemical Weapons Convention* (Martinus Nijhoff, 1994) 13; A Gioia, 'The Chemical Weapons Convention and its Application in Time of Armed Conflict', in M Bothe, N Ronzitti, and A Rosas (eds), *The New Chemical Weapons Convention—Implementation and Practice* (Kluwer, 1998) 379, 382.
[508] Article II(a). For the definition of toxic chemicals, see Article II(2).
[509] Article II(9)(d).
[510] Article I(5). Riot control agents are defined as 'any chemical not listed in a Schedule, which can produce rapidly in humans sensory irritation or disabling physical effects which disappear within a short time following termination of exposure': Article II(7).
[511] See also Krutzsch and Trapp, above note 507, 42; Boothby, *Weapons*, above note 462, 136.
[512] On the juxtaposition generally, see Melzer, above note 205.
[513] Customary International Humanitarian Law, Rule 75.

position is also supported by Executive Order 11850 of the United States, which 'renounces, as a matter of national policy ... first use of riot control agents in war except in defensive military modes to save lives such as: (a) Use of riot control agents in riot control situations in areas under direct and distinct U.S. military control, to include controlling rioting prisoners of war'.[514] The wording of the Order is ambiguous for it would seem to allow for the use of riot control agents even as a method of warfare, provided such use is in a defensive mode to save lives, which would go against the Convention prohibition. Regardless of the correctness of that position, the Order illustrates the idea of riot control agents being used to control disturbances even during armed conflicts. This was noted explicitly in the letter of transmittal from the US President to the Senate, which provided that the Chemical Weapons Convention 'does not apply to all uses of RCAs [riot control agents] in time of armed conflict. Use of RCAs solely against noncombatants for law enforcement, riot control, or other noncombatant purposes would not be considered as a "method of warfare" and therefore would not be prohibited'.[515]

A prohibition on '[e]mploying asphyxiating, poisonous or other gases, and all analogous liquids, materials or devices' is a war crime in non-international armed conflict.[516] The Resolution amending the Rome Statute of the International Criminal Court provides that such employment is a serious violation 'of the laws and customs applicable in armed conflict not of an international character, as reflected in customary international law'.[517] The phrase stems from the 1925 Geneva Gas Protocol, which has been interpreted as including chemical weapons. Accordingly, the war crime should include chemical weapons within its scope.[518] However, agreement was reportedly reached at the 1998 Rome Conference and confirmed at the 2010 review conference of the Rome Statute that the phrase 'asphyxiating, poisonous or other gases' would not cover chemical weapons for the purposes of the ICC.[519] If that is the case, that would be an unfortunate narrowing of the accepted meaning of the term, albeit for the purposes of the Court. It would also represent another example of the international criminal law prohibition being narrower than that of the associated prohibition in international humanitarian law.[520] The conclusion posited above, that riot control agents may be used during a non-international armed conflict for law-enforcement purposes, is confirmed for the purposes of the ICC through the Elements of Crimes, which provide that '[t]he gas, substance or device was such that it causes death or serious damage to health *in the ordinary course of events*, through its asphyxiating or toxic properties'.[521]

---

[514] Executive Order 11850.
[515] Message from the President of the United States transmitting the Convention on the Prohibition of Development, Production, Stockpiling and Use of Chemical Weapons and on their Destruction, 23 June 1994, reproduced in (1994) 88 *AJIL* 753, 754.
[516] Resolution RC/Res.5, 10 June 2010.
[517] Ibid.
[518] See also, reaching this conclusion, A Cassese, *International Criminal Law* (Oxford University Press, 2008) 95; K Dörmann, 'War Crimes under the Rome Statute of the International Criminal Court, with a Special Focus on the Negotiations on the Elements of Crimes' (2003) 7 *Max Planck Yearbook of United Nations Law* 341, 346.
[519] See A Alamuddin and P Webb, 'Expanding Jurisdiction over War Crimes under Article 8 of the ICC Statute' (2010) 8 *JICJ* 1219, 1226–8.
[520] See generally above, 79–81.
[521] Elements of Crimes, Article 8(2)(e)(xiv) (emphasis added).

3.3.4 Incendiary weapons

In the late 1960s and early 1970s, considerable concern was expressed on the part of the international community over the use of napalm and other incendiary weapons in armed conflicts. For example, a resolution of the International Conference on Human Rights in Tehran in 1968 considered 'napalm bombing [to] erode human rights'.[522] Such a view was reiterated in General Assembly Resolution 2932A (XXVII), which also provided that 'incendiary weapons have always constituted a category of arms viewed with horror'.[523] The background to this concern and these resolutions was, in particular, the conflict in Vietnam, which was raging at the time and which saw the use of napalm.

In 1980, within the framework of the Convention on Certain Conventional Weapons, a protocol was adopted on the prohibition and restriction of certain uses of incendiary weapons. The Incendiary Weapons Protocol, Protocol III to the Convention, provides that '[i]t is prohibited in all circumstances to make the civilian population as such, individual civilians or civilian objects the object of attack by incendiary weapons'.[524] The Protocol does not 'prohibit the use of incendiary weapons against combat personnel',[525] nor does it prohibit the use of incendiary weapons against military objectives aside from the situations discussed below.[526] Thus, the approach of the Protocol is to apply the general rules on targeting to the specific case of incendiary weapons. In this sense, it 'adds little'.[527] However, it does provide a useful indication as to what constitutes an incendiary weapon.

Incendiary weapons are defined as 'any weapon or munition which is primarily designed to set fire to objects or to cause burn injury to persons through the action of flame, heat, or a combination thereof, produced by a chemical reaction of a substance delivered on the target'.[528] The definition is almost the same as that drawn up by the Working Group on Incendiary Munitions Classification of the Lucerne Conference of Government Experts.[529] An illustrative list of the forms that incendiary weapons take is set out in the Convention. The list includes, 'for example, flame throwers, fougasses, shells, rockets, grenades, mines, bombs and other containers of incendiary substances'.[530] Incendiary weapons do not include '[m]unitions which may have incidental incendiary effects, such as illuminants, tracers, smoke or signalling systems'.[531] Nor do they include '[m]unitions designed to combine penetration, blast or fragmentation effects with an additional incendiary effect, such as armour-piercing projectiles, fragmentation shells, explosive bombs and similar combined-effects munitions in which the incendiary effect is not specifically designed to cause burn injury to persons, but to be used against military objectives, such as armoured vehicles, aircraft and installations

---

[522] International Conference on Human Rights, Human Rights in Armed Conflicts, Resolution XXIII, 12 May 1968.
[523] GA Res 2932A (XXVII) (1972).
[524] Convention on Certain Conventional Weapons, Protocol on Prohibitions or Restrictions on the Use of Incendiary Weapons (Protocol III), Article 2(1).
[525] FJ Hampson, 'Means and methods of warfare in the conflict in the Gulf', in P Rowe (ed), *The Gulf War 1990–91 in International and English Law* (Routledge, 1993) 89, 102.
[526] *Abella*, above note 25, para 187.
[527] Greenwood, Current Issues, above note 99, 445.
[528] Article 1.
[529] See Lucerne Conference Report, above note 442, Annex 5.
[530] Article 1(a).
[531] Article 1(b)(i). See also Lucerne Conference Report, above note 442, Annex 5; Kalshoven, Arms, above note 102, 221–2.

or facilities'.⁵³² The non-inclusion of the latter category is an important limitation on the definition, given that a 'substantial number of modern incendiary weapons are in fact combined-effects munitions'.⁵³³

One way in which the Protocol deviates from the ordinary rules on targeting is its prohibition 'in all circumstances to make any military objective located within a concentration of civilians the object of attack by air-delivered incendiary weapons'.⁵³⁴ The departure occurs through the prohibition of *all* such attacks, even those that would be discriminate and respect the principle of proportionality, such attacks being lawful under the ordinary rules of targeting. There is a danger that this encourages 'the establishment of military objectives... within cities, towns, and villages (all concentrations of civilians) thus immunizing the military objective from attack by air-delivered incendiary weapons'.⁵³⁵ However, this would be in violation of the customary rule on the obligation to take precautions against the effects of attack.⁵³⁶ Thus, the United States has indicated that it 'would reserve the right to use incendiaries against military targets located in concentrations of civilians where it is judged that such use would cause fewer casualties and less collateral damage than alternative weapons'.⁵³⁷ The advantage of the position taken by the Protocol is the additional protection that is afforded to the civilian population. The formulation of the Protocol reflects a compromise between those that were in favour of a complete prohibition on the use of incendiary weapons and those that were against a complete prohibition.⁵³⁸ Indeed, negotiation of the Protocol was reportedly difficult due to the distance between the various positions taken by delegates.⁵³⁹

The Protocol also prohibits the making of 'any military objective located within a concentration of civilians the object of attack by means of incendiary weapons other than air-delivered incendiary weapons, except when such military objective is clearly separated from the concentration of civilians and all feasible precautions are taken with a view to limiting the incendiary effects to the military objective and to avoiding, and in any event to minimizing, incidental loss of civilian life, injury to civilians and damage to civilian objects'.⁵⁴⁰ It also provides that '[i]t is prohibited to make forests or other kinds of plant cover the object of attack by incendiary weapons except when such natural elements are used to cover, conceal or camouflage combatants or other military objectives, or are themselves military objectives'.⁵⁴¹

---

⁵³² Article 1(b)(ii).
⁵³³ WJ Fenrick, 'New Developments in the Law Concerning the Use of Conventional Weapons in Armed Conflict' (1981) 19 *Canadian Yearbook of International Law* 229, 249.
⁵³⁴ Article 2(2).
⁵³⁵ HS Levie, 'Prohibitions and Restrictions on the Use of Conventional Weapons' (1994) 68 *St John's Law Review* 643, 664.
⁵³⁶ See above, 356.
⁵³⁷ Message From the President of the United States Transmitting Protocols to the 1980 Convention on Prohibitions or Restrictions on the Use of Certain Conventional Weapons Which May Be Deemed to Be Excessively Injurious or to Have Indiscriminate Effects: the Amended Protocol on Prohibitions or Restrictions on the Use of Mines, Booby-traps and Other Devices (Protocol II or the Amended Mines Protocol); the Protocol on Prohibitions or Restrictions on the Use of Incendiary Weapons (Protocol III or the Incendiary Weapons Protocol); and the Protocol on Blinding Laser Weapons (Protocol IV), reproduced in (1998) 1 *YIHL* 566, 569.
⁵³⁸ MJ Matheson, 'The Revision of the Mines Protocol' (1997) 91 *AJIL* 158, 159.
⁵³⁹ Fenrick, Conventional Weapons, above note 533, 248; Parks, Incendiary Weapons, above note 155, 537–8.
⁵⁴⁰ Article 2(3).
⁵⁴¹ Article 2(4).

The Customary International Humanitarian Law study indicates that there is a further obligation in customary international law to take precautions when using incendiary weapons.[542] This is simply an application of the general customary rule on precautions to the particular weapon.

The Protocol does not contain any particular sphere of application. Accordingly, reference must be made to the framework Convention to ascertain in which situations the Protocol applies. Article 1 of the framework Convention originally provided for application to international armed conflicts alone. It was amended during the Second Review Conference in 2001 to apply also 'to situations referred to in Article 3 common to the 1949 Geneva Conventions'.[543] The Protocol thus applies to non-international armed conflicts in respect of states that ratify the amendment.

3.3.5 Laser weapons designed to cause permanent blindness

Regulation of the use of laser weapons was a topic for consideration at the Lucerne Conference of Government Experts in 1974. However, at that time, the use of laser weapons during armed conflicts was considered only a theoretical issue and, at any rate, not at levels that would be damaging to vision. Accordingly, their regulation was not pursued.[544] Around the time that laser weapons were starting to be developed for use in armed conflict, the 1995 Protocol on Blinding Laser Weapons, Protocol IV to the 1980 Convention on Certain Conventional Weapons, was adopted. The Protocol provides that '[i]t is prohibited to employ laser weapons specifically designed, as their sole combat function or as one of their combat functions, to cause permanent blindness to unenhanced vision, that is to the naked eye or to the eye with corrective eyesight devices'.[545] The specific design of the laser weapon is thus an important element of the prohibition, as '[b]linding as an incidental or collateral effect of the legitimate military employment of laser systems, including laser systems used against optical equipment, is not covered by the prohibition'.[546] Thus, lasers which identify targets to aid precision-guided munitions would not be covered by the prohibition, as they have a combined military-humanitarian purpose and are not designed to cause blindness.[547] The other key element of the prohibition is the causing of permanent blindness, defined as 'irreversible and uncorrectable loss of vision which is seriously disabling with no prospect of recovery'.[548] Thus weapons designed to cause temporary blindness in the enemy are excluded from the prohibition.

---

[542] Customary International Humanitarian Law, Rule 84.

[543] Article 2. There was no opposition to the extension; numerous states spoke in favour of it. See 'Second Review Conference of the States Parties to the Convention on Prohibitions or Restrictions on the Use of Certain Conventional Weapons which may be Deemed to be Excessively Injurious or to have Indiscriminate Effects', CCW/CONF.II/2. On the history of the efforts, see D Kaye and SA Solomon, 'The Second Review Conference of the 1980 Convention on Certain Conventional Weapons' (2002) 96 *AJIL* 922, 928.

[544] Lucerne Conference Report, above note 442, 73, paras 261–2. Cf Lugano Conference Report, above note 445, 19, para 54.

[545] Article 1. For background to the Protocol, see L Doswald-Beck, 'New Protocol on Blinding Laser Weapons' (1996) 36 *IRRC* 272; Doswald-Beck, Obstacles, above note 457, 107.

[546] Article 3. On different meanings of 'specifically designed', see MC Zöckler, 'Commentary on Protocol IV on Blinding Laser Weapons' (1998) 1 *YIHL* 333, 335–6.

[547] BM Carnahan and M Robertson, 'The Protocol on "Blinding Laser Weapons": A New Direction for International Humanitarian Law' (1996) 90 *AJIL* 484, 487.

[548] Protocol, Article 4.

As with the Incendiary Weapons Protocol, the scope of application of the Blinding Laser Weapons Protocol is not contained in the Protocol itself. Accordingly, regard must be had to the framework Convention. Following the 2001 amendment to the scope of application clause of the framework Convention, and for those states parties accepting the amendment, the Protocol applies to international and non-international armed conflicts alike.[549] For those states parties that have not accepted the amendment, the situation is rather murkier. Some take the view that the Protocol is applicable to non-international armed conflict regardless of the amendment to the framework Convention,[550] while others disagree.[551] As far as the text of the Protocol is concerned, there is nothing to suggest its applicability to non-international armed conflict. However, the drafting history reveals a different story.[552] The Protocol was intended to have the same sphere of application as the amended Mines Protocol, which was being negotiated at the same time and which was expected to extend to non-international armed conflict.[553] When the talks on the amended Mines Protocol broke down, its envisaged scope of application clause was not available for use in the Blinding Laser Weapons Protocol. Rather than postpone adoption of the Protocol, it was adopted without a scope of application clause. Its scope of application is thus that of the framework Convention. However, its intended scope of application is evident from the Final Declaration of the Review Conference, which referenced 'the need for achieving the *total prohibition* of blinding laser weapons',[554] and the declaration of a number of states upon ratification of the Protocol, again that it applies 'in all circumstances'.[555] For its part, the United States has taken the view that the Protocol does not apply to all armed conflicts as a matter of law; however, 'it is U.S. policy to apply the Protocol to all such conflicts'.[556] That, on balance, seems to be the correct position. The prohibition has been posited as a norm of customary international law, a position that has also been doubted.[557]

3.3.6 Explosive bullets

The 1868 St Petersburg Declaration, the first major international agreement to outlaw the use of a particular weapon in time of war, provides that '[t]he Contracting Parties engage mutually to renounce, in case of war among themselves, the employment by

---

[549] See above, 399.
[550] Doswald-Beck, Blinding Laser Weapons, above note 545.
[551] L Maresca, 'Second Review Conference of the Convention on Certain Conventional Weapons' (2002) 845 *IRRC* 255.
[552] See Doswald-Beck, Blinding Laser Weapons, above note 545, 286–8; A Roberts and R Guelff, *Documents on the Laws of War* (Oxford University Press, 2000) 518.
[553] Report of Main Committee III, CCW/CONF.I/4, in Review Conference of the States Parties to the Convention on Prohibitions on Restrictions on the Use of Certain Conventional Weapons which may be Deemed to be Excessively Injurious or to have Indiscriminate Effects: Final Report, CCW/CONF.I/16 (Part II), para 5 and Annex.
[554] Review Conference of the States Parties to the Convention on Prohibitions on Restrictions on the Use of Certain Conventional Weapons which may be Deemed to be Excessively Injurious or to have Indiscriminate Effects: Final Report, CCW/CONF.I/16 (Part I), 36 (emphasis added).
[555] Australia, Austria, Belgium, Canada, Germany, Greece, Ireland, Israel, Italy, Liechtenstein, Netherlands, South Africa, Sweden, Switzerland, and the United Kingdom. See the various declarations in Roberts and Guelff, above note 552, 553–60.
[556] Report from US Secretary of State Warren Christopher on the three Protocols, accompanying President's letter of transmittal to the Senate, reproduced in (1997) 91 *AJIL* 325, 348.
[557] Customary International Humanitarian Law, Rule 86. Cf Boothby, *Weapons*, above note 462, 330; Haines, Weapons, above note 460, 277–8.

their military or naval troops of any projectile of a weight below 400 grammes, which is either explosive or charged with fulminating or inflammable substances'.⁵⁵⁸ The Declaration only applies 'in case of war among themselves', limiting application to conflicts between states parties. However, the prohibition applies to non-international armed conflicts through the rule on unnecessary suffering and through customary international law.⁵⁵⁹ Thus, the United Kingdom has taken the view that, as a solid bullet would disable the enemy, explosion of the bullet upon impact with the enemy would aggravate the injury unnecessarily.⁵⁶⁰ Along similar lines, during the US civil war of 1861–5, General Grant condemned the use of explosive musket balls by the Confederates as they produced 'increased suffering without any corresponding advantage to those using them'.⁵⁶¹ The customary status of the prohibition has been challenged by the United States. However, that challenge is based, in part, on the notion that the United Kingdom shares its view,⁵⁶² an argument which is misplaced as the UK military manual accepts that the prohibition applies to non-international armed conflicts through the prohibition on unnecessary suffering.⁵⁶³

The particular weight limit of 400 grammes was rather arbitrary.⁵⁶⁴ As a result, the customary prohibition is not considered to be in respect of explosive projectiles under 400 grammes, but the 'anti-personnel use of bullets which explode within the human body'.⁵⁶⁵ Debate exists as to the precise scope of the prohibition. The Customary International Humanitarian Law study frames the prohibition as one of effect, while others contend the prohibition is one of design.⁵⁶⁶ It is likely that the prohibition falls in between the two, relating to the nature of the bullet. This is consistent with the general principles on weapons use, which relate to the nature of the weapon.⁵⁶⁷ It is more limited than an effects-based approach, which is potentially too broad, but broader than a design-based approach, which is potentially too narrow, as the nature of the weapon excludes instances of misuse while including mis-design.

3.3.7 Expanding bullets

It is prohibited to use 'bullets which expand or flatten easily in the human body, such as bullets with a hard envelope which does not entirely cover the core or is pierced with incisions'.⁵⁶⁸ The prohibition covers bullets that are manufactured along those lines, for example with incisions, as well as those that are altered along those lines, for example

---

⁵⁵⁸ Declaration Renouncing the Use, in Time of War, of Explosive Projectiles Under 400 Grammes Weight.
⁵⁵⁹ Customary International Humanitarian Law, Rule 78.
⁵⁶⁰ UK *Manual*, above note 43, 109. See also Spaight, above note 483, 75.
⁵⁶¹ Winthrop, above note 484, 785.
⁵⁶² JB Bellinger, III and WJ Haynes, II, 'A US Government Response to the International Committee of the Red Cross Study *Customary International Humanitarian Law*' (2007) 89 *IRRC* 443, 465.
⁵⁶³ See UK *Manual*, above note 43, 397 in conjunction with 109. See also Boothby, *Weapons*, above note 462, 326.
⁵⁶⁴ Kalshoven, Arms, above note 102, 207.
⁵⁶⁵ Customary International Humanitarian Law, Rule 78. See also, with a slightly different formulation, Oeter, above note 454, 138.
⁵⁶⁶ See Bellinger and Haynes US Government Response', above note 562, 460–5; *Customary International Humanitarian Law, Volume I: Rules*, above note 84, 273; Boothby, *Weapons*, above note 462, 144.
⁵⁶⁷ See above, 390.
⁵⁶⁸ The language is taken from Hague Declaration IV(3) Concerning Expanding Bullets of 1899.

'by cutting notches in it with a knife in the course of combat'.[569] The classic example of such a bullet is the dum-dum bullet.

Some doubt has been cast on the applicability of the prohibition to non-international armed conflict. In 1899, the British delegate to the Hague Peace Conference opined that expanding bullets were needed in wars against 'savages' whom ordinary bullets did not stop. The delegate opined: 'there is a difference in war between civilized nations and that against savages.'[570] This was met with the response from the Russian delegate that '[i]t is impermissible to make a distinction between a savage and a civilized enemy; both are men who deserve the same treatment'.[571] Although the non-international armed conflict was not mentioned in the exchange, it was the colonial conflict that the British delegate had in mind. Although Great Britain dissented from the Declaration prohibiting the use of expanding bullets in 1899, it recalled dum-dum ammunition from South Africa during the Boer war and protested against its use by Boer forces, seemingly influenced by the prohibition in the Hague Declaration.[572]

A century later, the prohibition was considered inapplicable to non-international armed conflict on the basis that the use of expanding bullets was lawful during peacetime and situations of internal tensions and disturbances.[573] Expanding bullets are also considered useful as they cause less danger to surrounding individuals than ordinary bullets.[574] Contesting the analogy, it has been suggested that in times of peace, expanding bullets are fired by police from handguns and deposit far less kinetic energy than expanding bullets fired from rifles in times of armed conflict.[575] Regardless, the fact that expanding bullets are permitted to be used in times of peace does not support their continued use during times of non-international armed conflict. What is permitted in time of peace is not necessarily permitted in time of armed conflict. Hence there is authority for the proposition that the 'employment of bullets which expand or flatten easily in the human body' is prohibited in non-international armed conflict.[576] With the amendment to the Rome Statute prohibiting the employment of 'bullets which expand or flatten easily in the human body, such as bullets with a hard envelope which does not entirely cover the core or is pierced with incisions',[577] the matter can now be considered settled. The prohibition applies to non-international armed conflict as a matter of customary international law.[578]

---

[569] H McCoubrey, *International Humanitarian Law* (Dartmouth, 1990) 157.
[570] *Proceedings*, above note 432, 286. See also at 343.
[571] Ibid, 343.
[572] See Spaight, above note 483, 79–80.
[573] See eg Headquarters, Department of the Army, Office of the Judge Advocate General, DAJA-IA Memorandum 1985/7026, Subject: Use of Expanding Ammunition by US Military Forces in Counterterrorist Incidents, 23 September 1985, cited in WH Parks, 'Special Forces' Wear of Non-Standard Uniforms' (2003) 4 *Chicago JIL* 493, 524.
[574] Hampson Study, above note 55, para 32; IIHL *Manual*, above note 55, 35. See also the intervention of the Philippines during the Review Conference, as recounted in Alamuddin and Webb, above note 519, 1225.
[575] *Customary International Humanitarian Law, Volume I: Rules*, above note 84, 270. See R Coupland and D Loye, 'The 1899 Hague Declaration concerning Expanding Bullets: A Treaty Effective for More than 100 Years Faces Complex Contemporary Issues' (2003) 85 *IRRC* 135.
[576] *Constitutional Conformity of Protocol II*, above note 5, para 23; IIHL Declaration, above note 52, B2.
[577] Resolution RC/Res.5, 10 June 2010.
[578] See also Customary International Humanitarian Law, Rule 77.

Rather more difficult is whether there are any exceptions to the prohibition. As with riot control agents, it needs to be considered whether expanding bullets may be used, for example, to control a riot that breaks out in a detention centre housing captured fighters during a non-international armed conflict, or in the context of a mission to rescue hostages being held by one of the parties to a non-international armed conflict. The Resolution amending the Rome Statute provides that the prohibition relates to the employment of the bullets 'in the context of and ... associated with an armed conflict, *which consequently confirm the exclusion from the Court's jurisdiction of law enforcement situations*'.[579] As the Court has jurisdiction over law-enforcement situations during an armed conflict, for example in respect of detention centres housing captured fighters and hostage-rescue operations, the Resolution indicates that the juxtaposition here is between law enforcement in the sense of internal tensions and disturbances and times of peace, and armed conflict. Thus, the use of expanding bullets is prohibited in the hypothetical situations mentioned above when they are associated with an armed conflict. Expanding bullets can be used in situations that are not 'associated with' the armed conflict, for example to control a riot in an ordinary prison or in a hostage rescue mission unrelated to the armed conflict. This is perhaps surprising in light of the fact that the use of riot control agents is allowed in such situations.[580] Furthermore, if the use of expanding bullets is considered necessary, for example to stop suicide bombers,[581] this will be the case in situations of peace, international armed conflict, and non-international armed conflict alike. It is the situation at hand that should be determinative and not the characterization of the broader violence. In this sense, the sometimes unclear distinction between internal tensions and a non-international armed conflict is of less importance.[582]

The Resolution amending the Rome Statute seems to address the point through a different route. The Preamble to the Resolution provides that 'the crime is committed only if the perpetrator employs the bullets to uselessly aggravate suffering or the wounding effect upon the target of such bullets, as reflected in customary international law'.[583] This element was also stressed by a number of states following the adoption of the amendment.[584] On this basis, it would seem that the individual who uses expanding bullets in a non-international armed conflict with the view that it puts bystanders at less risk would not be guilty of the war crime. However, given that such an individual would violate the language of the Article 8(2)(e)(xv) provision, and would likely satisfy the ICC Elements of Crimes—the Elements simply providing that the perpetrator be '*aware* that the nature of the bullets was such that their employment would uselessly aggravate suffering or the wounding effect'[585]—irrespective of the Preamble to the Resolution, the individual would be committing a war crime.

---

[579] Resolution RC/Res.5, 10 June 2010 (emphasis added). For a different reading of the italicized words, see R Geiß, 'Poison, Gas and Expanding Bullets: The Extension of the List of Prohibited Weapons at the Review Conference of the International Criminal Court in Kampala' (2010) 13 *YIHL* 337, 346.

[580] See above, 395. See also, supporting such an exception, Melzer, above note 205, 375–8; K Watkin, 'Chemical Agents and Exploding Bullets: Limited Law Enforcement Exceptions or Unwarranted Handcuffs?' (2006) 36 *IYHR* 43, 67.

[581] Haines, above note 460, 272.

[582] Cf IIHL *Manual*, above note 55, 34–5.

[583] Resolution RC/Res.5, 10 June 2010.

[584] Alamuddin and Webb, above note 519, 1225; Geiß, above note 579, 346–7.

[585] ICC Elements of Crimes, Article 8(2)(e)(xv)-3.

3.3.8 Booby-traps and anti-personnel mines

Mines have long been used in times of armed conflict, and their use long condemned. It was written in 1911 that '[t]he question of mines is of much less importance in land war than in naval war; but it would be no loss of time and words if it were given some consideration at a future Hague Conference, with a view to the laying down of some definite principles on the subject'.[586] It would take many a decade before any proscriptions would be set out. The Amended Mines Protocol to the Convention on Certain Conventional Weapons is a complex affair consisting of numerous detailed provisions. The Protocol applies the general rules on weapons to the specific case of mines and booby-traps, namely the prohibition 'in all circumstances' on the use of 'any mine, booby-trap or other device which is designed or of a nature to cause superfluous injury or unnecessary suffering' or which is used in an indiscriminate manner.[587]

Booby-traps

The general issue considered above, namely whether to ban specific weapons or to lay out general rules that are applicable to all weapons,[588] was raised at the micro level in the context of booby-traps. At the Lugano Conference of Government Experts, it was noted that 'the detailed list of uses of booby-traps singled out for prohibition ... was not, and never could be, complete ... that the attempt to draw up such a list was misguided ... [and] that a general formula was to be preferred'.[589] However, this approach was not followed. The Amended Mines Protocol defines a booby-trap as 'any device or material which is designed, constructed, or adapted to kill or injure, and which functions unexpectedly when a person disturbs or approaches an apparently harmless object or performs an apparently safe act'.[590] It is unlawful for booby-traps to be 'attached to or associated with', *inter alia*, protective emblems, the dead, animals, medical equipment, children's toys, food, cultural objects, and religious items.[591] Many of these specific proscriptions are based on the prohibition of perfidious conduct.[592] Letter bombs, booby-trapped corpses, and the dropping of booby-traps in the shape of small animals—all documented in non-international armed conflicts[593]—are thus prohibited. The prohibition on the use of certain booby-traps is considered to have customary status.[594]

Anti-personnel mines

One of the principal problems with the use of anti-personnel mines is their potential indiscriminate effect,[595] both during conflicts and subsequent to the conclusion of conflicts. For example, in 1998, the Taliban took the view that 'the presence of

---

[586] Spaight, above note 483, 83.
[587] Convention on Certain Conventional Weapons, Amended Protocol II, Article 3(3).
[588] Above, 386–7.
[589] Lugano Conference Report, above note 445, 13, para 31.
[590] Article 2(4).
[591] Article 7.
[592] See Kalshoven, Arms, above note 102, 255.
[593] For documentation of their use, see Green, above note 83, 139 fn 121; BM Carnahan, 'The Law of Land Mine Warfare: Protocol II to the United Nations Convention on Certain Conventional Weapons' (1984) 105 *Military Law Review* 73, 90; Report on the Situation of Human Rights in Afghanistan prepared by the Special Rapporteur, E/CN.4/1985/21, 19 February 1985, para 108.
[594] Customary International Humanitarian Law, Rule 80; *Constitutional Conformity of Protocol II*, above note 5, para 23.
[595] Oeter, above note 136, 142.

landmines in large numbers is... one of the main problems of Afghanistan'. They are also 'a major threat to the reconstruction of Afghanistan and repatriation of the refugees and displaced persons to their homes'.[596] Anti-personnel mines are also prohibited for other reasons. After witnessing the effects of a mine on a Union soldier during the US civil war (1861–5), General Sherman described mines as 'not war, but murder';[597] however, forces under Sherman's command also used mines. Mines also contaminate the areas in which they are sown and upon conclusion of a conflict, land remains uninhabitable. Further compounding the situation is the fact that, oftentimes, records are not kept as to the locations in which mines have been sown. However, mines are also considered an important tool in the prevention of enemy advances and are used to aid the defence of certain areas.[598] Thus, armed groups that have committed to a ban on the use of anti-personnel mines occasionally continue to argue that mines may be used for defensive purposes.[599] Another group has not committed to the ban for precisely this reason, stating in 2006 that:

> [w]e abhor the use of landmines in warfare and understand the international condemnation of the use of landmines because of the high risk to civilians. However in certain circumstances we use them to defend our troops as we lack alternative means of defence. Our use of landmines is extremely limited and steps are taken to avoid civilian casualties. We only use them in military zones, not in civilian areas. The Karenni army does not place landmines on roads and in other areas used by innocent civilians. They are used for defensive purposes and we have no intention of placing them in war-free-zones.[600]

The Amended Mines Protocol

The Amended Mines Protocol prohibits the use of certain mines. It also requires states parties to take feasible precautions to protect civilians from the effects of mines, and to give a warning to the civilian population should mines be emplaced unless circumstances do not permit. Provision is made for the recording of mined areas, the removal of mines, and cooperation and assistance in the removal of mines.[601] Certain aspects of the Amended Mines Protocol, notably the prohibition on the indiscriminate use of mines,[602] the requirement of precautions,[603] the requirement of recording mine fields,[604] and the removal, rendering harmless, or facilitating removal of mines at the end of active hostilities have been posited as being of customary international law status.[605] The two former obligations are certainly of customary international law status, applying as they do the general customary rules to the specific case of anti-personnel mines.[606] As to the two latter obligations, there is growing practice pointing in this direction.

---

[596] Statement of the Islamic Emirate of Afghanistan on the Problem of Landmines, 6 October 1998.
[597] WT Sherman, *Memoirs of General WT Sherman, Volume II* (Charles Webster, 1891) 194.
[598] APV Rogers, 'A Commentary on the Protocol on Prohibitions or Restrictions on the Use of Mines, Booby-Traps and Other Devices' (1987) 26 *Military Law and the Law of War Review* 185, 186. See also Spaight, above note 483, 81–2.
[599] Geneva Call, Engaging Armed Non-State Actors in a Landmine Ban: The Geneva Call Progress Report (2000–2007) 20.
[600] KNPP, Statement on the Use of Landmines, Statement No 02/06, 31 August 2006.
[601] Article 1(2).
[602] EECC Partial Award, above note 73, para 15.
[603] Customary International Humanitarian Law, Rule 81.
[604] EECC Partial Award, above note 73, para 15; Customary International Humanitarian Law, Rule 82 ('arguably'; and 'as far as possible').
[605] Customary International Humanitarian Law, Rule 83.
[606] See above, 347–8 and 351–6.

The key obligations set out in the (original) Mines Protocol were accepted by a number of non-state armed groups. For example, in 1988, the FMLN of El Salvador justified its use of mines by reference to the (original) Mines Protocol, noting, *inter alia*, that it does not use mines 'in an indiscriminate manner or to directly attack the civilian population'.[607]

It also stated that it was 'attempting to increase to a maximum the effectiveness of the preventive measures aimed at protecting noncombatants'.[608] The FMLN also set out the precautionary measures it had taken, which included placing mines 'in unpopulated areas shortly before government military troops pass through', preparing 'a map of the mines placed', '[w]arning through FMLN radio stations and in other forms in what zones there are mined fields', and using mines that do 'not operate unless a weight of more than 80 pounds is applied. In this way the FMLN seeks to prevent children from being affected by land mines'.[609] Other groups have also accepted the various rules.

For example, the 1998 'Acuerdo de Puerta del Cielo' in respect of the Ejército de Liberación Nacional (ELN) of Colombia provided that '[n]o mines shall be used to deliberately kill or mutilate civilians'.[610]

During the conflict in Croatia, the Memorandum of Understanding concluded between representatives of the Republic of Croatia, the Republic of Serbia, and the Federal Republic of Yugoslavia of 27 November 1991, brought into effect the (unamended) Mines Protocol to the conflict.[611] The same was true of the Agreement of 22 May 1992 relating to the conflict in Bosnia.[612] For its part, the CNF of Burma provides in its Code that landmines are to be 'avoided as much as possible' due to the effect they can have on civilians. The Code goes on to note that when mines are used, 'as per the necessity of war, the place of the mines buried should be recorded and a copy of the record must be sent to the head office. Moreover, at the end of the war, these mines should be immediately removed'.[613]

The (original) Mines Protocol, like the framework Convention on Certain Conventional Weapons itself, originally applied to international armed conflicts alone. This was recognized as a significant limitation as the majority of casualties of anti-personnel mines resulted from non-international armed conflicts. As Spain noted at the Review Conference, speaking on behalf of the European Union, 'it was precisely in such conflicts, the most common kind at present, that the indiscriminate use of anti-personnel mines occurred most frequently and had the most devastating effects on innocent civilians'.[614] Thus, upon ratification of the framework Convention, the United States declared that it would apply it 'to all armed conflicts referred to in Article 2 and 3 common to the Geneva Conventions of 12 August 1949'.[615] Israel and

---

[607] FMLN, above note 26, 10–14.
[608] Ibid, 14.
[609] Ibid, 24.
[610] Acuerdo de Puerta del Cielo con el ELN, 15 de Julio de 1998, Article 15.D. The original reads: 'No se utilizarán minas para matar o mutilar deliberadamente a civiles.'
[611] Article 6.
[612] Article 2.5.
[613] Chin National Front, Code, above note 26, Article 30 (unofficial translation).
[614] CCW/CONF.I/SR.2 (1996) 4, para 16, in Review Conference of the States Parties to the Convention on the Prohibitions or Restrictions on the Use of Certain Conventional Weapons which may be Deemed to be Excessively Injurious or to have Indiscriminate Effects, Final Document, Part II, CCW/CONF.I/16 (Part II). See also Matheson, Mines Protocol, above note 538, 159; JA McCall Jr, 'Infernal Machines and Hidden Death: International Law and Limits on the Indiscriminate Use of Land Mine Warfare' (1994–5) 24 *Georgia Journal of International and Comparative Law* 229, 264.
[615] Reproduced in (1994) 88 *AJIL* 748, 751.

France made similar declarations.[616] Furthermore, in giving its advice and consent as to ratification of the Convention, which included the Mines Protocol, the US Senate considered extending the scope of application of the Protocol to include internal armed conflicts a priority for strengthening the Protocol.[617] The Protocol was subsequently amended to apply to the 'situations referred to in Article 3 common to the four Geneva Conventions of 12 August 1949'.[618]

During the Review Conference that adopted the Amended Mines Protocol, there was considerable support for extending the scope of application of the Protocol to all circumstances, namely times of armed conflict and peace alike.[619] This was considered necessary to prevent states from denying the existence of a non-international armed conflict on their territory and thereby failing to apply the Protocol.[620] However, a few states objected to such a scope of application clause, arguing that certain weapons were prohibited in times of armed conflict but allowed during times of peace.[621] Accordingly, the scope of application of the Protocol was extended to include non-international armed conflicts but excluded situations of internal tensions and disturbances. Much like common Article 3, the Amended Protocol provides that, in the case of 'armed conflicts not of an international character occurring in the territory of one of the High Contracting Parties, each party to the conflict shall be bound to apply the prohibitions and restrictions of this Protocol'.[622]

The Ottawa Convention

The Ottawa Convention on Anti-Personnel Mines contains more protective provisions in respect of anti-personnel mines than does the Amended Mines Protocol. States parties undertake 'never under any circumstances' to use, develop, produce, acquire, stockpile, retain or transfer anti-personnel mines, or to 'assist, encourage or induce . . . anyone to engage' in such activity.[623] States parties also undertake to destroy the relevant mines.[624] Furthermore, the Convention contains obligations in respect of clearance of mines, assistance to victims of mines, and mine-risk education.[625] The inclusion of the phrase 'never under any circumstances' was considered to render unnecessary a scope of application clause,[626] and includes non-international armed conflicts.

One difficulty with the Ottawa Convention is its lack of reference to parties to the conflict or non-state armed groups. Whereas the obligations contained in the Amended Mines Protocol are incumbent on 'each party to the conflict', the obligations resulting

---

[616] Declaration made on accession of Israel, in Schindler and Toman, above note 95, 218; Reservation made on signature of France, ibid, 217.
[617] Cited in Matheson, Mines Protocol, above note 538, 160.
[618] Article 1(2).
[619] See the 'Chairman's Rolling Text', Article 1, Alternative A, CCW/CONF.I/GE/23, 11.
[620] K Dörmann, 'The First Review Conference to the 1980 Convention on Prohibitions or Restrictions on the Use of Certain Conventional Weapons Which May Be Deemed to Be Excessively Injurious or to Have Indiscriminate Effects—A Story of Failure?' (1995) 8 *Humanitäres Völkerrecht* 203, 204.
[621] Ibid, 204.
[622] Article 1(3).
[623] 1997 Convention on the Prohibition of the Use, Stockpiling, Production and Transfer of Anti-Personnel Mines and on Their Destruction, Article 1(1).
[624] Article 1(2).
[625] Articles 5 and 6.
[626] S Maslen, *Commentaries on Arms Control Treaties: Volume I* (Oxford University Press, 2005) 75–6.

from the Ottawa Convention are framed in terms of states parties alone. The absence of reference to non-state armed groups, or parties to the conflict, was raised during the drafting of the Convention.[627] However, it remained framed in terms of states parties. This led to the creation of the NGO 'Geneva Call' which engages armed non-state actors on humanitarian norms, in particular the prohibition on anti-personnel mines and mine action.[628]

The importance of the prohibition on the use of anti-personnel mines in non-international armed conflicts, as well as mine action, is evidenced by the number of armed groups that have expressed their commitment to adhere to the relevant obligations. At the time of writing some 41 armed non-state actors had signed the Geneva Call Deed of Commitment, through which they commit to a 'total ban' on anti-personnel mines; to co-operate in and undertake destruction of stockpiles, clearance of mines, and provision of assistance to victims of mines; and to allow and co-operate in the verification of their commitments under the Deed.[629] The commitment to the prohibition on the use of anti-personnel mines is particularly important given that mines are traditionally considered a 'poor man's weapon' in light of their relative inexpensive nature, their being readily obtainable, and easily made. They are thus considered a useful counterpart to the more expensive weaponry that may be available to states. The fact that a number of armed groups have committed not to use them thus signals that the factual asymmetry of non-international armed conflicts is not an inherent obstacle to legal regulation or compliance with the law on the part of armed groups.[630]

Non-signatory non-state armed groups have also indicated that they do not use anti-personnel mines, with the NDFP of the Philippines indicating in 2010 that its armed wing, the NPA, 'does not use and has never used mines which are not command-detonated and directed against military vehicles and personnel'.[631] Similarly, the National Transitional Council of Libya indicated in a 2011 communiqué:

Recognising that landmines indiscriminately kill and maim both during and after armed conflict, and also impede humanitarian aid and socio-economic development as well as post-conflict reconstruction, the NTC hereby stresses the following:

The Libyan National Transitional Council (NTC) announces to the people of Libya that no forces under the command and control of the NTC will use antipersonnel or anti-vehicle landmines.

Forces under the command and control of the NTC shall be requested to destroy all landmines in their possession, including mines recovered during operations. This ban shall be transmitted to all combatants under the command and control of the National Transitional Council.

The NTC agrees to cooperate in the provision of mine clearance, risk education and victim assistance.

We believe that any future Libyan government should relinquish landmines and join the 1997 Mine Ban Treaty.[632]

---

[627] Ibid, 63–4 and 75.
[628] On which see below, 538–42.
[629] Geneva Call Deed of Commitment for Adherence to a Total Ban on Anti-Personnel Mines and for Cooperation in Mine Action. see below, 539.
[630] On asymmetry, see above, 245–6.
[631] NDFP Human Rights Monitoring Committee, 'NDFP denies use of anti-personnel mines, emphasizes adherence to international humanitarian law', 24 April 2010.
[632] Communiqué by the Libyan National Transitional Council Regarding Landmines, undated, available at the website of Human Rights Watch <http://www.hrw.org>.

3.3.9 Cluster munitions

States parties to the Convention on Cluster Munitions are prohibited, *inter alia*, from using, developing, producing, acquiring, stockpiling, retaining, or transferring cluster munitions, and from assisting anyone with those acts.[633] Obligations arise under the Convention also in respect of the clearance and destruction of remnants of cluster munitions, and providing assistance to victims of cluster munitions.[634] Cluster munitions are defined as 'a conventional munition that is designed to disperse or release explosive submunitions each weighing less than 20 kilograms, and includes those explosive submunitions'.[635] It does not include munitions or submunitions designed to dispense flares or smoke, designed to produce electrical effects, or are of a particular form in order to avoid having indiscriminate effects.[636] Cluster munitions are considered problematic given that, depending on the situations in which they are used, they may not be able to discriminate between civilians and fighters, or civilian objects and military objectives. Furthermore, cluster munitions may fail to explode, with dormant remnants causing death and injury to civilians and contamination of the land sometimes many years after a conflict concludes.[637] In certain respects, then, the regulation of cluster munitions has a parallel with the regulation of anti-personnel mines.

The Cluster Munitions Convention applies in non-international armed conflicts given its application 'under any circumstances',[638] a reference by this stage common to weapons treaties. Even prior to a prohibition on the use of cluster munitions, the Revolutionary United Front of Sierra Leone indicated in 1995 that '[t]he constant use of heavy artillery and cluster bombs have devastated the countryside'.[639] Likewise, the Sudan People's Liberation Movement indicated in 1996 that it was '[d]eeply concerned over the tragic consequences of indiscriminate use of Anti-personnel mines in particular and the presence of unexploded sub-munitions from cluster bombs and unexploded ordnance' and that it was '[p]articularly alarmed at the significant increase in the number of mines and sub-munition victims among the civilian population'.[640] The Preamble to the Cluster Munitions Convention contains an explicit reference to non-state armed groups, the first international humanitarian law instrument directly to do so. The Preamble provides: '*Resolved* also that armed groups distinct from the armed forces of a State shall not, under any circumstances, be permitted to engage in any activity prohibited to a State Party to this Convention.' However, this preambular reference is the only reference to non-state armed groups in the Convention and the Convention itself is framed in terms of states parties. A lack of reference to non-state armed groups or to parties to the conflict is unfortunate given that the use of cluster

---

[633] Article 1(1).
[634] Articles 4 and 5, respectively. See B Docherty, 'Breaking New Ground: The Convention on Cluster Munitions and the Evolution of International Humanitarian Law' (2009) 31 *HRQ* 934, 949–55.
[635] Article 2(2).
[636] Article 2(2)(a)–(c).
[637] This is recognized in the Preamble to the Convention. See also B Docherty, 'The Time is Now: A Historical Argument for a Cluster Munitions Convention' (2007) 20 *Harvard Human Rights Journal* 53, 61–3; Docherty, New Ground, above note 634, 938.
[638] Article 1(1). See K Hulme, 'The 2008 Cluster Munitions Convention: Stepping Outside the CCW Framework Convention (Again)' (2009) 58 *ICLQ* 219, 222.
[639] RUF, 'Footpaths to Democracy: Toward a New Sierra Leone', 1995.
[640] SPLM, Resolution on the Problem Posed by Proliferation of Anti-Personnel Mines in Liberated Parts of New Sudan, 1 November 1996, Preamble, reproduced in Mine Ban Education Workshop in Southern Sudan: Report of Proceedings and Recommendations (Geneva Call, 2003) Annex B.

munitions is by no means limited to states. Non-state armed groups have used cluster munitions, for example during the armed conflicts in Afghanistan (1990s), Bosnia (1992–5), Croatia (1991–5), and, arguably, Tajikistan (1992–7).[641]

At the time of writing, the prohibition on the use of cluster munitions applies in respect of states parties and does not reflect customary international law. Nonetheless, widespread condemnation followed reports that forces loyal to President Gaddafi used cluster munitions during the violence in Libya in 2011, including from non-states parties to the Convention. For example, the Contact Group on Libya 'deplored its reported use of cluster munitions and pledged these criminal actions will not go unpunished'.[642] The Libyan Government also denied using cluster munitions, stating that '[w]e can never do this, morally, legally'.[643] Although these reactions represent policy and propaganda as much as law, they suggest that the law is moving in the direction of prohibiting the use of cluster munitions as a matter of customary international law.

3.3.10 Non-detectable fragments

The Protocol on Non-Detectable Fragments, Protocol I to the Convention on Certain Conventional Weapons, provides that '[i]t is prohibited to use any weapon the primary effect of which is to injure by fragments which in the human body escape detection by X-rays'.[644] The focus of the Protocol is thus on fragments, primarily plastic, glass, and wooden fragments, which would not be detected by X-rays, thus preventing or impeding medical care. The prohibition is based on the unnecessary suffering principle.[645]

The prohibition covers only those weapons 'the primary effect of which' is to injure by non-detectable fragments. This has been interpreted as covering 'weapons which were *designed* to injure by such fragments'.[646] However, such an interpretation unreasonably narrows the weapons that are prohibited by the Convention, for the Convention explicitly adopts an effects-based test rather than an intention-based test to ascertain the prohibited weapons. At the Lugano Conference of Government Experts, it was made clear that '[t]he use of such weapons would cause unnecessary suffering, and it was immaterial whether the indiscriminate effects were brought about intentionally or not'.[647] Thus, weapons that were not designed to injure by fragments but nevertheless have that as their primary effect would fall foul of the prohibition. That said, the prohibition necessarily contains limits. As was also noted at Lugano, weapons may by chance give rise to fragments that are difficult to detect: 'it was convenient, for

---

[641] Human Rights Watch, *Timeline of Cluster Munition Use* (April 2010); G Nystuen and SC Maslen, *The Convention on Cluster Munitions: A Commentary* (Oxford University Press, 2010) 66.
[642] Contact Group on Libya: Chair's Conclusions, 5 May 2011.
[643] Government Spokesman, Moussa Ibrahim, quoted in H Sherwood, 'Libya: Gaddafi Forces "Using Cluster Bombs in Misrata"', *The Guardian* (UK), 15 April 2011.
[644] For its precursor, see Lugano Conference Report, above note 445, 123, para 79.
[645] Y Sandoz, 'A New Step Forward in International Law: Prohibitions or Restrictions on the Use of Certain Conventional Weapons' (1981) 21 *IRRC* 3, 11; JA Roach, 'Certain Conventional Weapons Convention: Arms Control or Humanitarian Law?' (1984) 105 *Military Law Review* 3, 69. Cf Boothby, *Weapons*, above note 462, 197.
[646] Roach, Conventional Weapons, above note 645, 70, drawing on discussions at the 1974–7 Diplomatic Conference.
[647] Lugano Conference Report, above note 445, 18, para 49.

example, to use plastic parts rather than metal ones in some munitions.'[648] Thus, not all non-detectable materials are prohibited; plastic casings or detonators, for example, would not be caught by the prohibition.[649] In any event, the prohibition is of little significance, given that such weapons neither exist nor are planned for development.[650] Indeed, the framework Convention on Certain Conventional Weapons requires a state to accept at least two of the annexed Protocols precisely in order to prevent a state from becoming party to the Protocol on Non-Detectable Fragments alone.[651]

The Protocol does not contain its own sphere of application. For this, reference must be made to the framework Convention, Article 1 of which, as amended during the Second Review Conference, applies 'to situations referred to in Article 3 common to the 1949 Geneva Conventions'. The Protocol is thus applicable to non-international armed conflicts in respect of those states that accept the amendment. The customary status of the prohibition has also been posited.[652]

3.3.11 *Explosive remnants of war*

The aftermath of a conflict often reveals millions of unexploded and abandoned shells, mortars, and grenades. These explosive remnants of war are unexploded ordnances that 'may have been fired, dropped, launched or projected and should have exploded but failed to do so', as well as those abandoned explosive ordnances that have been 'left behind or dumped by a party to an armed conflict'.[653] These cause further losses of life and injury to civilians, damage to civilian objects, and turn vast tracts of land into no-go areas. Protocol V to the Convention on Certain Conventional Weapons contains detailed provisions on the clearance, removal, and destruction of such remnants. For example, pursuant to Article 3(2) of the Protocol, '[a]fter the cessation of active hostilities and as soon as feasible, each High Contracting Party and party to an armed conflict shall mark and clear, remove or destroy explosive remnants of war in affected territories under its control'. There are also provisions on the recording of information 'to the maximum extent possible and as far as practicable',[654] and on the sharing of such information. Most provisions are directed towards all parties to the conflict. However, some are directed to High Contracting Parties alone, namely those relating to interaction with states and international organizations.[655]

Despite the amendment to the framework Convention, the Protocol on Explosive Remnants of War would not have been applicable automatically to non-international armed conflict given that Article 1(7) of the framework Convention provides that the amended scope of application would not necessarily apply to protocols concluded after

---

[648] Ibid, 122, para 78. See also the proposal made in this regard to use the language of weapons 'which rely for their injurious effects on': COLU/216, reproduced in Annex A.15.
[649] Roberts and Guelff, above note 552, 517.
[650] Fenrick, Conventional Weapons, above note 533, 242; LC Green, ' "Unnecessary Suffering", Weapons Control and the Law of War', in LC Green (ed), *Essays on the Modern Law of War* (Transnational, 1999) 329, 366.
[651] Y Sandoz, 'A New Step Forward in International Law: Prohibitions or Restrictions on the Use of Certain Conventional Weapons' (1981) 21 *IRRC* 3, 9.
[652] Customary International Humanitarian Law, Rule 79. Cf Boothby, *Weapons*, above note 462, 327.
[653] Article 2(2)–(4).
[654] Article 4(1).
[655] See eg Article 7, which uses the term 'states non-party' rather than 'non-state parties' which may have caused confusion.

1 January 2002.⁶⁵⁶ However, the Protocol is applicable to non-international armed conflicts through its scope of application clause, such scope proving uncontroversial.⁶⁵⁷

4. Methods of combat

Methods of combat relate to the tactics that are used in warfare. As with the means of combat, certain general rules apply to their regulation. Methods of combat are also subject to particular rules, which form the subject of this part. These rules include the denial of quarter, the prohibition on the use of certain emblems, the prohibition on certain perfidious conduct, the prohibition on taking human shields, and the prohibition on the starvation of civilians as a method of combat.

4.1 Denial of quarter

It is prohibited to order that there shall be no survivors, to threaten an adversary therewith, and to conduct hostilities on such a basis.⁶⁵⁸ The prohibition is an important one, as all the rules for the benefit of captured fighters depend on compliance with it. The rule also 'constitutes in essence a logical expression of the principle that the legal use of military violence is strictly limited to what is required by military necessity; clearly there is no necessity to kill persons *hors de combat*'.⁶⁵⁹

The rule applies to non-international armed conflict as a matter of conventional law. Additional Protocol II provides, in a rather simpler form: '[i]t is prohibited to order that there shall be no survivors.'⁶⁶⁰ The prohibition of conducting hostilities on that basis is a 'logical corollar[y] of the general ban'.⁶⁶¹ The rules also apply to non-international armed conflict as a matter of customary international law, with the Rome Statute criminalizing '[d]eclaring that no quarter will be given'.⁶⁶² The rule was set out as far back as the Lieber Code: '[n]o body of troops has the right to declare that it will not give ... quarter.'⁶⁶³ It has also been suggested that 'it is most unlikely that anyone would challenge' the 'existence or content' of the rule.⁶⁶⁴

In practice, orders are occasionally given that there shall be no survivors. Hostilities are also known to have been conducted on the basis of a denial of quarter. For example, during the American-Philippines war of 1899–1902, a US general was court-martialled in respect of his orders 'I want no prisoners' and 'I wish you to kill and burn. The more you kill and burn, the better you will please me'.⁶⁶⁵ Along similar lines, during the

---

⁶⁵⁶ There was much discussion at the Review Conference at which the amendment was discussed as to the application of the amendment to future Protocols. See D Kaye and SA Solomon, 'The Second Review Conference of the 1980 Convention on Certain Conventional Weapons' (2002) 96 *AJIL* 922, 930.
⁶⁵⁷ See L Maresca, 'A New Protocol on Explosive Remnants of War: The History and Negotiation of Protocol V to the 1980 Convention on Certain Conventional Weapons' (2004) 86 *IRRC* 815, 823.
⁶⁵⁸ Customary International Humanitarian Law, Rule 46.
⁶⁵⁹ Oeter, above note 454, 192–3.
⁶⁶⁰ Additional Protocol II, Article 4(1).
⁶⁶¹ Cassese, Geneva Protocols, above note 1, 79.
⁶⁶² Rome Statute, Article 8(2)(e)(x). See also Customary International Humanitarian Law, Rule 46; Darfur Commission Report, above note 25, para 166.
⁶⁶³ Article 60.
⁶⁶⁴ WJ Fenrick, 'Specific Methods of Warfare', in E Wilmshurst and SC Breau (eds), *Perspectives on the ICRC Study on Customary International Humanitarian law* (Cambridge University Press, 2007) 238, 241.
⁶⁶⁵ Quoted in L Friedman, *The Law of War: A Documentary History, Volume I* (Random House, 1972) 799, 801.

armed conflict in Sierra Leone (1991–2002), high-ranking officials of the Civil Defence Forces instructed newly trained recruits at a passing out parade: 'there is no place to keep captured or war prisoners', which was interpreted by some persons present as an injunction 'not to spare the vulnerables'. This interpretation was confirmed by the statement: 'a rebel is a rebel; surrendered, not surrendered, they're all rebels... [t]he time for their surrender had long since been exhausted, so we don't need any surrendered rebel.'[666]

Persons who are in the process of surrendering are in the transitory state between fighter and protected person. This 'brief period, often amounting to no more than minutes or seconds, when a combatant is or might be passing into the power of his adversary is one in which he is extremely vulnerable'.[667] Thus, the prohibition on the killing or wounding of members of the armed forces or armed group who have expressed a desire to surrender or are in the process of surrendering is closely related to the prohibition on the denial of quarter. Indeed, the protection of enemies in the process of surrendering is the final stage of application of the rule on the denial of quarter.[668] Thus, the Inter-American Commission on Human Rights implicitly considered refusal to accept an offer of surrender to be 'tantamount to a denial of quarter'.[669] The prohibition extends to soldiers and fighters who, incapacitated by their wounds, are unable to fight.[670] Accordingly, the rule on surrender applies to non-international armed conflict through the rule on the denial of quarter and as a matter of customary international law.[671]

There is no set means by which a desire to surrender has to be indicated, although classically, this has taken the form of waving a white flag or discarding weapons and placing hands on heads.[672] It is crucial, for practical reasons, that the intention to surrender be made clear and in a manner which does not leave any room for misunderstanding.[673] Provided the communication of the desire to surrender is unambiguous, the modalities of indicating surrender are of secondary importance.

There is much by way of practice that comports with the law and, in some cases, goes above and beyond that which the law requires. For example, during the attempted secession of Biafra, the Federal Government of Nigeria instructed its forces in 1967: '[d]uring the operations of Federal Government troops against the rebel troops many soldiers and civilians will surrender... Soldiers who surrender will not be killed. They are to be disarmed and treated as prisoners of war. They are entitled in all circumstances to humane treatment and respect for their person and their honour.'[674] The ONLF of Ethiopia indicated that it 'shall offer clemency to all combatants who surrender on the battlefield and willingly comply with international norms of battlefield combat'.[675] The 1947 Manifesto of the Chinese People's Liberation Army (CPLA) similarly provided:

---

[666] *CDF* Trial Judgment, above note 230, para 321.
[667] Baxter, Combatants, above note 390, 124.
[668] ICRC, *Commentary on the Additional Protocols*, above note 6, 1371.
[669] *Abella*, above note 25, paras 180, 185, and 190.
[670] Ibid, para 189; UK *Manual*, above note 43, 58; Customary International Humanitarian Law, Rule 47(B).
[671] *Abella*, above note 25, para 180; Customary International Humanitarian Law, Rule 47(B). See also IIHL *Manual*, above note 55, 40.
[672] Ibid; *Customary International Humanitarian Law, Volume I: Rules*, above note 84, 168. For other examples, see Spaight, above note 483, 95.
[673] See eg the facts of *Case of Korbely v Hungary*, Application No 9174/02, Judgment, 19 September 2008.
[674] Operational Code of Conduct for the Nigerian Army, above note 60.
[675] Political Programme of the Ogaden National Liberation Front (ONLF).

'[o]ur army will not kill or humiliate any of Chiang Kai-shek's army officers and men who lay down their arms, but will accept them into our service if they are willing to remain with us or send them home if they wish to leave.'[676] However, it should be noted that Mao Tse-Tung elsewhere advocated the killing of prisoners: '[i]t is best to require the prisoners first to hand over their weapons, and then to disperse them, or to execute them.'[677] The NRA of Uganda's Code of Conduct provided: '[n]ever kill... any captured prisoners, as the guns should only be reserved for armed enemies or opponents.'[678] The Ejército Zapatista de Liberación Nacional (EZLN) of Mexico issued an order in 1994 to its forces to '[r]espect the lives of prisoners and turn in the wounded to the International Red Cross for medical attention'.[679] Prior to undertaking a raid in 2005, a commander of the Communist Party of Nepal-Maoist (CPN-M) instructed the forces under his command: '[i]t is not allowed to behave indecently and kill the captured and surrendered people.'[680] The Code of the CNF of Burma provides that '[t]he command to finish or kill all enemies after attacking them is against the code of war, and therefore prohibited. Threatening enemies with this command is also prohibited'.[681] The SPLM indicated in 1998 that it 'believes that the object of combat is not necessarily to kill the enemy soldier, but rather to render the opponent non-combative, and hence, whenever an enemy soldier is disarmed or unarmed, his/her life must be spared, protected, respected, and considered as a Prisoner of War (POW)'.[682] A particularly instructive example is that of the 1958 address by Fidel Castro, in his capacity as Commander in Chief of the rebel forces, to encircled troops of President Batista, in which Castro stated:

Soldiers,

The rebel army, convinced that resistance is useless and would only lead to greater bloodshed... offers you surrender on the following terms:

1. Only arms will be taken. All other personnel possessions will be respected.
2. The wounded will be handed over to the Red Cross, as is currently the case for the wounded soldiers taken prisoner during the battle of Santo Domingo.
3. All prisoners—soldiers, rank and file, officers—will be freed within 15 days.
4. Until handed over to the Red Cross, the wounded will be cared for in our hospitals by competent doctors and surgeons.
5. All members of this troop under siege will immediately receive cigars, food and everything they need.
6. No prisoner will be interrogated, maltreated or humiliated, by word or by deed; [on the contrary, every soldier captured[683]] will receive the generous and humane treatment which we have always afforded to soldiers taken prisoner.

---

[676] Manifesto of the Chinese People's Liberation Army, in M Tse-Tung, *Selected Works of Mao Tse-Tung, Volume IV* (Foreign Languages Press, 1969) 147, 151.
[677] M Tse-Tung, *Basic Tactics* (Pall Mall Press, 1967) 98.
[678] The National Resistance Army Code of Conduct, reprinted in OO Amaza, *Museveni's Long March from Guerrilla to Statesman* (Kampala, 1998) 246.
[679] 'Declaration of War of the Zapatista National Liberation Army (EZLN)', Communique of 2 January 1994, reproduced and translated in B Clarke and C Ross (eds), *Voice of Fire: Communiqués and Interviews from the Zapatista National Liberation Army* (Freedom Voices, 2000) 31, 32.
[680] Pasang, *Red Strides of History* (Agnipariksha Janaprakashan Griha, 2008) 206.
[681] Chin National Front, Code, above note 26, Article 4 (unofficial translation).
[682] Fifteen Point Programme of the SPLM, Point 13, in Vision and Programme of the Sudan People's Liberation Movement (SPLM), SPLM Political Secretariat, March 1998.
[683] Words in square brackets added to the Perret translation to reflect the original statement.

7. We shall immediately inform by radio the wife, mother, father and other members of the family of each one of you—all those who are at this moment weeping, in despair at having no news of you and not knowing what has become of you.
8. If you accept these conditions, send a man carrying a white flag and saying out loud that he wishes to parley.⁶⁸⁴

Raul Castro addressed captured Batistianos along similar lines.⁶⁸⁵

In the practice of conflict, it will not always be possible to accept surrender. For example, it may prove impossible to distinguish persons who are continuing their fight from those who are wishing to surrender. Fighting in the vicinity, for example in the context of an ambush, may make the acceptance of surrender impossible. However, where possible, surrender must be accepted, and the difficulties that arise with surrender should not disguise the absolute nature of the rule. This is demonstrated in a 2011 statement of the State Department Legal Advisor following the US targeting of Osama bin Laden, in what branches of the US Government consider a non-international armed conflict:

[C]onsistent with the laws of armed conflict and U.S. military doctrine, the U.S. forces were prepared to capture bin Laden if he had surrendered in a way that they could safely accept. The laws of armed conflict require acceptance of a genuine offer of surrender that is clearly communicated by the surrendering party and received by the opposing force, under circumstances where it is feasible for the opposing force to accept that offer of surrender.⁶⁸⁶

Contrary to this practice, a number of armed groups have indicated to the ICRC that they execute prisoners as they are unable to detain them.⁶⁸⁷ Not all parties to conflicts thus heed the sentiment that 'the evil of increasing the strength of the enemy is less than that of violating the dictates of humanity'.⁶⁸⁸

4.2 Flags of truce and surrender

As intimated above, a rule that is closely related to that of surrender relates to the use of a white flag. A white flag may be used in order to request communication relating to the negotiation of a truce or surrender. Today, it also relates to the communication of the surrender itself. Improper uses of the white flag are prohibited. It is also prohibited to attack persons raising the white flag, unless they engage in hostilities.⁶⁸⁹ The rules are applicable to non-international armed conflict through customary international law.⁶⁹⁰ Indeed, it has been suggested that 'the applicability of the rule to non-international armed conflict is unlikely to be questioned'.⁶⁹¹ The rule is of longstanding origin, with the Lieber Code providing that:

---

⁶⁸⁴ Statement of Fidel Castro, Commander-in-Chief of the Rebel Forces, 16 July 1958, ICRC Archives 200 060. The English translation is taken from F Perret, 'Activities of the International Committee of the Red Cross in Cuba 1958–1962' (1998) 38 *IRRC* 655, 659–62.
⁶⁸⁵ See above, 300–1.
⁶⁸⁶ HH Koh, 'The Lawfulness of the US Operation against Osama bin Laden', Opinio Juris Blog, 19 May 2011. Reports on point are contradictory; for example N Schmidle, 'Getting Bin Laden', *The New Yorker*, 8 August 2011, quotes a special-operations officer as stating: 'There was never any question of detaining or capturing him—it wasn't a split-second decision. No one wanted detainees.'
⁶⁸⁷ See *Customary International Humanitarian Law, Volume II: Practice*, above note 84, 976–7.
⁶⁸⁸ Hall, *International Law*, 397, quoted in Spaight, above note 483, 89.
⁶⁸⁹ See also IIHL *Manual*, above note 55, 41.
⁶⁹⁰ Customary International Humanitarian Law, Rule 58.
⁶⁹¹ Fenrick, Methods of Warfare, above note 664, 250.

[i]f it be discovered, and fairly proved, that a flag of truce has been abused for surreptitiously obtaining military knowledge, the bearer of the flag thus abusing his sacred character is deemed a spy.

So sacred is the character of a flag of truce, and so necessary is its sacredness, that while its abuse is an especially heinous offense, great caution is requisite, on the other hand, in convicting the bearer of a flag of truce as a spy.[692]

More recently, the CNF of Burma included in its Code the provision that '[a]ttacking the enemies after deceitfully waving a white flag or other signals of surrender is strictly prohibited'.[693]

Violations of the law relating to the white flag are not uncommon. For example, in a controversial and contested incident during the final stages of the Sri Lankan conflict in May 2009, there are reports that Sri Lankan forces killed LTTE fighters who had indicated their desire to surrender in advance through neutral intermediaries, and who made their way to government troops 'waving a white flag'.[694] Surrender along these lines was reportedly prearranged between the LTTE and the Government of Sri Lanka through intermediaries, with a text message sent by the then Secretary to the Ministry of Foreign Affairs indicating: 'Just walk across to the troops, slowly! With a white flag and comply with instructions carefully. The soldiers are nervous about suicide bombers.'[695] Along similar lines, during the Libyan armed conflict of 2011, Libyan rebels reported that a group of state armed forces 'raised the white flag. We thought they no longer wanted to fight for Gaddafi... But when we approached, they opened fire. It was a trick... Everyone knows the white flag if [sic] for surrender. There are Gaddafi's dirty tricks'.[696] Over a century earlier, during the Boer war of 1899–1902, use of the flag of truce to shoot an officer had been condemned.[697]

4.3 Improper use of emblems and uniforms

4.3.1 Neutral or protected emblems and uniforms

The law of non-international armed conflict contains a rule to the effect that '[i]t is prohibited to make improper use of protected distinctive emblems or neutral military emblems, insignia, flags, or uniforms'.[698] Such emblems include those of the Red Cross, the United Nations, and the emblem for the protection of cultural property. The rule applies as a matter of customary international law,[699] and, with respect to 'the distinctive emblem of the red cross, red crescent or red [crystal]', also as a matter of

---

[692] Article 114.
[693] Chin National Front, Code, above note 26, Article 27 (unofficial translation).
[694] US Report on Sri Lanka, above note 26, 45–6.
[695] Quoted in B Doherty, '"Walk to the troops": SMS sent Tamils to their death', *The Saturday Age* (Australia), 14 May 2011, 1. The former Secretary told '*The Saturday Age* that while he sent the text message it was not a guarantee of safety. "Absolutely not. This would be have been [sic] way beyond my authority to promise"'. He also indicated that 'the text message was not part of any negotiations with the Tigers. He did not believe the group tried to surrender. "The text is likely to have been in response to an inquiry, but not from anyone associated with the LTTE. This was not an effort to arrange a surrender, which I had no authority to do"'. Ibid, 4. See also M Colvin, 'Tigers Begged me to Broker Surrender', *The Times* (UK), 24 May 2009.
[696] Suliman Abdul Mula, a rebel fighter, quoted in C McGreal, 'Libyan Rebels Encounter Fierce Fighting and "Dirty Tricks" from Gaddafi's Troops', *The Guardian* (UK), 28 March 2011.
[697] See Spaight, above note 483, 87–8.
[698] IIHL *Manual*, above note 55, 41.
[699] Customary International Humanitarian Law, Rules 59 (in respect of the ICRC), 60 (in respect of the UN), 61 (other internationally recognized emblems).

treaty law.[700] All improper usages of these emblems, insignia, flags, and uniforms are prohibited given that such uses endanger genuine uses. This is also reflected in the practice. For example, the JEM of Darfur alleged in 2009 that the Government of Sudan flew surveillance planes with 'UN/AU colours and logos' and noted that that 'undoubtedly puts UNAMID forces in danger and must be strongly condemned and stopped'.[701] Likewise, the Lieber Code provided that '[i]t is justly considered an act of bad faith, of infamy or fiendishness, to deceive the enemy by flags of protection. Such act of bad faith may be good cause for refusing to respect such flags'.[702] For similar reasons, use of the Red Cross emblem during the 2008 rescue mission to free Ingrid Betancourt and her fellow hostages resulted in an apology from the President of Colombia to the ICRC and an explanation that it was worn by a single soldier who, in doing so, had violated 'official orders'.[703]

4.3.2 Enemy emblems and uniforms

It is a matter of debate whether the law of non-international armed conflict contains a prohibition on the improper use of enemy military emblems, insignia, flags, and uniforms.[704] The reason for the hesitancy is that in some non-international armed conflicts, the parties, or at least armed group parties, do not wear a uniform or have any distinctive markings. Thus, the Customary International Humanitarian Law study provides that '[i]t can be argued that [the rule] *should*... apply in non-international armed conflicts when the parties to the conflict do in fact wear uniforms'.[705] The point is well made, as although some armed groups do not wear uniforms or do not have particular insignia, many in fact do wear or do have such identifying insignia. For example, the National Liberation Army (NLA) that fought in the former Yugoslav Republic of Macedonia in 2001 indicated that it 'has its own uniforms, ranks and insignia, which are worn in accordance with the Rules on the Wearing of Uniforms'.[706] The EZLN of Mexico stated in 1994: '[w]e are using the colors of red and black on our uniform, symbols of the working people in their struggles and strikes. Our flag carries the letters "EZLN", Zapatista National Liberation Army and we will always take this flag into our battles.'[707] The Provisional Government of the Algerian Republic indicated during the Algerian war of independence (1954–62) that the Armée de Libération Nationale (ALN) employed 'a distinctive sign to be worn by soldiers'.[708]

---

[700] Additional Protocol II, Article 12. The Protocol refers to the red lion and sun. However, that emblem has not been used since 1980. In 2005, a third Additional Protocol was concluded relating to the red crystal. See Protocol Additional to the Geneva Conventions of 2 August 1949, and Relating to the Adoption of an Additional Distinctive Emblem (Protocol III), of 8 December 2005.

[701] 'GOS Flies Surveillance Planes with UN Colour over Darfur', 31 January 2009.

[702] Instructions for the Government of Armies of the United States in the Field (Lieber Code), 24 April 1863, Article 117.

[703] 'Betancourt Rescuer wore Red Cross', *BBC News*, 17 July 2008; M Tran, 'Colombia Apologises over Use of Red Cross Symbol in Betancourt Rescue', *The Guardian* (UK), 16 July 2008.

[704] For an affirmative view, see IIHL *Manual*, above note 55, 41–2; Fenrick, Methods of Warfare, above note 664, 251.

[705] Customary International Humanitarian Law, Rule 62 (emphasis added).

[706] Ali Ahmeti, Political Representative, UÇK General Staff, Untitled Document, 8 May 2001, Exhibit P00507.E in ICTY *Boškoski* trial.

[707] 'Declaration of War of the Zapatista National Liberation Army (EZLN)', communiqué of 2 January 1994, reproduced and translated in B Clarke and C Ross (eds), *Voice of Fire: Communiqués and Interviews from the Zapatista National Liberation Army* (Freedom Voices, 2000) 31, 32.

[708] *White Paper on the Application of the Geneva Conventions of 1949 to the French-Algerian Conflict* (Algerian Office, 1960) 24.

Improper use of enemy uniforms was reportedly made by the FMLN of El Salvador, the Sendero Luminoso of Peru, and the Sandinista Government in Nicaragua.[709] During the second Boer war (1899–1902), an attempt to kidnap a high-ranking British official by an individual dressed in a British military uniform led to his trial before a military court and subsequent execution.[710] Accordingly, if it is not already a rule, the Customary International Humanitarian Law study is quite correct to note that it should be a rule. Difficult questions then arise as to the temporal scope of the prohibition.[711]

4.4 Perfidy

A rule that is associated with each of the aforementioned rules is that it is prohibited to kill, injure, and possibly capture an adversary by resort to perfidy. Perfidy may be defined as 'acts inviting the confidence of an adversary to lead him to believe that he is entitled to, or is obliged to accord, protection under the rules of international law applicable in armed conflict, with intent to betray that confidence'.[712] During the 1974–7 Diplomatic Conference there was a long debate as to the term to be used to describe such acts,[713] and the term 'treachery' is sometimes used to describe the practice in non-international armed conflict.[714] However, 'treachery' and 'perfidy' are essentially interchangeable terms.[715]

The reasoning behind the prohibition on certain perfidious conduct is that committing acts in violation of the rule will decrease respect for the law of armed conflict in the future.[716] Perfidious conduct manipulates the law of armed conflict and turns it into a tactic of conflict. This may lead the other party to disregard the law due to distrust, resulting in a downward spiral of lack of respect for the law. Thus, the Lieber Code provided that 'the common law of war allows even capital punishment for clandestine or treacherous attempts to injure an enemy, because they are so dangerous, and it is difficult to guard against them'.[717]

In light of the reasoning behind the prohibition, it is surprising that the prohibition is limited to killing or injuring an adversary through perfidious means. Parties may engage in perfidious conduct to force the other side, for example, to 'submit to tactical or operational measures which will be to their disadvantage',[718] to destroy property,[719]

---

[709] Documented in Parks, Air War, above note 82, 77.
[710] See Spaight, above note 483, 88.
[711] For the differing views, see V Jobst III, 'Is the Wearing of the Enemy's Uniform a Violation of the Laws of War' (1941) 35 *AJIL* 435, 436–7; D Fleck, 'Ruses of War and Prohibition of Perfidy' (1974) 13 *Military Law and the Law of War Review* 269, 279–82. The difference is longstanding: see Winthrop, above note 484, 785.
[712] Additional Protocol I, Article 37. See ICC Elements of Crimes, Article 8(2)(e)(ix); IIHL Declaration, above note 52, A4; UK *Manual*, above note 43, 392.
[713] See above, 70–1.
[714] See eg Statute of the ICC, Article 8(2)(e)(ix); UK *Manual*, above note 43, 391.
[715] See the view expressed in Reaffirmation and Development of the Laws and Customs Applicable in Armed Conflicts: Report submitted by the International Committee of the Red Cross (May 1969) 80; Green, above note 83, 146. Cf ICRC, *Commentary on the Additional Protocols*, above note 6, 432, taking the view that 'treachery' is narrower than 'perfidy'.
[716] Dinstein, above note 75, 201; JC Dehn, 'Permissible Perfidy? Analysing the Colombian Hostage Rescue, the Capture of Rebel Leaders and the World's Reaction' (2008) 6 *JICJ* 627, 633.
[717] Article 101.
[718] ICRC, *Commentary on the Additional Protocols*, above note 6, 432.
[719] Dinstein, above note 75, 201.

or 'with the motive not of attacking the enemy but of surviving to fight another day'.[720] Whether the prohibition extends to capture is unclear, with authority in support of both competing positions.[721] Accordingly, the Government of Colombia's 2008 mission to rescue hostages, including Ingrid Betancourt, from FARC captivity and the capture of FARC rebels during the mission may not have constituted a violation of the prohibition of perfidy, although it did violate other rules.[722] The Customary International Humanitarian Law study observes that, 'it can be argued that killing, injuring or capturing by resort to perfidy is illegal under customary international law but that only acts that result in serious bodily injury, namely killing or injuring, would constitute a war crime'.[723] The formulation 'it can be argued' suggests that the prohibition on capture through perfidy is not a customary rule at present. However, the division between the humanitarian law standard and the criminal law standard is consistent with the discussion above on the methodological aspects of the regulation of non-international armed conflict.[724]

The prohibition on certain perfidious conduct must be contrasted with the lawfulness of ruses. War 'is no stranger to cunning, skill, ingenuity, stratagems and artifices, in other words, to ruses of war, or the use of deception'.[725] Indeed, according to the Lieber Code, 'deception in war is admitted as a just and necessary means of hostility, and is consistent with honourable warfare'.[726] A line thus has to be drawn between perfidy and ruses, with the former being prohibited and the latter permitted. Both perfidy and ruses intend to mislead the adversary or induce the adversary to act in a reckless manner. However, perfidy also invites the confidence of the adversary with respect to the law whereas ruses do not, and it is that which constitutes the essential difference between the two. Ruses that have been used in non-international armed conflicts and which do not constitute a violation of the law include the Confederate shaping of logs and mounting them on wheels in order to deceive Union forces as to the strength of their artillery during the US civil war (1861–5), and the British use of dummy movements and issuance of dummy commands in order to deceive Boer forces during the Boer war (1899–1902).[727]

Although, today, the prohibition on killing, injuring, and possibly capturing an adversary by resort to perfidy is accepted as part of the customary international law of non-international armed conflict,[728] this was not always the case. At the 1974–7 Diplomatic Conference, a lengthy debate took place as to whether or not to prohibit certain perfidious conduct in non-international armed conflict, with many states taking the view that the concept of perfidy was applicable in international armed conflicts

---

[720] UK *Manual*, above note 43, 59 fn 36.
[721] It is omitted from the Statute of the ICC, Article 8(2)(e)(ix); UK *Manual*, above note 43, 391; IIHL *Manual*, above note 55, 43. However, it is included in Additional Protocol I, Article 37; *Constitutional Conformity of Protocol II*, above note 5, para 23; Customary International Humanitarian Law, Rule 65; IIHL Declaration, above note 52, A4. See also the mixed practice in *Customary International Humanitarian Law, Volume II: Practice*, above note 52, 1380–6.
[722] See above, 417. See, on this incident, Dehn, above note 716.
[723] *Customary International Humanitarian Law, Volume I: Rules*, above note 84, 225.
[724] See above, 79–81.
[725] ICRC, *Commentary on the Additional Protocols*, above note 6, 440.
[726] Instructions for the Government of Armies of the United States in the Field (Lieber Code), 24 April 1863, Article 101.
[727] Spaight, above note 483, 153–4.
[728] Statute of the ICC, Article 8(2)(e)(ix); *Tadić* Decision on Interlocutory Appeal on Jurisdiction, above note 25, para 125; *Constitutional Conformity of Protocol II*, above note 5, para 23; IIHL Declaration, above note 52, A4.

alone.⁷²⁹ A provision on perfidy was criticized for suggesting that 'there were two ways of rebelling against a legitimate Government: a legal way of killing, injuring or capturing soldiers belonging to the government forces, and an illegal way'.⁷³⁰ The question of using police forces in armed conflict, who would wear their ordinary uniform or civilian clothing, was also raised.⁷³¹ The prohibition of perfidious conduct was also considered superfluous given that members of the armed group could be arrested and punished regardless of their perfidious conduct.⁷³² Two decades later, the holding of the ICTY Appeals Chamber in *Tadić* that the prohibition on certain perfidious conduct applied in non-international armed conflict as a matter of customary international law was met with doubt on the part of commentators.⁷³³ However, some states spoke out in favour of the rule applying to non-international armed conflicts as a matter of customary international law, with the United States supporting it 'as a desirable customary law rule' as early as 1991.⁷³⁴ The prohibition has also been supported in practice, with the Ogaden Human Rights Committee accusing the Ethiopian Government in 2005 of violating the prohibition of perfidy in the killing and capturing of members of the ONLF delegation returning from peace negotiations.⁷³⁵ At any rate, as of 1998, with the prohibition criminalized in the Rome Statute, it quite clearly applies to non-international armed conflict through customary international law, even if that custom only crystallized during the Rome Conference, although the Rome Statute proscription is limited to the 'combatant adversary'.⁷³⁶

4.5 Human shields

4.5.1 Involuntary human shields

It is prohibited to use civilians and captured fighters to shield military objectives and military operations. The rule has been accepted as applying to non-international armed conflict through customary international law.⁷³⁷ For example, in discussing the customary international humanitarian law applicable to the Sri Lankan armed conflict in 2009, the United States noted that '[t]he civilian population must not be used to shield military objectives or operations from attack'.⁷³⁸ The prohibition follows from the requirement that 'the civilian population and individual civilians shall enjoy general protection against the dangers arising from military operations'.⁷³⁹ The use of human shields may also amount to inhuman treatment.⁷⁴⁰

Although the most frequent form of human shields used in times of armed conflict are persons who are forcibly located around a military objective, for example a military

---

⁷²⁹ *Official Records*, above note 8, Vol 14, 312, para 15 (Canada); Vol 15, 112, para 23 (Japan).
⁷³⁰ Ibid, Vol 15, 217, para 49 (Canada); 215, para 35 (FRG). See above, 70.
⁷³¹ Ibid, Vol 14, 312, para 15 (Canada); Vol 15, 215, para 38 (UK).
⁷³² Ibid, Vol 15, 215, para 34 (FRG); 215, para 37 (UK).
⁷³³ C Greenwood, 'International Humanitarian Law and the *Tadić* Case' (1996) 7 *EJIL* 265, 278; Turns, Vanishing Point, above note 9, 138.
⁷³⁴ 'Application of Humanitarian Law in Noninternational Armed Conflicts: Remarks by J Ashley Roach' (1991) 85 *ASIL Proceedings* 83, 98, 99.
⁷³⁵ Ogaden Human Rights Committee, Ogaden: Traditional Leaders' Peace Initiative and the Upcoming Elections, Ref: OHRC/1PR/05, 15 August 2005.
⁷³⁶ Article 8(2)(e)(ix).
⁷³⁷ Customary International Humanitarian Law, Rule 97.
⁷³⁸ US Report on Sri Lanka, above note 26, 7.
⁷³⁹ Additional Protocol II, Article 13(1).
⁷⁴⁰ See *Prosecutor v Blaskić*, IT-95-14-T, Judgment, 3 March 2000, para 716; *Prosecutor v Kordić and Čerkez*, IT-95-14/2-T, Judgment, 26 February 2001, para 256.

unit, in order to seek to prevent that objective or unit from being targeted by the other party, the notion of the human shield takes various forms. For example, it includes preventing persons from leaving the area of fighting and using them as a buffer, as was done by the LTTE in 2009 during the final stages of the armed conflict in Sri Lanka.[741] That this type of practice also falls within the notion of human shields is evident from the treaty provisions in the law of international armed conflict. Additional Protocol I, for example, provides that '[t]he presence or movements of the civilian population or individual civilians shall not be used to render certain points or areas immune from military operations'.[742] This has been interpreted as prohibiting taking advantage of voluntary movements of persons, as well as the forcing of persons into particular locations.[743] Similarly, the war crime in international armed conflict relates to the moving or otherwise taking advantage of the location of persons.[744] Another form of human shields, equally prohibited, is tasking captured fighters with searching for explosive devices. For example, during the US civil war (1861–5), after discovering mines impeding his path, General Sherman instructed Confederate prisoners of war to march at the head of Union forces 'so as to explode their own torpedoes, or to discover and dig them up'.[745] The ICRC has taken the position that this, too, constitutes an instance of taking human shields, with an appeal being made to the parties to an unnamed internal armed conflict after it became aware of 'instances in which civilians, including women and children, were compelled to walk in front of the troops along the railway track in order to protect the soldiers from the mines possibly laid there... After receiving a protest from the ICRC, the authorities issued instructions to immediately cease such practices'.[746] It is unfortunate, then, that the most frequent *type* of human shield has been transformed into the very *notion* of a human shield, with the commentary to the Customary International Humanitarian Law study indicating that 'the use of human shields requires an intentional colocation of military objectives and civilians or persons *hors de combat* with the specific intent of trying to prevent the targeting of those military objectives'.[747] This description was used by the Secretary-General's Panel of Experts on Accountability in Sri Lanka to require 'deliberately moving civilians towards military targets to protect the latter from attacks' and thus find that using civilians as a buffer did not constitute the use of human shields.[748] However, the open language of the Customary International Humanitarian Law study *rule* is to be preferred over the description in the commentary as better reflecting the customary proscription.

Using human shields is often condemned by one party or another, indicating their acceptance of the rule. For example, in 2009, the FDLR condemned 'the crimes against civilians and practices of the coalition of the FARDC, RPA, and MONUC [the armed forces of the DRC and Rwanda and the UN forces in Congo] of using civilians as

---

[741] See US Report on Sri Lanka, above note 26, 15.
[742] Article 51(7). See also Henderson, above note 74, 212.
[743] ICRC, *Commentary on the Additional Protocols*, above note 6, 627; Bothe, Partsch, and Solf, above note 93, 316.
[744] ICC Elements of Crimes, Article 8(2)(b)(xxiii).
[745] WT Sherman, *Memoirs of General WT Sherman, Volume II* (Charles Webster, New York, 1891) 194. For a more recent allegation of the same practice, see Amnesty International, *Crimes Against Humanity in Eastern Myanmar* (2008).
[746] ICRC Archive Document, quoted in *Customary International Humanitarian Law, Volume II: Practice*, above note 84, 2302. The example is contained in the section devoted to human shields.
[747] *Customary International Humanitarian Law, Volume I: Rules*, 340.
[748] Report of the Secretary-General's Panel of Experts on Accountability in Sri Lanka, 31 March 2011, para 237.

shields of war in eastern DRC'.[749] A prohibition on point may also be the subject of an ad hoc agreement concluded between the warring parties. For example, in 2002, the Government of Sudan and the SPLM committed themselves in a bilateral agreement 'to refrain from endangering the safety of civilians by intentionally using them as "human shields" or by using civilian facilities such as hospitals or schools to shield otherwise lawful military targets'.[750] It may also be found in internal codes. For example, the CNF Code provides that '[t]he use of civilians or prisoners of war as human shields to protect from attack or from getting hurt is strictly prohibited'.[751]

Rather more controversial is the impact of the use of involuntary human shields on the attacker. In the context of international armed conflicts, Additional Protocol I provides that violation of the prohibition 'shall not release the Parties to the conflict from their legal obligations with respect to the civilian population and civilians'.[752] Such a rule is also appropriate for non-international armed conflicts. Thus, the presence of involuntary human shields may affect the decision to target a particular military objective, particularly insofar as the proportionality analysis is concerned. In considering whether the expected loss of civilian life and injury to civilians would be excessive in relation to the military advantage anticipated, the presence of human shields would have to be ascertained, as involuntary shields cannot be considered taking a direct part in hostilities.[753] The question then becomes precisely what weight should be given to their presence. If they are treated as ordinary, that is to say non-shield, civilians, the defender would benefit from violation of the rule and could prevent an attack taking place. Thus, according to some, their presence should be given less weight in the proportionality calculation: 'the appraisal whether civilian casualties are excessive in relation to the military advantage anticipated must make allowances for the fact that—if an attempt is made to shield military objectives with civilians—civilian casualties will be higher than usual.'[754] However, it is submitted that, given that human shields are civilians who are not taking a direct part in hostilities and who are themselves victims of the defending state, their presence should not be discounted or given less weight in the proportionality analysis than would the presence of non-shield civilians.[755] Nonetheless, the test remains one of proportionality and the military advantage anticipated from an attack may be such that even the presence of involuntary human shields will not prevent the attack from taking place. The facts will be determinative.

4.5.2 Voluntary human shields

The issue of voluntary human shields is also a controversial one. In this context, it is submitted that civilians who voluntarily act as human shields are in a different position from involuntary human shields. They may be considered to be taking a direct part in hostilities in an appropriate situation.[756] Their presence, even if passive, can cause

---

[749] FDLR Press Release Nr 04/SE/CD/AUGUST2009, 20 August 2009.
[750] Agreement between the Government of the Republic of Sudan and the Sudan People's Liberation Movement to Protect Non-Combatant Civilians and Civilian Facilities from Military Attack, 10 March 2002, Article 1.
[751] Chin National Front, Code, above note 26, Article 24 (unofficial translation).
[752] Article 51(8).
[753] Schmitt, Fault Lines, above note 81, 300. Cf Parks, Air War, above note 82, 163.
[754] Dinstein, above note 75, 131. See also APV Rogers, 'Zero-Casualty Warfare' (2000) 82 *IRRC* 165, 179.
[755] See Henderson, above note 74, 214–16.
[756] *Public Committee against Torture*, above note 2, para 36; IIHL *Manual*, above note 55, 44. See, in particular, the nuanced discussion in Henderson, above note 755, 217–18.

actual harm to the other side depending on the site being shielded.[757] Accordingly, in this situation, the presence of voluntary human shields can be discounted, or at least reduced,[758] in the proportionality analysis. However, as it is not the shields per se but their shielding of the relevant site that poses the threat, they themselves may not be attacked, only the site they seek to protect.[759]

Although there may be difficulties in ascertaining whether or not an individual is acting voluntarily as opposed to through coercion,[760] once that determination is made, the issue is resolved. In the period prior to making that determination, the individual must be presumed to be acting involuntarily. Such a presumption is akin to the presumption of civilian status utilized in other areas of the law.[761]

4.6 Starvation of civilians

The starvation of civilians and of the civilian population as a method of combat is prohibited.[762] Accordingly, it is 'prohibited to attack, destroy, remove or render useless, for that purpose, objects indispensable to the survival of the civilian population, such as foodstuffs, agricultural areas for the production of foodstuffs, crops, livestock, drinking water installations and supplies and irrigation works'.[763] The Protocol II provision is 'a simplified version' of the equivalent provision in Additional Protocol I,[764] suggesting that interpretation of that article may provide guidance. The failure of the Rome Conference to criminalize the prohibition on starvation of civilians as a method of combat has been heavily criticized,[765] suggesting that in the view of many it reflects a norm of customary international law. This view has also been taken in the Customary International Humanitarian Law study and expressed by relevant bodies.[766]

4.6.1 Starvation

The prohibition on the starvation of civilians is a relatively recent one. The Lieber Code provided that '[i]t is lawful to starve the hostile belligerent, armed or unarmed, so that it leads to the speedier subjection of the enemy'.[767] Similarly, during the attempted secession of Biafra (1967–70), a Nigerian governmental official stated that 'starvation is a legitimate weapon of war'.[768] Likewise, a British Foreign Secretary once remarked

---

[757] ICRC *Interpretive Guidance*, above note 5, 56. But see 57.
[758] Rogers, Military Target, above note 80, 169.
[759] MN Schmitt, 'Targeting and Humanitarian Law: Current Issues' (2004) 34 *IYHR* 59, 95–7.
[760] RS Schondorf, 'The Targeted Killings Judgment: A Preliminary Assessment' (2007) 5 *JICJ* 301, 308.
[761] See eg Additional Protocol I, Article 50(1); ICRC *Interpretive Guidance*, above note 5, 75–6.
[762] Additional Protocol II, Article 14.
[763] Ibid.
[764] Article 54. See ICRC, *Commentary on the Additional Protocols*, above note 6, 1456.
[765] See eg D Momtaz, 'War Crimes in Non-International Armed Conflicts Under the Statute of the International Criminal Court' (1999) 2 *YIHL* 177, 186; D Robinson and H von Hebel, 'War Crimes in Internal Armed Conflicts: Article 8 of the ICC Statute' (1999) 2 *YIHL* 193, 208; C Kress, 'War Crimes Committed in Non-International Armed Conflict and the Emerging System of International Criminal Justice' (2000) 30 *IYHR* 103, 134.
[766] Customary International Humanitarian Law, Rule 53; Darfur Commission Report, above note 25, para 166.
[767] Instructions for the Government of Armies of the United States in the Field (Lieber Code), 24 April 1863, Article 17.
[768] Chief Anthony Enahoro, Feederal Commissioner for Information and Labour of Nigeria, quoted in L Garrison, 'The "Point of No Return" for the Biafrans', *New York Times Magazine*,

that, 'in the whole history of warfare, any nation which has been in a position to starve its enemy out has done so'.[769] However, today, it is accepted that the prohibition is a norm of customary international law.[770]

Starvation is 'the action of subjecting people to famine, i.e., extreme and general scarcity of food'.[771] It is only the starvation of civilians *as a method of combat* that is prohibited. The scarcity of provisions during times of non-international armed conflict inevitably subjects civilians to deprivation, but this would not constitute a violation of the law. Likewise, starvation as an incidental effect of the armed conflict would not fall foul of the prohibition,[772] for example through 'cutting off enemy supply routes which are also used for the transportation of food, or if civilians through fear of military operations abandon agricultural land or are not prepared to risk bringing food supplies into areas where fighting is going on'.[773] However, care needs to be taken, for what may seem to be an incidental effect of an armed conflict may prove to be a covert method of combat. Even in situations of starvation as an incidental effect of the conflict, the matter is a delicate one, as certain other rules come into play, such as an obligation to allow humanitarian relief actions subject to considerations of military necessity.[774] Nonetheless, difficulties arise in the relationship between the prohibition on starvation and siege warfare.[775]

4.6.2 Objects indispensable to the survival of the civilian population

As noted above, it is not starvation alone that is prohibited; so too is attacking, destroying, removing, and rendering useless objects indispensable to the survival of the civilian population. Ad hoc commitments have been made to this effect during armed conflicts. For example, in a 2009 agreement between the Government of the Philippines and the MILF, the parties committed to '[r]efrain from targeting or intentionally attacking civilian properties or facilities such as ... health and food distribution centers, or relief operations, or objects or facilities indispensable to the survival of the civilian population and of a civilian nature'.[776] Along similar lines, in 2002, the Government of Sudan and the SPLM committed themselves in a bilateral agreement 'to refrain from targeting or intentionally attacking ... health and food distribution centres, or relief operations, or objects or facilities indispensable to the survival of the civilian population and of a civilian nature'.[777]

---

8 September 1968, 102, cited in GA Mudge, 'Starvation as a Means of Warfare' (1969–70) 4 *International Lawyer* 228, 228.

[769] Statement of British Foreign Secretary, *Hansard* Vol 786 No 143 c 953, cited in, E Rosenblad, 'Starvation as a Method of Warfare—Conditions for Regulation by Convention' (1973) 7 *International Lawyer* 252, 253.

[770] Customary International Humanitarian Law, Rule 53. See EECC Partial Award, above note 73, para 105.

[771] ICRC, *Commentary on the Additional Protocols*, above note 6, 1456.

[772] IIHL *Manual*, above note 55, 46. See also IDI Resolution on Distinction, above note 45, para 5.

[773] UK *Manual*, above note 43, 74.

[774] See above, 329–34.

[775] See Dinstein, above note 75, 133–7; Rogers, above note 1, 101–3; KJ Riordan, 'Shelling, Sniping and Starvation: The Law of Armed Conflict and the Lessons of the Siege of Sarajevo' (2010) 41 *Victoria University of Wellington Law Review* 149, 168–72.

[776] Agreement on the Civilian Protection Component of the International Monitoring Team, 27 October 2009, Article 1.

[777] Agreement between the Government of the Republic of Sudan and the Sudan People's Liberation Movement to Protect Non-Combatant Civilians and Civilian Facilities from Military Attack, 10 March 2002, Article 1.

The prohibition is a corollary of the prohibition on starvation. The particular verbs used 'cover all eventualities, including pollution of water supplies by chemical agents or the destruction of a harvest by defoliants'.[778] A proposal had been made to draw up an exhaustive list of objects that it was prohibited to destroy.[779] However, an illustrative approach was adopted so as not to exclude other indispensable objects that may have been overlooked.[780]

The objects appearing on the Additional Protocol II list all relate to food and water. Thus, it has been suggested that it is difficult to argue that objects unrelated to food and water 'are intended to be protected by the Article'.[781] If the provision is seen as a derivation of the prohibition of starvation, as has been the case for many years, and is evident from the language of the Additional Protocol II provision itself, this may well be the case. However, if the provision is seen as a derivation from the protections afforded to the civilian population, as is the case with the equivalent provision in Additional Protocol I, it would include other objects that are indispensable to the survival of the civilian population,[782] for example medicines and implements for shelter. The latter interpretation is to be preferred. On this basis, the FMLN alleged in 1988 that the Government of El Salvador violated international humanitarian law through '[m]ilitary encirclements around villages inhabited by civilians to blockade or limit the entry of medicine and food'.[783] The 2011 report of the Turkel Commission on the Gaza Flotilla also interpreted the Additional Protocol I provision in this manner, and as including clothing, bedding, shelter, and oil for transport.[784] On either interpretation, supplies intended solely for the armed forces or the armed group may be destroyed as being military objectives.[785] Destruction of supplies would also not be unlawful if an incidental effect of a lawful attack on a military objective.

The prohibition also prevents scorched earth tactics,[786] by which one party to the conflict burns everything in its wake in order to prevent the other side from benefitting from the land and its resources. The prohibition thus affords greater protection than in international armed conflicts, with the latter allowing scorched earth tactics when 'the area affected belongs to the belligerent Party and is under its control (in contradistinction to enemy territory or even part of the national territory which is under the enemy's control)'.[787] Such an interpretation would not prove workable in non-international armed conflict as it would allow the state to engage in such tactics but not the non-state armed group, territory under the control of the armed group not 'belonging' to them.

---

[778] ICRC, *Commentary on the Additional Protocols*, above note 6, 1458.

[779] *Official Records*, above note 8, Vol 14, 148, para 31 (UK).

[780] ICRC, *Commentary on the Additional Protocols*, above note 6, 655, on the equivalent provision in Additional Protocol I.

[781] Bothe, Partsch, and Solf, above note 93, 340 fn 17 (on the Additional Protocol I provision); CA Allen, 'Civilian Starvation and Relief during Armed Conflict: the Modern Humanitarian Law' (1989) 19 *Georgia Journal of International and Comparative Law* 1, 64.

[782] See IIHL Manual, above note 55, 45. See also ICRC, *Commentary on the Additional Protocols*, above note 6, 55, on the equivalent provision in Additional Protocol I.

[783] FMLN, above note 26, 5.

[784] The Public Commission to Examine the Maritime Incident of 31 May 2010: Report, Part One, para 78.

[785] ICRC, *Commentary on the Additional Protocols*, above note 6, 1458; Doswald-Beck, Value, above note 91, 160; Dinstein, above note 75, 132.

[786] *Customary International Humanitarian Law, Volume I: Rules*, above note 84, 193; UK *Manual*, above note 43, 408 fn 123.

[787] Y Dinstein, 'Siege Warfare and the Starvation of Civilians', in AJM Delissen and GJ Tanja (eds), *Humanitarian Law of Armed Conflict, Challenges Ahead: Essays in Honour of Frits Kalshoven* (Nijhoff, 1991) 145, 149–50.

The relevant exception is also to be found in Additional Protocol I but not Additional Protocol II.[788]

4.7 Pillage

The terms pillage, plunder, spoliation, and looting tend to be used interchangeably.[789] Pillage, in all its forms, whether organized or as a result of indiscipline, whether widespread or isolated, and whether committed by fighters or civilians, is prohibited. Pillage may be defined as the 'unlawful appropriation of private or public property',[790] protecting both state and private property. Violence is not necessary in order to constitute pillage,[791] appropriation being the crucial element. There is some dispute as to whether the appropriation must be for private or personal purposes. This is the view of the ICC Elements of Crimes,[792] leaving requisitioning for military purposes lawful.[793] Other jurisprudence considers the limitation to be an 'unwarranted restriction'.[794] The debate is an important one given that it relates to the scope of the offence. However, the terminology used in the debates is unhelpful as private purposes are contrasted with military purposes. Yet, it is suggested that it is not military purposes that render the appropriation lawful but military necessity. Along these lines, the Elements of Crimes provide, in a footnote, that, as 'indicated by the use of the term "private or personal use", appropriations justified by military necessity cannot constitute the crime of pillaging'.[795] That, it is submitted, is where the emphasis lies and not the notion of private or personal use of the appropriated property. It recognizes the importance of respecting ownership of property while appreciating that, in certain situations, such property may have to be used in the course of the fighting.[796] Nonetheless, the rules relating to the requisition of property, particularly in territory under the control of an armed group, is an area in which much work remains to be done.

A second important definitional element relates to the notion of appropriation. Appropriation in this context is shorthand for appropriation without the consent of the legal owner. The question that this raises is the identity of the owner particularly in respect of natural resources in the territory of the state. As international law does not take a position on the identity of the lawful owner, the matter has to be judged by reference to national law, and insofar as natural resources are concerned, the owner will be the state. The consequence of this is that armed groups' use of natural resources will inherently be considered a case of pillage whereas such use by the state will not. This is

---

[788] Additional Protocol I, Article 54(5).
[789] *Hadžihasanović* Decision on Appeal of Rule 98*bis* Decision, above note 51, para 37; *Kordić* Appeal Judgment, above note 22, para 79; *CDF* Trial Judgment, above note 230, para 158; UK *Manual*, above note 43, 395.
[790] *CDF* Trial Judgment, above note 230, para 158. See also *Kordić* Appeal Judgment, above note 22, para 79.
[791] L Moir, 'Conduct of Hostilities—War Crimes', in J Doria, H-P Gasser, and MC Bassiouni (eds), *The Legal Regime of the International Criminal Court: Essays in Honour of Professor Igor Blishchenko* (Martinus Nijhoff, 2009) 487, 528; JG Stewart, *Corporate War Crimes: Prosecuting the Pillage of Natural Resources* (Open Society Institute, 2010) 16.
[792] ICC Elements of Crimes, Article 8(2)(e)(v)-2.
[793] UK *Manual*, above note 43, 395.
[794] *CDF* Trial Judgment, above note 230, para 160; *Prosecutor v Brima, Kamara, and Kanu*, SCSL-04-16-T, Judgment, 20 June 2007, para 754.
[795] ICC Elements of Crimes, Article 8(2)(e)(v)-2, fn.
[796] The point is controversial, especially in light of the extension to public property. See K Dörmann, *Elements of War Crimes under the Rome Statute of the International Criminal Court: Sources and Commentary* (Cambridge University Press, 2003) 272; Stewart, above note 791, 21.

unfortunate and it has accordingly been remarked that 'the policy arguments for allowing rebel groups to seize certain types of property during war are sometimes strong—there is little basis for expecting rebel groups to comply with the laws of war without offering certain privileges'.[797]

The prohibition on pillage applies in non-international armed conflicts, both as a matter of conventional and customary international law.[798] The prohibition is an important one given the not infrequent instances of pillage in non-international armed conflicts. Indeed, because of the commonplace nature of pillage in time of armed conflict, the codes of conduct issued to armed forces and armed groups frequently contain a prohibition on pillage. In the Code of Conduct issued by the Federal Government of Nigeria in 1967 during the attempted secession of Biafra, it is provided that there is to be '[n]o looting of any kind (a good soldier will never loot)'.[799] The prohibition is expressed in everyday language in the codes of conduct of armed groups. For example, the 1947 Three Main Rules of Discipline of the CPLA contained the provision: '[d]on't take a single needle or piece of thread from the masses.'[800] The CPLA's 1947 Eight Points of Attention similarly contained injunctions including: '[p]ay fairly for what you buy', '[r]eturn everything you borrow', '[p]ay for anything you damage', and '[d]ont damage crops.'[801] It is notable that of the Eight Points of Attention, four of the points related to the issue of pillage. This was a deliberate attempt on the part of the CPLA to seek to address one of the main challenges it faced, namely pillage on the part of its forces. Thus, violations of the Points should not be taken to suggest that the Points were purely in the nature of propaganda.[802]

Both the Three Main Rules of Discipline and the Eight Points of Attention have been adopted by several armed groups in the period following issuance by the CPLA. These groups include the NPA, the armed wing of the NDFP,[803] the RUF of Sierra Leone,[804] and the NRA of Uganda.[805] Accordingly, the codes of conduct of each of these groups also contained provisions on the prohibition of pillage, and President Museveni of Uganda, previously Head of the NRA, has recounted the importance of the prohibition.[806] The Code of Conduct of the NRA provided in greater detail '[n]ever take anything in the form of money or property from any member of the public, not even somebody's sweet bananas or sugar-cane on the grounds that it is a mere sugar-cane, without paying for the same', '[p]ay promptly for anything you take in cash', and '[r]eturn anything you borrow from the public'.[807] Museveni, as head of the NRA, noted that '[w]e paid for everything because we did not want to use "voluntary contributions" from the peasants for fear of the system being abused'.[808] The Eight

---

[797] Ibid, 21–2.
[798] Additional Protocol II, Article 4(2)(g); ICTR Statute, Article 4(f); SCSL Statute, Article 3; Statute of the ICC, Article 8(2)(e)(v); Hague Convention for the Protection of Cultural Property, Article 4 (via Article 19); *Hadžihasanović* Decision on Appeal of Rule 98*bis* Decision, above note 51, para 37.
[799] Operational Code of Conduct for the Nigerian Army, above note 60, para 4(h).
[800] Three Main Rules of Discipline, in M Tse-Tung, *Selected Works of Mao Tse-Tung, Volume IV* (Foreign Languages Press, 1969) 155.
[801] The Eight Points for Attention, in ibid.
[802] O Bangerter, *'Do As You Are Told': On Codes of Conduct of Insurgents and Other Measures to Enforce Behaviour* (Small Arms Survey, Geneva Call, forthcoming 2012).
[803] Basic Rules of the New People's Army, above note 211, Principle IV.
[804] *RUF* Trial Judgment, above note 197, para 705.
[805] National Resistance Army Code of Conduct, above note 678.
[806] Museveni, Strategy, above note 31, 9.
[807] National Resistance Army Code of Conduct, above note 678.
[808] YK Museveni, *Sowing the Mustard Seed* (MacMillan, 1997) 132.

Points of the RUF were vitiated entirely by initiatives such as 'Operation Pay Yourself' by which salaries of fighters would be paid through their looting.[809] For his part, Che Guevara indicated that '[m]erchandise that cannot be paid for in cash will be paid for with bonds; and these should be redeemed at the first opportunity'.[810] For its part, the 1982 Code of Conduct for members of the Sendero Luminoso of Peru included the injunctions '[d]o not steal', '[r]eturn what you borrow', and '[r]espect the property of farmers'.[811] The CNF of Burma also has provisions in its internal Code on the prohibition of 'taking the properties or possessions of civilians'.[812] Along similar lines, the 2006 Taliban Code of Conduct provided that 'Mujahideen have no right to confiscate money or personal possessions of civilians'.

4.8 Wanton destruction

The prohibition on the destruction or seizure of property of the adversary, subject to imperative military necessity, is a rule of customary international law.[813] The Customary International Humanitarian Law study suggests that this prohibition is 'essentially the same as' the prohibition on attacking civilian objects.[814] However, it is submitted that the two are distinct from one another, albeit related. While the present prohibition is limited to the property of the adversary, the prohibition on attacking civilian objects is of more general application. Similarly, this prohibition is subject to notions of military necessity, while the prohibition on attacking civilian objects is subject to such notions only to the extent that it becomes a military objective.

The prohibition is an important one. As Francis Lieber remarked to General Halleck in 1863, during the US civil war, wanton destruction 'does incalculable injury. It demoralizes our troops; it annihilates wealth irrecoverably, and makes a return to a state of peace more and more difficult'.[815] Lieber was commenting on wanton destruction more generally rather than the wanton destruction of the property of the adversary, but the point is much the same. A prohibition on the 'wanton destruction of cities, towns or villages, or devastation not justified by military necessity' is also to be found in the Statute of the ICTY.[816]

5. Conclusion

A substantial body of law exists relating to the conduct of hostilities. Although common Article 3 is silent on point and Additional Protocol II contains only a minimum of relevant norms, a whole host of other rules are applicable to non-international armed conflicts. Numerous weapons treaties apply to international and non-international armed conflicts alike. The Rome Statute contains rules on targeting, the prohibition

---

[809] On 'Operation Pay Yourself', see *RUF* Trial Judgment, above note 197, paras 782–4.
[810] Guevara, above note 191, 46.
[811] Code of 1982, reproduced in J Weinstein, *Inside Rebellion: The Politics of Insurgent Violence* (Cambridge University Press, 2007) 152.
[812] Chin National Front, Code, above note 26, Article 19 (unofficial translation).
[813] Rome Statute, Article 8(2)(e)(xii); Customary International Humanitarian Law, Rule 50; Darfur Commission Report, above note 25, para 166.
[814] *Customary International Humanitarian Law, Volume I: Rules*, above note 84, 597.
[815] Letter from Francis Lieber to General Halleck, 20 May 1863, reproduced in GB Davis, 'Doctor Francis Lieber's Instructions for the Government of Armies in the Field' (1907) 1 *AJIL* 13, 21.
[816] Article 3(b). See *Strugar* Trial Judgment, above note 50, para 228; *Hadžihasanović* Decision on Appeal of Rule 98*bis* Decision, above note 51, paras 29–30.

on the use of certain weapons, and the prohibition on certain methods of combat. Other rules apply at the level of customary international humanitarian law. The rules have been identified and developed by the international criminal tribunals and accepted by states. The law on point has changed rather dramatically as compared with the views expressed at the 1974–7 Diplomatic Conference.

The methodological approach set out in Part I is demonstrated in the law relating to the conduct of hostilities, as it was in the context of the law on humane treatment. Treaties created in the period since the mid-1990s apply to non-international armed conflicts as a matter of course. The Convention on Certain Conventional Weapons, its Protocol II, and the Rome Statute have all been amended so as to apply to, or develop, the law of non-international armed conflict. It was through the jurisprudence of the international criminal tribunals that the customary law on point was identified and the relevant rules fleshed out. This customary international humanitarian law developed, in turn, through analogy to the law of international armed conflict.

The concerns identified in Chapter 3 also play out in the law in this area. The standard of international criminal law is narrower than that of international humanitarian law, certainly in the notion of the disproportionate attack, and possibly also in the prohibition on certain perfidious conduct. Analogy to the law of international armed conflict has taken insufficient account of the involvement of armed groups as is evident from the failure to reference parties to the conflict in the Ottawa Convention. It has also weakened certain protections, such as that afforded to works and installations containing dangerous forces. Tagging on non-international armed conflicts at the end of conventional instruments has led to their scope not always being the model of clarity, as is the case with the Hague Convention on Cultural Property.

The particularities of the law of non-international armed conflict are also important. For example, 'scorched earth' tactics are prohibited in non-international armed conflicts, but are not prohibited in certain limited circumstances in international armed conflicts. Uncertainties surrounding the scope of application of the prohibition on riot control agents and expanding bullets also relate to the specificities of non-international armed conflict and the desire to treat them as analogous to situations of internal tensions and disturbances rather than armed conflicts. That insufficient attention has been paid to the involvement of armed groups is evident also from the notion of direct participation in hostilities. Historically, the notion of an armed group was essentially contested for fear of affording that group a certain status. This meant that members of the armed group were considered civilians taking a direct part in hostilities. This has changed in recent years, primarily with the 2009 Interpretive Guidance of the ICRC. However, that guidance defines membership based on a continuous combat function in an armed group, with *de jure* membership not being considered. The capacities of the parties to the conflict are also brought to bear in such areas as the requirement to investigate certain losses of life.

These various issues also play out, albeit in very different ways, in the implementation and enforcement of the law of non-international armed conflict.

10

Implementation and Non-Judicial Enforcement

1. Introduction

Implementation and enforcement are widely perceived to be the weak points of the law of armed conflict. This is particularly true of the law of non-international armed conflict.[1] Indeed, it has been observed that the system of implementation and enforcement 'as a whole has been devised for international conflicts; it cannot simply be switched over to non-international conflicts, whose basic data are completely different'.[2] There is much truth in this insight. As with the substantive law of non-international armed conflict, to use the non-judicial enforcement mechanisms that are designed for the law of international armed conflict to enforce the law of non-international armed conflict is to ignore the crucial differences that exist between the two sorts of conflict.

Mechanisms for implementation and non-judicial enforcement of the law are largely of three types. First, there are the mechanisms that are internal to the parties to the conflict, be it the state or the non-state armed group. These include dissemination, instruction, and legal advice; the drafting of codes of conduct and internal regulations; and sanctioning instances of non-compliance. Second, there are the mechanisms that consist of responses to the actions of the opposing party, principally the doctrine of belligerent reprisals. Third, there are the activities of entities that are external to the conflict, such as Protecting Powers, the International Humanitarian Fact-Finding Commission, United Nations and other intergovernmental bodies, the International Committee of the Red Cross (ICRC), and non-governmental organizations.

Legal mechanisms for ensuring compliance with the law of non-international armed conflict are only part of the picture. Of equal importance, perhaps even of greater importance, are other mechanisms such as public opinion, reputation, and personal conviction.[3] Personal connections may also prove important, as was the case with Jonas Savimbi of the União Nacional para a Independência Total de Angola (UNITA) and his former teacher, and French Prime Minister Pierre Mendès-France and his cousin the ICRC delegate based in Paris, the latter individual in both examples proving

---

[1] See eg GIAD Draper, 'The Implementation and Enforcement of the Geneva Conventions of 1949 and of the Two Additional Protocols of 1978' (1979-III) 164 *RdC* 1, 28; H-P Gasser, 'Ensuring Respect for the Geneva Conventions and Protocols: The Role of Third States and the United Nations', in H Fox and MA Meyer (eds), *Armed Conflict and the New Law, Volume II: Effecting Compliance* (BIICL, 1993) 15, 17; GH Aldrich, 'Compliance with the Law: Problems and Prospects', in ibid, 3, 4; S Oeter, 'Civil War, Humanitarian Law and the United Nations' (1997) 1 *Max Planck Yearbook of United Nations Law* 195, 210.

[2] Y Sandoz, 'Implementing International Humanitarian Law', in UNESCO, *International Dimensions of Humanitarian Law* (UNESCO, 1988) 259.

[3] See M Veuthey, *Guerrilla et Droit Humanitaire* (CICR, 1983) 338–9; R Wolfrum and D Fleck, 'The Enforcement of International Humanitarian Law', in D Fleck (ed), *The Handbook of International Humanitarian Law* (Oxford University Press, 2008) 675, 686–7.

influential in convincing the former individual to apply international humanitarian law.[4] However, the focus of this chapter is on the legal mechanisms of implementation and enforcement, as the law must also play its part.

2. Internal mechanisms

2.1 Dissemination

2.1.1 Importance of dissemination

In order for the law of non-international armed conflict to be applied, it must first be understood. Accordingly, one of the most important aspects of the implementation of the law is dissemination of, education about, and training on, the law. This is as true for members of the armed forces as it is members of armed groups and civilians.

The importance of dissemination has long been recognized. In 1869, Gustave Moynier, one of the founders of the ICRC, noted to the Second International Conference of the Red Cross: '[i]f the Convention is to be implemented, its spirit must be introduced into the customs of soldiers and of the population as a whole. Its principles must be popularized through extensive propaganda.'[5] When considering revisions to the 1864 Geneva Convention, Moynier suggested the inclusion of an additional provision: '[t]he High Contracting Parties undertake to introduce in their military regulations the modifications that have now become indispensable as a result of their adherence to the present Convention. They will give orders for them to be explained to the troops in peace time, and included in the general orders in times of war.'[6] Reflecting this idea, the preface to the Oxford Manual of 1880, which was largely drafted by Moynier, reads in relevant part:

... it is not sufficient for sovereigns to promulgate new laws. It is essential, too, that they make these laws known among all people, so that when a war is declared, the men called upon to take up arms to defend the causes of the belligerent States, may be thoroughly impregnated with the special rights and duties attached to the execution of such a command.[7]

The value of dissemination is also recognized in a number of international humanitarian law instruments. The 1949 Geneva Conventions, for example, provide that '[t]he High Contracting Parties undertake, in time of peace as in time of war, to disseminate the text of the present Convention as widely as possible in their respective countries'.[8] Given that common Article 3 is an integral part of the Geneva Conventions, the obligation to disseminate the law extends to that Article.[9] This also applies to the Hague Convention on Cultural Property, which contains a dissemination clause similar to that contained in the Geneva Conventions,[10] and of which Article 19 on

---

[4] See M Veuthey, 'Learning from History: Accession to the Conventions, Special Agreements, and Unilateral Declarations' (2003) 27 *Collegium* 139, 139–40 and 145.

[5] Quoted in WV Dunlap, 'Dissemination and International Humanitarian Law in Modern Social Conflict', in J Carey, WV Dunlap, and RJ Pritchard (eds), *International Humanitarian Law: Challenges* (Transnational, 2004) 15, 17–18.

[6] P Boissier, *From Solferino to Tsushima: History of the International Committee of the Red Cross* (Henry Dunant Institute, 1985) 203.

[7] The Laws of War on Land, Oxford, 9 September 1880.

[8] Articles 47, 48,127, and 144.

[9] L Moir, *The Law of Internal Armed Conflict* (Cambridge University Press, 2002) 243. Cf Draper, Implementation and Enforcement, above note 1, 27.

[10] Article 25.

non-international armed conflicts is an integral part. For its part, Additional Protocol II provides that the Protocol 'shall be disseminated as widely as possible'.[11] The importance of dissemination is also evidenced by Security Council Resolution 1894 (2009), which calls for 'the widest possible dissemination of information' on humanitarian norms.

2.1.2 States, non-state armed groups, and civilians

Given that the obligations mentioned above apply to the 'parties to the conflict', the obligation of dissemination applies to states as well as non-state armed groups.[12] Commitments drawn up by third parties and signed by non-state armed groups thus frequently contain a provision on dissemination. The Geneva Call Deed of Commitment, for example, commits the armed non-state actor signatory to issue 'the necessary orders and directives to our commanders and fighters for the implementation and enforcement of our commitment under the foregoing paragraphs, including measures for information, dissemination and training, as well as disciplinary sanctions in case of non-compliance'.[13] Ad hoc bilateral agreements concluded between the parties may also contain a provision on dissemination. In this regard, the National Democratic Front of the Philippines (NDFP) indicated in 2005 that it:

> has launched educational campaigns on CARHRIHL [Comprehensive Agreement on Respect for Human Rights and International Humanitarian Law] among its forces. It has caused the translation of the CARHRIHL into Filipino, Cebuano and Ilokano and has widely distributed and conducted studies on these reading materials within its mass organizations and the people in its territories and among its allies. The CARHRIHL has become a basic study material in the CPP, NPA, the revolutionary mass organizations and the organs of political power.[14]

The obligation to disseminate exists during times of peace and does not arise only upon the commencement of an armed conflict.[15] The obligation to disseminate is thus one of the few provisions of international humanitarian law that are applicable in peacetime. When viewed in this manner, the primary obligation of dissemination is vested in the state, as it arises at a time in which the non-state armed group may not exist. Upon the commencement of a non-international armed conflict, however, the obligation also vests in the armed group.

The obligation extends to dissemination to the civilian population and is not limited to dissemination to members of the armed forces and the armed group.[16] Dissemination in peacetime to the civilian population serves to inform persons who may later constitute members of the armed group of their obligations. For example, prior to 1977, Somali military schools taught classes on the law of war and individuals benefitting from such classes went on to become high-ranking members of the National

---

[11] Article 19.
[12] See also J-M Henckaerts and L Doswald-Beck, *Customary International Humanitarian Law, Volume I: Rules* (Cambridge University Press, 2005) 505–8; Institut de Droit International, 'Application of International Humanitarian Law and Fundamental Human Rights, in Armed Conflicts in which Non-State Entities are Parties' (Berlin, 1999) Article XII.
[13] Deed of Commitment under Geneva Call for Adherence to a Total Ban on Anti-Personnel Mines and for Cooperation in Mine Action, para 4. On Geneva Call, see below, 538–42.
[14] NDFP, *Praymer Hinggil sa CARHRIHL* (Booklet Number 5, December 2005) 80.
[15] See eg the language of the 1949 Geneva Conventions, Articles 47, 48, 127, and 144.
[16] See *Customary International Humanitarian Law, Volume I: Rules*, above note 12, 505–8.

Security Service and the Rahanwein Resistance Army.[17] For this reason, some states may be reluctant to educate their populations on the law of armed conflict, taking the view that such education may foment unrest.[18] Other states may take the view that a non-international armed conflict will not break out on their territory and thus no measures of dissemination need be taken. For example, in its report to UNESCO pursuant to the Hague Convention on Cultural Property, Poland remarked: '[w]e do not foresee on our territory any armed conflict not of an international character, and therefore we do not see the necessity for proceeding to take measures providing for the application of the provisions of Article 19',[19] Article 19 being the provision that regulates non-international armed conflicts. Even states that are willing to disseminate the law may not have the necessary resources to do so in any comprehensive manner.

Accordingly, although the primary obligation of dissemination rests with states, the ICRC and other entities play an important role.[20] As of 1996, the ICRC's Advisory Service on international humanitarian law has been providing legal advice to states on the implementation of international humanitarian law.[21] In relation to non-international armed conflicts, the work of the ICRC's Advisory Service could usefully be extended to non-state armed groups.[22] Dissemination by the ICRC also takes place at the level of universities,[23] and in a number of different and innovative ways.[24]

2.1.3 Modalities of dissemination

The modalities of dissemination are left to states and non-state armed groups. Traditionally, dissemination takes place through 'orders, courses of instructions, commentaries or manuals' in relation to the principles and norms of international humanitarian law.[25] However, dissemination is not, nor should it be, limited to handing out written copies of texts. It is of little use to the ordinary fighter to read detailed provisions that

---

[17] OA Alasow, *Violations of the Rules Applicable in Non-International Armed Conflicts and Their Possible Causes* (Martinus Nijhoff, 2010) 208–9.

[18] Conference of Government Experts on the Reaffirmation and Development of International Humanitarian Law Applicable in Armed Conflicts (Second Session, 3 May–3 June 1972): Report on the Work of the Conference, Volume I (July 1972) 96, para 2.325.

[19] UNESCO, *Information on the Implementation of the Convention for the Protection of Cultural Property in Case of Armed Conflict* (UNESCO, 1967) 31. See also UNESCO, *Information on the Implementation of the Convention for the Protection of Cultural Property in Case of Armed Conflict* (UNESCO, 1979) 27.

[20] See eg Resolution 21(IV) of the 1977 Diplomatic Conference, *Official Records of the Diplomatic Conference on the Reaffirmation and Development of International Humanitarian Law Applicable in Armed Conflicts, Geneva (1974–1977)* (Federal Political Department, 1978) Vol 1, 214. See also Statutes of the International Red Cross and Red Crescent Movement, Article 5(1).

[21] P Berman, 'The ICRC's Advisory Service on International Humanitarian Law: the Challenge of National Implementation' (1996) 36 *IRRC* 338.

[22] M Sassòli, 'The Implementation of International Humanitarian Law: Current and Inherent Challenges' (2007) 10 *YIHL* 45, 65.

[23] See AA Bouvier and KE Sams, 'Teaching International Humanitarian Law in Universities: the Contribution of the International Committee of the Red Cross' (2002) 5 *YIHL* 381; E David, 'Dissemination of International Humanitarian Law at University Level' (1987) 257 *IRRC* 155.

[24] See eg N Farrell, 'Dissemination in Bosnia and Herzegovina Lessons Learned' (1997) 37 *IRRC* 409; R Bigler, 'Disseminating International Humanitarian Law in Colombia: Dissemination is Everyone's Job—A Firsthand Report by an ICRC Delegate' (1997) 37 *IRRC* 421; É Baeriswyl and A Aeschlimann, 'Reflections on a Dissemination Operation in Burundi—Declaration for Standards of Humanitarian Conduct: Appeal for a Minimum of Humanity in a Situation of Internal Violence' (1997) 37 *IRRC* 385.

[25] Ministry of Defence, *The Manual of the Law of Armed Conflict* (Oxford University Press, 2004) 414.

are formulated in complicated legal terms. Without legal training—and even with—these provisions can be difficult to comprehend. Ordinary fighters only need to understand the principles that underlie the rules, as well as the basic rules themselves, both of which should be made readily understandable to all.[26] Means of communication with which fighters are familiar should be utilized as far as possible, even at the expense of books and manuals to which lawyers would instinctively turn. Norms could be presented pictorially if there is a high level of illiteracy among fighters or soldiers, or if child soldiers are known to be used. For example, when the ICRC distributed comic books on humanitarian rules to children in the Philippines, these were reportedly 'readily accepted and quickly found their way to their parents and other individuals, most notably combatants'.[27] If, as in many places, radio is the predominant means of communication, radio broadcasts could be used to convey humanitarian law ideals, not through lessons but through soap operas and the like.[28] Indeed, one armed group, the Armée Populaire pour la Restauration de la République et la Démocratie (APRD) of the Central African Republic, has itself suggested the launching of a radio and television campaign on the law relating to child soldiers.[29] ICRC appeals are sometimes carried out in this manner, for example the radio broadcast, including on insurgent-held radio, of ICRC delegate Herbert Beckh during the Hungarian uprising of 1956.[30] Alternatively, humanitarian norms could be distributed by text message if mobile telephones are commonplace.

Despite the efforts in the area over the years, dissemination remains crucial. In some states, such as Colombia, it has been suggested that 'no matter where, even in the most remote valleys of the Andes and in the hot and humid Amazon forests everyone spoke of Protocol II Additional to the Geneva Conventions, international humanitarian law and universal human rights'.[31] However, in other states, such as Somalia, it has been said that '[v]irtually no one with a weapon had heard of the Geneva Conventions'.[32] A survey published in 1999 of individuals in states that had experienced armed conflict, carried out for the ICRC, found that some 39 per cent of persons had heard of the Geneva Conventions, but of these, only 60 per cent had knowledge of their content.[33] This figure needs to be improved.

2.2 Instruction

Dissemination is not the same as instruction. Instruction allows individuals to ask questions, engage in dialogue, and resolve misunderstandings with a knowledgeable entity. It also allows the making of contacts, the formation of entry points, and the

---

[26] Sassòli, Implementation, above note 22, 47.
[27] M Veuthey, 'Remedies to Promote the Respect of Fundamental Human Values in Non-International Armed Conflicts' (2000) 30 *IYHR* 37, 52.
[28] Ibid.
[29] Geneva Call (ed), *In Their Words: Perspectives of Armed Non-State Actors on the Protection of Children from the Effects of Armed Conflict* (Geneva Call, 2010) 14.
[30] See F Perret, 'ICRC Action in Hungary in 1956' (1996) 36 *IRRC* 413, 417.
[31] R Bigler, 'Disseminating International Humanitarian Law in Colombia: Dissemination is Everyone's Job—A Firsthand Report by an ICRC Delegate' (1997) 37 *IRRC* 421.
[32] J Leaning, 'When the System Doesn't Work: Somalia in 1992', in KM Cahill (ed), *A Framework for Survival: Health, Human Rights and Humanitarian Assistance in Conflicts and Disasters* (Routledge, 1994) 31, 40. See also Situation of Human Rights in Somalia: Report of the Independent Expert, E/CN.4/2002/119, 14 January 2002, para 90.
[33] Greenberg Research Inc, *The People on War Report: ICRC Worldwide Consultation on the Rules of War* (ICRC, 1999) xi.

establishment of working relationships. Instruction may take the form of education and training. Thus, traditional means of education, such as presentations and question-and-answer sessions, play an important role. However, ensuring 'effective compliance during the stress of combat' will require non-classroom forms of training or instruction.[34] The breadth and depth of the instruction afforded will vary according to the level, mandate, and nature of the individuals being engaged.[35] The Security Council has recognized the importance of providing instruction to state armed forces and non-state armed groups, with Resolution 1894 (2009) calling for 'all parties concerned ... to provide training for members of armed forces and armed groups'.[36] The obligation to provide instruction has also been considered an obligation under customary international law and in respect of states and non-state armed groups alike.[37]

The ICRC and the International Institute of Humanitarian Law, in particular, have introduced courses on international humanitarian law for members of armed forces. These courses include instruction on aspects of the law of non-international armed conflict. If instruction is as important as is made out, and it is suggested that it is, courses should also be convened for members of armed groups. These should be tailored to the specificities of a particular group and a particular conflict in order that concrete issues that are raised by that conflict can be explored. Although there is a danger that such initiatives may (incorrectly) be considered to amount to providing material support to 'terrorist groups',[38] instruction is already provided to armed groups on an ad hoc basis. This type of engagement with non-state armed groups has developed, particularly over the last 10 years.[39] For example, the ICRC has conducted training sessions on international humanitarian law to, among others, the Moro Islamic Liberation Front (MILF) of the Philippines and its armed wing, the Bangsamoro Islamic Armed Force (BIAF); Geneva Call has done likewise on the ban on anti-personnel mines and mine action.[40] The training was carried out at the request of the MILF and BIAF and with the full support of the Government of the Philippines.[41] Further sessions were held for Bangsamoro youth and Bangsamoro women.[42] Geneva Call has also provided training on international humanitarian law and the anti-personnel mine ban to commanders of certain Iranian Kurdish armed groups,[43] along with the International Institute for Humanitarian Law to Polisario of Western Sahara,[44] and is increasingly requested by armed groups to provide training workshops on international humanitarian law, human rights, and mine action.[45] Indeed, armed groups that are signatories to Geneva Call's Deed of Commitment have requested training on

---

[34] *Customary International Humanitarian Law, Volume I: Rules*, above note 12, 503.
[35] See the various approaches in F de Mulinen, *Handbook on the Law of War for Armed Forces* (ICRC, 1987).
[36] See also GA Res 3032 (XXVII) (1972).
[37] Customary International Humanitarian Law, Rule 142. Cf D Turns, 'Implementation and Compliance', in E Wilmshurst and SC Breau (eds), *Perspectives on the ICRC Study on Customary International Humanitarian Law* (Cambridge University Press, 2007) 354, 362.
[38] See below, 533.
[39] O Bangerter, 'Reasons Why Armed Groups Choose to Respect IHL or Not' (2011) 93 *IRRC* 353.
[40] See Geneva Call, *Training of Trainers Workshop* (Geneva Call, 2005). On Geneva Call, see below, 538–42.
[41] Ibid, 2–3.
[42] Geneva Call, Annual Report 2006, 21.
[43] Geneva Call, Newsletter, Volume 7(2), November 2009, 2.
[44] See Geneva Call, Communiqué, 20 May 2011.
[45] Geneva Call, Annual Report 2006, 1.

humanitarian norms more generally.[46] The ICRC has also organized trainings on the law of armed conflict to the Karen National Union (KNU) of Burma.[47] On occasion, individuals may provide instruction on international humanitarian law, as was reportedly done by a professor of international humanitarian law at the University of Prishtina to members of the Kosovo Liberation Army (KLA).[48] Questions posed to instructors are revealing, for they indicate that non-state armed groups' knowledge of the law can be rather advanced. For example, questions posed to Geneva Call at a training session for Kurdish armed groups included: '[i]s a spy a civilian or a military person?' and does '[a] target need[] to be 100% military, not used for any civilian purpose. Even a tractor pulling a tank, or a civilian house that becomes a military base?'[49] Despite these examples, the provision of instruction to armed groups on international law standards remains limited. For example, in 2010, the Justice and Equality Movement (JEM) of Sudan indicated that it had 'approached several international bodies for further training [on issues relating to children]...but has received no response'.[50] Instruction is provided very much on an ad hoc basis.

Perhaps more important than external instruction is instruction from within the group. The impact of external trainings on the law of armed conflict, although necessary, can prove limited: '[i]t seems much more efficient to have respect of IHL enforced by those who exert...an important influence than by outsiders who try to convince each and every individual fighter to comply.'[51] It is not only efficiency that is impacted but the likelihood that the training is taken seriously. When viewed in this manner, helping armed groups help themselves is far more useful.[52] Accordingly, Geneva Call has engaged in 'training of trainers' workshops in order to train military and political officers of the relevant armed group who would then go on to train other members of the group. Such an approach was adopted as 'the principles could be appropriated by the group rather than being seen as imposed by the outside' making them more likely to being accepted.[53] Members of armed groups do, from time to time, train fellow members on international standards. For example, the JEM of Sudan has indicated that it 'provides training to all its commanders regarding protection of children who happen to pass though its camps'.[54] A briefing on point is also given to 'all new recruits'.[55] Likewise, the KNU of Burma has stated that it 'has included the topic of education on child soldiers and the protection of civilians in every basic military training and military officer's trainings'.[56] Other groups, such as the Forces Démocratiques de Libération du Rwanda (FDLR) in the Democratic Republic of the

---

[46] Declaration of the Second Meeting of Signatories to Geneva Call's 'Deed of Commitment for Adherence to a Total Ban on Anti-Personnel Mines and for Cooperation in Mine Action', 19 June 2009.
[47] *In Their Words*, above note 29, 22–3.
[48] HH Perritt Jr, *Kosovo Liberation Army: The Inside Story of an Insurgency* (University of Illinois Press, 2008) 107.
[49] Geneva Call, Annual Report 2009, 24.
[50] *In Their Words*, above note 29, 18.
[51] O Bangerter, 'Disseminating and Implementing International Humanitarian Law within Organized Armed Groups: Measures Armed Groups Can Take to Improve Respect for International Humanitarian Law', in International Institute of Humanitarian Law (ed), *Non-State Actors and International Humanitarian Law* (FrancoAngeli, 2010) 187, 193.
[52] Ibid, 188–9.
[53] Geneva Call, *Training of Trainers Workshop* (Geneva Call, 2006) 2.
[54] *In Their Words*, above note 29, 18.
[55] Ibid.
[56] Ibid, 23.

Congo and the Naxalites in India, are reported as having military academies with elaborate systems of training.[57]

2.3 Legal advice

The law of international armed conflict requires the employment of legal advisers to advise military commanders on the application of the Geneva Conventions and Additional Protocol I.[58] It also requires the employment of legal advisers on the part of national liberation movements.[59] It has been suggested that the employment of legal advisers is also 'implicit in the 1949 Geneva Conventions',[60] but that seems to be a stretch too far. The Customary International Humanitarian Law study posits that the employment of legal advisers is a norm of customary international law for states in respect of international and non-international armed conflicts alike.[61] Regardless of the customary nature of the obligation, legal advisers have certainly been utilized in non-international armed conflicts. For example, in 1997, during the conflict in Sri Lanka, a Directorate of International Humanitarian Law was established within the Sri Lankan Army.[62] Similarly, there are indications that at least one commander of a Colombian paramilitary group was assigned a lawyer to advise on issues of international humanitarian law.[63] Although it may seem curious to suggest that non-state armed groups should also seek the benefit of legal advice—and the Customary International Humanitarian Law study notes that 'no practice was found requiring such groups to have legal advisers'[64]—many armed groups do so. In practice, during the 2011 violence in Libya, the National Transitional Council requested a group of expatriate Libyan lawyers to advise it on 'the applicable rules of the law of armed conflict'. They, in turn, consulted others on the preparation of 'basic guidelines for use in the field'.[65] Furthermore, certain statements of non-state armed groups simply could not have been written without the benefit of such advice, for example the White Paper on the application of the Geneva Conventions issued by the Provisional Government during the Algerian war of independence (1954–62).[66] Indeed, in its 24-page booklet, *The Legitimacy of Our Methods of Struggle*, published in 1988, the Frente Farabundo Martí para la Liberación Nacional (FMLN) of El Salvador thanks 'the contributions that have been made to us by the experts in humanitarian law that we have consulted'.[67] Thus, even if non-state armed groups do not formally employ legal advisers in the same way as do states, there is not infrequently a close relationship between certain non-state armed groups and the provision of legal advice. This is to be encouraged.

---

[57] O Bangerter, *'Do As You Are Told': On Codes of Conduct of Insurgents and Other Measures to Enforce Behaviour* (Small Arms Survey, forthcoming 2012).
[58] Additional Protocol I, Article 82. See GIAD Draper, 'Role of Legal Advisers in the Armed Forces' (1978) 18 *IRRC* 6.
[59] Additional Protocol I, Article 82.
[60] H McCoubrey, *International Humanitarian Law* (Aldershot, 1990) 207.
[61] Customary International Humanitarian Law, Rule 141.
[62] MH Hoffman, 'The Application of International Humanitarian Law in Sri Lanka: A Compliance Based Case Study on the Rules of War' (2000) 30 *IYHR* 209, 213.
[63] F Kalshoven, 'Protocol II, the CDDH and Colombia', in K Wellens (ed), *International Law: Theory and Practice, Essays in Honour of Eric Suy* (Kluwer Law International, 1998) 597, 615.
[64] *Customary International Humanitarian Law, Volume I: Rules*, above note 12, 501.
[65] See I Scobbie, 'Operationalising the Law of Armed Conflict for Dissident Forces in Libya', EJIL: Talk! Blog, 31 August 2011.
[66] *White Paper on the Application of the Geneva Conventions of 1949 to the French-Algerian Conflict* (Algerian Office, 1960).
[67] FMLN, *The Legitimacy of Our Methods of Struggle* (Inkworks Press, 1988) 1.

2.4 Manuals, codes of conduct, and internal regulations

2.4.1 State measures

The military manuals of states have proven important in the creation and development of international humanitarian law.[68] They are referred to frequently in judgments of international courts and tribunals,[69] and are used as evidence of state practice and *opinio juris* in identifying customary norms.[70] The content of the military manual of one state may influence that of another; and states themselves may play a role in the preparation of other states' manuals. For example, the United Kingdom takes on board the views of the United States in preparing its military manual.[71] Similarly, the United States solicits the views of the United Kingdom, among other states, in the preparation of its own manual. Manuals emanating from institutions have also played a crucial role in the development of the law, for example, the *Oxford Manual on the Laws of War on Land* (1880) prepared by the Institut de Droit International and the *San Remo Manual on International Law Applicable to Armed Conflicts at Sea* (1994) drawn up under the auspices of the International Institute of Humanitarian Law to name but two.

States involved in non-international armed conflicts may also utilize instructions or codes of conduct to regulate the conduct of their forces in that conflict. This was true, for example, of the armed forces of the Federal Government of Nigeria during the attempted secession of Biafra (1967–70) and the armed forces of Tajikistan in 1996 against 'illegal armed units'.[72] These instructions and codes may prove useful for reminding the forces that they are fighting against their fellow nationals and that once the conflict concludes they will have to live alongside one another once again.[73] They may also enable individual soldiers who violate the instructions or codes to be disciplined. Most importantly, these regulations may be followed by the armed forces. For example, the Observer Team, which was invited by the Federal Government of Nigeria to look into the conduct of its armed forces, reported that 'Federal troops were for the most part aware of the instructions in "The Code of Conduct" and were following these instructions'.[74]

2.4.2 Non-state armed group measures

Non-state armed groups also draw up codes of conduct and issue internal regulations on issues pertaining to the law of armed conflict. For example, the Chin National Front (CNF) of Burma has a military 'Code of Conduct' which is based on the Geneva Conventions and Additional Protocols.[75] According to a 1988 publication of the

---

[68] See MH Hoffman, 'Can Military Manuals Improve the Law of War? The San Remo Manual on the Law of Non-International Armed Conflict considered in relation to Historical and Contemporary Trends' (2007) 37 *IYHR* 241.

[69] See eg *Prosecutor v Galić*, IT-98-29-A, Judgment, 30 November 2006, para 89.

[70] See generally *Customary International Humanitarian Law, Volume II: Practice*; Report of the International Commission of Inquiry on Darfur to the Secretary-General, S/2005/60, 1 February 2005, para 166.

[71] See C Garraway, 'The Use and Abuse of Military Manuals' (2004) 7 *YIHL* 425, 435.

[72] Operational Code of Conduct for the Nigerian Army, reproduced in AHM Kirk-Greene, *Crisis and Conflict in Nigeria: A Documentary Sourcebook 1966–1969, Volume I* (Oxford University Press, 1971) 455; E La Haye, *War Crimes in Internal Armed Conflicts* (Cambridge University Press, 2008) 60.

[73] See eg above, 28.

[74] Report of the Observer Team to Nigeria, 24 September to 23 November 1968, Cmnd 3878 (HMSO, 1969) 12.

[75] Chin National Front, Code, undated but attributed to 1998.

FMLN of El Salvador, the FMLN issued internal regulations *inter alia* on the interaction between FMLN fighters and the civilian population.[76] The BIAF, the armed wing of the MILF of the Philippines, has a Code of Conduct as well as various internal regulations dealing with humanitarian norms.[77] A spokesperson for the KLA stated in 1998 that the KLA had internal regulations which 'clearly lay down that the UCK recognizes the Geneva Convention and the conventions governing the conduct of war'.[78] The JEM of Sudan indicated in 2009 that its Army Penal Code provides that 'international Human Rights and Geneva Conventions and its Protocols have supremacy over JEM laws'.[79] Other groups that have adopted internal regulations or codes of conduct include the National Liberation Army (ELN) of Colombia, and the Fuerzas Armadas Revolucionarias de Colombia (FARC);[80] the Revolutionary United Front (RUF) of Sierra Leone;[81] the Sudan People's Liberation Movement (SPLM);[82] the National Resistance Army (NRA) of Uganda,[83] Sendero Luminoso of Peru;[84] the Taliban of Afghanistan;[85] and the NDFP.[86] Accordingly, it has been suggested that '[h]umanitarian provisions are to be found in . . . the internal directives of *most* guerrilla movements'.[87]

Assuming codes of conduct and internal regulations of armed groups meet international standards, they could prove rather important for a number of reasons. First, measures that are internal to the group, such as codes, regulations, and orders, are crucial as they are drafted in language understandable by ordinary fighters.[88] International instruments tend not to be helpful in this regard for want of clarity on the part of the everyday individual. It is crucial that the norms are captured in simple language understandable to all, for 'brevity and simplicity [are] the secret of success'.[89] Second, it is through such internal measures that the international norms are translated across

---

[76] See FMLN, above note 67, 6.

[77] *In Their Words*, above note 29, 25; General Order No 2 (2006); Supplemental General Order for General Orders Nos 1 and 2 (2010).

[78] 'Krasniqi Explains UCK's Origins, Structure', Pristina *Koha Ditore*, 12 July 1998, KLA Communiques and Political Declarations from 1997–9, Exhibit P48 in ICTY *Limaj* trial (ICTY translation).

[79] 'Report of the Panel of Experts established pursuant to Resolution 1591 (2005) concerning the Sudan Issues 29 October 2009: A Response from JEM', 18 November 2009.

[80] FARC, Normas de comportamiento con las masas (released in 1998); ELN, Código Guerrillero, 1995.

[81] RUF, Eight Codes of Conduct, reproduced in *Prosecutor v Sesay, Kallon and Gbao*, SCSL-04-15-T, Judgment, 2 March 2009, para 705.

[82] For example, the SPLA Act 2003, which repealed the SPLA Act 1994, and the SPLM Penal and Disciplinary Laws 1984.

[83] National Resistance Army Code of Conduct, reprinted in OO Amaza, *Museveni's Long March from Guerrilla to Statesman* (Kampala, 1998) 246.

[84] Eight Principles; Norms of Behaviour for a Sendero Luminoso Commander, reproduced in JM Weinstein, *Inside Rebellion* (Cambridge University Press, 2007) 152 and 375.

[85] Code of Conduct for the Mujahedin (2006, 2009, 2010).

[86] Basic Rules of the New People's Army, 13 May 1969, reproduced as Annex C to NDFP, *Declaration of Undertaking to Apply the Geneva Conventions of 1949 and Protocol I of 1977* (NDFP Human Rights Monitoring Committee Booklet No 6) 85.

[87] M Veuthey, 'Guerrilla Warfare and Humanitarian Law' (1976) 16 *IRRC* 277, 290 (emphasis added). For a collection of codes of conduct and internal regulations, see Bangerter, *Codes of Conduct*, above note 57.

[88] See also M Sassòli, 'Taking Armed Groups Seriously: Ways to Improve their Compliance with International Humanitarian Law' (2010) 1 *International Humanitarian Legal Studies* 5, 32.

[89] Conference of Government Experts on the Reaffirmation and Development of International Humanitarian Law Applicable in Armed Conflicts (Second Session, 3 May–3 June 1972): Report on the Work of the Conference, Volume I (Geneva, July 1972) 62.

from the group's political wing to fighters. Not infrequently, it is the political wing that engages with international actors and commits the group to abiding by the norms. However, by itself, this is not enough. The political wing may not be based in the state in which the fighting takes place,[90] and the norms must be understood and followed by the military wing if they are to be respected. Furthermore, the norms cannot be limited to the military elite but have to be understood by the rank and file. Internal measures allow the norms to be passed down the chain of command from the military elite to the rank and file. The importance of this latter point is well-described in the instructions issued by General Dufour during the Swiss civil war (1847), in which he wrote, '[l]et the superior officers apply themselves to instil [the] principles into the minds of their subordinates, who shall do the same to the lower-ranking officers, and similarly to the troops, so that they should become a law unto the entire federal army'.[91] Similarly, an order issued in 1919 during the Russian civil war provided that '[t]he military revolutionary councils of the armies in the east shall give the widest possible publicity to this order, shall disseminate it throughout the army units on the eastern front, and shall hand it to commanding officers and commissars so that no one may claim to have been unaware of it'.[92] Third, transmittal of the order down the chain of command is particularly important in light of the possible disconnect between commanders of the group and the rank and file. For example, leaders of a group may wish to comply with the law while lower level troops may not. Along these lines, it has been noted that local guerrilla commanders of the FARC 'resented the ICRC's forwarding of [violations] to their national general secretariat, whose commanders were keen on "humanizing" the practice [of hostage-taking], or on keeping it at least selective, and who occasionally remonstrate with them for their excesses'.[93] Internal regulations thus reduce the possibility of disparity of conduct. Fourth, internal measures of armed groups help the group train its fighters on legal standards. As the National Transitional Council of Libya indicated in 2011:

We recognize that many of those men and women who have taken up arms in opposition to the Qadhafi regime are not combatants who have been formerly trained in the laws of armed conflict. As such . . . guidelines were requested in order to help instruct them, as rapidly as possible, in the fundamental rules which they must respect . . .[94]

Finally, it is through internal measures that the norms are internalized rather than being seen as something that emanates from the outside. The armed group becomes invested in the process, enforcing its own rules, rather than something that is the creation of the other. This creates a sense of ownership over the relevant norms, aiding compliance. Thus, studies have suggested that non-state armed groups that have codes of conduct are more likely to comply with humanitarian standards than non-state armed groups that do not.[95]

---

[90] For example, the LTTE's political wing was based in London. The NDFP leadership is based in the Netherlands.
[91] Instructions of General Dufour, 4 November 1847, reproduced in 'An Example of Humanity' (1976) 16 *IRRC* 94, 96.
[92] Order of the Day No 92, 1 May 1919, quoted in M Veuthey, 'Military Instructions on the Treatment of Prisoners in Guerrilla Warfare' (1972) 12 *IRRC* 125, 133.
[93] P Gassmann, 'Colombia: Persuading Belligerents to Comply with International Norms', in S Chesterman (ed), *Civilians in War* (Lynne Rienner Publishers, 2001) 67, 75.
[94] National Transitional Council, 'Press Release No. 21', quoted in Scobbie, above note 65.
[95] International Council on Human Rights Policy, *Ends and Means: Human Rights Approaches to Armed Groups* (ICHRP, 2000) 52.

These various factors are reflected in the internal code of one armed group—the CNF of Burma. The CNF Code notes explicitly that:

> [t]he objective of writing this law is to let all the CNF members understand it. In other words, this law is meant for the people who practice it. The Geneva [Conventions are] written by international legal experts using relevant legal terms. Therefore, translating the original version of the Geneva [Conventions] into Burmese and distributing among the CNF members would be lengthy and boring and would not help in practical usage. If the members are to be made aware of the precepts of the Geneva Agreement and made to follow it, then it is necessary to make it easy to read and understand and present it in a practicable way.[96]

In order that codes of conduct and internal regulations constitute a useful means of enforcement, they need to be consistent with international standards. Many regulations are indeed consistent, with some reportedly being of a higher standard than that required by the law of armed conflict.[97] However, consistency with international standards cannot be assumed, and some regulations violate international standards. For example, the 2009 Code of Conduct of the Taliban provided that

> [i]f the captive is a Director (in a governmental office), a Commander, a District Administrator, or a higher ranking official than them, or a foreign Muslim, the Imam and his deputy will decide whether the captive will be punished, executed or released in the framework of prisoners exchange...
>
> If an infidel warrior has been captured, his fate (execution, release in prisoner exchange, release following negotiations, or release upon payment in case the Muslims need money) will be decided by the Imam and his deputy...
>
> If the Mujahideen who captured the enemy were not able to transfer them to their own centres, if they faced danger outside the centre, or if they could not manage to transfer the captives in secure places, then the Mujahideen can kill them—provided that the captives are prisoners of war or members of the authority from the other side.[98]

Similarly, while the ELN of Colombia committed to international humanitarian law in 1995,[99] it has defined the taking of hostages in such a manner as to allow certain actions which the law of armed conflict would consider prohibited. It has stated that it is 'permissible to recover war taxes, and to detain persons who refuse to pay them as a form of pressure in order to obtain payment. These detentions cannot be considered "hostage-taking", because we never use these persons as shields during hostilities'.[100] This transforms a potentially useful means of enforcement into something problematic and the absence of internal measures is to be preferred over problematic measures for the very same reasons as those outlined above.

For internal measures to be at their most useful, codes of conduct on humanitarian norms should not be separate from their military codes. Rather, a single code should contain military and humanitarian components.[101] The danger with separate codes is that a hierarchy of codes will be created, with the military code trumping

---

[96] Chin National Front, Code, above note 75 (unofficial translation).
[97] This was the view of Geneva Call on certain regulations of Iranian Kurdish armed groups: Geneva Call, Newsletter, Volume 7(2), November 2009, 2.
[98] Code of Conduct for the Mujahideen, 9 May 2009, reproduced and translated in M Sassòli, AA Bouvier, and A Quintin, *How Does Law Protect in War? Volume III* (ICRC, 2011) 2325.
[99] See 'Declaración sobre el Derecho Internacional Humanitario', 15 July 1995.
[100] N Rodríguez Bautista, 'Qué es humanizar el conflicto colombiano?', 1 May 1996, quoted in P Gassmann, 'Colombia: Persuading Belligerents to Comply with International Norms', in S Chesterman (ed), *Civilians in War* (Lynne Rienner Publishers, 2001) 67, 73. See further above, 270.
[101] Bangerter, Measures, above note 51, 201.

the humanitarian code. For example, '[h]olding an enemy captive or caring for a wounded opponent when resources are scarce for your own men is less difficult if that rule has been incorporated into military procedure as a part of strategy. If such is not the case, ethical considerations will not carry enough weight and are unlikely to be accepted and applied by the combatants'.[102] Codes that are unrelated to the law may also have a role to play in enforcement of the law. For example, in the early 1990s, armed groups operating in the north of Mali were reported to apply 'strict accounting of their weapons and ammunition stockpiles' and this accounting is considered to have contributed to the relatively low civilian casualty rate of the time.[103]

Measures that are internal to an armed group may have an impact beyond that group alone. In particular, they may be adopted by unrelated armed groups. The classic example on point is the 1947 instructions of the Chinese People's Liberation Army (CPLA), namely its Three Main Rules of Discipline and Eight Points of Attention.[104] These instructions were adopted decades later by groups unrelated to the CPLA and to China. These groups include the RUF of Sierra Leone,[105] the New People's Army (NPA), the armed wing of the NDFP,[106] and the NRA of Uganda.[107] Along similar lines, according to the *Boškovski* Trial Chamber, the rules and regulations used by the National Liberation Army (NLA), which fought in the former Yugoslav Republic of Macedonia (FYROM) in 2001, were 'merely copies' of those used by the Kosovo Liberation Army, Kosovo Protection Corps, and others, and 'had not been devised for or adapted to the circumstances in FYROM or the needs of the NLA'.[108] For these reasons, the Trial Chamber was rather dismissive of the NLA's rules and regulations. However, adopting the instructions of another group should not be taken to mean that the adopting group lacks willingness to comply with the rules. Adapting and tailoring the adopted rules to meet the specificities of the conflict in question is certainly a more useful means of regulating conduct. However, even regulations that are adopted without more have the potential to be useful. In any event, internal codes and regulations are important both for the conduct of the group in question and potentially also for other groups.

2.5 Unilateral declarations and bilateral agreements

Unilateral declarations and bilateral agreements on international humanitarian law also have a role to play in the implementation of the law. These are particularly important when states commit to rules while not being party to the relevant treaty. For non-state armed groups, unilateral declarations and bilateral agreements are important as, although bound by the law of armed conflict, they are not bound by virtue of their own consent.[109] Commitments to respect the law are thus useful as they avoid arguments along the lines that, as the group was not involved in the creation of the

---

[102] JC Lacayo, 'International Humanitarian Law and Irregular Warfare: Lessons Learned in Latin America' (2000) 82 *IRRC* 941, 946–7.
[103] N Florquin, K Lynge, and KL Pedersen, 'Beyond Weapons Collection: Promoting Safe and Responsible SA/LW Management' (2009) 13 *Journal of ERW and Mine Action* 1.
[104] The Three Rules of Discipline were issued in 1928 and reissued as the Three Main Rules of Discipline in 1947. Likewise the Eight Points of Attention reissued in 1947 were first issued in 1928 as the Six Points of Attention.
[105] *RUF* Trial Judgment, above note 81, para 705.
[106] Basic Rules of the New People's Army, above note 86.
[107] National Resistance Army Code of Conduct, above note 83.
[108] *Prosecutor v Boškoski and Tarčulovski*, IT-04-82-T, Judgment, 10 July 2008, para 273.
[109] See above, 240–1.

rule, it is not bound by it.[110] For both parties, the commitments are important should they bring into force rules that are not strictly applicable in non-international armed conflicts. For example, commitments have been made that bring into force the Geneva Conventions as a whole, and which have included a commitment to treat captured fighters as prisoners of war.[111]

These commitments are also useful as they restate the party's obligation to abide by the relevant norms in times of actual armed conflict. The conduct of the party can then be judged against their commitments, by various actors such as UN human rights mechanisms or non-governmental organizations. Commitments concluded during armed conflicts may also be useful for engaging with local commanders, mid-level officials, and ordinary fighters, more so than basing the engagement on an international convention that may have been ratified by a different government many years prior to the conflict breaking out. Commitments of non-state armed groups, in particular, provide entry points for dialogue on humanitarian issues. For example, an ICRC effort to conclude an agreement during the Bosnian conflict was aborted at one stage, but relations with interested persons were maintained and utilized at appropriate points.[112]

Explicit provision is made for special agreements in international humanitarian law instruments.[113] The conclusion of bilateral agreements on humanitarian norms may also serve as a confidence-building measure and may ultimately lead to the conclusion of a peace agreement. Indeed, a number of peace agreements include as a component a bilateral agreement on human rights or international humanitarian law that was concluded at an earlier stage.[114]

The conclusion of a bilateral agreement or the issuance of a unilateral declaration may also contribute to the development of the law of non-international armed conflict. This takes place at a number of levels. In respect of the conflict in question, a more substantive body of law may enter into force than would otherwise be the case. Parties to other conflicts may also model their commitments on those previously issued in unrelated conflicts.[115] At a much broader level, ad hoc commitments may contribute to the development of the law. For example, ad hoc commitments were utilized in the *Tadić* Decision on Interlocutory Appeal on Jurisdiction to demonstrate the acceptance of certain rules in non-international armed conflict and this led to the development of the law of non-international armed conflict.[116] The Customary International Humanitarian Law study also refers to certain bilateral agreements and commitments on the part of armed groups.[117] In this, there is nothing new, for conventional international humanitarian law instruments, albeit those applicable in international armed conflicts, have long been influenced by ad hoc agreements concluded between the warring

---

[110] For just such an argument, see above, 240.
[111] See eg the 22 May 1992 Agreement concluded during the conflict in Bosnia.
[112] 'Panel Discussion: Ways to Bind Non-State Actors to International Humanitarian Law' (2003) 27 *Collegium* 167, 168. See also Report of the Secretary-General on the Protection of Civilians in Armed Conflict, S/2009/277, 29 May 2009, para 45.
[113] Common Article 3; Hague Convention for the Protection of Cultural Property, Article 19.
[114] The Peace Agreement between the Government of El Salvador and the FMLN includes as a component part the Agreement on Human Rights. Likewise, the Government of Rwanda/RPF Arusha Accords includes as a component the Protocol on the Rule of Law. See C Bell, *Peace Agreements and Human Rights* (Oxford University Press, 2000).
[115] See eg above, 128–9.
[116] *Prosecutor v Tadić*, IT-94-1-AR72, Decision on the Defence Motion for Interlocutory Appeal on Jurisdiction, 2 October 1995, paras 96–127.
[117] See eg *Customary International Humanitarian Law, Volume II: Practice*, above note 12, 589, 606, 870.

parties, as was the case of the 1864 Geneva Convention and the 1929 Geneva Convention on Prisoners of War.[118]

It is sometimes suggested that these commitments are made for political purposes and have no effect on the ground. While it is certainly true that commitments could be made for political purposes and without any intention on the part of the party making the commitment to comply with them, the danger is always present for any party making any commitment. For example, it is equally true of some states and their ratification of the Geneva Conventions.[119] It is also the case that some commitments are followed. For example, in the armed conflict in Afghanistan during the Cold War (1979–89), a commitment was provided by resistance movements to the ICRC relating to the treatment of detainees. According to the Special Rapporteur on human rights in Afghanistan, 'witnesses stated that since then the resistance movements had endeavoured to ensure that foreign prisoners were not tortured or assassinated'.[120]

Another difficulty arises in that an exhortation to conclude a special agreement may be considered 'interference with the position of the High Contracting Parties' and as such 'unjustified...unnecessary and impracticable'. Such was the view of Burma during the 1949 Diplomatic Conference.[121] When the ICRC, in 1958, presented the Government of France and the Front de Libération Nationale (FLN) with a draft bilateral agreement committing both sides to comply with common Article 3, to avoid reprisals, and to treat prisoners humanely,[122] neither side responded.[123] The Provisional Government of the Algerian Republic proposed to France to conclude an agreement on humanitarian law, but France did not accept.[124] However, in other conflicts, the government may offer to conclude bilateral agreements on issues of international humanitarian law. For example, the Government of Colombia, under the Samper administration, set out the Urabá agenda, which included the possibility of concluding bilateral agreements on child soldiers, land-mines, the taking of hostages, disappearances, the protection of cultural property, and natural resources.[125] A similar approach was taken in 1999 under the Pastrana Government.[126] Bilateral agreements between the state and the non-state armed group certainly are concluded, as Chapter 4 indicated,[127] usually after the fighting has raged for an extended period of time or has reached a certain level of intensity. Prisoners may be exchanged pursuant to bilateral agreements concluded between the parties to the conflict,[128] as may the wounded and

---

[118] JS Pictet (ed), *The Geneva Conventions of 12 August 1949: Commentary, III Geneva Convention Relative to the Treatment of Prisoners of War* (ICRC, 1960) 78–9; R Provost, *International Human Rights and Humanitarian Law* (Cambridge University Press, 2002) 130–1.

[119] F Bugnion, '*Jus ad Bellum, Jus in Bello* and Non-International Armed Conflicts' (2003) 6 YIHL 167, 194. See above, 108.

[120] Report on the Situation of Human Rights in Afghanistan prepared by the Special Rapporteur, E/CN.4/1985/21, 19 February 1985, para 104.

[121] *Final Record*, Vol II-B, 329–30.

[122] M Bedjaoui, *Law and the Algerian Revolution* (International Association of Democratic Lawyers, 1961) 211.

[123] E van Cleef Greenberg, 'Law and the Conduct of the Algerian Revolution' (1970) 11 *Harvard International Law Journal* 37, 51.

[124] Bedjaoui, above note 122, 216–17.

[125] D García-Peña Jaramillo, 'Humanitarian Protection in Non-International Conflicts: A Case Study of Colombia' (2000) 30 I*YHR* 179, 185–6.

[126] 'Agenda Comun por el Cambio Hacia una Nueva Colombia', cited in ibid, 194.

[127] See above, 124–33.

[128] See eg Exchange of Prisoners Agreement between the Republic of Croatia and the Armed Forces of the SFRY, 6 November 1991, reproduced in J-F Berger, *The Humanitarian Diplomacy of the ICRC and the Conflict in Croatia 1991–2* (ICRC, Geneva, 1995) Annex 3. See also the Salamanca Agreement, concluded between the ICRC and the Burgos Government, 19 October 1936.

sick.¹²⁹ On occasion, the two sides will not sign the same sheet of paper, thus the agreement will be signed on two different documents, as was the case with the Mujahedeen and the Government of Afghanistan in 1982.¹³⁰ Parallel commitments whereby the two sides commit, usually to the ICRC, to undertake the same obligation, are better considered parallel unilateral declarations,¹³¹ as violation of the commitment by one side would not vitiate the other side's commitment. However, they are certainly akin to bilateral agreements.

A contentious issue relates to whether violation of these agreements should result in international criminal prosecution. The International Criminal Tribunal for the former Yugoslavia (ICTY) has taken the view that violation of agreements on issues of international humanitarian law concluded between parties to the conflict may be subject to criminal prosecution.¹³² The advantage of this position is that such agreements will only be concluded if the parties intend to abide by them. However, the very real danger is that it will lead to a reduction in the number of such agreements being concluded.¹³³

2.6 Sanctions

Sanctions express the sentiment that certain actions will not be tolerated.¹³⁴ They punish wrongful conduct, serve as a warning to those considering similar action, and send a message to victims. Thus, President Museveni of Uganda noted of his leadership of the NRA:

[I]n case one of our soldiers commits a mistake, especially killing people, he must be punished where the mistake was committed, in front of the people. If you take him away to punish him somewhere else, you are in trouble with the population, especially a population which is not educated. Because they will not know whether you punished him or not, they will think that you have just covered him up.¹³⁵

Accordingly, the NRA utilized courts-martial and unit disciplinary committees.¹³⁶ Sanctions also serve a military purpose, with commanders of armed groups sometimes stressing the importance of sanctioning failure to obey orders.¹³⁷ They thus enable commanders to instil discipline in low-level officials. The MILF of the Philippines has considered this especially important as many of its members joined 'not out of convention' but because family members had been killed by government soldiers. Accordingly, it noted in 2010 that '[o]ne of the most common causes of . . . disciplinary problems is the low ideological, political, and organizational consciousness of both political and military workers of the MILF'.¹³⁸ Along similar lines, Kwame Nkrumah

---

¹²⁹ Government-FARC Humanitarian Exchange Accord, 2 June 2001.
¹³⁰ Veuthey, History, above note 4, 141.
¹³¹ See above, 114–18.
¹³² *Tadić* Decision on Interlocutory Appeal on Jurisdiction, above note 116, paras 143–5.
¹³³ See above, 82.
¹³⁴ A-M La Rosa and C Wuerzner, 'Armed Groups, Sanctions and the Implementation of International Humanitarian Law' (2008) 90 *IRRC* 327, 334.
¹³⁵ YK Museveni, 'The Strategy of Protracted People's War: Uganda' [November–December 2008] *Military Review* 4, 9.
¹³⁶ National Resistance Army Code of Conduct, above note 83. See also YK Museveni, *Sowing the Mustard Seed* (MacMillan, 1997) 147.
¹³⁷ See eg the view of Brigadier General Malual Ayom Dor of the Sudan People's Liberation Army (SPLA), in Bangerter, Measures, above note 51, 208. See also E Guevara, *Guerrilla Warfare* (Penguin, 1969) 117.
¹³⁸ 'MILF Organizes Military Court', 9 October 2010.

observed that '[t]here must be no abuse of power of any kind. A freedom fighter who steals, loots, rapes or commits any other crime against the community must be tried and severely punished. It should be explained that such a breakdown in discipline endangers the whole revolutionary movement'.[139] Sanctioning wrongful conduct, particularly conduct that violates the law, also allows the armed group to distinguish itself from groups that intend to terrorize, engage in ethnic cleansing, and the like.[140] Furthermore, sanctioning wrongful conduct on the part of members of the armed group allows superiors to demonstrate that they punished violations of the law, thus satisfying their obligations under the principle of command responsibility. At least one local commander of an armed group has indicated that he has kept records along these lines for precisely this purpose.[141] This example also illustrates the impact that criminal prosecution has had on enforcement of the law.

Sanctions utilized by armed groups tend to be of five sorts—disciplinary sanctions, including reprimands, warnings, confiscation of weapons, demotion, and dismissal from the group; financial sanctions, including fines, suspension of pay, and compensation to victims; curtailing of movement, ranging from imprisonment to house arrest; corporal sanction, such as drill exercises or beatings; and criminal sanctions, including capital punishment.[142] Many of the sanctions that are used in practice are not to be encouraged given that they do not meet international standards; however, the examples that follow provide a useful sense of the types of sanctions that are actually instituted in the practice of armed groups.

During the conflict in El Salvador (1980–91), the FMLN reported that it imposed various sanctions including 'admonishment, detention, demotion, removal of rank, [and] expulsion'.[143] For its part, the Hêzên Parastina Gel (HPG) of Kurdistan reported in 2010 that, following trial in an HPG court, it sentenced two members of the group to a term of imprisonment and indicated their expulsion from the group following the serving of their term. The HPG also declared the deceased victims martyrs, apologized to their families, and awarded them compensation.[144] Likewise, the Communist Party of Nepal-Maoist (CPN-M) stated in 2006 that it had expelled members who were involved in detonating an explosion on a bus.[145] In 1992, the Liberation Tigers of Tamil Eelam (LTTE) of Sri Lanka stated that '[i]t has taken care to instruct its cadres' on 'the importance of acting, at all times, in accordance with the humanitarian law of armed conflict' and that 'breaches in this regard are inquired into and suitable punishment meted out'.[146] Following on from this, in 2006, the LTTE reported that junior fighters had made a 'serious mistake' in abducting children from school and that they were 'taking strict disciplinary action', expelling the relevant fighters from the movement.[147] For its part, the MILF of the Philippines reported in 2010 that a

---

[139] K Nkrumah, *Handbook of Revolutionary Warfare* (Panaf Books, London, 1968) 112.
[140] La Rosa and Wuerzner, above note 134, 331.
[141] See A Bellal, G Giacca, and S Casey-Maslen, 'Towards Engagement, Compliance and Accountability' (2011) 37 *Forced Migration Review* 4, 5.
[142] Bangerter, Measures, above note 51, 207; La Rosa and Wuerzner, above note 134, 334–5. Judicial sanctions, including the courts of armed groups, are considered in Chapter 12.
[143] FMLN, above note 67, 6.
[144] The Military Tribunal of HPG, 'The Sentence of the Court of HPG concerning the compartment of BATMAN', 23 November 2010.
[145] 'Prachanda Interview: Full Transcript', *BBC News*, 13 February 2006. Prachanda was the head of the CPNM in Nepal.
[146] Press Release, International Secretariat, Liberation Tigers of Tamil Eelam, 18 February 1992.
[147] LTTE military spokesman, Rasaiah Ilanthirayan, quoted in 'Tamil Tigers Kidnap 21 Children', *BBC News*, 19 December 2006.

'reconciliation committee' considers cases of lack of discipline and imposes penalties ranging from 'punishment to educating the erring MILF members'.[148] The MILF also suspended an officer after an investigation found that he had been involved in the burning of civilian property.[149] Also in 2010, the JEM of Darfur stated that '[s]oldiers and commanders found in breach of relevant rules [on child soldiers] are disciplined and punished in proportion to their offences' and may be expelled from the Movement.[150] The Mouvement pour la Libération du Congo (MLC) 'suspended two commanders who were suspected of pillaging' and referred others to trial.[151] The group Liberians United for Reconciliation and Democracy (LURD) is reported in 2002 to have given 'strict orders not to abuse human rights' and appointed 'a provost marshal with responsibility for addressing cases of abuse of authority in... LURD-held areas'.[152] LURD fighters who committed atrocities against civilians have been executed, or punished by using them as 'cannon fodder' during frontline attacks.[153] In 2001, commanders of the FARC indicated that two FARC fighters who had been found guilty of killing three US civilians were sentenced to digging a ditch and clearing land,[154] while the ELN indicated that it utilized sanctions that included reparations to victims, demotion, suspension, and death.[155] According to the internal rules of the NPA, the armed wing of the NDFP, the NPA metes out various sanctions, including a strong warning, a strong warning coupled with transfer to another area of work, demotion, suspension, expulsion from the group, and expulsion and death.[156] The latter category is limited to the offences of 'treachery, capitulation, abandonment of post, espionage, sabotage, munity, inciting for rebellion, murder, theft, rape, arson, and severe malversation of people's funds'.[157] For its part, the Sudan People's Liberation Army (SPLA), in its 2003 SPLA Act, provided for a whole host of sanctions, including death, imprisonment, fines, forfeiture of property, 'field punishment' (hard labour), and whipping.[158] The SPLA also used disciplinary sanctions, either as an alternative to the punishments listed above or in addition to them. These disciplinary sanctions included dismissal, reprimand, demotion, detention, prohibiting the carrying of a firearm, loss of seniority, extra work, and pay cuts.[159] The sanctions envisaged by the Act were usually imposed in relation to military misconduct—desertion, absence without leave, insubordination, and the like—but also included matters that would amount to violations of the law, namely plunder or offences against civilian objects.[160]

---

[148] 'MILF Organizes Military Court', 9 October 2010.
[149] 'MILF suspends BIAF officer for burning houses in Maguindanao Town', 16 July 2010.
[150] *In Their Words*, above note 29, 18.
[151] *Prosecutor v Jean-Pierre Bemba Gombo*, ICC-01/05-01/08, Decision Pursuant to Article 61(7)(a) and (b) of the Rome Statute on the Charges of the Prosecutor Against Jean-Pierre Bemba Gombo, 15 June 2009, paras 471 and 472.
[152] Human Rights Watch, *Back to the Brink: War Crimes by Liberian Government and Rebels* (May 2002) 8.
[153] Ibid, 8–9.
[154] See Letter from Human Rights Watch to Commander Manuel Marulanda, General Secretariat, FARC, 9 July 2001.
[155] Human Rights Watch Interview with Francisco Galán and Felipe Torres, 3 July 1996, cited in Human Rights Watch, *War without Quarter: Colombia and International Humanitarian Law* (1998) Chapter V.
[156] Basic Rules of the New People's Army, above note 86, Principle IV, Point 6.
[157] Ibid, Principle IV, Point 8.
[158] Chapter VI, section 47.
[159] Chapter VI, section 48.
[160] SPLA Act (2003), Chapter V, section 20(1)(h) and 20(2)(e) and (f).

Despite these host of examples, a report of a meeting with non-state armed groups notes that '[h]olding violators accountable was not the norm among most' and that when violators were held accountable, the predominant form of accountability was corporal punishment with little consideration being given to proportionality of sanction to the underlying wrong. The sanctions were also 'often tantamount to egregious human rights violations'.[161]

The group as a whole may also apologize to the civilian population for its conduct. For example, in 2003, UNITA of Angola came 'forward before the people to beg for pardon because many lives were lost'. It 'assume[d] responsibility for much [sic] of the errors produced during the armed conflict', and stated that '[w]e assume responsibility for our errors. We ask for forgiveness for the period of war that this country endured since 1975'.[162] For its part, the RUF of Sierra Leone delivered a somewhat self-serving 'Apology to the Nation' in 1997 in which it stated that:

[f]or the past six years or so, we have been living in an environment of hatred and divisiveness. We looked at our brothers and killed them in cold blood, we removed our sisters from their hiding places to undo their femininity, we slaughtered our mothers and butchered our fathers. It was really a gruesome experience which has left a terrible landmark in our history. But the atrocities that occurred must not be taken in the context of a personal vendetta. They were the result of the rottenness of a system which could not be uprooted except by brutal means...

In the process of cleaning the system, however, we have wronged the great majority of our countrymen. We have sinned both in the sight of our Sierra Leonean brothers and sisters, for all the terror and the mayhem we unleashed on you in our bid to make Sierra Leone a country that all Sierra Leoneans would be proud of.[163]

The counterpart to sanctions are the rewards that are given to members of the armed group. These are of the same sorts as the sanctions themselves—disciplinary rewards, including such things as promotion, praise, and the awarding of medals; financial rewards, including monetary awards, salary increase, or licence to plunder; extra leave; and tasks that are associated with a more senior position.[164] Rewards may be viewed as importantly as sanctions from the perspective of the fighter as they too incentivize compliance and encourage fighters to continue along the same lines as those for which they were rewarded.[165]

3. Responses to the other side: belligerent reprisals

A second category of enforcement measures are those that are carried out by one party as a response to violations committed by the other side. Such enforcement measures primarily take the form of belligerent reprisals. A belligerent reprisal is 'an act in breach of a rule of the law of armed conflict, directed by one belligerent party against the other

---

[161] Geneva Call, Women in Armed Opposition Groups in Africa and the Promotion of International Humanitarian Law and Human Rights: Report of a Workshop organized in Addis Ababa by Geneva Call and the Program for the Study of International Organization(s), 23–26 November 2005, 3. See also at 18–19.
[162] 'UNITA Apologises for Partaking in Angolan War', *AfrolNews*, 8 January 2003, quoted in J Doria, 'Angola: A Case Study in the Challenges of Achieving Peace and the Question of Amnesty or Prosecution of War Crimes in Mixed Armed Conflicts' (2002) 5 *YIHL* 3, 34 fn 135.
[163] Revolutionary United Front's Apology to the Nation, 18 June 1997.
[164] Bangerter, Measures, above note 51, 207.
[165] See, in the context of the LRA, R Haer, L Banholzer, and V Ertl, 'Create Compliance and Cohesion: How Rebel Organizations Manage to Survive' (2011) 22 *Small Wars and Insurgencies* 415, 426–7.

with a view to inducing the latter party to stop violating that or another rule of this branch of international law'.[166] Were the act not undertaken with such a view in mind, it would be unlawful.

3.1 Prohibited belligerent reprisals

In the law of international armed conflict, certain actions are prohibited even by way of belligerent reprisal. The 1949 Geneva Conventions prohibit belligerent reprisals against persons and objects in the power of the adversary, be they the wounded, sick, and shipwrecked; medical personnel, units, and transports; prisoners of war; or civilians and civilian objects.[167] The Hague Convention on Cultural Property protects cultural property from belligerent reprisals.[168] The Amended Mines Protocol prohibits the use of certain mines as a belligerent reprisal against civilians and civilian objects.[169] Additional Protocol I prohibits belligerent reprisals against persons in the power of the adversary, be they the wounded, sick, and shipwrecked; or medical and religious personnel, units, and transports.[170] It also prohibits certain uses of belligerent reprisals in the conduct of hostilities, namely against civilians and civilian objects; cultural property; objects indispensable to the survival of the civilian population; the natural environment; and works and installations containing dangerous forces.[171] The result of the various restrictions is that, unless a reservation has been made, states parties to Additional Protocol I are limited in their use of belligerent reprisals, essentially to combatants.[172]

The extent to which the law of non-international armed conflict prohibits the use of belligerent reprisals is altogether less clear. Prior to the 1949 Geneva Conventions, states were of the view that they had the right to resort to belligerent reprisals. For example, during the Spanish civil war (1936–9), the Minister for Foreign Affairs in the Republican Government indicated that it was entitled to use belligerent reprisals,[173] a position that was reiterated at the League of Nations and went unchallenged.[174] The example is an important one given that belligerency was not recognized during the war; however, it may be of limited weight given the intervention of outside states.[175] Thus, the notion that there was no place in the law of non-international armed conflict for a prohibition on belligerent reprisals, as expressed during the 1974–7 Diplomatic

---

[166] F Kalshoven, 'Belligerent Reprisals Revisited' (1990) 21 *NYIL* 43, 44. See also *Prosecutor v Martić*, IT-95-11-T, Judgment, 12 June 2007, para 465.
[167] First Geneva Convention, Article 46; Second Geneva Convention, Article 47; Third Geneva Convention, Article 13; Fourth Geneva Convention, Article 33.
[168] 1954 Hague Convention on Cultural Property, Article 4.
[169] Amended Mines Protocol, Article 3(7).
[170] Additional Protocol I, Article 20.
[171] Additional Protocol I, Articles 51(6), 52(1), 53, 54(4), 55(2), 56(4).
[172] FJ Hampson, 'Belligerent Reprisals and the 1977 Protocols to the Geneva Conventions of 1949' (1988) 37 *ICLQ* 818, 828–9; C Greenwood, 'The Twilight of the Law of Belligerent Reprisals' (1989) 20 *NYIL* 35, 65.
[173] (1938) 1 *La Protection de la Population Civile* 172–3, in A Cassese, 'The Spanish Civil War and the Development of Customary Law concerning Internal Armed Conflict', in A Cassese (ed), *Current Problems in International Law* (1975) 287, 312.
[174] League of Nations, Official Journal, Special Supplement No 186, Records of the XIXth Ordinary Session of the Assembly, Minutes of the IIIrd Committee, 19; League of Nations, Official Journal, February 1939, 87, cited in A Cassese, above note 173, 312.
[175] See eg L Oppenheim, *International Law: A Treatise, Volume II* ((H Lauterpacht ed) (Longman, 1952) 251; AVW Thomas and AJ Thomas Jr, 'International Legal Aspects of the Civil War in Spain, 1936–39', in RA Falk, *The International Law of Civil War* (Johns Hopkins Press, 1971) 111.

Conference, is misplaced. A distinction needs to be drawn in this context between belligerent reprisals against persons in the power of the adversary and belligerent reprisals in the context of the conduct of hostilities.

As with much of the international humanitarian law of non-international armed conflict, things changed with the adoption and interpretation of common Article 3. Although that Article does not contain a prohibition on the use of belligerent reprisals, such a prohibition has been read into its text by some commentators, in relation to persons protected by that Article, ie persons who are in the power of the adversary.[176] According to this view, common Article 3 is considered to prohibit the use of belligerent reprisals through its prohibition on collective punishments.[177] However, it is submitted that the one does not follow from the other. Belligerent reprisals may be carried out while still respecting the prohibition on collective punishments, as the object of the reprisal may be the very individuals who committed the original unlawful act. Belligerent reprisals are also of a different nature to collective punishments, a point that was appreciated at the 1899 Hague Peace Conference. At that Conference, when the prohibition on collective fines was extended to include all collective punishments, the rapporteur, Henri Rolin, observed that the extension was without prejudice to the question of reprisals.[178] A prohibition on collective punishments and a prohibition on belligerent reprisals were thus recognized as being separate issues. A more compelling argument is that, as common Article 3 provides that the acts prohibited therein (violence to life, torture, and the like) 'are and shall remain prohibited at any time', this includes belligerent reprisals 'which entail[] one of these acts' in relation to the persons protected.[179] However, the 'implicit waiver of such a power cannot lightly be assumed' and it may be queried whether a belligerent reprisal that results in death constitutes murder or violation of the principle of humane treatment.[180] Thus, for example, the Commission of Experts appointed to investigate violations of international humanitarian law committed in the former Yugoslavia took the view that 'there is no ban on reprisals contained in common article 3 and Additional Protocol II applicable to internal armed conflict'.[181]

Even if it is accepted that the acts that are prohibited in common Article 3 cannot be undertaken as belligerent reprisals against persons covered by that Article, it does not follow, as is often thought to be the case,[182] that *all* belligerent reprisals against civilians are prohibited, including through acts that are not prohibited by common Article 3, for example attacks against the civilian population in the context of the conduct of hostilities. This conclusion can be reached through two different lines of reasoning.

---

[176] For a broader view of the protective scope of common Article 3, see above, 246–9.

[177] See eg Y Sandoz, C Swinarski, and B Zimmermann (eds), *Commentary on the Additional Protocols of 8 June 1977 to the Geneva Conventions of 12 August 1949* (ICRC, 1987) 1372–3; *Prosecutor v Martić*, IT-95-11-R61, Decision, 8 March 1996, para 16 (referring to the Additional Protocol II prohibition); E Crawford, *The Treatment of Combatants and Insurgents under the Law of Armed Conflict* (Oxford University Press, 2010) 88.

[178] JB Scott (ed), *The Proceedings of the Hague Peace Conferences, Volume I: The Conference of 1899* (Oxford University Press, 1920) 431.

[179] JS Pictet (ed), *The Geneva Conventions of 12 August 1949, Commentary: IV Geneva Convention Relative to the Protection of Civilian Persons in Time of War* (ICRC, 1958) 39–40; *Customary International Humanitarian Law, Volume I: Rules*, above note 12, 526. See also Veuthey, Remedies, above note 27, 48–9; Greenwood, Belligerent Reprisals, above note 172, 67–8.

[180] F Kalshoven, *Belligerent Reprisals* (AW Sijthoff, 1971) 269 and 267. See generally, 266–70.

[181] Final Report of the Commission of Experts established pursuant to Security Council Resolution 780 (1992), S/1994/674, 27 May 1994, para 66.

[182] See eg 1995 Yearbook of the International Law Commission, Volume II Part Two, A/CN.4/Ser.A/1995/Add.1 (Part 2) 72, para 18; Moir, *Internal Armed Conflict*, above note 9, 239–40.

First, as common Article 3 does not relate to the means and methods of warfare, and does not, for example, prohibit the targeting of civilians,[183] equally it cannot prohibit the targeting of civilians as a belligerent reprisal.[184] Rather, the prohibition on the use of belligerent reprisals through common Article 3 has to be limited to the acts prohibited by that Article. Second, if common Article 3 did contain a complete prohibition on belligerent reprisals against civilians in the conduct of hostilities, given that common Article 3 is of customary status and also applies in international armed conflicts,[185] the customary law of international armed conflict would also contain a complete prohibition on belligerent reprisals against the civilian population. Yet the notion that the customary law of international armed conflict contains a prohibition on the use of belligerent reprisals against the civilian population has proven extremely controversial,[186] suggesting that the position cannot be such. Thus, it is difficult to conclude that common Article 3 prohibits belligerent reprisals against civilians in the conduct of hostilities.[187]

The idea that the use of belligerent reprisals is prohibited through Additional Protocol II is equally problematic. During the 1974–7 Diplomatic Conference, it was suggested that there was no place in the law of non-international armed conflict for a prohibition on belligerent reprisals.[188] However, this suggestion encompassed two diametrically opposed positions: both the view that the use of belligerent reprisals was permitted,[189] and the view that an explicit prohibition was unnecessary given that belligerent reprisals had no place in non-international armed conflicts.[190] For example, on ratifying Additional Protocols I and II, Egypt declared, in respect of both Protocols, that it 'upholds the right to react against any violation by any party of the obligations imposed by Additional Protocols I and II with all means admissible under international law in order to prevent any further violation'.[191] Other states supported the inclusion of a prohibition on the use of belligerent reprisals in non-international armed conflict.[192] The ICRC reads into Additional Protocol II an implicit prohibition on belligerent reprisals, its Commentary providing that '[t]he list of prohibited acts is fuller than that of common Article 3. That being so, and because of the absolute character of these prohibitions, which apply at all times and in all places, there is in fact no room left at all

---

[183] See above, 336.
[184] F Kalshoven, 'Reprisals and the Protection of Civilians: Two Recent Decisions of the Yugoslavia Tribunal', in LC Vohrah et al (eds), *Man's Inhumanity to Man: Essays on International Law in Honour of Antonio Cassese* (Kluwer Law International, 2003) 481, 489–90.
[185] *Military and Paramilitary Activities in and against Nicaragua*, [1986] ICJ Rep 14, para 218.
[186] See below, 452.
[187] See also S Darcy, 'The Evolution of the Law of Belligerent Reprisals' (2003) 175 *Military Law Review* 184, 219; S Darcy, *Collective Responsibility and Accountability under International Law* (Transnational, 2007) 148. APV Rogers, *Law on the Battlefield* (Manchester University Press, 2004) 235, describes the position as 'a matter of debate'.
[188] See eg *Official Records*, above note 20, Vol 7, 108, para 7 (United States); Vol 8, 330, para 37 (Iran); Vol 7, 108, para 8 (India); Vol 9, 318, para 80 (Mexico); Vol 11, 342, para 18 (Nigeria); Vol 14, 176, para 38 (Australia).
[189] Ibid, Vol 9, 455 (Cameroon); Vol 9, 456–7 (Yugoslavia).
[190] Ibid, Vol 7, 122 (Nigeria); Vol 11, 339–40, para 4 (Mongolia). See Darcy, *Collective Responsibility*, above note 187, 166–71.
[191] Declaration made upon ratification, 9 October 1992.
[192] See eg *Official Records*, above note 20, Vol 8, 324, para 7 (Finland); Vol 11, 291, para 62 (New Zealand); 336, para 51 (Sweden); Vol 14, 151, para 3 (USSR); 67, para 65 (Finland); Vol 11, 343, para 23 (Iran); 343, para 21 (USSR); 343, para 25 (Bangladesh); Vol 14, 178, para 50 (Sweden); Vol 11, 291, para 63 (ICRC).

for carrying out "reprisals" against protected persons'.[193] However, for the reasons outlined above in respect of common Article 3, this overstates the case. At the very most, Additional Protocol II can only prohibit as a belligerent reprisal the acts prohibited in Article 4 of that Protocol.

Other acts are prohibited as belligerent reprisals in non-international armed conflict through conventional law. This is true of the protection for cultural property, through the Hague Convention on Cultural Property and the prohibition on the use of certain mines as a belligerent reprisal through the Amended Mines Protocol.[194]

A better case can be made for the prohibition on the use of belligerent reprisals in non-international armed conflict through customary international law. The provisions of Article 4 of the Hague Convention on Cultural Property have customary status and given that Article 4 contains a prohibition on the use of belligerent reprisals against cultural property, that prohibition applies as a rule of customary international law.[195] The prohibition on the use of belligerent reprisals against the wounded and sick and medical and religious personnel in the law of international armed conflict may have extended to include non-international armed conflict.[196] The prohibition on the use of belligerent reprisals against prisoners of war in the law of international armed conflict cannot have customary status in non-international armed conflict given that, as a matter of law, prisoner of war status does not exist.[197] However, the prohibition may well extend to captured fighters.[198] A similar claim cannot be made in respect of belligerent reprisals against the civilian population. Although General Assembly Resolution 2675 (XXV) provides that '[c]ivilian populations, or individual members thereof, should not be the object of reprisals',[199] and the Resolution has been considered to reflect principles of customary international humanitarian law applicable to international and non-international armed conflict alike,[200] a similar conclusion reached by the ICTY[201] met with disapproval on the part of certain states. The United Kingdom, for example, has expressed the view that 'the court's reasoning is unconvincing and the assertion that there is a prohibition in customary law flies in the face of most of the state practice that exists. The UK does not accept the position as stated in this judgment'.[202] The ICTY has also retreated from its earlier position.[203] Thus, although the Customary International Humanitarian Law study takes the view that belligerent reprisals are prohibited in non-international armed conflicts as a matter of customary international humanitarian law,[204] this may be overstating the existing position. Nonetheless, such a position is certainly a desirable one and foolish would be the

---

[193] ICRC, *Commentary on the Additional Protocols*, above note 177, 1372. See also *Martić* Rule 61 Decision, above note 177, para 16. See further Greenwood, Belligerent Reprisals, above note 172, 68 (agreeing with the position of the ICRC).
[194] Article 4(4); Article 3(7).
[195] Above, 375. Customary International Humanitarian Law, Rule 147.
[196] Kalshoven, Belligerent Reprisals Revisited, above note 166, 78.
[197] See below, 521.
[198] Kalshoven, Belligerent Reprisals Revisited, above note 166, 78.
[199] GA Res 2675 (XXV) (1970) para 7.
[200] *Tadić* Decision on Interlocutory Appeal on Jurisdiction, above note 116, para 112.
[201] *Prosecutor v Kupreškić et al*, IT-95-16-T, Judgment, 14 January 2000, paras 521–36.
[202] UK *Manual*, above note 25, 43 fn 62. See also Kalshoven, Reprisals, above note 184, 481; CJ Greenwood, 'Belligerent Reprisals in the Jurisprudence of the International Criminal Tribunal for the Former Yugoslavia', in H Fischer, C Kreß, and S Rolf Lüder (eds), *International and National Prosecution of Crimes Under International Law: Current Developments* (Springer, 2001) 539.
[203] See *Martić* Trial Judgment, above note 166, paras 465–8; *Prosecutor v Martić*, IT-95-11-A, Judgment, 8 October 2008, paras 263–7.
[204] Customary International Humanitarian Law, Rule 148.

state that undertakes belligerent reprisals against its own population in a non-international armed conflict.

3.2 Restrictions on the use of belligerent reprisals

Certain belligerent reprisals are thus not prohibited by international humanitarian law. However, their use is limited by a number of restrictions. According to the *Kupreškić* Trial Chamber, these are:

(a) the principle whereby they must be a last resort in attempts to impose compliance by the adversary with legal standards (which entails, amongst other things, that they may be exercised only after a prior warning has been given which has failed to bring about the discontinuance of the adversary's crimes); (b) the obligation to take special precautions before implementing them (they may be taken only after a decision to this effect has been made at the highest political or military level; in other words they may not be decided by local commanders); (c) the principle of proportionality (which entails not only that the reprisals must not be excessive compared to the precedent unlawful act of warfare, but also that they must stop as soon as that unlawful act has been discontinued) and; (d) 'elementary considerations of humanity'.[205]

These restrictions have a long and distinguished history.[206]

The first requirement relates to belligerent reprisals being used as a means of last resort. Accordingly, prior to resorting to belligerent reprisals, steps must be taken to stop the other side's violation through means other than reprisals.[207] If it is apparent that nothing other than the use of reprisals will stop the violation, reprisals may be carried out without undertaking any other measure.[208] However, the futility of alternative measures cannot be lightly assumed.[209] In all situations, prior to resort to reprisals, a formal warning has to be given.[210] The warning must indicate that belligerent reprisals will be used unless the relevant, stated, violation ceases. The warning should allow sufficient time to allow the party to desist; quite how much time is required will depend on the situation at hand.[211] It should also be addressed to the highest political and military authorities,[212] rather than a local commander or a mid-level official. If the party does so desist, belligerent reprisals cannot then be used.[213]

The second requirement is that prior authorization must be granted before belligerent reprisals are utilized. Precisely who is entitled to authorize the use will depend on the state and the party in question. What is clear is that not each and every commander is entitled to so authorize, let alone a low-ranking member of the armed forces or armed

---

[205] *Kupreškić* Trial Judgment, above note 201, para 535. See also *Customary International Humanitarian Law, Volume I: Rules*, above note 12, 515–18.
[206] See eg The Laws of War on Land, Oxford Manual, 1880, Articles 85 and 86.
[207] UK *Manual*, above note 25, 421–2; R Bierzanek, 'Reprisals as a Means of Enforcing the Laws of Warfare: the Old and the New Law', in A Cassese (ed), *The New Humanitarian Law of Armed Conflict* (Editoriale Scientifica, 1979) 232, 236; Y Dinstein, *The Conduct of Hostilities Under the Law of International Armed Conflict* (Cambridge University Press, 2004) 221; M Bothe, KJ Partsch, and WA Solf, *New Rules for Victims of Armed Conflicts* (Martinus Nijhoff, 1982) 312.
[208] Kalshoven, *Belligerent Reprisals*, above note 180, 340; Dinstein, above note 207, 221.
[209] Greenwood, Twilight, above note 172, 47.
[210] *Martić* Trial Judgment, above note 166, para 466. See also Dinstein, above note 207, 221; Bothe, Partsch, and Solf, above note 207, 312.
[211] UK *Manual*, above note 25, 421–2.
[212] See *Martić* Trial Judgment, above note 166, para 468 fn 1264.
[213] UK *Manual*, above note 25, 422; Dinstein, above note 207, 221; Bothe, Partsch, and Solf, above note 207, 312.

group. Reprisals must be authorized at 'the highest political or military level',[214] whether the commander-in-chief[215] or 'the highest level of government'.[216] For the non-state armed group, this will amount to the head of the group or the leader of the political or military wing. Although it has been suggested that this requirement is 'more a matter of military discipline than international law',[217] it does serve to ensure that decisions are not taken in the heat of the moment,[218] that the requirements attaching to the use are complied with,[219] and that the full political, legal, and moral ramifications of the use are considered.[220]

A third limitation on the use of belligerent reprisals is the element of proportionality. Proportionality in this context relates to proportionality to the initial violation rather than to the goal of re-establishing compliance with the law.[221] As with many other instances in which the proportionality test is used, the equation is a difficult one. The difficulties are not insurmountable, however, as demonstrated from the following excerpt from a letter of Francis Lieber to General Halleck written during the US civil war (1861–5):

Is the threat of General Burnside true, that he would hang ten Confederate officers for every Union officer hung by the Confederates? Whether true or not, you are aware that this is the spirit which generally shows itself when a barbarous outrage is committed, but which it is very necessary promptly to stop. The wanton insolence of our enemy has been growing so fast, and is so provoking, that I am plainly and simply for quick and stern retaliation; but in retaliation it is necessary strictly to adhere to sections twenty-seven and twenty-eight of General Order 100, to the elementary principle which prevails all the world over—tit for tat, or eye for eye—and not to adopt ten eyes for one eye. If one belligerent hangs ten men for one, the other will hang ten times ten for the ten; and what a dreadful geometrical progression of skulls and cross-bones we should have.[222]

Things prove difficult, however, when the act carried out as a reprisal is of a different sort to the original violation, as it may well be.[223] This is particularly true of many non-international armed conflicts, with the differing capabilities and resources of the two opposing actors making retaliation in kind—aerial bombardment, for example—very difficult indeed.[224] Furthermore, with the prohibition on certain forms of belligerent reprisals, the proportionality equation becomes even more difficult. For these reasons, proportionality in this context has been interpreted as meaning 'the absence of obvious disproportionality, as opposed to strict proportionality'.[225] Related to the requirement

---

[214] *Martić* Trial Judgment, above note 166, para 466. See also Bierzanek, above note 207, 241 (commander-in-chief or government); Dinstein, above note 207, 221 (authority higher than individual combatant).
[215] The Laws of War on Land, Oxford Manual, 1880, Article 86.
[216] UK *Manual*, above note 25, 421–2.
[217] Greenwood, Twilight, above note 172, 40 fn 16.
[218] P Suter, 'The Continuing Role for Belligerent Reprisals' (2008) 13 *JCSL* 93, 100.
[219] Darcy, Belligerent Reprisals, above note 187, 193.
[220] S Oeter, 'Methods and Means of Combat', in D Fleck (ed), *The Handbook of International Humanitarian Law* (Oxford University Press, 2008) 233.
[221] *Martić* Trial Judgment, above note 166, para 467; UK *Manual*, above note 25, 421–2. Cf MS McDougal and FP Feliciano, *The International Law of War: Transnational Coercion and World Public Order* (New Haven Press, 1994) 682; Greenwood, Twilight, above note 172, 43–4.
[222] Letter from Francis Lieber to General Halleck, reproduced in GB Davis, 'Doctor Francis Lieber's Instructions for the Government of Armies in the Field' (1907) 1 *AJIL* 13, 21.
[223] UK *Manual*, above note 25, 421–2; Dinstein, above note 207, 221. Cf Hampson, Belligerent Reprisals, above note 172, 822–4.
[224] Bierzanek, Reprisals, above note 207, 244; Moir, *Internal Armed Conflict*, above note 9, 238.
[225] Kalshoven, *Belligerent Reprisals*, above note 180, 341–2. See also Greenwood, Twilight, above note 172, 40 and 44, using the language of 'reasonably proportionate'.

of proportionality, and following on from the very purpose of belligerent reprisals, once the original violation ceases so too must the reprisals.[226]

The final requirement that stems from the *Kupreškić* Trial Judgment is that belligerent reprisals must respect 'the laws of humanity and dictates of public conscience'.[227] Quite what this means is unclear. The requirement may have proven useful at a time when there was no category of persons or objects against which belligerent reprisals could not be used. However, in light of the present-day prohibition on the use of belligerent reprisals against various classes of persons and objects, the requirement does not serve a useful purpose. The *Martić* Trial Chamber interpreted it to mean that 'reprisals must be exercised, to the extent possible, in keeping with the principle of the protection of the civilian population in armed conflict and the general prohibition of targeting civilians'.[228] However, this interpretation confuses matters, for either civilians may be made the subject of belligerent reprisals or they may not. It is unworkable to suggest that belligerent reprisals may be carried out against civilians but that the party undertaking the reprisal should respect the protections afforded to civilians as far as possible.

As the purpose of a belligerent reprisal is to compel the other party to the conflict to observe the law, it is evident that a prior violation of the law of armed conflict must have been committed to which the belligerent reprisal is then directed.[229] The enforcement function of the doctrine also means that, 'if one party to an armed conflict breaches the law but then expresses regret, declares that it will not be repeated, and takes measures to punish those immediately responsible, then any action taken by another party in response to the original unlawful act cannot be justified as a reprisal'.[230] The *Martić* Trial Chamber has suggested that '[r]eprisals are...drastic and exceptional measures employed by one belligerent for the *sole* purpose of seeking compliance with the law of armed conflict by the opposite party'.[231] However, it is submitted that this overstates the point. While reprisals must be undertaken to enforce compliance with the law on the part of the opposing party, they may be taken also for other reasons, for example to satisfy public pressure,[232] or a particular domestic constituency. Likewise, the form that the reprisal takes may be motivated by military concerns. These other reasons do not render unlawful the use of belligerent reprisals. The relevant test should be whether the employment of belligerent reprisals was for the *primary* purpose of seeking compliance with the law by the opposing party.

3.3 Continued use of belligerent reprisals

Even the lawful use of belligerent reprisals is highly controversial given that it tends to penalize the innocent.[233] As the *Kupreškić* Trial Chamber noted, they are 'not directed

---

[226] *Martić* Trial Judgment, above note 166, para 467. See also UK *Manual*, above note 25, 421–2; Greenwood, Twilight, above note 172, 45.
[227] See also *Martić* Trial Judgment, above note 166, para 467. See also Bierzanek, Reprisals, above note 207, 236.
[228] *Martić* Trial Judgment, above note 166, para 467. See also Bierzanek, Reprisals, above note 207, 236.
[229] UK *Manual*, above note 25, 421–2; Hampson, Belligerent Reprisals, above note 172, 822–4; Greenwood, Twilight, above note 172, 39–40.
[230] UK *Manual*, above note 25, 421–2.
[231] *Martić* Trial Judgment, above note 166, para 465 (emphasis added).
[232] Darcy, Belligerent Reprisals, above note 187, 191.
[233] The Laws of War on Land, Oxford Manual, 1880, Article 84. See also RR Baxter, 'The Geneva Conventions of 1949' (1980) 62 *International Law Studies* 220, 229; SE Nahlik, 'Belligerent Reprisals As Seen in the Light of the Diplomatic Conference on Humanitarian Law, Geneva, 1974–1977'

specifically at the individual authors of the initial violation', instead, being directed at 'more vulnerable individuals or groups...who may not even have any degree of solidarity with the presumed authors of the initial violation; they may share with them only the links of nationality and allegiance to the same rulers'.[234] They may also be considered contrary to human rights ideals.[235] Furthermore, their effectiveness has been doubted.[236] They are considered so open to abuse[237] that they have been described as providing 'the chief loophole for the evasion, violation, and nullification of the laws of war'.[238] They may also lead to, if not invite, escalation and purported counter-reprisals.[239] Indeed, the Lieber Code notes that '[u]njust or inconsiderate retaliation removes the belligerents farther and farther from the mitigating rules of regular war, and by rapid steps leads them nearer to the internecine war of savages'.[240]

All that being said, the question remains whether there are sufficient alternative mechanisms by which the law of non-international armed conflict can be enforced such that resort to belligerent reprisals is rendered unnecessary. On this question, the *Kupreškić* Trial Chamber suggested that:

> while reprisals could have had a modicum of justification in the past, when they constituted practically the only effective means of compelling the enemy to abandon unlawful acts of warfare and to comply in future with international law, at present they can no longer be justified in this manner. A means of inducing compliance with international law is at present more widely available and, more importantly, is beginning to prove fairly efficacious: the prosecution and punishment of war crimes and crimes against humanity by national or international courts. This means serves the purpose of bringing to justice those who are responsible for any such crime, as well as, albeit to a limited extent, the purpose of deterring at least the most blatant violations of international humanitarian law.[241]

However, criminal prosecution tends to be retrospective in nature rather than ending violations existing at the time resort is had to belligerent reprisals.[242] Thus, although written well before the age of international criminal law, the Lieber Code aptly notes that '[t]he law of war can no more wholly dispense with retaliation[243] than can the law of nations, of which it is a branch...A reckless enemy often leaves to his opponent no other means of securing himself against the repetition of barbarous outrage'.[244]

(1978) 42 *Law and Contemporary Problems* 36, 37; F Kalshoven, 'Reprisals in the CDDH', in RJ Akkerman, PJ van Krieken, and CO Pannenborg, *Declarations on Principles: A Quest for Universal Peace* (AW Sitjhoff, 1977) 195, 209.

[234] *Kupreškić* Trial Judgment, above note 201, para 528.

[235] Ibid, para 529. See also Bierzanek, above note 207, 244; Dinstein, above note 207, 225.

[236] Kalshoven, CDDH, above note 233, 209; Kalshoven, Belligerent Reprisals Revisited, above note 166, 79; Oeter, above note 220, 232; S Darcy, 'What Future for the Doctrine of Belligerent Reprisals?' (2002) 5 *YIHL* 107, 112. Cf Hampson, Belligerent Reprisals, above note 172, 841.

[237] Bierzanek, above note 207, 237, quoting *History of the UN War Crimes Commission and the Development of the Law of War* (1948) 29; Baxter, Geneva Conventions, above note 233, 229; Kalshoven, CDDH, above note 233, 209.

[238] M Greenspan, *The Modern Law of Land Warfare* (University of California Press, 1959) 408.

[239] EC Stowell, 'Military Reprisals and the Sanctions of the Laws of War' (1942) 36 *AJIL* 643, 649; Kalshoven, Belligerent Reprisals Revisited, above note 166, 79; Darcy, Future, above note 236, 112; Oeter, above note 220, 232. See also Kalshoven, *Belligerent Reprisals*, above note 180, 367–78; Aldrich, above note 1, 8; Moir, *Internal Armed Conflict*, above note 9, 237–8.

[240] Article 28.

[241] *Kupreškić* Trial Judgment, above note 201, para 530. See also Bierzanek, above note 207, 245–6.

[242] Suter, above note 218, 119.

[243] Retaliation in this context should be read as referring to belligerent reprisals.

[244] Article 27. See also BVA Röling, 'Aspects of the Criminal Responsibility for Violations of the Laws of War', in A Cassese (ed), *The New Humanitarian Law of Armed Conflict* (Editoriale Scientifica, 1979) 199.

Nevertheless, resort to belligerent reprisals remains an unfortunate means by which to enforce the law.

4. Third parties

4.1 Protecting Powers

Upon the outbreak of an international armed conflict, it is not at all uncommon for the warring states to suspend or terminate diplomatic contact. In such situations, 'Protecting Powers' may be appointed to safeguard the interests of one state in the other,[245] and to serve as an intermediary between the two states.[246] The Protecting Powers system has a long history and it is not limited to situations of armed conflict.[247] It was first incorporated into conventional international humanitarian law in the 1929 Geneva Convention Relative to the Treatment of Prisoners of War and was later consolidated and developed in the 1949 Geneva Conventions and in Additional Protocol I.[248] However, it has rarely been utilized in the practice of armed conflicts since 1945. Indeed, the contrast between the law and practice is striking. The Protecting Powers system was designed to be a 'crucial part of the law',[249] and '[t]he corner-stone of the system of implementation'.[250] It has even been suggested that '[t]o talk of the regular application of international humanitarian law without the effective functioning of some Protecting Power system... is idle chatter'.[251] Yet, since 1949, Protecting Powers have only been used during the Suez crisis (1956), in Goa (1961), in the conflict between India and Pakistan (1970–1), and in the Falklands/Malvinas conflict (1982).[252] Given the limited use of the Protecting Powers regime, the ICRC has taken on a somewhat substitute role.[253]

The Protecting Power system does not apply to non-international armed conflicts. Conceivably, it could, as a neutral state may be able to carry out the role on behalf of the armed group. There is one instance of this in practice. During the Boer war (1899–1902), at the request of the British Government, the US Consul in Pretoria took charge of Britain's interests in the Transvaal Republic and Orange Free State. It was agreed that

---

[245] See J Pictet (ed), *The Geneva Conventions of 12 August 1949, Commentary: I Geneva Convention for the Amelioration of the Condition of the Wounded and Sick in Armed Forces in the Field* (ICRC, 1952) 86.

[246] G Best, *War and Law Since 1945* (Clarendon Press, 1994) 371.

[247] See DP Forsythe, 'Who Guards the Guardians: Third Parties and the Law of Armed Conflict' (1976) 70 *AJIL* 41; G Abi-Saab, 'The Implementation of Humanitarian Law', in A Cassese (ed), *The New Humanitarian Law of Armed Conflict* (Editoriale Scientifica, 1979) 310, 311–14; GAB Peirce, 'Humanitarian Protection for the Victims of War: The System of Protecting Powers and the Role of the ICRC' (1980) 90 *Military Law Review* 89.

[248] 1929 Geneva Convention, Article 86; 1949 First, Second, and Third Geneva Conventions, Articles 8–11; 1949 Fourth Geneva Convention, Articles 9–12; Additional Protocol I, Article 5. See also 1954 Hague Convention, Article 21.

[249] Forsythe, Third Parties, above note 247, 41.

[250] Abi-Saab, Implementation, above note 247, 311.

[251] GIAD Draper, 'Implementation of International Law in Armed Conflict' (1972) 48 *International Affairs* 46, 47.

[252] Best, above note 246, 372; Forsythe, Third Parties, above note 247, 46–7. K Dörmann, 'Dissemination and Monitoring Compliance of International Humanitarian Law', in W Heintschel von Heinegg and V Epping (eds), *International Humanitarian Law Facing New Challenges: Symposium in Honour of Knut Ipsen* (Springer, 2007) 227, 236, includes the 1962 conflict between France and Tunisia.

[253] Sandoz, above note 2, 274–5.

the Government of the South African Republic could request the US Consul to extend a similar function on behalf of the Boer and Afrikaaner prisoners held by Great Britain. However, the characterization of that conflict is open to question,[254] and, in any event, the Consul was able to do little more than provide a pipe and tobacco to prisoners, and forward money, letters, and parcels.[255] Furthermore, it is noteworthy that the example dates from over a century ago.

It is highly unlikely that, today, the system can be extended to non-international armed conflict. Indeed, one of the principal objections to extending the law applicable to non-international armed conflict was that a Protecting Power would be appointed on behalf of the armed group and this would confer upon the group a certain status.[256] Criticism was also made at the 1948 International Conference of the Red Cross at which time the possible intervention of a Protecting Power in a non-international armed conflict was characterized as 'interfering in the internal affairs' of the state.[257] In a memorandum issued by Greece immediately prior to the 1949 Diplomatic Conference, the Greek Delegation took the view that:

It can hardly be imagined that a legal State would, in the case of any armed conflict, be willing to have mutineers, rebels and even outlaws placed under the protection of a foreign Power, which would assume the duties of a Protecting Power... [258]

At the 1949 Diplomatic Conference, application of the Protecting Power system to non-international armed conflict was criticized as 'impair[ing] the sovereignty of governments' and it was even suggested that it 'might incite political opponents to take up arms against a legitimate government'.[259] It is particularly unworkable given that, in essence, individuals would be represented by a foreign state in respect of their government.[260] Thus, an early draft of common Article 3 extended the Geneva Conventions to certain non-international armed conflicts, but noted of the Protecting Powers regime: '[t]he provisions relating to the Protecting Powers shall, however, not be applicable, except in the instance of special agreement between the Parties to the conflict. An impartial humanitarian body, such as the International Committee of the Red Cross, may offer to the Parties to the conflict to undertake the duties conferred by the present Convention on the Protecting Powers.'[261] The role of the ICRC and other impartial humanitarian bodies in times of non-international armed conflict is considered below.[262]

---

[254] Cf J Dugard, 'The Treatment of Rebels in Conflicts of A Disputed Character: The Anglo-Boer War and the "ANC-Boer" War Compared', in AJM Delissen and GJ Tanja (eds), *Humanitarian Law of Armed Conflict, Challenges Ahead: Essays in Honour of Frits Kalshoven* (Nijhoff, 1991) 447, 448–9, with A Cassese, 'Civil War and International Law', reprinted in A Cassese, *The Human Dimension of International Law: Collected Papers* (Oxford University Press, 2008) 110, 114.

[255] See WM Franklin, *Protection of Foreign Interests* (United States Government Printing Office, 1946) 68–73; Peirce, above note 247, 95.

[256] Abi-Saab, Implementation, above note 247, 322. See also *Final Record*, above note 121, Vol II-B, 10–11 (Greece).

[257] *Seventeenth International Red Cross*, Stockholm, 1948, 72.

[258] *Propositions and Observations of the Governments for the Diplomatic Conference for the Establishment of International Conventions for the Protection of War Victims Convened at Geneva on April 21st, 1949 by the Swiss Federal Council: Memorandum by the Greek Government*, 2.

[259] See, respectively, *Final Record*, above note 121, Vol II-B, 99 (France); Vol II-B, 11 (Greece).

[260] F Siordet, 'The Geneva Conventions and Civil War' (1950) 3 *IRRC Supplement* 201, 203.

[261] *Final Record*, above note 121, Vol II-B, 124.

[262] See below, 467 et seq.

4.2 Fact-finding

4.2.1 The International Humanitarian Fact-Finding Commission

Fact-finding has long been envisaged as a useful means by which to enforce the law of armed conflict. The 1929 Geneva Convention for the Amelioration of the Condition of the Wounded and Sick in Armies in the Field provided for the possibility of enquiry on alleged violations of the Convention in a manner agreed by the relevant parties.[263] However, the requirement of agreement between the relevant parties constituted a significant hurdle to the conclusion of an enquiry. Along similar lines as the 1929 Geneva Convention, the 1949 Geneva Conventions provide that 'an enquiry shall be instituted in a manner to be decided between the interested Parties concerning any alleged violation of the Convention'. Should an agreement fail to be reached, 'the Parties should agree on the choice of an umpire who will decide on the procedure to be followed'.[264] However, this enquiry procedure has never been used successfully,[265] principally due to the lack of automaticity in bringing the fact-finding procedure into force.

In light of the importance of a fact-finding procedure and the difficulties with the procedures then in existence, an International Humanitarian Fact-Finding Commission (the Commission) was established pursuant to Article 90 of Additional Protocol I.[266] Article 90(2)(c) provides that the Commission shall be competent to:

(i). Enquire into any facts alleged to be a grave breach as defined in the [1949 Geneva] Conventions and this Protocol or other serious violation of the Conventions or of this Protocol;

(ii). Facilitate, through its good offices, the restoration of an attitude of respect for the Conventions and this Protocol.[267]

The Commission's mandate is thus two-fold. First, it has the competence to enquire into alleged grave breaches or other serious violations of the Geneva Conventions or Additional Protocol I. Neither the Geneva Conventions nor Additional Protocol I mention a category of 'serious violations'. Accordingly, the Commission will have to determine the meaning of the term for itself. It may be able to draw on the term in the international criminal law context, for example the idea in the *Tadić* Decision on Interlocutory Appeal on Jurisdiction that a serious violation of international humanitarian law constitutes 'a breach of a rule protecting important values, and the breach must involve grave consequences for the victim'.[268] However, a certain care needs to be taken, for what is a serious violation for the purposes of an international criminal

---

[263] Article 30.
[264] First Geneva Convention, Article 52; Second Geneva Convention, Article 53; Third Geneva Conventino, Article 132; Fourth Geneva Convention, Article 149.
[265] Requests have been made by one or other party. See J Pictet, *Humanitarian Law and the Protection of War Victims* (Sijthoff, 1975) 73; F Krill, 'The International Fact-Finding Commission' (1991) 31 *IRRC* 190, 192.
[266] See F Kalshoven, 'The International Humanitarian Fact-Finding Commission: Its Birth and Early Years', in F Kalshoven (ed), *Reflections on the Laws of War: Collected Essays* (Nijhoff, 2007) 793; F Hampson, 'Fact-Finding and the International Fact-Finding Commission', in H Fox and MA Meyer (eds), *Armed Conflict and the New Law, Volume II: Effecting Compliance* (BIICL, 1993) 53; A Mokhtar, 'Will this Mummification Saga Come to an End? The International Humanitarian Fact-Finding Commission: Article 90 of Protocol I' (2003–4) 22 *Pennsylvania State International Law Review* 243.
[267] Additional Protocol I, Article 90(2)(c).
[268] *Tadić* Decision on Interlocutory Appeal on Jurisdiction, above note 116, para 94(3).

tribunal may be too high a threshold for a serious violation for the purposes of the Commission.

A significant limitation on this aspect of the Commission's mandate is that an enquiry can only take place if the requesting state, which need not be the victim state, and the state against which a complaint is made have accepted the competence of the Commission.[269] The latter state may give its ad hoc consent to the enquiry process.[270] Some 72 states, at the time of writing, have submitted declarations accepting the competence of the Commission. A few declarations were submitted while the state in question was a party to an armed conflict, for example Croatia (11 May 1992), Bosnia and Herzegovina (31 December 1992), and Colombia (17 April 1995).[271]

The second aspect of the Commission's mandate is to use its good offices to facilitate the restoration of respect for the Geneva Conventions and Additional Protocol I. In this context, good offices refers to 'the communication of conclusions on the points of fact, comments on the possibilities of a friendly settlement, written and oral observations by States concerned', and the like.[272] This aspect of the Commission's work is equally as important as its undertaking of enquiries.[273]

Crucially, it has been suggested that the Commission has competence over international armed conflicts alone.[274] Despite the existence of these distinguished views, that position cannot be correct. Given that the Commission has competence over the Geneva Conventions, this necessarily includes common Article 3.[275] However, this does mean that the Commission is not competent to assess serious violations of Additional Protocol II, an unfortunate limitation given the limited scope of common Article 3 and its lack of rules on the means and methods of warfare. The Commission itself has indicated 'its willingness to enquire into alleged violations of humanitarian law, including those arising in non-international armed conflicts, so long as all Parties to the conflict agree'.[276] On this basis, it has offered its services to states involved in non-international armed conflicts.[277] Furthermore, a training exercise carried out by the Commission and staged by Sweden was premised on 'a fictional armed conflict between the Swedish government and a separatist movement that exercised control over part of the territory and sought recognition as an independent state',[278] that is to say, a non-international armed conflict.

---

[269] Additional Protocol I, Article 90(2)(a).
[270] Article 90(2)(d).
[271] F Kalshoven, 'The International Humanitarian Fact-Finding Commission: A Sleeping Beauty?', in F Kalshoven (ed), *Reflections on the Laws of War: Collected Essays* (Nijhoff, 2007) 836.
[272] ICRC, *Commentary on the Additional Protocols*, above note 177, 1046.
[273] Kalshoven, Birth, above note 266, 805; JA Roach, 'The International Fact-Finding Commission' (1991) 31 *IRRC* 167, 175; Dörmann, Dissemination, above note 252, 239.
[274] Steering Committee for Human Rights, *Study on Human Rights Protection during Situations of Armed Conflict, Internal Disturbances and Tensions*, DH-DEV(2002)1, 18 March 2001 (Document prepared by F Hampson) para 111; Bothe, Partsch, and Solf, above note 207, 543; Hampson, Fact-Finding, above note 266, 76; Dörmann, Dissemination, above note 252, 238 (implicitly); C Greenwood, 'International Humanitarian Law (Laws of War)', in C Greenwood, *Essays on War in International Law* (Cameron May, 2006) 134 (implicitly).
[275] Kalshoven, Birth, above note 266, 806; A Reinisch, 'The International Fact-Finding Commission According to Art. 90 Additional Protocol I to the Geneva Conventions and its Potential Enquiry Competence in the Yugoslav Conflict' (1996) 65 *Nordic Journal of International Law* 241, 246–9.
[276] Report of the International Fact-Finding Commission 1991–1996.
[277] See the Reports of the International Fact-Finding Commission, available at <http://www.ihffc.org>.
[278] Report of the International Fact-Finding Commission 1997–2001. See also 'Training Chamber, Stockholm, September 1998'.

Application of the enquiry procedure to non-international armed conflict raises certain difficulties. Pre-existing declarations of states that accept the competence of the Commission would not apply to non-international armed conflict. Rather, the state in question, as well as the non-state armed group, would have to provide the Commission with its ad hoc consent before an enquiry can take place.[279] Any other position allows the non-state armed group to benefit from the state's declaration while the state would not be able to benefit likewise. As to whether or not a complaint could be initiated by a non-state armed group, the ICRC Commentary takes the view that '[t]here is no doubt that only States are competent to submit a request for an enquiry to the Commission'.[280] It is submitted that this would be unfortunate both as a matter of law and as a matter of practice. As a matter of law, it is one-sided, disadvantageous to the armed group, and goes against ideas of equality of obligation, albeit obligations in relation to enforcement of the law. It also goes against the language of the provision itself. Whereas Article 90(2)(a) refers solely to High Contracting Parties in recognizing the competence of the Commission in advance, thereby limiting such recognition to states alone, Article 90(2)(c) refers to ad hoc requests and ad hoc consent on the part of parties to the conflict, thus including non-states parties. In practice, the Commission has been approached by a number of non-state armed groups. These approaches did not reach fruition, not because the Commission took the view that the process could not be instigated by armed groups, but because the groups became aware of the requirement of consent on the part of the opposing state as well as the possibility of a counter-request by the state in relation to the conduct of the group.[281] Accordingly, it is submitted that any party to a non-international armed conflict should be able to initiate an enquiry, states and non-state armed groups alike; however, both parties will have to consent to the process.

At the time of writing, the Commission has never been used. It has been described as an 'almost toothless body' and it has been suggested that '[i]t is most unlikely ... that the [Commission] will ever amount to an effective mechanism for the enforcement of the law'.[282] This author is rather less pessimistic. The Commission has been close to becoming involved in non-international armed conflicts. For example, the LTTE was reportedly interested in the Commission looking into alleged violations on the part of the Government of Sri Lanka, but became disinterested when it realised that the Government could then request an enquiry in respect of the LTTE's actions.[283] Armed groups fighting in Chechnya 'invited the Commission to investigate violations allegedly committed by Russian forces' but on the basis that Chechnya was a state and that the conflict was an international one,[284] and this proved unacceptable to the Commission. In Colombia, between 1995 and 1999, the Government and the ELN came close to reaching agreement on submitting particular incidents to the Commission. However, the election of a new President prevented the conclusion of any

---

[279] Report of the International Fact-Finding Commission 1997–2001. See also Kalshoven, Birth, above note 266, 806.
[280] Y Sandoz, C Swinarski, and B Zimmermann (eds), *Commentary on the Additional Protocols of 8 June 1977 to the Geneva Conventions of 12 August 1949* (ICRC, Geneva, 1987) 1044. See also Bothe, Partsch, and Solf, above note 207, 543; Roach, above note 273, 176.
[281] Report of the International Fact-Finding Commission 1997–2001.
[282] Greenwood, Twilight, above note 172, 57.
[283] Kalshoven, Sleeping Beauty, above note 271, 839.
[284] Ibid, 839.

agreement on point.²⁸⁵ Thus, although the situation has proved fruitless to date, hope remains that the Commission will be utilized.

4.2.2 Other fact-finding initiatives

Rather than utilizing a standing fact-finding mechanism, such as the International Humanitarian Fact-Finding Commission, a party to a conflict may request that an ad hoc fact-finding mission be convened. During the attempted secession of Biafra (1967–70), for example, the Federal Government of Nigeria invited the UN, the Organization for African Unity, as well as certain governments to send representatives to Nigeria to assess the conduct of the Federal Army's operations in 1968.²⁸⁶ The invitations were issued in response to reports that the Federal Government had massacred civilians and intended to commit genocide against the Ibo people.²⁸⁷ The Federal Government specifically requested investigation into the killing and wounding of ICRC officials and other relief workers.²⁸⁸ For their part, the Biafran authorities invited the observers to inspect the conduct of their forces. However, the invitation of the Biafran authorities was not accepted.²⁸⁹ This is unfortunate, for it would have been of greater utility to assess the conduct of both parties to the conflict. Nonetheless, the invitation of one of the parties, coupled with the work of the observers, provides a useful example of monitoring compliance with the law of non-international armed conflict.

Various other states and non-state armed groups have issued invitations to outside observers in respect of monitoring and verification of conduct. The practice on point is by no means inconsiderable. For example, in 1964, during the post-independence violence in the Democratic Republic of the Congo (DRC), the Prime Minister of the DRC invited the ICRC to 'designate an impartial observer to come at once to Leopoldville, in order to observe and verify compliance of my Government with [my declaration to comply with international humanitarian law]'.²⁹⁰ The Prime Minister continued, '[s]imilarly, I urge you to make every effort to send an observer to Stanleyville for similar purposes and to verify compliance of rebel authorities there with the applicable provisions of the Geneva Conventions'.²⁹¹ Some years later, according to the then UN High Commissioner for Human Rights, during his visit to Rwanda in May 1994, '[b]oth sides accepted the idea of an international investigation into human rights violations'.²⁹²

Insofar as non-state armed groups are concerned, in 2002, the Aceh Sumatra National Liberation Front (ASNLF) of Indonesia denied using anti-personnel mines and 'invited Geneva Call to conduct a verification mission'.²⁹³ Similarly, in 2008, the HPG of Kurdistan 'called for an international fact-finding mission to investigate its

---

²⁸⁵ Report of the International Fact-Finding Commission 1997–2001. See also Kalshoven, Sleeping Beauty, above note 271, 839.
²⁸⁶ See Report of the Observer Team, above note 74.
²⁸⁷ Ibid, 3.
²⁸⁸ Ibid, 13.
²⁸⁹ AHM Kirk-Greene, *Crisis and Conflict in Nigeria: A Documentary Sourcebook 1966–1969, Volume II* (Oxford University Press, 1971) 81.
²⁹⁰ 'Letter from Prime Minister Dr Moise Tshombe of the Democratic Republic of the Congo to the President of the International Committee of the Red Cross', 22 October 1964, reproduced in (1965) 59 *AJIL* 615.
²⁹¹ Ibid.
²⁹² Report of the United Nations High Commissioner for Human Rights, Mr José Ayala Lasso, on his mission to Rwanda, 11–12 May 1994, E/CN.4/S-3/3, 19 May 1994, para 21.
²⁹³ Geneva Call, Annual Report 2002, 8. See also Geneva Call, Annual Report 2003, 10.

actions' also in relation to allegations of the use of anti-personnel mines.²⁹⁴ Similar practice exists in relation to child soldiers. In Burma, the KNU reported in 2010 that it had 'sent a letter of invitation to the UN Special Representative of the Secretary-General for Children and Armed Conflict to visit us, but there has not been a response' and that it would 'welcome the UN agencies or the team concerned to come and visit KNU/KNLA [Karen National Liberation Army] areas to make sure that the KNU/KNLA has a clear policy and does not recruit child soldiers'.²⁹⁵ For its part, the Karenni National Progressive Party (KNPP) of Burma made similar statements.²⁹⁶ Along similar lines, also in 2010, the JEM of Sudan reported that it 'has invited numerous organizations to visit its areas to discuss adherence to child protection codes. The invitation is still open and JEM is ready to facilitate that at any time'.²⁹⁷

More generally, during the violence in Kosovo, in 1998, the KLA indicated that '[t]he General Staff repeats the demand for the dispatch of teams of international experts to investigate crimes of all kinds in Kosova, and in this it will have the help of every member of the UCK'.²⁹⁸ Around the same time, the RUF of Sierra Leone stated that '[i]t is time the International Community set up an investigation into whom are the perpetrators of amputations',²⁹⁹ amputations being characteristic of the conflict in Sierra Leone and attributed to the RUF. More recently, in 2010, the Taliban of Afghanistan proposed the creation of a committee comprising representatives of the 'Islamic Conference, UN's human rights organizations [*sic*] as well as representatives from ISAF forces and Islamic... Emirate of Afghanistan' to consider the issue of civilian casualties and the conduct of investigations into civilian casualties.³⁰⁰

There is also considerable practice relating to various armed groups fighting in and around the DRC in particular. In an interview in 2008, Laurent Nkunda, then leader of the National Congress for the Defence of the People (CNDP), stated that, after he heard accusations that the CNDP were recruiting child soldiers, 'I called for Unicef to come and verify it'.³⁰¹ Also in the DRC, Jean-Pierre Bemba Gombo allegedly wrote to the Special Representative of the Secretary-General for the DRC asking for UN involvement in the conduct of certain investigations.³⁰² Similarly, when the Special Representative of the Secretary-General for Children and Armed Conflict expressed concern about the targeting of civilians in the DRC, the Rally for Congolese Democracy (RCD) indicated that it was undertaking its own investigations but 'accepted the

---

²⁹⁴ General Command of Kongra Gel/HPG, Letter to Geneva Call, 29 October 2008, cited in E Decrey Warner, J Somer, and P Bongard, 'Armed Non-State Actors and Humanitarian Norms: Lessons from the Geneva Call Experience', in B Perrin (ed), *Modern Warfare: Armed Groups, Private Militaries, Humanitarian Organizations, and the Law* (University of British Columbia Press, 2012) 73, 80.
²⁹⁵ *In Their Words*, above note 29, 24. See also KNU Press Statement on Report of UNSG, 27 April 2009.
²⁹⁶ Press Release No 02/09, Appeal for the Karenni Army's name to be removed from the list of non-state armed groups making use of child soldiers in armed conflict, 18 April 2009.
²⁹⁷ *In Their Words*, above note 29, 19.
²⁹⁸ Political Statement No 11 of the Kosova Liberation Army, 5 October 1998, reproduced as 'UCK Confirms Respect for International Conventions', Pristina *Koha Ditore*, 6 October 1998, KLA Communiques and Political Declarations from 1997–9, Exhibit P48 in *Limaj* trial (ICTY translation).
²⁹⁹ RUF Political Leadership-Kailahun District, 'RUF Calls for Independent Investigations', 15 January 1999.
³⁰⁰ Response of the spokesman of the Islamic Emirate of Afghanistan about civilian casualties' survey, 15 August 2010.
³⁰¹ L Nkunda, 'Fighting for Peace', *The Guardian Weekly* (UK), 22 April 2008.
³⁰² *Prosecutor v Bemba Gombo*, ICC-01/05-01/08, Conclusions de la Défense en Réponse à l'Acte d'Accusation Amendé du 30 Mars 2009, 24 April 2009, para 239.

participation of international experts to assist in the process'.[303] For its part, the Executive Secretary of the FDLR told one reporter in 2009 that '[w]e have consistently called for an international investigation so that they can identify the authors of those [relevant] abuses and bring them to justice. That is our policy'.[304] In a press release issued some months earlier, the FDLR 'call[ed] once more for the set up of an independent international commission of inquiry to shed light on the various crimes committed in the Great Lakes Region of Africa and to bring to justice their perpetrators'.[305]

Some of these invitations may well be 'bluffs', with the armed group having no real intention to comply with the invitation were it accepted by the international community. However, if that is the case, the bluff needs to be called. In that way, parties that are genuinely committed to looking into allegations of violations and to enforcing the law can be distinguished from those that do not have any such intention.

States and non-state armed groups occasionally engage with reports of fact-finding mechanisms. For example, the NDFP has criticized a report of the UN Secretary-General on Children and Armed Conflict in the Philippines, arguing that, by applying the Paris Principles, standards were being imposed upon it that went beyond those of the Convention on the Rights of the Child and the relevant Optional Protocol thereto.[306] These exchanges are to be encouraged, with one exchange of views between a government and a UN special rapporteur being described by that special rapporteur as 'a model of the way in which relations between a government and a special procedure mandate-holder should be conducted in the event that there is a dispute not just as to the factual elements of a case but as to the applicable law'.[307] Exchanging views on the law with non-state armed groups is equally important, as it could lead to points of entry within the group on other legal issues and it improves the awareness and knowledge of the legal obligations of the group. Other states and armed groups have dismissed allegations made against them out of hand and have not engaged in reasoned explanation or constructive engagement.[308] These reactions are far less useful. Still others, for example the JEM of Sudan and the NDFP, have criticized UN reports for not seeking information from them and for not allowing them a right of reply to allegations contained in the relevant report.[309] These are equally important points, as the advantages that could be gained from engagement are lost. It also bolsters the view that certain norms are being foisted upon the group without the group being a participant in

---

[303] Protection of Children Affected by Armed Conflict, Report of the Special Representative of the Secretary-General for Children and Armed Conflict, A/54/430, Annex, 1 October 1999, para 93(b).

[304] Quoted in 'FDLR Inc: Congo's Multinational Rebels', *BBC News*, 18 November 2009.

[305] FDLR Press Release Nr 04/SE/CD/AUGUST2009, 20 August 2009.

[306] NDFP Letter to UN Secretary-General Ban Ki-Moon, 24 November 2008. See also, as examples of engagement, 'KNU [Karen National Union] Press Statement on Report of UNSG', 27 April 2009; 'Report of the Panel of Experts established pursuant to Resolution 1591 (2005) concerning the Sudan Issued 2 October 2009: A Response from JEM', 16 November 2009.

[307] P Alston, J Morgan-Foster, and W Abresch, 'The Competence of the UN Human Rights Council and its Special Procedures in relation to Armed Conflicts: Extrajudicial Executions in the "War on Terror"' (2008) 19 *EJIL* 183, 190.

[308] See eg 'Las FARC-EP responden a la carta que HRW dirigió al Comandante Manuel Marulanda Velez, Comunicado del Estado Mayor Central de las FARC-EP', 21 July 2001, in Human Rights Watch, *Colombia: Beyond Negotiation, International Humanitarian Law and its Application to the Conduct of the FARC-EP* (August 2001) 20–1.

[309] 'Report of the Panel of Experts established pursuant to Resolution 1591 (2005) concerning the Sudan Issued 2 October 2009: A Response from JEM', 16 November 2009; NDFP Letter to UN Secretary-General Ban Ki-Moon, 24 November 2008.

the process. Just as a state the subject of a report may be given access to the report prior to its publication, so too could the non-state armed group the subject of the report. The diversity in reactions of non-state armed groups to reports also demonstrates the importance of not assuming that there will never be any proper engagement on the part of these groups.

The possibility of an external verification mechanism is an important one. Not only may it prove that certain violations have been committed, it may also disprove such allegations. Certain non-state armed groups have expressed their unwillingness to sign up to humanitarian commitments for fear that allegations of non-compliance may be made against them but may not be disproved should the government fail to allow a verification mission to take place. This was true, for example, of the Aceh-Sumatra National Liberation Front/Free Aceh Movement (ASNLF/GAM) in respect of Geneva Call's Deed of Commitment.[310] This is not a hypothetical concern on the part of armed groups. For example, the Government of Myanmar has not allowed UN entities to engage with the KNU or the KNPP on issues of child soldiers,[311] and this has been described by the UN as 'a major obstacle to the collection and verification of data and reports received'.[312] For its part, the KNPP wrote to the Special Representative of the Secretary-General for Children and Armed Conflict 'highlighting the fact that they have invited the United Nations on several occasions to monitor its military bases and areas of operations and have offered open and independent access for compliance verification, as well as expressed their willingness to dialogue with the United Nations'.[313] Third-party fact-finding missions are thus a crucial means by which to enforce the law.

4.3 United Nations entities

4.3.1 The Security Council

The Security Council has utilized international humanitarian law in a number of different ways.[314] It has called upon parties to non-international armed conflicts, states and non-state armed groups alike, to respect international humanitarian law.[315] It has also condemned violations of international humanitarian law.[316] Still other Security Council resolutions recall the obligation to prosecute violations of international

---

[310] Geneva Call, An Inclusive Approach to Armed Non-State Actors and International Humanitarian Norms: Report of the First Meeting of Signatories to Geneva Call's Deed of Commitment, 24.
[311] Children and Armed Conflict: Report of the Secretary-General, A/62/609-S/2007/757, 21 December 2007, para 158.
[312] Report of the Secretary-General on Children and Armed Conflict in Myanmar, S/2007/666, 16 November 2007, para 18.
[313] Report of the Secretary-General on Children and Armed Conflict in Myanmar, S/2009/278, 1 June 2009, para 25.
[314] See C Bourloyannis, 'The Security Council of the United Nations and the Implementation of International Humanitarian Law' (1991–2) 20 *Denver Journal of International Law and Policy* 335; R Cryer, 'The Security Council and International Humanitarian Law', in SC Breau and A Jachec-Neale (eds), *Testing the Boundaries of International Humanitarian Law* (BIICL, 2006) 245; G Nolte, 'The Different Functions of the Security Council with Respect to Humanitarian Law', in V Lowe et al (eds), *The United Nations Security Council and War* (Oxford University Press, 2008) 519.
[315] See eg Liberia, SC Res 950 (1994).
[316] See eg Liberia, SC Res 950 (1994); Burundi, SC Res 1012 (1995); Sierra Leone, SC Res 1231 (1999).

humanitarian law.[317] The Security Council has authorized the creation of fact-finding missions to consider violations of international humanitarian law,[318] authorized the creation of international criminal tribunals,[319] and referred situations to the International Criminal Court.[320] More recently, it has adopted resolutions on particular thematic issues, notably child soldiers, the protection of civilians in armed conflict, and sexual violence against civilians in armed conflict.[321] Sanctions have also been imposed on high-level officials for violations of international humanitarian law. This has been done, *inter alia*, in respect of senior UNITA officials,[322] a commander of the Sudan Liberation Army (SLA) as well as a number of other persons,[323] the leadership of the Armed Forces Revolutionary Council (AFRC) and RUF in the Sierra Leonean armed conflict,[324] and various individuals and entities involved in the fighting in the DRC.[325]

4.3.2 The General Assembly

The General Assembly has also utilized international humanitarian law in different ways, for example calling on parties to non-international armed conflicts to respect the law and condemning violations of the law.[326] The General Assembly has called on states not parties to international humanitarian law instruments to consider becoming parties to them, and called on states parties to instruments to disseminate them.[327] Two important General Assembly Resolutions—General Assembly Resolutions 2444 (XXIII) and 2675 (XXV)—have also shaped the substantive law, the principles contained in them being considered to reflect customary international law.[328] General Assembly Resolution 2444 was also pivotal in the rejuvenation of international humanitarian law.[329] General Assembly resolutions adopted in the late 1960s and 1970s were also important for their position on the treatment of captured fighters in what some states considered to be wars of national liberation.[330] More recently, certain General Assembly resolutions have been considered important for their purportedly considering armed groups to have human rights obligations.[331]

---

[317] See eg SC Res 1291 (2000) (DRC), SC Res 1565 (2004) (DRC); SC Res 1479 (2003) (Ivory Coast); SC Res 794 (1992) (Somalia).
[318] SC Res 780 (1992) (Yugoslavia); SC Res 935 (1994) (Rwanda); SC Res 1012 (1995) (Burundi); SC Res 1564 (2004) (Darfur).
[319] SC Res 808 and 827 (1993) (ICTY); SC Res 955 (1994) (ICTR); SC Res 1315 (2000) (requesting the Secretary-General to negotiate an agreement with Sierra Leone for the establishment of a Special Court).
[320] SC Res 1593 (2005) (Darfur); SC Res 1970 (2011) (Libya).
[321] SC Res 1261 (1999), 1314 (2000), 1379 (2001), 1460 (2003), 1539 (2004) (child soldiers); SC Res 1265 (1999), 1296 (2000) (protection of civilians); SC Res 1820 (2008), 1888 (2009), 1889 (2009) (sexual violence).
[322] SC Res 1127 (1997); SC Res 1135 (1997).
[323] SC Res 1591 (2005); SC Res 1672 (2006).
[324] SC Res 1171 (1998).
[325] SC Res 1807 (2008).
[326] See eg GA Res 41/157 (4 December 1986) (El Salvador).
[327] GA Res 65/29 (2011).
[328] See above, 44–6.
[329] Ibid.
[330] See above, 213.
[331] See D Fleck, 'Humanitarian Protection Against Non-State Actors', in JA Fowein et al (eds), *Verhandeln fur fen Frieden—Negotiating for Peace: Liber Amicorum Tono Eitel* (Springer, 2003) 69. See generally above, 95–6.

4.3.3 Human rights mechanisms

United Nations human rights mechanisms also have a role to play in the enforcement of the law of non-international armed conflict. For example, in the universal periodic review process of the Human Rights Council, states undergo review of their human rights record and the review 'take[s] into account applicable international humanitarian law'.[332] Quite what is meant by this phrase is unclear. If it is a reference to international humanitarian law being used as an interpretive device, no such reference was needed; and if states are to be judged as against their international humanitarian law obligations, this should have been made clearer. Nevertheless, international humanitarian law is clearly relevant to the work of the Council.

The special procedures mechanisms have also considered issues of the law of non-international armed conflict in their work. For example, the then Commission on Human Rights, in renewing the mandate of the Special Representative on the situation of human rights in El Salvador in 1984, noted that the Special Representative should 'pay special attention in his report to the question of humanitarian law in armed conflicts and to violations of such law'.[333] The Special Representative, in turn, considered the practice of the Government and the non-state armed group and judged their conduct against international humanitarian law standards. International humanitarian law has also been a feature of the work of certain other special rapporteurs, for example the Special Rapporteur on Extrajudicial Executions. However, not all states have accepted such a role for the special procedures mechanisms, the United States, for example, considering that their mandates do not extend to the law of armed conflict.[334]

Human rights treaty bodies have also engaged with issues of international humanitarian law. For example, the Committee on the Rights of the Child monitors the Convention on the Rights of the Child and the Optional Protocol thereto on the Involvement of Children in Armed Conflict. States parties to the Optional Protocol are required to report to the Committee on measures taken to implement the provisions of the Optional Protocol, including the meaning they have given to 'direct participation in hostilities' in their domestic legislation.[335] The Committee has also pronounced on the age limit above which states may recruit children into the armed forces.[336]

4.4 The International Committee of the Red Cross

4.4.1 The institution

The ICRC is an impartial, neutral, and independent organization. It has as its mission the protection of the lives and the dignity of victims of armed conflict and other situations of violence and the provision of assistance to them. The ICRC also seeks to promote and strengthen international humanitarian law.[337] The history of the ICRC was initially intertwined with the history of the 'Geneva aspects' of the law of armed

---

[332] Human Rights Council Resolution 5/1 (2007) para 2.
[333] Commission on Human Rights Resolution 1984/52, E/1984/14, 87–9.
[334] See eg the exchange between the Government of the United States and the Special Rapporteur on Extrajudicial Executions recounted in Alston, Morgan-Foster, and Abresch, above note 307, 189.
[335] Guidelines regarding Initial Reports of States Parties to the Optional Protocol to the Convention on the Rights of the Child on the Involvement of Children in Armed Conflict, CRC/OP/AC/1, 12 October 2001.
[336] See above, 320.
[337] ICRC mission statement, available at <http://www.icrc.org>.

conflict.[338] Henry Dunant's call for the creation of relief societies that would provide care to the wounded in wartime led to the formation of a Group of Five to look into Dunant's ideas. The Group of Five, which would later become the ICRC, convened an international conference in 1863, which formalized the creation of national committees to assist the war wounded and adopted a 'uniform distinctive sign', namely a red cross on a white armlet.[339] The following year, at the request of the Group, the Government of Switzerland convened a diplomatic conference at which the first Geneva Convention for the Amelioration of the Condition of the Wounded in Armies in the Field was adopted. Over the years, the ICRC has been instrumental in the adoption of numerous other international humanitarian law treaties, including the 1949 Geneva Conventions and the two Protocols of 1977 Additional thereto, as well as of other legal instruments.

4.4.2 Activities

The ICRC is mandated, *inter alia*, to prepare the development of international humanitarian law.[340] It convenes meetings of experts to examine various issues of international humanitarian law, and prepares drafts of treaties for consideration by diplomatic conferences when mandated to do so. Its delegates also participate as observers in diplomatic conferences or other processes tasked with the adoption of international humanitarian law instruments, and are frequently called upon to offer their opinions on issues of international humanitarian law in various public and non-public fora. The ICRC Commentaries on the Geneva Conventions and Additional Protocols have been cited on innumerable occasions, so frequently that they are almost treated as authoritative. This can prove problematic as some passages are open to question.[341] Nonetheless, the Commentaries are rightly influential. The 2005 Customary International Humanitarian Law study prepared by the ICRC pursuant to a mandate given to the organization by the International Conference of the Red Cross and Red Crescent is also influential, and has been cited by leading courts, tribunals, and other important bodies almost immediately upon its publication.

The ICRC has played a critical role in the development of international humanitarian law applicable in non-international armed conflict. Although the Group of Five initially considered that it would not play a role in such conflicts, the Group changed its mind shortly after adopting that position.[342] Over the years, the ICRC has sought to develop the international humanitarian law of non-international armed conflict on numerous occasions, usually being ahead of the willingness of states in this regard.[343] The Customary International Humanitarian Law study is but a recent example of the ICRC's contribution to the development of the international humanitarian law of

---

[338] On the history, see P Boissier, *From Solferino to Tsushima: History of the International Committee of the Red Cross* (Henry Dunant Institute, 1985); A Durand, *From Sarajevo to Hiroshima: History of the International Committee of the Red Cross* (Henry Dunant Institute, 1984); F Bugnion, *The International Committee of the Red Cross and the Protection of War Victims* (ICRC, 2003). For a more recent account of the work, see SR Ratner, 'Law Promotion Beyond Law Talk: The Red Cross, Persuasion, and the Laws of War' (2011) 22 *EJIL* 459.
[339] Resolutions of the Geneva International Conference, Article 8.
[340] Statutes of the International Committee of the Red Cross, Article 4(1)(g).
[341] See eg above, 162. A former ICRC Director for International Law and Cooperation has also taken this view. Bugnion, above note 338, 344.
[342] See above, 30–1.
[343] See generally Chapter 2.

non-international armed conflict. Indeed, that study was undertaken in part because of the relative lack of conventional regulation of non-international armed conflict.[344]

The ICRC also assists in the conclusion of bilateral agreements on the law of non-international armed conflict between the warring parties, and if that does not prove possible, it encourages the issuance of unilateral declarations on the part of a willing party. The ICRC also issues public statements and appeals to the parties to respect international humanitarian law.[345] The ICRC conducts numerous dissemination activities and provides trainings on international humanitarian law for states and non-state armed groups.[346]

Pursuant to common Article 3, '[a]n impartial humanitarian body, such as the International Committee of the Red Cross, may offer its services to the Parties to the conflict'.[347] On this basis, any body may offer its services to the parties to the conflict provided it is impartial and humanitarian; in practice, it tends to be the ICRC. During the 1949 Diplomatic Conference, a stronger provision was suggested, requiring the parties to the conflict to accept the services of the humanitarian body: '[p]rovided that the other Party to the conflict is also prepared to do so, the High Contracting Party concerned shall accept, if offered, the services of an impartial humanitarian body, such as the International Committee of the Red Cross.'[348] However, such wording was considered too onerous, not least as it would have the effect of obliging the state 'to accept the services of a humanitarian body chosen by the insurgents'.[349] Accordingly, it was suggested that, instead, the words 'may offer its [services]' be replaced by 'shall be requested to furnish its [services]'.[350] However, this too was rejected, this time by the delegate of the ICRC, who took the view that the independence of the ICRC would be jeopardized by a mandatory clause of such a nature.[351]

The common Article 3 provision may be considered to be a fairly weak basis for ICRC action. However, the ICRC Commentary considers it to be 'of great moral and practical value' and to reflect a reduced version of the equivalent provision in the law of international armed conflict.[352] It should be noted in this regard that the 1929 Geneva Convention on Prisoners of War 'did not give the Committee any more definite basis of action; it was nevertheless sufficient during [the Second World] war to permit eleven thousand camp visits, to relieve millions of prisoners, and to transport and issue supplies worth 3,400 million Swiss francs in the camps'.[353] Thus, although the common Article 3 clause has its flaws, it is nonetheless of value. It is particularly valuable given that an equivalent provision, intended for inclusion in Additional Protocol II, did not find its way into the final text.[354]

While common Article 3 authorizes the ICRC to 'offer its services to the Parties to the conflict', such an offer does not amount to interference in the internal affairs of the state concerned. Nonetheless, states sometimes view offers in this manner. By way of

---

[344] *Customary International Humanitarian Law, Volume I: Rules*, above note 12, xxxiv–xxxv.
[345] See eg 'Public Statement by the ICRC on the Situation in Kosovo' (1998) 38 *IRRC* 725.
[346] See above, 435–6.
[347] Common Article 3. See also Customary International Humanitarian Law, Rule 124B.
[348] *Final Record*, above note 121, Vol II-B, 90 (UK).
[349] Ibid, 95 (United States).
[350] Ibid.
[351] Ibid, 95 (ICRC). See also F Siordet, 'The Geneva Conventions and Civil War' (1950) 3 *IRRC* Supplement 201, 215.
[352] Pictet, *Commentary on the First Geneva Convention*, above note 245, 58.
[353] Siordet, above note 351, 215.
[354] On the drafting process, see above, 49–52.

historical example, in 1923, the ICRC sent a telegram to the Minister of Foreign Affairs of the Irish Free State:

> International Committee of the Red Cross reminds the Irish Free State government of the absolute need to always be inspired by all the international conventions in their spirit and in their letter and to ensure that the political struggles that currently trouble Ireland do not lead to harsh measures contrary to the principles solemnly recognised by the Geneva Conventions and the Hague Conventions.[355]

It received a frosty telegram in response:

> refuse to discuss measures considered necessary by my government to repress rebellion in Ireland... your attempt at intervention an unfriendly act can only be excused by ignorance of facts or false information from anti Irish source[356]

The ICRC could only respond with a general statement: 'The International Committee without unfriendly intention acted in accordance with its traditions in a purely humanitarian and not political aim.'[357] It also decided to send a delegate to Ireland to meet with the Minister of Foreign Affairs.[358]

Apart from reliance on common Article 3 in non-international armed conflicts, the ICRC may also exercise its right of humanitarian initiative in any other situation of violence, including situations below the threshold of armed conflict, based on a mandate granted to the organization under the Statutes of the International Red Cross and Red Crescent Movement.[359] States may accept the ICRC's services on a similar basis. Thus, the United Kingdom allowed the ICRC to visit detainees in Cyprus (1955) and Kenya (1957) while not recognizing the existence of an armed conflict in either situation.[360] Indeed, in the very case of Ireland the subject of the exchange of telegrams above, Ireland did allow an ICRC delegate to visit prisons in which detainees were being housed. However, this was done as a matter of courtesy and not as a matter of obligation:

> The Irish government has authorised me to tell you it does not recognise any right of the ICRC to meddle in an Irish domestic issue.

---

[355] Telegram, 20 January 1923, ICRC Archives CR 22(84). The original reads: 'Comité International de la Croix-Rouge se permet rappeler au Gouvernement Etat Libre dIrlande nécéssité absolue de sinspirer toujours de toutes les conventions internationales dans leur espirit comme dans leur letter et de veiller ace que les lutte politiques qui troublent actuellement l'Irlande naboutissent pas aides measures de riguer contraires aux principes solennellement reconnus par les Conventions de Geneve et de la Haye.'
[356] Telegram from the Minister of Foreign Affairs, Desmond Fitzgerald, to President of the International Committee of the Red Cross, Gustave Ador, 23 January 1923, ICRC Archives CR 22 (84)/89. The original reads: 'refusons discuter measures considerées nécéssaires par mon gouvernement pour reprimer rebellion en irlande... votre essai dintervention actre inimical que lignorance des faits ou les faux renseignements de provenance anti irlandaise peuvent seuls excuser'.
[357] Telegram of 1 February 1923, from the ICRC to the Minister of Foreign Affairs, Desmond Fitzgerald, ICRC Archives CR 22 (84)/94. The original reads: 'Comite International sans aucune intention inamicale a agi conformement a ses traditions dans but exclusivement humanitaire et non politique.'
[358] Letter from the President of the ICRC to the Minister of Foreign Affairs, Desmond Fitzgerald, 9 April 1923, ICRC Archives, CR 22(84)/112.
[359] Article 5(3).
[360] See M Veuthey, 'Les Conflits Armés de Caractère Non-International et le Droit Humanitaire', in A Cassese (ed), *Current Problems of International: Essays on UN Law and on the Laws of Armed Conflict* (Giuffrè, 1975) 179, 246–7. On Kenya, see above, 200, and ICRC, *Rapport D'Activité 1957* (ICRC, 1958) 39–40.

But as an act of courtesy to the Committee's delegates, it has authorised me to show you the conditions in our barracks, our camps and our hospitals...³⁶¹

The activities that are engaged in by the ICRC pursuant to an offer of services are multifaceted. They include such things as visits to detainees, with the aim of preventing violations of law such as disappearances or torture, improving the conditions of detention, transmitting family news via Red Cross messages, tracing missing persons, providing aid to medical facilities, evacuating the wounded and sick, and instituting actions aimed at the protection of the civilian population. Various forms of humanitarian assistance, including the provision of food and water, are also undertaken. However, nothing prevents the independent and impartial humanitarian organization from undertaking whatever other humanitarian activity may be necessary, in agreement with the party in question. For example, the draft article intended for inclusion within Additional Protocol II provided that '[t]he parties to the conflict may call upon a body offering all guarantees of impartiality and efficacy, such as the International Committee of the Red Cross, to co-operate in the observance of the provisions of the... Protocol'.³⁶² The Commentary to the provision noted that it was drafted along these lines in light of the inapplicability of the Protecting Powers system.³⁶³

4.4.3 Modalities

The ICRC work, including its field operations, are guided by the Fundamental Principles of the International Red Cross and Red Crescent Movement—humanity, impartiality, neutrality, independence, voluntary service, unity, and universality³⁶⁴—of which the first four may be considered the most important. It is just as important for the ICRC to be perceived as being neutral as actually being neutral,³⁶⁵ for if the confidence of the parties to the conflict in the ICRC is lost, ICRC access to persons in need and its involvement in ensuring that international humanitarian law obligations are respected may be jeopardized. It is for this reason that confidentiality is the ICRC's preferred working method.

The ICRC thus does not engage in 'naming and shaming'. It endeavours to effect compliance with the law through a confidential dialogue with the parties to the conflict, thus making its approach distinct from that of many other organizations.³⁶⁶ The ICRC does, on occasion, and under defined conditions, make public pronouncements on violations of the law, including if the violations are 'major and repeated or likely to be

---

³⁶¹ Letter from Major-General Francis Morrin, Directeur du Service Médical de L'Armée, to the ICRC delegate in Ireland, quoted in Note from the ICRC Delegate in Ireland to the ICRC concerning visit to prisoners and camps, 19 April 1923, ICRC Archives CR 22(84)/119. The original reads: 'Le Gouvernement Irlandais m'a autorisé de vous dire qu'il ne reconnait aucun droit du CICR de se mêler dans une question domestique irlandaise.
Mais par acte de courtoisie envers les délégues du Comité il m'a autorisé de vous montrer les conditions qui existent dans nos casernes, nos camps d'internement et nos hopitaux...'
³⁶² Article 39, in ICRC, *Draft Additional Protocols to the Geneva Conventions of August 12, 1949: A Commentary* (October 1973) 170.
³⁶³ Ibid, 170. On the Protecting Powers system, see above, 457–8.
³⁶⁴ Statutes of the International Committee of the Red Cross, Article 4(1)(a). See J Pictet, 'The Fundamental Principles of the Red Cross: Commentary' (1979) 19 *IRRC* 130; (1979) 19 *IRRC* 184; (1979) 19 *IRRC* 255; (1979) 19 *IRRC* 301; (1980) 20 *IRRC* 29; (1980) 20 *IRRC* 70; (1980) 20 *IRRC* 129; (1980) 20 *IRRC* 193; (1980) 20 *IRRC* 250.
³⁶⁵ DP Forsythe, *The Humanitarians: The International Committee of the Red Cross* (Cambridge University Press, 2005) 178.
³⁶⁶ Cf below, 472–3.

repeated' and if the confidential procedure failed.³⁶⁷ It has also happened in a few instances that confidential ICRC reports have been leaked by one of the parties to a conflict or other actors. When an ICRC report on French torture of Algerian detainees during the Algerian war of independence was leaked in 1960, media reporting led to a change in behaviour on the part of France.³⁶⁸ This led to discussion within the ICRC as to whether its position on confidentiality should be modified but it was decided that this working method should be retained.³⁶⁹ Hence, the ICRC enforces the law of non-international armed conflict in a very particular manner. It does not take the form of public condemnation, but a 'behind the scenes' approach. This complements other forms of enforcement undertaken by other actors and mechanisms. The value of the ICRC's approach has been recognized. For example, the ICTY has determined that the ICRC has a right under customary international law to non-disclosure of confidential information in the possession of ICRC employees.³⁷⁰

4.5 Human rights non-governmental organizations

In recent years, human rights non-governmental organizations (NGOs) have taken the view that international humanitarian law and situations of non-international armed conflict fall within their purview. This entry into international humanitarian law is a relatively recent departure.³⁷¹ Traditionally, human rights NGOs left the enforcement of the law of non-international armed conflict to other bodies, considering international humanitarian law different from international human rights law.³⁷² Those NGOs that now work in the area of non-international armed conflict have adopted the approach that they use in their human rights work, namely 'naming and shaming' violations of the law. This 'naming and shaming' approach has a role to play in the enforcement of the law of non-international armed conflict. For example, UN Secretary-General Kofi Annan has noted that:

[i]n today's world, parties to conflict cannot operate as islands unto themselves. The viability and success of their political and military projects depend on networks of cooperation and good will that link them to the outside world, to their immediate neighbourhood as well as to the wider international community. There are, consequently, powerful factors that can influence all parties to conflict: the force of international and national public opinion; ... the growing strength and vigilance of international and national civil societies; and media exposure.³⁷³

The 'naming and shaming' approach also serves as a useful complement to the other enforcement mechanisms, such as that of the ICRC.³⁷⁴ Some NGOs, particularly Human Rights Watch, have gone beyond the traditional 'naming and shaming'

---

³⁶⁷ 'Action by the International Committee of the Red Cross in the Event of Violations of International Humanitarian Law or of Other Fundamental Rules Protecting Persons in Situations of Violence' (2005) 87 *IRRC* 393.
³⁶⁸ Forsythe, above note 365, 60.
³⁶⁹ Ibid.
³⁷⁰ *Prosecutor v Simić et al*, IT-95-9-PT, Decision on the Prosecution Motion under Rule 73 for a Ruling Concerning the Testimony of a Witness, 27 July 1999.
³⁷¹ See RK Goldman, 'International Humanitarian Law: Americas Watch's Experience in Monitoring Internal Armed Conflicts' (1993) 9 *American University Journal of International Law and Policy* 49.
³⁷² R Brett, 'Non-Governmental Human Rights Organizations and International Humanitarian Law' (1998) 38 *IRRC* 531, 532.
³⁷³ Children and Armed Conflict: Report of the Secretary-General, A/59/695-S/2005/72, 9 February 2005, para 77.
³⁷⁴ Cf above, 471.

approach and have extracted commitments from armed groups on humanitarian norms. For example, the Houthi rebels in Yemen responded to a letter from Human Rights Watch in which they committed to respecting international humanitarian law, international human rights law, and the Guiding Principles on Internal Displacement.[375] This followed a letter from Human Rights Watch to the Houthi rebels. The importance of such commitments, engagement with the parties on them, and their monitoring should not be underestimated.[376]

Human rights NGOs may be particularly well-placed to engage with parties to conflicts, given their likely presence in the state in question during times of peace and internal tensions and disturbances. In the build-up to an armed conflict, the NGO may have reported on violations by the state and by the emerging non-state armed group. However, difficulties may arise if the NGO focuses exclusively on violations committed by one side or another. For example, focusing on human rights violations by the government may lead to the NGO being accused of being sympathetic to the armed group when, in reality, the NGO may simply be adopting the position that only states can commit human rights violations. Focusing on violations by the non-state armed group may likewise see the NGO being accused of being sympathetic to the state. A fine line has to be drawn in this regard, particularly if the actual scale of violations on both sides is unequal.

5. Conclusion

The principal drawback to regulating non-international armed conflict by analogy to the law of international armed conflict is the failure to regulate the situation if a relevant analogy cannot be drawn. This is most apparent in the implementation and non-judicial enforcement of the law. The Protecting Power institution was deemed inappropriate for non-international armed conflict and as such does not comprise a part of that law. There has been much debate as to whether the International Humanitarian Fact-Finding Commission can be used to enforce the law of non-international armed conflict given that it is a creation of Additional Protocol I. Nonetheless, as the Commission is able to enforce the Geneva Conventions, it is submitted that, by necessity, it has competence over common Article 3. However, this is limited given the lack of rules pertaining to the conduct of hostilities in that Article and the vast number of other rules which pertain to non-international armed conflicts. The applicability of the enforcement mechanism of belligerent reprisals to non-international armed conflict has also been questioned given its lack of mention in the key conventional instruments. That mechanism is in fact applicable; however, its use is not to be encouraged. By and large, the implementation and enforcement mechanisms of international humanitarian law have proven insufficient for carrying out their task.

In this regard, international human rights law has played an important role. Human rights organizations have turned their attention also to violations of the law of non-international armed conflict. This has expanded over time, in the case of Human Rights Watch in particular, with engagement with the parties taking place over their respect for the law, and soliciting commitments to apply the law. Various UN entities have done likewise, with the General Assembly and the Security Council calling on parties to

---

[375] Letter from Abd al-Malik Badr al-Din Al-houthi to Human Rights Watch, 29/Jumada II/1430.
[376] See below, 542–6.

abide by relevant norms. The various UN human rights mechanisms, in particular, have reported on violations of the law of non-international armed conflict.

Aside from the work of the ICRC, there remains relatively little by way of systematic engagement with armed groups on their compliance with the law of non-international armed conflict and involvement of armed groups in the enforcement of the law. For example, disagreements surrounded whether the International Humanitarian Fact-Finding Commission could even institute an enquiry as a result of a request by a non-state armed group. Armed groups not infrequently issue invitations to UN agencies and NGOs to verify their compliance with the law; however, these invitations are usually ignored or not accepted. This is unfortunate and reflects continued anxiety over engagement with such actors even on humanitarian norms. This is a matter that will be re-considered in Chapter 12. Even on such matters as instruction of non-state armed groups on the law of non-international armed conflict, no systematic approaches are to be found, with the ICRC undertaking activities in this regard on a somewhat ad hoc basis. In light of this lack of engagement, and the general overlooking of ad hoc commitments,[377] a potentially useful form of implementation and enforcement has been overlooked, namely that of codes of conduct of armed groups, and their unilateral declarations and bilateral agreements. As the previous chapters have shown, each of these various ad hoc commitments has been, and has the potential to be, important.

---

[377] See Chapter 4.

11
Judicial Enforcement

1. Introduction

A significant addition to the traditional means of enforcing the law of non-international armed conflict is judicial enforcement. Judicial enforcement takes a number of forms, of which the most developed are criminal courts and tribunals. It has been suggested that the growth of criminal enforcement has affected resort to the other means of enforcement.[1] It has even been suggested that 'the rule of international humanitarian law *depends* on its enforcement through the prosecution and punishment of its offenders'.[2] Even if such a strong position is not adopted, enforcement of the law of non-international armed conflict through criminal prosecution is of undoubted importance. Criminal enforcement is limited in one respect in that it necessarily relates to violations that have already taken place. As such, it can only act as a complement to other forms of enforcement and implementation. In addition to criminal courts, the law of non-international armed conflict is enforced by other judicial bodies, regional human rights courts being the primary example. These courts have enforced both international humanitarian law and human rights law in non-international armed conflicts. Finally, a non-judicial alternative, namely that of amnesties, has played an important role in this area, albeit one that goes against notions of enforcement of the law. Each of these forms of enforcement (or lack thereof) is considered in this chapter. It commences with the relationship between international humanitarian law and international criminal law.

2. War crimes

Violations of certain provisions of the 1949 Geneva Conventions and Additional Protocol I applicable in international armed conflict are classified as 'grave breaches'. In respect of these grave breaches, states are required to enact domestic penal legislation, search for suspects, and prosecute them or hand them over to another state for trial.[3] Violation of common Article 3 is not one such grave breach. Despite the view expressed at the 1949 Diplomatic Conference that violations of common Article 3 constituted 'war crimes',[4] this was very much the minority opinion. Additional Protocol II also fails to contain any provisions on grave breaches. Indeed, there is no indication on the face of any of these provisions that their breach constitutes a war crime. Accordingly, the orthodox view that existed up until the mid-1990s was that the international humanitarian law of non-international armed conflict did 'not provide for

---

[1] *Prosecutor v Kupreškić et al*, IT-95-16-T, Judgment, 14 January 2000, para 530.
[2] A Cassese, 'On the Current Trends towards Criminal Prosecution and Punishment of Breaches of International Humanitarian Law' (1998) 9 *EJIL* 2, 17 (emphasis added).
[3] First Geneva Convention, Article 49; Second Geneva Convention, Article 50; Third Geneva Convention, Article 129; Fourth Geneva Convention, Article 146.
[4] *Final Record of the Diplomatic Conference of Geneva of 1949* (Federal Political Department, Berne) Vol II-B, 49 (Italy).

international penal responsibility of persons guilty of violations'.[5] Writing in 1994, the Commission of Experts tasked with looking into violations of international humanitarian law committed during the armed conflict in the former Yugoslavia noted in its final report: 'there does not appear to be a customary international law applicable to internal armed conflicts which includes the concept of war crimes.'[6] Likewise, one year earlier, the International Committee of the Red Cross (ICRC), commenting on the draft Statute of the International Criminal Tribunal for the former Yugoslavia (ICTY), noted that, 'according to International Humanitarian Law as it stands today, the notion of war crimes is limited to situations of international armed conflict'.[7]

With the benefit of hindsight, there was no reason to interpret the international humanitarian law of non-international armed conflict in this manner. The fact that common Article 3 and Additional Protocol II were silent as to their violation being considered war crimes should not have led to the questioning of the very concept of war crimes in non-international armed conflict. Certainly since the International Military Tribunal at Nuremberg took the view that violations of certain provisions of the Hague Conventions gave rise to criminal responsibility despite the lack of explicit statement to that effect,[8] the requirement that there be an explicit characterization in the instrument was open to question. To argue that violation of the international humanitarian law of non-international armed conflict cannot give rise to criminal responsibility is to 'confuse criminality with jurisdiction and penalties...the question of what actions constitute crimes must be distinguished from the question of jurisdiction to try those crimes'.[9] As the ICTY would later affirm, '[t]he fact that the Geneva Conventions themselves do not expressly mention that there shall be criminal liability for violations of common Article 3 clearly does not in itself, preclude such liability'.[10]

Furthermore, grave breaches were characterized as such, and not as 'grave crimes', in part to allow states a measure of discretion in respect of their domestic criminal law.[11] Thus, states could, if they saw fit, consider violations of common Article 3 to be crimes, albeit there was no obligation upon them to do so.[12] This is evident from the Geneva Conventions themselves, which provide that states parties 'shall take measures

---

[5] D Plattner, 'The Penal Repression of Violations of International Humanitarian Law Applicable in Non-International Armed Conflicts' (1990) 30 *IRRC* 409, 414. See also P Rowe, 'Liability for "War Crimes" during a Non-International Armed Conflict' (1995) 34 *Military Law and the Law of War Review* 149; T Meron, 'War Crimes in Yugoslavia and the Development of International Law' (1994) 88 *AJIL* 78, 80; D Shraga and R Zacklin, 'The International Criminal Tribunal for the former Yugoslavia' (1994) 5 *EJIL* 360, 366 fn 20.

[6] Final Report of the Commission of Experts established pursuant to Security Council Resolution 780 (1992), S/1994/674, 27 May 1994, para 52. See also 'Report of the Group of Experts for Cambodia established pursuant to General Assembly Resolution 52/135', S/1999/231, 16 March 1999, para 75.

[7] 'Some Preliminary Remarks by the International Committee of the Red Cross on the Setting-Up of an International Tribunal for the Prosecution of Persons Responsible for Serious Violations of International Humanitarian Law Committed on the Territory of the Former Yugoslavia', DDM/JUR/442b, 25 March 1993, para 4, reprinted in V Morris and MP Scharf, *An Insider's Guide to the International Criminal Tribunal for the Former Yugoslavia: Volume 2* (Transnational, 1995) 391, 392.

[8] *Trial of the Major War Criminals before the International Military Tribunal, Nuremberg, 14 November 1945–1 October 1946, Volume I* (Nuremberg, 1947) 253.

[9] T Meron, 'International Criminalization of Internal Atrocities' (1995) 89 *AJIL* 554, 561. See also C Greenwood, 'International Humanitarian Law and the *Tadić* Case' (1996) 7 *EJIL* 265, 279–80.

[10] *Prosecutor v Delalić et al*, IT-96-21-T, Judgment, 16 November 1998, para 308.

[11] See eg *Final Record*, above note 4, Vol II-B, 86 (United States); 356 (United Kingdom). See also 116–17 (Fourth Report drawn up by the Special Committee of the Joint Committee (Report on Penal Sanctions in Case of Violations of the Convention)).

[12] E La Haye, *War Crimes in Internal Armed Conflicts* (Cambridge University Press, 2008) 109.

necessary for the suppression of all acts contrary to the provisions of the present Convention other than the grave breaches'.[13] Such measures included criminal prosecution. Thus, the ICRC Commentary on the First Geneva Convention of 1949 provides that, '[a]t the very least, the Contracting Powers, having arranged for the repression of the various grave breaches and fixed an appropriate penalty for each, must include a general clause in their national legislative enactments, providing for the punishment of *other* breaches of the Convention'.[14] Accordingly, the ICRC model Geneva Conventions Implementation Act contains precisely such a clause. The model Act provides that '[a]ny person ... who ... commits, or aids, abets or procures any other person to commit, a breach of any of the Conventions or Protocols not covered by section 3 [on grave breaches], is guilty of an indictable offence'.[15] Furthermore, a few states did criminalize violations of common Article 3.[16] Grave breaches are, then, 'a species of a larger *genus* which is war crimes'.[17] Accordingly, even though grave breaches have been affirmed as being applicable only to international armed conflicts,[18] it does not follow that the law of non-international armed conflict cannot be enforced through criminal means.

There remains the question as to *which* violations of international humanitarian law amount to war crimes. On one, largely historical, view, all violations of international humanitarian law are war crimes.[19] A second view holds that not all violations of international humanitarian law amount to war crimes given that international humanitarian law contains some provisions that are of a rather technical nature,[20] for example the provision in the law of international armed conflict which requires the posting of a copy of the Geneva Conventions in every prisoner of war camp.[21] Rather, all *serious* violations of international humanitarian law amount to war crimes.[22] Factors that go to severity include the values protected by the norm and the gravity of the act.[23] A third view is that, for a violation of international humanitarian law to amount to a war crime, 'one should prove not only the existence of the violated rule in international law, but also the parallel existence of a secondary rule, usually a customary one, ascribing to the

---

[13] Common Articles 49(3), 50(3), 129(3), and 146(3).

[14] J Pictet (ed), *The Geneva Conventions of 12 August 1949, Commentary: I Geneva Convention for the Amelioration of the Condition of the Wounded and Sick in Armed Forces in the Field* (ICRC, 1952) 368 (emphasis added).

[15] Article 4(1).

[16] See below, 490–2.

[17] G Abi-Saab, 'The Concept of "War Crimes"', in S Yee and W Tieya (eds), *International Law in the Post-Cold War World* (Routledge, 2001) 99, 114.

[18] *Prosecutor v Tadić*, Decision on the Defence Motion for Interlocutory Appeal on Jurisdiction, IT-94-1-AR72, 2 October 1995, para 84. Cf para 83; Separate Opinion of Judge Abi-Saab, 4–6; *Delalić* Trial Judgment, above note 10, para 202; *Prosecutor v Aleksovski*, IT-95-14/1-T, Judgment, 25 June 1999, Dissenting Opinion of Judge Rodrigues, para 32. See generally, S Boelaert-Suominen, 'Grave Breaches, Universal Jurisdiction and Internal Armed Conflict: Is Customary Law Moving Towards a Uniform Enforcement Mechanism for All Armed Conflicts?' (2000) 5 *JCSL* 63; L Moir, 'Grave Breaches and Internal Armed Conflicts' (2009) 7 *JICJ* 763.

[19] This was the view of the International Military Tribunal at Nuremberg: *Trial of the Major War Criminals before the International Military Tribunal, Nuremberg, 14 November 1945–1 October 1946, Volume I* (Nuremberg, 1949) 253.

[20] H Lauterpacht, 'The Law of Nations and the Punishment of War Crimes' (1944) 21 *BYIL* 58, 78–9; H McCoubrey, 'War Crimes: The Criminal Jurisprudence of Armed Conflict' (1992) 31 *Military Law and the Law of War Review* 167, 174–7.

[21] Geneva Convention III, Article 41.

[22] Greenwood, *Tadić*, above note 9, 279–80; R Cryer, '*Prosecutor v. Galić* and the War Crime of Terror Bombing' (2005–6) 2 *IDF Law Review* 75, 93–7.

[23] *Tadić* Decision on Interlocutory Appeal, above note 18, para 94(iii). See also Meron, Internal Atrocities, above note 9, 562.

former rule this special legal effect in case of violation'.[24] It is this latter approach that has been adopted by the ICTY.

The Appeals Chamber in the *Tadić* Decision on Interlocutory Appeal on Jurisdiction adopted a test by which a violation of international humanitarian law amounted to a war crime for the purposes of the ICTY Statute if four conditions were satisfied: (1) a rule of international humanitarian law must have been violated; (2) the rule must have been a rule of customary international law, or, if a rule of conventional international law, it must have been binding on the parties to the conflict at the time of the offence and not in conflict with a peremptory norm of international law; (3) the violation must have been serious; and (4) the violation must entail individual criminal responsibility.[25] However, this test has been criticized. Some criticize the second condition and argue that the rule in question must be a rule of customary international law; conventional international law not sufficing.[26] Others tackle the third condition and argue that the requirement of severity is 'question-begging'.[27] Still others target the fourth condition and question its utility.[28] Regardless of the correctness of these critiques, the *Tadić* approach allowed the ICTY to determine whether allegations of violation of particular rules of international humanitarian law amounted to war crimes. On this basis, the ICTY was able to identify the war crimes applicable in non-international armed conflict, and given that war crimes are the criminalized versions of international humanitarian law, the ICTY was also able to identify, by implication, the international humanitarian law of non-international armed conflict.[29] This approach has also meant that a certain care needs to be taken when considering both areas of law given that international humanitarian law and international criminal law are not identical.[30]

Today, there remains no serious debate that certain violations of international humanitarian law in non-international armed conflict amount to war crimes. After all, '[t]here is no moral justification, and no truly persuasive legal reason, for treating perpetrators of atrocities in internal conflicts more leniently than those engaged in international wars'.[31] That this is the orthodox position today is in large part due to the creation and work of the ICTY and the creation of the International Criminal Tribunal for Rwanda (ICTR).

3. International criminal courts and tribunals

3.1 The International Criminal Tribunal for the former Yugoslavia

Prior to the creation of the ICTY, various views existed as to the nature of the armed conflict(s) in the former Yugoslavia. Many persons were of the view that the conflict was of an international character, or, at least, that it should be governed by the law of international armed conflict.[32] However, in creating the ICTY, the UN

---

[24] Abi-Saab, War Crimes, above note 17, 112.
[25] *Tadić* Decision on Interlocutory Appeal on Jurisdiction, above note 18, paras 94 and 143. See generally, paras 94–137.
[26] See *Prosecutor v Kordić and Čerkez*, IT-95-14/2-A, Judgment, 17 December 2004, para 45. Cf para 46.
[27] Abi-Saab, War Crimes, above note 17, 112.
[28] Greenwood, *Tadić*, above note 9, 279–80; Cryer, *Galić*, above note 22, 93–7.
[29] See generally above, 77–8.
[30] See above, 78–81.
[31] Meron, Internal Atrocities, above note 9, 561. See also Greenwood, *Tadić*, above note 9, 280.
[32] Interim Report of the Commission of Experts established pursuant to Security Council Resolution 780 (1992), S/25274, 10 February 1993, para 45; Final Report of the Commission of Experts

Secretary-General made clear that 'no judgement as to the international or internal character of the conflict is being exercised',[33] and the ICTY Statute was left neutral on point. The Statute included an article on grave breaches of the Geneva Conventions (Article 2) and an article on violations of the laws and customs of war (Article 3). The latter contained a list of violations drawn from the 1907 Hague Convention (IV) respecting the Laws and Customs of War on Land and the Regulations attached thereto, as interpreted by the International Military Tribunal at Nuremberg,[34] but its Preamble explicitly noted that the list of violations was not exhaustive.[35] Although neither common Article 3 nor Additional Protocol II was mentioned in Article 3 of the Statute, there was some indication that that Article was intended to include those provisions. For example, at the adoption of the Security Council Resolution that created the ICTY, the representative of the United States stated that the reference to the 'laws or customs of war' in Article 3 of the Statute included 'all obligations under humanitarian law agreements in force in the territory of the former Yugoslavia at the time the acts were committed, including common article 3 of the 1949 Geneva Conventions, and the 1977 Additional Protocols to these Conventions'.[36]

When the matter came to be decided by the ICTY, the Appeals Chamber confirmed that the Statute did not refer to the law of international armed conflict alone.[37] The Appeals Chamber held that 'Article 3 is a general clause covering all violations of humanitarian law not falling under Article 2 or covered by Articles 4 or 5' and that it included 'violations of common Article 3 and other customary rules on internal conflicts'.[38] While this conclusion initially proved controversial,[39] within a few years the controversy had died down. The approach was followed explicitly in subsequent ICTY cases, and implicitly through the creation of International Criminal Court (ICC).

3.2 The International Criminal Tribunal for Rwanda

The ICTR was established after the creation of the ICTY but before the ICTY Appeals Chamber handed down its influential Decision on Interlocutory Appeal on Jurisdiction in *Tadić*. One of the major advances arising out of the creation of the ICTR was the *express* criminalization of violations of the international humanitarian law of non-international armed conflict.

---

established pursuant to Security Council Resolution 780 (1992), S/1994/674, 27 May 1994, paras 42–4; Meron, Internal Atrocities, above note 9, 556. See generally, C Gray, 'Bosnia and Herzegovina: Civil War or Inter-State Conflict? Characterization and Consequences' (1997) 68 *BYIL* 155.

[33] Report of the Secretary-General pursuant to Paragraph 2 of Security Council Resolution 808 (1993), S/25704, 3 May 1993, para 62.

[34] Ibid, paras 41–3.

[35] Article 3 provides: '[s]uch violations shall include, but not be limited to' those listed therein.

[36] S/PV.3217, 25 May 1993, 15. See also, with varying degrees of clarity, 11 (France); 19 (UK); 20 (Hungary). See further, Annual Report of the International Tribunal for the Prosecution of Persons Responsible for Serious Violations of International Humanitarian Law committed in the Territory of the former Yugoslavia since 1991, A/49/342-S/1994/1007, 29 August 1994, para 19.

[37] *Tadić* Decision on Interlocutory Appeal on Jurisdiction, above note 18, paras 71–8.

[38] Ibid, para 89. See generally paras 86–93.

[39] See eg ibid, Separate Opinion of Judge Li, para 13; GR Watson, 'The Humanitarian Law of the Yugoslavia War Crimes Tribunal: Jurisdiction in *Prosecutor v Tadić*' (1995–6) 36 *Virginia Journal of International Law* 687, 709–18; C Warbrick and P Rowe, 'The International Criminal Tribunal for Yugoslavia: The Decision of the Appeals Chamber on the Interlocutory Appeal on Jurisdiction in the *Tadić* Case' (1996) 45 *ICLQ* 691, 699–701.

At the time of the creation of the ICTR, there was general agreement that the armed conflict in Rwanda was a non-international one. The Commission of Experts mandated to consider evidence relating to grave violations of international humanitarian law committed in Rwanda concluded that the 'armed conflict between 6 April and 15 July 1994 qualifies as a non-international armed conflict' and that common Article 3 and Additional Protocol II had been violated 'on a systematic, widespread and flagrant basis'.[40] Accordingly, when the ICTR was created, its Statute expressly included rules of international humanitarian law applicable in non-international armed conflict.

As noted above, during the period in question, there was considerable doubt as to whether common Article 3 and Additional Protocol II attracted individual criminal responsibility under international law. Cognizant of the debate, Secretary-General Boutros Boutros-Ghali noted that:

> the Security Council has elected to take a more expansive approach to the choice of the applicable law than the one underlying the statute of the Yugoslav Tribunal, and included within the subject-matter jurisdiction of the Rwanda Tribunal international instruments regardless of whether they were considered part of customary international law or whether they have customarily entailed the individual criminal responsibility of the perpetrator of the crime. Article 4 of the statute, accordingly, includes violations of Additional Protocol II, which, as a whole, has not yet been universally recognized as part of customary international law, and for the first time criminalizes common article 3 of the four Geneva Conventions.[41]

Unlike the Secretary-General's report on the ICTY Statute, his report on the ICTR Statute was issued after the adoption of the Statute and thus cannot be considered a part of the *travaux préparatoires*. Nonetheless, it remains an influential statement, and just months after the report was issued, the ICTY affirmed in the *Tadić* Decision on Interlocutory Appeal on Jurisdiction that violations of the law of non-international armed conflict could lead to individual criminal responsibility.

The Statute of the ICTR provides that the ICTR 'shall have the power to prosecute persons committing or ordering to be committed serious violations of Article 3 common to the Geneva Conventions of 12 August 1949 for the Protection of War Victims, and of Additional Protocol II thereto of 8 June 1977'.[42] These violations 'shall include, but shall not be limited to':

(a) Violence to life, health and physical or mental well-being of persons, in particular murder as well as cruel treatment such as torture, mutilation or any form of corporal punishment;
(b) Collective punishments;
(c) Taking of hostages;
(d) Acts of terrorism;
(e) Outrages upon personal dignity, in particular humiliating and degrading treatment, rape, enforced prostitution and any form of indecent assault;
(f) Pillage;

---

[40] Preliminary Report of the Independent Commission of Experts established in accordance with Security Council Resolution 935 (1994), S/1994/1125, 4 October 1994, paras 91 and 107; Final Report of the Commission of Experts established pursuant to Security Council Resolution 935 (1994), S/1994/1405, 9 December 1994, paras 108 and 124.

[41] Report of the Secretary-General pursuant to Paragraph 5 of Security Council Resolution 955 (1994), S/1995/134, 13 February 1995, para 12.

[42] Article 4.

(g) The passing of sentences and the carrying out of executions without previous judgment pronounced by a regularly constituted court, affording all judicial guarantees which are recognized as indispensable by civilized peoples;

(h) Threats to commit any of the foregoing acts.[43]

The specific mention of the non-exhaustive nature of the list is important given that the listed war crimes are taken solely from Article 4 of Additional Protocol II and common Article 3. The reference in the chapeau of the provision, to the power to prosecute violations of Additional Protocol II more broadly, allows the ICTR to prosecute violations of Additional Protocol II other than Article 4. Despite this breadth, the *Akayesu* Trial Chamber seemed to limit the scope of the ICTR's power to Article 4 of Additional Protocol II alone.[44] The applicable law was also limited in that it was confined to violations of common Article 3 and Additional Protocol II. Other international humanitarian law rules applicable in non-international armed conflict, for example, on weapons or cultural property, to the extent that they were not to be found in common Article 3 or Additional Protocol II, were thus excluded from prosecution before the ICTR.[45]

Ultimately, the key contribution of the ICTR to this area of the law relates to the explicit criminalization in its Statute of rules applicable in non-international armed conflict.[46] As the vast majority of charges brought by the Prosecutor relate to genocide and crimes against humanity, the ICTR's jurisprudential contributions to the law of non-international armed conflict have been limited.

3.3 The International Criminal Court

When it came to the drafting of the Rome Statute of the International Criminal Court (Rome Statute), there continued to be debate surrounding war crimes in non-international armed conflict, in particular whether the ICC should have jurisdiction over such crimes. Indeed, as with the Diplomatic Conferences of 1949 and 1974–7, the law of non-international armed conflict proved to be one of the most controversial issues.[47] For some states, it was crucial for the Court to have jurisdiction over war crimes in non-international armed conflict, as it went to the very relevance of the Court.[48] The 'raison d'être',[49] 'credibility',[50] and 'integrity and rationale'[51] of the Court depended on it. Other states, too, spoke out strongly in favour of including provisions on war crimes in non-international armed conflict,[52] while still others indicated their approval of this

---

[43] Article 4.
[44] *Prosecutor v Jean-Paul Akayesu*, ICTR-96-4-T, Judgment, 2 September 1998, paras 605–10.
[45] See LJ van den Herik, *The Contribution of the Rwanda Tribunal to the Development of International Law* (Nijhoff, 2005) 206; R Cryer, *Prosecuting International Crimes* (Cambridge University Press, 2005) 267.
[46] van den Herik, above note 45, 244.
[47] T Graditzky, 'War Crime Issues Before the Rome Diplomatic Conference on the Establishment of an International Criminal Court' (1999) 5 *University of California Davis Journal of International Law and Policy* 199, 208; MH Arsanjani, 'The Rome Statute of the International Criminal Court' (1999) 93 *AJIL* 22, 32.
[48] A/CONF.183/C.1/SR.4, para 72 (Denmark); A/CONF.183/C.1/SR.4, para 74 (Sweden).
[49] A/CONF.183/C.1/SR.26, para 54 (Republic of Korea).
[50] Ibid, para 72 (Togo).
[51] Ibid, para 97 (United States).
[52] See eg A/CONF.183/C.1/SR.25, para 10 (South Africa, on behalf of member states of the Southern African Development Community); para 14 (Austria, on behalf of member states of the European Union); para 19 (New Zealand); para 62 (Trinidad and Tobago); A/CONF.183/C.1/

position. Included in this respect were states then involved in non-international armed conflict.[53] However, certain states expressed reservations about including provisions on war crimes in non-international armed conflict.[54] Some did so as, in their view, the provisions did not reflect customary international law;[55] others in the fear that it would lead to interference in the domestic affairs of states.[56] Still others supported inclusion of a provision based on common Article 3 but not one based on Additional Protocol II.[57] Others yet took the view that the provisions would be applicable only in instances in which the state,[58] or government,[59] had collapsed. Ultimately, the states that were in favour of including provisions on war crimes in non-international armed conflict prevailed and the Rome Statute contains two lists of war crimes that are applicable in non-international armed conflict. The first is based on violations of common Article 3 (Article 8(2)(c) of the Statute) and the second contains other serious violations of the laws and customs applicable in non-international armed conflict (Article 8(2)(e) of the Statute). The latter is based on the list of war crimes applicable in international armed conflict.[60]

The two lists of war crimes should not be considered to constitute an exhaustive list of war crimes that are applicable in non-international armed conflict. They are only exhaustive insofar as the ICC is concerned; outside that context, as the UK Military Manual puts it, they are, at best, 'indicative of current international thinking in this area'.[61] Article 10 of the Rome Statute thus provides that '[n]othing in this Part shall be interpreted as limiting or prejudicing in any way existing or developing rules of international law for purposes other than this Statute'. Both these points are demonstrated through the amendment of the Statute some years after it was first adopted to include the employment in non-international armed conflict of poison and poisoned weapons, 'asphyxiating, poisonous or other gases, and all analogous liquids, materials or devices', and expanding bullets.[62] As discussed in Chapter 3, the amendment was

SR.26, para 66 (Mali); A/CONF.183/C.1/SR.27, para 27 (Hungary); A/CONF.183/C.1/SR.5, para 54 (Japan); para 108 (Canada); para 110 (New Zealand); para 114 (Brazil); A/CONF.183/C.1/SR.25, para 33 (Jordan); A/CONF.183/C.1/SR.26, para 44 (Lithuania); para 58 (Chile); para 116 (Georgia); A/CONF.183/C.1/SR.27, para 13 (Colombia); para 18 (Nicaragua); para 68 (Philippines); para 71 (Ecuador); para 80 (Venezuela).

[53] See eg A/CONF.183/C.1/SR.25, para 55 (Sierra Leone); A/CONF.183/C.1/SR.28, para 77 (Guinea-Bissau).

[54] A/CONF.183/C.1/SR.I, para 66 (UAE); para 70 (Bahrain); A/CONF.183/C.1/SR.5, para 107 (Turkey); para 115 (India); A/CONF.183/C.1/SR.27, para 2 (Iraq); para 65 (Vietnam); A/CONF.183/C.1/SR.28, para 9 (Pakistan); para 51 (Thailand); para 104 (Libyan Arab Jamahiriya).

[55] A/CONF.183/C.1/SR.26, para 102 (Islamic Republic of Iran); A/CONF.183/C.1/SR.25, para 36 (China).

[56] A/CONF.183/C.1/SR.27, para 5 (Algeria); A/CONF.183/C.1/SR.28, para 88 (Saudi Arabia).

[57] A/CONF.183/C.1/SR.4, para 76 (Sudan); A/CONF.183/C.1/SR.25, para 59 (Azerbaijan); para 65 (Mexico).

[58] A/CONF.183/C.1/SR.27, para 62 (Yemen).

[59] A/CONF.183/C.1/SR.28, para 92 (Oman).

[60] M Bothe, 'War Crimes', in A Cassese, P Gaeta, and JRWD Jones (eds), *The Rome Statute of the International Criminal Court: A Commentary* (Oxford University Press, 2002) 379, 417–18; A Zimmermann, 'Preliminary Remarks on para. 2(c)–(f) and para. 3: War crimes committed in an armed conflict not of an international character', in O Triffterer (ed), *Commentary on the Rome Statute of the International Criminal Court: Observers' Notes, Article by Article* (Beck, 2008) 475, 476–7; H von Hebel and D Robinson, 'Crimes within the Jurisdiction of the Court', in RS Lee (ed), *The International Criminal Court: The Making of the Rome Statute, Issues, Negotiations, Results* (Kluwer, 1999) 79, 119.

[61] Ministry of Defence, *The Manual of the Law of Armed Conflict* (Oxford University Press, 2004) 429.

[62] Resolution RC/Res.5.

justified on the basis that the prohibited conduct was already listed in the Rome Statute as a war crime in international armed conflict, and by implication, that there was no reason why it should not be extended to non-international armed conflict.[63] This is analogous to the position taken by the ICTY Appeals Chamber in its important Decision on Interlocutory Appeal on Jurisdiction in *Tadić*.[64]

Accordingly, as things stood at the time of writing, the following conduct was listed as a war crime applicable in non-international armed conflict and may be prosecuted as such before the ICC: violence to life and person, outrages upon personal dignity, the taking of hostages, the passing of sentences and carrying out of executions without fair trial, intentionally directing attacks against the civilian population and against certain specified civilian objects, intentionally directing attacks against humanitarian personnel and objects and peacekeeping personnel and objects provided that they are of a civilian nature, pillage, sexual violence, recruitment of children under the age of 15 or using them to participate actively in hostilities, ordering the displacement of the civilian population subject to certain exceptions, '[k]illing or wounding treacherously a combatant adversary', '[d]eclaring that no quarter will be given', physical mutilation or subjecting individuals to medical or scientific experiments, wanton destruction, employing poison or poisoned weapons, employing asphyxiating, poisonous, or associated gases and liquids, and using expanding bullets.[65]

From this list, it is apparent that there are some notable omissions—intentionally starving civilians as a method of warfare, intentionally attacking civilian objects, and intentionally launching a disproportionate attack, to name but three—all of which are criminalized in international armed conflict. The substance of the war crimes has already been analyzed through the lens of international humanitarian law, as have the situations in which they apply.[66] Accordingly, they will not be pursued here. Many useful texts have also been published on the ICC. As such, only two aspects of the ICC's work that are of particular importance to the law of non-international armed conflict are considered below. These are the manner in which allegations of war crimes committed in non-international armed conflict come before the Court; and the relationship between the ICC and non-international armed conflicts.

3.3.1 Jurisdiction

The Court may exercise jurisdiction over allegations of war crimes committed in non-international armed conflicts in three instances. First, a state party may refer a situation to the Prosecutor, such a situation involving war crimes in non-international armed conflict.[67] Second, the Security Council may refer a situation to the Prosecutor, such a situation again involving war crimes in non-international armed conflict.[68] Third, the Prosecutor may initiate an investigation *proprio motu* over war crimes in non-international armed conflict.[69]

The first few situations before the Court arose as a result of state referrals to the Prosecutor. This was true of the situations in Uganda, the Democratic Republic of the Congo, and the Central African Republic, the governments of which were fighting armed conflicts at the time of their referral.[70] The referrals caught many observers by

---

[63] See above, 63–4.   [64] See above, 57.   [65] Article 8.
[66] See Chapters 8, 9, and 7 respectively.
[67] Articles 13(a) and 14.   [68] Article 13(b).   [69] Articles 13(c) and 15.
[70] ICC Press Release, President of Uganda Refers Situation Concerning the Lord's Resistance Army (LRA) to the ICC, 29 January 2004; ICC Press Release, Prosecutor Receives Referral of the Situation

surprise. However, self-referring states may seek prosecution of the armed groups against which they are in conflict to the exclusion of their own forces. For example, the Government of Uganda referred the 'situation concerning the Lord's Resistance Army' to the ICC rather than the situation in 'northern Uganda'.[71] In light of the one-sided nature of the referral, the Prosecutor interpreted it to mean 'crimes within the situation of northern Uganda by whomever committed'.[72] Nonetheless, the early arrest warrants were issued in respect of members of armed groups rather than members of state forces,[73] and it has been suggested that this tendency will only increase.[74] Referrals may also take place for other reasons of self-interest, for example as an element of domestic politics.[75]

The second approach, that of referral by the Security Council, has also taken place in respect of non-international armed conflicts, namely the conflict in Darfur between the Government of Sudan and non-state armed groups including the Justice and Equality Movement (JEM) and the Sudan Liberation Movement/Army (SLM/A), and in respect of the 2011 violence in Libya.[76] The Security Council Resolution referring the situation in Darfur to the ICC was neutral in terms of parties to the armed conflict, and arrest warrants and summonses appear to have been issued in respect of state officials and members of armed groups alike. The Security Council Resolution referring the situation in Libya to the ICC was similarly neutral, at least in respect of the referral aspects of the Resolution.

With respect to the third approach, namely initiation of investigations by the Prosecutor, the Prosecutor has indicated that he is conducting investigations into the armed conflicts in Afghanistan, Colombia, and the Ivory Coast, among others. It remains to be seen what will happen in each.

3.3.2 Impact

The work of the ICC has had a concrete impact on non-international armed conflicts. Three issues, in particular, stand out. Members of various Darfuri armed groups—Abu Garda (United Resistance Front (URF)), Banda (JEM), and Jerbo (SLA-Unity)—have appeared voluntarily before the ICC without arrest warrants being issued. In a statement released by JEM in 2009, in addition to welcoming the issuance of an arrest warrant against President Al-Bashir of Sudan, JEM 'renew[ed] its commitment and full

---

in the Democratic Republic of Congo, 19 April 2004; ICC Press Release, Prosecutor Receives Referral Concerning Central African Republic, 7 January 2005. The precise characterization of the conflicts is open to question.

[71] ICC Press Release, President of Uganda Refers Situation Concerning the Lord's Resistance Army (LRA) to the ICC, 29 January 2004.

[72] Letter by the Chief Prosecutor to the President [of the ICC] dated 17 June 2004, annexed to ICC-02/04, Decision Assigning the Situation in Uganda to Pre-Trial Chamber II, 5 July 2004.

[73] Situation in the Democratic Republic of the Congo: Lubanga (Union des Patriotes Congolais (UPC) and Forces Patriotiques pour la Libération du Congo (FPLC)), Katanga (Force de Résistance Patriotique en Ituri (FRPI)), Chui (Front des nationalistes et intégrationnistes (FNI)), Ntaganda (Forces Patriotiques pour la Libération du Congo (FPLC) and Congrès National pour la Défense du Peuple (CNDP)); Situation in the Central African Republic: Bemba (Mouvement de libération du Congo (MLC)); Situation in Uganda: Kony (Lord's Resistance Army (LRA)), Otti (LRA), Odhiambo (LRA), Ongwen (LRA), Lukwiya (LRA).

[74] A Clapham, 'Non-State Actors', in D Moeckli, S Shah, and S Sivakumaran (eds), *International Human Rights Law* (Oxford University Press, 2010) 561, 572.

[75] See, with respect to the DRC referral, W Burke-White, 'Complementarity in Practice: The International Criminal Court as Part of a System of Multi-level Global Governance in the Democratic Republic of the Congo' (2005) 18 *LJIL* 557, 563–8.

[76] SC Res 1593 (2005); SC Res 1970 (2011).

cooperation with the Court'.⁷⁷ These voluntary appearances have been used by the armed groups to put pressure on the arrest of state officials in respect of whom warrants remain outstanding. For example, also in 2009, JEM condemned 'in the strongest possible terms the [African Union] decision not to cooperate with the ICC Arrest Warrant against Al-Bashir',⁷⁸ commended 'the surrender of Abu Garda to the ICC and hope[d that] this will encourage President Albashir to heed to the inevitable and hand over himself to the ICC with dignity and honour', and urged 'all others who are wanted by the ICC to emulate the courageous move of Abu Garda and surrender themselves to the Court'.⁷⁹ Other armed groups have called on the ICC and its Prosecutor to look into the relevant conflicts and issue arrest warrants, as was the case, for example, with the National Transitional Council of Libya in 2011.⁸⁰

Likewise, with respect to the ICTY, the National Liberation Army (NLA), which fought in the 2001 conflict in the former Yugoslav Republic of Macedonia, indicated that '[t]he General Staff will undertake all necessary measures for cooperation with the Hague Tribunal, as being the legitimate organ in this respect, against all those who abuse their function within the UÇK and whose conduct violates the rules in force within the UÇK, and also valid laws, and war crimes in particular'.⁸¹ For its part, the Kosovo Liberation Army (KLA) indicated in 1999 that '[t]he members of the tribunal in The Hague must have free reign and every opportunity to carry out investigations, contact individuals, and obtain the necessary documents. The UÇK will support all necessary measures that will lead to the exposure of the crimes against humanity and genocide carried out in Kosova by the Belgrade regime'.⁸² Things proved rather different a number of years following the conclusion of the conflict, when a re-trial had to be ordered in the case of *Haradinaj* in light of witness intimidation.⁸³

Of course, not every armed group has taken a positive approach to engagement, and some members of armed groups in respect of whom arrest warrants are outstanding have not assisted the ICC with its work. Nonetheless, these instances of compliance again contradict the assumption that non-state armed groups will not comply with mechanisms to enforce the law of non-international armed conflict.⁸⁴

Insofar as the admissibility of cases is concerned, measures taken by the state and the non-state armed group may have important effects. For example, in 2007, the Government of Uganda and the Lord's Resistance Army (LRA) signed an Agreement on Accountability and Reconciliation.⁸⁵ The Annexure to that Agreement, concluded in early 2008, provided for the creation of a 'special division of the High Court of Uganda' 'to try individuals who are alleged to have committed serious crimes during the conflict'.⁸⁶ This has given rise to uncertainty over the admissibility of cases against members of the LRA in light of the complementarity provisions of the Rome Statute. The view of the Government of Uganda as to the relationship between the special

---

⁷⁷ JEM, 'JEM Welcomes Al-Bashir's Arrest Warrant', 4 March 2009.
⁷⁸ JEM, 'AU on ICC Warrant and Mbeki's Panel on Darfur', 8 July 2009.
⁷⁹ JEM, 'JEM Welcomes Appearance of Abu Garda at the ICC', 18 May 2009.
⁸⁰ Interim Transitional National Council, 'Statement regarding Eman Al-Obaidi', 27 March 2011.
⁸¹ Ali Ahmeti, Political Representative, UÇK General Staff, Untitled Document, 8 May 2001, Exhibit P00507.E in ICTY *Boškoski* trial.
⁸² 'Political Declaration No 30 of the KLA', 8 February 1999, in KLA Communiques and Political Declarations from 1997–9, Exhibit P48 in *Limaj* trial.
⁸³ See *Prosecutor v Haradinaj, Balaj, and Brahimaj*, IT-04-84-A, Judgment, 19 July 2010, paras 14–51.
⁸⁴ See also above, 462–4.
⁸⁵ Agreement on Accountability and Reconciliation, 29 June 2007.
⁸⁶ Annexure to the Agreement on Accountability and Reconciliation, 19 February 2008, Article 7.

division of the High Court and the ICC is unclear.[87] At the time of writing, the peace process had not reached its conclusion, and, according to the Government of Uganda, the Accountability Agreement and its Annexure are not in force: '[t]he Agreement on Accountability and Reconciliation and all the other protocols that were agreed upon during the negotiations were only signed to signify the negotiators' acknowledgement that a given agenda item had been agreed upon and concluded. Therefore, in the absence of a comprehensive peace agreement signed by Mr Joseph Kony himself, the protocols are of no legal force.'[88] On this basis, in 2009, the Pre-Trial Chamber held that the cases against certain members of the LRA were admissible.[89] Should matters change, it remains to be seen what will be the response of the Prosecutor and Chambers, especially given that the Agreement on Implementing and Monitoring Mechanisms provides that, in terms of accountability and reconciliation, 'the Government shall give priority to commencing criminal investigations and establishing the special division of the High Court' and that the Government shall request the Security Council to adopt a resolution under Chapter VII of the Charter requesting the ICC to defer all investigations and prosecutions against leaders of the LRA.[90]

Also related to issues of admissibility is the principle of *ne bis in idem* and its relationship with courts of armed groups. Courts of armed groups as a possible mechanism by which to enforce the law of non-international armed conflict are considered in Chapter 12.[91] At this stage, it suffices to note that numerous armed groups convene courts to try, *inter alia*, war crimes. Provided fair trials are held by these courts, in respect of the same conduct as that in issue before the ICC, the principle of *ne bis in idem* may work to the effect that the ICC is prevented from trying the individual a second time.[92] It has been suggested that, given that the ICC works on the basis of complementarity, and the idea of complementarity is in respect of 'national' courts, courts of armed groups would not prevent the ICC from taking jurisdiction on the basis of complementarity.[93] This is true in that the relevant provision on complementarity is framed in terms of 'states' courts.[94] However, the *ne bis in idem* provision is framed rather more broadly in terms of an 'other court',[95] and it is submitted that this could be interpreted to include courts of armed groups. In this regard, the focus should not be on the identity of the particular institution—whether it is a state or non-state armed group institution—but on whether the required statutory conditions are met, namely whether the domestic proceedings were intended to shield the relevant individual from trial before the ICC, and whether the court was independent and impartial.[96] Should this

---

[87] See Letter of the Solicitor-General of Uganda to the Registrar of the ICC dated 27 March 2008, ICC-02/04-01/05-286-Anx2; Letter of the Solicitor-General of Uganda to the Registrar of the ICC dated 16 February 2009, ICC-02/04-01/05-369-Anx2.
[88] Letter of the Solicitor-General of Uganda to the ICC Registrar dated 18 November 2008, ICC-02/04-01/05-354-Anx2 (emphasis omitted).
[89] *The Prosecutor v Joseph Kony, Vincent Otti, Okot Odhiambo, Dominic Ongwen*, ICC-02/04-01/05, 10 March 2009.
[90] Agreement on Implementing and Monitoring Mechanisms, 29 February 2008.
[91] See below, 549 et seq.
[92] Rome Statute, Article 20(3).
[93] P Rowe, 'War Crimes', in D McGoldrick, P Rowe, and E Donnelly (eds), *The Permanent International Criminal Court* (Hart, 2004) 203, 227.
[94] Article 17(1)(a) and (b).
[95] Article 20(3). See also Article 17(1)(c).
[96] Article 20(3). See also JK Kleffner, 'The Law and Policy of Complementarity in Relation to "Criminal Proceedings" Carried Out by Non-State Organized Armed Groups', in C Stahn and M El Zeidy (eds), *The International Criminal Court and Complementarity* (Cambridge University Press, 2011) 707.

prove not to be the case, the ICC may be prevented from trying the relevant individual. It is submitted that there should not be anything objectionable about such a conclusion, providing the requisite conditions and fair trial guarantees are met.

3.4 The Special Court for Sierra Leone

The Statute of the Special Court for Sierra Leone (SCSL or Special Court) contains two articles on war crimes—Article 3, entitled '[v]iolations of Article 3 common to the Geneva Conventions and of Additional Protocol II' and Article 4, entitled 'Other serious violations of international humanitarian law'. Article 3 of the Statute is largely identical to the equivalent provision in the ICTR Statute. Accordingly, as with that Statute, the list is exhaustive in one way and non-exhaustive in another.[97]

Article 4 of the Statute of the Special Court provides in its chapeau that '[t]he Special Court shall have the power to prosecute persons who committed the following serious violations of international humanitarian law'. The listed violations are:

(a) Intentionally directing attacks against the civilian population as such or against individual civilians not taking direct part in hostilities;
(b) Intentionally directing attacks against personnel, installations, material, units or vehicles involved in a humanitarian assistance or peacekeeping mission in accordance with the Charter of the United Nations, as long as they are entitled to the protection given to civilians or civilian objects under the international law of armed conflict;
(c) Conscripting or enlisting children under the age of 15 years into armed forces or groups or using them to participate actively in hostilities.

The fact that these are described as 'other' serious violations reveals that they are not taken from common Article 3 or Additional Protocol II. Rather, they are taken from the Rome Statute of the International Criminal Court, which was concluded prior to the creation of the Special Court. Utilizing the Rome Statute in this manner proved controversial in one respect, namely whether the conduct proscribed in Article 4(c) of the Statute was criminal during the period in which the conflict in Sierra Leone took place. This resulted in a split decision of the Appeals Chamber of the Special Court, with the majority taking the view that the conduct was criminal at the time in question and the dissenting justice taking the view that it was only criminal as of the time of the adoption of the Rome Statute in July 1998.[98] However, apart from that one controversy, criminalizing violations of the international humanitarian law of non-international armed conflict proved unproblematic.

Once the ICTY, ICTR, and SCSL conclude their work, unless new ad hoc international criminal tribunals are created—and they have been proposed, with the Final Act of the Inter-Congolese Political Negotiations '[r]esolv[ing] that a request be made to the UN Security Council...with a view to establishing an International Criminal Court for the Democratic Republic of Congo'[99]—the ICC will be the only

---

[97] See above, 481.
[98] *Prosecutor v Norman*, SCSL-2004-14-AR72(E), *Decision on Preliminary Motion Based on Lack of Jurisdiction (Child Recruitment)*, 31 May 2004, Dissenting Opinion of Justice Robertson. See also Report of the Secretary-General on the Establishment of a Special Court for Sierra Leone, S/2000/915, 4 October 2000, paras 17–18.
[99] Inter-Congolese Political Negotiations, Final Act, 2 April 2003, Resolution No DIC/CPR/05, On the Establishment of an International Criminal Court, Preamble.

international criminal tribunal which has jurisdiction over war crimes committed in non-international armed conflict. Given the limited resources of the ICC, and its functioning on the basis of the principle of complementarity, prosecution at the national level will be crucial.

4. Domestic criminal courts

Domestic prosecution takes a number of different forms. Prosecutions may be instituted in respect of ordinary crimes rather than war crimes, for example 'grievous bodily harm' instead of 'torture', or 'robbery' as opposed to 'pillage'. On this basis, a number of states have taken the view that their domestic criminal legislation suffices for the prosecution of war crimes and grave breaches of the Geneva Conventions.[100] Prosecutions for acts committed in a non-international armed conflict have proven to be more numerous if the charges do not involve a war crime, but are framed as a violation of a different norm of international law. For example, there have been a greater number of prosecutions for torture, disappearances, crimes against humanity, and genocide, than there have been for war crimes, even if those other crimes were committed in a non-international armed conflict.[101]

Domestic legislation on war crimes itself takes different forms. Lists of war crimes may be reproduced from specific articles of the Geneva Conventions and Additional Protocols and characterized as war crimes. Alternatively, no specific list of violations may be set out but the legislation in question may criminalize 'war crimes' in the abstract, requiring reference to international law to elucidate the point. At an even more general level, domestic law may simply refer to 'violations of international law conventions ratified by the state' or which the state is under an obligation to punish. This, too, requires reference to international law.

Up until the mid-1990s, there were relatively few prosecutions at the national level for violations of the law of non-international armed conflict. A few states had enacted legislation which criminalized breaches of the law of non-international armed conflict,[102] and there were even fewer instances of actual prosecution, although both are more numerous than generally thought. Things changed with the creation of the ICTY and ICTR, after which point states increasingly began to enact or amend legislation to criminalize breaches of the international humanitarian law of non-international armed conflict. This increased further with the adoption of the Rome Statute and the enactment of legislation implementing the Rome Statute into domestic law. However, actual trials continue to be relatively few in number, with those that do take place tending to relate to the conflicts in the former Yugoslavia and Rwanda.[103]

---

[100] See eg the response of South Africa and Iraq to the ICRC, in Respect of the Geneva Conventions: Measures taken to Repress Violations, Report submitted by the International Committee of the Red Cross (April 1965).

[101] Mention can be made of the majority of the Ethiopian trials, on which see below, 492; the Rwandan genocide cases, on which see V Thalmann, 'Rwandan Genocide Cases', in A Cassese (ed), *The Oxford Companion to International Criminal Justice* (Oxford University Press, 2009) 498; prosecutions in Argentina after the 2005 nullification of the amnesty laws, on which see SR Ratner, JS Abrams, and JL Bishoff, *Accountability for Human Rights Atrocities in International Law* (Oxford University Press, 2009) 187–90; and ad hoc prosecutions for torture in third states, on which see C Ryngaert, 'Universal Criminal Jurisdiction over Torture' (2005) 23 *NQHR* 571.

[102] La Haye, above note 12, 171.

[103] M Sassòli, 'Humanitarian Law and International Criminal Law', in A Cassese (ed), *The Oxford Companion to International Criminal Justice* (Oxford University Press, 2009) 111, 114.

4.1 1860s to mid-1990s
4.1.1 Prosecutions

An early example of a trial for violation of the laws and customs of war in a civil war was that of Captain Henry Wirz in 1865 following the conclusion of the US civil war. Wirz, a member of the Confederates, was the Commandant of the Andersonville military prison, which held numerous detainees of the Union forces.[104] Wirz was charged with two counts of violation of the laws and customs of war. The first related to the conditions in which detainees were housed, with some 10,000 dying as a result, as well as to the cruel punishments and inhuman medical treatment administered to detainees, which resulted in the deaths of hundreds more persons.[105] The second was that of '[m]urder, in violation of the laws and customs of war' in respect of 13 prisoners.[106] The trial took place before a special military commission and Wirz was found guilty and sentenced to death.[107] A second example of a war crimes trial was that of Major-General John H Gee, again arising out of the US civil war. As with Wirz, the conduct related to prison conditions and the murder of detainees.[108] The trial took place before a military commission and Gee was found not guilty of the charges.[109] Even prior to the *Wirz* and *Gee* trials, investigations had taken place during the civil war in order to establish whether the law of war had been violated. For example, in 1864, upon the order of a Union commander, an investigation was launched in order to determine whether a captured Confederate general had violated the law of war by 'destroying or injuring the works, armament, and munitions at Ft. Morgan, Alabama, of which he was then commander, after he had abandoned the defense of the Fort and indicated his intention to surrender by hoisting the white flag'.[110]

As belligerency was recognized in the US civil war, the consequences that can be drawn from these two cases are limited. However, in the century following the *Wirz* and *Gee* trials, courts-martial for violations of the laws and customs of war took place in respect of conduct taking place in other non-international armed conflicts, albeit on an isolated basis. During and following the American–Philippines war of 1899–1902, a few US soldiers were court-martialled in respect of violations of the law of war. For example, General Smith was court-martialled in respect of his orders: 'I want no prisoners' and 'I wish you to kill and burn. The more you kill and burn, the better you will please me.'[111] Major Edwin Glenn was court-martialled in respect of subject-

---

[104] One study puts the figure at 33,000 prisoners, at a prison designed to hold 10,000. See LL Laska and JM Smith, '"Hell and the Devil": Andersonville and the Trial of Captain Henry Wirz, C.S.A., 1865' (1975) 68 *Military Law Review* 77, 81.
[105] *Trial of Henry Wirz*, HR Ex Doc No 23, 40th Cong, 2nd Sess (1867) 3–5.
[106] Ibid, 5–8.
[107] Ibid, 807–8.
[108] On the *Gee* trial, see G Mettraux, 'A Little-known Case from the American Civil War' (2010) 8 *JICJ* 1059.
[109] Ibid, 1065.
[110] MH Hoffman, 'The Customary Law of Non-International Armed Conflict: Evidence from the United States Civil War' (1990) 30 *IRRC* 322, 327, referring to General Order 50, Headquarters, Military Division of West Mississippi, 4 September 1864.
[111] Quoted in L Friedman, *The Law of War: A Documentary History, Volume I* (Random House, 1972) 799, 801. See also G Mettraux, 'US Courts-Martial and the Armed Conflict in the Philippines (1899–1902): Their Contribution to National Case Law on War Crimes' (2003) 1 *JICJ* 135, 139. See also GD Solis, *The Law of Armed Conflict* (Cambridge University Press, 2010) 63–5.

ing prisoners to 'water cure',[112] a practice akin to 'water-boarding'. Around the same time, during the Boer war (1899–1902), a number of individuals were tried for violations of the laws and customs of war. One individual was tried for 'placing prisoners in the firing line' and 'driving prisoners on foot with mounted commando and starving them'.[113] Another was tried for the misuse of the white flag.[114] Decades later, in 1966, Belgian soldier GW was court-martialled for an unlawful killing during the armed conflict in the Democratic Republic of the Congo.[115] Courts-martial were also undertaken in the late 1960s by the Nigerian Federal Government during the attempted secession of Biafra, including in respect of the execution of a surrendered Biafran fighter in violation of the Code of Conduct issued to armed forces.[116] Thus, some prosecutions were undertaken in respect of the law of non-international armed conflict. However, instances of prosecution remained relatively few and far between.

4.1.2 National legislation

In many respects this relative lack of prosecution is unsurprising. In the non-international armed conflicts that took place subsequent to the US civil war, there was little by way of applicable international law. There were very few conflicts in which the armed group was recognized as a belligerent, thus bringing into play the law of international armed conflict.[117] The ad hoc regulation that there was frequently failed to contain provisions on criminal prosecution. Even after the adoption of the 1949 Geneva Conventions and Additional Protocol II, the majority view was that violation of the law of non-international armed conflict did not attract criminal sanction.[118] Accordingly, the legislation in all but a few states simply did not provide for criminal prosecution for violations of the law of non-international armed conflict.

The legislation of a few states, however, did provide for criminalization. The Act for the Enforcement of the Geneva Convention relative to the Treatment of Prisoners of War of 12 August 1949, enacted in Thailand in 1955, related primarily, as its name suggests, to violations of the Third Geneva Convention. However, the Act also provided that, '[i]n the case of armed conflict not of an international character, whoever commits any of the acts specified in Section[s 12–14] of this Act with respect to persons listed in Article 3 of the Convention shall be liable to the punishment provided in those sections'. The acts mentioned in sections 12–14 were the subjection of a prisoner of war to 'medical, biological or scientific experiments of any kind which are not justified by the medical treatment of the prisoner concerned'; threatening, insulting, or subjecting a prisoner of war to humiliating or degrading treatment; the infliction of 'physical or mental torture or any other form of coercion on a prisoner of war to secure information of any kind whatsoever, or threatens, insults or exposes a prisoner of war who refuses to answer to any unpleasant or disadvantageous treatment of any kind

---

[112] Friedman, above note 111, 814. See also Mettraux, above note 111, 143–6; Solis, above note 111, 67–71.
[113] JW Spaight, *War Rights on Land* (1911) 274.
[114] Ibid, 319 fn 4.
[115] *Public Prosecutor v GW*, Conseil de Guerre (Brussels), Judgment of 18 May 1966, reproduced and translated in M Sassòli, AA Bouvier, and A Quintin, *How Does Law Protect in War? Volume II* (ICRC, 2011) 938.
[116] See *Tadić* Decision on Interlocutory Appeal on Jurisdiction, above note 18, para 106; J-M Henckaerts and L Doswald-Beck, *Customary International Humanitarian Law: Volume II: Practice* (Cambridge University Press, 2005) 959 and 2087.
[117] See generally above, 17–20.
[118] See above, 475–6.

whatsoever'. As the Act extended its protections to persons listed in common Article 3, it was not only prisoners of war who were covered but any person *hors de combat*. The Act also criminalized the taking of hostages in armed conflicts not of an international character.[119] As such, although the Act criminalized relatively few violations of common Article 3, it constitutes an example of early domestic legislation which explicitly criminalized violations of international humanitarian law applicable in non-international armed conflict.

A second example is that of the 1973 International Crimes (Tribunals) Act of Bangladesh. The Act was intended to enable the prosecution of crimes against peace, genocide, crimes against humanity, war crimes, violations of the 1949 Geneva Conventions, and 'any other crimes under international law'.[120] The provision on the Geneva Conventions related to 'violation of *any* humanitarian rules applicable in armed conflicts laid down in the Geneva Conventions of 1949'.[121] Although utilizing neutral language, the Act was specifically enacted in order to prosecute atrocities committed during the secession of Bangladesh from Pakistan and it was indicated that certain Pakistani nationals would be tried for 'genocide, war crimes, crimes against humanity, breaches of Article 3 of the Geneva Conventions, murder, rape and arson'.[122]

A third example is that of the Ethiopian Criminal Code of 1957 which criminalized in domestic law certain violations of the 1949 Geneva Conventions. For example, a provision on 'war crimes against the civilian population' provided that '[w]hosoever, in time of war, armed conflict or occupation, organizes, orders or engages in, against the civilian population and in violation of the rules of public international law and of international humanitarian conventions [certain listed acts] is punishable with rigorous imprisonment from five years to life, or, in cases of exceptional gravity, with death'.[123] Importantly, the Criminal Code did not distinguish between violations committed in international and non-international armed conflict.[124]

Other states criminalized violations of the law in a neutral manner by means of a general reference to the laws and customs of war. For example, the 1987 Law of Military Crimes Act of Mozambique defined as crimes against humanitarian rules: violation of generally accepted humanitarian rules in armed conflicts, in particular the use of prohibited means of combat; acts of cruelty against the civilian population, the wounded or sick, or the detained; and attacks against transports of the wounded, sick, and shipwrecked, or of the detained.[125] Accordingly, much turned on how the phrase 'generally accepted humanitarian rules' was understood. Likewise, the Netherlands Criminal Law in Wartime Act (1952) referred to 'violations of the laws and customs of war'.[126] The same is true of the 1957 Military Criminal Code of Switzerland, which provided that '[w]hoever acts contrary to the provisions of international agreements on the conduct of hostilities and the protection of persons and property, [and] whosoever violates other recognized laws and customs of war, shall . . . be

---

[119] Section 19.
[120] Article 3.
[121] Article 3(e) (emphasis added).
[122] Press Release of 17 April 1973, quoted in JJ Paust and AP Blaustein, 'War Crimes Jurisdiction and Due Process: the Bangladesh Experience' (1978) 11 *Vanderbilt Journal of Transnational* Law 1, 2.
[123] Article 282. The listed acts can be found in Articles 283–94.
[124] Office of the Special Prosecutor, 'The Special Prosecution Process of War Criminals and Human Rights Violators in Ethiopia', February 1994, reproduced in NJ Kritz (ed), *Transitional Justice, Volume III* (US Institute for Peace, 1995) 559, 570 fn 1.
[125] Lei No 17/87, 21 December 1987, Article 83.
[126] Article 8.

punished by imprisonment'.[127] The normal scope of application of that provision is 'declared wars and other armed conflicts between two or more states',[128] that is to say, international armed conflicts. However, the Code also provided that '[t]he violation of international agreements is furthermore punishable if provision is made in those agreements for a broader scope of application',[129] thus potentially covering the law of non-international armed conflict. The Criminal Code of the then Socialist Federal Republic of Yugoslavia (SFRY), which was adopted in 1976 and entered into force in July 1977, is a further example. The Code provided for punishment in respect of violations of listed rules of international law applicable in time of war or armed conflict, for example Article 142 on war crimes against the civilian population. Prior to the armed conflict in the former Yugoslavia, no cases had been prosecuted on the basis of Article 142 of the Criminal Code.[130]

Accordingly, prior to the 1990s, some states, albeit very few, criminalized violations of the law of non-international armed conflict *expressly* or sought to prosecute violations of that law on the basis of their legislation. A few more states enacted legislation that was drafted in a neutral manner, leaving much to turn on international law conceptions of war crimes. Given that the prevailing understanding of a war crime was, at that time, linked to violations of the law of international armed conflict, actual prosecutions of violations of the law of non-international armed conflict were few and far between. This changed in the mid-1990s, with the creation of the ICTY, with states interpreting their neutral legislation in a manner that included violations of the law of non-international armed conflict.

Thus, it would take until the mid-1990s for prosecutions to be brought in Ethiopia. In 1992, the Transitional Government of Ethiopia established a Special Prosecutor's Office 'to conduct investigation[s] and institute proceedings in respect of any person having committed or [being] responsible for the commission of an offence by abusing his position in the party, the government or mass organization under the Dergue-WPE regime'.[131] The prosecutions related, *inter alia*, to violations of international humanitarian law committed during the armed conflicts between the armed forces of the Dergue regime (the Government) and various non-state armed groups during the period roughly between 1975 and 1991.[132] The Transitional Government considered itself under a 'duty...to bring to justice' persons accused of 'serious violations...of international law',[133] and prosecutions were brought for genocide, crimes against humanity, war crimes, murder, disappearances, torture, and wilful bodily injury.[134]

---

[127] Article 109(1). English translation in (1996) 78 *IRRC* 499.
[128] Article 108(1). English translation in ibid.
[129] Article 108(2). English translation in ibid.
[130] *Prosecutor v Kunarac, Kovac and Vukovic* IT-96-23-T and IT-96-23/1-T, Judgment, 22 February 2001, para 835.
[131] Special Public Prosecutor's Office Establishment Proclamation No 22/1992, 8 August 1992, reproduced in Kritz, above note 124, 556, 557.
[132] T Sverdrup Engelschiøn, 'Ethiopia War Crimes and Violations of Human Rights' (1995) 34 *Military Law and the Law of War Review* 9; D Turns, 'War Crimes Without War? The Applicability of International Humanitarian Law to Atrocities in Non-International Armed Conflicts' (1995) 7 *African Journal of International and Comparative Law* 804.
[133] Letter dated 28 January 1994 from the Permanent Representative of the Transitional Government of Ethiopia to the United Nations Office at Geneva addressed to the Assistant Secretary-General for Human Rights, E/CN.4/1994/103, 3 February 1994, 4.
[134] See FK Tiba, 'The Mengistu Genocide Trial in Ethiopia' (2007) 5 *JICJ* 513, 514. See also Office of the Special Public Prosecutor, Statement of the Chief Special Public Prosecutor, 13 February 1997, quoted in *Customary International Humanitarian Law, Volume II: Practice*, above note 116, 3664.

When the Special Prosecutor's Office was created in 1992, prior to the establishment of the ICTY but at the same time as discussions as to its creation were taking place in the Security Council, the Special Prosecutor pointed to the discussions surrounding the creation of the ICTY in order to garner support for his Office.[135] Along associated lines, it would take a further 40 years for prosecutions to take place pursuant to the 1973 International Crimes (Tribunals) Act of Bangladesh.[136]

How the phrase 'violations of the laws and customs of war' the phrase used in the Netherlands Act of 1952 was to be understood arose in 1996, in the case of *Knesević*, in respect of whom an investigation was opened on violations of common Article 3 committed during the armed conflict in Bosnia in 1992. The Arnhem District Court confirmed that violations of common Article 3 could indeed be prosecuted under the Wartime Offences Act.[137] A few years later, in 2005, in the case of *X and Y*, the Hague District Court held that the Netherlands could exercise universal jurisdiction over violations of common Article 3 pursuant to its Wartime Offences Act.[138] In the case of the Swiss Military Code, it took until the late 1990s for cases to be brought pursuant to Articles 108 and 109 of the Code. In the case of *G*, violations of the Fourth Geneva Convention, Additional Protocol I, and Additional Protocol II were alleged to have been committed during the armed conflict in Bosnia. The Court held that the conflict was an international armed conflict and that there was insufficient evidence on which to convict the individual.[139] However, the Court also indicated that it was competent to deal with the case pursuant to its Criminal Code regardless of the nature of the conflict.[140] In the later case of *Niyonteze*, the defendant was charged with, and convicted for, war crimes, namely violations of common Article 3 and Additional Protocol II, in respect of conduct undertaken during the Rwandan armed conflict and genocide.[141] With respect to the SFRY Criminal Code, in 1992, in the case of *Martin Sablić and Others*, the defendants were charged, *inter alia*, with war crimes against civilians pursuant to Article 142 of the Code in relation to acts committed during the armed conflict in Croatia. The Military Court in Belgrade, holding the armed conflict to be of a non-international character, found the accused guilty of war crimes.[142] Accordingly, even states that had legislation in place that criminalized violations of the

---

[135] Office of the Special Prosecutor, 'The Special Prosecution Process of War Criminals and Human Rights Violators in Ethiopia', February 1994, reproduced in Kritz, above note 124, 559.

[136] See S Linton, 'Completing the Circle: Accountability for the Crimes of the 1971 Bangladesh War of Liberation' (2010) 21 *Criminal Law Forum* 191.

[137] Arnhem District Court, Military Chamber, Decision No 05/07805-95, 21 February 1996. The decision was overturned on other grounds. At a subsequent appeal, the Hoge Raad noted that the point was not at issue before it. See *Prosecutor v Knesević*, Hoge Raad der Nederlanden, Strafkamer (Supreme Court of the Netherlands, Criminal Division) No 3717, 11 November 1997, reproduced and translated at (1998) 1 *YIHL* 600, 605.

[138] *Prosecutor v X and Y*, Hague District Court, 14 October 2005, on which see G Mettraux, 'Dutch Courts' Universal Jurisdiction over Violations of Common Article 3 *qua* War Crimes' (2006) 4 *JICJ* 362.

[139] Military Tribunal, Division 1, Lausanne, 18 April 1997, reproduced and translated in M Sassòli, AA Bouvier, and A Quintin, *How Does Law Protect in War? Volume III* (ICRC, 2011) 2221, on which see the case-note by AR Ziegler (1998) 92 *AJIL* 78.

[140] Ibid.

[141] Military Tribunal, Division 2, Lausanne, 30 April 1999; Military Appeal Tribunal 1A, Geneva, 26 May 2000; Cassation Military Tribunal, 27 April 2001, reproduced and translated in Sassòli, Bouvier, and Quintin, above note 139, 2208, on which see the case-note by L Reydams, (2002) 96 *AJIL* 231.

[142] *Prosecutor v Martin Sablić and Others*, No 112/92, Military Court in Belgrade, 26 June 1992, on which see the case-note by A Strippoli, in A Cassese et al (eds), *The Oxford Companion to International Criminal Justice* (Oxford University Press, 2009) 899.

laws and customs of war only used that legislation to prosecute violations of the law of non-international armed conflict in the 1990s.

Further compounding the issue was the fact that many of the states that had legislation in place would have had to institute prosecutions on the basis of universal jurisdiction. During the period in question, universal jurisdiction for war crimes other than grave breaches was controversial and would have added an extra level of complexity to any prosecution.

4.2 Mid-1990s to present
4.2.1 Conventional law

As with the substantive law of non-international armed conflict, the criminal enforcement of that law changed significantly in the mid-1990s. Instruments adopted during and since the mid-1990s not only regulate non-international armed conflicts, but routinely require states parties to enact domestic legislation criminalizing violations of the instrument. This is true of the 1993 Chemical Weapons Convention,[143] the 1996 Amended Mines Protocol,[144] the 1997 Ottawa Convention on Anti-Personnel Mines,[145] the 1999 Second Protocol to the Hague Convention on Cultural Property,[146] and the 2008 Cluster Munitions Convention.[147]

4.2.2 Domestic legislation

Numerous domestic criminal codes drafted, or amended, since the mid-1990s also criminalize violations of international humanitarian law applicable in non-international armed conflict.[148] Legislation enacted during this period and implementing the Geneva Conventions also routinely criminalizes violations of that law.[149] Other, ad hoc, legislation is similarly broad.[150] However, a few states continue to criminalize violations of international humanitarian law applicable in international armed conflict alone.[151]

Following the adoption of the Rome Statute in 1998 and its entry into force in 2002, domestic criminalization of violations of the law of non-international armed conflict has increased significantly. A number of states parties to the Rome Statute have enacted implementing legislation, reproducing the crimes contained in the Rome Statute.[152] Others have amended their domestic penal codes to reflect the crimes contained in the Rome Statute.[153] Still others have gone further and criminalized violations of the law of

---

[143] Article VII.   [144] Article 14(1) and (2).
[145] Article 9.   [146] Articles 15–21.   [147] Article 9.
[148] See eg Georgia, Criminal Code 1999, Articles 411 and 413. See generally La Haye, above note 12, 153.
[149] See eg Loi du 16 juin 1993 relative à la répression des infractions graves aux Conventions internationales de Genève du 12 août 1949 et aux Protocoles I et II du 8 juin 1977, additionnels à ces Conventions (Belgium); Geneva Conventions (Amendment) Act 1998, section 4 (Ireland); Geneva Conventions Amendment Act 2003 (Mauritius), section 4.
[150] See eg Law No 33Bis/2003, Law repressing the Crime of Genocide, Crimes against Humanity and War Crimes 2003, Articles 8 and 10 (Rwanda); Act on Crimes against International Humanitarian Law, Genocide, and other Crimes against Humanity, section 3(c) and 4(c) (Philippines).
[151] See eg Geneva Conventions Act 2003, section 2 (Namibia).
[152] See eg Crimes against Humanity and War Crimes Act (2000), sections 4 and 6 (Canada); International Criminal Court Act 2001, sections 50(1) and 51 (United Kingdom).
[153] See eg Criminal Code of Bosnia-Herzegovina 2003, Articles 173–84; Criminal Code of the Republic of Slovenia 2005, Articles 374–86; Criminal Code 2004, Chapter IX, section 74 (Latvia); Criminal Code 2003, Articles 158–68 (Croatia).

non-international armed conflict which are not listed as war crimes in the Rome Statute. For example, the implementing legislation of some states criminalize violation of the prohibition on starvation of civilians as a method of warfare;[154] serious violations of the law relating to cultural property;[155] the use of biological weapons;[156] the use of anti-personnel mines in violation of the Ottawa Convention;[157] the use of incendiary weapons, laser weapons, and 'weapons the primary effect of which is to injure by fragments which in the human body escape detection by X-rays', all in violation of the Convention on Certain Conventional Weapons;[158] the use of weapons that cause unnecessary suffering or superfluous injury;[159] attacks against civilian objects;[160] disproportionate attacks;[161] violation of the prohibition on deportation and forcible transfer;[162] and the improper use of distinctive insignia and emblems.[163] Other domestic legislation also contains broader protections. For example, the approach taken in the Samoan implementing legislation provides that 'a "war crime" means an act specified in Article 8(2) of the Statute and any other act committed during an armed conflict which, at the time and in the place of its commission, constitutes a war crime according to customary international law or conventional international law applicable to armed conflicts, whether or not it constitutes a contravention of the law in force at the time and in the place of its commission'.[164] Thus, the legislation is in place in numerous states to prosecute violations of the law of non-international armed conflict, oftentimes broader than the list of violations subject to prosecution before the ICC.

---

[154] Act to Introduce the Code of Crimes against International Law (2002), Part 2, Chapter 2, section 11(5) (Germany); Loi relative aux violations graves du droit international humanitaire, 5 August 2003, Article 8 (Belgium); Penal Code, Chapter 16, section 106(b) (Norway); Adaptation of Criminal Legislation to ICC Statute, Chapter II, section II, Article 11(f) (Portugal).

[155] Loi relative aux violations graves du droit international humanitaire, 5 August 2003, Article 8 (Belgium); Criminal Code, as amended in 2003, Article 613 (Spain).

[156] Act on the Punishment, etc. of Crimes within the Jurisdiction of the International Criminal Court, Article 14(1) (Korea); Act to Introduce the Code of Crimes against International Law (2002), Part 2, Chapter 2, section 12 (Germany); Penal Code, Chapter 16, section 107(b) (Norway).

[157] Adaptation of Criminal Legislation to ICC Statute, Chapter II, Section II, Article 12(2)(d) (Portugal).

[158] Adaptation of Criminal Legislation to ICC Statute, Chapter II, Section II, Article 12(2)(f), (g), and (h) (Portugal).

[159] Loi relative aux violations graves du droit international humanitaire, 5 August 2003, Article 8 (Belgium); Penal Code, Chapter 16, section 107(d) (Norway); Adaptation of Criminal Legislation to ICC Statute, Chapter II, Section II, Article 12(1) and (2)(b) (Portugal); Criminal Code, as amended in 2003, Article 610 (Spain).

[160] Act on the Punishment, etc. of Crimes within the Jurisdiction of the International Criminal Court, Article 13(2) (Korea); Act to Introduce the Code of Crimes against International Law (2002), Part 2, Chapter 2, section 11(2) (Germany); Loi relative aux violations graves du droit international humanitaire, 5 August 2003, Article 8 (Belgium); Adaptation of Criminal Legislation to ICC Statute, Chapter II, Section II, Article 11(b) (Portugal).

[161] Act on the Punishment, etc. of Crimes within the Jurisdiction of the International Criminal Court, Article 13(3) (Korea); Act to Introduce the Code of Crimes against International Law (2002), Part 2, Chapter 2 section 11(3) (Germany); Loi relative aux violations graves du droit international humanitaire, 5 August 2003, Article 8 (Belgium); Penal Code, Chapter 16, Section 106(c) (Norway); Criminal Code, as amended in 2003, Article 611 (Spain).

[162] Code of Crimes Against International Law (2002), Part 2, Chapter 2, section 8(1)(6) (Germany); Loi relative aux violations graves du droit international humanitaire, 5 August 2003, Article 8 (Belgium); Penal Code, Chapter 16, section 103(h) (Norway); Adaptation of Criminal Legislation to ICC Statute, Chapter II, Section II, Article 10(1)(i) (Portugal); Criminal Code, as amended in 2003, Article 611 (Spain).

[163] Adaptation of Criminal Legislation to ICC Statute, Chapter II, Section II, Article 14 (Portugal).

[164] International Criminal Court Act 2007, section 7(2) (Samoa).

4.2.3 Trials in national courts

In addition to the legislative framework being in place, trials are increasingly conducted in the states in which armed conflicts occur, albeit some years after the conflicts end. For example, in the case of *Osvaldo Romo Meno*, the defendant was prosecuted for the kidnapping, torture, and killing of an individual during what was characterized by the Court as an internal armed conflict in Chile in 1974.[165] As noted above, at the time of writing, trials were also taking place in respect of violations committed during the secession of Bangladesh from Pakistan in 1971.[166] Prosecutions are also being carried out in respect of ongoing armed conflicts. In the Democratic Republic of the Congo (DRC), for example, Major Jean-Pierre Biyoyo of the Mudondo Forty armed group was convicted for the recruitment and use of children in armed conflict.[167] Also in the DRC, individuals have been brought before a mobile court in respect of rape as a crime against humanity in the context of the armed conflict.

War crimes trials have also taken place with varying degrees of involvement on the part of outside actors. Following the armed conflict in the Federal Republic of Yugoslavia in 1999, the United Nations Interim Administration in Kosovo (UNMIK) had responsibility for the maintenance of law and order in Kosovo.[168] The creation of a tribunal to prosecute serious violations of international humanitarian law and serious ethnically motivated crimes had been suggested; however, for various reasons, including that of funding, the proposed tribunal was not established. Instead, the UNMIK authorized the appointment of international judges and prosecutors,[169] and international judges sat alongside their domestic counterparts on panels that formed part of the court system of Kosovo. A number of war crimes trials have since taken place.[170]

A similar scheme was adopted in East Timor. The United Nations Transitional Administration in East Timor (UNTAET) was endowed 'with overall responsibility for the administration of East Timor' and empowered to 'exercise all legislative and executive authority, including the administration of justice'.[171] The UNTAET established the structure of East Timor's court system and vested the District Court in Dili with exclusive jurisdiction over certain listed serious offences, which included war crimes.[172] The Special Panels comprised international and national judges, of which the international judges formed the majority.[173] These Special Panels tried the war crimes set out in UNTAET Regulation 2000/15, which reflected the list of war crimes contained in the Rome Statute.[174] Following the transition of East Timor to independence and the

---

[165] *Osvaldo Romo Meno*, Appeal Court of Santiago, No 13.597-94, 26 September 1994, reproduced and translated in M Sassòli and AA Bouvier, *How Does Law Protect in War: Volume II* (ICRC, 2006) 1357.
[166] See above, 493.
[167] Report of the Special Representative of the Secretary-General for Children and Armed Conflict, A/HRC/4/45, 9 February 2007, para 17.
[168] SC Res 1244 (1999).
[169] UNMIK Regulations 1999/1, 2000/6, and 2001/34.
[170] See the summaries in OSCE Mission in Kosovo, *Kosovo's War Crimes Trials: A Review* (September 2002) and in the various issues of the *YIHL*.
[171] SC Res 1272 (1999).
[172] UNTAET Regulation 2000/11 on the Organization of Courts in East Timor; UNTAET Regulation 2000/15 on the Establishment of Panels with Exclusive Jurisdiction over Serious Criminal Offences.
[173] UNTAET Regulation 2000/15, sections 22.1 and 22.2.
[174] Ibid, section 6.

conclusion of the UNTAET, war crimes trials continued pursuant to East Timor's Constitution.[175] A number of trials have taken place, but principally for domestic crimes or for crimes against humanity.[176]

The Iraqi Special Tribunal is of a different character. It, too, forms part of the domestic court system of the state in question; however, it was created in 2003 largely by the Coalition Provisional Authority.[177] The Special Tribunal has jurisdiction over war crimes committed in non-international armed conflict as well as other crimes, international as well as domestic.[178] The war crimes provision contained in the Statute of the Special Tribunal is taken from the Rome Statute, and various war crimes trials have taken place.[179]

In Bosnia, Croatia, and Serbia war crimes trials have taken place in respect of the armed conflicts in the former Yugoslavia. In Croatia, numerous war crimes trials have been conducted.[180] War crimes trials have also taken place in Serbia. In 2003, the War Crimes Chamber of the Belgrade District Court was established. This Chamber, a purely national Chamber, can and does prosecute war crimes. In Bosnia and Herzegovina, war crimes trials were carried out pursuant to the Rome Agreement between the warring factions in the Yugoslav conflict.[181] Paragraph 5 of the Agreement provided that '[p]ersons other than those already indicted by the Tribunal, may be arrested and detained for serious violations of international humanitarian law only pursuant to a previously issued order, warrant or indictment that has been reviewed and deemed consistent with international legal standards by the International Tribunal'. Thus, between 1996 and 2004, war crimes trials in Bosnia operated on the basis that the ICTY Office of the Prosecutor would approve war crimes prosecutions, which would then be carried out by local courts.[182] In 2005, a War Crimes Chamber of the State Court was established, comprising international and national judges and serving as the focal point for war crimes prosecutions. War crimes trials in Bosnia, Croatia, and Serbia have increased as a result of referrals by the ICTY. Whereas the ICTY initially operated on the basis of the principle of deferral, pursuant to which it had primacy over state prosecutions, it now operates also on the basis of referral, pursuant to which it may refer cases to state courts for prosecution.[183] The principle of referral is also applicable to the

---

[175] Constitution of the Democratic Republic of East Timor, Article 163(1).
[176] See the collation of judgments and decisions in, A Klip and G Sluiter (eds), *Annotated Leading Cases of International Criminal Tribunals, Volumes 13 and 16* (Intersentia, 2008 and 2009).
[177] See I Bantekas, 'The Iraqi Special Tribunal for Crimes Against Humanity' (2005) 54 *ICLQ* 237, 239; M Scharf, 'Is it International Enough? A Critique of the Iraqi Special Tribunal in Light of the Goals of International Justice' (2004) 2 *JICJ* 330, 331–2.
[178] Statute, Articles 11–14.
[179] See eg Iraqi High Tribunal, *Al Anfal*, Case No 1/CSecond/2006, 24 June 2007.
[180] I Josipović, 'Responsibility for War Crimes before National Courts in Croatia' (2006) 88 *IRRC* 145, 152. For one example, see *Prosecutor v Rajko Radulovic and Others*, K-15/95, Judgment of 26 May 1997, reproduced and translated in M Sassòli and AA Bouvier, *How Does Law Protect in War: Volume II* (ICRC, 2006) 2071.
[181] Rome Agreement, 18 February 1996.
[182] J Manuell and A Kontić, 'Transitional Justice: The Prosecution of War Crimes in Bosnia and Herzegovina under the "Rules of the Road"' (2002) 5 *YIHL* 331. However, reportedly, in many cases this was not complied with: U Garms and K Peschke, 'War Crimes Prosecution in Bosnia-Herzegovina (1992–2002)' (2006) 4 *JICJ* 258, 262–3.
[183] Rules of Procedure and Evidence, Rule 11*bis*. See also SC Res 1534 (2004). See eg *Prosecutor v Stanković*, IT-96-23/2-PT, Decision on Referral of Case under Rule 11*bis*, 17 May 2005 [referral to Bosnia]; *Prosecutor v Ademi and Norac*, IT-04-78-PT, Decision for Referral to the Authorities of the Republic of Croatia pursuant to Rule 11*bis*, 14 September 2005 [referral to Croatia]; *Prosecutor v Kovačević*, IT-01-42/2-I, Decision on Referral of Case pursuant to Rule 11*bis*, 17 November 2006 [referral to Serbia].

ICTR; and, after a number of attempts, the ICTR has referred a case to Rwanda.[184] The ICTR has also referred cases to other states for prosecution.[185] However, even here it has encountered difficulty, in light of the state in question possibly not having jurisdiction over international crimes.[186]

Trials have also taken place that have arisen out of the involvement of state forces in non-international armed conflicts in other states. For example, in Belgium and Canada, members of the armed forces have been prosecuted or court-martialled for certain acts carried out while United Nations Operation in Somalia (UNOSOM) peacekeepers. In both states, international humanitarian law was considered inapplicable to the activities of the peacekeepers in question.[187] Regardless of the correctness of those conclusions, it is noteworthy that proceedings were brought in respect of violations of common Article 3 and Additional Protocol II by the states in question, again demonstrating that by the mid-1990s, prosecutions were being brought in national courts for violations of the law of non-international armed conflict.

The practice should not be overstated. There remain a great many states in which trials have not taken place for violations of the law of non-international armed conflict. However, since the mid-1990s, there has been a clear trend towards criminal prosecution at the domestic level.

4.2.4 Trials in courts of states not involved in the conflict

A further development that has emerged over the same period of time is the use of universal jurisdiction to bring prosecutions for war crimes committed in non-international armed conflict. At the level of conventional law, neither common Article 3 nor Additional Protocol II provides for universal jurisdiction. Despite some states advocating for the position, the International Criminal Court does not operate on the basis of universal jurisdiction.[188] However, the Second Protocol to the Hague Convention on Cultural Property and the Convention on the Safety of United Nations and Associated Personnel, both of which apply in non-international armed conflict, do provide for universal jurisdiction.[189]

Outside conventional law, and in the realm of customary international law, things are in a state of flux. A resolution of the Institut de Droit International notes that '[u]niversal jurisdiction may be exercised over international crimes identified by international law as falling within that jurisdiction in matters such as... serious violations of international humanitarian law committed in... non-international armed conflict' but

---

[184] *Prosecutor v Jean Uwinkindi*, ICTR-2001-75-R11*bis*, Decision on Prosecutor's Request for Referral to the Republic of Rwanda, 28 June 2011. Cf *Prosecutor v Gatete*, ICTR-2000-61-R11*bis*, Decision on Prosecutor's Request for Referral to the Republic of Rwanda, 17 November 2008.

[185] See eg *Prosecutor v Munyeshyaka*, ICTR-2005-87-I, Decision on Prosecutor's Request for Referral of Wenceslas Munyeshyaka's Indictment to France, 20 November 2007.

[186] *Prosecutor v Bagaragaza*, ICTR-2005-86-R11*bis*, Decision on the Prosecution Motion for Referral to the Kingdom of Norway, 19 May 2006; *Prosecutor v Bagaragaza*, ICTR-2005-86-11*bis*, Decision on Prosecutor's Extremely Urgent Motion for Revocation of the Referral to the Kingdom of the Netherlands pursuant to Rule 11*bis*(F)&(G), 17 August 2007.

[187] *Ministère Public and Others v B and C*, Belgian Military Court, Judgment of 20 November 1997, on which see note by M Cogen in (1998) 1 *YIHL* 415; *R v Brocklebank*, Judgment of 2 April 1996, reproduced in Sassòli, Bouvier, and Quintin, above note 139, 1681.

[188] See O Bekou and R Cryer, 'The International Criminal Court and Universal Jurisdiction: A Close Encounter?' (2007) 56 *ICLQ* 49.

[189] Article 16(1)(c) and Article 10(4) respectively.

the Resolution does not go on to identify any such crimes itself.[190] One view holds that states may exercise universal jurisdiction over war crimes committed in non-international armed conflict as a matter of customary international law.[191] A competing view, expressed some years earlier, holds that 'national legislation and case law... is neutral as to exercise of universal jurisdiction'.[192] Still another view is that there is a 'good amount' of state practice and *opinio juris* that supports the exercise of universal jurisdiction, but not yet enough to amount to a norm of customary international law.[193]

This uncertainty has not prevented states from prosecuting war crimes committed in non-international armed conflict on the basis of universal jurisdiction. Most famously, Belgium's 1993 law allowed Belgian courts to prosecute violations of the law of non-international armed conflict on the basis of universal jurisdiction.[194] In the *Butare four* case, relating to the armed conflict and genocide in Rwanda, charges were brought in Belgium against the defendants for violations of common Article 3 and Additional Protocol II.[195] Numerous other cases have been brought pursuant to the 1993 law.[196] However, Belgium subsequently amended its legislation to require a more tangible jurisdictional link between Belgium and the offence in question.[197]

Belgium was not the only state to utilize universal jurisdiction as the basis on which to prosecute violations of the law of non-international armed conflict. The cases of *Knezević* and *X and Y* in the Netherlands, and *Niyonteze* and *Gabrez* in Switzerland, which have already been discussed,[198] also proceeded on the basis of universal jurisdiction. In Denmark, in the case of *Refik Sarić*, the Eastern Division of the High Court found various provisions of the Third and Fourth Geneva Conventions to have been violated in respect of treatment meted out to detainees held at a camp in Bosnia in 1993.[199] The court had jurisdiction over the offences pursuant to the Danish Penal Code, which provided for universal jurisdiction over *inter alia* the grave breaches provisions of the Geneva Conventions. Accordingly, it may be assumed that the court found the conflict to be an international one.[200] However, the view has been expressed that the grave breaches provisions were applied irrespective of the nature of

---

[190] Institut de Droit International, 'Universal Criminal Jurisdiction with regard to the Crime of Genocide, Crimes against Humanity and War Crimes' (Krakow, 2005) Article 3(a).
[191] Customary International Humanitarian Law, Rule 157; AU-EU Technical Ad hoc Expert Group on the Principle of Universal Jurisdiction, 15 April 2009, para 9.
[192] *Case Concerning the Arrest Warrant of 11 April 2000 (Democratic Republic of the Congo v Belgium)* [2002] ICJ Rep 3, Joint Separate Opinion of Judges Higgins, Kooijmans and Buergenthal, 76, para 45.
[193] La Haye, above note 12, 255. See generally, 227–56.
[194] Act concerning the punishment of grave breaches of the Geneva Conventions of 12 August 1949 and their Additional Protocols I and II of 18 June 1977, 16 June 1993.
[195] Assize Court of Brussels, 8 June 2001, on which see L Reydams, 'Belgium's First Application of Universal Jurisdiction: the *Butare Four* Case' (2003) 1 *JICJ* 428.
[196] See L Reydams, *Universal Jurisdiction* (Oxford University Press, 2003) 109–18; D Vandermeersch, 'Prosecuting International Crimes in Belgium' (2005) 3 *JICJ* 400, 403–8.
[197] *Loi relative aux violations grave du droit humanitaire*, 5 August 2003. See L Reydams, 'Belgium Reneges on Universality: The 5 August 2003 Act on Grave Breaches of International Humanitarian Law' (2003) 1 *JICJ* 679.
[198] Above, 493.
[199] Judgment of 22 November 1994, summarized in (1998) 1 *YIHL* 431. See also Judgment of the Supreme Court, 15 August 1995.
[200] La Haye, above note 12, 247; Boelaert-Suominen, 'Grave Breaches, Universal Jurisdiction and Internal Armed Conflict: Is Customary Law Moving Towards a Uniform Enforcement Mechanism for All Armed Conflicts?' (2000) 5 *JCSL* 63, 95–6; F Harhoff, 'Sarić', in A Cassese et al (eds), *The Oxford Companion to International Criminal Justice* (Oxford University Press, 2009) 901.

the armed conflict.[201] Ultimately, as the court did not establish the character of the conflict, the *Sarić* case remains inconclusive. In France, in the cases of *Javor* and *Munyeshyaka*, the Cour de Cassation confirmed that French courts may exercise jurisdiction in respect of war crimes committed in the former Yugoslavia and Rwanda, pursuant to French legislation implementing Security Council Resolution 827 (on the ICTY) and Security Council Resolution 955 (on the ICTR), provided the accused were present in France.[202] The facts of *Munyeshyaka* did not concern war crimes; however, the principle derived from the judgment can be extended to war crimes. Likewise, the facts of *Javor* do not necessarily assume a non-international armed conflict; however, again, the principle derived from the judgment can be extended to war crimes in the armed conflicts in the former Yugoslavia. In the absence of domestic legislation incorporating the universal jurisdiction provisions of the Geneva Conventions, French courts would have considerably more difficulty establishing jurisdiction over war crimes committed in non-international armed conflicts other than those of the former Yugoslavia and Rwanda. Many more states also have legislation in place through which violations of international humanitarian law committed in non-international armed conflict may be prosecuted on the basis of universal jurisdiction.[203]

Instances of prosecution of war crimes committed in non-international armed conflict in states other than the parent state are still relatively few. In many ways, this is not surprising given that, historically, states have had little interest in prosecuting crimes that do not affect them or their citizens directly.[204] The prosecutions that do exist tend to relate to the armed conflicts in the former Yugoslavia and Rwanda.[205] It remains to be seen to what extent the establishment of the ICC will influence prosecutions in unaffected states, especially given that a number of states' legislation implementing the Rome Statute into domestic law provide for universal jurisdiction.[206]

5. Human rights courts

Criminal prosecution is the primary judicial means by which to enforce international humanitarian law. However, judicial enforcement is not limited to criminal prosecution alone. Human rights courts have enforced international humanitarian law applicable in non-international armed conflict as well as human rights law applicable in such conflicts, with individuals, or more exceptionally states, instituting proceedings before a regional human rights court. The applicability of human rights law to situations of

---

[201] *Tadić* Decision on Interlocutory Appeal on Jurisdiction, above note 18, para 83; A McDonald, 'The Year in Review' (1998) 1 *YIHL* 113, 122–3.

[202] See *In re Javor*, Cour de Cassation, 26 March 1996, reproduced and translated in Sassòli and Bouvier, above note 165, 2060; *Munyeshyaka*, Cour de Cassation, 6 January 1998. See B Stern (1999) 93 *AJIL* 525; A Cassese, 'Javor and Others', in A Cassese et al (eds), *The Oxford Companion to International Criminal Justice* (Oxford University Press, 2009) 732; A Cassese, 'Munyeshyaka', in ibid, 828.

[203] See generally T Graditzky, 'Individual Criminal Responsibility for Violations of International Humanitarian Law Committed in Non-International Armed Conflicts' (1998) 38 *IRRC* 29; Boelaert-Suominen, above note 200, 89–93; La Haye, above note 12, 150–60; *Customary International Humanitarian Law, Volume II: Practice*, above note 116, 3894–912.

[204] RR Baxter, 'The Municipal and International Law Basis of Jurisdiction over War Crimes' (1951) 28 *BYIL* 382, 392.

[205] Sassòli, Humanitarian law, above note 103, 114.

[206] For example, International Crimes and International Criminal Court Act 2000, section 8(1)(c) (New Zealand); International Crimes Act 2003, section 2(1)(a) (Netherlands). See generally La Haye, above note 12, 230–5.

armed conflict is useful as much for its enforcement mechanisms as for its substantive content.²⁰⁷ Indeed, on one view, '[t]he most important result of the convergence of the two systems of protection' are the enforcement possibilities afforded by human rights law.²⁰⁸

5.1 Enforcement of international humanitarian law

If human rights law is being applied with the primary aim of utilizing its enforcement mechanisms, an alternative approach to applying the substantive law of human rights would be to bypass the applicable law and use its enforcement mechanisms to monitor not human rights law but humanitarian law. For a while, the Inter-American Commission on Human Rights did precisely this, applying international humanitarian law directly to several matters before it. In a series of cases, the Commission explicitly condemned violations of international humanitarian law, for example holding that Colombia had committed a 'flagrant violation of common Article 3',²⁰⁹ that Peru 'violated common Article 3',²¹⁰ and that El Salvador 'violated common Article 3 . . . as well as Article 4 of [Additional] Protocol II'.²¹¹ However, in other cases, the Commission was less explicit, indeed rather ambiguous, holding that Colombia 'violated the right to life enshrined in Article 4 of the American Convention as well as the *standards* of common Article 3',²¹² and that El Salvador 'violated the right to life enshrined in Article 4 of the American Convention, together with the *principles* recognized in common Article 3'.²¹³

The Commission squarely addressed its competence 'to apply directly' international humanitarian law.²¹⁴ However, these arguments have been persuasively critiqued,²¹⁵ and can be set out in brief. The Commission noted that the American Convention and the Geneva Conventions 'share a common nucleus . . . and a common purpose' and

---

²⁰⁷ On the content, see above, 87–93. See also T Meron, 'The Humanization of Humanitarian Law' (2000) 94 *AJIL* 239, 247; H-J Heintze, 'The European Court of Human Rights and the Implementation of Human Rights Standards during Armed Conflicts' (2002) 45 *GYIL* 60, 60.

²⁰⁸ AH Robertson, 'Humanitarian Law and Human Rights', in C Swinarski (ed), *Studies and Essays on International Humanitarian Law and Red Cross Principles in Honour of Jean Pictet* (ICRC, 1984) 793, 800 (emphasis added). See also the discussion in NK Modirzadeh, 'The Dark Sides of Convergence: A Pro-Civilian Critique of the Extraterritorial Application of Human Rights Law in Armed Conflict' (2010) 86 *International Law Studies* 350, 389–93.

²⁰⁹ *Avilan et al v Colombia*, Case 11.142, Report No 26/97, 30 September 1997, OEA/Ser.L/V/II.98, doc.6 rev, 13 April 1998, para 202.

²¹⁰ *Hugo Bustios Saavedra v Peru*, Case 10.548, Report No 38/97, 16 October 1997, OEA/Ser.L/V/II.98, doc.6 rev, 13 April 1998, para 88.

²¹¹ *Lucio Parada Cea et al v El Salvador*, Case 10.480, Report No 1/99, 27 January 1999, para 82.

²¹² *Colombia v Jose Alexis Fuentes Guerrero et al*, Case 11.519, Report No 61/99, OEA/Ser.L/V/II.95, Doc.7 rev 446, 1998, para 43 (emphasis added).

²¹³ *Ignacio Ellacuria et al v El Salvador*, Case 10.488, Report No 136/99, 22 December 1999, para 237 (emphasis added). See also *Monsignor Oscar Arnulfo Romero y Galdamez v El Salvador*, Case 11.481, Report No 37/00, 13 April 2000, para 72.

²¹⁴ *Juan Carlos Abella v Argentina*, Case 11.137, OEA/Ser.L/V/II.98, doc.6 rev, 13 April 1998, para 157.

²¹⁵ See L Zegveld, 'The Inter-American Commission on Human Rights and International Humanitarian Law: A Comment on the Tablada Case' (1998) 38 *IRRC* 505; L Moir, 'Law and the Inter-American Human Rights System' (2003) 25 *HRQ* 182; C Byron, 'A Blurring of the Boundaries: The Application of International Humanitarian Law by Human Rights Bodies' (2006–7) 47 *Virginia Journal of International Law* 839; EJ Buis, 'The Implementation of International Humanitarian Law by Human Rights Courts: The Example of the Inter-American Human Rights System', in R Arnold and N Quenivet (eds), *International Humanitarian Law and Human Rights Law* (Martinus Nijhoff, 2008) 269.

that the rules of common Article 3 are 'essentially pure' human rights law.[216] However, the fact that certain provisions may be common to the various instruments or are of a similar nature is immaterial to the competence of the Commission. The Commission also noted that it may not be able to resolve allegations as to violations of the right to life in situations of armed conflict 'because the American Convention contains no rules that either define or distinguish civilians from combatants' and that 'the Commission must necessarily look to and apply definitional standards and relevant rules of humanitarian law as sources of authoritative guidance'.[217] This is an important point and the relevant rule of international human rights law may have to be interpreted by reference to international humanitarian law. However, it does not follow that the Commission would then be enforcing international humanitarian law. Rather, it would have to interpret and apply the relevant rule of the American Convention. The Commission also considered that the American Convention itself required international humanitarian law to be applied in appropriate situations.[218] However, here too the Commission overstated its case. The justifications provided by the Commission thus proved rather weak.

The direct enforcement of international humanitarian law on the part of human rights courts has been considered to raise issues of lack of expertise and the overstepping of mandates.[219] The former objection does not hold much weight, for although the two bodies of law are different from one another, lack of expertise is not an inherent difficulty—expertise may be gained and *amicus curiae* briefs may be entertained. The latter objection is, however, important and for that reason, the Inter-American Court of Human Rights held that neither it nor the Inter-American Commission had the competence to apply international humanitarian law directly.[220] Following that holding, the Commission altered its position, referring to violations of the American Convention and not of international humanitarian law.[221] Thus, both the Court and the Commission are limited to using international humanitarian law to interpret the American Convention on Human Rights.[222] On this basis, the Inter-American Court has interpreted the content of the American Convention provision on freedom of movement and residence by reference to the Additional Protocol II provisions on displacement as well as the Guiding Principles on Internal Displacement.[223] Similarly, the Court used the Additional Protocol II provisions on the protection of the civilian population to interpret Article 31 of the American Convention on the recognition of other rights.[224] Rather curiously, the Court has also suggested that it is entitled to 'observe' that acts that violate the American Convention 'also violate other

---

[216] *Abella*, above note 214, para 158.
[217] Ibid, para 161. See also *Guerrero*, above note 212, para 35 fn 24.
[218] *Abella*, above note 214, paras 164–5, 168–70.
[219] 'Response of the United States to Request for Precautionary Measures—Detainees in Guantanamo Bay, Cuba' (2002) 41 *ILM* 1015, 1019. See also Meron, Humanization, above note 207, 247; Byron, above note 215, 882.
[220] *Las Palmeras v Colombia*, Preliminary Objections, Ser C No 67, 4 February 2000, paras 32–4.
[221] See eg *Riofrio Massacre (Colombia)*, Case 11.654, Report No 62/01, 6 April 2001, paras 53–8.
[222] *Bámaca-Velásquez v Guatemala*, Merits, Ser C No 70, 25 November 2000, para 209; *Las Palmeras v Colombia*, Preliminary Objections, Judgment of 4 February 2000, Separate Opinion of Judge AA Cancado Trindade, para 3; *Serrano-Cruz Sisters v El Salvador*, Preliminary Objections, Judgment of 23 November 2004, paras 119; *Mapiripan Massacre v Colombia*, Merits, Reparations and Costs, Judgment of 15 September 2005, paras 114–15; *Ituango Massacres v Colombia*, Preliminary Objections, Merits, Reparations and Costs, Judgment of 1 July 2006, para 179.
[223] *Mapiripan Massacre*, para 171; *Ituango Massacres*, paras 208–9.
[224] *Ituango Massacres*, paras 180–2.

international instruments for the protection of the individual, such as the 1949 Geneva Conventions and, in particular, common Article 3'.[225] If this is indeed the case, it is not far removed from the earlier position adopted by the Commission, although few consequences could follow from the 'observation'.

The African Commission has also directly applied, and enforced, international humanitarian law. The Commission held that Articles 60 and 61 of the African Charter on Human and Peoples' Rights, with its reference to drawing inspiration from international law instruments and using such instruments to determine principles of law, allowed it to take the Geneva Conventions and Additional Protocols 'into consideration in the determination of the case'.[226] This it is certainly entitled to do. However, the Commission went on to use international humanitarian law not only to find a violation of the Charter, but also to find a violation of international humanitarian law itself.[227] Whether it is entitled to do so is rather less clear. The situation is different insofar as the African Court on Human and Peoples' Rights is concerned. That Court is mandated to enforce not only the African Charter on Human and Peoples' Rights but any human rights instrument that binds the relevant state,[228] and this would include the instruments of international humanitarian law. Ultimately, the competence of the relevant human rights body is determined by its constituent instrument and many such constituent instruments limit enforcement to the relevant regional human rights treaty.

The more orthodox position of interpreting human rights law by reference to international humanitarian law would go a long way towards the enforcement of the latter body. Although violations of international humanitarian law would not be found, the very fact that that body of law was being used to identify and interpret human rights law would come close to its enforcement. The considerable merits of this approach should not be overlooked.

5.2 Enforcement of human rights law

An alternative approach, which has been adopted by a different regional human rights court, has been to regulate non-international armed conflict directly through international human rights law. As noted in Chapter 3, this human rights law of non-international armed conflict holds that non-international armed conflict should be regulated by human rights law rather than international humanitarian law.[229] The two *Isayeva* judgments of the European Court of Human Rights have been cited in support of this notion.[230]

In its early years, the European Court of Human Rights had little occasion on which to utilize international humanitarian law, as it rarely heard cases involving armed conflicts. On the occasions that the Court could have used international humanitarian law, it chose not to do so, aside from the occasional borrowing of language.[231] For example, in *Ergi*, the Court noted that state responsibility may arise when state agents 'fail to take all feasible precautions in the choice of means and methods of a security

---

[225] *Bamaca-Velasquez*, paras 208–9.
[226] Communication 227/1999, DRC/Burundi, Rwanda, Uganda, 20th Report of the African Commission on Human and People's Rights, EX.CL/279(IX), paras 70, 78.
[227] Ibid, paras 79–87.
[228] Statute of the African Court of Justice and Human Rights, Article 28.
[229] See above, 93–4.
[230] Ibid.
[231] See A Reidy, 'The Approach of the European Commission and Court of Human Rights to International Humanitarian Law' (1998) 38 *IRRC* 513; Heintze, above note 207.

operation mounted against an opposing group with a view to avoiding and, in any event, to minimising, incidental loss of civilian life'.[232] Aside from the substitution of the phrase 'security operation mounted against an opposing group' for the word 'attack', the language is taken from Additional Protocol I.[233] However, this deliberate substitution is important, as it suggests that the Court was of the view that the situation was a security operation rather than an armed conflict, taking it outside the scope of international humanitarian law.[234] In requiring that precautions have to be taken in the context of security operations, the Court extends the humanitarian law requirement to a situation of law enforcement.

The non-application of international humanitarian law is arguably taken further in the *Isayeva* cases. In those judgments, the Court seems to suggest the existence of a non-international armed conflict, referring to measures being needed 'to suppress the illegal armed insurgency'[235] and referring to 'the conflict in Chechnya at the relevant time'.[236] However, the recognition of an armed conflict is not entirely clear given that, at other times, the Court refers to the armed group's 'active resistance to the law-enforcement bodies'[237] and 'the degree of caution expected from a law-enforcement body in a democratic society'.[238] Still, the literature accepts that the Court viewed the situation as a non-international armed conflict, and separate opinions in other cases suggest likewise.[239] Assuming that to be the case, the Court opts for regulation of non-international armed conflict through human rights law.

This human rights law of non-international armed conflict gives rise to certain difficulties. The principal difficulty arises at the level of the rules themselves, in particular in situations in which the human rights law norm differs from the equivalent humanitarian law norm. This was discussed in Chapter 3.[240] Another difficulty relates to whether, and if so, in which situations human rights obligations attach to non-state armed groups, a question also discussed in Chapter 3.[241] A related issue, and one that concerns the enforcement of the law by human rights courts, is that of jurisdiction. The jurisdiction of human rights courts is limited to states alone. This means that the courts will be able to consider allegations made only against the state party to the conflict. This in turn could lead to a perception of bias as it is necessarily one-sided.[242] In this regard, the Organization of American States has called upon the Inter-American Commission to address the issue of human rights violations by armed groups.[243] For its part, the Inter-American Commission on Human Rights had previously considered the issue, the statement of which is worth quoting in large part:

[I]f the Commission, in violation of its mandate, were to agree to process a denunciation involving some alleged acts of terrorism, in doing so it would implicitly place terrorist organizations on an equal footing with government[s], as the Commission would have to transmit the

---

[232] *Ergi v Turkey*, Judgment of 28 July 1998, para 79.
[233] Article 57(2)(a)(ii). See Byron, above note 215, 853 fn 61.
[234] Cf G Gaggioli and R Kolb, 'A Right to Life in Armed Conflicts? The Contribution of the European Court of Human Rights' (2007) 37 *Israel Yearbook on Human Rights* 115, 141.
[235] *Isayeva et al v Russia*, Judgment of 24 February 2005, para 178.
[236] Ibid, para 181.
[237] *Isayeva v Russia*, Judgment of 24 February 2005, para 180.
[238] Ibid, para 191.
[239] See above, 93–4.
[240] See above, 89–90.
[241] See above, 95–8.
[242] K Watkin, 'Controlling the Use of Force: A Role for Human Rights Norms in Contemporary Armed Conflict' (2004) 98 *AJIL* 1, 30; Byron, above note 215, 883.
[243] OAS General Assembly Resolution AG/Res 1043 (XX-0/90).

denunciation to the subversive organization which allegedly is responsible for the act and request that it make such observations as it deems appropriate. Undoubtedly, such organizations would be very pleased to be dealt with as if they were government[s]. But, what government in the hemisphere could tolerate an implicit recognition of quasi-governmental status for an organization of this kind?[244]

Enforcement of the law by human rights bodies is another area in which non-state armed groups tend to be overlooked.

6. Non-enforcement: amnesties

A common alternative to the prosecution of war crimes committed in non-international armed conflicts has been that of amnesty. The idea of an amnesty being declared at the conclusion of a non-international armed conflict is not a new one. Early examples include the amnesty granted by President Lincoln in 1863 during the US civil war, the 1902 amnesty granted by President Roosevelt following the conclusion of the American-Philippine war, and the amnesty contained in the 1902 Peace Treaty that concluded the Boer war.[245] Amnesties are wide-ranging.[246] Some are sweeping, while others exclude war crimes from their purview.[247] Still others are general but exclude specific acts that may be of particular relevance to the conflict in question.[248] Some amnesties are reciprocal, applying to all parties involved in the armed conflict,[249] while others are limited to the party that granted the amnesty,[250] or to the opposing side.[251] Others are limited to particular actors without being party-specific,[252] while still others are broadly inclusive but contain specific exclusions.[253] Some amnesties are unconditional; others require that certain actions be undertaken by the beneficiary of the obligation, such as renunciation of violence or disarmament and demobilization.[254]

---

[244] Inter-American Commission on Human Rights, Report on the Situation of Human Rights in the Republic of Colombia, OEA/Ser.L/V/II.53 doc.22, 30 June 1981, Introduction. See also Inter-American Commission on Human Rights, Annual Report of the Inter-American Commission on Human Rights 1990–1991, OEA/Ser.L/V/II.79.rev.1 Doc.12, 22 February 1991, Chapter V, Part 2.
[245] Proclamation of Amnesty and Reconstruction, 8 December 1863; Proclamation of Amnesty, 4 July 1902; Peace Treaty of Vereeniging, 31 May 1902.
[246] See generally, A O'Shea, *Amnesty for Crime in International Law and Practice* (Kluwer, 2002); L Mallinder, *Amnesty, Human Rights and Political Transitions* (Hart, 2008); M Freeman, *Necessary Evils: Amnesties and the Search for Justice* (Cambridge University Press, 2009).
[247] Examples of the latter include: Quadripartite Agreement on Voluntary Return of Refugees and Displaced Persons, 4 April 1994, Article 3(c) (Georgia); Linas-Marcoussis Agreement, 23 January 2003, Annex (Ivory Coast), as implemented by Loi portant amnistie, 6 August 2003, Article 4; Amnesty Law, 6 May 2009, Articles 2 and 3 (DRC).
[248] Ley 37 de 1981 por la cual se declara una amnistía condicional, 23 March 1981, Article 1 (Colombia, which excludes *inter alia* the poisoning of water sources); Ordonnance No 06-01 du 28 Moharram 1427 correspondant au 27 Février 2006 portant mise en oeuvre de la Chartre pour la paix et la réconciliation nationale, Article 10 (Algeria, which excludes collective massacres, rape, use of explosives in public places).
[249] Law on Amnesty to the Participants of the Political and Military Confrontation in the Republic of Tajikistan, July 1997; Cotonou Accord, 25 July 1993, Section G, Article 19 (Liberia); Tripoli Agreement, 23 December 1976, Article 3(12) (Philippines).
[250] Décret No 62–328, 22 Mars 1962 portant amnistie de faits commis dans le cadre des opérations de maintien de l'ordre dirigées contre l'insurrection algérienne (France/Algeria).
[251] Amnesty Act 2000, section 3 (Uganda); Memorandum of Understanding between the Government of the Republic of Indonesia and the Free Aceh Movement, 15 August 2005, Article 3, as implemented by Presidential Decree No 22/2005.
[252] Townsville Peace Agreement, 15 October 2000, Part 2, Article 3 (Solomon Islands).
[253] Linas-Marcoussis Agreement, 23 January 2003 (Ivory Coast) (certain soldiers).
[254] Amnesty Act 2000 section 4, (Uganda).

Some amnesties are limited by temporal or geographical scope of application.[255] Some serve to prohibit criminal prosecutions but not civil damages;[256] others to prohibit even investigations;[257] still others extending to the vacation of existing sentences.[258] Of primary concern to this book are those amnesties that are granted to fighters for taking part in hostilities, as akin to combatant immunity,[259] and those that purport to cover war crimes.

Certain types of amnesties are not problematic. They may be granted at the end of a conflict for good reason. Thus, UN Secretary-General Kofi Annan noted in 2000 that 'amnesty is an accepted legal concept and a gesture of peace and reconciliation at the end of a civil war or an internal armed conflict' and that '[c]arefully crafted amnesties can help in the return and reintegration of [displaced civilians and fighters] and should be encouraged'.[260] Amnesties may also prevent further violence. For example, the Sierra Leone Truth and Reconciliation Commission noted in its report that '[d]isallowing amnesty in all cases would be to deny the reality of violent conflict and the urgent need to bring such strife and suffering to an end'.[261]

More difficult are the amnesties that purport to extend to war crimes. There exists little by way of conventional law on the legality of such amnesties. The UN Principles on extra-legal executions prohibit the granting of 'blanket immunity from prosecution ... to any person allegedly involved in extra-legal, arbitrary or summary executions'.[262] The UN Declaration on Enforced Disappearances prohibits 'any special amnesty law or similar measures that might have the effect of exempting' persons 'who have or are alleged to have committed' disappearances 'from any criminal proceedings or sanction'.[263] However, both instruments are of a soft-law nature. When a clause on amnesties has been suggested for inclusion during treaty drafting processes, the issue has proven contentious. For example, it has been reported that, when the issue was raised during the drafting of the Disappearances Convention, it nearly led to the breakdown of negotiations,[264] and when the issue was raised during the drafting of the Rome Statute, it led to conflicting views.[265]

One treaty that does explicitly mention amnesties is Additional Protocol II, Article 6(5) of which provides that, '[a]t the end of hostilities, the authorities in power shall endeavour to grant the broadest possible amnesty to persons who have participated in the armed conflict, or those deprived of their liberty for reasons related to the armed

---

[255] Tripoli Agreement (GRP/MNLF), 23 December 1976; Amnesty Law, 6 May 2009, Article 1 (DRC [limited to North and South Kivu]).
[256] Amnesty Law, 6 May 2009, Article 4 (DRC).
[257] Ley de Amnistía, 22 January 1994, Article 4 (Mexico).
[258] General Amnesty Law for the Consolidation of the Peace, Decree No 486, 20 March 1993, Article 4 (El Salvador).
[259] See below, 514–20.
[260] See respectively, Report of the Secretary-General on the Establishment of a Special Court for Sierra Leone, S/2000/915, 4 October 2000, para 22; The Rule of Law and Transitional Justice in Conflict and Post-Conflict Societies: Report of the Secretary-General, S/2004/616, 23 August 2004, para 32. In both reports, the Secretary-General notes the exception for amnesties in the cases of genocide, crimes against humanity, and war crimes.
[261] Witness to Truth: Report of the Sierra Leone Truth and Reconciliation Commission, Volume 3B, Chapter 6, para 11.
[262] Principles on the Effective Prevention and Investigation of Extra-Legal, Arbitrary and Summary Executions, E/1989/89 (1989), Article 19.
[263] Declaration on the Protection of All Persons from Enforced Disappearances, Article 18(1), GA Res 47/133, 18 December 1992.
[264] Freeman, above note 246, 33.
[265] D Robinson, 'Serving the Interests of Justice: Amnesties, Truth Commissions and the International Criminal Court' (2003) 14 *EJIL* 481, 483.

conflict, whether they are interned or detained'. This provision has been used by a number of domestic courts to uphold the legality of amnesties, including amnesties for war crimes. For example, in the *AZAPO* case, the South African Constitutional Court noted that:

> there is no obligation on the part of a contracting state to ensure the prosecution of those who might have performed acts of violence or other acts which would ordinarily be characterised as serious invasions of human rights. On the contrary, article 6(5) of Protocol II to the Geneva Conventions of 1949 provides that '[a]t the end of hostilities, the authorities in power shall endeavour to grant the broadest possible amnesty to persons who participated in the armed conflict, or those deprived of their liberty for reasons related to the armed conflict, whether they are interned or detained.'
>
> The need for this distinction is obvious. It is one thing to allow the officers of a hostile power which has invaded a foreign state to remain unpunished for gross violations of human rights perpetrated against others during the course of such conflict. It is another thing to compel such punishment in circumstances where such violations have substantially occurred in consequence of conflict between different formations within the same state.[266]

The provision has also been stressed in the literature as supportive of amnesties, even for war crimes.[267]

However, the reference to 'the broadest possible amnesty' in Article 6(5) of Additional Protocol II has been misunderstood and it does not purport to include violations of international humanitarian law. The provision cannot be read in isolation but needs to be placed in context. During the 1971 Conference of Government Experts, a proposal was made to include a provision on a general amnesty at the end of hostilities in order that 'normal life ... be resumed as soon as possible' but it was expressly noted that such a provision was 'not at all intended to eliminate penal prosecution of war criminals'.[268] Accordingly, a provision was included in the draft Protocol that '[a]t the end of hostilities, the authorities in power shall endeavour to grant amnesty to as many as possible of those who have participated in the armed conflict, in particular those whose liberty has been restricted for reasons in relation to the armed conflict, whether they are interned or detained'.[269] A variation of this proposal found its way into the final Protocol.

Both the drafting history of the proposal and the construction of the initial language indicate that the provision was drawn up in respect of persons 'merely' taking a part in the armed conflict. The amnesty provision was designed to mitigate the effects of the lack of combatant immunity in non-international armed conflicts.[270] The winning party is thus encouraged not to try individuals for taking part in the hostilities. While

---

[266] *Azanian Peoples Organization (AZAPO) and Others v President of the Republic of South Africa and Others*, CCT 17/96, 25 July 1996, paras 30 and 31. While relying on the provision, the Court held it doubtful that international humanitarian law was applicable to the events in question: para 29.

[267] See eg K Gallagher, 'No Justice, No Peace: The Legalities and Realities of Amnesty in Sierra Leone' (2000–1) 23 *Thomas Jefferson Law Review* 149, 176–8; Mallinder, above note 246, 126 and 227.

[268] Conference of Government Experts on the Reaffirmation and Development of International Humanitarian Law Applicable in Armed Conflicts (1971) Part V, 59–60.

[269] Draft Article 10(6). See ICRC, *Draft Additional Protocols to the Geneva Conventions of August 12, 1949: Commentary* (1973) 141. See also *Official Records of the Diplomatic Conference on the Reaffirmation and Development of International Humanitarian Law Applicable in Armed Conflicts, Geneva (1974–1977)* (Federal Political Department, 1978) Vol I, Part 3, 36.

[270] Customary International Humanitarian Law, Rule 159. See also *Constitutional Conformity of Protocol II*, C-225/95, para 42, reproduced and translated in Sassòli, Bouvier, and Quintin, above note 139, 2240.

the element of reconciliation is an important one,²⁷¹ the combatant immunity aspect should not be lost, for it is that which gives an indication as to the intended scope of the provision. Thus, while it is true that 'the article places no explicit limits on the right to amnesty but instead encourages one form of its usage',²⁷² the point should not be taken to extremes. In this light, the Inter-American Commission on Human Rights has noted that the provision 'cannot be interpreted in the sense of supporting amnesty for violations of humanitarian law'.²⁷³ Indeed, as early as the US civil war, amnesties were viewed as not extending to violations of the laws and customs of war. The Judge Advocate in the *Wirz* trial argued on the scope of the relevant amnesty and pardon that:

[t]he most that could, with any plausibility, be claimed is that all acts of war committed by this prisoner as a belligerent, and coming within the usages of civilized warfare, may be considered as pardoned, but it cannot be admitted for one moment that anything short of a special pardon by the President of the United States, setting forth precisely the offences pardoned, can give exemption from trial for acts in violation of the laws and customs of civilized warfare, especially when they involve crimes so enormous and atrocious as those charged upon the prisoner here arraigned.²⁷⁴

Likewise, the amnesty contained in the 1902 Peace Treaty that concluded the Boer war provided:

No proceedings, civil or criminal, will be taken against any of the burghers so surrendering or so returning for any Acts in connection with the prosecution of the War. The benefit of this Clause will not extend to certain Acts contrary to the usage[s] of War which have been notified by the Commander in Chief to the Boer Generals, and which shall be tried by Court Martial immediately after the close of hostilities.²⁷⁵

Along similar lines, following the conclusion of the armed conflict in the plebiscite of Upper Silesia in 1921, the Inter-Allied Commission governing the territory 'published a decree ... granting a general amnesty for all participants of the uprising excluding only those who committed common crimes'.²⁷⁶

Given the scope of Article 6(5) of Additional Protocol II and the lack of other conventional law on point, it becomes necessary to consider whether the prohibition on amnesties for war crimes has passed into customary international law. UN Secretary-General Kofi Annan, for example, has spoken of the 'illegality' in international law of amnesties for international crimes,²⁷⁷ presumably as a matter of customary international law. A similar view was taken by Justice Robertson of the SCSL in *Kondewa*. In his view, customary international law prohibited amnesties for 'crimes against humanity (genocide and widespread torture) and the worst war crimes (namely those in common Article 3 of the Geneva Conventions)'.²⁷⁸ The Customary International

---

²⁷¹ See Y Sandoz, C Swinarski, and B Zimmermann (eds), *Commentary on the Additional Protocols of 8 June 1977 to the Geneva Conventions of 12 August 1949* (ICRC, 1987) 1402.
²⁷² Freeman, above note 246, 56.
²⁷³ *Lucio Parada Cea*, above note 211, para 116.
²⁷⁴ *Wirz*, above note 105, 15.
²⁷⁵ Peace Treaty of Vereeniging, 31 May 1902.
²⁷⁶ Report No 13 from ICRC Delegate Cuénod to the ICRC in Geneva, 3 July 1921, ICRC Archives CR 22-5/114. The original reads: 'a fait afficher hier un décret accordant une amnistie générale pour tous les participants de l'insurrection n'exceptant que ceux ayant commis des crimes de droit commun.'
²⁷⁷ Report of the Secretary-General on the Establishment of a Special Court for Sierra Leone, S/2000/915, 4 October 2000, para 24.
²⁷⁸ *Prosecutor v Kondewa*, SCSL-2004-14-AR72(E), Decision on Lack of Jurisdiction/Abuse of process: Amnesty Provided by the Lomé Accord, Separate Opinion of Justice Robertson, para 51.

Humanitarian Law study likewise provides: '[a]t the end of hostilities, the authorities in power must endeavour to grant the broadest possible amnesty to persons who have participated in a non-international armed conflict, or those deprived of their liberty for reasons related to the armed conflict, with the exception of persons suspected of, accused of or sentenced for war crimes.'[279] However, these claims are somewhat overstated. The SCSL Appeals Chamber held in 2004 that a norm to the effect that governments cannot grant amnesties for international crimes may be in the process of crystallization but had not yet crystallized.[280] At the time of writing, the position had not moved on from that set out by the Appeals Chamber. UN practice on point certainly has changed. In years gone by, the UN would encourage amnesties in order to seek to put an end to armed conflicts,[281] and agreements containing amnesty provisions would be welcomed by the General Assembly.[282] This should be contrasted with more recent UN practice, which maintains that amnesties cannot be granted for international crimes.[283] However, this change in position has not led to a clear trend at the state level. Studies have shown that, although in recent years, an increasing number of amnesties have excluded crimes under international law from their scope, a significant number of amnesties make no such exclusion. According to one such study, during the period between July 1999 and December 2007, 34 amnesty laws excluded international crimes or a subset thereof, while 28 did not.[284] Furthermore, states not involved in the relevant armed conflict are sometimes instrumental in the conclusion of amnesties, even those that do not contain exceptions for international crimes, suggesting that their *opinio juris* is not such as to evidence a customary prohibition.[285] There is, however, a growing trend towards the conclusion of amnesties that do not cover international crimes and this in itself is an important step forward.

7. Conclusion

Judicial enforcement of the law of non-international armed conflict takes different forms. War crimes may be, and have been, enforced at the international level, first with the work of the ad hoc international criminal tribunals and later with the creation of the ICC. War crimes may also be enforced at the domestic level. Indeed, complementarity with domestic courts is the basis on which the ICC operates. Both the international criminal enforcement of the law and the national criminal enforcement of the law are largely constructs of the period starting from the mid-1990s. This was due to the previously existing uncertainty as to the concept of war crimes in non-international armed conflict.

---

[279] Customary International Humanitarian Law, Rule 159.
[280] *Prosecutor v Kallon and Kamara*, SCSL-2004-15-AR72(E), Decision on Challenge to Jurisdiction: Lomé Accord Amnesty, 13 March 2004, para 82. See also A Cassese, *International Criminal Law* (Oxford University Press, 2003) 315.
[281] OHCHR, *Rule of Law Tools for Post-Conflict States: Amnesties* (UN, 2009) 2.
[282] See E Crawford, *The Treatment of Combatants and Insurgents under the Law of Armed Conflict* (Oxford University Press, 2010) 108.
[283] See eg Report of the Secretary-General on the Establishment of a Special Court for Sierra Leone, S/2000/915, 4 October 2000, para 22; The Rule of Law and Transitional Justice in Conflict and Post-Conflict Societies: Report of the Secretary-General, S/2004/616, 23 August 2004, para 10.
[284] Mallinder, above note 246, 122.
[285] For example in his separate opinion in *Kondewa*, Justice Robertson refers to the offer of amnesty made by the US and UK to Saddam Hussein: above note 278, para 30.

Criminal prosecution of war crimes is not the sole form of judicial enforcement. Human rights law has also played an important role, with the regional human rights courts enforcing the law. The law that they have enforced has been of different sorts. For a while, the Inter-American Commission of Human Rights enforced international humanitarian law; the European Court of Human Rights has enforced human rights law in situations of non-international armed conflict. Although the enforcement of the law of non-international armed conflict by human rights bodies is important, the difficulties are also important, whether they relate to questions of mandate or to applicable law. The specificities of the law of non-international armed conflict, and the involvement of non-state armed groups therein, again feature, with human rights mechanisms having jurisdiction over states but not non-state armed groups.

PART III
MOVING FORWARD

12
Developments Needed in the Law

1. Introduction

The law of non-international armed conflict has developed considerably since the mid-1990s. The methodology by which the law is created and interpreted has changed over time, and the substantive content of the law as it exists today is vastly different from that which existed previously.[1] The mechanisms of implementation and enforcement of the law have also started to change.[2] Despite this immense growth of law in a very short space of time, a number of gaps continue to exist in two principal areas, namely the substantive norms and the mechanisms of implementation and enforcement. The methodology by which the law is created is also open to revision. These gaps and this methodological concern are the focus of this chapter, which aims to provide concrete and realistic proposals for moving forward.

2. Substantive norms

In the realm of the substantive law, three particular areas are in need of further consideration. These are notions of combatant immunity and prisoners of war; protection of the natural environment; and the regulation of relations between a non-state armed group and persons and objects in territory under its control. Each is considered in turn.

2.1 Combatant immunity and prisoners of war

Combatant immunity and prisoner of war status are not to be found in the international humanitarian law of non-international armed conflict. No treaty provision that is applicable to non-international armed conflict mentions either concept. At the Diplomatic Conference of 1949, an attempt to introduce a rule that prohibited prosecution for taking part in a non-international armed conflict did not succeed.[3] At the Diplomatic Conference of 1974–7, a proposal to introduce prisoner of war status into the international humanitarian law of non-international armed conflict similarly failed.[4] This is one of the few areas of real difference between international and non-international armed conflicts also at the level of customary international law,[5]

---

[1] See Parts I and II respectively.
[2] See Chapters 10 and 11.
[3] *Final Record of the Diplomatic Conference of Geneva of 1949* (Federal Political Department, Berne) Vol II-B, 44 (Norway). See also 49 (UK); Vol II-A, 322 (Norway). For criticism of the proposal, see Vol II-B, 50 (Burma); 99 (Denmark).
[4] *Official Records of the Diplomatic Conference on the Reaffirmation and Development of International Humanitarian Law Applicable in Armed Conflicts, Geneva (1974–1977)* (Federal Political Department, 1978) Vol 5, 91, para 6 (Norway); Vol 8, 359, para 15 (Sweden); Vol 5, 187, paras 20–21 (Bangladesh). For criticism of the proposal, see Vol 8, 293, para 41 (Burundi).
[5] See J-M Henckaerts and L Doswald-Beck, *Customary International Humanitarian Law, Volume I: Rules* (Cambridge University Press, 2005) 384–95.

and there is near-unanimity among commentators that this is the exclusive domain of the law of international armed conflict.[6] Domestic courts have taken the same view.[7]

2.1.1 Combatant immunity

The greatest benefit of combatant and, in turn, prisoner of war, status is the notion of combatant immunity.[8] This is the idea that persons will not be subject to prosecution under domestic law for taking part in the armed conflict and for committing lawful acts of war. It is combatant immunity that is the most controversial aspect of transplanting the law of international armed conflict into the law of non-international armed conflict.[9] States view members of non-state armed groups against which they are in conflict as criminals or traitors, and, increasingly, terrorists,[10] thus making it extremely unlikely that combatant immunity would be granted in advance and as a matter of course. Nonetheless, immunity from prosecution for taking part in hostilities is a crucial incentive for compliance with the law of non-international armed conflict, a point which is widely recognized.[11]

Combatant immunity had been proposed for inclusion in the conventional international humanitarian law instruments that govern non-international armed conflict. During the 1949 Diplomatic Conference, Norway proposed a provision by which 'application of the Conventions...would not prevent the lawful government from instituting regular procedure for the prosecution of the rebels. The latter, however, could not be punished on the sole grounds of having taken part in the conflict'.[12] Similarly, the United Kingdom considered it 'anomalous to protect insurgents by a Convention during the rebellion and treat them as traitors at the close of it'. Accordingly, it suggested that '[i]t might, therefore, be necessary to suggest that the signatory countries agree to amend their penal law to prevent them from condemning vanquished rebels on the sole grounds of having borne arms against the legal government'.[13] However, these suggestions did not meet with unanimous approval, with

---

[6] See eg Y Sandoz, C Swinarski, and B Zimmermann (eds), *Commentary on the Additional Protocols of 8 June 1977 to the Geneva Conventions of 12 August 1949* (ICRC, 1987) 1332; M Bothe, KJ Partsch, and WA Solf, *New Rules for Victims of Armed Conflicts* (Martinus Nijhoff, 1982) 671–2; WA Solf, 'The Status of Combatants in Non-International Armed Conflicts under Domestic Law and Transnational Practice' (1983) 33 *American University Law Review* 53, 57–9; LC Green, *The Contemporary Law of Armed Conflict* (Manchester University Press, 2000) 318; D Fleck, 'The Law of Non-International Armed Conflicts', in D Fleck (ed), *The Handbook of International Humanitarian Law* (Oxford University Press, 2008) 605, 627. An exception is E Crawford, *The Treatment of Combatants and Insurgents under the Law of Armed Conflict* (Oxford University Press, 2010).

[7] See Constitutional Court of Colombia, Decision C-291/07, reproduced and translated in M Sassòli, AA Bouvier, and A Quintin, *How Does Law Protect in War? Volume III* (ICRC, 2011) 2255.

[8] Bothe, Partsch, and Solf, above note 6, 243–4; D Jinks, 'The Declining Significance of POW Status' (2004) 45 *Harvard International Law Journal* 367, 436.

[9] C Greenwood, 'International Humanitarian Law (Laws of War)', in C Greenwood, *Essays on War in International Law* (Cameron May, 2006) para 5.16.

[10] See above, 204–5.

[11] See eg 'Protection of Victims of Non-International Conflicts' (1969) 9 *IRRC* 343, 348–51; 'Determining Customary International Law Relative to the Conduct of Hostilities in Non-International Armed Conflicts: Remarks of WJ Fenrick' (1987) 2 *American University Journal of International Law and Policy* 471, 474; Fleck, Non-International Armed Conflicts, above note 6, 633; M Sassòli, 'Taking Armed Groups Seriously: Ways to Improve their Compliance with International Humanitarian Law' (2010) 1 *International Humanitarian Legal Studies* 5, 26–7.

[12] *Final Record*, above note 3, Vol II-B, 44. See also Vol II-A, 322.

[13] Ibid, Vol II-B, 49. Cf Vol II-A, 322.

some states taking the view that 'rebels usually acted with full cognizance in advance of the risk they were running to incur penal sanctions',[14] and others that '[i]t seemed impossible to apply to insurgents the régime of prisoners of war'.[15] In light of this opposition, proposals to introduce combatant immunity into the international humanitarian law of non-international armed conflict proved unsuccessful. Similar proposals were made by the International Committee of the Red Cross (ICRC) to the Conference of Government Experts in 1969 and 1971,[16] and by certain states at the 1974–7 Diplomatic Conference,[17] but these too failed.

Pursuant to international humanitarian law applicable in international armed conflict, combatants who violate that law are, at least in theory, prosecuted for war crimes, but those who respect the law are immune from prosecution. This should be contrasted with the situation in non-international armed conflicts, in which fighters may be prosecuted under the state's domestic law for taking up arms and for any act committed in the course of the conflict, regardless of whether or not that act was lawful under international humanitarian law. As such, there is little incentive on the part of the fighter to comply with the law. At the 1947 Conference of Government Experts, it was noted that limitation of partisans' right to prisoner of war status 'might induce them to disregard the laws of war, thus making the position of the occupying Power more difficult and the conflict more pitiless'.[18] This is equally true of members of non-state armed groups fighting in non-international armed conflicts. A 2009 report of UN Secretary-General Ban Ki-Moon thus provides that granting amnesty to members of armed groups for taking part in hostilities may incentivize compliance with the law of armed conflict.[19] This is a crucial issue that needs further consideration on the part of the international community.

Although states may prove resistant to the idea, there is some practice suggesting that the principle of combatant immunity can be applied in certain non-international armed conflicts. This is particularly true of non-international armed conflicts that are of a significant magnitude and extended duration. Indeed, while the question of combatant immunity has been considered 'particularly delicate at the beginning of the conflict, at a point when the State feels the first attacks upon its existence and its integrity, and when, naturally, it is tempted to take energetic steps . . . when the hostilities have continued for a certain time, and when it seems that they will continue, perhaps it would be possible to obtain acceptance of the limitation proposed by the ICRC'.[20] Thus, during the US civil war, pursuant to the terms of surrender between Generals Grant and Lee, and between Generals Sherman and Johnston, both in April 1865, Confederate officers and fighters were not subjected to criminal prosecution. This was also the effect of

---

[14] Ibid, Vol II-B, 50 (Burma).
[15] Ibid, 99 (Denmark).
[16] Reaffirmation and Development of the Laws and Customs Applicable in Armed Conflicts: Report submitted by the International Committee of the Red Cross (May 1969) 104; Conference of Government Experts on the Reaffirmation and Development of International Humanitarian Law Applicable in Armed Conflicts, Geneva, 24 May–12 June 1971, Submitted by the International Committee of the Red Cross (1971) Part V: Protection of Victims of Non-International Armed Conflicts, 61–2.
[17] See eg *Official Records*, above note 4, Vol 8, 359, para 15 (Sweden).
[18] ICRC, Report on the Work of the Conference of Government Experts for the Study of the Conventions for the Protection of War Victims (Geneva, April 14–26, 1947) (1947) 110.
[19] Report of the Secretary-General on the Protection of Civilians in Armed Conflict, S/2009/277, 29 May 2009, para 44.
[20] Protection of Victims of Non-International Armed Conflicts, above note 16, 56–7.

President Johnson's Proclamation of Amnesty and Reconciliation of 29 May 1865. The consequences to be drawn from this practice are limited given that belligerency was recognized during the US civil war. However, the amnesty granted at the conclusion of the 1899–1902 Boer war was to a similar effect.[21]

Likewise, in 1958, a few years into the Algerian war of independence, France issued an order which provided that, '[p]roposals for prisoners to be brought before courts will be systematically avoided, except for those who have committed atrocities or have shown fanaticism to a degree which is likely to be detrimental to the development of a favourable state of mind of the prisoners as a whole'.[22] This followed an earlier Order which provided that:

[t]he attitude of rebels taken prisoner in the course of fighting and who have not engaged in extortion is not of the odious nature associated with banditry and terrorism... They should receive treatment which is as nearly as possible identical to that which prisoners of war are granted...[23]

This was done, in part, for military reasons:

Rebels fighting with their backs to the wall often show a tenacity which leads to their extermination...

Interrogation of prisoners has in fact shown that the 'moudjahidines' are given dire warning during their training of the risk they run in the event of surrender. French troops massacring prisoners after torturing them...

The fear nurtured must be allayed as much as possible, with the objective of reducing our losses.

One means of doing this is to grant prisoners as liberal a treatment as possible and to let it be known that we are doing this.[24]

However, it was also made clear that the detainees 'should not be considered as prisoners of war'.[25] Thus, they were being afforded treatment akin to that afforded to prisoners of war, but were not considered prisoners of war. A letter from the French military command in Algeria to the French Ministry of Justice dated November 1959 similarly provided that:

rebels captured with guns in their hands, guiltless of any crimes of terrorism before joining a rebel group, are not prosecuted but are interned in military camps. They are treated as members of an enemy army.[26]

Following this, for some time at least, captured fighters of the Front de Libération Nationale (FLN) were not prosecuted for taking part in the conflict.[27] Indeed, France

---

[21] Peace Treaty of Vereeniging, 31 May 1902.
[22] Superior Army Command, 10th Military Region, Memorandum of 19 March 1958, ICRC Archives B AG 225 008-009. Translation of ICRC.
[23] Service Order [marked 'Secret'], 24 November 1957, ICRC Archives B AG 225 008-009. Translation of ICRC.
[24] Memorandum of 19 March 1958.
[25] Ibid.
[26] Letter of November 1959, quoted in M Bedjaoui, *Law and the Algerian Revolution* (International Association of Democratic Lawyers, 1961) 149. The original, quoted in M Veuthey, 'La guérilla: Le problème du traitement des prisonniers' (1972) 3 *Annales d'etudes internationales* 119, 130, reads: 'les rebelles pris les armes à la main, qui ne sont coupables d'aucun crime terroriste avant leur incorporation dans un groupe rebelle, ne sont pas poursuivis, mais internés dans des camps militaires. Ils sont ainsi assimilés aux membres d'une armée ennemie.'
[27] A Fraleigh, 'The Algerian Revolution as a Case Study in International Law', in RA Falk (ed), *The International Law of Civil War* (Johns Hopkins University Press, 1971) 179, 196; A Rosas, *The Legal Status of Prisoners of War* (Suomalainen Tiedeakatemia, 1976) 149.

denied that captured FLN members had been executed solely for bearing arms against France.[28]

Along similar lines, at the conclusion of the conflict following the attempted secession of Biafra (1967–70), despite the Federal Government being victorious, it did not prosecute members of the rebel forces, instead it released all captured prisoners.[29]

More recently, during the conflict in the former Yugoslavia, an Agreement on the Release and Transfer of Prisoners was reached in 1992 between various conflicting parties which provided that '[a]ll prisoners not accused of, or sentenced for, grave breaches of International Humanitarian Law... will be unilaterally and unconditionally released'. Persons accused of, or sentenced for, grave breaches benefitted 'from the judicial guarantees as set out in Arts 82–108 of the Third Geneva Convention if they are captured combatants, and Arts 71–76 of the Fourth Geneva Convention if they are civilians'.[30] Likewise, in numerous ad hoc agreements concluded between the parties to conflicts, provision is made for '[p]olitical prisoners and detainees held due to the conflict' to be 'released unconditionally'.[31] Such provisions are broader than the case at hand, given that they relate to political prisoners and detainees in general; however, in many cases, they include detained fighters. For example, the 1985 Nairobi Peace Agreement between the Government of Uganda and the National Resistance Movement (NRM) included a clause which provided that '[a]ll political detainees who are known to be members of the National Resistance Movement shall be immediately released'.[32] Provision was likewise made for the release of detainees in the 1996 Abidjan Peace Agreement between the Government of Sierra Leone and the Revolutionary United Front (RUF).[33] Following the Peace Agreement, the RUF took the view that:

an important first step in the process of the peace we are inaugurating would be the immediate and unconditional release of the RUF/SL leader, Cpl. Foday Saybana Sankoh. All charges against him should be dropped, thus signposting a move away from the path of politics of revenge and recrimination into the highway of healing and national reconciliation. In the same vein, there shall be a blanket amnesty for all AFRC [Armed Forces Revolutionary Council] personnel and

---

[28] Fraleigh, above note 27, 198.
[29] 'Note from the Nigerian Minister of Defence to the ICRC delegation in Lagos, 14 May 1970, ICRC Archives, file 219 (186)', cited in F Bugnion, '*Jus ad bellum, jus in bello* and non-international armed conflicts', (2003) 6 *YIHL* 167, 181.
[30] Agreement on the Release and Transfer of Prisoners, 1 October 1992, Articles 3(1) and 4(1).
[31] The N'Sele Ceasefire Agreement between the Government of the Rwandese Republic and the Rwandese Patriotic Front, as amended at Gbadolite, 16 September 1991, and at Arusha, 12 July 1992, Article II(4). See also Memorandum of Understanding between the Government of Indonesia and the Free Aceh Movement, 15 August 2005, Article 3.1.2; Cotonou Accord between between Interim Government of National Unity (IGNU) of Liberia, National Patriotic Front of Liberia (NPFL) and the United Movement of Liberia for Democracy (ULIMO), 25 July 1993, Section I, Article 10; Agreement to Create a Conducive Atmosphere for Peace between the Government of Sudan and the Eastern Sudan Front, 19 June 2006, Article 8(b); Eastern Sudan Peace Agreement, 14 October 2006, Appendix A, para 19; Agreement on Humanitarian Ceasefire on the Conflict in Darfur between the Government of Sudan and the Justice and Equality Movement (JEM), 8 April 2004, Article 5; Agreement between the Government of Sudan, the Sudan Liberation Movement, and the Justice and Equality of Movement', 25 April 2004, Article 4(f); Protocol between the Government of Sudan (GoS), the Sudan Liberation Movement/Army (SLM/A) and the Justice and Equality Movement (JEM) on the Enhancement of the Security Situation in Darfur in Accordance with the N'Djamena Agreement, 9 November 2004, Article 4; Acte d'Engagement, Article III [between various armed groups in the DRC].
[32] Nairobi Peace Agreement, 17 December 1985, Article 1(h).
[33] Abidjan Peace Agreement, 30 November 1996, Article 19.

so-called sympathizers or collaborators, and all combatants with effect from the signing of the Agreement.[34]

To be sure, in many other conflicts, combatant immunity was not afforded to members of the armed group. To take but two examples, following the Spanish civil war (1936–9) and the armed conflict in Nicaragua in the 1980s, prosecutions took place.[35] More recently, the United States has prosecuted individuals for participating in what it considers to be a non-international armed conflict. In one case, that of *Khadr*, the stipulation of fact provided, *inter alia*:

Khadr is an alien unprivileged enemy belligerent as defined by the 2009 Military Commissions Act and at no time relevant to the charged offenses did he have any legal basis to commit any war-like acts, to include all of the acts described above in this stipulation. During the charged timeframe, Khadr knowingly and intentionally engaged in hostilities against the United States.[36]

The charges against Khadr included murder and attempted murder of US soldiers. Furthermore, the 2009 Military Commission Act defined the notion of an alien unprivileged enemy belligerent as:

an individual (other than a privileged belligerent) who—

(A) has engaged in hostilities against the United States or its coalition partners;
(B) has purposefully and materially supported hostilities against the United States or its coalition partners; or
(C) was a part of al Qaeda at the time of the alleged offense under this chapter.[37]

Thus, this recent practice of the United States goes directly against affording notions of combatant immunity in non-international armed conflict.

Recognizing that some sort of combatant immunity provides an incentive for members of the armed group to comply with the law, but also appreciating that states may not be willing to provide combatant immunity in the abstract and in advance of a conflict, alternative ways ahead need to be canvassed. One way of approaching the issue is to recognize that the choice is not simply between treating fighters as lawful combatants who have been captured and treating them as common criminals. For example, during the 1899–1902 Boer war, an exchange of letters took place between Great Britain and the Boer Republic. Lord Roberts, on the British side, expressed his concern that captured British fighters were being treated as criminals and were being housed in prison. The President of the Boer Republic denied this, observing that only persons who had violated the laws and customs of war and persons who had tried to escape were housed in prison and even then separate from the usual prisoners. Subject to one exception, this was accepted by Lord Roberts.[38] Thus, it was accepted by all concerned that captured fighters were not ordinary criminals and were not to be treated as ordinary criminals. Along similar lines, in 1970, UN Secretary-General U Thant proposed that '[e]fforts should be pursued towards gradual assimilation of [captured fighters and civilian detainees] to prisoners of war under Geneva Convention III and

---

[34] 'Lasting Peace in Sierra Leone: The Revolutionary United Front Sierra Leone (RUF/SL) Perspective and Vision', undated.
[35] See Bugnion, *Jus ad bellum*, above note 29, 189.
[36] *United States of America v Omar Ahmed Khadr*, Stipulation of Fact, 13 October 2010.
[37] Section 948a(7).
[38] See generally JW Spaight, *War Rights on Land* (1911) 280–1.

civilian detainees under Convention IV through the further elaboration of Special Minimum Rules for "political" or "non-delinquent" prisoners'.[39]

Furthermore, in the case of *Mrkšić*, the Appeals Chamber of the International Criminal Tribunal for the former Yugoslavia (ICTY) held that common Article 3 'reflects the same spirit of the duty to protect members of armed forces who have laid down their arms and are detained as the specific protections afforded to prisoners of war in Geneva Convention III as a whole, particularly in its Article 13'.[40] Although this cannot be read as holding that captured fighters are to be treated as prisoners of war, with all the benefits that come with such treatment,[41] it does recognize that fighters should not be treated in the same way as criminals. Similarly, the ICRC Commentary to the Third Geneva Convention takes the view that 'once the fighting reaches a certain magnitude and the insurgent armed forces meet the criteria specified in Article 4(A)(2) [of the Third Geneva Convention], the spirit of Article 3 certainly requires that members of the insurgent forces should not be treated as common criminals'.[42] Some non-state armed groups have attempted to meet the requirements of Article 4(A)(2) or at least the slightly more relaxed requirements of Article 44 of Additional Protocol I. For example, according to the National Liberation Army (NLA), Chief of Staff members of the NLA, which fought in the Former Yugoslav Republic of Macedonia in 2001, 'were obliged to wear uniforms'. According to him, '[i]t was forbidden for the personnel when carrying a weapon to gather in groups without uniforms. This was the rule, since this was a requirement of the international law. A person without a uniform would be considered a criminal, not a combatant. We were aware of this situation, and were very careful in this respect'.[43] Likewise, the Fuerzas Armadas Revolucionarias de Colombia (FARC) has indicated that its fighters meet the requirements to be considered combatants.[44] This *sui generis* approach whereby fighters are not treated as prisoners of war but nor are they treated as common criminals may prove more acceptable to states.

A second way of approaching the issue, which avoids any semblance of status, is to encourage non-prosecution for taking part in hostilities. Oftentimes during non-international armed conflicts, captured fighters are detained without prosecution, trials being considered to inflame the situation. In such cases, detainees are held 'in a legal limbo for the duration of the hostilities' and are treated as if they are in a *sui generis* situation.[45] Upon the conclusion of the conflict, they may be released. Amnesties or their equivalents have also been granted in numerous conflicts, usually being included in ceasefire or peace agreements.[46] These take a variety of forms and

---

[39] Respect for Human Rights in Armed Conflicts: Report of the Secretary-General, A/8052, 18 September 1970, para 156.

[40] *Prosecutor v Mrkšić, Radić, and Šljivančanin*, IT-95-13/1-A, Judgment, 5 May 2009, para 70.

[41] Cf A Cassese, 'Should Rebels be Treated as Criminals?' in A Cassese (ed), *Realizing Utopia: The Future of International Law* (Oxford University Press, 2012) 519, 522; G Pinzauti, 'Protecting Prisoners of War: The *Mrkšić et al* Appeal Judgment' (2010) 8 *JICJ* 199, 210.

[42] JS Pictet (ed), *The Geneva Conventions of 12 August 1949: Commentary, III Geneva Convention Relative to the Treatment of Prisoners of War* (ICRC, 1960) 40.

[43] Witness Statement of Gzim Ostreni, Chief of NLA General Staff, para 39, Exhibit P00497.E in ICTY *Boškoski* trial.

[44] FARC-EP Comisión Interacional, *Beligerancia: Suplemento*, 12.

[45] Cassese, Rebels, above note 41.

[46] See eg Accord de Paix entre le Gouvernement de la République Centrafricaine et le mouvements politico-militaires ci-apres designes: Front Democratique du Peuple Centrafricain (FDPC), Union des Forces Démocratiques pour le Rassemblement (UFDR), Article 4; Peace Agreement between the Government of the Republic of Chad and the Movement for Democracy and Justice in Chad,

some refer explicitly to members of the armed group or military activities. For example, in the dialogue between the Government of Nepal and the Communist Party of Nepal-Maoist (CPN-M), it took the form of withdrawal of charges.[47] In the 2005 Memorandum of Understanding between the Government of Indonesia and the Free Aceh Movement (GAM), amnesty was granted 'to all persons who have participated in GAM activities'.[48] Likewise, in the 1996 Abidjan Peace Agreement between the Government of Sierra Leone and the RUF, provision was made that 'no official or judicial action [be] taken against any member of the RUF/SL in respect of anything done by them in pursuit of their objectives as members of that organization'.[49] In the 2003 Peace Agreement between the Government of Liberia, the Liberians United for Reconciliation and Democracy (LURD), and the Movement for Democracy in Liberia (MODEL), provision was made for consideration of an amnesty 'to all persons and parties engaged or involved in military activities during the Liberian civil conflict'.[50] Along similar lines, in the 2007 Ouagadougou Agreement between the Government of the Ivory Coast and the Forces Nouvelles, an amnesty was set out in respect of 'crimes and offences related to national security'.[51] Although amnesties are by no means the same as combatant immunity—amnesties exist after the fact while combatant status and immunity exists at the outset—amnesties are, in many ways, a functional equivalent of combatant immunity in that both prevent fighters from being prosecuted under domestic law for taking part in the conflict and for committing lawful acts of war. This type of amnesty is to be encouraged and greater use could be made of Article 6(5) of Additional Protocol II in this regard.[52] Indeed, an argument could be made that, pursuant to Article 6(5), at the end of the hostilities the relevant authorities are obliged, if not actually to grant amnesties, actively to *consider* the granting of amnesties. This, in turn, means that parties should be encouraged not to exercise the death penalty during times of conflict, instead waiting until the conflict ends, at which time passions may not be as inflamed and amnesty may be granted. This would be a significant step forward.

As the examples above suggest, combatant immunity or its functional equivalent is more embedded in the practice of non-international armed conflicts than the law suggests. Furthermore, it is not simply a choice between common criminality and prisoner of war status; it is possible to navigate an intermediate course. It is worth quoting the statement of the US Supreme Court in the *Prize Cases* in this regard, in which it opined that, '[s]hould the sovereign conceive he has a right to hang up his prisoners as rebels, the opposite party will make reprisals, &c, &c; the war will become cruel, horrible, and every day more destructive to the nation'.[53]

---

7 January 2002, Article 2; Cotonou Accord, 25 July 1993, Section G Article 19; Lincoln Agreement on Peace, Security and Development on Bougainville, 23 January 1998, Article 10.

[47] Understanding between Seven Political Parties Alliance and the CPN (Maoist), Article I(4).

[48] Memorandum of Understanding between the Government of Indonesia and the Free Aceh Movement, 15 August 2005, Article 3.1.1.

[49] Abidjan Peace Agreement, 30 November 1996, Article 14.

[50] Peace Agreement between the Government of Liberia (GOL), The Liberians United for Reconciliation and Democracy (LURD), The Movement for Democracy in Liberia (MODEL) and the Political Parties Accra, Ghana, 18 August 2003, Article XXXIV.

[51] Ouagadougou Agreement, 4 March 2007, Article 6.3.

[52] See also above, 506–8.

[53] *Prize Cases* (1862) 67 US 635, 667.

2.1.2 Prisoners of war

As with combatant immunity, no mention of prisoners of war is to be found in the law of non-international armed conflict. However, there is an important distinction between prisoner of war *status* and *treatment* of individuals as prisoners of war. Members of the military wing of the non-state armed group (fighters) who are captured do not benefit from prisoner of war status as a matter of law. However, suggestions have been made to afford them treatment akin to that of prisoners of war. Along these lines, the UK Military Manual provides that '[w]herever possible, treatment equivalent to that accorded to prisoners of war should be given'.[54] The statement is one of policy, it being provided that captured fighters do not benefit from prisoner of war status as a matter of law; nonetheless, the point is an important one. As early as 1923, the ICRC delegate in Ireland recounted, in relation to the treatment of prisoners, that:

> [i]n summary, I can say that the treatment of prisoners is devoid of any spirit of hostility and that the general principles adopted by the Tenth International Red Cross Conference are observed to the letter. The government denies prisoners 'POW' status but in effect grants them an equivalent status.[55]

In many respects, treatment akin to that afforded to prisoners of war can be given to captured fighters, the relevant rules finding a parallel in the law of non-international armed conflict.[56] For example, in such areas as humane treatment, conditions of detention, and due process guarantees, equivalent rules in the law of non-international armed conflict already exist.[57] The rules on the treatment of captured persons, in both types of conflict, have also come much closer, regardless of the identity of the captured individual. However, some aspects of the treatment of prisoners of war may be difficult, if not impossible, to transpose, for example the rules relating to the identification of prisoners of war or the provisions relating to the financial resources of prisoners of war.[58] In this regard, it should be recalled that '[a]ssimilating a rebel to a prisoner of war for one purpose does not dictate assimilating him to a prisoner of war for all purposes'.[59] Given that the prisoners of war regime is a composite category, it is important to break down the category into its component parts in order to ascertain which rules are suitable for transposition to non-international armed conflicts and which are not. This comes through from the comments of certain states to the 1949 Diplomatic Conference, even if they eventually opted for a blanket non-application of the rules.[60]

---

[54] Ministry of Defence, *The Manual of the Law of Armed Conflict* (Oxford University Press, 2004) 390.
[55] Rapport General de M R Haccius, Délégué en Irlande, ICRC Archives CR 22(84)/134. The original reads: 'En résumé, je puis dire que le traitement des prisonniers est dépourvu de tout esprit d'hostilité et que les principes généraux adoptés par la Xème Conférence International des Croix-Rouge sont observés à la lettre. Le gouvernement refuse aux prisonniers la qualité de "PG" mais les met effectivement au bénéfice du regime correspondant.' Ireland considered the situation an internal manner. See further above, 34. The finding of the ICRC delegate was disputed by various entities in light of the lack of visits to other places of detention and the inability to speak to detainees. See ICRC Archives, CR 22(84)/148, /155, and/161.
[56] See Crawford, above note 6, 78–117.
[57] Common Article 3; Additional Protocol II, Articles 4 and 6.
[58] Third Geneva Convention, Articles 4 and 58–68.
[59] JE Bond, 'Internal Conflict and Article Three of the Geneva Conventions' (1971–2) 48 *Denver Law Journal* 263, 283. See also JE Bond, *The Rules of Riot* (Princeton University Press, 1974) 116–17.
[60] See *Final Record*, above note 3, Vol II-B, 13 (Canada); 99 (France).

There is also some practice, principally from certain older conflicts, which suggest that captured fighters are to be treated as prisoners of war. For example, prisoner of war treatment, and status, was afforded during the US civil war. An 1862 order of Major-General Grant provided that '[p]ersons acting as guerrillas without organization and without uniform to distinguish them from private citizens are not entitled to the treatment of prisoners of war when caught, and will not receive such treatment'.[61] The order thus suggested that those persons who acted as part of an organized group and wore uniforms were entitled to treatment as prisoners of war. A bilateral agreement concluded a few weeks later, between Generals Dix and Hill of the Union and Confederate Armies, confirmed the applicability of prisoner of war status to the US civil war with its detailed provisions on the exchange and release of prisoners of war.[62] The Lieber Code of 24 April 1863 confirmed the practice with its numerous detailed rules on prisoners of war.[63] Given that belligerency was recognized in the US civil war, the conclusions to be drawn from the affording of prisoner of war treatment and status are limited. However, such treatment was also afforded in many other non-international armed conflicts.

Some 50 years after the conclusion of the US civil war, during the Hungarian revolution of 1919, the head of the Italian Military Mission argued to the People's Commissar that it was 'entirely legitimate that [detainees] be given the same treatment as that stipulated by the Geneva Convention for prisoners of war'.[64] This was rejected by the People's Commissar for Foreign Affairs, who replied: 'I do not believe that the intention of your government is to see or apply the provisions of the Geneva Convention to bandits of the counterrevolution and to free their hands for other assaults against women and children and to organise pogroms.'[65] Although rejected, the exchange demonstrates the view of one outside state at the time.

At around the same time, during the violence in Ireland in 1922, the Irish Republican Army stated:

As your 'Parliament' and your headquarters know perfectly well, we have always complied with the recognised rules of war. In the early days of this war, we made hundreds of men of your forces prisoners, but we gave them all the rights of Prisoners of War, and furthermore treated them as compatriots and former comrades. Several of your soldiers were released by us up to three times, though they were carrying arms each time.[66]

---

[61] General Orders No 60, 3 July 1862, reproduced in United States War Department, *The War of the Rebellion: A Compilation of the Official Records of the Union and Confederate Armies, Series 1, Volume 17, Part 2* (Government Printing Office, 1886) 69.

[62] 'The "Dix-Hill Cartel" for the General Exchange of Prisoners of War Entered into Between the Union and Confederate Armies', 22 July 1862, reproduced in HS Levie (ed), *Documents on Prisoners of War* (Volume 60 International Law Studies, Naval War College Press, 1979) 34. See also the Statement of the United States, *Compte-Rendu de la Neuvième Conférence Internationale de la Croix-Rouge Tenue à Washington du 7 au 17 mai 1912*, ICRC Archives CR 22/32.

[63] Section III.

[64] Letter from Lieutenant-Colonel G Romanelli, Chef de la mission italienne à Budapest to Béla Kun, Commissaire du peuple aux Affaires Etrangères, 26 June 1919, ICRC Archives Mis 4.5/120. English translation taken from A Durand, *From Sarajevo to Hiroshima: History of the International Committee of the Red Cross* (Henry Dunant Institute, 1984) 132.

[65] Letter from Béla Kun to Lieutenant-Colonel G Romanelli, 27 June 1919, ICRC Archives Mis 4.5/120. The original reads: 'je ne crois pas que l'intention de votre gouvernement soit que vous désiriez voir appliquer les dispositions de la Convention de Genève aux bandits de la contre-révolution, et leur laisser les mains libres pour d'autres aggressions contre des femmes et des enfants, et pour l'organisation de pogroms.'

[66] Lettre de Protestation addressée au 'Président du Parlement Provisoire de l'Irlande du Sud' par le Chef d'Etat Major de l'Armée Républicaine Irlandaise, 1 December 1992, annexed to Mémoire du

At the outset of the Spanish civil war, in 1936, the central Government agreed in a declaration to the ICRC that it would, *inter alia*, co-operate in the setting up of a prisoner of war information agency.[67] The central Government also announced that 4,000 prisoners would be 'treated in accordance with the military code providing for the handling of prisoners of war'.[68] For their part, the rebels declared themselves 'ready to observe and respect the Geneva Convention concerning the war wounded, the sick and the prisoners'.[69] Indeed, they went as far as declaring that they 'respect[ed] and caus[ed] to be respected, with the utmost scrupulousness, the laws and customs of warfare'.[70] Neither side lived up to their declarations, however, although some exchanges of prisoners did take place.[71]

During the Algerian war of independence, France initially tried and executed captured FLN fighters. However, on 19 March 1958, special camps were created for detaining 'combatants captured while bearing weapons openly',[72] and some detained fighters, previously housed in ordinary prisons, were transferred to these special camps.[73] France made it clear that these individuals were not being considered prisoners of war but that they were being treated akin to prisoners of war.[74] In the view of the ICRC, prisoners detained in the camps received treatment 'closely related to that of the prisoner-of-war camps'.[75] For its part, the FLN indicated its willingness to apply the provisions of the Geneva Conventions from an early stage of the conflict. In a letter to the ICRC of 23 February 1956, the FLN indicated its willingness to apply this to all French prisoners of war taken by the FLN 'on condition of reciprocity on the part of the Government of France'.[76] Throughout the conflict, the FLN insisted 'that it had conferred upon captured French soldiers the status of prisoners of war'.[77] Internal FLN regulations also contained detailed rules on the law of war in general and the treatment

---

Gouvernement de la République Irlandaise au Comité International de la Croix-Rouge, 13 mars 1922, ICRC Archives CR 22 (84)/1. The original reads: 'Comme le savent parfaitement bien votre "Parlement" et votre Quartier-Général, nous nous sommes toujours conformés aux règles reconnues de la guerre. Dans les premiers jours de cette guerre, nous fîmes prisonniers des centaines d'hommes de vos forces, mais leur avons accordé tous les droits de Prisonniers de Guerre, et les avons traités, en plus, comme compatriotes et anciens camarades. Plusieurs de vos soldats ont été relâchés par nous jusqu'à trois fois, quoique pris à chaque occasion les armes à la main.'

[67] Accord de José Giral, Le Président du Conseil des Ministres, 3 September 1936, reproduced in (1936) 18 *RICR* 749, Annex II.
[68] NJ Padelford, 'International Law and the Spanish Civil War' (1937) 31 *AJIL* 226, 226, citing a report in the *New York Times*, 10 August 1936. See also AVW Thomas and AJ Thomas, 'International Legal Aspects of the Civil War in Spain, 1936–39', in RA Falk (ed), *The International Law of Civil War* (Johns Hopkins Press, 1971) 111, 122.
[69] Miguel Cabanellas, Junte de Défense Nationale d'Espagne, 15 September 1936, reproduced in (1936) 18 *RICR* 749, Annex IV.
[70] Quoted in NJ Padelford, *International Law and Diplomacy in the Spanish Civil Strife* (Macmillan, 1939) 597.
[71] See M Junod, *Warrior Without Weapons* (Jonathan Cape, 1951) Spain, Chapter II.
[72] Bugnion, *Jus ad bellum*, above note 29, 195. See also ICRC, *The ICRC and the Algerian Conflict* (1962) 6.
[73] Fraleigh, above note 27, 196; Rosas, above note 27, 149.
[74] Rosas, ibid, 149.
[75] *ICRC and the Algerian Conflict*, above note 72, 6.
[76] Lettre de la délégation algérienne au Caire à David de Traz, 23 février 1956, quoted in F Perret, 'L'action du Comité International de la Croix-Rouge pendant la Guerre d'Algérie (1954–1962)' (2004) 86 *IRRC* 917, 926. The original reads 'sous réserve de réciprocité de la part du Gouvernement de la République Française'.
[77] Fraleigh, above note 27, 196.

of prisoners of war in particular.[78] The Provisional Government of the Algerian Republic (GPRA) also published a *White Paper on the Application of the Geneva Conventions of 1949 to the French-Algerian Conflict* in which it reiterated its willingness to 'accept and apply the Geneva Conventions' and dealt in some detail with the application of common Article 3 and Article 4 of the Third Geneva Convention to the conflict.[79] The FLN allowed prisoners to receive parcels, to send messages to their families, and, from time to time, lists of names of prisoners were sent to the ICRC.[80] Prisoners were also released through the ICRC.[81]

Some years later, during the attempted secession of Biafra, the 1967 Operational Code of Conduct issued by the Federal Government to the armed forces provided that '[s]oldiers who surrender will not be killed. They are to be disarmed and treated as prisoners of war. They are entitled in all circumstances to humane treatment and respect for their person and their honour'.[82] The Federal Government housed captured Biafran fighters in *de facto* prisoner of war camps and treated them as prisoners of war. The ICRC visited the camps and interviewed detainees. On the Biafran side, *de facto* prisoner of war camps were also established and visits were undertaken by the ICRC.[83]

Along similar lines, the 22 May 1992 Agreement concluded during the conflict in Bosnia provided that '[c]aptured combatants shall enjoy the treatment provided for by the Third Geneva Convention' relative to the treatment of prisoners of war and that '[t]he International Committee of the Red Cross (ICRC) shall have free access to all captured combatants in order to fulfil its humanitarian mandate according to the Third Geneva Convention of 12 August 1949'.[84] The 1991 Memorandum of Understanding concluded between the Republic of Croatia, the Republic of Serbia, and the Federal Republic of Yugoslavia likewise provided that '[c]aptured combatants shall enjoy the treatment provided for by the Third Geneva Convention' relative to the treatment of prisoners of war.[85] Similar commitments were made at various points and by various parties during the other conflicts in the former Yugoslavia.[86]

For its part, in 1996, the National Democratic Front of the Philippines (NDFP) indicated that it 'will treat any captured personnel of the military, police and paramilitary forces of the GRP [Government] as prisoners of war and demands that the GRP likewise treat as prisoners of war any captured personnel of the NPA [New People's Army] and other forces represented herein by the NDFP'.[87] Most recently, during the

---

[78] Bedjaoui, above note 26, 215 fn 17; Fraleigh, above note 27, 196; M Veuthey, *Guérilla et Droit Humanitaire* (CICR, 1983) 202.

[79] *White Paper on the Application of the Geneva Conventions of 1949 to the French-Algerian Conflict* (Algerian Office, 1960).

[80] Rosas, above note 27, 147.

[81] *ICRC and the Algerian Conflict*, above note 72, 9; Rosas, above note 27, 148; Bedjaoui, above note 26, 216.

[82] Operational Code of Conduct for the Nigerian Army, July 1967, para 4(e), reproduced in AHM Kirk-Greene, *Crisis and Conflict in Nigeria: A Documentary Sourcebook 1966–1969, Volume I* (Oxford University Press, 1971) 455, 456.

[83] See 'Help to War Victims in Nigeria' (1969) 9 *IRRC* 119.

[84] Agreement of 22 May 1992, para 2.4, in M Sassòli, AA Bouvier, and A Quintin, *How Does Law Protect in War? Volume III* (ICRC, 2011) 1717.

[85] Memorandum of Understanding, 27 November 1991, Article 3, in ibid, 1713.

[86] See eg Order of Lieutenant General Panić, 18 November 1991, Exhibit 00415 in ICTY *Mrkšić* trial; Agreement regarding Evacuation of Vukovar Hospital, annexed to Fax Message of EC Monitor Mission, 19 November 1991, Exhibit 00315 in ICTY *Mrkšić* trial.

[87] NDFP Declaration of Undertaking to Apply the Geneva Conventions of 1949 and Protocol I of 1977, 5 July 1996, reproduced in NDFP, *Declaration of Undertaking to Apply the Geneva I of 1977* (NDFP Human Rights Monitoring Committee Booklet No 6).

2011 violence in Libya, the Transitional National Council issued a statement indicating that 'its policies strictly adhere to the "Geneva Convention relative to the treatment of Prisoners of War"'.[88]

Another instructive example, of a slightly different type, comes from the armed conflict in Afghanistan during the Cold War (1979–89). In 1982 an agreement was concluded between the Afghan resistance and the ICRC on the 'conditions for the internment of foreign prisoners... under which the resistance expressed its intention to respect the spirit of the provisions of the Geneva Convention relative to the Treatment of Prisoners of War'.[89] The parties also 'agreed to the transfer and internment in a neutral country of Soviet soldiers detained by the Afghan opposition movements, in application, by analogy, of the Third Geneva Convention, relative to the treatment of prisoners of war'.[90] Pursuant to this agreement, 11 USSR nationals who had been captured in Afghanistan were transferred to Switzerland. Switzerland agreed to hold the individuals and the parties to the conflict agreed to the procedure.[91] Given that this is the procedure foreseen by Article 111 of the Third Geneva Convention, the example demonstrates that the essence of certain provisions of the law of international armed conflict, even in the area of prisoners of war, can be applied in situations of non-international armed conflict with the agreement of the parties to the conflict.[92] A similar possibility was canvassed, although not implemented, during the armed conflict in the former Yugoslavia.[93]

Thus, in practice, in some large-scale non-international armed conflicts, captured fighters are in fact afforded a functional equivalent to combatant immunity and/or treated as prisoners of war and this is done despite the lack of binding law to that effect. However, it should be noted that these examples principally relate to older, large-scale conflicts and are distinct from the smaller, more recent conflicts in which armed groups have tended to be characterized as terrorists as a matter of course. Furthermore, in the context of the 'war on terror', in 2002, the United States stated explicitly that captured members of Al-Qaeda and the Taliban 'do not qualify as prisoners of war'. Instead, they were characterized as 'unlawful combatants'.[94]

It is widely recognized that the notion of combatant immunity, or some sort of functional equivalent, is desirable for the law of non-international armed conflict in order to incentivize compliance with the law on the part of non-state armed groups. While states may be reluctant to declare in advance of a conflict that they will afford such immunity, they should be encouraged to do so during a conflict, in particular conflicts of a significant intensity and duration. Advocates of this position could usefully point to historical practice in this regard. At the very least, states should be encouraged not to sentence fighters to capital punishment during non-international armed conflicts, given that, in many such conflicts, some sort of amnesty for taking part in hostilities tends to be granted at its conclusion. Treating captured fighters in a *sui*

---

[88] Interim Transitional National Council, 'The Treatment of Detainees and Prisoners', 25 March 2011.
[89] Report of the situation of human rights in Afghanistan, E/CN.4/1985/21, 19 February 1985, para 104. See also para 163.
[90] 'External Activites' (1984) 24 *IRRC* 239, 240.
[91] Ibid.
[92] The character of the conflict is, however, open to question.
[93] See The London International Conference: Programme of Action on Humanitarian Issues Agreed between the Co-Chairmen to the Conference and the Parties to the Conflict, 27 August 1992.
[94] Memorandum for the Vice President and Others from the President, 7 February 2002, reproduced in KJ Greenberg and JL Dratel (eds), *The Torture Papers: The Road to Abu Ghraib* (Cambridge University Press, 2005) 134.

generis manner, as has been proposed above, may meet the concerns of the state while also leaving open the possibility that such individuals will benefit from more lenient treatment as part of the negotiations that end hostilities.

2.2 The natural environment

A second area of the substantive law that is in need of development is the law relating to the protection of the natural environment in situations of non-international armed conflict. As discussed in Chapter 3, the content of the law of non-international armed conflict consists primarily of international humanitarian law, which has developed by reference to the international humanitarian law of international armed conflict, and joined by international human rights law and international criminal law.[95] Other bodies of international law, however, have remained relatively untouched. For example, international humanitarian law rules on the protection of the natural environment have not generally been interpreted by reference to international environmental law. Unlike specific rules of international human rights law, specific rules of international environmental law have not been considered to form the *lex specialis* of the more general international humanitarian law provisions on the protection of the environment.

International humanitarian law provisions on the protection of the natural environmental tend to focus on aspects of the environment that impact upon humans rather than envisage the environment as an object itself in need of protection. For example, the prohibition on pillage, the prohibition on the destruction of dams and dykes that may cause the release of dangerous forces and thus cause severe losses among the civilian population, and the prohibition on the destruction of 'foodstuffs, crops, livestock, drinking water installations and supplies and irrigation works',[96] all serve primarily to protect persons rather than the environment. These rules are by no means unimportant insofar as protection of the environment itself is concerned. However, if international environmental law definitions of the environment were considered, air, water, soil, flora, and fauna would all be protected in their own right. These objects tend to benefit from little protection in non-international armed conflict, with defoliants sometimes being used and other measures taken to make land inhospitable to one side or another.[97]

Certain international humanitarian law provisions do protect the environment itself. Additional Protocol I provides that '[i]t is prohibited to employ methods or means of warfare which are intended, or may be expected, to cause widespread, long-term and severe damage to the natural environment', and that '[c]are shall be taken in warfare to protect the natural environment against widespread, long-term and severe damage'.[98] However, the requirement of 'widespread, long-term *and* severe damage', coupled with the meaning given to those terms, means that they will likely have little impact.[99] Another set of protections relate to modification of the natural environment. The Environmental Modification (ENMOD) Convention prohibits all 'hostile use of environmental modification techniques having widespread, long-lasting or severe

---

[95] Above, 77–99.
[96] Additional Protocol II, Articles 4(2)(g), 14, and 15.
[97] A Roberts, 'The Law of War and Environmental Damage', in JE Austin and CE Bruch (eds), *The Environmental Consequences of War* (Cambridge University Press, 2000) 47, 75.
[98] Articles 35(3) and 55(1) respectively.
[99] Emphasis added. Bothe, Partsch, and Solf, above note 6, 348; Final Report to the Prosecutor by the Committee Established to Review the NATO Bombing Campaign Against the Federal Republic of Yugoslavia (2000) 39 *ILM* 1257, 1262, para 15.

effects as the means of destruction, damage or injury' to the adversary.[100] This is considerably limited in its definition of environmental modification techniques and in the notion of widespread, long-lasting, or severe effects.[101] The applicability of both the foregoing provisions to non-international armed conflict is also questionable. The ENMOD Convention only applies in international armed conflict and even then only as between states parties.[102] There is some suggestion that customary international humanitarian law contains a rule by which '[t]he use of methods or means of warfare that are intended, or may be expected, to cause widespread, long-term and severe damage to the natural environment is prohibited', and that '[d]estruction of the natural environment may not be used as a weapon'.[103] However, the suggestion is very much an equivocal one; and the rules apply only 'arguably' to non-international armed conflict.[104] That said, it is surely correct that 'even if this rule is not yet customary, present trends towards further protection of the environment and towards establishing rules applicable in non-international armed conflicts mean that it is likely to become customary in due course'.[105] The existence of rules along these lines would be welcome in light of, for example, the Government of Iraq's draining of marshlands in the early 1990s reportedly to assist in the fight against insurgents.

Certain protections in respect of the natural environment also come about through other rules. For example, when the law of targeting limits attacks to military objectives, the natural environment would be protected insofar as it amounts to a civilian object.[106] Similarly, protection of the natural environment would have to be taken into account in the proportionality calculation.[107] Indeed, 'attacks against military targets which are known or can reasonably be assumed to cause grave environmental harm' require 'a very substantial military advantage in order to be considered legitimate'.[108]

Protection of the environment has also had a role to play in the development of the law of non-international armed conflict. Certain rules relating to weapons have come about, at least in part, due to concern for the protection of the environment. Commitments to the prohibition on anti-personnel mines, for example, have stemmed in part due to the effect of these mines on the environment.[109] Likewise, the Incendiary Weapons Protocol provides that 'it is prohibited to make forests or other kinds of plant cover the object of attack by incendiary weapons except when such natural elements are used to cover, conceal or camouflage combatants or other military objectives, or are themselves military objectives'.[110] While human rights law is only starting to deal with the environment as such, the Cairo Declaration on Human Rights

---

[100] Article I.
[101] Article II; Understandings Regarding the Convention, reproduced in D Schindler and J Toman, *The Laws of Armed Conflict* (Nijhoff, 2004) 168.
[102] Article 1.
[103] Customary International Humanitarian Law, Rule 45.
[104] Ibid.
[105] *Customary International Humanitarian Law, Volume I: Rules*, 157.
[106] Customary International Humanitarian Law, Rule 43A.
[107] *Legality of the Threat or Use of Nuclear Weapons*, Advisory Opinion [1996] ICJ Rep 226, para 30.
[108] Final Report on NATO, above note 99, 1263, para 22; Customary International Humanitarian Law, Rule 43C.
[109] See eg Declaration of the Rebolusyonaryong Partido ng manggagawa—Pilipinas and the Revolutionary Proletarian Army—Alex Boncayao Brigade against the use and Production of Landmines, 21 March 2000.
[110] Article 2(4).

in Islam provides that, in time of armed conflict, '[i]t is prohibited to fell trees [and] to damage crops or livestock'.[111]

On occasion, ad hoc agreements or declarations of the parties will contain provisions on protection for the environment. A notable example of this is the 2006 commitment of the Lord's Resistance Army (LRA) relating to protection of certain endangered species located in the Garamba National Park in the Democratic Republic of the Congo. The agreement provided an assurance to the rangers of the Garamba Park that, 'provided they properly identify themselves and not attack us, we undertake to fully cooperate with them'.[112] Reportedly, the Head of the LRA delegation to the Juba peace talks, then taking place between the LRA and the Government of Uganda, stated that '[t]he statistics we were shown [on the dangers posed to the endangered species] shocked us, and so we have given a tacit commitment that we will do whatever possible to live in harmony with the animals' and that '[w]e will act as their curators and do everything possible to see that they are not harmed for posterity'.[113] Despite the commitment, in subsequent years, the LRA continued to launch attacks inside the park and killed park rangers.

If there is truly to be a holistic law of non-international armed conflict, areas of international environmental law need to be embraced more fully than is the case at present, to the extent that they are relevant. Some aspects of international environmental law could be incorporated relatively easily. As a starting point, existing provisions of the law of non-international armed conflict could be extended to cover the natural environment. For example, depending on the situation at hand, nature reserves could be considered akin to 'demilitarized zones or other protected areas'.[114] This is similar to a proposal made at the 1974–7 Diplomatic Conference but which was not taken up.[115] Clean-up operations during times of non-international armed conflict could be considered akin to humanitarian assistance missions, at least insofar as affording protection to those persons involved in the operations is concerned.[116] Endangered species could be treated akin to cultural property and thus benefitting from particular protections. Reference could be made to the Convention on the Law of the Sea which contains obligations to protect and preserve the marine environment, and to prevent and reduce pollution of the marine environment.[117] Similarly, the principle in the Stockholm Declaration on the Environment could be taken on board, by which states—modified to parties to reflect the principal actors involved in non-international armed conflicts—have a 'responsibility to ensure that activities within their jurisdiction or control do not cause damage to the environment of other States or of areas beyond the limits of national jurisdiction'.[118] The more general point is that, in order for there truly to be a law of non-international armed conflict, all relevant areas need to be considered. That international human rights law and international criminal law have a role to play is

---

[111] Cairo Declaration on Human Rights in Islam, Article 3(b).
[112] Quoted in 'LRA Rebels Vow to Protect Rare Wildlife', *Independent Online* (South Africa), 21 August 2006. See also D Adam, 'The Elephant Man', *The Observer* (UK), 22 February 2009.
[113] Statement of Martin Ojul, Head of the LRA Delegation to the Juba Peace Talks, quoted in LRA Rebels, above note 112. See also Adam, above note 112.
[114] A Bouvier, 'Recent Studies on the Protection of the Environment in Time of Armed Conflict' (1992) 32 *IRRC* 554, 558. See also P Antoine, 'International Humanitarian Law and the Protection of the Environment in Time of Armed Conflict' (1992) 32 *IRRC* 517, 532–3.
[115] See ICRC, *Commentary on the Additional Protocols*, above note 6, 664.
[116] A Roberts, 'Environmental Destruction in the 1991 Gulf War' (1992) 32 *IRRC* 538, 553.
[117] United Nations Convention on the Law of the Sea, Articles 192 and 194.
[118] Declaration of the United Nations Conference on the Human Environment, Principle 21. See also USA/Canada, *Trail Smelter Arbitration*, III RIAA 1905.

widely accepted; however, to date, there has been little movement beyond those two areas of the law.

2.3 Territory under the control of the non-state armed group

A third aspect of non-international armed conflict that suffers from a particular dearth of legal attention is the regulation of relations between a non-state armed group and the persons and objects in territory under its control. As the international humanitarian law of non-international armed conflict has developed through analogy to the international humanitarian law of international armed conflict,[119] in instances in which no appropriate analogy could be drawn, there has been little by way of legal regulation.

Resort could have been made to the law of belligerent occupation; however, the orthodox view is that the law of belligerent occupation is particular to international armed conflict.[120] Reflecting such orthodoxy, the rules relating to belligerent occupation in the Customary International Humanitarian Law study apply to international armed conflict alone.[121] This may be for good reason. Some of the rules that comprise the law of belligerent occupation reflect a careful balance between the three principal actors, namely the occupying power, the people of the occupied territory, and the displaced sovereign. For example, the rules relating to the requisitioning of property reflect the competing interests of the different actors. The occupying power can take into its possession certain property belonging to the sovereign 'which may be used for military operations' but requisitions from the general population are prohibited 'except for the needs of the army of occupation'.[122] As regards 'public buildings, real estate, forests, and agricultural estates belonging to the hostile State, and situated in the occupied country', the occupying power acts as usufruct.[123] This tripartite division between occupier, occupied, and sovereign cannot be mapped neatly onto situations of non-international armed conflict. Furthermore, states may be unlikely to accept that the tripartite relationship applies at all vis-à-vis non-state armed groups. This is a controversial issue, both as a matter of law and as a matter of politics. As such the situation is generally considered to end there.

No rules of international humanitarian law have been developed to regulate relations between a non-state armed group and the persons and objects in territory under its control. Yet, not infrequently, non-state armed groups control sizeable tracts of territory. For example, mention can be made of the recently concluded conflicts in Nepal, Sri Lanka, and Sudan, in which the Communist Party of Nepal-Maoist (CPN-M), the Liberation Tigers of Tamil Eelam (LTTE), and the Sudan People's Liberation Movement/Army (SPLM/A), respectively controlled sizeable tracts of territory. It is difficult to comprehend that, once territory falls under the control of a non-state armed group, international humanitarian law has little or nothing to offer.

---

[119] See above, 55–65.
[120] *Prosecutor v Sesay, Kallon and Gbao*, SCSL-04-15-T, Judgment, 2 March 2009, para 982; Y Dinstein, *The International Law of Belligerent Occupation* (Cambridge University Press, 2009) 33–4; H-P Gasser, 'Protection of the Civilian Population', in D Fleck (ed), *The Handbook of International Humanitarian Law* (Oxford University Press, 2008) 272; RR Baxter, 'Jus in Bello Interno', in JN Moore (ed), *Law and Civil War in the Modern World* (Jonhs Hopkins University Press, 1974) 531; Greenwood, International Humanitarian Law, above note 9, para 5.16. Cf Fleck, Non-International Armed Conflicts, above note 6, 628.
[121] See Rules 41, 129A, 130.
[122] Regulations respecting the Laws and Customs of War on Land, annexed to Convention (IV) respecting the Laws and Customs of War on Land, The Hague, 1907, Articles 53 and 52 respectively.
[123] Ibid, Article 55.

It may be that, in such situations, international human rights law is considered better placed to regulate the relations, and in recent years, international human rights law has stepped in to fill the gap. Special procedures mechanisms of the UN Human Rights Council, in particular, have taken the view that, where non-state armed groups exercise control over territory and have a political structure, they can be expected to comply with human rights standards.[124] However, this remains controversial.

Yet, it is submitted that there is no reason why there should be a gap in international humanitarian law. The law of belligerent occupation is, in reality, a composite category that contains a number of different rules. The composite category could be broken down into its component parts in order to ascertain which rules can be applied to territory under the control of non-state armed groups and which cannot. Certain general protections and prohibitions contained in the law of belligerent occupation—for example, the protections afforded to the wounded and sick; the protection of civilian hospitals; the principle of humane treatment; the prohibition of collective penalties, pillage, and reprisals; the taking of hostages; the prohibitions of deportation and forcible transfer; and the right to due process and judicial guarantees—are already applicable to non-international armed conflicts, whether through comparable treaty provisions or through customary international law.[125] These would remain applicable.[126] The principles behind other rules, although more controversial, may be equally applicable. Take, as an example, the maintenance of law and order in the territory under the control of the armed group. The principle expressed in Article 43 of the Hague Regulations could have some role to play in non-international armed conflict: '[t]he authority of the legitimate power having in fact passed into the hands of the occupant, the latter shall take all the measures in his power to restore and ensure, as far as possible, public order and safety, while respecting, unless absolutely prevented, the laws in force in the country.' The alternative would be that there is no entity both responsible and able to maintain law and order in the territory in question. An analogy could also be drawn to the situation concerning unrecognized governments. Acts of unrecognized governments are given legal effect from time to time if failing to do so would be 'to the detriment of the inhabitants of the [t]erritory'.[127] Following the conclusion of the US civil war, in the context of certain Confederate legislation, the US Supreme Court opined that:

> acts necessary to peace and good order among citizens... which would be valid if emanating from a lawful government, must be regarded in general as valid when proceeding from an actual, though unlawful government; and... acts in furtherance or support of rebellion... or intended to defeat the just rights of citizens, and other acts of the like nature, must, in general, be regarded as invalid and void.[128]

In a later case, the Supreme Court indicated:

> The existence of a state of insurrection and war did not loosen the bonds of society, or do away with civil government or the regular administration of the laws. Order was to be preserved, police regulations maintained, crime prosecuted, property protected, contracts enforced, marriages

---

[124] See in particular, the view of the Special Rapporteur on extrajudicial, summary or arbitrary executions, E/CN.4/2005/7, 22 December 2004, para 76; ibid, Mission to Sri Lanka, E/CN.4/2006/53/Add.5, 27 March 2006, paras 26–7. See above, 96.
[125] See generally Chapter 8.
[126] See also Fleck, Non-International Armed Conflicts, above note 6, 628.
[127] *Legal Consequences for States of the Continued Presence of South Africa in Namibia (South West Africa) notwithstanding Security Council Resolution 276 (1970)* [1971] ICJ Rep 16, para 125.
[128] *Texas v White* (1868) 74 US 700, 733. See further below, 560.

celebrated, estates settled, and the transfer and descent of property regulated precisely as in time of peace. No one that we are aware of seriously questions the validity of judicial or legislative acts in the insurrectionary states touching these and kindred subjects where they were not hostile in their purpose or mode of enforcement to the authority of the national government and did not impair the rights of citizens under the Constitution.[129]

The Supreme Court also held that, although currency issued by the Confederates was illegal, contracts concluded during the war and using that currency should be upheld.[130] This conclusion was reached even though the Court found that 'the Confederate notes were issued in furtherance of an unlawful attempt to overthrow the government of the United States by insurrectionary force'.[131] Although belligerency was recognized during the US civil war, it is unclear whether, and if so to what extent, this influenced the Supreme Court. On a more general note, the situation demonstrates that, if drawing on analogies, analogy should not be limited to the international humanitarian law of international armed conflict. Other bodies of law could also prove useful.

This is not to suggest that the entirety of the law of belligerent occupation can be transposed *ipso facto* and without more to regulate the territory controlled by non-state armed groups. Other rules of the law of belligerent occupation may remain inapplicable. Issues relating to taxation or the requisitioning of property may prove difficult to apply, although here, too, there has been suggestion that 'the policy arguments for allowing rebel groups to seize certain types of property during war are sometimes strong' and that 'there is little basis for expecting rebel groups to comply with the laws of war without offering certain privileges'.[132] Indeed, this is an area that is in particular need of regulation. Other rules yet may presume the capacities of a state occupier.[133] To apply still other rules of the law of belligerent occupation to situations of non-international armed conflict may be to take them out of context. However, in general, all this demonstrates the need to move beyond the idea that the entire category of 'the law of belligerent occupation' has no applicability to non-international armed conflict. Despite the potential controversy that may ensue, the legal regulation of the situation in territory under the control of an armed group needs to be considered.

Just occasionally, there is practice on point. The 1820 Treaty on the Regularization of the War, concluded during the Colombian war of independence, provided that '[t]he inhabitants of villages which are alternately occupied by the forces of both Governments shall be highly respected and will enjoy extensive and absolute freedom and security whatever their opinions, positions, services or conduct with respect to the belligerent parties may be or may have been'.[134] The Lieber Code of 1863 contained provisions on territory controlled by the Confederate forces, including those relating to legislation, the work of local officials, and oaths of loyalty.[135] Ratko Mladić, in a 1994

---

[129] *Horn v Lockhart* (1873) 84 US 570, 580.
[130] *Thorington v Smith* (1868) 8 Wall 1.
[131] Ibid, 7.
[132] JG Stewart, *Corporate War Crimes: Prosecuting the Pillage of Natural Resources* (Open Society Initiative, 2010) 21–2.
[133] See, in the context of national liberation movements, A Roberts, 'What is a Military Occupation?' (1984) LV *BYIL* 249, 293.
[134] Tratado de Regularización de la Guerra, 26 November 1820, Article 11. French version published in (1820–1) 71 *Consolidated Treaty Series* 291. The original reads: 'Los habitantes de los pueblos que alternativamente se ocuparen por las armas de ambos gobiernos serán altamente respetados, y gozarán de una absoluta libertad y seguridad, sean cuales fueren o hayan sido sus opiniones, destinos, servicios y conducta con respecto a las partes beligerantes.'
[135] Lieber Code, Articles 6, 26, and 39.

order to his forces, which transmitted the contents of a ceasefire agreement, provided that '[t]he parties shall agree to protect the human rights of persons living in territories under their control. In accordance with international standards, including therein the international humanitarian law, all persons, regardless of their age, sex or ethnic origin, shall have the right to live in the place of their choice. The state of human rights in all areas shall be subject to international monitoring and surveillance'.[136] Perhaps more importantly, an ICTY Trial Chamber in the *Martić* case utilized the rules relating to belligerent occupation in the Hague Regulations without considering whether the conflict in question was an international or non-international one.[137] In general, this is an area in which further work needs to be carried out.

3. Enforcement and implementation of the law

As discussed in Chapter 10, it is in the area of implementation and non-judicial enforcement that international humanitarian law is considered to be at its weakest. This is particularly true of situations of non-international armed conflict, the enforcement mechanisms in respect of which are simply those of the law of international armed conflict. The importance of tailoring the relevant enforcement mechanism to the specificities of non-international armed conflicts is starting to be recognized, and in recent years, novel forms of implementation and enforcement have been established. These recognize, in particular, the need to take into account non-state armed groups and to engage with them on their respect for the law. The importance of engagement with non-state armed groups more generally is evident from a 2009 statement of UN Secretary-General Ban Ki-Moon, who observed that '[w]e need urgently to develop a comprehensive approach towards improving compliance by all these [non-state armed] groups with the law, encompassing actions that range from engagement to enforcement'.[138] The Secretary-General continued: 'while engagement with non-State armed groups will not always result in improved protection, the absence of systematic engagement will almost certainly mean more, not fewer, civilian casualties in current conflicts.'[139] Writing one year later, the Secretary-General expressed himself in stronger terms, noting that '[i]mproved compliance with international humanitarian law and human rights law will always remain a distant prospect in the absence of, and absent acceptance of the need for, systematic and consistent engagement with non-State armed groups'.[140]

However, engagement with non-state armed groups is controversial. The characterization of armed groups as terrorists has impacted concretely on the work of various parties. For example, 'staff members of particular nationalities can risk prosecution in their home countries' and 'restrictive clauses in funding agreements constrain certain activities'.[141] On occasion, the state may expel entities from its territory for engaging

---

[136] Ratko Mladić, Order to Commands [transmission of ceasefire agreement], 23 December 1994, Exhibit 5D01043.E in ICTY *Popović* trial.
[137] *Prosecutor v Martić*, IT-95-11-T, Judgment, 12 June 2007, paras 100–4.
[138] Report of the Secretary-General on the Protection of Civilians in Armed Conflict, S/2009/277, 29 May 2009, para 39.
[139] Ibid, para 40.
[140] Report of the Secretary-General on the Protection of Civilians in Armed Conflict, S/2010/579, 11 November 2010, para 52.
[141] K Thorne, 'Terrorist Lists and Humanitarian Assistance' (2007) 37 *Humanitarian Exchange* 13, 13. See also N Florquin and E Decrey Warner, 'Engaging Non-State Armed Groups or Listing Terrorists? Implications for the Arms Control Community' (2008) 1 *Disarmament Forum* 17.

with an armed group, as was true of the Government of Ethiopia in respect of the ICRC's engagement with the Ogaden National Liberation Front (ONLF) in 2007.[142] To engage with armed groups, even on matters of the law of non-international armed conflict, may also be considered to constitute the provision of 'material support or resources to a foreign terrorist organization'.[143] Concern has been voiced publicly in this regard by UN Secretary-General Ban Ki-Moon.[144]

One of the particularly unfortunate aspects of the law of non-international armed conflict is that, historically, there has been relatively little by way of engagement with non-state armed groups on the implementation and enforcement of the law. There has been even less by way of encouraging armed groups to enforce the law *themselves*. Things have started to change somewhat in recent years, with two particular initiatives proving important—the work of the United Nations in the area of children and armed conflict and the work of the non-governmental organization 'Geneva Call'. Particular attention is paid to these two initiatives in what follows given their novel approaches to engagement with armed groups on the law. A more general discussion on the advantages and disadvantages of engagement with armed groups follows. One particular form of non-state armed group enforcement is also considered, namely the courts of non-state armed groups.

3.1 Office of the Special Representative of the Secretary General for Children and Armed Conflict and the Security Council Working Group on Children and Armed Conflict

United Nations initiatives in the area of children and armed conflict have recognized the importance of engaging with all parties to armed conflicts, whether states or non-state armed groups, on issues pertaining to children and armed conflict. The activities in this area are several. Security Council Resolution 1261 (1999) contained various issues relating to children and armed conflict, in particular calling on parties to conflicts to respect their legal obligations and calling on the Secretary-General to submit a report on the implementation of the Resolution to the Security Council.[145] Over time, the focus of the Secretary-General's report has centred on six grave violations, namely the killing or maiming of children, recruitment or use of children as child soldiers, attacks on schools and hospitals, rape and other grave sexual violence against children, abduction of children, and denial of humanitarian access.[146] In 2001, the Security Council requested that the report include as an annex a list of parties to conflicts that recruit and use child soldiers.[147] This listing was intended to be 'a naming and shaming exercise that would indicate to the world who the perpetrators are, their names and

---

[142] Florquin and Decrey Warner, ibid, 19.
[143] See, in the United States, 18 USC 2339B(a)(1) and *Holder, Attorney-General, et al v Humanitarian Law Project, et al* (2010) 130 S Ct 2705, although the point is by no means limited to the United States. See, for the position in other states, Harvard Program on Humanitarian Policy and Conflict Research, 'Humanitarian Action under Scrutiny: Criminalizing Humanitarian Engagement', HPCR Working Paper, February 2011, 23–5.
[144] Report of the Secretary-General on the Protection of Civilians in Armed Conflict, S/2010/579, 11 November 2010, para 55.
[145] SC Res 1261 (1999).
[146] See eg Children and Armed Conflict: Report of the Secretary-General, A/59/695-S/2005/72, 9 February 2005, para 68.
[147] SC Res 1379 (2001).

where they are located'.[148] Appearing on the annexed lists over the years have been state forces, paramilitary groups, and non-state armed groups.

In order to be de-listed from the annex, parties are required to prepare and implement action plans on the cessation of recruitment and use of child soldiers in collaboration with UN country teams.[149] These action plans 'provide a mechanism to engage parties in practical steps to fulfill their obligations in regard to children'.[150] Dialogue with the listed parties is envisaged as a means by which to end the recruitment and use of child soldiers and to assist in the development of the action plans.[151] Accordingly, various UN entities interact with listed parties on the issue of child soldiers. Several action plans have been drawn up,[152] pursuant to which numerous child soldiers have been disarmed, de-mobilized, and reintegrated into society. Some parties have been de-listed following the conclusion and implementation of action plans and monitoring to ensure compliance. This is true of the Forces Armées des Forces Nouvelles (now Forces de Défense et de Sécurité des Forces Nouvelles (FDS-FN)) and four militia groups, all active in the Ivory Coast.[153] The Ivory Coast example has been used to show other listed parties that de-listing is possible through submission of, and compliance with, an action plan.[154] Parties may be re-listed should they recruit or use child soldiers at a later point in time.[155]

A further development took place in 2005 with the creation of a Security Council Working Group on Children and Armed Conflict, comprising all members of the Security Council.[156] The Security Council Working Group considers country reports and formulates conclusions and recommendations on them.[157] The conclusions and recommendations then feed into the work of the Office of the Special Representative of the Secretary-General for Children and Armed Conflict (SRSG-CAAC) as well as other interested actors. The Council may impose targeted measures on actors that have not drawn up or implemented action plans, measures that include 'the imposition of travel restrictions on leaders, their exclusion from any governance structures and amnesty provisions, a ban on the export or supply of small arms, a ban on military assistance,

---

[148] R Coomaraswamy, 'The Security Council and Children and Armed Conflict: An Experiment in the Making', Public Lecture, 12 April 2010, Centre on Human Rights in Conflict, University of East London School of Law.
[149] SC Res 1539 (2004).
[150] Report of the Special Representative of the Secretary-General for Children and Armed Conflict, A/62/228, 13 August 2007, para 35.
[151] SC Res 1460 (2003).
[152] For example Action Plan between the Moro Islamic Liberation Front (MILF) and the United Nations in the Philippines regarding the Issue of Recruitment and Use of Child Soldiers in the Armed Conflict in Mindanao, 1 August 2009; Action Plan between the Sudan People's Liberation Army (SPLA) and the United Nations regarding Children Associated with the SPLA in Southern Sudan, 20 November 2009; Action Plan between the Government of Nepal, the Unified Communist Party of Nepal-Maoist, and the United Nations in Nepal regarding the Discharge of Disqualified Maoist Army Personnel and Related Tasks, 16 December 2009. See also the Memorandum of Understanding between the Justice and Equality Movement (JEM) and the United Nations regarding Protection of Children in Darfur, 21 July 2010.
[153] Annual Report of the Special Representative of the Secretary-General for Children and Armed Conflict, A/HRC/9/3, 27 June 2008, para 16.
[154] See eg the statement of the Security Council Working Group to the LTTE: Working Group on Children and Armed Conflict, Conclusions on Children and Armed Conflict in Sri Lanka, S/AC.51/2008/11, 21 October 2008, para 5.
[155] Children and Armed Conflict: Report of the Secretary-General, A/63/785-S/2009/158, 26 March 2009, para 9.
[156] SC Res 1612 (2005); Article 2, Terms of Reference of the Working Group of the Security Council on Children and Armed Conflict, S/2006/275.
[157] Coomaraswamy, above note 148.

restrictions on the flow of financial resources to offending parties and a ban on illicit trade in natural resources'.[158] However, in practice, targeted measures are rarely imposed and some parties have remained listed for years.[159] The Security Council Working Group also issues letters, statements, and démarches to the parties concerned, states and armed groups alike. These have included the Forces Nouvelles of the Ivory Coast;[160] the Sudan Liberation Army (SLA) and the Justice and Equality Movement (JEM), both of Sudan;[161] the Forces Nationales de Libération of the Palipehutu, of Burundi;[162] the NPA, the armed wing of the NDFP, and the Moro Islamic Liberation Front (MILF), both of the Philippines;[163] the LTTE of Sri Lanka;[164] the Lord's Resistance Army (LRA) of Uganda;[165] and the Taliban of Afghanistan.[166]

The UN's work on child soldiers suggests that engagement with an actor is crucial to that actor's compliance with the relevant norm. The importance of engagement with non-state armed groups has been stressed and is reiterated in the various reports of the SRSG-CAAC.[167] The SRSG-CAAC has also recommended that '[c]ontact between the United Nations and non-State parties for dialogue towards the implementation of specific commitments to protect and release children should be encouraged in the best interest of the children involved'.[168] Although concerns surrounding legitimacy and legal status may arise as a result of engagement,[169] UN engagement with non-state armed groups is expressly noted as taking place without prejudice to the legal status, political status, and legitimacy of the groups in question.[170]

Importantly, the UN approach is not solely one of engagement; it is also a process that involves naming and shaming, pressure, and threats. The naming and shaming, through the listing, plays a crucial role, given that certain actors have expressed their desire to be removed from the annexed list in light of their intention to play a part in the governance of their country at a future point in time. The involvement of the

---

[158] Children and Armed Conflict: Report of the Secretary-General, A/59/695-S/2005/72, 9 February 2005, para 115. See also S/2006/724, Addendum, Option 5.
[159] Report of the Special Representative of the Secretary-General for Children and Armed Conflict, A/63/227, 6 August 2008, para 25.
[160] Security Council Working Group on Children and Armed Conflict Conclusions on Côte d'Ivoire, S/2007/93, Annex, 15 February 2007, para 4.
[161] Working Group on Children and Armed Conflict, Conclusions on Children and Armed Conflict in Chad, S/AC.51/2007/16, 24 September 2007, para 16.
[162] Working Group on Children and Armed Conflict, Conclusions on parties to the situation of armed conflict in Burundi, S/AC.51/2008/6, 5 February 2008, para 13.
[163] Working Group on Children and Armed Conflict, Conclusions on Children and Armed Conflict in the Philippines, S/AC.51/2008/10, 3 October 2008, para 5.
[164] Working Group on Children and Armed Conflict, Conclusions on Children and Armed Conflict in Sri Lanka, S/AC.51/2008/11, 21 October 2008, para 5.
[165] Working Group on Children and Armed Conflict, Conclusions on Children and Armed Conflict in Uganda, S/AC.51/2008/13, 5 December 2008, para 11.
[166] Working Group on Children and Armed Conflict, Conclusions on Children and Armed Conflict in Uganda Afghanistan, S/AC.51/2009/1, 13 July 2009, para 15.
[167] See eg Report of the Special Representative of the Secretary-General for Children and Armed Conflict, A/64/254, 6 August 2009, para 19; Report of the Special Representative of the Secretary-General for Children and Armed Conflict, A/63/227, 6 August 2008, para 8; Report of the Special Representative of the Secretary-General for Children and Armed Conflict, A/60/335, 7 September 2005, para 51.
[168] Report of the Special Representative of the Secretary-General for Children and Armed Conflict, A/64/254, 6 August 2009, para 76.
[169] See below, 546–9.
[170] See eg Report of the Special Representative of the Secretary-General for Children and Armed Conflict, A/62/228, 13 August 2007, para 27; Report of the Special Representative of the Secretary-General for Children and Armed Conflict, A/63/227, 6 August 2008, para 8.

Security Council and the threat of sanction also have a role to play in compliance with the law. Each of these elements has been raised in conservations between the SRSG-CAAC and various armed parties. In 2010, the SRSG-CAAC recounted:

> It is true that a number of parties do not care, and sometimes are unaware, if they are listed by the Secretary-General, but in many cases the listing process has resulted in compliance. For example in 2008 I visited the Central African Republic and met with Commandant Laurent of the APRDC [the Armée Populaire pour la Restauration de la République et la Démocratie]. He lived deep in the bush and did not have much access to international news. I informed him that he was on the annexes of the Secretary-General's annual report and since it was after Security Council resolution 1612, that there was a possibility of targeted measures being used against him in the near future. He was initially taken aback and gave me a long lecture, his unique version of the history of the United Nations. However, even though he was a rebel now, he had aspirations of leading the country one day. He did not want to be on any list. He made a commitment to release the children as long as there were proper programmes for their care. He is currently releasing the children in a structured manner and all separated children have been reintegrated into their communities... A similar change of heart took place in Nepal. After prolonged negotiations, in February this year the Nepalese Maoists released their minors who had been held in the cantonments. Again, they felt that as a past and possible future ruling party they should not be on the Secretary-General's list.[171]

Thus, the naming and shaming element, and the threat of sanctions are both important. However, it is equally apparent that these are not the only drivers of the process given that, on occasion, it is the non-state armed group rather than the UN that will initiate the listing procedure, as was the case with the Chin National Front/Chin National Army (CNF/CNA) of Burma.[172]

Just as with the codes of conduct of non-state armed groups,[173] an armed group that enters into a commitment to abide by humanitarian norms may influence other armed groups also to enter into such commitments. Thus, UN Secretary-General Ban Ki-Moon has observed that, '[i]t is anticipated that the precedent set by the commitment of the SLA (Minawi) [Sudan Liberation Army (Minawi)] faction in Darfur to an action plan [on child soldiers] will generate momentum for other armed groups to follow suit'.[174] Similarly, the Government of the Philippines was 'encouraged' by the submission of an action plan on child soldiers by the MILF 'and was optimistic that this action plan could be the springboard of similar negotiations with other non-State actors to halt the recruitment and use of children'.[175] Engagement with armed groups on the issue of child soldiers has also led to engagement on other humanitarian norms concerning children,[176] as well as on humanitarian norms more broadly.[177]

These UN initiatives on children and armed conflict are significant. In addition to the concrete results that they have achieved, they suggest that there is a very real role for engaging parties to a conflict on humanitarian norms, be they states or non-state armed groups, coupled with the threat of sanction. Nevertheless, certain shortcomings in the

---

[171] Coomaraswamy, above note 148.
[172] Report of the Secretary-General on Children and Armed Conflict in Myanmar, S/2009/278, 1 June 2009, para 17.
[173] See above, 442.
[174] Report of the Secretary General on Children and Armed Conflict in the Sudan, S/2007/520, 29 August 2007, para 36.
[175] Report of the Secretary General on Children and Armed Conflict in the Philippines, S/2010/36, 21 January 2010, para 47.
[176] Children and Armed Conflict: Report of the Secretary-General, A/63/785-S/2009/158, 26 March 2009, para 159.
[177] Ibid, para 38.

process are evident. First, the consent of the relevant state is required even to engage the non-state armed group. While, oftentimes, such consent is forthcoming, on occasion it is not, as was the case with the Governments of Colombia and Myanmar.[178] When consent is not provided, UN entities are not able to engage with the relevant armed groups. This is problematic as it renders monitoring difficult. If armed groups are already listed in the annex, it may also mean that they are unable to be de-listed. For example, in 2009, the Karenni National Progressive Party (KNPP) wrote to the SRSG-CAAC inviting monitoring of its bases, requesting dialogue with the UN, and de-listing.[179] For its part, in 2010, the JEM of Darfur indicated that the '[i]nsistence of relevant organizations to work with sovereign states to the exclusion of rebels' is a major problem as well as the '[i]nability and unwillingness of these organizations to visit JEM areas and discuss and evaluate with them ways of implementing these conventions on the ground and assess the degree of conformity of JEM and others to these rules'.[180] However, other entities may be able to engage with the actors concerned. For example, while the Governments of Colombia and Myanmar have been reluctant to allow UN entities to meet with non-state armed groups fighting against them on issues of child soldiers, both states have, to varying degrees, allowed Geneva Call to meet with the very same groups on issues relating to mine action and the ban on anti-personnel mines, with the Vice-President of Colombia stating that '[t]he national government of Colombia offers guarantees to Geneva Call to engage illegal armed groups'.[181] The reason the state does not allow the UN to engage with armed groups may relate to the formality and prestige of the UN. These same issues tend not to surround engagement on the part of NGOs. This highlights the need for different forms of engagement and enforcement to take place, at different levels of formality.

The second shortcoming—which also reflects the importance of the initiative—is that the process is limited largely to child soldiers. The 2009 extension of the process to include the killing or maiming of children and the rape or sexual violence against children[182] is thus to be welcomed. Parties that engage in those atrocities are also to be included in the annexes to the report to the Security Council. A similar process is underway in respect of rape and sexual violence in armed conflict more generally.[183] However, it seems unlikely that a process of this type will ever be able to cover all aspects of the law of non-international armed conflict. As indicated above, it does, however, provide a useful complement to other enforcement mechanisms.

The third shortcoming relates to the lack of involvement of relevant parties at the early stages of the process. When an initial listing report relates to state armed forces,

---

[178] Children and Armed Conflict: Report of the Secretary-General, A/62/609-S/2007/757, 21 December 2007, para 158. On interaction with the Government of Myanmar, see Report of the Secretary-General on Children and Armed Conflict in Myanmar, S/2007/666, 16 November 2007, paras 48–52; Report of the Secretary-General on Children and Armed Conflict in Myanmar, S/2009/278, 1 June 2009, paras 45–52.

[179] Report of the Secretary-General on Children and Armed Conflict in Myanmar, S/2009/278, 1 June 2009, para 25. See Press Release No 02/09, Appeal for the Karenni Army's name to be removed from the list of non-state armed groups making use of child soldiers in armed conflict, 18 April 2009.

[180] Geneva Call (ed), *In Their Words: Perspectives of Armed Non-State Actors on the Protection of Children from the Effects of Armed Conflict* (Geneva Call, 2010) 19.

[181] Statement of Francisco Santos, Vice-President of Colombia, June 2004, excerpted in Geneva Call, Annual Report 2004, 25. On Geneva Call, see below, 538–42.

[182] SC Res 1882 (2009).

[183] SC Res 1960 (2010).

the state concerned can challenge information contained in the report at the draft stage; however, the same is not true of non-state armed groups. Similarly, while the Security Council Working Group may invite the state the subject of its considerations to the relevant meeting to hear its observations,[184] no invitations are extended to the armed groups concerned. There are obvious reasons that explain this divergence in treatment. Yet, if the state concerned is unable to attend the meeting, it is able to provide the Working Group with written comments on the report.[185] This possibility could usefully be extended to non-state armed groups. The point is an important one given that armed groups have objected to being listed in the annex without any prior discussion or notification, as was the case with the United Wa State Army (UWSA) of Burma.[186] Others, including the Armée Populaire pour la Restauration de la République et la Démocratie (APRD) of the Central African Republic, have indicated that they only found out about their being listed through reading the reports of the Secretary-General.[187] Still others, including the NDFP, have criticized the fact that a report may be issued 'without hearing the side' of the armed group 'as required by standards and fundamental rules of fairness and due process'.[188]

Despite these shortcomings, and in comparison with traditional enforcement mechanisms such as the Protecting Powers regime and the International Humanitarian Fact-Finding Commission,[189] the results that have been achieved are significant. Above all, it demonstrates the importance of tailoring an enforcement mechanism to the specificities of the situation in which it is being applied.

3.2 Geneva Call

A second initiative that has made important progress in engaging armed groups on humanitarian norms is that of 'Geneva Call'. Geneva Call is a Geneva-based NGO that seeks to engage compliance with humanitarian norms on the part of 'armed non-state actors'. Armed non-state actors are those actors that are 'involved in situations of armed conflict that operate outside effective State control and are primarily motivated by political goals'. They include 'armed movements, de facto authorities, and non-internationally recognized States'.[190] Established in 2000, the origins of Geneva Call lie in the recognition of the challenges posed by the state-centric nature of international law coupled with the realization that the problem of anti-personnel mines 'would not be effectively addressed unless ANSAs [armed non-state actors] were included in the solution'.[191]

---

[184] Article V, Terms of Reference of the Working Group of the Security Council on Children and Armed Conflict, S/2006/275.
[185] This was the case for Somalia: Working Group on Children and Armed Conflict, Conclusions on Children and Armed Conflict in Somalia, S/AC.51/2007/14, 20 July 2007, para 1.
[186] Report of the Secretary-General on Children and Armed Conflict in Myanmar, S/2009/278, 1 June 2009, para 51.
[187] *In Their Words*, above note 180, 14.
[188] Letter to UN Secretary General Ban Ki-Moon on Children in Armed Conflict from LG Jalandoni, Member of the NDFP National Executive Committee and Chairperson of the NDFP Negotiating Panel, 24 November 2008. See also 'Report of the Panel of Experts established pursuant to Resolution 1591 (2005) concerning the Sudan Issues 29 October 2009: A Response from JEM', 18 November 2009.
[189] See above, 457–8 and 459–62.
[190] <http://www.genevacall.org/about/about.htm>; <http://www.genevacall.org/about/mission.htm>.
[191] <http://www.genevacall.org/about/about.htm>.

3.2.1 The Deed of Commitment

Compliance is engaged, in part, through a Deed of Commitment, which provides for obligations similar to those contained in the Ottawa Convention on Anti-Personnel Mines. Deeds are concluded by armed non-state actors and usually signed in the Alabama Room, the room in which the 1864 Geneva Convention was signed.[192] The Deed provides for three principal obligations. First, signatories are required 'to adhere to a total ban on anti-personnel mines', namely 'a complete prohibition on all use, development, production, acquisition, stockpiling, retention, and transfer of such mines, under any circumstances. This includes an undertaking on the destruction of all such mines'.[193] Second, there is an obligation 'to cooperate in and undertake stockpile destruction, mine clearance, victim assistance, mine awareness, and various other forms of mine action, especially where these programs are being implemented by independent international and national organizations'.[194] The 'other forms of mine action' include such things as the mapping and marking of mine fields, and the recording and classification of stockpiles. Third, signatories are required 'to issue the necessary orders and directives to ... commanders and fighters for the implementation and enforcement of [their] commitment under the foregoing paragraphs, including measures for information dissemination and training, as well as disciplinary sanctions in case of non-compliance'.[195] Sanctions have included '[d]emotion, suspension, expulsion and imprisonment'.[196]

Further dialogue on the obligations takes place between Geneva Call and the armed non-state actor signatory. Although there are no formal next steps or deadlines by which certain activities are required to be undertaken, discussion between the two actors relates to these issues. In the case of the MILF of the Philippines, a confidential submission was required to be made to Geneva Call disclosing 'maps of its occupied areas and possible mine-contaminated areas for joint mine clearance'.[197] With respect to measures of implementation, the MILF was required to issue 'written orders and directives' to its armed wing, the Bangsamoro Islamic Armed Force (BIAF), to undertake 'effective information dissemination to the BIAF rank and file', to make 'changes in BIAF military doctrine to remove the use of APMs', to conduct 'various trainings starting with technical briefings and seminar-workshops for the BIAF general staff and field commanders, mine and humanitarian education programs which reach the foot soldiers', and to ensure 'BIAF military disciplinary sanctions for violations or non-compliance'.[198] This was designed to address a misconception on the part of the MILF as to precisely which mines were prohibited.

3.2.2 Monitoring

The Deed of Commitment also requires monitoring of the armed non-state actor undertakings. It provides:

---

[192] Geneva Call, Annual Report 2003, 11.
[193] Deed of Commitment, para 1 (emphasis omitted).
[194] Ibid, para 2 (emphasis omitted).
[195] Ibid, para 4 (emphasis omitted).
[196] Geneva Call, Engaging Armed Non-State Actors in a Landmine Ban: The Geneva Call Progress Report (2000–2007), 19. See generally above, 445–8.
[197] Implementing Guidelines for the Moro Islamic liberation Front (MILF) pursuant to its 'Deed of Commitment under Geneva Call for Adherence to a Total Ban on Anti-Personnel Mines and for Cooperation in Mine Action', Section D.
[198] Ibid, Section C.

TO ALLOW AND COOPERATE in the monitoring and verification of our commitment to a total ban on anti-personnel mines by Geneva Call and other independent international and national organizations associated for this purpose with Geneva Call. Such monitoring and verification include visits and inspections in all areas where antipersonnel mines may be present, and the provision of the necessary information and reports, as may be required for such purposes in the spirit of transparency and accountability.[199]

Monitoring takes place at three levels. First, monitoring is undertaken by the armed non-state actor signatory itself. This self-monitoring takes the form of submitting reports to Geneva Call on the measures the signatory has taken to implement its obligations arising from the Deed,[200] the challenges it has faced in complying with the Deed, as well as details on stockpiles, mine action undertaken, and any incidents involving mines.[201] The standard reporting forms are modelled on the Ottawa Convention transparency reports.[202] Self-reporting is important as it contributes to a sense of ownership of the Deed on the part of the armed group,[203] provides an indication of the willingness (or not) of the armed group to comply with its obligations,[204] and leads to greater knowledge of the relevant norms, on the part of the armed group. The self-monitoring aspect of the Deed has been welcomed by signatories, who also recognize that that, by itself, is insufficient.[205]

Accordingly, the second level of monitoring is undertaken by Geneva Call, through third parties, namely 'local networks and partners that are familiar with the [armed non-state actor], the affected communities and the mine issue in the region'.[206] These bodies, with their specialist knowledge and field presence, have proved important in ascertaining signatories' compliance with the Deed. For example, these third parties have ascertained that certain allegations of mine use have, in fact, involved mines that are not prohibited by the Deed, were planted by state forces rather than by armed non-state actor signatories, or were laid decades prior to signature.[207] However, there are also limits to the use of this type of third party monitoring. Some third parties may be partial to one party to the conflict or the other; others may be unwilling to share information; still others may be distrusted by the signatory and not be provided with the necessary information or access to the relevant area.[208]

The third level of monitoring takes place through Geneva Call missions. There are two types of missions: routine follow-up missions, and verification missions undertaken in response to credible allegations of serious violations which could not be resolved through the second level of monitoring. Three verification missions have been undertaken—twice in respect of the MILF of the Philippines in relation to the use and production of anti-personnel mines, and once in respect of the Puntland administration

---

[199] Deed of Commitment, para 3.
[200] Geneva Call, An Inclusive Approach to Armed Non-State Actors and International Humanitarian Norms: Report of the First Meeting of Signatories to Geneva Call's Deed of Commitment, 19. See also Geneva Call, Annual Report 2004, 21; Geneva Call, Annual Report 2006, 14.
[201] Geneva Call, Engaging Armed Non-State Actors in a Landmine Ban: The Geneva Call Progress Report (2000–2007) 25.
[202] Geneva Call, Inclusive Approach, above note 200, 20. See P Bongard and J Somer, 'Monitoring Compliance of Armed Non-State Actors: A Look at International Mechanisms and the Example of Geneva Call Deed of Commitment' (2011) 93 *IRRC* 673.
[203] Geneva Call, Engaging Armed Non-State Actors, above note 201, 25.
[204] Ibid.
[205] Geneva Call, Inclusive Approach, above note 200, 20.
[206] Ibid.
[207] Geneva Call, Engaging Armed Non-State Actors, above note 201, 26 fn 59.
[208] Ibid, 29.

in Somalia in relation to the acquisition of mines. The Puntland administration was found not to have violated the Deed.[209] A violation was found in respect of the first set of allegations against the MILF in 2000, although this resulted from a misunderstanding as to the nature of the mines that were prohibited.[210] A verification mission in respect of the second allegation found that it was not proven that the mines had been planted by the MILF.[211] Allegations of violation of the Deed have also been raised against three other signatories, namely the Jowhar administration of Somalia, regarding the acquisition of mines; the SPLM/A, concerning the use of mines; and the Kurdistan Workers' Party (PKK), also regarding the use of mines. However, in the case of these three signatories, the allegations were withdrawn or the second form of monitoring established that no violation had taken place. All five signatories accepted verification on the part of Geneva Call and its local partners.[212] This demonstrates that enforcement of the law of non-international armed conflict through consensual verification missions is indeed possible and that parties may well allow monitoring of their compliance. By contrast, despite reports of violations of the Ottawa Convention, no verification missions have taken place pursuant to Article 8 of that Convention.

The Deed provides that Geneva Call may publicize instances of compliance or non-compliance with the Deed on the part of the signatory.[213] Publicizing instances of compliance, in particular, is important. As with much of the law of non-international armed conflict, instances of violation are publicized, leading to a perception that the law is something which is neglected or ignored. Non-state armed groups in particular are criticized for violating the law. This approach assists in the re-orientation of such a perception, giving credit where it is due.[214]

3.2.3 Beyond anti-personnel mines

While initially focusing on anti-personnel mines, Geneva Call has viewed the particular case of mines as a step towards greater engagement on other humanitarian norms. Thus, the Deed of Commitment provides that armed non-state actor signatories treat 'this commitment as one step or part of a broader commitment in principle to the ideal of humanitarian norms, particularly of international humanitarian law and human rights, and to contribute to their respect in field practice as well as to the further development of humanitarian norms for armed conflicts'.[215]

Armed non-state actor signatories have themselves encouraged Geneva Call to expand its work beyond anti-personnel mines.[216] The 'Children and Armed Non-State Actor' programme was launched in 2008 following exploratory missions and

---

[209] Report of the Geneva Call follow up mission to Puntland, Hiran and Bakol regions, 15–27 September 2004 (Geneva Call, Geneva, 2005). See Bongard and Somer, above note 202.
[210] Report of the Geneva Call Mission to the Moro Islamic Liberation Front (MILF) in Central Mindanao, Philippines (30 April 2002).
[211] Report of the 2009 Verification Mission to the Philippines to Investigate Allegations of Anti-Personnel Landmine Use by the Moro Islamic Liberation Front (2010).
[212] Geneva Call Newsletter, Volume 6(3) (2008) 3.
[213] Deed of Commitment, Article 7.
[214] See above, 4.
[215] Deed of Commitment, para 5. See also the Statutes of Geneva Call, Article 3.
[216] Declaration of the Second Meeting of Signatories to Geneva Call's 'Deed of Commitment for Adherence to a Total Ban on Anti-Personnel Mines and for Cooperation in Mine Action', 19 June 2009.

discussions with armed non-state actors.[217] A Deed of Commitment has been drawn up,[218] in a process that has been supported by signatories to the Deed on anti-personnel mines.[219] The Deed is important, *inter alia*, for its adoption of the age of 18 for armed non-state actor signatories as compared with the varying ages used by the differing human rights and humanitarian law instruments. The Deed also imposes a 'total ban' on the use of children in hostilities rather than a ban on their direct or active participation,[220] reflecting the Additional Protocol II standard. At the time of writing, Geneva Call was in the process of drafting a third Deed of Commitment on sexual and gender-based violence.

The difficulty with the approach taken by Geneva Call is that verification missions are dependent on the consent of the party to the Deed and of the relevant state. If the state is unwilling to grant consent for Geneva Call to undertake a mission, the mission will not be able to take place. A second difficulty is that a slight tension exists between encouraging the armed non-state actor to implement and enforce its commitments and an outside observer doing so. A fine line has to be drawn between the two and that line may have to vary as between different groups and different obligations. Despite these difficulties, Geneva Call has made important progress, using novel means, as compared with the traditional modalities of implementing and enforcing the law of non-international armed conflict.

3.3 Engaging compliance

The work of Geneva Call and the Office of the Special Representative of the Secretary-General for Children and Armed Conflict raises broader issues relating to engagement with non-state armed groups on humanitarian norms.

3.3.1 Influencing others

Engagement with armed groups on humanitarian norms has had a direct effect on compliance with these norms on the part of *other* actors. This effect has taken place at different levels.

Engagement with an armed group on humanitarian law norms has had an impact on the state against which the armed group is in conflict.[221] States may refrain from ratifying a treaty because the opposing non-state armed group is unable to do so. Although state ratification of a treaty binds the non-state armed group as a matter of law,[222] the state may view ratification as binding itself but not the armed group. Accordingly, when an armed group commits itself to abiding by particular norms, this may ameliorate the state's concern and allow the state to ratify the treaty. The Government of Sudan's approach to the Ottawa Convention usefully illustrates the point. The SPLM/A signed Geneva Call's Deed of Commitment in October 2001 and, a year later, the SPLM/A and the Government of Sudan signed a Memorandum of

---

[217] Geneva Call, Annual Report 2008, 7.
[218] Deed of Commitment under Geneva Call for the Protection of Children from the Effects of Armed Conflict, November 2010.
[219] Declaration of the Second Meeting of Signatories, above note 216.
[220] Deed of Commitment, Article 1. See above, 316.
[221] See, for further details, A Roberts and S Sivakumaran, 'Lawmaking by Non-State Actors: Engaging Armed Groups in the Creation of International Humanitarian Law' (2012) 37 *Yale Journal of International Law* 107.
[222] See above, 240–1.

Understanding with the UN on mine action. The following year, in October 2003, the Government of Sudan ratified the Ottawa Convention. According to the former Director of the UN Mine Action Service, '[i]t is clear from conversations with senior officials of the Government, that they would not have felt able to ratify the Treaty, if the SPLM/A had not already made a formal commitment to observe its provisions in the territory under its control'.[223] Along similar lines, the Government of Sri Lanka indicated that 'it would be willing to sign the Mine Ban Treaty if the LTTE takes on a similar commitment'.[224] Accordingly, it is not uncommon for state ratification of the Ottawa Convention to be linked to non-state armed group signature of Geneva Call's Deed of Commitment. For example, a 2006 European Parliament Resolution on Sri Lanka provided that the European Parliament 'urges both sides, as an immediate gesture of goodwill, to cease the use of anti-personnel landmines and to assist in their removal, and considers that, to this end, the Government of Sri Lanka should set an example by signing the Ottawa Convention and the LTTE should sign the Geneva Call "Deed of Commitment"'.[225]

Armed groups may sign Geneva Call's Deed, in part, in order to influence the state into making a similar commitment or to implement their commitments. On the occasion of signature of the Deed, the armed non-state actor often makes a statement setting out the reasons why it has decided to sign the Deed. In these statements, several armed groups have called upon the government against which they are fighting to commit to, or implement, the Ottawa Convention. For example, in 2003 the National Council for the Defence of Democracy-Forces for the Defence of Democracy (CNDD-FDD) of Burundi urged 'the government to respect and quickly implement its obligations' under the mine ban treaty.[226] In 2007, the Palaung State Liberation Front (PSLF) of Burma stated that it 'would like to appeal to the Government and other armed groups to desist from planting landmines'.[227] In 2001, the SPLM/A stated that, 'as we stand committed to deposit our Deed of Commitment, we raise our voice to the international community to bring pressure to bear on the government of the Sudan to ratify the Ottawa Convention... and to allow free access for co-ordinated cross-conflict mine action operations'.[228]

The influence is not felt solely at the level of the opposing state. Armed groups influence one another, such influence also operating at a number of levels. Indeed, Geneva Call operates, in part, on the idea that one armed group may influence another. The Deed of Commitment on Anti-Personnel Mines thus provides: '[w]e see the desirability of attracting the adherence of other armed groups to this *Deed of Commitment* and will do our part to promote it.'[229] Signatories themselves have recognized the need to influence armed non-state actor non-signatories to desist from using

---

[223] M Barber, 'Preface', in Geneva Call, *Armed Non-State Actors and Landmines: Volume I* (2005) 1.
[224] Ibid, 31. See also Geneva Call, Annual Report 2002, 8.
[225] 18 May 2006, para 12.
[226] Geneva Call, Annual Report 2003, 9.
[227] Statement made by Mai Aik Phone, General Secretary of the Palaung State Liberation Front (PSLF), on the Occasion of Signing the *Deed of Commitment* to Ban Anti-Personnel Mines Held, 16 April 2007.
[228] Statement made by Cdr Nhial Deng Nhial, Chairman of the Commission for External Relations, Information and Humanitarian Affairs of the Sudan People's Liberation Movement/Army on the Occasion of the Signing and Depositing to Geneva Call Deed of Commitment to Ban Anti-Personnel Mines, 4 October 2001 (emphasis omitted).
[229] Deed of Commitment, para 8.

anti-personnel mines.[230] Geneva Call has noted that engaging armed non-state actors that have not yet signed the Deed 'can only be achieved through a collaborative effort. Peer pressure is a useful tool in this context: armed groups that have signed the Deed of Commitment can have a significant effect on other groups if they explain their reasons for adhering to the ban and share their experience, especially in the area of mine action'.[231] Signatories have followed through on this statement, advocating to other armed non-state actors the importance of a prohibition on anti-personnel mines. This is true, for example, of the Arakan Rohingya National Organization (ARNO) and CNF in Burma, the National Socialist Council of Nagalim-Isaac/Muivah (NSCN-IM) in India, and the United Somali Congress/Somali National Alliance/Somalia Reconciliation and Restoration Council (USC/SNA/SRRC) in Somalia.[232] The SPLM/A has also shared its experience, 'notably with Colombian, Angolan and other Sudanese' armed non-state actors.[233]

This peer influence operates at both the local and the international levels. If several armed groups are involved in the same armed conflict, even if they are not formally related to one another, they may have links and these links may allow mutual influence. For example, the Implementing Guidelines of the Deed of Commitment of the MILF provide that 'the MILF shall take active steps in promoting this Deed with other non-state armed groups in the Philippines'.[234] Along similar lines, at the signing of the Deed of Commitment in 2007, the Lahu Democratic Front (LDF) of Burma stated that '[w]e will do our best to advocate to other armed Lahu groups to also stop using anti-personnel mines. . . . [w]e will use our position within the National Democratic Front (NDF) to encourage other armed opposition groups to ban anti-personnel mines'.[235] During the armed conflict in Colombia, for a time, the various armed groups arranged themselves under an umbrella organization known as the Coordinadora Guerrillera Simón Bolivar for peace talks. The Ejército de Liberación Nacional (ELN) reportedly brought international humanitarian law to the fore of discussions between the armed groups, introducing some of its concepts to the FARC and other groups.[236] The ELN, in turn, had reportedly been influenced by its contacts 'with the academic world, and its contacts, in the 1980s, with the Salvadoran and Nicaraguan insurgencies, both of which had made public commitments to abide by IHL'.[237]

---

[230] See eg Geneva Call, Workshop Report: Towards a Mine Free World, Dimapur, Nagaland, India, 16 March 2005, 4.
[231] Geneva Call, Inclusive Approach, above note 200, 23. See also Declaration to the Nairobi Summit made by the Signatories of the Geneva Call's Deed of Commitment for Adherence to a Total Ban on Antipersonnel Mines and for Cooperation in Mine Action, December 2004. See also Declaration by Signatories to the 'Deed of Commitment under Geneva Call for Adherence to a Total Ban on Anti-Personnel Mines and for Cooperation in Mine Action' to the Cartagena Summit on a Mine-Free World, 30 November to 4 December 2009 (19 June 2009).
[232] Geneva Call, *Armed Non-State Actors and Landmines, Volume II: A Global Report of NSA Mine Action* (Geneva Call, 2006) 79–81.
[233] Ibid, 81.
[234] Implementing Guidelines for the Moro Islamic Liberation Front (MILF) pursuant to its 'Deed of Commitment under Geneva Call for Adherence to a Total Ban on Anti-Personnel Mines and for Cooperation in Mine Action', Section F1 (emphasis omitted).
[235] Statement Made by Aik Long Kham Mwe, Chairman and General Secretary of the Lahu Democratic Front (LDF), on the Occasion of Signing the Deed of Commitment to Ban Anti-Personnel Mines Held, 16 April 2007.
[236] D García-Peña Jaramillo, 'Humanitarian Protection in Non-International Conflicts: A Case Study of Colombia' (2000) 30 *IYHR* 179, 197.
[237] P Gassmann, 'Colombia: Persuading Belligerents to Comply with International Norms', in S Chesterman (ed), *Civilians in War* (Lynne Rienner Publishers, 2001) 67, 79.

This potential for peer-influence is by no means limited to locally situated groups. Groups unrelated to the conflict in question, operating in very different parts of the world, may influence one another. For example, the African National Congress is reported to have influenced the Irish Republican Army (IRA) in its decommissioning of arms.[238] In the context of anti-personnel mines, the Ban Landmines Campaign Nepal and Geneva Call organized a seminar on the role of the Communist Party of Nepal (Maoist) in the mine ban. The Chairman of the MILF Coordinating Committee for the Cessation of Hostilities attended, sharing the MILF's perspective on the mine ban and on 'the benefits for confidence-building that this measure has brought to relations between the MILF and the Government of the Republic of the Philippines'.[239] Similarly, the Executive Director of the New Sudan Mine Action Directorate, an entity of the SPLM/A, sent a letter to the ELN of Colombia in 2004 setting out the use of landmines in Sudan and explaining the reasons behind the SPLM/A ban. He appealed to the ELN, the Government, and other armed groups 'to go on with your politics, but to save Colombia... from further landmines contamination'.[240] This peer influence has had concrete results. Geneva Call has indicated that '[i]n at least one case it appears that NSAs [non-state actors] wish to become involved in mine action because they would like to follow the example of other NSAs'.[241]

The idea of impacting other actors takes place at yet another level, namely if the armed group succeeds in becoming the government or creating a new state. In such instances, the policy adopted while an armed group may be continued while in government. For example, the Code of Conduct used by the National Resistance Army (NRA) of Uganda under Museveni was later used by the Ugandan armed forces under the Presidency of Museveni.[242] Along similar lines, the Deputy Prime Minister and Minister of the Interior of the Transitional Federal Government of Somalia has stated that '[i]t is the intention of the Transitional Federal Government to follow in the principles of the Ottawa Convention and outlaw anti-personnel landmines. This is already the case in some regions as many of the former faction leaders, now my colleagues in Government, including myself, have signed the Geneva Call "Deed of Commitment"'.[243] More concrete are the cases of Burundi, Iraq, and South Sudan. In Burundi, in 2003, the CNDD-FDD signed Geneva Call's Deed of Commitment. In 2005, the CNDD-FDD became the Government of Burundi and, in 2008, Parliament enacted legislation implementing the Ottawa Convention.[244] In Iraq, two signatories to Geneva Call's Deed, the Kurdistan Democratic Party (KDP) and the Patriotic Union of Kurdistan (PUK), became part of the government. They encouraged ratification of the Ottawa Convention and Iraq became party to the Convention in 2007.[245] Following the newly created state of South Sudan by the SPLM in 2011, the

---

[238] See H McDonald, 'ANC Brokered IRA Peace Offer', *The Observer* (UK), 14 May 2000.
[239] Geneva Call, *Armed Non-State Actors and Landmines, Volume II*, above note 232, 80. See also Geneva Call, Annual Report 2006, 5.
[240] Letter sent by a Commandant of the Sudan People Liberation Army to the ELN, June 2004.
[241] Geneva Call, *Armed Non-State Actors and Landmines, Volume II*, above note 232, 14.
[242] YK Museveni, *Sowing the Mustard Seed* (MacMillan, 1997) 146–7.
[243] Eng. Mohamed Hussein Aideed, quoted in Geneva Call, Annual Report 2005, 4.
[244] Loi No 1/30 du 10 Octobre 2008 portant mise en oeuvre de la Convention sur l'Interdiction de l'Emploi, du Stockage, de la Production et du Transfert des Mines Antipersonnel et sur leur Destruction signée à Ottawa le 3 December 1997 (10 October 2008).
[245] Geneva Call, Engaging Armed Non-State Actors in a Landmine Ban: The Geneva Call Progress Report (2000–2007) 8–9.

Government of South Sudan ratified the Ottawa Convention, also in 2011. The SPLM had signed Geneva Call's Deed several years earlier.

3.3.2 Legitimacy concerns

One of the principal concerns of states in allowing third parties to engage with armed groups, even on issues of the law of armed conflict, is that this may serve to legitimize the group. Accordingly, states sometimes restrict access to, or prohibit engagement with, non-state armed groups on the basis that any such access or engagement by outside actors affords the group a measure of legitimacy. For example, during a 2009 Security Council debate on the protection of civilians in armed conflict, Vietnam stated that '[r]eality has proved that, while possibly effective in certain cases, dialogue with non-State armed groups must be carefully considered and approached in the overall framework of cooperation with the States in question in order to avoid the unintended legitimization of illegal or even internationally recognized terrorist groups'.[246] More forcefully, the Russian Federation stated:

We believe that the contact of humanitarian organizations with non-State armed groups can be established only with the consent of the Government of the relevant States. Moreover, the practice of such contacts must be approached with great caution so as not to legitimize existing outlawed units. We believe that it is unacceptable to consider terrorist organizations, especially the Taliban and Al-Qaida, as some sort of armed opposition groups with which one could allegedly conduct a dialogue on humanitarian matters.[247]

In the particular case of the Taliban, in 2008, the Government of Afghanistan indicated concern about engagement on the part of the international community, as this 'would reduce the Government from being a sovereign to being a mere faction in a civil war'.[248] During the same period, the Special Rapporteur on extra-judicial executions noted that he was 'aware that various actors had reservations about the political implications' of his meeting with the Taliban while on mission to Afghanistan.[249] He continued that although he abided by these reservations, '[i]n retrospect, this was a mistake. Taking account of information provided by such sources would permit a more nuanced understanding of Taliban and other AGE [anti-government element] strategies'.[250]

These insights have importance beyond engagement specifically with the Taliban. Indeed, as indicated above, the importance of engagement with non-state armed groups is starting to be recognized. For example, on the 60th anniversary of the 1949 Geneva Conventions, UN Secretary-General Ban Ki-Moon stated:

We must...focus more attention on compliance with international humanitarian law by non-State armed groups. Unpalatable as it may be for some States, engagement with such groups is critical. The United Nations must be able to talk to all warring parties, including armed groups. Failure to do so is always likely to mean more, not fewer, civilians killed and wounded. I urge Member States to accept this necessity.

---

[246] Security Council, 6151st meeting, 26 June 2009, Protection of Civilians in Armed Conflict, S/PV.6151, 26 June 2009, 9.
[247] Ibid, 17.
[248] Report of the Special Rapporteur on Extrajudicial, Summary or Arbitrary Executions, Mission to Afghanistan, A/HRC/11/2/Add.4, 6 May 2009, para 43. The Government has since entered into talks with the Taliban.
[249] Ibid, fn 38.
[250] Ibid, para 42.

We know from experience that regular engagement, monitoring and reporting creates a culture in which both States and non-State groups are increasingly being made aware of the need to respect international humanitarian law.[251]

UN special procedure mandate-holders are also cognizant both of the importance of engaging non-state armed groups and of the problem of such contact potentially affording legitimacy to the groups. Thus, a draft of the manual for special procedures mandate-holders provided that it should be made clear that 'the involvement of the mandate-holder is not understood as an endorsement of any particular claim made by the non-State actor as to representativity, legitimacy, or other matters'.[252]

In some respects, concerns surrounding legitimacy are related to those surrounding legal status. Thus, the concepts of legitimacy and legal status are sometimes treated together. For example, the African Union Convention on Internally Displaced Persons provides in relevant part that '[t]he provisions of this Article shall not, in any way whatsoever, be construed as affording legal status or legitimizing or recognizing armed groups'.[253] The Special Representative of the Secretary-General for Children and Armed Conflict has similarly noted that 'the engagement in dialogue with an insurgency group does not confer legitimacy or a particular legal status on that group'.[254] To the extent that the concerns are related, reference can be made to the discussion on legal status and armed groups.[255]

In other respects, legitimacy-related concerns surrounding engagement of non-state armed groups are of a different order to those relating to legal status. States often actively seek to de-legitimize armed groups, describing them as criminals, traitors, or terrorists. For example, the Government of Turkey stated in 2005, maintaining its longstanding position, that the PKK is not a non-state armed group but a terrorist organization and that '[t]he use of terms such as "rebels" or "armed non-state actors"' to describe the PKK gives 'a wrong indication about the real nature of a terrorist organization'.[256] Similarly, also in 2005, a former President of Colombia stated that 'in Colombia there is a very serious social problem that we must solve, but the actions of the violent groups cannot be framed nor defined as actions within an internal armed conflict. It is a terrorist threat'.[257]

At a different, but no less important, level, a 2010 judgment of the US Supreme Court suggests that training non-state armed groups ('terrorist organizations') even on international humanitarian law standards may amount to 'knowingly providing material support or resources to a foreign terrorist organization', in turn amounting to a domestic crime.[258] The reasoning is that, providing material support, even for

---

[251] 'Honouring Geneva Conventions, Secretary-General says Debate "No Longer between Peace and Justice but between Peace and What Kind of Justice', SG/SM/12494, 26 September 2009. See also Security Council, 6151st meeting, 26 June 2009, Protection of Civilians in Armed Conflict, S/PV.6151, 26 June 2009, 4 (Under-Secretary General for Humanitarian Affairs).

[252] Manual of the United Nations Human Rights Special Procedures (Draft), June 2006, para 83.

[253] Article 7(1).

[254] Report of the Special Representative of the Secretary-General for Children and Armed Conflict, A/60/335, 7 September 2005, para 51.

[255] See above, 205–9.

[256] Letter from Ambassador Türkekul Kurttekn in response to the characterization of the PKK in Landmine Monitor Report 2005, 15 December 2005.

[257] Intervention of President Uribe, Forum on 'Internal Conflict or Terrorist Threat?', Chía, Colombia, 26 April 2005, quoted in D Roa-Castro, 'Mine Action in the Midst of Internal Conflict: The Colombian Case', in Geneva Call, *Mine Action in the Midst of Internal Conflict* (2005) 17. See above, 204–5.

[258] *Humanitarian Law Project*, above note 143; 18 USC §2339B(a)(1).

peaceful purposes, could 'free[] up other resources within the organization that may be put to violent ends. It also importantly helps lend legitimacy to foreign terrorist groups—legitimacy that makes it easier for those groups to persist, to recruit members, and to raise funds—all of which facilitate more terrorist attacks'.[259]

The impact of listing armed groups fighting in non-international armed conflicts as terrorist groups has been felt by those seeking to engage with armed groups on humanitarian norms.[260] For example, a 2004 report of UN Secretary-General Kofi Annan noted that '[t]he designation of certain non-State armed groups as terrorist organizations has had an adverse impact on opportunities for humanitarian negotiations. The prohibition on dialogue with armed groups in Colombia, for example, has resulted in severe restrictions on access to populations in need'.[261] One representative of an armed group indicated in 2011 that listing as a terrorist group may have the effect of saying to the armed group 'what do I have to lose?'.[262] Accordingly, listing may serve to suggest that there is no incentive to comply with the law.

However, the position is far more nuanced than simply to assert that states are reluctant to allow engagement with armed groups on humanitarian norms for fear of affording them legitimacy. Many states do allow outside entities—foreign states, the UN, or NGOs—to have access to non-state armed groups. Others will purport to grant access but then deny visas or indicate that security considerations make any visit impossible.[263] Others yet may prohibit direct interaction on the part of outside entities but allow local partners to meet with armed groups.[264] Still others will actively facilitate access to the armed group, for example allowing the outside entity to meet imprisoned leaders of the group, even releasing those leaders for short periods of time to allow them to promote compliance with humanitarian norms.[265] Some states may place various armed groups on their lists of terrorists, yet fund the work of third parties who seek to engage with the listed groups on humanitarian norms or actively praise the work of these third parties.[266] There is a general recognition, at least by certain states, that even listed groups cannot be ignored and have to be engaged. Invariably, despite state pronouncements on point, secret channels exist between the state and the opposing armed group, which may, over time, give rise to the commencement of a peace process.[267] Furthermore, as noted above, no less an entity than the Security Council

---

[259] *Humanitarian Law Project*, ibid, 2725. Cf the opinion of Justice Breyer, dissenting (joined by Ginsburg J and Sotomayor J).

[260] See above, 532–3.

[261] Report of the Secretary-General to the Security Council on the protection of civilians in armed conflict, S/2004/431, 28 May 2004, para 41.

[262] Information provided to author.

[263] See eg Geneva Call, Annual Report 2005, 16 (India); Geneva Call, Annual Report 2007, 24 (Sri Lanka).

[264] Geneva Call, Engaging Armed Non-State Actors in a Landmine Ban: The Geneva Call Progress Report (2000–2007) 11.

[265] See Geneva Call, Annual Report 2003, 11; Geneva Call, Annual Report 2004, 23–4; E Reusse-Decrey, 'The Struggle against Landmines: An Opening for Peace Talks in Colombia' (2005) 16 *Conciliation Resources: Accord* 48.

[266] Cf Council Common Position 2009/67/CFSP, 26 January 2009, updating Common Position 2001/931/CFSP on the application of specific measures to combat terrorism and repealing Common Position 2008/586/CFSP, Official Journal of the European Union, 27 January 2009, L.23/37, with Geneva Call, Annual Report 2009, 32 (list of donors). See also European Parliament Resolution on measures to promote a commitment by non-State actors to a total ban on anti-personnel landmines, 6 September 2001.

[267] Consider, for example, the history of the Declaration of Principles on Interim Self-Government Arrangements (1993) (the Oslo Accords). Consider also the history of the Northern Ireland peace process, on which see C Bell, *Peace Agreements and Human Rights* (Oxford University Press, 2000) 60.

has called for the training of members of armed groups on humanitarian norms.[268] As also noted above, the precise nature of the outside entity and the particular humanitarian issue may have an impact on the approach taken.[269]

Similarly, the very issue of legitimacy is a contested one, and a distinction needs to be drawn between legitimacy under the law, political legitimacy, and other forms of legitimacy.[270] The issue is usually presented as a comparison between the legitimacy of the armed group and the legitimacy of the state, with the armed group being considered inherently illegitimate and the state inherently legitimate. Less frequently asked, but critical, is from whose perspective legitimacy is being assessed. From the perspective of civilians, things may be altogether different. For example, a US soldier reports that, in relation to the armed conflict in Afghanistan, '[t]he most common complaint we hear from Afghans...is that we haven't seen the government in "X" number of years'.[271] In such situations, particularly if it is the armed group that is providing health and education services, enforcing the law, and adjudicating disputes, it may well be the armed group that is deemed the more legitimate in the eyes of the local population. In conflicts with an ethnic, racial, or religious character, the ethnicity, race, or religion of the parties will also likely have a role to play in perceptions of legitimacy.

The issue of legitimacy and legitimization is thus an important one, perhaps the most difficult hurdle to engaging with non-state armed groups on humanitarian norms. However, it is also a highly nuanced issue. In light of the possible benefits of engaging with parties to the conflict, it is an issue that needs to be addressed. As with legal status,[272] it is to be hoped that a caveat that engagement is taking place without any notion of legitimacy will serve to assuage state concerns in this area. It should also not distract from the essential point, which is that there needs to be engagement with armed groups on their respect for humanitarian norms.

3.4 Courts of non-state armed groups

Another mechanism by which the law of non-international armed conflict could be enforced, and which involves armed groups taking responsibility for enforcement themselves, is to use courts of armed groups. Armed groups frequently establish courts. The convening of these courts is usually justified as being in the interests of the populace, couched in the language of 'people's courts' and 'popular revolutionary trials'. The international community views these courts in far less favourable terms, dismissing them as illegitimate and inconsistent with fair trial standards. The concern is that courts of non-state armed groups amount to 'a veneer of legality to what would better be termed vigilantism', as the Special Rapporteur on extra-judicial executions has put it, in the context of courts set up by the NDFP.[273] States the territory on which the courts are based are even more critical, viewing the convening of courts by armed groups as an encroachment on their sovereignty, and disputing the characterization of the decisions of these courts as 'law'. Accordingly, outside actors rarely engage with

---

[268] SC Res 1894 (2009). See generally above, 434–7.
[269] See above, 537.
[270] On legitimacy in international law generally, see TM Franck, *The Power of Legitimacy Among Nations* (Oxford University Press, 1990).
[271] Lt-Col DG Fivecoat, quoted in CJ Chivers, 'In Eastern Afghanistan, at War with the Taliban's Shadowy Rule', *New York Times*, 6 February 2011.
[272] See above, 209.
[273] Report of the Special Rapporteur on extrajudicial, summary or arbitrary executions, A/HRC/8/3/Add.2, 16 April 2008, para 32.

armed groups on the creation and operation of their courts. When they do engage, the two sides usually speak past one another rather than engaging in any sustained dialogue. Yet, it is submitted that the courts of armed groups have the potential to constitute an alternative to summary execution, to contribute to the maintenance of law and order in territory controlled by the armed group, and to reduce the climate of impunity that so often exists in times of non-international armed conflict. Courts of non-state armed groups also have the potential to be a mechanism by which to enforce the law of non-international armed conflict.

3.4.1 Examples

That armed groups establish courts is sometimes met with some surprise.[274] Yet, armed groups have always convened courts. In situations of recognized belligerency, prize courts were convened in order to determine whether or not ships were lawfully seized and their contraband sold. These courts were *required* to be convened and were recognized by outside states.[275] Prize courts are, of course, of a different nature to other courts operated by non-state armed groups and which are convened in existing non-international armed conflicts. However, even more traditional courts were convened by armed groups in historical conflicts and were recognized by outside states. For example, during the US civil war, the illegal abduction and subsequent enslavement of a British citizen in territory under the control of Confederate forces gave rise to a statement on the part of the British Law Officers that 'the Southern Government is ... bound to take proper measures for the purpose of bringing to justice the offender, if found within the limits over which it exercises *de facto* authority'.[276]

In many non-international armed conflicts, non-state armed groups have convened courts. In the Philippines, the NDFP convenes 'people's courts'. It has argued that, through the 1998 Comprehensive Agreement on Respect for Human Rights and International Humanitarian Law, the Government of the Philippines 'itself has recognized the separate authority of the NDFP to take actions pertaining to suspected violators of human rights and international humanitarian law, who can be arrested, investigated and, if the evidence warrants, subjected to prosecution and trial'.[277] The NDFP 'Guide for Establishing the People's Democratic Government' provides that 'people's courts' are to be created at the provincial, district, municipal, and barrio levels.[278] A panel of three judges sits on 'minor and simple' cases and a panel of nine judges on 'major and complex' cases, in particular those involving the death penalty.[279] A right of appeal exists to a higher court, and cases involving the death penalty are

---

[274] See eg *Official Records*, above note 4, Vol 8, 362, para 28 (Spain).

[275] See eg Report of the Law Officers (Atherton, Palmer, and Phillimore), 'The Legality of the Sinking of Neutral Merchant Ships by a Belligerent, and the Question whether the Remedy should be sought in the Prize Court or Diplomatically', 12 November 1862, reproduced in A McNair, *International Law Opinions, Selected and Annotated, Volume Three* (Cambridge University Press, 1956) 359; Opinion of the Law Officers (Atherton, Palmer, and Phillimore), 17 January 1863, reproduced in ibid, Vol One, 139; Opinion of the Law Officers (Atherton, Palmer, and Phillimore), 16 September 1863, reproduced in ibid, 140.

[276] Opinion of the Law Officers (Atherton, Palmer, and Phillimore), 12 September 1863, reproduced in ibid, 146, 147.

[277] JM Sison, 'Introduction', in NDFP, *Declaration of Undertaking to Apply the Geneva Conventions of 1949 and Protocol I of 1977* (NDFP Human Rights Monitoring Committee Booklet No 6) 4.

[278] NDFP 'Guide for Establishing the People's Democratic Government', October 1972, Part II, Chapter III, Article 2, reproduced in ibid, 78.

[279] Ibid, Part II, Chapter III, Article 2.

automatically appealed.[280] Trials are 'ordinarily' held in public.[281] An article on, what may be considered to be, due process guarantees provides:

> The people's court shall require specification of charges and sufficient investigation of the case prior to trial and shall always inquire into the side of the complainant as well as the accused. The opposite sides of any case shall be given ample hearing and shall be entitled to counsel as well as the presentation of witnesses and evidence.[282]

However, NDFP courts have been criticized as being 'either deeply flawed or simply a sham' due to the lack of due process guarantees afforded by them. They are also considered to lack 'anything that could reasonably be characterized as a penal code'.[283]

'People's courts' were convened by the CPN-M during the armed conflict in Nepal and flourished in the period immediately after the conclusion of the ceasefire.[284] The increase in the number of CPN-M courts paralleled the establishment of a CPN-M administration. Indeed, the CPN-M regarded their courts as the heart of their government.[285] The courts applied the CPN-M public legal code, which provided that, '[i]nvestigations shall be carried out by the security organ, prosecutions by the People's Prosecutor and decisions by the Peoples Court. The organs of the state shall rely on the people, based on evidence and criterion of law'.[286] Many cases heard by CPN-M courts involved minor disputes over land, money, and familial relationships.[287] 'Informers' were also tried before people's courts.[288] Judges were given training, however, only for a day or two. This was considered sufficient as, in the words of one judge, 'these cases are often a matter of common sense'.[289]

In Indonesia, officials of the Free Aceh Movement (GAM) reported to Human Rights Watch that, if:

> GAM leaders believed a person had committed a crime... they did not exercise summary punishment, but convened a council or *majelis* at the village, subdistrict, or district level. Village councils, they said, mostly handled petty crimes, but if a person were accused of 'interaction with the enemy' or involvement with Indonesian security forces, one of the higher level councils would be convened. Each such council, they said, was composed of four or five persons, but, they rarely handed out punishments: rather, usually, they discussed the crime with the accused, secured his or her repentance and a promise of no further wrongdoing, and then released the person. If arrested for theft, the person would have to return the stolen property.[290]

During the armed conflict in Sierra Leone (1991–2002), the RUF convened 'people's courts'. The RUF recounted:

---

[280] Ibid, Article 6.
[281] Ibid, Article 4.
[282] Ibid, Article 3.
[283] Report of the Special Rapporteur on extrajudicial, summary or arbitrary executions, A/HRC/8/3/Add.2, 16 April 2008, para 32.
[284] United Nations Office of the High Commissioner for Human Rights in Nepal, *Human Rights Abuses by the CPN-M: Summary of Concerns* (2006), 4; J Somer, 'Jungle Justice: Passing Sentence on the Equality of Belligerents in Non-International Armed Conflict' (2007) 89 *IRRC* 655, 681.
[285] C Haviland, 'Parallel justice, Maoist style', *BBC News*, 14 October 2006.
[286] Article 2, Paragraph 9 of the Public Legal Code, 2060 (2003/2004).
[287] See 'Judged by the people', *The Economist*, 5 October 2006; C Haviland, 'Parallel justice, Maoist style', *BBC News*, 14 October 2006.
[288] 'Prachanda Interview: Full Transcript', *BBC News*, 13 February 2006. Prachanda was the head of the CPN-M in Nepal.
[289] Maoist judge, in C Haviland, 'Parallel justice, Maoist style', *BBC News*, 14 October 2006.
[290] Human Rights Watch, *Indonesia: The War in Aceh* (2001) 22.

A few RUF fighters in the bush went on the rampage and as their own way of stating their objection to the planned elections, they proceeded on a campaign to cut off the hands of innocent villagers as a message that no voting should occur. This was how the amputation of hands started in Sierra Leone by desperate RUF men... Pa Foday Sankoh, the RUF leader was especially chagrined at the actions taken by these few RUF fighters. Our leader is aware that in war, atrocities occur especially when young disenfranchised men are revolting against an oppressive system. However, Pa Sankoh has never condoned acts of violence against civilians by RUF fighters. Pa Foday Sankoh immediately set up a special investigative Tribunal. This Tribunal was set up by the RUF War & Peace Council to look into the actions of and subsequently discipline the RUF fighters who performed these amputations. After the tribunal, all those fighters found guilty of this were publicly executed.[291]

During the armed conflict in El Salvador (1980–91), the Frente Farabundo Martí para la Liberación Nacional (FMLN) set out a detailed explanation as to the legal basis for its convening of courts. The FMLN took the view that international humanitarian law 'indisputably presupposes that either of the contending parties has the authority to try and sanction penal infractions committed in relation to the armed conflict'.[292] The FMLN argued that the Additional Protocol II requirement, that the courts offer the 'essential guarantees of independence and impartiality', did not require the courts to be established 'according to the government law in effect'. According to the FMLN:

Nor is it necessary that guilt be proven by the standards of the government law; rather Protocol II presupposes the coexistence 'of national legislation of the State with insurgent legislation'. Consequently, under this interpretation, each of the contending parties shall be able to try according to their own applicable laws.[293]

FMLN courts tried, *inter alia*, violations of international humanitarian law. Following the shooting of two wounded US service-personnel by an FLMN fighter, the FMLN 'admitted to what happened and... said that those responsible have been charged with committing a war crime by violating the FMLN's code of conduct and the Geneva Conventions'. The FMLN indicated that 'the trial of the accused will be open and independent observers will participate'.[294]

FMLN courts were criticized for failing to provide the requisite due process guarantees. The United Nations Observer Mission in El Salvador (ONUSAL) held that the courts lacked impartiality, lacked legal training on the part of the decision-makers, and failed to afford all the necessary rights and means of defence, including the right to appeal.[295] For its part, Americas Watch took the courts to task for failing to provide legal training to those involved with the courts and for not disclosing the identity of defence counsel to the accused.[296] The FMLN responded to these criticisms, contending that its procedural law did afford fair trial guarantees, including the presumption of innocence and the prohibitions on retroactive trials, coerced testimony, and enforced guilty pleas. However, in the view of the FMLN, the particular type of tribunal and

---

[291] RUF Political Leadership-Kailahun District, 'RUF Calls for Independent Investigations', 15 January 1999.
[292] FMLN, *Legitimacy of Our Methods of Struggle* (Inkworks Press, 1988) 17.
[293] Ibid, 19–20 (internal citation omitted).
[294] Inter-American Commission on Human Rights, 'Annual Report of the Inter-American Commission on Human Rights 1990–1991', Doc. OEA/Ser.L/V/II.79.rev.1 Doc. 12, 22 February 1991, 442.
[295] Third Report of the United Nations Observer Mission in El Salvador, A/46/876-S/23580, 19 February 1992, paras 112–14.
[296] Americas Watch, *Violations of Fair Trial Guarantees by the FMLN's Ad Hoc Courts* (Americas Watch, 1990) 21.

legislation required by Additional Protocol II had to be 'adapted to the conditions and capacity' of the warring parties. Realism dictated that 'the particular mechanisms necessary for defense' had to be 'adjusted to the real possibilities of the zone where the trial is held'. By way of example, the FMLN observed that defence counsel could not be required to be a licensed attorney if there were no licensed attorneys in the region. Instead, in such a situation, 'defense counsel should be selected by virtue of his conduct and the solidity [sic] of his ethical principles'.[297] The FMLN also argued that, in certain circumstances, the identity of jurors and defence counsel could not be disclosed so as to avoid reprisals being carried out against them.[298]

An example of a particularly developed court system is that of the courts established by the LTTE during the conflict in Sri Lanka (1983–2009). In the early 1990s, the LTTE began establishing a system of courts in the north and east of Sri Lanka, on the territory under its control. The chief of the LTTE legal and administration division pointed to two principal reasons for the LTTE's convening of courts. First, the system was intended to aid a smooth administration of the territory: '[w]e have to maintain law and order in the areas controlled by us. For this purpose we need the court system.'[299] Second, the will of the people demanded it: '[t]he people in the north and east have lost faith in the legal system of the country. Therefore this [LTTE court] system should continue.'[300]

At its most developed, the court system consisted of some 17 courts organized in a hierarchical structure, including six district courts, two High Courts, an Appeals Court, and a Special Bench that was akin to a Supreme Court. Those sentenced to capital punishment could also have recourse to a 'Review Committee on Appeal for Pardon'.[301] By late 2004, LTTE courts had heard some 23,000 cases, many of which related to land disputes and financial matters. Others involved LTTE cadres, although some of these were referred to specialist military courts.[302] The courts enforced the Tamil Eelam Penal and Civil Codes, both of which were enacted in 1994. These codes, like the rest of the LTTE legal system, were based on a mixture of Sri Lankan, Indian, and British law.[303] The LTTE also established a 'law college'. Initially open to LTTE cadres alone, the college was later opened to the wider population. The course was of five years' duration, consisting of three years' academic study and a two-year apprenticeship.[304] Lawyers from any part of Sri Lanka could appear before LTTE courts, but had to take an oath before doing so.[305]

Prior to this high watermark, things were very different. As explained by the Chief of the LTTE Legal Division:

---

[297] FMLN, above note 292, 20.
[298] Ibid. See also Letter from Head of the FMLN Secretariat for the Promotion and Protection of Human Rights to Americas Watch, excerpted in Americas Watch, above note 296, 11.
[299] C Kamalendran, 'The Inside Story of "Eelam Courts"', *Sunday Times* (Sri Lanka), 14 November 2004.
[300] Ibid. See also Interview with E Pararajasingham, 'Tamil Eelam—a de facto State: Tamil Eelam Legal System', 30 October 2003, available at <http://tamilnation.org>.
[301] Ibid. For a slightly different structuring, see 'LTTE Courts structure', *Sunday Times* (Sri Lanka), 14 November 2004.
[302] S Gurunathan, 'LTTE courts open to all lawyers', *Sunday Times* (Sri Lanka), 14 November 2004; 'We have an independent system says "District Court Judge"', *Sunday Times* (Sri Lanka), 14 November 2004; Kamalendran, above note 299; Pararajasingham, above note 300.
[303] Pararajasingham, ibid; Kamalendran, above note 299.
[304] Kamalendran, above note 299.
[305] Gurunathan, above note 302.

[I]n the beginning we established mediation boards (Inakka Saphai) at the village level. These functioned from 1984 to 1992. But the mediation board system was a failure mainly because there was no legal code as [a] basis for adjudication and because many of those who sat on the mediation boards weren't educated and trained in law. It created a lot of problems for the Liberation Movement and led to frictions with society.[306]

In response to the question as to why, then, the mediation boards continued to operate for close to eight years, the legal chief answered:

In the beginning we were a guerrilla organisation, engaging in hit and run tactics against the Sri Lankan armed forces. We had no stable control over large territories or populations. Therefore we neither had the resources nor the environment to set up and run a proper judicial system.[307]

Mirroring the view of the FMLN, the LTTE's approach was that the facts on the ground dictated the way in which the courts could operate:

[T]he contours of the space within which our legal system has to function is quite limited by political, economic and military pressures. But as this space expands in the future we would be in a position to adopt measures that would perfect our legal system to match international standards.[308]

The SPLM operated a system of courts in the territory under its control in the south of Sudan. The court structure comprised a Court of Appeal, a High Court for each region, county courts, as well as chiefs' courts of appeal, chiefs' regional courts, and chiefs' courts.[309] An Attorney-General's Chambers, comprising a civil division, criminal division, and legislation and drafting division was also created,[310] and an extensive penal code specified the criminal law applicable in 'SPLM/SPLA controlled areas'.[311] The Mouvement pour la Libération du Congo (MLC) operates a 'military judicial system'.[312] The MLC has adopted a Code of Conduct which sets out rules of military discipline and outlines the framework of the Martial Court and Disciplinary Board system.[313] The Disciplinary Board has the competence to try junior officers for any offence except those of murder, theft, rape, and certain others. Such cases are to be referred to the Martial Court.[314] For its part, the Kosovo Liberation Army (KLA) utilized a military court. Investigative judges, assistants, and a president operated the court. The court applied 'international conventions . . . KLA rules . . . former laws used in the VJ [Yugoslav Army] and international laws'.[315] One KLA order provided that '[i]mmediate measures of isolation, disarmament and escort to the KLA organs of military justice are to be undertaken against the perpetrators of criminal offences or violations of military discipline'.[316]

---

[306] Pararajasingham, above note 299.
[307] Ibid.
[308] Ibid.
[309] Resolution 9: Establishment of an Independent Judiciary, in SPLM, *A Major Watershed: SPLM/SPLA First National Convention, Resolutions, Appointments and Protocol* (SPLM, New Sudan, March/April 1994) 10–11.
[310] Ibid, 12.
[311] The New Sudan Penal Code, 1994, Chapter I, section 3.
[312] *Prosecutor v Jean-Pierre Bemba Gombo*, ICC-01/05-01/08, Decision Pursuant to Article 61(7)(a) and (b) of the Rome Statute on the Charges of the Prosecutor Against Jean-Pierre Bemba Gombo, 15 June 2009, para 461.
[313] Ibid, para 462.
[314] Ibid.
[315] *Prosecutor v Đorđević*, IT-05-87/1-T, Judgment, 23 February 2011, para 1574.
[316] Kosovo Liberation Army General Staff, Order, 28 November 1998, Exhibit P441 in ICTY *Đorđević* Trial.

In Turkey, the Hêzên Parastina Gel (HPG) opened an investigation into the use of mines which resulted in the death of four civilians. When that investigation pointed to the planting of anti-vehicle mines by two members of the armed group, they were tried in a HPG court.[317] The Naxalites in India also convene people's courts, known as 'jan adalats', in order to try and punish offenders, but these have been criticized for failing to meet fair trial standards.[318] During the attempted secession of Biafra (1967–70), various non-Nigerian individuals were captured and tried in Biafra for crimes against the Republic of Biafra.[319] They were tried by a High Court judge and represented by counsel.[320] A former judge of the International Court of Justice, Sir Louis Mbanefo, was the Chief Justice of Biafra.[321] During the Algerian war of independence (1954–62), the Armée de Libération Nationale (ALN) operated a system of military courts, including a military appeal court. It adopted regulations on general discipline and military law, and enacted a Code of Military Law.[322] In the period leading up to the civil war in Ireland (1922–3), the Republicans created a separate legal system and system of courts.[323] For its part, the MILF of the Philippines convenes a military court composed of five persons 'to deal with crimes committed by members of its military establishment'.[324] In Colombia, both the ELN and the FARC have established courts.[325] The Karen National Union (KNU) of Burma has indicated that '[i]f somebody breaks the [KNU] law he will be sent to [a KNU] court' and that '[t]here is a civilian court and a military court'.[326] Yet another armed group indicated in 2011 that it has a criminal law, a disciplinary code, and a civil law; and voluntary lawyers appear before the courts of that armed group.[327] Armed groups thus frequently convene courts.

3.4.2 Potential importance

The potential importance of courts of non-state armed groups has been recognized in certain quarters. The international community frequently calls on all parties to a conflict to enforce international humanitarian law. The Security Council, for example, has required all warring factions, regardless of their governmental or non-governmental status, to enforce international humanitarian law, to end impunity, and to bring alleged perpetrators to justice.[328]

---

[317] The Military Tribunal of HPG, 'The Sentence of the Court of HPG concerning the compartment of BATMAN', 23 November 2010.
[318] See Human Rights Watch, *Being Neutral is Our Biggest Crime: Government, Vigilante and Naxalite Abuses in India's Chhattisgarh State* (July 2008) 98–9.
[319] AHM Kirk-Greene, *Crisis and Conflict in Nigeria: A Documentary Sourcebook 1966–1969, Volume II* (Oxford University Press, 1971) 399–400.
[320] El Nwogugu, 'The Nigerian Civil War: A Case Study in the Law of War' (1974) 14 *Indian Journal of International Law* 13, 46–7.
[321] J de St Jorre, *The Nigerian Civil War* (Hodder and Stoughton, 1972) 13 and 397.
[322] See Bedjaoui, above note 26, 50–1.
[323] See D Foxton, *Revolutionary Lawyers: Sinn Féin and Crown Courts in Ireland and Britain 1916–1923* (Four Courts Press, 2008) 187–97.
[324] 'MILF Organizes Military Court', 9 October 2010.
[325] See Inter-American Commission on Human Rights, 'Third Report on the Human Rights Situation in Colombia', OEA/Ser.L/V/II.102, Doc.9 Rev.1, 26 February 1999, Chapter IV, para 51; Letter from Human Rights Watch to Commander Manuel Marulanda, General Secretariat, FARC, 10 July 2001.
[326] Geneva Call, *In Their Words*, above note 180, 21.
[327] Information provided to author.
[328] See eg SC Res 1479 (2003) on Ivory Coast; SC Res 1509 (2003) on Liberia. See also the statements of the Security Council Working Group on Children and Armed Conflict, for example, S/AC.51/2005/15, 3-4; S/AC.51/2009/1, 2.

At times, the leaders of armed groups are explicitly called upon to ensure the accountability of their members for any violations committed. For example, in 1996, the Special Rapporteur on human rights in Sudan called upon the senior leadership of the Sudan People's Liberation Army and the South Sudan Independence Army to deter violations of international humanitarian law by 'investigating the cases brought to their attention and holding the perpetrators responsible'.[329] Similarly, the SLA, JEM, and other armed groups have been called upon to 'take every appropriate measure to prevent *and punish* human rights abuses and violations of international humanitarian law by rebel commanders and combatants'.[330] The report of the International Commission of Inquiry into the violence in Libya in 2011 contained as a recommendation to the non-state armed group: 'conduct exhaustive, impartial and public investigations into all allegations of international human rights law and international humanitarian law violations, and in particular... investigate *with a view to prosecuting* cases of extrajudicial, summary or arbitrary executions and torture with full respect of judicial guarantees.'[331] The report of the UN Fact-Finding Mission on the Gaza Conflict, albeit not in respect of a traditional non-international armed conflict, notes that 'the responsibility to investigate violations of international human rights and humanitarian law, *prosecute if appropriate and try* perpetrators belongs in the first place to domestic authorities and institutions. This is a legal obligation incumbent on States and State-like entities'.[332] This approach was continued in the follow-up procedure to assess the measures taken by the relevant state and state-like entities.[333] Rather more obliquely, the Inter-American Commission on Human Rights has opined that armed groups should, 'through their command and control structures, respect, implement and enforce the rules governing hostilities set forth in international humanitarian law'.[334] In a related manner, when the Special Rapporteur on extra-judicial executions assessed and criticized the courts of the NDFP, his recommendation was that the NDFP 'should stop using people's courts that do not comply with human rights and humanitarian law standards' rather than that the NDFP should stop using people's courts altogether.[335] Similarly, the Special Rapporteur on human rights in Somalia has recommended that '[a]ssistance should be given' to Somaliland courts in the area of training and the provision of legal materials.[336]

---

[329] Report of the Special Rapporteur on the situation of human rights in Sudan, E/CN.4/1996/62, 20 February 1996, para 87.

[330] Report of the Special Rapporteur on the Human Rights Situation in the Sudan, E/CN.4/2006/111, 11 January 2006, para 81(d) (emphasis added).

[331] Report of the International Commission of Inquiry to investigate all alleged violations of international human rights law in the Libyan Arab Jamahiriya, A/HRC/17/44, 1 June 2011, para 269 (emphasis added).

[332] Report of the United Nations Fact-Finding Mission on the Gaza Conflict, A/HRC/12/48, 25 September 2009, para 1963 (emphasis added). The reference to domestic authorities is to distinguish it from international justice mechanisms rather than non-state armed group authorities. See also the view of R Goldstone, who led the Gaza mission, in 'Justice in Gaza', *New York Times*, 17 September 2009.

[333] Report of the Committee of independent experts in international humanitarian and human rights laws to monitor and assess any domestic, legal or other proceedings undertaken by both the Government of Israel and the Palestinian side, in the light of General Assembly resolution 64/254, including the independence, effectiveness, genuineness of these investigations and their conformity with international standards, A/HRC/15/50, 23 September 2010.

[334] Inter-American Commission on Human Rights, 'Third Report on the Human Rights Situation in Colombia', OEA/Ser.L/V/II.102, Doc.9 Rev.1, 26 February 1999, Chapter IV, I. Recommendations.

[335] Report of the Special Rapporteur on extrajudicial, summary or arbitrary executions, A/HRC/8/3/Add.2, 16 April 2008, para 77.

[336] Report on the Situation of Human Rights in Somalia, E/CN.4/1997/88, 3 March 1997, para 84.

The application of the doctrine of command responsibility to non-international armed conflicts also suggests a need for the creation of courts of non-state armed groups.[337] A non-international armed conflict, requiring as it does a certain level of organization on the part of the armed group, 'implies responsible command and that responsible command in turn implies command responsibility'.[338] This mode of liability applies to state and non-state armed groups alike. Accordingly, commanders of armed groups would be criminally responsible if they knew or had reason to know that their subordinate had committed a prohibited act and they failed to take the necessary and reasonable measures to punish the subordinate.[339] For the most part, the obligation will be satisfied through referral of the incident to the competent judicial authorities.[340] However, given that armed groups are unlikely to refer the matter to state authorities—indeed to do so may be considered an act of betrayal or treachery— the authorities in question will likely have to be those of the armed group. Thus, the ICC has considered that 'the availability of a functional military judicial system within the [armed group] through which [a commander] could have punished crimes committed and prevented their future repetition' is an important element of the duty to punish crimes of subordinates.[341]

3.4.3 Legitimacy and recognition

As noted above, the principal criticism of courts of armed groups on the part of the international community is that they fail to afford due process guarantees.[342] Indeed, there are those who cannot envisage the possibility of their being able to so provide.[343] This issue was considered in Chapter 8 and will not be discussed here. Insofar as the state the territory on which the courts are based is concerned, the principal objection to courts of armed groups is one of legitimacy.

Insofar as state courts are concerned, the presumption is one of legitimacy; for courts of armed groups, the presumption seems to be one of illegitimacy. Thus, state officials dismiss out of hand the very notion of courts of armed groups. For example, reacting to the LTTE's convening of courts, the Chief Justice of Sri Lanka remarked: '[j]udicial power is part of the sovereignty of the people and it cannot be exercised by any other person than those who are vested with it.'[344] The Chief Justice also stated: '[t]he LTTE can have a conciliation mechanism if they want, like if two neighbours are at dispute then settling such a dispute in an amicable manner is all right. But they have no judicial

---

[337] M Sassòli, 'Possible Legal Mechanisms to Improve Compliance by Armed Groups with International Humanitarian Law and International Human Rights Law', Paper submitted at the Armed Groups Conference (Vancouver, 2003) 12; Somer, above note 284, 685.

[338] *Prosecutor v Hadžihasanović, Alagić, and Kubura*, IT-01-47-AR72, Decision on Interlocutory Appeal Challenging Jurisdiction in Relation to Command Responsibility, 16 July 2003, para 17. See above, 174–6.

[339] Ibid, para 18.

[340] *Prosecutor v Kordić and Čerkez*, IT-95-14/2-T, Judgment, 26 February 2001, para 446.

[341] *Bemba Gombo*, above note 312, para 501.

[342] See eg above, 551.

[343] JE Bond, 'Application of the Law of War to Internal Conflicts' (1973) 3 *Georgia Journal of International and Comparative Law* 345, 373; P Rowe, 'War Crimes', in D McGoldrick, P Rowe, and E Donnelly (eds), *The Permanent International Criminal Court* (Hart, 2004) 203, 226–7; P Rowe, *The Impact of Human Rights Law on Armed Forces* (Cambridge University Press, 2006) 197 and 201; International Council on Human Rights Policy, *Ends and Means: Human Rights Approaches to Armed Groups* (ICHRP, 2000) 52.

[344] L Nasry, 'Interview with Chief Justice Sarath N de Silva: LTTE has no judicial authority—CJ', *Sunday Times* (Sri Lanka), 14 November 2004.

authority.'³⁴⁵ Likewise, when the FLN convened military tribunals to try captured French soldiers during the Algerian war of independence, France stated that it could not recognize 'the jurisdiction of a rebellious act'.³⁴⁶ Similarly, when the FMLN proposed trying certain of its members for executing two wounded US service-personnel, the President of the Supreme Court of El Salvador 'warned that any foreigner or Salvadoran national participating in a [FMLN] tribunal to judge the guerrillas would be subject to criminal proceedings under Salvadoran law'.³⁴⁷ Referring to the same incident, a high-level US official stated that '[t]here are two properly constituted judicial systems already in place to try the murderers of the two US servicemen, those in El Salvador and the United States. The FMLN lacks the legal authority to carry out a proper investigation, prosecution or appellate process that would deserve recognition or legitimacy under international law or the law of any sovereign state'.³⁴⁸ Furthermore, when Human Rights Watch indicated that it would observe the proposed FMLN trial, the United States 'complained that observation of the trial would lend it legitimacy'.³⁴⁹

The concern of affording courts of armed groups a certain legitimacy and armed groups themselves some semblance of status also forms part of the explanation as to why the international community fails to engage with these courts. A proposed judicial monitoring system of LTTE courts, originally envisaged to be based on the Judicial System Monitoring Programme in East Timor, was not enacted for fear of legitimizing the courts. Fear of legitimization may also explain why the United Nations Observer Mission in El Salvador (ONUSAL) failed to offer constructive suggestions to the FMLN on improving its courts.³⁵⁰ For the International Council on Human Rights Policy, which is otherwise in favour of engaging with non-state armed groups on humanitarian norms, 'the fact that it is possible to work with armed groups (to improve their knowledge of international standards, to advise them on "judicial" matters, and on training programmes for their military commanders) does not mean that it is desirable to do so' as it may legitimize their control over the population and support secessionist aims.³⁵¹

It is not a coincidence that, in conflicts in which an armed group exercises territorial control, the establishment of courts takes place alongside the provision of education, health services, and the like. This is often a conscious effort on the part of the armed group to afford services that are traditionally provided by the state in an attempt to normalize the situation, to present the image of a stable and functioning regime, and to create a quasi-state. The LTTE, for example, viewed the development of a legal framework as 'an important aspect' of establishing its authority and power.³⁵² To the

---

³⁴⁵ Ibid.
³⁴⁶ Quoted in Fraleigh, above note 27, 199.
³⁴⁷ Human Rights Watch, 1992 Annual Report (1993) Section on El Salvador. See also A-M La Rosa and C Wuerzner, 'Armed Groups, Sanctions and the Implementation of International Humanitarian Law' (2008) 90 *IRRC* 327, 338.
³⁴⁸ Quoted in 'Application of Humanitarian Law in Noninternational Armed Conflicts: Remarks by Theodor Meron' (1991) 85 *ASIL Proceedings* 83, 83–4.
³⁴⁹ Human Rights Watch, 1992 Annual Report (1993) Section on El Salvador, fn 55.
³⁵⁰ On the omission, see TF Acuña, *The United Nations Mission in El Salvador: A Humanitarian Law Perspective* (Kluwer Law International, 1995) 60; L Zegveld, *The Accountability of Armed Opposition Groups in International Law* (Cambridge University Press, 2002) 74.
³⁵¹ International Council on Human Rights Policy, above note 343, 50 (emphases omitted).
³⁵² 'This is Our Country', *Sunday Times* (Sri Lanka), 14 November 2004. See also C Kamalendran, 'The Inside Story of "Eelam Courts"', *Sunday Times* (Sri Lanka), 14 November 2004.

CPN-M, the courts were at the very heart of its government.³⁵³ These institutions are thus designed to provide the armed group with legitimacy, at least in relation to the local population. The concerns of states and the international community is thus a fair one. However, these concerns have to be balanced against the counterweight provided by the courts to the disorder and chaos that would otherwise reign in the territory under armed group control. For example, in 2010, a journalist described certain areas under PKK control as 'a place without government, yet also without disorder'.³⁵⁴ Even in territory under governmental control, the existence of an armed conflict can lead to general lawlessness with criminal gangs flourishing and operating in a climate of impunity. Significant benefits accrue to the civilian population if law and order is maintained. Without trials, summary executions, a practice already prevalent in armed conflict, including those in which armed groups have established their own courts,³⁵⁵ may become the norm. Accordingly, while giving legitimacy to the courts of armed groups is a concern, some of these courts may well have a claim to legitimacy.

Such a claim is strengthened upon recognition that the courts may offer a forum for prosecution when none would otherwise exist. It is both impractical and unrealistic to require the armed group to have recourse to the state judicial system. An armed group is simply not going to be willing to transfer those of its members who are suspected of having committed violations of the law of non-international armed conflict to the state against which it is in conflict for prosecution.³⁵⁶ Indeed, alleged discrimination on the part of the state, including the judicial system of the state, may have been a reason for the taking up of arms. It is equally untenable to suggest that state personnel captured by the armed group will be transferred to the state to stand trial for any alleged violation. Although such transfer is sometimes required,³⁵⁷ realism dictates otherwise. The courts of states other than the parent state have been suggested as an alternative forum for prosecution,³⁵⁸ but this presumes a good relationship between the armed group and the relevant state as well as the consent of all parties involved. Resort to international criminal courts has also been posited,³⁵⁹ but these are subject to jurisdictional constraints and have limited capabilities. Accordingly, a court of the armed group may be the only forum in which violations of international humanitarian law will actually be prosecuted. This has implications for the doctrine of command responsibility, as it not only suggests that fair trials in courts of armed groups would satisfy the duty to punish on the part of the superior, but they may well represent a useful practical means by which to do so.³⁶⁰

---

³⁵³ C Haviland, 'Parallel justice, Maoist style', *BBC News*, 14 October 2006.
³⁵⁴ N Abdulla, 'A Kurdish Village Governed by None', *New York Times*, 24 August 2010.
³⁵⁵ See eg *RUF* Trial Judgment, above note 120, para 712 fn 1333.
³⁵⁶ A possible exception is the handing over of one member of the Mai-Mai, suspected of being involved in mass sexual violence, to UN peacekeepers, who then handed him over to the DRC. However, it is unclear whether the Mai-Mai were aware that he would be handed over to the Government of the DRC, as a spokesperson for the Mai-Mai has stated that '[w]e gave [the accused] to the UN so that he can be investigated by the *international criminal court* for his actions against the local population': X Rice, 'Milita Commander Mayele Arrested After Mass Rape of Congo Villagers', *The Guardian* (UK), 6 October 2010.
³⁵⁷ This was the view of United Nations Observer Mission in El Salvador. See Acuña, above note 350, 61 fn 247.
³⁵⁸ *Prosecutor v Bemba Gombo*, ICC-01/05-01/08-406, Amicus Curiae Observations of Amnesty International on Superior Responsibility submitted pursuant to Rule 103 of the Rules of Procedure and Evidence, 20 April 2009, para 25.
³⁵⁹ Ibid.
³⁶⁰ See also *Bemba Gombo*, above note 312, para 501.

It may even be that armed groups are under an *obligation* to preserve law and order in the territory they control. For example, in 2006, UN Secretary-General Kofi Annan indicated that he was 'deeply concerned by the absence of a system for the administration of justice in areas under the control of the Forces Nouvelles' of the Ivory Coast.[361] Courts of armed groups may also, on occasion, compare favourably to state courts, which do not always hold up well in time of armed conflict, ceasing to operate or becoming of questionable legitimacy. All these factors militate in favour of recognizing as legitimate certain courts of armed groups in certain circumstances.

There is an abundance of authority from a different, but related, context—that of the unrecognized government—which supports recognizing certain acts as official or having legal effect even if those acts emanate from an unrecognized or unlawful entity. The key test is whether failure so to recognize would be 'to the detriment of the inhabitants of the [t]erritory'.[362] Typically, the example given to illustrate the proposition is 'the registration of births, deaths and marriages'.[363] However, courts have been careful not to make any sweeping determinations and have stressed the desirability of ascertaining precisely which matters may be considered to have the status of law on a case-by-case basis.[364] A useful test may be that set out by the US Supreme Court in considering the status of certain Confederate legislation, which was noted above.[365] As examples of things recognized as valid, the Court listed 'actions sanctioning and protecting marriage and the domestic relations, governing the course of descents, regulating the conveyance and transfer of property, real and personal, and providing remedies for injuries to person and estate'.[366] Given that many of the cases before courts of armed groups relate to familial and property disputes and petty crime, these examples are important. The US Supreme Court noted of these sorts of matters:

That what occurred or was done in respect of such matters under the authority of the laws of these local *de facto* governments should not be disregarded or held invalid merely because those governments were organized in hostility to the Union established by the national constitution; this because the existence of war between the United States and the Confederate states did not relieve those who were within the insurrectionary lines from the necessity of civil obedience, nor destroy the bonds of society, nor do away with civil government or the regular administration of the laws, and because transactions in the ordinary course of civil society as organized within the enemy's territory, although they may have indirectly or remotely promoted the ends of the *de facto* or unlawful government organized to effect a dissolution of the Union, were without blame 'except when proved to have been entered into with actual intent to further invasion or insurrection.'[367]

Reasoning along these lines would also suggest that trials for violations of the law of non-international armed conflict would be equally regarded as valid whereas politically motivated prosecutions would not. The difficulty is identifying where to draw the line.

The recognition of, and legal effect accorded to, certain decisions of unrecognized entities suggests that decisions of courts of non-state armed groups are neither universally invalid nor categorically legitimate. It is submitted that the question should not be

---

[361] Report of the Secretary-General on Children and Armed Conflict in Côte d'Ivoire, S/2006/835, 25 October 2006, para 51.
[362] *Namibia*, above note 127, para 125.
[363] Ibid. See also *Loizidou v Turkey*, Application No 15318/89, para 45 (1996).
[364] Ibid.
[365] *Texas v White*, above note 128, 733. See further above, 530–1.
[366] Ibid.
[367] *Baldy v Hunter* (1969) 171 US 388, 400.

whether decisions may be recognized as law but *which* decisions are to have legal effect. The same is true of the courts themselves.

A related issue concerns the 'legislation' and 'law' of the non-state armed group. The unwillingness of states to accept any such characterization should come as little surprise given the close relationship between the establishment of a judicial system and state sovereignty.[368] Accordingly, it may be difficult for a state to accept that courts that are established by an armed group against which it is in conflict are able to enact law. Indeed, during the 1974–7 Diplomatic Conference, Iraq asked 'under what concepts the terms "offence", "penal law" and "court" should be interpreted when applied to the rebel party?' and queried how the principle of non-retroactivity could be applied to the rebel party,[369] while Argentina considered it unlikely that the state would 'recognize the ideas of rebels as "national law"'.[370]

While it is thus true that a number of states opposed the characterization of the outputs of armed groups as law, it is equally true that other states take the view that the outputs may be characterized in such a manner. The position of the United Kingdom, for example, is that 'the use of the bare word "law" [in Article 6(2)(c) of Additional Protocol II] must be taken to include both national and international law. It could also be wide enough to cover "laws" passed by an insurgent authority'.[371] Indeed, the term 'national law' was omitted from the final text of Article 6 precisely because of the uncertainty surrounding whether the term was wide enough to cover the 'law' of the armed group.[372] This, in turn, suggests that the 'law' of the armed group can be covered by the reference to law.[373] Along similar lines, at the 1974–7 Diplomatic Conference, the USSR recommended that 'it would be wise to take a look at history. The lesson to be learned from for example, the Napoleonic Wars or the Russian Civil War or the Spanish Civil War was that both parties could adopt their own laws...the armed conflicts in question were those in which the anti-government forces had their own machinery, authority or administration and could therefore make their own laws'.[374] Hungary agreed with the recommendation of the USSR and noted that the laws of the armed group 'might be more in harmony with the demands of the time and more humanitarian than the laws in force prior to the beginning of the conflict'.[375] Unsurprisingly, armed groups have also taken this view, with the FMLN arguing that it is not 'necessary that guilt be proven by the standards of the government law'.[376] The practice of ONUSAL, in assessing the laws of the FMLN against the provisions of Additional Protocol II, would support such a position.[377] For its part, the ICRC Commentary notes the complexity involved in the parallel application of two systems of national law but does not deny its acceptability,[378] while another authoritative commentary opines:

---

[368] See eg above, 557.
[369] *Official Records*, above note 4, Vol 8, 355, para 69 (Iraq).
[370] Ibid, Vol 9, 314, para 54 (Argentina).
[371] UK *Manual*, above note 54, 404. See also P Rowe, 'Liability for "War Crimes" during a Non-International Armed Conflict' (1995) 34 *Military Law and the Law of War Review* 149, 154.
[372] Bothe, Partsch, and Solf, above note 6, 651–2.
[373] Ibid.
[374] *Official Records*, above note 4, Vol 11, 441, para 83 (in a different context).
[375] Ibid, 442, para 88 (in a different context).
[376] FMLN, above note 292, 19–20.
[377] Third Report of the United Nations Observer Mission in El Salvador, A/46/876-S/23580, 19 February 1992, para 113.
[378] ICRC, *Commentary on the Additional Protocols*, above note 6, 1399.

'[t]here is no basis for the concept that the rebels are prevented from changing the legal order existing in the territory where they exercise factual power.'[379]

3.4.4 Towards greater engagement

It is no longer true, if it ever were, that '[c]ases where rebel factions have conducted trials are rare'.[380] Indeed, many armed groups establish courts and conduct trials. Rather than ignoring them, or criticizing them without offering concrete suggestions for improvement, the international community needs to grapple with them and consider how best they may be utilized in order to aid enforcement of the law.[381] Courts of armed groups exist and will continue to exist regardless of the views of third parties. At the very least, a court that is established by law, conducts fair trials, and contributes to the maintenance of peace and good order among citizens warrants engagement on the part of the international community.

Engagement does have the potential to lead to difficulties. Establishing that these courts satisfy fair trial standards may legitimize them and that will not be in the interests of the state. However, as noted above, in certain situations, the courts may well have a claim to legitimacy. In any event, the tension between engagement and legitimacy is ingrained in the law of non-international armed conflict, and its existence should not lead to turning a blind eye to courts of armed groups. That would be a wasted opportunity when such opportunities are few and far between. Without minimizing the seriousness of the difficulties, engagement with the courts of armed groups is needed in order to encourage enforcement of the law. Just as the prohibition on the use of force did not stop the development of the law of war/armed conflict,[382] the fact that the state is seeking to defeat the armed group should not prevent engagement on the part of the international community with the courts of armed groups. In many respects, issues surrounding the courts of armed groups are an allegory to broader issues of the law of non-international armed conflict, which run throughout this book.

4. Methodology: armed groups and the creation of the law

A more general area in which further thinking needs to be done relates not so much to substantive rules but to the methodology by which the rules are created. In particular, the international community needs to consider whether, and if so, to what extent, non-state armed groups should have a role to play in the creation and development of the law of non-international armed conflict.[383]

There may be good reason for allowing for such a role. For example, some armed groups have argued that they are not bound by international humanitarian law as they did not participate in its creation. This was true of the National Liberation Front (FLN) of Viet Nam, which informed the ICRC in 1965 that it 'did not participate in the Geneva Conventions for the protection of war victims and is not bound by the Conventions'.[384] The FARC of Colombia has made a similar point over the years in

---

[379] Bothe, Partsch, and Solf, above note 6, 651. See also Rowe, War Crimes, above note 371, 154–5.
[380] GIAD Draper, 'The Geneva Conventions of 1949' (1965-I) 114 *RdC* 63, 98.
[381] See also Acuña, above note 350, 60–2.
[382] Although, see *1949 Yearbook of the International Law Commission* (UN, 1956) 281, para 18.
[383] For greater detail, see Roberts and Sivakumaran, above note 221.
[384] Letter from Chef de la Représentation Permanente du FLN du Sud-Vietnam en URSS to Representative of the ICRC, 16 October 1965, ICRC Archives B AG 202 223-005 (Russian original

relation to Additional Protocol II. A member of its Secretariat opined in 1999 that '[i]t is supposed that for one to have to abide by the norms set forth in a pact, one should have participated in its drafting, in its discussion and should be in agreement with its conclusions. We have not been there, were never invited to any forum or event of the international community to discuss this topic'.[385] However, the FARC has committed to certain humanitarian norms despite not being involved in their formation.[386] The FMLN of El Salvador also made similar arguments on specific norms.[387] The same was true of various national liberation movements in the 1970s.[388] More generally, some members of certain armed groups have taken the view that international humanitarian law is 'law defined by states and violated by the same'.[389]

By including armed groups in the creation of the relevant norm, there may also be a greater likelihood of their compliance with that norm. The International Council on Human Rights Policy has reported, for example, that its research and consultations suggest that where armed groups commit themselves to written codes of conduct, this encourages them to respect human rights.[390] A report of ICRC expert seminars has suggested along similar lines that, 'better accountability by armed groups for international humanitarian law might be achieved by granting them an opportunity to express their consent to be bound by the rules'.[391] Other entities also stress the relationship between engagement with armed groups, commitments by armed groups, and levels of compliance.[392] This reflects the idea that 'it is psychologically easier to have [international humanitarian law norms] accepted and respected by persons who were involved—or represented—in their development' as this promotes a sense of 'ownership' over them.[393] It also makes the law more realistic, geared to the difficulties faced by the parties to the conflict.[394] Thus, when the FLN of Viet Nam informed the ICRC that it did not consider itself bound by the Geneva Conventions, it stated that the Conventions 'contain articles which neither strictly correspond to our action, nor to the

---

and French translation). The French translation reads: 'le Front National de Libération du Vietnam du Sud n'ait pas participé aux Conventions de Genève pour la protection des victimes de la guerre et ne soit pas lié par les Conventions.'

[385] 'Reaparece Cano', Cambio No 704, 8–15 de Noviembre de 1999, Bogota, quoted in D García-Peña Jaramillo, 'Humanitarian Protection in Non-International Conflicts: A Case Study of Colombia' (2000) *IYHR* 179, 189–90. See also Letter from Human Rights Watch to Commander Manuel Marulanda, General Secretariat, FARC, 10 July 2001; Human Rights Watch, *Colombia: Beyond Negotiation, International Humanitarian Law and its Application to the Conduct of the FARC-EP* (August 2001) 6–7; Human Rights Watch, *War Without Quarter: Colombia and International Humanitarian Law* (1998) text at fn 34.

[386] For example, the Trabajo de Masas, undated; Normas de Comportamiento con las Masas, 1998.

[387] Second Report of the United Nations Observer Mission in El Salvador, A/46/658, 15 November 1991, paras 64–5; Zegveld, above note 350, 17.

[388] M Veuthey, *Guerilla et droit humanitaire* (CICR, 1983) 61; D Fleck, 'Ruses of War and Prohibition of Perfidy' (1974) 13 *Military Law and the Law of War Review* 269, 297.

[389] See O Bangerter, 'Talking to Armed Groups' (2011) 37 *Forced Migration Review* 7, 8.

[390] International Council on Human Rights Policy, above note 343, 52.

[391] ICRC, *Improving Compliance with International Humanitarian Law: ICRC Expert Seminars* (October 2003) 21. See also Zegveld, above note 350, 28.

[392] See above, 533–8 and 542–6.

[393] Sassòli, Possible Legal Mechanisms, above note 337, 6. See also G de Beco, 'Compliance with International Humanitarian Law by Non-State Actors' (2005) 18 *Humanitäres Völkerrecht* 190, 193; ICRC, *Increasing Respect for International Humanitarian Law in Non-International Armed Conflicts* (ICRC, February 2008).

[394] LC Green, 'The New Law of Armed Conflict' (1977) 15 *Canadian Yearbook of International Law* 3, 8; M Sassòli, 'The Implementation of International Humanitarian Law: Current and Inherent Challenges' (2007) 10 *YIHL* 45, 64.

organisation of the armed forces of the FLN, which is why the FLN cannot mechanically apply the Convention[s]'.³⁹⁵ It should not go unnoticed that various national liberation movements participated in the 1974–7 Diplomatic Conference and in the years that followed committed to abide by international humanitarian law.³⁹⁶ Involvement of the armed group in the creation of norms may also have an impact on other armed groups, and on the state against which the armed group is in conflict.³⁹⁷

Against this, the opposing view stresses the potentially negative implications of giving armed groups a role in creating international humanitarian law. One argument against giving armed groups any such role is the danger that humanitarian law standards may be weakened.³⁹⁸ Another concern is that acknowledging the practice of such groups as relevant to law-making would lend legitimacy and status to these groups, many of which states view as no more than criminals or terrorists.³⁹⁹

Nonetheless, the disadvantage of the existing situation is that the law appears to be moving along two parallel tracks, which, aside from a few exceptions, do not meet. Treaties and custom are sources of international law, but benefit from little participation on the part of non-state armed groups. Materials emanating from armed groups are necessarily heavy in armed group participation but carry little normative weight. The disjunction between the two tracks is potentially problematic. Furthermore, a role for non-state armed groups in the creation of the law of non-international armed conflict could be constructed in such a way that does not downgrade existing standards nor affords them legal status or legitimacy, but does give them a sense of ownership over the rules, potentially leading to increased compliance.⁴⁰⁰ The methodology by which the law is created is thus a further aspect that needs greater consideration.

5. A concrete proposal

As Part I demonstrated, the law of non-international armed conflict has gone through a wholesale transformation in recent years. However, this chapter has shown that gaps in, and difficulties with, the law remain. Questions also arise as to the methodology by which the law of non-international armed conflict has been, and is, created. This section seeks to provide a concrete proposal that addresses the various concerns and allows us to move forward.⁴⁰¹

Armed groups are bound by international humanitarian law but international humanitarian law presupposes the existence of an armed conflict. Given the partial disinclination of states to recognize the existence of an armed conflict, and in the absence of a binding independent assessor, international humanitarian law may prove inapplicable to the situation at hand. Insofar as states are concerned, this is not overly

---

³⁹⁵ Letter from Chef de la Représentation Permanente du FLN du Sud-Vietnam en URSS to Representative of the ICRC, 16 October 1965, ICRC Archives B AG 202 223-005 (Russian original and French translation). The French translation reads: '[c]es Conventions contiennent des articles qui ne correspondent absolument pas à notre action, ni à l'organisation des forces armées du FNL, et c'est pourquoi le FNL ne peut pas appliquer mécaniquement cette Convention.'
³⁹⁶ See above, 118.
³⁹⁷ See above, 542–6.
³⁹⁸ See generally, Roberts and Sivakumaran, above note 221, 137–41.
³⁹⁹ See above, 546–9.
⁴⁰⁰ For various approaches, see Roberts and Sivakumaran, above note 221, 141–51.
⁴⁰¹ This section is based on S Sivakumaran, 'How to Improve upon the Faulty Legal Regime of Internal Armed Conflicts', in A Cassese (ed), *Realizing Utopia: The Future of International Law* (Oxford University Press, 2012) 525.

problematic as international human rights law fills any normative gap. With respect to armed groups, however, there may be a gap in protection insofar as international law is concerned. That armed groups have human rights obligations is a contested issue and one progressive view limits human rights obligations to armed groups that exercise territorial control.[402] However, it is unlikely that armed groups would exercise territorial control in situations of low intensity violence. Accordingly, in such situations, a normative gap exists. A new instrument designed to bind armed groups in all situations ought to be concluded with armed groups remaining bound by their pre-existing obligations. A different approach would be to conclude a treaty on point that is open to states and armed groups alike. However, the 'right' moment in time would have to be found in order to prevent any such treaty proving regressive.

The proposed instrument would draw from all relevant areas of international law—international humanitarian law, international human rights law, international environmental law, and so on. It would also bring together the patchwork of treaty norms that pertain to non-international armed conflicts, customary international law, as well as certain soft law standards such as the Guiding Principles on Internal Displacement. Drawing up such an instrument would also afford an opportunity to assess the existing state of affairs, including considering such issues as the workability of particular rules in non-international armed conflicts, the need for new norms, and whether both parties to such conflicts, states and non-state armed groups alike, are able to enforce the various rules.[403]

The 'Fundamental Standards of Humanity' initiative could form a useful starting point in this regard.[404] However, it would be but a starting point. It is crucial that armed groups be involved in the formulation of any new instrument that concerns them, for, as has been aptly remarked, '[n]o one would suggest revising the law of naval warfare without speaking with the navies'.[405] Inclusion of representatives of armed groups in the drafting process would provide certain actors within the armed group with increased exposure to international humanitarian law. It would also afford the international community points of contact within the group for engagement on humanitarian issues at a later stage.[406] More importantly, the international community would get a better sense of the norms that armed groups find controversial, those norms that they have difficulty meeting, and those that are uncontested. This is not to suggest that the normative content should be sacrificed or watered down in light of the comments of armed groups. Indeed, the text should be drawn up by a group of experts. However, ultimately, the involvement of armed groups would imbue the rules with a greater realism.

Armed groups should also be able to sign up to the instrument, given that signature coupled with participation in the process may afford armed groups a greater sense of investment in the process as well as the norms that result from that process. This has the potential to aid levels of compliance.[407] This is not to suggest that states should not be involved in the creation of the instrument. On the contrary, they too should play an important role, whether in the form of separate meetings of state representatives, government experts, or as participating observers in meetings of armed groups. Particular use should be made of the views of those governments or states that were, until recently, armed groups, for example Kosovo (KLA), East Timor (FRETILIN), Rwanda

---

[402] See above, 95–6. [403] See generally Chapter 3.
[404] On which see above, 52.
[405] Sassòli, Implementation, above note 394, 64.
[406] See above, 443. [407] See above, 440. See also above, 532–42.

(RPF), and South Sudan (SPLM/A). It is unfortunate that more use is not made of the knowledge of such states in the period immediately after they gain statehood and prior to their mindset changing to that of states. Regardless of how the instrument is characterized—as a treaty, a hybrid treaty, an agreement subject to international law, or something altogether different—it would be binding on its signatories.

The instrument would need to contain strong provisions on implementation, dissemination, and enforcement. The instrument should require its signatories to 'translate' the instrument into orders, regulations, or directives internal to the armed group and in language that is understood by its members.[408] The instrument should also contain provisions on dissemination. Creative thinking is needed in this regard. For example, dissemination need not be limited to the written form. Rather, means of communication with which fighters are familiar should be utilized as far as possible. Norms could be presented pictorially if there is a high level of illiteracy among fighters, for example in the form of comic books aimed at child soldiers. They could be broadcast by radio if, as in many places, radio is the predominant means of communication. Alternatively, they could be distributed by text message, if mobile phones are commonplace but writing materials are in short supply. Indeed, the latter approach was reportedly the one adopted by the National Transitional Council (NTC) during the 2011 conflict in Libya in respect of the NTC's 'frontline manual on the fundamental rules of armed conflict'.[409]

Monitoring and enforcement of the instrument is, of course, crucial. This should take place through a number of complementary means, not being reliant on any single one alone. Signatories to the instrument should have obligations of self-reporting.[410] This would include the submission of progress reports on the obligations of translation and dissemination. More importantly, there would be an obligation to submit periodic reports responding to allegations of violation of the instrument. It would also be incumbent on the armed group to explain the measures it has taken in response to the allegations. These allegations could come from the state, a third state, NGO's, or individual victims. This self-monitoring has the potential to continue fostering a sense of investment in the humanitarian law process and may lead to greater exposure of humanitarian norms amongst a broader community. It would also counter the idea that enforcement always comes from the outside, whether the state, NGOs, or international organizations.

Of course, self-monitoring cannot be relied upon alone for enforcement of the instrument. Rather, there needs to be an external monitoring mechanism in place to complement self-monitoring. Armed groups have to be aware that signing the instrument brings with it certain responsibilities and commitments that have to be honoured. Accordingly, there would be no possibility of opting out of the monitoring mechanism; with signature comes monitoring. There are various possible modalities for this external monitoring. Monitoring could be carried out by a standing body created by the instrument for that specific purpose. It could be a neutral body but with input from a representative of the armed group provided confidentiality allows. The armed group could even select the composition of the neutral monitoring body from a list of designated experts or organizations.

---

[408] See above, 439–40.
[409] See I Scobbie, 'Operationalising the Law of Armed Conflict for Dissident Forces in Libya', EJIL: Talk! Blog, 31 August 2011.
[410] See the approach of Geneva Call in this regard, above, 540.

To be sure, not all armed groups will sign on to an instrument. Others may sign on but with no intention of complying with their obligations. In this respect, armed groups are not unlike states parties to treaties. However, a mechanism that separates out those armed groups that take their obligations seriously from those that do not, and one which differentiates between those groups that claim to respect the law of non-international armed conflict and those that actually do so, would be an accomplishment in and of itself.

Conclusion

The law of non-international armed conflict is a substantial body of law. At the level of conventional law, its core content can be found in common Article 3 and Additional Protocol II. However, conventional law stretches far beyond these two instruments, and includes the Hague Convention on Cultural Property and its Second Protocol as well as numerous weapons treaties. Relevant treaties also exist at the regional level, such as the African Union Convention on internal displacement. A variety of other instruments are also of import, such as the Guiding Principles on Internal Displacement and the Optional Protocol to the Convention on the Rights of the Child on Children and Armed Conflict.[1] The customary law of non-international armed conflict is even more substantial. In particular, it includes a whole host of rules relating to targeting and the means and methods of warfare.[2]

The substance of the law of non-international armed conflict is largely accepted by states and non-state armed groups alike. Although there continues to be debate as to the applicability of particular norms to non-international armed conflict, the idea that there is a substantial body of law that governs non-international armed conflict is not seriously questioned. Insofar as states that are actually involved in non-international armed conflict are concerned, the position is even clearer with some of them concluding bilateral agreements with the non-state armed groups against which they are in conflict. These agreements bring into force 'international humanitarian law', the Geneva Conventions, or particular rules set out in the agreement. On occasion, the rules go beyond that which is strictly required and commits the state to affording, for example, prisoner of war treatment to captured fighters. Insofar as non-state armed groups are concerned, they too indicate their acceptance of the law. This takes place through the bilateral agreements just mentioned, as well as bilateral agreements with UN entities and, more commonly, unilateral declarations or commitments to the ICRC. Internal regulations or codes of conduct of non-state armed groups also tend to have components that reflect ideas of the law of non-international armed conflict.[3]

Aside from a couple of exceptions, the law of non-international armed conflict is not dissimilar to the law of international armed conflict. This is unsurprising when it is recognized that the law of non-international armed conflict has been modelled on the law of international armed conflict. Indeed, the standards of the law of international armed conflict have been the standards to which the law of non-international armed conflict has aspired. At the level of conventional law, non-international armed conflicts are often tagged on at the end of an instrument designed specifically for international armed conflicts.[4] Insofar as customary international law is concerned, as the

---

[1] See above, 101–2. [2] See above, 105–7. See generally Chapters 8 and 9.
[3] See Chapter 4. [4] See above, 61–5.

International Criminal Tribunal for the former Yugoslavia put it in the *Tadić* Decision on Interlocutory Appeal on Jurisdiction: 'what is inhumane and consequently prohibited in international wars, cannot but be inhumane and inadmissible in civil strife.'[5] Nonetheless the exceptions are important, and, in one respect, that of combatant immunity, lack of an equivalent impedes compliance with the law.[6]

Although the law of non-international armed conflict has been modelled, in large part, on the law of international armed conflict, it is not made up of international humanitarian law alone. International humanitarian law forms the core of the law of non-international armed conflict, but international human rights law and international criminal law play a significant role.[7] These bodies of law have contributed to the law of non-international armed conflict in a variety of ways. They have provided substantive content, for example in the area of the requisite due process guarantees; assisted in the interpretation of key terms, as with the definition of torture; and even regulated non-international armed conflicts directly, in the case of when persons may be lawfully targeted.[8] Insofar as international criminal law is concerned, it was through the lens of war crimes that the law of non-international armed conflict developed so considerably in the 1990s.[9] Other bodies of international law, such as international environmental law, also have a role to play; however, to date, they have been under-utilized.[10]

The impact of the law of international armed conflict on the law of non-international armed conflict, and the resort to international human rights law and international criminal law, has led to considerable advancements. Without the modelling approach, the international humanitarian law applicable in non-international armed conflict would have remained stunted. However, it has not been entirely positive. On occasion, norms are transplanted from one body of law to another without sufficient appreciation of context. Thus, greater protection afforded by the humanitarian law of non-international armed conflict is vitiated by the application of norms of international armed conflict, as in the cases of child soldiers and protection afforded to certain works and installations containing dangerous forces.[11] At other times, when a counterpart cannot be found in one of the other branches of the law or the counterpart is deemed inappropriate, the situation remains unregulated. This is true of combatant immunity and of the regulation of relations between an armed group and persons and objects in territory under the control of the armed group.[12] When drawing on human rights law, as in the case of norms on child soldiers, the principle of equality of obligation of belligerents has not been respected.[13] Insofar as international criminal law is concerned, substantive provisions are sometimes framed more narrowly than in international humanitarian law, as is the case with the prohibitions on disproportionate attacks and forcible transfer of persons.[14] At still other times, insufficient regard is had for the parties that are involved in non-international armed conflicts, with the consequence that the capabilities of non-state armed groups are overlooked. This is symptomatic of a broader point.

Non-international armed conflicts are fought between states and armed groups or between armed groups. Armed groups are thus present in each and every non-international armed conflict that takes place. Yet the law of non-international armed

---

[5] *Prosecutor v Tadić*, IT-94-1-AR72, Decision on the Defence Motion for Interlocutory Appeal on Jurisdiction, 2 October 1995, para 97. See above, 55–61.
[6] For proposals for moving forward, see above, 514–20.
[7] See above, 77–99.   [8] See generally Chapters 8 and 9.   [9] See above, 57–8.
[10] See above, 526–9.   [11] See above, 68–9.   [12] See above, 514–20 and 529–32.
[13] See above, 88.   [14] See above, 79–81.

conflict focuses, either explicitly or implicitly, on states parties to conflicts, ignoring in a number of salient respects armed groups parties to conflicts. The ability of armed groups to implement and enforce the law has not traditionally played a central role in the development of new rules.[15] The occasional rule is framed in a manner that makes it difficult for armed groups to comply with it, as in the case of the prohibition on pillage of natural resources.[16] Armed groups are rarely consulted on their views of the law, and their statements on point tend to be overlooked and ignored.[17] There is also a lack of knowledge and understanding of the sanctions imposed by armed groups for violations of their internal regulations, including their convening of courts.[18]

While there is a tension between non-state armed groups and notions of legality and legitimacy, particularly insofar as the opposing state is concerned, the fact that armed groups are parties to conflicts means that they have to be taken seriously. Insofar as compliance with the law of non-international armed conflict is concerned, little is achieved by turning a blind eye to them, their practice, or their views.

The law of non-international armed conflict bears a heavy burden, tasked as it is with regulating a situation which gives rise to many of the worst atrocities committed today. It has developed significantly particularly since the mid-1990s. However, there remains some way to go. It is to be hoped that, with certain amendments to its substance and to its approach, it can better meet its obligations.

---

[15] See above, 562–4. [16] See above, 426–7.
[17] On which see Chapter 4. [18] See above, 445–8 and 549–62.

Select Bibliography

ACADEMIC LITERATURE

Abi-Saab, G, 'Wars of National Liberation and the Laws of War' (1972) 3 *Annales d'Etudes Internationales* 93.
—— 'Wars of National Liberation and the Development of Humanitarian Law', in RJ Akkerman, PJ van Krieken, and CO Pannenborg (eds), *Declarations on Principles: A Quest for Universal Peace* (AW Sijthoff, Leyden, 1977).
—— 'Wars of National Liberation in the Geneva Conventions and Protocols' (1979-IV) 165 *RdC* 353.
—— 'Non-International Armed Conflicts', in UNESCO (ed), *International Dimensions of Humanitarian Law* (UNESCO, Paris, 1988).
—— 'The Concept of War Crimes', in S Yee and W Tieya (eds), *International Law and the Post-Cold War World: Essays in Honour of Li Haopei* (Routledge, London, 2001).
Abi-Saab, R, 'Humanitarian Law and Internal Conflicts: The Evolution of Legal Concern', in AJM Delissen and GJ Tanja (eds), *Humanitarian Law of Armed Conflict, Challenges Ahead: Essays in Honour of Frits Kalshoven* (Nijhoff, Dordrecht, 1991).
Abresch, W, 'A Human Rights Law of Internal Armed Conflict: The European Court of Human Rights in Chechnya' (2005) 16 *EJIL* 741.
Ador, G, and Moynier, G, 'Les Destinées de la Convention de Genève pendant la Guerre de Serbie' (1876–October) *Bulletin International des Sociétés de Secours aux Militaires Blessés* 165.
African Union-European Union Technical Ad hoc Expert Group on the Principle of Universal Jurisdiction, 15 April 2009.
Akande, D, 'Clearing the Fog of War? The ICRC's Interpretive Guidance on Direct Participation in Hostilities' (2010) 59 *ICLQ* 180.
Alam, S, 'Indian Intervention in Sri Lanka and International Law' (1991) 38 *Netherlands International Law Review* 246.
Alamuddin, A and Webb, P, 'Expanding Jurisdiction over War Crimes under Article 8 of the ICC Statute' (2010) 8 *JICJ* 1219.
Alasow, OA, *Violations of the Rules Applicable in Non-International Armed Conflicts and Their Possible Causes* (Martinus Nijhoff, Leiden, 2010).
Aldrich, GH, 'Application of Humanitarian Law in Noninternational Armed Conflicts: Remarks' (1991) 85 *ASIL Procs* 93.
—— 'Compliance with the Law: Problems and Prospects', in H Fox and MA Meyer (eds), *Armed Conflict and the New Law, Volume II: Effecting Compliance* (BIICL, London, 1993).
—— 'The Laws of War on Land' (2000) 94 *AJIL* 42.
—— 'Customary International Humanitarian Law—An Interpretation on Behalf of the International Committee of the Red Cross' (2005) LXXVI *BYIL* 503.
Allen, CA, 'Civilian Starvation and Relief during Armed Conflict: the Modern Humanitarian Law' (1989) 19 *Georgia Journal of International and Comparative Law* 1.
Alston, P, Morgan-Foster, J, and Abresch, W, 'The Competence of the UN Human Rights Council and its Special Procedures in relation to Armed Conflicts: Extrajudicial Executions in the "War on Terror"' (2008) 19 *EJIL* 183.
Americas Watch, *Violations of Fair Trial Guarantees by the FMLN's Ad Hoc Courts* (Americas Watch, New York, 1990).
Antoine, P, 'International Humanitarian Law and the Protection of the Environment in Time of Armed Conflict' (1992) 32 *IRRC* 517.
Arai-Takahashi, Y, *The Law of Occupation* (Martinus Nijhoff, Leiden, 2009).
Arimatsu, L, 'Territory, Boundaries and the Law of Armed Conflict' (2009) 12 *YIHL* 157.

Arnold, R, 'War Crimes—para. 2(b)(iv)', in O Triffterer (ed), *Commentary on the Rome Statute of the International Criminal Court: Observers' Notes, Article by Article* (Beck, München, 2008).

—— and N Quénivet (eds), *International Humanitarian Law and Human Rights Law* (Martinus Nijhoff, Leiden 2008).

Arsanjani, MH, 'The Rome Statute of the International Criminal Court' (1999) 93 *AJIL* 22.

Baeriswyl, É and Aeschlimann, A, 'Reflections on a Dissemination Operation in Burundi—Declaration for Standards of Humanitarian Conduct: Appeal for a Minimum of Humanity in a Situation of Internal Violence' (1997) 37 *IRRC* 385.

Bagshaw, S, 'Internally Displaced Persons at the Fifty-Fourth Session of the United Nations Commission on Human Rights, 16 March–24 April 1998' (1998) 10 *IJRL* 549.

Bangerter, O, 'Reasons Why Armed Groups Choose to Respect International Humanitarian Law or Not' (2011) 93 *IRRC* 353.

—— 'Disseminating and Implementing International Humanitarian Law within Organized Armed Groups: Measures Armed Groups can Take to Improve Respect for International Humanitarian Law', in International Institute of Humanitarian Law, *Non-State Actors and International Humanitarian Law, Organized Armed Groups: A Challenge for the Twenty-First Century* (FrancoAngeli, Milano, 2010).

—— 'Talking to Armed Groups' (2011) 37 *Forced Migration Review* 7.

Bantekas, I, 'The Iraqi Special Tribunal for Crimes Against Humanity' (2004) 54 *ICLQ* 237.

Basdevant, J, 'A Little-Known Convention on the Law of War' (1974) 160 *IRRC* 344.

Bassiouni, MC, *The Legislative History of the International Criminal Court* (Transnational, Ardsley, 2005).

—— and Manikas, P, *The Law of the International Criminal Tribunal for the Former Yugoslavia* (Transnational, Irvington-on-Hudson, 1996).

Baxter, RR, 'The Municipal and International Basis of Jurisdiction over War Crimes' (1951) 28 *BYIL* 382.

—— 'The First Modern Codification of the Law of War: Francis Lieber and General Orders No 100' (1963) 3 *IRRC* 171.

—— 'Forces for Compliance with the Law of War' (1964) 58 *ASIL Procs* 82.

—— 'Multilateral Treaties as Evidence of Customary International Law' (1965–6) 41 *BYIL* 275.

—— 'Ius in Bello Interno: The Present and Future Law', in JN Moore (ed), *Law and Civil War in the Modern World* (Johns Hopkins University Press, Baltimore, 1974).

—— 'Some Existing Problems of Humanitarian Law' (1975) 14 *Military Law and the Law of War Review* 297.

—— 'Humanitarian Law or Humanitarian Politics? The 1974 Diplomatic Conference on Humanitarian Law' (1975) 16 *Harvard International Law Journal* 1.

—— 'The Geneva Conventions of 1949 and Wars of National Liberation', in MC Bassiouni (ed), *International Terrorism and Political Crimes* (Thomas, Springfield, 1975).

—— 'The Geneva Conventions of 1949' (1980) 62 *International Law Studies* 220.

—— 'The Duties of Combatants and the Conduct of Hostilities (Law of The Hague)', in UNESCO (ed), *International Dimensions of Humanitarian Law* (UNESCO, Paris, 1988).

Beale Jr, JH, 'The Recognition of Cuban Belligerency' (1895–6) 9 *Harvard Law Review* 406.

Bedjaoui, M, *Law and the Algerian Revolution* (International Association of Democratic Lawyers, Brussels, 1961).

Bekou, O and Cryer, R, 'The International Criminal Court and Universal Jurisdiction: A Close Encounter?' (2007) 56 *ICLQ* 49.

Bell, C, *Peace Agreements and Human Rights* (Oxford University Press, Oxford, 2000).

—— 'Peace Agreements: Their Nature and Legal Status' (2006) 100 *AJIL* 373.

—— *On the Law of Peace* (Oxford University Press, Oxford, 2008).

Bellal, A, 'Towards Engagement, Compliance and Accountability' (2011) 37 *Forced Migration Review* 4.
—— Giacca, G, and Casey-Maslen, S, 'International Law and Armed Non-State Actors in Afghanistan' (2011) 93 *IRRC* 47.
Bellinger III, JB and Haynes II, WJ, 'A US Government Response to the International Committee of the Red Cross Study *Customary International Humanitarian Law*' (2007) 89 *IRRC* 44.
—— and Padmanabhan, VM, 'Detention Operations in Contemporary Conflicts: Four Challenges for the Geneva Conventions and other Existing Law' (2011) 105 *AJIL* 201.
Benoit, JP, 'Mistreatment of the Wounded, Sick and Shipwrecked by the ICRC Study on Customary International Humanitarian Law' (2008) 11 *YIHL* 175.
Berger, J-F, *The Humanitarian Diplomacy of the ICRC and the Conflict in Croatia 1991–2* (ICRC, Geneva, 1995).
Berman, P, 'The ICRC's Advisory Service on International Humanitarian Law: the Challenge of National Implementation' (1996) 36 *IRRC* 338.
Best, G, *Humanity in Warfare* (Methuen, London, 1983).
—— *War and Law Since 1945* (Clarendon Press, Oxford, 1994).
Bierzanek, R, 'Humanitarian Law in Armed Conflicts: The Doctrine and Practice of Polish Insurgents in the 19th Century' (1977) 17 *IRRC* 128.
—— 'Reprisals as a Means of Enforcing the Laws of Warfare: the Old and the New Law', in A Cassese (ed), *The New Humanitarian Law of Armed Conflict* (Editoriale Scientifica, Napoli, 1979).
Bigler, R, 'Disseminating International Humanitarian Law in Colombia: Dissemination is Everyone's Job—A Firsthand Report by an ICRC Delegate' (1997) 37 *IRRC* 421.
Bílková, V, 'Treat Them as They Deserve?! Three Approaches to Armed Opposition Groups under Current International Law' (2010) 4 *Human Rights and International Legal Discourse* 1.
Bindschedler-Robert, D, *The Law of Armed Conflict* (Carnegie Endowment for International Peace, New York, 1971).
Birganie, AB, 'An African Initiative for the Protection of the Rights of Internally Displaced People' (2010) 10 *HRLR* 179.
Blix, H, 'Means and Methods of Combat', in UNESCO (ed), *International Dimensions of Humanitarian Law* (Martinus Nijhoff, Dordrecht, 1988).
Blum, G, 'Re-envisaging the International Law of Internal Armed Conflict: A Reply to Sandesh Sivakumaran' (2011) 22 *EJIL* 265.
Boelaert-Suominen, S, 'Grave Breaches, Universal Jurisdiction and Internal Armed Conflict: Is Customary Law Moving Towards a Uniform Enforcement Mechanism for All Armed Conflicts?' (2000) 5 *JCSL* 63.
Boissier, P, *From Solferino to Tsushima: History of the International Committee of the Red Cross* (Henry Dunant Institute, Geneva, 1985).
Bond, JE, 'Internal Conflict and Article Three of the Geneva Conventions' (1971–2) 48 *Denver LJ* 263.
—— 'Application of the Law of War to Internal Conflicts' (1973) 3 *Georgia Journal of International and Comparative Law* 345.
—— *The Rules of Riot* (Princeton University Press, Princeton, 1974).
Boothby, WH, *Weapons and the Law of Armed Conflict* (Oxford University Press, Oxford, 2009).
—— 'Direct Participation in Hostilities—A Discussion of the ICRC Interpretive Guidance' (2010) 1 *Journal of International Humanitarian Legal Studies* 143.
—— '"And For Such Time As": The Time Dimension to Direct Participation in Hostilities' (2010) 42 *New York University Journal of International Law and Politics* 741.
Bothe, M, 'Article 3 and Protocol II: Case Studies of Nigeria and El Salvador' (1981–2) 31 *American University Law Review* 899.

Bothe, M, 'Relief Actions: The position of the Recipient State', in F Kalshoven (ed), *Assisting the Victims of Armed Conflict and Other Disasters* (Martinus Nijhoff, Dordrecht, 1989).

—— 'War Crimes', in A Cassese, P Gaeta, and JRWD Jones (eds), *The Rome Statute of the International Criminal Court: A Commentary* (Oxford University Press, Oxford, 2002).

—— 'Customary International Humanitarian Law: Some Reflections on the ICRC Study' (2005) 8 *YIHL* 143.

—— Partsch, KJ, and Solf, WA, *New Rules for Victims of Armed Conflicts* (Martinus Nijhoff Publishers, The Hague, 1982).

Bourloyannis, C, 'The Security Council of the United Nations and the Implementation of International Humanitarian Law' (1991–2) 20 *Denver Journal of International Law and Policy* 335.

Bouvier, A, 'Recent Studies on the Protection of the Environment in Time of Armed Conflict' (1992) 32 *IRRC* 554.

—— and Sams, KE, 'Teaching International Humanitarian Law in Universities: the Contribution of the International Committee of the Red Cross' (2002) 5 *YIHL* 381.

Bowring, B, 'Fragmentation, *Lex Specialis* and the Tensions in the Jurisprudence of the European Court of Human Rights' (2009) 14 *JCSL* 485.

Boylan, PJ, Review of the Convention for the Protection of Cultural Property in the Event of Armed Conflict, UNESCO Doc. CLT-93/WS/12 (1993).

Boyle Jr, WE, 'Under the Black Flag: Execution and Retaliation in Mosby's Confederacy' (1994) 144 *Military Law Review* 148.

Branche, R, 'The French in Algeria: Can There be Prisoners of War in a "Domestic" Operation?', in S Scheipers (ed), *Prisoners in War* (Oxford University Press, Oxford, 2010).

Brett, R, 'Non-Governmental Human Rights Organizations and International Humanitarian Law' (1998) 38 *IRRC* 531.

Briggs, HW, *The Law of Nations* (Crofts, New York, 1938).

Bugnion, F, *The International Committee of the Red Cross and the Protection of War Victims* (ICRC, Geneva, 2003).

—— '*Jus ad Bellum, Jus in Bello* and Non-International Armed Conflicts' (2003) 6 *YIHL* 167.

Buis, EJ, 'The Implementation of International Humanitarian Law by Human Rights Courts: The Example of the Inter-American Human Rights System', in R Arnold and N Quenivet (eds), *International Humanitarian Law and Human Rights Law* (Martinus Nijhoff, Leiden, 2008).

Burke-White, W, 'Complementarity in Practice: The International Criminal Court as Part of a System of Multi-Level Global Governance in the Democratic Republic of the Congo' (2005) 18 *LJIL* 557.

Byron, C, 'Armed Conflicts: International or Non-International?' (2001) 6 *JCSL* 63.

—— 'A Blurring of the Boundaries: The Application of International Humanitarian Law by Human Rights Bodies' (2006–7) 47 *Virginia JIL* 839.

—— *War Crimes and Crimes against Humanity in the Rome Statute of the International Criminal Court* (Manchester University Press, Manchester, 2009).

Carnahan, BM, 'Reason, Retaliation, and Rhetoric: Jefferson and the Quest for Humanity in War' (1993) 139 *Military Law Review* 83.

—— and Robertson, M, 'The Protocol on "Blinding Laser Weapons": A New Direction for International Humanitarian Law' (1996) 90 *AJIL* 484.

Carr, S, 'From Theory to Practice: National and Regional Application of the Guiding Principles' (2009) 21 *IJRL* 34.

Carrillo-Suárez, A, '*Hors de Logique*: Contemporary Issues in International Humanitarian Law as Applied to Internal Armed Conflict' (1999) 15 *American University International Law Review* 1.

Cassese, A, 'The Spanish Civil War and the Development of Customary Law concerning Internal Armed Conflicts', in A Cassese (ed), *Current Problems of International Law: Essays on UN Law and the Law of Armed Conflict* (Giuffrè, Milan, 1975).

—— 'The Prohibition of Indiscriminate Means of Warfare', in RJ Akkerman, PJ van Krieken, and CO Pannenborg (eds), *Declarations on Principles: A Quest for Universal Peace* (AW Sijthoff, Leyden, 1977).

—— 'A Tentative Appraisal of the Old and the New Humanitarian Law of Armed Conflict', in A Cassese (ed), *The New Humanitarian Law of Armed Conflict* (Editoriale Scientifica, Napoli, 1979).

—— 'Means of Warfare: The Traditional and the New Law', in A Cassese (ed), *The New Humanitarian Law of Armed Conflict* (Editoriate Scientifica, Napoli, 1979).

—— 'The Status of Rebels under the 1977 Geneva Protocol on Non-International Armed Conflicts' (1981) 30 *ICLQ* 416.

—— 'The Geneva Protocols of 1977 on the Humanitarian Law of Armed Conflict and Customary International Law' (1984) 3 *UCLA Pacific Basin Law Journal* 55.

—— 'Wars of national liberation and humanitarian law', in C Swinarski (ed), *Studies and Essays on International Humanitarian Law and Red Cross Principles in Honour of Jean Pictet* (ICRC, Geneva, 1984).

—— 'On the Current Trends towards Criminal Prosecution and Punishment of Breaches of International Humanitarian Law' (1998) 9 *EJIL* 2.

—— 'The Statute of the International Criminal Court: Some Preliminary Reflections' (1999) 10 *EJIL* 144.

—— 'The Special Court and International Law: The Decision Concerning the Lomé Agreement Amnesty' (2004) 2 *JICJ* 1130.

—— 'The *Nicaragua* and *Tadić* Tests Revisited in Light of the ICJ Judgment on Genocide in Bosnia' (2007) 18 *EJIL* 649.

—— *International Criminal Law* (Oxford University Press, Oxford, 2008).

—— 'Weapons Causing Unnecessary Suffering: Are They Prohibited?', reprinted in A Cassese, *The Human Dimension of International Law: Selected Papers* (Oxford University Press, Oxford, 2008).

—— 'Civil War and International Law', reprinted in A Cassese, *The Human Dimension of International Law: Collected Papers* (Oxford University Press, Oxford, 2008).

—— et al (eds), *The Oxford Companion to International Criminal Justice* (Oxford University Press, Oxford, 2009).

—— 'Should Rebels be Treated as Criminals? Some Modest Proposals for Rendering Internal Armed Conflicts Less Inhumane', in A Cassese (ed), *Realizing Utopia: The Future of International Law* (Oxford University Press, Oxford, 2012).

Castrén, E, 'Recognition of Insurgency' (1965) 5 *Indian Journal of International Law* 443.

—— *Civil War* (Suomalainen Tiedeakatemia, Helsinki, 1966).

Chamberlain, K, *War and Cultural Heritage* (Institute of Art and Law, Leicester, 2004).

Chapelle, D, 'How Castro Won', in TN Greene, *The Guerrilla—And How to Fight Him* (Praeger, New York, 1967).

Chen, T, *The International Law of Recognition* (Stevens and Sons, London, 1951).

Chimni, BS, 'The Incarceration of Victims: Deconstructing Safety Zones', in N Al-Nauimi and R Meese, *International Legal Issues Arising under the United Nations Decade of International Law* (Martinus Nijhoff, The Hague, 1995).

Ciobanu, D, 'The Concept and the Determination of the Existence of Armed Conflicts Not of an International Character' (1975) 58 *Rivista di Diritto Internazionale* 43.

Clapham, A, *Human Rights Obligations of Non-State Actors* (Oxford University Press, Oxford, 2006).

—— 'Human Rights Obligations of Non-State Actors in Conflict Situations' (2006) 88 *IRRC* 491.

Clapham, A, 'The Rights and Responsibilities of Armed Non-State Actors: The Legal Landscape and Issues Surrounding Engagement', Ownership of Norms Project—Toward a Better Protection of Civilians in Armed Conflicts, February 2010.

—— 'Non-State Actors', in D Moeckli, S Shah, and S Sivakumaran (eds), *International Human Rights Law* (Oxford University Press, Oxford, 2010).

Cohen, R, 'The Guiding Principles on Internal Displacement: An Innovation in International Standard Setting' (2004) 10 *Global Governance* 459.

Condorelli, L, 'War Crimes and Internal Conflicts in the Statute of the International Criminal Court', in M Politi and G Nesi (eds), *The Rome Statute of the International Criminal Court: A Challenge to Impunity* (Ashgate, Aldershot, 2001) 107.

Coomaraswamy, R, 'The Security Council and Children and Armed Conflict: An Experiment in the Making', *Public Lecture*, 12 April 2010, Centre on Human Rights in Conflict, University of East London School of Law.

Cottier, M, 'Article 8(2)(b)(xxvi)', in O Triffterer (ed), *Commentary on the Rome Statute of the International Criminal Court* (Beck, München, 2008).

Coupland, RM (ed), *The SIrUS Project: Towards a Determination of Which Weapons Cause 'Superfluous Injury or Unnecessary Suffering'* (ICRC, Geneva, 1997).

Crawford, E, 'Unequal before the Law: The Case for the Elimination of the Distinction between International and Non-International Armed Conflicts' (2007) 20 *LJIL* 441.

—— *The Treatment of Combatants and Insurgents under the Law of Armed Conflict* (Oxford University Press, Oxford, 2010).

Cryer, R, *Prosecuting International Crimes* (Cambridge University Press, Cambridge, 2005) 283.

—— '*Prosecutor v. Galić* and the War Crime of Terror Bombing' (2005–6) 2 *IDF Law Review* 75.

—— 'The Security Council and International Humanitarian Law', in SC Breau and A Jachec-Neale (eds), *Testing the Boundaries of International Humanitarian Law* (BIICL, London, 2006).

—— 'The Fine Art of Friendship: *Jus in Bello* in Afghanistan' (2007) 7 *JCSL* 37.

—— et al, *An Introduction to International Criminal Law and Procedure* (Cambridge University Press, Cambridge, 2008).

—— 'The Definitions of International Crimes in the *Al Bashir* Arrest Warrant Decision' (2009) 7 *JICJ* 283.

—— 'The Interplay of Human Rights and Humanitarian Law: The Approach of the ICTY' (2010) 14 *JCSL* 511.

Cuadra Lacayo, J, 'International Humanitarian Law and Irregular Warfare: Lessons Learned in Latin America' (2000) 82 *IRRC* 941.

Cullen, A, 'Key Developments Affecting the Scope of Internal Armed Conflict in International Humanitarian Law' (2005) 183 *Military Law Review* 66.

—— *The Concept of Non-International Armed Conflict in International Humanitarian Law* (Cambridge University Press, Cambridge, 2010).

Cullen, H, *The Role of International Law in the Elimination of Child Labour* (Martinus Nijhoff, Leiden, 2007).

Danner, AM, 'When Courts Make Law: How the International Criminal Tribunals Recast the Laws of War' (2006) 59 *Vanderbilt Law Review* 1.

Darcy, S, 'What Future for the Doctrine of Belligerent Reprisals?' (2002) 5 *YIHL* 107.

—— 'The Evolution of the Law of Belligerent Reprisals' (2003) 175 *Military Law Rev* 184.

—— *Collective Responsibility and Accountability under International Law* (Transnational, Leiden, 2007).

—— 'Prosecuting the War Crime of Collective Punishment' (2010) 8 *JICJ* 29.

David, E, 'Dissemination of International Humanitarian Law at University Level' (1987) 257 *IRRC* 155.

—— *Principes de Droit des Conflits Armés* (Bruylant, Bruxelles, 2002).
Davis, GB, 'Doctor Francis Lieber's Instructions for the Government of Armies in the Field' (1907) 1 *AJIL* 13.
de Beco, G, 'Compliance with International Humanitarian Law by Non-State Actors' (2005) 18 *Humanitäres Völlkerecht* 190.
de Mulinen, F, *Handbook on the Law of War for Armed Forces* (ICRC, Geneva, 1987).
de St Jorre, J, *The Nigerian Civil War* (Hodder and Stoughton, London, 1972).
de Vattel, E, *The Law of Nations or the Principles of Natural Law, Volume 3* (CG Fenwick trans) (Carnegie Institution, Washington DC, 1916).
de Zayas, AM, 'International Law and Mass Population Transfers' (1975) 16 *Harvard ILJ* 207.
Decrey Warner, E, 'The Struggle against Landmines: An Opening for Peace Talks in Colombia' (2005) 16 *Conciliation Resources: Accord* 48.
—— Somer, J, and Bongard, P, 'Armed Non-State Actors and Humanitarian Norms: Lessons from the Geneva Call Experience', in B Perrin (ed), *Modern Warfare: Armed Groups, Private Militaries, Humanitarian Organizations, and the Law* (University of British Columbia Press, 2012).
Deeks, AS, 'Administrative Detention in Armed Conflict' (2009) 40 *Case Western Reserve Journal of International Law* 403.
Dehn, JC, 'Permissible Perfidy? Analysing the Colombian Hostage Rescue, the Capture of Rebel Leaders and the World's Reaction' (2008) 6 *JICJ* 627.
Delissen, AJM, 'Legal Protection of Child-Combatants after the Protocols: Reaffirmation, Development or a Step Backwards?', in C Swinarski (ed), *Studies and Essays on International Humanitarian Law and Red Cross Principles in Honour of Jean Pictet* (ICRC, Geneva, 1984).
Dennis, MJ, 'Application of Human Rights Treaties Extraterritorially in Times of Armed Conflict and Military Occupation' (2005) 99 *AJIL* 119.
Detter, I, *The Law of War* (Cambridge University Press, Cambridge, 2000).
Dinstein, Y, 'Commentary' (1981–2) 31 *American University Law Review* 849.
—— 'Siege Warfare and the Starvation of Civilians', in AJM Delissen and GJ Tanja (eds), *Humanitarian Law of Armed Conflict, Challenges Ahead: Essays in Honour of Frits Kalshoven* (Nijhoff, Dordrecht, 1991).
—— *The Conduct of Hostilities under the Law of International Armed Conflict* (Cambridge University Press, Cambridge, 2004).
—— 'International Humanitarian Law as *Lex Specialis*', in G Ravasi and GL Beruto (eds), *International Humanitarian Law and Other Legal Regimes: Interplay in Situations of Violence* (Nagard, Milano, 2005).
—— 'The ICRC Customary International Humanitarian Law Study' (2006) 36 *IYHR* 1.
—— 'The Interaction between Customary International Law and Treaties' (2006) 322 *RdC* 243.
—— *The International Law of Belligerent Occupation* (Cambridge University Press, Cambridge, 2009).
Docherty, B, 'The Time is Now: A Historical Argument for a Cluster Munitions Convention' (2007) 20 *Harvard Human Rights Journal* 53.
—— 'Breaking New Ground: The Convention on Cluster Munitions and the Evolution of International Humanitarian Law' (2009) 31 *HRQ* 934.
Doria, J, 'Angola: A Case Study in the Challenges of Achieving Peace and the Question of Amnesty or Prosecution of War Crimes in Mixed Armed Conflicts' (2002) 5 *YIHL* 3.
Dörmann, K, 'The First Review Conference to the 1980 Convention on Prohibitions or Restrictions on the Use of Certain Conventional Weapons Which May Be Deemed to Be Excessively Injurious or to Have Indiscriminate Effects—A Story of Failure?' (1995) 8 *Humanitäres Völkerrecht* 203.

Dörmann, K, 'Preparatory Commission for the International Criminal Court: the Elements of War Crimes' (2000) 82 *IRRC* 771.

—— *Elements of War Crimes under the Rome Statute of the International Criminal Court: Sources and Commentary* (Cambridge University Press, Cambridge, 2003).

—— 'War Crimes under the Rome Statute of the International Criminal Court, with a Special Focus on the Negotiations on the Elements of Crimes' (2003) 7 *Max Planck Yearbook of United Nations Law* 341.

—— 'Dissemination and Monitoring Compliance of International Humanitarian Law', in W Heintschel von Heinegg and V Epping (eds), *International Humanitarian Law Facing New Challenges: Symposium in Honour of Knut Ipsen* (Springer, Berlin, 2007).

Doswald-Beck, L, 'The Value of the 1977 Geneva Protocols for the Protection of Civilians', in MA Meyer (ed), *Armed Conflict and the New Law* (BIICL, London, 1989).

—— 'Obstacles to Regulating New Weaponary: Battlefield Laser Weapons', in H Fox and MA Meyer (eds), *Armed Conflict and the New Law, Volume II: Effecting Compliance* (BIICL, London, 1993).

—— 'New Protocol on Blinding Laser Weapons' (1996) 36 *IRRC* 272.

—— 'The Right to Life in Armed Conflict: Does International Humanitarian Law Provide All the Answers?' (2006) 88 *IRRC* 881.

—— and Vité, S, 'International Humanitarian Law and Human Rights Law' (1993) 33 *IRRC* 94.

Draper, GIAD, *The Red Cross Conventions* (Stevens and Sons, London, 1958).

—— 'The Geneva Conventions of 1949' (1965-I) 114 *RdC* 63.

—— 'Role of Legal Advisers in the Armed Forces' (1978) 18 *IRRC* 6.

—— 'The Implementation and Enforcement of the Geneva Conventions of 1949 and of the Two Additional Protocols of 1978' (1979-III) 164 *RdC* 1.

—— 'Humanitarian Law and Internal Armed Conflicts' (1983) 13 *Georgia Journal of International and Comparative Law* 253.

—— 'Humanitarian Law and Human Rights', in MA Meyer and H McCoubrey (eds), *Reflections on Law and Armed Conflicts: The Selected Works on the Laws of War by the late Professor Colonel GIAD Draper OBE* (Kluwer, The Hague, 1998).

Droege, C, 'The Interplay between International Humanitarian Law and International Human Rights Law in Situations of Armed Conflict' (2007) 40 *Israel Law Review* 310.

—— 'Elective Affinities? Human Rights and Humanitarian Law' (2008) 90 *IRRC* 501.

Dunant, H, *A Memory of Solferino* (reprinted and translated, ICRC, Geneva, 1986).

Dunlap, WV, 'Dissemination and International Humanitarian Law in Modern Social Conflict', in J Carey, WV Dunlap, and RJ Pritchard (eds), *International Humanitarian Law: Challenges* (Transnational, Ardsley, 2004).

Durand, A, *From Sarajevo to Hiroshima: History of the International Committee of the Red Cross* (Henry Dunant Institute, Geneva, 1984).

Duxbury, A, 'Drawing Lines in the Sand—Characterising Conflicts for the Purposes of Teaching International Humanitarian Law' (2007) 8 *Melbourne JIL* 259.

Eide, A, 'The New Humanitarian Law in Non-International Armed Conflict', in A Cassese (ed), *The New Humanitarian Law of Armed Conflict* (Editoriale Scientifica, Napoli, 1979).

Elder, DA, 'The Historical Background of Common Article 3 of the Geneva Conventions of 1949' (1979) 11 *Case Western Journal of International Law* 37.

Elliott, HW, 'Dead and Wounded', in R Gutman, D Reiff, and A Dworkin (eds), *Crimes of War* (WW Norton and Co, New York, 2007).

Falk, R, 'Janus Tormented: The International Law of Internal War', in JN Rosenau (ed), *International Aspects of Civil Strife* (Princeton University Press, Princeton, 1964).

—— (ed), *The Vietnam War and International Law, Volumes I–IV* (Princeton University Press, Princeton, 1968–1976).

Farer, T, 'Humanitarian Law and Armed Conflicts: Toward the Definition of "International Armed Conflict"' (1971) 71 *Columbia Law Review* 37.

Farrell, N, 'Dissemination in Bosnia and Herzegovina Lessons Learned' (1997) 37 *IRRC* 409.

Fenrick, WJ, 'New Developments in the Law Concerning the Use of Conventional Weapons in Armed Conflict' (1981) 19 *Canadian YIL* 229.

—— 'The Rule of Proportionality and Protocol I in Conventional Warfare' (1982) 98 *Military Law Review* 91.

—— 'Determining Customary International Law Relative to the Conduct of Hostilities in Non-International Armed Conflicts: Remarks' (1987) 2 *American University Journal of International Law and Policy* 471.

—— 'The Law Applicable to Targeting and Proportionality After Operation Allied Force: A View from the Outside' (2000) 3 *YIHL* 53.

—— 'The Prosecution of Unlawful Attack Cases before the ICTY' (2004) 7 *YIHL* 153.

—— 'Specific Methods of Warfare', in E Wilmshurst and SC Breau (eds), *Perspectives on the ICRC Study on Customary International Humanitarian Law* (Cambridge University Press, Cambridge, 2007).

—— 'ICRC Guidance on Direct Participation in Hostilities' (2009) 12 *YIHL* 287.

Fleck, D, 'Ruses of War and Prohibition of Perfidy' (1974) 13 *Military Law and the Law of War Review* 269.

—— 'Humanitarian Protection in Non-International Armed Conflicts: The New Research Project of the International Institute of Humanitarian Law' (2000) 30 *IYHR* 1.

—— 'Humanitarian Protection Against Non-State Actors', in JA Fowein et al (eds), *Verhandeln fur fen Frieden—Negotiating for Peace: Liber Amicorum Tono Eitel* (Springer, Berlin, 2003).

—— (ed), *The Handbook of International Humanitarian Law* (Oxford University Press, Oxford, 2008).

—— 'The Law of Non-International Armed Conflicts', in D Fleck (ed), *The Handbook of International Humanitarian Law* (Oxford University Press, Oxford, 2008).

Fleiner-Gerster, T and Meyer, MA, 'New Developments in Humanitarian Law: A Challenge to the Concept of Sovereignty' (1985) 34 *ICLQ* 267.

Flores Acuña, T, *The United Nations Mission in El Salvador: A Humanitarian Law Perspective* (Kluwer, The Hague, 1995).

Florquin, N and Decrey Warner, E, 'Engaging Non-State Armed Groups or Listing Terrorists? Implications for the Arms Control Community' (2008) 1 *Disarmament Forum* 17.

—— Lynge, K, and Pedersen, KL, 'Beyond Weapons Collection: Promoting Safe and Responsible SA/LW Management' (2009) 13 *Journal of ERW and Mine Action* 1.

Forsythe, DP, 'The 1974 Diplomatic Conference on Humanitarian Law: Some Observations' (1975) 69 *AJIL* 77.

—— 'Who Guards the Guardians: Third Parties and the Law of Armed Conflict' (1976) 70 *AJIL* 41.

—— 'Legal Management of Internal War: The 1977 Protocol on Non-International Armed Conflicts' (1978) 72 *AJIL* 272.

—— 'The International Committee of the Red Cross and Humanitarian Assistance—A Policy Analysis' (1996) 36 *IRRC* 512.

—— *The Humanitarians: The International Committee of the Red Cross* (Cambridge University Press, Cambridge, 2005).

Fraleigh, A, 'The Algerian Revolution as a Case Study in International Law', in RA Falk (ed), *The International Law of Civil War* (Johns Hopkins University Press, Baltimore, 1971).

Franklin, WM, *Protection of Foreign Interests* (US Government Printing Office, Washington DC, 1946).

Freeman, M, *Necessary Evils: Amnesties and the Search for Justice* (Cambridge University Press, Cambridge, 2009).

Friedman, L, *The Law of War: A Documentary History, Volume I* (Random House, New York, 1972).

Gaggioli, G and Kolb, R, 'A Right to Life in Armed Conflicts? The Contribution of the European Court of Human Rights' (2007) 37 *IYHR* 115.

Gallagher, K, 'No Justice, No Peace: The Legalities and Realities of Amnesty in Sierra Leone' (2000–1) 23 *Thomas Jefferson Law Review* 149.

García-Peña Jaramillo, D, 'Humanitarian Protection in Non-International Conflicts: A Case Study of Colombia' (2000) 30 *IYHR* 179.

Gardam, JG, *Non-Combatant Immunity as a Norm of International Humanitarian Law* (Martinus Nijhoff, Dordrecht, 1993).

—— *Necessity, Proportionality and the Use of Force by States* (Cambridge University Press, Cambridge, 2004).

—— 'The Neglected Aspect of Women and Armed Conflict—Progressive Development of the Law' (2005) LII *NILR* 197.

—— 'Crimes involving Disproportionate Means and Methods of Warfare under the Statute of the International Criminal Court', in J Doria, H-P Gasser, and MC Bassiouni (eds), *The Legal Regime of the International Criminal Court: Essays in Honour of Professor Igor Blishchenko* (Martinus Nijhoff, Leiden, 2009).

—— and Charlesworth, H, 'Protection of Women in Armed Conflict' (2000) 22 *HRQ* 148.

—— and Jarvis, MJ, *Women, Armed Conflict and International Law* (Kluwer, The Hague, 2001).

Garms, U and Peschke, K, 'War Crimes Prosecution in Bosnia-Herzegovina (1992–2002)' (2006) 4 *JICJ* 258.

Garner, JW, 'Questions of International Law in the Spanish Civil War' (1937) 31 *AJIL* 66.

Garraway, C, 'The Use and Abuse of Military Manuals' (2004) 7 *YIHL* 425.

Gasser, H-P, 'The Protection of Journalists Engaged in Dangerous Professional Missions' (1983) 23 *IRRC* 3.

—— 'Internationalized Non-International Armed Conflicts: Case Studies of Afghanistan, Kampuchea, and Lebanon' (1983–4) 33 *American University Law Review* 145.

—— 'Customary Law and Additional Protocol I to the Geneva Conventions for Protection of War Victims: Future Directions in Light of the U.S. Decision Not to Ratify: Remarks' (1987) 81 *ASIL Procs* 26.

—— 'Determining Customary International Law Relative to the Conduct of Hostilities in Non-International Armed Conflicts: Remarks' (1987) 2 *American University Journal of Inernational Law and Policy* 471.

—— 'Ensuring Respect for the Geneva Conventions and Protocols: The Role of Third States and the United Nations', in H Fox and MA Meyer (eds), *Armed Conflict and the New Law, Volume II: Effecting Compliance* (BIICL, London, 1993).

—— 'International Humanitarian Law and Human Rights Law in Non-international Armed Conflict: Joint Venture or Mutual Exclusion?' (2002) 45 *GYIL* 149.

—— 'Protection of the Civilian Population', in D Fleck (ed), *The Handbook of International Humanitarian Law* (Oxford University Press, Oxford, 2008).

Gassmann, P, 'Colombia: Persuading Belligerents to Comply with International Norms', in S Chesterman (ed), *Civilians in War* (Lynne Rienner Publishers, London, 2001).

Geiß, R, 'Armed Violence in Fragile States: Low-Intensity Conflicts, Spillover Conflicts, and Sporadic Law Enforcement Operations by Third Parties' (2009) 91 *IRRC* 127.

Geneva Call, Deed of Commitment for Adherence to a Total Ban on Anti-Personnel Mines and for Cooperation in Mine Action.

—— Deed of Commitment under Geneva Call for the Protection of Children from the Effects of Armed Conflict.

—— Engaging Non-State Actors Toward Compliance with Humanitarian Norms: Summary Report (2001).
—— Mine Ban Education Workshop in Southern Sudan: Report of Proceedings and Recommendations (Geneva Call, Geneva, 2003).
—— An Inclusive Approach to Armed Non-State Actors and International Humanitarian Norms: Report of the First Meeting of Signatories to Geneva Call's Deed of Commitment (2004).
—— Workshop Report: Towards a Mine Free World, Dimapur, Nagaland, India, 16 March 2005.
—— Women in Armed Opposition Groups in Africa and the Promotion of International Humanitarian Law and Human Rights: Report of a Workshop organized in Addis Ababa by Geneva Call and the Program for the Study of International Organization(s), 23–26 November 2005.
—— *Armed Non-State Actors and Landmines: Volume I* (Geneva Call, Geneva, 2005).
—— *Armed Non-State Actors and Landmines, Volume II: A Global Report of NSA Mine Action* (Geneva Call, Geneva, 2006).
—— *Training of Trainers Workshop* (Geneva Call, Geneva, 2006).
—— Engaging Armed Non-State Actors in a Landmine Ban: The Geneva Call Progress Report (2000–2007).
—— *Women in Armed Opposition Groups Speak on War, Protection and Obligations under International Humanitarian and Human Rights Law* (Geneva Call, Geneva, 2008).
—— (ed), *In Their Words: Perspectives of Armed Non-State Actors on the Protection of Children from the Effects of Armed Conflict* (Geneva Call, Geneva, 2010).
—— Annual Reports.
—— Newsletters.
—— Communiqués.
Gillard, E-C, 'The Role of International Humanitarian Law in the Protection of Displaced Persons' (2005) 24 *Refugee Survey Quarterly* 37.
Gioia, A, 'The Chemical Weapons Convention and its Application in Time of Armed Conflict', in M Bothe, N Ronzitti, and A Rosas (eds), *The New Chemical Weapons Convention—Implementation and Prospects* (Kluwer, The Hague, 1998).
Goldman, RK, 'International Humanitarian Law: Americas Watch's Experience in Monitoring Internal Armed Conflicts' (1993) 9 *American University Journal of International Law and Policy* 49.
Gomulkiewicz, RW, 'International Law Governing Aid to Opposition Groups in Civil War: Resurrecting the Standards of Belligerency' (1988) 63 *Washington Law Review* 43.
Goulding, M, 'The Evolution of United Nations Peacekeeping' (1993) 69 *International Affairs* 451.
Graditzky, T, 'Individual Criminal Responsibility for Violations of International Humanitarian Law Committed in Non-International Armed Conflicts' (1998) 38 *IRRC* 29.
—— 'War Crime Issues Before the Rome Diplomatic Conference on the Establishment of an International Criminal Court' (1999) 5 *University of California Davis Journal of International Law and Policy* 199.
Gray, C, 'Bosnia and Herzegovina: Civil War or Inter-State Conflict? Characterization and Consequences' (1997) 68 *BYIL* 155.
Green, LC, 'The New Law of Armed Conflict' (1977) 15 *Canadian Year Book of International Law* 3.
—— 'Low-Intensity Conflict and the Law' (1996–7) 3 *ILSA Journal of International and Comparative Law* 493.
—— *Essays on the Modern Law of War* (Transnational, Ardsley, 1999).
—— '"Unnecessary Suffering", Weapons Control and the Law of War', in LC Green (ed), *Essays on the Modern Law of War* (Transnational, Ardsley, 1999).

Green, LC, *The Contemporary Law of Armed Conflict* (Manchester University Press, Manchester, 2000).

Greenspan, M, *The Modern Law of Land Warfare* (University of California Press, Berkeley, 1959).

Greenwood, C, 'The Relationship between *Jus ad Bellum* and *Jus in Bello*' (1983) 9 *Review of International Studies* 221.

—— 'The Twilight of the Law of Belligerent Reprisals' (1989) 20 *NYIL* 35.

—— 'Customary Law Status of the 1977 Geneva Protocols', in AJM Delissen and GJ Tanja (eds), *Humanitarian Law of Armed Conflict Challenges Ahead: Essays in Honour of Frits Kalshoven* (Nijhoff, Dordrecht, 1991).

—— 'Battlefield Laser Weapons in the Context of the Law on Conventional Weapons', in L Doswald-Beck (ed), *Blinding Weapons* (ICRC, Geneva, 1993).

—— 'Scope of Application of Humanitarian Law', in D Fleck (ed), *The Handbook of Humanitarian Law in Armed Conflicts* (Oxford University Press, Oxford, 1995).

—— 'International Humanitarian Law and the *Tadić* Case' (1996) 7 *EJIL* 265.

—— 'Current Issues in the Law of Armed Conflict: Weapons, Targets and International Criminal Liability' (1997) 1 *Singapore Journal of International and Comparative Law* 441.

—— 'The Law of Weaponry at the Start of the New Millennium' (1998) 71 *International Law Studies* 185.

—— 'The Development of International Humanitarian Law by the International Criminal Tribunal for the Former Yugoslavia' (1998) 2 *Max Planck Yearbook of United Nations Law* 97.

—— 'International Humanitarian Law and United Nations Military Operations' (1998) 1 *YIHL* 3.

—— 'A Critique of the Additional Protocols to the Geneva Conventions of 1949', in H Durham and TLH McCormack (eds), *The Changing Face of Conflict and the Efficacy of International Humanitarian Law* (Martinus Nijhoff, The Hague, 1999).

—— 'The Applicability of International Humanitarian Law and the Law of Neutrality to the Kosovo Campaign' (2002) 78 *International Law Studies* 35.

—— 'International Humanitarian Law: Laws of War', in C Greenwood, *Essays on War in International Law* (Cameron May, London, 2006).

Guevara, E, *Guerrilla Warfare* (Penguin Books, Middlesex, 1969).

Gutteridge, JAC, 'The Geneva Conventions of 1949' (1949) 26 *BYIL* 294.

Haines, S, 'Weapons, Means and Methods of Warfare', in E Wilmshurst and SC Breau (eds), *Perspectives on the ICRC Study on Customary International Humanitarian Law* (Cambridge University Press, Cambridge, 2007).

Hall, WE, *A Treatise on International Law* (A Pearce Higgins (ed)) (Clarendon Press, Oxford, 1924).

Halleck, HW, *International law: or rules regulating the intercourse of states in peace and war* (S Baker (ed)) (C Kegan Paul, London, 1878).

Hampson, FJ, 'Belligerent Reprisals and the 1977 Protocols to the Geneva Conventions of 1949' (1988) 37 *ICLQ* 818.

—— 'Means and methods of warfare in the conflict in the Gulf', in P Rowe (ed), *The Gulf War 1990–91 in International and English Law* (Routledge, London, 1993).

—— 'Fact-Finding and the International Fact-Finding Commission', in H Fox and MA Meyer (eds), *Armed Conflict and the New Law, Volume II: Effecting Compliance* (BIICL, London, 1993).

—— 'Fundamental Guarantees', in E Wilmshurst and SC Breau (eds), *Perspectives on the ICRC Study on Customary International Humanitarian law* (Cambridge University Press, Cambridge, 2007).

Happold, M, *Child Soldiers in International Law* (Manchester University Press, Manchester, 2005).

Harding, I, 'The Origins and Effectiveness of the Geneva Conventions for the Protection of War Victims' (1973) 13 *IRRC* 283.

Hartigan, RS, *Lieber's Code and the Law of War* (Precedent, Chicago, 1983).

Heintze, H-J, 'The European Court of Human Rights and the Implementation of Human Rights Standards during Armed Conflicts' (2002) 45 *GYIL* 60.

Helle, D, 'Optional Protocol on the Involvement of Children in Armed Conflict to the Convention on the Rights of the Child' (2000) 82 *IRRC* 797.

Henckaerts, J-M, 'New Rules for the Protection of Cultural Property in Armed Conflict' (1999) 81 *IRRC* 593.

—— 'Binding Armed Opposition Groups through Humanitarian Treaty Law and Customary Law' (2003) 27 *Collegium* 123.

—— 'Study on Customary International Humanitarian Law: A Contribution to the Understanding and Respect for the Rule of Law in Armed Conflict' (2005) 87 *IRRC* 175.

—— 'Customary International Humanitarian Law: A Response to US Comments' (2007) 89 *IRRC* 473.

—— and Doswald-Beck, L, *Customary International Humanitarian Law: Volumes I and II* (Cambridge University Press, Cambridge, 2004).

Henderson, I, *The Contemporary Law of Targeting* (Nijhoff, Leiden, 2009).

Higgins, N, *Regulating the Use of Force in Wars of National Liberation: The Need for a New Regime* (Martinus Nijhoff, Leiden, 2010).

Higgins, R, 'Internal War and International Law', in CE Black and RA Falk (eds), *The Future of the International Legal Order, Volume III: Conflict Management* (Princeton University Press, Princeton, 1971).

Hladik, J, 'The Review Process of the 1954 Hague Convention for the Protection of Cultural Property in the Event of Armed Conflict and its Impact on International Humanitarian Law' (1998) 1 *YIHL* 313.

Hoffman, MH, 'The Customary Law of Non-International Armed Conflict' (1990) 30 *IRRC* 322.

—— 'The Application of International Humanitarian Law in Sri Lanka: A Compliance Based Case Study on the Rules of War' (2000) 30 *IYHR* 209.

—— 'Can Military Manuals Improve the Law of War? The San Remo Manual on the Law of Non-International Armed Conflict considered in relation to Historical and Contemporary Trends' (2007) 37 *IYHR* 241.

Hoffman, T, 'The Gentle Humanizer of Humanitarian Law—Antonio Cassese and the Creation of the Customary Law of Non-International Armed Conflict', in C Stahn and L van den Herik (eds), *Future Perspectives on International Criminal Justice* (TMC Asser Press, The Hague, 2010).

Holland, J, 'Military Objective and Collateral Damage: Their Relationship and Dynamics' (2004) 7 *YIHL* 35.

Hull, IV, 'Prisoners in Colonial Warfare: The Imperial German Example', in S Scheipers (ed), *Prisoners in War* (Oxford University Press, Oxford, 2010).

Hulme, K, 'The 2008 Cluster Munitions Convention: Stepping Outside the CCW Framework (Again)' (2009) 58 *ICLQ* 219.

Human Rights Watch, 1992 Annual Report (1993).

—— *War Without Quarter: Colombia and International Humanitarian Law* (1998).

—— *Colombia: Beyond Negotiation, International Humanitarian Law and its Application to the Conduct of the FARC-EP* (August 2001).

—— *Indonesia: The War in Aceh* (2001).

—— *Back to the Brink: War Crimes by Liberian Government and Rebels* (May 2002).

—— *Being Neutral is Our Biggest Crime: Government, Vigilante and Naxalite Abuses in India's Chhattisgarh State* (July 2008).

Hyde, CC, *International Law Chiefly as Interpreted and Applied by the United States* (Little, Brown, and Co, London, 1922).
Independent International Fact-Finding Mission on the Conflict in Georgia, Report, Two Volumes (September 2009).
Institut de Droit International, 'Droits et devoirs des Puissances étrangères, au cas de mouvement insurrectionnel, envers les gouvernements établis et reconnus qui sont aux prises avec l'insurrection' (Neuchâtel, 1900).
—— 'The Distinction Between Military Objectives and Non-Military Objects in General and Particularly the Problems Associated with Weapons of Mass Destruction' (Edinburgh, 1969).
—— 'Conditions of Application of Humanitarian Rules of Armed Conflict to Hostilities in which United Forces May be Engaged' (Zagreb, 1971).
—— 'Conditions of Application of Rules, other than Humanitarian Rules, of Armed Conflict to Hostilities in which United Forces may be engaged' (Wiesbaden, 1975).
—— 'The Application of International Humanitarian Law and Fundamental Human Rights, in Armed Conflicts in which Non-State Entities are Parties' (Session of Berlin, 1999).
—— 'Humanitarian Assistance' (Bruges, 2003).
—— 'Universal Criminal Jurisdiction with regard to the Crime of Genocide, Crimes against Humanity and War Crimes' (Krakow, 2005).
Inter-American Commission on Human Rights. 'Annual Report of the Inter-American Commission on Human Rights 1990–1991', OEA/Ser.L/V/II.79 Doc.12 rev.1, 22 February 1991.
—— 'Third Report on the Human Rights Situation in Colombia', OEA/Ser.L/V/II.102 Doc.9 rev.1, 26 February 1999.
—— Report on Terrorism and Human Rights, OEA/Ser.L/V/II.116 Doc.5 rev.1 corr, 22 October 2002, para 59.
International Council on Human Rights Policy, *Ends and Means: Human Rights Approaches to Armed Groups* (ICHRP, 2000).
International Criminal Court, Press Release, President of Uganda Refers Situation Concerning the Lord's Resistance Army (LRA) to the ICC, 29 January 2004.
—— Press Release, Prosecutor Receives Referral of the Situation in the Democratic Republic of Congo, 19 April 2004.
—— Letter by the Chief Prosecutor to the President, 17 June 2004, annexed to ICC-02/04, Decision Assigning the Situation in Uganda to Pre-Trial Chamber II, 5 July 2004.
—— Press Release, Prosecutor Receives Referral Concerning Central African Republic, 7 January 2005.
International Criminal Tribunal for the former Yugoslavia, Final Report to the Prosecutor by the Committee Established to Review the NATO Bombing Campaign Against the Federal Republic of Yugoslavia (2000) 39 *ILM* 1257.
International Fact-Finding Commission, Annual Reports.
—— 'Training Chamber, Stockholm, September 1998'.
International Institute of Humanitarian Law (Council of the), Declaration on the Rules of international humanitarian law governing the conduct of hostilities in non-international armed conflicts (San Remo, 7 April 1990).
—— Guiding Principles on the Right to Humanitarian Assistance.
—— *The Manual on the Law of Non-International Armed Conflict With Commentary* (Sanremo, 2006).
International Law Association Committee on the Use of Force, *Final Report on the Meaning of Armed Conflict in International Law* (2010).
Jakovljević, B, 'The Agreement of May 22, 1992, on the Implementation of International Humanitarian Law in the Armed Conflict Bosnia-Herzegovina' [1992] *Jugoslovenska Revija Za Medunarodno Pravo* 212.

—— and Patrnogić, J, 'The Urgent Need to Apply the Rules of Humanitarian Law to So-Called Internal Armed Conflicts' (1961) 1 *IRRC* 250.
Jessup, PC, 'The Spanish Rebellion and International Law' (1936–7) 15 *Foreign Affairs* 260.
Jinks, D, 'The Temporal Scope of Application of International Humanitarian Law in Contemporary Conflicts', Background Paper prepared for the Informal High-Level Expert Meeting on the Reaffirmation and Development of International Humanitarian Law, Cambridge, 27–29 January 2003.
—— 'The Declining Significance of POW Status' (2004) 45 *Harvard ILJ* 367.
Jobst III, V, 'Is the Wearing of the Enemy's Uniform a Violation of the Laws of War' (1941) 35 *AJIL* 435.
Josipović, I, 'Responsibility for War Crimes before National Courts in Croatia' (2006) 88 *IRRC* 145.
Junod, M, *Warrior Without Weapons* (Jonathan Cape, London, 1951).
Junod, S, 'Additional Protocol II: History and Scope' (1983–4) 33 *American University Law Review* 29.
Kälin, W, *Guiding Principles on Internal Displacement: Annotations* (American Society of International Law, Washington DC, 2008).
Kallenberger, J, 'Sixty Years of the Geneva Conventions: Learning from the Past to Better Face the Future', Address at the Ceremony to Celebrate the 60th Anniversary of the Geneva Conventions, 12 August 2009.
Kalshoven, F, *Belligerent Reprisals* (Sijthoff, Leiden, 1971).
—— 'The Conference of Government Experts on the Reaffirmation and Development of International Humanitarian Law Applicable in Armed Conflicts, 24 May–12 June, 1971' (1971) 2 *NYIL* 68.
—— 'The Conference of Government Experts on the Reaffirmation and Development of International Humanitarian Law Applicable in Armed Conflicts (Second Session), 3 May–2 June, 1972' (1972) 3 *NYIL* 18.
—— 'The First Session of the Diplomatic Conference on Reaffirmation and Development of International Humanitarian Law Applicable in Armed Conflicts, Geneva, 20 February–29 March 1974' (1974) 5 *NYIL* 3.
—— 'Reaffirmation and Development of International Humanitarian Law Applicable in Armed Conflicts: The Diplomatic Conference, Geneva, 1974–1977, Part I: Combatants and Civilians' (1977) 8 *NYIL* 107.
—— 'Reprisals in the CDDH', in RJ Akkerman, PJ van Krieken, and CO Pannenborg, *Declarations on Principles: A Quest for Universal Peace* (AW Sitjhoff, Leiden, 1977).
—— 'The Soldier and his Golf Clubs', in C Swinarski (ed), *Studies and Essays on International Humanitarian Law and Red Cross Principles in Honour of Jean Pictet* (ICRC, Geneva, 1984).
—— 'Arms, Armaments and International Law' (1985-II) 191 *RdC* 183.
—— *Constraints on the Waging of War* (ICRC, Geneva, 1987).
—— 'Conventional Weaponry: the Law from St Petersburg to Lucerne and Beyond', in MA Meyer (ed), *Armed Conflict and the New Law* (BIICL, London, 1989).
—— 'Belligerent Reprisals Revisited' (1990) 21 *NYIL* 43.
—— 'Protocol II, the CDDH and Colombia', in K Wellens (ed), *International Law: Theory and Practice, Essays in Honour of Eric Suy* (Kluwer, The Hague, 1998).
—— 'Reprisals and the Protection of Civilians: Two Recent Decisions of the Yugoslavia Tribunal', in LC Vohrah et al (eds), *Mans Inhumanity to Man: Essays on International Law in Honour of Antonio Cassese* (Kluwer, The Hague, 2003).
Kalshoven, F, 'International Humanitarian Law and Violation of Medical Neutrality', in F Kalshoven, *Reflections on the Law of War: Collected Essays* (Nihoff, Leiden, 2007).
—— 'The International Humanitarian Fact-Finding Commission: Its Birth and Early Years', in F Kalshoven (ed), *Reflections on the Laws of War: Collected Essays* (Nijhoff, Leiden, 2007).

—— 'The International Humanitarian Fact-Finding Commission: A Sleeping Beauty?', in F Kalshoven (ed), *Reflections on the Laws of War: Collected Essays* (Nijhoff, Leiden, 2007).

Kaye, D and Solomon, SA, 'The Second Review Conference of the 1980 Convention on Certain Conventional Weapons' (2002) 96 *AJIL* 922.

Keen, D, *Conflict and Collusion in Sierra Leone* (International Peace Academy, New York, 2005).

Kelsen, H, *Principles of International Law* (Rinehart and Co, New York, 1952).

Kirk-Greene, AHM, *Crisis and Conflict in Nigeria, A Documentary Sourcebook 1966–1969* (Oxford University Press, London, 1971).

Klabbers, J, '(I Can't Get No) Recognition: Subjects Doctrine and the Emergence of Non-State Actors', in J Petman and J Klabbers (eds), *Nordic Cosmopolitanism: Essays in International Law for Martti Koskenniemi* (Martinus Nijhoff, Leiden, 2003).

Kleffner, JK, 'From "Belligerents" to "Fighters" and Civilians Directly Participating in Hostilities—On the Principle of Distinction in Non-International armed Conflicts One Hundred Years After the Second Hague Peace Conference' (2007) LIV *NILR* 315.

—— 'Protection of the Wounded, Sick, and Shipwrecked', in D Fleck (ed), *The Handbook of International Humanitarian Law* (Oxford University Press, Oxford, 2008).

—— 'The Collective Accountability of Organized Armed Groups for System Crimes', in H van der Wilt and A Nollkaemper (eds), *System Criminality in International Law* (Cambridge University Press, Cambridge, 2009).

—— 'The Law and Policy of Complementarity in relation to "Criminal Proceedings" carried out by Non-State Organized Armed Groups', in C Stahn and M El Zeidy (eds), *The International Criminal Court and Complementarity* (Cambridge University Press, Cambridge, 2011).

Klip, A and Sluiter, G (eds), *Annotated Leading Cases of International Criminal Tribunals, Volumes 1* (Intersentia, Antwerp, various).

Koh, HH, 'The Obama Administration and International Law', Speech at the Annual Meeting of the American Society of International Law, 25 March 2010.

—— 'The Lawfulness of the US Operation against Osama bin Laden', Opinio Juris Blog, 19 May 2011.

Kolb, R, 'The Relationship between International Humanitarian Law and Human Rights Law: A Brief History of the 1948 Universal Declaration of Human Rights and the 1949 Geneva Convention' (1998) 38 *IRRC* 409.

Kooijmans, PH, 'In the Shadowland between Civil War and Civil Strife: Some Reflections on the Standard-Setting Process', in AJM Delissen and GJ Tanja (eds), *Humanitarian Law of Armed Conflict, Challenges Ahead: Essays in Honour of Frits Kalshoven* (Nijhoff, Dordrecht, 1991).

Kosirnik, R, 'Application of Humanitarian Law in Noninternational Armed Conflicts: Remarks' (1991) 85 *ASIL Procs* 83.

Kotzsch, L, *The Concept of War in Contemporary History and International Law* (Droz, Geneva, 1956).

Kress, C, 'War Crimes Committed in Non-International Armed Conflict and the Emerging System of International Criminal Justice' (2000) 30 *IYHR* 103.

—— 'The 1999 Crisis in East Timor and the Threshold of the Law on War Crimes' (2002) 13 *Criminal Law Forum* 409.

—— 'Some Reflections on the International Legal Framework Governing Transnational Armed Conflicts' (2010) 15 *JCSL* 245.

Kretzmer, D, 'Rethinking the Application of IHL in Non-International Armed Conflicts' (2009) 42 *Israel Law Review* 8.

Krieger, H, 'A Conflict of Norms: The Relationship between Humanitarian law and Human Rights Law in the ICRC Customary Law Study' (2006) 11 *JCSL* 265.

Krill, F, 'The Protection of Women in International Humanitarian Law' (1985) 25 *IRRC* 337.

—— 'The International Fact-Finding Commission' (1991) 31 *IRRC* 190.

Kritsiotis, D, 'The Tremors of *Tadić*' (2010) 43 *Israel Law Review* 262.

Krutzsch, W and Trapp, R, *A Commentary on the Chemical Weapons Convention* (Martinus Nijhoff, Dordrecht, 1994).

Kwakwa, E, 'Belligerent Reprisals in the Law of Armed Conflict' (1990) 27 *Stanford JIL* 49.

La Haye, E, *War Crimes in Internal Armed Conflicts* (Cambridge University Press, Cambridge, 2008).

La Rosa, A-M, and Wuerzner, C, 'Armed Groups, Sanctions and the Implementation of International Humanitarian Law' (2008) 90 *IRRC* 327.

Laska, LL and Smith, JM, '"Hell and the Devil": Andersonville and the Trial of Captain Henry Wirz, SA, 1865' (1975) 68 *Military Law Review* 77.

Lauterpacht, H, 'The Law of Nations and the Punishment of War Crimes' (1944) 21 *BYIL* 58.

—— *Recognition in International Law* (Cambridge University Press, Cambridge, 1947).

—— 'The Limits of the Operation of the Law of War' (1953) 30 *BYIL* 206.

—— *International Law: Collected Papers, Volume 5, Disputes, War and Neutrality* (E Lauterpacht (ed)) (Cambridge University Press, Cambridge, 2004).

Lavoyer, J-P, 'Comments on the Guiding Principles on Internal Displacement' (1998) 38 *IRRC* 467.

Lawrence, TJ, *The Principles of International Law* (MacMillan, London, 1895).

Leaning, J, 'When the System Doesn't Work: Somalia in 1992', in KM Cahill (ed), *A Framework for Survival: Health, Human Rights and Humanitarian Assistance in Conflicts and Disasters* (Routledge, New York, 1994).

Levie, HS, 'Prohibitions and Restrictions on the Use of Conventional Weapons' (1994) 68 *St John's Law Review* 643.

Lindroos, A, 'Addressing Norm Conflicts in a Fragmented Legal System: The Doctrine of *Lex Specialis*' (2005) 74 *Nordic Journal of International Law* 27.

Lindsey, C, *Women Facing War: ICRC Study on the Impact of Armed Conflict on Women* (ICRC, Geneva, 2001).

Linton, S, 'Completing the Circle: Accountability for the Crimes of the 1971 Bangladesh War of Liberation' (2010) 21 *Criminal Law Forum* 191.

Lootsteen, YM, 'The Concept of Belligerency in International Law' (2000) 166 *Military Law Review* 109.

Luard, E, 'Civil Conflicts in Modern International Relations', in E Luard (ed), *The International Regulation of Civil Wars* (Thames and Hudson, London, 1972).

Lubell, N, 'Challenges in Applying Human Rights Law to Armed Conflict' (2005) 87 *IRRC* 737.

—— *Extraterritorial Use of Force Against Non-State Actors* (Oxford University Press, Oxford, 2010).

Lunze, S, 'Serving God and Caesar: Religious personnel and their protection in armed conflict' (2004) 86 *IRRC* 69.

Lysaght, C, 'The Attitude of Western Countries', in A Cassese (ed), *The New Humanitarian Law of Armed Conflict* (Editoriale Scientifica, Napoli, 1979).

—— 'The Scope of Protocol II and its Relation to Common Article 3 of the Geneva Conventions of 1949 and other Human Rights Instruments' (1983) 33 *American University Law Review* 9.

Macalister-Smith, P, 'Rights and duties of the agencies involved in providing humanitarian assistance and their personnel in armed conflict', in F Kalshoven (ed), *Assisting the Victims of Armed Conflict and Other Disasters* (Martinus Nijhoff, Dordrecht, 1989).

Machel, G, *The Impact of War on Children* (Hurst, London, 2001).

MacLeod, IJ and Rogers, APV, 'The Use of White Phosphorus and the Law of War' (2007) 10 *YIHL* 75.

Mallinder, L, *Amnesty, Human Rights and Political Transitions* (Hart, Oxford, 2008).

Manuell, J and Kontić, A, 'Transitional Justice: The Prosecution of War Crimes in Bosnia and Herzegovina under the "Rules of the Road"' (2002) 5 *YIHL* 331.

Maresca, L, 'Second Review Conference of the Convention on Certain Conventional Weapons' (2002) 845 *IRRC* 255.

—— 'A New Protocol on Explosive Remnants of War: The history and negotiation of Protocol V to the 1980 Convention on Certain Conventional Weapons' (2004) 86 *IRRC* 815.

Martin, FF, 'Using International Human Rights Law for Establishing a Unified Use of Force Rule in the Law of Armed Conflict' (2001) 64 *Saskatchewan Law Review* 347.

Maslen, S, *Commentaries on Arms Control Treaties* (Oxford University Press, Oxford, 2005).

Matheson, MJ, 'The Revision of the Mines Protocol' (1997) 91 *AJIL* 158.

McCall Jr, JA, 'Infernal Machines and Hidden Death: International Law and Limits on the Indiscriminate Use of Land Mine Warfare' (1994–5) 24 *Georgia Journal of International and Comparative Law* 229.

McCarthy, C, 'Legal Conclusion or Interpretive Process? *Lex Specialis* and the Applicability of International Human Rights Standards', in R Arnold and N Quenivet (eds), *International Humanitarian Law and Human Rights Law* (Martinus Nijhoff, Leiden, 2008).

McCormack, T, 'From Solferino to Sarajevo: A Continuing Role for International Humanitarian Law' (1997) 21 *Melbourne University Law Review* 612.

McCoubrey, H, *International Humanitarian Law* (Dartmouth, Aldershot, 1990).

—— 'War Crimes: The Criminal Jurisprudence of Armed Conflict' (1992) 31 *Military Law and the Law of War Review* 167.

McDougal, MS and Feliciano, F, *The International Law of War: Transnational Coercion and World Public Order* (New Haven Press, New Haven, 1994).

McNair, A, *International Law Opinions, Selected and Annotated, Three Volumes* (Cambridge University Press, Cambridge, 1956).

—— and Watts, A, *The Legal Effects of War* (Cambridge University Press, Cambridge, 1966).

Melzer, N, *Targeted Killing in International Law* (Oxford University Press, Oxford, 2008).

—— 'Keeping the Balance between Military Necessity and Humanity: A Response to Four Critiques of the ICRC's Interpretive Guidance on the Notion of Direct Participation in Hostilities' (2010) 42 *New York University Journal of International Law and Politics* 831.

Mercier, M, *Crimes without Punishment: Humanitarian Action in the Former Yugoslavia* (Pluto Press, London, 1995).

Meron, T, 'On the Inadequate Reach of Humanitarian and Human Rights Law and the Need for a New Instrument' (1983) 77 *AJIL* 589.

—— *Human Rights in Internal Strife: Their International Protection* (Grotius Publications, Cambridge, 1987).

—— *Human Rights and Humanitarian Norms as Customary Law* (Clarendon Press, Oxford, 1989).

—— 'Application of Humanitarian Law in Noninternational Armed Conflicts: Remarks' (1991) 85 *ASIL Procs* 83.

—— 'War Crimes in Yugoslavia and the Development of International Law' (1994) 88 *AJIL* 78.

—— 'International Criminalization of Internal Atrocities' (1995) 89 *AJIL* 554.

—— 'Convergence of International Humanitarian Law and Human Rights Law', in D Warner (ed), *Human Rights and Humanitarian Law* (Nijhoff, The Hague, 1997).
—— *War Crimes Law Comes of Age* (Oxford University Press, Oxford, 1998).
—— 'Francis Lieber's Code and Principles of Humanity' (1998) 36 *Columbia Journal of Transnational Law* 269.
—— 'Classification of Armed Conflict in the Former Yugoslavia: *Nicaragua's* Fallout' (1998) 92 *AJIL* 236.
—— 'The Humanization of Humanitarian Law' (2000) 94 *AJIL* 239.
Mettraux, G, 'US Courts-Martial and the Armed Conflict in the Philippines (1899–1902): Their Contribution to National Case Law on War Crimes' (2003) 1 *JICJ* 135.
—— *International Crimes and the ad hoc Tribunals* (Oxford University Press, Oxford, 2005).
—— 'A Little-known Case from the American Civil War' (2010) 8 *JICJ* 1059.
Meyer, JM, 'Tearing Down the Façade: A Critical Look at the Current Law on Targeting the Will of the Enemy and Air Force Doctrine' (2001) 51 *Air Force Law Review* 143.
Meyer, MA, 'Development of the Law Governing Relief Operations', in MA Meyer (ed), *Armed Conflict and the New Law: Aspects of the 1977 Geneva Protocols and the 1981 Weapons Convention* (BIICL, London, 1989).
Meyrowitz, H, 'The Principle of Superfluous Injury or Unnecessary Suffering' (1994) 34 *IRRC* 98.
Milanović, M, 'State Responsibility for Genocide' (2006) 17 *EJIL* 553.
—— 'Norm Conflicts, International Humanitarian Law and Human Rights Law' (2009) 14 *JCSL* 459.
Modirzadeh, NK, 'The Dark Sides of Convergence: A Pro-Civilian Critique of the Extraterritorial Application of Human Rights Law in Armed Conflict' (2010) 86 *International Law Studies* 350.
Moir, L, *The Law of Internal Armed Conflict* (Cambridge University Press, Cambridge 2002).
—— 'Law and the Inter-American Human Rights System' (2003) 25 *HRQ* 182.
—— 'Towards the Unification of International Humanitarian Law?', in R Burchill, ND White, and J Morris (eds), *International Conflict and Security Law: Essays in Memory of Hilaire McCoubrey* (Cambridge University Press, Cambridge, 2005).
—— 'Violations of Common Article 3 of the Geneva Conventions', in J Doria, H-P Gasser, and MC Bassiouni (eds), *The Legal Regime of the International Criminal Court: Essays in Honour of Professor Igor Blishchenko* (Martinus Nijhoff, Leiden, 2009).
—— 'Conduct of Hostilities—War Crimes', in J Doria, H-P Gasser, and MC Bassiouni (eds), *The Legal Regime of the International Criminal Court: Essays in Honour of Professor Igor Blishchenko* (Martinus Nijhoff, Leiden, 2009).
—— 'Grave Breaches and Internal Armed Conflicts' (2009) 7 *JICJ* 763.
Mokhtar, A, 'Will this Mummification Saga Come to an End? The International Humanitarian Fact-Finding Commission: Article 90 of Protocol I' (2003–4) 22 *Pennsylvania State International Law Review* 243.
Momtaz, D, 'War Crimes in Non-International Armed Conflicts Under the Statute of the International Criminal Court' (1999) 2 *YIHL* 177.
Moore, JB, *Digest of International Law, Volume 1* (Government Printing Office, Washington DC, 1906).
Moore, JN, 'Ratification of the Geneva Protocol on Gas and Bacteriological Warfare: A Legal and Political Analysis' (1972) 58 *Virginia Law Review* 419.
—— (ed), *Law and Civil War in the Modern World* (Johns Hopkins University Press, Baltimore, 1974).
Moreillon, J, 'The International Committee of the Red Cross and the Protection of Political Detainees' (1975) 15 *IRRC* 171.
Morris, V, *The International Criminal Tribunal for Rwanda* (Transnational, Irvington-on-Hudson, 1998).

Morris, V and Scharf, MP, *An Insider's Guide to the International Criminal Tribunal for the Former Yugoslavia, Two Volumes* (Transnational, Irvington-on-Hudson, 1995).

Moynier, G, *Etude sur la Convention de Genève* (1870).

—— *La Croix-Rouge: Son Passé et Son Avenir* (Paris, Sandoz and Thuillier, 1882).

Mudge, GA, 'Starvation as a Means of Warfare' (1969–70) 4 *International Lawyer* 228.

Museveni, YK, *Sowing the Mustard Seed* (MacMillan, London, 1997).

—— 'The Strategy of Protracted People's War: Uganda' [November–December 2008] *Military Review* 4.

Nahlik, SE, 'Belligerent Reprisals As Seen in the Light of the Diplomatic Conference on Humanitarian Law, Geneva, 1974–1977' (1978) 42 *Law and Contemporary Problems* 36.

Neff, S, *War and the Law of Nations: A General History* (Cambridge University Press, Cambridge, 2005).

Nkrumah, K, *Handbook of Revolutionary Warfare* (Panaf Books, London, 1968).

Nolte, G, 'The Different Functions of the Security Council with Respect to Humanitarian Law', in V Lowe et al (eds), *The United Nations Security Council and War* (Oxford University Press, Oxford, 2008).

Noone Jr, MF, 'Unprivileged Belligerency: The IRA' [September–October 2005] *Military Review* 58.

Nwogugu, EL, 'The Nigerian Civil War: A Case Study in the Law of War' (1974) 14 *Indian Journal of International Law* 13.

Nystuen, G and Maslen, SC, *The Convention on Cluster Munitions: A Commentary* (Oxford University Press, Oxford, 2010).

O'Keefe, R, *The Protection of Cultural Property in Armed Conflict* (Cambridge University Press, Cambridge 2006).

—— 'Protection of Cultural Property', in D Fleck (ed), *The Handbook of International Humanitarian Law* (Oxford University Press, Oxford, 2008).

O'Rourke, V, 'Recognition of Belligerency and the Spanish War' (1937) 31 *AJIL* 398.

O'Shea, A, *Amnesty for Crime in International Law and Practice* (Kluwer, The Hague, 2002).

Oeter, S, 'Civil War, Humanitarian Law and the United Nations' (1997) 1 *Max Planck Yearbook of United Nations Law* 195.

—— 'Methods and Means of Combat', in D Fleck (ed), *The Handbook of International Humanitarian Law* (Oxford University Press, Oxford, 2008).

Olson, LM, 'Practical Challenges of Implementing the Complementarity between International Humanitarian and Human Rights Law—Demonstrated by the Procedural Regulation of Internment in Non-International Armed Conflict' (2007–9) 40 *Case Western Reserve Journal of International Law* 437.

Oppenheim, L, *International Law, A Treatise: Volume II* (Lauterpacht (ed)) (Longmans, London, 1952).

Padelford, NJ, 'International Law and the Spanish Civil War' (1937) 31 *AJIL* 226.

—— *International Law and Diplomacy in the Spanish Civil Strife* (Macmillan, New York, 1939).

Parks, WH, 'Air War and the Law of War' (1990) 32 *Air Force Law Review* 1.

—— 'The Protocol on Incendiary Weapons' (1990) 30 *IRRC* 535.

—— 'Special Forces' Wear of Non-Standard Uniforms' (2003) 4 *Chicago JIL* 493.

—— 'Combatants', in MN Schmitt (ed), *The War in Afghanistan: A Legal Analysis* (Volume 85, International Law Studies, Naval War College, Newport, Rhode Island, 2009) 247.

—— 'Part IX of the ICRC "Direct Participation in Hostilities" Study: No Mandate, No Expertise, and Legally Incorrect' (2010) 42 *New York University Journal of International Law and Politics* 769.

Partsch, KJ, 'Protection of Cultural Property', in D Fleck (ed), *The Handbook of International Humanitarian Law* (Oxford University Press, Oxford, 1995).

Paulus, A and Vashakmadze, M, 'Asymmetrical Warfare and the Notion of Armed Conflict—A Tentative Conceptualization' (2009) 91 *IRRC* 95.

Paust, JJ and Blaustein, A, 'War Crimes Jurisdiction and Due Process: the Bangladesh Experience' (1978) 11 *Vanderbilt Journal of Transnational Law* 1.

Peirce, GAB, 'Humanitarian Protection for the Victims of War: The System of Protecting Powers and the Role of the ICRC' (1980) 90 *Military Law Review* 89.

Pejić, J, 'Procedural Principles and Safeguards for Internment/Administrative Detention in Armed Conflict and Other Situations of Violence' (2005) 87 *IRRC* 375.

—— 'The Protective Scope of Common Article 3: More than Meets the Eye' (2011) 93 *IRRC* 189.

Perna, L, *The Formation of the Treaty Law of Non-International Armed Conflicts* (Martinus Nijhoff, Leiden, 2006).

Perret, F, 'ICRC Action in Hungary in 1956' (1996) 36 *IRRC* 413.

Perritt Jr, HH, *Kosovo Liberation Army: The Inside Story of an Insurgency* (University of Illinois Press, Urbana, 2008).

Pfirter, D, 'Article 8(2)(b)(iv)', in RS Lee (ed), *The International Criminal Court: Elements of Crimes and Rules of Procedure and Evidence* (Transnational, Ardsley, 2001).

Phuong, C, *The International Protection of Internally Displaced Persons* (Cambridge University Press, Cambridge, 2004).

Pictet, JS, (ed), *The Geneva Conventions of 12 August 1949, Commentary: I Geneva Convention for the Amelioration of the Condition of the Wounded and Sick in Armed Forces in the Field* (ICRC, Geneva, 1952).

—— *The Geneva Conventions of 12 August 1949, Commentary: IV Geneva Convention Relative to the Protection of Civilian Persons in Time of War* (ICRC, Geneva, 1958).

—— *The Geneva Conventions of 12 August 1949: Commentary, II Geneva Convention for the Amelioration of the Condition of Wounded, Sick and Shipwrecked Members of Armed Forces at Sea* (ICRC, Geneva, 1960).

—— *The Geneva Conventions of 12 August 1949: Commentary, III Geneva Convention Relative to the Treatment of Prisoners of War* (ICRC, Geneva, 1960).

—— *Humanitarian Law and the Protection of War Victims* (Sijthoff, Leiden, 1975).

—— *Development and Principles of International Humanitarian Law* (Nijhoff, Dordrecht, 1985).

—— 'The Fundamental Principles of the Red Cross: Commentary' (1979) 19 *IRRC* 130; (1979) 19 *IRRC* 184; (1979) 19 *IRRC* 255; (1979) 19 *IRRC* 301; (1980) 20 *IRRC* 29; (1980) 20 *IRRC* 70; (1980) 20 *IRRC* 129; (1980) 20 *IRRC* 193; (1980) 20 *IRRC* 250.

Pinzauti, G, 'Protecting Prisoners of War: The *Mrkšić et al* Appeal Judgment' (2010) 8 *JICJ* 199.

Plattner, D, 'The Penal Repression of Violations of International Humanitarian Law Applicable in Non-International Armed Conflicts' (1990) 30 *IRRC* 409.

—— 'Assistance to the Civilian Population: The Development and Present State of International Humanitarian Law' (1992) 32 *IRRC* 249.

Provost, R, *International Human Rights and Humanitarian Law* (Cambridge University Press, Cambridge, 2002).

Prud'homme, N, '*Lex Specialis:* Oversimplifying a More Complex and Multifaceted Relationship?' (2007) 49 *Israel Law Review* 356.

Quéguiner, JF, 'Precautions under the law governing the conduct of hostilities' (2006) 88 *IRRC* 793.

Quenivet, N, 'The Moscow Hostage Crisis in the Light of the Armed Conflict in Chechnya' (2001) 4 *YIHL* 348.

Rakate, PK, 'The Shelling of Knin by the Croatian Army in August 1995: A Police Operation or a Non-International Armed Conflict?' (2000) 82 *IRRC* 1037.

Ranjeva, R, 'Peoples and National Liberation Movements', in M Bedjaoui, *International Law: Achievements and Prospects* (Martinus Nijhoff, Dordrecht, 1991).

Ratner, SR, Abrams, JS, and Bishoff, JL, *Accountability for Human Rights Atrocities in International Law* (Oxford University Press, Oxford, 2009).

Reidy, A, 'The Approach of the European Commission and Court of Human Rights to International Humanitarian Law' (1998) 324 *IRRC* 513.

Reinisch, A, 'The International Fact-Finding Commission According to Art. 90 Additional Protocol I to the Geneva Conventions and its Potential Enquiry Competence in the Yugoslav Conflict' (1996) 65 *Nordic JIL* 241.

Reisman, WM and Silk, J, 'Which Law applies to the Afghan Conflict?' (1988) 82 *AJIL* 459.

Reverdin, O, *La Guerre du Sonderbund vue par le Général Dufour, Juin 1847–Avril 1848* (Éditions du Journal de Genève, Genève, 1987).

Reydams, L, 'Belgium Reneges on Universality: The 5 August 2003 Act on Grave Breaches of International Humanitarian Law' (2003) 1 *JICJ* 679.

—— *Universal Jurisdiction* (Oxford University Press, Oxford, 2003).

Roach, JA, 'Certain Conventional Weapons Convention: Arms Control or Humanitarian Law?' (1984) 105 *Military Law Review* 3.

—— 'The International Fact-Finding Commission' (1991) 31 *IRRC* 167.

Roberts, A, 'What is a Military Occupation?' (1984) LV *BYIL* 249.

—— 'Environmental Destruction in the 1991 Gulf War' (1992) 32 *IRRC* 538.

—— 'Land Warfare: From Hague to Nuremberg', in M Howard, GJ Andreopoulos, and MR Shulman (eds), *The Laws of War: Constraints on Warfare in the Western World* (Yale University Press, New Haven, 1994).

—— 'The Law of War and Environmental Damage', in JE Austin and CE Bruch (eds), *The Environmental Consequences of War* (Cambridge University Press, Cambridge, 2000) 47.

—— and Guelff, R, *Documents on the Laws of War* (Oxford University Press, Oxford, 2000).

Roberts, AE and Sivakumaran, S, 'Lawmaking by Non-State Actors: Engaging Armed Groups in the Creation of International Humanitarian Law' (2012) 37 *Yale JIL* 107.

Robertson, AH, 'Humanitarian Law and Human Rights', in C Swinarski (ed), *Studies and Essays on International Humanitarian Law and Red Cross Principles in Honour of Jean Pictet* (ICRC, Geneva, 1984).

Robinson, D, 'Serving the Interests of Justice: Amnesties, Truth Commissions and the International Criminal Court' (2003) 14 *EJIL* 481.

—— 'The Identity Crisis of International Criminal Law' (2008) 21 *LJIL* 925.

—— and von Hebel, H, 'War Crimes in Internal Armed Conflicts: Article 8 of the ICC Statute' (1999) 2 *YIHL* 193.

Rodley, NS, 'Can Armed Opposition Groups Violate Human Rights?', in KE Mahoney and P Mahoney, *Human Rights in the Twenty-first Century* (Martinus Nijhoff, Dordrecht, 1993).

Rogers, APV, 'A Commentary on the Protocol on Prohibitions or Restrictions on the Use of Mines, Booby-Traps and Other Devices' (1987) 26 *Military Law and the Law of War Review* 185.

—— 'Zero-Casualty Warfare' (2000) 82 *IRRC* 165.

—— *Law on the Battlefield* (Manchester University Press, Manchester, 2004).

—— 'Unequal Combat and the Law of War' (2004) 7 *YIHL* 3.

—— 'What is a Legitimate Military Target?', in R Burchill, ND White, and J Morris (eds), *International Conflict and Security Law: Essays in Memory of Hilaire Mcoubrey* (Cambridge University Press, Cambridge, 2005).

Röling, BVA, 'Aspects of the Criminal Responsibility for Violations of the Laws of War', in A Cassese (ed), *The New Humanitarian Law of Armed Conflict* (Editoriale Scientifica, Napoli, 1979).

Romano, CPR, Nollkaemper, A, and Kleffner, JK (eds), *Internationalized Criminal Courts* (Oxford University Press, Oxford, 2004).

Rosas, A, *The Legal Status of Prisoners of War* (Suomalainen Tiedeakatemia, Helsinki, 1976).

Rosenblad, E, 'Starvation as a Method of Warfare –Conditions for Regulation of Convention' (1973) 7 *International Lawyer* 252.

Rowe, P, 'Liability for "War Crimes" during a Non-International Armed Conflict' (1995) 34 *Military Law and the Law of War Review* 149.

—— 'War Crimes', in D McGoldrick, P Rowe, and E Donnelly (eds), *The Permanent International Criminal Court: Legal and Policy Issues* (Hart, Oxford, 2004).

—— *The Impact of Human Rights Law on Armed Forces* (Cambridge University Press, Cambridge, 2006).

—— 'The Obligation of a State under International Law to Protect Members of its Own Armed Forces during Armed Conflict or Occupation' (2006) 9 *YIHL* 3.

Ryngaert, C, 'Universal Criminal Jurisdiction over Torture' (2005) 23 *NQHR* 571.

—— 'Human Rights Obligations of Armed Groups' (2008) 41 *RBDI* 361.

Sandoz, Y, 'A New Step Forward in International Law: Prohibitions or Restrictions on the Use of Certain Conventional Weapons' (1981) 21 *IRRC* 3.

—— 'Implementing International Humanitarian Law', in UNESCO (ed), *International Dimensions of Humanitarian Law* (UNESCO, Paris, 1988).

—— 'The Establishment of Safety Zones for Persons Displaced within their Country of Origin', in N Al-Nauimi and R Meese, *International Legal Issues Arising under the United Nations Decade of International Law* (Martinus Nijhoff, The Hague, 1995).

—— Swinarski, C and Zimmermann, B, (eds), *Commentary on the Additional Protocols of 8 June 1977 to the Geneva Conventions of 12 August 1949* (ICRC, Geneva, 1987).

Sandvik-Nylund, M, *Caught in Conflicts: Civilian Victims, Humanitarian Assistance and International Law* (Institute for Human Rights, Turku/Abo, 1998).

Santos Jr, S, 'A Critical Reflection on the Geneva Call Instrument and Approach in Engaging Armed Groups on Humanitarian Norms: A Southern Perspective', 31 October 2002.

Sassòli, M, 'The legal qualification of the conflicts in the former Yugoslavia: double standards or new horizons for international humanitarian law?', in S Yee and W Tieya (eds), *International Law in the Post-Cold War World: Essays in Memory of Li Haopei* (Routledge, London, 2001).

—— 'Possible Legal Mechanisms to Improve Compliance by Armed Groups with International Humanitarian Law and International Human Rights Law', Paper submitted to the Armed Groups Conference, Vancouver, 13–15 November 2003.

—— 'Transnational Armed Groups and International Humanitarian Law', Harvard University Program on Humanitarian Policy and Conflict Research, Occasional Paper Series, Winter 2006, No 6.

—— 'The Implementation of International Humanitarian Law: Current and Inherent Challenges' (2007) 10 *YIHL* 45.

—— '*Ius ad Bellum* and *Ius in Bello*: The Separation between the Legality of the Use of Force and Humanitarian Rules to be Respected in Warfare—Crucial or Outdated?', in M Schmitt and J Pejić (eds), *International Law and Armed Conflict: Exploring the Faultlines, Essays in Honour of Yoram Dinstein* (Martinus Nijhoff, Leiden, 2007).

—— 'Humanitarian Law and International Criminal law', in A Cassese et al (eds), *The Oxford Companion to International Criminal Justice* (Oxford University Press, Oxford, 2009).

—— 'Taking Armed Groups Seriously: Ways to Improve their Compliance with International Humanitarian Law' (2010) 1 *International Humanitarian Legal Studies* 5.

—— and Bouvier, AA, *How Does Law Protect in War: Volume II* (ICRC, Geneva, 2006).

—— and Olson, LM, 'The Relationship between International Humanitarian and Human Rights Law Where it Matters: Admissible Killing and Internment of Fighters in Non-International Armed Conflicts' (2008) 90 *IRRC* 599.

Schabas, W, *The International Criminal Court* (Oxford University Press, Oxford, 2010).

Scharf, M, 'Is it International Enough? A Critique of the Iraqi Special Tribunal in Light of the Goals of International Justice' (2004) 2 *JICJ* 330.

Scheipers, S (ed), *Prisoners in War* (Oxford University Press, Oxford, 2010).

Schindler, D, 'State of War, Belligerency, Armed Conflict', in A Cassese (ed), *The New Humanitarian Law of Armed Conflict* (Editoriale Scientifica, Napoli, 1979).

—— 'The Different Types of Armed Conflicts According to the Geneva Conventions and Protocols' (1979-II) 163 *RdC* 121.

—— 'Human Rights and Humanitarian Law' (1981–2) 31 *American University Law Review* 935.

—— and Toman, J, *The Laws of Armed Conflict* (Nijhoff, Dordrecht, 2004).

Schmitt, MN, '"Direct Participation in Hostilities" and 21st Century Armed Conflict', in H Fischer et al (eds), *Crisis Management and Humanitarian Protection: Festschrift für Dieter Fleck* (Berliner Wissenschafts-Verlag, Berlin, 2004).

—— 'Targeting and Humanitarian Law: Current Issues' (2004) 34 *IYHR* 59.

—— 'Humanitarian Law and Direct Participation in Hostilities by Private Contractors or Civilian Employees' (2005) 5 *Chicago JIL* 511.

—— 'Precision attack and international humanitarian law' (2005) 87 *IRRC* 445.

—— 'Fault Lines in the Law of Attack', in SC Breau and A Jachec-Neale (eds), *Testing the Boundaries of International Humanitarian Law* (BIICL, London, 2006).

—— 'The Interpretive Guidance on the Notion of Direct Participation in Hostilities: A Critical Analysis' (2010) 1 *Harvard National Security Journal* 5.

—— 'Deconstructing Direct Participation in Hostilities: The Constitutive Elements' (2010) 42 *New York University Journal of International Law and Politics* 697.

—— 'Investigating Violations of International Law in Armed Conflict' (2011) 2 *Harvard National Security Journal* 31.

Schondorf, RS, 'Extra-State Armed Conflicts: Is there a Need for a New Legal Regime?' (2004) 37 *New York University Journal of International Law and Politics* 1.

—— 'The Targeted Killings Judgment: A Preliminary Assessment' (2007) 5 *JICJ* 301.

Schwarzenberger, G, *International Law as Applied by International Courts and Tribunals, Volume II: The Law of Armed Conflict* (Stevens and Sons, London, 1968).

Scobbie, I, 'Operationalising the Law of Armed Conflict for Dissident Forces in Libya', EJIL: Talk! Blog, 31 August 2011.

Scott, JB, (ed), *The Proceedings of the Hague Conferences: The Conference of 1899* (Oxford University Press, New York, 1920).

Shraga, D, 'The United Nations as an Actor Bound by International Humanitarian Law', in L Condorelli, A-M La Rosa, and S Scherrer (eds), *Les Nations Unies et le Droit International Humanitaire* (Pedone, Paris, 1996).

—— and Zacklin, R, 'The International Criminal Tribunal for the former Yugoslavia' (1994) 5 *EJIL* 360.

Siordet, F, 'The Geneva Conventions and Civil War' (1950) III *RICR Supplement* 132.

Siotis, J, *Le Droit de la Guerre et les Conflits Armés d'un Caractère Non-International* (Librairie Général de Droit et de Jurisprudence, Paris, 1958).

Sivakumaran, S, 'Torture in International Human Rights and International Humanitarian Law: The Actor and the Ad Hoc Tribunals' (2005) 18 *LJIL* 541.

—— 'Binding Armed Opposition Groups' (2006) 55 *ICLQ* 369.

—— 'Sexual Violence against Men in Armed Conflict' (2007) 18 *EJIL* 253.

—— 'Courts of Armed Opposition Groups: Fair Trials or Summary Justice?' (2009) 7 *JICJ* 489.

—— 'Identifying an Armed Conflict Not of an International Character', in C Stahn and G Sluiter (eds), *The Emerging Practice of the International Criminal Court* (Nijhoff, Leiden, 2009).
—— 'War Crimes before the Special Court for Sierra Leone' (2010) 8 *JICJ* 1009.
—— 'Re-envisioning the International Law of Internal Armed Conflict' (2011) 22 *EJIL* 219.
—— 'Lessons for the Law of Armed Conflict from Commitments of Armed Groups: Identification of Legitimate Targets and Prisoners of War' (2011) 93 *IRRC* 463.
Smith, C, 'Special Agreements to Apply the Geneva Conventions in Internal Armed Conflicts: The Lessons of Darfur' (2007) 2 *Irish Yearbook of International Law* 91.
Smith, HA, *Great Britain and the Law of Nations, Volume I: States* (King and Son, London, 1932).
—— 'Some Problems of the Spanish Civil War' (1937) 18 *BYIL* 17.
Solf, WA, 'The Status of Combatants in Non-International Armed Conflicts under Domestic Law and Transnational Practice' (1983) 33 *American University Law Review* 53.
—— 'Development of the protection of the wounded, sick and shipwrecked under the Protocols Additional to the 1949 Geneva Conventions', in C Swinarski (ed), *Studies and Essays on International Humanitarian Law and Red Cross Principles in Honour of Jean Pictet* (ICRC, Geneva, 1984).
Solis, GD, *The Law of Armed Conflict* (Cambridge University Press, Cambridge, 2010).
Somer, J, 'Jungle Justice: Passing Sentence on the Equality of Belligerents in Non-International Armed Conflict' (2007) 89 *IRRC* 655.
Spaight, JW, *War Rights on Land* (Macmillan, London, 1911).
Speiker, H, 'Twenty-five Years after the Adoption of Additional Protocol II: Breakthrough or Failure of Humanitarian Legal Protection?' (2001) 4 *YIHL* 129.
Spinedi, M, 'On the Non-Attribution of the Bosnian Serbs' Conduct to Serbia' (2007) 5 *JICJ* 829.
Stewart, JG, 'Towards a single definition of armed conflict in international humanitarian law: A critique of internationalized armed conflict' (2003) 85 *IRRC* 313.
—— *Corporate War Crimes: Prosecuting the Pillage of Natural Resources* (Open Society Initiative, New York, 2010).
Stoffels, RA, 'Legal Regulation of Humanitarian Assistance in Armed Conflict: Achievements and Gaps' (2004) 86 *IRRC* 515.
Stowell, EC, 'Military Reprisals and the Sanctions of the Laws of War' (1942) 36 *AJIL* 643.
Suter, K, *An International Law of Guerrilla Warfare* (St Martins Press, New York, 1974).
Suter, P, 'The Continuing Role for Belligerent Reprisals' (2008) 13 *JCSL* 93.
Sverdrup Engelschiøn, T, 'Ethiopia War Crimes and Violations of Human Rights' (1995) 34 *Military Law and the Law of War Review* 9.
Talmon, S, *Recognition of Governments in International Law* (Clarendon Press, Oxford, 1998).
Tanca, A, *Foreign Armed Intervention in Internal Conflict* (Martinus Nijhoff, Dordrecht, 1993).
Thalmann, V, 'Rwandan Genocide Cases', in A Cassese (ed), *The Oxford Companion to International Criminal Justice* (Oxford University Press, Oxford, 2009).
Thomas, AVW and Thomas, AJ, *Legal Limits on the Use of Chemical and Biological Weapons* (Southern Methodist University Press, Dallas, 1970).
—— 'International Legal Aspects of the Civil War in Spain, 1936–39', in RA Falk (ed), *The International Law of Civil War* (Johns Hopkins University Press, Baltimore, 1971).
Thorne, K, 'Terrorist Lists and Humanitarian Assistance' (2007) 37 *Humanitarian Exchange* 13.
Tiba, FK, 'The Mengistu Genocide Trial in Ethiopia' (2007) 5 *JICJ* 513.
Toman, J, *The Protection of Cultural Property in the Event of Armed Conflict* (Aldershot, Dartmouth, 1996).
—— 'The Status of Al Qaeda/Taliban Detainees under the Geneva Conventions' (2003) 32 *IYHR* 271.
—— *Cultural Property in War: Improvement in Protection* (UNESCO Publishing, Paris, 2009).

Tomuschat, C, 'The Applicability of Human Rights Law to Insurgent Movements', in H Fischer, et al (eds), *Krisensicherung und Humanitärer Schutz—Crisis Management and Humanitarian Protection: Festschrift fur Dieter Fleck* (Berliner Wissenschaftsverlag, Berlin, 2004).
—— *Human Rights: Between Idealism and Realism* (Oxford University Press, Oxford, 2008).
—— 'Human Rights and International Humanitarian Law' (2010) 21 *EJIL* 15.
Torrelli, M, 'From Humanitarian Assistance to "Intervention on Humanitarian Grounds"' (1992) 32 *IRRC* 228.
Tse-Tung, M, *On Guerilla Warfare* (Anchor Press, New York, 1978).
—— *Basic Tactics* (Pall Mall Press, London, 1966).
Turns, D, 'War Crimes without War? The Applicability of International Humanitarian Law to Atrocities in Non-International Armed Conflicts' (1995) 7 *African Journal of International and Comparative Law* 804.
—— 'At the "Vanishing Point" of International Humanitarian Law: Methods and Means of Warfare in Non-International Armed Conflicts' (2002) 45 *GYIL* 115.
—— 'Implementation and Compliance', in E Wilmshurst and SC Breau (eds), *Perspectives on the ICRC Study on Customary International Humanitarian law* (Cambridge University Press, Cambridge, 2007).
—— 'The Law of Armed Conflict (International Humanitarian Law)', in MD Evans (ed), *International Law* (Oxford University Press, Oxford, 2010).
UNESCO, *Information on the Implementation of the Convention for the Protection of Cultural Property in Case of Armed Conflict* (UNESCO, Paris, 1967).
—— *Information on the Implementation of the Convention for the Protection of Cultural Property in Case of Armed Conflict, The Hague 1954* (UNESCO, Paris, 1970).
—— *Information on the Implementation of the Convention for the Protection of Cultural Property in Case of Armed Conflict* (UNESCO, Paris, 1979).
—— (ed), *International Dimensions of Humanitarian Law* (UNESCO, Paris, 1988).
—— Diplomatic Conference on the Second Protocol to the Hague Convention for the Protection of Cultural Property in the Event of Armed Conflict: Summary Report (Paris, 1999).
UNICEF, *The State of the World's Children 1996* (Oxford University Press, Oxford, 1997).
Valencia Villa, A, *La Humanización de la Guerra: Derecho Internactional Humanitario y Conflicto Armado en Colombia* (Ediciones Uniandes, 1991).
Valencia Villa, H, 'The Law of Armed Conflict and its Application in Colombia' (1990) 30 *IRRC* 5.
van Bueren, G, 'The International Legal Protection of Children in Armed Conflicts' (1994) 43 *ICLQ* 809.
van Cleef Greenberg, E, 'Law and the Conduct of the Algerian Revolution' (1970) 11 *Harvard International Law Journal* 37.
van den Herik, LJ, *The Contribution of the Rwanda Tribunal to the Development of International Law* (Nijhoff, Leiden, 2005).
Vandermeersch, D, 'Prosecuting International Crimes in Belgium' (2005) 3 *JICJ* 400.
Verma, DP, 'Humanitarian Assistance to the Tamils in Sri Lanka', in F Kalshoven (ed), *Assisting the Victims of Armed Conflict and Other Disasters* (Martinus Nijhoff, Dordrecht, 1989).
Veuthey, M, 'The Red Cross and Non-International Conflicts' (1970) 10 *IRRC* 411.
—— 'Military Instructions on the Treatment of Prisoners in Guerrilla Warfare' (1972) 12 *IRRC* 125.
—— 'Les Conflits Armés de Caractère Non-International et le Droit Humanitaire', in A Cassese (ed), *Current Problems of International: Essays on UN Law and on the Laws of Armed Conflict* (Giuffrè, Milan, 1975).
—— 'Guerrilla Warfare and Humanitarian Law' (1976) 16 *IRRC* 277.

—— *Guerilla et droit humanitaire* (CICR, Genève, 1983).
—— 'Guerrilla Warfare and Humanitarian Law' (1983) 23 *IRRC* 115.
—— 'Remedies to Promote the Respect of Fundamental Human Values in Non-International Armed Conflicts' (2000) 30 *IYHR* 37.
—— 'Learning from History: Accession to the Conventions, Special Agreements, and Unilateral Declarations' (2003) 27 *Collegium* 139.
Vierucci, L, '"Special Agreements" between Conflicting Parties in the Case-law of the ICTY', in B Swart, A Zahar, and G Sluiter (eds), *The Legacy of the International Criminal Tribunal for the former Yugoslavia* (Oxford University Press, Oxford, 2011).
von Glahn, G, 'The Protection of Human Rights in Armed Conflicts' (1971) 1 *IYHR* 208.
von Hebel, H and Robinson, D, 'Crimes within the Jurisdiction of the Court', in RS Lee (ed), *The International Criminal Court: The Making of the Rome Statute, Issues, Negotiations, Results* (Kluwer, The Hague, 1999).
Walker, TA, *Science of International Law* (CJ Clay and Sons, London, 1893).
Warbrick, C and Rowe, P, 'The International Criminal Tribunal for Yugoslavia: The Decision of the Appeals Chamber on the Interlocutory Appeal on Jurisdiction in the *Tadić* Case' (1996) 45 *ICLQ* 691.
Watkin, K, 'Controlling the Use of Force: A Role for Human Rights Norms in Contemporary Armed Conflict' (2004) 98 *AJIL* 1.
—— 'Assessing Proportionality: Moral Complexity and Legal Rules' (2005) 8 *YIHL* 3.
—— 'Chemical Agents and Exploding Bullets: Limited Law Enforcement Exceptions or Unwarranted Handcuffs?' (2006) 36 *IYHR* 43.
—— 'Opportunity Lost: Organized Armed Groups and the ICRC "Direct Participation in Hostilities" Interpretive Guidance' (2010) 42 *New York University Journal of International Law and Politics* 641.
Watson, GR, 'The Humanitarian Law of the Yugoslavia War Crimes Tribunal: Jurisdiction in *Prosecutor v Tadić*' (1995–6) 36 *Virginia JIL* 687.
Weinstein, JM, *Inside Rebellion: The Politics of Insurgent Violence* (Cambridge University Press, Cambridge, 2004).
Weisburd, AM, *Use of Force: The Practice of States since World War II* (Pennsylavnia State University Press, Pennsylvania, 1997).
Westlake, J, *International Law, Part II: War* (Cambridge University Press, Cambridge, 1913).
Wheaton, H, *International Law* (Dana (ed)), (8th edn, 1866).
Wilms, J, 'Without Order, Anything Goes? The Prohibition of Forced Displacement in Non-International Armed Conflict' (2009) 91 *IRRC* 547.
Wilmshurst, E and Breau, S (eds), *Perspectives on the ICRC Study on Customary International Humanitarian Law* (Cambridge University Press, Cambridge, 2007).
Wilson, HA, *International Law and the Use of Force by National Liberation Movements* (Clarendon Press, Oxford, 1988).
Winthrop, W, *Military Law and Precedents* (Government Printing Office, Washington, 1920).
Wolfrum, R and Fleck, D, 'The Enforcement of International Humanitarian Law', in D Fleck (ed), *The Handbook of International Humanitarian Law* (Oxford University Press, Oxford, 2008).
Wood, EJ, 'Variation in Sexual Violence during War' (2006) 34 *Politics and Society* 307.
Wright, Q, *A Study of War, Two Volumes* (University of Chicago Press, Chicago, 1942).
Yingling, R and Ginnane, GW, 'The Geneva Conventions of 1949' (1952) 46 *AJIL* 393.
Zahar, A, 'Civilizing Civil War: Writing Morality as Law at the ICTY', in B Swart, A Zahar, and G Sluiter (eds), *The Legacy of the International Criminal Tribunal for the former Yugoslavia* (Oxford University Press, Oxford, 2011).
Zeender, G, 'Engaging Armed Non-State Actors on Internally Displaced Persons Protection' (2005) 24 *Refugee Survey Quarterly* 96.

Zegveld, L, 'The Inter-American Commission on Human Rights and International Humanitarian Law: A Comment on the Tablada Case' (1998) 324 *IRRC* 505.
Zegveld, L, *The Accountability of Armed Opposition Groups in International Law* (Cambridge University Press, Cambridge, 2002).
Zimmermann, A, 'War Crimes', in O Triffterer (ed), *Commentary on the Rome Statute of the International Criminal Court: Observers' Notes, Article by Article* (Beck, München, 2008).
Zöckler, MC, 'Commentary on Protocol IV on Blinding Laser Weapons' (1998) 1 *YIHL* 333.
Zorgbibe, C, *La Guerre Civile* (Presses Universitaires de France, Paris, 1975).
—— 'Sources of the Recognition of Belligerent Status' (1977) 17 *IRRC* 111.

INTERNATIONAL CONFERENCES OF THE RED CROSS

Compte-Rendu de la Neuvième Conférence Internationale de la Croix-Rouge Tenue à Washington du 7 au 17 mai 1912, ICRC Archives CR 22/32.
Sixteenth International Red Cross Conference, London, 1938: Report.
Seventeenth International Red Cross Conference: Stockholm, 1948: Report.
XVIIe Conférence Internationale de la Croix-Rouge (Stockholm, août 1948) Commission Juridique, Sténogramme des Séances (janvier 1949).
XXIst International Conference of the Red Cross, Istanbul, 1969: Report.

INTERNATIONAL COMMITTEE OF THE RED CROSS

Report on the Interpretation, Revision and Extension of the Geneva Convention of July 27, 1929 (June 1938).
'Le Role et l'Action de la Croix-Rouge en Temps de Guerre Civile' (1938) 230 *RICR* 97.
ICRC, Report on the Work of the Preliminary Conference of National Red Cross Societies for the study of the Conventions and of various Problems relative to the Red Cross (Geneva, 26 July–3 August 1946) (Geneva, 1947).
ICRC, Report on the Work of the Conference of Government Experts for the Study of the Conventions for the Protection of War Victims (Geneva, 14–26 April 1947) (Geneva, 1947).
ICRC, *Draft Revised or New Conventions for the Protection of War Victims* (ICRC, Geneva, 1948).
ICRC, *Revised and New Draft Conventions for the Protection of War Victims* (Geneva, 1948).
CICR, *Projets de Conventions Revisées ou Nouvelles Protégeant les Victimes de la Guerre* (CICR, Genève, May 1948).
Remarks and Proposals submitted by the International Commission of the Red Cross: Document for the Consideration of Governments invited by the Swiss Federal Council to attend the Diplomatic Conference at Geneva (April 21, 1949) (Geneva, 1949).
ICRC, *The Geneva Conventions of August 12, 1949: Analysis for the Use of National Red Cross Societies, Volume II* (ICRC, Geneva, 1950).
Commission of Experts for the Examination of the Question of Assistance to Political Detainees, Geneva, June 9–11, 1953.
Commission of Experts for the Study of the Question of the Application of Humanitarian Principles in the Event of Internal Disturbances, Geneva, October 3–8, 1955.
Final Record Concerning the Draft Rules for the Limitation of the Dangers Incurred by the Civilian Population in Time of War (ICRC, Geneva, April 1958).
'Humanitarian Aid to the Victims of Internal Conflicts: Meeting of a Commission of Experts in Geneva' (1963) 3 *IRRC* 79.
ICRC, Respect of the Geneva Conventions: Measures taken to Repress Violations, Report submitted by the International Committee of the Red Cross (Geneva, April 1965).

Reaffirmation and Development of the Law and Customs Applicable in Armed Conflicts: Report submitted by the International Committee of the Red Cross (Geneva, May 1969).

'Protection of Victims of Non-International Conflicts' (1969) 9 *IRRC* 343.

ICRC, Conference of Red Cross Experts on the Reaffirmation and Development of International Humanitarian Law Applicable in Armed Conflicts (The Hague, 1–6 March 1971) Report on the Work of the Conference (Geneva, April 1971).

Conference of Government Experts on the Reaffirmation and Development of International Humanitarian Law Applicable in Armed Conflicts (Geneva, 24 May–12 June 1971): Submitted by the International Committee of the Red Cross (Geneva, 1971).

Conference of Government Experts on the Reaffirmation and Development of International Humanitarian Law Applicable in Armed Conflicts (Geneva, 24 May–12 June 1971): Report on the Work of the Conference (ICRC, Geneva, August 1971).

ICRC, *Conference of Government Experts on the Reaffirmation and Development of International Humanitarian Law Applicable in Armed Conflicts, Geneva, 3 May–3 June 1972 (second session): I Basic Texts, Documentary Material Submitted by the International Committee of the Red Cross* (Geneva, January 1972).

ICRC, *Conference of Government Experts on the Reaffirmation and Development of International Humanitarian Law Applicable in Armed Conflicts, Geneva, 3 May–3 June 1972 (second session): II Commentary, Part Two, Documentary Material Submitted by the International Committee of the Red Cross* (Geneva, January 1972).

Conference of Government Experts on the Reaffirmation and Development of International Humanitarian Law Applicable in Armed Conflicts (Second Session, 3 May–3 June 1972): Report on the Work of the Conference, Volume I (Geneva, July 1972).

'Reaffirmation and Development of International Humanitarian Law Applicable in Armed Conflicts: Conference of Government Experts [Second Session]' (1973) 13 *IRRC* 61.

ICRC, *Draft Additional Protocols to the Geneva Conventions of August 12, 1949: Commentary* (Geneva, October 1973).

Report on the Study by the XXIInd International Conference of the Red Cross of the Draft Additional Protocols to the Geneva Conventions of August 12, 1949 (Geneva, January 1974).

ICRC, Conference of Government Experts on the Use of Certain Conventional Weapons (Lucerne, 24.9–18.10.1974): Report (ICRC, Geneva, 1975).

ICRC, Conference of Government Experts on the Use of Certain Conventional Weapons (Second Session—Lugano, 28.1–26.2.1976): Report (ICRC, Geneva, 1976).

ICRC, Report of the International Committee of the Red Cross for the Review Conference of the 1980 United Nations Convention on Prohibitions or Restrictions on the Use of Certain Conventional Weapons which May be Deemed to be Excessively Injurious or to have Indiscriminate Effects (ICRC, February 1994) 123.

'Meeting of the Intergovernmental Group of Experts for the Protection of War Victims, Geneva (23–27 January 1995)' (1995) 77 *IRRC* 33.

ICRC. 'Armed Conflicts Linked to the Disintegration of State Structures, Preparatory Document Drafted by the ICRC for the First Periodical Meeting on International Humanitarian Law' (Geneva, 19–23 January 1998).

ICRC, The People on War Report: ICRC Worldwide Consultation on the Rules of War (ICRC, Geneva, 1999).

'Internally Displaced Persons: The Mandate and Role of the International Committee of the Red Cross' (2000) 82 *IRRC* 491.

ICRC, Improving Compliance with International Humanitarian Law: ICRC Expert Seminars (Geneva, October 2003).

'Application of International Humanitarian Law and International Human Rights Law to UN-Mandated Forces: Report on the Expert Meeting on Multinational Peace Operations' (2004) 86 *IRRC* 207.

'Action by the International Committee of the Red Cross in the Event of Violations of International Humanitarian Law or of Other Fundamental Rules Protecting Persons in Situations of Violence' (2005) 87 *IRRC* 393.

'International humanitarian law and the challenges of contemporary armed conflicts', Document prepared by the International Committee of the Red Cross for the 30th International Conference of the Red Cross and Red Crescent, Switzerland, 26–30 November 2007' (2007) 89 *IRRC* 719.

ICRC, *Increasing Respect for International Humanitarian Law in Non-International Armed Conflicts* (ICRC, Geneva, February 2008).

'How is the Term "Armed Conflict" Defined in International Humanitarian Law?: International Committee of the Red Cross (ICRC) Opinion Paper', March 2008.

ICRC, Interpretive Guidance on the Notion of Direct Participation in Hostilities under International Humanitarian Law (ICRC, Geneva, May 2009).

'Expert Meeting on Procedural Safeguards for Security Detention in Non-International Armed Conflict' (2009) 91 *IRRC* 859.

Annual Reports

Bulletin International.
Revue International de la Croix-Rouge.
International Review of the Red Cross.

Archive documents

STATE AND NON-STATE ARMED GROUPS

General

Declaration to the Nairobi Summit made by the Signatories of the Geneva Call's *Deed of Commitment for Adherence to a Total Ban on Antipersonnel Mines and for Cooperation in Mine Action*, December 2004.

Declaration by Signatories to the 'Deed of Commitment under Geneva Call for Adherence to a Total Ban on Anti-Personnel Mines and for Cooperation in Mine Action' to the Cartagena Summit on a Mine-Free World, 30 November to 4 December 2009 (19 June 2009).

AFGHANISTAN

Taliban

Statement of the Islamic Emirate of Afghanistan on the Problem of Landmines, 6 October 1998.

Code of Conduct, 2006.

Code of Conduct for the Mujahideen, 9 May 2009, reproduced and translated in M Sassòli, AA Bouvier, and A Quintin, *How Does Law Protect in War? Volume III* (ICRC, Geneva, 2011) 2325.

Response of the spokesman of the Islamic Emirate of Afghanistan about civilian casualties' survey, 15 August 2010.

ALGERIA

France

(1955) 10 *United Nations General Assembly Official Records* 193.
(1956) *United Nations Security Council Official Records* 5.

Letter from P Mendès-France to Monsieur WH Michel, Comité International de la Croix-Rouge, 2 Feburary 1955, ICRC Archives B AG 225 008–002.
Communiqué de presse [of Prime Minister Guy Mollet, 23 June 1956], ICRC Archives B AG 202 008–001.

Algerian Rebels/Provisional Government

Lettre de la Délégation Algérienne, représentant le Front de Libération Nationale et l'Armée de Libération Nationale à Monsieur David de Traz, Représentant Spécial du Comité International de la Croix-Rouge, 23 February 1956, ICRC Archives B AG 202 008–001.
White Paper on the Application of the Geneva Conventions of 1949 to the French-Algerian Conflict (Algerian Office, New York, May 1960).
Instruments of Accession of the Algerian Republic to the Geneva Conventions of August 12, 1949 (registered at Berne, 20 June 1960).
Memorandum on the Accession of the Algerian Republic to the 1949 Geneva Conventions, reproduced in M Bedjaoui, *Law and the Algerian Revolution* (International Association of Democratic Lawyers, Brussels, 1961) 189.

ANGOLA

UNITA

Declaration by UNITA, 25 July 1980 [to ICRC] (1980) 20 *IRRC* 320.

FLEC

Statement of Rodrigues Mingas, Secretary-General of the FLEC, in 'Togo footballers were attacked by mistake, Angolan rebels say', *The Guardian* (UK), 11 January 2010.

BOSNIA

Agreement of 22 May 1992, reproduced in M Sassòli and AA Bouvier, *How Does Law Protect in War? Volume II* (ICRC, Geneva, 2006) 1765.
Agreement on the Release and Transfer of Prisoners, 1 October 1992.

BURMA/MYANMAR

Government

Letter from Myanmar to Human Rights Watch, 12 September 2007, reproduced as an Appendix to Human Rights Watch, *Sold to be Soldiers: The Recruitment and Use of Child Soldiers in Burma* (2007).

CNF

Deed of Commitment, 10 March 2009.

KNU/KNLA

Deed of Commitment, 4 March 2007.
Press Statement on Report of UNSG, 27 April 2009.

KNPP/KNA

Deed of Commitment, 13 April 2007.
Press Release No 02/09, Appeal for the Karenni Army's name to be removed from the list of non-state armed groups making use of child soldiers in armed conflict, 18 April 2009.

Lahu Democratic Front

Statement Made by Aik Long Kham Mwe, Chairman and General Secretary of the Lahu Democratic Front (LDF), on the Occasion of Signing the Deed of Commitment to Ban Landmines Held, 16 April 2007.

Palaung State Liberation Front

Statement made by Mai Aik Phone, General Secretary of the Palaung State Liberation Front (PSLF), on the Occasion of Signing the *Deed of Commitment* to Ban Landmines Held, 16 April 2007.

BURUNDI

Comprehensive Ceasefire Agreement between the Government of the Republic of Burundi and the Palipehutu-FNL, 7 September 2006.

CENTRAL AFRICAN REPUBLIC

Accord de Paix entre le Gouvernement de la République Centrafricaine et le mouvements politico-militaires ci-après désignés: Front Democratique du Peuple Centrafricain (FDPC), Union des Forces Démocratiques pour le Rassemblement, 21 June 2008.

CHAD

Peace Agreement between the Government of the Republic of Chad and the Movement for Democracy and Justice in Chad, 7 January 2002.

CHINA

M Tse-Tung, *Selected Works of Mao Tse-Tung, Four Volumes* (Foreign Languages Press, Peking, 1969).
Three Main Rules of Discipline, in M Tse-Tung, *Selected Works of Mao Tse-Tung, Volume IV* (Foreign Languages Press, Peking, 1969) 155.
The Eight Points for Attention, in ibid.
Three Main Rules of Discipline, 1927.
Six Points for Attention, 1928.
Four Policies for the Lenient Treatment of Captives, 1928.

COLOMBIA

Bolívar/Méndez

Tratado de Armisticio y Suspensión de Armas, 25 November 1820 (1820–1) 71 *Consolidated Treaty Series* 281.
Tratado de Regularización de la Guerra, 26 November 1820 (1820–1) 71 *Consolidated Treaty Series* 291.
Proclamation of 25 April 1821.

Confederación Granadina/Cipriano de Mosquera

Pacto de Chinchiná, 27 August 1860.
Esponsión de Manizales, 29 August 1860.
Armisticio de Chaguani, 3 March 1861.

Government

Ministry of Foreign Affairs of Colombia. 'Recognition of State of War Respecting the FARC (Fuerzas Armadas Revolucionarias de Colombia)', 16 June 1999, reprinted in (1999) 2 *YIHL* 440.

'Answer of H.E. the Minister of Foreign Affairs Guillermo Fernando to the questions as posed in the proposal of summons no. 142, Recognition of state of war respecting the FARC', reproduced in (1999) 2 *YIHL* 440.

Intervention of President Uribe, Forum on 'Internal Conflict or Terrorist Threat?', Chía, Colombia, 26 April 2005, quoted in D Roa-Castro. 'Mine Action in the Midst of Internal Conflict: The Colombian Case', in Geneva Call, *Mine Action in the Midst of Internal Conflict* (2005).

Government-FARC Humanitarian Exchange Accord, 2 June 2001.

ELN

Código de Guerra, 15 July 1995.
Nuestra Ética En La Doctrina Militar, 1996.
Foro Internacional: Minas antipersonales y Acuerdos Humanitarios, 4 June 2004.

FARC

Normas de Comportamiento con las Masas, 1998.

'Reaparece Cano', Cambio No 704, 8–15 de Noviembre de 1999, Bogota, quoted in D García-Peña Jaramillo. 'Humanitarian Protection in Non-International Conflicts: A Case Study of Colombia' (2000) 30 *IYHR* 179.

A La Poblacion Civil, in FARC-EP Comisión Internacional, *Beligerencia: Suplemento*, 10.

'Communiqué of 26 April 2000', quoted in P Gassmann, 'Colombia: Persuading Belligerents to Comply with International Norms', in S Chesterman (ed), *Civilians in War* (Lynne Rienner Publishers, London, 2001) 73.

Trabajo de Masas, undated.

CROATIA

Exchange of Prisoners Agreement between the Republic of Croatia and the Armed Forces of the SFRY, 6 November 1991.

Croatia/Yugoslav People's Army, Agreement on Humanitarian Convoy to Evacuate Wounded and Sick from Vukovar Hospital, 18 November 1991.

Memorandum of Understanding, 27 November 1991.

CUBA

Telegram from Fidel Castro, Commander-in-Chief of the Rebel Army, 3 July 1958, ICRC Archives B AG 200 060, reproduced in F Perret, 'Activities of the International Committee of the Red Cross in Cuba 1958–1962' (1998) 38 *IRRC* 655.

Telegram from Fidel Castro, 6 July 1958, ICRC Archives B AG 200 060.

Statement of Fidel Castro, Commander-in-Chief of the Rebel Forces, 16 July 1958, ICRC Archives 200 060, reproduced in F Perret, 'Activities of the International Committee of the Red Cross in Cuba 1958–1962' (1998) 38 *IRRC* 655.

Letter from Fidel Castro, 24 July 1958, ICRC Archives B AG 200 060.

Oral Commitment of Fidel Castro to the ICRC Delegate in Cuba, 10 January 1959, In: Rapport No 3 de P Jequier à CICR, 14 January 1959, ICRC Archives B AG 200 060.

DOMINICAN REPUBLIC

Oral commitment of General Imbert and Junta Government, noted in Telegram from ICRC Delegate Jequier to the ICRC in Geneva, 19 May 1965, ICRC Archives B AG 251 170.

DRC

FDLR

FDLR Press Release Nr 04/SE/CD/AUGUST2009, 20 August 2009.

Government

Letter from Minister of Foreign Affairs, Republic of Congo, to Political Department, Berne, 20 February 1961, ICRC Archives B AG 202 229–00.
Public Statement of the Prime Minister, Dr Moise Tshombe, 21 October 1964, ICRC Archives B AG 202 229–006, reproduced in (1965) 59 *AJIL* 616.
Letter from Premier Dr Moise Tshombe of the Democratic Republic of the Congo to the President of the International Committee of the Red Cross, 22 October 1964, ICRC Archives B AG 202 229–006, reproduced in (1965) 59 *AJIL* 615.

Various

Inter-Congolese Political Negotiations, Final Act, 2 April 2003, Resolution No DIC/CPJ/03, Relating to the Enshrinement of Democratic Principles, Preamble.
Acte d'Engagement.

MLC

Statuts du Mouvement de Libération du Congo, 30 Juin 1999.

EL SALVADOR

Government

Agreement on Human Rights, 26 July 1990, A/44/971-S/21541, Annex, 16 August 1990.

FMLN

The Legitimacy of Our Methods of Struggle (Inkworks Press, Berkeley, 1988).

ETHIOPIA

Government

Office of the Special Prosecutor. 'The Special Prosecution Process of War Criminals and Human Rights Violators in Ethiopia', February 1994, reproduced in NJ Kritz, *Transitional Justice, Volume III* (United States Institute for Peace, Washington DC, 1995) 559.
Special Public Prosecutor's Office Establishment Proclamation No. 22/1992, 8 August 1992, reproduced in NJ Kritz, *Transitional Justice, Volume III* (United States Institute for Peace, Washington DC, 1995) 556.
Letter dated 28 January 1994 from the Permanent Representative of the Transitional Government of Ethiopia to the United Nations Office at Geneva addressed to the Assistant Secretary-General for Human Rights, E/CN.4/1994/103, 3 February 1994, 4.

OLF

Oromo Liberation Front. 'Major Policies'.

ONLF

'Political Programme of the Ogaden National Liberation Front (ONLF)'.

FORMER YUGOSLAV REPUBLIC OF MACEDONIA

National Liberation Army

Witness Statement of Gzim Ostreni, Chief of NLA General Staff, Exhibit P00497.E in ICTY *Boškoski* trial. Ali Ahmeti, Political Representative, UCK General Staff, Untitled Document, 8 May 2001, Exhibit P00507.E in ICTY *Boškoski* trial.

GEORGIA

Declaration on Measures for A Political Settlement of the Georgian/Abkhaz Conflict Signed on 4 April 1994, Article 9.

Quadrapartite Agreement on Voluntary Return of Refugees and Displaced Persons signed on 4 April 1994, S/1994/397.

GERMANY

'Reply by the Federal Government to the written question submitted by Bundestag member Vera Wollenberger and the parliamentary party of the Alliance 90/Greens', reproduced and translated in M Sassòli and AA Bouvier, *How Does Law Protect in War: Volume II* (ICRC, Geneva, 2006).

GUATEMALA

Government

Letter from the Consul Général Représentant Permanent de Guatemala auprès de l'Office Européen des Nations Unies to M. Gallopin, Directeur du CICR, 25 June 1954, ICRC Archives, B AG 200 086.

Admission of Guatemala as to its liability for war crimes: (2000) 3 *YIHL* 516.

Comprehensive Agreement on Human Rights between the Government of Guatemala and the Unidad Revolucionaria Nacional Guatemalteca, 29 March 1994.

Armed group

Telegram from Carlos Salazar, Secretario de relaciones exteriores and Luis Valladares y Aycinena, Secretaro de gobernacion to ICRC, 26 June 1954, ICRC Archives, B AG 200 086.

HUNGARY

Government

Ordonnance du Commissariat du people pour les Affaires Étrangères No 2086 concernant la Situation juridique de la Croix Rouge International de Genève dans la République des Conseils de Hongrie, 10 April 1919, ICRC Archives Mis.4 5/67, reproduced in (1919–May) 1 *RICR* 604.

Letter from Béla Kun to Lieutenant-Colonel G Romanelli, 27 June 1919, ICRC Archives Mis 4.5/120.

INDONESIA

Government

Memorandum of Understanding between the Government of the Republic of Indonesia and the Free Aceh Movement, 15 August 2005.

ASNLF

'The Aims of the ASNLF'.

FRETILIN

Counter-Attacks Indon[esian] Forces, annexed to A/39/345-S/16668, 16 July 1984.

IRELAND

Mémoire du Gouvernement de la République Irlandaise au Comité International de la Croix-Rouge, 13 Mars 1923, ICRC Archives CR 22 (84)/1.

Lettre de Protestation addressée au 'Président du Parlement Provisoire de l'Irlande du Sud' par le Chef d'Etat Major de l'Armée Républicaine Irlandaise, 1 December 1992, annexed to Mémoire du Gouvernment de la République Irlandaise au Comité International de la Croix-Rouge, 13 March 1922, ICRC Archives CR 22 (84)/1.

Letter from Major-General Francis Morrin, Directeur du Service Médical de l'Armée, to the ICRC Delegate in Ireland, quoted in Note from the ICRC Delegate in Ireland to the ICRC concerning visit to prisoners and camps, 19 April 1923, ICRC Archives CR 22(84)/119.

Telegram, 20 January 1923, ICRC Archives CR 22(84).

Telegram from the Minister of Foreign Affairs, Desmond Fitzgerald, to President of the International Committee of the Red Cross, Gustave Ador, 23 January 1923, ICRC Archives CR 22(84)/89.

Telegram of 1 February 1923, from the ICRC to the Minister of Foreign Affairs, Desmond Fitzgerald, ICRC Archives CR 22 (84)/94.

IVORY COAST

Linas-Marcoussis Agreement, 23 January 2003.

Ivory Coast/FNA, Ouagadougou Agreement, 4 March 2007.

KOSOVO

KLA

'Krasniqi Explains UCK's Origins, Structure', Pristina Koha Ditore, 12 July 1998, KLA Communiques and Political Declarations from 1997–9, Exhibit P48 in ICTY *Limaj* trial.

Political Statement of the KLA, 27 April 1998, Exhibit P328, Annex 12, in ICTY *Haradinaj* trial.

Political Statement No 11 of the Kosova Liberation Army, 5 October 1998, reproduced as 'UCK Confirms Respect for International Conventions', Pristina Koha Ditore in Albanian, 6 October 1998, exhibit P48 in ICTY Limaj trial.

'Memorandum of the General Staff of the Kosova Liberation Army Sent to the Relevant Institutions of the International Community' (undated), reproduced in 'UCK Sends "Memorandum" to International Community', Pristina Bujku, 17 October 1998, ibid.

Kosovo Liberation Army General Staff, Order, 28 November 1998, Exhibit P441 in ICTY *Dordević* trial.

'Political Declaration No 30 of the KLA', 8 February 1999, in KLA Communiques and Political Declarations from 1997–9, Exhibit P48 in Limaj trial.
Communique of the KLA General Staff, reproduced as 'Text of Ceku Communique Urging Serbs to Remain', 18 August 1999, Exhibit P48 in ICTY Limaj trial.

LIBERIA

First Policy Statement of Mr Charles Ghankay Taylor, Leader of the National Patriotic Front of Liberia, 1 January 1990.
Cotonou Accord between between Interim Government of National Unity (IGNU) of Liberia, National Patriotic Front of Liberia (NPFL) and the United Movement of Liberia for Democracy (ULIMO), 25 July 1993.
Agreement on Ceasefire and Cessation of Hostilities between the Government of the Republic of Liberia and Liberians United for Reconciliation and Democracy and the Movement for Democracy in Liberia, 17 June 2003.
Peace Agreement between the Government of Liberia (GOL), The Liberians United for Reconciliation and Democracy (LURD), The Movement for Democracy in Liberia (MODEL) and the Political Parties, 18 August 2003.

LIBYA

Interim Transitional National Council

The Interim Transitional National Council Statement, 22 March 2011.
The Treatment of Detainees and Prisoners, 25 March 2011.
Statement regarding Eman Al-Obaidi, 27 March 2011.
Urgent Press Release, 6 April 2011.
Communiqué regarding Landmines, undated.
A Vision of a Democratic Libya, undated.

MEXICO

EZLN

'Revolutionary Women's Law'.
Letter from Insurgent Comandante Marcos to 'Asma Jahangir, Special Correspondent [sic] of the UN for Extrajudicial, Summary or Arbitrary Executions', 19 July 1999, reproduced in B Clarke and C Ross (eds), *Voice of Fire: Communiqués and Interviews from the Zapatista National Liberation Army* (Freedom Voices, San Francisco, 2000) 116.
Speech by an Indigenous Guerrilla, later published in La Jornada, 19 January 1994, reproduced and translated in B Clarke and C Ross (eds), *Voice of Fire: Communiqués and Interviews from the Zapatista National Liberation Army* (Freedom Voices, San Francisco, 2000) 39.

MOZAMBIQUE

RENAMO/Government of Mozambique, Guiding Principles of Humanitarian Assistance, 16 July 1992.

NAMIBIA

SWAPO

South West Africa People's Organisation, Declaration to the International Committee of the Red Cross, 15 July 1981.

NEPAL

Government

Ceasefire Code of Conduct, 25 May 2006.
Action Plan between the Government of Nepal, the Unified Communist Party of Nepal—Maoist, and the United Nations in Nepal regarding the Discharge of Disqualified Maoist Army Personnel and Related Tasks, 16 December 2009.

CPN-M

Public Legal Code, 2060 (2003/2004).
Appeal of the Communist Party of Nepal (Maoist), 16 March 2004.
Understanding between Seven Political Parties Alliance and the CPN (Maoist), 16 June 2006.
12-Point Understanding between Parties and Maoists, 22 November 2006.

NICARAGUA

Definitive cease-fire agreement between the Government of the Republic of Nicaragua and the 'YATAMA' Atlantic Front of the Nicaraguan Resistance under the auspices of His Eminence Miguel Cardinal Obando y Bravo, Annex, Act Establishing the Demilitarized Zone, 18 April 1990, A/44/941-S/21272, 25 April 1990.

NIGERIA

Government

Declaration of War of 12 August 1967.
Operational Code of Conduct for the Nigerian Army, undated, reproduced in AHM Kirk-Greene, *Crisis and Conflict in Nigeria: A Documentary Sourcebook 1966–1969, Volume I* (Oxford University Press, London, 1971).
Statement of 2 September 1968, in AHM Kirk-Greene, *Crisis and Conflict in Nigeria: A Documentary Sourcebook 1966–1969: Volume II* (Oxford University Press, London, 1971).
Federal Government of Nigeria Policy Statement on Relief Supplies to Displaced Persons and Other Civilian Victims of the Civil War, 30 June 1969, reproduced in T Hentsch, *Face au Blocus: la Croix-Rouge International dans Le Nigeria en Guerre (1967–1970)* (Graduate Institute, 1973).
'Partners in Crime', Lagos Radio talk, in AHM Kirk-Greene, *Crisis and Conflict in Nigeria: A Documentary Sourcebook 1966–1969: Volume II* (Oxford University Press, London, 1971).

PHILIPPINES

Government

Tripoli Agreement (GRP/MNLF), 23 December 1976.
Comprehensive Agreement on Respect for Human Rights and International Humanitarian Law, 16 March 1998.
Implementing Guidelines on the Humanitarian, Rehabilitation and Development Aspects of the GRP-MILF Tripoli Agreement on Peace of 2001, 7 May 2002.
Agreement on the Civilian Protection Component of the International Monitoring Team, 27 October 2009.

NDFP

NDFP, Rules in the Investigation and Prosecution of Suspected Enemy Spies, 1989.

NDFP Declaration of Undertaking to Apply the Geneva Conventions of 1949 and Protocol I of 1977, addressed to the Swiss Federal Council, 5 July 1996.

NDFP Declaration of Undertaking to Apply the Geneva Conventions of 1949 and Protocol I of 1977, addressed to the ICRC, 5 July 1996.

'Basic Rules of the New People's Army', reproduced in NDFP, *Declaration of Undertaking to Apply the Geneva Conventions of 1949 and Protocol I of 1977* (NDFP Human Rights Monitoring Committee Booklet No 6).

NDFP Human Rights Monitoring Committee, *Praymer Hinggil sa CARHRIHL* (Booklet Number 5, December 2005).

NDF-P, *NDFP's Defense of the Rights of the Filipino Child* (NDFP Human Rights Monitoring Committee 2005, Booklet No 7).

Letter to UN Secretary General Ban Ki-Moon on Children in Armed Conflict from LG Jalandoni, Member of the NDFP National Executive Committee and Chairperson of the NDFP Negotiating Panel, 24 November 2008.

NDFP Human Rights Monitoring Committee, 'NDFP denies use of anti-personnel mines, emphazises adherence to international humanitarian law', 24 April 2010.

Letter to Ms Coomaraswamy [Special Representative of the Secretary-General for Children and Armed Conflict] from the Chairperson of the NDFP Human Rights Monitoring Committee, 7 April 2011.

MILF

Implementing Guidelines for the Moro Islamic liberation Front (MILF) pursuant to its 'Deed of Commitment under Geneva Call for Adherence to a Total Ban on Anti-Personnel Mines and for Cooperation in Mine Action'.

'Resolution to reiterate MILF policy of strongly and continuously condemning all kidnap for ransom activities in Mindanao and everywhere, and to take drastic action against the perpetrators of this heinous crime in all MILF areas', 6 February 2002.

Action Plan between the Moro Islamic Liberation Front (MILF) and the United Nations in the Philippines regarding the Issue of Recruitment and Use of Child Soldiers in the Armed Conflict in Mindanao, 1 August 2009.

'MILF suspends BIAF officer for burning houses in Maguindanao Town', 16 July 2010.

'MILF Organizes Military Court', 9 October 2010.

Rebolusyonaryong Partido ng manggagawa

Declaration of the Rebolusyonaryong Partido ng manggagawa—Pilipinas and the Revolutionary Proletarian Army—Alex Boncayao Brigade against the Use and Production of Landmines, 21 March 2000.

PERU

Sendero Luminoso

'Norms of Behaviour for a Sendero Luminoso Commander', reproduced in JM Weinstein, *The Politics of Insurgent Violence* (Cambridge University Press, Cambridge, 2007) 375.

POLAND

Instructions for Doctors in the Field, 14 April 1863.

RUSSIA

Order of the Day No 92, 1 May 1919.
Order of the Day No 126, 18 July 1919.

RWANDA

The N'Sele Ceasefire Agreement between the Government of the *Rwandese* Republic and the Rwandese Patriotic Front, as amended at Gbadolite, 16 September 1991, and at Arusha, 12 July 1992, Article 2(5).

SIERRA LEONE

Government

Agreement, 10 November 2000.

RUF

RUF, 'Footpaths to Democracy: Toward a New Sierra Leone', 1995.
'Lasting Peace in Sierra Leone: The Revolutionary United Front Sierra Leone (RUF/SL) Perspective and Vision', undated.
Revolutionary United Front's Apology to the Nation, 18 June 1997.
RUF Political Leadership-Kailahun District, 'RUF Calls for Independent Investigations', 15 January 1999.
Eight Codes of Conduct, reproduced in *Prosecutor v Sesay, Kallon and Gbao*, SCSL-04–15-T, Judgment, 2 March 2009.

SOLOMON ISLANDS

Townsville Peace Agreement, 15 October 2000.

SOMALIA

Agreement between the TFG and the ARS, 9 June 2008.

SPAIN

Accord de José Giral, Le Président du Conseil des Ministres, 3 Septemer 1936, reproduced in (1936) *RICR* 749, Annex II.
Miguel Cabanellas, Junte de Défense Nationale d'Espagne, 15 September 1936, reproduced in (1936) *RICR* 749, Annex IV.

SRI LANKA

Government

Memorandum of Understanding among the Government of the Socialist Republic of Sri Lanka and the Office of the United Nations High Commissioner for Refugees relating to the Repatriation of Sri Lankan Refugees and Displaced Persons, 1 February 1993.
Agreement on a Ceasefire between the Government of the Democratic Socialist Republic of Sri Lanka and the Liberation Tigers of Tamil Eelam, 22 February 2002.
L Nasry, 'Interview with Chief Justice Sarath N de Silva: LTTE has no judicial authority—CJ', *Sunday Times* (Sri Lanka), 14 November 2004.

LTTE

Letter dated 24 February 1988 from Vellupillai Prabhakaran to Members and Observers, United Nations Commission on Human Rights.
Press Release, International Secretariat, Liberation Tigers of Tamil Eelam, 18 February 1992.
Letter from Velummylum Manoharan, Representative, LTTE International Secretariat, to Honourable Judges of the US Court of Appeal District of Colombia Circuit (undated), published in *Sunday Times* (Sri Lanka), 16 November 1997.
Political Committee of the LTTE, Special Press Release, 10 October 1997.
Interview with E Pararajasingham, 'Tamil Eelam—a de facto State: Tamil Eelam Legal System', 30 October 2003, previously available at <tamilnation.org>.
LTTE, Tamil Eelam Child Protection Act (Act No 3 of 2006).
Liberation Tigers of Tamil Eelam Peace Secretariat, Press Release, 15 June 2006, in Report of the Special Rapporteur on extrajudicial, summary or arbitrary executions, Follow-up to Country Recommendations, A/HRC/8/3/Add.3, 14 May 2008.
'Charter of the North East Secretariat on Human Rights'.

SUDAN (SOUTH SUDAN REGION)

Government

Agreement between the Government of the Republic of Sudan and the Sudan People's Liberation Movement to Protect Non-Combatant Civilians and Civilian Facilities from Military Attack, 10 March 2002.

SPLM/A

New Sudan Penal Code, 1994.
A Major Watershed: SPLM/SPLA First National Convention, Resolutions, Appointments and Protocol (SPLM, New Sudan, March/April 1994).
SPLM/Operation Lifeline Sudan, Agreement on Ground Rules, 3 July 1995.
SPLM-United/Operation Lifeline Sudan, Agreement on Ground Rules, May 1996.
Resolution on the Problem Posed by Proliferation of Anti-Personnel Mines in Liberated Parts of New Sudan, 1 November 1996.
Vision and Programme of the Sudan People's Liberation Movement, March 1998.
Statement of the Sudan People's Liberation Movement/Army on the Occasion of the Signing and Depositing to Geneva Call Deed of Commitment to Ban Landmines, 4 October 2001.
SPLA Act 2003.
Formation of New Sudan Authority on Landmines, 9 May 2004.
Letter sent by a Commandant of the Sudan People Liberation Army to the ELN, June 2004.
Action Plan between the Sudan People's Liberation Army (SPLA) and the United Nations regarding Children Associated with the SPLA in Southern Sudan, 20 November 2009.

SSIM

South Sudan Independence Movement Operation/Lifeline Sudan, Agreement on Ground Rules, 5 August 1995.

SUDAN (DARFUR REGION)

Government

Agreement on Humanitarian Ceasefire on the Conflict in Darfur, 8 April 2004.
Protocol on the Establishment of Humanitarian Assistance in Darfur, Annex, ibid.

Agreement between the Government of Sudan, the Sudan Liberation Movement, and the Justice and Equality of Movement', 25 April 2004.
Protocol between the Government of Sudan (GoS), the Sudan Liberation Movement/Army (SLM/A) and the Justice and Equality Movement (JEM) on the Improvement of the Humanitarian Situation in Darfur, 9 November 2004.
Protocol between the Government of Sudan (GoS), the Sudan Liberation Movement/Army (SLM/A) and the Justice and Equality Movement (JEM) on the Enhancement of the Security Situation in Darfur in Accordance with the N'Djamena Agreement, 9 November 2004.
Darfur Peace Agreement, May 2006.

JEM

Statement by the Opposition Movements [JEM and SLM-Unity], undated (published on 11 July 2008).
GOS Flies Surveillance Planes with UN Colour over Darfur, 31 January 2009.
JEM Welcomes Al-Bashir's Arrest Warrant, 4 March 2009.
JEM Welcomes Appearance of Abu Garda at the ICC, 18 May 2009.
A Letter from JEM Prisoners of War in Khartoum to the UN Human Rights Rapporteur to Sudan, 3 June 2009.
AU on ICC Warrant and Mbeki's Panel on Darfur, 8 July 2009.
Report of the Panel of Experts established pursuant to Resolution 1591 (2005) concerning the Sudan Issues 29 October 2009: A Response from JEM, 18 November 2009.
Memorandum of Understanding between the Justice and Equality Movement (JEM) and the United Nations regarding Protection of Children in Darfur, 21 July 2010.

SLM

Darfur Rebel Leader Praises UNAMID Refusal to Handover Kalma Residents, 5 August 2010.

SUDAN (EASTERN SUDAN)

Eastern Sudan Front

Agreement to Create a Conducive Atmosphere for Peace, 19 June 2006.
Eastern Sudan Peace Agreement, 14 October 2006.

SWITZERLAND

Recommendations to the division commanders with respect to the conduct to adopt toward the inhabitants and soldiers of the Sonderbund, 4 November 1847.
Proclamation to the Army, 5 November 1847.
'Law of Armed Conflicts: Conditions Governing the Application of Protocol II Additional to the 1949 Geneva Conventions (case of El Salvador)' (1987) 43 *Annuaire Suisse de Droit International* 185.

TAJIKISTAN

Order of the Commander and Head of the Department of the Interior Troops of the Ministry of Internal Affairs of the Republic of Tajikistan, 23 April 1996, in E La Haye, *War Crimes in Internal Armed Conflicts* (Cambridge University Press, Cambridge, 2008).
Protocol on Refugees [Tajikistan/United Tajik Opposition], 21 January 1997.

TURKEY

Government

Letter from Ambassador Türkekul Kurttekn in response to the characterization of the PKK, *Landmine Monitor Report*, 15 December 2005.

PKK/HPG

PKK Statement to the United Nations, 24 January 1995.

General Command of Kongra Gel/HPG, Letter to Geneva Call, 29 October 2008, cited in P Bongard, E Decrey Warner, and J Somer, 'Influencing Armed Non-State Actors to Respect Humanitarian Norms: Lessons from the Geneva Call Experience', in B Perrin (ed), *Modern Warfare: Armed Groups, Private Militaries, Humanitarian Organizations, and the Law* (University of British Columbia Press, Vancouver, 2012).

The Military Tribunal of HPG, 'The Sentence of the Court of HPG concerning the compartment of BATMAN', 23 November 2010.

UGANDA

Government

Government of Uganda/National Resistance Movement (NRM), Nairobi Peace Agreement, 17 December 1985.

NRA

The National Resistance Army Code of Conduct, in OO Amaza, *Museveni's Long March from Guerrilla to Statesman* (Kampala, Fountain, 1998) 246; abridged version in JM Weinstein, *The Politics of Insurgent Violence* (Cambridge University Press, Cambridge, 2007).

Government

Cessation of Hostilities Agreement between the between the Government of the Republic of Uganda and Lord's Resistance Army/Movement, Addendum I, 1 November 2006.

Agreement on Accountability and Reconciliation, 29 June 2007.

Annexure to the Agreement on Accountability and Reconciliation, 19 February 2008.

Agreement on a Permanent Ceasefire, 23 February 2008.

Letter of the Solicitor-General of Uganda to the Registrar of the ICC, 27 March 2008, ICC-02/04–01/05–286-Anx2.

Letter of the Solicitor-General of Uganda to the ICC Registrar, 18 November 2008, ICC-02/04–01/05–354-Anx2.

Letter of the Solicitor-General of Uganda to the Registrar of the ICC, 16 February 2009, ICC-02/04–01/05–369-Anx2.

LRA

Statement of Martin Ojul, Head of the LRA Delegation to the Juba Peace Talks, quoted in 'LRA Rebels Vow to Protect Rare Wildlife', *Independent Online* (South Africa), 21 August 2006.

UNITED KINGDOM

The Law of War on Land being Part III of the Manual of Military Law (HMSO, London, 1958).

Ministry of Defence, *The Manual of the Law of Armed Conflict* (Oxford University Press, Oxford, 2004).

Statement of Secretary of State for International Development, Douglas Alexander, 15 May 2009.

UNITED STATES

General Orders (various).
Instructions for the Government of Armies of the United States in the Field (Lieber Code), 24 April 1863.
US War Department, *The War of the Rebellion: A Compilation of the Official Records of the Union and Confederate Armies* (Government Printing Office, Washington, 1886).
WT Sherman, *Memoirs of General WT Sherman, Two Volumes* (Charles Webster, New York, 1891).
Special Message of President Grant, 13 June 1870, reproduced in JB Moore, *Digest of International Law, Volume 1* (Government Printing Office, Washington DC, 1906).
Seventh Annual Message of President Grant, 7 December 1875, reproduced in JB Moore, *Digest of International Law, Volume 1* (Government Printing Office, Washington DC, 1906).
Letter from Francis Lieber to General Halleck, 20 May 1863, reproduced in GB Davis, 'Doctor Francis Lieber's Instructions for the Government of Armies in the Field' (1907) 1 *AJIL* 13.
US statement at the discussion preceding adoption of the resolution: GAOR, 23rd Session, Third Committee, 1634th Meeting, UN Doc. A/C.3/SR.1634 (1968).
Letter from the US Department of Defence, excerpted in (1973) 67 *AJIL* 122.
'Report of the US Delegation to the 1974–77 Diplomatic Conference to the Secretary of State' (1978) 72 *AJIL* 405.
The 'Dix-Hill Cartel' for the General Exchange of Prisoners of war entered into between the Union and Confederate Armies, 22 July 1862, reproduced in HS Levie (ed), *Documents on Prisoners of War* (60 International Law Studies, Naval War College Press, Rhode Island, 1979).
Message from the President of the United States Transmitting the Protocol II Additional to the Geneva Conventions of August 12, 1949, and Relating to the Protection of Victims of Non-international Armed Conflicts, Concluded at Geneva on June 10, 1977 (US Government Printing Office, Washington, 1987).
'The Position of the United States on Current Law of War Agreements: Remarks of Judge Abraham D Sofaer, Legal Adviser, United States Department of State, January 22, 1987' (1987) 2 *American University Journal of International Law and Policy* 460.
'The United States Position on the Relation of Customary International Law to the 1977 Protocols Additional to the 1949 Geneva Conventions: Remarks of Michael J Matheson' (1987) 2 *American University Journal of International Law and Policy* 419.
Department of the Army, Office of the Judge Advocate General of the Army, Memorandum of Law: Executive Order 12333 and Assassination', 2 November 1989 (written by WH Parks, as reissued).
Report from US Secretary of State Warren Christopher on the three Protocols, accompanying President's letter of transmittal to the Senate, reproduced in (1997) 91 *AJIL* 325.
[United States] *Annotated Supplement to the Commander's Handbook on the Law of Naval Operations* (Naval War College, Newport, 1997).
US Department of Justice, Application of Treaties and Laws to Al Qaeda and Taliban Detainees, 9 January 2002; Presidential Order, 7 February 2002.
Operational Law Handbook (2005).
US Department of State, Report to Congress on Incidents During the Recent Conflict in Sri Lanka (2009).

UPPER SILESIA

Letter from Korfanty to ICRC Delegates, 1 June 1921, ICRC Archives CR 22–5/26, reproduced in (1921) 3 *RICR* 691, Annex 1.

Letter from Hoefer to ICRC Delegates, 1 June 1921, ICRC Archives CR 22–5/76, reproduced in (1921) 3 *RICR* 691, Annex 2.

Letter from Korfanty to the ICRC in Oppeln, 27 June 1921, ICRC Archives CR 22–5/85, reproduced in (1921) 3 *RICR* 691, Annex 17.

Oral commitment of General Hoefer reported in the Telegram of the ICRC Delegate in Oppeln to the ICRC in Geneva, 30 June 1921, ICRC Archives CR 22–5/128ter, reproduced in (1921) 3 *RICR* 691, Annexes 17bis.

VIETNAM

Letter from Chef de la Représentation Permanente du FLN du Sud-Vietnam en URSS to Representative of the ICRC, 16 October 1965, ICRC Archives B AG 202 223–005.

YEMEN

Letter from El-Badr to the President of the ICRC, 2 January 1963, ICRC Archives B AG 200 226.

Written Statement from Président de la République arabe yéménite, Al-Mousir Abdullah El-Sallal, 28 January 1963, ICRC Archives B AG 200 226.

Letter from Abdulmalik al Houthi to Dr Mohammed Al-Mikhlafi (Head of the Yemeni Observatory for Human Rights), undated (published on 4 September 2009).

Letter from Abd al-Malik Badr al-Din Al-houthi to Human Rights Watch, 29/Jumada II/1430.

Agreement on a Cease-Fire in the Republic of Yemen, 30 June 1994, annexed to S/1994/778.

UN DOCUMENTS

Secretary-General

Respect for Human Rights in Armed Conflicts: Report of the Secretary-General, A/7720, 20 November 1969.

Respect for Human Rights in Armed Conflicts: Report of the Secretary-General, A/8052, 18 September 1970.

Report of the Secretary-General pursuant to Paragraph 2 of Security Council Resolution 808 (1993), S/25704, 3 May 1993.

Report of the Secretary-General pursuant to Paragraph 5 of Security Council Resolution 955 (1994), S/1995/134, 13 February 1995.

Minimum Humanitarian Standards: Analytical Report of the Secretary-General submitted pursuant to Commission on Human Rights Resolution 1997/21, E/CN.4/1998/87, 5 January 1998.

Report of the Secretary-General pursuant to General Assembly Resolution 53/35: The Fall of Srebrenica, A/54/549, 15 November 1999.

Report of the Secretary-General on the establishment of a Special Court for Sierra Leone, S/2000/915, 4 October 2000.

Women, Peace and Security, Study Submitted by the Secretary-General Pursuant to Security Council Resolution 1325 (2000) (United Nations, New York, 2002).

The Rule of Law and Transitional Justice in Conflict and Post-Conflict Societies: Report of the Secretary-General, S/2004/616, 23 August 2004.

'Honouring Geneva Conventions, Secretary-General says Debate "No Longer between Peace and Justice but between Peace and What Kind of Justice"', SG/SM/12494, 26 September 2009.
Reports of the Secretary-General on Children and Armed Conflict.
Reports of the Secretary-General on the Protection of Civilians in Armed Conflict.

Reports of Representatives of the Secretary-General

Report of the Representative of the Secretary-General for Internally Displaced Persons. 'Compilation and Analysis of Legal Norms', E/CN.4/1996/52/Add.2, 5 December 1995.
Reports of the Representative of the Secretary-General on internally displaced persons.
Reports of the Special Representative of the Secretary-General for Children and Armed Conflict.
ST/SGB/1999/13, 6 August 1999.

Reports of Commissions of Inquiry to the Secretary-General

Report of the International Commission of Inquiry on Darfur to the Secretary-General, S/2005/60, 1 February 2005.
Report of the Secretary-General's Panel of Experts on Accountability in Sri Lanka, 31 March 2011.

OHCHR

Report of the United Nations High Commissioner for Human Rights, Mr José Ayala Lasso, on his mission to Rwanda, 11–12 May 1994, E/CN.4/S-3/3, 19 May 1994.
Office of the High Commissioner for Human Rights in Nepal, *Human Rights Abuses by the CPN-M: Summary of Concerns* (2006).
'Outcome of the Expert Consultation on the Issue of Protecting the Human Rights of Civilians in Armed Conflict: Report of the Office of the United Nations High Commissioner for Human Rights', A/HRC/11/31, 4 June 2009.
OHCHR, *Rule of Law Tools for Post-Conflict States: Amnesties* (United Nations, Geneva, 2009).

Human Rights Council/(Former) Commission on Human Rights

Final Report on the Situation of Human Rights in El Salvador, E/CN.4/1985/18, 1 February 1985.
Report of the situation of human rights in Afghanistan, E/CN.4/1985/21, 19 February 1985.
Report of the Special Rapporteur on torture and other cruel, inhuman or degrading treatment or punishment, E/CN.4/1991/17, 10 January 1991.
Report of the Special Rapporteur on extrajudicial, summary or arbitrary executions, Mission to Rwanda, E/CN.4/1994/7/Add.1, 11 August 1993.
Report of the Special Rapporteur on the situation of human rights in Sudan, E/CN.4/1996/62, 20 February 1996.
Statement of the Commission on Human Rights of 24 April 1996, Situation of Human Rights in the Republic of Chechnya of the Russian Federation, E/CN.4/1996/177.
Report on the situation of human rights in Somalia, E/CN.4/1997/88, 3 March 1997.
Situation of Human Rights in Somalia: Report of the Independent Expert, E/CN.4/2002/119, 14 January 2002.

Final Report of the Special Rapporteur on Terrorism and Human Rights, E/CN.4/Sub.2/2004/40, 25 June 2004.
Report of the Special Rapporteur on Extrajudicial, Summary or Arbitrary Executions, E/CN.4/2005/7, 22 December 2004.
Report of the Special Rapporteur on the Human Rights Situation in the Sudan, E/CN.4/2006/111, 11 January 2006.
Report of the Special Rapporteur on Extrajudicial, Summary or Arbitrary Executions, E/CN.4/2006/53, 8 March 2006.
Report of the Special Rapporteur on Extrajudicial, Summary or Arbitrary Executions, Mission to Sri Lanka, E/CN.4/2006/53/Add.5, 27 March 2006.
Report of four Special Rapporteurs, Mission to Lebanon and Israel, A/HRC/2/7, 2 October 2006.
Report of the Special Rapporteur on Extrajudicial, Summary or Arbitrary Executions, A/HRC/8/3/Add.2, 16 April 2008.
'Human Rights Situation in Palestine and Other Occupied Arab Territories', combined report, A/HRC/10/22, 20 March 2009.
Report of the Special Rapporteur on Extrajudicial, Summary or Arbitrary Executions, Mission to Afghanistan, A/HRC/11/2/Add.4, 6 May 2009.
'Human Rights in Palestine and Other Occupied Arab Territories', Report of the United Nations Fact-Finding Mission on the Gaza Conflict, A/HRC/12/48, 25 September 2009.
Report of the Special Rapporteur on Extrajudicial, Summary or Arbitrary Executions: Study on Targeted Killings, A/HRC/14/24/Add.6, 28 May 2010.
Report of the Committee of independent experts in international humanitarian and human rights laws to monitor and assess any domestic, legal or other proceedings undertaken by both the Government of Israel and the Palestinian side, In: the light of General Assembly resolution 64/254, including the independence, effectiveness, genuineness of these investigations and their conformity with international standards, A/HRC/15/50, 21 September 2010.
Report of the International Commission of Inquiry to investigate all alleged violations of international human rights law in the Libyan Arab Jamahiriya, A/HRC/17/44, 1 June 2011.

Human Rights Committee

Human Rights Committee, *General Comment No 29: States of Emergency (Article 4)*, CCPR/C/21/Rev.1/Add.11, 31 August 2001.
General Comment No 31. 'Nature of the General Legal Obligation Imposed on States Parties to the Covenant', CCPR/C/21/Rev.1/Add.13, 2004.

Committee on the Rights of the Child

Concluding Observations: Bhutan, CRC/C/15/Add.157, 9 July 2001.
Guidelines regarding Initial Reports of States Parties to the Optional Protocol to the Convention on the Rights of the Child on the Involvement of Children in Armed Conflict, CRC/OP/AC/1, 12 October 2001.
Concluding Observations: Chad, CRC/C/TCD/CO/2, 12 February 2009.

ONUSAL

Second Report of the United Nations Observer Mission in El Salvador, A/46/658-S/23222, 15 November 1991.
Third Report of the United Nations Mission in El Salvador, A/46/876-S/23580, 19 February 1992.

Security Council

Interim Report of the Commission of Experts established pursuant to Security Council Resolution 780 (1992), S/25274, 10 February 1993.

Final Report of the Commission of Experts established pursuant to Security Council Resolution 780 (1992), S/1994/674, 27 May 1994.

Preliminary Report of the Independent Commission of Experts established in accordance with Security Council Resolution 935 (1994), S/1994/1125, 4 October 1994.

Terms of Reference of the Working Group of the Security Council on Children and Armed Conflict, S/2006/275.

Reports and Conclusions of the Security Council Working Group on Children and Armed Conflict.

Index

active participation in hostilities *see* direct/active participation in hostilities
ad hoc regulation 2, 9–29
  advantages and drawbacks 28–9, 54
  agreements 20, 25–9
  belligerency, recognition of 9–20, 28–9
  instructions 20, 21–4, 28–9
  systematic regulation 53
ad hoc statements and press releases of armed groups 141–2
Additional Protocol I to Geneva Conventions
  belligerent reprisals 449, 451
  capital punishment 311, 525
  cessation of protection 69
  child soldiers 69
  civilian objects, attacks on 344
  combatant immunity 519
  commentaries 468
  contents 51
  customary international law 58–9
  dams, dykes, and nuclear electrical generating stations 382–3
  disproportionate attacks 79
  domestic criminal courts 493
  drafting 49, 51
  due process 307–8
  human rights 86, 503–4
  human shields 421–2
  International Criminal Tribunal for the former Yugoslavia 58
  International Humanitarian Fact-Finding Commission 459–60
  international humanitarian law 69
  intra-party protection 248
  manuals, codes of conduct, and internal regulations 438–9
  missing persons 284
  national liberation, wars of 118, 219–20, 222
  Red Cross, International Committee of the 468–70
  reservations 69
  starvation of civilians 423, 425–6
  systematic regulation 49, 51
  targeting of certain listed objects 69
  transnational/extra-state armed conflicts 233
  war crimes 475
  wounded, sick, and shipwrecked 274–5
Additional Protocol II to Geneva Conventions
  Additional Protocol I 64
  adoption 184
  amnesties 506–8
  belligerency, recognition of 190–1
  belligerent reprisals 450–2
  capacity to comply 74–6, 188–9, 191
  cessation of protection 69
  children 68, 79, 315, 317
  civilian objects, attacks on 344
  collective punishments 272
  combatant immunity 520
  commentaries 468
  commitments 111–12
  common Article 3 51, 192–3
  conduct of hostilities 336–7, 428
  contents 49–51, 66
  courts of non-state armed groups 552–3, 561
  criminal process, persons subject to 305–6
  criticism 52
  cultural property 376–7, 379
  customary international law 56–9, 61, 66–7, 105, 192
  dams, dykes, and nuclear electrical generating stations 381, 383
  dead persons, protection of 280
  detained persons 292–3, 295
  differentiation between NIACs and IACs 70, 72, 74–6
  diplomatic conferences 49, 66–7, 182, 184–5, 189–90, 192–3
  discrimination 258
  displaced persons 285–6
  disproportionate attacks 79–80, 349
  dissemination 432, 434
  domestic criminal courts 490, 493, 498–9
  drafting history 49–51, 182–5, 189, 192, 207–8
  due process 307–10
  environment 526
  fair trials 75–6
  Geneva Conventions 49–50
  geographical scope of application 250–1
  government/state armed forces, definition of 184, 191
  human rights 83, 86, 87, 91, 94, 501–3
  humane treatment 257–8, 334
  humanitarian assistance 329–32
  identification of NIACs 162, 182–93, 210
  implementation 185–7, 188–91
  intensity 169, 188, 190
  International Committee of the Red Cross 36–7, 66, 174, 178, 182–3, 468–70
  International Criminal Court 188, 210, 482
  International Criminal Tribunal for Rwanda 480–1
  International Criminal Tribunal for the former Yugoslavia 57–9, 60, 66, 188, 192, 479
  International Humanitarian Fact-Finding Commission 460
  international humanitarian law 64, 66–8
  interned and detained persons 292–3, 295
  intra-party protection 248
  levels of protection 68
  loss of protection 365–7
  medical and religious personnel 278–9
  medical units and transports 373–4
  methods of combat 428
  national liberation, wars of 217

620 Index

Additional Protocol II to Geneva Conventions (*cont.*)
  NIACs, definition of 155, 164–6, 181–3
  organized armed groups 174, 178, 184–5, 189
  peacekeeping missions 325–6
  perfidy 70
  precautions 351
  protecting powers system 457
  protracted armed conflicts, definition of 192–3
  provisions versus principles 50–1, 53
  quarter, denial of 412
  ratification 190–2
  reciprocity 189, 244
  regularly constituted courts 305–6
  reservations 69
  responsible command 183, 184–5, 189, 191
  scope of application clause 182–4, 190–2, 196–7
  sexual violence 264–5
  simplification 50–1, 54
  starvation of civilians 423, 425–6
  sustained and concerted military operations 188
  systematic regulation 49–54, 67
  targeting 69, 338
  temporal scope of application 252–3
  territorial control 97, 185–7, 188, 191, 193, 210, 244
  threshold of application 51–2, 66–7
    reading out threshold for application 66–7
  transnational/extra-state armed conflicts 229–32
  violence, characterization of 196, 207–8
  war crimes 79, 475–6
  women 313–14
  wounded, sick, and shipwrecked 74, 273, 276
adequate time and facilities for defence 309
Afghanistan *see also* Afghanistan, Taliban in
  agreements 445
  Cold War conflict 259, 444–5, 525
  commitments 444–5
  cultural property 378
  humane treatment 259
  prisoners of war 525
Afghanistan, Taliban in
  anti-personnel mines 404–5
  code of conduct 139
  education and training 549
  engaging compliance 546–7
  fact-finding missions 463
  interned and detained persons 297, 299
  manuals, codes of conduct, and internal regulations 439, 441
  medical units and transports 375
  NATO 222
  organization of non-state armed groups, level of 174
  pillage 428
  precautions 352
  Red Cross, International Committee of the 114
  troops, intervention through use of 222
  war on terror 233–4
AFRC 272, 318, 319, 466, 517
African Charter on Human and Peoples' Rights 83, 503

African Union Convention on Internally Displaced Persons 290–1
age of child soldiers 315–17, 320–3, 361, 467
agreements 118–25
  ad hoc regulation 20, 25–9
  advantages and drawbacks 28–9
  belligerency, recognition of 28
  bilateral agreements 9, 28, 96–7, 107, 109–14, 133, 144–52, 442–5
  ceasefires 256, 261, 267–8, 270, 292, 305, 340–1
  civilians, attacks on 240–1
  combatant immunity 517
  commitments 107, 109, 111, 113, 124–33
  common Article 3 124
  customary international law 109, 443
  dead persons, protection of 280–1
  development of law 443–4
  displaced persons 290, 292
  dissemination 432
  environment 528
  exchanges of persons 277
  Geneva Conventions 444
  hostages, taking 270
  human rights 97, 129–32
  humane treatment 256–7, 334–5
  humanitarian assistance 333–4
  internal mechanisms for implementation and enforcement 442–5
  International Criminal Tribunal for the former Yugoslavia 82
  international humanitarian law 26–7, 125–31, 133, 443–5
  interned and detained persons 295
  medical and religious personnel 279
  non-state armed groups, agreements between 133
  peace agreements 125, 253, 256–7, 292, 305, 443
  peacekeeping missions 327
  precautions 352–3
  prisoner exchanges 444–5
  Red Cross, International Committee of the 127–8, 469
  starvation of civilians 424
  Tadić decision 82, 107
  trilateral agreements 107, 132–3
  violence, characterization of 204
  war crimes 82–3
  war, law of 25–6
  wounded and sick, exchanges of 444–5
aid *see* humanitarian assistance
air, relief provided by 333–4
Al Qaeda 103, 232–3, 251, 353–4, 525
Algerian War of Independence
  agreements 444
  blockades 19
  combatant immunity 516–17
  courts of non-state armed groups 555, 558
  emblems and uniforms, improper use of 417
  Geneva Conventions 54, 119
  instructions, codes of conduct, and internal regulations 134

Index

interned and detained persons 293–4, 297
legal advice 437
prisoners of war 523–4
Red Cross, International Committee of the 472
transnational/extra-state armed conflicts 230
violence, characterization of 197–8, 203–4
ALN 173, 197, 230, 293–4, 417, 555
American Civil War
  amnesties 515–16
  anti-personnel mines 405
  belligerency, recognition of 17–18
  belligerent reprisals 454
  civilian objects, attacks on 345
  combatant immunity 515–16
  courts of non-state armed groups 550, 560
  domestic criminal courts 489, 490
  explosive bullets 401
  human shields 421
  instructions or declarations, regulation by 23–4
  Lieber Code 33–4
  military necessity, definition of 23
  poison and poisoned weapons 392–3
  precautions 355
  prisoners of war 522
  ruses 419
  territorial control 530–1
American Convention on Human Rights 501–3
amnesties 475, 505–9
  Additional Protocol II 506–8
  capital punishment 525
  combatant immunity 506, 507–8
  conditions 505–6
  customary international law 508–9
  Disappearances Convention 506
  Inter-American Commission on Human Rights 508
  International Criminal Court 506
  limits 506
  prisoners of war 525
  soft law 506
  summary executions 506
  treaties and conventions 506–7
  United Nations 509
  war crimes 505–9
ANC 201, 545
ANC-ZAPU 118
Angola 220, 430–1, 448
anti-personnel mines 404–8
  children 406
  civilians 405–6
  commitments 110, 238, 408
  common Article 3 406–7
  contamination of land 405
  Conventional Weapons Convention, Amended Mines Protocol to 62, 404–7
  cooperation and assistance in removal 405, 407
  customary international law 405
  defensive use 405
  engaging compliance 543–6
  environment 527

Geneva Call Deed of Commitment 113, 243–4, 408, 538–45
Geneva Conventions 406–7
indiscriminate use 392, 404–5, 406
instruction 435
Ottawa Convention on Anti-Personnel Mines 238, 240, 407–8
  commitments 238
  differentiation between NIACs and IACs 62
  engaging compliance 543, 545–6
  Geneva Call 539, 541
  indiscriminate use of weapons 392
  scope of application clause 407
  unnecessary suffering or superfluous injury 390
personal scope of application 238, 240
precautions 405, 406
records of locations 405
unilateral declarations 113
unnecessary suffering or superfluous injury 390, 404
warnings 405, 406
apologies of armed groups 448
APRD 316, 319, 322, 434, 536, 538
armed conflict, identification of *see* **identification of NIACs**
armed forces of states *see* **government/state forces**
arrest warrants 483–4
ASNLF 218, 462, 465
attacks *see* civilians, attacks on; civilian objects, attacks on
AUC 358

bacteriological weapons 393
bandits 162, 178, 204–5, 370, 522
Bangladesh 491, 493, 496
Belgium 498, 499
belligerency, recognition of 9–20
  ad hoc regulation 9–20, 28–9
  Additional Protocol II 190–1
  agreements 28
  appeals to be recognised 195–6
  blockades 18–19
  civil wars accompanied by state of general hostilities 11
  combatants, armed groups treated as 16
  concept of recognition 9–14
  conditions of recognition 11–14
  consequences of recognition 14–16
  courts of non-state armed groups 550
  definition 181–2
  diplomatic conferences 41
  diplomatic relations 14, 15
  differentiation between NIACs and IACs 70, 212, 234
  general hostilities, definition of 11
  general principle, statements of 10–11
  Geneva Conventions 19–20
  Havana Convention, Protocol to 20
  humanitarian protection 15–16
  identification of NIACs 157–9, 161, 195–6
  independence, recognition of 17

belligerency, recognition of (*cont.*)
  instances of recognition 17–20
  instructions 20, 21–4, 28–9
  insurgency, comparison with 9–10
  levels of violence 9–10
  neutrality, law of 10, 15, 17–19
  observance of law and customs of war 11, 12
  occupation and orderly administration 11, 12
  political organization of insurgents 10
  rebellion, comparison with 9–10
  recognition by third States 11, 12–18, 29
  regulation 9–20, 28–9, 41
  restricted belligerence 196
  self-interest 16, 29
  status of armed groups, enhancing 16
  terminology 70
  territorial control 531
  traitors, armed groups as 15
  violence, characterization of 206–9
  war, law of 10, 12, 14–16
belligerent occupation, law of 529–31
belligerent reprisals 448–57
  Additional Protocol I 449, 451
  Additional Protocol II 450–2
  adversary, persons in the power of the 450
  authorization 453–4
  civilians, attacks on 450–3, 455
  collective punishment 450
  common Article 3 450–1
  conduct of hostilities 450–1
  continued use 455–7
  Conventional Weapons Convention, Amended Mines Protocol to 449, 452
  criminal prosecutions 456
  customary international law 55–6, 104, 451–3
  definition 448–9
  General Assembly resolutions 55–6
  Geneva Conventions 449
  Hague Convention on Cultural Property 449, 452
  Hague Peace Conference 1899 450
  human rights 456
  humane treatment 450
  implementation and non-judicial enforcement 430, 448–57
  International Criminal Tribunal for the former Yugoslavia 77, 104, 452–3, 455–6
  international humanitarian law 450, 453
  last resort, as a 453
  Lieber Code 456
  prohibited reprisals 449–53
  proportionality 454–5
  Red Cross, International Committee of the 451
  restrictions 453–7
  war crimes 83
  warnings 453
beneficiaries of protection 357–86
  categories of persons 359–63
  civilian objects 357–9
  collaborators, notion of 358–9
  combatant status 359
  context 357–9
  continuous combat function 360–3, 429
  customary international law 359, 362
  direct part in hostilities 360–5, 372, 429
  international humanitarian law 359–60, 362
  Interpretative Guidance (ICRC) 359–61, 363–4, 429
  logistical roles, persons with 361–2
  loss of protection 365–72
  military objectives 357–8
  military wings of armed groups 359–62, 372, 429
  Red Cross, International Committee of the 359–61, 363–4, 429
  state armed forces, members of 359–62, 372
  targeting 357–86
BIAF 315, 322, 435, 439, 447, 539
Biafran conflict
  agreements 28
  belligerency, recognition of 17
  children 315
  civilian objects, attacks on 342–3
  codes of conduct 54, 133–4, 261, 438
  combatant immunity 517
  courts of non-state armed groups 555
  cultural property 379
  domestic criminal courts 490
  fact-finding missions 462
  Geneva Conventions 120, 134, 203
  humanitarian assistance 333–4
  indiscriminate attacks 348
  murder 261
  pillage 427
  prisoners of war 524
  quarter, denial of 413
  sexual violence 267
  starvation of civilians 423–4
  violence, characterization of 202, 203
  wounded, sick, and shipwrecked 275
biological and bacteriological weapons 393
births, deaths and marriages, registration of 560
blindness, laser weapons designed to cause permanent 399–400
blockades 18–19
Boer War
  amnesties 505
  combatant immunity 518
  domestic criminal courts 490
  emblems and uniforms, improper use of 418
  expanding bullets 402
  flags of truce and surrender 416
  interned and detained persons 301
  protecting powers system 457–8
  ruses 419
booby traps 404
border regions *see* **transnational/extra-state armed conflicts**
Bosnia
  agreements 125, 126–7
  anti-personnel mines 406
  commitments 107, 443
  cultural property 378
  domestic criminal courts 493, 497, 499
  peacekeeping missions 327

safe area or havens 385
troops, intervention through use of 224, 225
unilateral declarations 117
wounded, sick, and shipwrecked 276
Brussels Declaration 294
buffers, people used as 421
Bulgaria 35
bullets
dum dum bullets 402
expanding bullets 71, 401–3
explosive bullets 400–1
Burma/Myanmar
agreements 444
anti-personnel mines 406, 543–4
children 316, 321–2, 536, 537, 538
civilian objects, attacks on 343
code of conduct 135–6, 438–9, 441
courts of non-state armed groups 555
dead persons, protection of 283
fact-finding missions 463, 465
flags of truce and surrender 416
instruction 436
interned and detained persons 298, 301
murder 261
pillage 428
precautions 354
quarter, denial of 414
wounded, sick, and shipwrecked 275
Burundi 543, 545

Cairo Declaration on Human Rights in Islam 101–2, 527–8
Cambodia 378
camps, placement in 290
Canada 498
capacity of non-state armed groups
Additional Protocol II 74–6, 188–9, 191
child soldiers 72
dead persons, protection of 283–4
derogation 75
diplomatic conferences 72–3, 75
due process 309
education and training 72
fair trials 75–6
Geneva Conventions 72–3, 157
human rights 124
identification of NIACs 157
insurgents 12
interned and detained persons 76, 293, 295–7
life, right to 373
loss of protection 371–2
organization of non-state armed groups, level of 177–8
wounded and sick 74–5
capital punishment
Additional Protocol I 310
amnesties 311, 525
children 310
combatant immunity 311
criminal process, persons subject to 310–11
International Covenant on Civil and Political Rights 311
international humanitarian law 310–11

perfidy 418
pregnant women 310, 314
prisoners of war 525
summary executions 506, 549–50, 559
termination of conflict, not exercised until after 51, 311, 520
women 314
Carlist Wars 23–4, 31
Castro, Fidel 275, 300
CDF 272, 317, 318, 319, 320, 322, 362, 413, 426
ceasefire agreements
civilians, attacks on 340–1
displaced persons 292
hostages, taking of 270
humane treatment 256
interned and detained persons 305
murder 261
sexual violence 267–8
Central African Republic 135, 316, 319, 322, 434, 538
Certain Conventional Weapons, Convention on *see* **Conventional Weapons Convention**
cessation of hostilities 252–3
Charter of UN 85–6, 218, 324–30
Chechnya 198, 201, 349, 461, 504
chemical weapons 61–2, 394–6
child soldiers 316–24
action plans for de-listing 534
active/direct participation 79, 81, 88, 316–19, 321, 361
Additional Protocol I 68
Additional Protocol II 79, 317
adult, age of becoming an 315–16
age 315–17, 320–3, 361, 467
capacity 72
commitments 535–6
Committee on the Rights of the Child 467
conscription 319–20
Convention on the Rights of the Child 87–8, 237–8, 317, 320–4, 464, 467
customary international law 317, 320
danger as a potential target, exposing children to real 318
de-listing from Secretary-General's report 534, 535–6
differentiation between NIACs and IACs 72
dissemination 434, 566
early stages, involvement of armed groups at 537–8
education 324
engaging with non-state armed groups 533–8
enlistment 319–20
equality of obligation 324
fact-finding missions 463–5
Geneva Call 113, 537
human rights 79, 87–8, 323–4
instruction 435
International Criminal Court 317, 320, 323
international criminal law 323
International Criminal Tribunal for Rwanda 318

child soldiers (*cont.*)
  international humanitarian law 68, 79, 81, 316, 319, 323–4
  intra-party protection 248
  listing 533–8
  naming and shaming 533–8
  Office of the Special Representative of the Secretary-General for Children and Armed Conflict 534–7, 542, 547
  Paris Principles 320–1
  personal scope of application 237–8
  pictorial presentation of information 434
  recruitment 319–24
  sanctions 536–7
  Security Council 533–5, 538
  Security Council Working Group on Children and Armed Conflict 534–5, 538
  support functions 318
  targeted measures 534–5
  treaties and conventions 316–17
  unilateral declarations 113
  United Nations 320–1, 533–8
  war crimes 79, 81, 323
children 315–24 *see also* **child soldiers**
  Additional Protocol II 315
  age 315–16
  anti-personnel mines 406
  capital punishment 310
  civilians and persons *hors de combat*, protection of 315–24
  customary international law 316
  education 315–16
  engaging compliance 533–8
  Geneva Call 541–2
  Geneva Conventions 315
  implementation and non-judicial enforcement 532–8
  international humanitarian law 315
  safer place, taking children to a 315–16
  United Nations 533–8, 537
Chile 17, 496
China
  codes of conduct 134, 442
  dignity, outrages upon personal 264
  humane treatment 256
  quarter, denial of 413–14
civil servants 365–8
civil wars
  belligerency, recognition of 11
  common Article 3 161
  general hostilities, civil wars accompanied by state of 11
  identification of NIACs 161
  transnational/extra-state armed conflicts 229–30
civilian objects, attacks on 342–7, 357–9
  Additional Protocol I 344
  Additional Protocol II 344
  customary international law 342, 344
  definition of civilian objects 344–7
  distinction, principle of 342
  dual-use objects 347
  infrastructure of state 350

International Criminal Court 342
International Criminal Tribunal for the former Yugoslavia 342
international humanitarian law 342, 347
location 344–6
military advantage 344, 346
military objectives, definition of 344–7
nature and purpose of objects 344–6
protections afforded to civilian objects 342–3
proximate nexus, need for 344–6
treaties and conventions 342
wanton destruction 428
civilians *see also* **civilian objects, attacks on; civilians and persons hors de combat, protection of; civilians, attacks on**
  anti-personnel mines 405–6
  apologies of armed groups 448
  direct part in hostilities, taking 362–8, 372
  displaced persons 285–92
  dissemination 432–3
  interned and detained persons 293
  non-state armed groups 429
  peacekeeping missions 324–8
  security 287
civilians and persons hors de combat, protection of 255–335 *see also* **humane treatment**
  ad hoc participation 367
  children 315–24
  criminal process, persons subject to 305–11, 335
  dams, dykes, and nuclear electrical generating stations 381–2
  dead persons 280–4
  definition 365–6
  detained persons 292–305, 334
  differentiation between NIACs and IACs 69–70
  diplomatic conferences 40–52, 307
  direct part in hostilities, taking a 365–8
  displaced persons 285–92
  drafting 39
  Geneva Conventions 24, 35, 39
  hospitals 274, 383–5
  human shields 420–3
  humanitarian assistance 328–34
  incendiary weapons 397
  instructions or declarations, regulation by 24
  interned and detained persons 292–305, 334
  journalists 311–13
  loss of protection 365–8
  medical and religious personnel 277–80
  missing persons 284–5
  particular protections, persons benefitting from 273–329
  peacekeeping missions 324–8
  police 368
  precautions 351–7
  prisoners, shooting 24
  starvation of civilians 423–6
  targeting 337–48
  women 313–14
  wounded, sick, and shipwrecked 273–80, 334–5

Index

civilians, attacks on 338–41
  ad hoc agreements 340–1
  belligerent reprisals 450–3, 455
  bilateral agreements 340–1
  ceasefire agreements 340–1
  cluster munitions 409
  customary international law 339
  disproportionate attacks 350
  distinction, principle of 44, 102–3, 105, 337–8, 342
  indiscriminate use of weapons 390–1
  International Criminal Court 339
  international criminal law 339
  International Criminal Tribunal for the former Yugoslavia 339, 341
  international humanitarian law 339
  military advantage 341
  targeting 338–41
  terrorizing civilians 341
  war crimes 339
cluster munitions 409–10
  civilians 409
  Convention on Cluster Munitions 62, 83, 238, 240, 409–10
  Convention on the Rights of Persons with Disabilities 83
  customary international law 410
  definition 409
  differentiation between NIACs and IACs 62
  human rights 83
  indiscriminate effects 409
  land, contamination of 409
  non-state armed groups 409–10
  personal scope of application 238, 240
CNA 536
CNDD-FDD 545
CNDP 463, 484
CNF 536, 135, 261, 267, 270, 275, 283, 284, 298, 301, 322, 343, 354, 406, 414, 416, 428, 438, 441, 536, 544
codes *see* instructions, codes of conduct, and internal regulations; manuals, codes of conduct, and internal regulations
collaborators 358–9
collective punishments 271–2, 450
Colombia
  Additional Protocol II 562–3
  agreements 24–7, 107, 444
  anti-personnel mines 406
  belligerency, recognition of 196
  beneficiaries of protection 358
  child soldiers 537
  civilian objects, attacks on 346
  codes of conduct 137–8, 439, 441
  creation of law 562–3
  dead persons, protection of 281
  dissemination 434
  emblems and uniforms, improper use of 417
  engaging compliance 544–5, 547–8
  existence of armed conflicts, acceptance of 111
  hostages, taking 270
  human rights courts 501

instructions, codes of conduct, and internal regulations 137–8
International Humanitarian Fact-Finding Commission 461–2
legal status of non-state armed groups 209
loss of protection 368
manuals, codes of conduct, and internal regulations 439, 441
national liberation, wars of 210
non-state armed groups, characterization of 205
peer pressure 544–5
perfidy 419
police 368
precautions 357
sanctions 447
territorial control 98, 531
transnational/extra-state armed conflicts 230, 231, 234
violence, characterization of 201–2
colonial domination, wars against 213, 216–20, 234
combatant immunity 513–20
  ad hoc agreements 517
  Additional Protocol I 519
  Additional Protocol II 520
  amnesties 506, 507–8, 515–16, 519–20
  belligerency, recognition of 16
  beneficiaries of protection 359
  capital punishment 311
  common Article 3 519
  differentiation between NIACs and IACs 71
  Geneva Conventions 517–19
  International Criminal Tribunal for the former Yugoslavia 519
  international humanitarian law 513, 514
  personal scope of application 243
  prisoners of war 515–20, 525
  Red Cross, International Committee of the 515
  troops, intervention through use of 223
  war crimes 515
command responsibility
  courts of non-state armed groups 557, 559
  cultural property 380
  International Criminal Court 557
  level of command 380
  organization of non-state armed groups, level of 175–6, 179
  sanctions 446
command structure 170, 172–80, 210
commanders *see also* command responsibility; command structure
  legal advice 437
  sanctions 445, 447
  targeting 366
  training 558
commitments 107–52
  ad hoc commitments 101, 107–52, 284, 375, 408, 474
  Additional Protocol II 111–12
  agreements 107, 109, 111, 113, 124–33
  anti-personnel mines 110, 238, 408
  bilateral agreements 107, 109
  child soldiers 535–6

commitments (*cont.*)
  common Article 3 111, 152
  compliance 112–13
  creation and development of law 106–8, 443–4
  criminal prosecutions for breach 445
  customary international law 109–12, 443
  distinction, principle of 337
  formation of law, participation in 107–8
  Geneva Conventions 111, 112, 443–4
  human rights 111
  implementation and non-judicial enforcement 474
  instructions, codes of conduct, and internal regulations 107, 133–9
  internal mechanisms for implementation and enforcement 442–5
  international humanitarian law 107
  internees and detainees 114
  interpretation 110–12
  list of commitments 144–52
  medical units and transports 375
  missing persons 284
  nature of commitments 108–13
  normative status 109–10
  parallel commitments 445
  personal scope of application 238
  propaganda 108, 112
  prosecutions 445
  Red Cross, International Committee of the 114, 443–5
  sources of NIACs 107, 124–33, 152
  Tadić decision 110–11, 443
  targeting 337–8
  territorial control 111
  unilateral declarations 107, 109–10, 113–24
common Article 3 of Geneva Conventions
  Additional Protocol II 51, 192–3
  agreements 124
  anti-personnel mines 406–7
  belligerent reprisals 450–1
  civil war, NIACs at level of 161
  collective punishment 271, 450
  combatant immunity 519
  commentaries 162, 180
  conduct of hostilities 336, 428
  Conventional Weapons Convention 62–3
  criminal process, persons subject to 305–6
  customary international law 57, 59, 61, 105
  detained persons 292
  differentiation between NIACs and IACs 74
  discrimination 258–9
  displaced persons 285
  domestic criminal courts 490–1, 493, 498–9
  due process 308–9
  gas and chemical weapons 394
  geographical scope of application 250
  hostages, taking 268–9
  human rights 87, 501–3
  humane treatment 255, 257–9, 334
  identification of NIACs 162
  incendiary weapons 399
  insurgency 162
  International Criminal Court 482
  International Criminal Tribunal for Rwanda 480–1
  International Criminal Tribunal for the former Yugoslavia 479
  International Humanitarian Fact-Finding Commission 460, 473
  international humanitarian law 66
  interned and detained persons 292
  intra-party protection 248–9
  medical and religious personnel 277–8
  methods of combat 428
  national liberation, wars of 213
  NIACs, definition of 164, 181
  organized armed groups 178–9, 185
  personal scope of application 239
  ratification 230
  Red Cross, International Committee of the 43–4, 48–9, 53, 162, 180, 469–71
  regularly constituted courts 305–6
  systematic regulation 43–4, 48–9, 53, 54
  transnational/extra-state armed conflicts 229, 230–1
  violence, characterization of 206–7
  war crimes 67, 78, 475–6
  women 313–14
  wounded, sick, and shipwrecked 74, 273, 275
complementarity 485, 488, 509
compliance *see* **capacity of non-state armed groups for enforcement and compliance; engaging compliance**
concerted and sustained military operations 188
conduct of hostilities 336–429 *see also* **targeting**
  Additional Protocol II 336–7, 428
  belligerent reprisals 450–1
  common Article 3 336, 428
  customary international law 337, 429
  humane treatment 336, 429
  methods of combat 412–28, 429
  weapons 386–412, 428–9
conferences *see* **diplomatic conferences**
confidentiality 279–80, 471–2, 566
Congo *see* **Democratic Republic of Congo**
conscription 319–20
consent
  courts of non-state armed groups 559
  displaced persons 289
  humanitarian assistance 330–4, 335
  International Humanitarian Fact-Finding Commission 460–1
contamination of land *see* **natural environment**
continuous combat function 360–3, 429
Convention on the Rights of Persons with Disabilities 83, 87
Conventional Weapons Convention
  Amended Mines Protocol 62, 404–7, 449, 452
  anti-personnel mines 404–7
  application to NIACs 429
  belligerent reprisals 449, 452
  booby traps 404
  common Article 3 62–3
  domestic criminal courts 495

Explosive Remnants of War, Protocol on 62, 411–12
incendiary weapons 397–9
instructions, codes of conduct and internal regulations 135
international humanitarian law 62–3
laser weapons designed to cause permanent blindness 399–400
non-detectable fragments 410–11
personal scope of application 236
Review Conference 62
scope of application clause 407
unnecessary suffering or superfluous injury 390
conventions *see also* **particular conventions; treaties and conventions**
correspondence 295
countermeasures *see* **belligerent reprisals**
courts *see* **courts of non-state armed groups; domestic criminal courts; fair trials; individual courts; international criminal tribunals; judicial enforcement**
courts of non-state armed groups 549–62
 accountability 556
 Additional Protocol II 552–3, 561
 belligerency, recognition of 550
 births, deaths and marriages, registration of 560
 capital punishment 310–11
 command responsibility 557, 559
 complementarity 485, 488
 consent 559
 criminal process, persons subject to 75–6, 305–11
 differentiation between NIACs and IACs 75–6
 due process 75–6, 305, 306–10, 335, 551–3, 557
 engaging compliance 549–62
 examples 550–5
 fair trials 75–6, 485–6, 549, 552–3, 559, 562
 human rights 556, 558
 importance 555–7
 impunity 550, 555
 Inter-American Commission on Human Rights 556
 International Criminal Court 485–6, 488
 international humanitarian law 552–9
 legislation and law of non-state armed groups 561
 legitimacy 557–62
 prize courts 550
 regularly constituted courts 75–6, 305–6, 335
 state sovereignty 561
 summary executions 549–50, 559
 territorial control 558–60
 training of judges 551
 transfers to state systems 559
 unrecognized governments 560–1
 vigilantism 549
CPLA 134, 256, 260, 264, 267, 297–8, 413, 427, 442
CPN-M 122, 123, 131, 132, 277, 284, 303, 304, 414, 446, 520, 529, 551, 559
creation and development of law of non-international armed conflict 2–3, 5, 30–53, 54–100
 agreements 443–4
 child soldiers 537–8
 codes of conduct 563
 commitments 106–8, 443–4
 early stages, involvement of armed groups at 537–8
 'Fundamental Standards of Humanity' initiative 52, 565–7
 human rights 2–3, 83–99
 international armed conflict, drawing on law of 55–77
 international criminal law 2–3, 77–83
 international humanitarian law 2–3
 methodology 65–77, 562–4
 national liberation movements 563
 non-state armed groups, participation of 106–8, 537–8, 562–4
 proposal for instrument binding states and non-state armed groups 565–6
 treaties and conventions 564
 unilateral declarations 443–4
criminal proceedings *see also* **criminal process, persons subject to; domestic criminal courts; fair trials; international criminal law; international criminal tribunals**
 belligerent reprisals 456
 commitments 445
 domestic criminal courts 488–9
 prosecutions 445, 456, 488–9
criminal process, persons subject to 305–11
 Additional Protocol II 305–6
 capital punishment 305, 310–11
 civilians and persons hors de combat, protection of 305–11, 335
 common Article 3 305–6
 customary international law 305–6
 differentiation between NIACs and IACs 75–6
 due process 75–6, 305, 306–10, 335
 fair trials 75–6
 human rights 306
 independence and impartiality 306
 international humanitarian law 305
 regularly constituted courts 75–6, 305–6, 335
 summary executions 305
Croatia
 agreements 125–6
 anti-personnel mines 406
 civilian objects, attacks on 343
 civilians, attacks on 340
 domestic criminal courts 493–4, 497
 interned and detained persons 299
 unilateral declarations 117
cruel and inhuman treatment 262–4
Cuba
 belligerency, recognition of 10, 11, 13, 17
 Geneva Conventions 120
 interned and detained persons 300–1
 quarter, denial of 414–15

Index

Cuba (cont.)
  Red Cross, International Committee of the 31
  wounded, sick, and shipwrecked 275–6
cultural property 375–81 *see also* Hague Convention on Cultural Property
  Additional Protocol II 376–7, 379
  application to non-international armed conflict 376–7
  customary international law 375–6, 378, 381, 452
  definition 376
  emblems and uniforms, improper use of 417–18
  enhanced protection 379–80
  ethnic character, conflicts with an 376
  general protection 377
  identity, destruction of 376
  imperative military necessity 377, 379–80
  International Criminal Court 377, 381
  international humanitarian law 375–7
  level of command 380
  precautions 380–1
  protections 377–80
  religious character, conflicts with a 376
  self-defence 380
  special protection 377
  targeting 375–81
  UNESCO, offers of services from 379
  warnings 380
  without prejudice clause 379
Customary International Humanitarian Law study, *see* customary international law
customary international law
  Additional Protocol I 58–9
  Additional Protocol II 56–9, 61, 66–7, 105, 192
  agreements 109, 443
  amnesties 508–9
  anti-personnel mines 405
  belligerent reprisals 55–6, 104, 451–3
  beneficiaries of protection 359, 362
  biological and bacteriological weapons 393
  booby traps 404
  burden of proof 104
  chemical weapons 394, 395–6
  children 316–17, 320
  civilian objects, attacks on 342, 344
  civilians, attacks on 339
  cluster munitions 410
  codes of conduct 139, 438–9, 441
  collective punishment 271
  commitments 109–12, 443
  common Article 3 57, 59, 61, 105
  conduct of hostilities 337, 429
  confidentiality 472
  criminal proceedings 305–6, 498–9
  cultural property 375–6, 378, 381, 452
  Customary International Humanitarian Law study 56, 58–9, 61, 65, 67, 69, 102, 104, 107
  dams, dykes, and nuclear electrical generating stations 382–3
  dead persons, protection of 280–3
  Declaration of the IIHL on Rules of IHL 105–6
  denials of parties 102–4
  dignity, outrages upon personal 263
  displaced persons 285, 287–9, 291
  disproportionate attacks 102–3, 349
  distinction, principle of 102–3, 105
  domestic criminal courts 498–9
  environment 527
  expanding bullets 402
  explosive bullets 401
  flags of truce and surrender 415
  gas and chemical weapons 394, 395–6
  General Assembly (UN) 55–6, 466
  Hague Convention on Cultural Property 56
  hostages, taking of 268
  human rights 98
  human shields 420–1
  humane treatment 255, 258, 334
  humanitarian assistance 329, 330
  incendiary weapons 398–9
  indiscriminate attacks 348, 390–1
  instructions, codes of conduct, and internal regulations 139
  Inter-American Commission on Human Rights 59
  International Court of Justice 55
  International Criminal Court 80, 106, 482
  International Criminal Tribunal for Rwanda 56
  International Criminal Tribunal for the former Yugoslavia 56–60, 102, 104, 107, 192, 452–3, 479
  international criminal tribunals 56–61, 429
  international humanitarian law 69
  interned and detained persons 292, 294–5
  intra-party protection 249
  jus cogens 478
  laser weapons 400
  legal advice 437
  manuals, codes of conduct, and internal regulations 438–9, 441
  medical and religious personnel 278–9
  medical units and transports 373–5
  methodology 102–3
  missing persons 284–5
  NIACs, definition of 155
  non-detectable fragments 410
  opinio juris 55, 57, 102, 105, 438
  outrages upon personal dignity 257
  peacekeeping missions 324
  perfidy 419–20
  personal scope of application 239
  pillage 427
  poison and poisoned weapons 302
  precautions 351, 353–6
  prisoners of war 513
  protected zones 383–5
  quarter, denial of 412
  Red Cross, International Committee of the 56, 59, 104, 468–9, 472
  regularly constituted courts 305–6
  regulation 2, 54, 55–61, 99

sexual violence 264–5
slavery and slave trade 268
sources of law of NIACs 102–7, 152
starvation of civilians 423–4
state practice 55, 57
Tadić 102, 104
territorial control 529–30
unilateral declarations 110
unnecessary suffering or superfluous injury 387–8
violence to life and persons 259–60
wanton destruction 428
war crimes 60, 106, 477–8
weapons, use of 106
wounded, sick, and shipwrecked 273, 275, 276–7

Cyprus 470

dams, dykes, and nuclear electrical generating stations 381–3, 526
Darfur, Sudan
capital punishment 311
child soldiers 322, 536
emblems and uniforms, improper use of 417
indiscriminate attacks 348
instructions, codes of conduct, and internal regulations 135
International Criminal Court 484–5
interned and detained persons 300
loss of protection 368
police 368
sanctions 447
dead persons, protection of 280–4
ad hoc agreements 280–1
Additional Protocol II 280
burial in decent manner 281–2
capacity 283–4
collection and evacuation 280
customary international law 280–3
despoliation 281
exhumation 284
graves, respect for 282–4
human rights 282–3
identification 283–4
marking graves 283–4
records 282–4
Red Cross, International Committee of the 283
rites 282
search for, obligation to 280, 283
death penalty *see* **capital punishment**
decentralized armed groups 175
declarations 20, 21–4, 28–30 *see also* **unilateral declarations**
defence, adequate time and facilities for preparation of 309
defensive use of weapons 405
definition of NIACs 155–82
actors participating in violence 165
ad hoc international criminal tribunals 167
Additional Protocol II 155, 164–6, 181–3
advantages and disadvantages of lack of definition 162–4
belligerency, recognition of 181–2

common Article 3 164, 181
customary international law 155
diplomatic conferences 180–1
flexibility 155
Geneva Conventions 1949 155
government forces, involvement of 181–2
governmental authorities 155 , 164, 180
identification of NIACs 155–82, 210
intensity of violence 164, 165–70, 181, 192, 210
International Criminal Court 92, 164, 166, 181, 192
International Criminal Tribunal for Rwanda 167
International Criminal Tribunal for former Yugoslavia 155–6, 164–7, 210
international humanitarian law 67–8, 155
motives of actors 182
non-definition approach 156–64, 192
non-requisites 180–2
organization of armed group 164, 165–7, 168, 170–82, 192, 210
Red Cross, International Committee of the 165–6, 180–1
Tadić decision 155–6, 164–80, 210
territorial control of armed group 180–1
violence 165
war crimes 78
demilitarized zones 383–5
Democratic Republic of Congo
civilian objects, attacks on 342
courts of non-state armed groups 554
displaced persons 292
domestic criminal courts 490, 496
environment 528
fact-finding missions 463–4
human shields 422
humane treatment 256
instruction 437
international criminal tribunals 487–8
Katanga 270–1, 374
medical units and transports 374
motivations for taking up arms, expressions of 143
peacekeeping missions 325
precautions 353
sanctions 447
Security Council (UN) 466
states, declarations of 113–14
denial of existence of armed conflicts 5, 102–4, 162–4, 200–4, 210
Denmark 499
deportation 68–9, 80, 286–7, 335
derogations 75, 83–4, 250
despoliation 281
detained persons *see* **interned and detained persons**
detention *see* **interned and detained persons**
development of law *see* **creation and development of law of non-international armed conflict**
differentiation between NIACs and IACs 69–77, 212–35

differentiation between NIACs and IACs (*cont.*)
  abolition of distinction 46, 49, 53, 54
  Additional Protocol II 70, 72, 74–6
  belligerency, recognition of 212, 234
  belligerent reprisals 70
  capacity of non-state armed groups to comply with rules 72–6
  Chemical Weapons Convention 61–2
  child soldiers 72
  Cluster Munitions Convention 62
  combatant immunity 71
  common Article 3 74
  criminal proceedings 75–6
  diplomatic conferences 70, 72–4, 75
  disproportionate attacks 70
  expanding bullets 71
  Explosive Remnants of War, Protocol on 62
  fair trial, right to a 75–6
  Geneva Conventions 49
  Hague Convention on Cultural Property, Second Protocol to 62
  hors de combat, humane treatment of persons who are 69–70
  indiscriminate use of weapons 391
  internment, review of 76
  International Criminal Court 70–1
  international humanitarian law 61–2, 65, 69–77
  military necessity 70
  national liberation, wars of 212–22, 234
  non-state armed groups 71–6, 99–100
  Ottawa Convention on Anti-Personnel Mines 1997 62
  outside states, intervention by 212, 222–8, 234
  perfidy 70–1
  raids into neighbouring territory 212
  state sovereignty 70–1
  Tadić decision 73
  transnational/extra-state armed conflicts 212, 228–34, 235
  wanton destruction 70–1
  war crimes, list of 70–1
  weapons, lawfulness of 71
  wounded and sick 74–5
dignity 86, 263–4, 334
diplomatic conferences 42–9
  Additional Protocol II 49, 66–7, 182, 184–5, 189–90, 192–3
  belligerency, recognition of 41
  bilateral agreements 444
  capacity 72–3, 75
  civilians and persons *hors de combat*, protection of 40–52, 307
  common Article 3
    acceptance of services of impartial humanitarian body 469
    bilateral agreements 444
    civilians and persons *hors de combat*, protection of 307
    human rights 87
    identification of NIACs 156, 161, 180–5, 192, 206–7
    international humanitarian law 78
    national liberation movements 213
    protecting powers, system of 458
    systematic regulation 30, 44, 47, 53
    war crimes 475
  differentiation between NIACs and IACs 70, 72–5
  extension to non-international armed conflicts 40–2
  Hague Conventions of 1907 40–2
  human rights 44–6, 52, 87
  identification of NIACs 155–85, 192, 206–7, 210
  intensity of violence 169
  international humanitarian law 40–2, 66, 78
  national liberation movements 213
  NIACs, definition of 180–1
  organized armed groups 174, 178, 184–5
  perfidy 70
  protecting powers, system of 458
  responsible command 184–5
  symbol of Red Cross 468
  systematic regulation 49–53
  treaties and conventions 468
  war crimes 78, 475
diplomatic relations 14, 15, 198, 209
direct/active participation in hostilities
  age 361
  beneficiaries of protection 360–5, 372, 429
  borderline situations 365
  child soldiers 79, 81, 88, 316–19, 321, 361
  civilians 362–8, 372
  continuous combat function 360–3
  criteria 361
  definition 362–5
  examples 364–5
  gender 361
  human shields 422–3
  international criminal law 363
  international humanitarian law 362
  journalists 312–13, 364–5
  loss of protection 365–8
  military wings of armed groups 360–2
  Red Cross, International Committee of the 360–2, 363–4
  support 364
  types of acts 364–5
  weapons 361
disabilities, persons with 83, 87
disappearances 87, 506
discipline 135, 171–6, 178–80, 427–8
discrimination (prohibition on) 258–9
discrimination in attacks *see* **indiscriminate attacks**
displaced persons 285–92
  ad hoc agreements 290, 292
  Additional Protocol II 285–6
  African Union Convention on Internally Displaced Persons 290–1
  bilateral agreements 290
  camps, placement in 290
  ceasefire agreements 292
  common Article 3 285

consent 289
customary international law 285, 287–9, 291
deportation 80, 286–7, 335
ethnic cleansing 285, 286–7
exceptions to prohibitions 287–8
forcible transfers 80, 286–9, 335
Geneva Conventions 285, 287
Guiding Principles on Internal Displacement 284, 288, 289–91
identification documents 290
imperative military reasons 287–8, 291
internment 290
International Criminal Court 80, 285, 288
international criminal law 287, 335
International Criminal Tribunal for the former Yugoslavia 289
international humanitarian law 80, 285, 287–90, 335
military necessity 287–8, 291
missing persons 284
modalities 288–9
non-state armed groups, recognition of 291
ordered or compelled displacement 285–6
peace agreements 292
return of 288, 291–2
security of civilians 287
soft law 288, 289–90
treatment of internally displaced persons 289–91
unilateral declarations 290
war crimes 80
disproportionate attacks 349–51
Additional Protocol I 79
Additional Protocol II 349
belligerent reprisals 454–5
civilian life, loss of 350
customary international law 80, 349
dams, dykes, and nuclear electrical generating stations 381
differentiation between NIACs and IACs 70
environment 527
human shields 422–3
incendiary weapons 398
infrastructure 350
International Criminal Court 79–80, 349, 350–1
international criminal law 429
international humanitarian law 79–80, 350–1
military advantage 349–50
military necessity 80
military objectives 349–50
precautions 353–5
targeting 349–51
unnecessary suffering or superfluous injury 389
wanton destruction 70
war crimes 79–80
dissemination 431–4
ad hoc bilateral agreements 432
Additional Protocol II 432, 434
child soldiers 434, 566
civilians 432–3
commentaries or manuals 433–4
courses of instruction 433–4
education and training 431–4
'Fundamental Standards of Humanity' initiative 566
Geneva Call Deed of Commitment 432
Geneva Conventions 431–2
Hague Convention on Cultural Property 431–2, 433
illiteracy 434, 566
importance of dissemination 431–2
internal mechanisms for implementation and enforcement 431–4
international humanitarian law 432
modalities 433–4
non-state armed groups 432–3
orders 433–4
pictorial presentation 434, 566
radio 434
Red Cross, International Committee of the 433, 434, 469
Security Council resolutions 432
states 432–3
television 434
distinction, principle of 44, 102–3, 105, 337–8, 342
domestic criminal courts 488–500
1860s to mid-1990s 489–94
mid-1990s to present 494–400
Additional Protocol I 493
Additional Protocol II 490, 493, 498–9
common Article 3 490–1, 493, 498–9
complementarity 509
conventional law 494
Conventional Weapons Convention 495
criminalization 488, 490–5
customary international law 498–9
Geneva Conventions 488, 490–1, 493–4, 499–500
grave breaches 488, 499–500
Hague Convention on Cultural Property, Second Protocol to 498
Institute of International Law, resolution of 498–9
International Criminal Court 494–5, 498, 509
International Criminal Tribunal for Rwanda 488, 497–8, 500
International Criminal Tribunal for the former Yugoslavia 488, 493, 497–8, 500
international humanitarian law 488, 494, 497–8
legislation 488, 490–5
prosecutions 488–9
Safety of UN and Associated Personnel Convention 498
third states not involved in conflicts, trials in courts of 498–500
treaties and conventions 494–5
trials in national courts 496–8
universal jurisdiction 494, 498–500
war crimes 488–9, 491–9
Dominican Republic 116, 277, 280
dual-use objects 347
due process guarantees 306–10

due process guarantees (cont.)
    adequate time and facilities for defence 309
    Additional Protocol I 307–8
    Additional Protocol II 307–10
    capacity of actors 309
    common Article 3 306–7
    content of obligations 308–9
    context 309–10
    courts of non-state armed groups 75–6, 305, 306–10, 335, 551–3, 557
    criminal process, persons subject to 75–6, 305, 306–10, 335
    fair trial, right to a 306–8
    Geneva Conventions 307–8
    human rights 307–8, 310
    ICC Elements of Crimes 307–9
    identification of obligations 306–7
    independence and impartiality 307
    intensity of the conflict 308
    International Covenant on Civil and Political Rights 307–8
    prisoners of war 521
    Red Cross, International Committee of the 307, 310
    territorial control 308–10
Dufour, General 21, 22, 28, 30
dum dum bullets 402
Dunant, Henry 28, 30
dykes 381–3, 526

EAM 119
East Timor 496–7, 558
education and training
    capacity 72
    children 315–16, 324
    courts of non-state armed groups 551
    dissemination 431–4
    engaging compliance 548–9
    illiteracy 434
    instruction 435–7
    judges 551
    organization of non-state armed groups, level of 171
    pictorial presentation of information 434
    Red Cross, International Committee of the 469
El Salvador
    Additional Protocol I 59
    Additional Protocol II 142
    agreements 131
    anti-personnel mines 406
    child soldiers 318
    civilian objects, attacks on 345–6
    courts of non-state armed groups 552–3, 558, 561
    creation of law of non-international armed conflict 563
    customary international law 59
    dams, dykes, and nuclear electrical generating stations 382
    disproportionate attacks 349
    human rights 131, 467, 501
    interned and detained persons 298

    legal advice 437
    loss of protection 368
    medical and religious personnel 279
    precautions 352, 355–6
    press releases and other ad hoc statements 142
    sanctions 446
    starvation of civilians 425
    wounded, sick, and shipwrecked 275
ELAS 119
ELN 121, 135–6, 205, 270, 276, 406, 439, 441, 447, 461–2, 544, 545, 555
emblems and uniforms, improper use of 416–18
    bad faith 417
    cultural property 416
    customary international law 417–18
    enemy emblems and uniforms 417–18
    Lieber Code 417
    neutral or protected emblems and uniforms 416–17
    Red Cross, Red Crescent or Red Crystal 416–17, 468
endangered species 528
enforcement see capacity of non-state armed groups for enforcement and compliance; implementation and non-judicial enforcement; judicial enforcement
engaging compliance
    anti-personnel mines 543–6
    child soldiers 533–8
    children 533–8
    commitments 112–13
    courts of non-state armed groups 549–62
    creation of law of non-international armed conflict 562–4
    education and training 548–9
    Geneva Call 538–46
    Geneva Conventions 546–7
    greater engagement, towards 562
    implementation and non-judicial enforcement 532–3, 542–9
    influencing others 542–6
    legitimacy concerns 546–9, 562
    listing armed groups 548
    Office of the Special Representative of the Secretary-General for Children and Armed Conflict 534–7, 542, 547
    peer pressure 544–5
    publicity 541
    Security Council Working Group on Children and Armed Conflict 534–5, 538
    terrorist organizations, training 547–8
    treaties and conventions 542–3, 564
enlistment 319–20
environment see natural environment
equality of obligations
    asymmetry 244, 245–6
    child soldiers 324
    Geneva Call Deed of Commitment on Anti-Personnel Mines 243–4
    human rights 95–7, 243
    International Humanitarian Fact-Finding Commission 461

personal scope of application 242–6
reciprocity 31, 37–9, 189, 244–5
unilateral declarations 118
Eritrea-Ethiopia Claims Commission 75
ESF 257
essential supplies, definition of 330
Ethiopia
civilians, attacks on 340
domestic criminal courts 491, 492–3
engaging compliance 532–3
Eritrea-Ethiopia Claims Commission 75
human rights 123
national liberation, wars of 218
perfidy 420
quarter, denial of 413
wounded and sick 75
ethnic cleansing 266, 285, 286–7
European Convention on Human Rights 92–4, 372
European Court of Human Rights 90–4, 503–4, 510
evacuation 277, 296
exchanges of persons 277, 301, 444–5, 523
exhumation 284
existence of NIACs *see* identification of NIACs 155
expanding bullets 71, 401–3
explosive bullets 400–1
explosive remnants of law 62, 411–12
extra-state armed conflicts *see* transnational/extra-state armed conflicts
EZLN 122, 141, 270, 275, 298, 305, 414, 417

fact-finding missions 459–65
ad hoc missions 462
child soldiers 463–5
Convention on the Rights of the Child 464
exchanges of views 464–5
Geneva Call's Deed of Commitment 465
International Humanitarian Fact-Finding Commission 459–62, 473
monitoring and verification of conduct 462–5
Red Cross, International Committee of the 462
responses to reports 141
sources of law of NIACs 141
fair trials
Additional Protocol II 75–6
capacity of actors 75–6
common Article 3 91
courts of non-state armed groups 75–6, 485–6, 549, 552–3, 559, 562
differentiation between NIACs and IACs 75–6
due process 306–8
International Criminal Court 485–6
intra-party protection 249
territorial control 186
FARC 20, 98, 127, 137, 196, 201, 202, 205, 208, 209, 219, 230, 231, 233, 234, 240, 242, 270, 277, 281, 287, 309, 314, 346, 357, 368, 419, 439, 440, 445, 447, 464, 519, 544, 555, 562–3

FDLR 286, 323, 357, 366, 421–2, 436, 464
feasibility, notion of 353–6
flags of truce and surrender 415–16
customary international law 415
Lieber Code 415–16
white flags 413, 415–16
FLEC 341
FLN 54, 72, 119, 197, 240, 241, 242, 245, 297, 444, 516–17, 523–4, 558, 562, 563–4
FMLN 73, 75–6, 106, 120, 131, 141, 142, 189, 197, 240, 242, 275, 279, 294, 298, 301, 312–13, 318, 339, 345–6, 349, 352, 355–6, 368, 382, 406, 418, 425, 437, 439, 443, 446, 552–3, 554, 558, 561, 563
FNLA 220
forcible transfers 285–9, 335
forests or plant cover, incendiary weapons and 398
former Yugoslavia *see also* **Bosnia; Croatia; International Criminal Tribunal for the former Yugoslavia; Kosovo; Macedonia**
belligerent reprisals 450, 452–3, 455–6
combatant immunity 517
displaced persons 286–7, 292
domestic criminal courts 488, 492–3, 496–8, 500
prisoners of war 524–5
Serbia 125, 369, 406, 497, 524
France 500 *see also* **Algerian War of Independence**
FRELIMO 73, 215
'Fundamental Standards of Humanity' initiative 52, 565–7

GAM 465, 520, 551
gas and chemical weapons 393–6
Gaza 425, 556
gender *see* **women**
General Assembly (UN)
customary international law 55–6, 466
distinction, principle of 105
human rights 44–5, 466
humanitarian assistance 329–30, 332
implementation and non-judicial enforcement 466
incendiary weapons 397
international humanitarian law 466
missing persons 284
national liberation, wars of 213–16
protected zones 383
resolutions 55–6, 105, 213–16, 284, 329–30, 332, 383, 397, 466
Geneva Call
anti-personnel mines 113, 243–4, 408, 538–45
children 113, 537, 541–2
Deed of Commitment 13, 243–4, 408, 432, 435, 465, 539–45
dissemination 432
engaging compliance 538–46
equality of obligations 243–4
fact-finding missions 465

Geneva Call (*cont.*)
  Geneva Conventions 539
  human rights 542
  implementation and non-judicial enforcement 538–46
  instruction 435
  international humanitarian law 541–2
  missions 540–1
  monitoring 539–41
  peer pressure 544
  publicity for instances of compliance 541
  routine follow-up missions 540–1
  self-monitoring 540
  sexual and gender-based violence 113
  unilateral declarations 113
  verification missions 540–1
Geneva Conventions 30–42 *see also* **Additional Protocol I to Geneva Conventions; Additional Protocol II to Geneva Conventions; common Article 3 of Geneva Conventions; diplomatic conferences**
  abolition of differentiation between NIACs and IACs 49
  agreements 444
  anti-personnel mines 406–7
  belligerency, recognition of 19–20
  belligerent reprisals 449
  capacity of actors to comply with 72–3, 157
  children 315
  civilians and persons *hors de combat*, protection of 24, 35, 39
  combatant immunity 517–19
  commentaries 78, 162, 180, 468
  commitments 111, 112, 443–4
  depositary 121
  displaced persons 285, 287
  dissemination 431–2
  domestic criminal courts 488, 490–1, 493–4, 499–500
  due process 307–8
  engaging compliance 546–7
  European Convention on Human Rights 90
  extension to NIACs 40–1
  Gas Protocol 393–6
  grave breaches 475–7, 479, 488, 499–500
  hostages, taking of 270
  human rights 86, 501–3
  identification of NIACs 157
  International Criminal Tribunal for the former Yugoslavia 479
  International Humanitarian Fact-Finding Commission 459–60, 473
  international humanitarian law 85, 99
  interned and detained persons 113
  intra-party protection 247–9
  legal advice 437
  legislation 140
  Lieber Code 27
  medical and religious personnel 278–9
  national liberation, wars of 212–16, 219–20
  NIACs, definition of 155
  non-state armed groups, purported accession by 118–19
  organization of non-state armed groups, level of 177
  peacekeeping missions 327
  personal scope of application 240–2
  Preamble 41–2
  precautions 352–3
  prisoners of war 37, 39, 518–19, 522–5
  protecting powers system 457
  ratification 4447
  reciprocity 31, 37, 39
  Red Cross, International Committee of the 30–9, 59, 78, 162, 180, 467–70, 475, 477, 515–16
  targeting 338
  unilateral declarations 116–22
  universal jurisdiction 499–500
  violence, characterization of 203, 206, 207–8
  war crimes 475–7
  wounded, sick, and shipwrecked 33, 39, 247–8, 273
geographical scope of application 250–2
  ad hoc international criminal tribunals 250
  Additional Protocol II 250–1
  boundaries, drawing of arbitrary 251
  common Article 3 250
  human rights treaties, derogations to 250
  International Criminal Tribunal for the former Yugoslavia 250
  international humanitarian law 250–2
  personal scope 252
  Red Cross, International Committee of the 251
Georgia 282
good offices 459, 460
government/state forces
  beneficiaries of protection 359–62, 372
  definition 184, 191
  identification of NIACs 184
  intensity of violence 169
  loss of protection 365–7
  NIACs, definition of 155, 164, 180
  police, use of 169
  Tadić decision 180
governments, unrecognized 560–1
GPRA 524
grave breaches
  domestic criminal courts 488, 499–500
  Geneva Conventions 475–7, 479, 488, 499–500
  International Criminal Tribunal for Rwanda 480
  International Criminal Tribunal for the former Yugoslavia 479
  war crimes 475–7
graves, respect for 282–4
Greece 11, 15, 17, 141–2
Guatemala 131, 243
Gulf War 1990–1 350

Hague Convention on Cultural Property 376–80, 429
  belligerent reprisals 449, 452

Index

customary international law 56
differentiation between NIACs and IACs 62
dissemination 431–2, 433
domestic criminal courts 498
enhanced protection 379–80
International Criminal Court 62
international humanitarian law 62, 63, 64
personal scope of application 236–7
Second Protocol 62, 237, 377, 379–80, 498
systematic regulation 42–3, 54
war crimes, list of 62
Hague Conventions of 1899 and 1907 34, 36, 40–2, 244, 287, 320, 470, 479
Haiti 17, 18
hardship 330, 338
Havana Convention on Duties and Rights of States in the Event of Civil Strife, Protocol to 20
heads of state and high-ranking officials, loss of protection of 366–7
Honduras 31
hors de combat, persons who are *see* civilians and persons *hors de combat,* protection of
hospitals
  protected zones, as 383–5
  wounded, sick, and shipwrecked, protection of 274
hostages, taking of
  ad hoc agreements 270
  ceasefire agreements 270
  common Article 3 268–9
  customary international law 268
  definition 269
  expanding bullets 403
  Geneva Conventions 270
  humane treatment 268–71
  international humanitarian law 268, 271
  Taking of Hostages, Convention against the 269
HPG 446, 462, 463, 555
human rights 83–99 *see also* **life, right to**
  Additional Protocol I 86, 503–4
  Additional Protocol II 83, 86, 87, 91, 94, 501–3
  African Charter on Human and Peoples' Rights 83, 503
  agreements 97, 129–32
  American Convention on Human Rights 501–3
  application 83–99
  Cairo Declaration on Human Rights in Islam 101–2, 527–8
  Capacity to respect 124
  Charter of the UN 85–6
  child soldiers 79, 87–8, 323–4
  Cluster Munitions Convention 83
  Commission on Human Rights (UN) 467
  commitments 111
  Committee on the Rights of the Child 467
  common Article 3 87, 501–3
  Convention on the Rights of Persons with Disabilities 83, 87
  Convention on the Rights of the Child 87–8

courts 904, 500–5, 510, 556, 558
creation of law of non-international armed conflict 2–3
criminal process, persons subject to 306
customary international law 98
dead persons, protection of 282–3
derogations 83–4, 250
dignity 86
diplomatic conferences 44–6, 52, 87
direct regulation by 93–9
Disappearances Convention 87
due process 307–8, 310
environment 526, 527–8
equality of obligations 243
European Convention on Human Rights 90–4, 372, 503–4, 510
fair trial, right to a 91
gaps in protection 564–5
General Assembly (UN) 44–5, 466
Geneva Call 542
Geneva Conventions 86, 501–3
geographical scope of application 250
Human Rights Council (HRC) (UN) 467
Human Rights Watch 472–3
humanitarian assistance 329–30
implementation and non-judicial enforcement 472–3, 500–5
Inter-American Commission on Human Rights 59, 501–5, 508, 556
Inter-American Court of Human Rights 502
International Council on Human Rights Policy 563
International Covenant on Civil and Political Rights 83–4, 87, 91, 307–8, 311
International Covenant on Economic, Social and Cultural Rights 85, 87
International Criminal Tribunal for the former Yugoslavia 89, 95
international humanitarian law 2, 84–99, 467, 472–3, 500–4
International Law Commission 85
internment 90–1
interpretation 88–99
judicial enforcement 500–5, 510
lex specialis rule 89–92
loss of protection 370–2
Martens Clause 86
medical experimentation 91
military necessity 87
missing persons 284
motivations for taking up arms, expressions of 143
naming and shaming 472–3
non-governmental organisations 472–3
non-state armed groups 95–8, 111
peace agreements 443
preambular references 132
precautions 352, 356
press releases and other ad hoc statements 142
Red Cross, International Committee of the 85
regulation 83–99
sanctions 448
Secretary-General (UN) 44–7

human rights (cont.)
  Security Council 467
  state responsibility 503–4
  targeting 337
  Tehran International Conference on Human Rights 44–5, 53, 86
  terminology 131
  territorial control 97–8, 530–2, 565
  torture, definition of 88–9
  treaties and conventions 83–7, 250, 467
  treaty bodies 467
  unilateral declarations 123–4
  United Nations 44–7, 53, 85, 467
  Universal Declaration of Human Rights 85, 86, 87, 123, 329
  war crimes 79
human shields 420–3
  Additional Protocol I 421–2
  buffers, used as 421
  civilians 420–3
  customary international law 420–1
  direct part on hostilities, taking a 422–3
  disproportionate attacks 422–3
  humane treatment 420
  involuntary shields 420–2
  Red Cross, International Committee of the 421
  voluntary shields 422–3
  war crimes 421
humane treatment 255–72
  ad hoc agreements 256–7, 334–5
  Additional Protocol II 257–8, 334
  belligerent reprisals 450
  ceasefire agreements 256
  collective punishments 271–2
  common Article 3 255, 257–9, 334
  conduct of hostilities 336, 429
  cruel and inhuman treatment 262–3
  customary international law 255, 258, 334
  differentiation between NIACs and IACs 69–70
  hostages, taking of 268–71
  human shields 420
  instructions and codes of conduct 255–6, 334–5
  international humanitarian law 255, 334
  murder 260–1
  nationality, discrimination on grounds of 259
  non-discrimination 258–9
  outrages upon personal dignity 263–4, 334
  peace agreements 256–7
  principle 255–8
  prisoners of war 521, 524
  Red Cross, International Committee of the 259
  sexual violence 264–8, 334
  slavery and slave trade 268
  specific prohibitions 259–72
  territorial control 530
  torture 261–2, 334
  violence to life and person 259–63
  wounded, sick, and shipwrecked 274–5
humanitarian assistance 328–34
  Additional Protocol II 329–32
  air, relief provided by 333–4
  bilateral agreements 333–4
  Charter of UN 328–30
  civilians, protection as 328–9
  consent 330–4, 335
  customary international law 329, 330
  detention 329
  distinction 330
  essential supplies, definition of 330
  General Assembly resolutions 329–30, 332
  Guiding Principles 330
  hardship 330
  human rights 329–30
  impartiality 330–2
  military necessity 331–2
  missions 328–9
  Nicaragua case 329–30
  Red Crescent 329
  Red Cross, International Committee of the 329, 333–4, 471
  refusal of offers 332–4
  relief societies 329–33
  starvation of civilians 424
  territorial control 332–3
  unilateral declarations 333–4
  Universal Declaration of Human Rights 329
humanitarian law *see* **international humanitarian law**
humanity, principle of 370–1
humiliating and degrading treatment 263–4
Hungary 33–4, 119–20, 140, 522

ICC Elements of Crimes
  displaced persons 288
  due process guarantees 307–9
  expanding bullets 403
  pillage 426
  regularly constituted courts 306
  sexual violence 265–6
identification *see* **identification of NIACs; identification of persons**
identification of NIACs 155–211 *see also* **distinction between NIACs and IACs**
  Additional Protocol II 162, 182–93, 210
  advantages and disadvantages of lack of definition 162–4
  agreements 111
  banditry, situations of 162, 178, 204–5
  belligerency, recognition of 157–9, 161, 195–6
  borderline cases 163
  capacity of non-state armed groups 157
  civil war, level of 161
  common Article 3 156–7, 160–3
  de jure governments 158
  denials of existence of armed conflicts 5, 102–4, 162–4, 200–4, 210
  diplomatic conferences 155–85, 192, 206–7, 210
  Geneva Conventions 156–64
  government/state forces 184
  identity of actors 156, 158
  insurgency, situations of 162
  intensity of violence 199

internal tensions and disturbances 161–2
International Criminal Court 192–5, 210
minimum rules 158–9
NIACs, definition of 155–82, 210
non-definition approach 156–64, 192
organized armed groups 184–5
prerequisites for particular rules to apply 182–96
protracted armed conflicts, definition of 192–5
Red Cross, International Committee of the 47
responsible command 184–5
territorial control 157, 185–7, 210
sustained and concerted military operations 188
United Nations, dispute admitted to Agenda of 158
violence, characterization of 196–209
war crimes 193–4

identification of persons
dead persons 283–4
destruction of identity 376
displaced persons 290
documents 290
journalists 312
loss of protection 367

illiteracy 434, 566
immunity *see* **combatant immunity**
impartiality *see* **neutrality**
imperative military necessity 287–8, 291, 377, 379–80
implementation and non-judicial enforcement 430–74, 532–49 *see also* **capacity of non-state armed groups for enforcement and compliance**
ad hoc commitments 474
belligerent reprisals 430, 448–57
bilateral agreements 442–5
children 533–8
commitments 442–5
compliance, engaging 532–8, 542–9
dissemination 431–4
fact-finding missions 459–65, 473
'Fundamental Standards of Humanity' initiative 566
General Assembly (UN) 466
Geneva Call 538–46
human rights 472–3, 500–5
instruction 434–7
internal mechanisms 430, 431–48, 474
manuals, codes of conduct, and internal regulations 438–42, 474
organization of non-state armed groups, level of 178–9, 210
personal convictions 430–1
protecting powers 457–8, 473
public opinion 430
Red Cross, International Committee of the 467–72, 474
reputation 430
sanctions 445–8
Security Council (UN) 465–6, 473–4
third parties 430, 457–74, 566
unilateral declarations 442–5

United Nations 465–7, 473–4
war crimes 77, 82–3
impunity 550, 555
incendiary weapons 397–9, 527
India 437, 555
indiscriminate attacks 338, 347–8
anti-personnel mines 392, 404–5, 406
booby traps 404
civilians 390–1
customary international law 348, 390–1, 409
distinction, principle of 44, 102–3, 105, 337–8, 342
incendiary weapons 398
International Criminal Court 391
International Criminal Tribunal of former Yugoslavia 391, 392
military objectives, failure to identify 347–8
non-detectable fragments 410
nuclear weapons 391
targeting 338, 347–8
weapons 390–2, 398, 404–6, 409–10
individual criminal responsibility 77, 79, 100, 475, 478
Indonesia
combatant immunity 520
courts of non-state armed groups 551
fact-finding missions 462–3, 465
national liberation, wars of 218
peace, spaces or zones of 386
informers 39
infrastructure 350
inhuman treatment *see* **humane treatment**
Institute of International Law (IIL) 44, 498–9
instruction as a mechanism for interpretation and enforcement 434–7
anti-personnel mines 435
child soldiers 436
customary international law 435
education and training 435–7
Geneva Call Deed of Commitment 435
international humanitarian law 435–6
Red Cross, International Committee of the 435–6
Security Council resolutions 435
terrorist groups, providing material support to 435
instructions, codes of conduct, and internal regulations 107, 133–9, 438–42
ad hoc regulation 20, 21–4, 28–30
Additional Protocol I 438–9
belligerency, recognition of 28
commentaries 433–4
commitments 107, 133–9
courses of instruction 433–4
creation of law of non-international armed conflict 563
customary international law 139, 438
dissemination 433–4
doctors in the field 24
Geneva Conventions 438–9, 441
group measures 438–42
humane treatment 255–6, 334–5

instructions, codes of conduct, and internal
    regulations (cont.)
  International Council on Human Rights
    Policy 563
  international humanitarian law 438, 441
  international standards, consistency with 440–1
  interned and detained persons 297–9
  Lieber Code 23–4, 28
  manuals 433–4
  military codes 441–2
  military necessity, definition of 23
  non-state armed groups 134, 438–42
  opinio juris 438
  Penal and Disciplinary Rules 135
  pillage 427–8
  political wings of armed groups 440
  precautions 355–6
  Red Cross, International Committee of the 440
  regulation 20, 21–4, 28–30
  sexual violence 267
  sources of law of NIACs 133–9
  state measures 438
insurgency
  belligerency, recognition of 9–10
  capacity 12
  common Article 3 162
  identification of NIACs 162
  levels of violence 9–10
  political organization 10
intelligence personnel 369
intensity of violence 164, 165–70
  Additional Protocol II 169, 188, 190
  armed forces rather than police, use by state of 169
  diplomatic conferences 169
  due process 308
  duration 167–9
  identification of NIACs 199
  indicia 167–70
  International Criminal Tribunal of former Yugoslavia 169
  large-scale violence 167–8
  national liberation, wars of 217, 222
  NIACs, definition of 164, 165–70, 181, 192, 210
  organization, elements of 167, 168–9, 177–8
  protracted violence 167–8, 188
  sustained and concerted military operations 188
  Tadić decision 167–9
  territorial control 186
  transnational/extra-state armed conflicts 232
  violence, characterization of 199
Inter-American Commission on Human
    Rights 59, 501–5, 508, 556
internal affairs of state, interference in 469–71
internal mechanisms for implementation and
    non-judicial enforcement 430, 431–48
  bilateral agreements 442–5
  commitments 442–5
  dissemination 431–4
  instruction 434–7
  legal advice 437

manuals, codes of conduct, and internal
    regulations 438–42, 474
sanctions 445–8
unilateral declarations 442–5
internal regulations *see* instructions, codes of
    conduct, and internal regulations
internal tensions and disturbances 161–2
International Committee of the Red Cross *see* Red
    Cross, International Committee of the
International Covenant on Civil and Political
    Rights 83–4, 87, 91, 307–8, 311
International Covenant on Economic, Social
    and Cultural Rights 85, 87
International Criminal Court *see* ICC Elements
    of Crime; International Criminal Court,
    Rome Statute of
International Criminal Court, Rome Statute
    of 482–5
  Additional Protocol II 188, 210, 506
  amendment 63
  amnesties 506
  application to NIACs 429
  arrest warrants 483–4
  child soldiers 317, 320, 323
  civilian objects, attacks on 342
  civilians, attacks on 339
  command responsibility 557
  common Article 3 482
  complementarity 485, 488, 509
  courts of armed groups 485–6, 488
  cruel and inhuman treatment 262–3
  cultural property 377, 381
  customary international law 80, 106, 482
    Baxter paradox 106
  definition of NIACs 92, 164, 166, 181, 192
  differentiation between NIACs and IACs 70–1
  dignity, outrages upon personal 263
  displaced persons 285, 288
  disproportionate attacks 79–80, 349, 350–1
  domestic criminal courts 494–5, 498
  drafting 481
  expanding bullets 71, 402–3
  fair trials 485–6
  forced displacement 80
  gas and chemical weapons 396
  Hague Convention on Cultural Property 62
  identification of NIACs 192–5, 210
  impact 484–5
  indiscriminate use of weapons 391
  international humanitarian law 62, 63–4, 66–7, 483
  intra-party protection 249
  jurisdiction 482–4
  list of war crimes 483
  medical and religious personnel 278–9
  ne bis in idem 485–6
  NIACs, definition of 165, 166, 181
  omissions 483
  organization of armed groups 175–7, 192
  perfidy 420
  precautions 351
  protracted armed conflict, definition of 192–5
  quarter, denial of 412

Security Council 483–4, 485
sexual violence 265
state referrals 483–4
sustained and concerted military
 operations 188
Tadić decision 483
targeting 429–30
universal jurisdiction 498
unnecessary suffering or superfluous
 injury 390
violence, characterization of 199
voluntary appearances 484–5
war crimes 79–81, 248–9, 323, 481–3,
 485, 487–8
 child soldiers 323
 customary international law 106
 differentiation between NIACs and IACs 70–1
 Hague Convention on Cultural Property 62
 international humanitarian law 62, 63–4
 medical units and transports 374
 protracted armed conflict, definition of 193–4
 unnecessary suffering or superfluous
  injury 390
 weapons 428–30
international criminal law 77–83
 see also **international criminal
  tribunals; war crimes**
 arrest warrants 483–4
 belligerent reprisals 77
 child soldiers 323
 civilians, attacks on 339
 creation of law of non-international armed
  conflict 2–3
 direct part in hostilities, taking 363
 displaced persons 287, 335
 disproportionate attacks 429
 environment 528–9
 gas and chemical weapons 396
 individual criminal responsibility 77, 79, 100,
  475, 478
 International Criminal Court 323
 international criminal tribunals 55
 international humanitarian law 2, 77
 perfidy 420, 429
 regulation 55, 77–83, 99
 sexual violence 267
 torture 261
International Criminal Tribunal for Rwanda
 Additional Protocol II 56, 480–1
 child soldiers 318
 common Article 3 480–1
 customary international law 56
 domestic criminal courts 488, 497–8, 500
 grave violations 480
 international humanitarian law 479, 481
 list of violations 480–1
 NIACs, definition of 167
 organization of non-state armed groups, level
  of 170, 175
 responsible command 175
 sexual violence 265
 Statute, report on the 480
 Tadić decision 479, 480

territorial control 186–7
transnational/extra-state armed conflicts 232
travaux préparatoires 480
unilateral declarations 109–10
violence, characterization of 199
war crimes 478, 480–1
**International Criminal Tribunal for the former
 Yugoslavia** *see also* ***Tadić* decision**
 ad hoc agreements 82
 Additional Protocol I 58
 Additional Protocol II 57–9, 60, 66, 188,
  192, 479
 belligerent reprisals 77
 civilian objects, attacks on 342
 civilians, attacks on 339, 341
 combatant immunity 519
 common Article 3 479
 cruel and inhuman treatment 262
 customary international law 56–60, 102, 104,
  107, 479
 deferral, operation on basis of 497–8
 dignity, outrages upon personal 263
 displaced persons 289
 domestic criminal courts 488, 493,
  497–8, 500
 Geneva Conventions, grave breaches of 479
 geographical scope of application 250
 Hague Convention 1907 479
 human rights 89, 95
 indiscriminate use of weapons 391, 392
 intensity of violence 169
 international humanitarian law 66
 journalists 313
 NIACs, definition of 155–6, 164–7, 210
 Nuremberg Military Tribunal 479
 organization of non-state armed groups, level
  of 170, 176, 177–80
 perfidy 420
 precautions 355
 referrals 497–8
 Security Council resolutions 479
 sexual violence 265–6
 territorial control 531–2
 torture, definition of 89
 troops, intervention through use of 223–5
 UN Secretary-General 478–9
 unilateral declarations 110
 voluntary appearances 485
 wanton destruction 428
 war crimes 60, 81, 82, 475, 478
international criminal tribunals 55 *see also*
 **International Criminal Court, Rome
  Statute of; International Criminal
  Tribunal for Rwanda; International
  Criminal Tribunal for the former
  Yugoslavia**
 ad hoc tribunals 167, 250
 authorization by Security Council 466
 customary international law 56–61, 429
 enforcement 478–88, 509
 geographical scope of application 250
 international humanitarian law 78
 loss of protection 366

international criminal tribunals (cont.)
  NIACs, definition of 167
  regulation 55
  Special Court for Sierra Leone 109, 166, 272, 487, 508–9
  war crimes 77–8
international human rights law see human rights
International Humanitarian Fact-Finding Commission 459–62
  Additional Protocol I 459–60
  Additional Protocol II 460
  common Article 3 460, 473
  consent, role of 460–1
  declarations 460–1
  enquiries 459–61
  equality of obligations 461
  Geneva Conventions 459–60, 473
  good offices 459, 460
  Red Cross, International Committee of the 461
  serious violations 459–60
  Tadić decision 459
international humanitarian law 1, 2–3, 61–77
  see also customary international law
  ad hoc regulation 2, 9–29, 53
  Additional Protocol I 68–9
  Additional Protocol II 51–2, 64, 66–9
  agreements 5, 26–7, 125–31, 443–5
  belligerent reprisals 450, 453
  beneficiaries of protection 359–60, 362
  bilateral agreements 5
  capital punishment 310–11
  Certain Conventional Weapons Convention 1980 62–3
  children 68, 79, 81, 315–16, 319, 323–4
  civilian objects, attacks on 342, 347
  civilians, attacks on 339
  combatant immunity 513, 514
  commitments 107
  common Article 3 of Geneva Conventions 66
  courts of non-state armed groups 552–9
  creation of law of non-international armed conflict 2–3
  criminal process, persons subject to 305
  cultural property 375–7
  customary international law 69
  Declaration on Minimum Humanitarian Standards 52
  Declaration on the Rules of International Humanitarian Law 52, 105–6
  definition of NIAC 67–8
  deportation 68–9
  dignity 86, 263–4
  diplomatic conferences 40–2, 66, 78
  direct part in hostilities, taking 362
  direct regulation 93–9
  displaced persons 285, 287–90, 335
  disproportionate attacks 350–1
  dissemination 432
  distinction between IACs and NIACs 61–2, 65, 69–77
  domestic criminal courts 488, 494, 497–8
  dual-use objects 347
  environment 526

forced displacement 80
gaps in protection 564–5
gas and chemical weapons 396
General Assembly (UN) 466
Geneva Call 541–2
Geneva Conventions 85, 99
geographical scope of application 250–2
Hague Convention on Cultural Property 1954 62, 63, 64
hostages, taking 268, 271
human rights 2, 84–99, 467, 472–3, 500–4
humane treatment 255, 334
instruction 435–6
international Covenant on Civil and Political Rights 87
International Criminal Court 62, 63–4, 66–7, 483
international criminal law 2, 77, 323
International Criminal Tribunal for Rwanda 479, 481
International Criminal Tribunal for the former Yugoslavia 66
interned and detained persons 90–1, 296
interpretation 79–82, 88–93
intra-party protection 247
judicial enforcement 475
legislation 140–1
levels of protection 68–9
lex specialis rule 89–92
Lieber Code 85
life, right to 85–6, 91–2, 373
loss of protection 370–1
manuals, codes of conduct, and internal regulations 438, 441
Martens Clause 86
medical experimentation 91
minimum standards 52
model of IACs 63–5
national liberation, wars of 214–16, 220, 222, 234
NIACs, definition of 155
peace agreements 443
peacekeeping missions 324–8
personal scope of application 236–49
precautions 356
primary rules 77, 81
prisoners of war 513
protected zones 385–6
protecting powers system 457
reciprocity 244–5
Red Cross, International Committee of the 468–71
regulation 2, 9–53, 61–77, 99
scope/content nexus of NIAC 66–8
secondary rules 77
Security Council (UN) 465–6
serious violations 77, 81
sexual violence 267, 314
slavery and slave trade 268
St Petersburg Declaration on Explosive Projectiles 85
state sovereignty 65
systematic regulation 30–53

Index

targeting 337
temporal scope of application 253–4
territorial control 97–8, 529–32
torture 261
treaties and conventions 61–5, 85, 87
United Nations 85, 328
violence 202–3, 206–9, 259–60
war crimes 67, 77–83, 475–8
women 313–14
International Institute of International Humanitarian Law (IIHL) 105–6, 435
Internationalization of armed conflict
see troops, intervention by outside states through use of
interned and detained persons 292–305
see also prisoners of war
abuse 292
Additional Protocol II 292–3, 295
bilateral agreements 295
Brussels Declaration 1874 294
capacity 76, 293, 295–7
ceasefire agreements 305
civilians and persons hors de combat, protection of 292–305, 334
codes of conduct 297–9
commitments 114
common Article 3 292
conditions 293–7
contact with families 295
correspondence 295
customary international law 292, 294–5
differentiation between NIACs and IACs 76
displaced persons 290
European Convention on Human Rights 90–1
evacuation 296
Geneva Conventions 90, 114
human rights 90–1
humanitarian assistance 329
international humanitarian law 90–1, 296
legal basis for security detention/internment 301–5
liberty and security, right to 90–1
location of places of detention 296
medical examinations and treatment 295, 296
medical experimentation 296
minimum obligations 293–5
peace agreements 305
peacekeeping missions 325
political detainees 34, 42
records of personal details 295
Red Cross, International Committee of the 42, 114
release 297, 300–1
religion 294
reviews 76
searches for missing persons 295
specificities of NIACs 296–300
statements 297–9
territorial control 186–7
treaties and conventions 294
treatment, standards of 293
visits 295
women, separation of 295, 314

intervention in a NIAC see troops, intervention by outside states through use of; outside states, intervention by
intra-party protection 246–9
investigative duty and right to life 92–3, 372–3
Iran
  instruction 435
  Kurds 316, 353, 435
Iraq
  courts of non-state armed groups 561
  domestic criminal courts 497
  engaging compliance 545
  environment 527
  gas and chemical weapons 394–5
  Geneva Call Deed of Commitment 545
  Gulf War 1990–1 350
  Iraqi Special Tribunal 497
  Kurds 394–5, 545
Ireland
  1922, civil war in 34, 35
  peer pressure 545
  press releases and other ad hoc statements 141
  prisoners of war 522
  Red Cross, International Committee of the 470–1
Israel 218, 370–1
Ivory Coast 520, 534, 560

JEM 109, 122–3, 124, 128, 132, 135, 141, 191, 202, 257, 268, 292, 300, 301, 316, 322, 333, 340, 343, 356, 417, 436, 439, 447, 463, 464, 484, 485, 517, 534, 535, 537, 538, 556
journalists 311–13
  accreditation 312
  armed forces, as members of the 311
  civilian protection 311–13
  dangerous professional missions 311–13
  definition 311–12
  direct part in hostilities, taking 312–13, 364–5
  embedded journalists 312–13
  equipment and buildings 313
  identity cards 312
  International Criminal Tribunal for the former Yugoslavia 313
  propaganda, broadcasting of 313
  taking part in hostilities 312–13
  war correspondents 311–13
judicial enforcement 475–510 see also courts of non-state armed groups
  amnesties 475, 505–9
  domestic criminal courts 488–500, 509
  human rights courts 500–5, 510
  international criminal courts and tribunals 478–88, 509
  international humanitarian law 475
  training of judges 551
  war crimes 475–8, 509–10
jus cogens 478

Katanga 270–1, 374
Kenya 200–1, 470
KLA 122, 135, 142, 178, 191, 223, 303, 369, 436, 439, 463, 485, 554, 565

KNA 322
KNLA 316, 322, 463
KNPP 322, 405, 463, 465, 537
KNU 141, 316, 322, 436, 463, 464, 465, 555
Kosovo
  codes of conduct 135, 442
  courts of non-state armed groups 554
  domestic criminal courts 496
  fact-finding missions 463
  Geneva Conventions 122
  human rights 142
  instructions, codes of conduct, and internal
    regulations 135
  International Criminal Tribunal for the former
    Yugoslavia 485
  journalists 313
  loss of protection 369–70
  manuals, codes of conduct, and internal
    regulations 442
  NATO involvement 223
  organization of non-state armed groups, level
    of 178
  press releases and other ad hoc statements 142
  troops, intervention through use of 223
Kurds
  children 316
  courts of non-state armed groups 559
  engaging compliance 545
  gas and chemical weapons 394–5
  Geneva Call Deed of Commitment 541, 545
  instruction 435
  Iran 316, 353, 435
  Iraq 394–5, 545
  loss of protection 368–9
  organization of non-state armed groups, level
    of 179
  precautions 353
  sanctions 446
  Turkey 368–9
  United Nations 121

land mines *see* anti-personnel mines
laser weapons designed to cause permanent
    blindness 399–400
Lebanon 116, 181–2, 203
legal advice 433, 437
legislation
  courts of non-state armed groups 561
  domestic criminal courts 488, 490–5
  Geneva Convention 1864 140
  Hungarian revolution of 1919 140
  international humanitarian law 140–1
  non-state armed groups, by 140–1
  Red Cross, International Committee of the 140
  Russian revolution and civil war 140
  sources of law of NIACs 140–1
  states, by 140–1
  territorial control 140–1
legitimacy
  courts of non-state armed groups 557–62
  engaging compliance 546–9, 562
  Lieber Code 206
  military objectives 351–2

non-state armed groups 9, 29, 205–9
  violence, characterization of 205–9
lex specialis rule 89–92
Liberia 97, 127, 131–2, 447, 520
liberty and security, right to 90–1
Libya
  anti-personnel mines 408
  belligerency, recognition of 20
  cluster munitions 410
  courts of non-state armed groups 556
  dead persons, protection of 283
  dissemination 466
  equality of obligation 245
  flags of truce and surrender 416
  International Criminal Court 484, 485
  interned and detained persons 295, 298–9
  legal advice 437
  manuals, codes of conduct, and internal
    regulations 440
  motivations for taking up arms, expressions
    of 143
  NATO involvement 222, 224–5
  non-state armed groups, characterization of 205
  organization of non-state armed groups, level
    of 172
  precautions 353
  press releases and other ad hoc statements 142
  prisoners of war 525
Lieber Code
  belligerent reprisals 456
  emblems and uniforms, improper use of 417
  flags of truce and surrender 415–16
  Geneva Conventions 27
  instructions or declarations, regulation
    by 23–4, 27–8
  international humanitarian law 85
  legitimacy of armed groups 206
  perfidy 418–19
  poison and poisoned weapons 392–3
  prisoners of war 522
  quarter, denial of 412
  ruses 419
  starvation of civilians 423
  territorial control 531
  unnecessary suffering or superfluous
    injury 388
  warnings 354
life, right to 91–4
  American Convention on Human Rights 501
  arbitrary deprivation of life 91
  capacity 373
  capture 370–1
  European Convention on Human
    Rights 90–4, 370, 373
  human rights courts 501–2
  International Court of Justice 91–2
  international Covenant on Civil and Political
    Rights 91
  international humanitarian law 85–6,
    91–2, 373
  investigative duty 92–3, 372–3
  loss of protection 370–1
  nuclear weapons, use of 91

targeting 372–3
logistical roles, persons with 361–2
loss of protection from attack 365–72
  ad hoc participation 367
  Additional Protocol II 365–7
  beneficiaries of protection 365–72
  capacity 371–2
  capture, feasibility of 370
  civil servants 369
  civilians 365–8
  direct part in hostilities, taking 365–8
  heads of state and high-ranking
    officials 366–7
  human rights 370–2
  humanity, principles of 370–1
  identification 367
  informers 369
  intelligence personnel 369
  international criminal tribunals 366
  international humanitarian law 370–1
  Interpretative Guidance (ICRC) 366, 370–1
  life, right to 370–1
  military commanders 366
  military necessity and humanity 366–7
  military wings of armed groups 365–7
  necessary, no more use of force than 370–1
  police force, members of 368
  political figures 366–7
  political wings of armed groups 367, 371
  Red Cross, International Committee of
    the 366, 370–1
  representatives of the state 366–7
  revolving door problem 367
  state armed forces, members of 365–7
  targeting 365–72
  territorial control 371
  views of armed groups 368–70
LRA 127, 230, 234, 448, 483, 484, 485, 486,
  528, 535
LTTE 73, 98, 103, 120, 122, 132, 205, 218,
  238, 245, 254, 256, 257, 281, 287, 291,
  303, 322, 323, 340–1, 366, 378, 383,
  386, 416, 421, 440, 446, 461, 529, 534,
  535, 543, 553, 554, 557, 558
LURD 131, 132, 292, 447, 520

Macedonia, former Yugoslav Republic of
  dead persons, protection of 281
  emblems and uniforms, improper use of 317
  Geneva Conventions 122
  International Criminal Tribunal for the former
    Yugoslavia 485
  manuals, codes of conduct, and internal
    regulations 442
  organization of non-state armed groups, level
    of 171, 172
  targeting 338
Malaya 200–1, 271
Mali 442
**manuals, codes of conduct, and internal
  regulations** 438–42
  Additional Protocol I 438–9
  customary international law 438

Geneva Conventions 438–9, 441
  instructions 438
  international humanitarian law 438, 441
  international standards, consistency with 440–1
  military codes, separation from 441–2
  non-state armed group measures 438–42
  opinio juris 438
  political wings of armed groups 440
  Red Cross, International Committee of
    the 440
  state measures 438
marine environment 528
maritime commerce, interference with 13, 16
maritime conflicts 438
markings of graves 283–4
Martens Clause 86
means of combat *see* **weapons**
media *see* **journalists**
medical and religious personnel 277–80
  Additional Protocol II 278–9
  bilateral agreements 279
  common Article 3 277–8
  confidentiality 279–80
  customary international law 278–9
  definition of medical personnel 278–9
  Geneva Conventions 278–9
  instructions or declarations, regulation by 24
  International Criminal Court 278–9
  religious personnel, definition of 278–9
  wounded, sick, and shipwrecked 274–5,
    277–80
medical examinations and treatment
  detention, in 295, 296
  hospitals 283–5, 274
medical experimentation 91, 296
medical units and transports 373–5
  ad hoc commitments 375
  Additional Protocol II 373–4
  customary international law 373–5
  definition 373–4
  Red Cross, Red Crescent or Red Crystal
    symbol 374–5
  war crimes 374
  warnings 374
  weapons, equipped with 374
  wounded and sick 373–4
methods of combat 412–28
  Additional Protocol II 428
  common Article 3 428
  emblems and uniforms, improper use of 416–18
  flags of truce and surrender 415–16
  human shields 420–3
  perfidy 418–20, 429
  pillage 426–8
  quarter, denial of 412–15
  starvation of civilians 423–6
  wanton destruction 428–9
Mexico
  emblems and uniforms, improper use of 417
  Geneva Conventions 122
  hostages, taking 270
  interned and detained persons 298
  quarter, denial of 414

Mexico (*cont.*)
  regularly constituted courts 305
  wounded, sick, and shipwrecked 275
MILF 72, 124, 127, 128, 131, 250, 270, 284, 292, 315, 320, 322, 333, 337, 340, 343, 351, 352, 424, 435, 439, 445, 446–7, 534, 535, 536, 539, 540, 541, 544, 545, 555
military advantage
  civilian objects, attacks on 344, 346
  civilians, attacks on 341
  disproportionate attacks 349–50
  environment 527
  precautions 354
  terrorizing civilians 341
military necessity
  cultural property 377, 379–80
  definition 23
  differentiation between NIACs and IACs 70
  displaced persons 287–8, 291
  disproportionate attacks 80
  human rights 87
  humanitarian assistance 331–2
  imperative military necessity 287–8, 291, 377, 379–80
  instructions or declarations, regulation by 23
  loss of protection 366–7
  pillage 426
  quarter, denial of 412
  starvation of civilians 424
  unnecessary suffering or superfluous injury 388–9
  wanton destruction 70, 428
military objectives *see also* targeting
  beneficiaries of protection 357–8
  civilian objects, attacks on 344–7
  dams, dykes, and nuclear electrical generating stations 382
  definition 344–7
  disproportionate attacks 349–50
  distinction, principle of 44, 102–3, 105, 337–8, 342
  failure to identify military objective 347–8
  indiscriminate attacks 347–8
  legitimate objectives 351–2
  precautions 351–2
military wings of armed groups
  beneficiaries of protection 359–62, 372, 429
  continuous combat function 360–2
  de facto membership 360–2, 365, 367, 372
  de jure membership 360–2, 365, 372, 429
  direct part in hostilities 360–2
  logistical roles, persons with 361–2
  loss of protection 365–7
mines *see* anti-personnel mines
missing persons 284–5
  ad hoc commitments 284
  Additional Protocol I 284
  customary international law 284–5
  General Assembly resolutions 284
  Guiding Principles on Internal Displacement 284
  human rights 284
  information, provision of 284–5
  searches 284–5, 295
MLC 135, 143, 256, 447, 484, 554
MNLF 506
MODEL 131, 292, 520,
monitoring 462–5, 539–41, 566
motivations for taking up arms
  expressions 143–51
  human rights 143
  NIACs, definition of 182
  non-state armed groups 143–51
Moynier, Gustave 30, 31
Mozambique 73, 75–6, 178, 491
MPLA 220
MRTA 122, 139
murder 260–1
Myanmar *see* Burma/Myanmar

naming and shaming 471–3, 533–8
napalm 397
national liberation, wars of 212–22, 234
  Additional Protocol I 118, 219–20, 222
  Additional Protocol II 217
  alien occupation, against 213, 216–20, 234
  colonial domination, against 213, 216–20, 234
  Common Article 3 213
  creation of law of non-international armed conflict 563
  definition 216–22, 234
  differentiation between NIACs and IACs 212–22, 234
  diplomatic conferences 213
  General Assembly resolutions 213–16
  Geneva Conventions 212–16, 219–20
  historical regulation 212–16
  intensity of violence 217, 222
  international humanitarian law 214–16, 220, 222, 234
  organization of non-state armed groups 222
  racist regimes, against 213, 217–20, 234
  Red Cross, International Committee of the 214, 221
  regional intergovernmental organizations, recognition by 221–2
  self-determination 216, 217–19
  territorial control 221
  unilateral declarations 118, 220–2
national liberation movements *see* national liberation, wars of
natural environment 526–9
  ad hoc agreements or declarations 528
  Additional Protocol II 526
  anti-personnel mines 405, 527
  Cairo Declaration on Human Rights in Islam 527–8
  cluster munitions 409
  customary international law 527
  dams and dykes, destruction of 526
  endangered species 528
  Environmental Modification Convention 526–7
  human rights 526, 527–9
  Incendiary Weapons Protocol 527

international criminal law 528–9
international humanitarian law 526
marine environment 528
nature reserves as demilitarized zones or protected areas 528
pillage 526
proportionality 527
Stockholm Declaration 528
substantial military advantage 527
weapons 527
natural resources, use of 426–7
nature of the law 2–3
nature reserves as demilitarized zones or protected areas 528
NDFP 88, 113, 120–1, 129, 133, 134, 141, 172, 179, 205, 209, 219, 221, 243, 256, 264, 267, 281, 299–300, 303, 304, 305, 321, 322–3, 337–8, 348, 357, 360, 369, 408, 427, 432, 439, 440, 442, 447, 464, 524, 535, 538, 549, 550–1, 556
ne bis in idem 485–6
necessity *see* military necessity
Nepal 122, 414, 446, 520, 545, 551
Netherlands 491, 493, 499
neutrality
 belligerency, recognition of 10, 15, 17–19
 decision-makers 196–9, 21
 emblems and uniforms, improper use of 416–17
 humanitarian assistance 330–2
 Red Cross, International Committee of the 416
 United Nations 416
Nicaragua 384, 518
Niger 256
Nigeria 438 *see also* **Biafran conflict**
NLA 122, 171, 172, 281, 338, 417, 442, 485, 519
non-detectable fragments 410–11
non-governmental organizations (NGOs) 107, 132, 430, 443, 472–3, 533, 555
 see also **particular organizations**
non-interference in other states *see* **outside states, intervention by**
non-international armed conflicts *see* **creation and development of non-international armed conflict law; definition of NIACs; differentiation between NIACs and IACs; identification of NIACs**
non-state armed groups *see also* **organization of non-state armed groups, level of; territorial control by non-state armed groups**
 agreements 124–5
 bandits 162, 178, 204–5, 370, 522
 capacity 124
 characterization 204–5
 civilians 429
 cluster munitions 409–10
 codes of conduct 134, 438–42
 courts of non-state armed groups 75–6, 549–62
 de facto states 73
 differentiation between NIACs and IACs 71–6, 99–100
 displaced persons 291

dissemination 432–3
enhancement of status 16
fact-finding missions 141
'Fundamental Standards of Humanity' initiative 565–7
Geneva Conventions, purported accession to 118–19
group measures 438–42
human rights 95–8, 111, 123–4
instructions, codes of conduct, and internal regulations 134
international law 3–4, 5
intra-party protection 246–9
legal status 205–9
legislation 140–1
legitimacy, granting 9, 29, 205–9
manuals, codes of conduct, and internal regulations 438–42
military wings of armed groups 359–62, 365–7, 372, 429
motivations for taking up arms, expressions of 143–51
outside states, control by 225–8, 234
participation in creation and development of law 106–8, 537–8, 562–4
personal scope of application 236–42
political wings 10, 367, 371, 440
practice of non-state armed groups 152
press releases and other ad hoc statements 141–2
proposal for instrument binding states and non-state armed groups 565–6
recognition 291
Red Cross, International Committee of the 119–20, 204, 429
rules, declarations on particular 122–3
terrorists 204–5
traitors 15
Twitter accounts 141
unilateral declarations 118–25
views of armed groups 368–70
violence, characterization of 204–5
websites 141
women 314
NPA 133, 134, 172, 205, 299–300, 321, 323, 324, 360, 361, 369, 408, 427, 432, 442, 447, 524, 535
NPFL 127–8, 143, 517
NRA 134, 256, 260, 267, 276, 298, 340, 343, 414, 427, 439, 442, 445, 545
NRM 132, 384, 517
NTC 20, 143, 225, 283, 284, 295, 300, 408, 566
nuclear electrical generating stations 381–3
nuclear weapons 91, 391
nullum crimen sine lege **principle** 81
Nuremberg Military Tribunal 475, 479

observance of law and customs of war 10–11, 12, 489–94
occupation
 belligerent occupation, law of 529–31
 national liberation, wars of 213, 216–20, 234

occupation (cont.)
  orderly administration 11, 12
Office of the Special Representative of the Secretary-General for Children and Armed Conflict 534–7, 542, 547
omissions 483
ONLF 123, 218, 340, 413, 420, 533
open relief centres 386
opinio juris 55, 57, 102, 105, 438
orders, dissemination of 433–4
organization of non-state armed groups, level of 170–82
  Additional Protocol II 174, 178, 184–5, 189
  capacity to comply with law 177–8
  command responsibility 175–6, 179
  command structure 170, 172–80, 210
  common Article 3 178–9
  decentralized groups 175
  degree of organization 185
  diplomatic conferences 174, 178, 184–5
  discipline 171–6, 178–80
  duration of conflicts 167, 177
  effective control 176
  enforcement of law 178–9, 210
  Geneva Conventions 177
  identification of NIACs 184–5
  implementation of law 178
  indicia of organization 170–8
  intensity of violence 167, 168–9, 177–8
  International Criminal Court 175–7
  International Criminal Tribunal for Rwanda 170, 175
  International Criminal Tribunal for the former Yugoslavia 170, 176, 177–80
  national liberation, wars of 222
  NIACs, definition of 164, 165–7, 168, 170–82, 192, 210
  parties to the conflict, notion of 177
  political organization 10
  practice, organization in 172–4
  rationale for organization 176–80
  responsible command, 174–6, 179–80, 210
  statements 171
  training 171
outrages upon personal dignity 263–4, 334
outside states, intervention by 222–8
  Cold War 222
  dependence and control test 227
  differentiation between NIACs and IACs 212, 222–8, 234
  effective control 226–8
  forms 222
  International Criminal Court 226–7
  International Criminal Tribunal for the former Yugoslavia 226–8
  internationalization 226
  non-state armed groups, outside state control of 225–8, 234
  organization and coordination test 227
  proxy, notion of 227
  rebellion 9–10
  Tadić decision 226–8
  troops, through use of 222–5, 234

Oxford Manual on the Laws of War on Land 438

Pairings approach 223–4
Pakistan and war on terror 233–4
parallel declarations 114–15
Paris Principles 320–1
participation of non-state armed groups in development of law 106–8, 537–8, 562–4
parties to the conflict, definition of 237
PDKI 316, 321, 353
peace agreements
  agreements 125, 256–7, 443
  displaced persons 292
  human rights 443
  humane treatment 256–7
  international humanitarian law 443
  interned and detained persons 305
  temporal scope of application 253
peace spaces or zones 386
peacekeeping missions 324–8
  Additional Protocol II 325–6
  agreements 327
  Charter of UN 324–7
  civilians, as 324–8
  customary international law 324
  definition 325
  detention 325
  Geneva Conventions 327
  international humanitarian law 324–8
  Safety of UN and Associated Personnel, Convention on 327
  self-defence, use of force in 325–6
  UN forces, application of international humanitarian law to 328
  violence, definition of 324–5
peer pressure 544–5
perfidy 418–20
  Additional Protocol II 70
  capital punishment 418
  customary international law 419–20
  definition 418
  diplomatic conferences 70
  International Criminal Court 420
  international criminal law 420, 429
  International Criminal Tribunal for the former Yugoslavia 420
  Lieber Code 418–19
  methods of combat 418–20, 429
  ruses 419
  state sovereignty 70
  Tadić decision 420
  war crimes 70–1, 419
personal convictions 430–1
personal scope of application 236–49
  asymmetry 244, 245–6
  child soldiers 237–8
  Cluster Munitions Convention 238, 240
  combatant immunity 243
  commitments 238
  common Article 3 239
  Convention on the Rights of the Child, Optional Protocol to 237–8

Index 647

Conventional Weapons Convention 236
customary international law 239
equality of obligation 242–6
Geneva Conventions 240–2
geographical scope of application 252
Hague Cultural Property Convention 236–7
individuals, treaties as being binding on 240–2
international humanitarian law 236–49
intra-party protection 246–9
non-state armed groups 236–42
Ottawa Convention on Anti-Personnel Mines 238, 240
parties to the conflict, definition of 237
reciprocity 244–5
Red Cross, International Committee of the 238, 241
territorial control 239
third parties, treaties as being binding on 240–2
treaties and conventions 236–41
Vienna Convention on the Law of Treaties 240

Peru
codes of conduct 134–5, 139, 439
Geneva Conventions 122
human rights courts 501
instructions, codes of conduct, and internal regulations 134–5, 139
interned and detained persons 298
manuals, codes of conduct, and internal regulations 439
pillage 428

Philippines
agreements 124, 128–31, 133
amnesties 505
anti-personnel mines 408, 539, 540–1
beneficiaries of protection 360–1
capacity 72
children 88, 315, 320, 322, 536
civilian objects, attacks on 343
civilians, attacks on 340
courts of non-state armed groups 550–1, 555
criminal process, persons subject to 305
dignity, outrages upon personal 264
disproportionate attacks 351
dissemination 432
domestic criminal courts 489–90
engaging compliance 544–5
equality of obligations 243
fact-finding missions 464
Geneva Call Deed of Commitment 539, 540–1, 544
Geneva Conventions 120–1
hostages, taking of 270
human rights 129–31
humane treatment 256
instruction 435
international humanitarian law 129–41, 133
interned and detained persons 299–300
loss of protection 369
manuals, codes of conduct, and internal regulations 439, 442
missing persons 284

national liberation, wars of 219
peer pressure 544–5
precautions 352, 357
press releases and other ad hoc statements 142
prisoners of war 524
protected zones 386
quarter, denial of 412
sanctions 445–7
starvation of civilians 424
targeting 338–9
United States, war with 412, 489–90, 505
pictorial presentation of information 434, 566
pillage 426–8
appropriation 426–7
codes of conduct and discipline 427–8
customary international law 427
definition 426
environment 526
ICC Elements of Crimes 426
military necessity 426
natural resources, use of 426–7
private or personal use 426
requisitioning 426
PKK 121, 179, 197, 201, 204–5, 368, 541, 547, 559
PLO 109, 118, 215
poison and poisoned weapons 392–3
Poland 24
police 169, 368
political detainees 34, 42
political figures, targeting 366–7
political wings of armed groups 10, 367, 371, 440
precautions 338, 351–7
ad hoc agreements 352–3
Additional Protocol II 351
anti-personnel mines 405, 406
bilateral agreements 352–3
carrying out attacks, in 351–6
civilians, protection of 351–7
cultural property 380–1
customary international law 351, 353–6
dams, dykes, and nuclear electrical generating stations 382
effect of attacks, against 356–7
feasibility, notion of 353–6
Geneva Conventions 352–3
human rights 352, 356
incendiary weapons 398–9
instructions 355–6
International Criminal Court 351
International Criminal Tribunal of the former Yugoslavia 355
international humanitarian law 356
legitimate military objectives 351–2
military advantage 354
planning 351–6
proportionality 353–5
targeting 338, 351–7
warnings 354–5
pregnant women 266–7, 310, 314
press releases and other ad hoc statements of armed groups 141–2

prisoners *see* interned and detained persons
prisoners of war 90, 294, 299–300 *see also* interned and detained persons
  agreements 444–5
  amnesties 525
  capital punishment during conflicts 525
  civilians and persons hors de combat, protection of 24
  combatant immunity 515–20, 525
  conditions of detention 521
  customary international law 513
  due process 521
  exchanges 301, 444–5, 523
  Geneva Conventions 39, 518–19, 522–5
  humane treatment 521, 524
  international humanitarian law 513
  Lieber Code 522
  Red Cross, International Committee of the 37, 523–5
  shooting prisoners 24
  status and treatment as prisoners of war, difference between 521–2
  substantive norms 513–14, 521–6
private initiatives, regulation through 52
prize courts 550
propaganda
  broadcasting 313
  commitments 108, 112
  Red Cross, International Committee of the 120
  unilateral declarations 120
prostitution, definition of enforced 266
protected zones 383–6
  customary international law 383–5
  demilitarized zones 383–5, 528
  General Assembly resolutions 383
  hospitals 383–5
  international humanitarian law 385–6
  nature reserves as demilitarized zones or protected areas 528
  open relief centres 386
  peace spaces or zones 386
  Red Cross, International Committee of the 383, 385
  safe areas or havens 385–6
  targeting 383–6
  unilateral declarations 383–4
proportionality *see* disproportionate attacks
protecting powers system 457–8, 471, 473
protection through provisions versus principles 37–8, 42, 50–1, 53
Protocol I Additional to Geneva Conventions *see* Additional Protocol I to Geneva Conventions
Protocol II Additional to Geneva Conventions *see* Additional Protocol II to Geneva Conventions
protracted violence 167–8, 188
PSLF 543
psychiatric injury 388
public opinion 430
publicity for compliance 541

quarter, denial of 412–15
  Additional Protocol II 412
  customary international law 412
  International Criminal Court, Rome Statute of 412
  Lieber Code 412
  military necessity 412
  Red Cross, International Committee of the 415
  surrender, persons in process of 413, 415

racist regimes, wars against 213, 217–20, 234
radio, dissemination by 434
raids into neighbouring territory 212
rape, definition of 265, 267
RCD 321–2, 464
rebellion 9–10
reciprocity 31, 37–9, 189, 244–5
recognition of belligerency *see* belligerency, recognition of
recruitment 319–24
Red Crescent 329, 374–5, 416–17, 468
Red Cross, International Committee of the 30–9 *see also* diplomatic conferences
  activities 468–71
  Additional Protocol I 468–70
  Additional Protocol II 36–7, 66, 174, 178, 182–3, 468–70
  Advisory Service 433
  belligerent reprisals 451
  beneficiaries of protection 359–61, 363–4, 439
  bilateral agreements 469
  civilians
    protection from targeting, draft rules on 42–3
    terrorizing civilians 341
  combatant immunity 515
  commentaries on Geneva Conventions 78, 162, 180, 468
  commitments 114, 443–5
  common Article 3 43–4, 48–9, 53, 162, 180, 469–71
  confidentiality 471–2
  customary international law 56, 59, 104, 468–9, 472, 519
  dead persons, protection of 283
  definition of NIACS 47–8
  diplomatic conferences 468
  direct part in hostilities, taking 360–2, 363–4
  dissemination 433, 434, 469
  due process 307, 310
  education and training 469
  emblems and uniforms, improper use of 416–17
  fact-finding missions 462
  First Geneva Convention 1864 30–1, 33
  Geneva Conventions 30–9, 59, 78, 162, 180, 467–70, 475, 477, 515–16
  geographical scope of application 251
  Group of Five 468
  Hague Conventions 470
  history 467–8
  human rights 85
  human shields 421
  humane treatment 259

humanitarian assistance 329, 333–4, 471
identification of existence of NIACs 47
implementation and non-judicial
  enforcement 467–72, 474
instruction 435–6
internal affairs, interference in 469–71
International Conference of the Red Cross and
  Red Crescent 468
international conferences 32–9, 40, 42–4,
  46–8, 53, 468
International Humanitarian Fact-Finding
  Commission 461
international humanitarian law 468–71
internees and detainees 114
Interpretive Guidance 359–61, 363–4, 366,
  370–1, 429
intra-party protection 248
legal advice 433
legislation 140
loss of protection 366, 370–1
manuals, codes of conduct, and internal
  regulations 440
medical units and transports 374–5
modalities 471–2
naming and shaming 471–2
national liberation, wars of 214, 221
national Red Cross societies, role of 31–7,
  44, 53
neutrality 416
NIACs, definition of 165–6, 180–1
non-state armed groups 119–20, 204, 429
opinions 468
personal scope of application 238, 241
political detainees 34, 42
principles 471
prisoners of war 37, 523–5
propaganda 120
protected zones 383, 385
protecting powers system 457–8, 471, 473
provisions versus principles 37–8, 42, 53
public pronouncements 471–2
quarter, denial of 514
reciprocity 37–9
resolutions 34–6, 43
special cases 48
symbol 383, 468
systematic regulation 30–9, 42–4, 46–8, 53
targeting, draft rules on protection from 42–3
terrorizing civilians 341
treaties 468, 470
unilateral declarations 109–10, 114–16,
  119–20, 469
United Nations 46–7
unnecessary suffering or superfluous
  injury 399
victims, protection of 42–4, 46–7
violence, characterization of 198–204, 207
wounded, sick, and shipwrecked 74, 277
Red Crystal 374–5, 416–17
regional organizations 198
regularly constituted courts 75–6, 305–6, 335
regulation 2–3 *see also* systematic regulation
  through international humanitarian law

ad hoc regulation 2, 9–29, 53
agreements 20, 25–9
belligerency, recognition of 9–20, 28–9, 41
body of international law, through a 54–100
customary international law 2, 54, 55–61, 99
direct regulation 93–9
human rights 93–9
instructions 20, 21–4, 28–9
international armed conflict, drawing on law
  of 55–77
international criminal law 55, 77–83, 99
international human rights law 83–99
international humanitarian law 61–77, 93–9
regulations *see* instructions, codes of conduct,
  and internal regulations
relief *see* humanitarian assistance
religion
  definition of religious personnel 278–9
  interned and detained persons 294
  personnel, protection of 277–80
RENAMO 178, 333
reprisals *see* belligerent reprisals
reputation 430
requisitioning 426, 529, 531
responses to the other side *see* belligerent reprisals
responsible command
  Additional Protocol II 183, 184–5,
    189, 191
  diplomatic conferences 184–5
  identification of NIACs 184–5
  International Criminal Tribunal for
    Rwanda 175
  organization of non-state armed groups, level
    of 174–6, 179–80, 210
rewards 448
riot control 393–6, 403, 429
Rome Statute *see* International Criminal Court,
  Rome Statute of
RPF 120, 252, 280, 443, 566
RUF 109, 123, 124, 132, 134, 179, 186, 187,
  247, 256, 257, 261, 264, 267, 269, 286,
  298, 299, 309, 322, 323, 325, 326, 329,
  358, 427, 428, 439, 442, 448, 463, 466,
  517, 520, 551–2
ruses 419
Russia
  Chechnya 198, 201, 349, 461, 504
  civil war and revolution 24, 33–4, 111, 440
  engaging compliance 546
  legislation 140
  manuals, codes of conduct, and internal
    regulations 440
  Red Cross, International Committee of
    the 33–4, 111
Rwanda *see also* International Criminal
  Tribunal for Rwanda
  dead persons, protection of 280–1
  displaced persons 286
  domestic criminal courts 488, 493,
    497–8, 500
  fact-finding missions 462
  instruction 436
  loss of protection 366

Rwanda (cont.)
  precautions 357
  propaganda, broadcasting 313

safe areas or havens 385–6
Safety of UN and Associated Personnel, Convention on the 327, 498
Samoa 495
San Remo Manual on International Law Applicable to Armed Conflicts at Sea 438
sanctions
  apologies to civilian population 448
  child soldiers 536–7
  command responsibility 446
  human rights 448
  internal mechanisms for implementation and enforcement 445–8
  rewards 448
  Security Council (UN) 466
  types of sanctions 446
scope of application 236–54
  geographical scope 250–2
  personal scope 236–49, 252
  scope/content nexus of NIAC 66–8
  temporal scope 252–4
scorched earth tactics 425–6, 429
sea, conflicts at 438
searches
  dead persons, protection of 280, 283
  interned and detained persons 295
  missing persons 284–5, 295
  wounded, sick, and shipwrecked 276
Secretary-General (UN)
  action plans for de-listing 534, 535–6
  child soldiers, listing of armed groups with 533–8
  human rights 44–7
  International Criminal Tribunal for the former Yugoslavia 478–9
  Office of the Special Representative of the Secretary-General for Children and Armed Conflict 534–7, 542, 547
Security Council (UN)
  children 533–5, 537–8
  dissemination 432
  gas and chemical weapons 395
  human rights 467
  implementation and non-judicial enforcement 465–6, 473–4
  instruction 435
  International Criminal Court 466, 483–4, 485
  International Criminal Tribunal for the former Yugoslavia 479
  international criminal tribunals 466
  international humanitarian law 465–6
  resolutions 432, 435, 479
  sanctions 466
  thematic issues, resolutions on 466
  Working Group on Children and Armed Conflict 534–5, 538
self-defence 325–6, 361, 380
self-determination 216, 217–19
self-interest 16, 29

self-reporting 566
Serbia 125, 369, 406, 497, 524
sexual and gender-based violence
  Additional Protocol II 264–5
  ceasefire agreements 267–8
  codes of conduct of non-state armed groups 267
  customary international law 264–5
  enforced prostitution, definition of 266
  enforced sterilization 267
  forced pregnancy 266–7
  Geneva Call Deed of Commitment 113
  humane treatment 264–8, 334
  International Criminal Court 265–6
  international criminal law 267
  International Criminal Tribunal for Rwanda 265
  International Criminal Tribunal for the former Yugoslavia 265–6
  international humanitarian law 267, 314
  intra-party protection 249
  rape, definition of 265, 267
  slavery 266
  unilateral declarations 113
  war crimes 265–7
shipwrecked persons see wounded, sick, and shipwrecked
sick persons see wounded, sick, and shipwrecked
siege warfare 424
Sierra Leone
  Additional Protocol II 487
  agreements 109
  amnesties 506, 508–9
  beneficiaries of protection 358–9
  child soldiers 322–3
  cluster munitions 409
  collective punishment 272
  combatant immunity 517–18, 520
  common Article 3 487
  courts of non-state armed groups 551–2
  fact-finding missions 463
  hostages, taking 269–70
  human rights 123–4, 132
  humanitarian assistance 329
  International Criminal Court 487
  international humanitarian law 487
  interned and detained persons 298
  list of violations 487
  manuals, codes of conduct, and internal regulations 439, 442
  NIACs, definition of 166
  peacekeeping missions 326
  quarter, denial of 413
  sanctions 448
  Security Council (UN) 466
  sexual violence 266
  Special Court for Sierra Leone 109, 166, 272, 487, 508–9
  war crimes 487
SLA 202, 268, 340, 343, 466, 535, 536, 556
slavery and slave trade 266, 268
SLM 109, 122, 124, 128, 132, 311, 356
SLM/A 187, 484
SLM/Unity 122, 124
soft law 288, 289–90, 506, 565

Solferino, Battle of 30
Somalia
  anti-personnel mines 540–1
  courts of non-state armed groups 556
  dissemination 432–3
  domestic criminal courts 498
  engaging compliance 545
  Geneva Call 540–1
  humanitarian assistance 332
  peacekeeping missions 326
  peer pressure 545
sources of law of NIAC 101–52
  ad hoc commitments 101, 107–52
  agreements 107, 124–33, 152
  custom 102–7, 152
  fact-finding missions, responses to reports of 141
  instructions, codes of conduct, and internal regulations 133–9
  legislation 140–1
  less traditional sources 101, 107–52
  motivations for taking up arms, expressions of 143
  practice of non-state armed groups 152
  press releases and other ad hoc statements 141–2
  state practice 152
  traditional sources 101–7
  treaties 101–2
  unilateral declarations 107, 113–24
South Africa see also Boer War
  amnesties 507
  apartheid 217–18
  national liberation, wars of 217–18
Soviet Union 259, 444–5, 525 see also Russia
Spanish-American War 17
Spanish Civil War
  belligerency, recognition of 15
  belligerent reprisals 449
  blockades 18–19
  combatant immunity 518
  commitments 112
  customary international law 103–4
  precautions 351–2
  prisoners of war 523
  Red Cross, International Committee of the 34, 35–6
  unilateral declarations 115–16
Special Court for Sierra Leone 109, 166, 272, 487, 508–9
Special Representative of the Secretary-General for Children and Armed Conflict, Office of the 534–7, 542, 547
SPLA 135, 173, 243, 360, 369, 447, 554
SPLM 98, 128, 132–3, 135, 142, 218–19, 322, 338, 340, 343, 352, 360, 369, 414, 422, 424, 439, 554
SPLM/A 73, 209, 238, 369, 370, 529, 541, 542, 543, 544, 545–6, 566
Sri Lanka
  air and sea capabilities 73
  anti-personnel mines 543
  child soldiers 322–3
  civilians, attacks on 340–1

courts of non-state armed groups 553–4, 557–9
cultural property 378
dead persons, protection of 281
displaced persons 291–2
distinction, principle of 102–3
disproportionate attacks 102–3, 249
flags of truce and surrender 416
Geneva Call Deed of Commitment 543
Geneva Conventions 120
human shields 420–1
humane treatment 256–7
humanitarian assistance 331–4
International Humanitarian Fact-Finding Commission 461
legal advice 437
loss of protection 366, 371
national liberation, wars of 218
non-state armed groups, characterization of 205
open relief centres 386
protected zones 383, 386
sanctions 446
temporal scope of application 253–4
territorial control 98
wounded, sick, and shipwrecked 277
St Petersburg Declaration on Explosive Projectiles 85, 388, 400–1
starvation of civilians 423–6
  ad hoc agreements 424
  Additional Protocol I 423, 425–6
  Additional Protocol II 423, 425–6
  criminalization 423
  customary international law 423–6
  definition 424
  destruction of supplies 424–5
  humanitarian assistance 424
  Lieber Code 423
  military necessity 424
  objects indispensable to survival of civilian population 424–6
  scorched earth tactics 425–6, 429
  siege warfare 424
  water 425
states see also government/state forces; third states
  de facto states 73
  dissemination 432–3
  fact-finding missions 141
  legislation 140–1
  manuals, codes of conduct, and internal regulations 438
  proposal for instrument binding states and non-state armed groups 565–6
  recognition of conflicts 200–4
  responsibility 77, 503–4
  sovereignty 50, 54, 65, 70–1, 209, 279, 561
  state practice 55, 57, 59, 105, 139, 364, 438, 452, 499
  unilateral declarations 113–14, 12
  unrecognized governments 560–1
sterilization, enforced 267
substantive norms 513–32

substantive norms (*cont.*)
    combatant immunity 513–20
    natural environment 526–9
    prisoners of war 513–14, 521–6
    territorial control 529–32
Sudan *see also* Darfur, Sudan
    agreements 109, 128
    anti-personnel mines 543, 545–6
    beneficiaries of protection 360
    capacity 73
    children 316, 322
    civilian objects, attacks on 343
    civilians, attacks on 340
    cluster munitions 409
    codes of conduct 135, 439
    Conventional Weapons Convention 135
    courts of non-state armed groups 554, 556
    engaging compliance 542–3, 545–6
    equality of obligations 243–4
    fact-finding missions 463
    human rights 132, 142
    human shields 422
    humane treatment 257
    humanitarian assistance 330–1
    instruction 436
    instructions, codes of conduct, and internal regulations 135
    loss of protection 370
    manuals, codes of conduct, and internal regulations 439
    precautions 352–3, 356
    press releases and other ad hoc statements 142
    sanctions 447
    Security Council (UN) 466
    sexual violence 268
    starvation of civilians 424
    targeting 338
    territorial control 187, 529
    transnational/extra-state armed conflicts 230, 234
    unilateral declarations 122–4
suicide bombers 403, 416
summary executions 506, 549–50, 559
superfluous injury *see* unnecessary suffering or superfluous injury
support functions 69, 169, 212, 225, 274, 318, 364
surrender
    acceptance 413, 415
    indications 413
    quarter, denial of 413, 415
    white flags 413, 415–16
sustained and concerted military operations
    ability to carry out operations 188
    Additional Protocol II 188
    identification of NIACs 188
    intensity 188
    International Criminal Court 188
    protracted violence 188
    territorial control 185–6
SWAPO 118
Switzerland
    domestic criminal courts 491–2, 493, 499
    humane treatment 255–6, 257
    manuals, codes of conduct, and internal regulations 440
    Swiss Civil War 21–2, 23, 255–6, 267, 440
systematic regulation through international humanitarian law 2, 30–53
    1949–74 42–9, 55
    1977, initiatives after 52, 54, 55
    abolition of distinction between international and non-international conflicts 46, 49, 53, 54
    ad hoc regulation 53
    Additional Protocol I on international armed conflicts 49, 51
    Additional Protocol II on non-international armed conflicts 49–51, 53, 54, 67
    common Article 3 of Geneva Conventions 43–3, 48–9, 53, 54
    Declaration on Minimum Humanitarian Standards 1990 52
    Declaration on the Rules of International Humanitarian Law (Institute of International Humanitarian Law) 52
    diplomatic conferences 40–2, 49–53
    Fundamental Standards of Humanity initiative 52
    Hague Convention on Cultural Property 1954 42–3, 54
    Institute of International Law resolution on Distinction between Military Objectives and Non-Military Objects 44
    judicial bodies 54–5
    legitimacy to rebels 40
    private initiatives 52
    Red Cross, International Committee of the 30–9, 42–4, 46–9, 53
    special cases 48
    state sovereignty 50, 54
    United Nations, human rights and 44–7, 53

tactics *see* methods of combat
Tadić decision
    agreements 107
    commitments 110–11, 443
    customary international law 102, 104
    definition of NIACs 210
    differentiation between NIACs and IACs 73
    government authorities 180
    intensity of violence 167–9
    International Criminal Court 483
    International Criminal Tribunal for Rwanda 479, 480
    International Humanitarian Fact-Finding Commission 461
    NIACs, definition of 155–6, 164–80, 210
    perfidy 420
    protracted armed conflicts, definition of 193–4
    temporal scope of application 253
    transnational/extra-state armed conflicts 231–2
    war crimes 78, 478
Tajikistan 202, 410, 438

Taliban *see* **Afghanistan, Taliban in**
targeting 337–86
  ad hoc commitments 337–8
  Additional Protocol I 69
  Additional Protocol II 69, 338
  avoiding or minimizing losses 338
  beneficiaries of protection 357–86
  child soldiers 534–5
  civilians 337–48
  commanders 366
  cultural property 375–81
  dams, dykes, and nuclear electrical generating stations 381–3, 526
  disproportionate attacks 349–51
  distinction, principle of 337–8
  Geneva Conventions 338
  hardship 338
  human rights 337
  incendiary weapons 398
  indiscriminate attacks 338, 347–8
  International Criminal Court 429–30
  international humanitarian law 337
  loss of protection 365–72
  losses of life, investigations relating to 372–3
  medical units and transports 373–5
  particular protections, objects benefiting from 373–86
  precautions 338, 351–7
  protected zones 383–6
  underlying principles 337–8
  weapons 429–30
Tehran International Conference on Human Rights 1968 44–5, 53, 86, 397
television, dissemination by 434
temporal scope of application 252–4
  Additional Protocol II 252–3
  cessation of hostilities 252–3
  international humanitarian law 253–4
  peace agreements 253
  Tadić decision 253
territorial control by non-state armed groups 529–32
  Additional Protocol II 97, 185–7, 188, 191, 193, 210, 244
  amount of territory 185
  belligerency, recognition of 531
  belligerent occupation, law of 529–31
  commitments 111
  courts of non-state armed groups 558–60
  customary international law 529–30
  detention 186–7
  due process 308–10
  duration 185
  fair trials 186
  general protections and prohibitions 530
  Hague Regulations 530, 532
  human rights 97–8, 530–2, 565
  humane treatment 530
  humanitarian assistance 332–3
  identification of NIACs 157, 185–7, 210
  implementation of Additional Protocol II 185–7
  intensity 186
  International Criminal Tribunal for Rwanda 186–7
  International Criminal Tribunal for the former Yugoslavia 531–2
  international humanitarian law 97–8, 529–32
  interned persons and detainees 186
  legislation 140–1
  Lieber Code 531
  loss of protection 371
  national liberation, wars of 221
  NIACs, definition of 180–1
  personal scope of application 239
  reciprocity 244
  requisitioning 529, 531
  sustained and concerted military operations 185–6
  transnational/extra-state armed conflicts 231
  tripartite relationships 529
terrorists
  Al Qaeda 103, 232–3, 251, 353–4, 525
  Bin Laden, shooting of 415
  education and training 547–8
  engaging compliance 547–8
  instruction 435
  non-state armed groups, characterization of 204–5
  quarter, denial of 415
  suicide bombers 403, 416
  support, providing 435
  training 547–8
  war on terror 232–4
terrorizing civilians 341
Thailand 490–1
third parties, implementation and non-judicial enforcement by 430–74
  fact-finding missions 459–65, 473
  'Fundamental Standards of Humanity' initiative 566
  human rights non–governmental organisations 472–3
  protecting powers 457–8, 471, 473
  Red Cross, International Committee of the 467–72, 474
  troops, intervention with use of 222–5, 234
  United Nations 465–7, 473–4
third states
  belligerency, recognition of 11, 12–18, 29
  interference in internal affairs 469–71
  intervention 212, 222–8, 234
  maritime commerce, interference with 13, 16
  non-state armed groups, control of 225–8, 234
  trials in third states 496–8
threshold of application of international humanitarian law *see* **identification of NIACs**
Togo 341
torture
  definition 88–9, 261
  human rights 88–9
  humane treatment 261–2, 334
  international criminal law 261
  International Criminal Tribunal for Rwanda 89

torture (cont.)
  International Criminal Tribunal for the former Yugoslavia 89
  international humanitarian law 261
  pain and suffering, severity of 262
  Torture Convention 89
training see education and training
traitors 15, 514, 547
transnational/extra-state armed conflicts 212, 228–34
  Additional Protocol I 233
  Additional Protocol II 229–32
  civil wars 229–30
  common Article 3 229, 230–1
  differentiation between NIACs and IACs 212, 228–34, 235
  intensity of violence 232
  International Criminal Tribunal for Rwanda 232
  overspill 230, 233–4, 235
  Red Cross, International Committee of the 229–30
  Tadić decision 231–2
  territorial control 231
  war on terror 232–4
transports see medical units and transports
Tratado de Regularización de la Guerra 1820 27–8, 283
treachery see perfidy
treaties and conventions see also particular conventions
  amendment 62–3
  amnesties 506–7
  child soldiers 316–17
  civilian objects, attacks on 342
  creation of law of non-international armed conflict 564
  derogations 250
  dignity, outrages upon personal 263
  diplomatic conferences 468
  drafts 468
  engaging compliance 542–3, 564
  examples of treaties 101–2
  'Fundamental Standards of Humanity' initiative 565–7
  human rights 83–7, 250, 467
  individuals, as binding on 240–2
  international humanitarian law 61–5, 85, 87
  interned and detained persons 294
  model of IACs 63–4
  personal scope of application 236–41
  proposal for instrument binding states and non-state armed groups 565–6
  ratification 542–3
  Red Cross, International Committee of the 468, 470
  soft law 565
  sources of NIACs 101–2
  third parties 240–2
  treaty bodies 467
tripartite relationships 529
troops, intervention by outside states through use of 222–5, 234
  combatant immunity 223

  International Criminal Tribunal for the former Yugoslavia 223–5
  internationalization approach 224
  outside states, intervention by 234
  pairings, theory of 223–4
truces 277 see also flags of truce and surrender
Tunisia 230, 297
Turkel Commission 19
Turkey
  courts of non-state armed groups 555
  engaging compliance 547
  Kurds 368–9
  loss of protection 368–9
  non-state armed groups, characterization of 204–5
Twitter accounts 151

Uganda
  civilian objects, attacks on 343
  civilians, attacks on 340
  engaging compliance 545
  humane treatment 256
  International Criminal Court 484, 485–6
  interned and detained persons 298
  manuals, codes of conduct, and internal regulations 439, 442
  murder 260
  peer pressure 545
  pillage 427–8
  protected zones 384
  quarter, denial of 414
  sanctions 445
  sexual violence 267
  transnational/extra-state armed conflicts 230, 234
  wounded, sick, and shipwrecked 276
UNESCO (UN Educational, Scientific and Cultural Organization) 42, 237, 328, 378–9, 433
uniforms see emblems and uniforms, improper use of
unilateral declarations 107, 113–24
  anti-personnel mines 113
  child soldiers 113
  commitments 107, 109–10, 113–24
  custom 110
  development of law 443–4
  displaced persons 290
  equality of obligations 118
  general declarations 120–2
  Geneva Call Deed of Commitment 113
  Geneva Conventions 116–22
  human rights 123–4
  humanitarian assistance 333–4
  internal mechanisms for implementation and enforcement 442–5
  International Criminal Tribunal for Rwanda 109–10
  International Criminal Tribunal for the former Yugoslavia 110
  national liberation, wars of 118, 220–2
  non-state armed groups 118–25
  parallel declarations 114–15

propaganda 120
protected zones 383–4
public at large, made to 121
reciprocity 245
Red Cross, International Committee of the 109–10, 114–16, 119–20, 469
rules, declarations on particular 122–3
sexual and gender-based violence 113
sources of NIACs 107, 113–24
states, declarations of 113–14, 124
United Nations 109–10, 121, 124
Universal Declaration of Human Rights 123
UNITA 118, 220, 430–1, 448, 466,
United Nations (UN) *see also* General Assembly (UN); Secretary-General (UN); Security Council (UN)
   Charter 85–6, 218, 324–30
   child soldiers 320–1, 533–8
   colonial domination, wars against 218
   Commission on Human Rights 467
   disputes submitted to UN 158
   emblems and uniforms 416
   Geneva Conventions 44
   human rights 44–7, 53, 85–6, 467
   Human Rights Council 467
   humanitarian assistance 328–30
   identification of NIACs 158
   implementation and non-judicial enforcement 465–7, 473–4
   international humanitarian law 85, 328
   neutrality 416
   peacekeeping missions 324–8
   Red Cross, International Committee of the 46–7
   Safety of UN and Associated Personnel, Convention on the 327, 498
   summary executions 506
   Tehran International Conference on Human Rights 1968 44–5, 53
   UNESCO 42, 237, 328, 378–9, 433
   unilateral declarations 109–10, 121, 124
United States *see also* American civil war
   Additional Protocol II 111–12
   Al Qaeda 103, 232–3, 251, 353–4, 525
   amnesties 505
   belligerency, recognition of 10–13, 15, 17–18
   Bin Laden, shooting of 415
   blockades 18
   combatant immunity 518, 520
   dams, dykes, and nuclear electrical generating stations 381–2
   dead persons, protection of 281
   engaging compliance 547–8
   gas and chemical weapons 396
   manuals, codes of conduct, and internal regulations 438
   medical and religious personnel 280
   Philippines, war with 412, 489–90, 505
   precautions 351, 353–4
   quarter, denial of 415
   Red Cross, International Committee of the 112
   Spanish-American War 17
   terrorist organizations, training of 547–8

Universal Declaration of Human Rights 85, 86, 87, 123, 329
universal jurisdiction 494, 498–500
unnecessary suffering or superfluous injury, weapons causing 387–90, 401, 403, 410
   anti-personnel mines 404
   booby traps 404
   Conventional Weapons Convention 390
   customary international law 387–8
   design of weapons 389
   expanding bullets 403
   explosive bullets 401
   International Criminal Court 390
   Lieber Code 388
   military necessity 388–9
   non-detectable fragments 410
   Ottawa Convention on Anti-Personnel Mines 1997 390
   proportionality 389
   psychiatric injury 388
   Red Cross, International Committee of the 388
   St Petersburg Declaration 388
   war crimes 390
unrecognized governments 560–1
Upper Silesia 34, 35, 114–15, 508
URNG 131

Vattel, E de 16
Venezuela 230, 231, 234
verification missions 462–5, 540–1
Vietnam 72–3, 397, 546, 562, 563–4
vigilantism 549
violence *see also* intensity of violence
   Additional Protocol II 196–7, 207–8
   belligerency, recognition of 206–9
   bilateral agreements 204
   characterization 196–210
   common Article 3 206–7
   cruel and inhuman treatment 262–3
   customary international law 259–60
   decision-makers, neutrality of 196–9, 210
   definition 324–5
   denials of existence of NIACs 200–4, 210
   Geneva Conventions 203, 206, 207–8
   humane treatment 259–63
   identification of NIACs 196–209
   intensity of violence 199
   International Criminal Court 199
   International Criminal Tribunal for Rwanda 199
   international humanitarian law 202–3, 206–9, 259–60
   international organizations 198
   legal status of armed groups 205–9
   legitimacy of armed groups 205–9
   life and persons to 259–63
   murder 260–1
   NIACs, definition of 165
   non-state armed groups, characterization of 204–5
   non-state armed groups, legal status and legitimacy of 205–9

violence (*cont.*)
  protracted violence 167–8, 188
  recognition by states of armed conflicts 200–4
  Red Cross, International Committee of the 198–204, 207
  regional organizations 198
  sexual and gender-based violence 113, 264–8
  torture 261–2

wanton destruction 428–9
  civilian objects, attacks on 428
  customary international law 428
  differentiation between NIACs and IACs 70–1
  disproportionate attacks 70
  International Criminal Tribunal for the former Yugoslavia 428
  military necessity 70, 428
  state sovereignty 70–1
  war crimes 70–1
war correspondents 311–13
war crimes
  ad hoc agreements, enforcement of 82–3
  Additional Protocol I 475
  Additional Protocol II 79, 475–6
  amnesties 505–9
  belligerent reprisals 83
  child soldiers 79, 81, 323
  civilians, attacks on 339
  combatant immunity 515
  common Article 3 69, 78, 475–6
  customary international law 60, 106, 477–8
  definition 78
  differentiation between NIACs and IACs 70–1
  dignity, outrages upon personal 264
  diplomatic conferences 78, 475
  disproportionate attack, crime of 79–80
  domestic criminal courts 488–9, 491–9
  enforcement function 77, 82–3
  expanding bullets 403
  forced displacement 80
  Geneva Conventions, grave breaches of 475–7
  Hague Convention on Cultural Property 62
  human shields 421
  individual criminal responsibility 77, 79, 100, 475, 478
  International Criminal Court 79–81, 248–9, 323, 481–3, 485, 487–8
    child soldiers 323
    customary international law 106
    differentiation between NIACs and IACs 70–1
    Hague Convention on Cultural Property 62
    international humanitarian law 62, 63–4
    medical units and transports 374
    protracted armed conflict, definition of 193–4
    unnecessary suffering or superfluous injury 390
  International Criminal Tribunal for Rwanda 478, 480–1
  International Criminal Tribunal for the former Yugoslavia 60, 81, 82, 475, 478
  international criminal tribunals 77–8
  international human rights law 79
  international humanitarian law 67, 77–83, 475–8
  interpretation 79–82, 100
  intra-party protection 248–9
  judicial enforcement 475–8, 509–10
  jus cogens 478
  list 62, 63–4, 67, 70–1
  medical units and transports 374
  methodological concerns 78–83
  ne bis in idem 485
  NIAC, definition of 78
  norms 79–81
  nullum crimen sine lege principle 81
  Nuremberg Military Tribunal 475
  perfidy 419
  primary rules of IHL 77, 81
  protracted armed conflicts, definition of 193–4
  secondary rules 77
  serious violations of IHL 77, 81
  sexual violence 265–7
  state responsibility 77
  state sovereignty 70–1
  Tadić decision 78, 478
  unnecessary suffering or superfluous injury 390
  wanton destruction 70–1
war, law of 10, 12, 14–16, 25–6
wars of national liberation *see* national liberation, wars of
warnings
  anti-personnel mines 405, 406
  belligerent reprisals 453
  cultural property 379
  Lieber Code 354
  medical units and transports 374
  precautions 354–5
water 425
weapons 386–412 *see also* anti-personnel mines; Conventional Weapons Convention
  biological and bacteriological weapons 393
  booby traps 404
  cluster munitions 62, 238, 240, 409–10
  conduct of hostilities 386–412, 428–9
  definition 386
  direct part in hostilities, taking 361
  environment 527
  expanding bullets 71, 401–3
  explosive bullets 400–1
  Explosive Projectiles, St Petersburg Declaration on 85
  explosive remnants of law 62, 411–12
  gas and chemical weapons 61–2, 394–6
  general rules 386–92
  Hague Peace Conference of 1899 387
  incendiary weapons 397–9, 527
  indiscriminate effects 390–2, 398, 404–6, 409–10
  International Criminal Court 428–9
  laser weapons designed to cause permanent blindness 399–400

medical units and transports equipped with
  weapons 374
methods of combat, distinguished from 386
motivations for taking up arms, expressions
  of 143
non-detectable fragments 410–11
nuclear weapons 91, 391
poison and poisoned weapons 392–3
self-defence 361
specific prohibitions 386, 392–12
targeting 429–30
unnecessary suffering or superfluous
  injury 387–90, 401, 403, 410
websites 141
Western Sahara 72, 218, 222, 435
white flags 413, 415–16
women
  Additional Protocol II 313–14
  common Article 3 313–14
  death penalty 314
  detention, separation in 314
  direct part in hostilities, taking 361
  enforced pregnancy 266–7
  international humanitarian law 313–14
  interned and detained persons 295
  non-state armed groups, as members of 314
  pregnant women and mothers of young
    children 266–7, 310, 314
  prostitution, definition of enforced 266
  sexual violence 264–8, 314
  sterilization 267
wounded, sick, and shipwrecked 273–7
  Additional Protocol I 274–5

Additional Protocol II 74, 273, 276
capacity 74–5
civilians and persons *hors de combat*, protection
  of 273–4, 334–5
common Article 3 74, 273, 275
customary international law 273, 275,
  276–7
definition 274
differentiation between NIACs and
  IACs 74–5
evacuation 277
exchanges, bilateral agreements on 277
Geneva Conventions 33, 39,
  247–8, 273
Hague Statement 1991 276
hospitals 274
humane treatment 274–5
intra-party protection 247–8
medical and religious personnel, protection
  of 277–80
medical care 274–5
medical units and transports 373–4
protection 274–6
Red Cross, International Committee of
  the 74, 277
respect 274, 373–4
search, obligation to 276
truces 277

Yemen 116–17, 123, 271
Yugoslavia *see* former Yugoslavia; International
  Criminal Tribunal for the former
  Yugoslavia

Lightning Source UK Ltd.
Milton Keynes UK
UKOW06f0615020514

230960UK00001B/1/P